The Face of the Deep

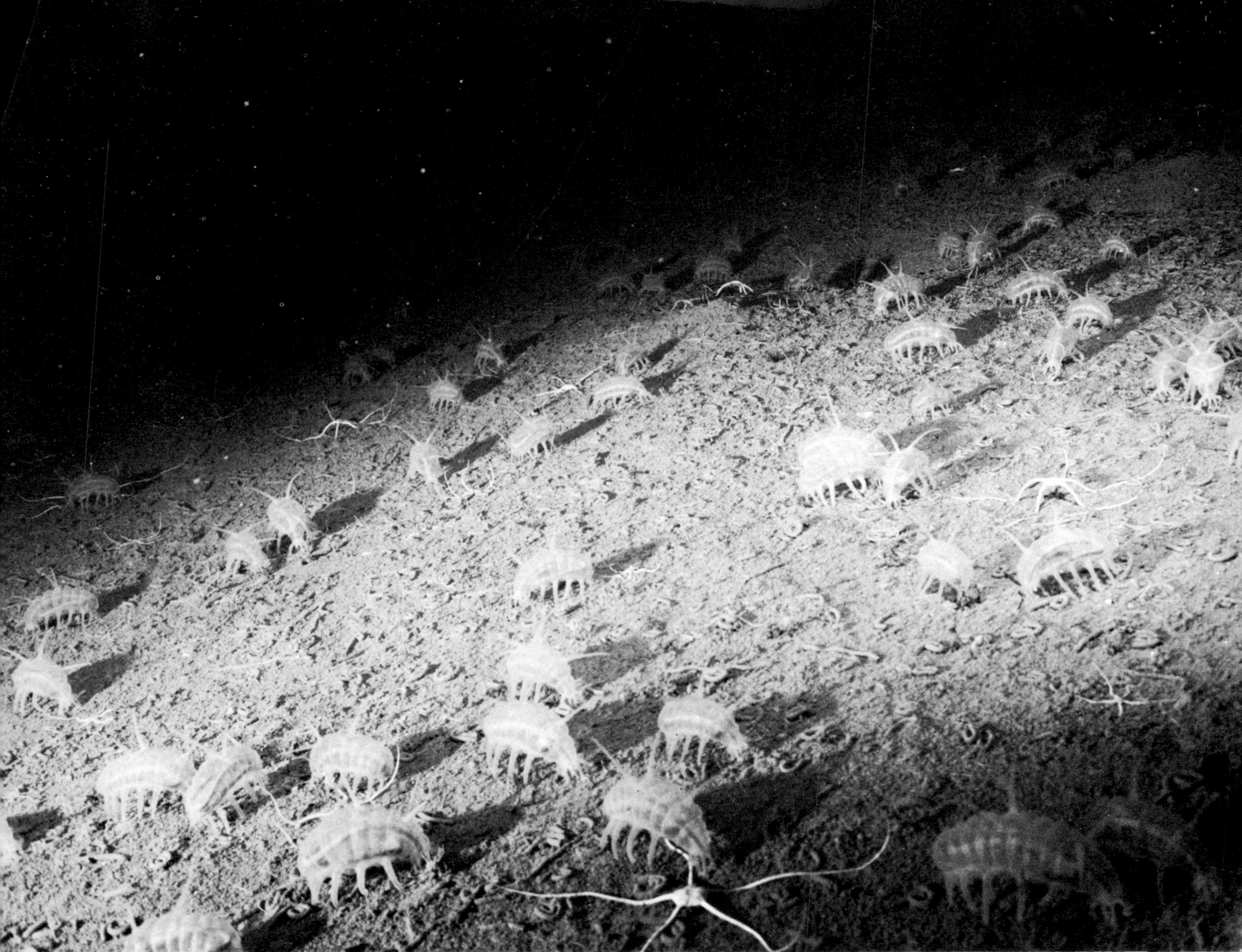

Sea cucumbers and brittle stars on the continental slope.

In the beginning the earth was without form and void . . . and darkness was upon the face of the deep.

THE FACE OF THE DEEP

BRUCE C. HEEZEN AND CHARLES D. HOLLISTER

NEW YORK · OXFORD UNIVERSITY PRESS · LONDON · TORONTO · 1971

Library of Congress Catalogue Card Number: 77-83038
Printed in the United States of America
Second printing, 1972

Preface

This illustrated natural history of the visible abyss was born out of pure curiosity. If we had realized the enormity of the task before us, we surely would never have started it, but once begun, we found that we could not put the vast dark deep abyss out of our minds.

Both of us began our careers in oceanography by studying photographs of the deep-sea floor. Both were beckoned by the puzzle and mystery of the visible abyss and both became addicted to the pursuit of answers and explanations of the curious features which the cameras record. We must confess that we did not begin this work in an attempt to solve major scientific problems; we were simply plagued by a frustrating curiosity as to what created the variety of generally vague features faintly and often poorly recorded by cameras seemingly held just a little too far from the scene.

Our study began in 1947 when one of us led a minor expedition which obtained two hundred photographs and bottom samples of the continental shelf and continental slope off New England. Although a variety of exciting discoveries was made, we could not identify or fully comprehend most of what was seen. Later, we searched through the records of the great deep-sea expeditions of the nineteenth and early twentieth century in order to determine what larger objects and beasts should be seen in the abyss. We plotted the courses of bottom currents and studied the geographical variations in bottom materials. We plotted earthquakes and volcanic eruptions. Every bit of available knowledge which we considered pertinent to the visible natural history of the abyss was assembled. Then we tried to imagine what visual effects the various known animals and the various predicted physical and chemical processes should have on the seascape, and we attempted to identify the resulting features and forms recorded in thousands upon thousands of deep-sea photographs. Although we are gratified by the progress in our understanding attained at sea, in the laboratory, and in the library over the past twenty years, it is with the full realization that even now much of what we see cannot be identified or fully explained.

We have used a minimum of technical terms and tried to avoid the jargon of specialists in order that all of those who have an interest in the abyss, whether pupil, student, scholar, biologist, chemist, geologist, physicist, engineer, mariner, or layman, may read the book without the aid of a technical dictionary.

The tiny fringe of shallow sunlit waters which has been so frequently treated in books and films is entirely excluded, for in this book we are concerned only with the sunless and little-known abyss which claims over half of the planet.

There is at the present time a great acceleration in oceanic exploration. Bathyscaphes, until recently, have been used largely by adventure-seeking "submarine mountain climbers" for the purpose of breaking depth records. Now that the greatest depth of the ocean has been reached by man, these submersibles are being equipped as useful research tools. More and more scientists will have the opportunity to view the deep-sea floor through the portholes of bathyscaphes and other deep submersibles. Many of the things which will be seen from future deep submersibles will be new to the world, yet perhaps the majority will have been previously recorded by automatic deep-sea cameras. Since the vast majority of existing deep-sea photographs remains unpublished, it seems now a particularly opportune time to present a summary of the knowledge so far gained through remote deep-sea photography.

The central idea of this book is very simple—to present a partially classified selection of the best photographs of the deep-sea floor for you to look at and contemplate. The text, a verbal accompaniment to the visual story presented in the assembled photographs, attempts to explain and interpret some of the more obvious aspects of the varying scene. The words, which provide an incomplete guide and are not intended to be read alone, may perhaps add to your enjoyment of the visual armchair journey through the abyssal world which we will now begin.

Beside the Tappan Zee B. C. H.
April 11, 1970 C. D. H.

Acknowledgments

The photographs reproduced in this book derive from three principal sources. Approximately one-third were obtained over the past few years in Antarctic waters by the National Science Foundation's Research Ship *Eltanin*. Another third were obtained by the authors over the past two decades from ships operating in the Atlantic and Pacific. The remaining third were contributed by scientists from many institutions in several countries.

Many people assisted, encouraged, and aided us, and it is difficult to select names from the many and impossible to order them in any fair and reasonable way. We have been assisted at sea by R. Anderson, J. O. Cason, J. E. Damuth, E. Escowitz, J. I. Ewing, D. W. Folger, J. Foster, P. J. Fox, B. Glass, J. Glass, E. Haff, J. Hirshman, T. Holcombe, W. Jahns, E. Johnson, G. L. Johnson, M. Langseth, A. S. Laughton, A. Lowrie, Jr., C. Macgruder, H. D. Needham, D. Ninkovich, J. Northrop, W. Ruddiman, W. B. F. Ryan, M. J. Schneck, E. D. Schneider, and R. E. Sheridan. Marie Tharp offered continuous encouragement and frequently advised on special problems. Hester Haring drew the sketches with care and enthusiasm. D. Johnson drafted several special illustrations. Special thanks are due K. O. Emery for his critical review of the manuscript. We also wish to express our thanks to Michael E. McKean.

We originally planned to write this book in collaboration with Professor R. J. Menzies, an old friend and collaborator, but unfortunately his heavy work schedule prevented him from participating in the work. We are grateful for his encouragement and generously contributed ideas, and for the preparation of an early draft of the second chapter. We owe a great debt to many others who contributed much but who wish to remain anonymous. Most of the photographs reproduced in this book were obtained on expeditions supported by the Office of Naval Research, the Naval Ships Systems Command and the Naval Oceanographic Office, United States Navy; the National Science Foundation; the U.S. Geological Survey; Cable and Wireless Ltd.; and the Bell Telephone System. The results of these investigations have been reported in scientific journals and contributed to the data banks of scientific and governmental institutions.

Contents

Everyone must know the feeling of triumph and pride which a grand view . . . communicates to the mind. In these little frequented [regions] there is also joined to it some vanity, that you are . . . the first man who ever . . . admired this view.

CHARLES DARWIN, 1845

The Face of the Deep

59°35′S 155°17′E

1.1 The living face of the deep. Sea cucumbers (center) skim off the upper film of sediment, pass it through their bodies, and leave the exhausted residue as knots of remolded sediment. Urchins (lower center) plow meandering furrows and other creatures create mounds and holes. All the while currents continuously wear these creations down and drift the mud into telltale streamers. Life is particularly evident in this photograph taken beneath the fertile circumpolar current of the southern ocean. Depth, 3250 m, Mid-Oceanic Ridge, south of New Zealand.

1
The Visible Abyss

Once beyond the edge of the shelf, as we visualize the steeper declivities of the continental slope, we begin to feel the mystery and alien quality of the deep sea—the gathering darkness, the growing pressure, the starkness of a seascape in which all plantlife has been left behind.

RACHEL CARSON

Three kilometers beneath the sunlit waters of the world ocean we reach the vast abyss,[1] a lonely dark underworld, sparingly peopled by strange beasts (1.1). Until recently its scenery, virgin and unseen, existed only in the imagination. Some of those who carefully examined the material brought up by dredges and trawls had constructed in their mind's eye a fairly accurate view, but until the invention of the deep-sea flash camera no one was completely certain what the sea floor really looked like (1.2).

In this seasonless abyssal world of total and eternal night, "scenery" acquires a special meaning. Mountains, plains, valleys, and canyons of the deep sea are neither smaller nor less impressive than those on land (1.3), but we simply cannot see them with our own eyes nor are they seen by the inhabitants of the sea. One cannot photograph a seamount in the same way as one can photograph Mount McKinley or the Matterhorn on a clear day. The restrictions imposed by the murkiness of sea water, even with the most powerful lights, allow one to see at a glance but a few square meters (1.4). Therefore, a full view of the larger features must be inferred from echo-soundings and it is, of necessity, abstract.

FOUNDATIONS OF THE DEEP

Until forty years ago, all knowledge of the form of the ocean floor was derived from widely spaced hemp and wire line soundings.[2] From this crude information, it was discovered that the surface of the earth lies at

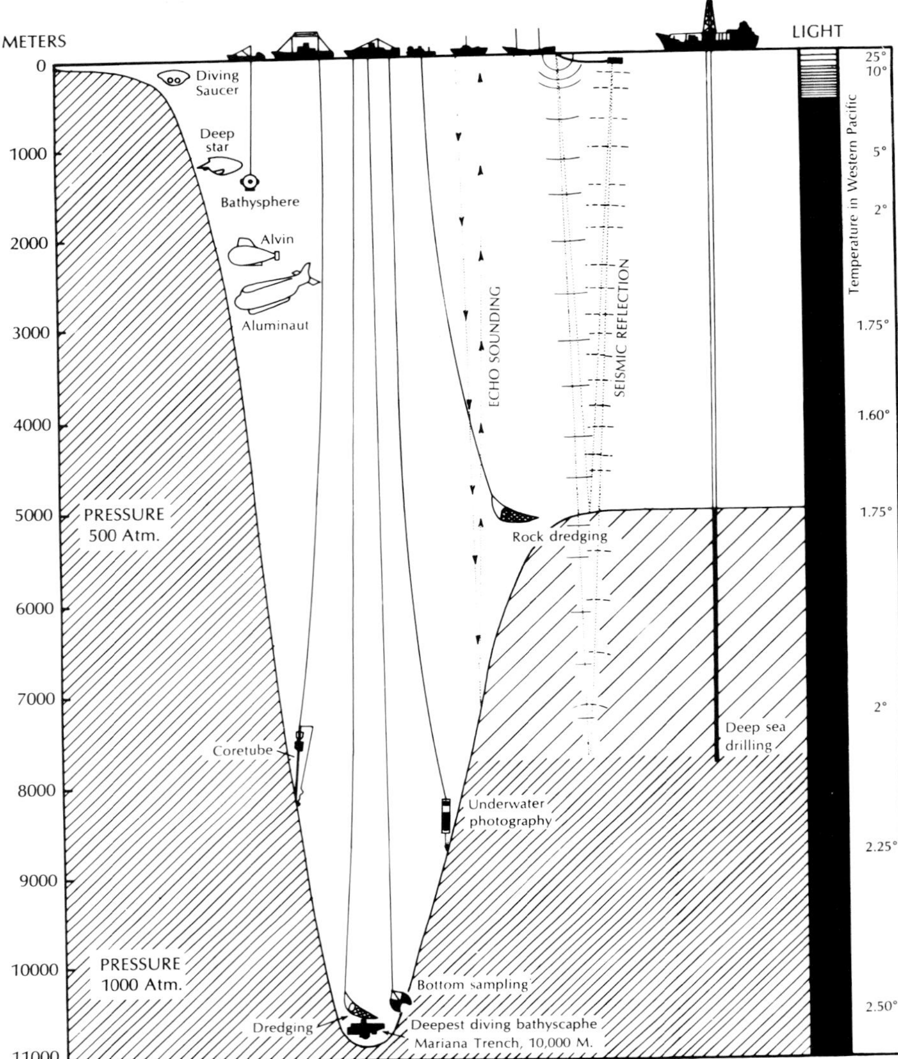

1.2 Methods of sampling and examining the deep-sea floor. Free diving vehicles, seismic reflection profiling, and rotary drilling have recently been added to the techniques of abyssal exploration. Corers capable of recovering nearly 100 feet of ooze have provided marine geologists with invaluable information concerning the evolution of microscopic marine animals, the rate of sediment accumulation, processes of deposition, absolute ages of geologic events, history of the earth's magnetic field, and global changes in patterns of ocean circulation. Recently, drilling rigs have been taken to sea in order to penetrate still deeper. Heat sensors attached to core tubes allow geologists to determine the rate of heat loss from the earth's interior. Bottom sampling devices, including dredges, are used to recover samples of rocks, mud, and animals that are on the sea floor.

two predominant elevations. One, approximating present sea level, represents the continents and their wetted edges while the other, 5000 meters deeper, represents the general level of the ocean basin floor. It was further discovered that deep, narrow, steep-walled trenches, approximately 10,000 meters deep, lie seaward of the arcuate island festoons of the Pacific and that median elevations exist in several of the major oceans. Modern knowledge of the form of the sea floor, however, emerged only during the past few decades following the invention of the continuously recording echo-sounder. Reflections of sound pulses sent out and recorded at one-second intervals provide detailed profiles of the ocean floor and allow the identification of a variety of bottom configurations. The mapping, investigation, and explanation of these physiographic features have occupied a whole generation of oceanographers, and the job has only just begun. Deep-sea cameras which have been in use for the past two decades permitted an even closer look at the sea floor and provided further insight into the processes that shape the ocean floor.

Those physiographic provinces associated with the transition from the shore to the abyss constitute the continental margins (1.5, 1.6). The monotonous continental shelf is but the wetted perimeter of the continent. The true boundary between continent and ocean is marked by the abrupt and relatively precipitous continental slope. Near or at the base of this dissected slope, we reach the abyss which claims the half of the earth's surface which is covered by more than 3000 meters of ocean water.[3] In the Atlantic and Indian Oceans, a broad subdued continental rise, a few hundred kilometers wide, sweeps out toward the basin floor. At its base, on the true ocean basin floor, lie the abyssal plains, the flattest surfaces on earth. The Pacific, however, is ringed with trenches, the gentle continental rise is only locally present, and abyssal plains are nearly absent. The centers of the Atlantic, Indian, and South Pacific Oceans are occupied by a continuous broad and rugged world-encircling mountain range known as the Mid-Oceanic Ridge (1.7). Its crest, which lies almost precisely in mid-ocean, is cleft by a deep median rift valley. Deep gashes cut into the sea floor nearly at right angles to the crest and flanks of the ridge and continue across the ocean basin floor until they are obscured beneath the sediments accumulated in the continental margins. Seamounts and islands lie in straight rows along these fracture zones, and together with the linear scarps and ridges which are parallel to the crest of the Mid-Oceanic Ridge, they impose a vivid fabric-like texture on the ocean floor.[4]

These rocky ribs of the solid earth which form the foundations of the deep are gradually being blanketed by an unremitting drift of sediment.

80°
75°
70°
65°
60°
55°
50°
45°
50°
45°
40°
35°
30°
25°
20°

1.3 The unseen abyssal scenery. Thousands of miles of continuous echo-sounding profiles were used to construct this abstract view of the sea floor. Abyssal scenery at this scale can be seen in no other way but in the mind's eye.

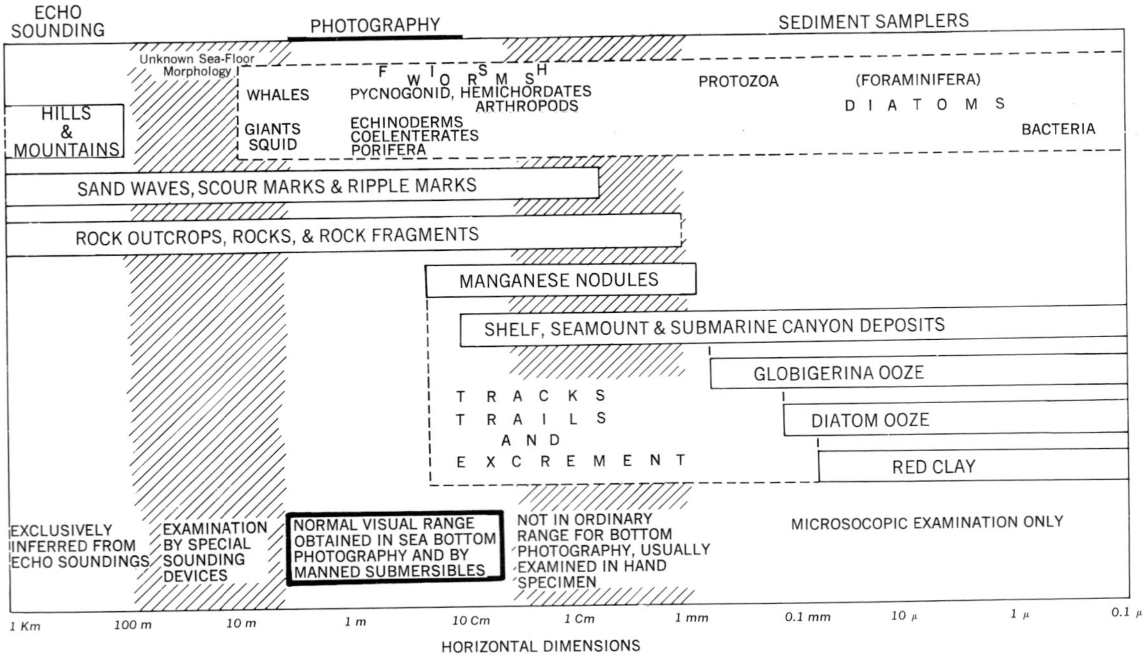

ECHO SOUNDING
PHOTOGRAPHY
SEDIMENT SAMPLERS
Unknown Sea-Floor Morphology
F W O R M S H
WHALES
PYCNOGONID, HEMICHORDATES
ARTHROPODS
PROTOZOA
(FORAMINIFERA)
D I A T O M S
HILLS & MOUNTAINS
GIANTS SQUID
ECHINODERMS
COELENTERATES
PORIFERA
BACTERIA
SAND WAVES, SCOUR MARKS & RIPPLE MARKS
ROCK OUTCROPS, ROCKS, & ROCK FRAGMENTS
MANGANESE NODULES
SHELF, SEAMOUNT & SUBMARINE CANYON DEPOSITS
GLOBIGERINA OOZE
T R A C K S
T R A I L S
A N D
E X C R E M E N T
DIATOM OOZE
RED CLAY
EXCLUSIVELY INFERRED FROM ECHO SOUNDINGS
EXAMINATION BY SPECIAL SOUNDING DEVICES
NORMAL VISUAL RANGE OBTAINED IN SEA BOTTOM PHOTOGRAPHY AND BY MANNED SUBMERSIBLES
NOT IN ORDINARY RANGE FOR BOTTOM PHOTOGRAPHY, USUALLY EXAMINED IN HAND SPECIMEN
MICROSOCOPIC EXAMINATION ONLY
1 Km 100 m 10 m 1 m 10 Cm 1 Cm 1 mm 0.1 mm 10 μ 1 μ 0.1 μ
HORIZONTAL DIMENSIONS

1.4 The visual window. Dimensions of features on the sea floor. Note the limited range of objects that can be visually observed. Under the normal procedure, most bottom dwelling organisms are too small to be seen in photographs. However, rock outcrops, ripple marks, scour marks, large organisms such as starfish, holothurians, sea urchins, and tracks and trails of large animals are satisfactorily photographed with the normal combination of film size, film grain, and lens-subject distance.

The cold dark watery surface of this growing blanket is the home of especially adapted animals whose tracks and burrows are the principal elements of submarine scenery. Currents sweep the sediment into drifts leaving a definite visible texture. Minerals, dissolved in the currents, migrate ion-by-ion from the land to the most remote portions of the abyss. The rocky cradle of the seas is still growing deeper and wider, and fresh additions to its framework, chilled by the frigid waters, are seen in the mid-oceanic rift valley. These are the few and simple themes which we wish now to explore and further develop through a thoughtful examination of the visible abyss.

THE VISIBLE ABYSS

One's first view of a photograph of the deep-sea floor is apt to be somewhat disappointing. In the first place, the photographs are visually confusing. The peculiar vertical angle traditionally used is so unfamiliar that at first one cannot distinguish highs from lows; usually there is nothing to indicate scale, and hardly ever is there any large or spectacular object or beast, save alone some soft rounded flocculent lumps and mounds of earth. One's dim memory demands: But where are all the monsters of the deep? Where are the rocky ribs of the earth? Where are those gems of purest ray serene, which the caves of ocean bear? Where are all the bizarre and romantic seascapes? Then, after this first shock of disappointment when one stops to adjust his eye and mind to the "nose to the ground perspective" and tries to understand what he sees, he will remember that the ocean is the earth's great cesspool, where the settling of sediments creates a vast soft blanket. Therefore, outlines are generally soft and relief low. But it is not conceivable that the scenery of two-thirds of the globe is completely dull and without interest, so we look at the photographs with greater care for detail. Again we are frustrated. One asks: Are all oceanographers stupid? Why can't they focus their cameras? Why don't they realize that the features are mostly too small to be recorded with the techniques they use? Why don't they take close-ups? Why have they standardized on such a frustrating angle and such a relatively great distance from the subect? Then, after looking through a few hundred exposures, we see a starfish. Our bearings are secured by this familiar animal, and perhaps, after looking through a few hundred more pictures,

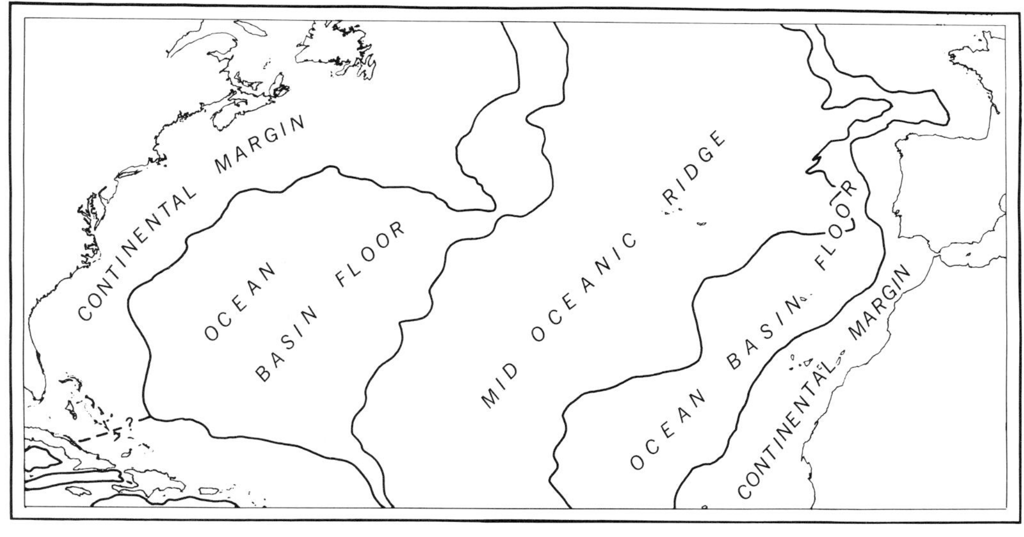

1.5 The three major physiographic divisions of the ocean floor.

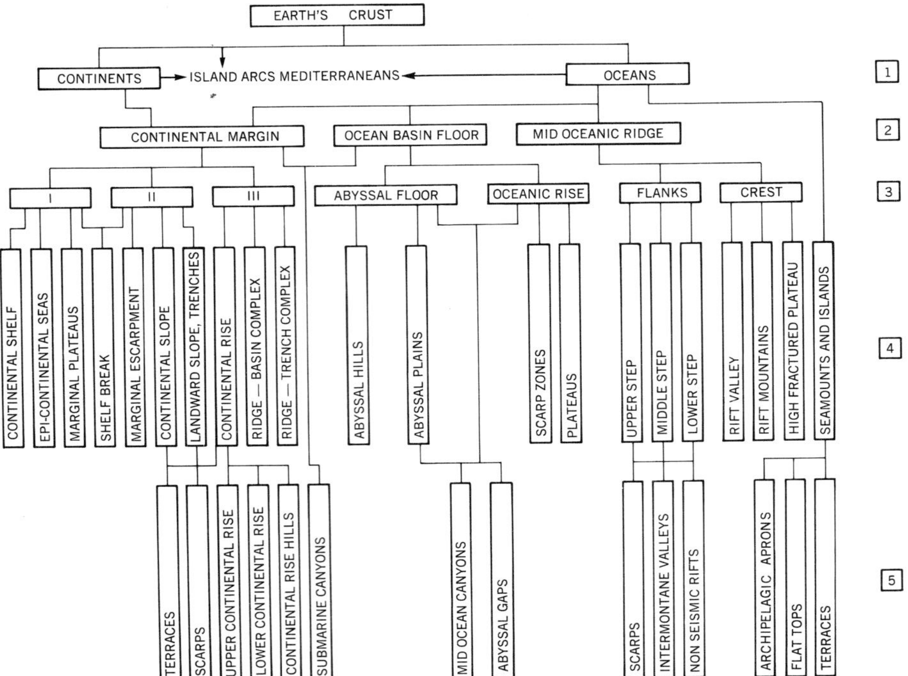

1.6 Outline of submarine topography. Line 1, first order features of the earth's crust; line 2, major topographic features of the ocean; line 3, categories of provinces and superprovinces; line 4, provinces; line 5, subprovinces and other important features. This system is used in all locality descriptions found in this book.

we begin to recognize tracks and trails. Now our curiosity is aroused and, despite the continuing frustration and frequent wonderments about our sanity, we look further through thousands upon thousands of photographs. We have an inexplicable desire to identify and understand the vague and vexing features of the sea floor.

The first underwater photographs were taken on the continental shelf through that thick greenish organic and inorganic soup which we call shelf water.[5] On the inner shelf, a white dinner plate, if held at a meter's distance, could rarely be seen and almost never could one see such a plate as far away as three meters. In the abyss, transparency increases and the camera can be placed farther from the scene, but even in the clearest water interpretable photographs cannot be taken from a distance of much more than five meters. The light is usually located close to the bottom and the camera farther away to cut down the path the light has to follow from the light source to the bottom and back to the camera. This reduces the amount of back scatter from suspended matter. Deep-sea cameras (1.8, 1.9, 1.10) are traditionally placed three or five meters

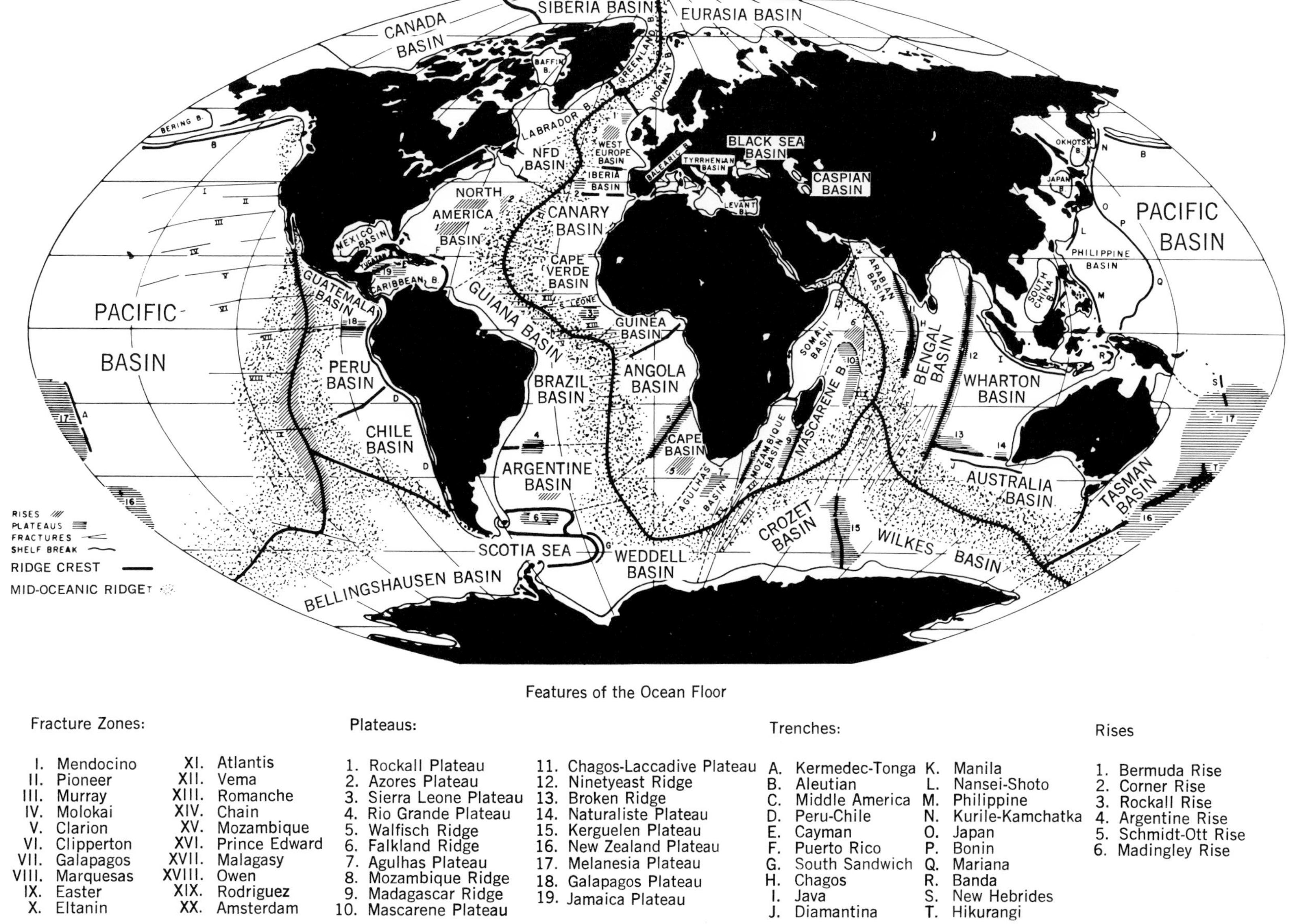
CANADA BASIN
SIBERIA BASIN
EURASIA BASIN
BAFFIN B.
GREENLAND B.
NORWAY B.
BERING B.
LABRADOR B.
NFD BASIN
WEST EUROPE BASIN
IBERIA BASIN
BALEARIC B.
TYRRHENIAN BASIN
BLACK SEA BASIN
CASPIAN BASIN
LEVANT B.
OKHOTSK B.
JAPAN B.
PACIFIC BASIN
PHILIPPINE BASIN
SOUTH CHINA B.
NORTH AMERICA BASIN
CANARY BASIN
MEXICO BASIN
YUCATAN
CARIBBEAN B.
CAPE VERDE BASIN
GUATEMALA BASIN
GUIANA BASIN
GUINEA BASIN
PACIFIC BASIN
PERU BASIN
BRAZIL BASIN
ANGOLA BASIN
ARABIAN BASIN
SOMALI BASIN
MASCARENE B.
BENGAL BASIN
WHARTON BASIN
CHILE BASIN
ARGENTINE BASIN
CAPE BASIN
AGULHAS BASIN
MOZAMBIQUE BASIN
AUSTRALIA BASIN
TASMAN BASIN
CROZET BASIN
WILKES BASIN
SCOTIA SEA
WEDDELL BASIN
BELLINGSHAUSEN BASIN
RISES
PLATEAUS
FRACTURES
SHELF BREAK
RIDGE CREST
MID-OCEANIC RIDGE
Features of the Ocean Floor
Fracture Zones:
I. Mendocino
II. Pioneer
III. Murray
IV. Molokai
V. Clarion
VI. Clipperton
VII. Galapagos
VIII. Marquesas
IX. Easter
X. Eltanin
XI. Atlantis
XII. Vema
XIII. Romanche
XIV. Chain
XV. Mozambique
XVI. Prince Edward
XVII. Malagasy
XVIII. Owen
XIX. Rodriguez
XX. Amsterdam
Plateaus:
1. Rockall Plateau
2. Azores Plateau
3. Sierra Leone Plateau
4. Rio Grande Plateau
5. Walfisch Ridge
6. Falkland Ridge
7. Agulhas Plateau
8. Mozambique Ridge
9. Madagascar Ridge
10. Mascarene Plateau
11. Chagos-Laccadive Plateau
12. Ninetyeast Ridge
13. Broken Ridge
14. Naturaliste Plateau
15. Kerguelen Plateau
16. New Zealand Plateau
17. Melanesia Plateau
18. Galapagos Plateau
19. Jamaica Plateau
Trenches:
A. Kermedec-Tonga
B. Aleutian
C. Middle America
D. Peru-Chile
E. Cayman
F. Puerto Rico
G. South Sandwich
H. Chagos
I. Java
J. Diamantina
K. Manila
L. Nansei-Shoto
M. Philippine
N. Kurile-Kamchatka
O. Japan
P. Bonin
Q. Mariana
R. Banda
S. New Hebrides
T. Hikurangi
Rises
1. Bermuda Rise
2. Corner Rise
3. Rockall Rise
4. Argentine Rise
5. Schmidt-Ott Rise
6. Madingley Rise

1.7 Main features of the bottom topography of the oceans.

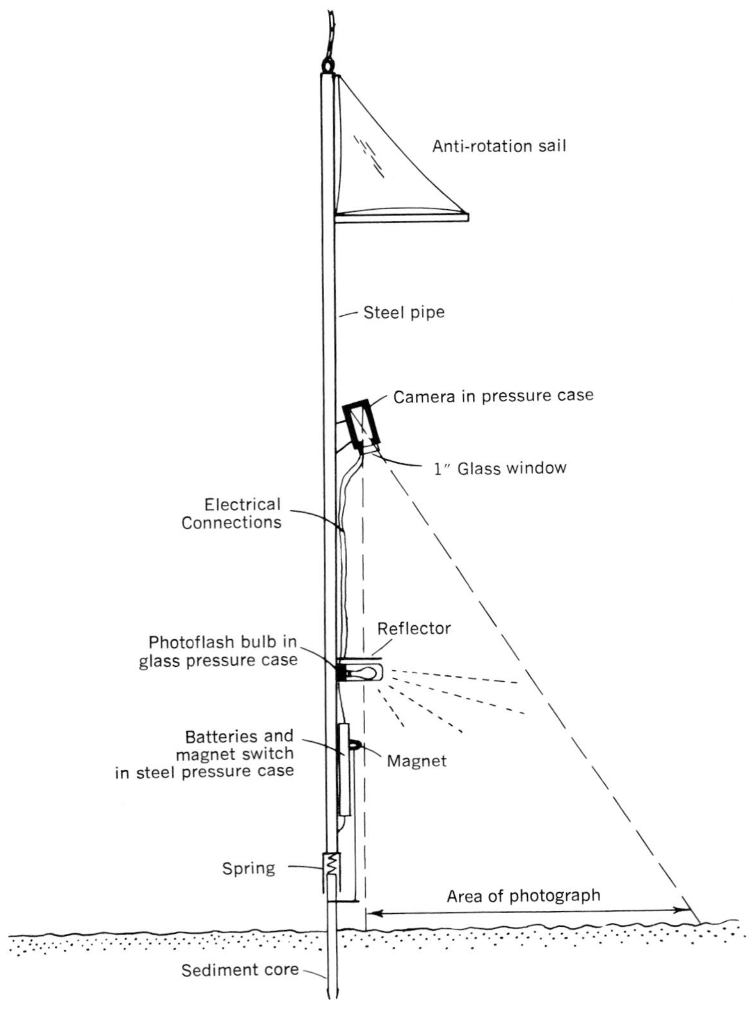

1.8 Early deep-sea camera. Several hundred photographs were obtained with cameras of this design between 1947 and 1952. A serious problem was shutter-light synchronization, for the duration of flash bulb illumination was sufficiently long that any motion of the camera would cause blurring. Various methods were employed to stabilize cameras including the asymmetrical sail, but with only limited success.

from the bottom, near the practical limit of useful photography. If fuller consideration were given to the subject matter, it would be more frequently realized that the standard lens-subject distance should be radically decreased, for the vast majority of the objects on the deep-sea floor are less than two centimeters in diameter. All the sediment is smaller than that, and thus most of the features within the area of each picture are too small to be resolved with the techniques normally employed. As a result, what in effect has been done is to explore the ocean for a few large and rare beasts, constructions, and features—such as ripples and scour marks. The vast majority of prints are rejected because they contain nothing that can be identified. Thus, in our study we have had to content ourselves with investigating those larger organisms and larger features which can, in fact, be seen with the techniques employed.

The area represented in each photograph may range from two to ten square meters (1.11), but the vast majority include about as much area as a bed sheet,[6] about six square meters. Until very recently, virtually all underwater cameras employed thirty-five millimeter film. This small negative size, even with the finest grain film available, imposes serious resolution limitations; an important need is the development and use of cameras which may attain greater resolution.

Since both the light source and the camera are generally attached relatively close together on a single supporting frame, shadows fall away from the observer.[7] Some people find difficulty in distinguishing highs from lows in near-vertical photographs with front lighting. If you have this trouble, turn the photograph upside down for a moment so that the shadows appear to fall toward you, and you can become adjusted to the scene with more conventional back lighting. In viewing photographs in this manner, however, you should have the feeling that you are looking at a ceiling rather than the floor of the ocean. Having secured your bearings, turn the photograph right side up and usually, if not always, a correct impression of shadows and depressions will be preserved.

"STAND BY TO LOWER AWAY"

A two-hundred-pound pressure-proof camera swings over the ship's rail, suspended from the end of a pencil-thin steel wire. The scientist makes his final check and then gives the order, "Lower away." The winch operator gradually speeds his machine until the camera is descending toward the abyssal plain at 100 meters per minute. The camera carries with it a water sampler, a sediment sampler, a current meter, a transparency meter, and a temperature recorder. After nearly an hour has passed the scientist gives further orders, "Stop and weigh at 5000 meters." The cable tension is read from the sensitive gauge and recorded in

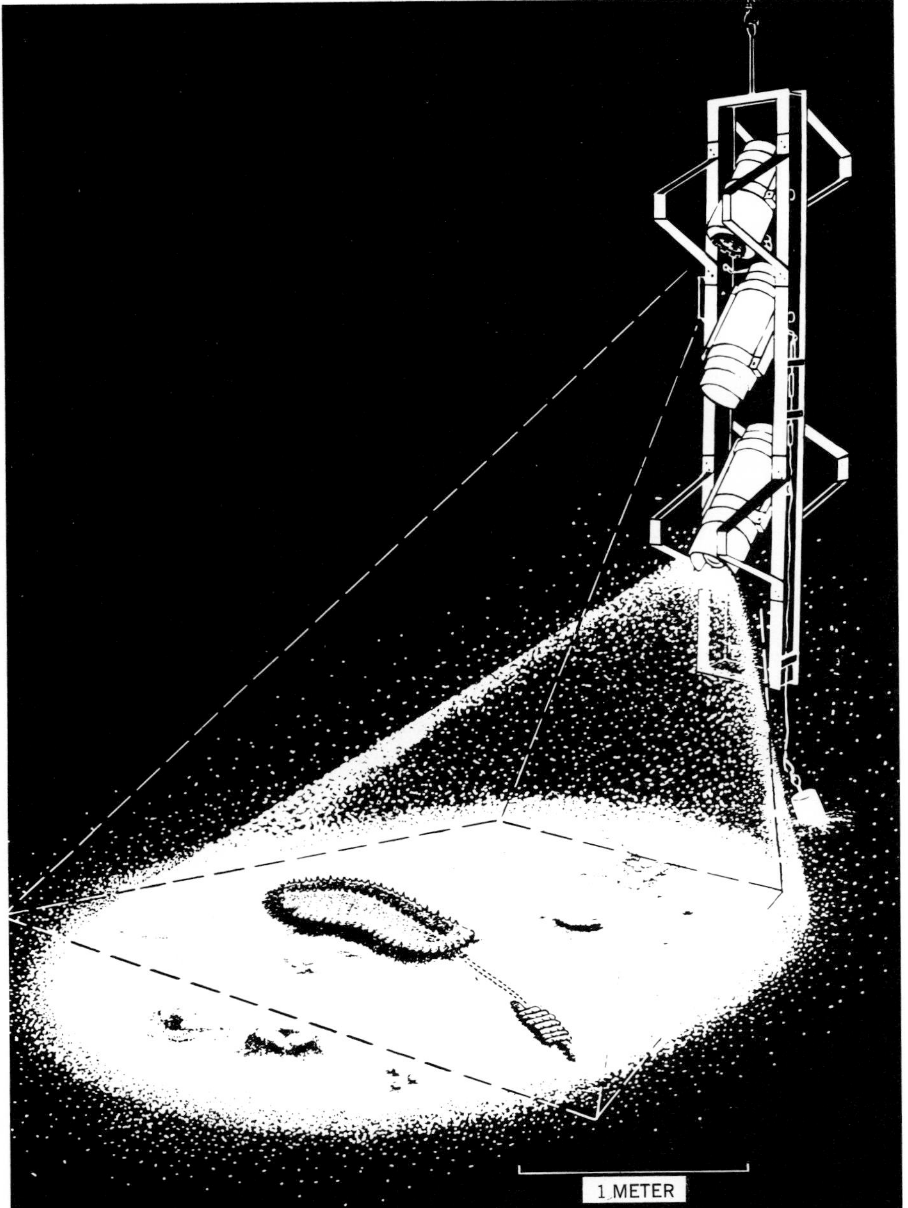

1.9 Deep-sea camera. Most of the photographs reproduced in this book were taken with cameras of this design. The upper pressure case contains a shutterless camera, the lower pressure case contains an electronic flash unit. The trigger weight is attached by a thin flexible wire to a switch located on the side of the camera frame. When the weight is released, the switch closes, triggering the electronic flash. This camera may be used with or without a sonic pinger. In this drawing, a pinger unit, allowing constant position control, is shown between the camera and light source. This camera and light source together, provided with sufficient power to take thirty photographs at a repetition rate of thirty seconds, weigh 150 pounds in water.[8]

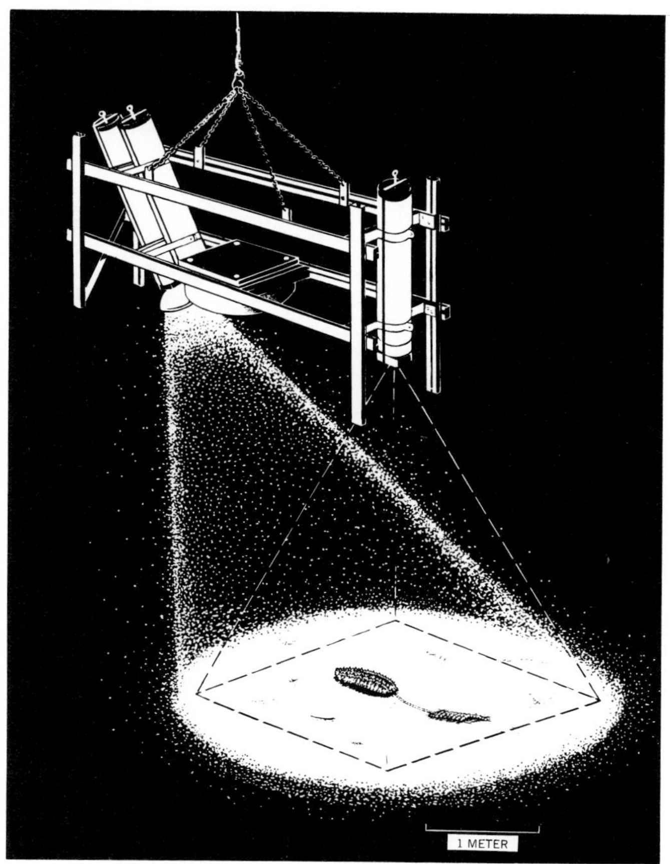

1.10 Another deep-sea camera. The electronic flash unit and the pinger unit are attached together at the left side. The pinger transducer is located in the middle, and the camera pointed vertically down is at the right side. Photographs are taken each ten seconds as the operator monitoring the ping on a suitable device attempts to keep the camera at a proper distance from the sea floor.[8]

a notebook. The scientist orders, "Lower at 50 meters per minute." His eyes glued to the tension gauge, he patiently waits for an indication of a contact with the sea floor. The tension needle makes a subtle motion, simultaneously he and the winch operator shout, "Hit." A kibitzing messman says, "I didn't see anything." The scientist insists, "Bring her up 10 meters." Someone says, "that hit was at fifty-two forty-six meters." Then for thirty minutes, as the ship slowly drifts through the water, the camera is repeatedly raised a few meters and then again lowered to the sea floor. Each time that the tension meter makes a characteristic wiggle the camera has touched the sea floor and flashed a picture of the bottom.[8] The time, wire out, and tension at each of the twenty hits is carefully recorded. The scientist finally declares, "That makes a station,[9] bring her

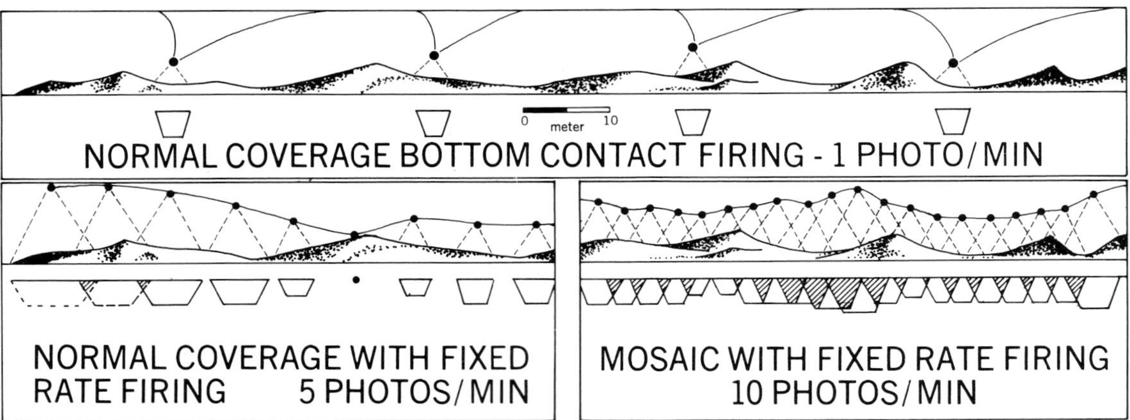

1.11 Photographic sampling of the sea floor. Two types of triggering are employed. In one case (U) a weight hanging at a set distance beneath the camera activates the electronic flash (1.9). This procedure produces photographs of nearly constant area. In another mode of operation the lights are flashed at fixed intervals and the operator by monitoring the signals sent by sonic pinger attempts to position the camera in range with the bottom (1.10). This method produces a series of photographs of constantly varying area, some of which do not show the bottom (LL, LR).

up." After another hour the camera nears the surface. Hands line the rail waiting for the first sign of the camera. The winchman calls out, "Ten meters to go"; a man at the rail shouts, "In sight," and the scientists scramble to make another check and to bring the heavy camera aboard.

After it is landed and secured on deck, the camera is unloaded, the film rushed to the dark room and developed; and in another half hour the scientist is standing in the dark room peering at the wet negative. His first interest is technical: "Did the film transport? Did the light flash? Was the compass in the picture? Was the film properly developed? What corrections must be made before the next lowering?" Then when these questions are satisfactorily answered he looks at the subject matter. "Are there ripple marks? Did we get any animals? What is the direction of the bottom current? How soon do we need to take the next picture?" The negative is scribed with the letters E7-67-2, the identifying station number. A few test prints are made for shipboard study and the negatives filed away. Meanwhile the camera is reloaded with film, the batteries are replaced, and pressure seals, which may need to withstand up to one thousand times more pressure than at the surface, are checked. The cameraman reports to the chief scientist: "Camera is ready for the next

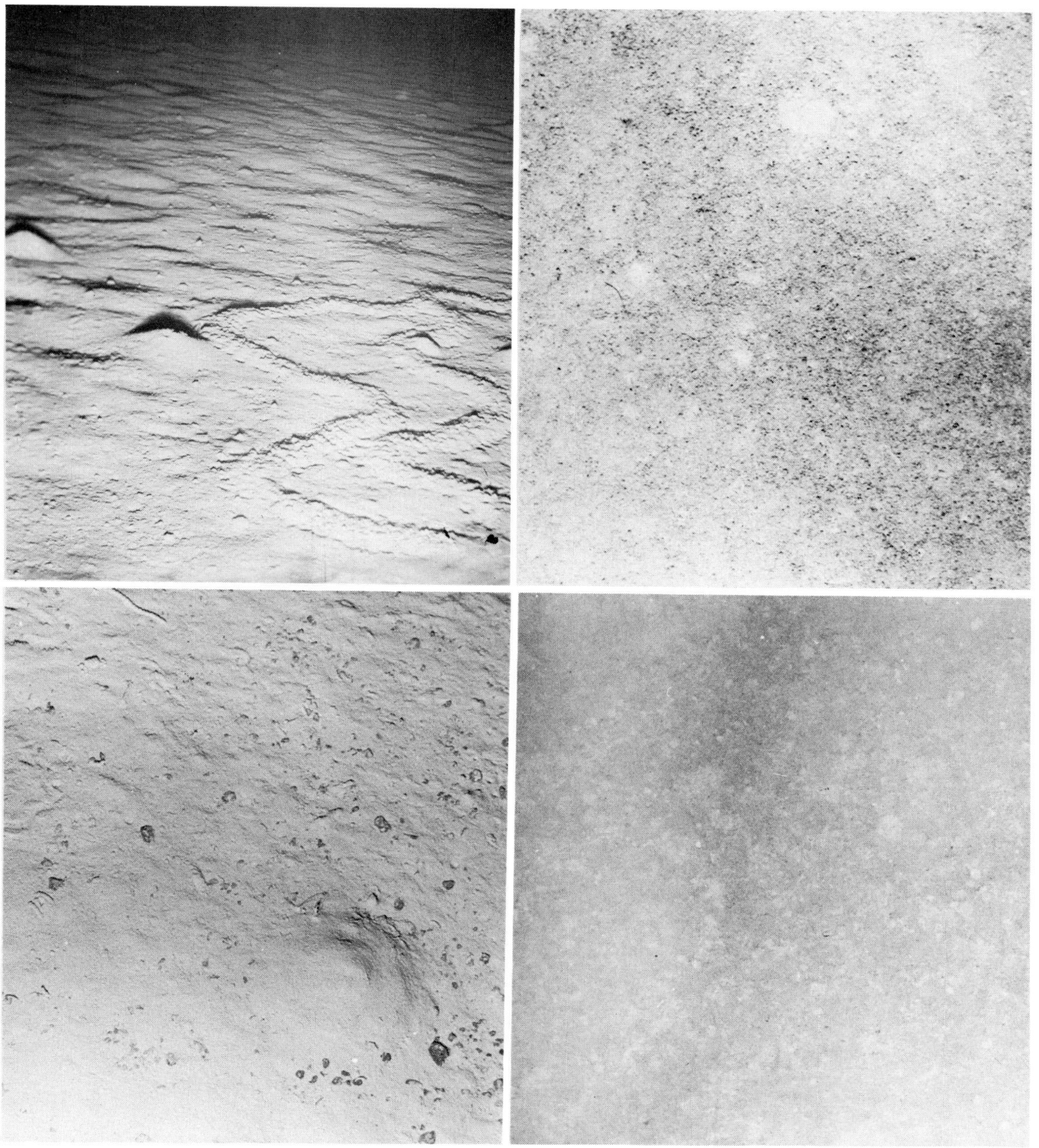

1.12 Oblique photographs (Left) are easiest to interpret. Low angle oblique photographs (UL) give the best resolution of subtle sea floor features. Standard oblique (LL) are less desirable due to lack of shadows. Vertical close-up photos (UR) or standard vertical photos (LR) are extremely difficult to interpret.

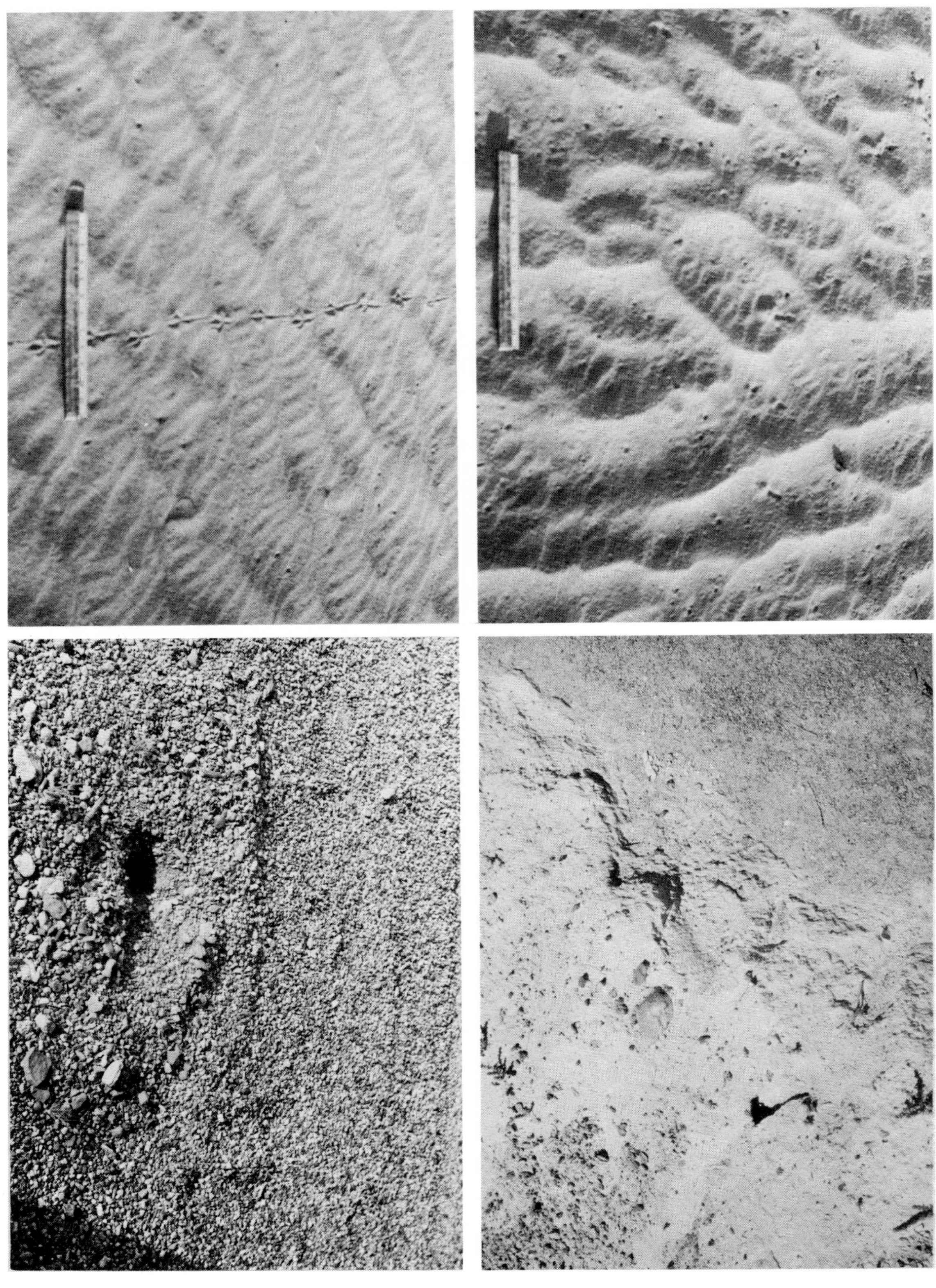

station." The chief scientist replies, "We will heave to and lower at 0300 on the flank of the Outer Ridge to check for bottom current direction. Better get an hour's sleep."

The watch, shaking the groggy scientist, says, "Station in ten minutes." As the ship slows down and stops, the camera is swung out over the rail and the scientist orders again: "Stand by to lower away."

Only recently have the authors joined the aquanauts in direct visual observation of the deep-sea floor (1.14). Neither of us will ever forget the thrill of our first dives to the abyss. Robert Dill arranged that one of us accompany him on a 1200 meter dive in *Deep Star* 4000 to the floor of La Jolla Submarine Canyon. The descent to the depths of the sea is a visually rewarding and exciting experience. With the floodlights off, a multitude of tiny bioluminescent sparks reveal the glowing drifting life which with the floodlights on becomes fuzzy snow. The density of this life is as unbelievable as the material itself is unresolvable by eye or camera. Despite the enormous quantity of material represented by the soup, there is, in fact, little in mid-depths which can be recorded on film save occasional fish and jellyfish. As the sea floor is approached, the snow becomes finer, and then in one glorious second the sea floor comes brilliantly into view. Anyone will find this sight tremendously exciting; but to one who has studied for twenty years in preparation, this is a breathtaking experience of a lifetime. We were able to look and poke away at the mysterious sea floor which for two decades we had seen only in fuzzy photos. At last we could feast our eyes on the oozy bed. We could see if the animals moved, what tracks they made, and could sometimes determine if the burrows were inhabited.

Much of the fuzzy background recorded by normal remote cameras turns out to be resolvable into identifiable features and creatures, but as might have been expected, even with bright lights and our eyes glued to the porthole a mere eighteen inches off the bottom, the majority of the features are still nondescript. Certainly one could use a huge hand lens to examine still more closely the enigmatic small features of the sea floor. One's curiosity is insatiable, and the answers bring new questions requiring new dives and new equipment. Angles, distances, and light intensity

◁ 1.13 The land above the sea. These views of the terrestrial surface taken at a similar angle to normal deep-sea photographs and from a point even closer to the subject clearly demonstrate the difficulty of identifying even familiar features in near-vertical photographs. It is not immediately obvious which is the crest and which the trough of the ripple marks (UL, UR), and the prairie-dog hole (LL) at first looks like a black lump, or object lying on the ground. The rock outcrop (LR) could as well be clay, and its composition remains a mystery.

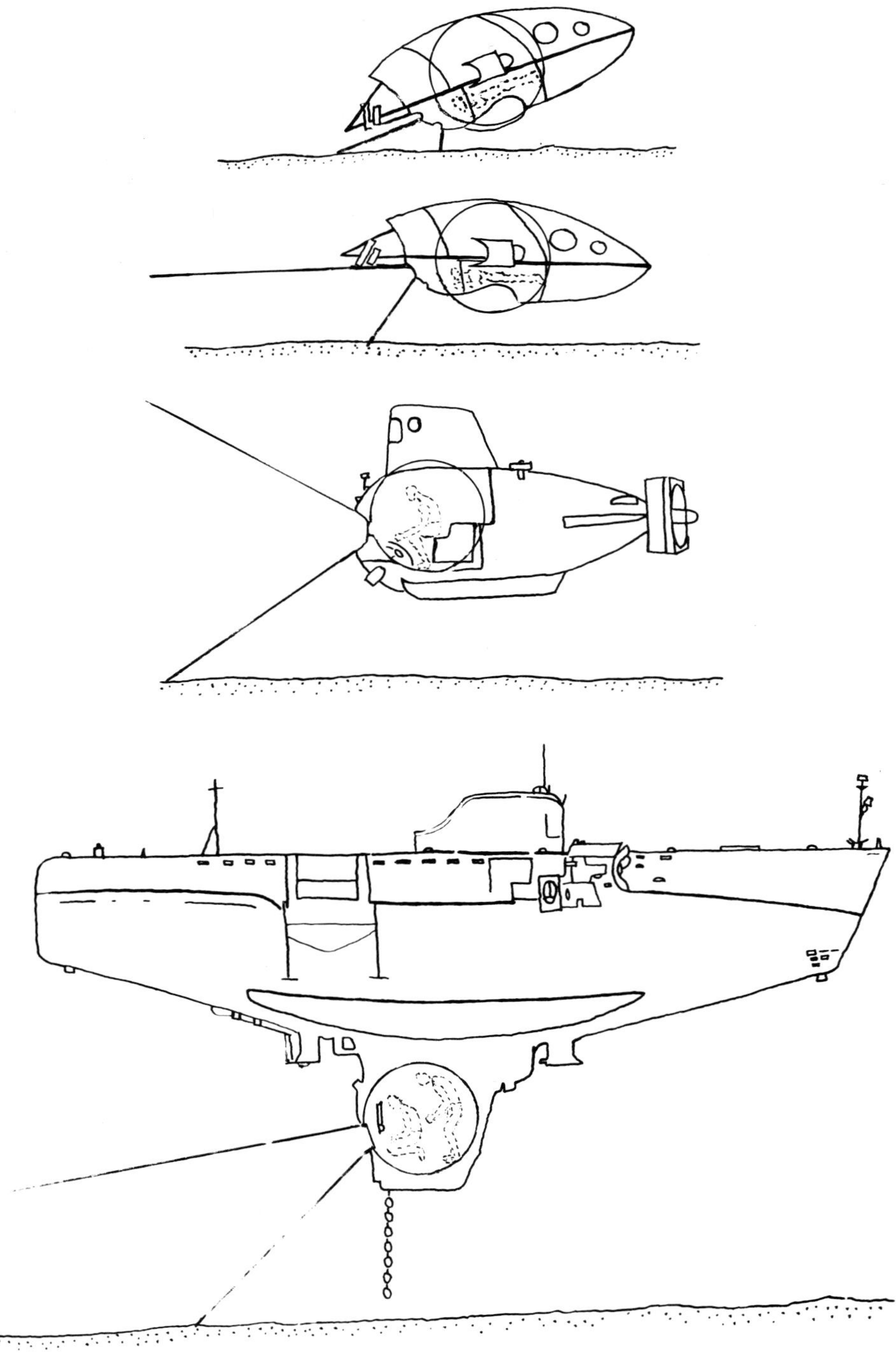

1.14 The deep submersibles such as *Deep Star 4000, Alvin, Archimède,* and their successors will allow man to examine the face of the deep. "Wouldst thou . . . learn the secrets of the sea? Only those who brave its dangers comprehend its mysteries." LONGFELLOW

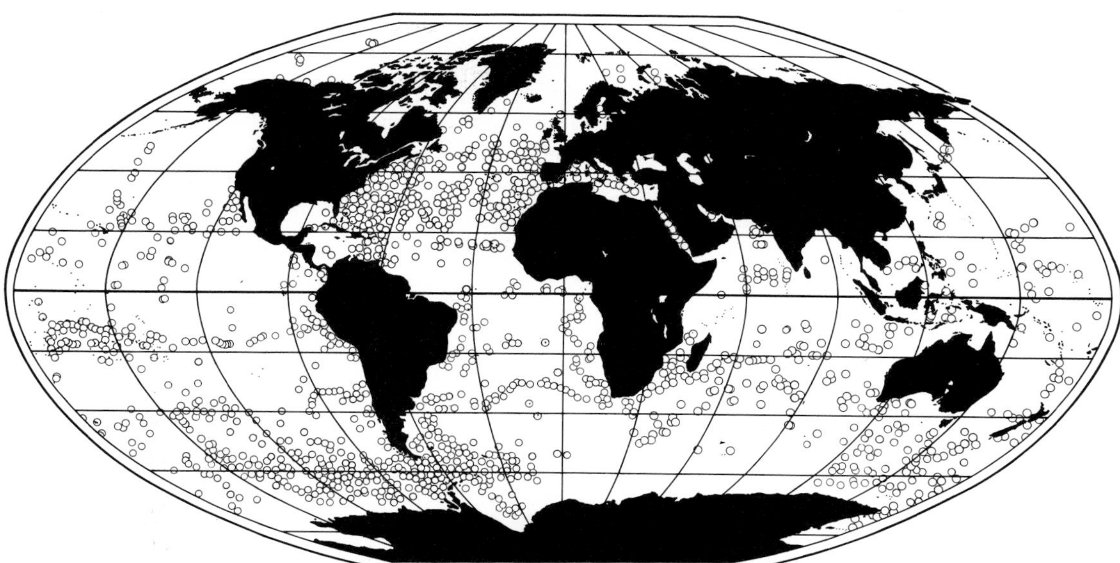

1.15 World distribution of abyssal photographs. Photographs from each of the more than 2000 locations indicated on this map have been studied by the authors. Several hundred thousand photographs have now been taken of the sea floor on the continental slope, continental rise, abyssal plain, seamounts, island slopes, Mid-Oceanic Ridge, in the floors of trenches, in straits, and in other diverse environments. The ocean floor has been photographed from the North Pole to the Antarctic continent and in all oceans and seas. Photographs have been taken beneath the marine deserts as well as beneath highly productive surface waters.

are easily and almost infinitely variable; but the favored position is a low oblique with the subject less than three feet away from eager eyes and camera.

The now obsolete and little-used deep-diving bathyscaphes are being replaced by more versatile devices which can cruise along the bottom, allowing the observer to examine and sample the sea floor.[10] As yet, these devices cannot descend below 2500 meters, and the scenery of the vast abyss is known only from remote photography[11] (1.15).

REFERENCES AND NOTES

1. Since animals seem more sensitive to temperature than to pressure, in a biological sense the boundary of the abyss varies between 1000 and 3000 meters, being roughly coincident with the four degree isotherm.
2. See Appendix 1 (page 616).
3. Of the 510 million square kilometers of the earth's surface 278 million lie in the abyss, below a depth of 3000 meters. All the oceans and seas comprise 361 million square kilometers and only 5 million lie below 6000 meters.

4. The fundamental morphology of the ocean floor, based on a study of continuously recorded echo profiles is summarized by: B. C. Heezen and H. W. Menard, 1963. Topography of the deep-sea floor. In: M. N. Hill (Editor), *The Sea.* Wiley, New York, 3:233-81; B. C. Heezen, M. Tharp, and M. Ewing, 1959. The floors of the Oceans, I. *Geol. Soc. Am., Spec. Paper 65,* 122 pp.; H. W. Menard. 1964. *Marine Geology of the Pacific.* McGraw-Hill, New York, 271 pp.; and G. B. Udintsev, G. V. Agapova, A. F. Bereznev, L. Ya. Boudanova, L. K. Zatonskiy, N. L. Zenkevitch, A. G. Ivanov, V. F. Kanaiev, I. P. Koutcherov, N. I. Larina, N. A. Marova, V. Mineiev, and E. I. Rantskiy, 1963. The new bathymetric map of the Pacific. *Okeanolog. Issled., Rez. Issled., Progr. Mezhd. Geofiz. Goda, Mezhd. Geofiz. Kom., Presidiume, Akad. Nauk, S.S.S.R.,* 9:60-101.

5. The first photographs of the sea floor were taken of the sunlit floor of the Mediterranean (L. Boutan. 1893. La photographie sous-marine. *Archives de la Zoologic Experimental,* 3(1):281-324). Although the present book is concerned exclusively with the abyss, we can suggest the following references to those readers seeking information on shallow water photography: H. Schenck, Jr. and H. Kendall. 1957. *Underwater Photography.* Cornell Maritime Press, Cambridge, Maryland, 160 pp.; J. Y. Cousteau and J. Dugan. 1963. *The Living Sea.* Harper, New York, 325 pp.; and Anon., 1968. Bibliography on underwater photography and photogrammetry. *Eastman Kodak Co., Pamphlet,* P124:23 pp.

6. Unless otherwise indicated, photographs in this book are reproduced at approximately 3 to 6 per cent of natural scale. The trimmed photographs are in general at the same scale as those reproduced in full.

7. Deep-sea cameras have traditionally been designed to take nearly vertical photographs (1.12). This procedure suppresses or eliminates the sense of relief and makes it difficult to study the texture of the bottom (1.13). Only on rare occasions have oblique photographs been made on purpose; however, occasionally a camera accidentally falls over and obtains beautiful low-oblique pictures.

8. Ocean-bottom photography was started about thirty years ago at the Woods Hole Oceanographic Institution by a group led by Maurice Ewing (M. Ewing, A. C. Vine, and J. L. Worzel, 1946. Photography of the Ocean Bottom. *J. Opt. Soc. Am.* 36: 307-321). The cameras developed by the group photograph the sea floor at a fixed distance when triggered by contact with the bottom. (E. M. Thorndike. 1959. Deep-sea cameras of the Lamont Observatory. *Deep-Sea Res.,* 5:234-37). Most of the photographs in this book were obtained with cameras of the Thorndike design, manufactured by Alpine Geophysical Associates. Both A. S. Laughton (in the United Kingdom) and N. L. Zenkevitch (in the U.S.S.R.) have built somewhat similar cameras (N. L. Zenkevitch. 1959. Automatic photography in great depths. *Oceanologia e Limnologia Sinica* (in Chinese), 2:16-25).

Professor H. E. Edgerton designed, at the Massachusetts Institute of Technology, cameras and light sources of the type illustrated in Fig. 1.10, which operate remotely at a fixed time interval (H. E. Edgerton. 1963. Underwater photography. In: M. N. Hill (Editor), *The Sea.* Wiley, New York, 3:473-75). Edgerton's cameras are commercially manufactured by EG&G, Inc. The photographs in this volume, obtained from R.V. *Chain,* C.S. *Long Lines,* C.S. *Stanley Angwin,* C.S.S. *Hudson,* R.V. *Atlantis,* and certain other research vessels, were taken with such apparatus.

9. Each camera station normally produces from 15 to 50 individual samples of the form of the bottom distributed along a line a few meters to a few thousand meters in length.

10. In August 1953, the first deep-diving dirigible (FNRS-3) descended 4000 meters to the floor of the Atlantic (G. Houot and P. Willm. 1955. *2000 Fathoms Down.* Dutton, New York, 249 pp.). In 1960 (J. Picard and R. S. Dietz, *Seven Miles Down.* Putnam, New York, 1961, 249 pp.) the floor of the deepest trench was observed. As important as these pioneer efforts were, little effective scientific work was accomplished. It was not until 1966 that efficient vehicles for the direct observations of the sea floor were available. *Deep Star 4000, Aluminaut,* and *Alvin* all allowed exploration of the continental shelf and upper continental slope (C. W. Covey (Editor). 1968. Oceanographic ships of the world–Submersibles. In: *UnderSea Technology, Handbook Directory.* Compass, Arlington, Va., pp. 1333-36). Submersibles for the visual exploration of the abyss were not available when this book was completed.

11. J. B. Hersey (Editor). 1967. Deep sea photography. *The Johns Hopkins Oceanographic Studies,* 3:310 pp. Dr. Hersey has been active in deep-sea-bottom photography since its early days. The most detailed account of the history, techniques, and applications of deep-sea photography is found in this well illustrated volume.

48°38′N 28°48′W

2.1 Life on the Mid-Atlantic Ridge. Sponges and gorgonians grow attached to rock outcrops near the crest of this great mountain range, 2629 m.

2
Abyssal Portraits

As we descend deeper and deeper . . . the inhabitants (of the sea) become more and more modified, and fewer and fewer, indicating our approach towards an abyss where life is extinguished or exhibits but a few sparks to mark its lingering presence.—It is in the exploration of this vast deep-sea region that the finest field for submarine discovery yet remains.

EDWARD FORBES, 1851

It is now time for us to turn away from the lush gardens and fertile pastures of the sun-nurtured sea and begin our visual journey to the underlying vast, black, and frigid watery Hades. We will first search through this nearly barren abyss for those few sparks of life which have somehow found a way to survive in a dark, bitter-cold environment.[1] Our principal interest will be the visual effects that the various animals may have on the sea floor. The lowly sessile forms which depend on currents to carry in food and carry away their waste contribute little, save their own decorative shapes, but the more advanced mobile beasts, particularly the larger ones, produce through their activities most of what can be seen by the eye on two-thirds of the planet (2.1, 2.2, 2.3). The animals living on the abyssal floor are rarely as large as a robin and only a few are as large as a mouse (Table 2.1). In fact, most deep-sea creatures are smaller than honeybees and thus are far too small to be seen in normal photographs. For example, clams, worms, and crustaceans are extremely common forms brought up in trawls with meshes finer than one-quarter millimeter, but only a few of these are large enough to be seen in photographs.

Of the many major groups of marine organisms, only slightly more than three dozen have abyssal representatives.[2] Nearly all of these groups include at least a few species large enough to be seen. However, most of the worms, crustaceans, brachiopods, and molluscs lie near or below the lower size limit for recognition and usually cannot be seen, or, if seen, cannot be identified. Only the sponges, fans, pens, anemones, corals, mosses, lilies, starfish, brittle stars, urchins, cucumbers, squid and octopuses, crabs, spiders, acorn worms, eels, squirts, and fish include a number of large identifiable forms.

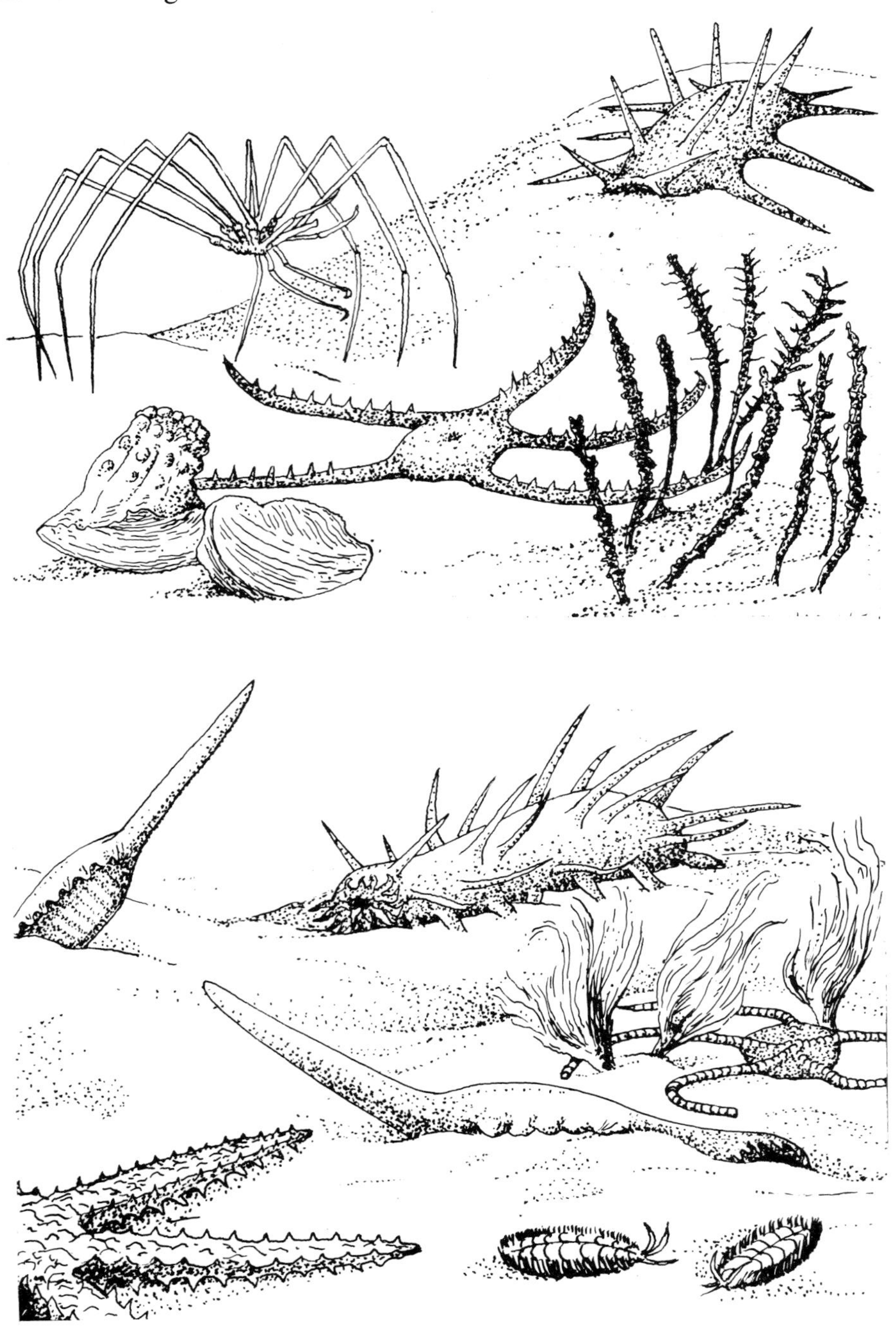

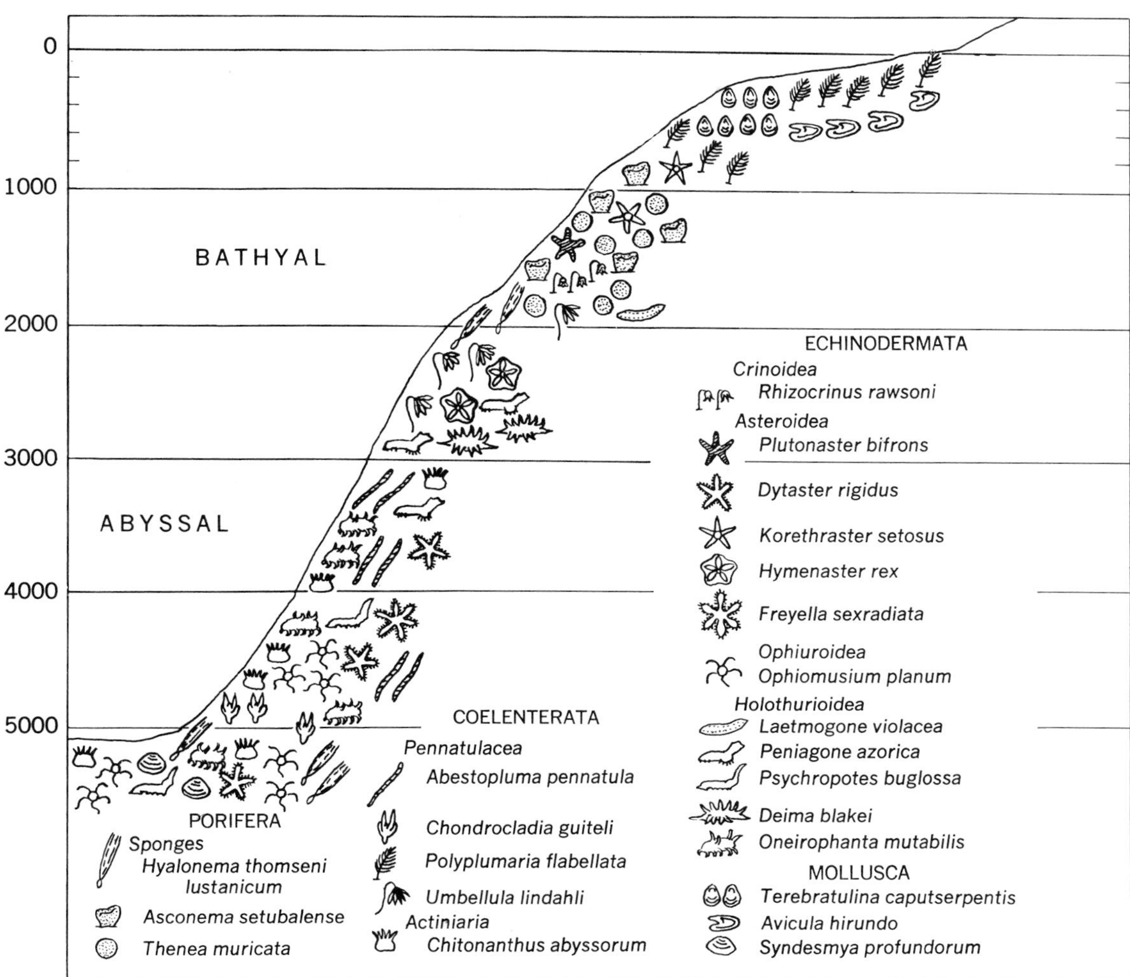

2.3 The descent into the abyss. This profile summarizes the results of trawling on the Atlantic continental margin of Europe. The echinoderms are clearly the dominant group of large animals.

"The animals inhabiting the depths of the sea are strange to all but a few specialists and are known only by Latin names of which even most zoologists are ignorant." ALEXANDER AGASSIZ

◁ 2.2 The predicted abyssal scene. These remarkably accurate sketches were prepared entirely on the basis of deep-sea trawlings before the first abyssal photographs of animal life were taken. The density of life is, however, misleading for rarely are two large organisms photographed in the same picture. (A) The animals between 2000 and 4000 meters: UL, sea spider; UR, sea cucumber; LL, bivalves, one with attached sea anemone; C, starfish; LR, stalked sponge. (B) The animals below 5000 meters on the continental margin of Europe: UL, UR, C, sea cucumbers; R, sponges and brittle star; LL, starfish; RC, bristle worms.

Table 2.1 Large deep-sea animals.

MARINE ANIMALS*																
				ABYSSAL ANIMALS												
				Captured						Photographed						
	PHYLUM A. SUBPHYLUM SUPERCLASS 1. CLASS I. Subclass (a) Order	Non-parasitic	> 200 meters	> 5000 meters	> 1 centimeter	> 10 centimeters	> 20 centimeters	Common	Abundant	Photographed	5-10 photos	> 10 photos	> 50 photos	Major Groups		
	PROTOZOA	■	■												Sponges	MOST ARE SESSILE
	PORIFERA, Sponges	■	■	■	■	■	■	■		■	■	■				
COELENTERATA	1. HYDROZOA, Hydroids	■	■	■	■	■	■			■					COELENTERATES	
COELENTERATA	2. SCYPHOZOA, Jellyfishes	■	■	■	■	■										
3. ANTHOZOA, I. ALCYONARIA	(a) Stolonifera	■														
3. ANTHOZOA, I. ALCYONARIA	(b) Telestacea	■														
3. ANTHOZOA, I. ALCYONARIA	(c) Alcyonacea	■														
3. ANTHOZOA, I. ALCYONARIA	(d) Coenothecalia	■														
3. ANTHOZOA, I. ALCYONARIA	(e) Gorgonacea	■	■	■	■	■	■	■		■	■			Gorgonians		
3. ANTHOZOA, I. ALCYONARIA	(f) Pennatulacea	■	■	■	■	■	■	■		■	■	■		Pennatulids		
3. ANTHOZOA, II. ZOANTHARIA	(a) Actinaria, Sea Anemones	■	■	■	■	■	■	■		■	■	■		Actinarians		
3. ANTHOZOA, II. ZOANTHARIA	(b) Madreporaria, Stony Coral	■														
3. ANTHOZOA, II. ZOANTHARIA	(c) Zoanthidea	■														
3. ANTHOZOA, II. ZOANTHARIA	(d) Antipatharia, Black Coral	■	■	■	■	■	■	■		■				Antipatharians		
3. ANTHOZOA, II. ZOANTHARIA	(e) Ceriantharia	■	■	■	■	■										
	CTENOPHORA, Comb Jellies	■	■													
	NEMERTINEA and ACANTHOCEPHALA	■	■	■	■	■	■	■								
	BRYOZOA	■	■	■	■	■	■			■						
	PHORONIDEA	■														
	BRACHIOPODA	■	■	■	■											
ECHINODERMATA	1. CRINOIDEA, Sea Lilies	■	■	■	■	■	■	■		■	■	■		Crinoids	ECHINODERMS	MOST ARE MOBILE
ECHINODERMATA	2. ASTEROIDEA, Starfishes	■	■	■	■	■	■	■		■	■	■		Asteroids		
ECHINODERMATA	3. OPHIUROIDEA, Brittle Stars	■	■	■	■	■	■	■	■	■	■	■	■	Ophiuroids		
ECHINODERMATA	4. ECHINOIDEA, Sea Urchins	■	■	■	■	■	■	■	■	■	■	■	■	Echinoids		
ECHINODERMATA	5. HOLOTHURIOIDEA, Sea Cucumbers	■	■	■	■	■	■	■	■	■	■	■	■	Holothurians		
	CHAETOGNATHA, Arrow Worms	■														
MOLLUSCA	1. MONOPLACOPHORA	■	■	■	■	■									MOLLUSCS	
MOLLUSCA	2. AMPHINEURA	■	■	■	■	■										
MOLLUSCA	3. SCAPHOPODA, Tooth Shells	■	■	■	■	■										
MOLLUSCA	4. GASTROPODA, Snails, Slugs	■	■	■	■	■										
MOLLUSCA	5. PELECYPODA, Bivalves	■	■	■	■	■										
MOLLUSCA	6. CEPHALOPODA, Squids, Octopuses	■	■	■	■	■	■			■				Cephalopods		
ANNELIDA	1. ARCHIANELLIDA	■													ANNELIDS	
ANNELIDA	2. POLYCHAETA, Sand Worms	■	■	■	■	■	■	■	■	■	■	■	■	Polychaets		
	SIPUNCULOIDEA, Peanut Worms	■	■	■	■	■	■									
	PRIAPULOIDEA	■	■	■	■	■										
	ECHIUROIDEA	■	■	■	■	■	■									
ARTHROPODA, 1. CRUSTACEA	I. Branchiopoda	■	■												ARTHROPODS	
ARTHROPODA, 1. CRUSTACEA	II. Ostracoda	■	■	■												
ARTHROPODA, 1. CRUSTACEA	III. Copepoda	■	■	■												
ARTHROPODA, 1. CRUSTACEA	IV. Cirripedia, Barnacles	■	■	■	■	■										
ARTHROPODA, 1. CRUSTACEA, V. Malacostraca	(a) Mysidacea	■	■	■	■	■										
ARTHROPODA, 1. CRUSTACEA, V. Malacostraca	(b) Cumacea	■	■	■												
ARTHROPODA, 1. CRUSTACEA, V. Malacostraca	(c) Tanaidacea	■	■	■												
ARTHROPODA, 1. CRUSTACEA, V. Malacostraca	(d) Isopoda	■	■	■	■			■		■				Isopods		
ARTHROPODA, 1. CRUSTACEA, V. Malacostraca	(e) Amphipoda	■	■	■												
ARTHROPODA, 1. CRUSTACEA, V. Malacostraca	(f) Stomatopoda	■														
ARTHROPODA, 1. CRUSTACEA, V. Malacostraca	(g) Euphausiacea	■	■	■	■											
ARTHROPODA, 1. CRUSTACEA, V. Malacostraca	(h) Decapoda	■	■	■	■	■	■			■				Decapods		
ARTHROPODA	2. ARACHNOIDEA, (Sea Spiders)	■	■	■	■	■	■			■				Arachnoids		
CHORDATA	A. POGONOPHORA	■	■	■	■	■	■			■						
CHORDATA	B. HEMICHORDATA	■	■	■	■	■	■			■				Hemichordates	CHORDATES	
CHORDATA	C. CEPHALOCHORDATA	■														
CHORDATA	D. AGNATHA	■	■	■	■	■										
CHORDATA	E. TUNICATA, 1. ASCIDIACEA	■	■	■	■	■				■				Tunicates		
CHORDATA	F. PISCES, (Fish)	■	■	■	■	■	■	■		■	■	■	■	Fish		
CHORDATA	G. TETRAPODA, 1. MAMMALIA (Whales)	■	■	■	■	■										

*Note: Read this key from left to right. Thus if an organism, regardless of size, is not found in deep water it is eliminated from subsequent columns.

Members of all nineteen of these major groups have been photographed and representative illustrations of each are included in this chapter. In addition, certain exceptionally large or distinctive worms, crustaceans, and molluscs have been identified and are also illustrated. Thus, large members of virtually all the classes and orders brought up from the abyssal depth in trawls have been photographed in their natural habitat.

Although the abyssal fauna is not fundamentally different from that of other cold-water regions of the sea, it does possess a few peculiarities which are apparently related to life on a dark, calm mud bottom. Creatures of the abyss tend to be uniformally colored in shades of gray and black. Many are delicately built. Some possess long slender legs, and the sessile animals often have relatively long stalks to raise them above the mud. Many crustaceans and fish are blind and some of the latter have developed especially long tactile fins. Another peculiarity of abyssal life is that with increasing depth the number of animals deriving their nourishment from the ooze, or filtering it from the water, increases as the number of scavengers and carnivores decreases. The density of life is extremly low (2.4). Whereas 5000 grams of living organisms can be found on a square meter of inshore sea floor and 200 grams might be recovered from a square meter of the continental shelf, in the mid-ocean abyss the amount drops to one milligram per square meter and the seascape appears stark and barren.

In the tens of thousands of photographs which have been taken in the water between the sunlit zone and the abyssal floor, hardly anything can

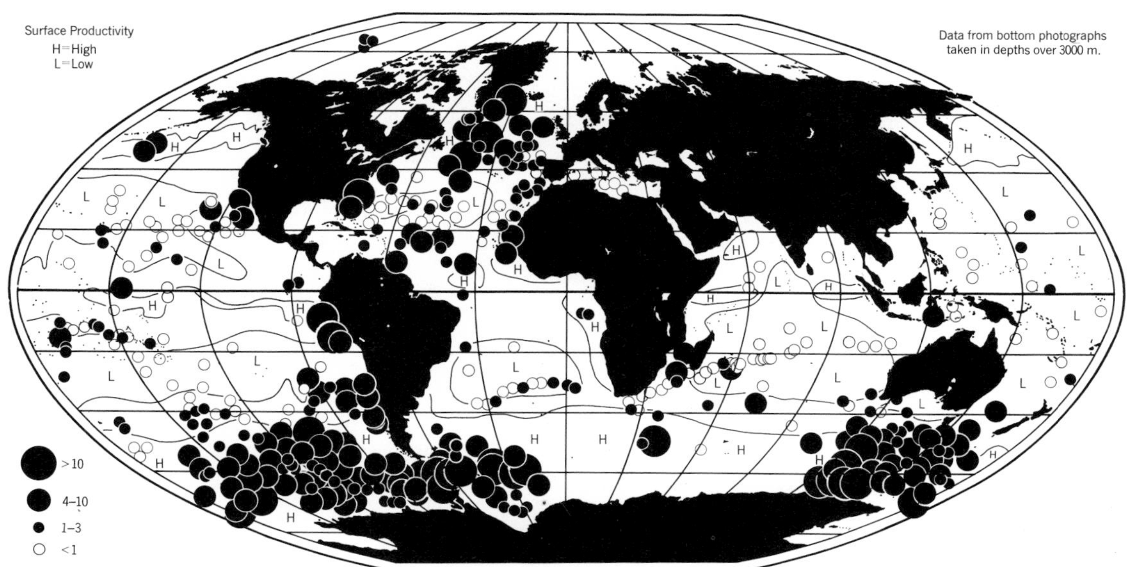

2.4 Density of large visible bottom-living organisms. Number of animals photographed for 10 square meters of the sea floor. Estimate based on 10 to 20 photographs per point. Life is sparse beneath the temperate deserts but abundant beneath the polar and coastal waters which support a large surface population.

be identified. Except for an occasional jellyfish, squid, or fish, the remainder consists of billions of fuzzy dots, some luminescent, some not, which are referred to as "snow" by the aquanauts. The vast majority of the animals that are visible or at least photographable in the abyss resides on the sea floor.

LIVING SCREENS

> *Food is brought to them, waste is taken away. For them in their eternal abyss, with its time-like stream, there is no hurry, there is no return. Such an organism becomes a mere living screen between the used half of the universe and the unused half—a moment of active metabolism between the unknown future and the exhausted past.*
>
> GEORGE BIDDER

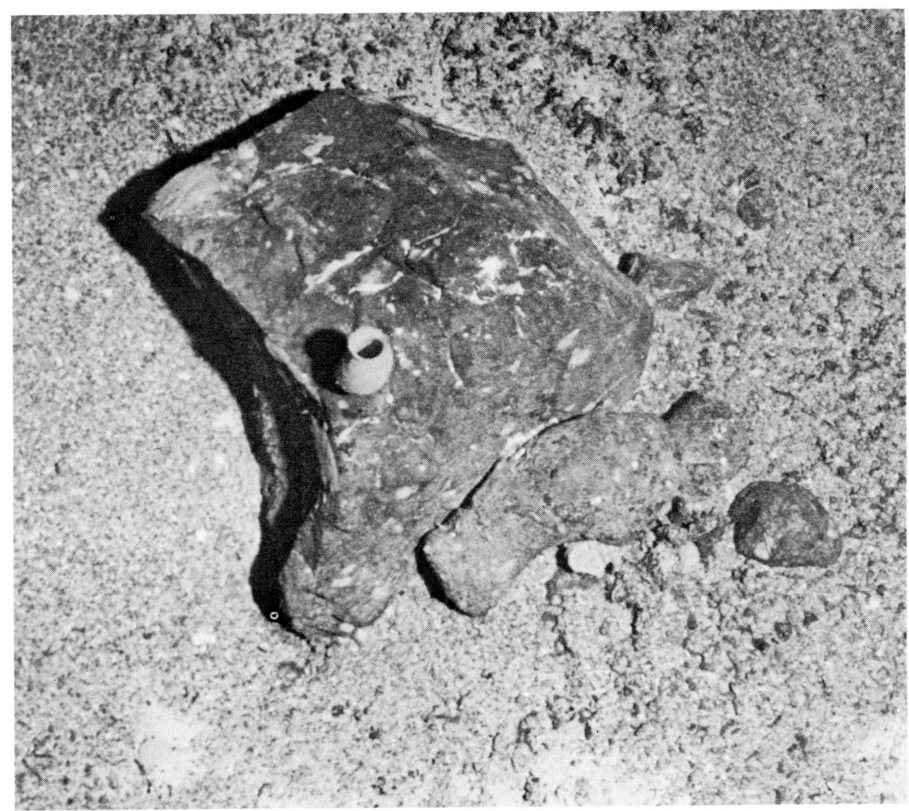

45°15′N 28°55′W

2.5 A, solitary sponge sits on a lava boulder high on the rift mountains in the North Atlantic. 2395 m, west side of Rift Valley, Mid-Atlantic Ridge.

From the continental shelf to the greatest depths of the ocean, the photogenic sponges are seen attached to the sea bottom. While the smallest individuals of this simple group are too small to be seen, the largest are enormous, measuring over two meters tall. Although the sponges found in shallow waters commonly grow irregularly in a plant-like manner, most of the deep-sea forms exhibit radial symmetry and have a vase-like shape (2.5).

Delicate glass sponges[3] are found in the deeper waters of the ocean, where they are often a dominant and dramatic aspect of the visual seascape. They are frequently so abundant that trawls come up looking as if they had "fouled a deep-sea haystack, with bundles of hay and an occasional bird's nest protruding from the bag."[4] The Venus flower basket (*Euplectella*), one of the most beautiful of the glass sponges, is a nearly transparent tower-like cylinder formed of a regular latticework of spicules (2.6, 2.7, 2.8).

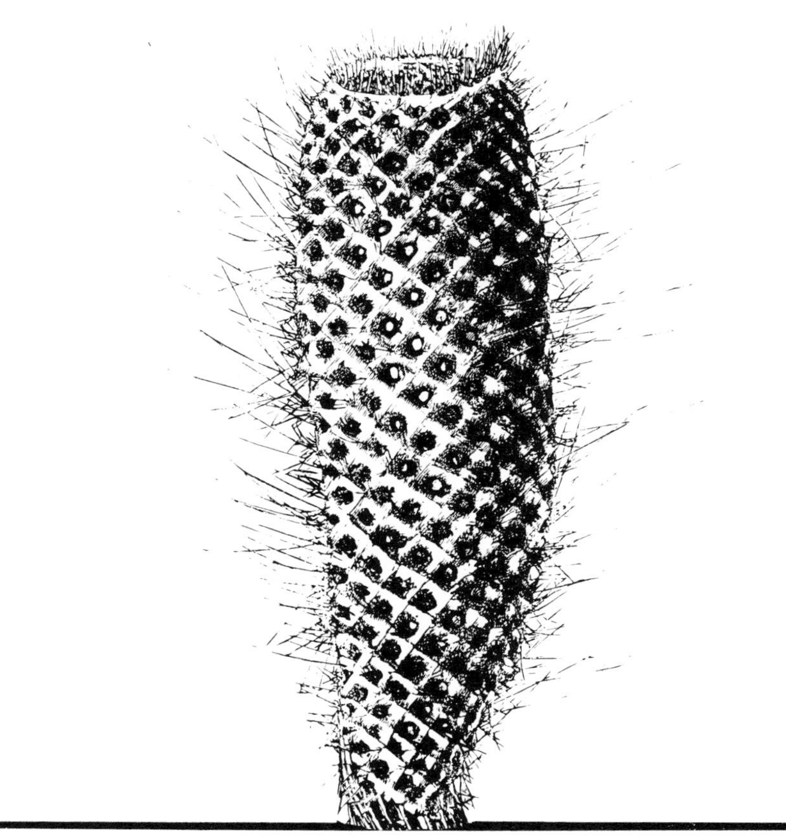

2.6 Venus flower basket (*Euplectella suberea*).

2.7 Graceful vase-shaped glass sponges. L, a trio of *Euplectella* sponges attached to a rock and R, short, round sponge covered with transparent filaments, 2726 m, continental rise off northwest coast of Africa.

The most common abyssal sponges (*Hyalonema*) are bowl- or funnel-shaped organisms at the end of a stout stalk through which runs a sheaf of siliceous needles which may be as much as 20 or 30 centimeters long (2.9, 2.10, 2.11). Some stalks are covered with colonies of sea anemones (2.10).

Most shallow-water sponges have a rather powerful hydraulic mechanism by which they pump water in and out of their bodies. "It is a puzzling fact, at first, that in most of the Hexactinellida we can detect no hydraulic evolution nor hydraulic efficiency, puzzling until we remember that in the great depths where they live, an unchanging current sweeps slowly from the poles to the equator. They have but to spread a net across it, and, whatever their mechanical inefficiency, they have incoming and outgoing streams 180° apart; the flagella have only to work the water through the many meshes formed by the feet of the collar-cells. The cavity of the Hexactinellida is no pressure chamber; it is even perforated to let the onflowing water sweep out that which is befouled."[5] George Bidder also inferred that deep-sea glass sponges must live in a curved attitude, facing downstream so that weak deep-sea currents could more easily remove the toxic excretory products. This curved attitude has been occasionally observed (2.11 UL, 2.12, 9.1, 9.48), but in weaker currents the glass sponges apparently stand erect. Although some sponges live attached to rock, most attach themselves to the sediment by a root-like tuft (2.11 LL, 2.13).

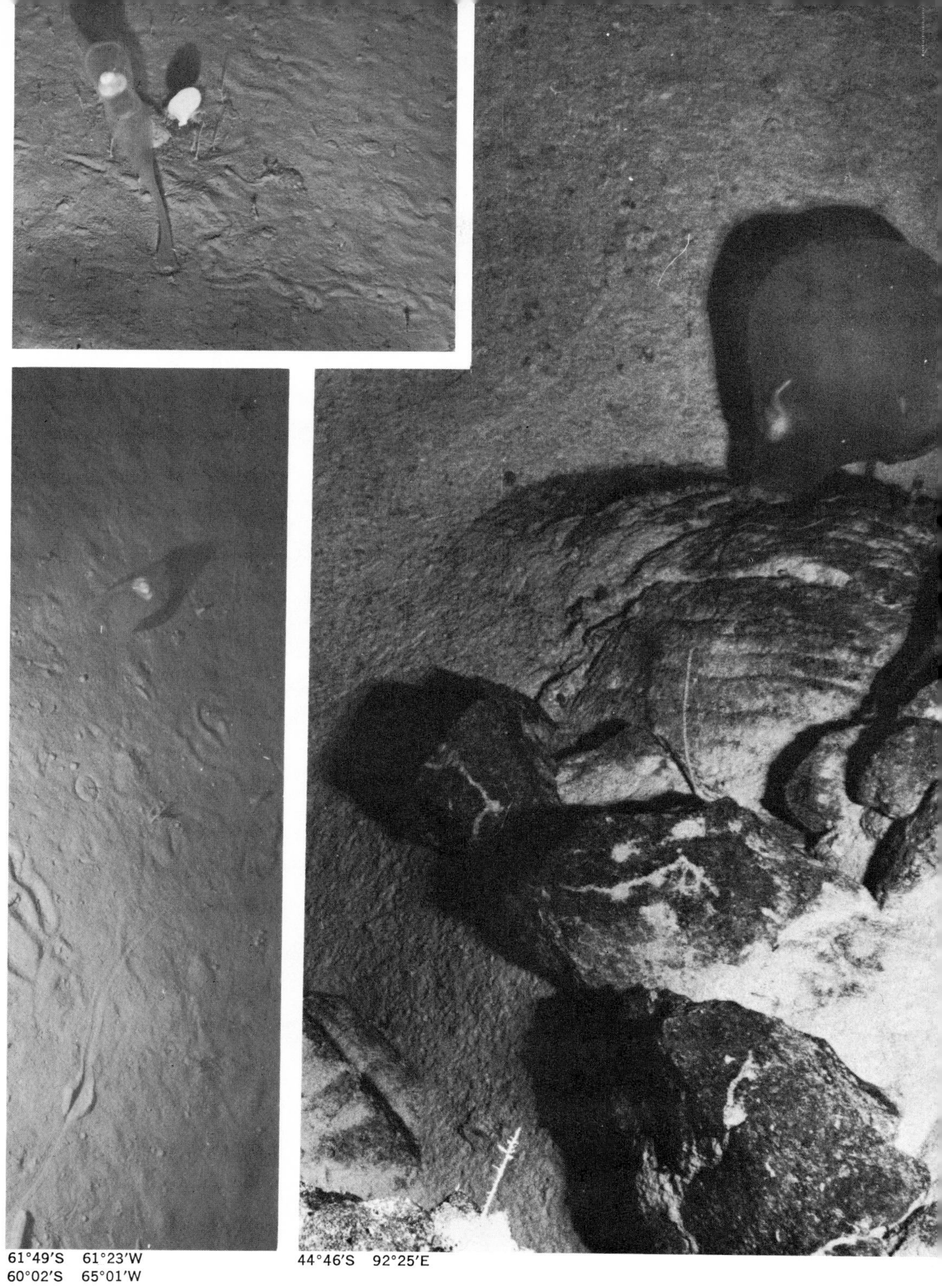

2.8 Living screens. UL and LL, Venus flower basket, 3269 m, 3792 m, Drake Passage. R, sponge attached to pillow basalt, 2785 m, Mid-Indian Ocean Ridge.

In the shallow waters of the continental shelf, on the upper continental slope, and on the crest of the Mid-Oceanic Ridge, huge light-

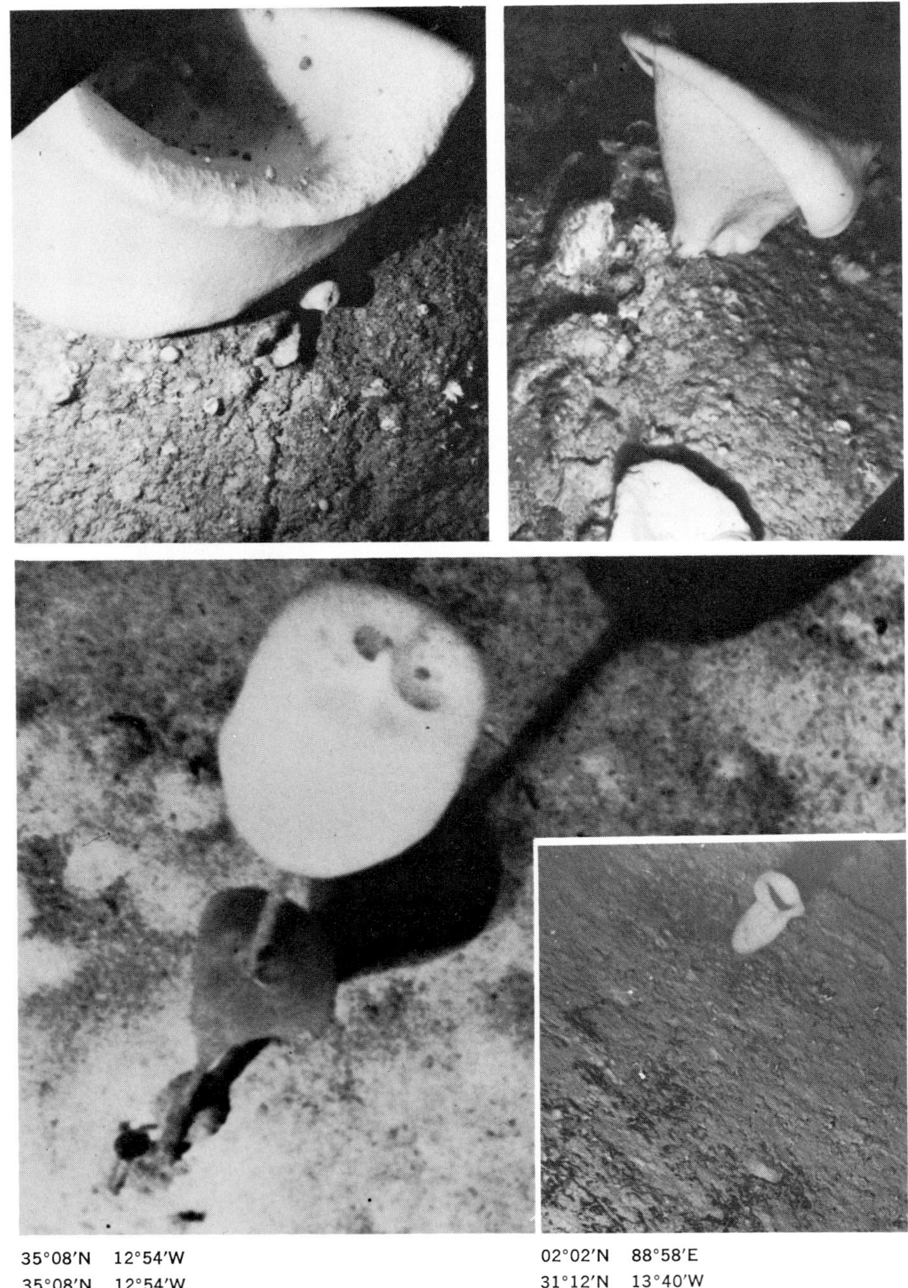

35°08′N 12°54′W
35°08′N 12°54′W

02°02′N 88°58′E
31°12′N 13°40′W

2.9 Sponges. UL, UR, cornucopia-shaped sponges, 529 m, near the top of Ampere Seamount, North Atlantic. LL, stalked *Hyalonema,* 3062 m, crest of Ninetyeast Ridge, Indian Ocean. LR, 301 m, slope of the Canary Islands, North Atlantic.

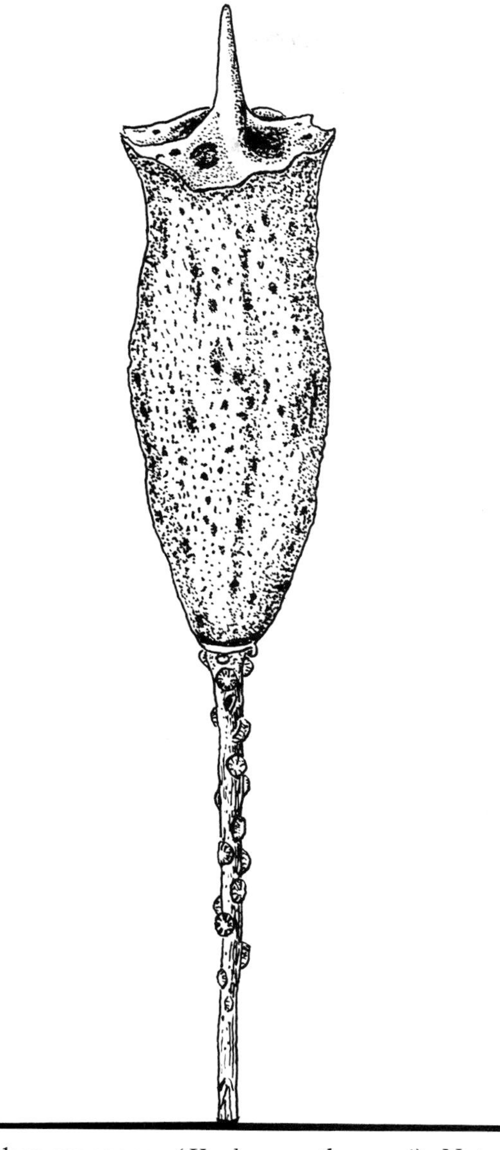

2.10 A tulip-shaped deep-sea sponge (*Hyalonema thomsoni*). Note sea anemones attached to stalk.

colored sombrero- or cornucopia-shaped sponges are frequently seen (2.11 UR, 2.14). These curvaceous animals are often so large as to completely fill the picture (2.9).

While the bath sponges are limited to the warmest shallow waters of the continental shelf, a few of their bizarre relatives are rather commonly found in the deep sea. *Cladorhiza,* a particularly dramatic one which somewhat resembles a space-age microwave antenna, was not uncommon

2.11 There is no hurry. Sponges in moderate depths. UL, 622 m, Blake Plateau. UR, 529 m, Ampere Seamount. LL, 301 m, slope of Canary Islands. LR, 584 m, Blake Plateau.

in the early dredge hauls of *Challenger* and *Blake* (2.15). Alexander Agassiz observed that "they are sponges with a long stem ending in ramifying roots, sunk deeply in the mud. The stem has nodes with four to six club-like appendages. They evidently cover like bushes extensive tracts of the bottom."[6] *Cladorhiza* has been photographed on a manganese-nodule-covered bottom in the Bellingshausen Sea (2.16). It is interesting to note that of sixteen pictures at this particular location only one such sponge was observed. Apparently the population was not as dense here as in areas where *Challenger* and *Blake* dredged. The Agassiz drawing shows the club-like appendages to be curved, the lower drooping down

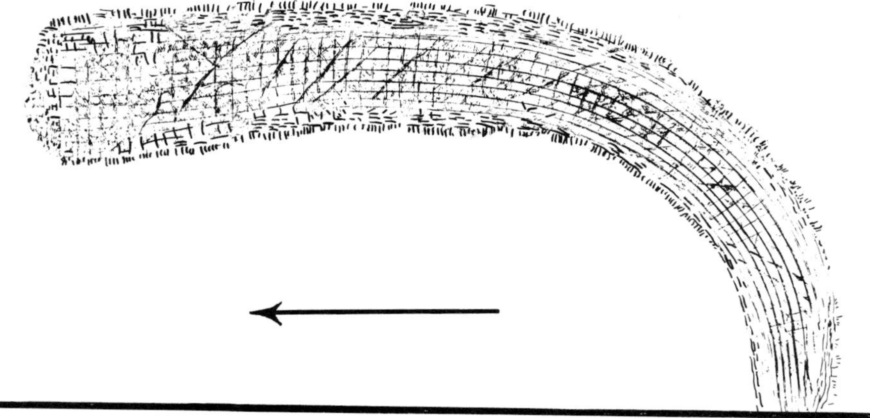

2.12 *Euplectella* spreads its net and bends with the current.

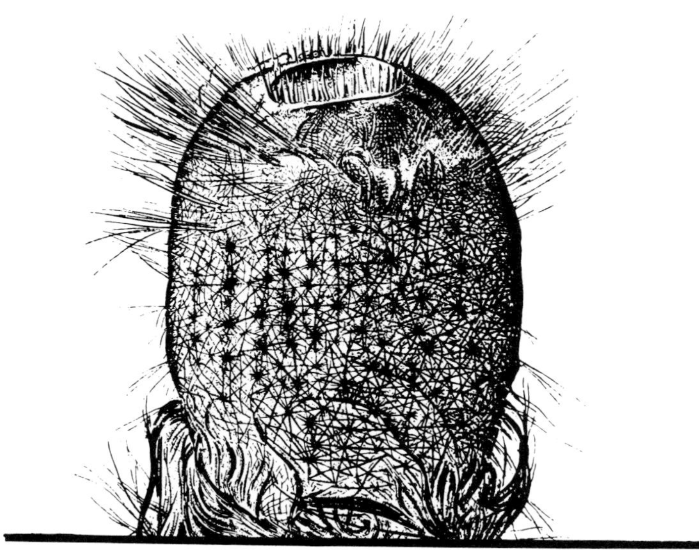

2.13 Cactus-like sponge (*Pheronema carpenteri*).

and the upper raised; whereas, in the photograph we see that this creature actually lives erect with the appendages oriented horizontally at right angles to the nearly straight vertical stem. The tips of the appendages show up so brightly in the photograph as to suggest that either they are of an extremely light color or that they phosphoresce.

Sponges must live in an appreciable bottom current, and it is not surprising that they are most commonly seen associated with moderate to strong physical indications of vigorous circulation such as ripple marks and bare rock.

45°41′N 27°59′W

2.14 Deep-sea sponges are commonly decorated with stalkless crinoids. 1973 m, west wall of Rift Valley, Mid-Atlantic Ridge.

FANS, FEATHERS, AND ANEMONES

Another photogenic group of animals that attach themselves to the deep-sea floor and gather food from the passing current is the tentacled animal flowers, collectively known as coelenterates.[7] Many, particularly the gorgonians, sea pens, and anemones, are large and attractive.

The horny corals (gorgonians) include the graceful, pastel-colored sea whips, sea feathers, and sea fans. Tough, horny, shrub-like branching fans are commonly seen on the pebble-strewn rock bottoms of the continental shelf, and sometimes are also observed in some profusion, attached to current-swept slopes of rocky ridges and seamounts (2.17). They attach themselves to any solid object, including deep-sea cables, and are regularly recovered from moderate depths by cable repair ships. Gorgonians occur in a vast variety, some colonies resembling shrubs while others look like long, unsprung bedsprings. The abyssal forms are

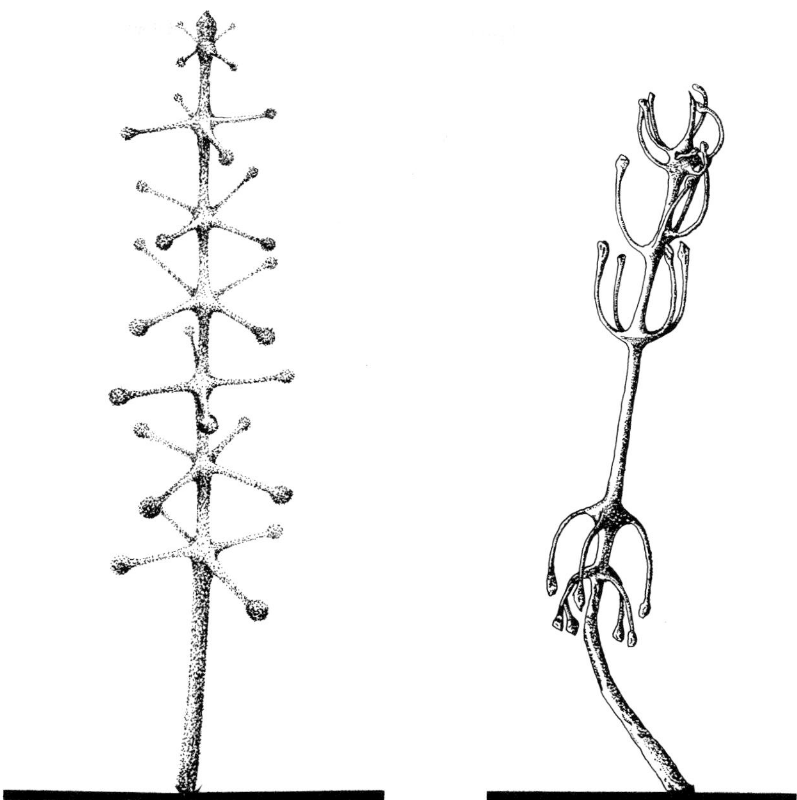

2.15 *Cladorhiza.* R, with clubs drooping as figured by early expeditions. L, straight and erect, from life (see 2.16).

all brightly luminescent; one distinctive shrub-like gorgonian glows with a soft, pale lilac light.

A particularly large and dramatic horny coral which has been dredged from greater depths is *Primnoa,* a plume-like form with regularly pinnate branchlets all in one plane (2.18). To this genus belongs the huge bush coral which grows "to the height of a man and has an axis as thick as a man's leg."[6] Several such fern-like fans have been photographed in the deep sea (2.19). The terminal ends of all branches drag in the sediment as the animal swings like a weathervane around its central point of attachment, thus creating an arcuate dragmark in the mud (4.11). Although most hydroids are too small to be recognized, there is at least one large form which inhabits the abyss and reaches two meters in length.[8]

The feathery, sometimes luminous, filter-feeding sea pens (pennatulids) are seen attached to the sea floor from the shallow depths of the continental shelf to the greatest depths of the sea (2.20, 2.21). They form more or less fleshy colonies, composed of the very elongate body

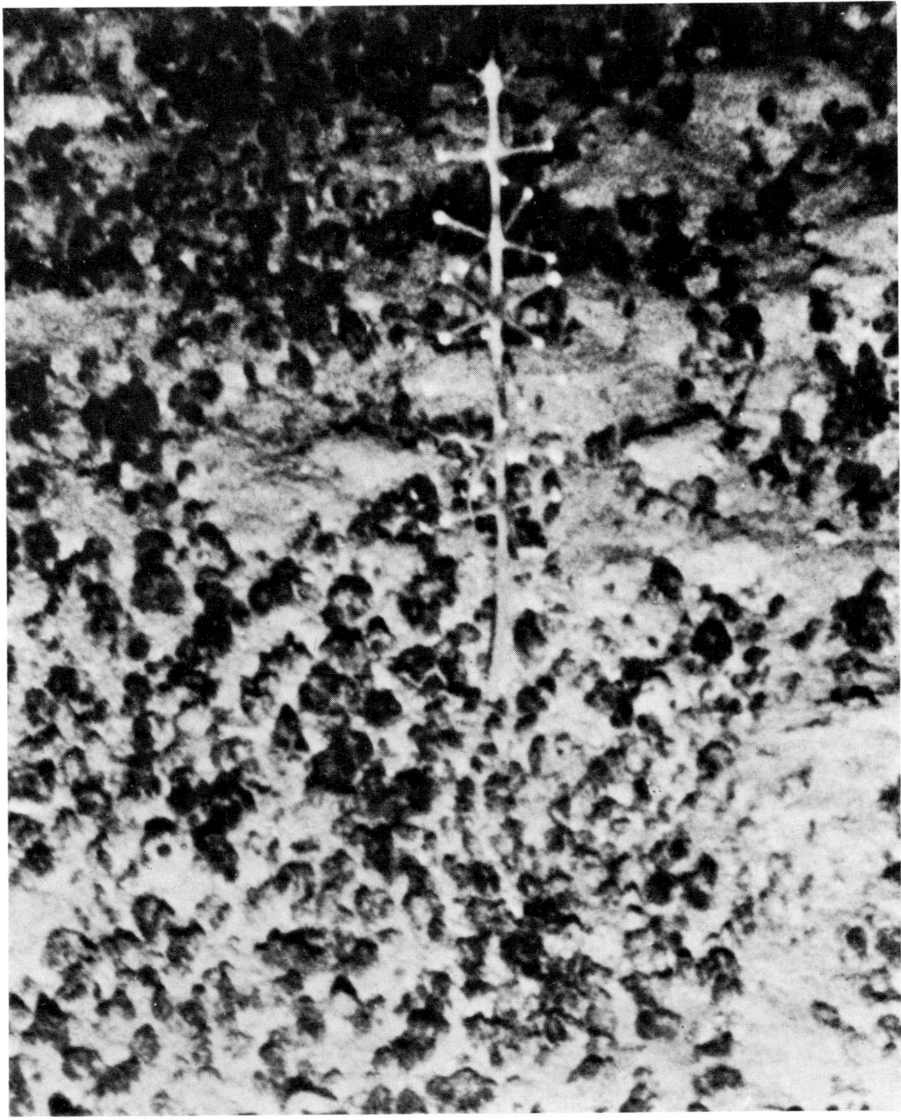

2.16 A bizarre antennae-like abyssal sponge. This sponge (*Cladorhiza*) stands erect, towering over the manganese nodules, 3904 m, Bellingshausen Basin, South Pacific.

of a primary axial polyp and numerous secondary polyps springing laterally from it. Sea pens stand up to a meter above the bottom, and the feathery ones cast a lacy shadow. Their color is usually yellow, brown, orange-red, or purple. Members of the genus *Pennatula* (2.22, 2.23, 2.24, 2.25) are the most ornate, while the club-like *Kophobelemn*

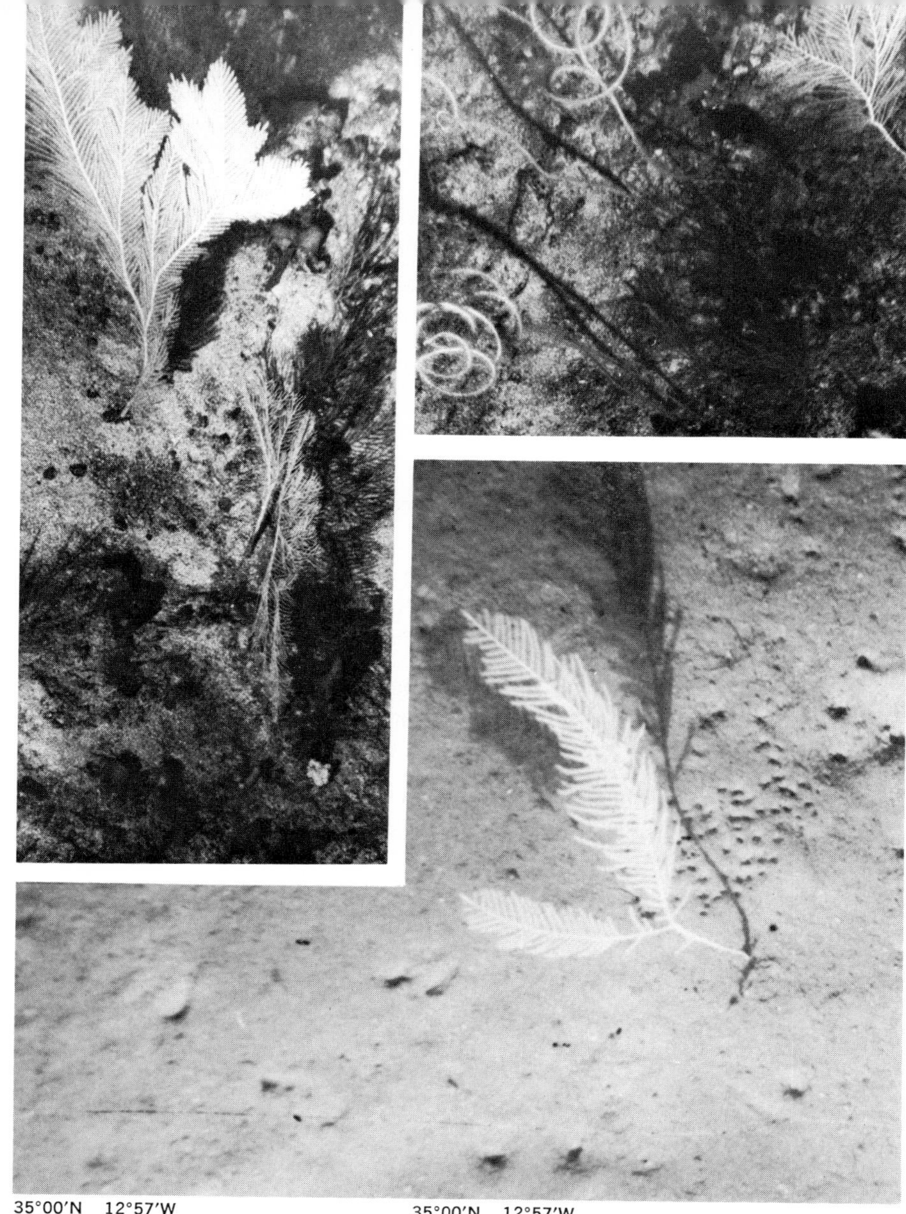

35°00′N 12°57′W
07°32′N 109°05′E

35°00′N 12°57′W

2.17 Pink magic. These large yellow, red, and purple sea fans which abound in warm shallow water may have been some of the first objects to be hauled up by the ancients who endowed them with magical powers. Perhaps the red color implied the blood of Uranus and the rise of Aphrodite from the foam. UL, UR, 143 m, top of Ampere Seamount, North Atlantic. L, 186 m, continental shelf, Vietnam.

(2.26) are short, erect post-like organisms whose surface detail is usually not discernible in underwater photographs.

Lily-like sea pens (*Umbellula*) closely resemble the stalked crinoids (2.27). Firmly attached to the sea floor, they are usually bent by a gentle current (2.28). Sir Wyville Thomson, describing a specimen of *Umbellula,* stated that "when taken from the trawl, the polyps and membranes covering the hard axis of the stem were brightly phosphorescent."[9] Sea pens are now noted for their bright luminescence in shades of blue, violet, green, and yellow.

The thread-like pens, together with the spring-like gorgonians, probably account for many of the springy or straight threads frequently seen protruding from the sea floor. The pilot of the bathyscaphe *FRNS-III* observed that "stationary fauna" although very beautiful are very rare. "I have encountered some only once at the bottom of the Setubal Canyon in the Atlantic off Portugal at about 1800 meters. Dark red pennatulids and orange gorgonians covered the ground at the rate of at least one colony per square meter. For once the bottom had lost its desert aspect, for these colonies of animals could easily be taken for finely serrated flowers."[10]

Black corals (antipatharians) form slender, branching, plant-like colonies (2.29) which, like gorgonians, consist of a skeletal axis covered with polyps. The lower end of the colony usually consists of a flat basal plate which adheres to some firm object, but is often simply thrust into the sediments. From this attachment rises a main stem which gives off a number of slender unbranched stems, but more commonly breaks up into branches. Some have a bottle-brush appearance, consisting of a main stem with numerous short lateral branches. Most of our knowledge of these thorny animals comes from the dredge hauls of oceanographic expeditions.

2.18 Plumose deep-sea gorgonian (*Primnoa pourtalesii*).

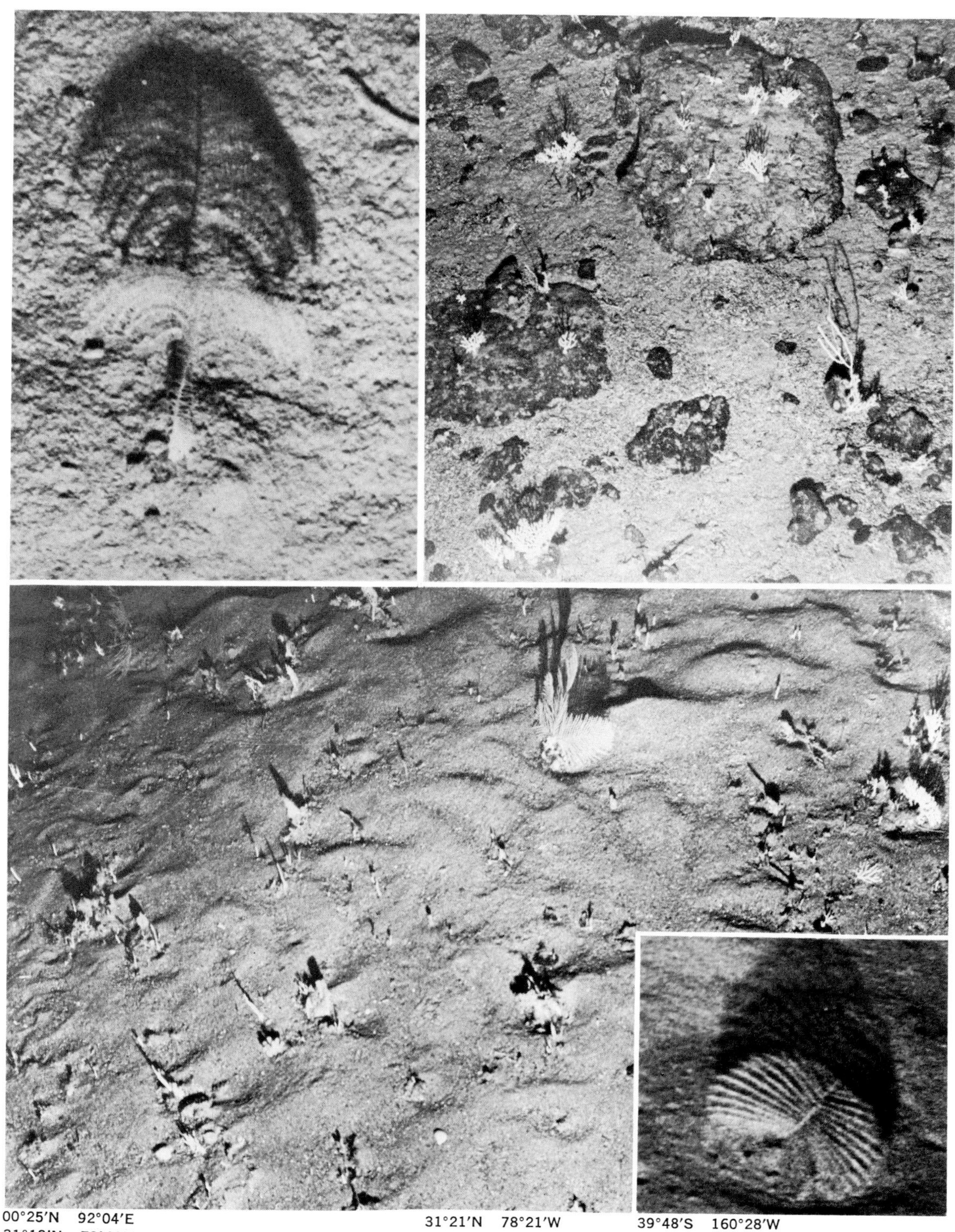

2.19 Fans. UL, 4483 m, east equatorial Indian Ocean. LR, 5013 m, western South Pacific. UR, LL, 622 m, 554 m, Blake Plateau.

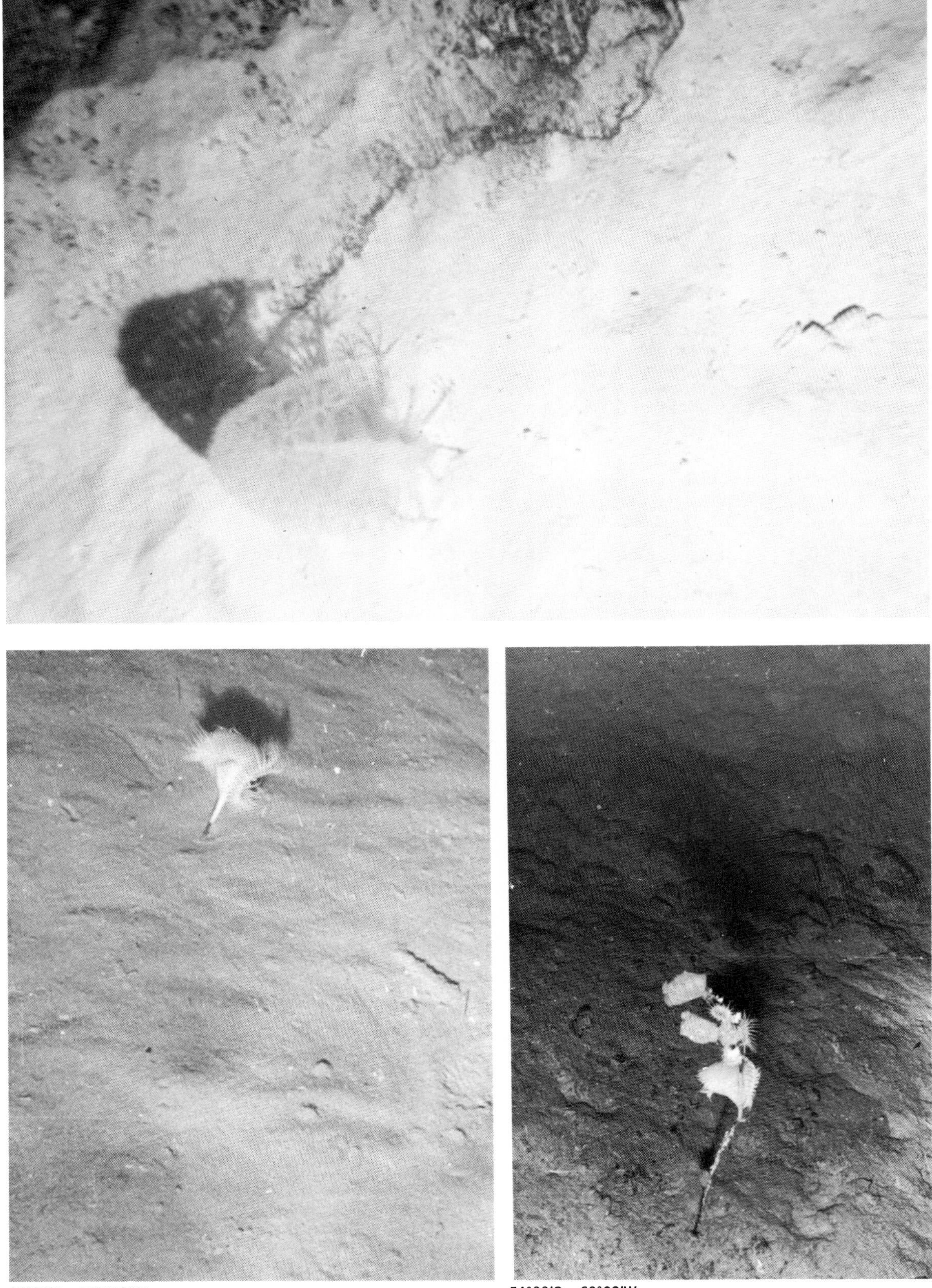

14°21′S 149°38′W
55°03′S 58°59′W

54°00′S 62°28′W

2.20 Feathers. U, 2490 m, Tuamotu Archipelago. LL and LR, 3092 m, 398 m, Falkland Plateau.

2.21 Coelenterates bending with the current. L, graceful pennatulid and multitude of small brittle stars rest on the cobble-covered sea floor, 430 m, peak on Mid-Oceanic Ridge, South Pacific; R, stalked sea pen, 5066 m, Sierra Leone Abyssal Plain, eastern Atlantic.

The squat thistle-shaped sea anemones or actinarians commonly are large evident forms, and they have been photographed and dredged from all depths of the ocean. They have a circular shape and bear many short hollow tentacles around a slit-like mouth (2.30). Practically always solitary and chiefly sessile, but never wholly fixed, they are known to be burrowers and may be responsible for some of the larger craters, mounds, and burrows seen in photographs (6.13, 6.31). Prevalent colors are white, flesh, tan, brown, olive, and green, but bright colors such as orange and red are not uncommon; and some are blue. The tentacles and oral disc may display complicated geometrical color patterns. Beautiful anemones have been photographed in the deep sea (2.31, 2.32), but they have not yet been recorded on color film; if the deep-sea varieties are as striking as those seen in shallow water, a treat is in store. Certain anemones habitually are fastened to snail shells inhabited by hermit crabs, to the stalks of sponges and sea pens, and on the tubes of polychaete worms.

Some of the deep-sea actinarians have developed a peculiar base, similar to the sea pens, which is adapted to life on sediment-covered bottoms. Anemones are difficult to preserve and the deep-sea forms are not well described. At least some deep-sea types secrete phosphorescent mucus from the tentacles and upper part of the column. The extremely light-colored tips of the tentacles of the anemone shown in Figure 2.30 probably denote phosphorescence. Tiny anemones have been found attached to rock dredged from 10,000 meters in the Philippine Trench. Many of the tiny circular light encrustations seen on outcrops, talus, and rafted debris may

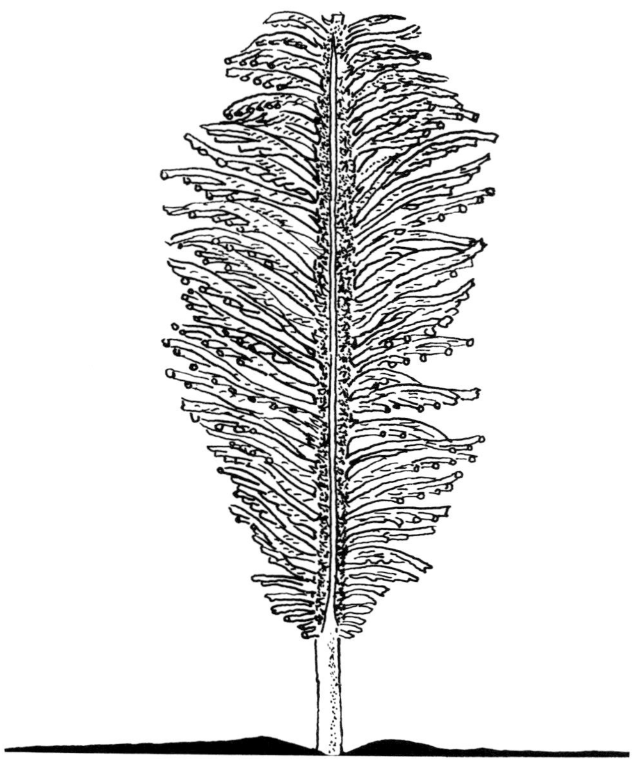

2.22 The feather. *Pennatula aculeata,* a common sea pen.

2.23 Sea pens spread feather-like nets to secure their food. 565 m, northeast wall of "the gully" on the continental slope east of Nova Scotia.

be abyssal anemones. The cerianthid, another anemone-like animal, has a smooth, muscular, elongated cylindrical body that is occasionally seen thrust into the sediment up to the oral disc which bears many slender tentacles (2.32 UL).

The stony corals are the builders of coral reefs and atolls and hence objects of great popular and scientific interest. They are mostly colonial, and are provided with a hard calcareous exoskeleton and thus may be

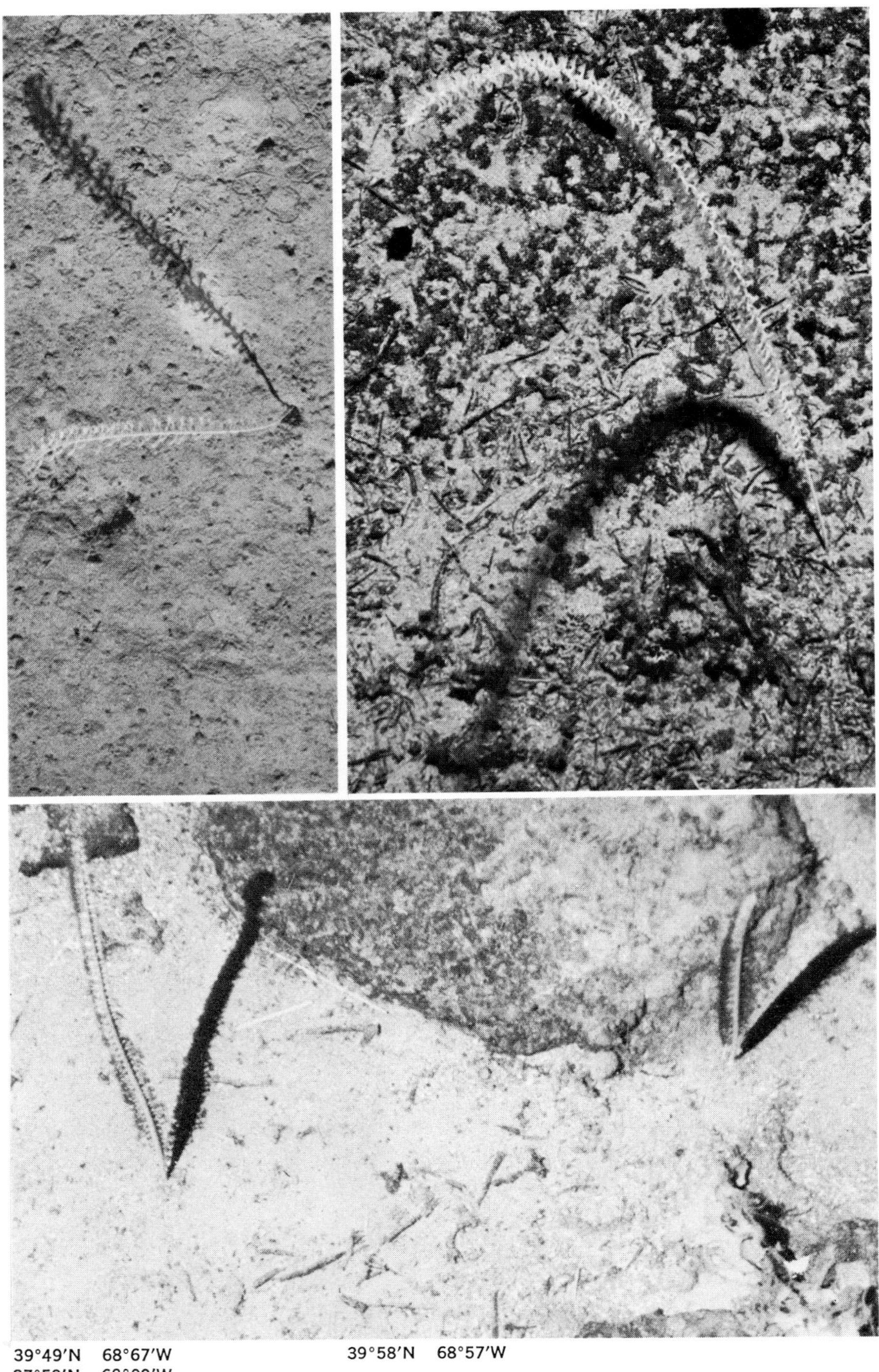

39°49′N 68°67′W 39°58′N 68°57′W
37°58′N 62°09′W

2.24 Feathers and whips in the deep sea. UL, UR, 2147 m, 1503 m, continental slope off New England. L, 4821 m, seamount in western Atlantic.

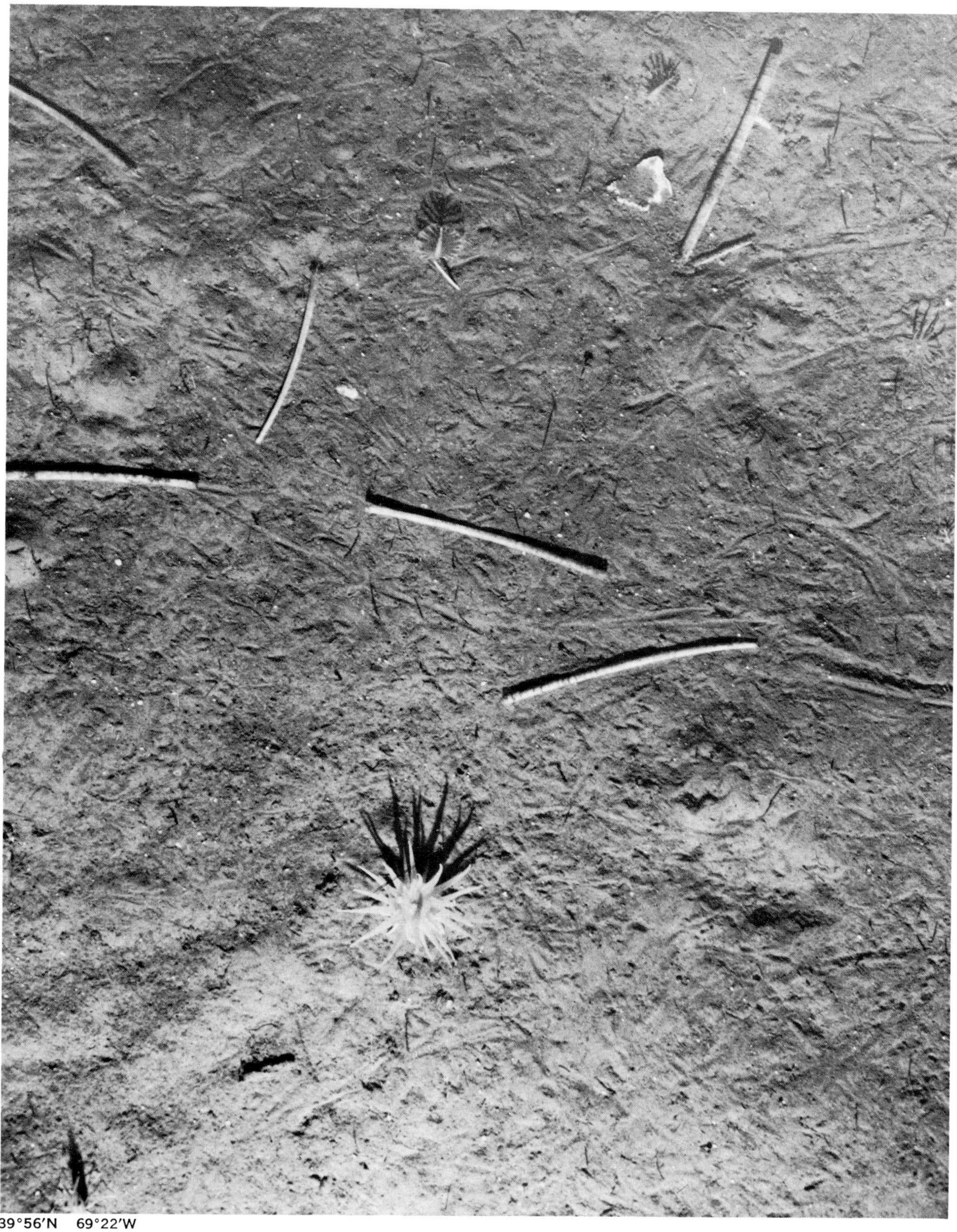

39°56′N 69°22′W

2.25 Pens, worm tubes, and anemones. 830 m, New England continental slope.

regarded as skeleton-forming anemones. The reef-building corals form a dramatic and overpowering seascape in warm sunlit waters, but since these beautiful, bright-colored animals cannot exist without sunlight or below temperatures of 18° C, they are found only in shallow tropical seas.

The non-reef-forming corals which grow as solitary cups or tall branching colonies have been photographed in relatively great depths and in high latitudes. Banks of deep-water coral occur off the Norwegian coast in several hundred meters' depth.[11] Solitary corals[12] are commonly photographed on current-swept environments of the continental shelf and slope (2.33) and crests of seamounts, where they are often seen attached to rocks.

The fans, pens, and corals, which feed on tiny animals swept up by their deadly fingers, require a moderate to appreciable bottom current. They are seen on seamounts, escarpments, the continental slope, and in other active areas, but are not seen in a completely tranquil environment.

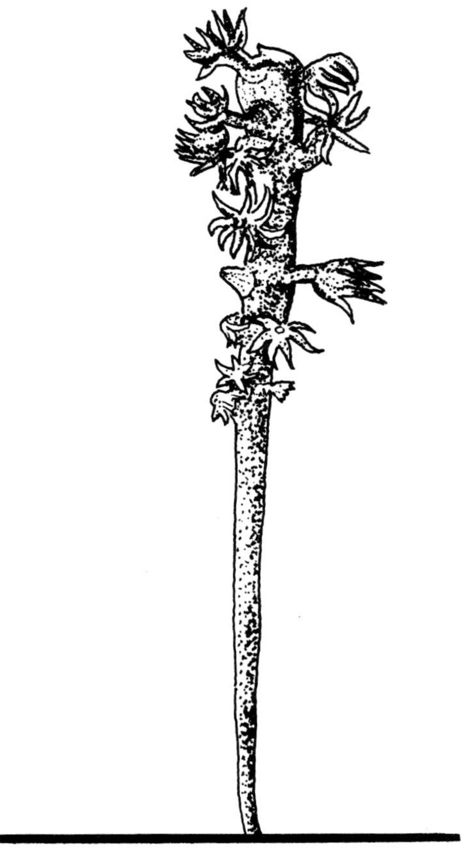

2.26 The club. *Kophobelemnon stelliferum,* a pennatulid.

The corals and gorgonians which usually are attached to rock require the swiftest currents, while the pens attach themselves to the sediment and inhabit somewhat quieter areas. The actinarians, which apparently rely on the capture of larger prey, are frequently seen in the more tranquil environment of the deep-sea floor. In burrowing, they mark and pit the bottom and thus contribute more than their own attractive shapes to the visual seascape.

MOSS

Bryozoans are moss-like animals which live attached to the sea floor. On certain ridges, seamounts, and other shallower and rockier current-swept areas, they have been dredged in considerable abundance, and

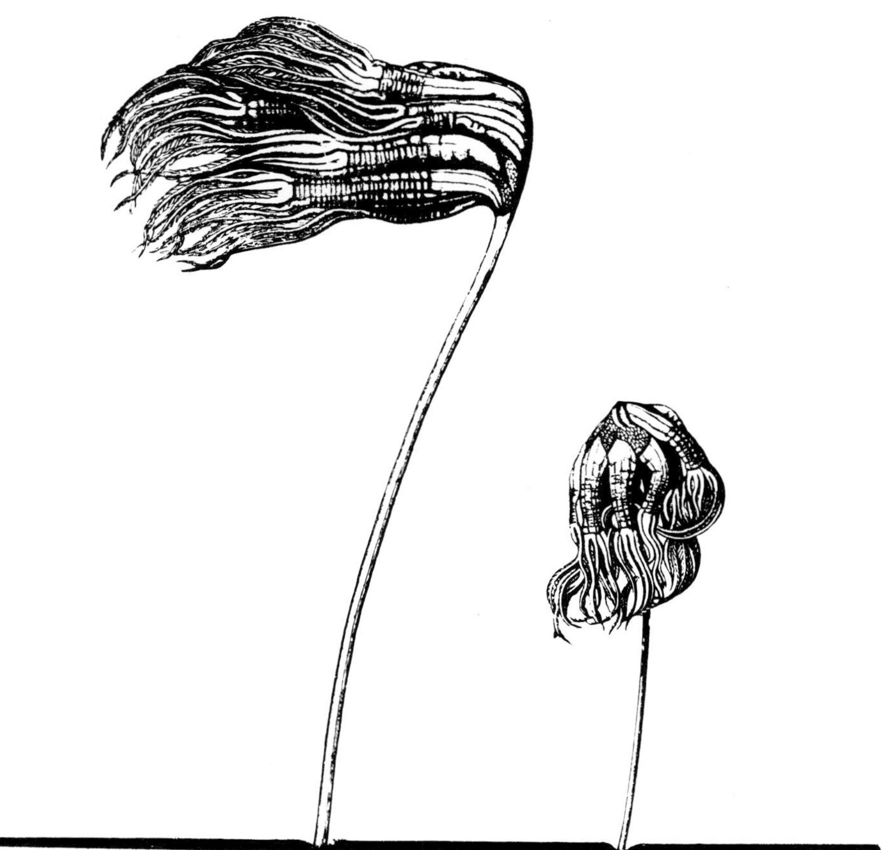

2.27 The bottle-brush. *Umbellula* have a very long slender bare stem up to 50 cm long topped by a cluster of large orange-red or purplish flower-like polyps. Some emit bluish light. In this drawing of preserved specimens the tentacles are clustered together in an unnatural way. These were drawn from preserved specimens.

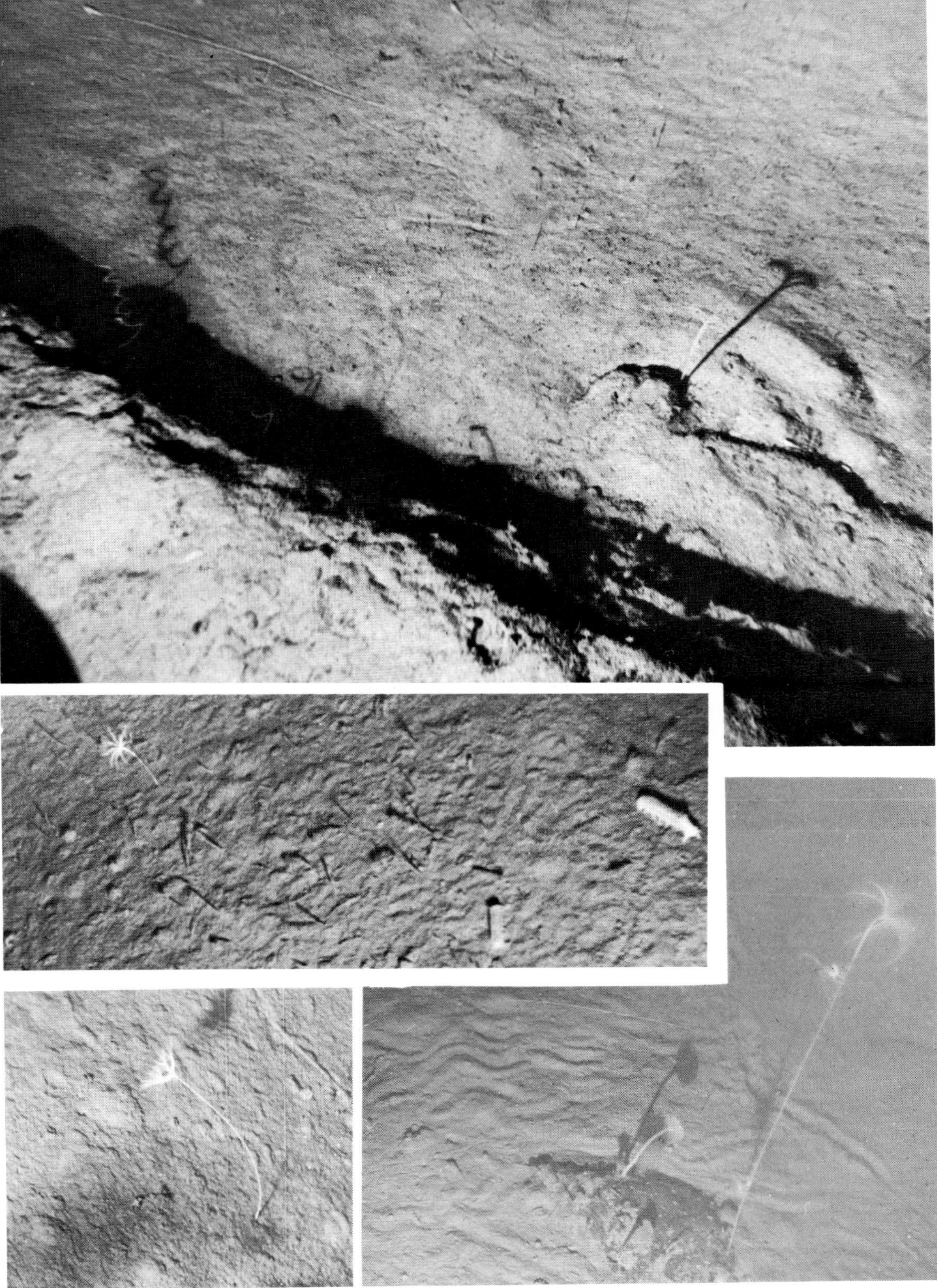

20°12′S 57°23′E
08°17′S 81°06′W
31°43′S 72°00′W

64°45′S 82°32′W

2.28 Lilies. Some sea pens resemble the stalked crinoid (LR). U, 605 m, slope of Réunion Island. LC, Sea cucumbers, worm tubes and a sea pen, 6238 m, floor of Peru-Chile Trench. LL, 5802 m, west wall of Peru-Chile Trench. LR, 4506 m, Pacific continental rise, Antarctic Peninsula.

bryozoan debris has been photographed on the flanks of seamounts (2.34, 2.35). Encrusting forms are found on shells, corals, and rocks. Bryozoans require an appreciable current and are limited to rocky and current-swept environments.

LILIES, STARS, URCHINS, AND CUCUMBERS

The deep sea is ruled by the spiny echinoderms, which are by far the most important animals decorating and marking the abyssal seascape. The feathery crinoids, although least abundant, are perhaps the most photogenic. Starfish, sea urchins, and sea cucumbers, which constitute the vast majority of the living animals seen in deep-sea photographs, are found in all seas, at all latitudes and to the greatest depths. As deep-sea animals go, all are relatively large. None are microscopic, and some

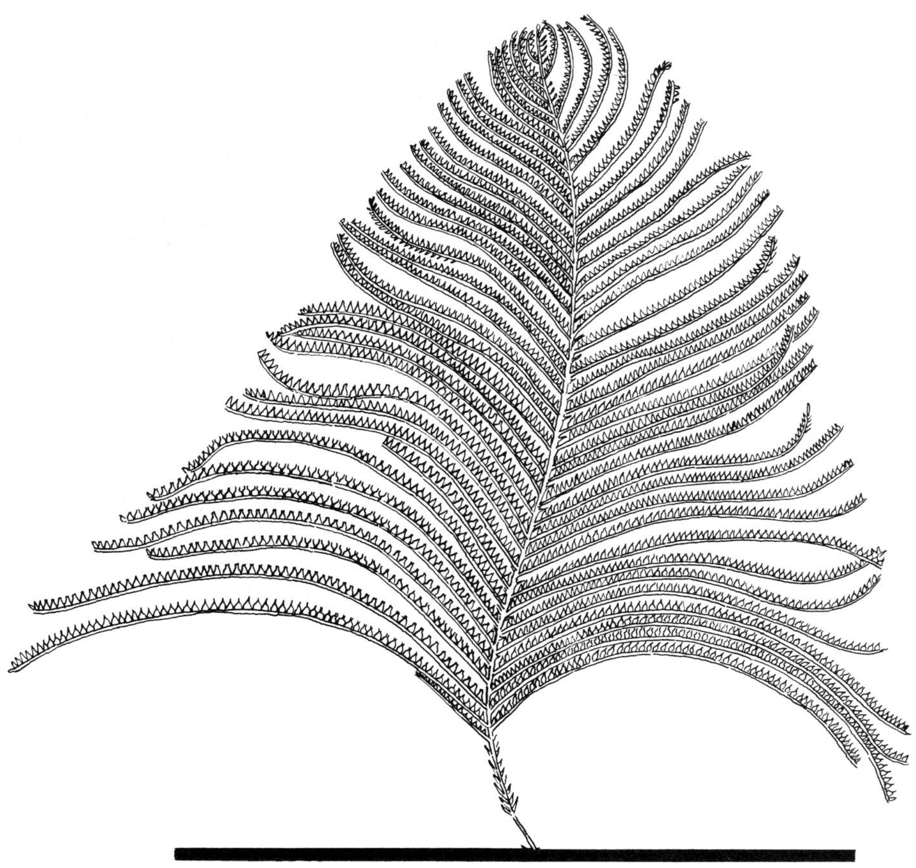

2.29 Plant-like black coral (Antipatharia).

42°24′S 140°49′E
36°08′S 111°29′E
28°52′S 104°12′E

06°38′N 76°25′E

2.30 Abyssal actinarians of the Indian Ocean. UL, 5061 m, Australia Basin. UR, 4854 m, Wharton Basin. LC, 4915 m, Diamantina Fracture Zone. L, 1912 m, continental slope of India.

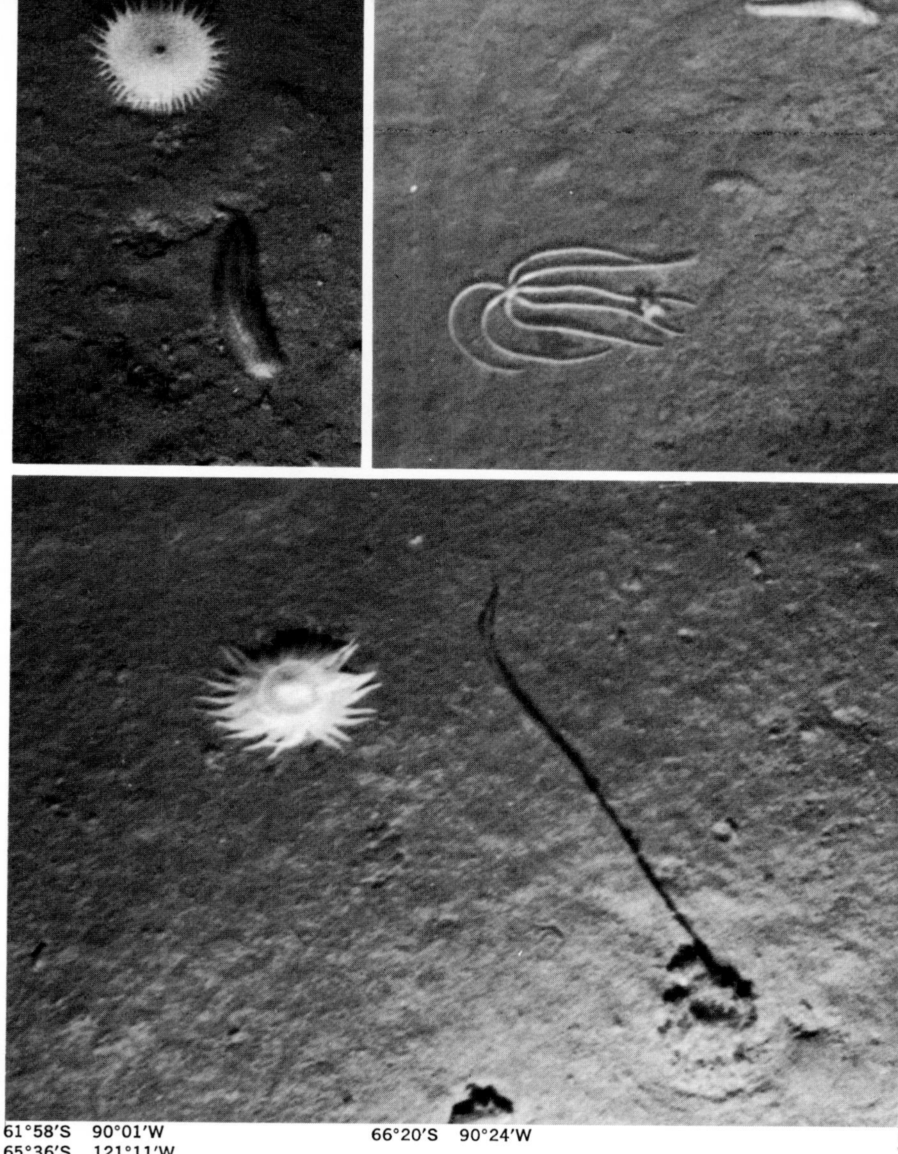

61°58′S 90°01′W 66°20′S 90°24′W
65°36′S 121°11′W

2.31 Antarctic life: actinarians, starfish, sea cucumbers, and fish. UL, 4840 m, UR, 4525 m, L, 4866 m, Antarctic continental rise, Marie Byrd Land.

giants attain the size of a kitten. Most are free-moving, although ancient, sessile stalked forms survive among the crinoids.

The crinoids, graceful living relics of the Paleozoic seas, are so abundant in some areas as to form veritable sea gardens and are seen bent by gentle currents in favored locations (2.36). The body disc is a small cup-shaped calyx of calcareous plates to which are attached five flexible arms that fork to form ten or more narrow appendages, each bearing many slender lateral pinnules arranged like barbs of a feather (2.37). A long jointed stem extends from the calyx and attaches the stalked crinoid to the sea bed. The attachments take the form of root-like outgrowths, grappling hooks, bulbous swellings, flat circular discs, or single finger-like projections.

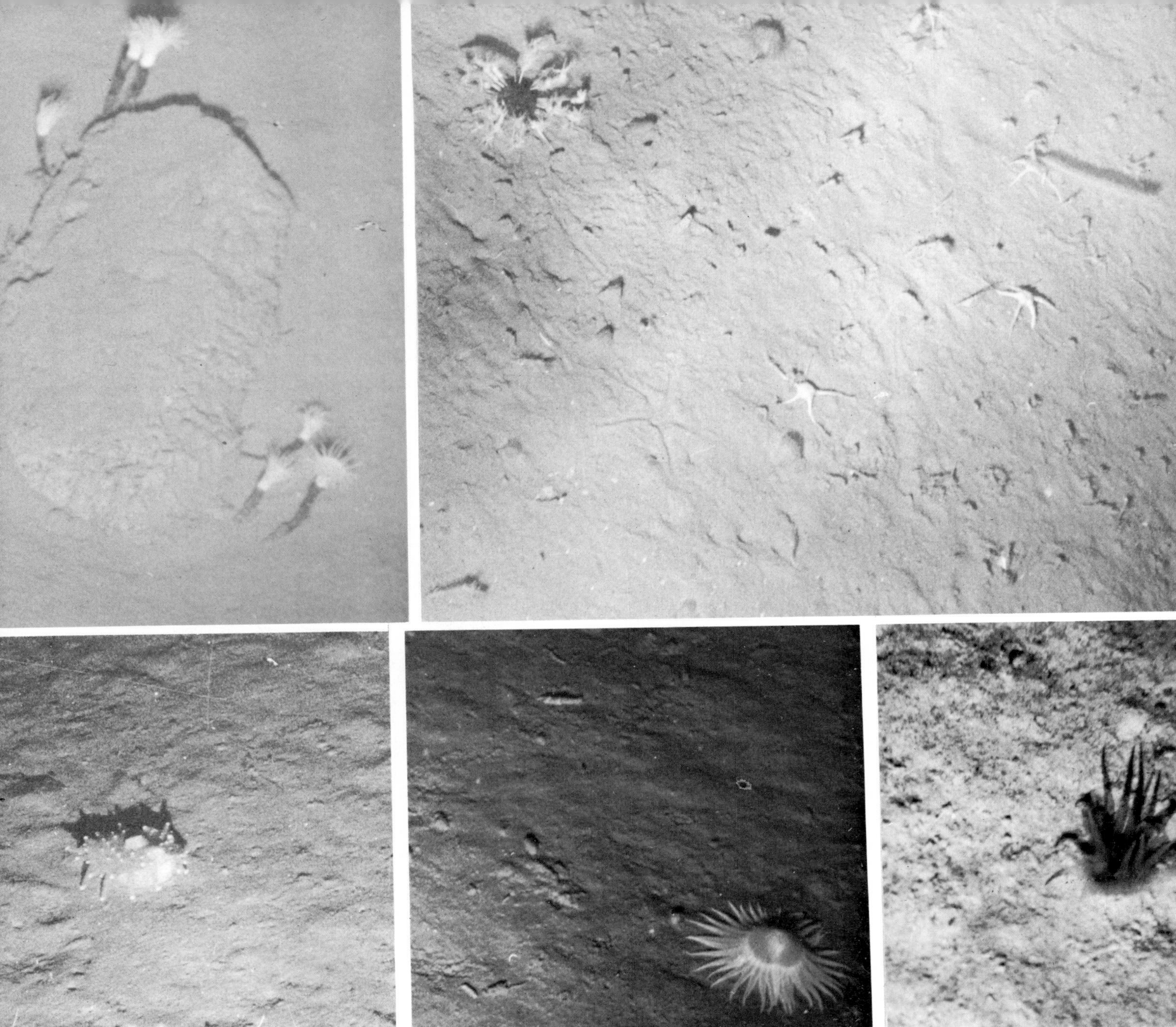

19°54′N 65°57′W
62°53′S 74°52′W

62°59′S 59°03′W
62°55′S 115°13′W

07°04′N 60°55′E

2.32 Actinarians. UL, Cerianthids attached to rock, 8143 m, north wall, Puerto Rico Trench. UR, Actinarians, worms, and brittle stars, 627 m, Pacific continental slope, Antarctic Peninsula. LL, 4153 m, Pacific continental rise, Antarctic Peninsula. LC, 5126 m, Bellingshausen Basin, South Pacific. LR, 2681 m, Carlsberg Ridge, Indian Ocean.

The stalkless crinoids attach themselves to the bottom by grasping rocks with their fingerlike cirri (2.38, 2.39). When detached, they swim gracefully by alternately raising and lowering some of their arms. Few

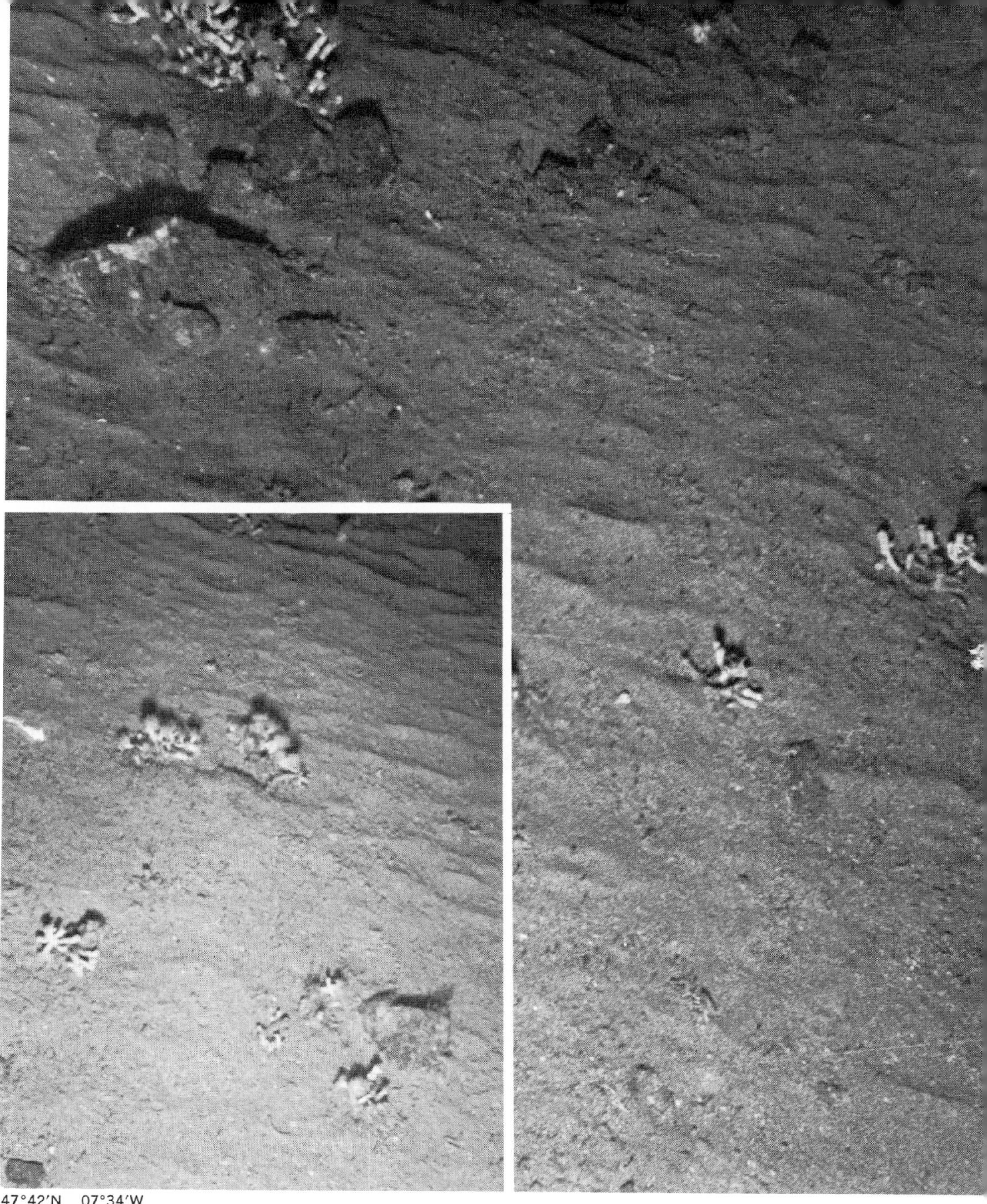

47°42′N 07°34′W
47°42′N 07°34′W

2.33 Solitary corals. 508 m, Atlantic continental slope of France.

species exceed eight inches in length. Most are brilliantly colored yellow, red, white, green, purple, or brown. Their food, microscopic plankton and detritus gathered from the passing current, is conveyed from the pinnules to the mouth by cilia.

Colonies of the free-living feather stars have been photographed on the continental margin in the North Atlantic (2.40), the South Pacific,

34°00′N 30°09′W

2.34 Bryozoan debris on the flanks of a seamount. This photograph, taken with an early single-shot camera, shows festoons of bryozoan debris. A simultaneous core obtained manganese-encrusted bryozoan fragments, 1015 m, Atlantis Seamount.

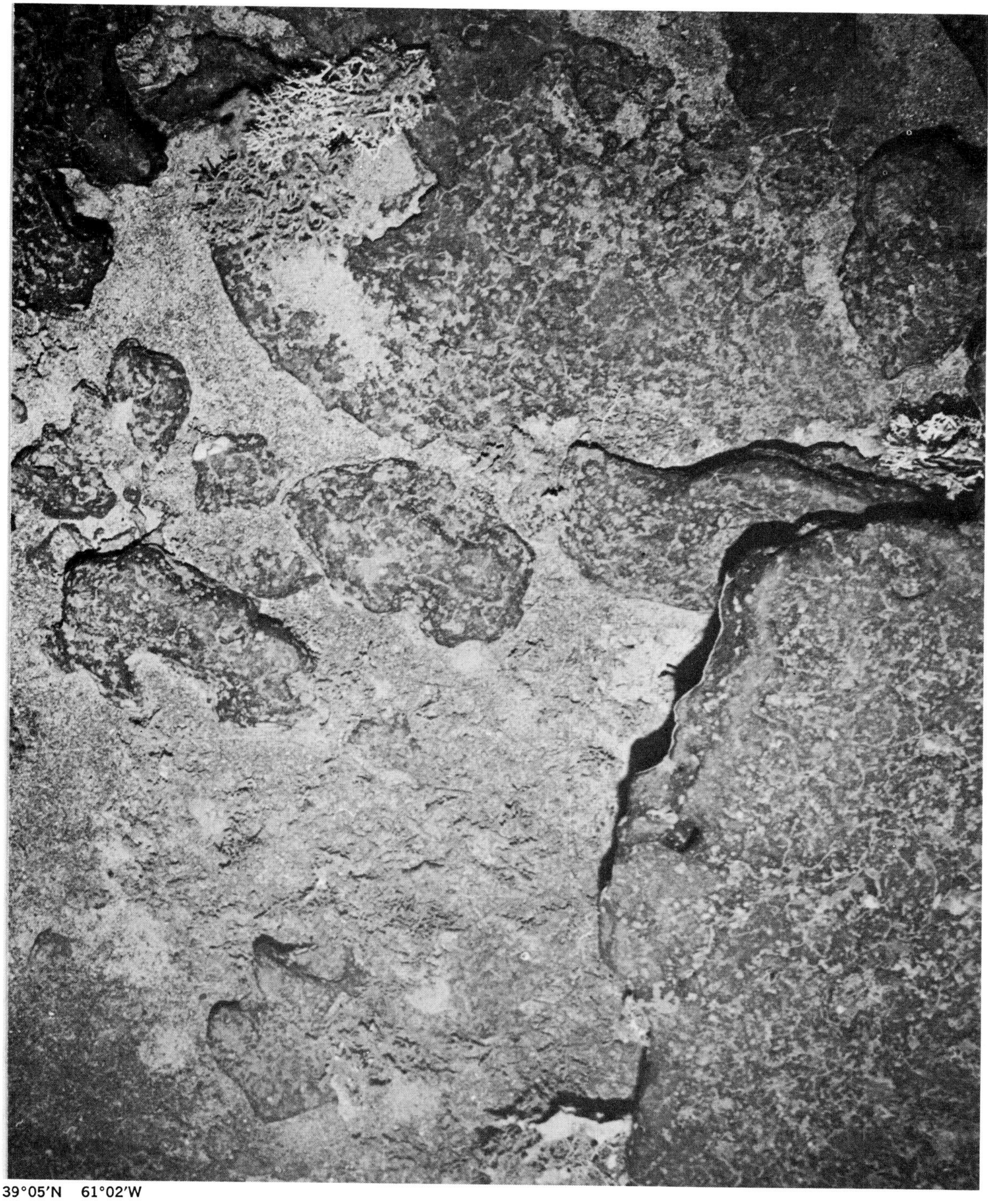

2.35 Colonies of coral and bryozoans frequently adorn stark, current-swept lava flows. 903 m, Kelvin Seamount Group, western North Atlantic.

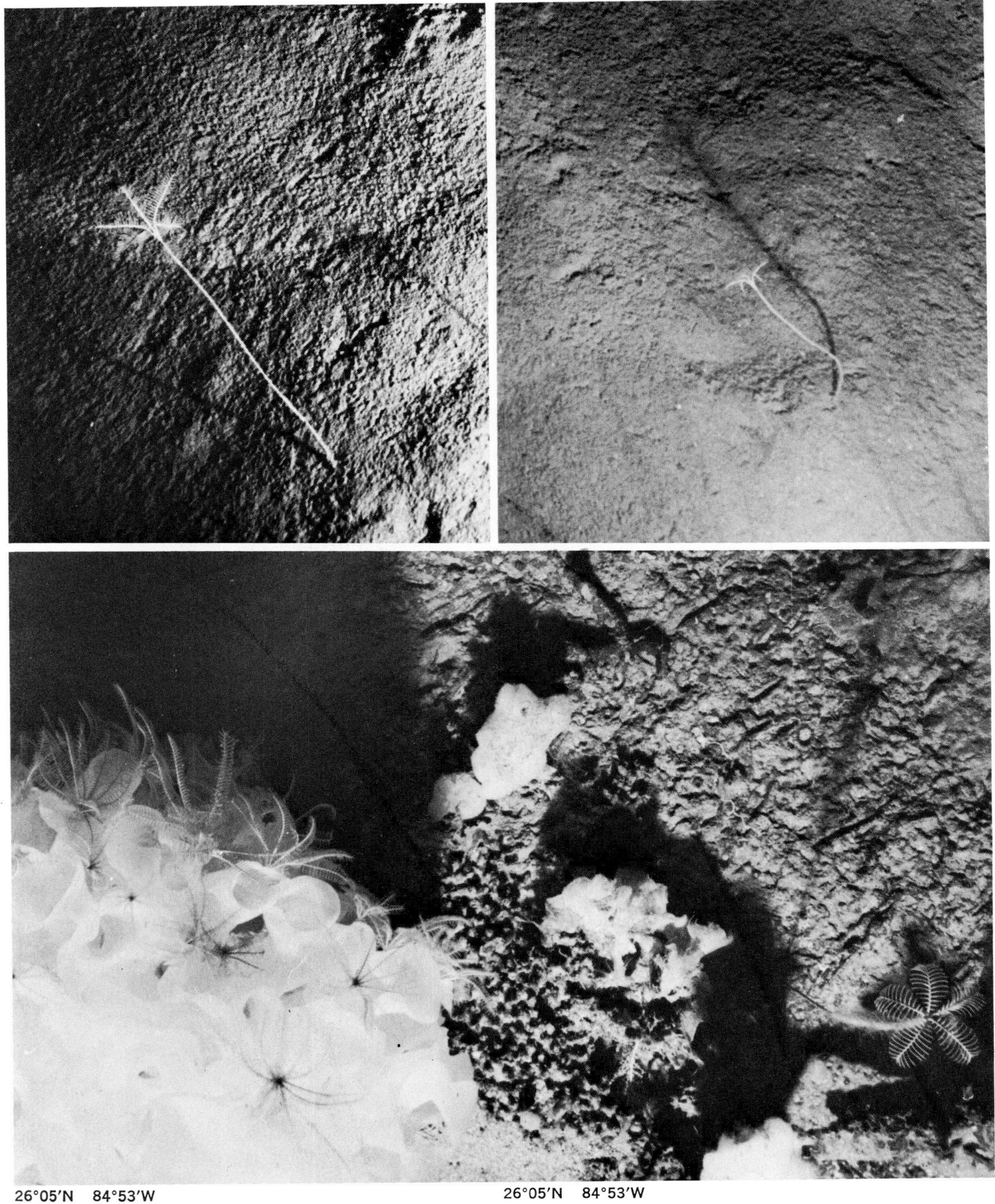

26°05′N 84°53′W
33°32′N 62°27′W

26°05′N 84°53′W

2.36 Stalked crinoids. UL, UR, stalked crinoids, 1602 m, Gulf of Mexico. L, free-living crinoids on sponges (left) and single-stalked crinoid (right), 1390 m, Muir Seamount, western Atlantic.

and the Antarctic. Dense colonies of stalked crinoids are known from coral reefs, but those photographed in the deep sea appear to be thinly scattered. They are generally attached to hard bottom,[13] although there are some cases where they are surely attached to soft sediment. Crinoids have been photographed in depths exceeding 6000 meters. However they have a spotty distribution for, like other large attached forms, they require at least a moderate current and are not found in the more tranquil environments.

Some of the most commonly photographed animals of the sea floor are the starfish (asteroids). These animals are familiar to every visitor of the seashore and occur from there to the abyss (2.41). Typically, they consist of a central disc with five tapering rays of length equal to two or three times the diameter of the disc. However, rays can vary widely in size and length, and in number from four to fifty (2.42).

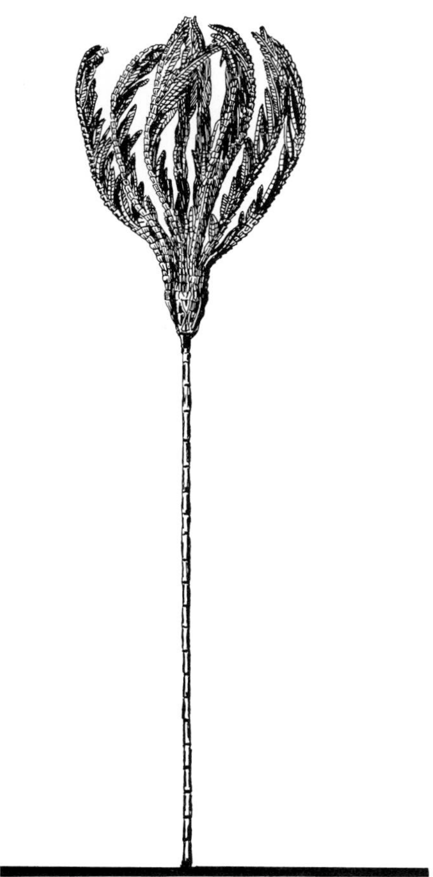

2.37 Stalked crinoid.

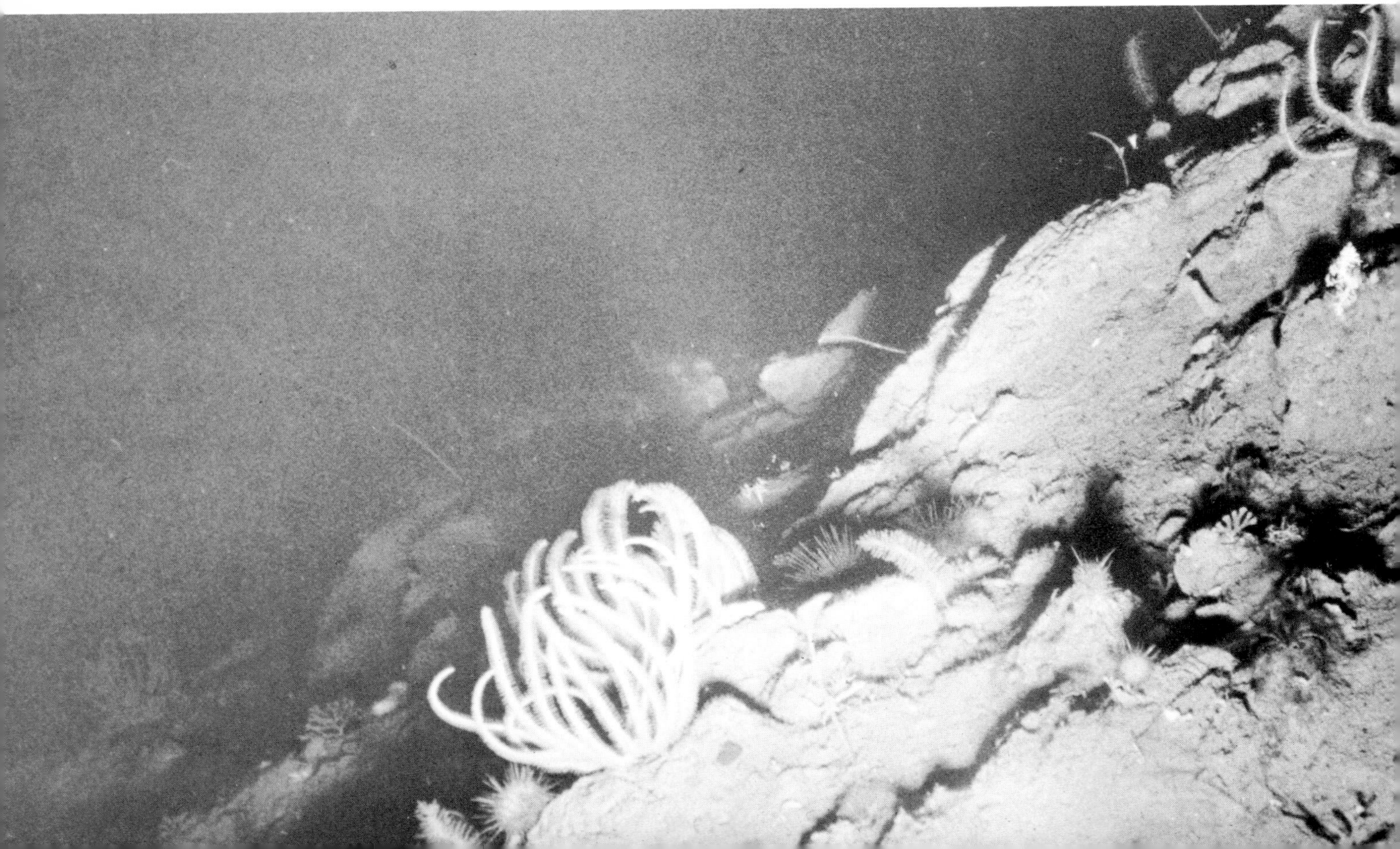

Brisingidae, a deep-water family with numerous long slender rays may have been mistaken for the similar appearing ophiuroids (2.44) in bottom photographs.

Many starfish are of a dull yellowish hue, but others are red, orange, blue, green, gray, and brown, sometimes in mottled and banded patterns of contrasting colors. Most asteroids are carnivores and feed voraciously on almost any available slowly moving or sessile animal, chiefly molluscs and other echinoderms. Carnivorous starfish capture their prey and digest it either within the body or externally. Many burrow into soft muddy bottoms where they pick out bivalve molluscs as their main source of food.

The deep-sea starfish belong predominantly to a peculiarly modified group of strong, rigid individuals having five short broad-based arms often lacking powerful suckers as well as mouth, intestines, and anus. In

62°35′S 59°59′W

2.39 Feather star (*Pentacrinus maclearanus*).

2.38 Free-living feather stars. U, stalkless crinoids and brittle stars, 91 m, continental shelf, Antarctic Peninsula. L, stalkless crinoids and sea pens, 994 m, continental slope, southern Chile.

48°54′S 75°49′W

fact all members of one dominant abyssal group (*Porcellanasteridae*) lack the intestine and must ingest and egest masses of mud. The effect of their passage should be very apparent in the abyssal seascape.

The spiny cushion stars (*Pterasteridae*), plump five-rayed starfish with short broad arms often appear peculiarly inflated (2.43). This deep-sea form has a special respiratory chamber between the upper surface of the exoskeleton and the covering membrane. This chamber is rhythmically inflated and deflated by the intake and outflow of water. One shallow-water representative was observed[14] to inflate four times per minute and to expel sixty-five milliliters of water with each pulse.

Starfish are often photographed on the continental shelf and the continental slope, and on insular shelves and slopes (2.43), but are infrequently seen on seamounts or on the Mid-Oceanic Ridge.

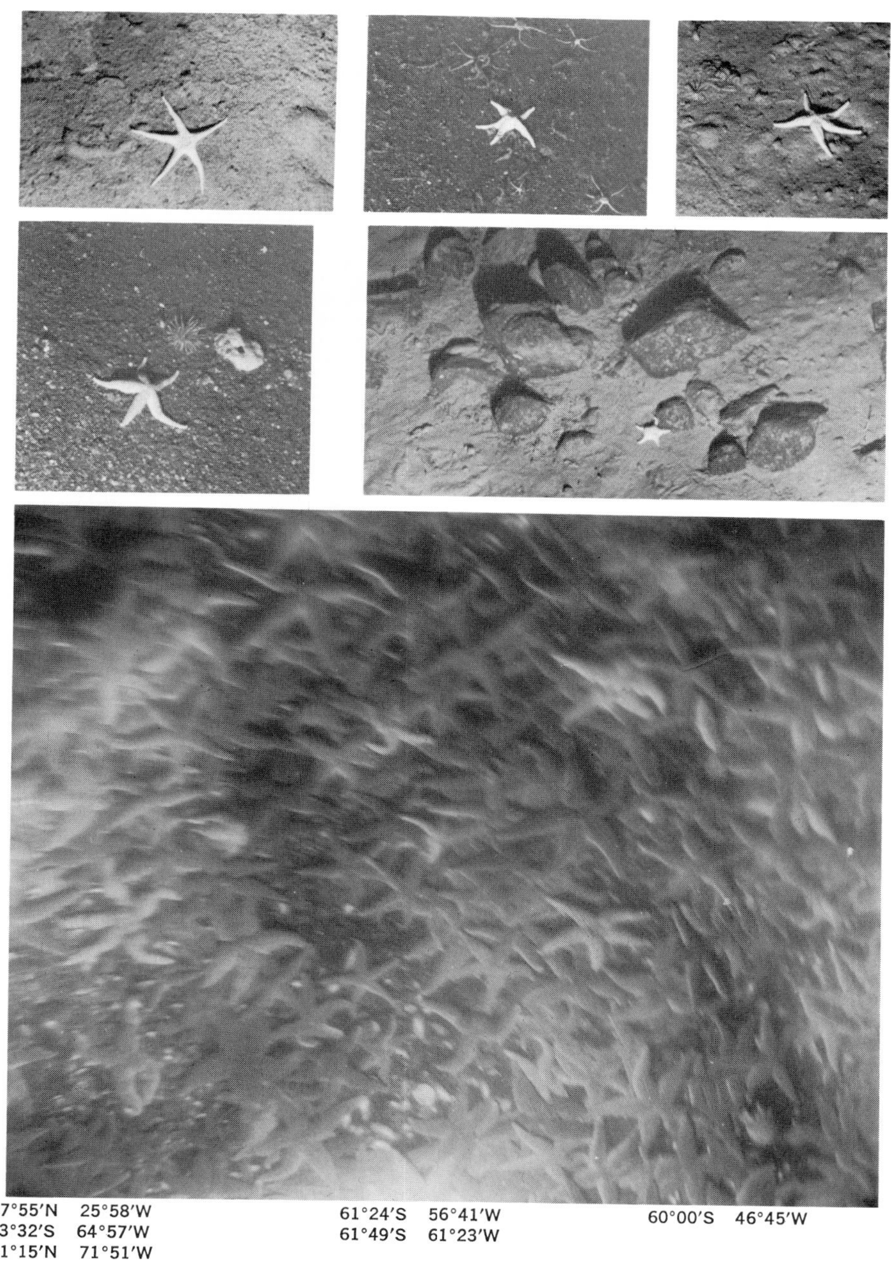

37°55′N 25°58′W
53°32′S 64°57′W
41°15′N 71°51′W
61°24′S 56°41′W
61°49′S 61°23′W
60°00′S 46°45′W

2.41 Starfish. UL, 1470 m, Azores. UC, 618 m, continental slope, Antarctic Peninsula. UR, 2442 m, eastern Scotia Sea. LC, 119 m, Falkland Plateau. RC, 3278 m, Drake Passage. L, 34 m, Vineyard Sound, Mass.

50°30′N 50°47′W

◁ 2.40 Feather garden. Free-living crinoids and anemones thrive in the nutrient-rich waters of the fishing grounds off the Grand Banks of Newfoundland, 331 m.

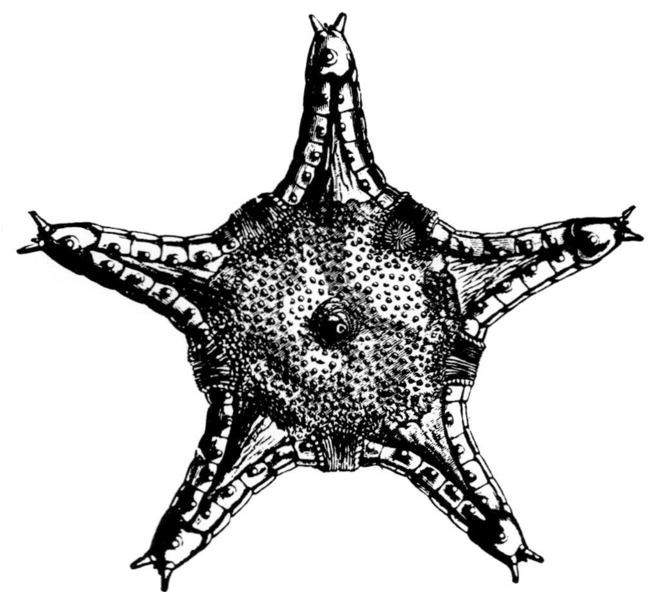

2.42 A deep-sea short-armed starfish (*Porcellanaster*).

Photographs of asteroids have been taken in very shallow water showing a layer several animals thick covering the entire sea floor, and their impressions are very common in softer sediments of the shelf and slope. They are seen in the greatest depths, although on the lower continental slope and continental rise they are apparently replaced as the most abundant form by the slender-rayed brittle stars.

Their radial impressions are readily recognized. In some cases asteroids are partially buried; in other cases the animal is seen on the surface of the sediment. They make a star impression similar to their own form by burrowing into the sediment with an almost vertical motion.

The commonly photographed brittle stars (ophiuroids) differ externally from starfish in having usually a small rounded disc with five distinct arms that are long (up to one-quarter meter), slender, jointed, and fragile (2.44). Brittle stars move by rowing. With one arm outstretched in the direction of movement and two arms pressing on each side, they leave distinctive marks that are convex forward. They may also move by snakelike movements, holding to objects by one or more rays and pushing with the others, so as to jerk the body along. Their food is small crustaceans, molluscs, and other animals and bottom debris. Although many are somber-colored, red, blue, green, yellow, and vermilion colors are seen in shallow water. Many of the deep-sea brittle stars are bright orange or red but the colors fade quickly in alcohol, and those which delighted the

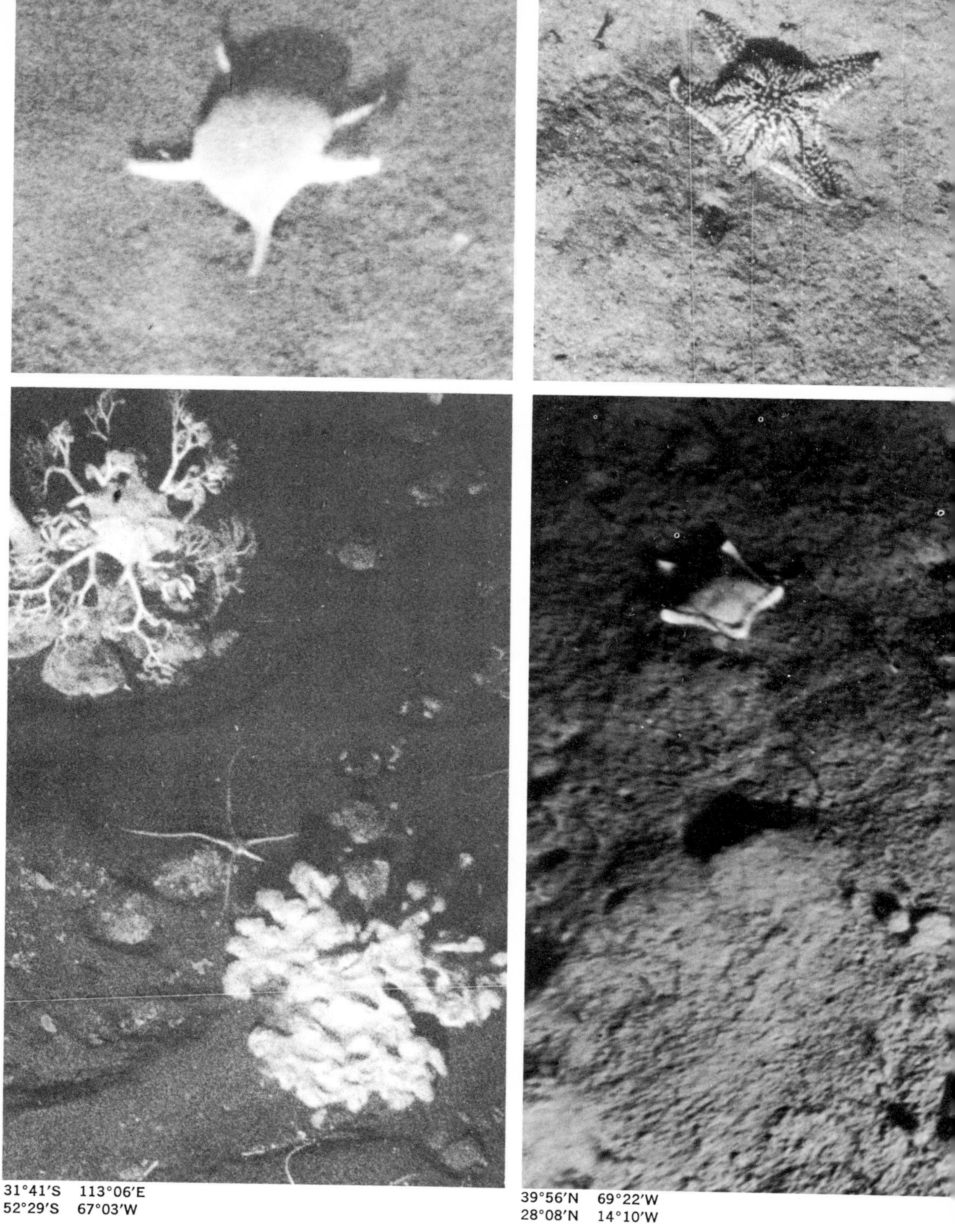

2.43 Short-armed starfish and basket stars. UL, Inflated abyssal starfish, 5029 m, Wharton Basin, Indian Ocean. UR, 279 m, New England continental slope. LL, basket star, 86 m, Argentine continental shelf. LR, 122 m, Canary Islands.

eye of the sea-going scientist were later described by specialists as dull. Basket stars, although rather uncommon, have been seen on the sandy ripple-marked continental shelf (2.43 LL).

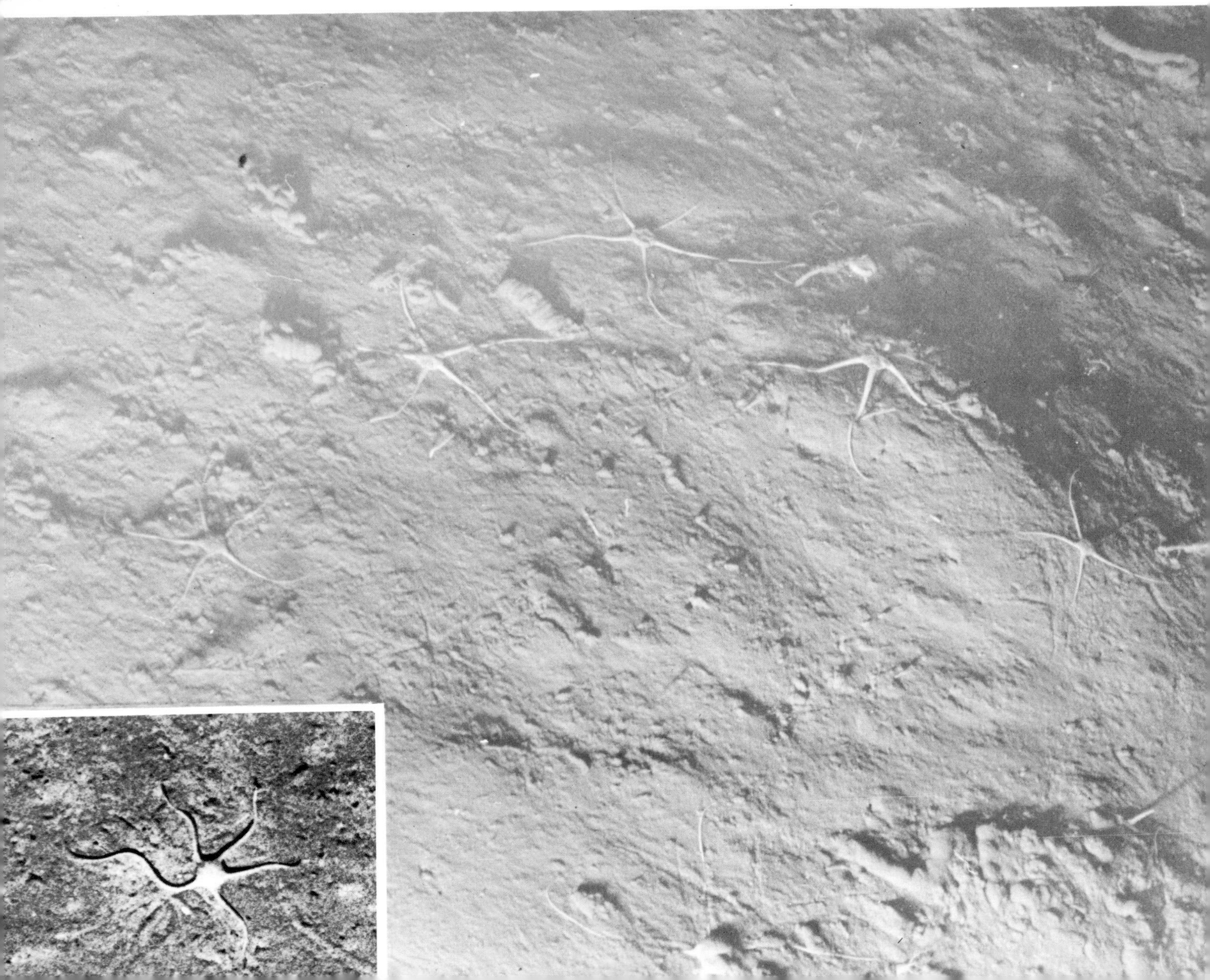

Brittle stars are second in importance only to holothurians in the visible abyss. They are found in all the world oceans, including the Arctic Ocean, and to the greatest depths. Eleven cosmopolitan species are known to occur in the Atlantic, Pacific, and Indian Oceans.

"The brittle-star's arm coils round the scrap of food like an elephant's trunk and draws it into the wide open mouth on the lower side of the disc, where the prey is dealt with by the teeth."[15] It had been suspected that carnivorous brittle stars live on the surface of the sea floor and do
60°46′S 49°20′W not burrow into it. Photographs of ophiuroids, in general, substantiate this view, although they do appear at times to burrow at least shallowly in the sediment, leaving a radial star-shaped burrow mark on the sea floor. A unique characteristic of ophiuroids is the tendency to stick one ray out of the sediment or, in other cases, to extend their rays into the sediment and elevate their central disc a few centimeters off the bottom.

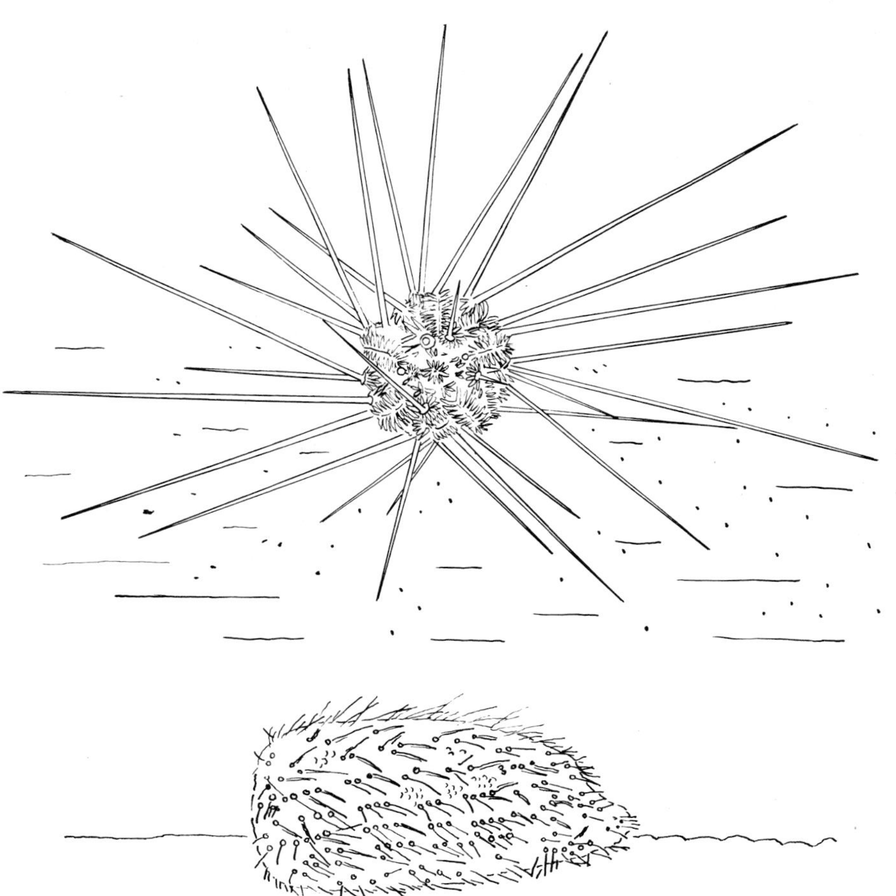

62°24′S 64°17′W

2.45 Regular (U, *Porocidaris elegans*) and irregular (L, *Pourtalesia hispida*) urchins.

◁ 2.44 Brittle stars. U, 2645 m, Scotia Sea. LL, 1815 m, Blake Escarpment. LR, 3677 m, Drake Passage.

32°01′N 76°54′W

30°59′N 73°32′W
31°50′N 77°38′W
12°14′N 45°48′W

Sea urchins (echinoids) have round bodies lacking free arms or rays and are thickly covered by many movable spines. They are separated into the symmetrical globose "regular" urchins and the elongate asymmetrical "irregular" urchins (2.45).

The frequently photographed and quite photogenic regular urchins move over the sediment by means of their podia or their spines or both, with any ray forward (2.46). They can reverse direction without turning around and frequently change the axis of forward locomotion. They feed on almost anything but tend to be carnivorous. The regular urchins feed by moving over the food, holding it with spines and podia, and chewing it into bits with their powerful Aristotle's lantern. Echinoids are usually colored uniformly in plain dark shades, most commonly green, olive, purple, brown, and black, although some are pale or nearly white and a few are red.

The infrequently photographed irregular urchins differ altogether in their habits, morphology, and physiology from regular urchins. Most live buried in the bottom sediments and their many structural peculiarities are related to this habit. In the symmetrical regular urchins, the centrally placed mouth is located in the center of the downward-facing oral surface. However, in the irregular urchins the mouth has migrated forward and the anus migrated aft. These echinoids, whose spines are swept back, can move only forward and cannot back up. Some groups of the irregular urchins have lost the lantern and thus the ability to devour larger food. They apparently live on small morsels found in the mud. Several irregular urchins of the shallow waters live in burrows with only a tuft of podia thrust through the surface hole.

The spiny globose regular echinoids are relatively common in the deep sea, although less so than the holothurians. They occur on all types of bottoms and in all depths. They range from small black dots to large, ornate, spiny forms (2.47). The largest urchins belong to the deep-sea family *Echinothuriidae* and attain a diameter of at least thirty-two centimeters (2.48). Urchins live in both current-swept and tranquil environments, but their presence is most noticeable in the tranquil areas where their furrows, created while feeding, are a common element of the abyssal scene.

Sea cucumbers (holothurians) are the largest and most numerous animals seen on the deep-sea floor (2.49, 2.50). Some reach one-half meter in length and they occur abundantly in all depths. Those that graze

◁ 2.46 Regular urchins. U, C, 856 m, 774 m, Blake Plateau. L, 1224 m, Mid-Atlantic Ridge.

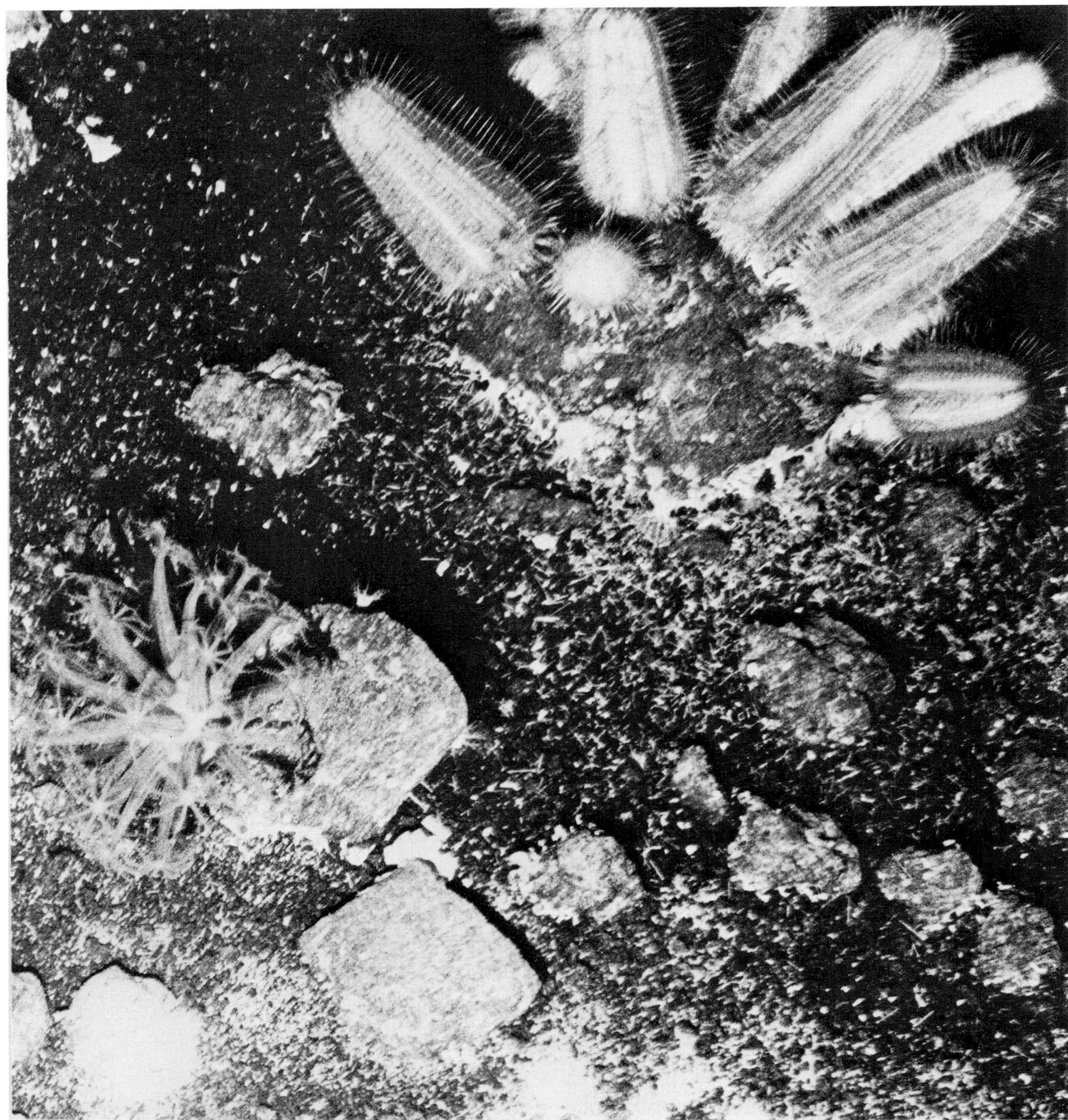

46°02′S 83°57′W

2.47 Urchins and a coelenterate on Eltanin Seamount. This is the only known life photograph of the cactus-like urchin, *Dermechinus horridus,* 388 m, peak on the Chile Ridge, southern Pacific.

on the ooze and clay, tracking the bottom and remolding the sediment, create prominent and characteristic features which over wide areas dominate the abyssal landscape. These large, conspicuous, elongated, soft-bodied creatures are covered with leathery skin containing microscopic calcareous spicules. The mouth, with a circle of tentacles, is near one end, and the anus, edged with papillae, is at the other (2.51). Most lie on one side which has differentiated as a flattened creeping sole, bears all the locomotory podia, and contrasts with the arched dorsal surface on which the podia are represented by vestigial warts and finger-like projections (2.52).

The five orders of holothurians are all represented in the deep-sea fauna (2.53). Although most species belonging to the orders Apoda and Dendrochirota are found in shallow sunlit waters, four species of each order are found in the deep sea. The Apoda are elongate burrowers with

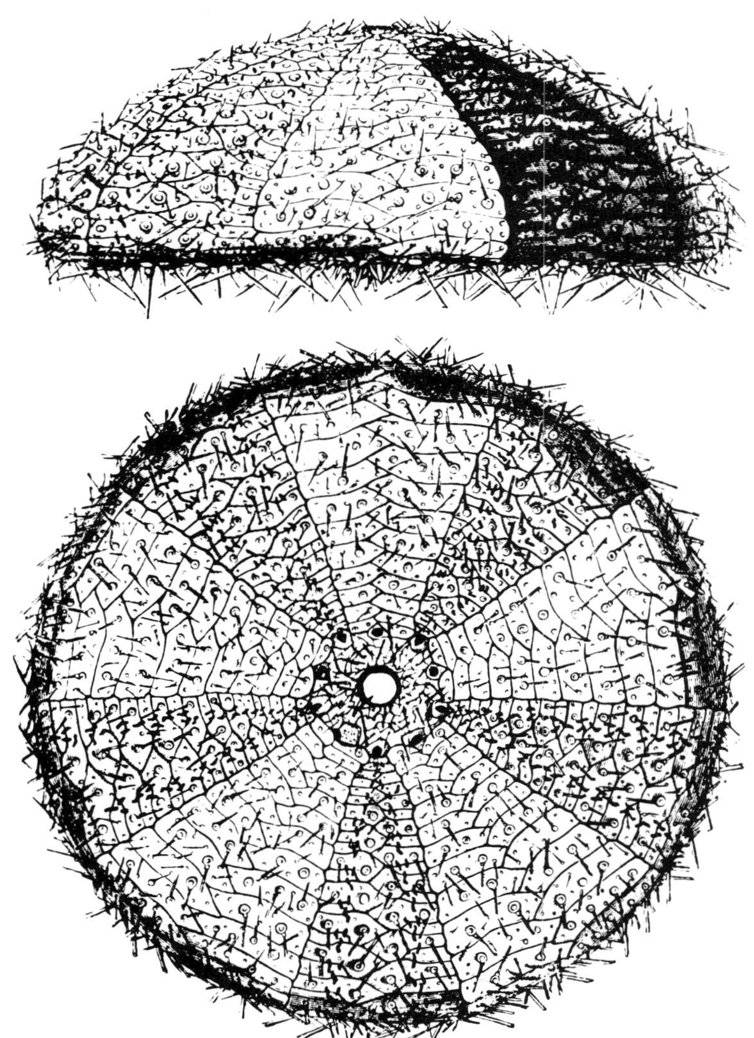

2.48 A large abyssal urchin (*Phormosoma uranus*).

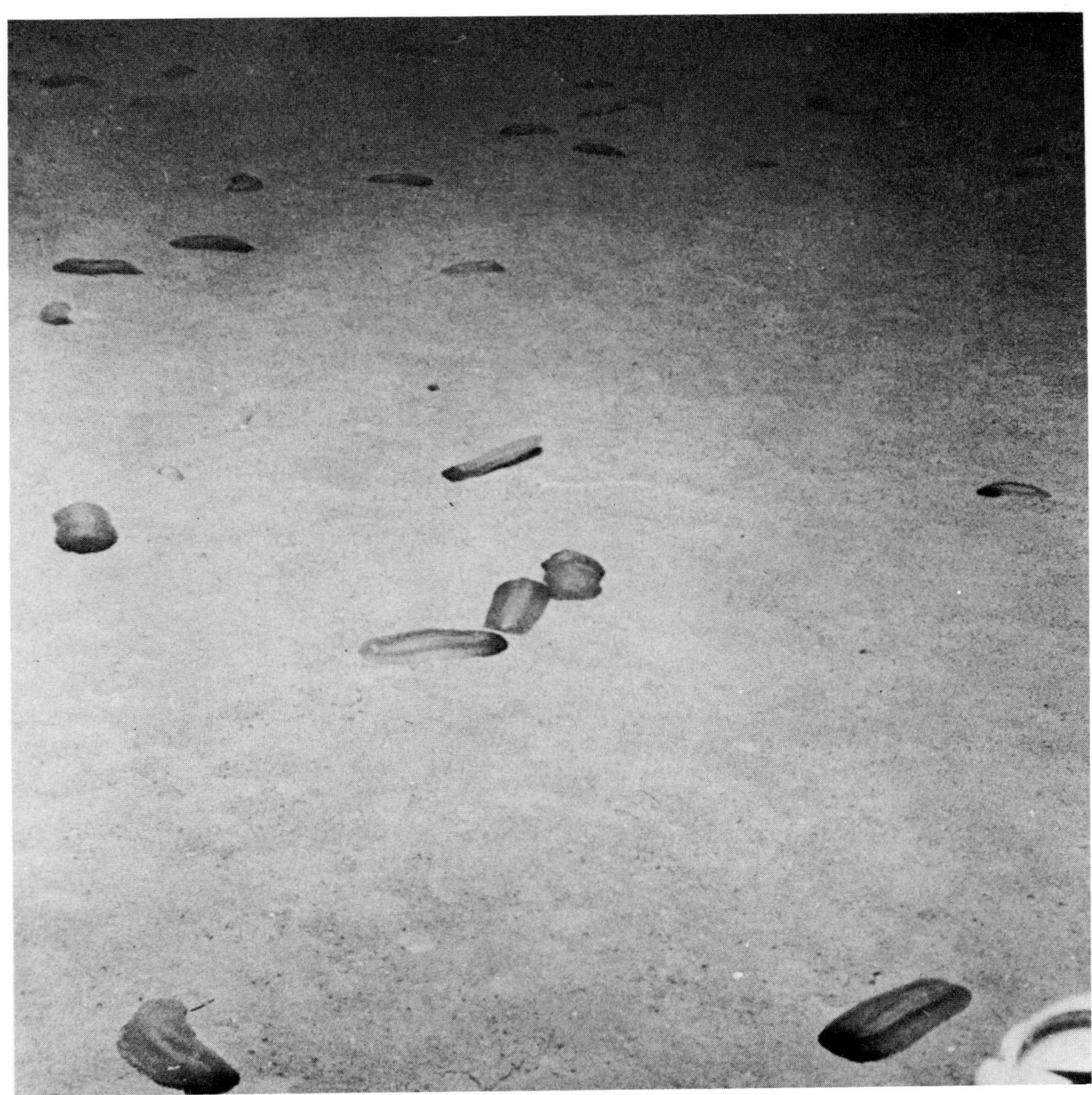

18°48'N 65°27'W

2.49 Holothurian army walking and swimming on the south wall of the Puerto Rico Trench. The majority of holothurians at this location were walking down the south wall of the trench, toward the bottom, 2193 m.

tentacles but no podia or creeping sole (2.53, 2.54, 2.55). The Dendrochirota are generally covered with many small podia, have branching tentacles and a creeping sole. They are filter feeders, and in some the locomotory podia have been altered for adhesion while the mouth and anus have migrated to the upper surface. Seven species of the order

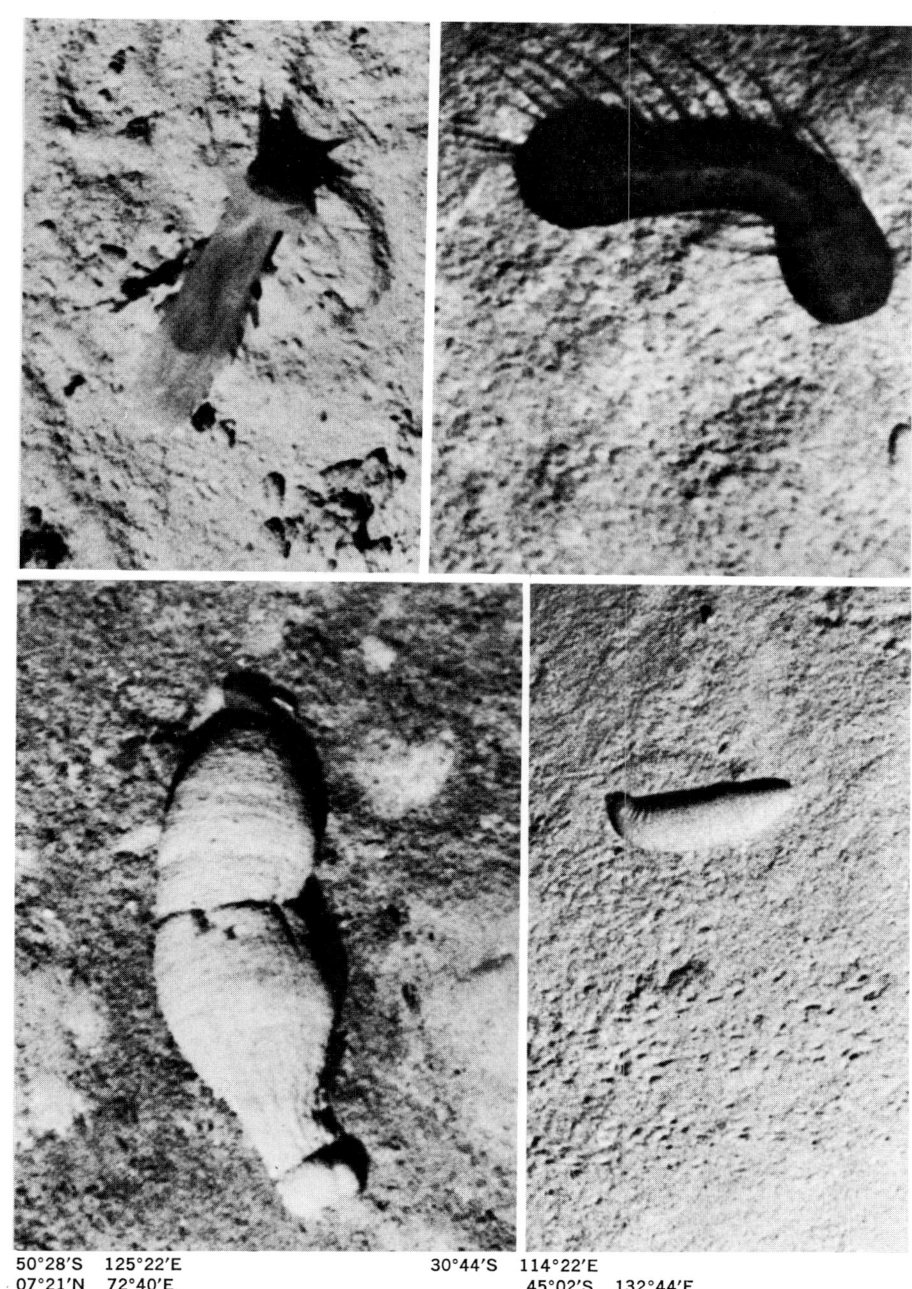

50°28′S 125°22′E 30°44′S 114°22′E
07°21′N 72°40′E 45°02′S 132°44′E

2.50 Holothurians from the Indian Ocean. UL, 3688 m, Mid-Indian Ocean Ridge. UR, 2516 m, western continental slope of Australia. LL, 1760 m, Maldive Islands. LR, 4670 m, Mid-Indian Ocean Ridge.

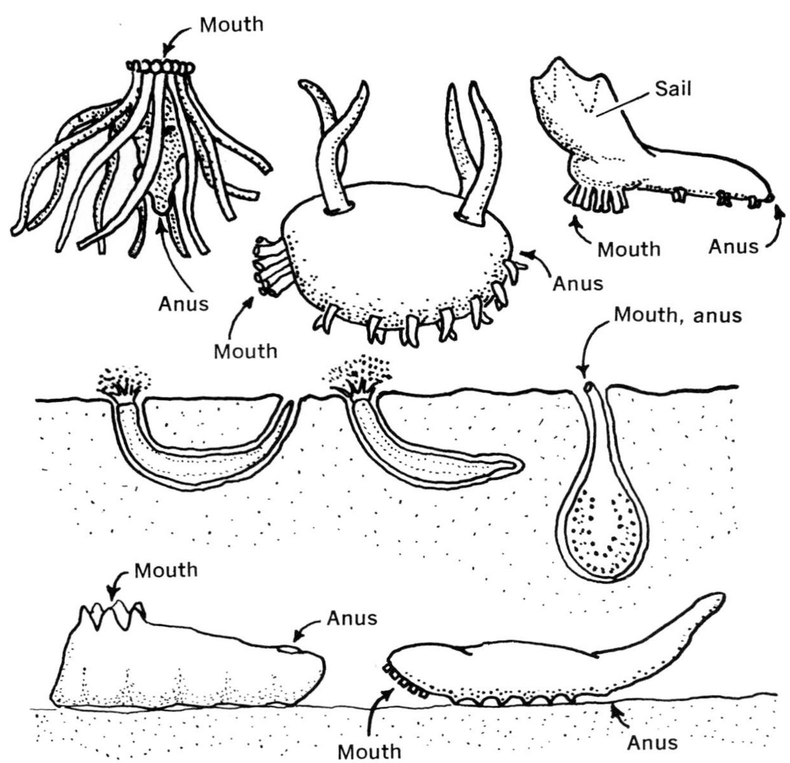

2.51 Mode of life of holothurians. UL, swimming elasipod (*Pelagothuria*); UC, UR, grazing elasipods (*Scotoplanes* and *Peniagone*); CL, C, burrowing Apoda; CR, burrowing Molpadonia; L, adaption to mode of life; LL, the mouth has migrated to upper surface of this filter feeder (*Psolus,* a Dendrochirota); LR, mouth has migrated down in a vacuum-cleaner-like arrangement of this grazer (*Psychropotes,* an Elasipoda).

Molpadonia are found in the deep sea. The burrowers of this order are stout, relatively smooth, and have neither podia nor a creeping sole (2.53).

The vast majority of the abyssal holothurians belong to the Aspidochirota (27 species) and the Elasipoda (88 species). Members of both orders have podia and a creeping sole. The more ornate Elasipoda have fewer but longer and more prominent podia than the Aspidochirota. Members of both orders have been photographed, but the large distinctive elasipods have been seen most frequently.

All elasipods are confined to the abyss. A ventral displacement of the mouth and anus is obvious in the elasipods in which the anterior end is shoved ventrally, facing the sediment surface (2.51). Such a vacuum cleaner configuration is ideally suited to skimming off the surface slime

2.52 Abyssal cucumbers. UL, 3585 m, Drake Passage. UR, 3115 m, Mid-Oceanic Ridge, southeast Pacific. LC, 2887 m, Carlsberg Ridge, Indian Ocean. RC, 4205 m, Pacific continental rise, Antarctic Peninsula. LL, 3792 m, Drake Passage. LR, 4134 m, Pacific continental rise, Antarctic Peninsula.

(2.56, 2.57, 2.58). A thin rim of fused podia which forms a lateral fringe in some elasipods is used in swimming (2.49).

Many deep-sea elasipods are vividly colored in bright translucent shades of purple, maroon, and violet; however, dull shades of gray, brown, olive, or black are characteristic of shallow-water holothurians.

ABYSSAL HOLOTHURIANS

List of Genera dredged from below 3000 m with sketches
of representative species of each order

ORDER APODA
*Protankyra, *Myriotrochus*

ORDER MOLPADONIA
*Gephyrothuria, Hedingia, Ceraplectana, *Molpadia*

ORDER DENDROCHIROTA
**Abyssicucumis, Ypsilothuria*

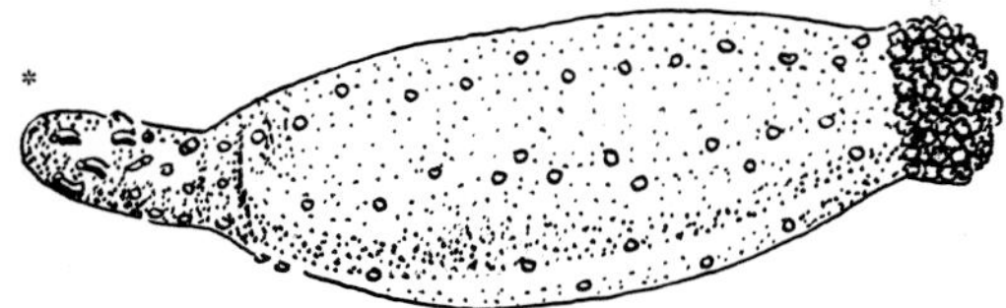

ORDER ASPIDOCHIROTA
*Bathyplotes, Benthothuria, Capheira, Mesothuria, *Paelopatides, Paroriza, **Pseudostichopus, Synallactes*

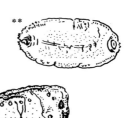

ORDER ELASIPODA
*Deima, Oneirophanta, Orphnurgus, Laetmogone, Achlyonice, Ellipinion, Elpidia, Kolga, Periamma, *Scotoplanes, Parelpidia, Peniagone, Scotoanassa, Benthodytes, Euphronides, Psycheotrephes, Psychropotes*

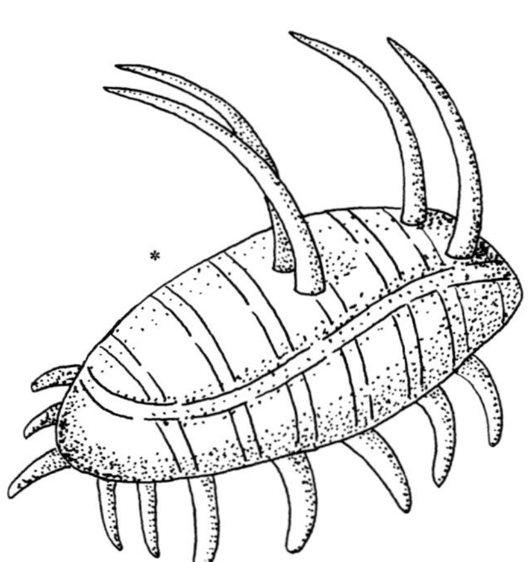

2.53 Abyssal holothurians.

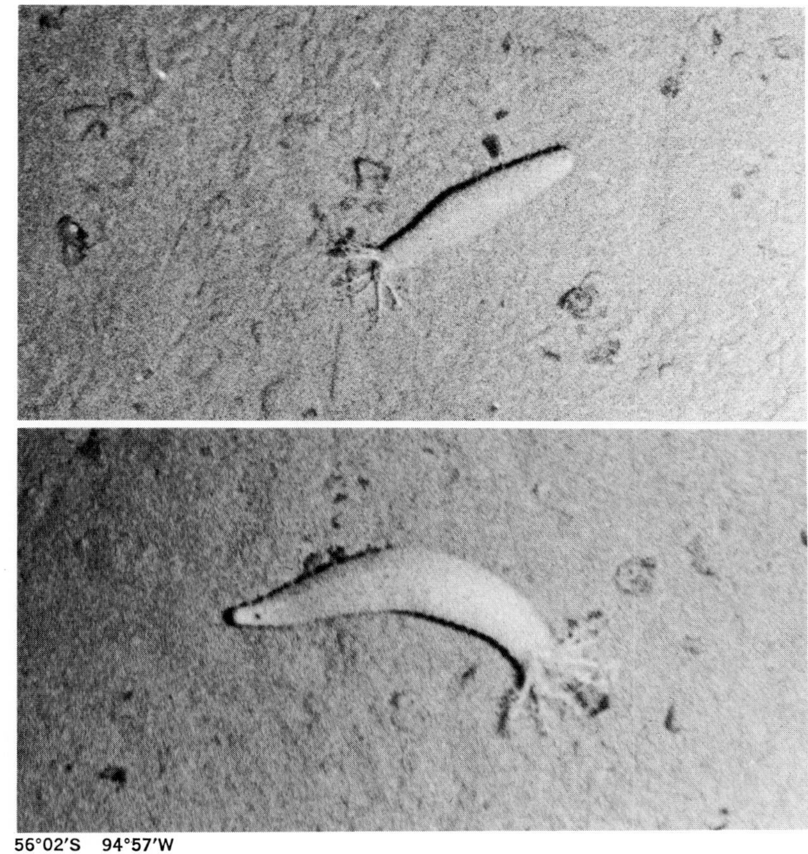

2.54 Apoda holothurians. These animals closely resemble *Myriotrochus* (2.53). U, L, 4757 m, Bellingshausen Basin, South Pacific.

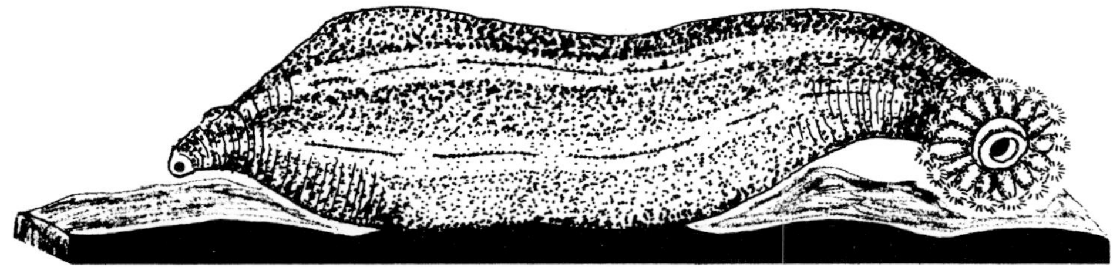

2.55 An abyssal Apoda holothurian (*Trochostoma arcticum*).

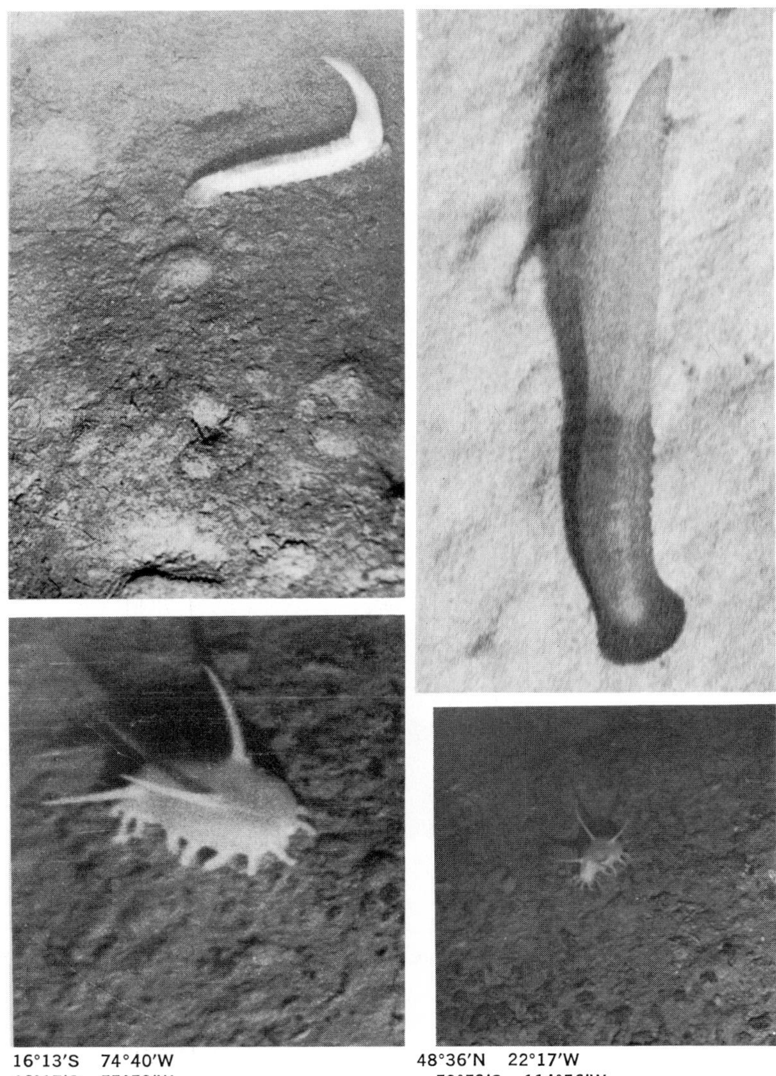

16°13′S 74°40′W
46°17′S 55°53′W
48°36′N 22°17′W
59°53′S 114°56′W

2.56 Abyssal elasipod holothurians. *Psychropotes* (top) and *Scotoplanes* (bottom). UL, 3045 m, east wall, Peru-Chile Trench. UR, 4014 m, Mid-Atlantic Ridge, eastern North Atlantic. LL, 5386 m, continental rise of Argentina. LR, 5195 m, Bellingshausen Basin.

Those which live within the sediments are pink, rose, orange, terra-cotta, violet, or transparent. Yellow, red, and orange hues are also seen among the dendrochirotes.

Veritable armies of holothurians are occasionally observed on the deep-sea floor (2.59). Photographs from the south wall of the Puerto Rico Trench (2.49) and from the continental slope off California,

(2.60) show large numbers of holothurians moving along the bottom. The holothurian most frequently photographed in the Puerto Rico Trench has a wide brim (2.61). It has been speculated that such brims

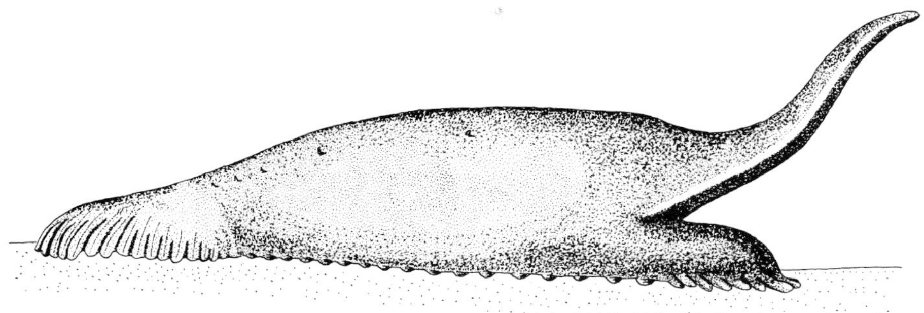

2.57 Side view of *Psychropotes;* A giant abyssal grazer which may reach half a meter in length. Mouth is on left.

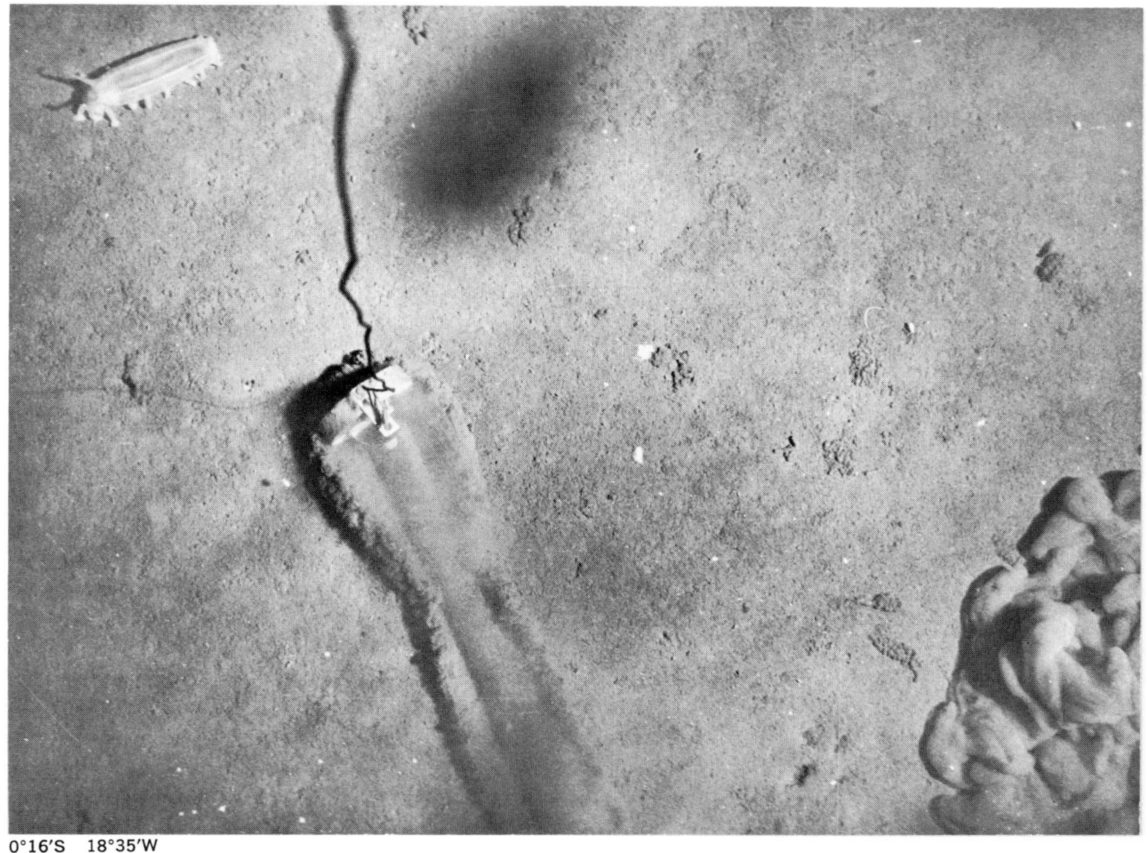

0°16′S 18°35′W

2.58 Holothurian walking across the floor of the Romanche Trench. Sediment cloud is stirred by trigger weight, 7325 m, equatorial Atlantic.

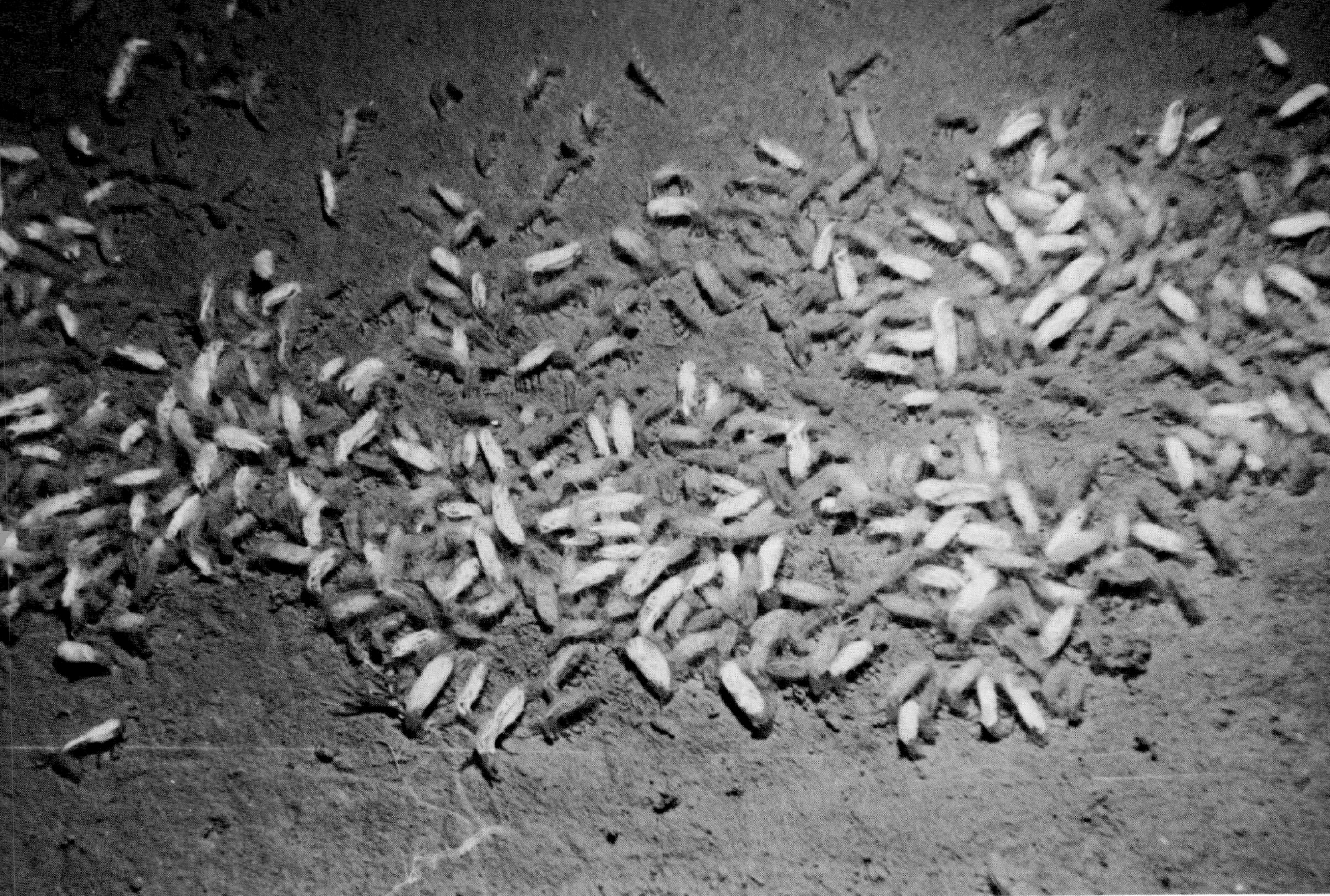

2.59 Varicolored holothurians swarm on the organic rich muds of the continental slope. 1615 m, east of Cape Hatteras.

are used in swimming and, indeed, they may be; for a biologist observed from the bathyscaphe *Archimède* what appeared to be a swimming holothurian of this type.[16] At one location on the south wall of the Puerto Rico Trench an average of ten or fifteen holothurians were observed in each of the thirty bottom photographs obtained. In several cases the holothurians lay with their anterior ends on the sediment and the whole posterior portions of their bodies inclined to the bottom at angles up to fifteen or twenty degrees. Whether this attitude resulted from swimming activities or whether they were inching along in the manner well known among shallow-water forms is not known. In several photographs pairs of holothurians are noticed lying side by side (2.61 LL). In the well-explored Kurile-Kamchatka Trench, holothurians (chiefly the small elasipod *Elpidia*) constitute as much as 80 per cent of the total weight of living organisms at depths below 8000 meters and over 30 per cent at lesser depths to 2500 meters.[17]

The ocean covers 73 per cent of the earth's surface and over 80 per cent of this surface is a soft-sediment-covered sea floor. This is the home of the abyssal holothurians. These animals are the most evident organisms seen in abyssal photographs (2.62) and the combination of these circumstances leads one to the inescapable conclusion that holothurians are the dominant large animals of the major part of the earth's surface. Holothurians feeding on bottom sediments mix and till the surface muds on an enormous scale, producing features more widespread and more visibly evident than those produced by any other animal on earth.

SNAILS, CLAMS, SQUIDS, AND OCTOPUSES

Except for the squid, octopus, and slug, most abyssal molluscs are relatively small and live partially or entirely buried in the mud. They are therefore difficult to photograph. Chitons, tooth shells, snails, slugs, bivalves, squids, and octopuses mostly live in shallow water, but a few

2.60 A holothurian herd. Elasipod holothurians (*Scotoplanes*) and brittle stars cover the sea floor. A shrimp was seen escaping into round hole lower right, 1100 m, Coronado Submarine Canyon off Southern California.

32°20′N 117°25′W

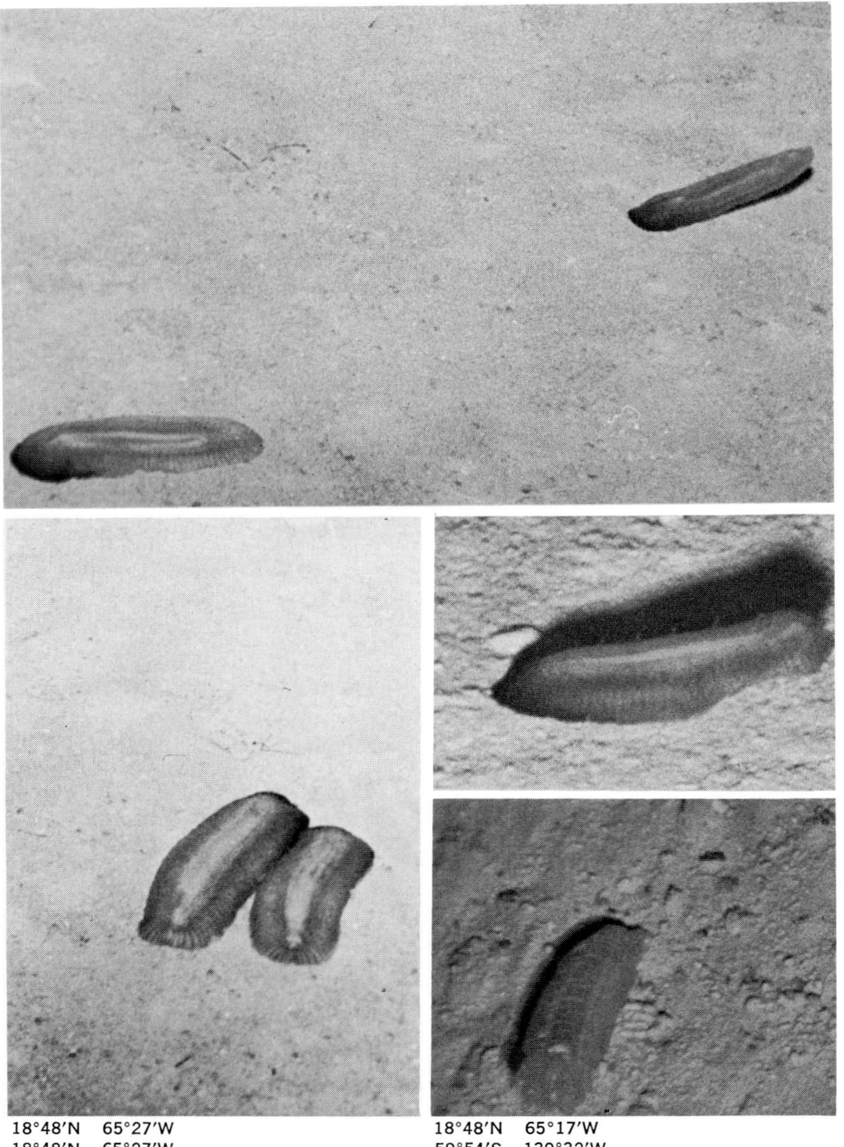

2.61 Large abyssal sea cucumbers. U, holothurian in upper right may be swimming, 2173 m. L, RC, 2173 m, and 2068 m, south wall, Puerto Rico Trench. LR, 4091 m, Mid-Oceanic Ridge, South Pacific.

representatives of each are found to the greatest depths. The deep-sea forms are even smaller than their shallow-water relatives and are much more fragile. In addition, an entire group of small (2 cm) primitive molluscs, *Neopolina,* is found only in the abyss.

The gastropods, which lead a roving life in search of prey, occur at

2.62 A giant abyssal Aspidochirote. Note large anal opening on right, 3657 m, Mid-Oceanic Ridge, South Pacific.

all depths; are generally small and rarely have been identified in photographs (2.63, 4.8). Although the brilliantly colored sea hares are common among the reefs, they have not yet been reported from the abyss.

Squid about three feet in length have been photographed in mid-water with a camera employing a bait-operated trigger.[18] Somewhat larger

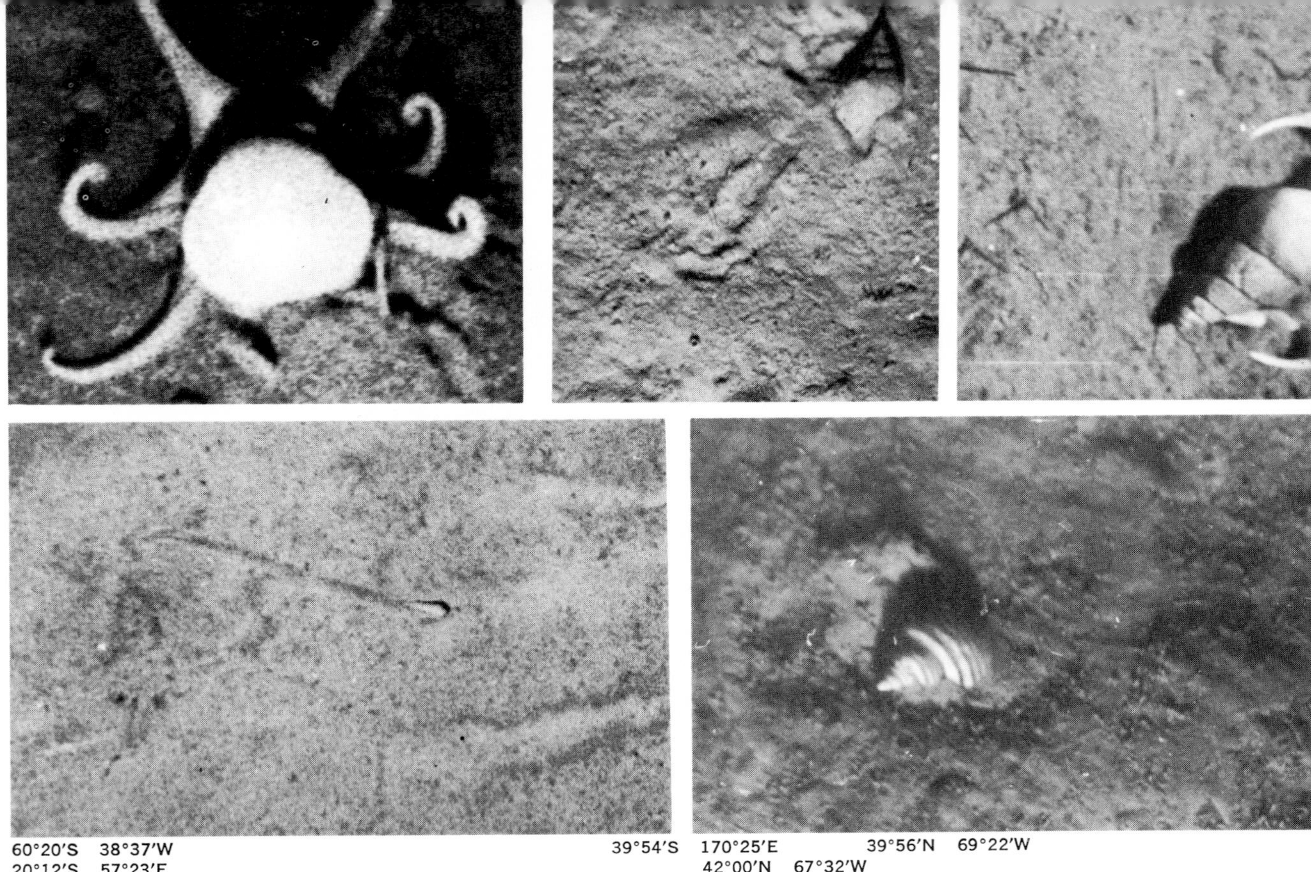

60°20′S 38°37′W
20°12′S 57°23′E

39°54′S 170°25′E
42°00′N 67°32′W

39°56′N 69°22′W

2.63 Snails and octopuses. UL, 3368 m, Scotia Sea. UC, 803 m, New Zealand Plateau. UR, hermit crab in abandoned snail shell, 448 m, continental slope off New England. LL, 605 m, slope of Réunion Island. LR, 80 m, Georges Bank.

squid have taken their own mid-water portraits by grasping the twenty-pound camera trigger weight in their beaks. Giant squids are the largest invertebrates living in the deep sea and are believed to reach thirty meters in length; however, these giants have never been photographed in the sea and knowledge of them has come almost entirely from sucker marks left on the skin of whales. Deep-sea octopuses and squids are chocolate brown, orange-brown, and purplish-brown in color. Most have large eyes and apparently keen vision. Octopuses have been photographed resting on muddy bottom (2.63 UL), and lurking behind rocks (2.64 U), but the marks which they must make in the sediment have not been identified.

The vampire squid is a pint-sized, blue-black animal which looks as much like an octopus as a squid. Its eight tentacles are linked together by a web. It has two enormous globular eyes which occupy more than a third of the body diameter, and it is covered by numerous light-producing organs of many shapes and sizes. This exotic squid is thought to be pelagic but it has been photographed swimming near the deep-sea floor in over 5000 meters depth (2.64 L).

Deep-sea bivalves, although plentiful, are generally quite small and live buried in the sediment. Bivalves account for 10 to 20 per cent of

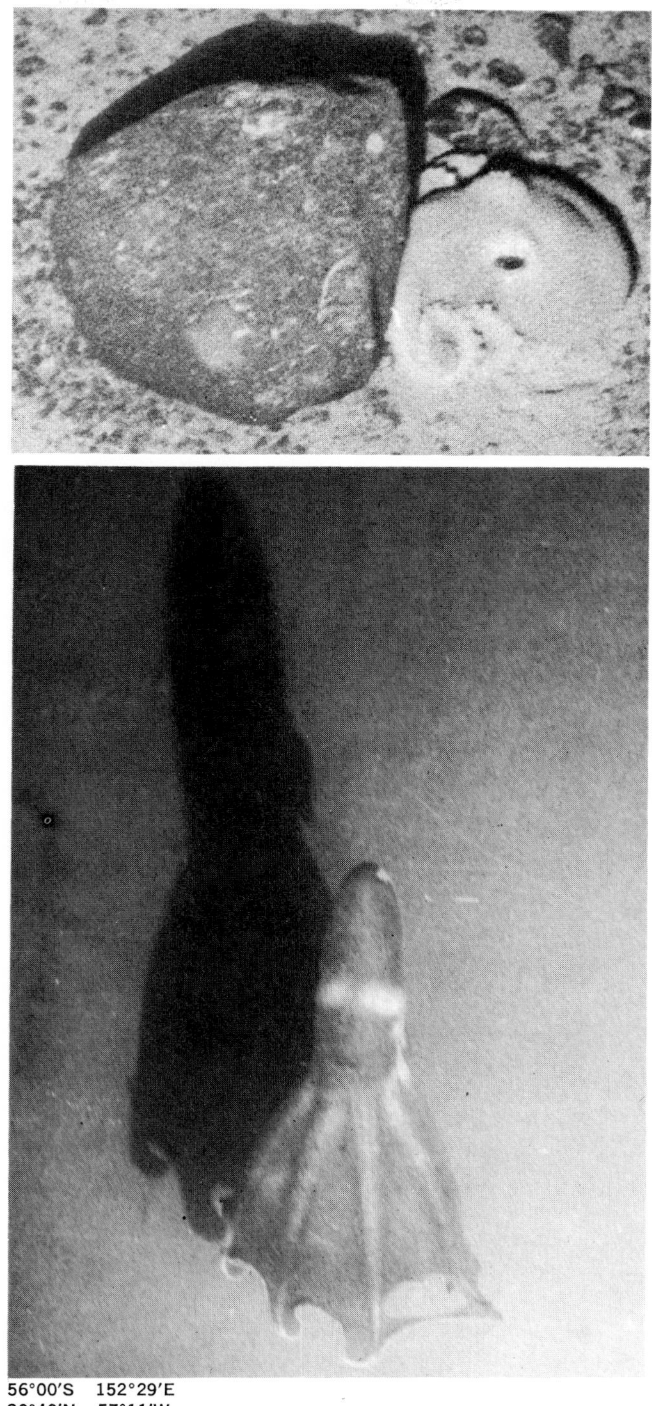

56°00′S 152°29′E
32°42′N 57°11′W

2.64 Shy octopus and bold squid. U, octopus hiding behind ice-rafted boulder, 3819 m, South Pacific. L, vampire squid, 5202 m, western Atlantic.

39°30′N 73°40′W

2.65 Broken mollusc shells and sand dollars litter the shallow current-swept continental shelf, 60 m. On the continental shelf most bivalve shells lie with their concave sides facing up. However, in the wave-washed zone off the beaches, they lie facing down. The latter position is most stable and is diagnostic of very high-velocity currents. On the open shelf, shells are thought to be turned over by scavengers.

the animal groups trawled in depths between 2000 and 6000 meters, and it is certain that some of the indistinct small objects seen in abyssal photographs are molluscs and their marks. The shallow depths of the continental shelf are littered with the shells of living bivalves as well as fossil shells of ice-age bivalves (2.65). Large scallops are commonly seen scooting along on the continental shelves, but large heavy-shelled molluscs are rarely seen in the abyss.

The brachiopods have lived on the floor of the oceans for 500 million years, slowly declining in number. These light-colored, pebble-sized organisms are found at all depths of the sea. Their shells are delicate, thin, and lamp-shaped, and they live in holes or attached by a short stalk to the bottom.

WORMS

Worms are abundant in the deep sea and it is curious that more visual evidence of them is not seen; however, their small size and their burrowing habit make many of them virtually impossible to see with present-day photographic methods. In highly productive areas, forests of fuzzy tufts are often seen. Many of these, no doubt, represent worms whose bodies are largely buried in the mud. Whereas most are annelid polychaetes, some must be echiuroids, sipunculids, priapuloids, and nemerteans, but until more close-up photographs are taken it will be difficult to see—let alone identify—the various small worms that inhabit the sea floor (2.66). Unusually large polychaete worm tubes have been dredged and photographed on the continental shelf and slope off New York and Massachusetts (2.67).

CRUSTACEANS AND SPIDERS

The infrequently photographed abyssal arthropods range in size from tiny leggy crustaceans less than one-quarter millimeter in length to large spiders and crabs whose legs span nearly 50 cm. Of all the many groups of crustaceans only the barnacles, isopods, and decapods have large abyssal representatives (2.68-2.73.).

Rather large beautiful red barnacles have been dredged from the deep sea, but to date none have been positively identified in underwater photographs. Only the isopods and decapods have bottom-living forms which are large enough to be seen. Isopods are abundant in the deep sea but

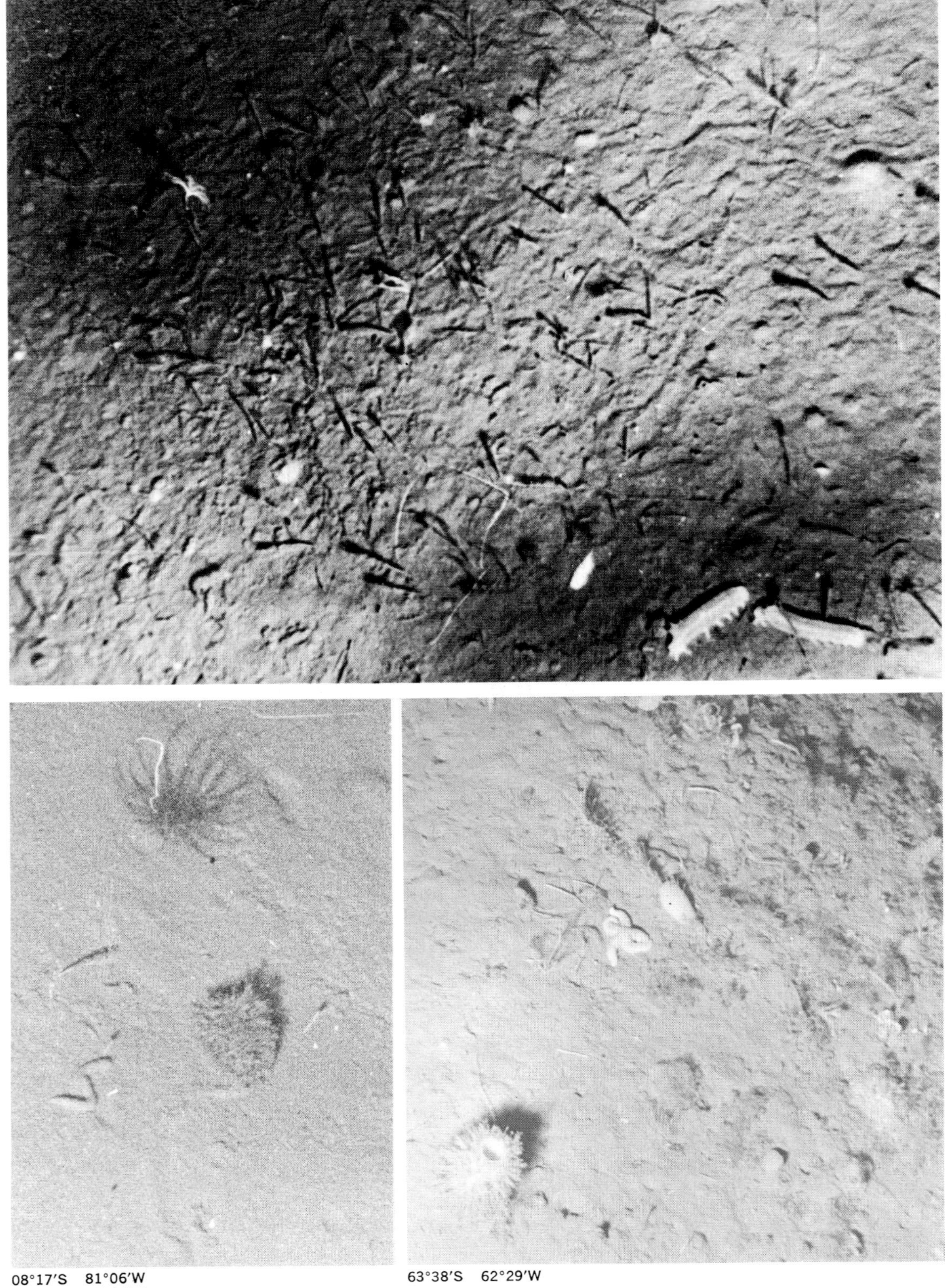

08°17′S 81°06′W
42°56′S 76°46′W

63°38′S 62°29′W

2.66 Abyssal worms. U, holothurians in a forest of worm tubes, 6238 m, floor of Peru-Chile Trench. LL, bristle worm, *Aphrodite,* crawling toward an actinarian, 3698 m, southern Peru-Chile Trench. LR, large worm tube and starfish, 284 m, continental shelf, Antarctic Peninsula.

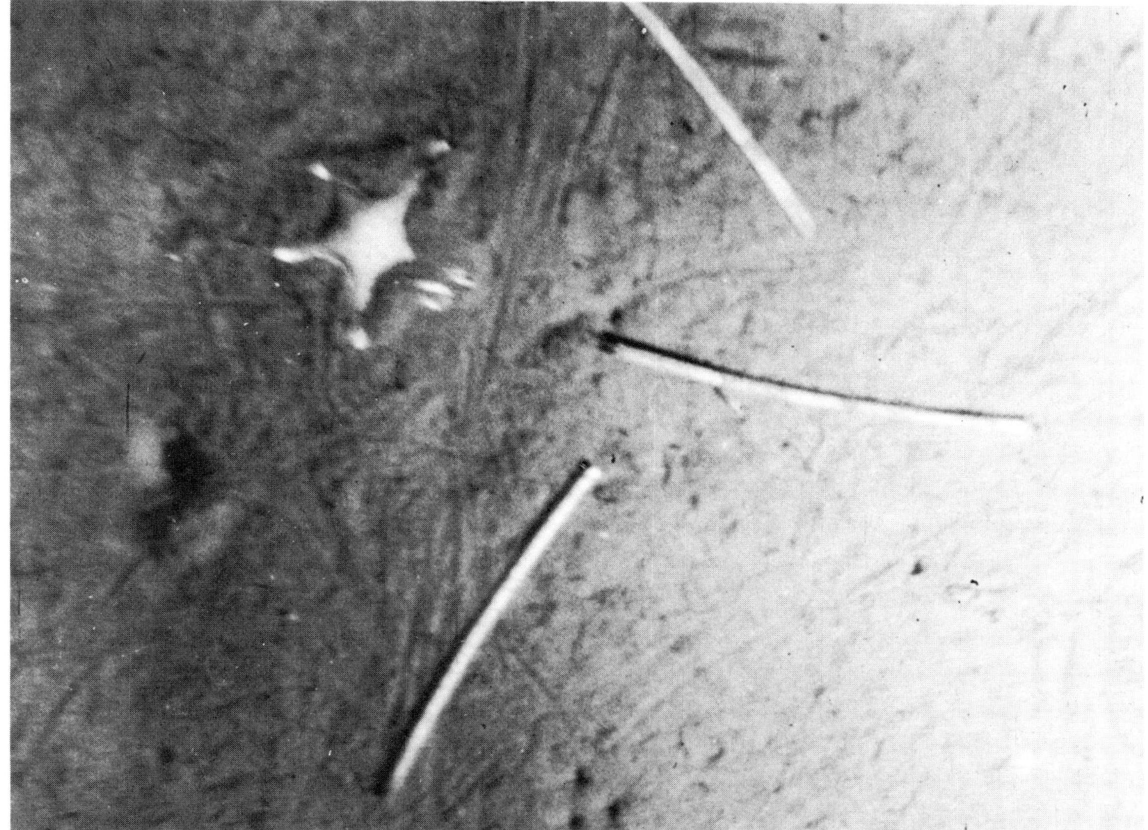

39°34′N 72°23′W
39°48′N 70°49′W

2.67 Armored worms. (*Hyalinoecia tubicola*). U, 450 m. L, 600 m, New England continental slope.

39°48′N 70°34′W

2.68 A crab challenges the *Alvin*. This pugnacious crab, *Geryon quinquidens,* is frequently seen on the continental slope, 1250 m, continental slope off New England.

most are very small organisms. However, a few are comparative giants, reaching the size of a toad. Three unusual photographs (2.73 UL, UR, RC) show giant isopods on the bottom of the ocean in depths of approximately 3000 meters.

Rather large crabs have been frequently dredged and phtographed from the deep sea. Although crabs are quite alert animals and usually assume a fighting stance (2.68, 2.69) on the approach of the camera, they have been occasionally photographed off guard (2.69 U).

Giant sea spiders (*Colendeis colossea*) (2.74), which have been dredged throughout the abyss, have been seen in several areas (2.75, 2.76). Shrimp-like crustaceans are occasionally seen swimming just above the sea floor (2.77). Some minute forms, commonly reported

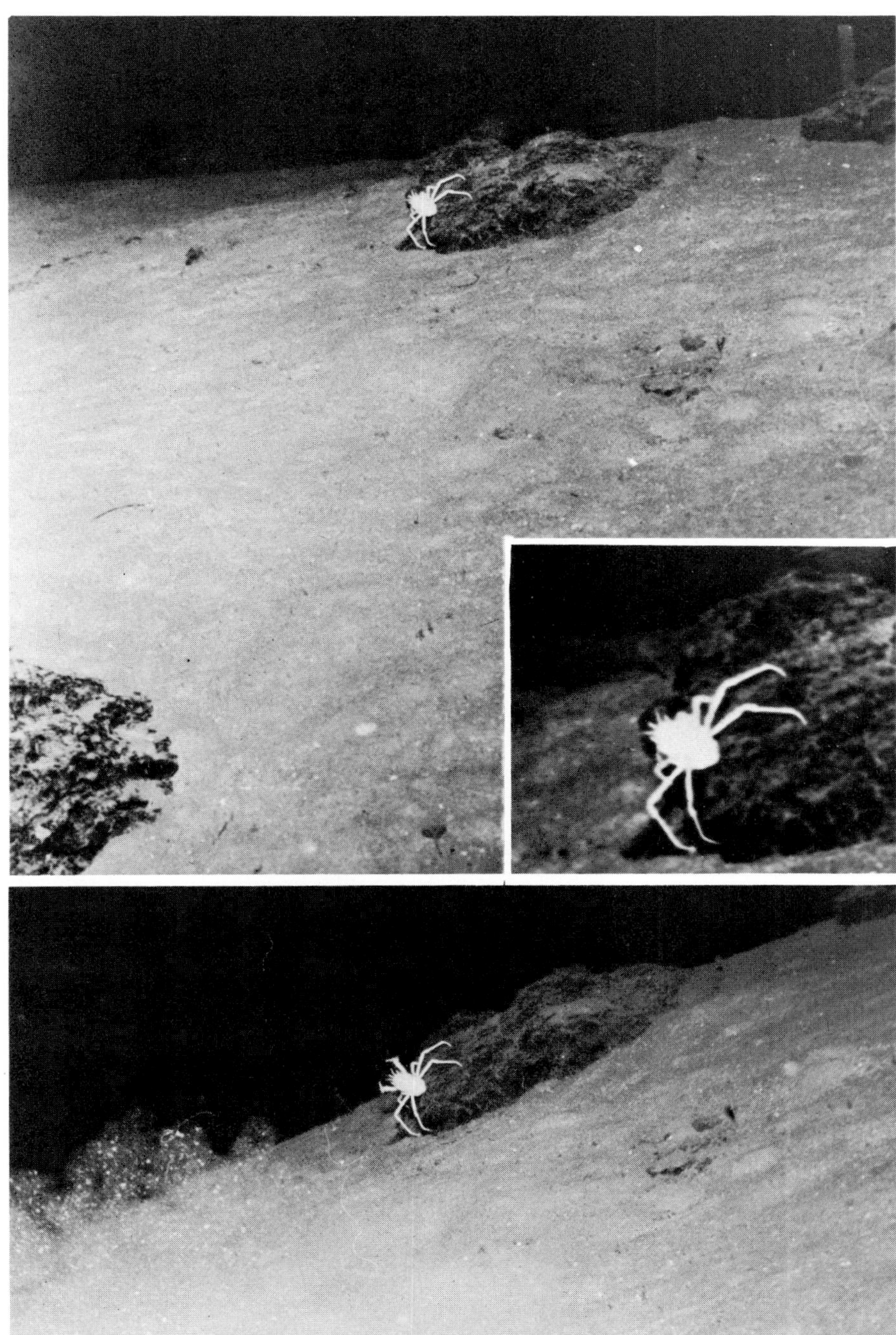

19°01′N 65°25′W

2.69 A light-colored crab and glass sponge decorate boulders in the ooze. U, this first of two photographs of the same crab shows the head and pincers depressed. L, photograph taken a few seconds later, 3607 m, south wall of Puerto Rico Trench.

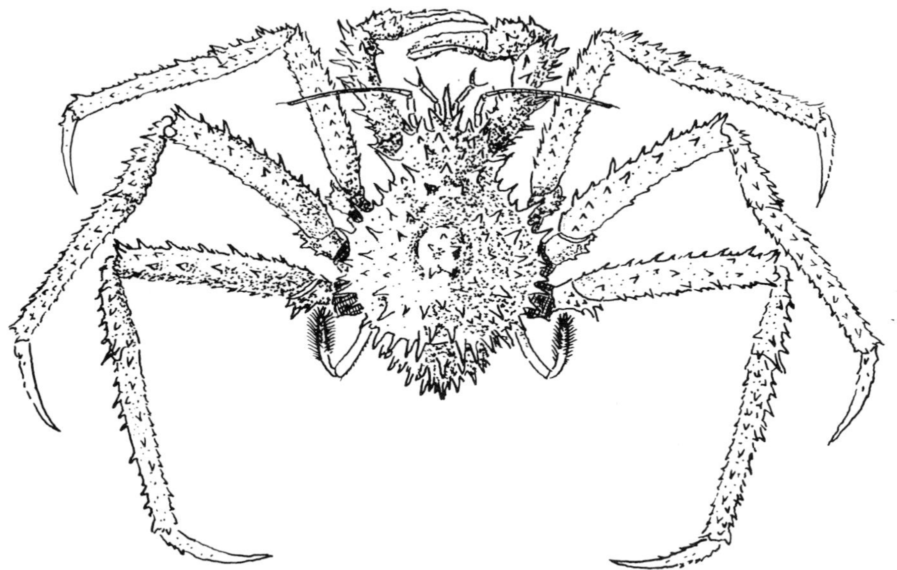

2.70 A deep-sea crab (*Lithodes agassizii*).

by aquanauts, remain unperturbed on the sea floor while others, attracted by the searchlights, swarm around the submersible and sometimes become so plentiful that they completely obscure the view.

Many crustaceans make their home within the bottom sediments. Some, in fact, are helpless when removed from their burrows. Those that live within the sediment, deriving their sustenance from digestible material, have a significant effect on the tilling of the substrate, and although of small size must have a widespread effect on the seascape.

Crustaceans too small to be seen in photographs must make small grooves when moving over the sea floor. The larger decapods walk (3.3) but the smaller ones either leave no mark or plow a fuzzy furrow; and although the furrows are recognized in shallow water, they could hardly be distinguished from those of other tiny animals in normal deep-sea photographs.

SQUIRTS, ACORN WORMS, AND BEARD-BEARERS

The lowly acorn worms, the squirts, beard-bearers, the lancelets, lampreys, sharks, rays, bony fishes, amphibians, reptiles, birds, and mammals are all chordates. There are no abyssal birds, amphibians, or reptiles, and of the mammals only the sperm whales enter the abyss.

The slender acorn worms range from the size of earthworms to the size of snakes. Most live in shallow water, but a few live in the abyss

2.71 Crabs. UL, UR, 3992 m, south wall, Puerto Rico Trench. LL, 3235 m, Mid-Oceanic Ridge, South Pacific. LR, 1117 m, continental slope off Nova Scotia.

and either burrow shallowly by means of a soft proboscis or crawl along the bottom. A sticky mucus secreted by glands in the skin causes the formation of a tubular case of sediment. Dramatic photographs of these hemichordates (5.1) show them creating large coils of remolded sedi-

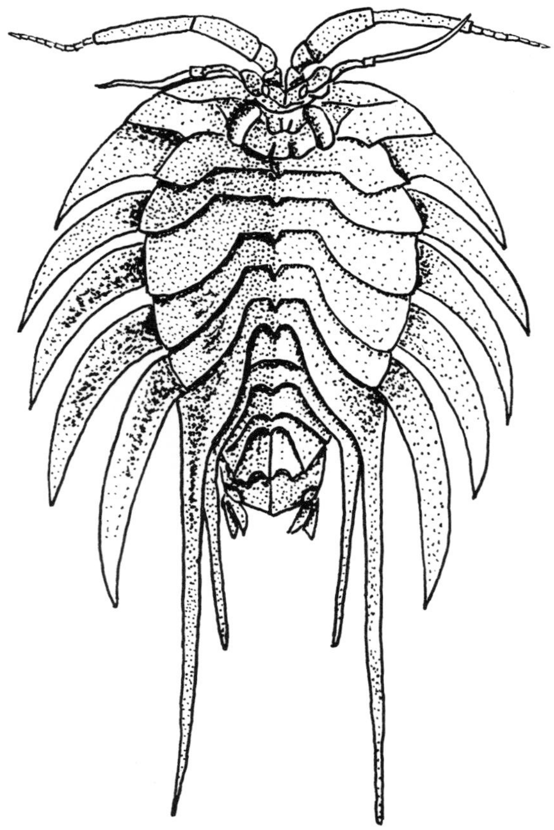

2.72 A giant abyssal isopod. (*Serolis*).

ment. These coils, found in all depths, are visually important over wide areas of the sea floor.

Tunicates, or sea squirts, another group of lowly chordates, inhabit the sea from the polar oceans to the tropics and from the beach to the greatest depths. Some are free-living and others are fixed; some are solitary, some colonial. They vary in size from microscopic to forms a foot in diameter, and on rare occasions they have been observed in abyssal photographs. The most evident of these probably belong to the genus *Culeolus* or to *Boltenia* (2.78); they resemble little balls attached to a golf tee. The two holes representing their incurrent and excurrent siphons can be discerned on the upper surface. These stalked ascidians have a bluish color and appear to phosphoresce. Like other attached animals, they prefer the current-swept environments (2.79).

The abyssal bread-bearers (Pogonophora) are a group of strange animals which were not discovered until this century.[19] They are thin, thread-like animals one-tenth of a millimeter to a centimeter in diameter,

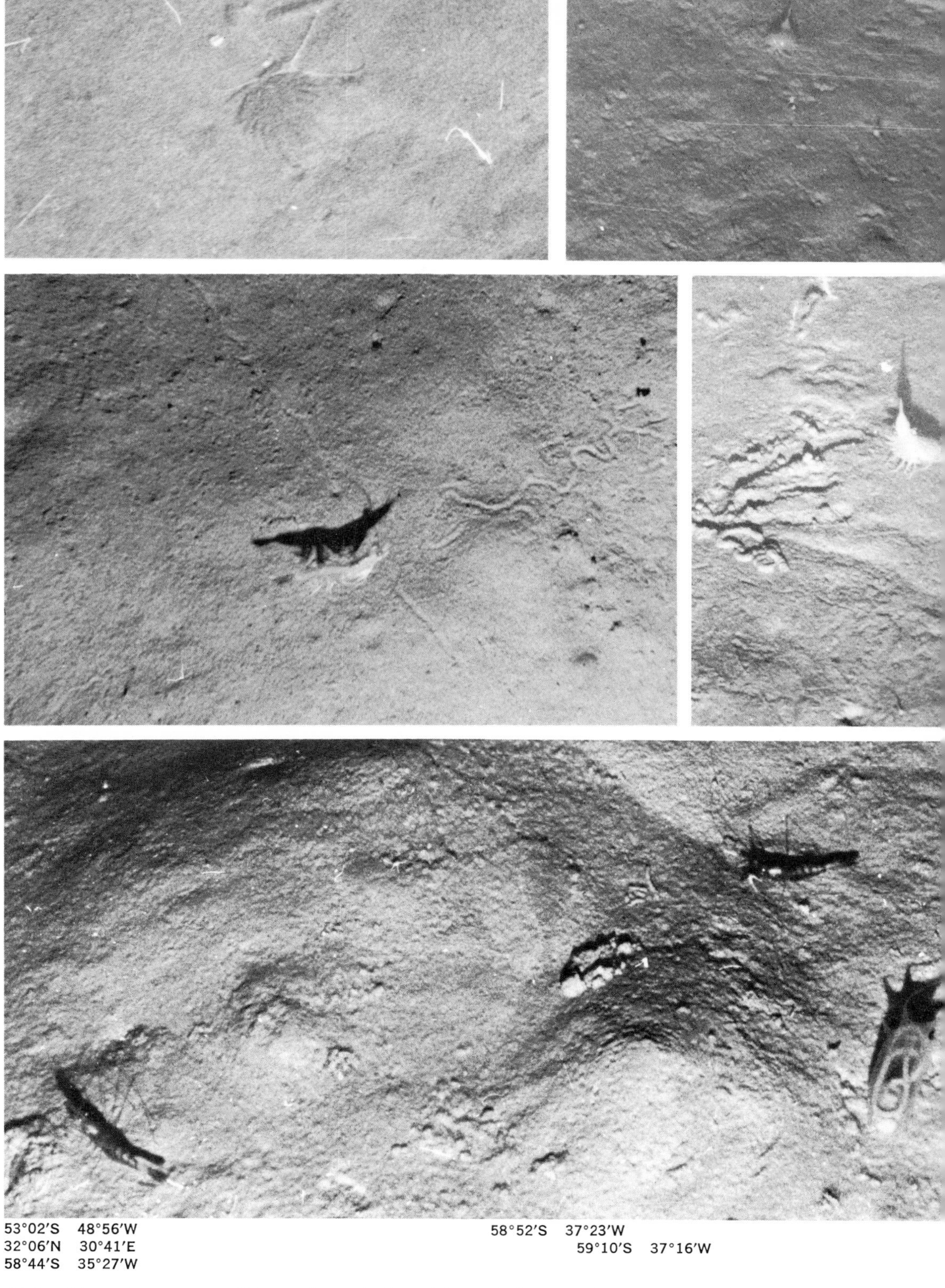

53°02′S 48°56′W
32°06′N 30°41′E
58°44′S 35°27′W

58°52′S 37°23′W
59°10′S 37°16′W

2.73 Abyssal crustacea. UL, an isopod (*Serolis*) partially covering an ophiuroid, 3181 m, Falkland Plateau. UR, an isopod with luminous white eyes, 2976 m, Scotia Sea. LC, shrimp swimming just above the sea floor, 670 m, eastern Mediterranean. RC, isopod with long tapered tail, 2835 m, Scotia Sea. L, two shrimp and an elasipod holothurian, 2054 m, Scotia Sea.

and they range from 10 to 35 cm in length. These chordates have no alimentary tract, and it is a mystery how they feed. They have not been positively identified in photographs, but judging from trawling results they should be seen on the walls of Pacific trenches.

FISH

The rat tails, brotulids, ray fins, and eels are the chief groups of bony fish that inhabit the deep sea (2.80), and representatives of each have been photographed. They range in size from tiny slivers to veritable monsters nearly three feet long. These deep-sea fish may be black, pink, or silvery.

Although most cartilaginous fish dwell in the sunlit waters, a few, such as sleeper sharks and dogfish, swim along the deep-sea floor. These large active fish are commonly seen by aquanauts. They are the largest animals yet seen in the abyss (2.81), and the baited cameras which have photographed them are called "monster" cameras. Chimaeras, another group of cartilaginous fish, are large-eyed creatures which live near the bottom in shelf and slope waters. One has a hoe-shaped appendage on its nose. Perhaps an aquanaut will discover its use.

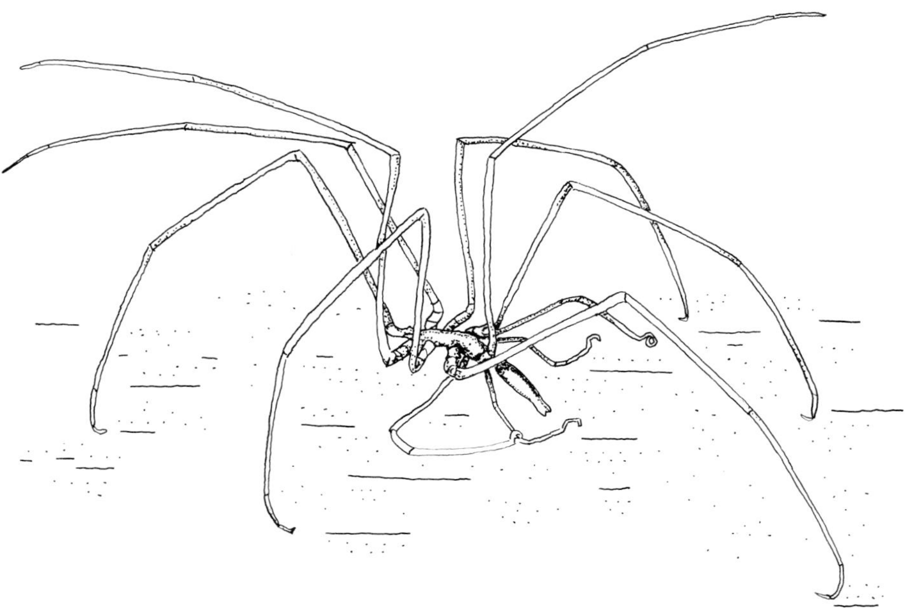

2.74 The sea spider (*Colossendeis colossea*).

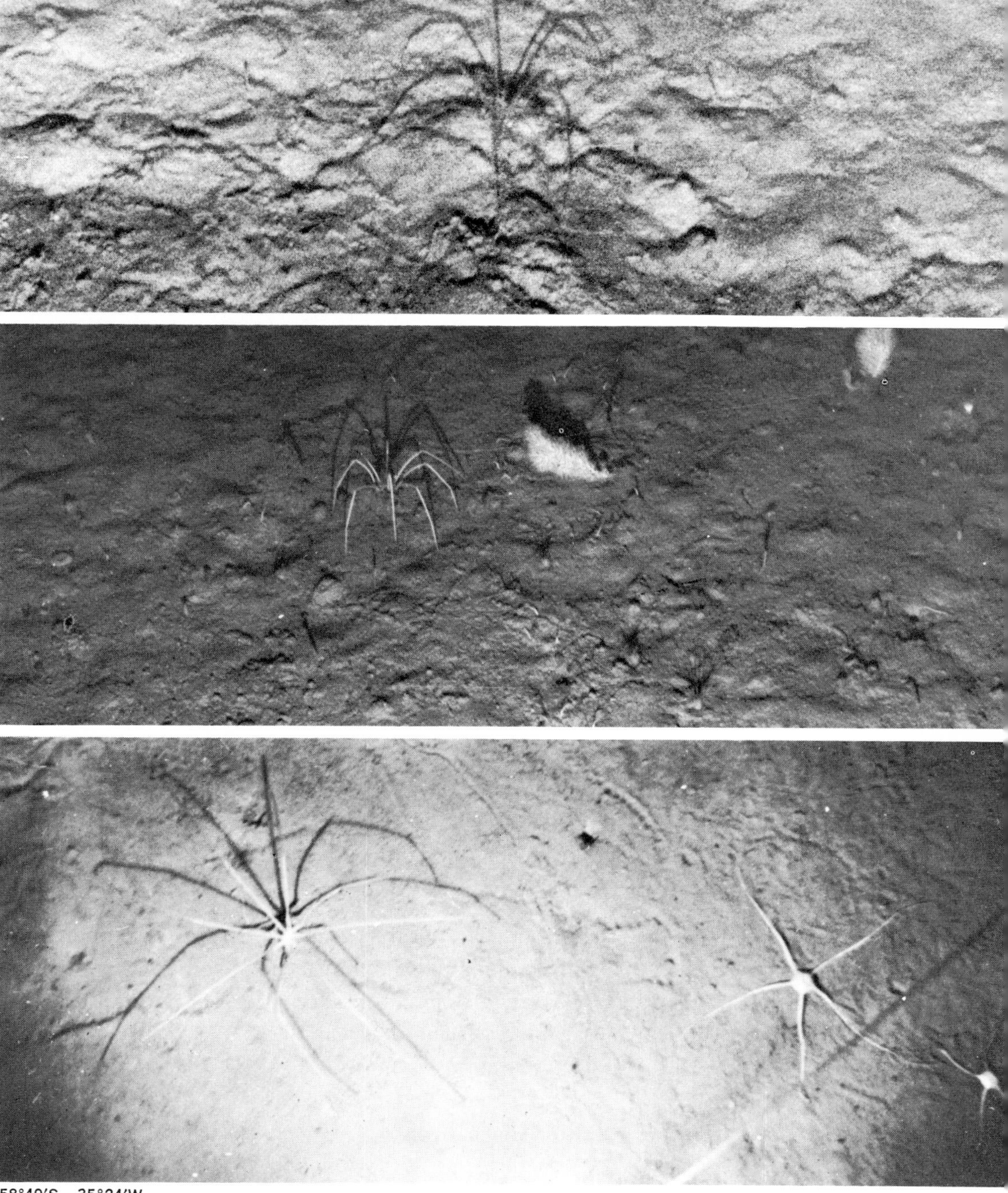

58°49′S 35°24′W
60°00′S 46°45′W
39°46′N 70°50′W

2.75 Spiders of the deep. U, C, 1591 m, 2437 m, Scotia Sea. L, *Collossendeis colossea,* 1833 m, New England continental slope.

On the continental slope, particularly between 1000 and 3000 meters, many hundreds of bony fish have been collected near the bottom, and a rich fauna has been described (2.82). However, relatively few have been trawled from abyssal depths. Up to 1952, only 118 specimens from 36 species of deep-sea fish had been captured at a grand total of 34 suc-

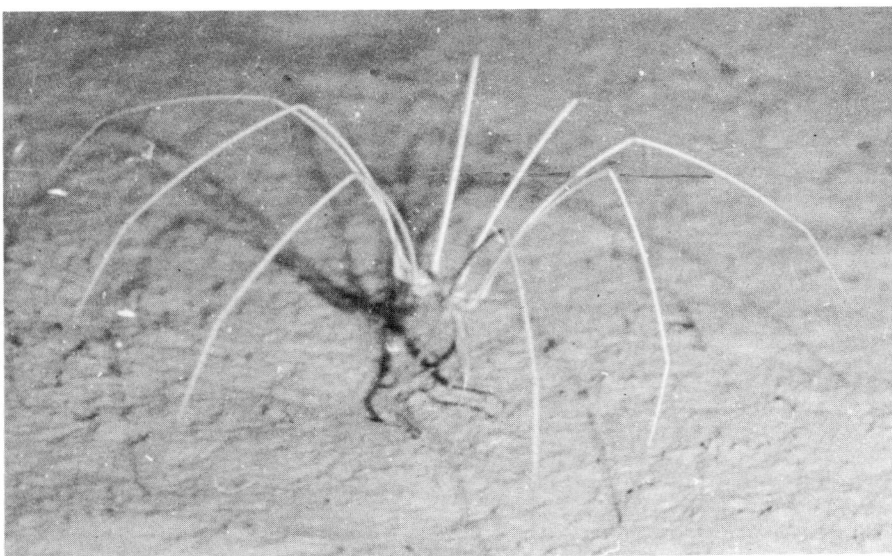

39°45′N 70°31′W

2.76 Giant abyssal sea spider (*Colossendeis colossea*). Photograph taken from *Alvin* with hand-held camera and telephoto lens, 1900 m, continental slope of New England.

cessful stations in depths greater than 3600 meters. The reader will recall illustrations of bizarre and specialized forms of lantern fish, hatchet fish, and other toothy monsters in dramatic color paintings and photographs reproduced by William Beebe[20] and other workers. Virtually all of these bizarre fish are tiny bathypelagic forms not yet found near the abyssal sea floor. Due to their small size they would be difficult, if not impossible, to recognize in normal sea-floor photographs. Fish have been photographed in depths in excess of 6000 meters and have been observed directly at the greatest depth in the ocean at the bottom of the Marianas Trench.[21]

Of the nine families of fish frequently captured from the greatest depths, the most common are the rat tails (Macrouridae) (2.83). This large-headed fish has a long tapering tail, large eyes, and a heavy armored head. Some grow to over three feet in length. Several have been photographed, but the best series of photographs by far was taken when the camera accidentally lay on the bottom in 4000 meters. While the strobe flashed every twelve seconds, the fish approached the lens and a series of fifty pictures was obtained while the fish, seemingly unperturbed, rooted about in the ooze. It seems peculiar that even with its large eyes, it was unconcerned by the bright, flashing strobe light (2.84).

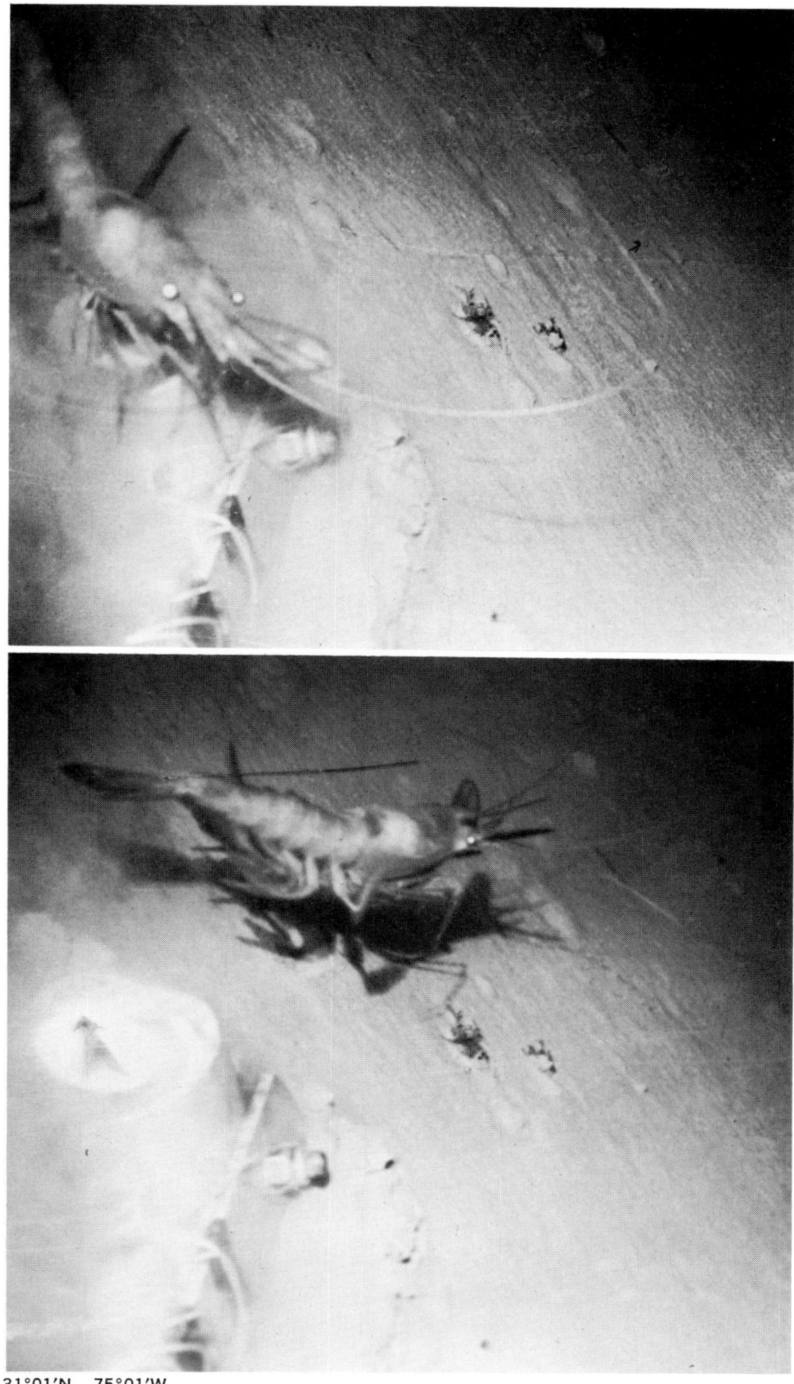

31°01′N 75°01′W
31°01′N 75°01′W

2.77 Abyssal crustacean investigating camera compass. U, L, 4000 m, Blake Bahama Outer Ridge.

Bathyscaphe divers have noted with amazement the lack of effect of bright lights on large-eyed abyssal fish. One asked the question: "Are abyssal fish blind? These animals have lived for millions of years in the realm of eternal night and appear to be totally insensitive to light. They pass back and forth in the beams of our searchlights, and they suffer the flare of our electronic flashes without the least tremor, whereas one would expect them to be blinded by such a vivid light."[10]

It is interesting to note that the rat-tail fish seen in the photographs wander nose down over the sediments, the long body axis being inclined at a slight angle to the bottom (2.83, 2.84). "In most macrourids the rays of the anal fin are considerably larger than those of the second dorsal. As the tail is undulated the side-to-side swing of the anal fin would generate a lift and depress the head . . . [thus] considering the dynamics of their fin pattern this attitude is to be expected."[22]

The Halosauridae and Notacanthidae are long-bodied fishes with a tapering tail and a long anal fin. Their jaws are set below a protruding snout and they adapt an inclined posture like the macrourids (2.85). It has been pointed out that this is to be expected on anatomical grounds

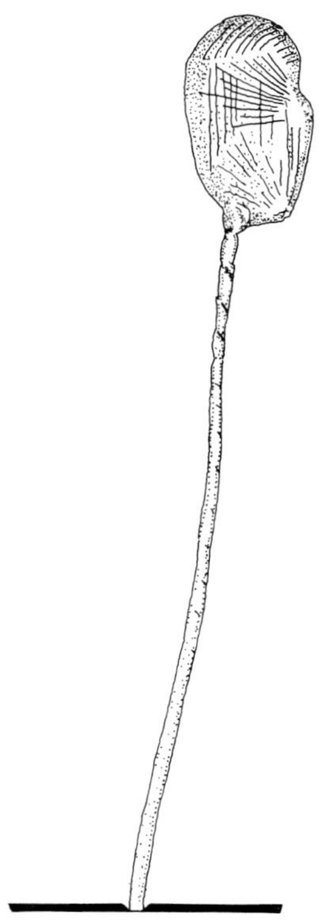

2.78 Tunicate (*Boltenia elegans*).

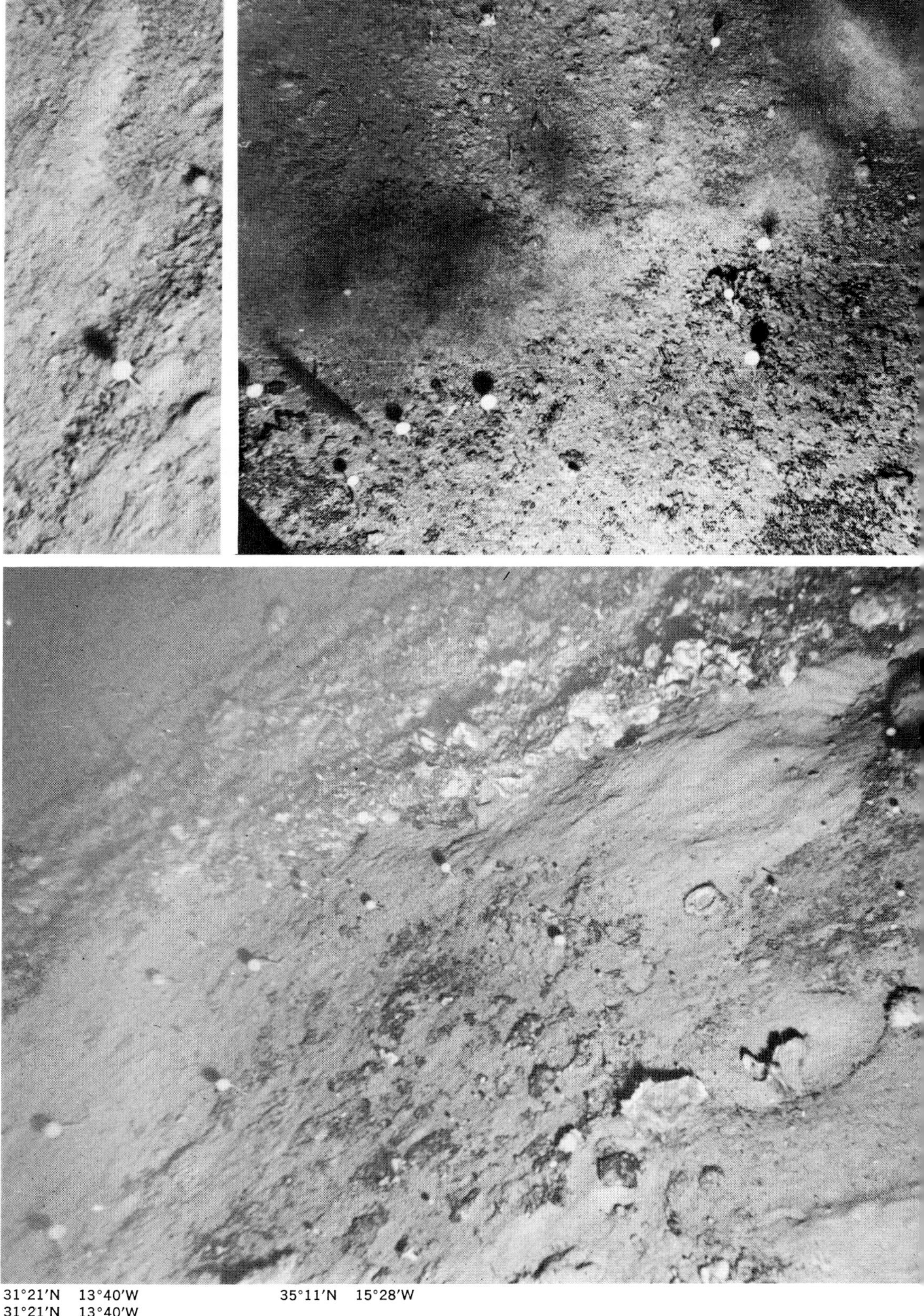

31°21′N 13°40′W
31°21′N 13°40′W
35°11′N 15°28′W

2.79 Golf balls. UL, L, stalked squirts on current-swept rocky bottom, 301 m, and UR, squirts and a glass sponge, 854 m, Whale Seamount, eastern North Atlantic.

since halosaurs also have a long tail and an anal fin with long rays but the single dorsal member has a short base. Undulations of the tail and anal fin will again drive the animal forward and incline its head down to the sediment. The photographs often show halosaurs with short-wave undulations passing down the posterior half to a third of the tail, but longer wave eel-like undulations have also been seen.[22]

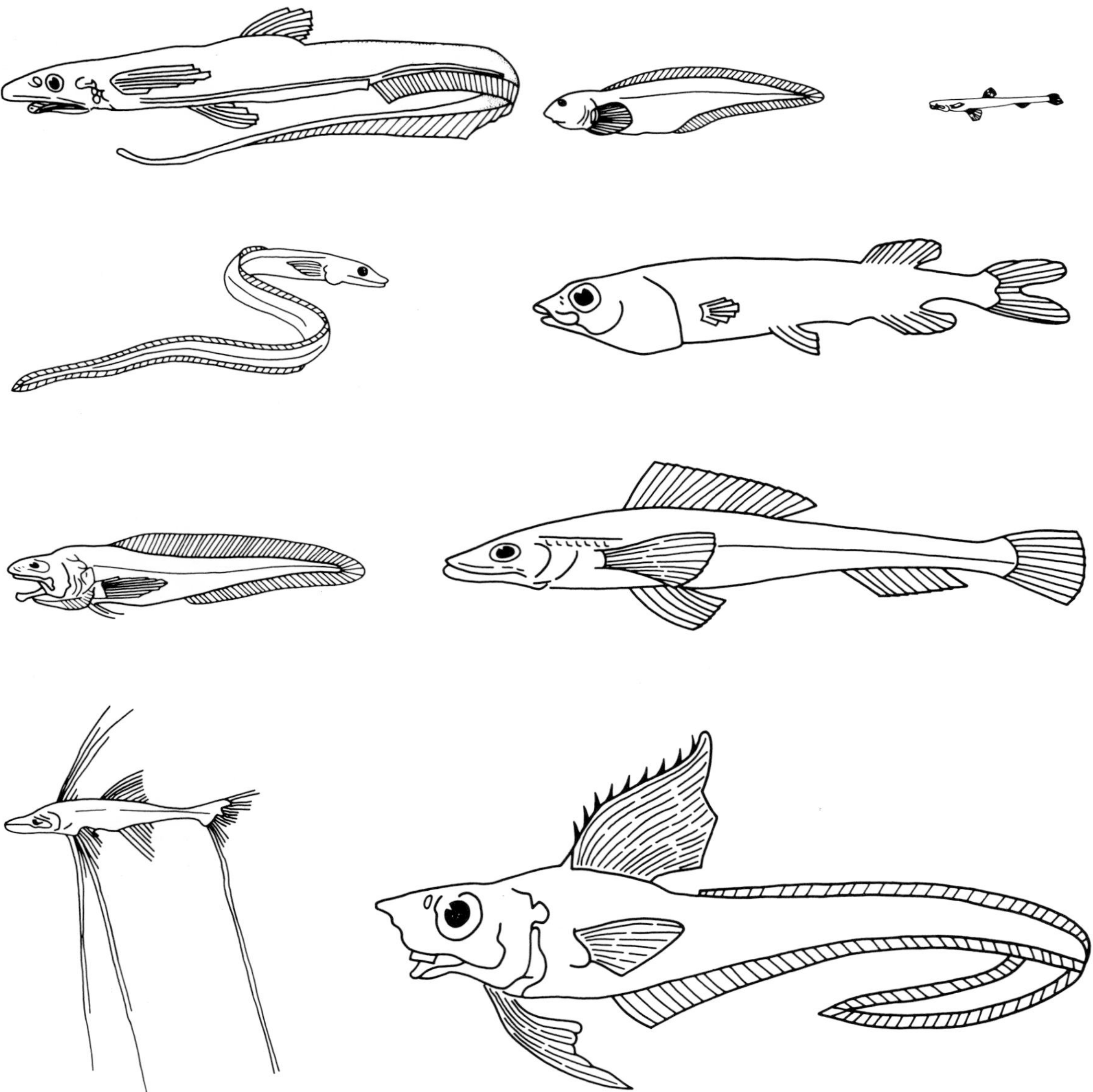

2.80 Boney fish captured below 3000 meters. UL, Halosaur, common, up to 65 centimeters long. UC, Liparid, rare, to 25 centimeters. UR, Ipnopid, rare, to 10 centimeters. UML, Synaphobranch, rare, to 60 centimeters. UMR, Alepocephalid, common, to 45 centimeters. LML, Brotulid, common, to 30 centimeters. LMR, Synodont, rare, to 50 centimeters. LL, Bathypteroid, rare, to 20 centimeters. LR, Macrourid, abundant, to 70 centimeters.

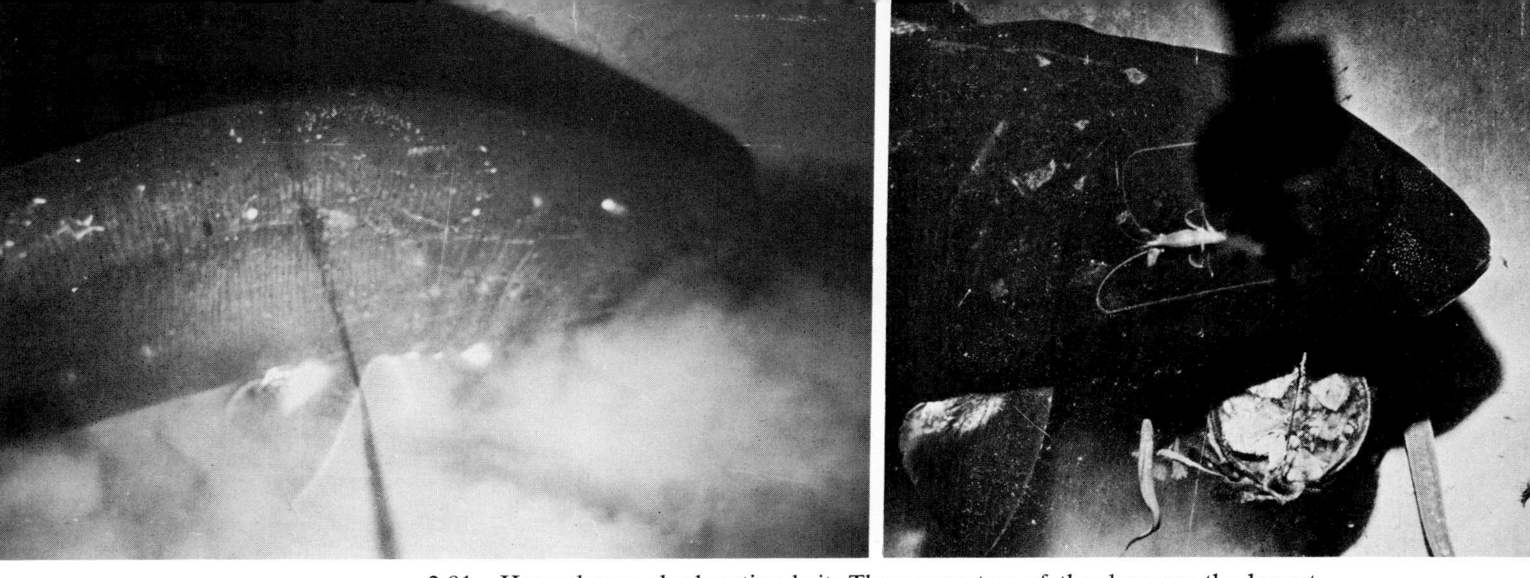

2.81 Huge sleeper shark eating bait. These monsters of the deep are the largest animals yet photographed on the deep-sea floor. L, 2039 m, continental slope off Baja, California. R, 1949 m, island slope off Hawaii.

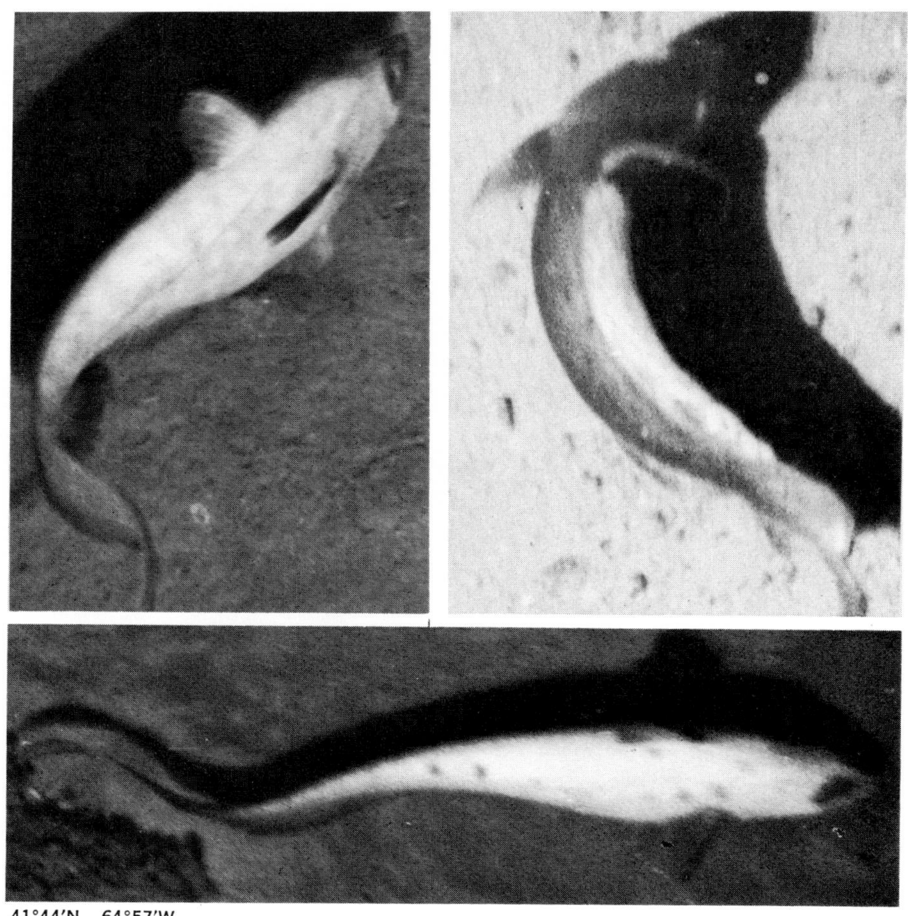

41°44′N 64°57′W

2.82 Rat tails (*Lionurus carapinus*) and a Morid (UR). Frequently, fish escape being photographed by getting out of the field and leaving a muddy cloud. Sometimes only the end of their tail shows in the photograph and with early flash-bulb photography their sudden movement frequently blurred their portrait, 2600 m, continental slope off New England.

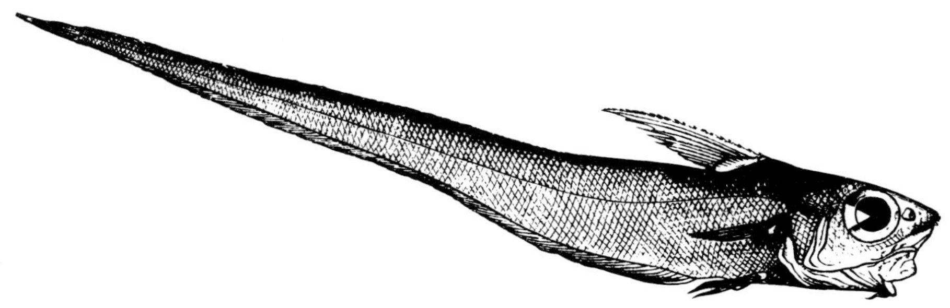

2.83 Rat tail (*Coryphoenides serratus*).

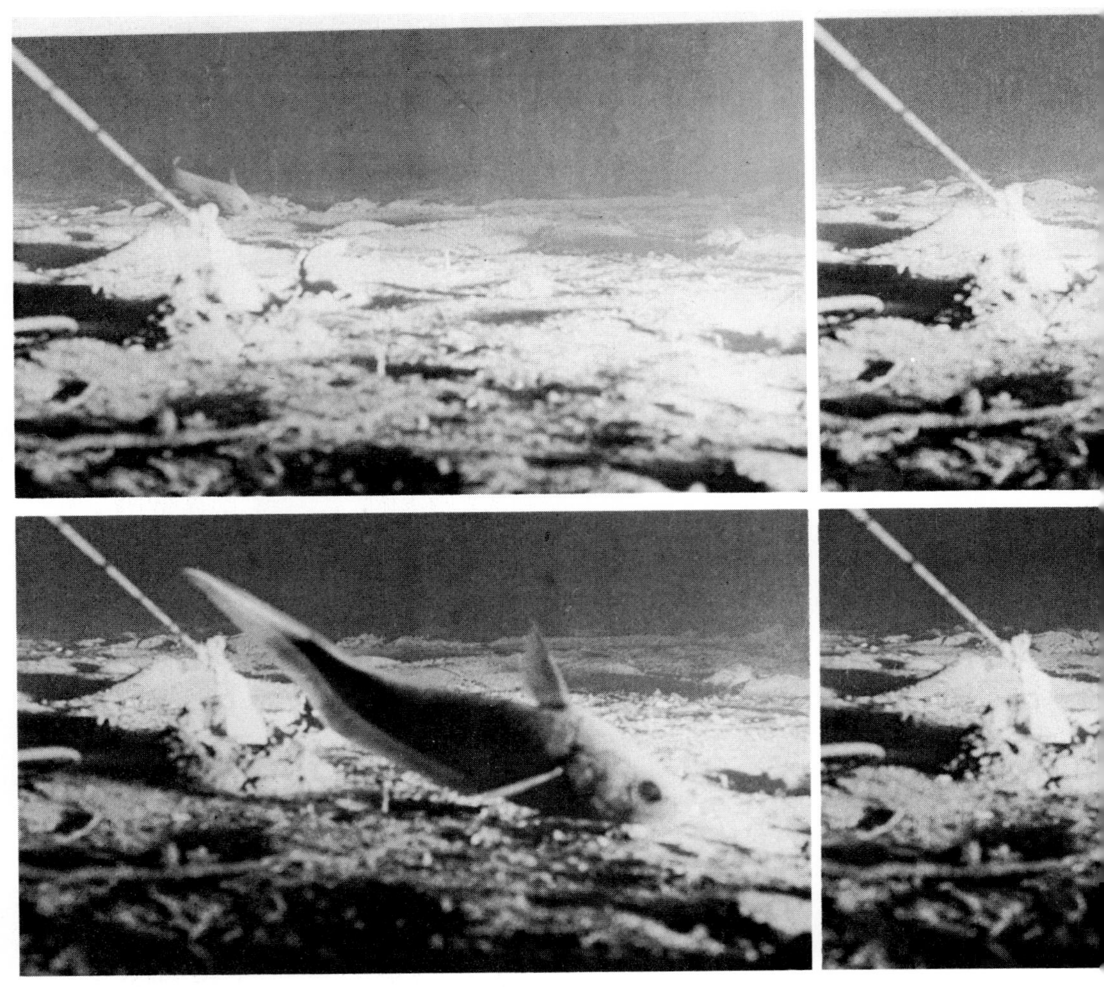

All halosaurs and most macrourids have the jaw suspended underneath the snout, and thus this head-down attitude is a useful adaptation for plucking organisms off the bottom. Moreover, the triangular armored snout can be used to root beneath the ooze after the ascidians, sponges, and foraminifera which have frequently been found in their gut.

Almost equally abundant in the deep-sea trawls are the blind, semitransparent brotulids which grow to a maximum size of one foot. Some of them, as well as some of the rat tails, have a horseshoe-shaped mouth which can be protruded like a shovel for sifting through the mud when the fish pursues a prey. *Typhlonus* is a brotulid with an immense, soft,

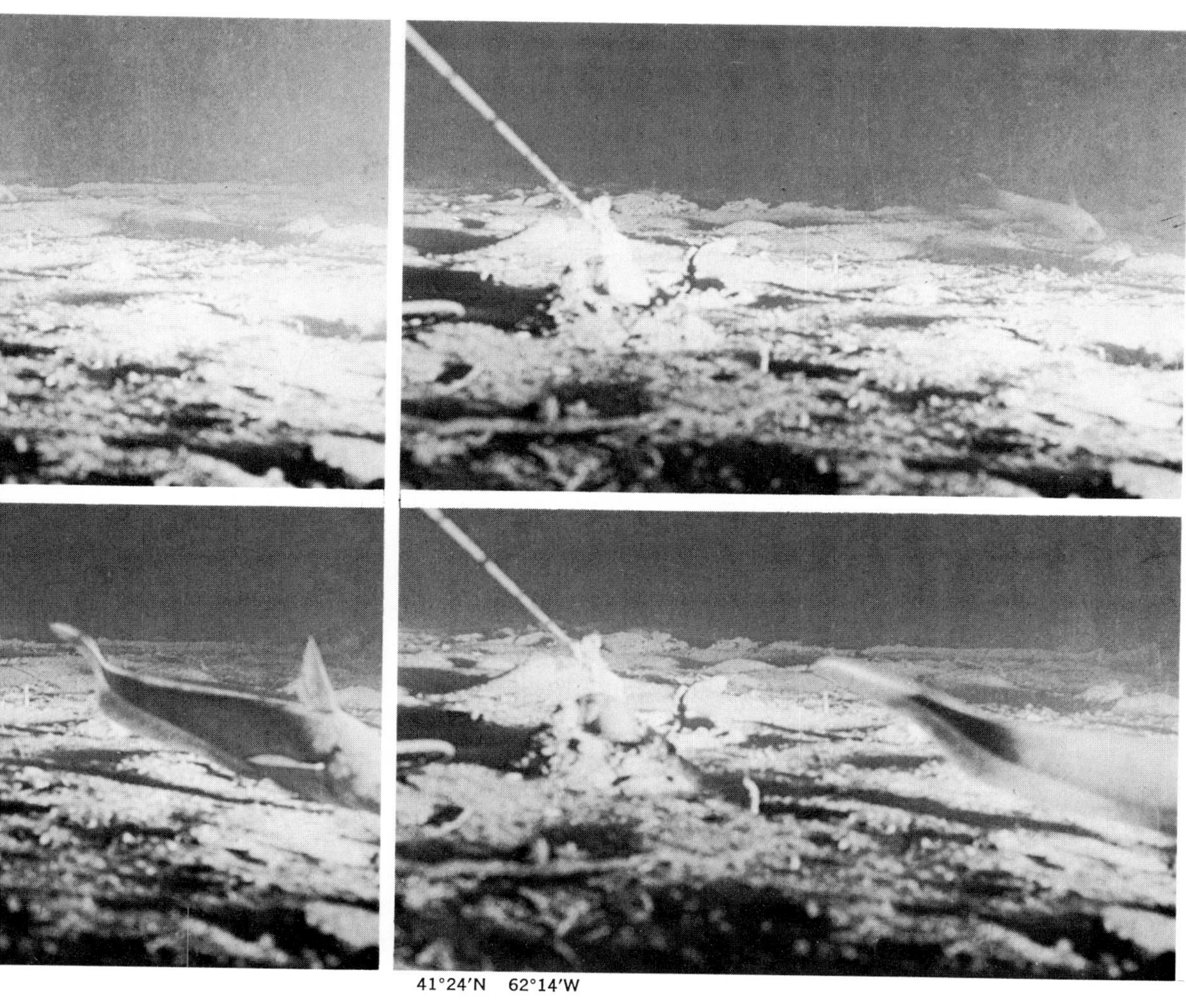

41°24′N 62°14′W

2.84 Rat tails probing the sea floor. The camera, lying on its side, took repeated silhouette portraits of these two fish as they searched the ooze for food. String in upper left marked in inches, 4030 m, continental rise off Nova Scotia.

2.85 The deep-sea halosaurs and rat tails swim nose down.

gelatinous head, a small semi-transparent body, and a long compressed tail. On the underside of the head is a horseshoe-shaped mouth which can be thrust out like a shovel for digging up the bottom mud in search of food—which should leave important marks on the bottom. However, neither the animals nor their traces have yet been identified in photographs.

The remarkable ray fins (Bathypteroidae) generally have long, articulated pectoral rays which extend both dorsally and ventrally (2.86, 3.5). They are compactly built, muscular, and apparently the most actively predacious fish of the abyss. The rays of *Benthosaurus* are enormously prolongated, but *Bathysaurus* and *Bathymicrops* lack the large pectoral ray fins. Another family related to the ray fins are the members of the Alepocephalidae. These distinctive and common deep-sea fish have a cod-like shape (2.87 C, R, 2.88 UR) and large eyes. Long, slender, sinuous deep-sea eels (Synaphobranchidae) are occasionally seen swimming near the sea floor (2.87 L, 2.89 UL, 290 UL).

A peculiar family of soft-bodied fish called sea snails (Liparidae) are known exclusively from the bathyal and abyssal regions. They are generally bottom dwelling and characteristically have a sucker formed by the belly fins for adhesion to stones and the like on the ocean floor.

The deep sea has been little explored, particularly in relation to its fish and it is probable that many more shallow-water families have representatives in the abyss.[23]

Normally, deep-sea trawls are not provided with a closing device that would prevent the capture of pelagic species during the haul to the surface. Thus, underwater photographs have been valuable in resolving certain doubts concerning the living spaces of deep-sea fish. Photographs

2.86 Bizarre tripod fish spreads a dark membraneous net in the gentle current. These exceptional photographs of *Bathypterois bigelowi* were taken from *Deepstar 4000*. UL, UR, L, 1200 m, De Soto Submarine Canyon, Gulf of Mexico. ▷

29°12′N 87°36′W

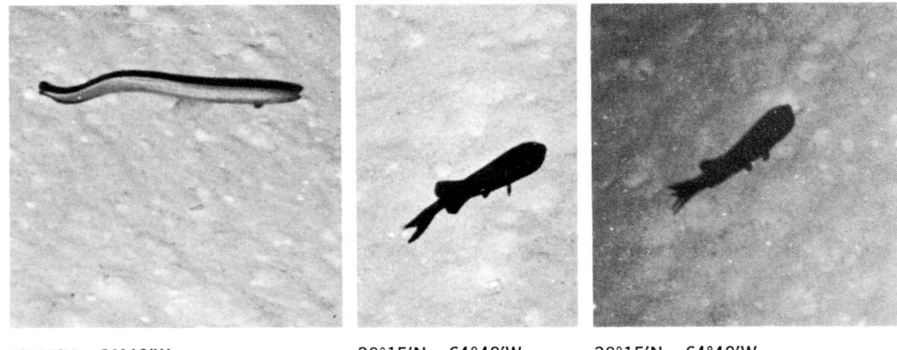

2.87 Fish from the Bermuda Pedestal. Deep-sea eel (L) and Alepocephalid fish. C, R, 1522 m, Bermuda Pedestal.

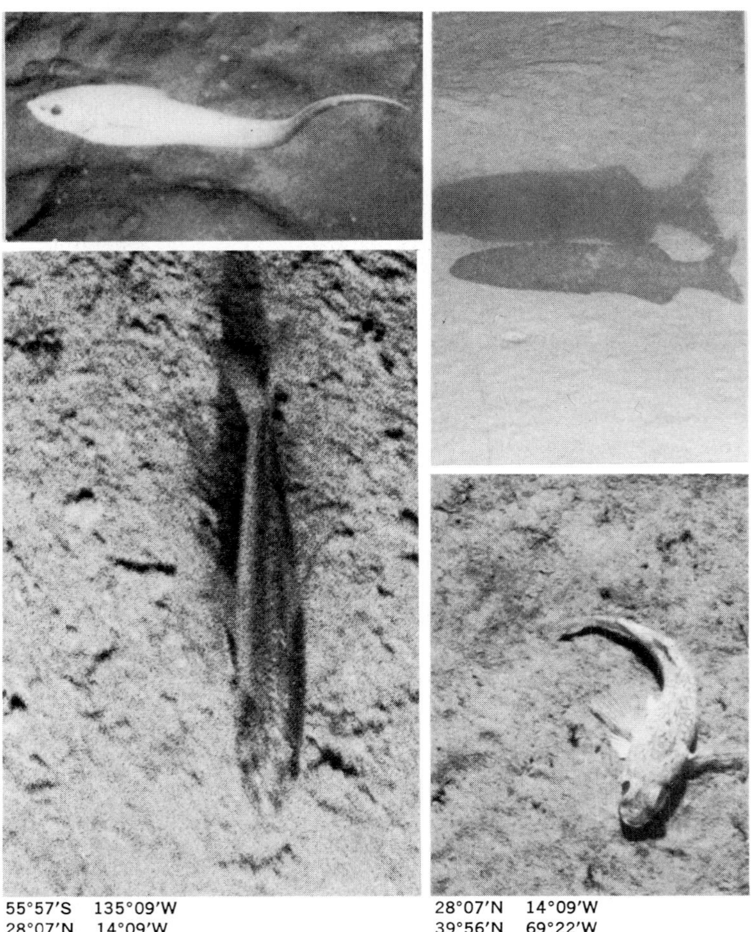

2.88 Fish portraits. UL, rat tail, 3276 m, Mid-Oceanic Ridge, South Pacific. UR, Alepocephalid and LL, Bathypteroid, 744 m, Canary Islands. LR, scorpion fish, 279 m, New England continental slope.

have also confirmed suspicions heretofore based largely on the form, fin pattern, and position of the mouth as to which groups are bottom dwelling.[22]

In spite of the impression of abundant life in the deep sea imparted by the numerous portraits presented in this chapter, it must be stressed that it is not the living organisms themselves, but the effect they have had on the sediment during the course of their lives that is the principal thing to be seen on most of the deep-sea floor. In the following four chapters we will examine the footprints, plow marks, excrement, holes, and mounds that comprise nearly all there is to see in the vast majority of abyssal photographs.

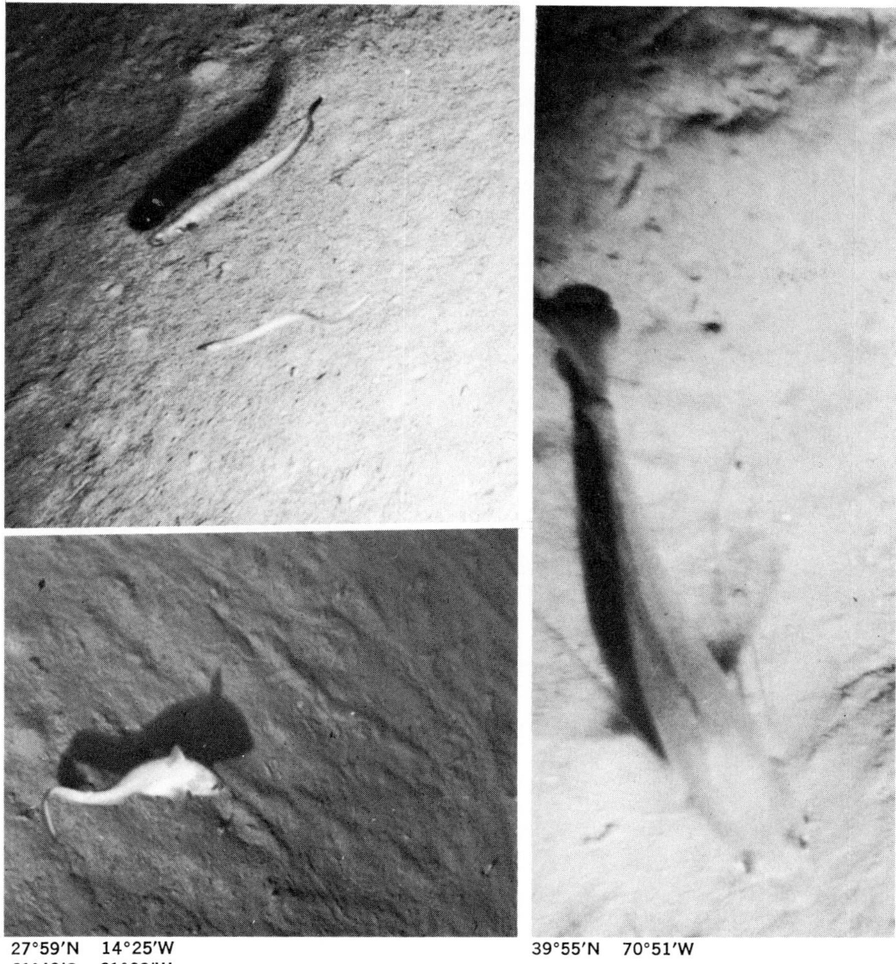

27°59′N 14°25′W
61°49′S 61°23′W
39°55′N 70°51′W

2.89 Fish portraits. UL, a deep-sea spiny eel (Notacanth), 1259 m, Canary Islands. R, sea robin, 700 m, New England continental slope. LL, rat tail, 3269 m, Scotia Sea.

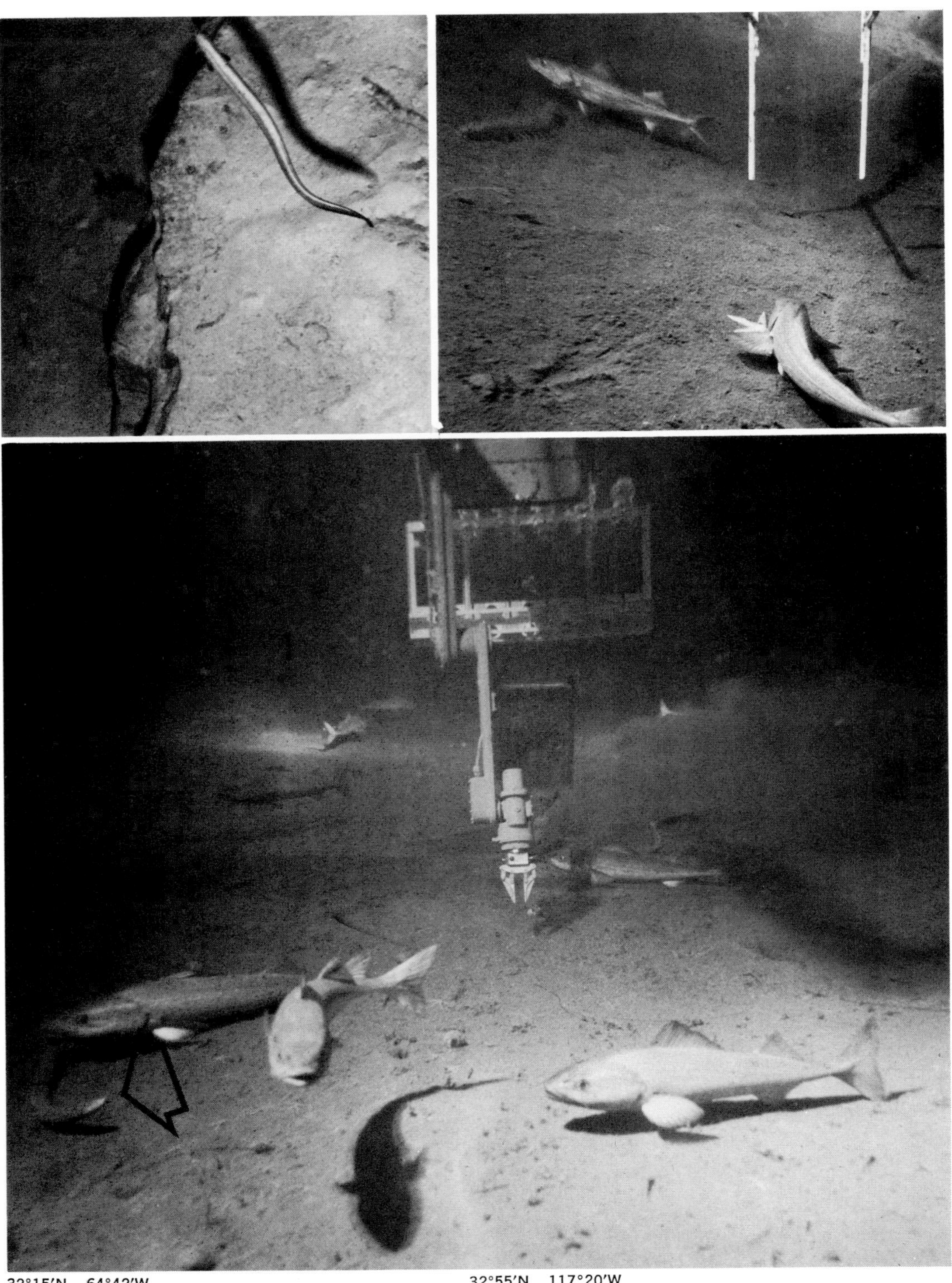

32°15′N 64°42′W
32°20′N 117°25′W

32°55′N 117°20′W

REFERENCES AND NOTES

1. The temperature over the greater part of the abyss ranges between 0.5°C and 2.5°C, is constant over wide geographical areas and has no seasonal variations. The salinity is virtually constant at 34.8 ± 0.2 parts per thousand. Bottom water contains sufficient oxygen for the support of animal life, ranging from 3 to 6 ml per liter.
2. Descriptions of the abyssal fauna are found in the references listed in Appendix 2 (p. 621). Appendix 3 (p. 623) is a list of publications containing particularly good photographs or drawings of larger abyssal animals.
3. On the basis of the character and composition of the skeletal network, sponges are divided into three classes: Calcarea (limey sponges), Hexactinellida (glass sponges), and Demospongia ("bath sponges").
4. A. Alcock. 1902. *A Naturalist in Indian Seas.* Murray, London. 328 pp.
5. G. P. Bidder. 1923. The relation of the form of a sponge to its currents. *Quarterly Journ. Micros. Sci., 67*:293-323.
6. A. Agassiz. 1888. *Three Cruises of the* Blake. Riverside Press, Cambridge, 2:21-36.
7. This group also includes the rarely photographed hydroids and jellyfish.
8. *Branchiocerianthus.*
9. C. W. Thomson. 1878. *The Atlantic: The Voyage of the H.M.S.* Challenger. Harper, New York, *1*:150-151.
10. G. Houot. 1958. Four years of diving to the bottom of the sea. *Natl. Geog. Mag., 113*:715-731.
11. C. Teichert. 1957. Cold and deep water coral banks. *Bull. Am. Assoc. Petrol. Geol., 42*:1064-1082.
12. The discovery, in the late nineteenth century, of a solitary coral attached to an under-sea cable in the Mediterranean at a depth of 2000 meters constituted one of the earliest irrefutable evidences for the existence of deep-sea life below 500 meters.
13. A photograph of stalked crinoids from the rocky continental slope (*ca.* 1200 meters) was published in 1952 by G. F. Jordan (Continental slope off Apalachicola River, Fla. *Bull. Am. Assoc. Petrol. Geol., 35*:1978-1993).
14. I. Rodenhouse and J. Guberlet. 1946. The morphology and behavior of the cushion star. *Univ. of Wash. Publ. Biol., 12.*
15. H. Blegvad. 1914. Food and conditions of nourishment among the communities of invertebrate animals found on or in the sea bottom in Danish waters. *Rep. Danish Biol. Sta., 22*:41-78.
16. J. M. Peres. 1965. Aperçu sur les résultats de deux plongées effectuées dans le ravin de Puerto Rico par le bathyscaphe, Archimède. *Deep-Sea Res., 12*:883-892.
17. L. Zenkevitch. 1963. *Biology of the Seas of the U.S.S.R.* George Allen and Unwin, Ltd., London, 955 pp.
18. A. C. Baker. 1957. Underwater photographs in the study of oceanic squid. *Deep-Sea Res., 4*:126-130.

◁ 2.90 Hag fish and sable fish. UL, eel, 1522 m, Bermuda Pedestal. UR, sable fish, 600 m, La Jolla Canyon. L, sable fish and hag fish (open arrow), 1200 m, Coronado Submarine Canyon.

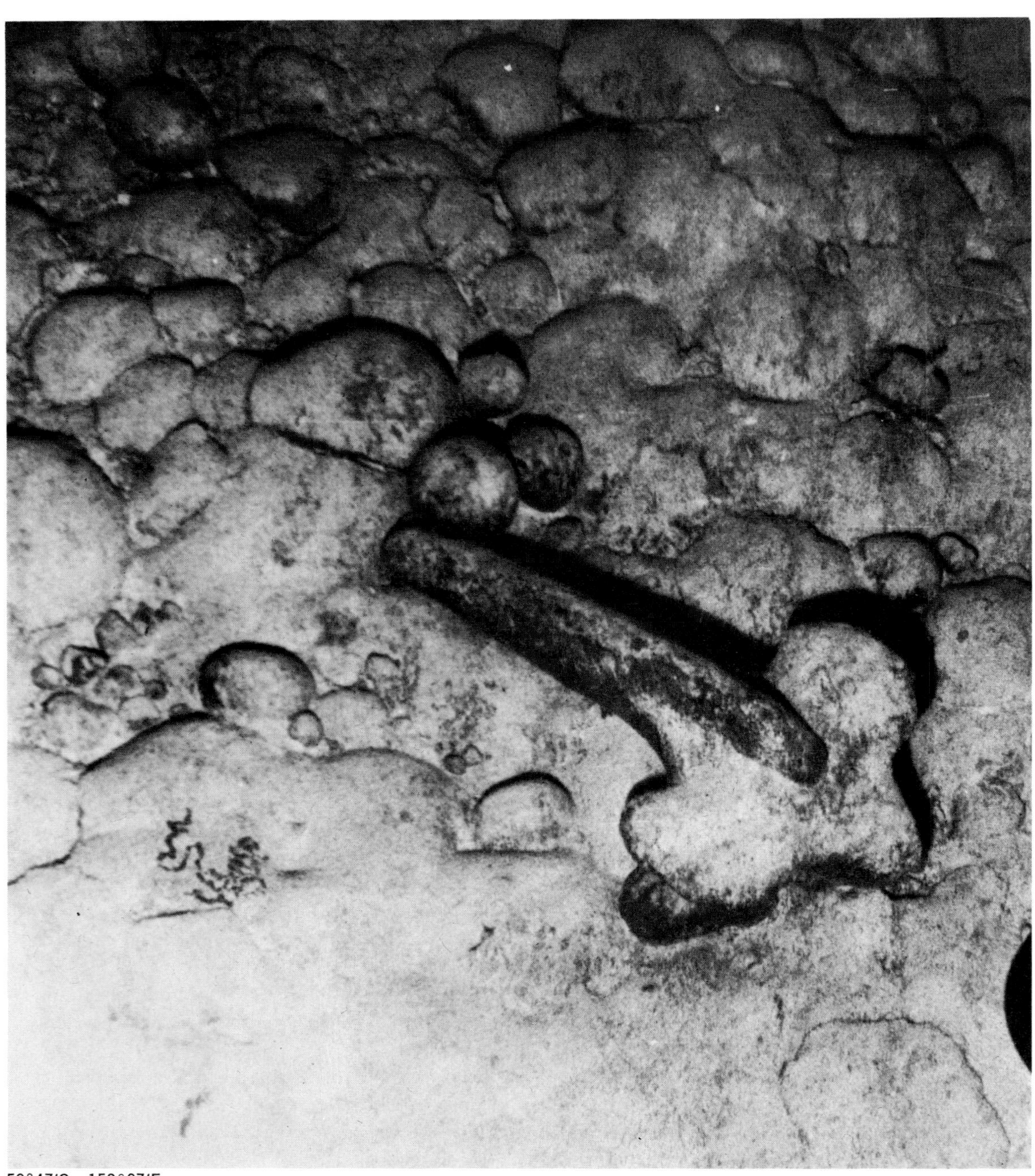

2.91 Whale bone on current-swept sea floor south of Tasmania, 3500 m.

17°50′N 64°45′W

2.92 Octopods hovering over the sea floor north of St. Croix Virgin Islands, 3800 m.

19. A. V. Ivanov. 1954. New Pogonophora from the far eastern seas. *System. Zool.*, 3:68.
20. Dramatic color paintings of small bizarre fish are found in: W. Beebe. 1932. The depths of the sea. Strange life-forms a mile below the surface. *Nat. Geog. Mag.*, *61*:65-88.
21. J. Piccard and R. S. Dietz. 1961. *Seven Miles Down.* Putnam, New York, 249 pp.
22. N. B. Marshall and D. W. Bourne. 1964. A photographic survey of benthic fishes in the Red Sea and Gulf of Aden, with observations on their population, density, diversity and habits. *Bull. Mus. Comp. Zool.*, *132*:223-244.
23. When it was established a century ago that life could exist in the abyss, a search began for living fossils—forms which might have survived with little change in the supposedly ancient and unchanging abyss. But these forms were never found. In fact few groups are peculiar to the abyss and those few are probably not particularly ancient. It appears that the deep sea has undergone a marked cooling during the last 100 million years and may consequently have been subjected to more drastic changes than the shallower environments. Thus it now appears that repeated penetration of shallower forms into the abyss can better account for the existing fauna and the dream of an abyssal fauna consisting of living fossils must be abandoned.

30°59′N 79°00′W

3.1 Decapod footprints on sandy rippled bottom. 789 m, Blake Plateau, western Atlantic.

3
Footprints

Hallo! said Piglet what are you doing?
Hunting, said Pooh.
Hunting what? said Piglet, coming closer.
That's just what I ask myself, I ask myself, What?
What do you think you'll answer?
I shall have to wait until I catch up with it, said Winnie-the-Pooh. Now, look there. He pointed to the ground in front of him. What do you see there?
Tracks, said Piglet. Paw-marks. He gave a little squeak of excitement. Oh, Pooh! Do you think it's a—a—a Woozle?
It may be, said Pooh. Sometimes it is, and sometimes it isn't. You never can tell with paw-marks.

A. A. MILNE

Throughout geologic time animals have left their footprints in the muds and sands over which they have moved, and the resulting tracks and trails preserved on the bedding planes of ancient sedimentary rocks have long intrigued geologists.[1] Observations of animal activity in the intertidal zone led long ago to the identification of many shallow-water track-and-trail makers, but the study of abyssal tracks and trails and their makers has only recently become possible. (3.1, 3.2).[2]

In the deep sea, deposition of sediment dominates over erosion and the resulting water-saturated muds and oozes are loosely assembled. The water content of the uppermost few centimeters of deep-sea sediment ranges from 60 up to 90 per cent, while the bearing capacity ranges from twenty-five down to five grams per square centimeter.[3]

In the vast areas of abyssal clay and ooze, compaction of sediment is nearly imperceptible even ten meters below the bottom. Such incoherent paste is easily marked and disturbed, yet the surface is distinct enough that marks, once formed, do not quickly disintegrate. Bearing capacities are sufficient that most animals do not sink into the mud but must excavate holes in order to penetrate the sediment.

3.2 It is not always possible to identify tracks, not even your very own.

The slowly accumulating abyssal red clays of the abyssal basins are laid down at rates of from less than one to about two millimeters per thousand years. The more rapidly deposited globigerina ooze of moderate mid-ocean depths collects at rates of from one to three centimeters per thousand years and the clays and silts of the continental margin are laid down at rates as high as sixty centimeters per thousand years.[4] Since some tracks are a few centimeters deep and many mounds are more than five centimeters high, it is obvious that animal traces seen in deep-sea photographs may be a few minutes to a few hundred years old. Most, however, are less than a few years old, for currents and the moving carpet of small animals soon blur and smooth the outlines of all but the most massive features (3.4).

3.3 Large decapods leave a trail of elongate footprints.

48°29′N 14°19′W
01°30′N 154°07′E
42°18′N 14°47′W

3.4 Where the "woozle" was. UL, "Caterpillar" or "Tread" track ending abruptly at asteroid impression, 4577 m, continental rise of Britain. UR, Lightly veiled meandering track, 5398 m, Iberian Abyssal Plain. L, It has been speculated by Soviet biologists that this track was created by a giant decapod, 2970 m, Solomon Rise, equatorial Pacific.

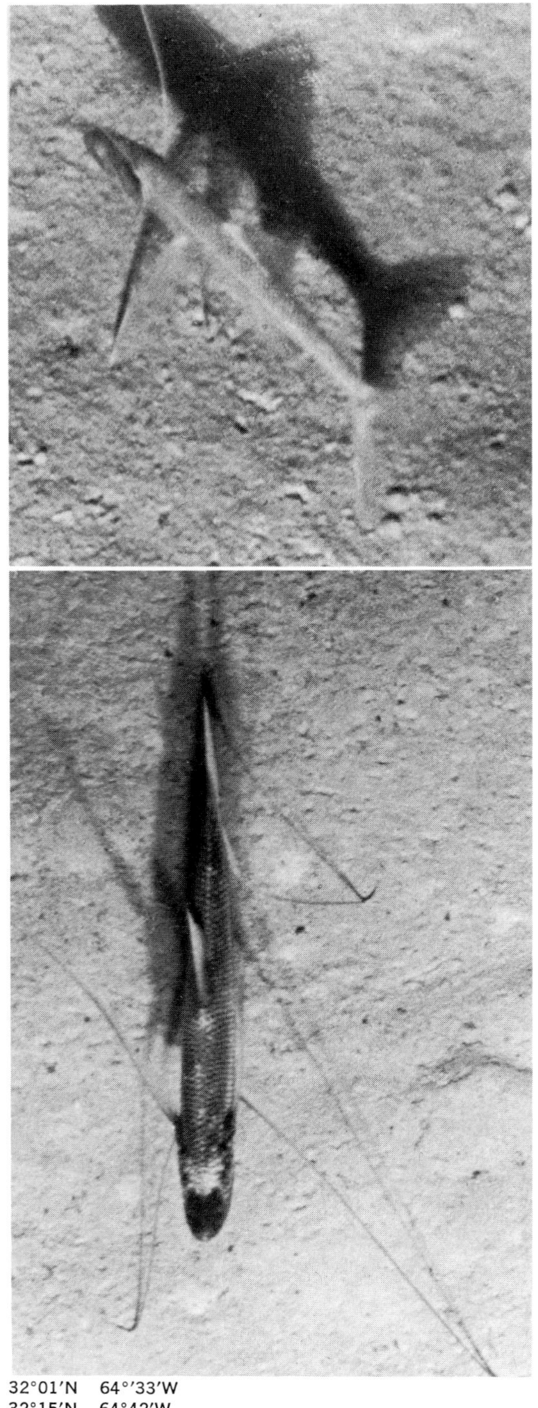

32°01′N 64°′33′W
32°15′N 64°42′W

3.5 Fish on stilts. U, Bathypterid fish standing on its ray fins, 3722 m, Bermuda Pedestal. L, Bathypterid leaving footprints in ooze, 1526 m, Bermuda Pedestal.

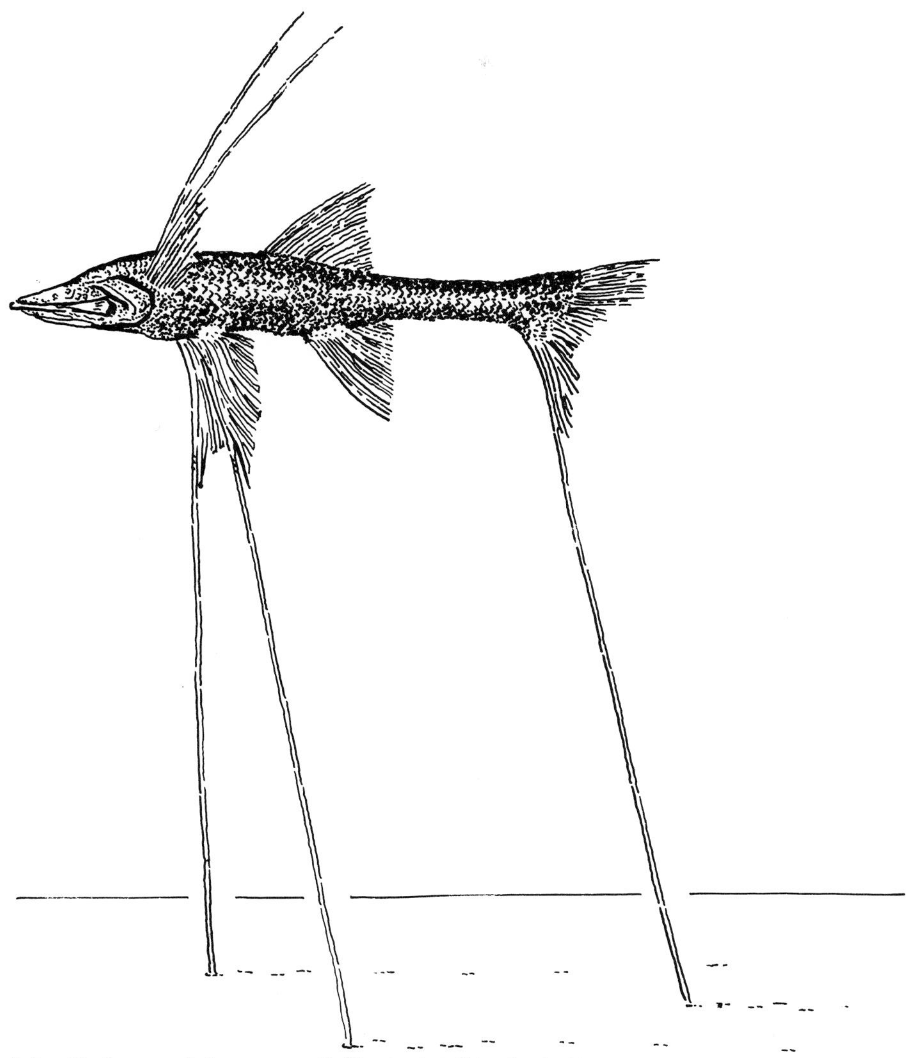

3.6 *Bathypterois* leaves small "footprints" in the bottom.

All of the larger discrete footprints seen on the deep-sea floor must be formed by echinoderms, arthropods, or chordates, for only within these groups do we find the large abyssal animals which walk on multiple feet with the body raised off the sea floor. The arthropods of the abyss have small sharp feet and must tread lightly on the ooze. Only a few isopods are large enough to be seen and these may have restricted distributions. Although sea spiders, as represented by the leggy pycnogonids, have been seen in bottom photographs (2.75, 2.76), these light animals have not been observed creating prominent tracks on the bottom. Crabs create very distinctive trails in shallow water (3.3), and their tracks have been photographed in moderate depths (3.1).

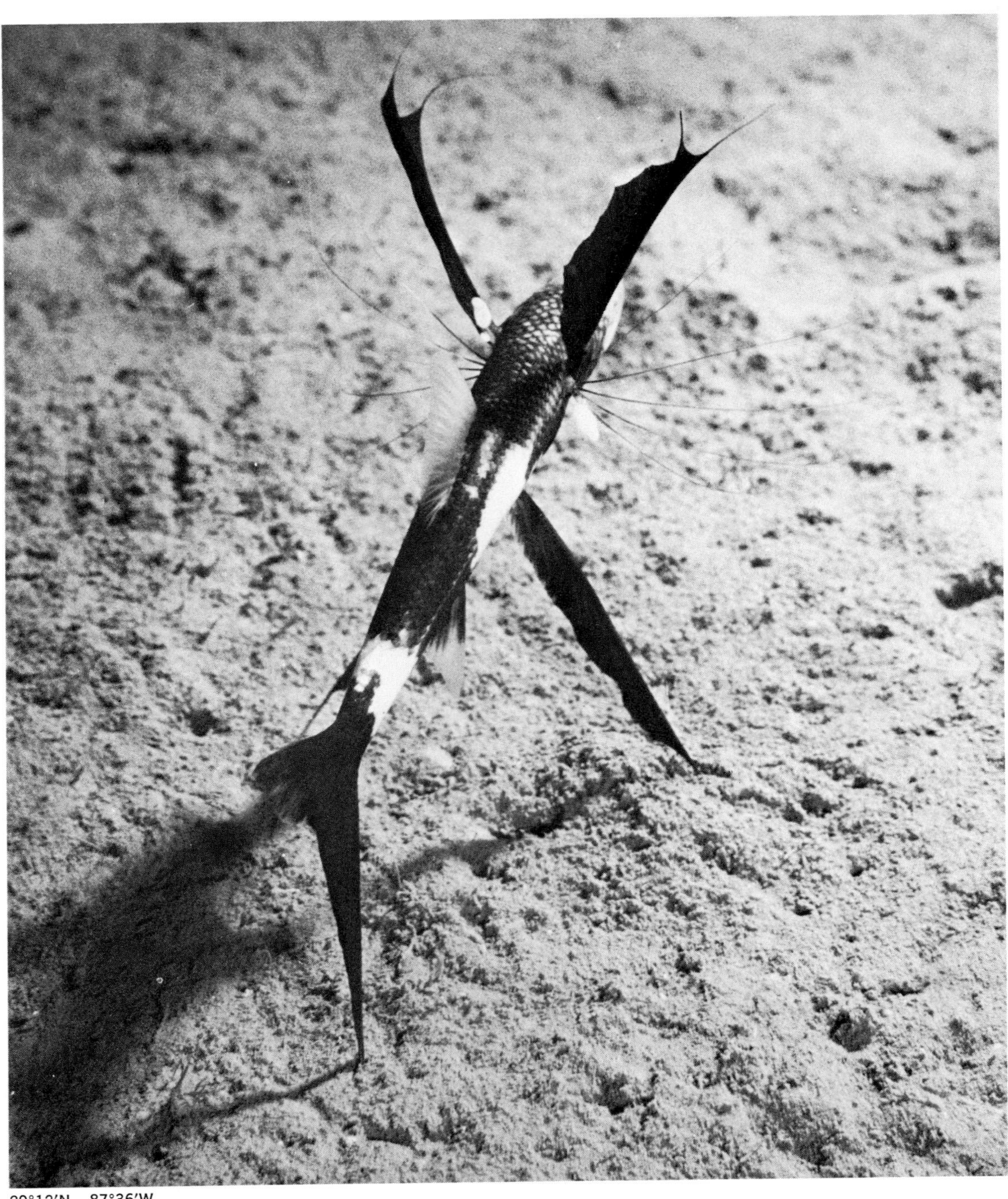

29°12′N 87°36′W

3.7 The tripod fish stands on the bottom in silent ambush. This bizarre fish, photographed from *Deepstar 4000,* was facing into the weak bottom current. Note the very pitted surface of the sea floor near the fish's "feet," De Soto Canyon, Gulf of Mexico, 1200 m.

Abyssal bathypteroid fish have been photographed resting near the sea floor with their long, slender ray-fins touching or probing the sediment (3.5). The structure of these fish has suggested that they live close to the deep-sea floor, probing the surface of the ooze with their long, stiff, independently movable feelers.[5] These fish are blind and it has been suggested[6] that they sail over the sea floor using the three long rays as feelers to report if there is anything worth investigating as possible food. *Benthosaurus* have been observed several times from a bathyscaphe. One of the most experienced pilots[7] reports, "I have never observed them in any other posture than sitting on their three projections. I see them on the bottom, 'legs' wide apart, the head a little higher than the tail, the nose into the current, without moving, like a statuette on a mantle piece . . . I even released ballast shot almost on its back, but it did not budge. If the fins had not been moving slightly, I might have believed it stuffed!"

The photographs of bathypteroids illustrated here show the fish standing on its ray fins unconcerned with the approach of the camera or the flashing of the light (3.5, 2.86). Although one observer inferred that they walk or hop along the bottom, he apparently never observed them moving. With the knowledge that these fish rest for long periods on their stilts (3.6, 3.7), it would seem probable that they play a "waiting game," feeding on animals which are carried along in the current.

The batfish[8] actually walks on the sea floor with large fins which might really be considered feet, but these curious creatures have not yet been found below 1200 meters' depth. However, if they live in the abyss they should leave dramatic footprints on the sea floor.

Long mysterious meandering trails consisting of a series of oval depressions transverse to the direction of motion are occasionally seen. These tiny, canoe-shaped depressions which may be made by a fish probing the ooze (3.8) are about the size of a cat's paw and occur single file at a regular spacing. There are in all probability many fish tracks yet to be identified on the deep-sea floor (3.9).

STAR TRACKS

Echinoderms, the rulers of the abyss, are responsible for all the large prominent tracks and trails seen on the deep-sea floor. In pulling themselves over the bottom,[9] brittle stars (ophiuroids) sometimes create a discrete series of partial body impressions which produce a feathery pinnate trail (3.10, 3.11). The starfish (asteroids) move with their tube feet entirely or walk with their arms alone, leaving long, blunt "footprints" in the sediment.

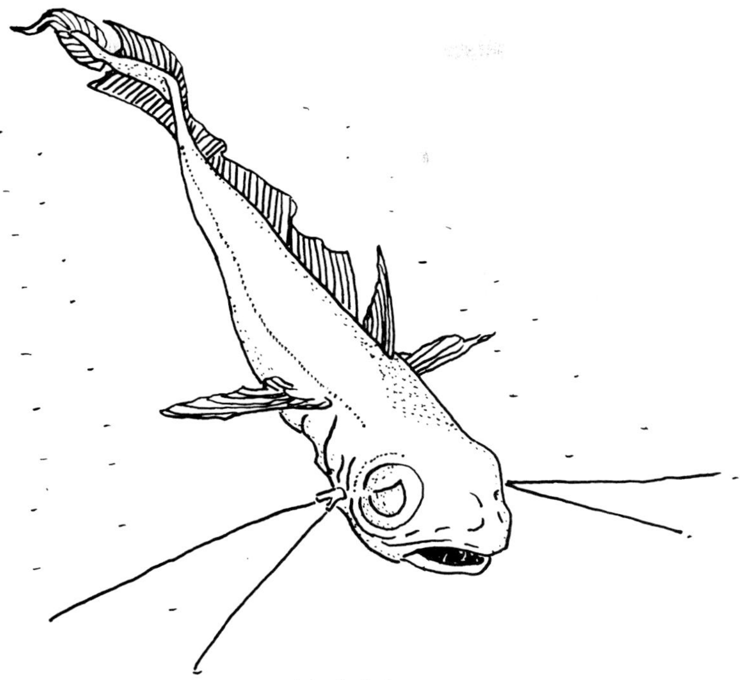

3.9 The morids probe the ooze with their long rays.

28°07′N 14°09′W

A group of relatively large mud-eating starfish, the Porcellanasteridae, inhabit the deep sea, having their greatest development in depths over 4000 meters. They possess rather rigid, broad-based, tapering, unsuckered rays, and the upper surface is generally broadly arched. They have no intestine or anus but take mud into their oral cavity, where mucus aids in digestion; and they later eject the exhausted sediment as little round balls. These animals should produce large and distinctive trails while feeding on the sea floor.

One of the most dramatic and mysterious of all deep-sea trails resembles the mold of a ribbed snowtire tread (3.4, 3.12, 3.13). These 20-centimeter-wide ribbed trails consist of a narrow longitudinal axial groove with lateral ridges and grooves which terminate in deep round or oval impressions about three centimeters in diameter. These "tread trails" characteristically begin or end abruptly. In several photographs a star impression occurs at the end of a "tread trail" (3.4 UL), and in one case (3.13 R) a "tread trail" ends in a deep cylindrical vertical hole. These trails are very seldom straight for more than one meter and typ-

◁ 3.8 Single-file footprints. U, L, The maker of these puzzling tracks has yet to be caught in the act, 686 m, Canary Islands.

28°07′N 14°09′W

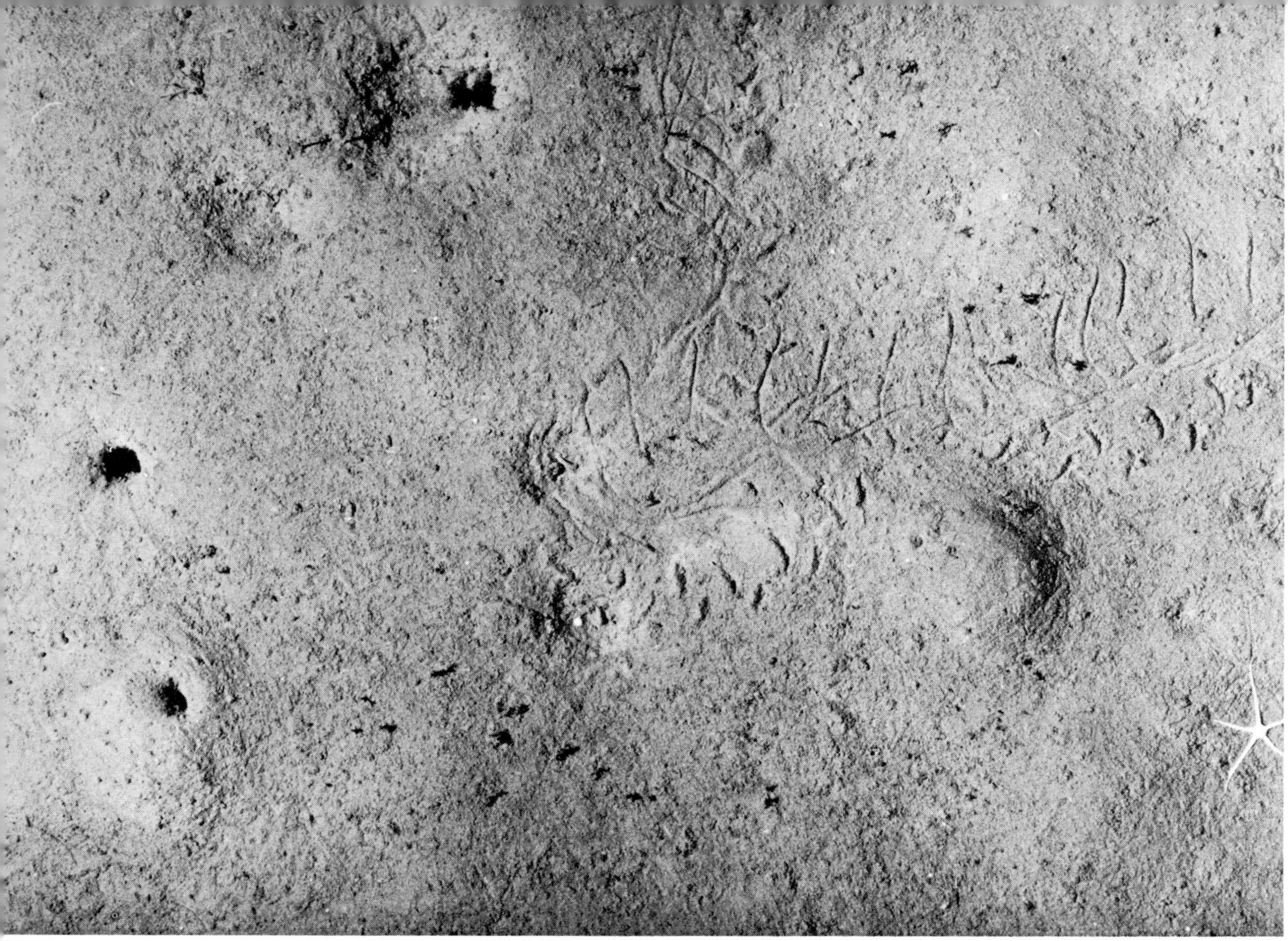

38°42′N 68°58′W

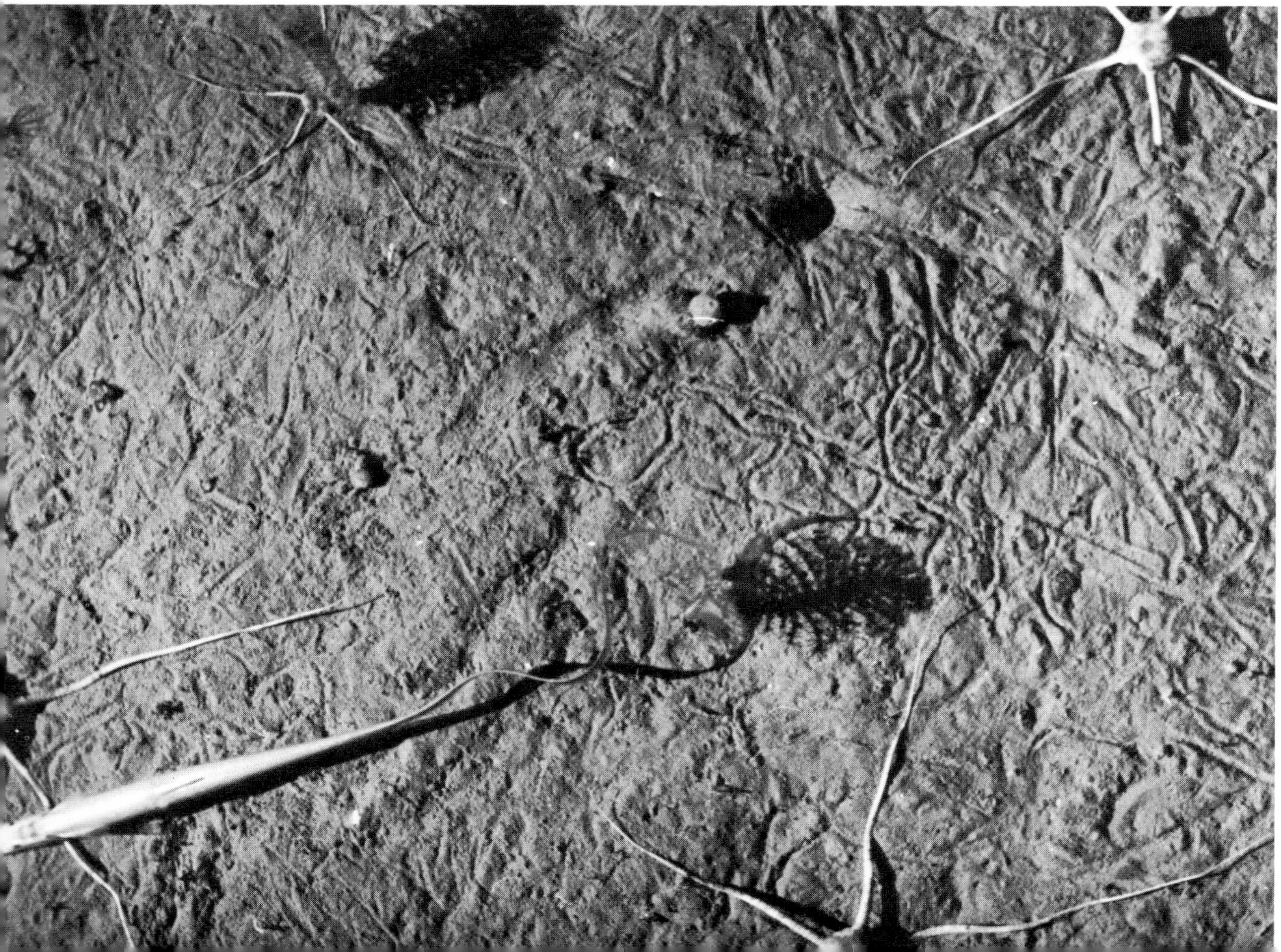

39°58′N 68°57′W

3.11 Brittle star tracks. Brittle stars produce feathery trails while rowing themselves over the sea floor.

ically meander, often recrossing. One may surmise that "tread trails" are the feeding traces of a large mud-eating asteroid; however, none have yet been caught in the act.

CUCUMBER TRAILS

The characteristic tracks of most asteroids and ophiuroids are easily recognized; the footprints of the various arthropods are mostly too small to be seen in normal photographs and real walking fish are not known in the abyss. Thus, only the holothurians can be responsible for most of the large prominent discrete footprints so commonly seen on the deep-sea floor. In view of their importance in the abyssal seascape, we will briefly discuss the size and arrangement of the podia on the ventral walking soles of the various holothurians (Table 3.1).[10]

The aspidochirotes possess numerous, generally small, podia, while the much more common elasipods have fewer but larger and longer ones (2.53). Considering the number and arrangement of podia, one would suspect that about half of the genera of these two orders should produce paths of holes often without discernible arrangement whereas the remainder, which significantly includes all the giants, should leave ordered rows of footprints.

◁ 3.10 Curvaceous tracks of brittle stars. U, Ophiuroids are the most common bottom markers on the continental margin, 3396 m, New England continental rise. L, Fish, sea pens, and ophiuroids creating tracks on the sea floor, 1476 m, New England continental slope.

Table 3.1 Abyssal holothurians. Genera dredged below 3000 m.

ABYSSAL HOLOTHURIANS List of Genera Dredged from Below 3000 m		Maximum size captured, cm	Location (1)	Color (2)	Arrangement of feet on walking sole Feet all around	Two rows of feet on both sides only	Two rows of feet near middle and feet on both sides
ORDER APODA	(many shallow water genera)						
Protankyra		2	A P	Y		No podia	
Myriotrochus		5	P	W, Y, Gr		No podia	
ORDER MOLPADONIA	(many shallow water genera)						
Gephyrothuria		5	P	R		No podia	
Hedingia		11	W	Gr		No podia	
Ceraplectana		8	P	Gr		No podia	
Molpadia		20	A P	Gr, V, Br		No podia	
ORDER DENDROCHIROTA	(many shallow water genera)						
Abyssicucumis		4-10	W	Y	One to three bands		
Ypsilothuria		2	I P	Gr	One to three bands		
ORDER ASPIDOCHIROTA							
Bathyplotes		15	I	Gr		X	
Benthothuria		11	I	Gr	X		
Capheira		10	P	Gr	X		
Mesothuria		13	W	Gr, W	X		
Paelopatides		30	A P	Br			X
Paroriza		23	A	Br, V		X	
Pseudostichopus		17	W	V, B, Y	X		
Synallactes		18	W	Gr		X	
ORDER ELASIPODA	(exclusively deep water)						
Deima		17	A I	Gr	X		
Oneirophanta		20	W	W, Y, V, Gr		X	
Orphnurgus		17	P	Gr		X	
Laetmogone		24	W	V		X	
Achlyonice		10	P	Gr	X		
Ellipinion		7	A I	W, Gr	X		
Elpidia		3	A I	Clear		X	
Kolga		5	A			X	
Periamma		13	W	W, V	X		
Scotoplanes		13	W	Gr	X		
Parelpidia		19	P	Gr, V	X		
Peniagone		10	W	Gr, V, B	X		
Scotoanassa		5	A I	W	X		
Benthodytes		34	W	B, V, R, Gr, Br			X
Euphronides		15	W	R, V			X
Psycheotrephes		3	P	V			X
Psychropotes		30	W	V, Br			X

(1) A = Atlantic P = Pacific I = Indian W = World
(2) B = Blue Br = Brown Gr = Gray Y = Yellow R = Red V = Violet W = White

Table 3.2 Walking abyssal holothurians.

WALKING ABYSSAL HOLOTHURIANS						
Type of Trail	Genus	Maximum Size of Captured Specimens, cm.				
		>10	>15	>20	>25	>30
FOUR ROW TRAIL	Benthodytes	■	■	■	■	■
	Psychropotes	■	■	■	■	■
	Paelopatides	■	■	■	■	■
	Euphronides	■	■			
	Psycheotrephes					
TWO ROW TRAIL	Laetmogone	■	■	■		
	Paroriza	■	■	■		
	Oneirophanta	■	■	■		
	Synallactes	■	■			
	Orphnurgus	■	■			
	Bathyplotes	■	■			
	Kolga					
	Elpidia					
PATH OF HOLES	Parelpidia	■	■			
	Pseudostichopus	■	■			
	Deima	■	■			
	Periamma	■				
	Scotoplanes	■				
	Mesothuria	■				
	Benthothuria	■				
	Capheira	■				
	Peniagone	■				
	Achlyonice	■				
	Ellipinion					
	Scotoanassa					

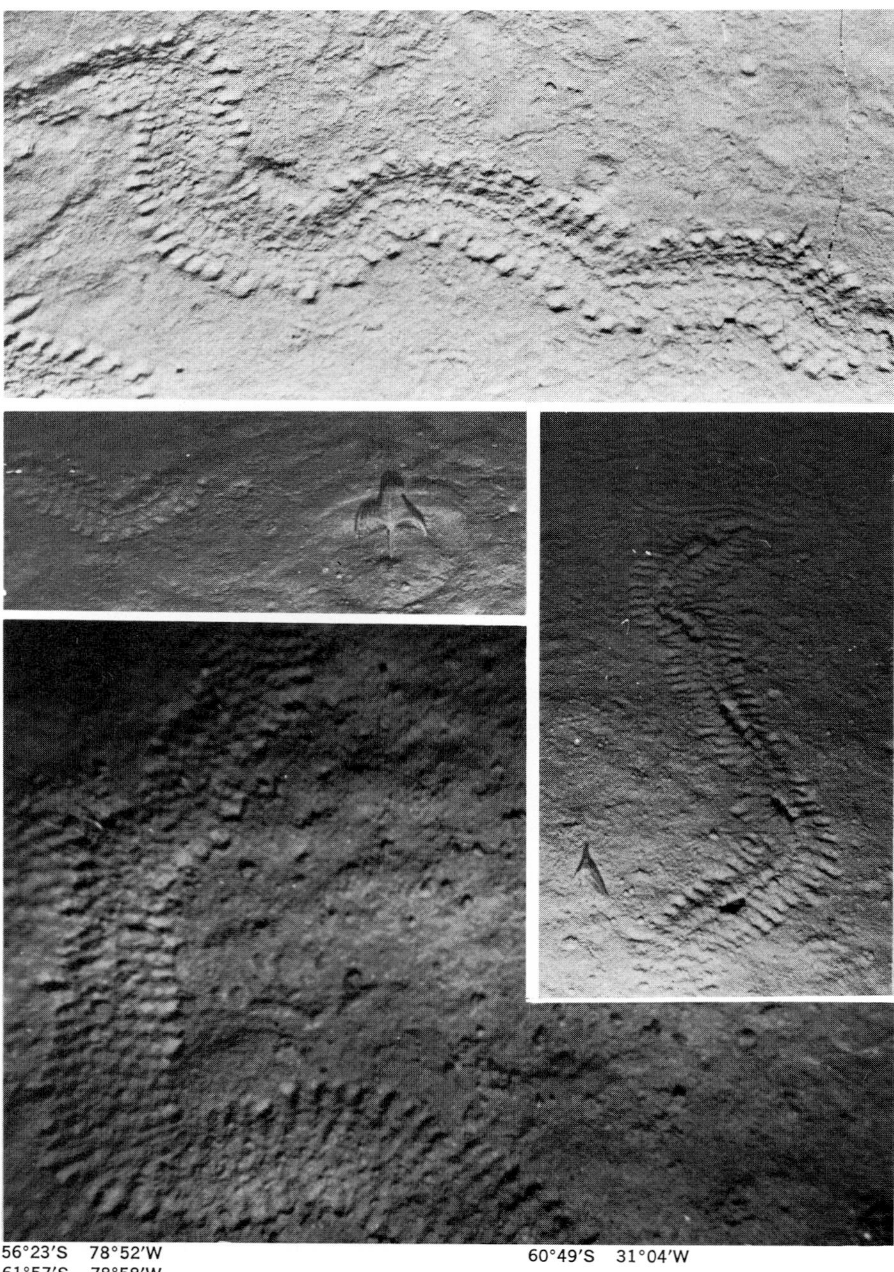

56°23′S 78°52′W
61°57′S 78°58′W
12°24′S 101°32′E

60°49′S 31°04′W

3.12 Large "tread trail" tracks. U, Meandering track with prominent lateral impressions, 4410 m, continental margin of southern Chile. CL, These tracks commonly terminate abruptly. Note gorgonian coral (sea fan) on right, 4798 m, Pacific continental rise of Antarctic Peninsula, Bellingshausen Basin. CR, 4276 m, Prominent median furrows are frequently observed in tread tracks, southeast Scotia Sea. L, Median furrow is not always prominent, 4839 m, Outer Ridge, Java Trench.

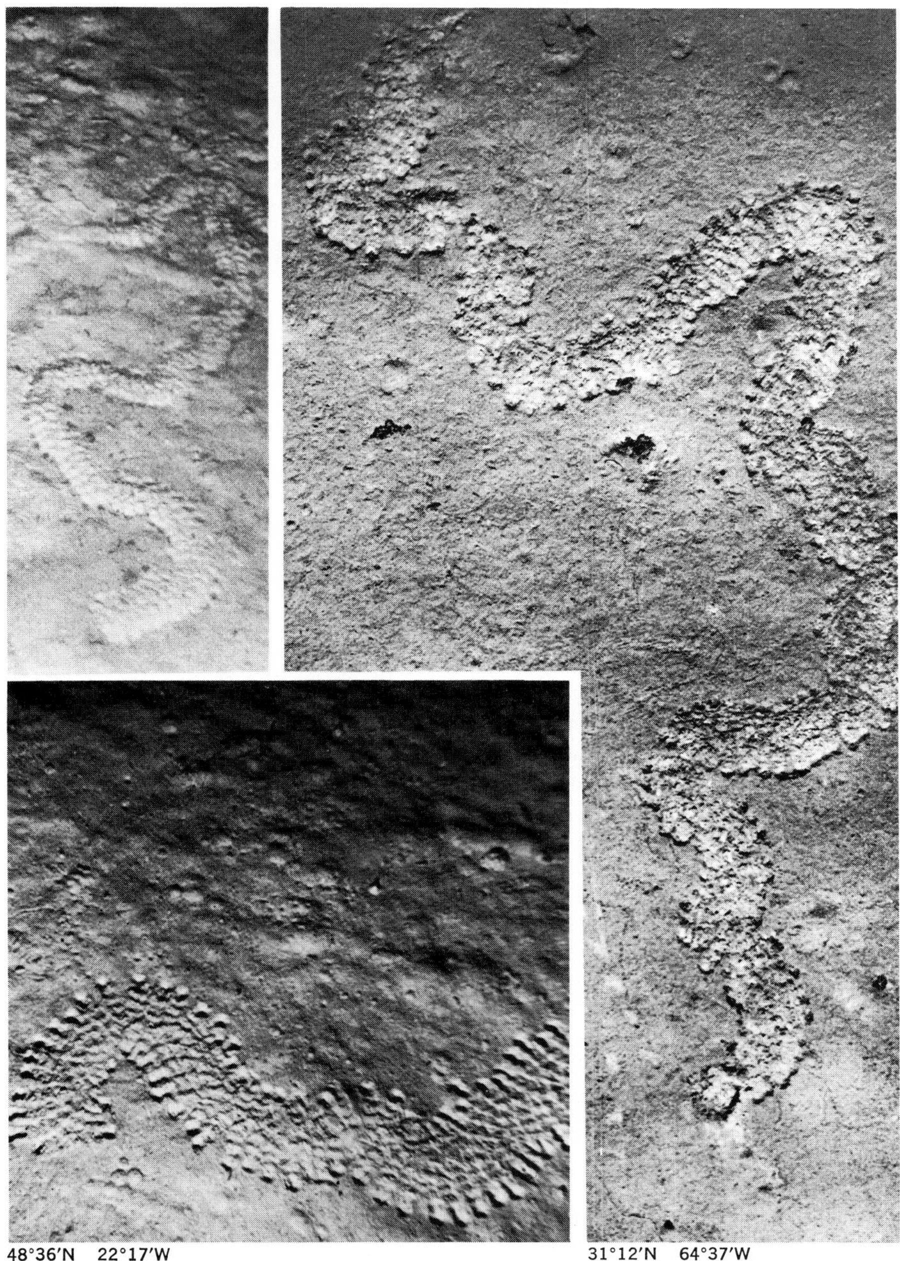

3.13 Tread tracks abruptly terminate. UL, Criss-crossing tracks, 4014 m, Mid-Atlantic Ridge, northeastern Atlantic. R, This fresh track ends abruptly in a deep vertical hole, 4608 m, central Bermuda Rise. LL, Tread track with an abrupt termination (or beginning) without hole, 3442 m, Mid-Oceanic Ridge, central South Pacific.

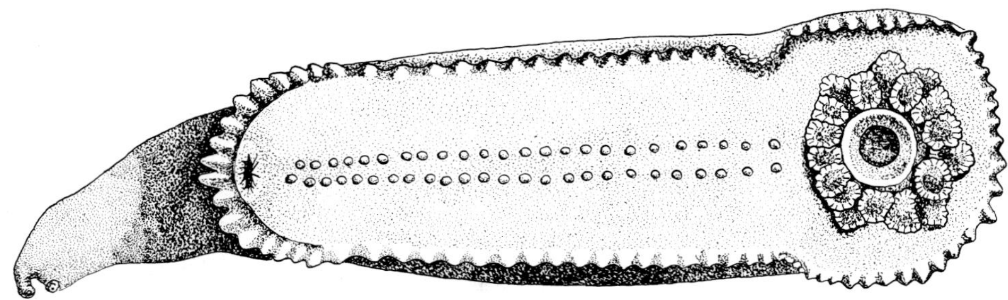

3.14 A giant holothurian. *Psychropotes,* one of the largest elasipods, leaves a wide track consisting of four parallel rows of holes.

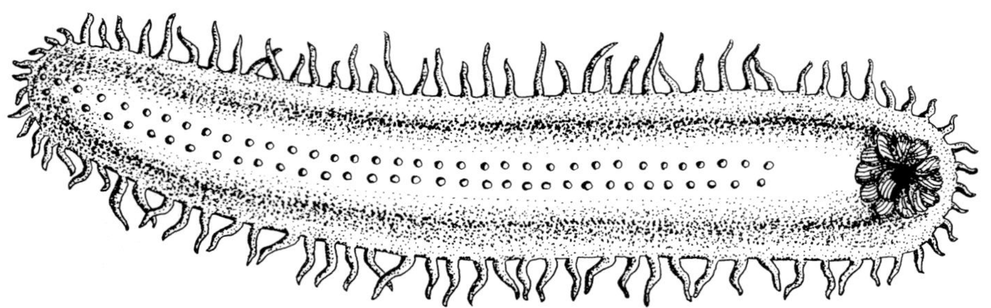

3.15 Another large tracker of the abyss. The holothurian *Benthodytes* leaves a four-row trail with the innermost rows closely spaced. The track should be about five centimeters across.

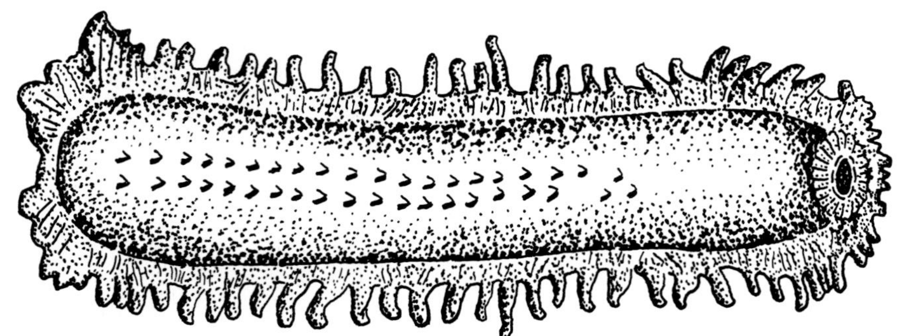

3.16 The abyssal aspidochirote holothurian, *Paelopatides,* should also make a four-row track.

Most abyssal holothurians do not exceed the size of a mouse, but a few of the largest reach the size of a kitten. Such giants occur in the related elasipod genera *Psychropotes* and *Benthodytes* and in the similar-appearing aspidochirote genus *Paelopatides* (Table 3.2). Curiously, all three (3.14, 3.15, 3.16) have a double row of podia in the central por-

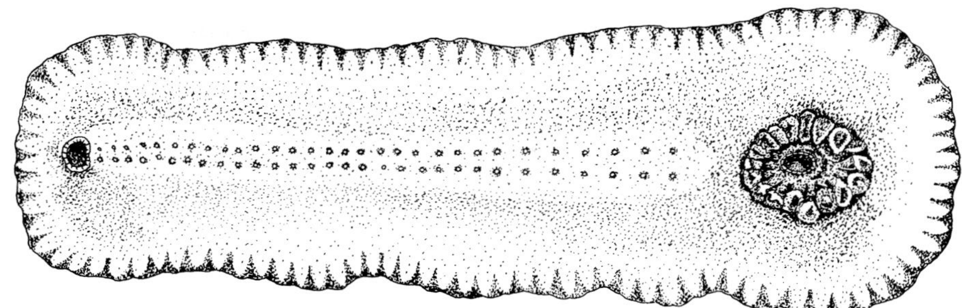

3.17 A large abyssal tracker (*Euphronides depressa*). This elasipod holothurian makes a double row of holes with tube feet and another outside double row of impressions with its crenulated mantle.

3.18 Four-row trails. Of the known genera of holothurians, only *Psychropotes, Paelopatides, Euphronides,* and *Benthodytes* can produce broad four-rowed trails. U, 4289 m, archipelagic apron near Tahiti; L, 4372 m, archipelagic apron near Bora Bora.

15°58′S 149°39′W
17°01′S 152°38′W

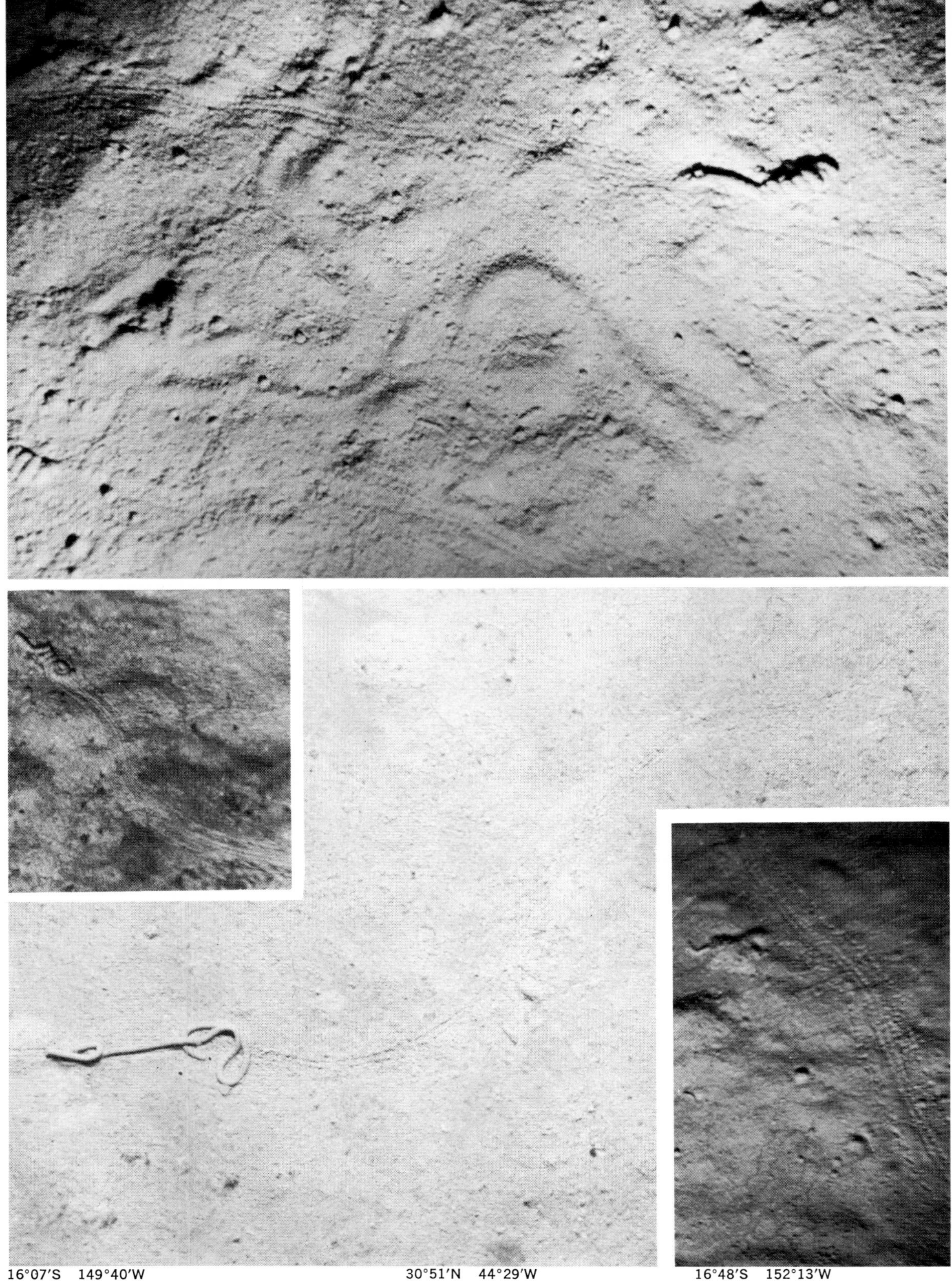

16°07′S 149°40′W
48°29′N 14°19′W

30°51′N 44°29′W

16°48′S 152°13′W

3.19 Feces and four-hole tracks. U, 4286 m, archipelagic apron near Tahiti. LC, 4577 m, continental rise of Britain. LL, 3705 m, Mid-Atlantic Ridge, western North Atlantic. LR, 3938 m, archipelagic apron near Bora Bora.

3.20 Giant abyssal "boxing glove" holothurian. This is the first life photograph of *Paelopatides gigantica* Verrill. Note its narrow double row of footprints. Photographed in 1947, identification by Elizabeth Deichmann; 2120 m, New England continental slope.

tion of their creeping sole, and all three have a fused mantle with more or less developed podia on the brim. These giants, together with the more moderate sized *Euphronides* (3.17), produce the 20-centimeter-wide distinctive and common walking trails which consist of four rows of tiny shallow holes (3.18, 3.19). The trails are usually straight or slightly curved and the outer tracks are often less perfectly aligned than the inner rows and are frequently elongate parallel to the track. These largest holothurian trails consist of a double row of closely spaced tracks with or without (3.20) two additional lateral rows of less distinct tracks produced by the lateral fused podia of the brim. The grazers responsible for these essentially four-row trails drop the large knotted feces that are frequently found aligned parallel to the direction of travel (3.19). Less dis-

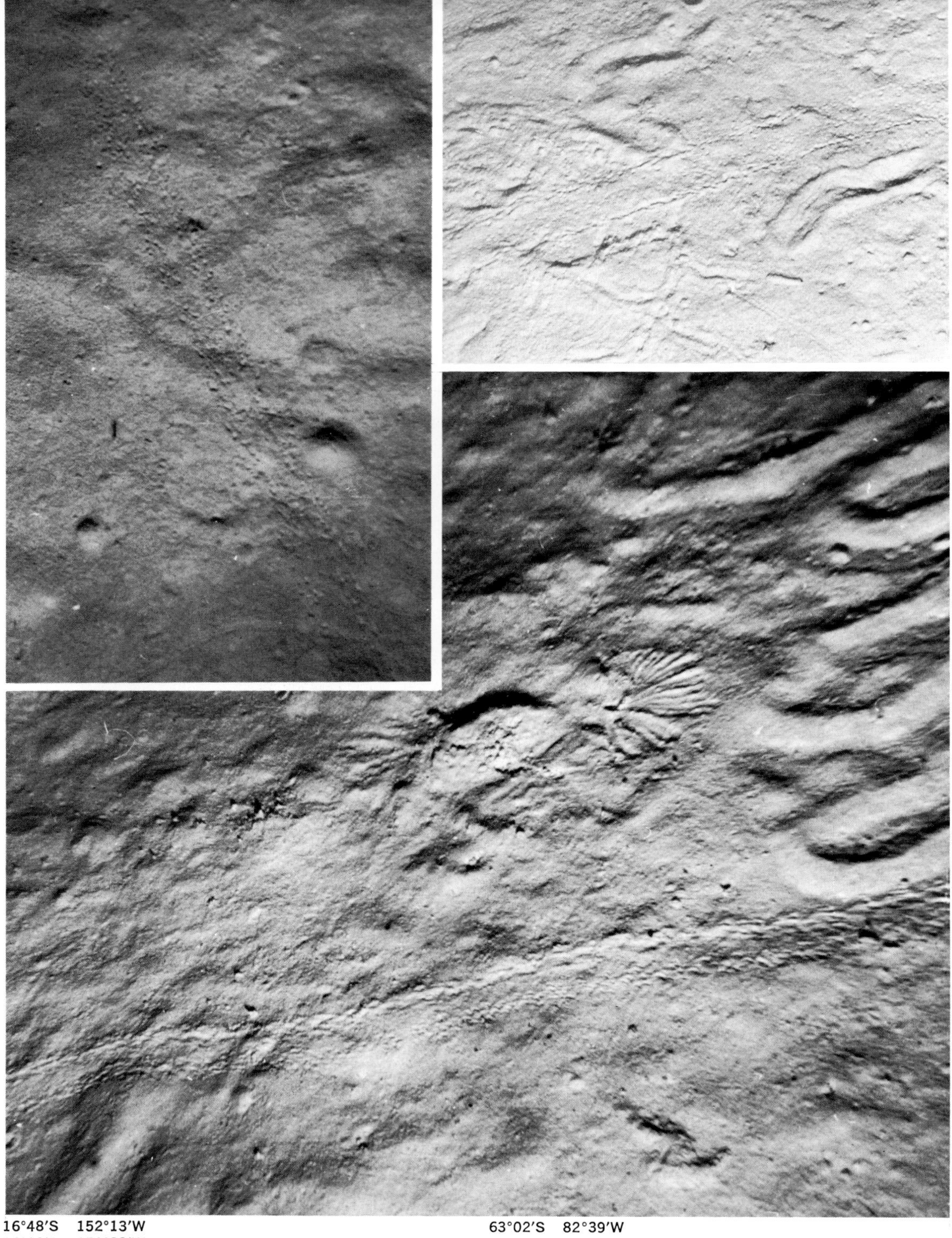

16°48′S 152°13′W
16°18′S 151°38′W

63°02′S 82°39′W

3.21 Tracks of giant holothurians. UL, 3938 m, archipelagic apron west of Bora Bora; UR, 4706 m, Bellingshausen Basin; L, 2328 m, near Bora Bora.

tinctive, small double-row tracks (3.21) are produced by six genera of moderately large abyssal holothurians. The most prominent traces are probably made by the long, slender *Laetmogone* (3.22), *Oneirophanta* (3.23), and the large *Paroriza*.

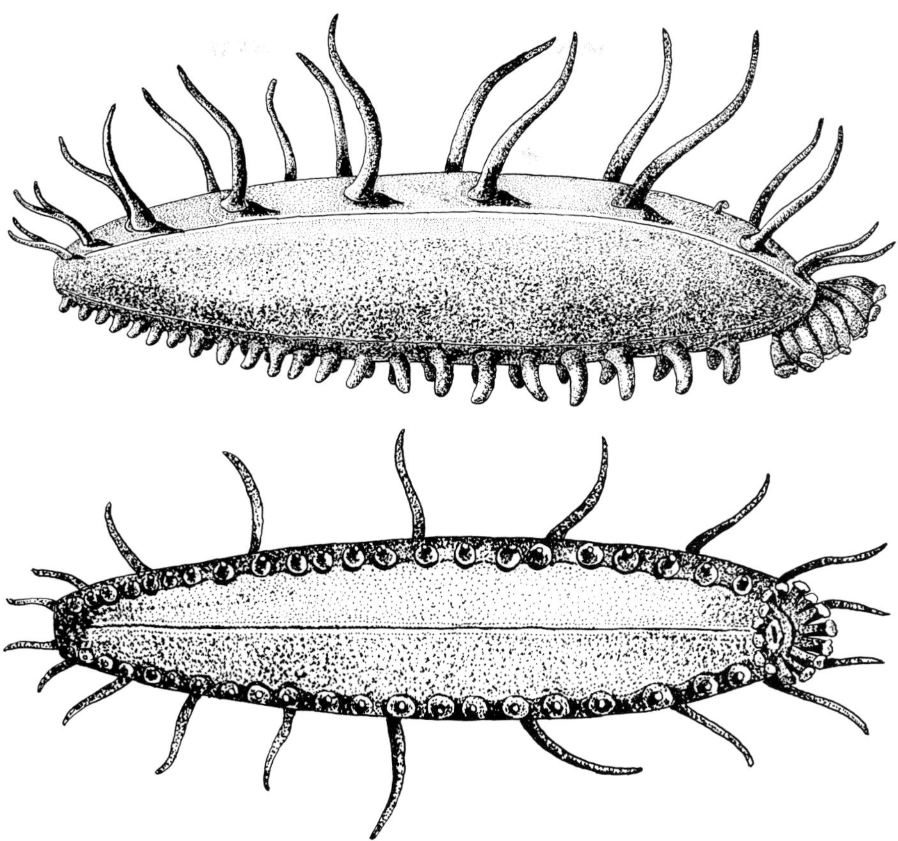

3.22 *Laetmogone.* This long, slender but ornate abyssal elasipod leaves a double-row trail.

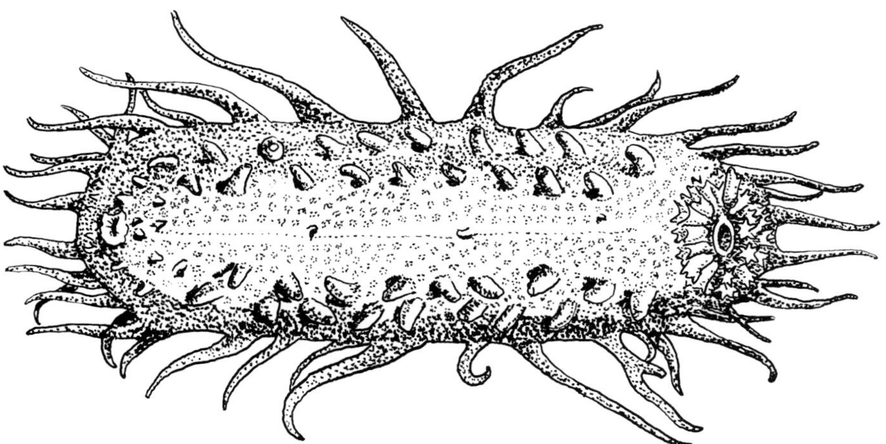

3.23 The relatively large elasipod *Oneirophanta* produces two rows of deep impressions.

3.24 *Peniagone*, a very common smaller holothurian, leaves multi-hole paths.

The dozen genera of abyssal holothurians which produce multi-holed paths are comparatively small; only four include individuals which reach fifteen centimeters in length. One of the most common of these is *Peniagone* (3.24, 3.25).[12] This genus has been found in all the world oceans and in depths exceeding 7000 meters. More *Peniagone*-type holothurians have been photographed than any other and some are occasionally seen associated with small circular impressions that are aligned in parallel rows. The horseshoe-shaped line of tube feet on the walking sole of *Peniagone,* as well as on the less common *Deima* (3.26, 3.27), and *Scotoplanes* (3.28), would leave a regularly spaced multi-hole path.

Trails that consist of multiple tracks, eight, ten, or twelve holes wide (3.29), are fairly common. They are not as easily recognized as the giant four-row or moderate-sized two-row trails, except under optimum conditions. The individual holes are arranged in cadences, sometimes parallel to, and sometimes transverse to, the apparent direction of motion. In one case (3.29), where the animal was apparently moving forward across the area photographed, the tracks are spaced transverse to the trail axis. The animal in this instance took three abrupt sidewise zigs. In these zigs the track rows are aligned parallel in the direction of travel, whereas in the main part of the trail the track-rows are aligned in a transverse position. This somewhat peculiar pattern is easily understood by examination of another photograph (3.25 LR), which shows a large *Peniagone* at the end of a broad belt of holes which it produced by side-stepping. Such holothurians, when walking straight ahead, produce a rhythmic track of eight, ten, or twelve holes, spaced in rows, transverse

63°02′S 82°39′W
62°24′S 64°17′W

58°52′S 37°23′W

3.25 Elasipod holothurians track the deep. U, A rabbit-eared cucumber, cf. *Peniagone,* is tracking an already well-tracked bottom, 4705 m, Pacific continental rise of Antarctic Peninsula. LL, A long, slender abyssal holothurian, cf. *Laetmagone,* 3677m, Drake Passage. LR, Abyssal side-stepping holothurian, 2976 m, Scotia Sea south of South Georgia Island.

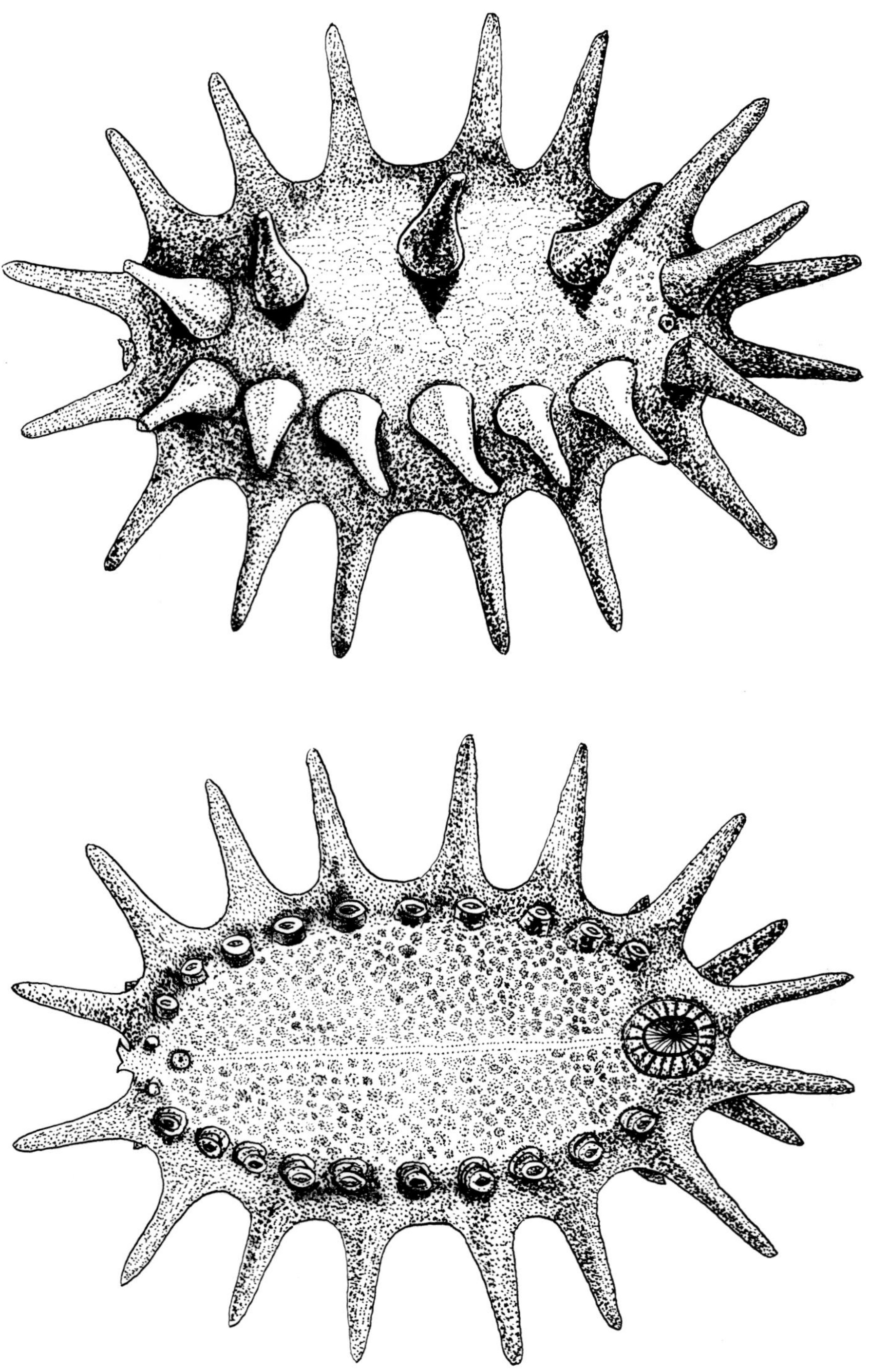

3.26 The abyssal elasipod holothurian, *Deima,* makes a path of holes. U, top, L, bottom.

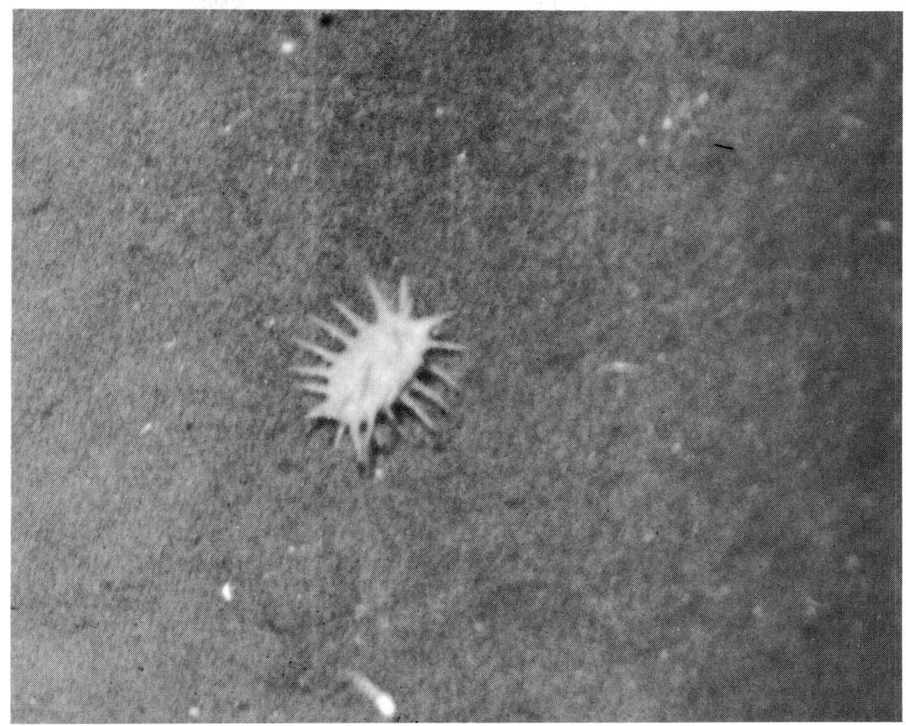

3.27 The abyssal holothurian, *Deima,* walking across the ooze. 4430 m, Hawaiian Archipelagic Apron.

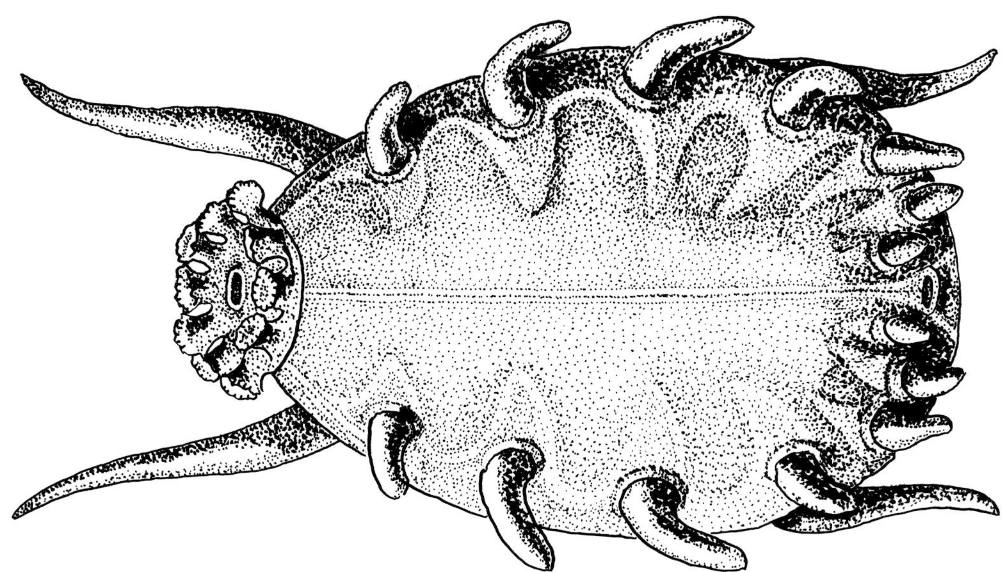

3.28 *Scotoplanes* leave a path of holes. This common abyssal elasipod holothurian is often likened to a pig. (bottom surface).

3.29 Holothurian tracks in the abyssal Pacific. Side-stepping holothurian trails, 4736 m, archipelagic apron west of Tahiti.

to the direction of motion, while the same animal when side-stepping produces tracks that are aligned in the direction of its sidewise motion. In other photographs (3.21 UR, L) similar cadence trails are seen in which the outer lateral tracks are somewhat deeper than the central ones.

The tube feet of holothurians are probably responsible for the vast majority of the recognizable walking trails. However, these same organisms at other times may plow or drag themselves through the sediment and produce plow marks. Occasionally, trails begin or end rather abruptly, and in certain cases, this may be due to the fact that the holothurian swam off or was carried away. Searching through over 50,000 photographs taken at more than 1200 locations on the deep-sea floor, it has been possible to find over one hundred animals caught in the act of producing tracks, trails and fecal deposits. Nevertheless, the animals responsible for many, if not most, abyssal tracks and trails still remain to be identified.

REFERENCES AND NOTES

1. The interest shown by geologists in tracks and trails is more than idle curiosity for they can be used to infer ancient environments and to identify overturned sequences of rocks. For an exhaustive treatment of organic and inorganic features preserved on the bedding planes of ancient rocks, see: R. R. Schrock. 1948. *Sequence in layered rocks.* McGraw-Hill, New York, 507 pp.
2. See Appendix 4 (p. 629).

3. The bearing capacity of sea-floor sediments has been studied during recent years in connection with the design and construction of structures to be placed on the ocean bottom (A. Richards (Editor). 1967. *Marine Geotechnique*. Univ. of Illinois Press, Chicago, 327 pp.).

4. The rate at which sediments accumulate can be directly determined by radiochemical studies on the sediments themselves or can be inferred by the identification of sediments resulting from dated events. This subject is treated further in Chapter 7. (See also, K. Turekian. 1968. *Oceans*, "Stratigraphy and Geochemistry of Deep-Sea Deposits, Prentice-Hall, Englewood Cliffs, N.J.).

5. N. B. Marshall. 1954. *Aspects of Deep Sea Biology*. Hutchinson, London, pp. 131-156; and N. B. Marshall and D. W. Bourne, 1964. A photographic survey of benthic fishes in the Red Sea and Gulf of Aden, with observations on their population, density, diversity and habits. *Bull. Mus. Comp. Zool., 132*(2):223-244.

6. A. F. Bruun. 1956. Animal life of the deep sea bottom. In: A. F. Bruun (Editor), *The* Galathea *Deep Sea Expedition, 1950-1952*. Macmillan, New York, 296 pp.

7. One of the six deep-sea bottom photographs reproduced by G. S. Houot (1958. Four years of diving to the bottom of the sea. *Nat. Geog. Mag., 113*:715-731.) shows a *Benthosaurus* resting on the floor of the Mediterranean.

8. J. Y. Cousteau. 1965. *World Without Sun*. Harper and Row, New York, 205 pp. This narrative of the film by the same name includes one photograph (p. 174) taken from the cinematic sequence that shows a batfish walking across the sea floor in 250 meters' depth.

9. A brittle star pulling itself along the sea floor (1300 m) at approximately one millimeter per second is reproduced in a one-page mosaic of six bottom photographs by J. G. Bruce (1962. Photographic record of a moving brittle star. *Deep-Sea Res., 9*:77.).

10. The following reports contain exceptionally good illustrations of the walking soles of holothurians: H. Theel. 1882. Report on the Holothuroidea. Challenger *Rept. Zool., 14*(XIII):176 pp.; H. Theel. 1885. Report on the Holothurioidea. Challenger *Rept. Zool.,* 14(XXXIX):310 pp.; H. Ludwig. 1894. The Holothurioidea. *Mem. Mus. Comp. Zool.,* 17(3): 183 pp; and E. Herouard. 1902. Holothuries provenant des campagnes de la *Princesse Alice. Res. Campagnes Sci. du Prince de Monaco. 21*:61 pp.

11. The list (Table 3.1) was taken directly from F. Madsen (1955. Holothurioidea *Repts. of the Swedish deep sea exped., 2*:149-175), but the descriptive characteristics were compiled largely from references listed in Appendix 3.

12. Photographs of *Peniagone* have been reproduced by R. J. Menzies (1963. General results of biological investigations USNS *Eltanin* Cruise 3. *Int. Rev. Ges. Hydrobiol., 48*:185-200) and B. C. Heezen, E. T. Bunce, J. B. Hersey, and M. Tharp (1965. Chain and Romanche fracture zones. *Deep-Sea Res., 11*:11-33). In the latter report a photograph in the floor of the Romanche Trench shows an elasipod holothurian *Peniagone incerta* walking across a soft mud bottom. The biological observations on the bottom and midwater of the Puerto Rico Trench is summarized by J. M. Peres (1965. Aperçu sur les résultats de deux plongées effectuées dans le ravin de Puerto Rico par la bathyscaphe *Archimède. Deep-Sea Res., 12*:883-891), who observed abundant holothurians which he believed to be *Synallactidae* and *Myriotrochus*.

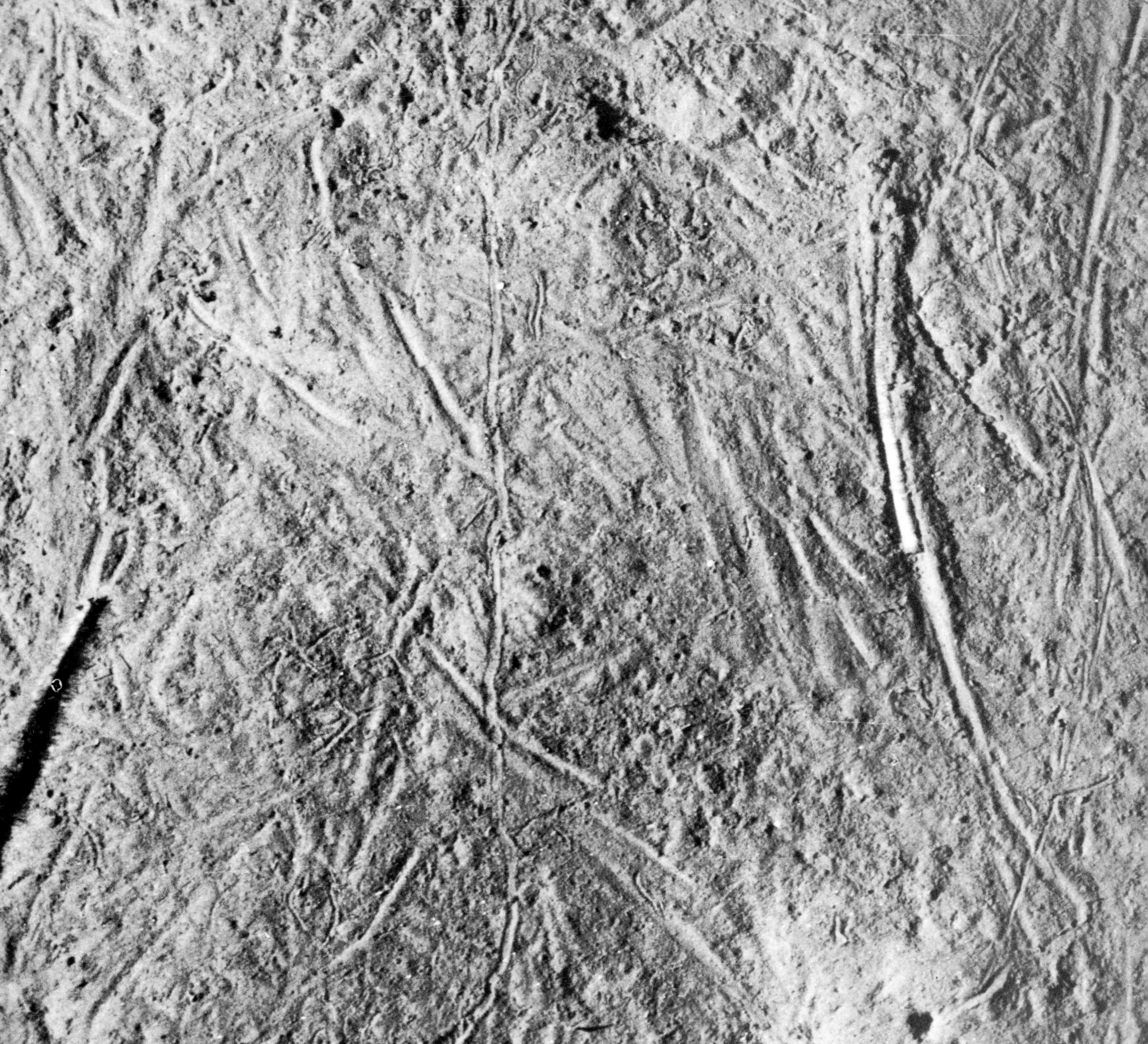

39°56′N 69°22′W

4.1 Large armored polychaete worms leave distinct plowmarks on the sea floor. 849 m, continental slope of New England.

4
Plow the Watery Deep

Mine be the dirt and dross
The dust and scum of the earth . . .
JOHN MASEFIELD

The smaller grooves, gouges, rills, and ridges that line the aging face of the deep are created by roving creatures which creep or crawl on or just beneath the soft and sensitive skin of the abyss (4.1, 4.2). The large heavy echinoderms are the principal plowers of the deep but certain vertebrates also leave their marks, and if one takes a closer look he will occasionally see the work of the numerous but generally tiny worms, molluscs and crustaceans which leave little grooves in their wake.

Although most of the large roving holothurians walk raised up on their podia, leaving footprints (Chapter 3), some creep along, plowing a furrow. *Pseudostichopus,* which has innumerable small feet all over its under-surface, produces a shallow, intermittent, broadly U-shaped groove as it inches its way across the sea floor (4.10) The locomotion of *Stichopus panimensis,* a similar shallow-water cucumber, has been studied. This large creature, twenty to thirty-five centimeters in length, normally attaches itself to the substrate by its creeping sole, whose three rows of tube feet are essential to locomotion.[1] Creeping is accomplished in part by a muscular wave that originates in the rear and sweeps forward (4.3). With the first appearance of this wave, the rear feet are loosened from the sea floor and the whole hind-end is lifted and then vigorously contracted (4.3b). Then the rear feet become re-attached to the sea floor, while the wave moves on to the middle of the animal (4.3c). As this portion is becoming attached, the wave reaches the head which is projected forward (4.3d) and finally re-attached to the sea floor. Individuals twenty-five centimeters long have been seen to creep a meter in about fifteen minutes, moving about seven centimeters with each locomotor wave.

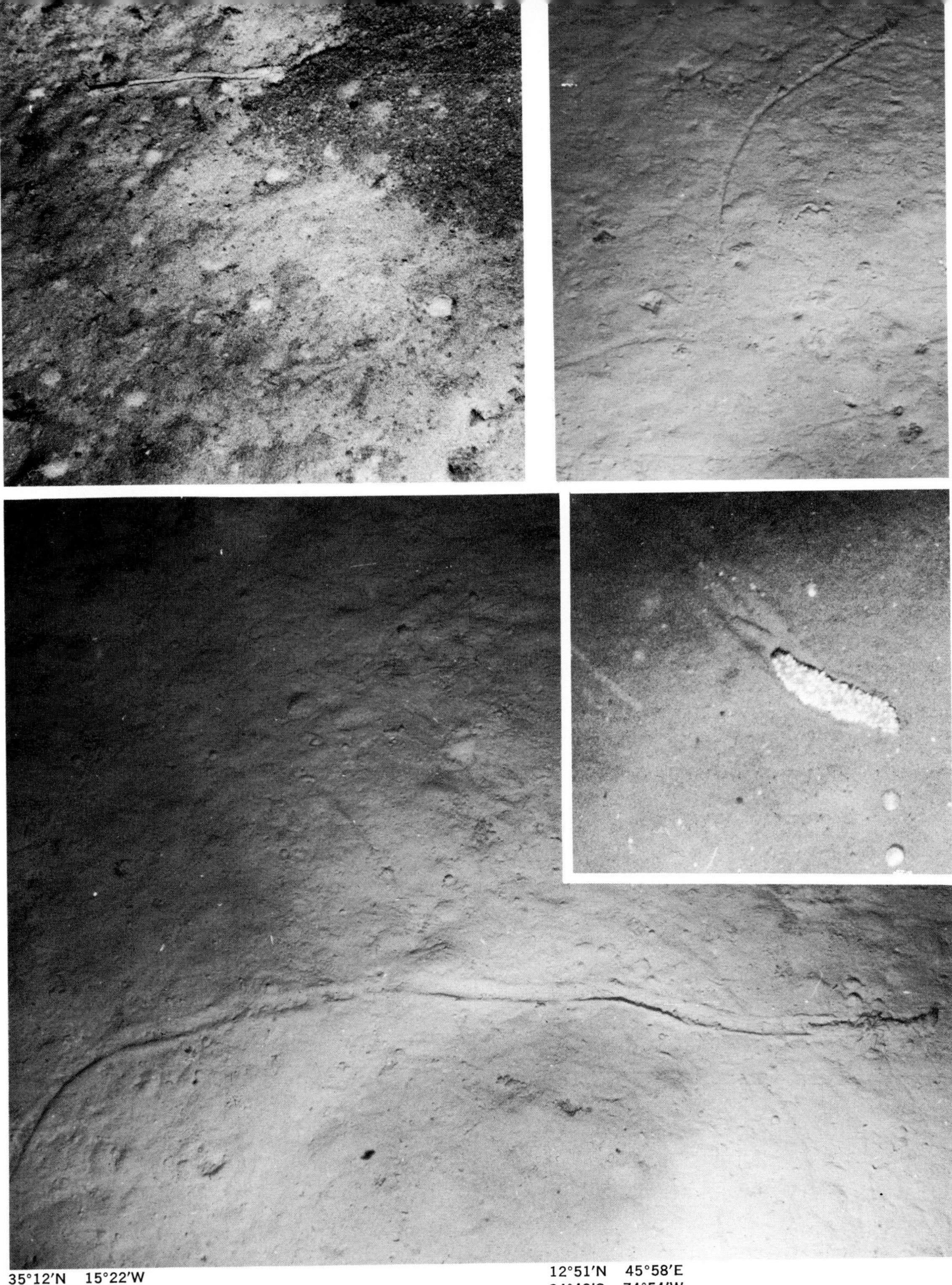

35°12′N 15°22′W
34°48′S 74°54′W

12°51′N 45°58′E
34°48′S 74°54′W

4.2 Plowers and plowmarks. Most plowers cannot be identified. UL, 1597 m, seamount, north of Madiera. UR and L, 4165 m, outer ridge off Central Chile. RC, plowing holothurian (cf. *Pseudostichopus*), 1288 m, Mid-Oceanic Ridge, Gulf of Aden. L, The plower at end of broad U-shaped plowmark somewhat resembles a large naked gastropod (sea hare or sea slug).

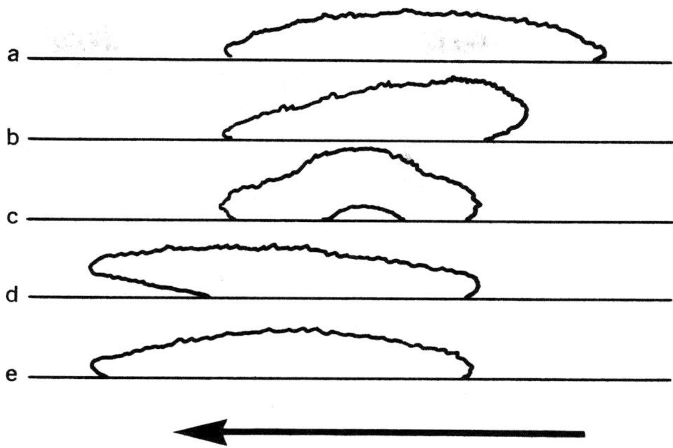

4.3 The motion of a plowing holothurian; (a) at rest; (b) rear lifts and contracts; (c) rear reattaches to bottom; (d) forward thrust; (e) at rest.

The locomotion of the snail (4.4) is known to be similar to that of plowing cucumbers; but abyssal snails are so small that one can rarely see their tiny marks. Among the few dramatic exceptions is a gastropod which was observed skimming the ooze off dark pillow basalts (4.5). Those soft-bellied hermit crabs which carry a gastropod or scaphopod shell to protect their abdomen (2.63) leave footprints and a shallow groove as they walk dragging their house with them. Although such marks have been frequently identified in shallow depths, they have not been recognized in the deep sea.

The relatively small free-moving bivalves plow freely through the soft bottom sediments often leaving a V-shaped furrow in their wake (4.6, 4.7). Those of the deep sea are small and fragile, rarely reaching four centimeters in breadth, yet they are frequently recovered in deep-sea trawls and are thus probably responsible for many of the narrow, V-shaped zigzag grooves[2] occasionally observed in exceptionally clear photographs (4.8, 4.9).

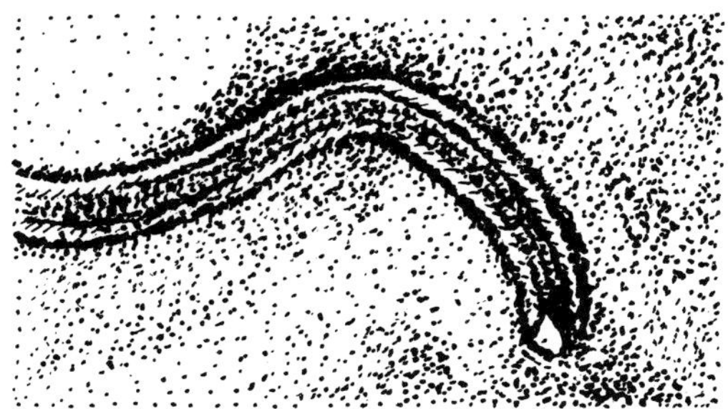

4.4 Gastropods plow furrows across tidal flats. Similar plow marks have been seen in the abyss and may have a similar origin.

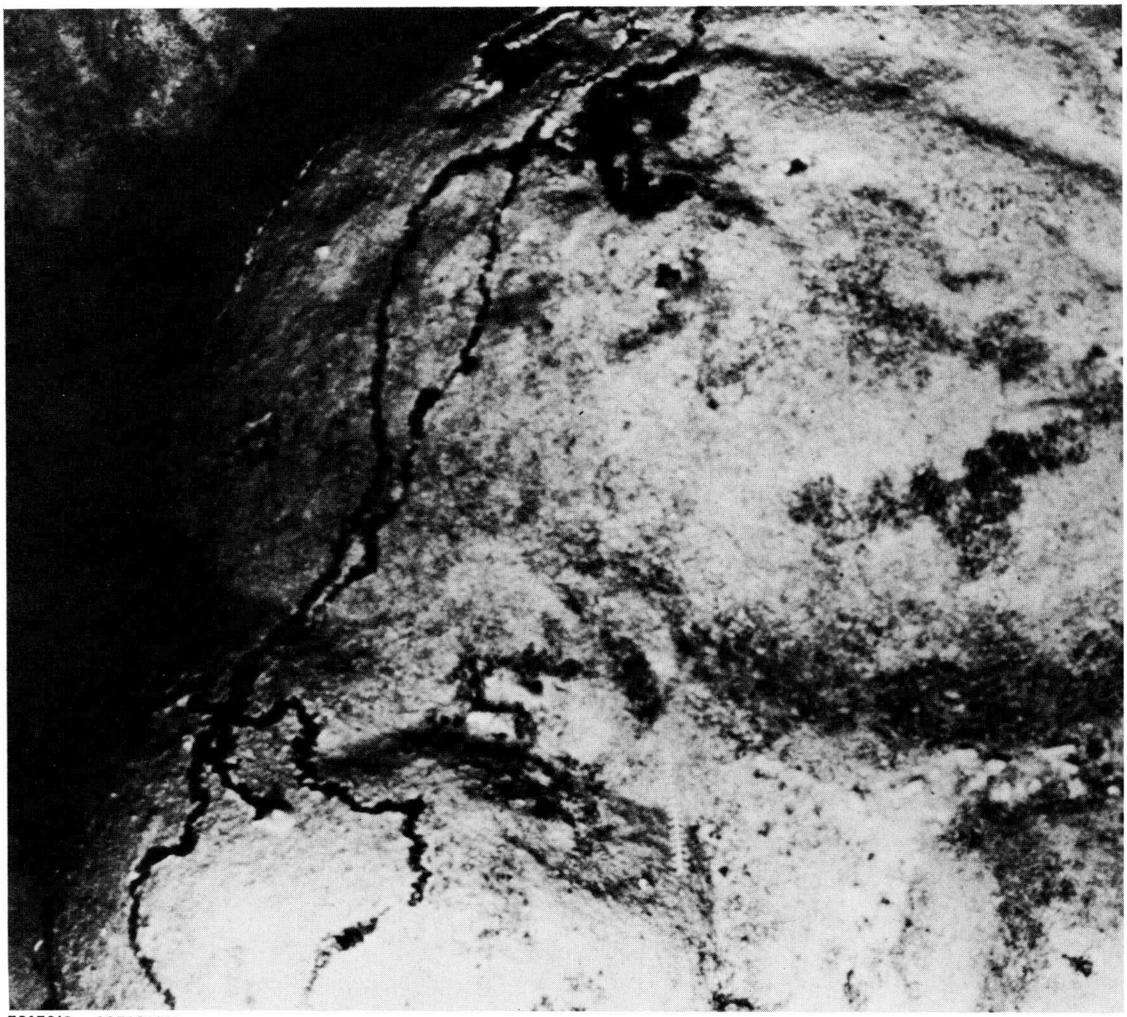

58°58′S 135°20′W

4.5 Plowing abyssal gastropod. The light dusting of ooze is being swept from the dark pillowed lava of the Mid-Oceanic Ridge by a small light-colored gastropod (lower left). A sea pen stands erect in lower center, 3794 m, Mid-Oceanic Ridge, south Pacific.

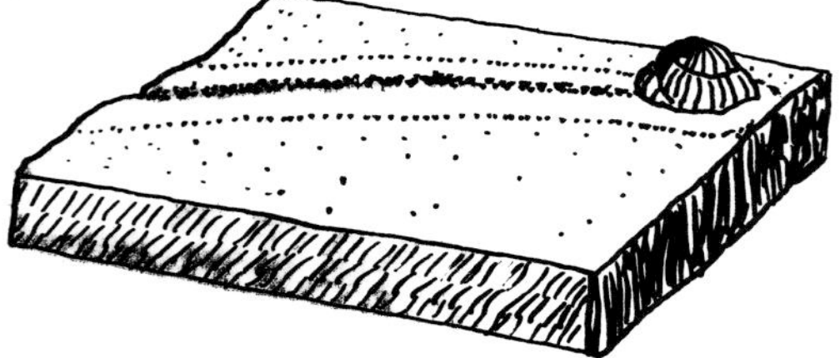

4.6 Bivalves have been caught-in-the-act plowing in the exposed muds of the seashore.

PATTERNS

The polychaete worms, free-moving, predaceous and mud-loving, are one of the most abundant animal groups of the deep-sea floor, yet very few are large enough to leave traces recognizable in the average sea-floor photograph. Exceptions to this rule are the elongate sticklike organisms up to one-half meter long which have been photographed lying flat on the sea floor along the continental shelf and slope (4.1, 2.67). The organism produces a slightly hyperboloid impression and apparently pulls it-

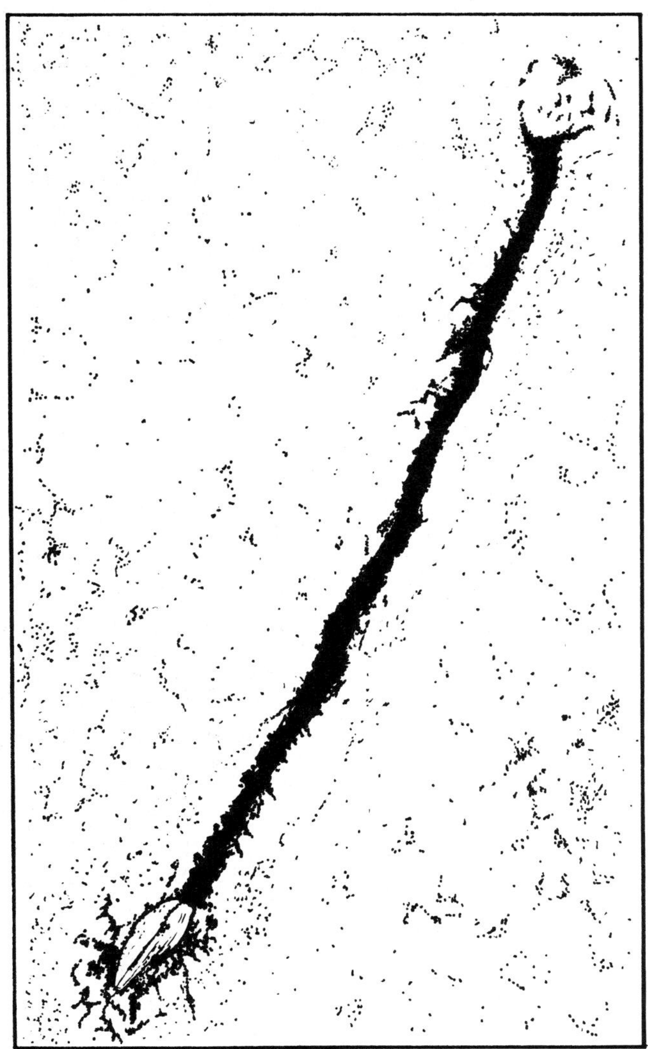

4.7 Bivalves have been seen plowing narrow V-shaped grooves in sandy beaches. Similar grooves have been photographed on the deep-sea floor (see 4.8).

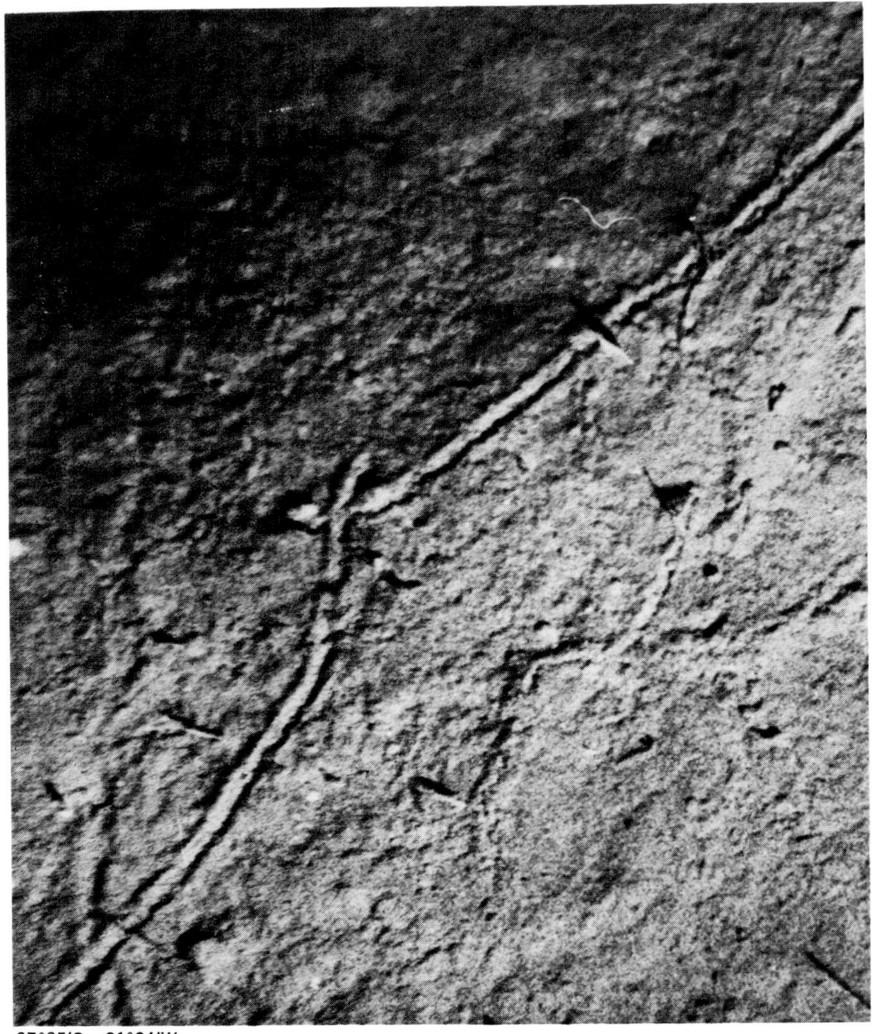

07°35′S 81°24′W

4.8 Mollusc grooves in the Peru-Chile Trench. Specimens of *Neopilina,* a living relic of the Paleozoic seas, were dredged nearby,[2] 5817 m, off northern Peru.

self along the sea floor, producing a series of intersecting, criss-crossing shallow grooves or impressions on the bottom. The exceptionally large tube-dwelling polychaete, *Hyalinoecia tubicola,* dredged in abundance in the areas where these photographs were taken, have been identified as the animal responsible for these distinctive marks.

One would not ordinarily think of the corals as plowers of the deep, but in fact some of them make circular drag or plowmarks as the current swings their attached fan-like bodies (4.11).

Decorative herringbone patterns of leaf-like depressions which project

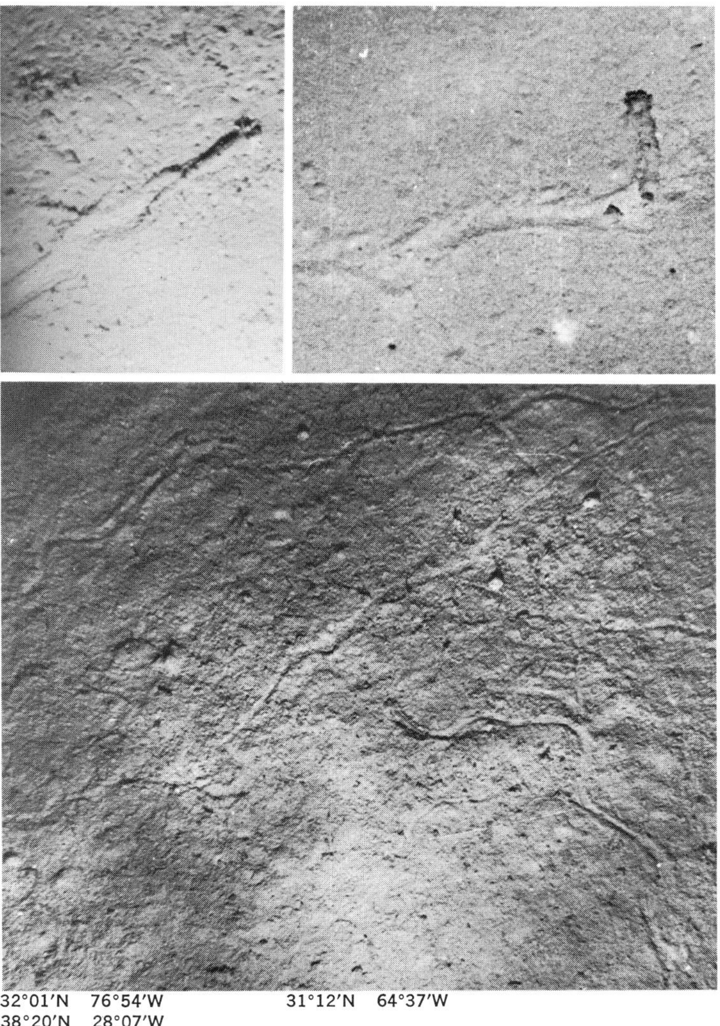

4.9 Abyssal plowers. UL, 1815 m, Blake Escarpment, western North Atlantic. UR, 4608 m, central Bermuda Rise. L, 1580 m, slope of Pico Island, Azores.

from narrow irregular furrowed ridges have occasionally been photographed (4.12-4.14). Since the maker of these curious trails has not been identified, one can only speculate on the manner in which they are produced. One might suppose that the long leaf-like depressions might be caused by the fins of a fish which at the same moment was creating the furrowed ridge by probing its mouth into the sediment. Rat-tailed, brotulid, sea-snail and bathypteroid fish, eels, and giant squid are known to live near the abyssal sea floor. Many of the deep-sea fish have large shovel-shaped mouths which biologists have suspected are used in plow-

33°15′N 75°54′W

4.10 Plowing holothurians. *Pseudostichopus,* a large abyssal sea cucumber, characteristically attaches bits of shells and debris to its surface. Inching along the sea floor, it thrusts itself forward a few centimeters at a time. The effect of successive thrusts is clearly evident in these photographs. U, L, 2792 m, crest of Blake Bahama Outer Ridge off North Carolina.

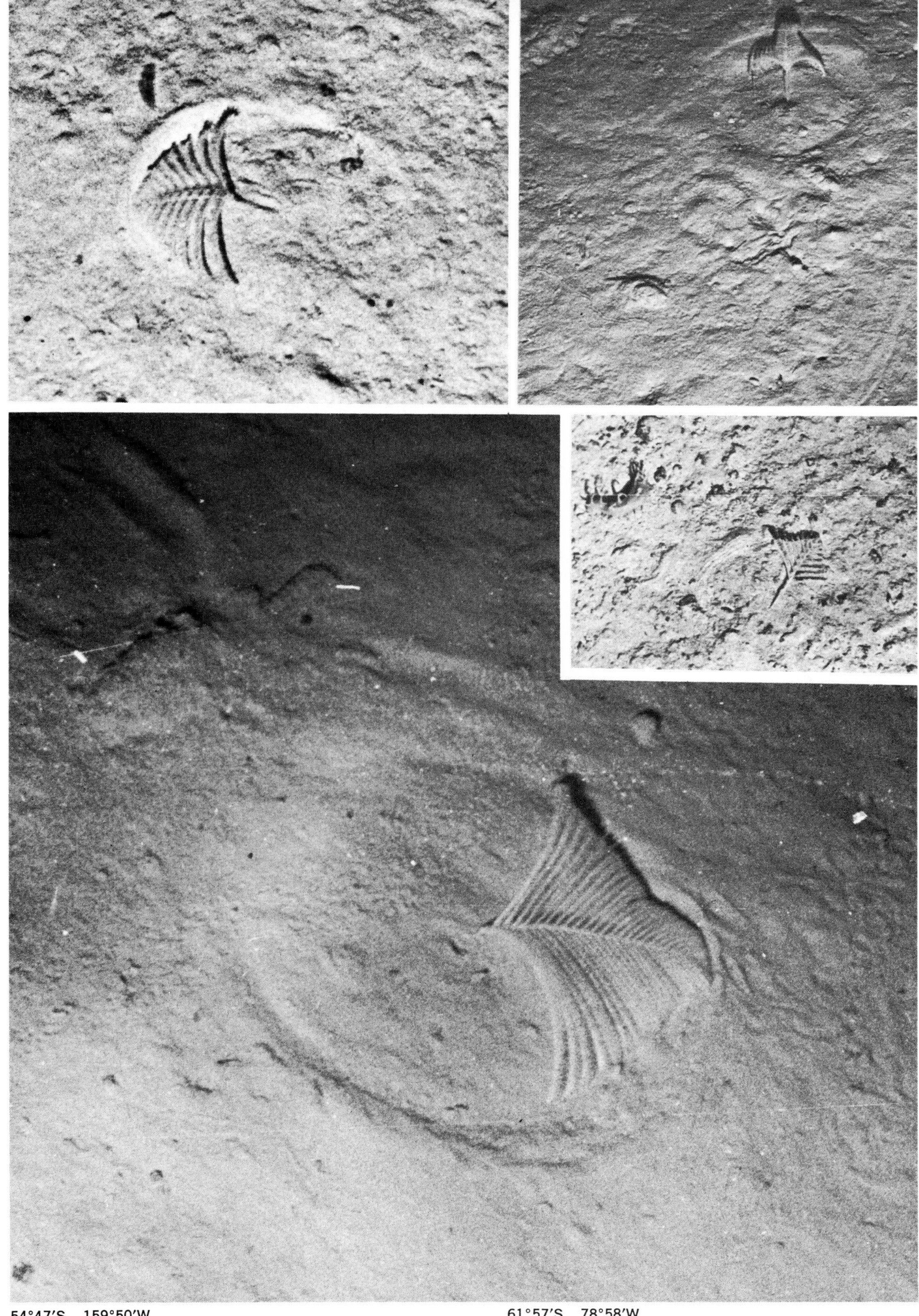

54°47′S 159°50′W
63°14′S 71°34′W

61°57′S 78°58′W
54°47′S 159°50′W

4.11 Circle scribers. Attached compass-like corals plow circular furrows as they swing with the shifting currents. UL, RC, 4287 m, Mid-Oceanic Ridge, southwest Pacific. UR, L, 4798 m, 3766 m, Pacific continental rise of Antarctic Peninsula.

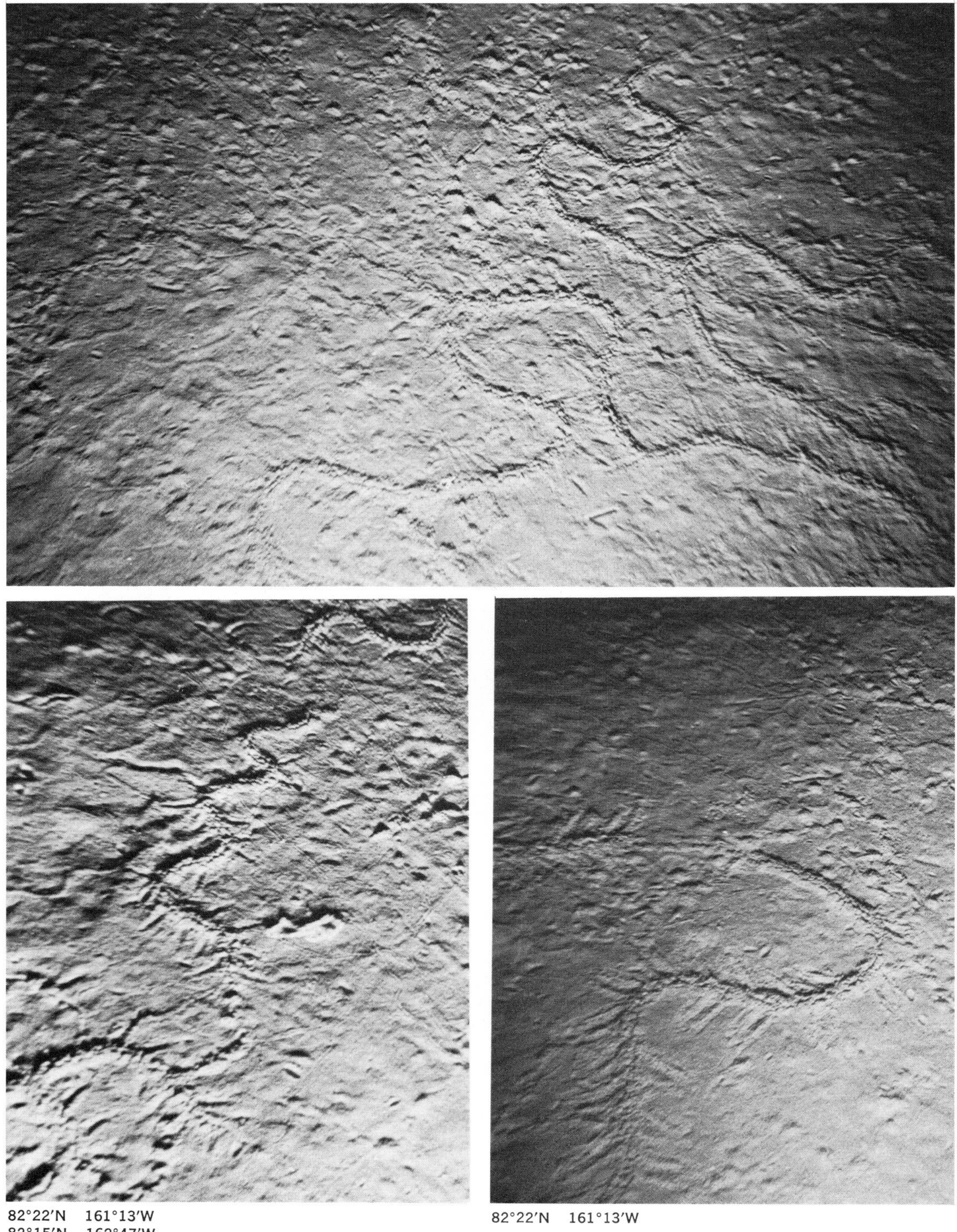

4.12 Arctic hieroglyphics. U, LL, LR, 3790 m, Canada Abyssal Plain.

ing.[3] The shape of their bodies suggests that they have adopted a mode of life similar to the holothurians, ingesting the surface layers into their mouths, or perhaps that they simply shovel through the sediment in search of prey.

MONSTER MARKS

Giant squid and sperm whales descend to the sea floor in depths of at least twelve hundred meters but the results of their bottom activities have never been identified. Sperm whales occasionally become entangled in deep-sea communication cables, which they may seriously damage.[4]

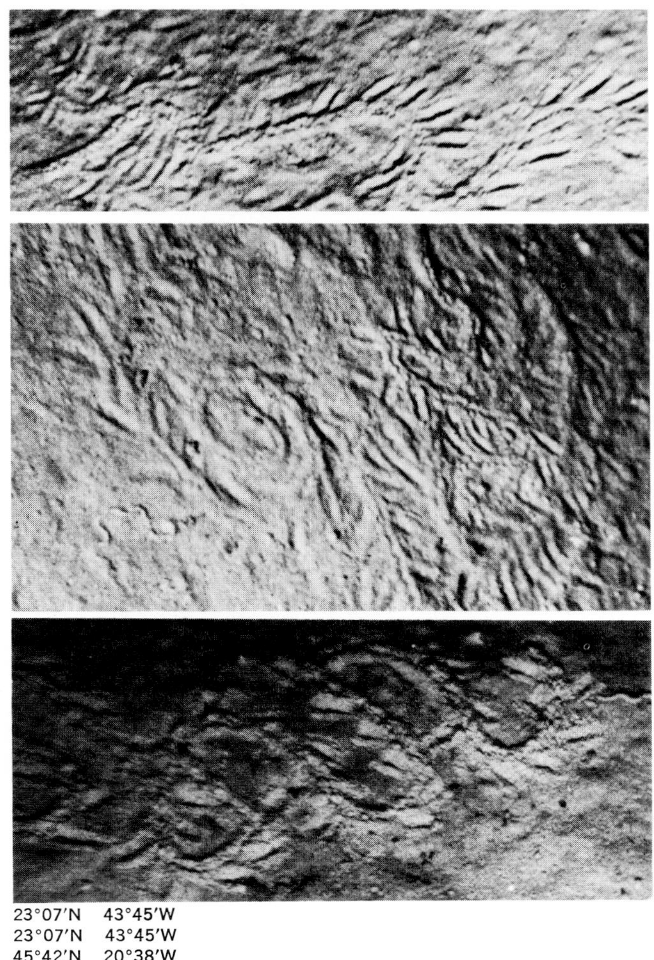

23°07′N 43°45′W
23°07′N 43°45′W
45°42′N 20°38′W

4.13 Atlantic hieroglyphics. U, C, L, 3982 m, 4732 m, Mid-Atlantic Ridge, eastern North Atlantic.

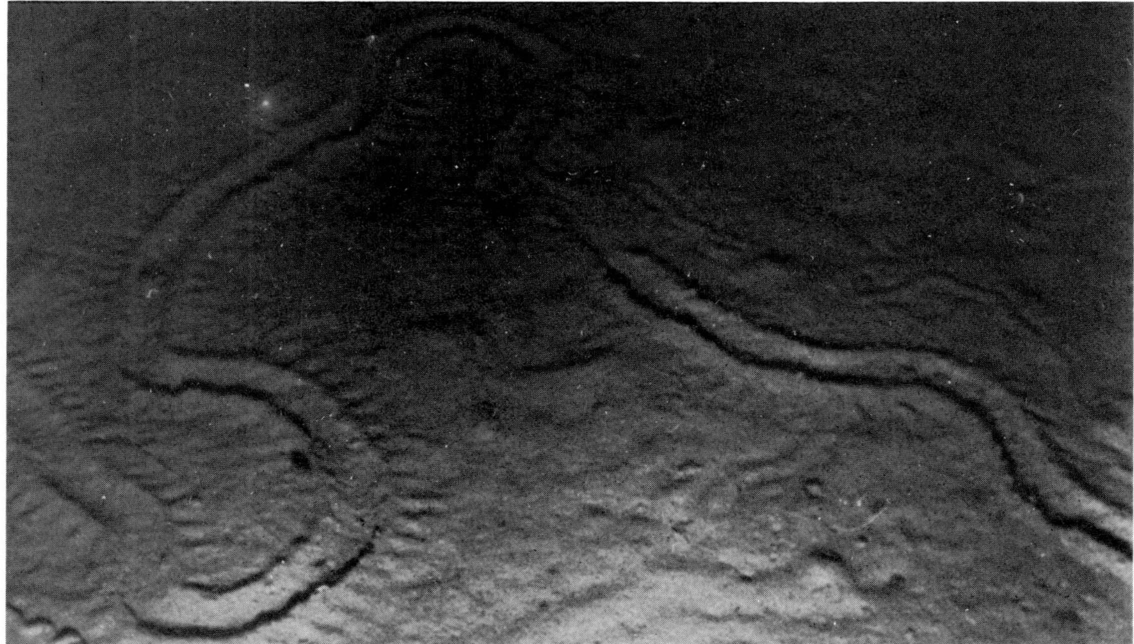

70°07′S 102°56′W
70°07′S 102°56′W

4.14 Giant antarctic crenulated plowmarks. U, L, 3840 m, Antarctic continental rise, Marie Byrd Land.

Their rotting carcasses have been recovered during cable repairs, the cable being tightly looped around the lower jaw and occasionally also around the tail and flippers (4.15, 4.16). Diving to the sea floor, they must plow through the bottom sediments, for bottom ooze by the cubic meter has been found in their alimentary tracts. These enormous creatures must till the substrate, breaking it into clods, and their trails should be readily discernible from those of the smaller animals.[5] In the process of repairing cables large grapnels are sent down to the bottom and dragged back and forth across the cable line until the cable is hooked

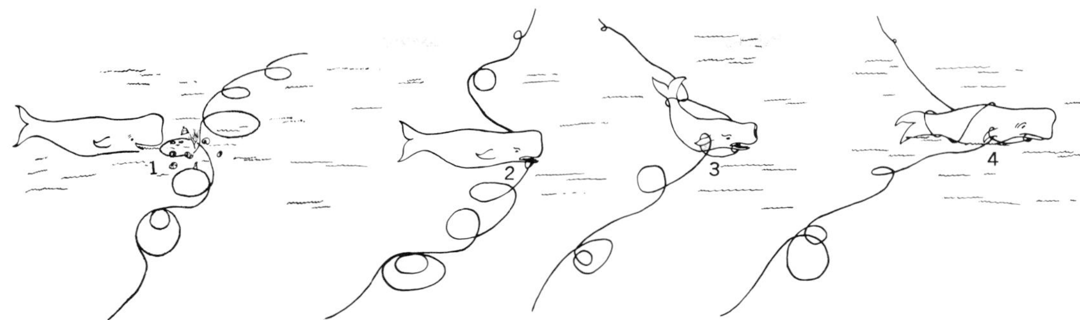

4.15 Plowing whale becomes entangled in submarine cable. (1) whale skimming along bottom with lower jaw in sediment searching for food; (2) whale gets lower jaw in loop of slack cable; (3) whale struggles and gets fin and flukes in adjacent loops of cable; (4) whale completely entangled dies on sea floor.

(4.17).[6] Although we have no photographs of the marks made by these instruments they must be distinctive and some day an oceanographer will puzzle over a photograph of strange and mysterious gouges made in this way. Oceanographers, fishermen and miners probing and scraping the sea floor with instruments suspended from thin steel wires have also created strange and puzzling marks (4.18 UR, UL). Deep and striking

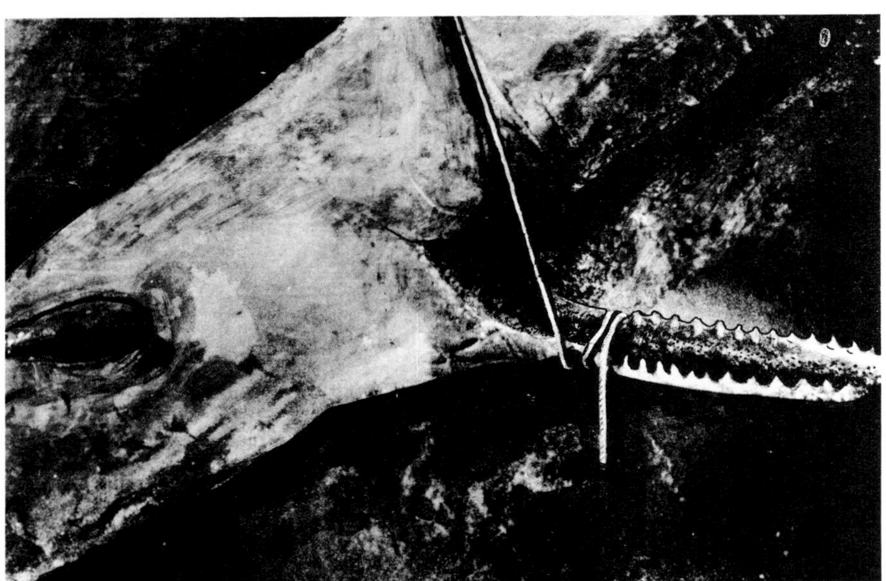

4.16 Submarine cables are occasionally damaged by plowing sperm whales. This whale became entangled in eleven hundred meters depth off Peru, seriously damaging the telegraph cable before the huge mammal drowned. The rotting carcas was hauled up by a cable repair ship a few days later.

plowmarks are occasionally made by the undersides of deep manned submersibles (4.18 L); however, for the time being, such plowmarks can be assumed to be very rare.

URCHIN FURROWS

In the dim geological past, nearly two hundred million years ago, some sea urchins began to plow and burrow deeply into the muds of the ocean floor. In adapting to this new mode of life their nearly perfect symmetry was gradually lost and their shape became more and more modified allowing them to push more efficiently through the sediment.[7] Their mouths migrated to one end, their anus to the other. Their spines became shorter and more specialized; some were swept back and others became

4.17 Cable grapnels plow the ocean depths. This grapnel plowed a long furrow in the sea floor before it hooked the faulty telegraph cable and brought it to the bows of the cable repair ship.

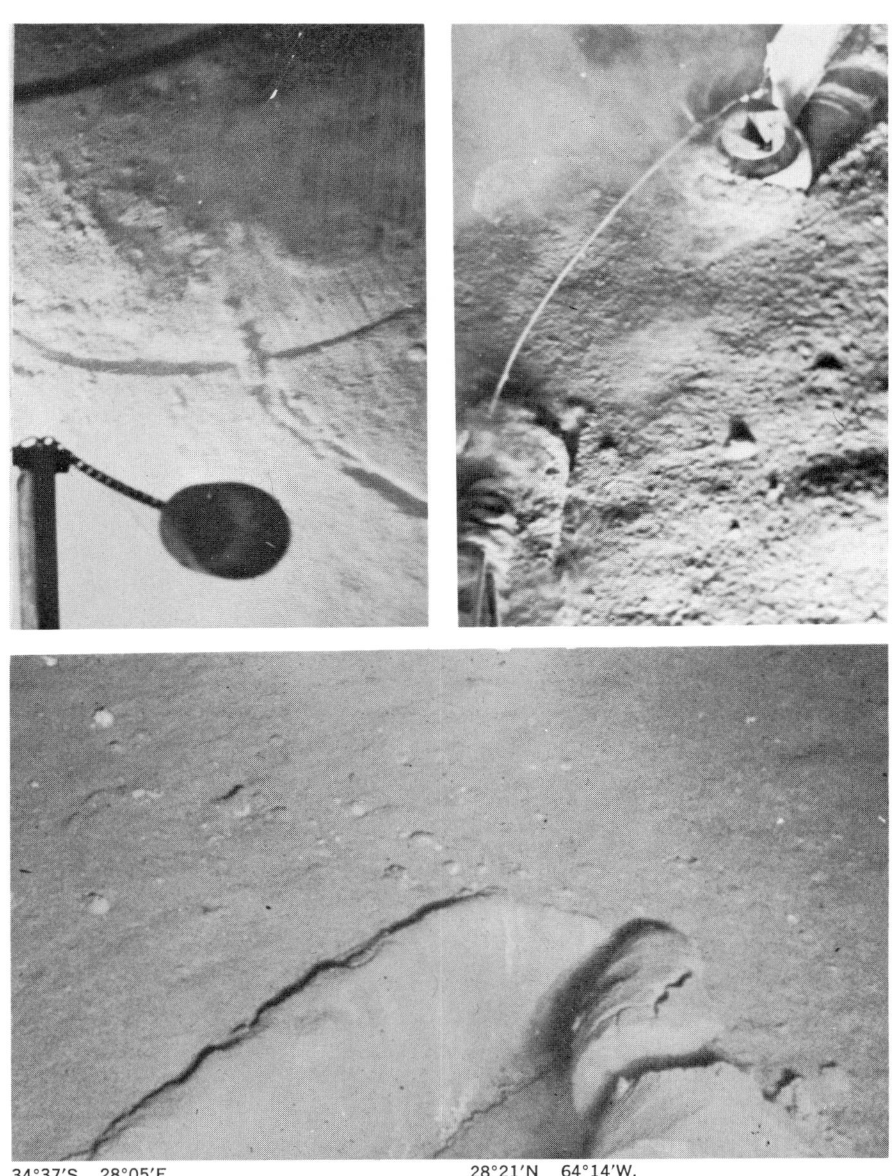

34°37′S 28°05′E
19°15′N 66°30′W
28°21′N 64°14′W,

4.18 The rarest plowmarks. UL & UR, Suspended compass dragging in the mud, 4054 and 4804 m. L, the bathyscaphe *Archimède* plowed this mark on the floor of the Puerto Rico Trench at 6000 meters.

little paddles with which they propelled themselves through the ooze. Some urchins began to depend entirely on fine food derived from the mud and, having no further need for a powerful chewing apparatus, gave up the Aristotle's lantern still retained by their carnivorous surface-living

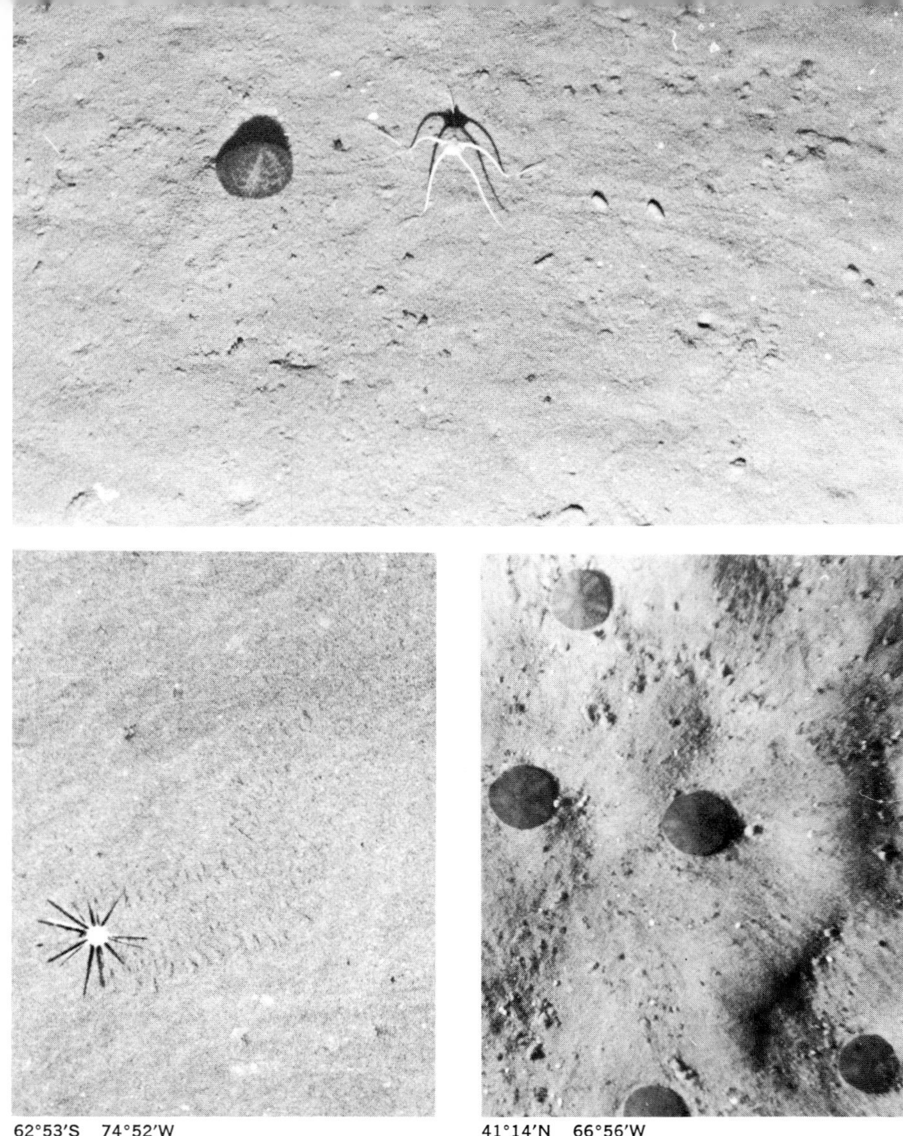

62°53′S 74°52′W
32°37′N 17°06′W

41°14′N 66°56′W

4.19 Urchin trails. U, a brittle star stands over the echinoid trail, 4153 m, Pacific continental rise, Antarctic Peninsula. LL, long radial spines of the regular urchins make fine pinnate trails, 1259 m, slope of Maderia, eastern North Atlantic. LR, sand dollars, 80 m, Georges Bank, south of Cape Cod.

relatives. Today the symmetrical modern descendants of the ancient regular urchins still tread lightly on the ooze, often leaving little evidence of their passing (4.19), while the modern descendants of the variously modified irregular urchins plow and burrow deeply through the mud, leaving telltale signs on the ocean floor (4.20-4.23).

The spines on the undersides of many irregular urchins are divided into three rows (4.24). A central longitudinal row of paddle-like spines which are used to lever the animal forward extend from mouth to anus. Rows of longer curved spines extend along each lateral margin of the animal's undersurface.[8] Due to this configuration the urchins when inch-

4.20 Sediment covered plower. Tracking irregular echinoid covered with its own excreta, 4747 m, Bellingshausen Basin.

ing lightly on the surface produce three rows of transverse crenulations (4.25). The two parallel narrow ridges result from the two nearly spineless areas which separate the three rows of active locomotory spines

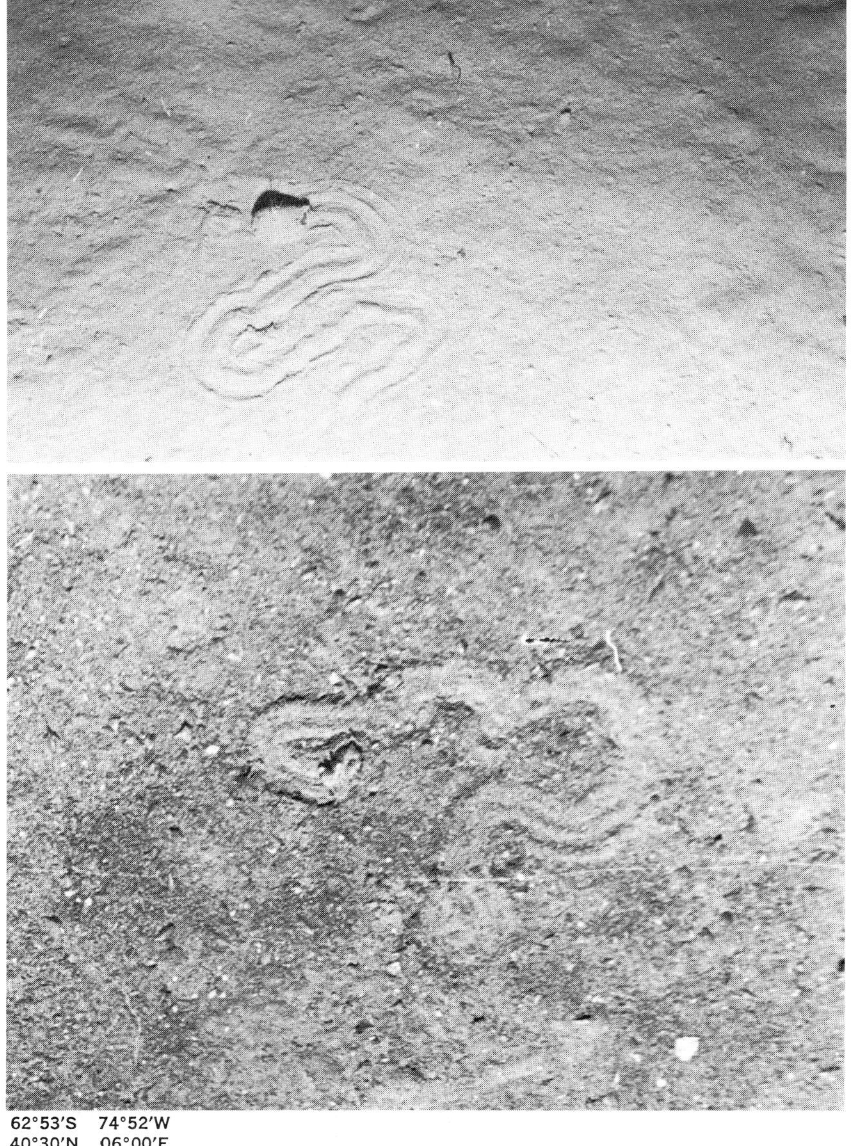

62°53′S 74°52′W
40°30′N 06°00′E

4.21 Meandering plowers. U, 4153 m, Pacific continental rise of Antarctic Peninsula. L, 2778 m, Balearic Abyssal Plain, Western Mediterranean.

(4.24) and the transverse crenulations record a regular rhythm of successive lurches and pauses in the animal's progress.

Thus when treading lightly a crenulate triple trail is imprinted on the bottom but when plowing more deeply a bolder, simpler and less ornamented sinuous U- or W-shaped groove is made (4.26). Such grooves sometimes terminate in a small sediment-covered mound, often with a dark hole in the center (4.27). This small black hole is the respiratory shaft of the buried echinoid.

Enormous ridges are sometimes seen meandering across the ocean floor (4.28, 4.29). The flanks of some are marked by transverse crenulations and bordered by smoothed depressions about as wide as the ridge itself (4.28 U). The crest of the ridge is faintly marked by a shallow

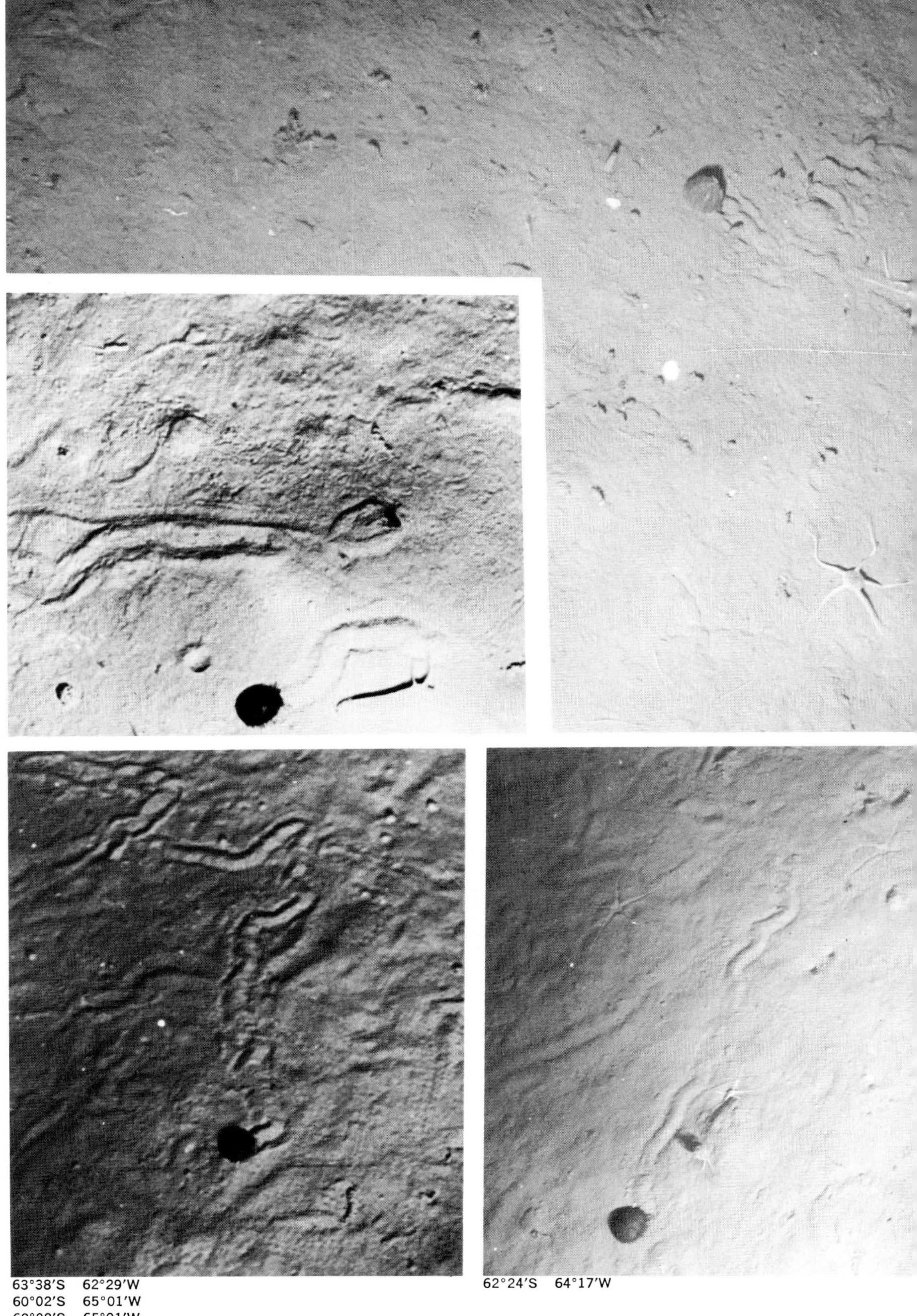

63°38′S 62°29′W
60°02′S 65°01′W
60°02′S 65°01′W

62°24′S 64°17′W

4.22 Plowing urchins. U, 275 m, continental shelf, Antarctic Peninsula. CL, LL, LR, 3792 m, 3792 m, and 3677 m, Drake Passage.

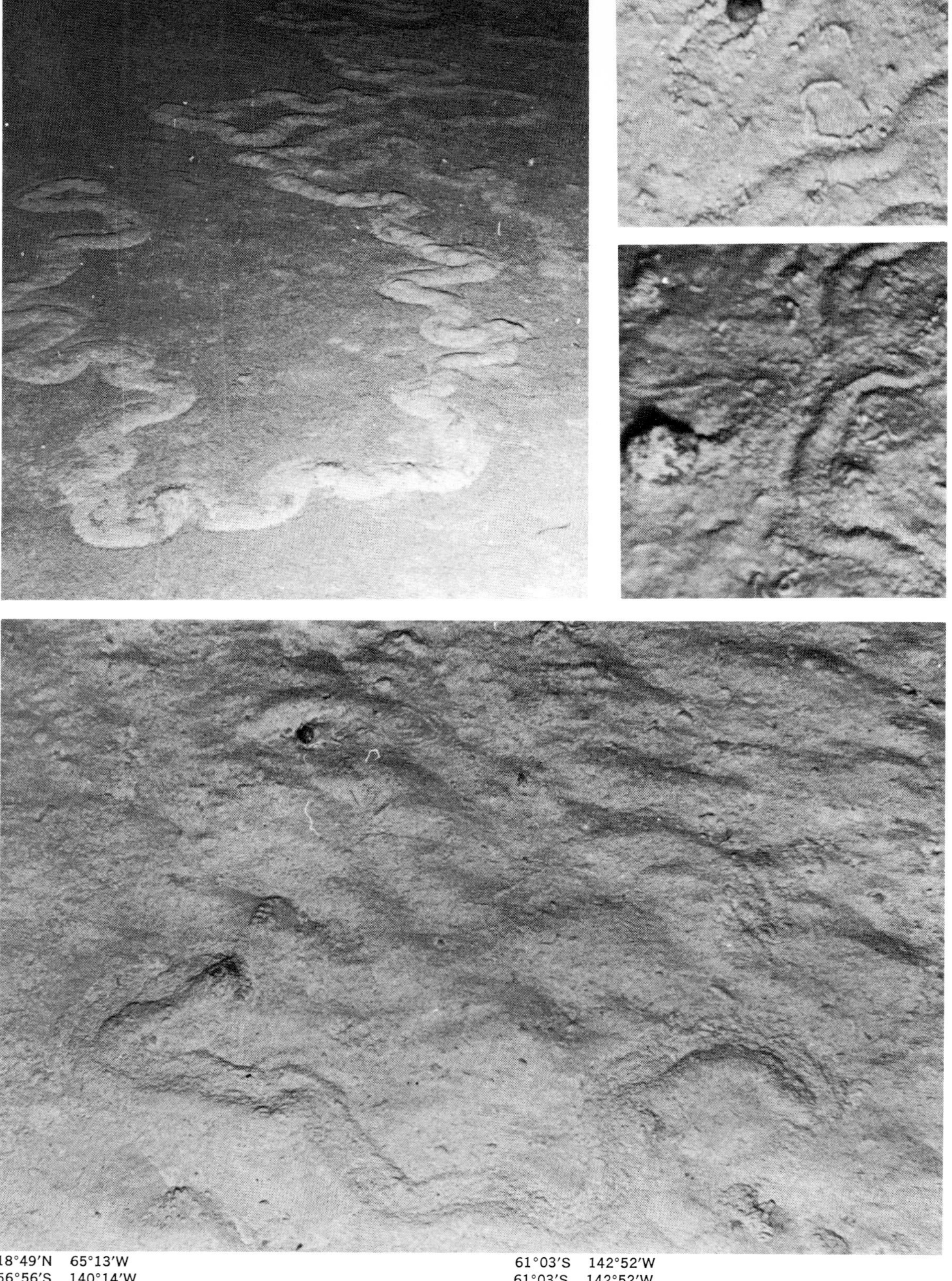

18°49′N 65°13′W
56°56′S 140°14′W

61°03′S 142°52′W
61°03′S 142°52′W

4.23 Plowers and meandering plowmarks. UL, echinoid trail, 1983 m, south wall, Puerto Rico Trench. UR, echinoid beginning to plow deeply, 3652 m. CR, plowmarks, 2711 m. L, meandering plower emerging, 4153 m, Mid-Oceanic Ridge, South Pacific.

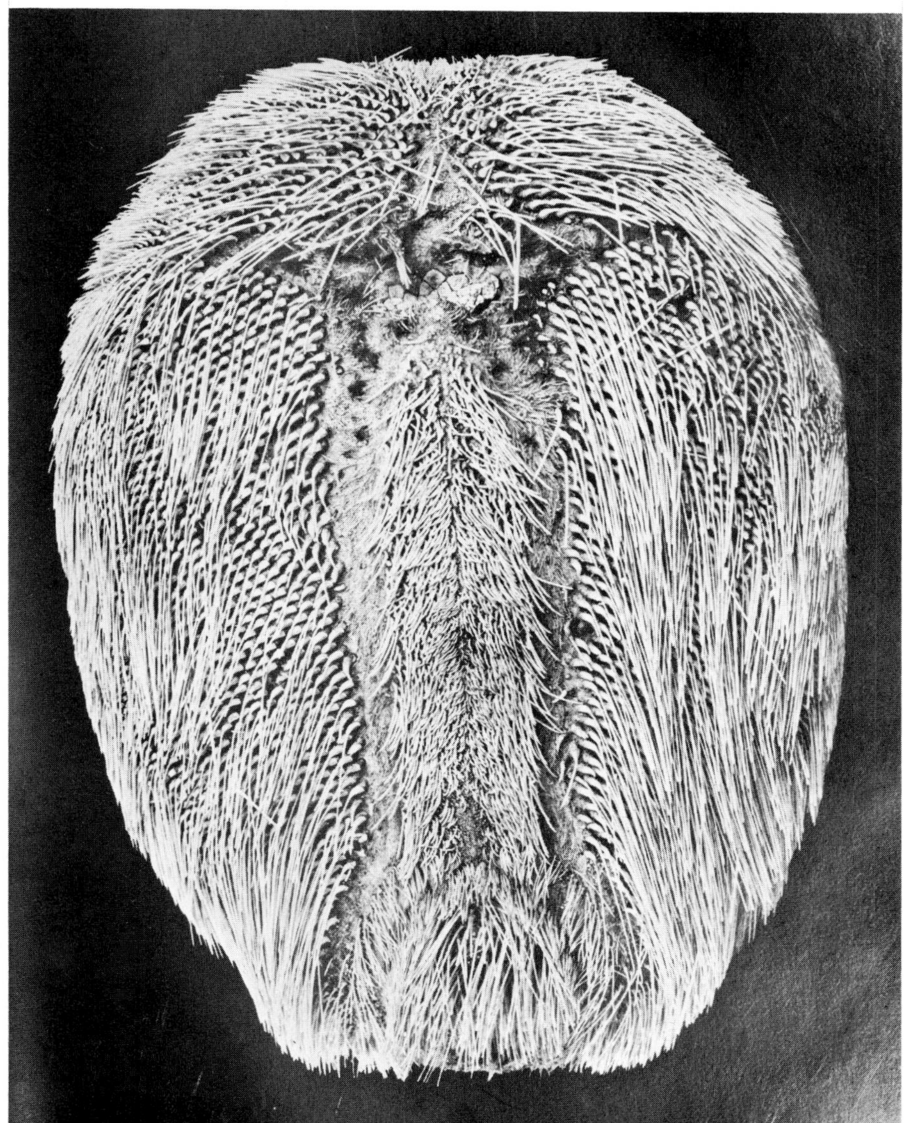

4.24 Large spatangoid urchins produce distinctive three-lobed furrows with their spines. Under side of *Plagiobrissus grandes.* Adult members of this genera reach 20 centimeters in length.

longitudinal groove (4.28 L). These as well as some of the giant furrows seen occasionally (4.29) may also be the work of giant echinoids.

The principal plowers identified in photographs are the urchins and it seems reasonable to suppose that the majority of the large plowing trails seen on the deep-sea floor have been formed by these animals as they lurch along searching for food.

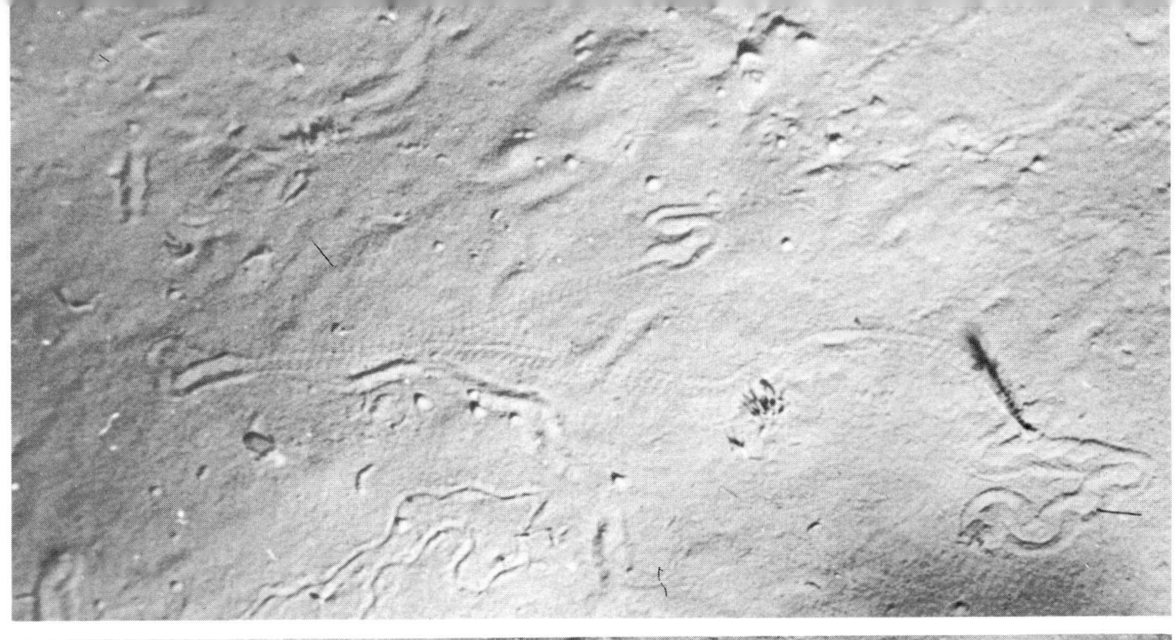

60°02′S 65°01′W
42°29′S 75°58′W

4.25 Trails to plowmarks. Crenulated trails intermittently become plowmarks. U, 3792 m, Drake Passage. L, 3626 m, outer ridge of Peru-Chile Trench.

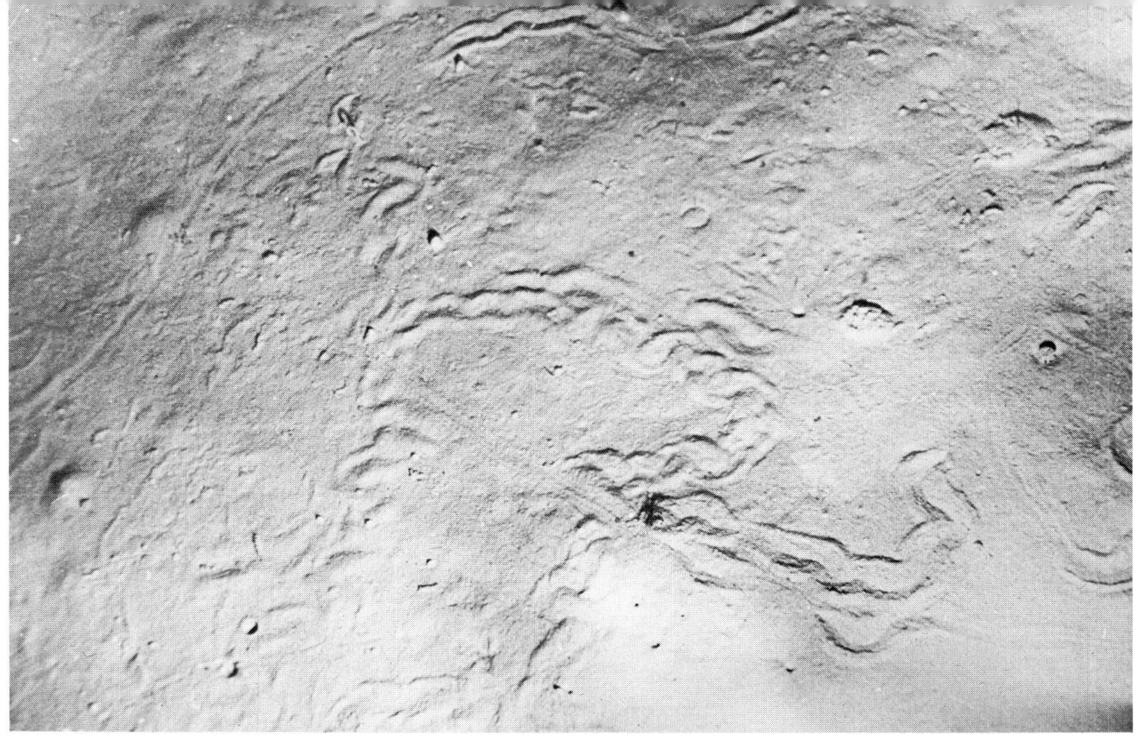

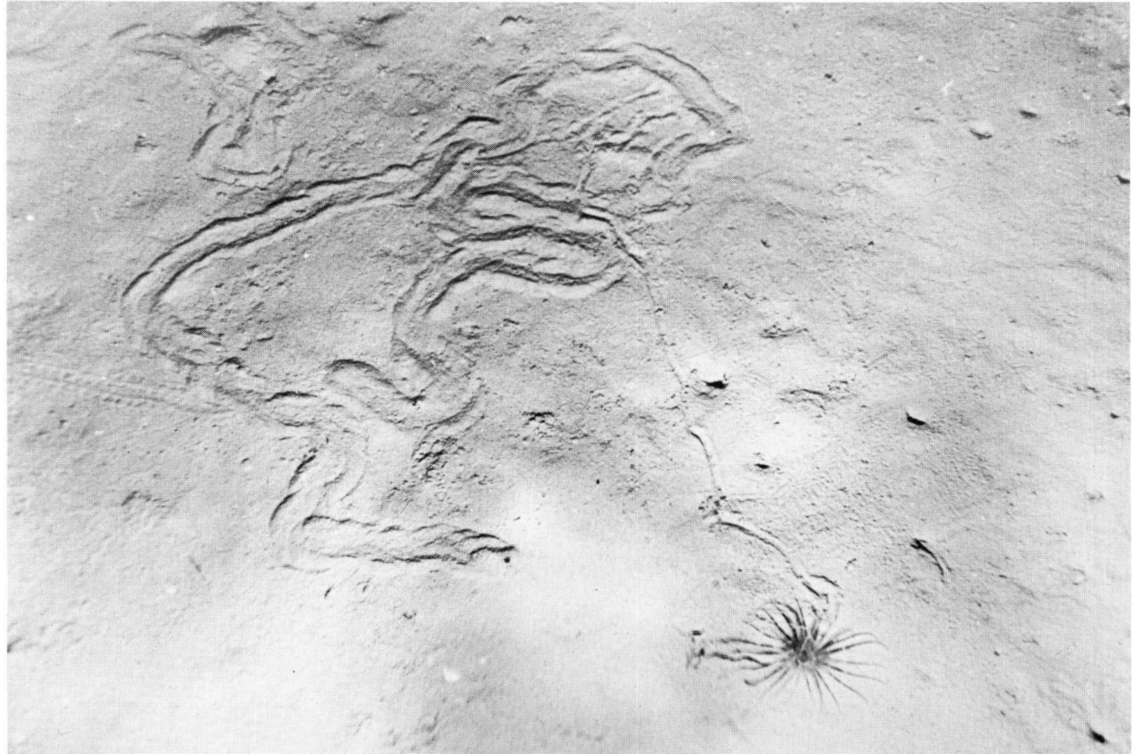

60°02′S 65°01′W
42°29′S 75°58′W

4.26 Walking, plowing and maneuvering. U, dark echinoid, center, has plowed from right to left and is recrossing earlier plowmark, 3792 m, Drake Passage. L, echinoid walked in from left, began plowing (center) and meandered toward upper right, circled left and is now in lower center. Actinarian has plowed across echinoid's trail and echinoid has crossed actinarian trail, 3626 m, outer ridge, southern Peru-Chile Trench.

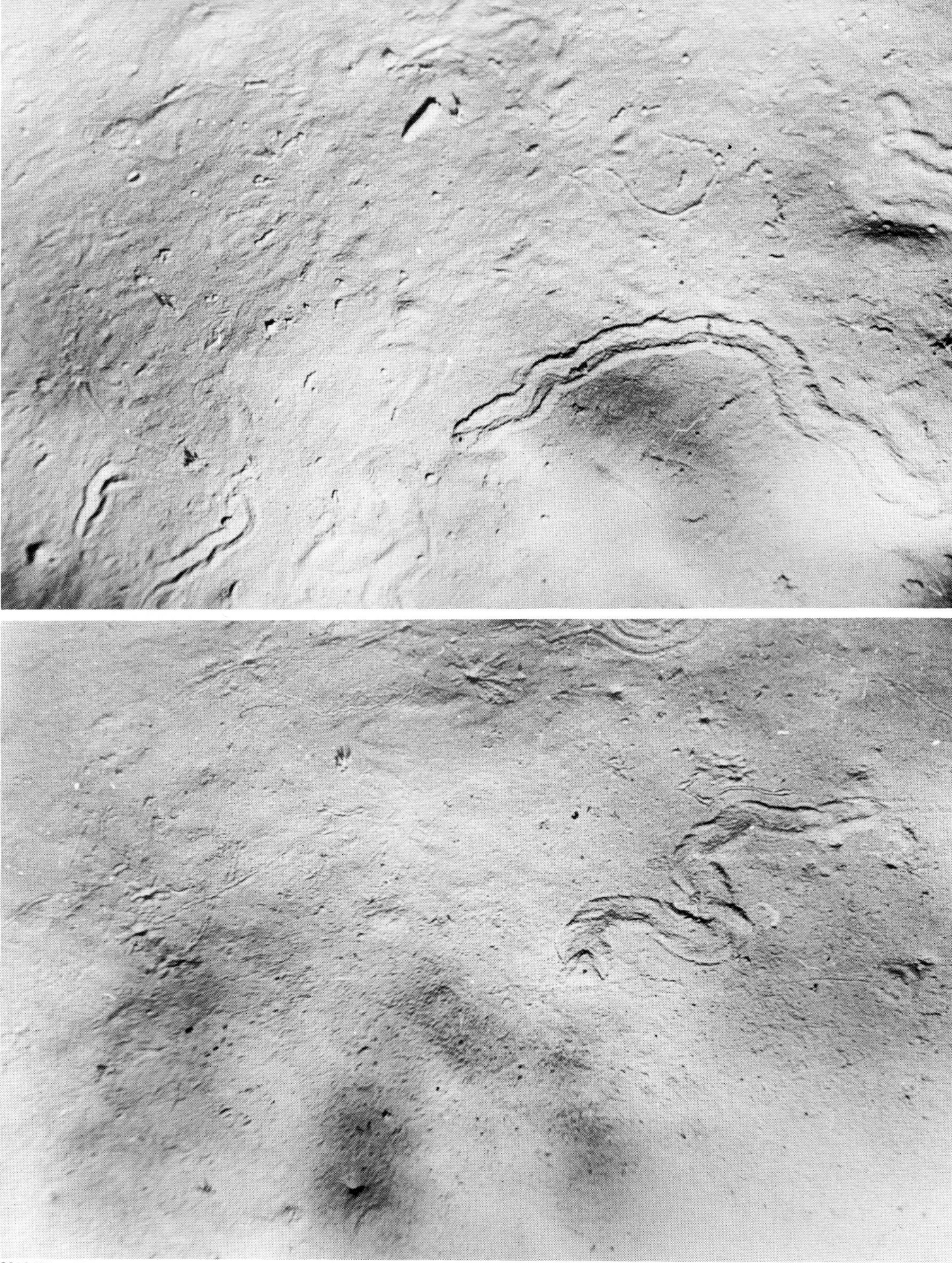

60°02′S 65°01′W
42°29′S 75°58′W

4.27 Caught in the act. Echinoids are the principal plowers of the deep. They lever themselves through the sediment by a series of specialized spines on their undersurfaces. The black dot on the small triangular mound is the tip of the animal's respiratory shaft. U, 3792 m, Drake Passage; L, 3626 m, outer ridge, southern end of Peru-Chile Trench.

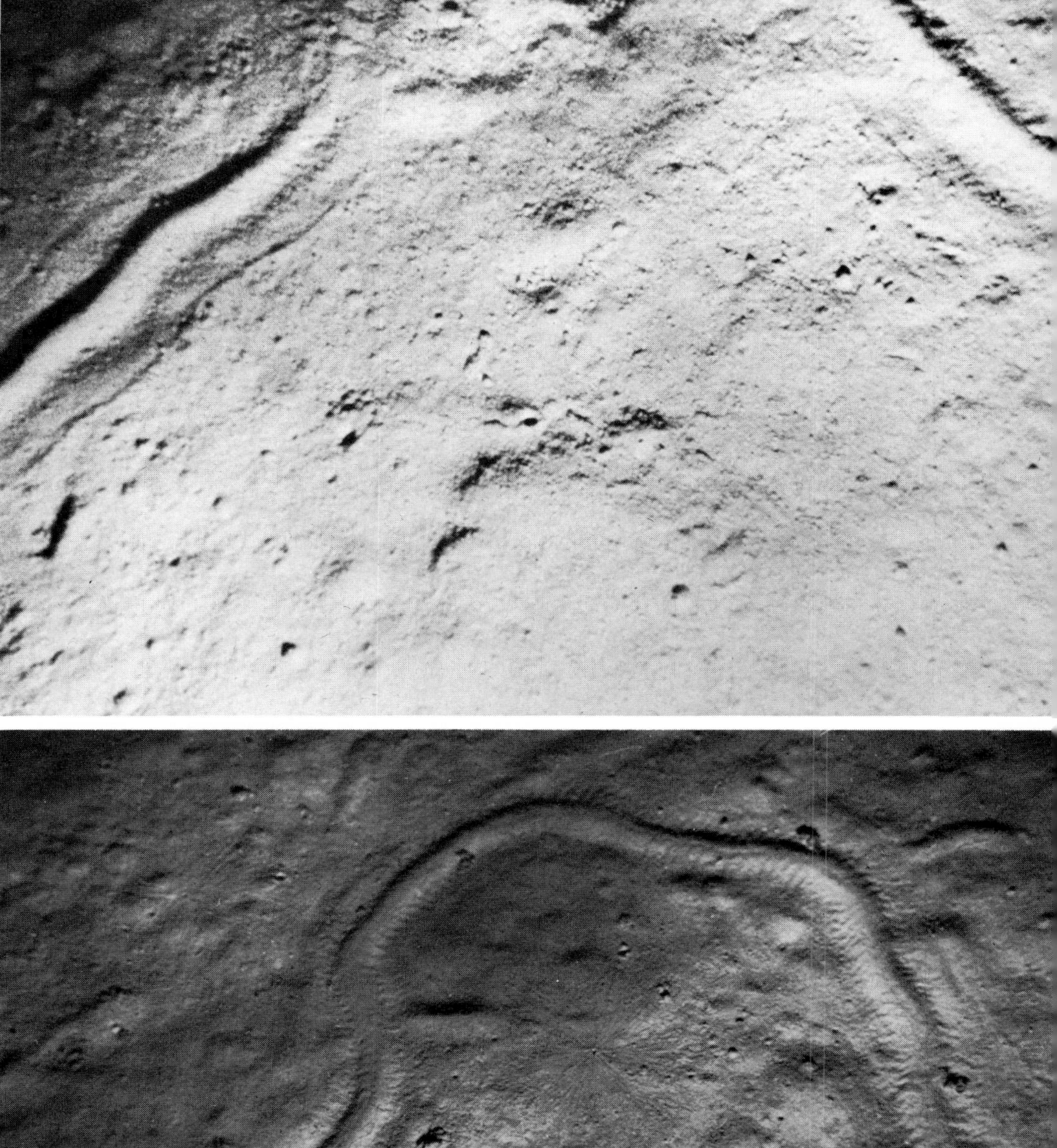

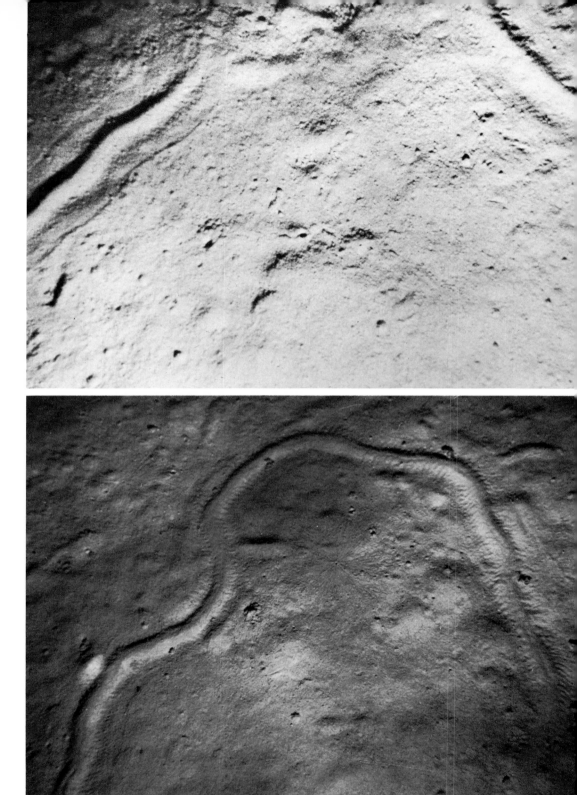

15°58′S 149°39′W
16°48′S 152°13′W

4.28 Sinuous crenulated plowmarks. U, 4289 m, archipelagic apron near Tahiti. L, 3938 m, archipelagic apron near Bora Bora.

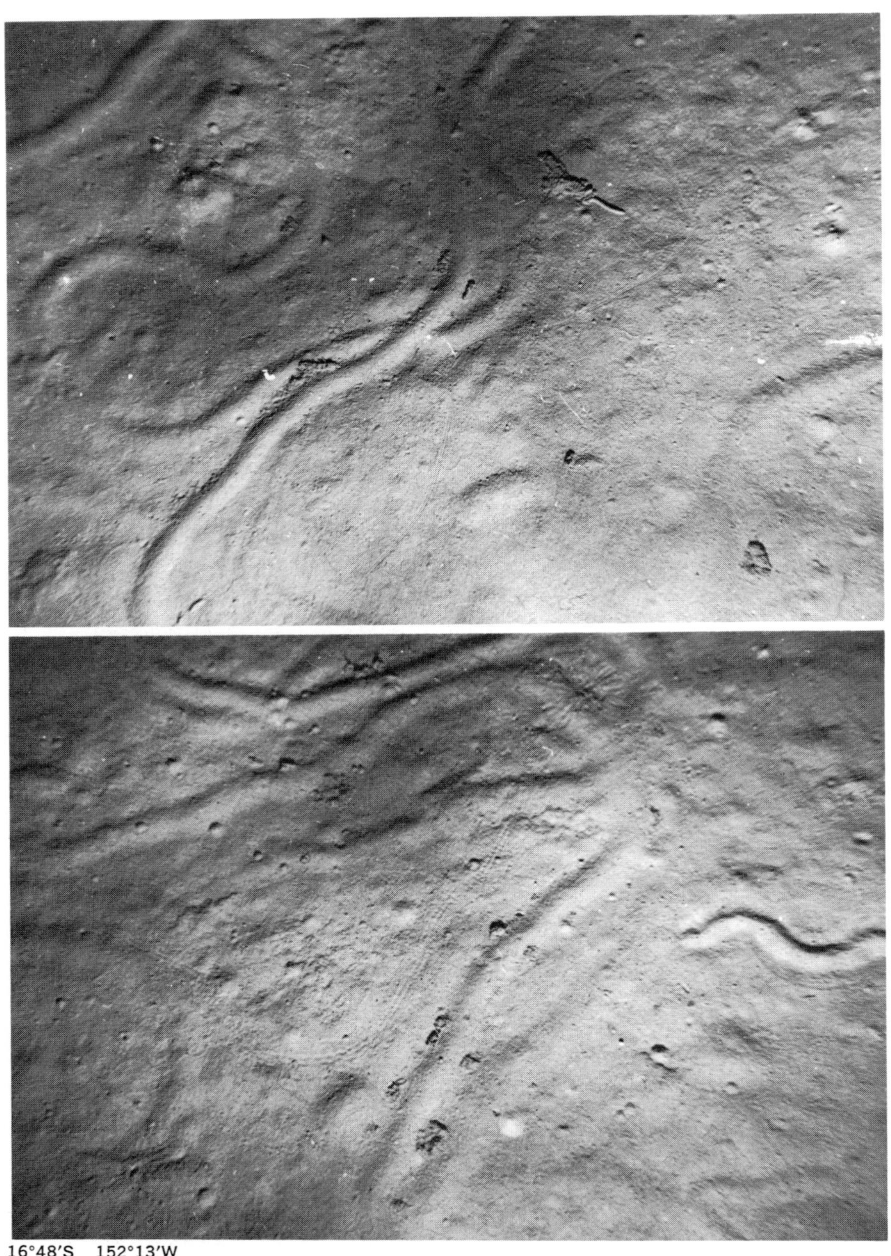

16°48′S 152°13′W
16°48′S 152°13′W

4.29 Old crenulated plowmark and holothurian tracks. U, L, 3938 m, near Bora Bora.

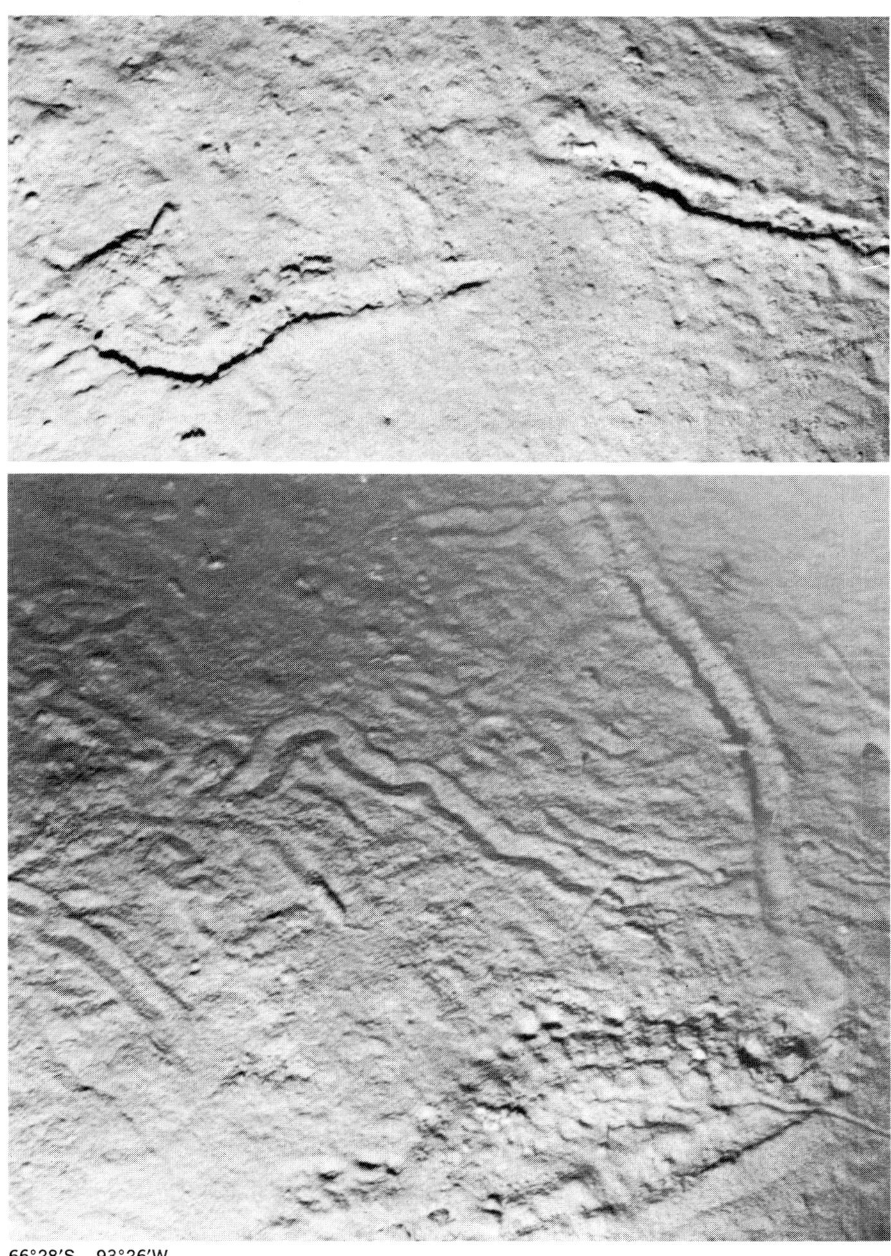

66°28′S 93°26′W
66°08′S 102°27′W

4.30 Discontinuous deep furrows. U, L, 4679 m, 4840 m, Antarctic continental rise, Marie Byrd Land.

Table 4.1 Abyssal echinoids (> 3000 m) (after Mortensen[8]).

CLASS ECHINOIDEA

Subclass REGULARIA (17 species)

Order Lepidocentroida

Mostly large, flattened, short-spined deep-sea forms with flexible leathery tests and hollow, hoof-life spines on the underside. Four species are known from the abyss, the largest is a giant reaching thirty centimeters in diameter.

Order Cidaroidea

Most live on the upper continental slope but there are some abyssal forms. Hard, globose, symmetrical forms with long, widely spaced primary spines. Two abyssal species.

Order Aulodonta

High, delicate, fragile test with long, thin, downwardly curved primary spines which touch the ground some distance from the test. Five abyssal species.

Order Stirodonta

Rounded small tests with long, thorny primary spines pointed upwards. Three abyssal species.

Order Camarodonta

Large red or green deep-water forms with short purple spines. Two abyssal species.

Subclass IRREGULARIA (26 species)

Order Spatangoida

Globose to elongate asymmetrical forms with either short spines or long spines swept parallel to the body. Some (the *Pourtalesiidae*) are bottle-shaped. Some have respiratory filaments which protrude from the upper surface. Most spatangoid genera are exclusively abyssal and all have lost the chewing lantern.

REFERENCES AND NOTES

1. The locomotion of a few shallow water organisms possessing a single creeping sole has been studied and these results are our principle guide to the methods employed by similar appearing deep-sea species (Parker, G. H., 1911. The mechanism of locomotion in Gastropods. *J. Morph.,* 22:155-170; Parker, G. H., 1917. Pedal locomotion in Actinians. *J. Exper. Zool.,* 24:111-124; Parker, G. H., 1921. The locomotion of the Holothurian, *Stichopus panimensis Clark. J. Exper. Zool.,* 33: 205-208.). In the future, geologists and biologists may hope to observe the habits and methods of deep-sea plowers in their natural habit from the portholes of deep submersibles.

2. Numerous V-shaped plowmarks are seen on the floor of the Peru-Chile Trench. R. J. Menzies, M. Ewing, J. L. Worzel, A. H. Clarke, Jr. (1959. Ecology of the Recent Monoplacophora. *Oikos,* 10:168-182.) presumed that they were made by a primitive "living fossil" mollusc, *Neopilina,* specimens of which were dredged nearby. A controversy developed when T. Wolff (1961. Animal life from a single abyssal trawling. *Galathea Rept.,* 5:129-162.) noted the similarity between the

supposed *Neopilina* plowmarks of Menzies et al. and the marks of the bivalve *Cardium* seen on the tidal flats of the Waddenzee. He concluded that *Neopilina,* which is much broader than the sharp-edged bivalve, should leave a more broad, open track than those photographed and that the narrow V-shaped tracks were probably made by an abyssal bivalve. Wolff also pointed out that many more bivalves than *Neopilina* were recovered by Menzies in the trawls and therefore one would have a greater chance of photographing bivalve traces. Clearly the application of close-up photography would help resolve this controversy concerning these minute plowers.

3. The brotulid *Typhlonus,* a potential plower that has "a horseshoe mouth which can be protruded almost like a shovel, and it is presumably used for shoveling into the mud when the fish perceives a prey," was recovered in a deep-sea trawl (Bruun, A. F., 1956. Animal life in the deep sea bottom. In: A. F. Bruun, S. V. Greeve, H. Mielche, and R. Sparck (Editors), *The Galathea Deep-Sea Expedition, 1950-1952.* Macmillan, New York, pp. 149-195).

4. Whales have become entangled in cable at depths up to 1200 m. The majority of reports come from the continental slope of Peru, but they have also been reported from the vicinity of Nova Scotia, Alaska, Brazil and West Pakistan (Heezen, B. C., 1957. Whales entangled in deep-sea cables. *Deep-Sea Res.,* 4:105-115).

5. Emery, K. O. and Ross, D. A., 1969. Topography and sediments of a small area of the continental slope south of Martha's Vineyard. *Deep-Sea Res.,* 15:415-422.

6. The techniques of grapling and raising communication cables have remained relatively unchanged since the late 19th century (Wilkinson, H. D., 1909. *Submarine Cable Laying and Repairing.* D. Van Nostrand Co., New York. 557 pp.).

7. Nichols, D., 1959. Mode of life and taxonomy in irregular sea urchins. In: A. J. Cain (Editor), Function and taxonomy. *Syst. Assoc. Publ.,* 3:61-80.

8. Many photographs of the underside of urchins are included in the over 3000 illustrations reproduced in this most complete work on the sea urchins: T. Mortensen, 1938-1951. *A Monograph of the Echinoidea.* C. Reitzel, Copenhagen, 5 vols., 4433 pp.

29°40′S 176°43′W

5.1 An abyssal acorn worm from the east wall of the Kermadec Trench. The animal's body ends shortly past the first bend where the long fecal coil begins. A similar feces is seen at the right of the picture, 4871 m. This 1962 photograph was the first record of an abyssal enteropneust since 1873 when *Challenger* first dredged three damaged specimens.

5
Excrement

The earth's a thief that feeds and breeds by composture stolen from general excrement.

SHAKESPEARE

We beg you to imagine for the moment that you are a farmer, for those who live off the fertile soil have a respect for animal feces not usually shared by the urban dweller. If for some reason you cannot accept a farmer's approach, you may, in admiring design and form, take an artist's or even an architect's view. Considering the abundance of relatively large tracks in the deep sea, it is not in the least surprising that large and prominent feces are frequently seen.

In general, carnivorous animals tend to produce feces of loose consistency; vegetable eaters, firmer ones, and deposit eaters, the most resistant of all. The large feces seen on the deep-sea floor are probably exclusively formed by deposit eaters. Tiny ovoid and rod-shaped fecal pellets generally less than one millimeter in diameter have been described,[1] but the larger feces of the abyss are rarely mentioned in scientific literature. Probably the principal reason for the lack of studies of fecal material is the difficulty in sampling. While the deep-sea dredge or trawl is being raised to the surface, the fecal strings are destroyed, and what is left is usually washed away with the fine material when the animals are sieved from the sediment. Possibly many fecal pellets in bottom samples and photographs go unrecognized because of a nondescript form.

Feces seen in photographs might properly be called remolded sediment for the bottom material is probably very little altered. The amount of organic matter and bacteria in the sediment is volumetrically small, and the detritus feeders must ingest huge volumes in order to derive a significant quantity of nutrients. In such a severe environment as the deep sea there probably is little organic waste since animals must utilize virtually every digestible item.

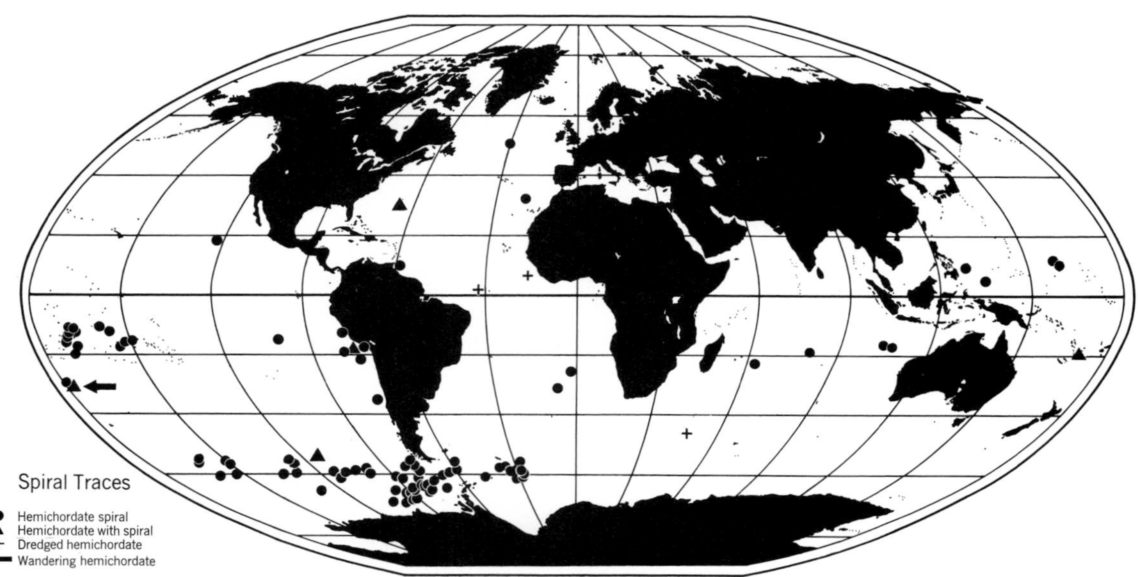

5.2 Coils of excrement photographed on the abyssal floor. Symbols: ●, spirals; ▲, animals associated with spirals; ←, wandering abyssal enteropneust (5.1); +, dredged abyssal enteropneusts.

5.3 Multicolored abyssal acorn worm: *Glandiceps abyssicola* from a sketch by von Willemenes Suhm. The proboscis was yellow; the collar, bright red; and the trunk, yellowish-red.

SPIRALS

Large and dramatic planispiral coils are quite frequently seen in the equatorial and South Pacific (5.1). On a research cruise between Wellington, New Zealand, and Tahiti, the camera recorded them at nearly every station made in depths greater than 4000 meters. They appeared in seventeen of these deep stations but were absent in sixty-nine shallower ones. Later, they were photographed in over 10 per cent of the more than 500 stations made in the southeast Pacific and Scotia Sea. Still more spirals have been found in pictures from the North Atlantic, Indian Ocean, and North Pacific. But they appear most often in pictures from the high southern latitudes and they are especially common in the South Pacific (5.2).

At the first photograph station made in the aforementioned South Pacific research cruise, the animal responsible for making these dramatic coils was caught in the act (5.1). It is a giant enteropneust or acorn worm (hemichordate) about one meter long and five centimeters thick,

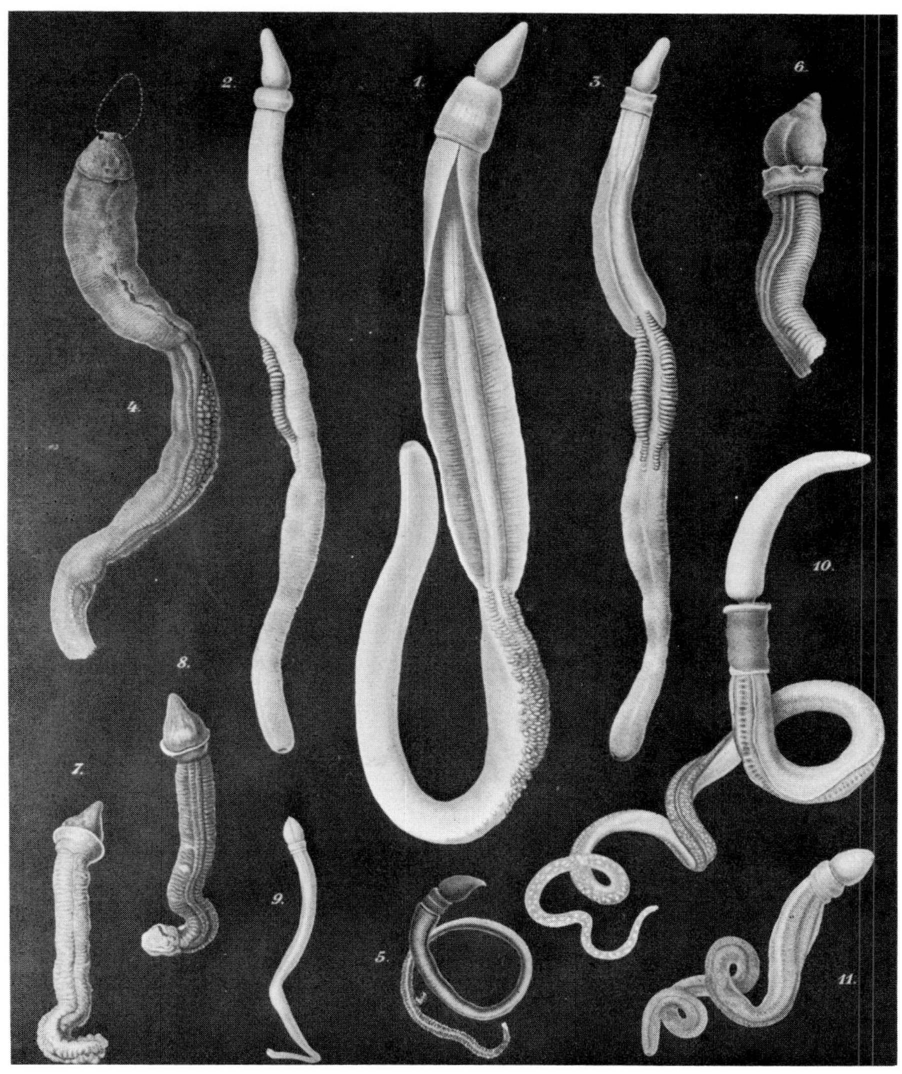

5.4 Acorn worms captured in dredges.

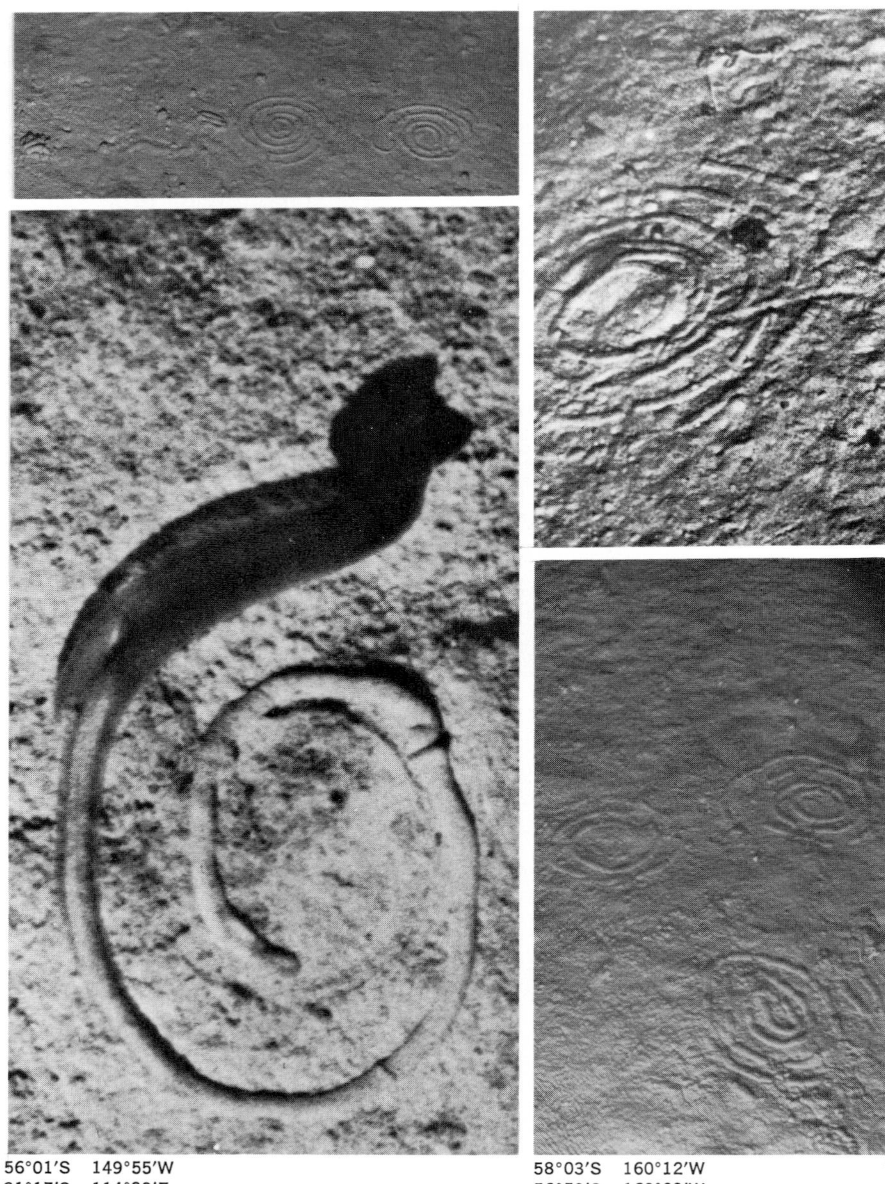

56°01′S 149°55′W
31°17′S 114°38′E
58°03′S 160°12′W
56°59′S 160°09′W

5.5 Coils and coil-maker. UL, 3311 m, Mid-Oceanic Ridge, central South Pacific; LL, 2018 m, western continental slope of Australia; UR, LR, 4360 m, 3129 m, Mid-Oceanic Ridge, central South Pacific.

or about the size of a large garden snake (5.3, 5.4).[2] This animal methodically covers a relatively small area as it feeds upon the ooze. Particles trapped in a strand of mucus which is secreted by its proboscis and by ciliary action are either passed into the mouth or ejected at the

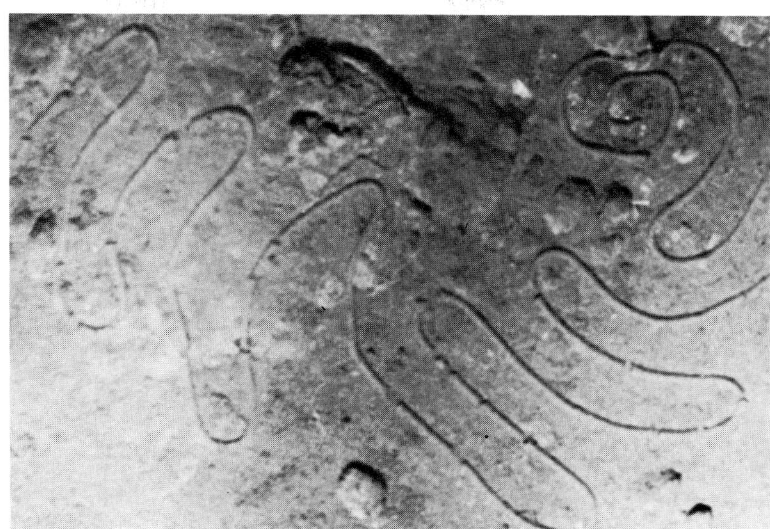

5.6 Coil- and loop-makers. The organism began his fecal trace with a coil and then proceeded to make switchback loops around the scattered rocks, 6725 m, New Hebrides Trench.

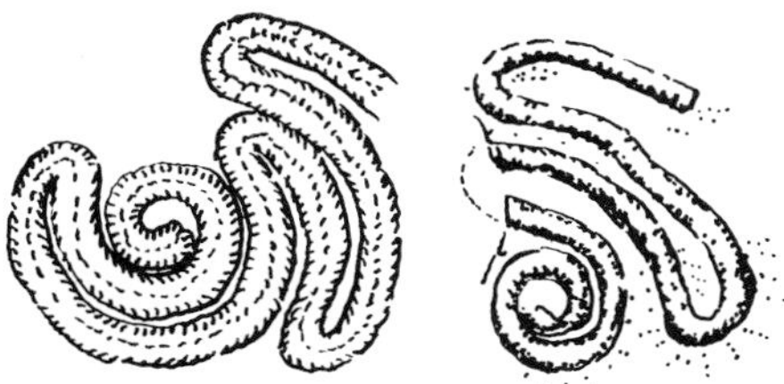

5.7 Fossil fecal coils from the Alps resemble those from the modern abyss.

collar.[3] A trace of that mucus mixed with bits of sediment can be seen to run back from the collar parallel to the fecal coil (5.1). The identification of this enteropneust was extremely difficult for hardly anyone has considered these acorn worms as significant members of the deep-sea fauna.[4] However, they are extremely fragile animals, unlikely to survive a trawling, thus their absence from collections may be simply the fault of fishing methods. In addition, very few trawls have been taken from the South Pacific and virtually none have been described.

Coil makers have been photographed in the Indian Ocean (5.5), the North Atlantic, the New Hebrides Trench (5.6), the Peru-Chile Trench, and the Bellingshausen Sea. Since fecal coils begin and end abruptly, it appears that the abyssal acorn worms either disappear as burrowers into the sediment, move over the bottom, having ceased ingesting sediment, or swim away.[5] Similar fecal coils have been found fossilized in ancient sedimentary rocks (5.7).

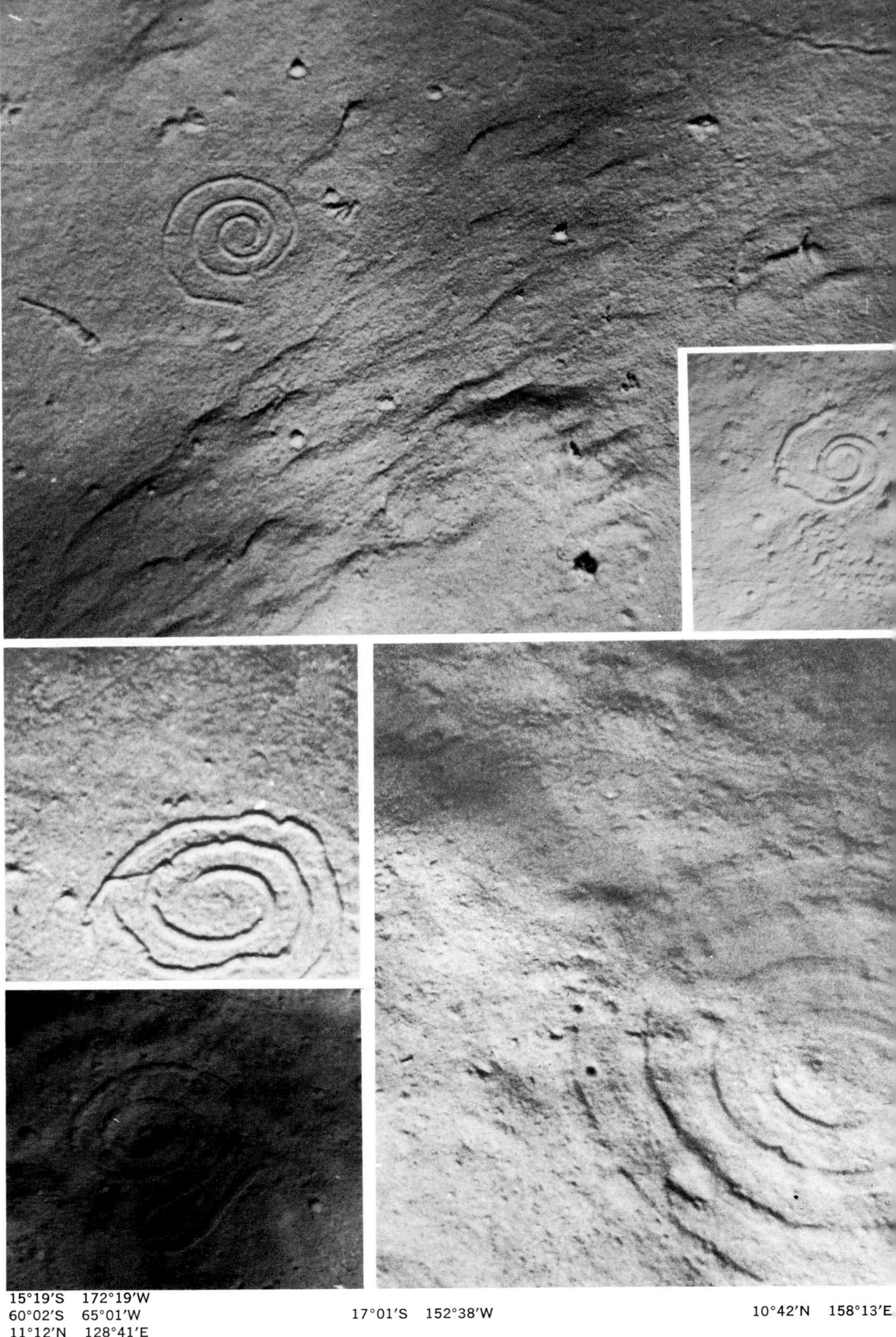

15°19′S 172°19′W
60°02′S 65°01′W
11°12′N 128°41′E

17°01′S 152°38′W

10°42′N 158°13′E

5.8 Pacific coils. UL, UR, 6613 m, 5646 m, Marshall Islands. LC, 3792 m, Drake Passage. LR, 4372 m, near Bora Bora. LL, 5595 m, outer ridge, Philippine Trench.

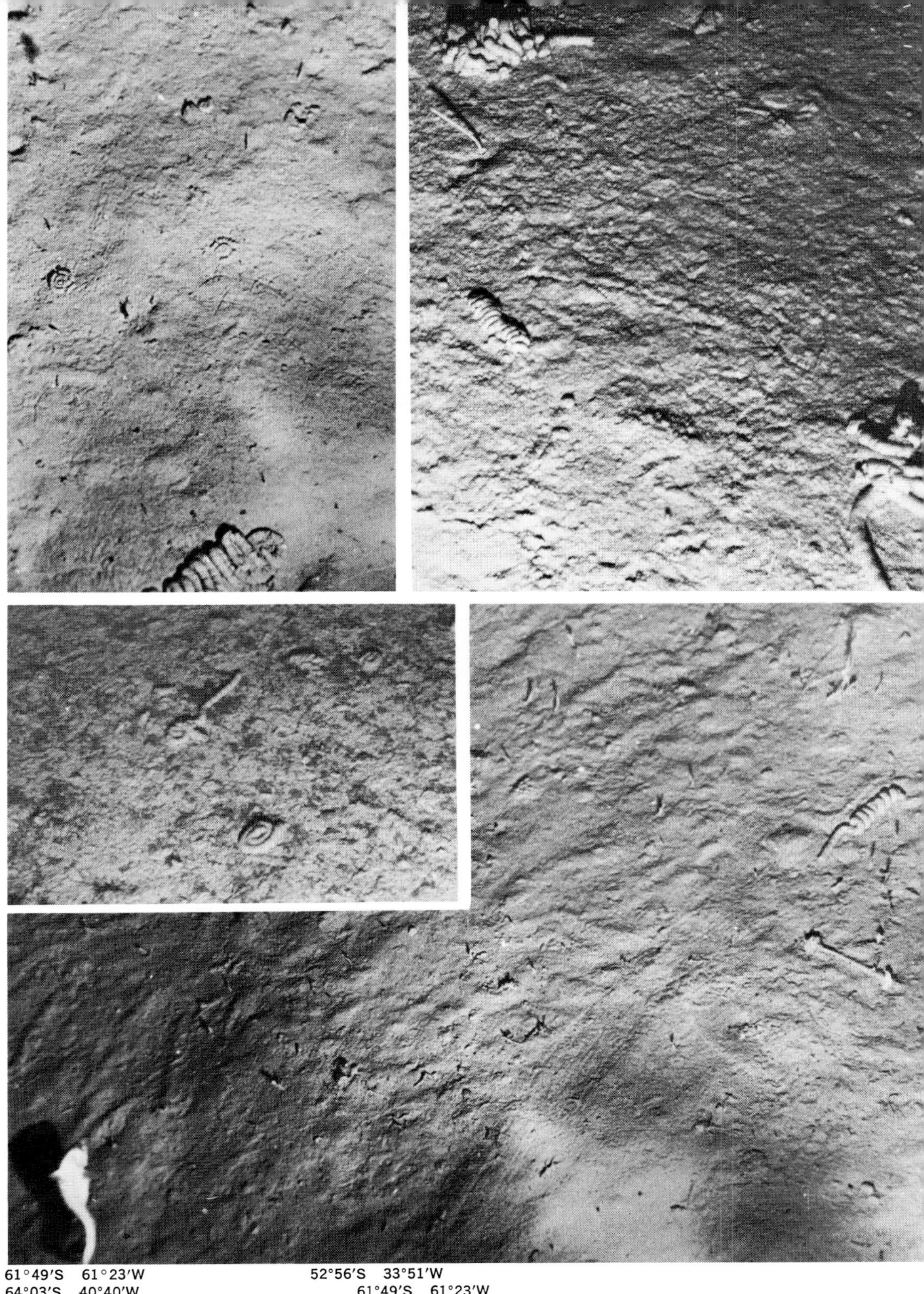

5.9 Knots, coils, and cylinders. UL, Tightly coiled spiral and holothurian knot, 3269 m, Drake Passage. UR, Holothurian knot and cylinder heaps, 2839 m, outer ridge, South Sandwich Trench. LC, Small tight coils, 4609 m, northern Weddell Sea. LR, Knot and trail probably left by the large abyssal holothurian, *Psychropotes*. Rat-tailed fish at left, 3269 m, Drake Passage.

The large planispiral and switchback fecal coils are easily identifiable in photographs and even those which are quite old and nearly buried show through a veneer of later sediment (5.8). Considering the rates of deposition in the southwest Pacific one would suspect that some of the coils which one sees are hundreds of years old. In the photograph reproduced as Figure 5.1, one can see behind and to the right of the proboscis a disturbance in the sediment created as the animal swung its front end to the right. The area covered by the animal is slightly rougher than the sediment surface on either side, indicating that these worms clean off the surface film and do not dig far into the sediment.

Small tightly coiled planispiral fecal coils of two or three complete turns (5.9 UL, CL) have been observed. Their size is near the lower limit of bottom photograph resolution, but the pattern appears to be distinctly different from the hemichordate spirals. The ratio of width of coiled material to intervening space is approximately ten to one, whereas in the larger hemichordate spirals the ratio is nearly one to four. Similar fossil coils have been found in ancient rocks.[6]

KNOTS, CYLINDERS, AND LOOPS

By far the most common recognizable excrement found throughout the world resembles a coiled piece of clothesline (3.19, 5.9 L, 5.10). Circular in cross section and evenly segmented, the strings may be knotted, thereby resembling a helicoid (5.9 L), irregularly piled, unevenly coiled, or lie in gentle loops on the sea floor. Tracks of giant holothurians are clearly associated with the knots and loops (3.19, 5.9, 5.10, 5.11), and holothurians have been photographed in the act of egesting these types of remolded sediment (5.12, 5.13).

The small apodia *Leptosynapta inhaerens* ejects its feces with great force.[7] These small animals shrink to one-third of their original length at the end of the violent discharge during which the excrement is thrown distances equivalent to two to eight times its body length (5.14). The initial discharges produced spirals while the closing stages produced more loosely looped coils. While this genus has not been found in the deep sea and would, in any case, be too small to see in photographs, this observation demonstrates the force which can be employed by holothurians in ejecting feces (5.15). The three holothurians shown in Figures 5.12 and 5.13 have ejected loops which extend one to three body lengths behind them. Perhaps the approach of the camera provoked them. The common large spindled cylinders approximately three to five centimeters in diam-

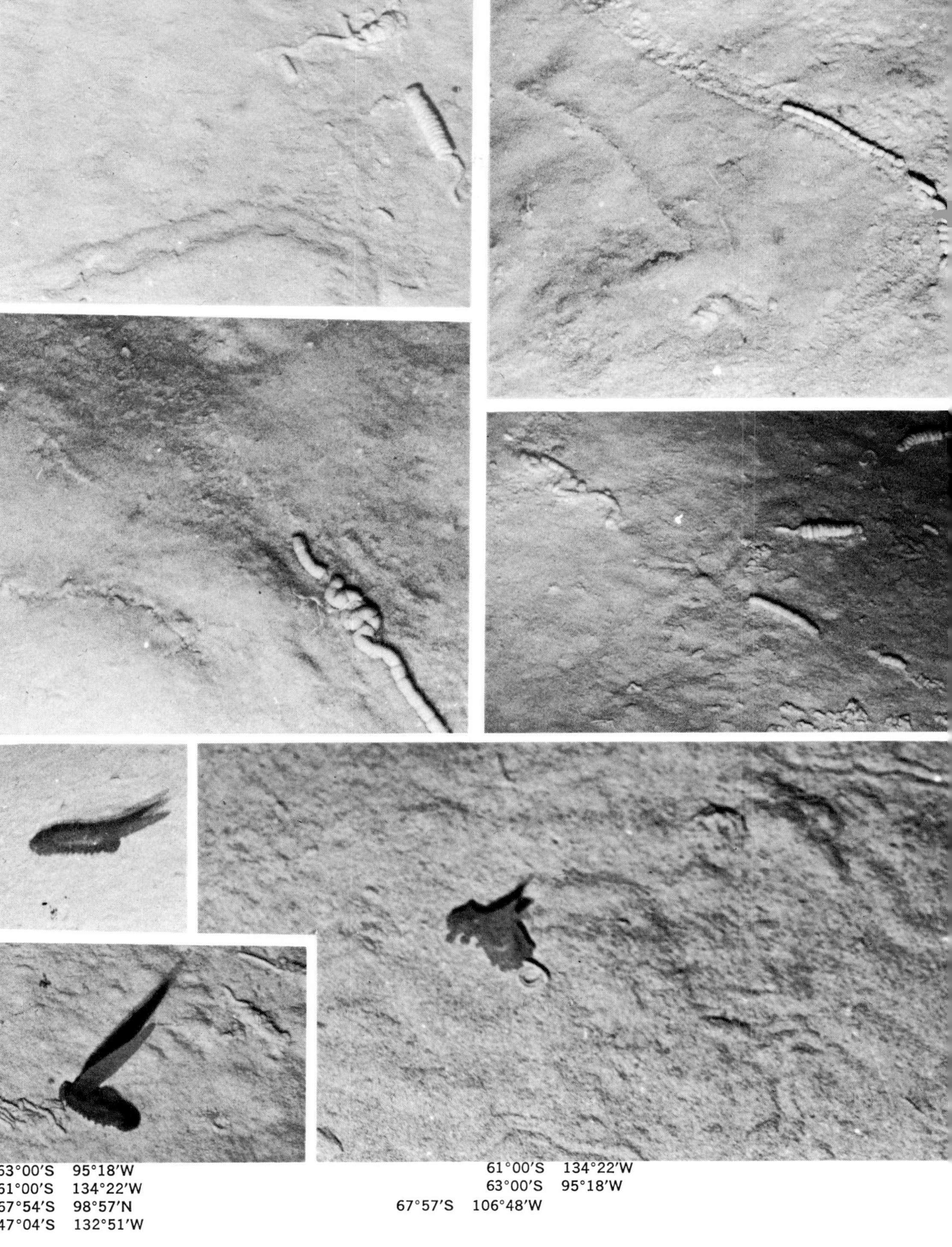

63°00′S 95°18′W
61°00′S 134°22′W
67°54′S 98°57′N
47°04′S 132°51′W

61°00′S 134°22′W
63°00′S 95°18′W
67°57′S 106°48′W

5.10 Holothurians, feces, and tracks. UL, Echinoid plow mark and holothurian fecal knots, 4975 m, Bellingshausen Basin; UR, LC, Holothurian tracks and feces, 4599 m, east flank Mid-Oceanic Ridge, South Pacific; RC, Cylinders and knots, 4975 m, Bellingshausen Basin; LLC, *Psychropotes,* one of the largest and commonest tracking holothurians, 4562 m, Pacific continental rise, Antarctica; LL, *Psychropotes* caught in the act, 4487 m, west flank Mid-Oceanic Ridge, South Pacific; LR, Holothurian producing tightly coiled fecal spiral, 4349 m, Pacific continental rise, Antarctica.

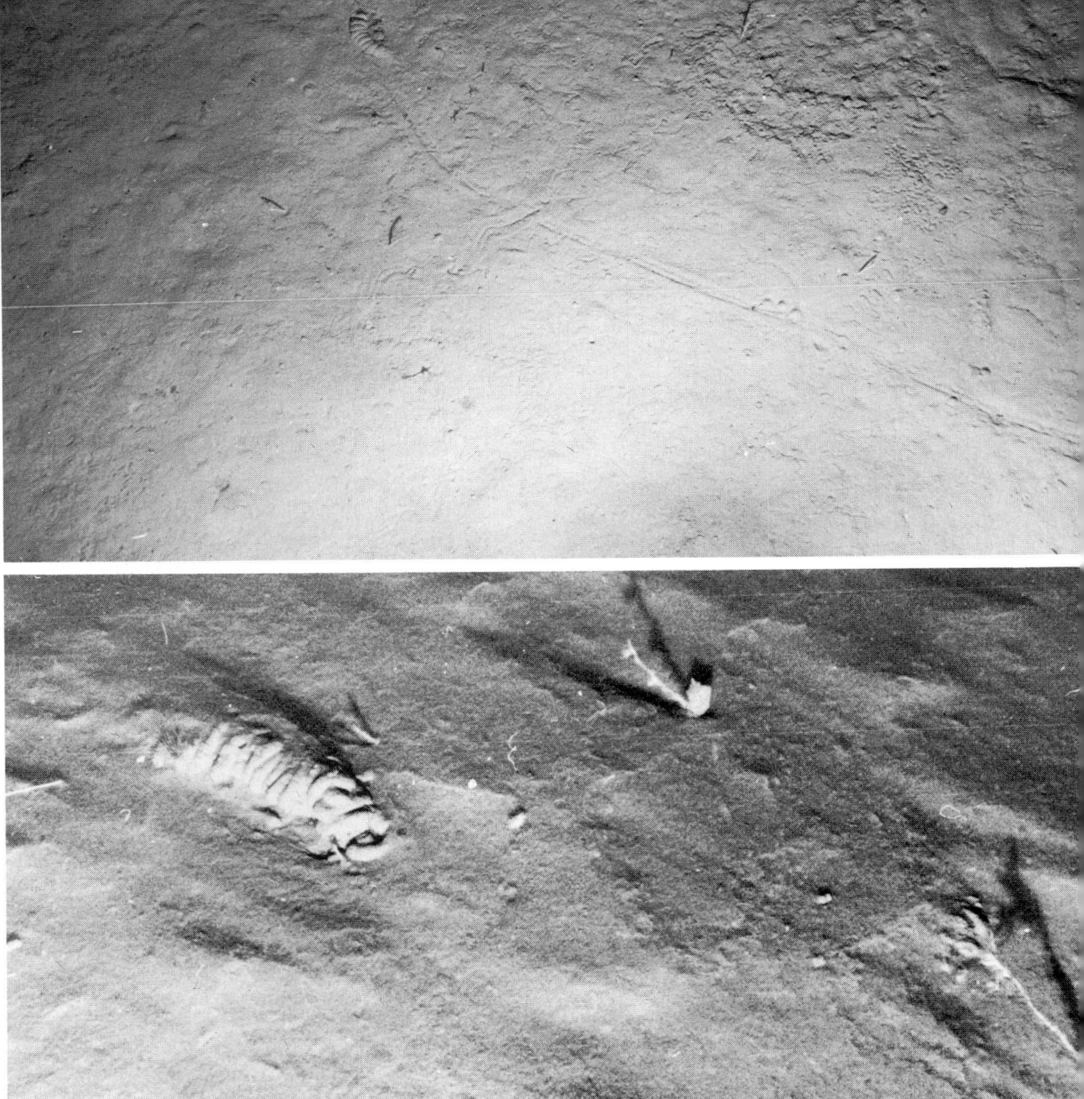

34°48′S 74°54′W
58°41′S 33°41′W

5.11 Knots. U, Holothurian left progressively deeper footprints just before leaving knot of remolded sediment on its trail, 4165 m, east wall, Peru-Chile Trench off central Chile. L, Holothurian knot nearly obliterated by vigorous current flowing from right to left, 3406 m, eastern Scotia Sea.

eter whose segments reach fifteen centimeters in length are probably also produced by sea cucumbers (5.9 UR).

Holothurians are the most common mud-eating benthic animals. They have been photographed throughout the world and knotted feces are frequently seen lying on their characteristic trails. The giants seen in abyssal photographs apparently skim only the very uppermost millimeter off the bottom, for one rarely sees any evidence of their passage except for their

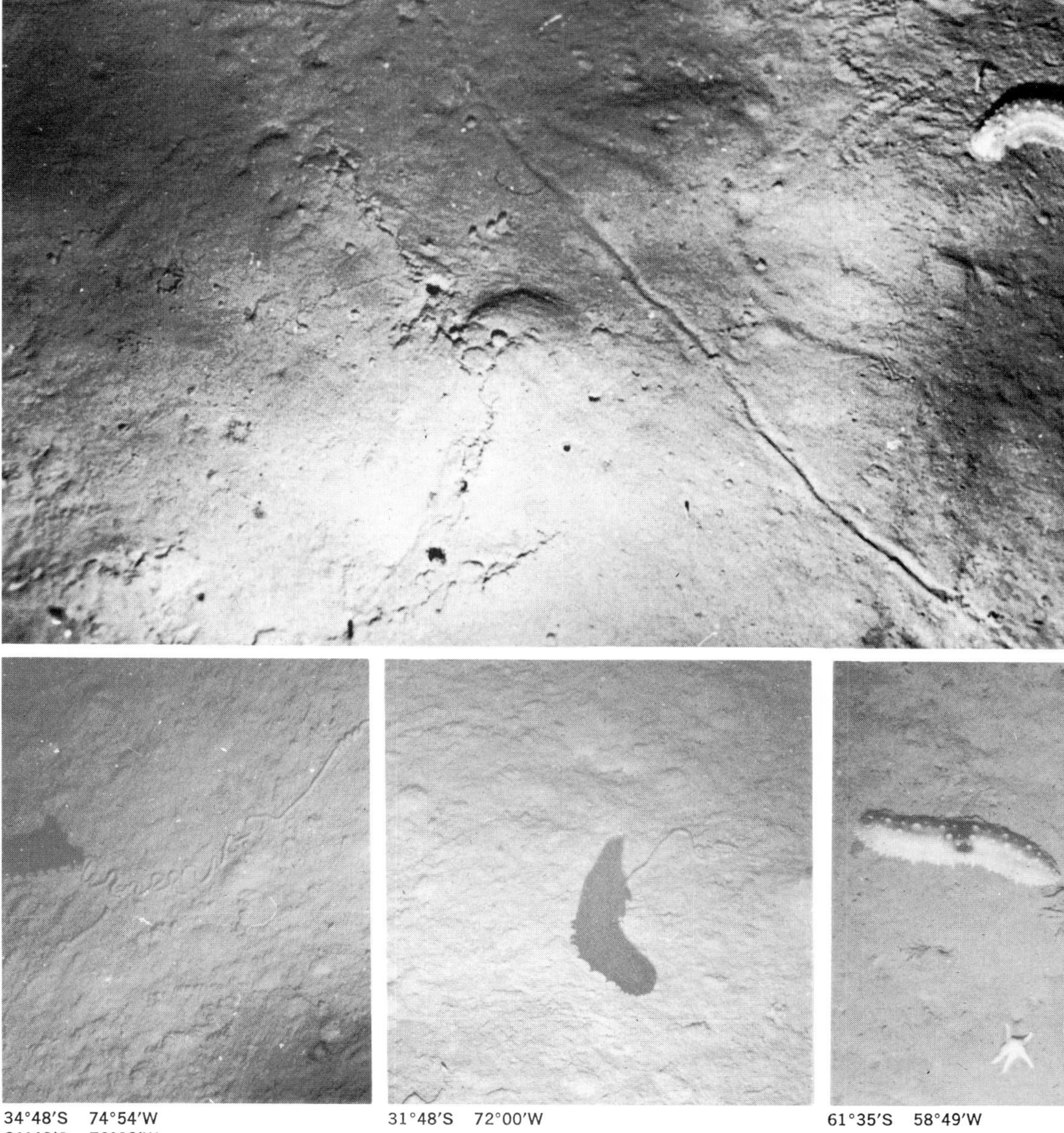

34°48′S 74°54′W
31°48′S 72°00′W
31°48′S 72°00′W
61°35′S 58°49′W

5.12 Holothurian loopers. U, 4165 m, LL, LC, 5802 m, Peru-Chile Trench off central Chile. LR, 1186 m, continental slope, Antarctic Peninsula.

tube-feet impressions (5.16). The tentacles which surround the mouth are used as fingers. Food is collected on their mucous coating and then the tentacle is thrust into the mouth, where it is licked clean. Thus their feeding is a selective process.

Their habit of ingesting sediment for a period, collecting it in their intestines and then ejecting it at intervals is apparent from the photographs, for in very few cases does one see a continuous fecal string. In most cases, all one sees is a discrete mass, either tightly coiled, free looped, or in a random pile (5.17, 5.18). A 25-centimeter-long individual of the shallow-water holothurian genus *Stichopus* can ingest and egest approximately one kilogram (dry weight) of bottom sediment each day.[8]

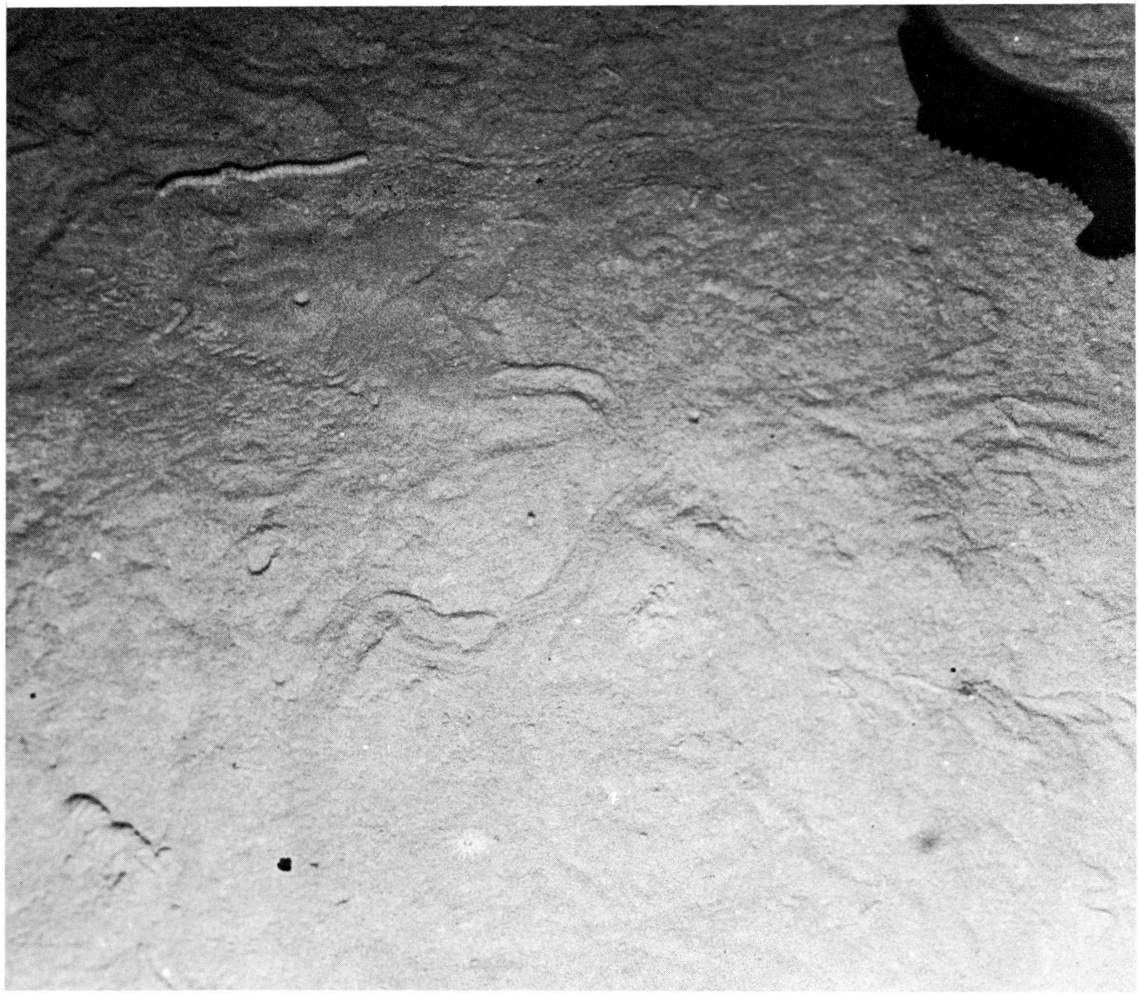

57°05′S 99°21′W

5.13 Rope, track, and holothurian. *Psychropotes* slurping up the surface slime has left its distinctive fecal rope and multi-holed path, 4490 m, Bellingshausen Basin.

The egested material is contained in two or three compact strings. It is not known whether the abyssal holothurians ingest sediment at a rate comparable with their shallow-water relatives, but if they do, a few holothurians could account for many strings measuring kilometers in length and weighing tons; for these fecal knots and strings are often a few centimeters high, and in most parts of the abyss, would take decades, centuries, or millennia to become completely buried.

On the deep-sea floor the characteristic knotted feces of the holothurians are frequently seen associated with trails consisting of tube-feet tracks. In examining a large number of photographs we have found many instances where the fecal castings lie on the trails. Frequently we see trails without castings and in other cases castings without evident tracks, but in no case has it been evident that two fecal castings were associated with a single trail within the area of one photograph. Thus, the distance traveled by the holothurian from the time it empties its gut until the gut becomes full again is necessarily more than five meters since this is approximately the maximum dimension seen in a single photograph. Since feces are associated with so many of the trails one might estimate that the distance between feces along one trail probably is in the order of ten meters. The larger knots are approximately ten centimeters in length and two or three centimeters in diameter. The volume of material contained in the larger feces is perhaps twenty-five to fifty cubic centimeters which is skimmed off the very uppermost film of sediment and compacted in the gut. The amount of sediment ingested by such an animal in traveling ten meters is difficult to estimate. However, assuming that the average feces contains fifty cubic centimeters, which would appear to be a high figure, and that the animal traveled ten meters between times that he emptied his gut, and then assuming that the animal is only ingesting sediment over a two-centimeter-wide path, which would appear to be an ultra-conservative figure, one would conclude that the thickness of the layer removed would be one-tenth of a millimeter thick, and, even assuming ten to one compaction of this surface film, the thickness of the layer removed would be only one millimeter. This conclusion

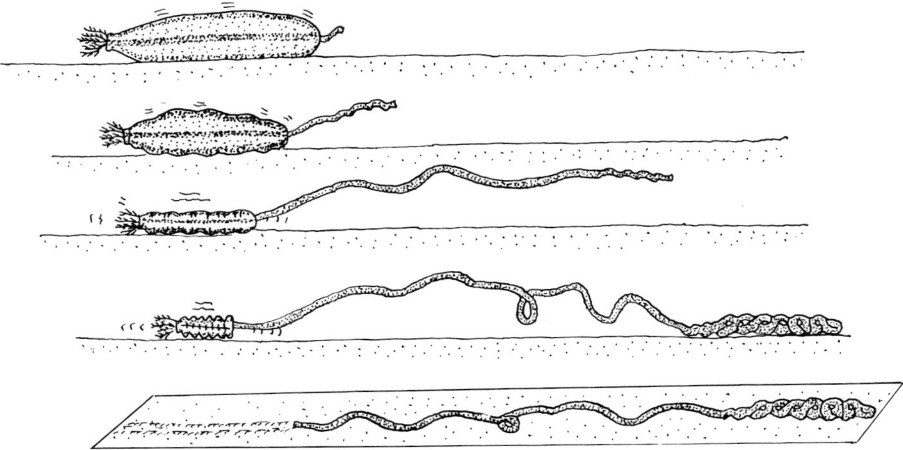

5.14 Shooting strings. Holothurians in shallow water have been observed to shoot fecal strings more than twice their body length.

5.15 Close-up photography reveals a sea floor partially covered with minute fecal logs. These unusual 1:1 pictures, taken from the drifting ice-station T-3, show that the Arctic Ocean floor is pitted and burrowed on a very fine scale. U, L, 3800 m, floor of Canada Basin, Arctic Ocean.

5.16 Holothurian tracks and feces beneath the Arctic ice pack. U, L, 2784 m, Canadian continental rise. One half natural size.

80°10′N 158°04′W

80°10′N 158°04′W

79°37′N 172°34′W

79°37′N 172°34′W

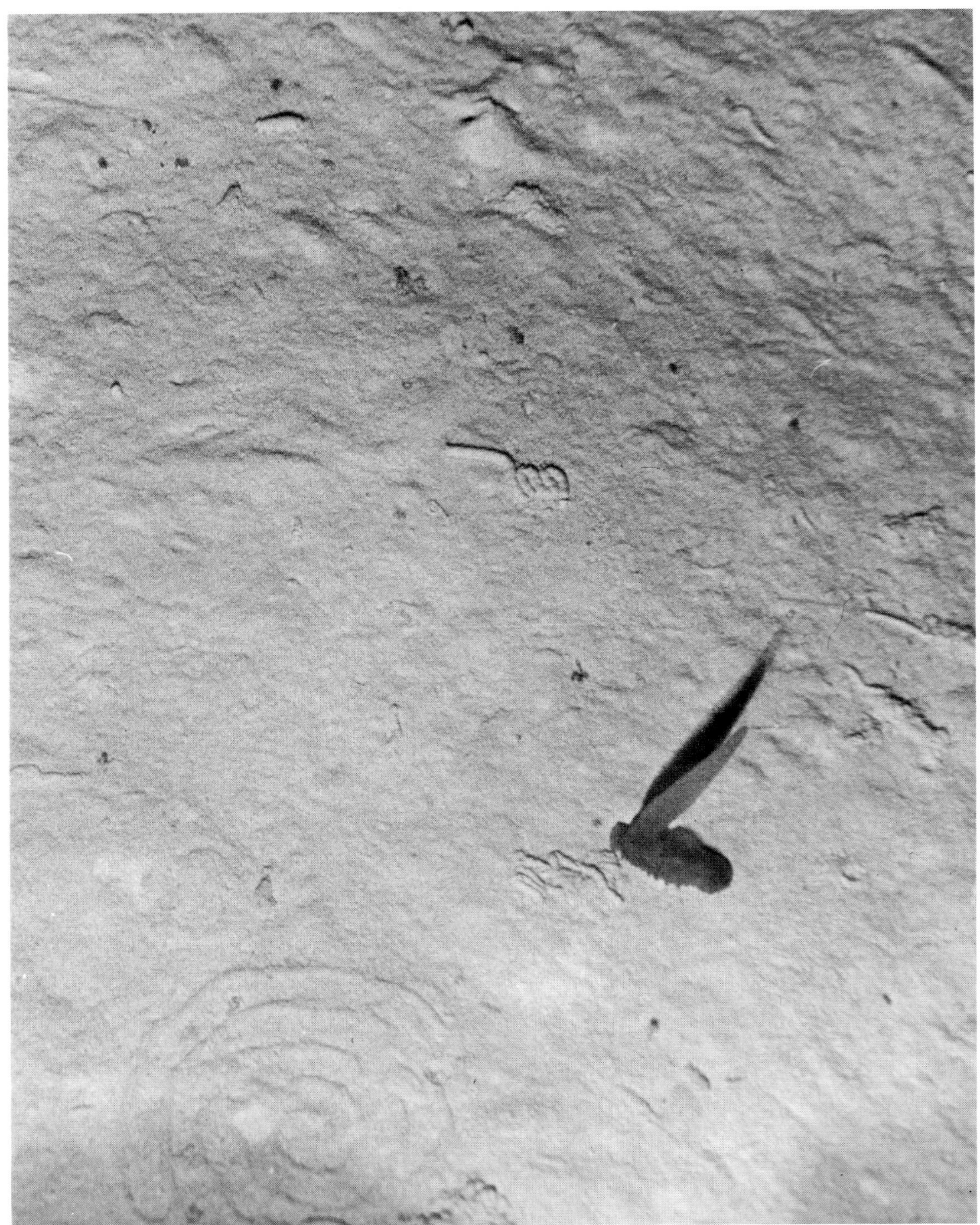

5.17 High-tailed knot maker. Abyssal elasipod, *Psychropotes,* making cylinders, 4512 m, Mid-Oceanic Ridge, South Pacific.

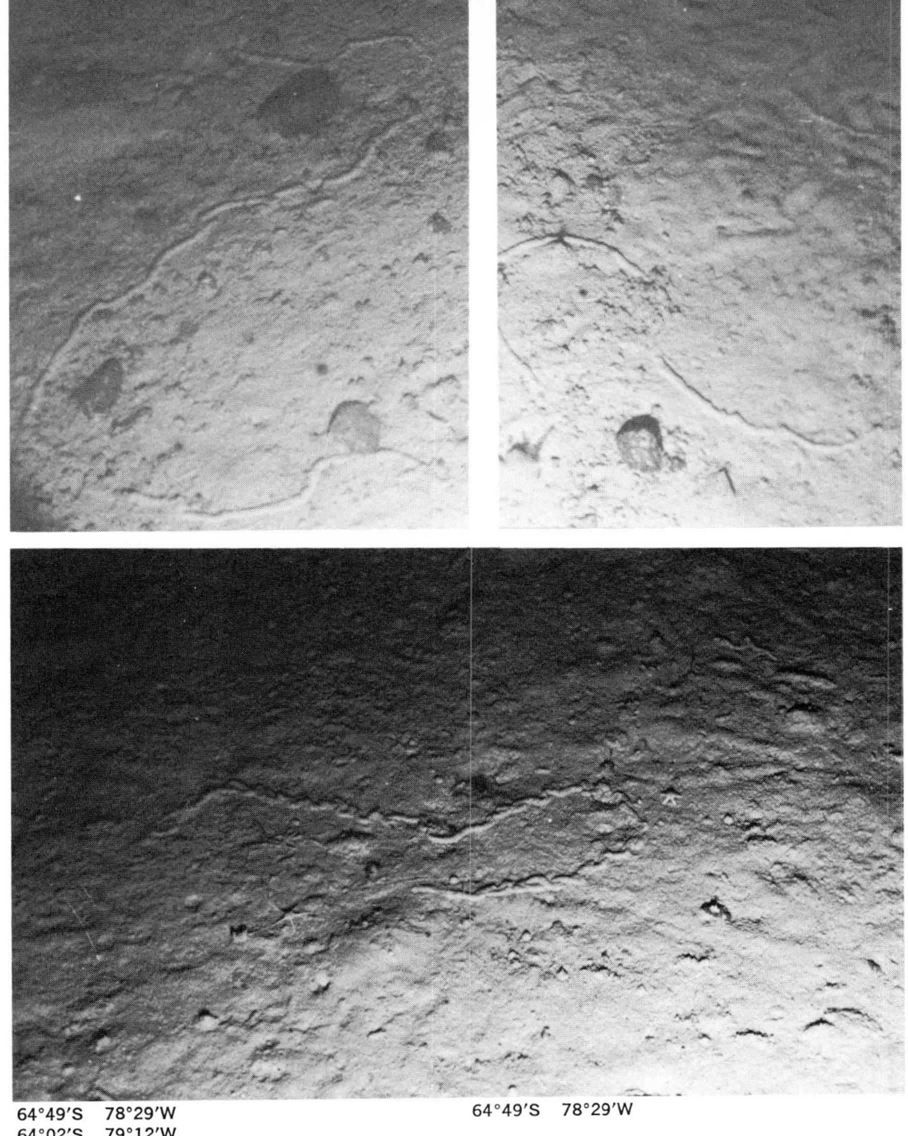

64°49′S 78°29′W
64°02′S 79°12′W

64°49′S 78°29′W

5.18 Giant loops and braided loops. UL, UR, 4205 m, and L, 4304 m, Pacific continental rise of Antarctic Peninsula.

is in keeping with the lack of any noticeable disturbance of the bottom by holothurians, save the tube-feet impressions, which is remarkable in view of the large feces and the obvious mode of life of these detritus-feeders. It appears, therefore, that they live on the latest material arriving on the sea floor and deal only with the topmost millimeter or less of the sediment. It has been widely assumed that these large holothurians plow indiscriminately through the sediment but since we have seen no evidence of this in photographs, we must conclude that they are selective skimmers rather than random plowers.

Their rate of movement across the bottom cannot be easily estimated. We can surmise, however, that these animals of the deep sea move at a slower rate than their shallow-water relatives. If, for instance, they

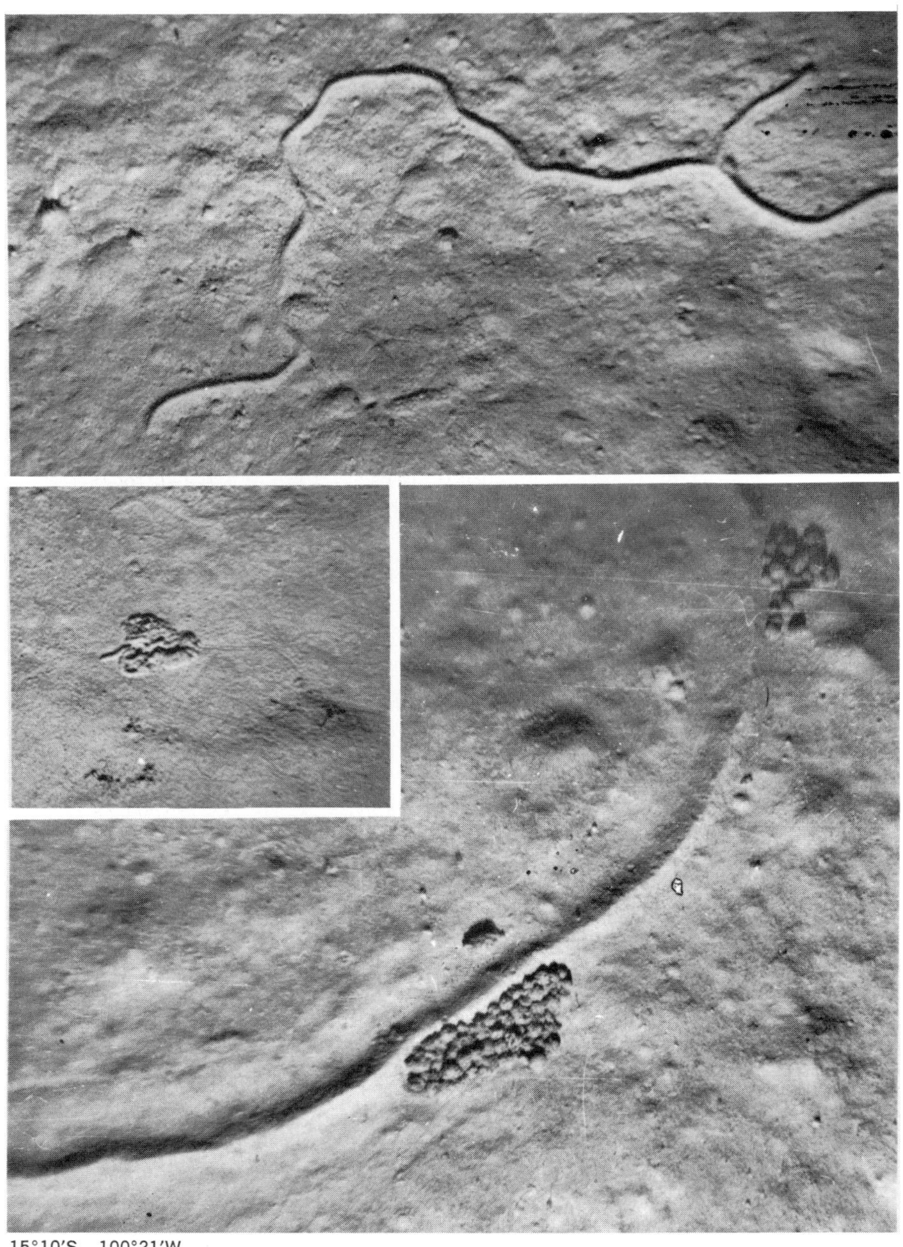

15°10'S 100°21'W
16°48'S 152°13'W
12°47'S 161°04'W

5.19 Ridges, spaghetti, and balls. U, Mysterious forked ridge, 3835 m, Mid-Oceanic Ridge, equatorial Pacific. LC, 3938 m, near Bora Bora. L, 3162 m, eastern scarp, Manihiki Plateau, equatorial Pacific.

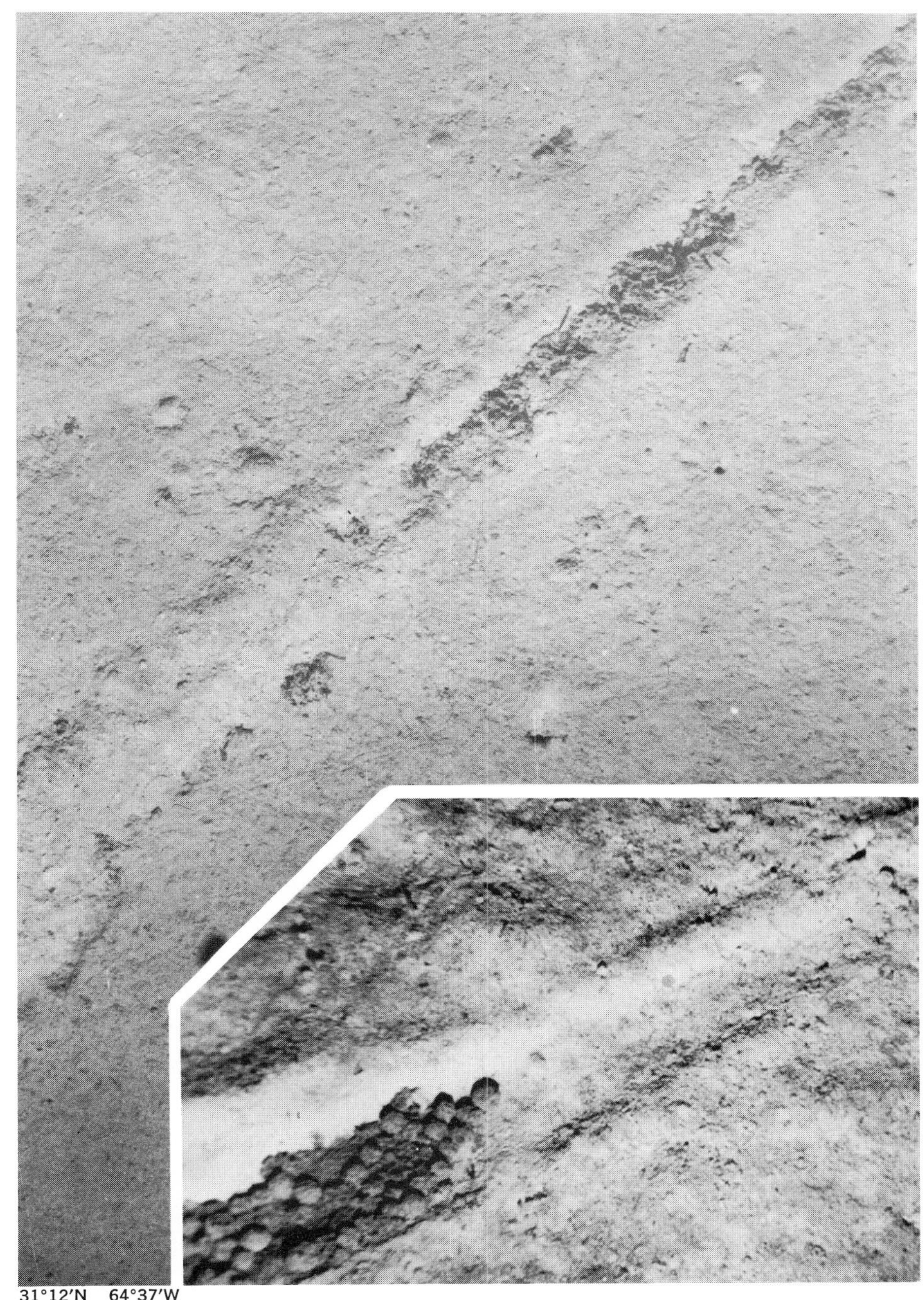

5.20 Grooves and balls. U, 4634 m, central Bermuda Rise. L, 2681 m, Carlsberg Ridge, Indian Ocean.

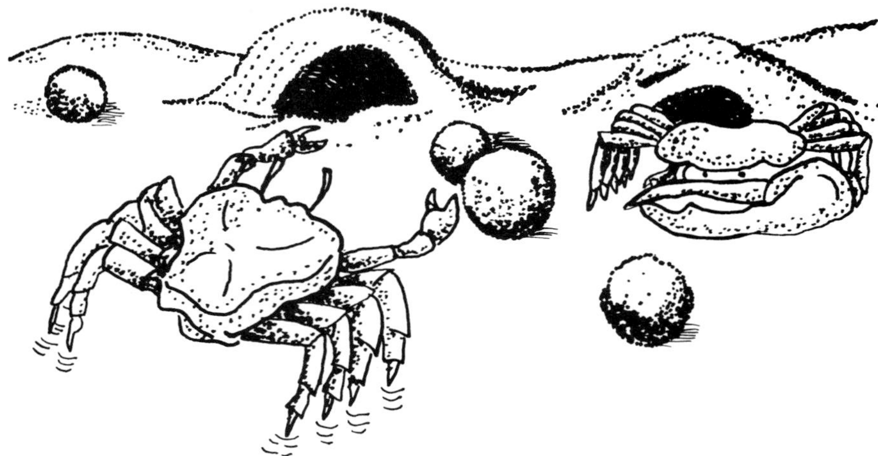

5.21 Crabs have been observed making fecal balls in shallow water.

emptied their gut twice a day as the shallow-water *Stichopus* does, and fecal castings were found ten meters apart, this would imply a rate of motion of about fifty centimeters per hour. Such a rate has been observed from the portholes of a bathyscaphe. In one case, an army of *Scotoplanes* moved at the rate of nearly forty centimeters per hour.[9]

RIDGES AND BALLS

Low meandering ridges which abruptly end and sometimes fork are an enigma (5.19 U). In most cases, it is not known either what the ridges are or what made them, for it is rather difficult to imagine how a single animal could produce a widely forked trail of feces. One dramatic photograph (5.19 L) gives the distinct impression that the ridge marks the trail of some large animal which may perhaps have been twenty or thirty centimeters wide. Associated with these broad ridges and furrows are piles of round or ovoid pellets approximately the size of golf balls (5.20). Some fiddler crabs work the sediment into round balls, and one might wonder if both the ridge and the balls were produced by some gigantic crab (5.21), but the deep-sea starfish *Porcellanaster* are also reported to form fecal pellets in the shape of their body cavity and to cast off digested balls on the sea floor. Rather than give the impression that all has been answered by our yet superficial investigations of the abyss, it might be more stimulating, and certainly more romantic, to suppose that the enormous tracks and the mysterious balls are the work of some still undiscovered sea monster.

REFERENCES AND NOTES

1. The only fecal materials from the deep-sea floor which have been described in the scientific literature are tiny pellets, (H. B. Moore, 1939. Fecal pellets in relation to marine deposits. In: P. D. Trask (Editor), *Recent Marine Sediments,* Am. Assn. Petroleum Geol., Tulsa, pp. 516-24); however, the geologic record contains fossil remains of large excreta which geologists refer to as coprolites (E. C. Dapples, 1938. The sedimentational effects of the work of marine scavengers. *Am.* Jour. Sci., 35:54-65).
2. D. W. Bourne and B. C. Heezen, 1965. A wandering enteropneust from the abyssal Pacific; and the distribution of "spiral" tracks on the sea floor. *Science,* 150:60-63.
3. A discussion of the feeding habits of the hemichordata and simple sketches of hemichordates is found in: E. Barrington, 1965. *The Biology of Hemichordata and Protochordata.* Oliver and Boyd, London, 176 pp.
4. Of the thousands of trawls recovered from the deep sea, acorn worms have only been reported from three locations. Four plates (one colored) showing entire specimens can be found in: J. W. Spengel, 1893. Die Enteropneusten. *Fauna u. Flora des Golfes von Neapel,* Berlin, 18:756 pp. A sketch of the head of *Balanglossus* and a short description of the species by Dr. W. Suhm is found in T. H. Tizard, H. N. Moseley, J. Y. Buchanan, and J. Murray, 1885. Challenger Repts. Narrative, 1(1):p. 195 (Fig. 78).
5. Shallow-water acorn worms do not crawl on the bottom but live exclusively in burrows and therefore their disappearance into a hole would be consistent with known behavior (G. Stiasny, 1910. Zur Kenntnis der lebensweise von *Balanoglossus clavigerus* Deele Chiaje. *Zoo. Anz.* 35:561-65).
6. A variety of spiral fecal traces frequently occur in certain ancient sediments (A. Seilacher, 1958. Flysch and Molasse als Faziestypen. *Ecologae Geol. Helv.,* 51:1062-1078; W. Hantzschel, 1962. Trace fossils and problematica. In: R. C. Moore (Editor), *Treatise on Invertebrate Paleontology, Part W, Miscellanae.* Geol. Soc. Am., New York, 177-245; and J. Hulsemann, 1966. Spiralfahrten und "gefuhrte Maander" auf dem Meeresboden. *Natur. und Museum, Frankfurt,* 96:449-455.
7. An experimental study of defecation by a small apodia holothurian was conducted by C. L. Fenton and M. A. Fenton (1934. *Lumbricaria;* a holothuroid casting? *Pan. Am. Geol.,* 61, 291-292).
8. The feeding and egesting activity of a holothurian from a shallow littoral bottom is described by W. J. Crozier (1918. The amount of bottom material ingested by holothurians (*Stichopus*). *Jour. Exp. Zool.,* 26:379-389).
9. The rate of movement of the holothurian *Scotoplanes* was observed by Eugene La Fond from the bathyscaphe Trieste in San Diego Trough.

6.1 Digging and heaping under way.

6
Dig and Heap

But in the mud and scum of things
There always, always something sings
EMERSON

If the creatures which live on and in the abyssal floor were able to count their blessings they surely would offer thanks to a provident heaven above for sending the life-giving gentle rain of organic particles which, ultimately, is their sole source of food. The remains of planktonic organisms and the lifeless bodies of bottom dwellers are broken down by bacteria and consumed by the roving scavengers and living screens which inhabit the floor of the abyss.[1]

Many, if not most, of the roving mud eaters probably feed upon bacteria in much the same way that cattle graze on grass and thus bacteria might be thought of as the grass of the abyss. The standing crop of bacteria in the uppermost thin film of most recently deposited sediment is at least one million individuals per milliliter, but it rapidly decreases with depth, rarely exceeding ten thousand at half a meter and falling to less than ten individuals per milliliter in depths greater than three meters. Several studies have even shown that the bacterial count drops as much as one hundredfold between the surface and a depth of only one centimeter.[2]

Of the animals that graze on the muds, those who skim off the very surface film must encounter the richest crop of bacteria and organic matter. Thus, the holothurians skim off the cream. The plowing echinoids graze only slightly deeper, whereas some worms and other organisms probe to the greatest depths. There would seem little incentive for animals to burrow to greater depths than ten to fifteen centimeters if their objective were to feed on bacteria or on the food bacteria are feeding on.

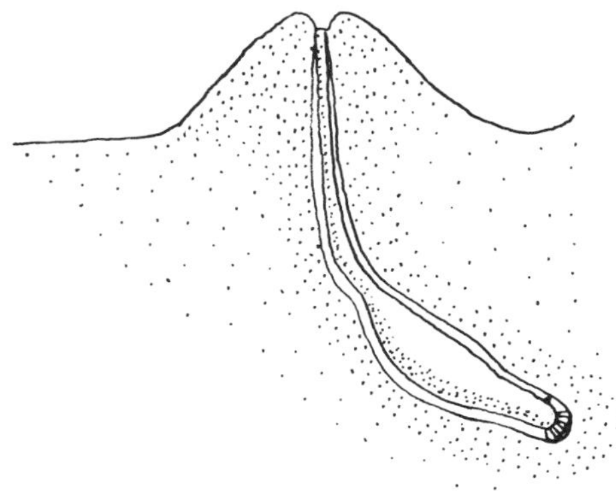

6.2 Some holothurians, by swallowing and egesting sediment, produce cone-shaped mounds with apical vent.

It is, therefore, not surprising that we find so many surface grazers in the deep sea. Forms such as the acorn worms, which in shallow water live in deep holes, have adopted a surface grazing habit; spatangoid urchins, which burrow deep in shallow water, often graze at the surface in the abyss, and holothurians have developed a whole order of large surface grazers (Elasipoda).

Many animals, however, do burrow (6.1, 6.2), as the numerous holes in the bottom and the filled burrows recorded in deep-sea cores[3] so clearly demonstrate (6.3-6.5), for burrowing is a splendid way to avoid many of the predators, and most worms and many crustaceans, molluscs, holothurians and fish hide in holes. These hiders reach out or, in the case of the crustaceans and fish, swim out of their holes for food only to retreat again when in danger. Of all the predators only the nemerteneans and a few annelids burrow in search of prey.

The majority of these benthic animals are extremely small creatures which live in the top few centimeters of the sediment. In normal bottom photography we cannot expect to see most of the effects of these tiny beasts but we can see the more massive constructions created by larger animals which build mounds and craters and create numerous, dramatic burrows and burrow fillings.

Animals burrow through the sediment in various ways. Elasipod holothurians which live on the sea floor skim off the surface film and remold it into compact fecal knots and strings. The echinoids, on the other hand, burrow a bit deeper and their feces are mixed in the sediment contained in their furrowed wake. Other creatures burrow through the ooze and leave as a subterranean trail a burrow filled with remolded sediment. In sediments recovered by coring it is often difficult to distinguish burrow fillings from feces since in many cases there really is little difference save

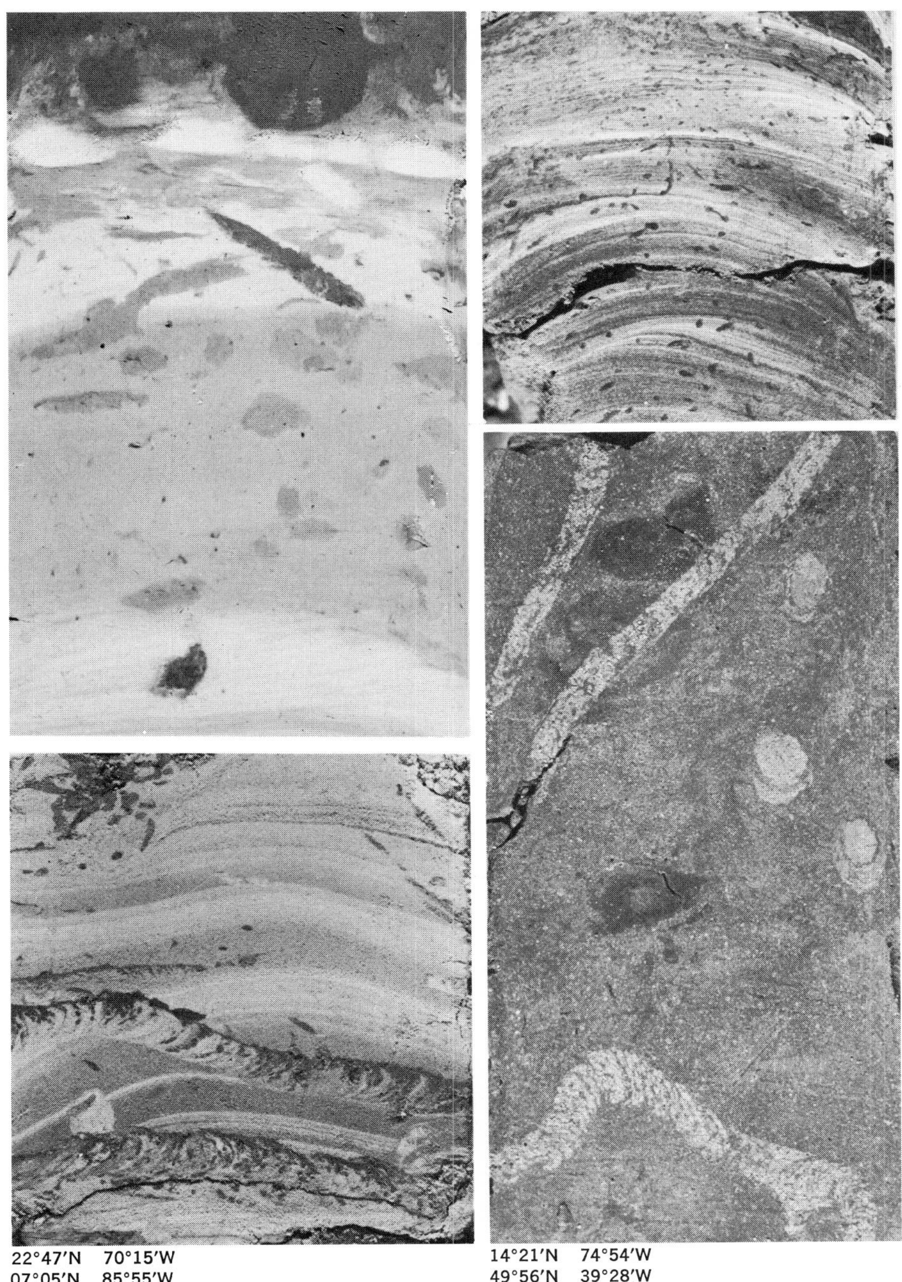

6.3 Burrows. Animals leave filled burrows in the deep-sea sediments. These vertical cross sections of portions of 6-centimeter-wide piston cores show some of the larger and more dramatic burrows that are well displayed by a strong contrast of color between successive layers. UL, Upper portion of graded limey sand layer, 5441 m, off Caicos Island. UR, Small dark burrows in upper portion of graded silt layer, 4118 m, Colombia Abyssal Plain. LL, Helical burrows in volcanic ash bed, 2860 m, equatorial Pacific. LR, Light-colored burrows in mud, 4300 m, Labrador Sea.

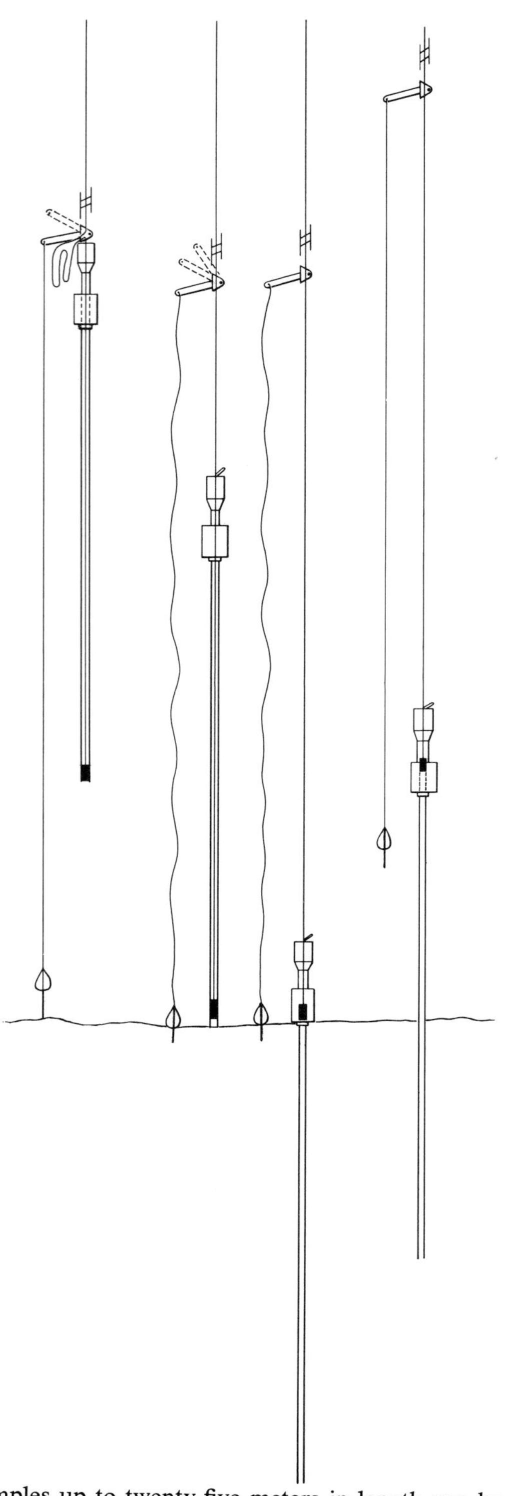

6.4 Sediment samples up to twenty-five meters in length can be recovered with a piston corer.

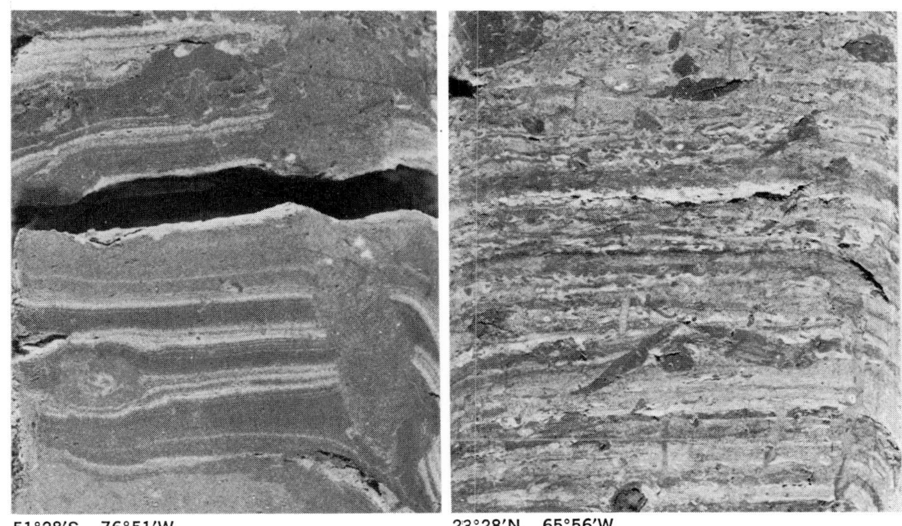

6.5 Burrowers destroy fine laminae. L, 3473 m, continental slope off Chile. R, 5836 m, Nares Abyssal Plain, North Atlantic.

the discontinuous nature of the feces and the fact that burrows cut across bedding planes. Burrows vary in diameter from less than one to over fifty millimeters and are often recognized by distinct contrasts in color or texture (6.3). In homogeneous sediments burrowing is detected by a subtle particle reorientation which may not be apparent except through microscopic inspection. Red clays from the ocean basin floor, particularly those deposited beneath the oceanic deserts such as the Sargasso Sea, contain relatively few burrows, and sediments of stagnant basins are totally lacking in burrows.

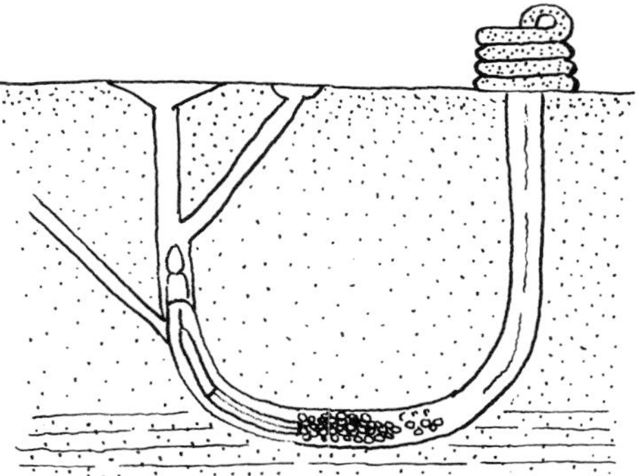

6.6 In shallow water acorn worms have been observed producing U-shaped holes and coiled mounds of discarded sediment. In the abyss, acorn worms have been seen in the process of leaving planispiral and meandering loops of egested material while they skim the surface muds without burrowing into the sea bottom (see Figure 5.1). Priapuloids also live in a U-shaped burrow and pump water through it.

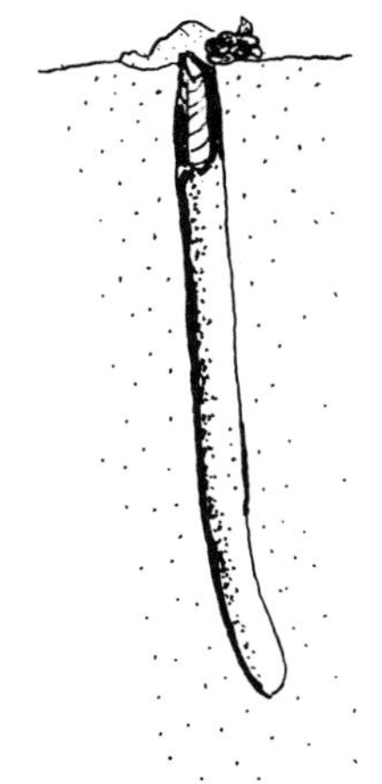

6.7 Small sand hoppers (crustaceans) dig into the beach sand and leave burrows and small mounds.

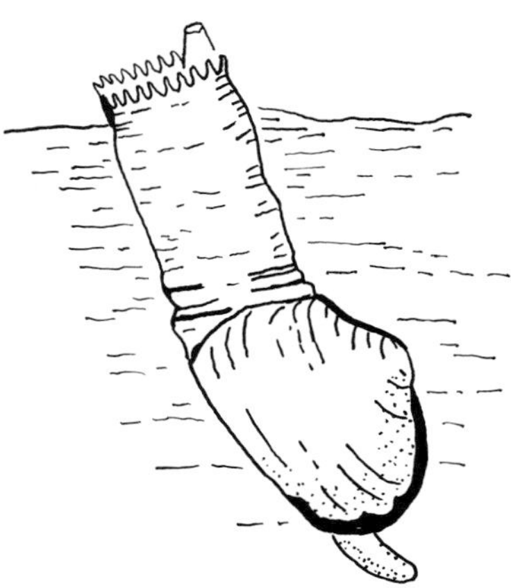

6.8 Pelecypods produce burrows by sticking their siphons out of the sea floor. When the siphon is retracted, one would see only a hollow burrow.

Molluscs, arthropods, echinoderms, and various worms account, no doubt, for many of the burrow mounds and holes. Among the individual groups which have been observed producing burrows are enteropneusts (6.6), crabs, amphipods (6.7), shrimp, worms, starfish, gastropods, holothurians (6.2), pelecypods (6.8), and even fish. At a depth of 10,000 feet in the Japan Trench, aquanauts "saw small crabs

6.9 Star burrows. UL, Deep sea burrowing starfish (cf. *Porcellanasteridae*), 5361 m, Wharton Basin, equatorial Indian Ocean. UR, Asteroids, star burrows, and sea pens, 93 m, New England continental shelf. L, Star burrows and tractor treads made by starfish, 4577 m, continental rise off Great Britain.

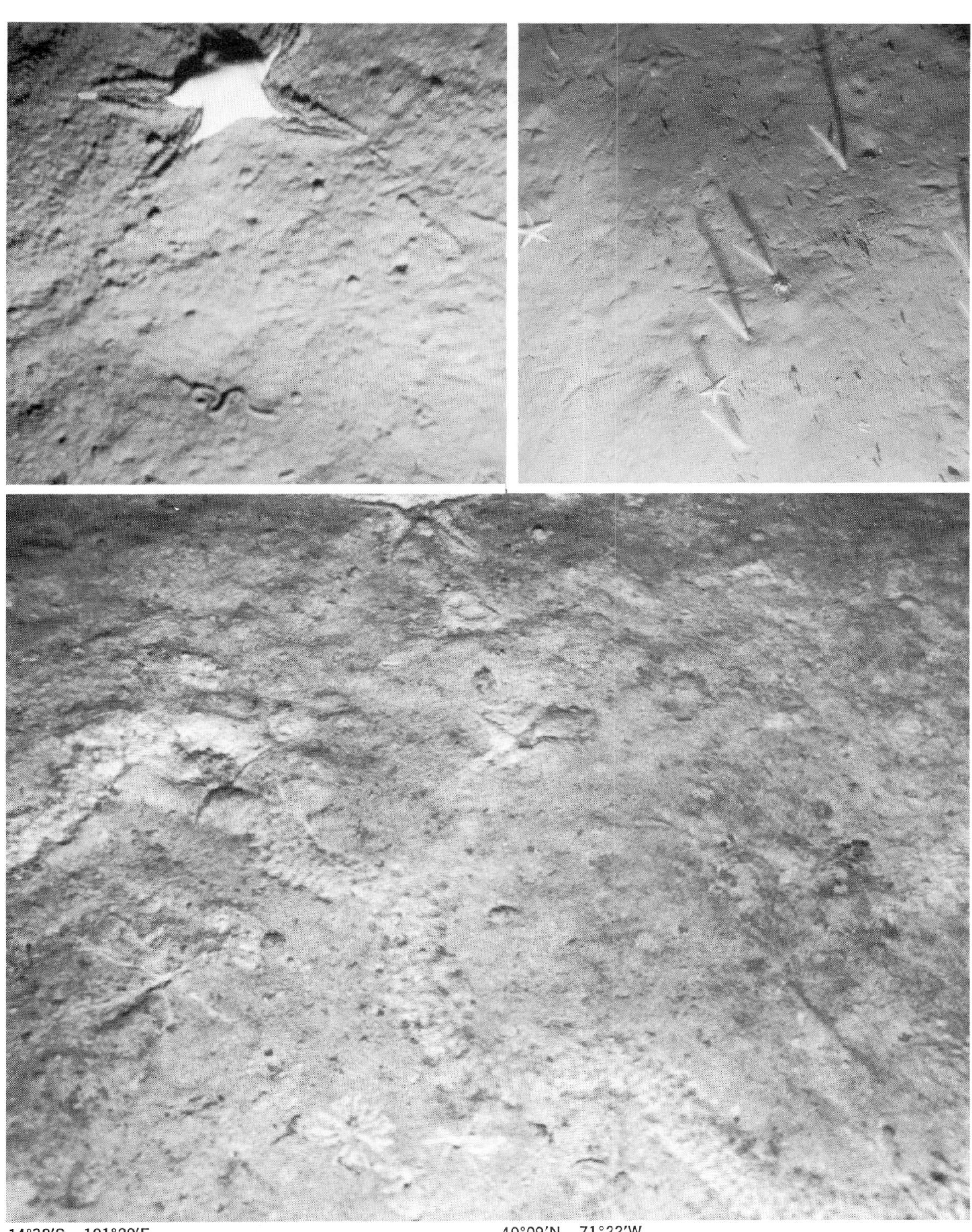

14°38′S 101°20′E
48°29′N 14°19′W

40°09′N 71°22′W

6.10 Star burrow and starfish are readily identified on the beach or in the abyss.

from one to three inches long, busily entering and emerging from holes in the ooze," and on the continental slope of California "a shrimp" was seen "living in a large round hole in the bottom." A large ray was attempting to chase the shrimp which thereupon disappeared into a burrow. On the basis of four years of experience in diving to the ocean floor, one bathyscaphe pilot states that: "At one time the mud is riddled with little holes; at another it reveals little cones, veritable volcanos in miniature, about fifteen to twenty inches high; and still again wide, gaping holes" which "compare with rabbit burrows. . . ." At another time he observed the large macrourid fish "*Trachyrhynchus scabrus* disappear from sight in a strange way. It seemed as though he vanished on contact with the bottom as if he had burrowed in."[4]

STARS AND SPOKES

Although it is extremely difficult and in most instances impossible to decide what organism made a particular hole or mound, there is one type of burrow in which there need never be any doubt (6.9). Both starfish (6.10) and brittle stars (6.11, 6.12) burrow into the bottom and the star shape of the burrow allows positive identification. Star burrows are best seen in soft mud bottoms, and asteroids have been seen in the process of burying themselves in the mud (6.9 UL). In some cases ophiuroids (6.11) bury themselves with only the tips of their rays visible above the surface; in other cases with only one ray protruding out, and in still other cases they are observed standing on all rays with their central disc elevated several centimeters above the bottom. Starfish impressions, al-

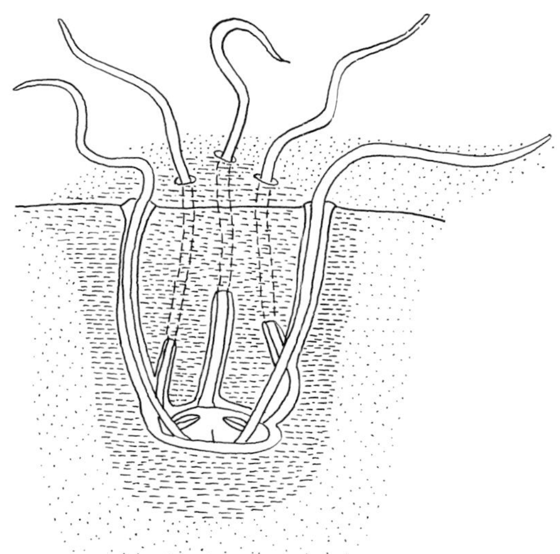

6.12 Burrowing brittle star. An underwater photograph would reveal only the white sinuous arms waving in the current.

◁ 39°58′N 68°57′W

6.11 Ophiuroids burrowing into the ooze. 1503 m, continental slope off New England.

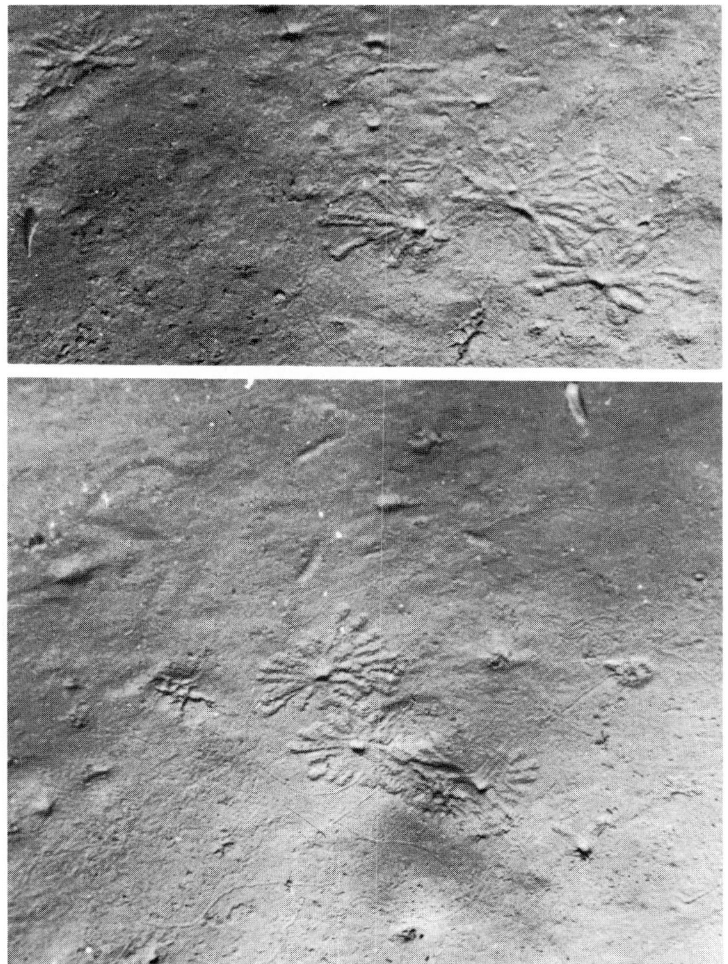

65°06'S 70°41'W

14°29'S 149°39'W

42°29'S 75°58'W
42°29'S 75°58'W

6.14 Spoke burrows. U, L, 3626 m, outer ridge, southern Peru-Chile Trench.

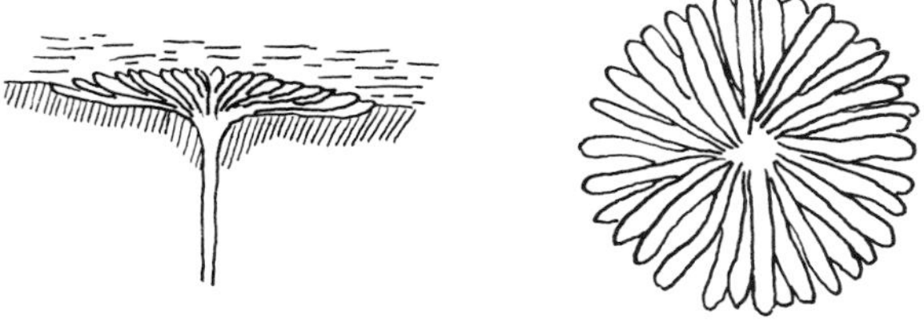

6.15 Four hundred million years ago a buried organism produced these spoke burrows.

◁ 6.13 Ray burrow and burrower. U, 4359 m, Tuamotu Archipelago. L, 3133 m, Pacific continental rise, Antarctic Peninsula.

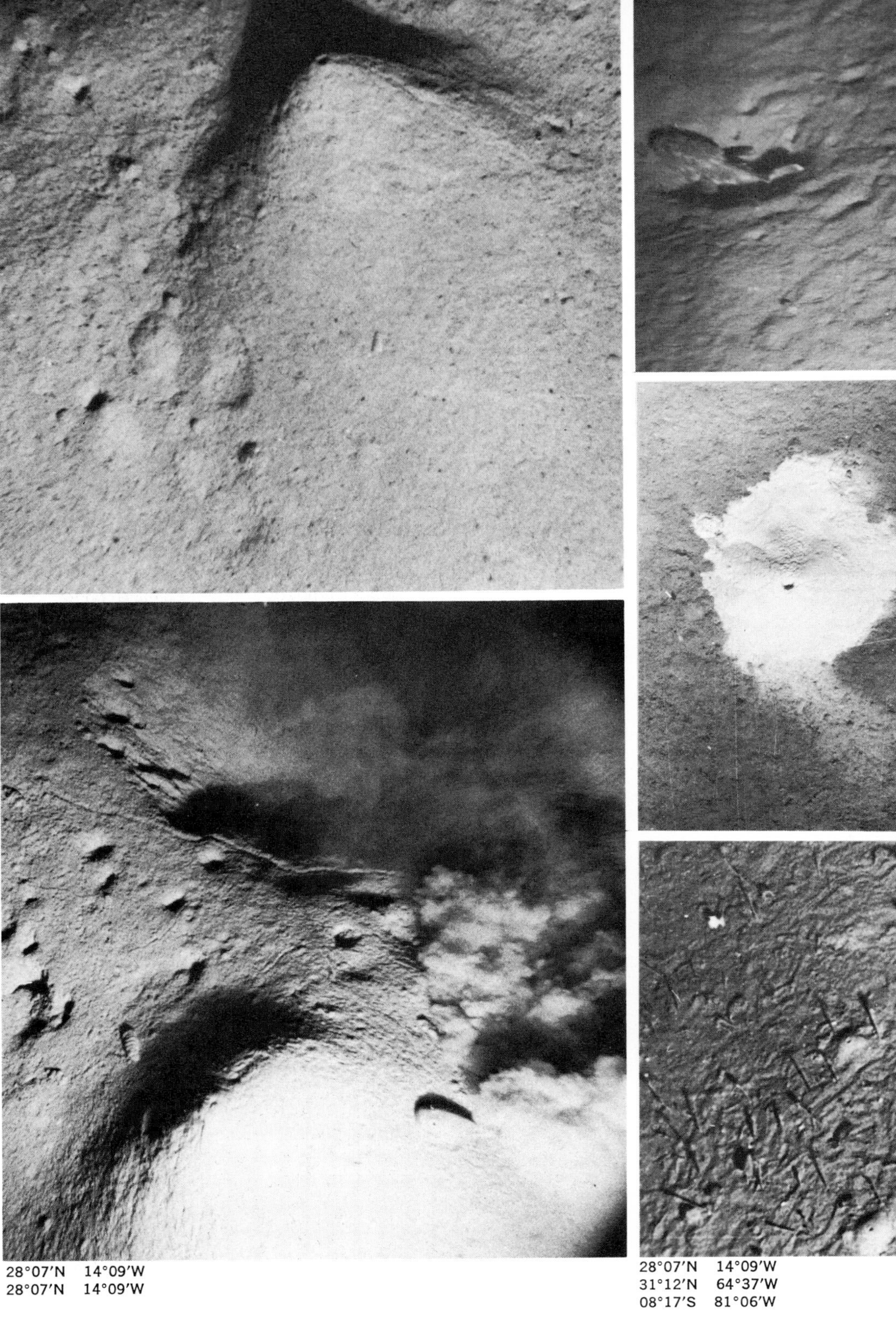

28°07′N 14°09′W
28°07′N 14°09′W

28°07′N 14°09′W
31°12′N 64°37′W
08°17′S 81°06′W

6.16 Animal volcanos. UL, Symmetrical cone with apical hole. UR, Fish in crater. LL, Fish emerging from crater, 686 m, Canary Islands. RC, Cone of white ooze ejected on dark sea floor, 4608 m, central Bermuda Rise. Light-colored material on the flank of the mound is streamed toward the lower right-hand corner of the picture. LR, Cones and worm tubes, 6238 m, floor of Peru-Chile Trench.

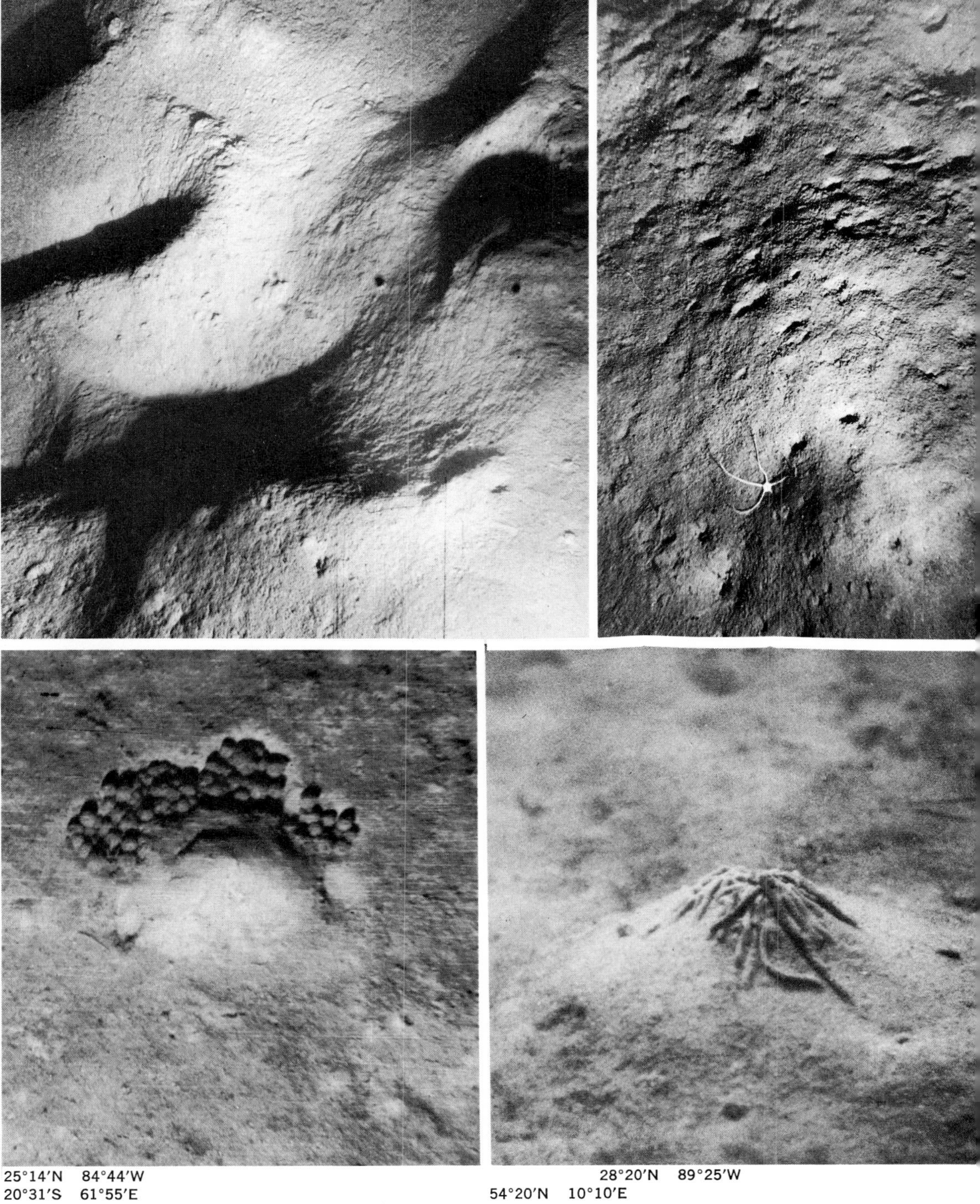

6.17 Cones, craters, and feces. UL, UR, 2003 m, Gulf of Mexico. LL, 3316 m, near Mauritius, western Indian Ocean. LR, 6 m, Baltic.

though certainly not the most common type of burrow, are so dramatic, so clear and so easily identified that they can be recorded under almost any condition of photography .

Sipunculids are worms about the size of a pencil which live in holes on the bottom. When feeding they spread a circle of tentacles on the surface of the mud and cause a current to flow by beating their cilia. Food

19°01′N 65°29′W

6.18 Symmetrical cones and log. 3988 m, south wall of Puerto Rico Trench.

is captured in the mucus covering their tentacles and carried to the mouth. When startled they contract into their burrow. Thus it is unlikely that they will be photographed although the holes and spoke-like impressions left by the tentacles in the mud may be commonly seen but unidentified. They move from place to place by burrowing through the sediment, leave but one hole in the bottom, and do not form tubes.

The echiuroids are unsegmented worms somewhat similar to the sipunculids but they live permanently in a U-shaped burrow through which they circulate water. The two openings may be from ten to one hundred centimeters apart. The burrows are kept clean and all debris is flushed out by powerful jets of water from the anus. A small cone is thus built

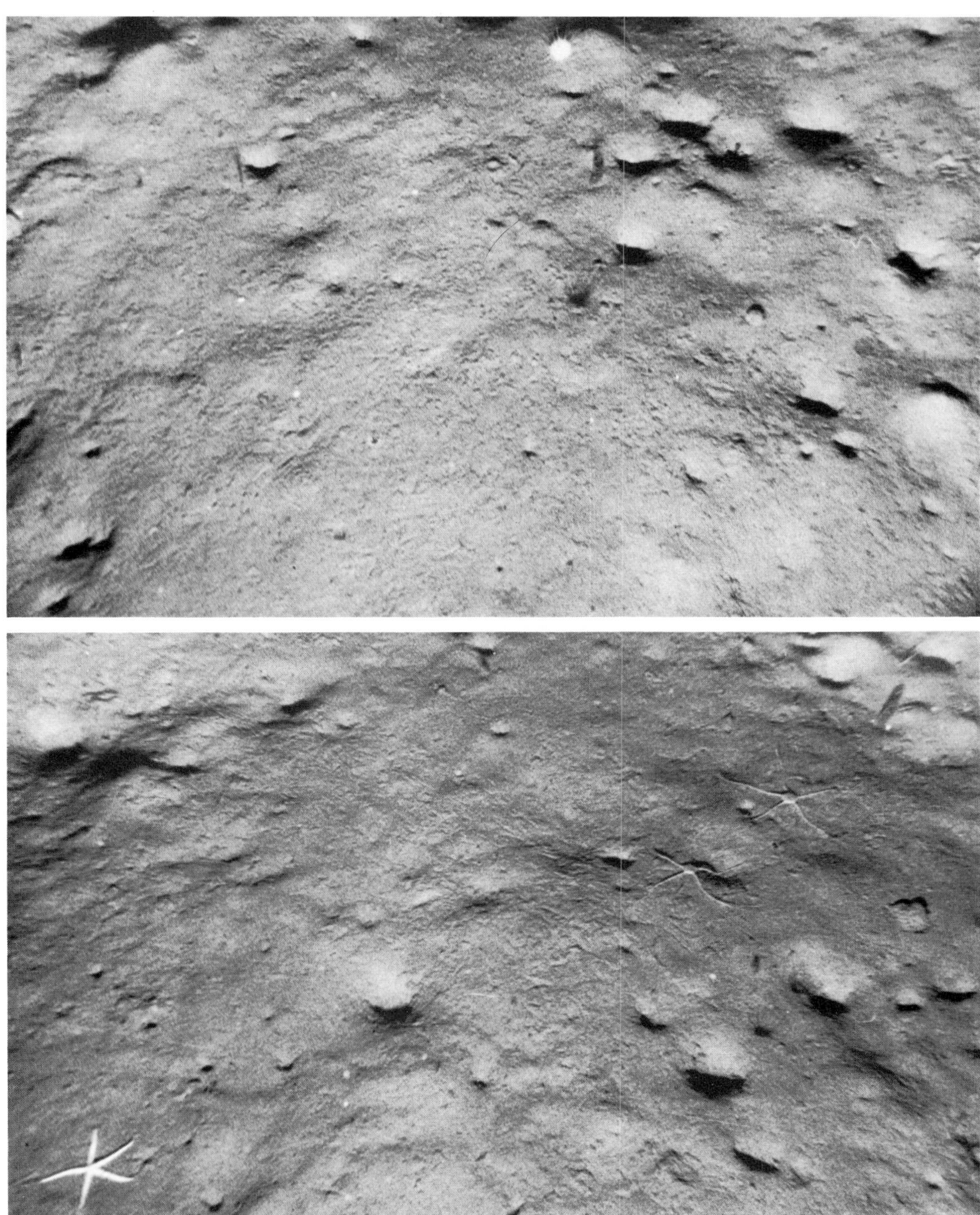

38°33'N 72°33'W
38°33'N 72°33'W

6.19 Rimless craters. The material excavated from these craters is nowhere to be seen. U, L, continental slope off New York, 2329 m.

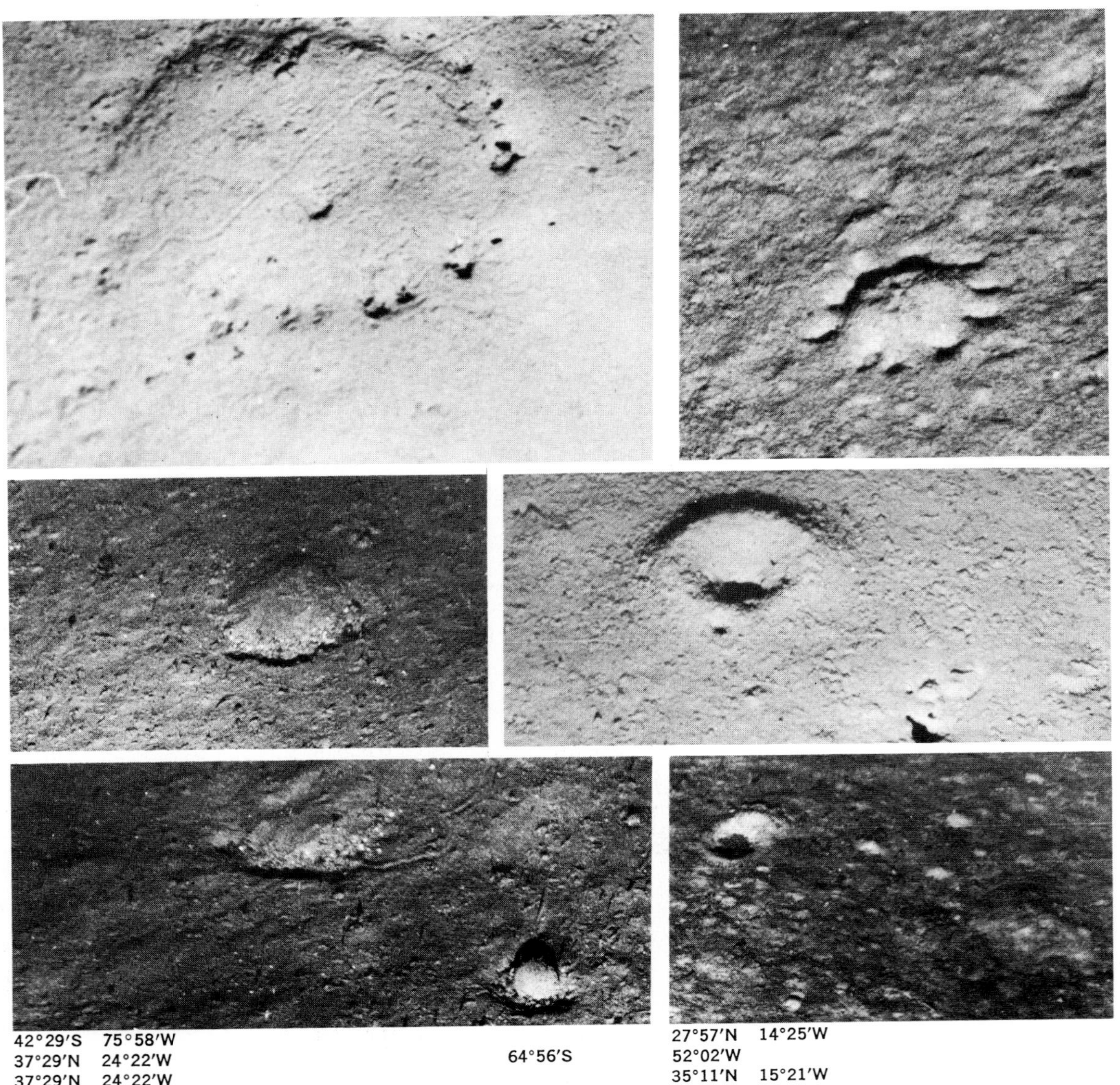

42°29′S 75°58′W
37°29′N 24°22′W
37°29′N 24°22′W
64°56′S
27°57′N 14°25′W
52°02′W
35°11′N 15°21′W

6.20 Craters and crater rings. UL, 3626 m, outer ridge, southern Peru-Chile Trench. UR, 1447 m, Canary Islands. LC, LL, 1222 m, Azores. LR, 2297 m, Whale Seamount, eastern North Atlantic. RC, 2916 m, Weddell Sea.

around one of the two holes. In feeding, the echiuroid slowly extends its proboscis from the burrow in one direction, capturing food in mucus which is drawn in stages to the mouth. The proboscis is then withdrawn and extended in another direction creating a spoke-like pattern on the sea floor. In fact one occasionally sees curious spoke-like patterns of impressions which radiate from a central hole (6.13, 6.14). The broad

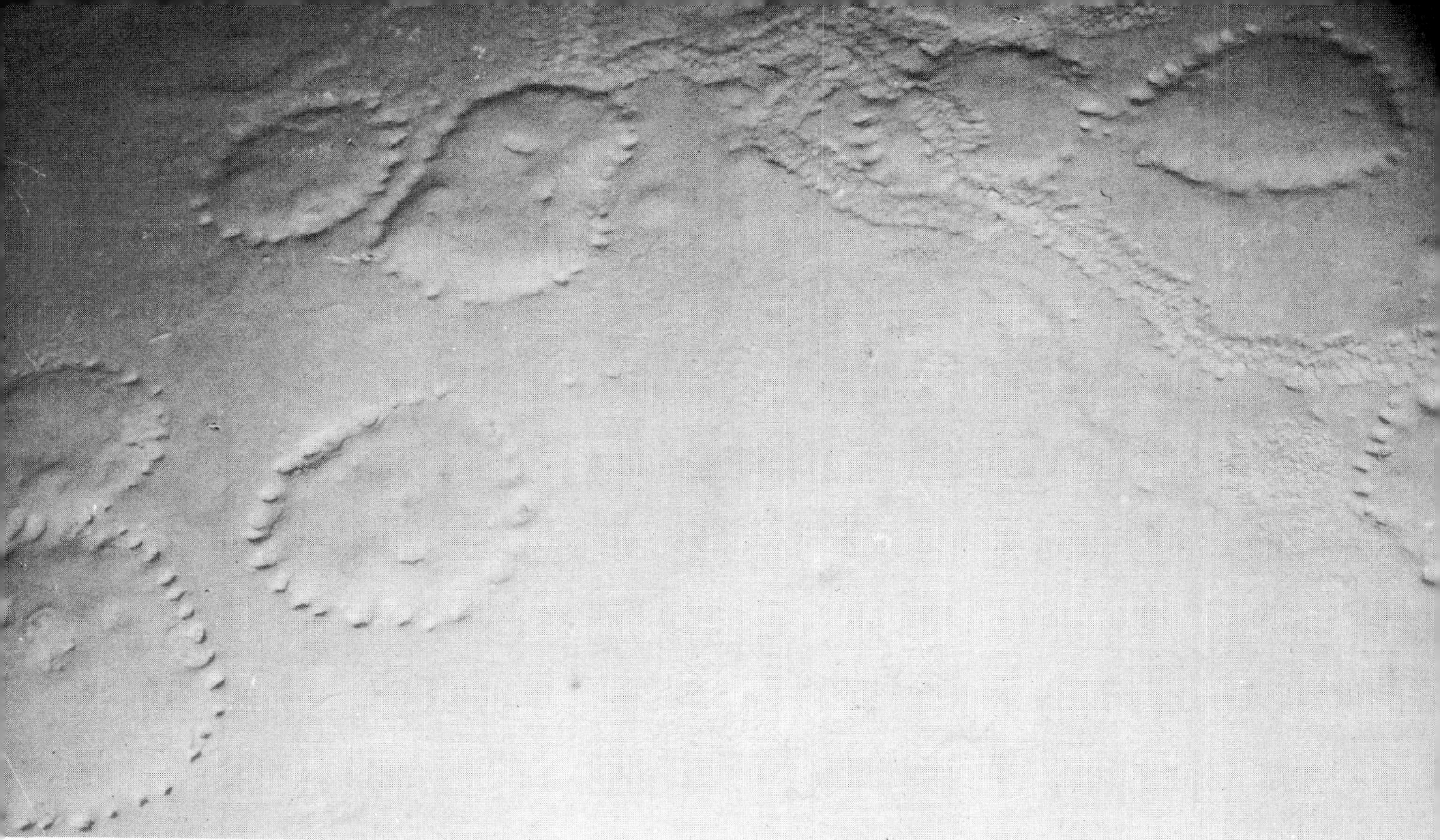

29°05′N 76°49′W

6.21 Crater rings and tread trails. 1810 m, Hatteras Outer Ridge, western Atlantic.

6.22 Cones and crater rings. Abundant echinoid plow marks, 3464 m, Mid-Oceanic Ridge, southwestern Pacific.

48°59′S 120°00′W

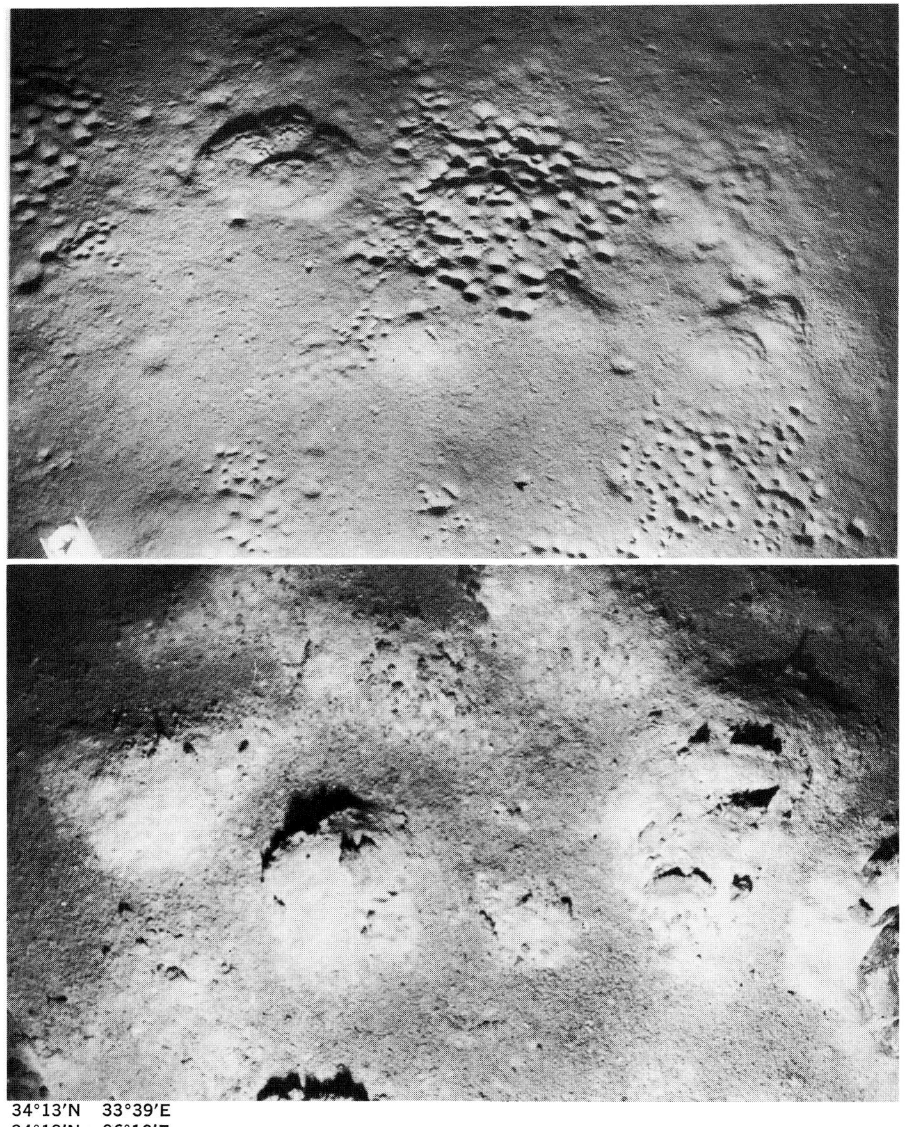

34°13′N 33°39′E
34°18′N 26°12′E

6.23 Crater fields and irregular mounds. U, 2683 m, Hecataeus Mountains south of Cyprus; L, 3099 m. Pliny Trench south of Crete.

shallow spokes are often from three to ten centimeters wide and up to fifty centimeters long. The animal responsible for this type of mark lives in the bottom beneath the central hole and occasionally probes the surrounding area with an appendage. Spoke patterns might also be created

6.24 Cones and holes. U, 686 m, Canary Islands. L, 1061 m, Red Sea. ▷

15°41′N 41°48′E

28°07′N 14°09′W

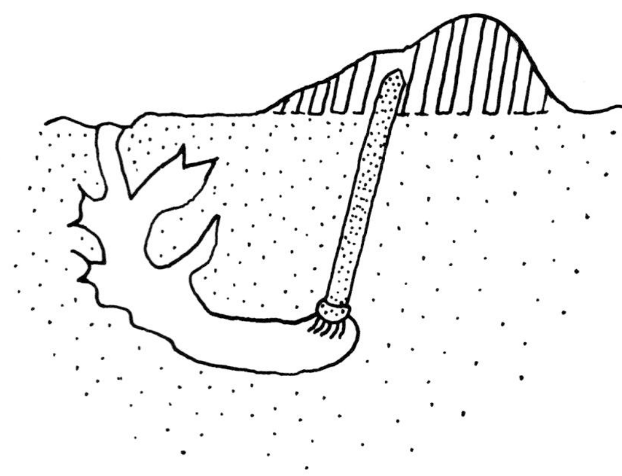

6.25 Worms produce both mounds and holes.

by the siphons of pelecypods (6.8). Similar patterns are found in ancient sediments (6.15).

Most of the annelids live on detritus or plankton and build permanent burrows lined with leathery tubes of mucus impregnated with bits of bottom material. They often withdraw one tentacle only to thrust it out again to continue feeding. This activity should produce a very fine radial pattern on the sea floor.

ANIMAL VOLCANOS

Some of the largest constructions seen in bottom photographs are miniature volcanic cones complete with apical vent (6.16, 6.17). Such cones have been observed in eruption in shallow waters (6.1). It can be expected that after the animal responsible for the cone dies or moves on the cone will remain visible on the sea floor for some time (6.18). As sediment gradually buries it the apical vent would certainly become filled and obliterated as the aging feature becomes a mere mound on the sea floor. Very often the material which has been excavated from beneath the bottom and thrown out from the vent is of a different color than the surrounding sediment (6.16 RC), and in some cases currents cause the mounds to become asymmetrical.

The vent of a perfect cone may be relatively small compared with the total size of the cone. However, there are other features on the sea floor which one might better describe as cone craters in which the crater is the dominant feature and large by comparison with the cone. Such cone

6.26 Cones and holes. 286 m, south of Great Inagua, Bahamas.

craters appear singly (6.19), in strange pock-like groups (6.20-6.22), scattered (6.23-6.26), or in curious straight rows (6.27) which end as mysteriously and abruptly as they begin. The volume of material contained in the cones surrounding the craters often appears to be less than the volume excavated; but in no case does the volume appear to be much greater. This, of course, suggests a shallow hole and a rather short blunt probe into the bottom; whereas cones suggest a rather deep and probing excavation (6.25). In the case of the cones and "cone craters" the material excavated resides in the cone or cone rim; however, other somewhat more mysterious craters are those in which no evidence of the ex-

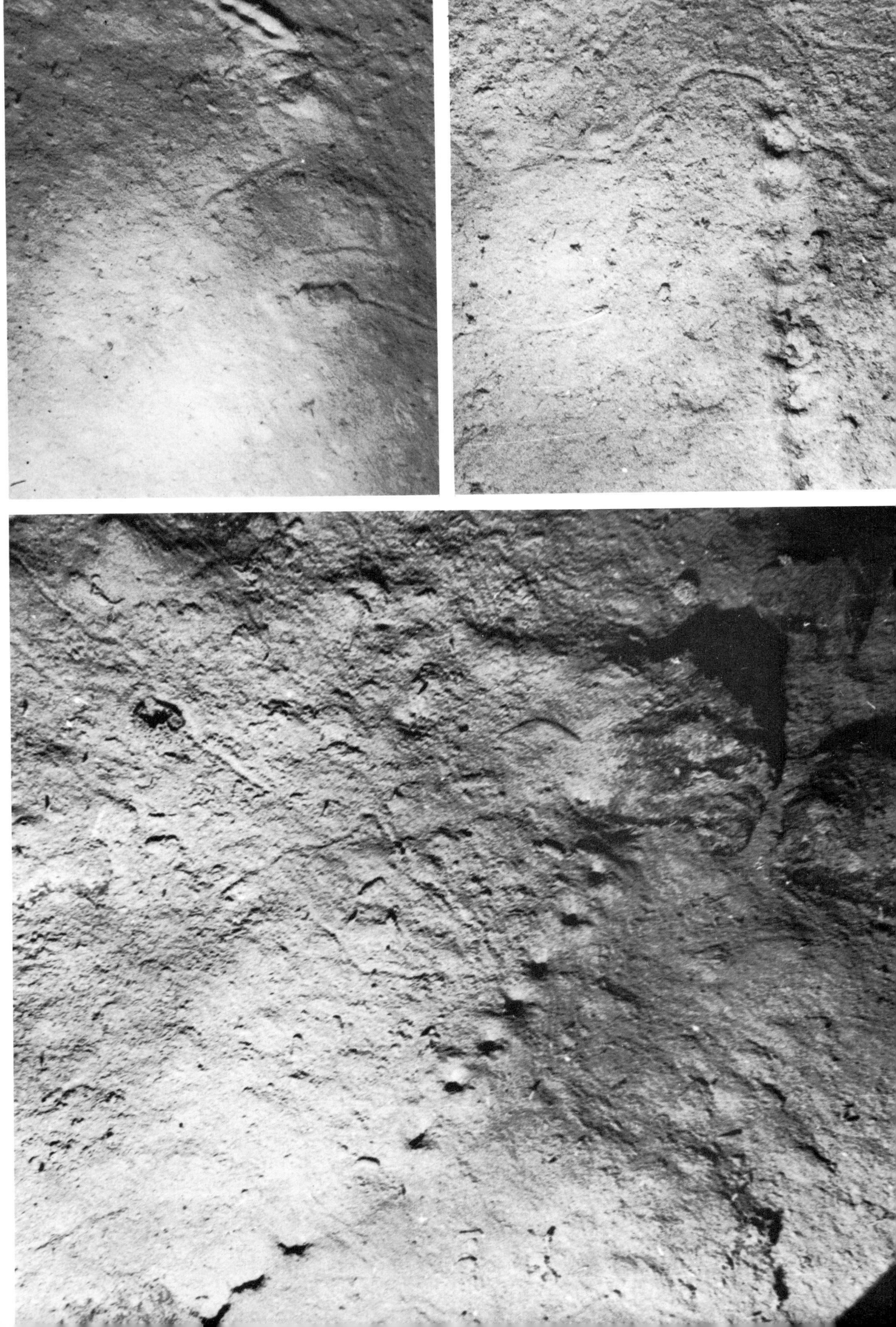

37°20′N 33°15′W
38°20′N 28°07′W

37°55′N 25°58′W

42°18′N 14°47′W
42°18′N 14°47′W

6.28 One-armed circle scriber. 5398 m, Iberia Abyssal Plain.

cavated sediments is seen (6.19). In exceptionally clear photographs one occasionally sees small circular drag marks that appear to be created by the bristles or tentacles of animals living in the mud (6.28-6.30) and there is some evidence that burrowing actinarians (6.31, 6.32) produce craters in the ooze.

◁ 6.27 Crater rows. UL, UR, L, 1723 m, 1580 m, 1471 m, Azores.

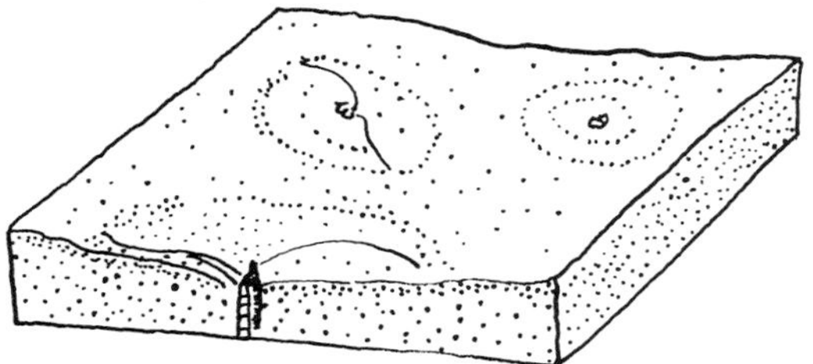

6.29 Circle-scribing bristle worm.

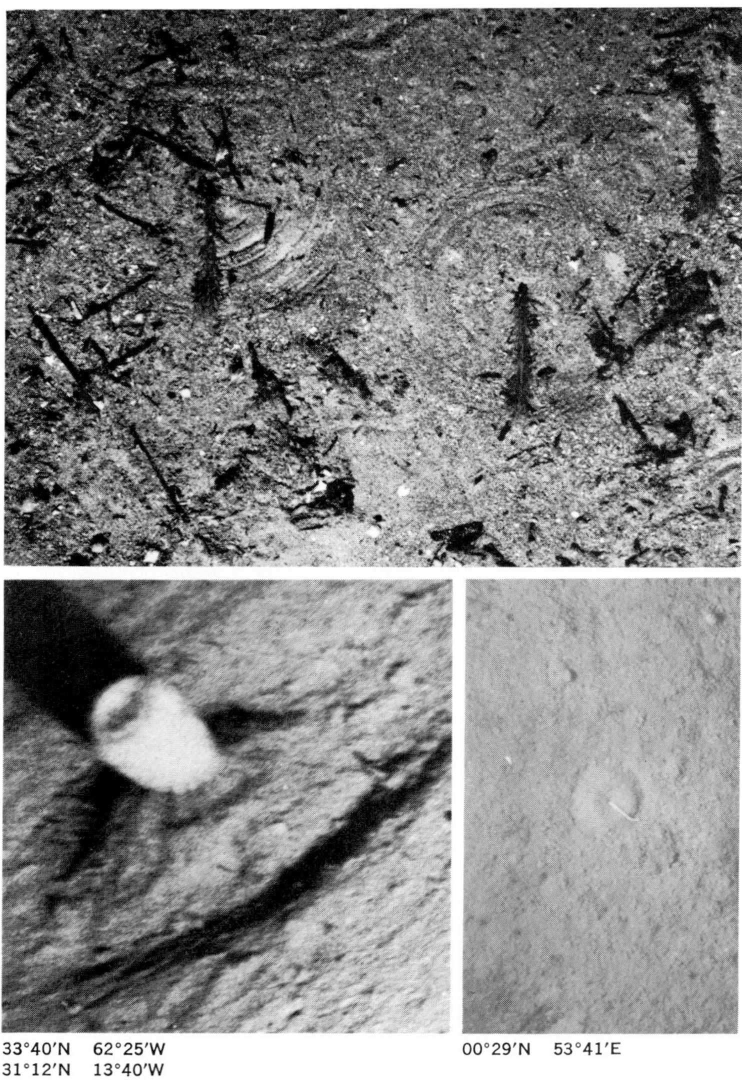

33°40′N 62°25′W
31°12′N 13°40′W

00°29′N 53°41′E

6.30 Circle scribers. U, 1602 m, Muir Seamount. LL, Sponge, 301 m, Dacia Seamount. LR, 4853 m, Somali Basin.

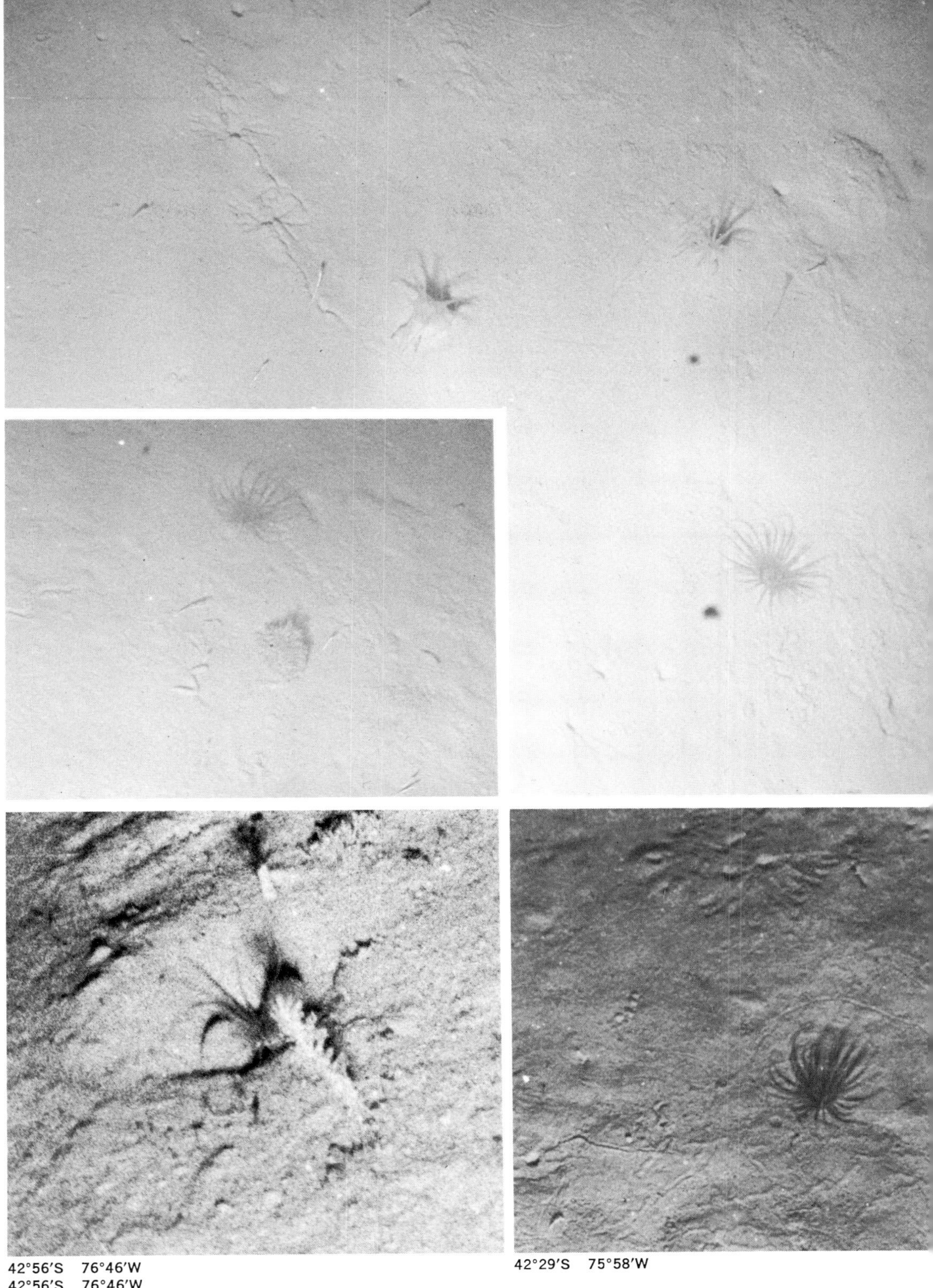

42°56′S 76°46′W
42°56′S 76°46′W
48°54′S 75°59′W

42°29′S 75°58′W

6.31 Spokes, craters, and grooves. U, Actinarians and spokes, LC, Actinarians and a bristle worm or sea mouse (cf. *Aphrodite*), 3698 m, outer ridge, southern Peru-Chile Trench. LL, Animal in crater, 994 m, continental slope, southern Chile. LR, Spokes and actinarian, 3626 m, outer ridge, southern Peru-Chile Trench.

39°49′N 68°57′W
48°59′S 120°00′W

6.32 Abyssal burrowing actinarians. U, 2147 m, continental slope off New England. L, 3461 m, Mid-Oceanic Ridge, South Pacific.

During our journey through the inhabited abyss we have viewed many animal markings. In some cases we have been able to attribute them to certain animals or even to specific functions such as walking, crawling, burrowing, or defecating. These few dozen exceptional views have been selected from about 100,000 photographs. Each is the best available and many are the only examples known. Thus, you may rightfully inquire:

6.33 Mounds and holes in the shallow water of the Cariaco Trench (U) contrasts sharply with the soft flocculent bottom (L) devoid of any evidence for recent bioturbations on the floors of this stagnant basin. Burrowing is absent in sediments cored from the trench floor, U, 360 m, east slope of trench wall; L, 905 m, floor of Cariaco Trench.

0°48′N 65°04′W

10°39′N 65°04′W

6.34 Animals in ventilated seas mix and till the muds whereas numerous fine stratifications are left intact where lack of oxygen prevents animals from flourishing. Cariaco Trench, 900 m.

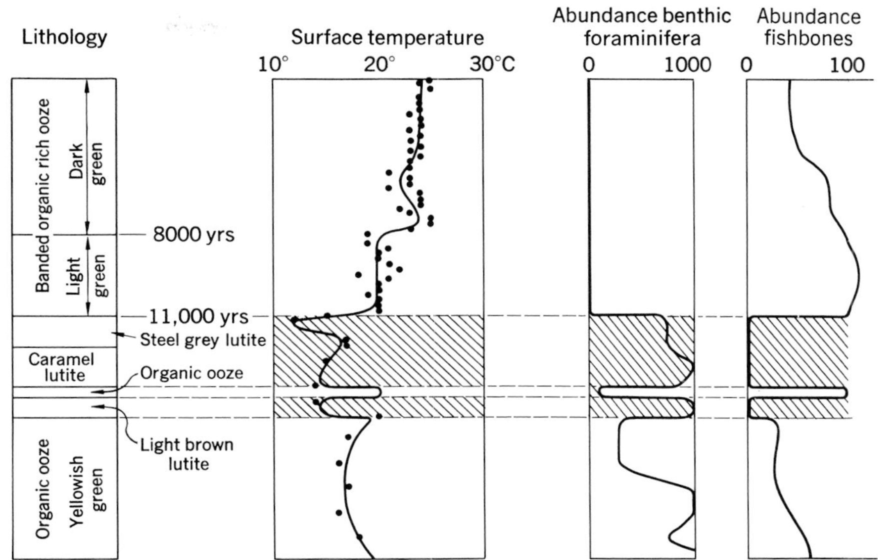

6.35 The rise of sea level at the end of the last ice age, ten thousand years ago, allowed cold waters to flow over the shallow sill into the Cariaco Trench. These dense waters prevented the oxygenated surface waters from reaching the sea floor. Soon the oxygen was exhausted, bottom life extinguished and subsequently thin annual layers accumulated undisturbed by bottom life.

"What about the rest of the photographs? What do they show?" They show mounds, bumps, vague impressions which cause the sea floor to be irregular on a scale of a few centimeters. These bumps of uncertain origin are the dominant features and in fact the only features seen in the vast majority of sea floor photographs. Some must be fecal pellets, some may actually be animals, others are the cones of burrowers in various stages of construction or destruction.[5] Most must result from the activity of animals for the black, lifeless floors of the stagnant basins have neither tracks, trails, cones, craters, burrows, nor large mounds (6.33, 6.34).

FEATURELESS FLOORS

It is difficult to ascertain at what concentration oxygen begins to control the benthic population.[6] Since the oxygen concentration in the bottom waters of the principal ocean basins seldom drops below 50 per cent of the oxygen concentration of the surface waters, this factor should not be

12°02′S 168°53′W

6.36, 6.37, 6.38 Animal traces in the abyssal Pacific. A representative station, 5331 m, equatorial Pacific. ▷

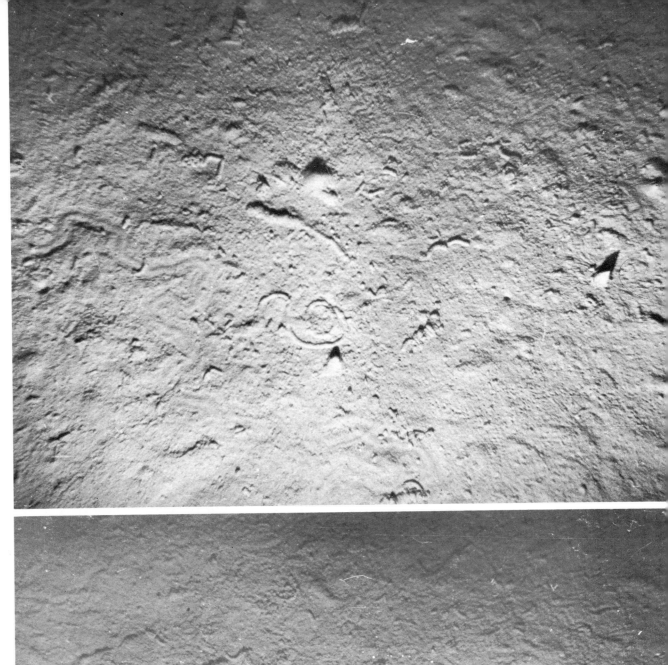

significant in the over-all form of the seascape. However, in the poorly ventilated Mediterranean and other isolated basins which have at times in the geologic past become stagnant, oxygen supply is a significant factor controlling the type and distribution of animal traces.

The stagnant floors are however not featureless but have a special character of their own (6.33). The flocculent surface has a coarse irregular appearance somewhat resembling the accumulation of lint and dust in an ill-kept bedroom. Curiously, it is covered by a continuous succession of low indistinct mounds. The flocculent appearance is quite understandable since in the absence of benthic organisms and without bottom currents there is nothing to break down or smooth out the accumulating organic and inorganic debris. The general background of low mounds is perhaps more puzzling; particularly so if one is prone to identify all the mounds in the inhabited abyss as animal excavations in various stages of construction or burial.

The sediments of one such stagnant basin are thinly stratified, each pair of thin laminae representing a year's accumulation. Five meters of this unburrowed ooze has collected since the Cariaco Trench stagnated at the end of the last glaciation (6.35). The unlaminated deposits laid down in this basin before the stagnation bear clear evidence of mixing and burrowing of benthic organisms. One explanation of the faint low mounds observed in the now barren seascape is that they reflect the smoothed outline of cones and bumps lying five or more meters below. Some must surely be of this origin. But can we so attribute all of them or must we look for an inorganic process which produces low mounds?

Mounds, mounds, mounds, mounds, that is about all one sees in the average ocean-floor photographs. To illustrate our point, we have reproduced six photographs from a random location in the equatorial Pacific (6.36-6.38) and four from a random location in mid-Atlantic (6.39, 6.40). No animals are seen, and indeed one should not expect to see any, for only one out of fifty mid-latitude abyssal photographs reveals an organism large enough to be recognized. Among the mounds one sees an occasional nearly obliterated furrow and here and there the barely recognizable outlines of holothurian feces. A few fairly clear plow marks are seen but no footprints; just mounds, mounds, mounds, mounds (6.41).

25°15′N 25°45′W

6.39, 6.40 Animal traces in the abyssal Atlantic. A representative station, 5292 m, eastern Atlantic. ▷

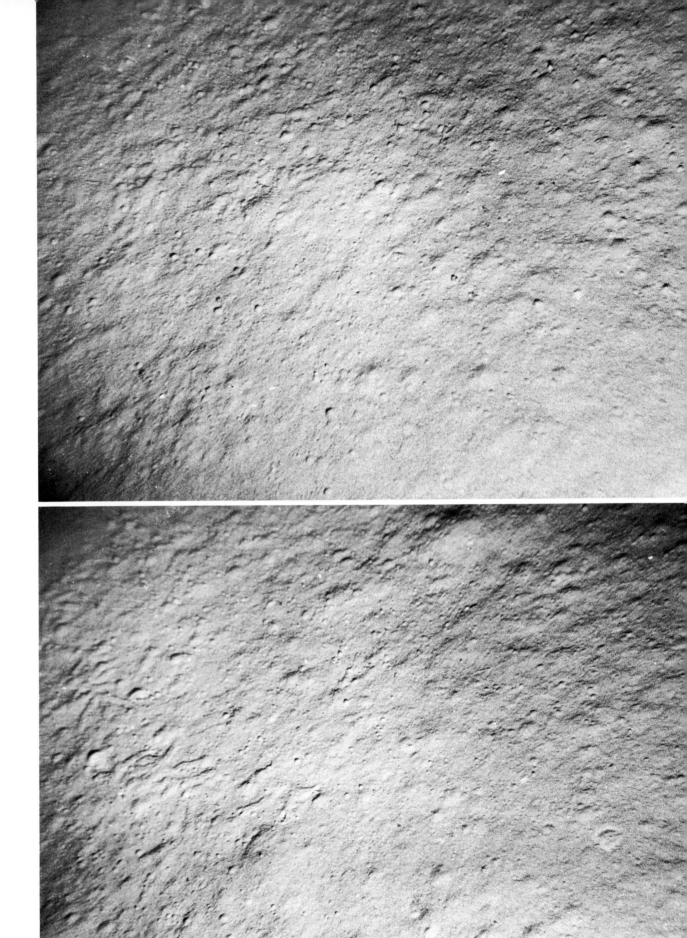

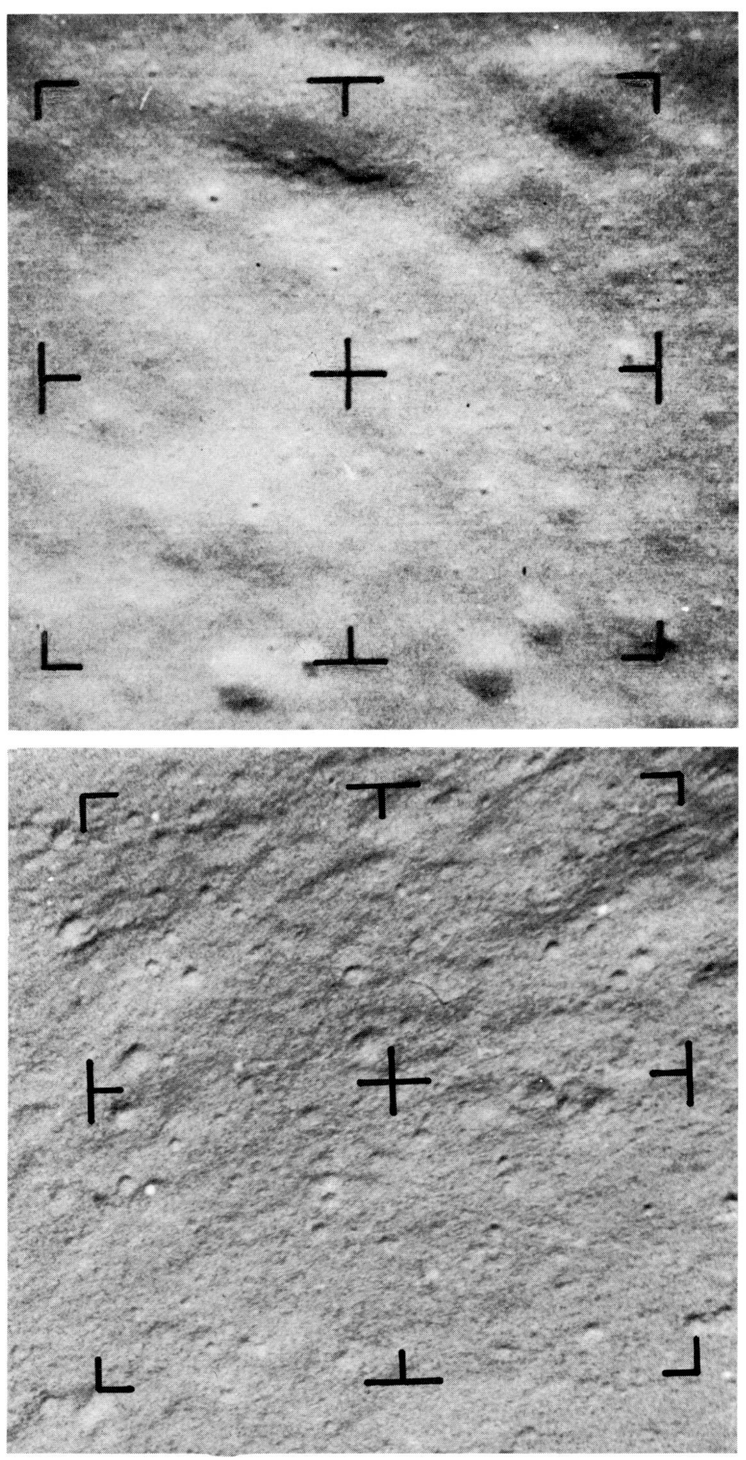

6.41 Which one is the moon?

REFERENCES AND NOTES

1. Zoologists distinguish between the animals living buried *in* the mud (infauna) and those living *on* the mud (epifauna). This chapter concerns the infauna and their work, particularly those larger species which create mounds and burrows (A. C. Hardy, 1959. *The Open Sea. Its Natural History*. Houghton Mifflin, Boston, Pt. 2:94-122). An extensive literature exists on the features left by worms, molluscs, and various other burrowing organisms. (W. H. Bucher, 1928. Observations on organisms and sedimentation on shallow sea-bottoms. *Amer. Midland Naturalist,* 11:235-42).

2. R. Y. Morita and C. E. Zobell, 1955. Occurrence of bacteria in pelagic sediments collected during the Mid-Pacific Expedition. *Deep-Sea Res.,* 3:66-73.

3. The first significant study of stratification in deep-sea cores with photographic illustrations and lithologic logs was published by M. N. Bramlette and W. H. Bradley (1941. Lithology and geologic interpretations. In W. H. Bradley, editor. Geology and Biology of North Atlantic Deep-Sea Cores between Newfoundland and Ireland. *U.S. Geol. Survey, Prof. Paper,* 196:1-32). Virtually all twenty-two cores illustrated by G. Arrhenius (1952. Sediment cores from the east Pacific. *Reports Swedish Deep Sea Exped.,* 5:244 pp.) show evidence of burrowing. Burrowing has a practical application to the study of stratification in that it tends to homogenize the upper few centimeters and those events recorded by extremely fine layers of sediments are often obliterated from the deep-sea stratigraphic record as revealed in sediment cores.

4. R. F. Dill told us of his observations of shrimp. The bathyscaphe pilot is again G. S. Houot (1960. Deep diving off Japan. *Nat. Geog. Mag.,* 117:138-50; and 1958. Four years of diving to the bottom of the sea. *Nat. Geog. Mag.,* 113:715-31).

5. A. S. Laughton (1963. Microtopography. In M. N. Hill, editor. *The Sea.* Wiley, New York, 3:437-73) has estimated from bottom photographs that about 5 to 10 per cent of the deep-sea floor and about 10 to 20 per cent of shallower bottoms on seamounts and the continental slope is covered with disturbances of three centimeters or larger. Three centimeters is about the resolution limit of modern photographs and the vast majority of deep-sea animals are much smaller and produce features smaller than this. One may expect that improvements in resolution will tend to increase the proportion of bottom which is visibly disturbed. Another illustrated discussion of microrelief is found in: C. J. Shipeck, 1966. Photoanalysis of sea-floor microrelief. *U.S. Navy Electronic Laboratory, Report,* 1374:70 pp.

6. There is generally an oxygen minimum in the ocean lying between 500 meters' and 1000 meters' depth. The fact that the organic content of the sediment where this minimum impinges on the sea floor is significantly higher suggests that the benthic population and the depth of penetration of burrowers there must be greatly diminished. In this region the visual seascape should contain fewer mounds, holes, and tracks (F. A. Richards and A. C. Redfield, 1954. A correlation between the oxygen content of seawater and the organic content of marine sediments. *Deep-Sea Res.,* 1:279-81; F. A. Richards, 1957. Oxygen in the ocean. *Geol. Soc. Am. Memoir,* 67:185-238).

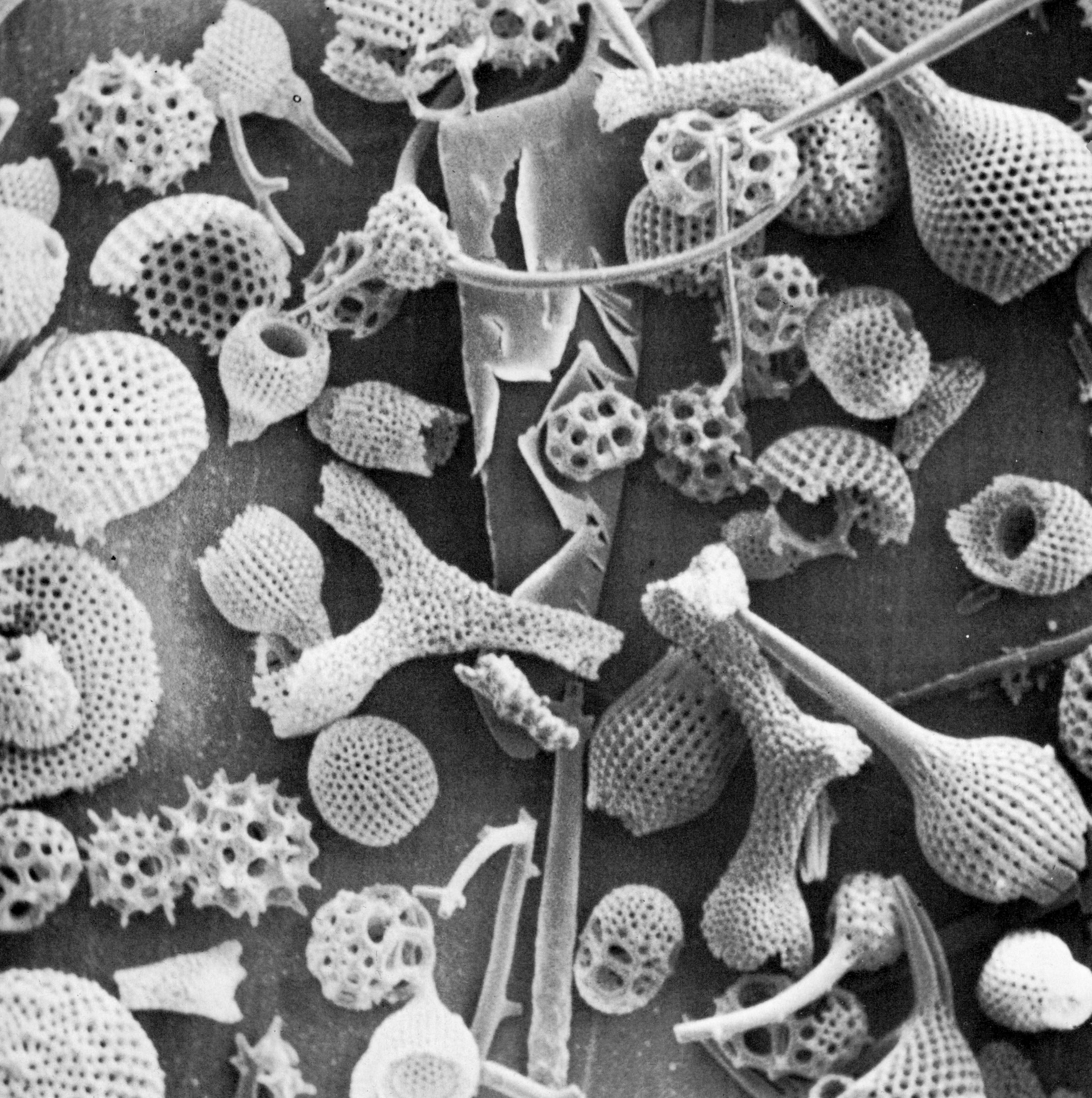

09°18′N 142°33′E

7.1 Planktonic Radiolaria. These delicate siliceous shells are common in abyssal sediments of the great depths. Scanning electron micrograph (x200), Lower Miocene from Deep-Sea Drilling Project hole 55, 80 meters below the sea floor in 4383m, Caroline Ridge.

7
The Deep Six

The wrecks dissolve above us; their dust drops down from afar—
Down to the dark, to the utter dark where the blind white sea snakes are
There is no sound, no echo of sound in the deserts of the deep
On the great grey level plains of ooze where the shell buried cables creep
Here in the womb of the world, here on the tie ribs of the earth
Words and the words of men flicker, and flutter and beat.

RUDYARD KIPLING

In addition to a gentle, voluminous, and unrelenting snowfall of clay and ooze (7.1),[1] the ocean floor intermittently receives consignments of a large size: rocks plucked from the land and later dropped from melting icebergs; stomach stones disgorged by sea lions; rocks borne to sea by rotting giant algae; garbage, paper, radioactively contaminated tools and waste[2]; junk, wrecks from peace and war; artillery projectiles; clinkers from coal-burning steamships; ballast; telephone and telegraph cables; beer bottles, tin cans (7.2), and much more, (7.3) imaginable, virtually unimaginable, and sometimes, unmentionable.

JUNK

So many clinkers were dumped in the North Atlantic during the time of coal-burning steam vessels that one frequently dredges them from the mid-Atlantic. Oceanographers lose wire, coring rigs, cameras, thermometers, water samplers (7.4), and all sorts of other valuable instruments. Dud explosives litter the sea floor. Yet despite the hundreds of wrecks and millions of bottles and cans which have been thrown into the sea, one rarely sees any evidence of these marks of man in the abyss (7.5).

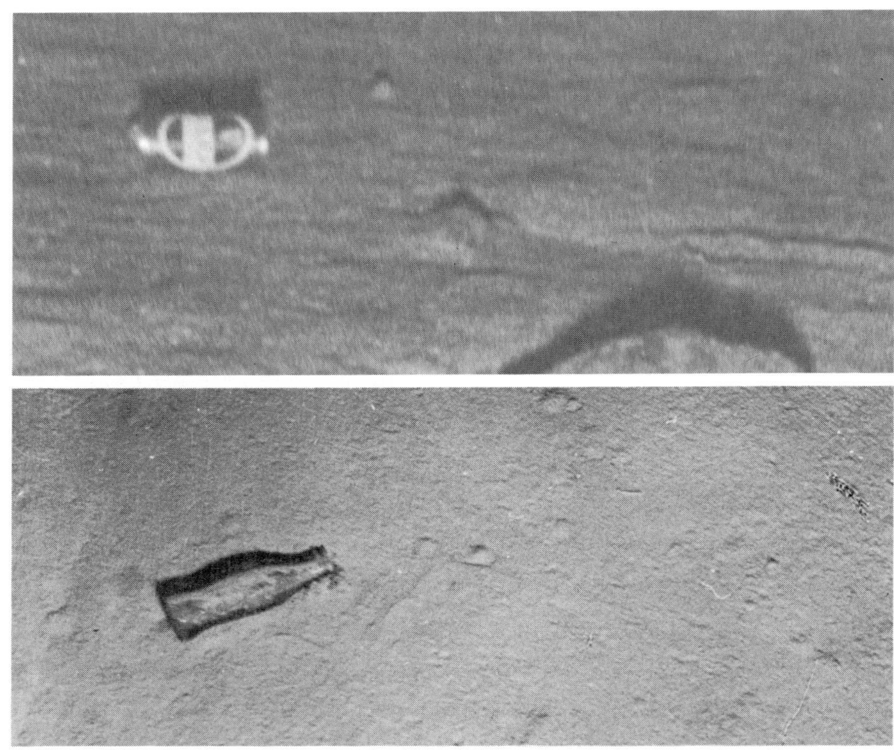

19°02′N 65°23′W
33°00′N 70°32′W

7.2 Bottle and can in Davey's Locker. U, empty Harp beer can, 3307 m, Puerto Rico Trench. L, Coca-Cola bottle, 5378 m, Hatteras Abyssal Plain.

32°44′N 117°22′W

7.3 Everything but. . . . This sink was photographed from *Deep Star 4000,* 250 m, continental slope off La Jolla, California.

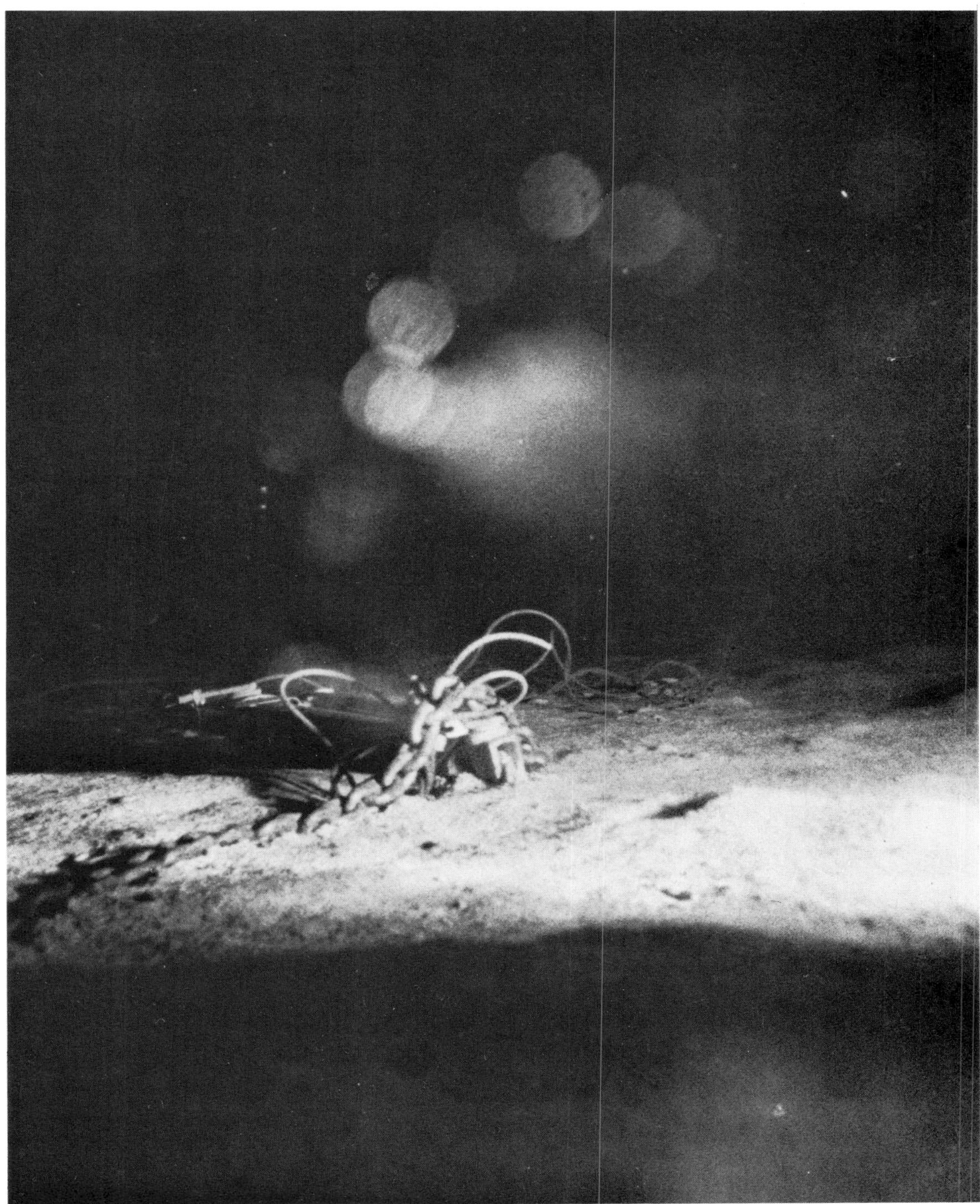

48°21′N 17°35′W

7.4 Tools of oceanographers. Thermometer and water sampler (Nansen bottle), wire rope and chain lying on the ooze, 4129 m, Mid-Atlantic Ridge.

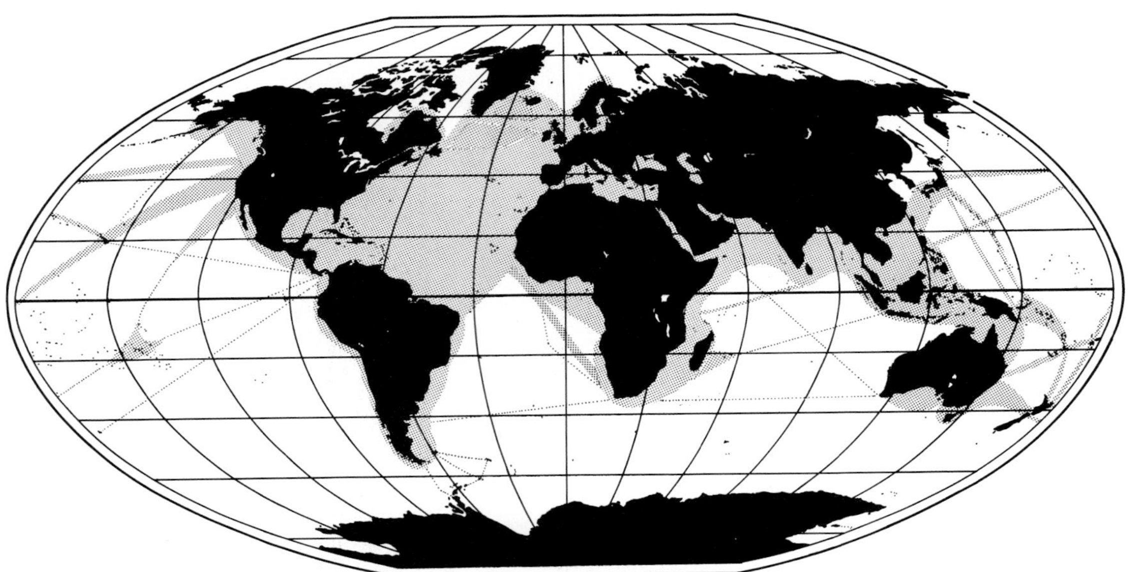

7.5 Trade routes. Man's debris litters the sea floor beneath the shipping lanes.

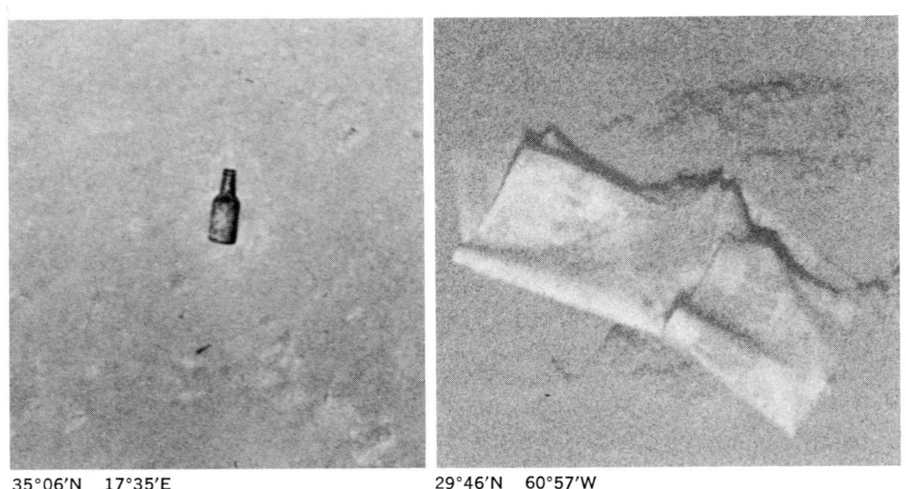

7.6 Bottles, and newspapers. R, folded newspaper, 5592 m, the western Atlantic. L, bottle, 2895 m, Ionian Sea.

Geologists often refer to various strata by their characteristic fossil remains. During the nineteenth and early twentieth centuries the bed of the North Atlantic received the clinker formation, but that era ended with the advent of petroleum-powered ships. Now we have entered a

7.7 Lost tools or dumped junk? 2068 m, Puerto Rico Trench. Note white crab-like animals living within the structure.

new era—that of the bottles and cans (7.6). Recently, a Coca-Cola bottle was photographed on an abyssal plain at over 5000 meters' depth (7.2 L). Since it will take considerable time for the glass to disintegrate, this will be a rather good fossil. In the Puerto Rico Trench we have photographed an empty can, which had contained Irish beer (7.2 U), and large fragments of structural steel (7.7). We suspect, however, that the accumulation of sediment is slow enough that beer cans will be largely destroyed by corrosion before they are buried.

WRECKS

Throughout the history of man's navigation of the oceans, ships have been lost and sunk to the bottom of the sea.[3] Wrecks are naturally fascinating subjects; the thought of ancient relics and gold bullion interests not only the archaeologist, but almost everyone. Recently, several groups

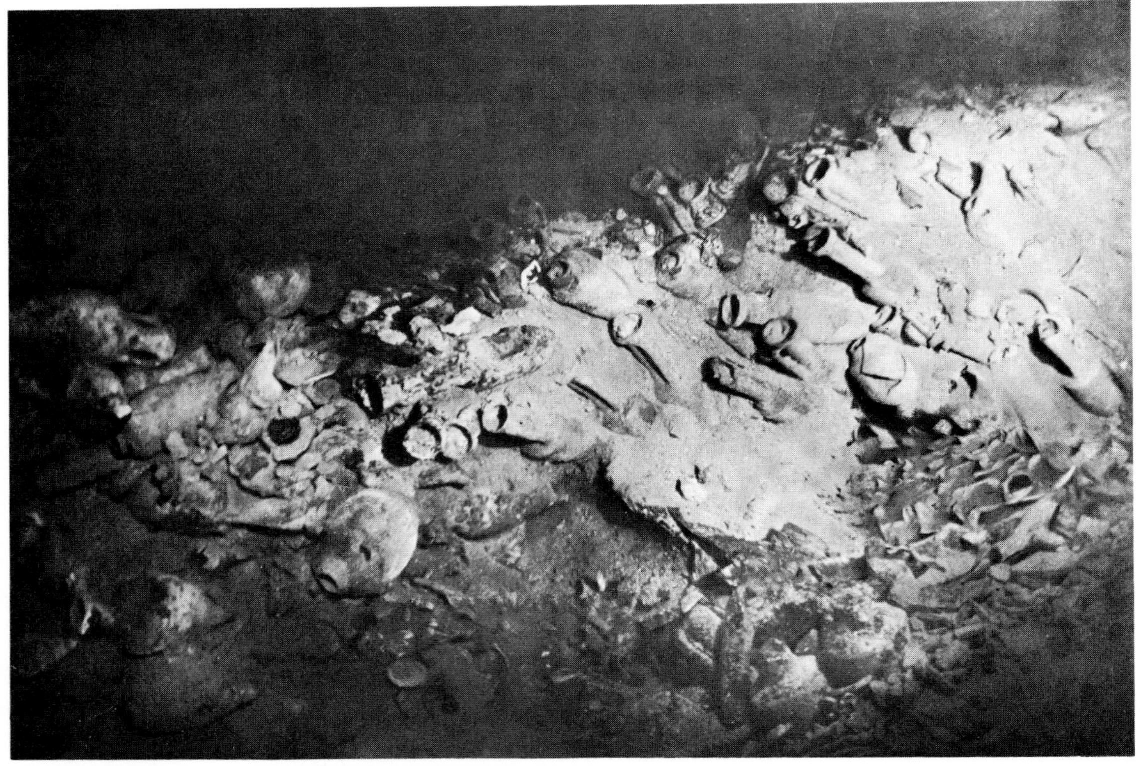

43°05′N 5°20′E

35°43′N 22°27′E

7.8 Amphora consigned to the deep. U, wine jars in the hold of a third century B.C. wine ship. Elongate jars are Roman; fuller-bellied ones are Greek, 45 m, continental shelf off Marseilles. L, amphora serves as the coffin of an unfortunate Greek, 3800 m, eastern Mediterranean Sea.

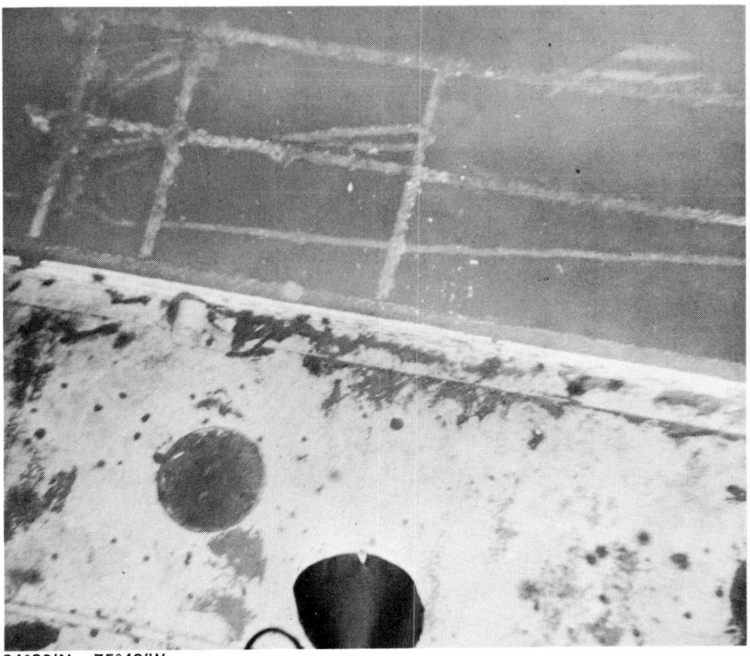

34°39′N 75°48′W
34°49′N 75°33′W

7.9 Torpedoed tankers off Cape Hatteras. These pictures were taken in mid-summer 1943 by scientists of the Woods Hole Oceanographic Institution. U, 44 m; L, 59 m.

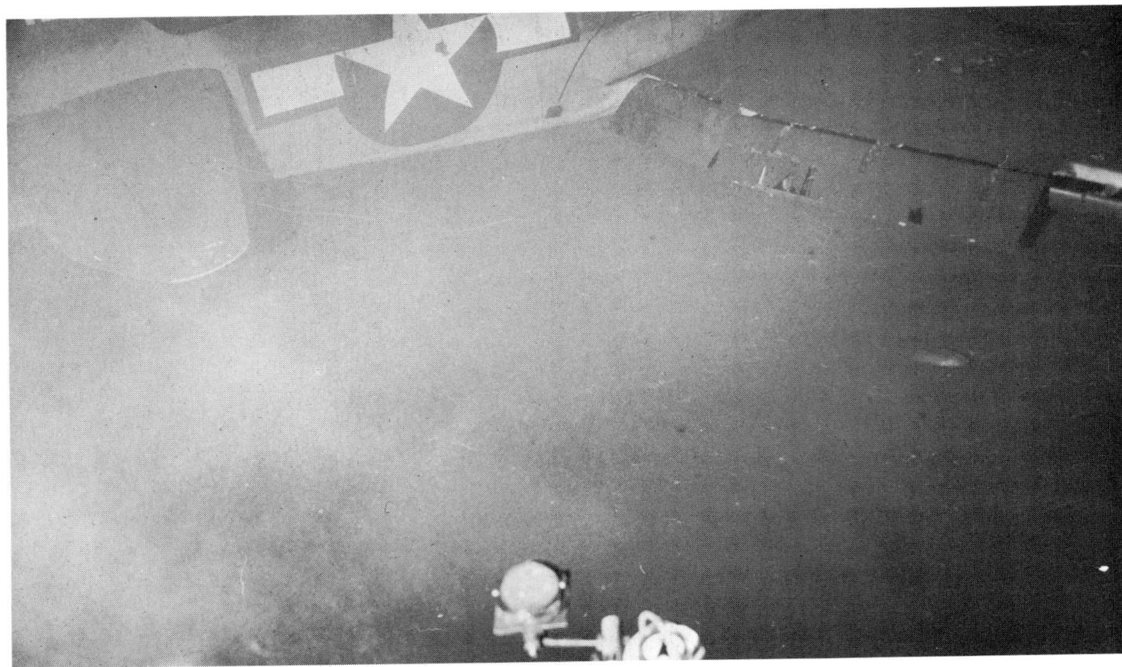

40°07′N 68°16′W

7.10 Fighter plane accidentally consigned to Davy Jones' locker. This Navy Hellcat, which crashed into the sea in 1944, was photographed 24 years later from a submersible, 1709 m, continental slope off New England.

have explored and recovered pre-Christian classical wrecks in the Mediterranean. Beautiful wine vessels known as amphora (7.8), which were recovered literally by the hundreds from a wreck not far from Marseilles, are now so well known that they are a diver's "trademark." Most wrecks which have been discovered, and almost all of those which have been explored, were found in extremely shallow water. During World War II, oceanographers were able to locate and identify the wrecks of many of the ships torpedoed off the eastern United States (7.9).

Although wrecks can be located easily in the shallow waters of the continental shelf, the same task in oceanic depths is difficult and in many areas impossible to accomplish with present-day equipment (7.10). The first wreck identification in abyssal depths was the crushed hull of the submarine *Thresher* detected in 2500 meters on the continental slope of eastern North America.[4] Subsequently, the hull of the lost submarine *Scorpion* was photographed in a depth over 4000 meters in the mid-Atlantic. The location of the *Thresher* by echo-soundings and magnetic surveys, the identification of it through dredging and photography (7.11), and the final confirmation by bathyscaphe observations provided a somber demonstration of the advanced state of the art of deep-sea exploration.

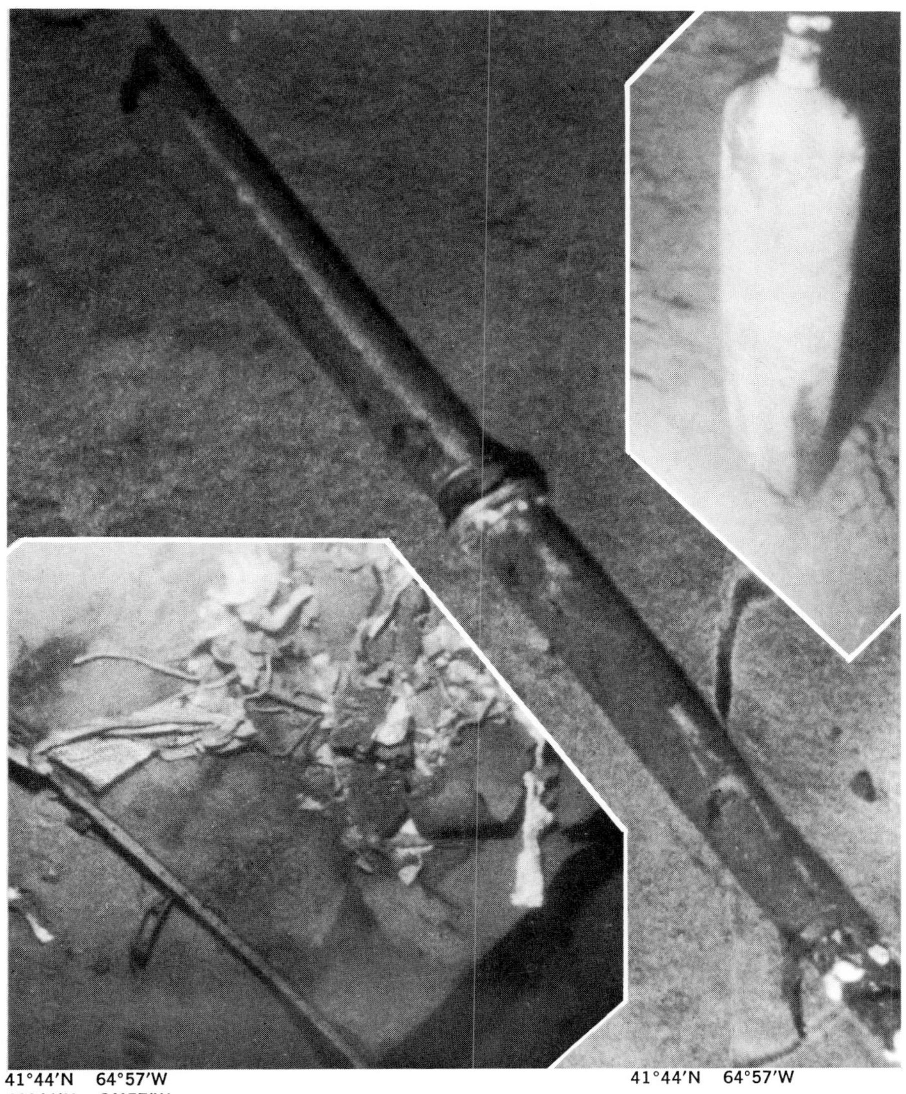

7.11 Fragments of the submarine *Thresher*. A large area of the seafloor off the entrance to the Gulf of Maine is covered with debris from the *Thresher,* lost with all hands April 10, 1963, in 2500 meters of water.

THE WORDS OF MEN

Over the last century a cable system (7.12) was steadily extended throughout all the oceans of the world, yet it was only a few years ago that cables were observed and photographed in their working environment on the sea floor (7.13, 7.14).[5]

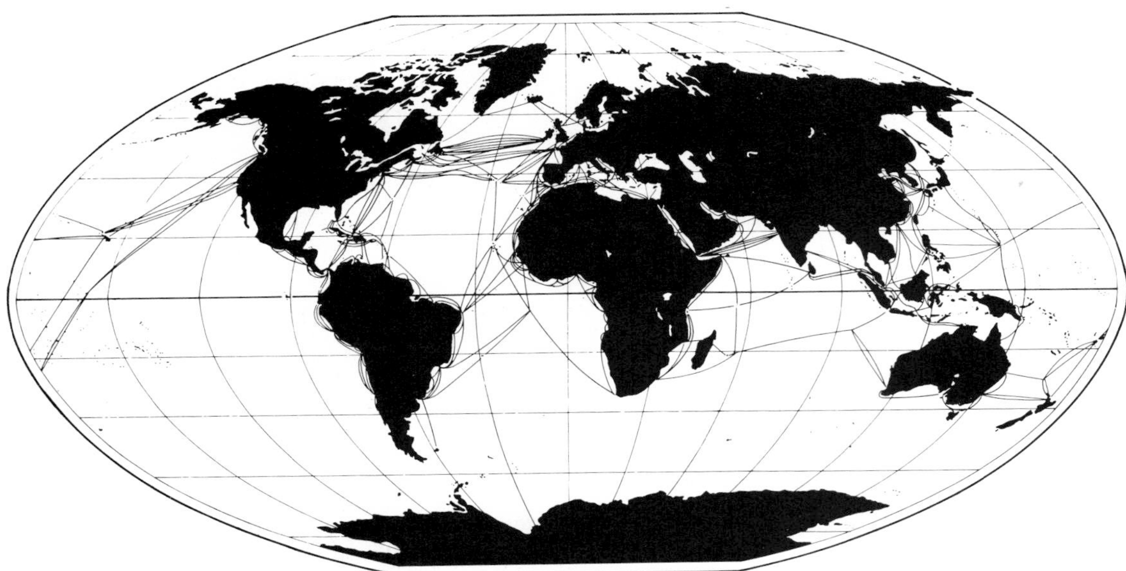

7.12 "Where the shell buried cables creep."

7.13 A transatlantic telephone cable. Continental shelf off New Jersey.

50°49′N 50°44′W

7.14 Transatlantic telephone cable. U, L, 413 m, Grand Banks of Newfoundland. ▷

Now that we have viewed the few startling but barely significant visible traces left by man in the abyss we shall turn to more significant contributions. Next we will examine the work of other large animals and plants which swim or float at the surface of the sea. Then we will consider volcanic and cosmic fall-out, ice, and, finally, the massive drift of dust which creates the substance of the seascape.

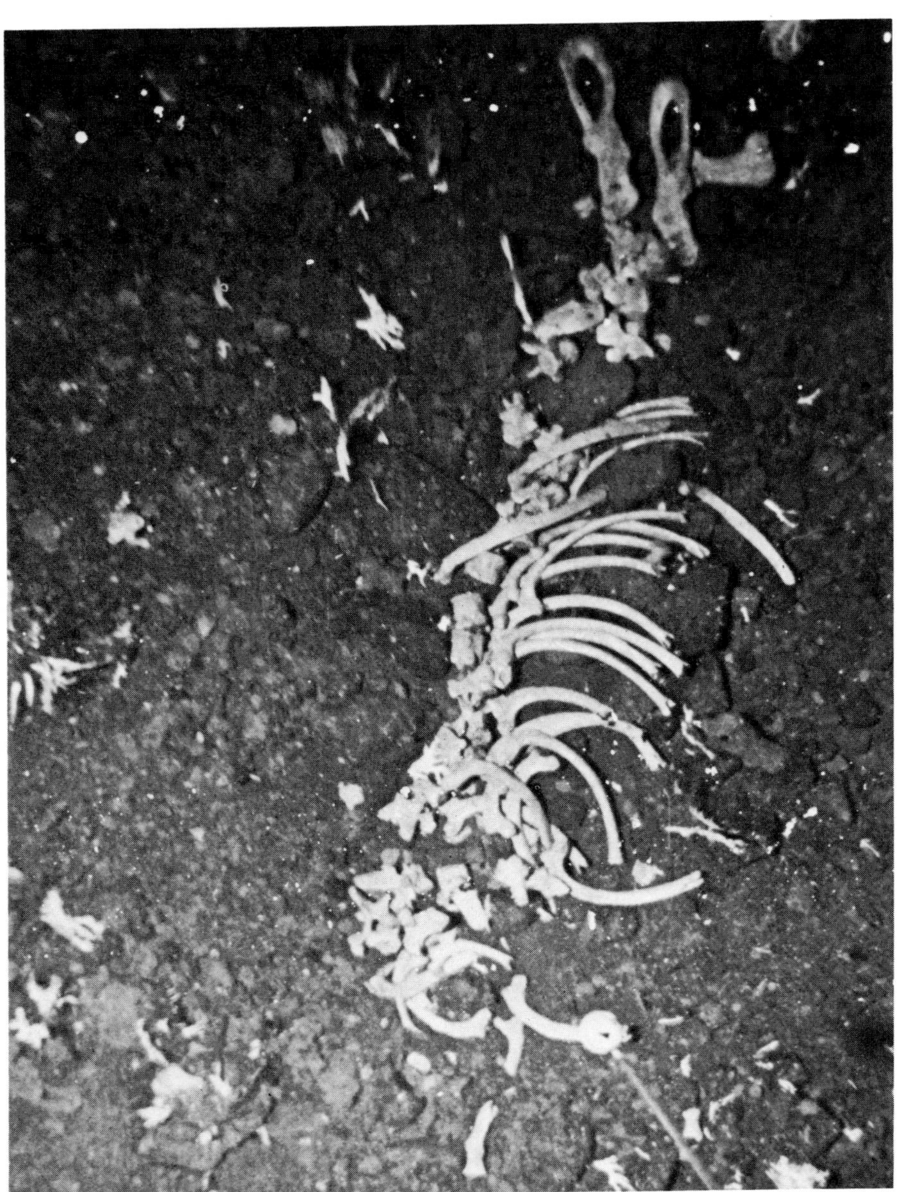

7.15 Fur seal skeleton. 600 m, Aleutian Islands.

BONANZAS

Most organic matter entering the abyss is cycled and recycled during its slow descent from the surface of the sea.[6] But the fall of some of the heavier and larger carcasses is far too rapid, and thus the dead bodies of seals (7.15), whales, squid, and the larger fish may reach the sea floor.

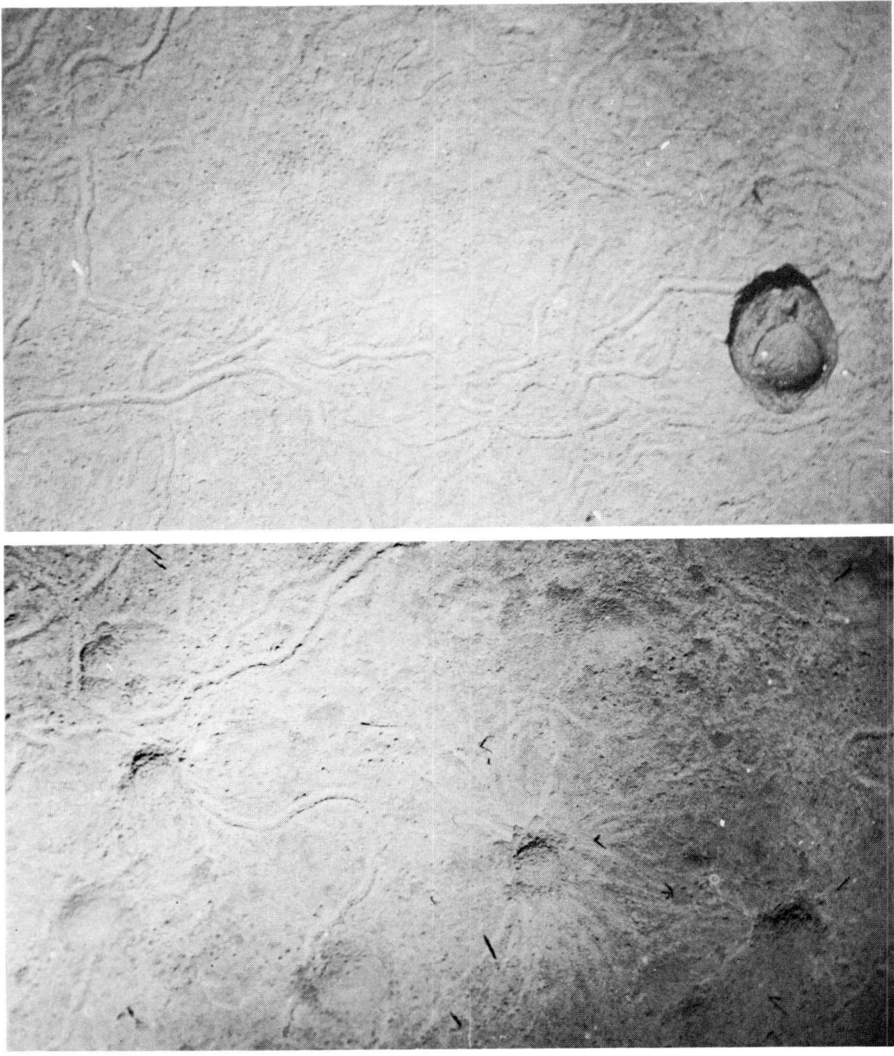

5°59′S 152°15′E
5°51′S 152°32′E

7.16 Opened coconut husk lies on the tracked floor of the New Britain Trench. U, 8235 m, flat floor of New Britain Trench; L, 7680 m, south wall New Britain Trench.

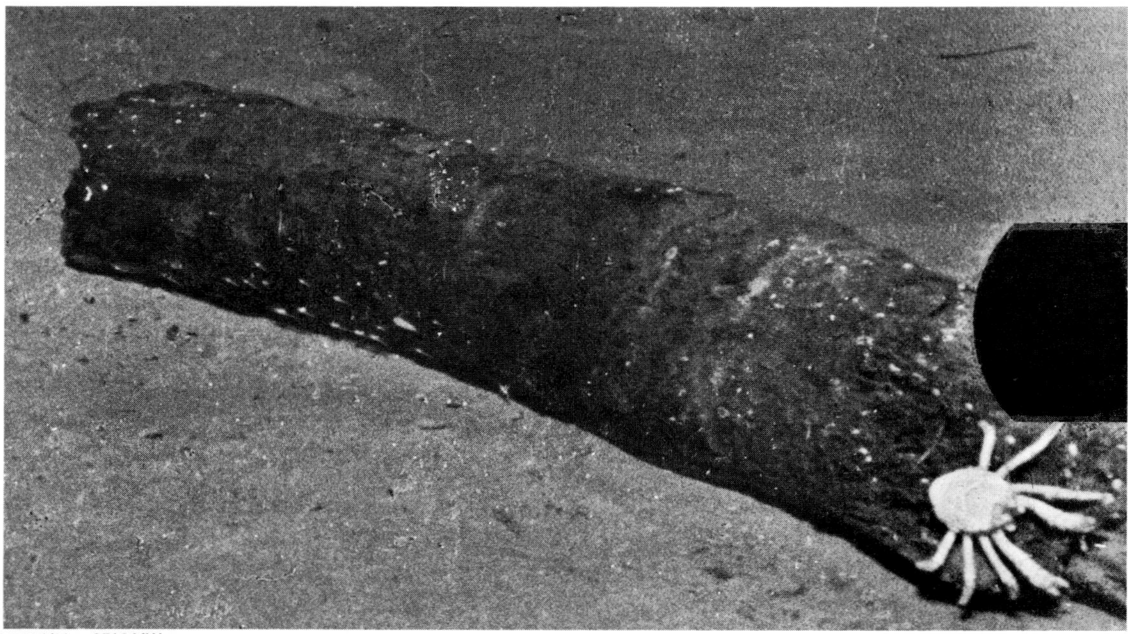

7.17 A large crab prowls a piece of sunken drift wood. 3988 m, Puerto Rico Trench.

In the very deep sea a dead whale would certainly take some time for the abyssal animals and bacteria to consume, and it has been suggested that spots of anomalously rich bottom life in the deep sea are caused by such windfalls. There have been remarkably few cases where large bodies have been found lying on the sea floor, yet some of the occasional nondescript irregular masses occasionally seen may represent bodies so decomposed that one cannot recognize the original beast. This, of course, could not be true of the bigger-boned animals, as the bones should clearly announce themselves. The early expeditions brought up a considerable number of sharks' teeth and whale earbones (otoliths), and such deposits were taken as characteristic of the deep sea. Many of the recovered sharks' teeth are much larger than those of any presently living shark (10.3). Thus, some of the large teeth we see on the present sea floor have either remained on the sediment surface for millions of years or have been buried and later re-excavated.[7]

Logs float out to the sea from most of the major rivers of the world and some are eventually cast up on the shore. But much of this floating debris, particularly the less resistant types, must sink to the bottom (7.16). Camera explorations along the south wall of the Puerto Rico Trench have revealed logs, cane, and palm fronds littering the sea floor;

and in dives to the floor of this trench, dead black leaves, remains of reeds, and branches of trees have been observed.[8] One could hardly believe that there could be a monograph written on the subject of wood-burrowing molluscs of the deep, yet Xylophaga have been found in abundance in the deep trenches of the Pacific, and a forty-seven-page monograph was written on them.[9] The large crab seen walking on top of a sunken log (7.17) was probably not interested in the decaying wood itself as much as in the various organisms that found food and refuge in this bonanza of the deep. During the extensive visual search for the lost submarine *Thresher* concentrations of regular urchins were noted on and near any organic debris. They had apparently congregated in order to consume the tons of organic matter carried to the deep-sea floor during the disaster.

STOMACH STONES

Many types of birds that fly over the sea collect small pebbles and coarse sand in their gizzards. Shear-waters, petrels, steamer ducks, oyster catchers, sheath bills, cape pigeons, ducks, and cormorants, all carry such gastroliths. Some of this material finds its way to the bottom of the sea.[10] Gallons of mud and rocks have been extracted from the stomachs of sperm whales which apparently root in the sea floor. Sea lions, sea elephants, fur seals, harbor seals, walruses, porpoises, and sea otters all

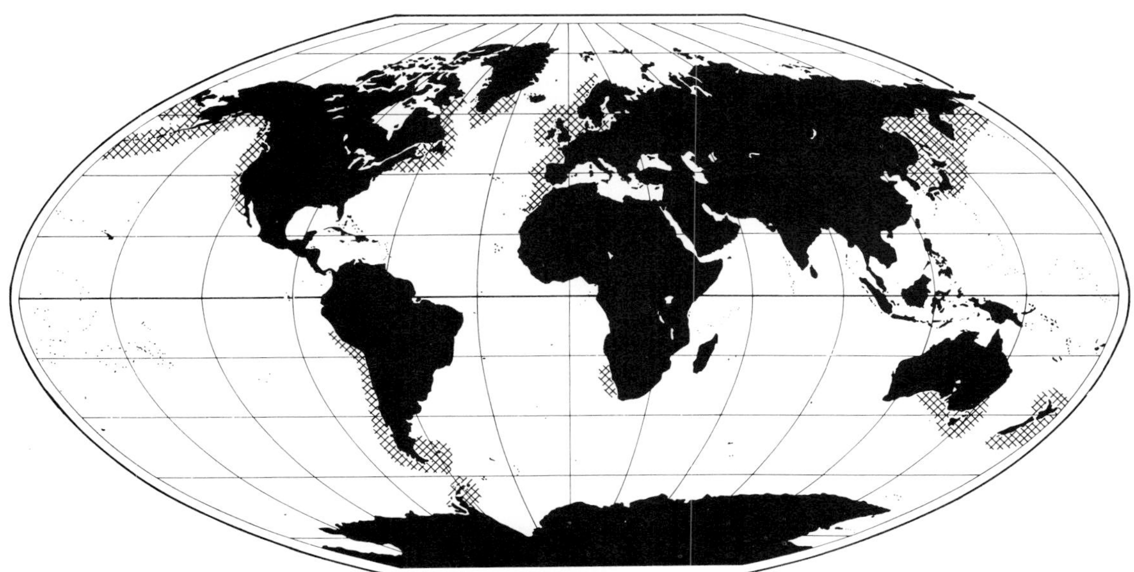

7.18 Areas which might receive stones transported by kelp.

carry stones in their stomachs and are therefore potential bombers of the deep. The large brown algae known as kelp have gas-filled floats and are equipped with root-like holdfasts which attach to rocks, boulders, and outcrops. Frequently the kelp breaks free with boulders attached (7.18). Nevertheless, rocks rafted by biological processes have never surely been identified in mid-ocean deposits, and their quantitative significance remains obscure.

VULCAN

In the initial phase of a volcanic eruption ejecta can be carried well up into the stratosphere.[11] The maximum size of the volcanic debris which falls to the ground or into the sea drops off sharply with distance from a

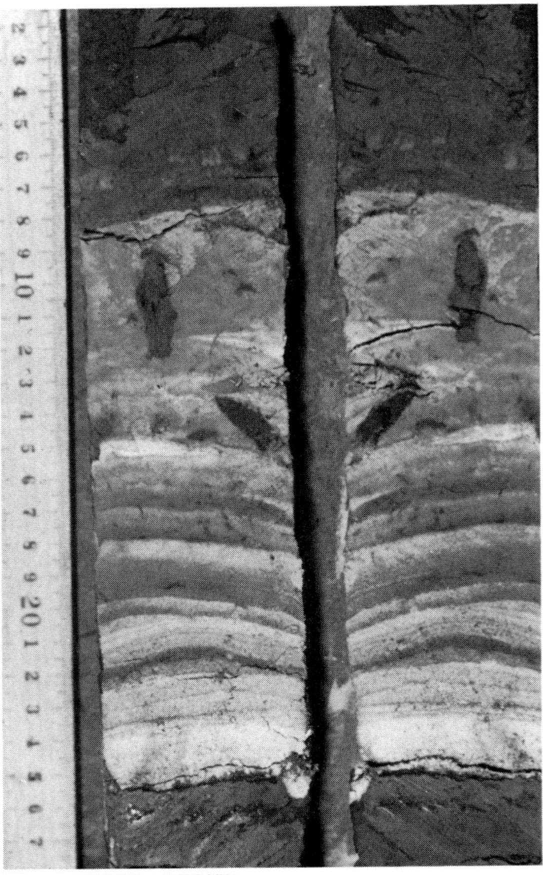

7.19 Laminated bed of volcanic ash. Bottom currents have winnowed and redeposited this ash layer producing the distinct bedding, and burrowers have left their traces near the top, 3083 m, north of Cocos Ridge, eastern equatorial Pacific.

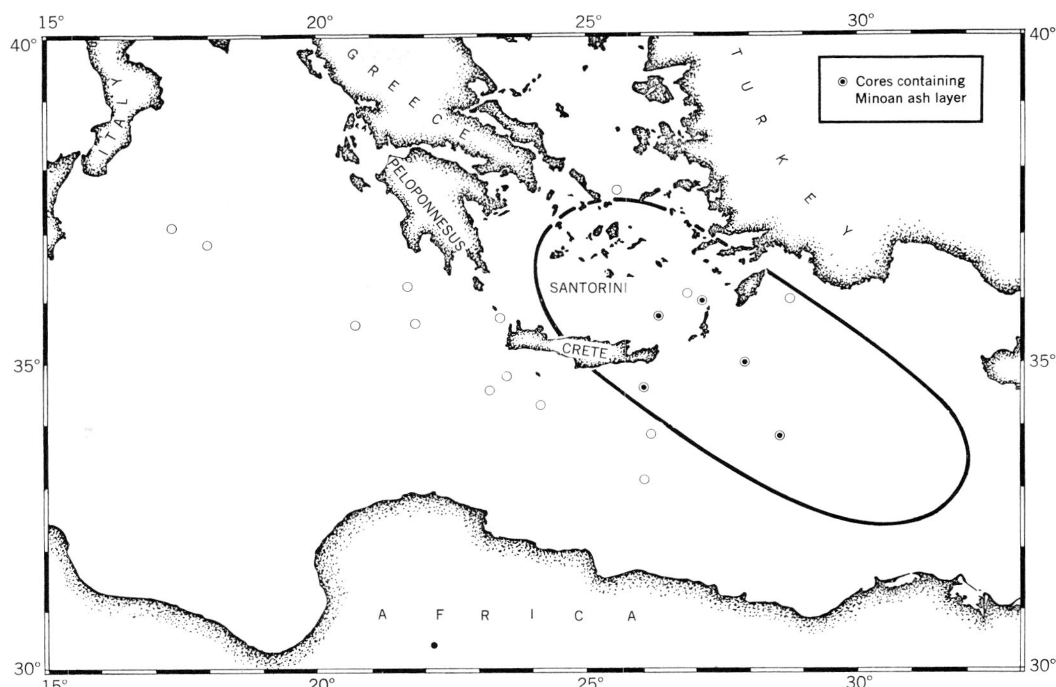

7.20 Extent of Minoan ash in Mediterranean sediments. A bed of ash several centimeters thick smothered life on the soils above and beneath the Mediterranean and drove the Minoans from Crete.

volcanic source.[12] Although blocks up to 50 cm in diameter may fall several kilometers from the vent, sizes larger than 3 mm are never found beyond 100 kilometers, and at 500 kilometers the grains are generally no larger than .03 mm. At 1000 kilometers the deposit is generally unrecognized, since the grain size at that distance has fallen to less than 0.01 mm and material of this size can be carried indefinitely in the atmosphere. The blocks of floating pumice eventually become water-soaked, and as the vesicles become permeated with water, sink to the sea floor. Pumice can be carried for vast distances from the volcanic source and might occasionally be seen in bottom photographs almost anywhere. However, as we noted above, airborne volcanic debris (tephra) of a size large enough to be seen in bottom photographs is limited to a very small area in the vicinity of the volcanic source, yet the fine wind-borne volcanic ash carried out by exceptionally ample eruptions often forms beds of appreciable thickness (7.19) which extend as much as 1000 kilometers from the volcano. In some regions this contribution can be a dominant component of bottom sediment and can have a significant visual effect on the seascape.

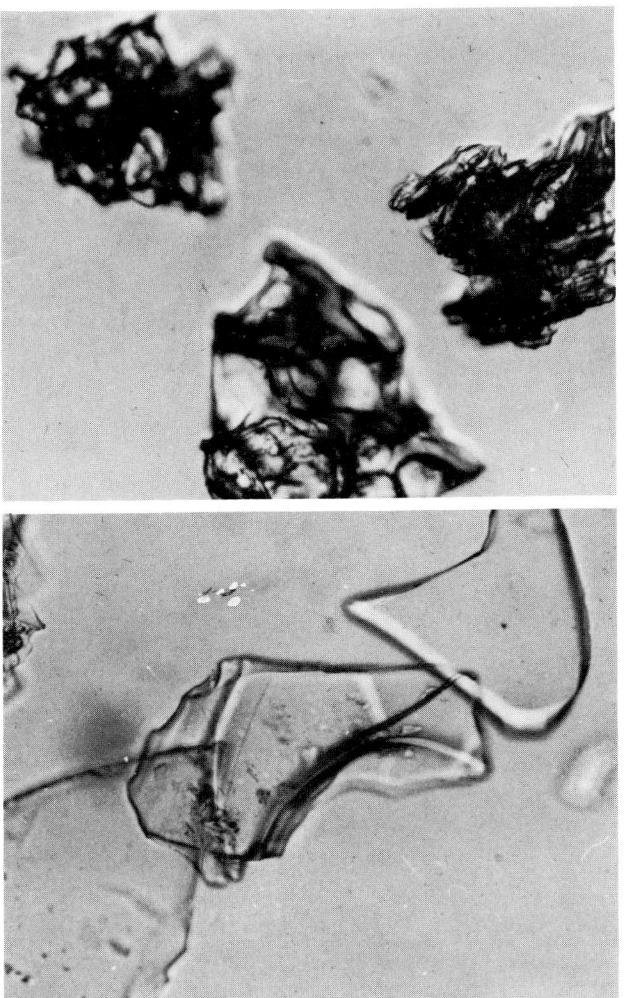

7.21 Glass shards of the Santorini Tephra.

It is not hard to imagine that the sudden fall of fine glass totalling several centimeters must have a catastrophic effect on the sea floor. The bottom animals would not only have to avoid being buried beneath the fall but even more disastrous would be the temporary devastation of the bacterial pastures. The fall of volcanic ash on the land has also had dramatic consequences. Several times over the past thousand years ash falls on Iceland have destroyed pastures and led to famine.[13] The enormous eruption of Santorini thirty-five centuries ago laid so much ash on Crete that the prosperous Minoans fled to Greece and abandoned their island empire. This ash (7.20, 7.21) is found throughout the northeastern Mediterranean and must have had as great an effect

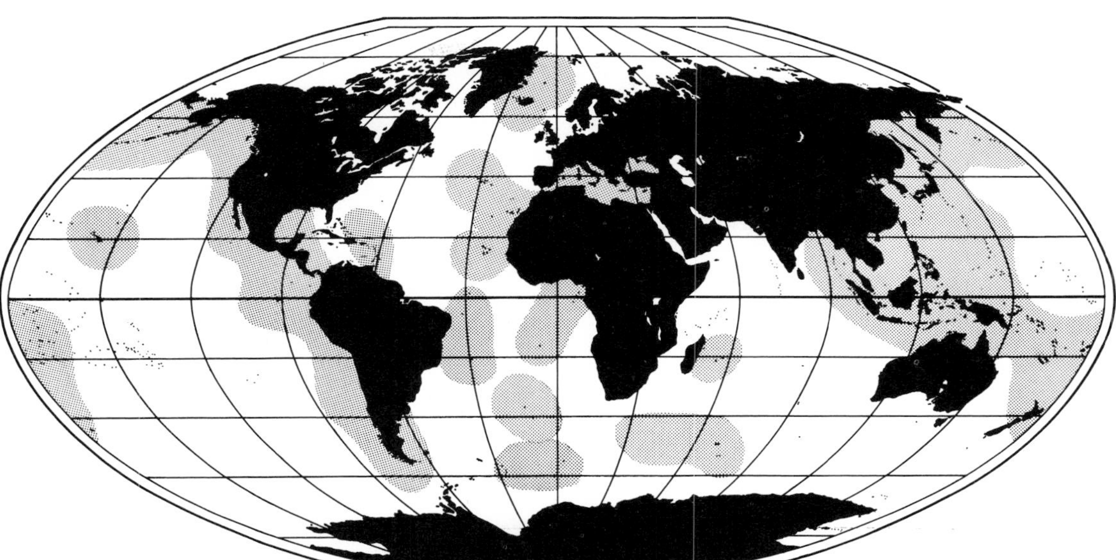

7.22 Areas where volcanic ash falls can blanket the sea floor. Thick deposits of ash are found only within 1000 km of a volcanic source.

on the abyssal scene as it did on Western civilization.[14] Just as the course of human history has been seriously altered by the catastrophic effects of gentle but deadly falls of ash which have destroyed pastures and gardens, so over the eons the animals at the bottom of the sea must have repeatedly experienced the deadly effects of heavy falls of ash (7.22).

FROM SPACE

Fine cosmic dust has been recognized as a small but significant component of deep-sea sediments. In the slowly depositing abyssal red clays, tiny metallic and glassy spherules are frequently found. This material, evidently arising from outer space, forms a detectable component only in those sediments which are being laid down at the very lowest rates.[15] But most of this cosmic dust is much too small to see with an unaided eye, let alone in a bottom photograph.

Tektites, curious nut-sized fragments of sculptured glass (7.23), are found scattered over Australia, Indonesia, the Philippines, Indo-China, and Thailand (7.24).[16] Off Saigon, one was recovered by the dredge from the current-swept continental slope of the South China Sea.[17] In the course of a search for faunal changes which might correlate with the last reversal[18] of the earth's magnetic field, microtektites less than one millimeter in diameter were discovered[19] in deep-sea cores from the Indian

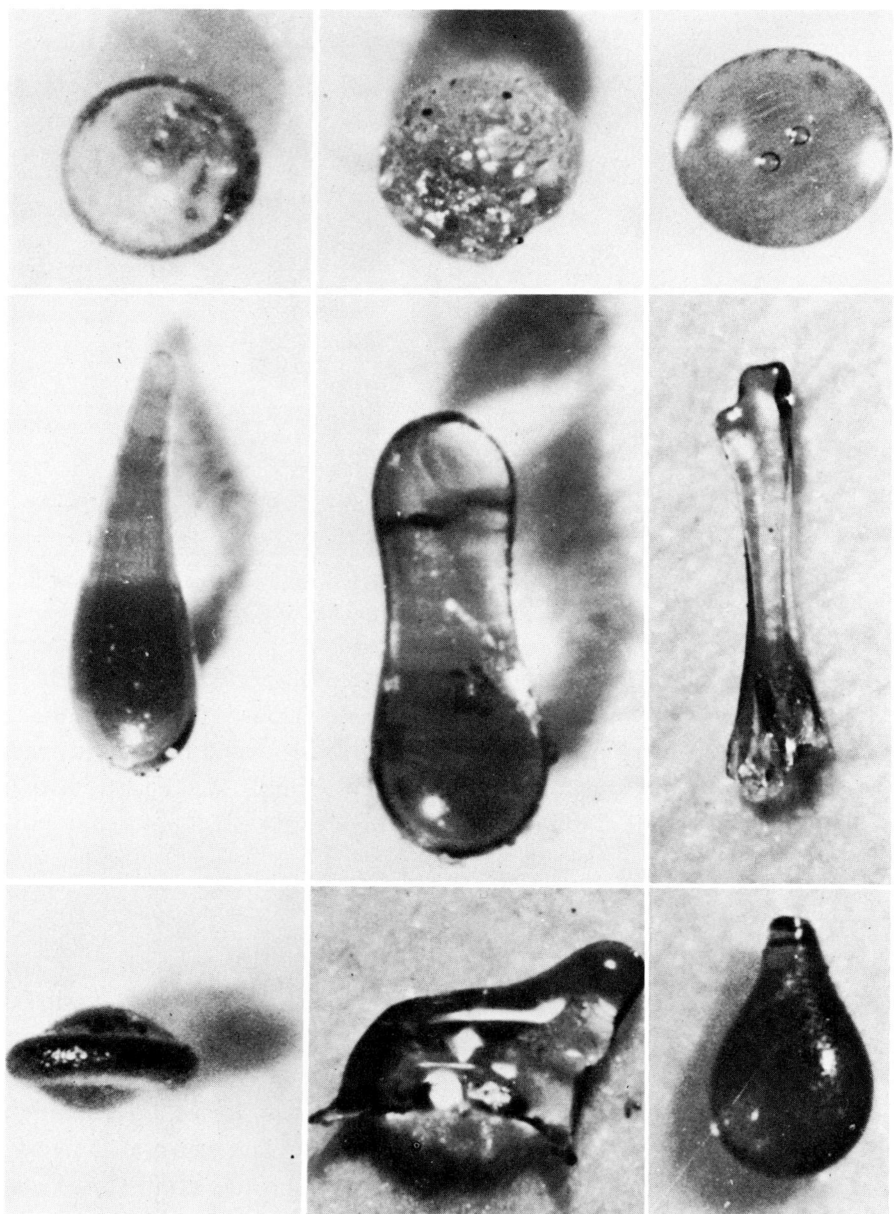

7.23 These tiny drops of sculptured glass fell into the Indian Ocean 700,000 years ago. These range from 0.2 to 0.8 millimeters, but glass dust much finer in size as well as hunks up to several centimeters in diameter also fell on the earth.

Ocean (7.25). This layer containing the cosmic glass which was deposited during a reversal of the earth's magnetic field 700,000 years ago lies from three to ten meters beneath the deep-sea floor. In this single cosmic catastrophe nearly a billion tons of tektites were consigned to the deep and now lie buried beneath the floor of the Indian Ocean.

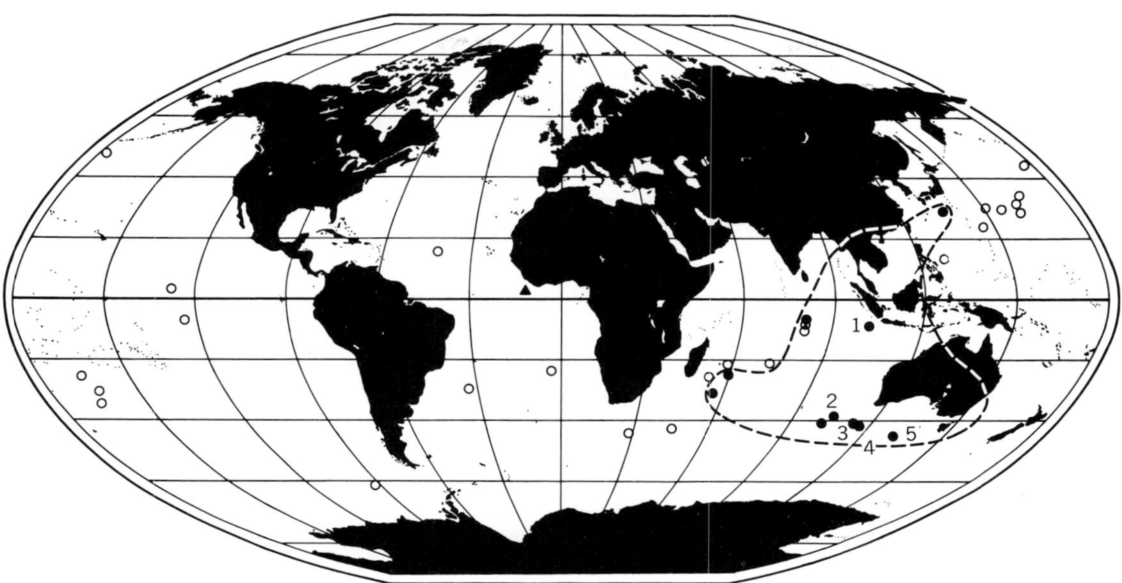

7.24 The debris of a cosmic encounter covers a twelfth of the earth's surface. Although generally buried beneath the ooze or clay, the larger tektites may lie directly on the sea floor in areas of scour and erosion (see Fig. 7.25 for core profiles).

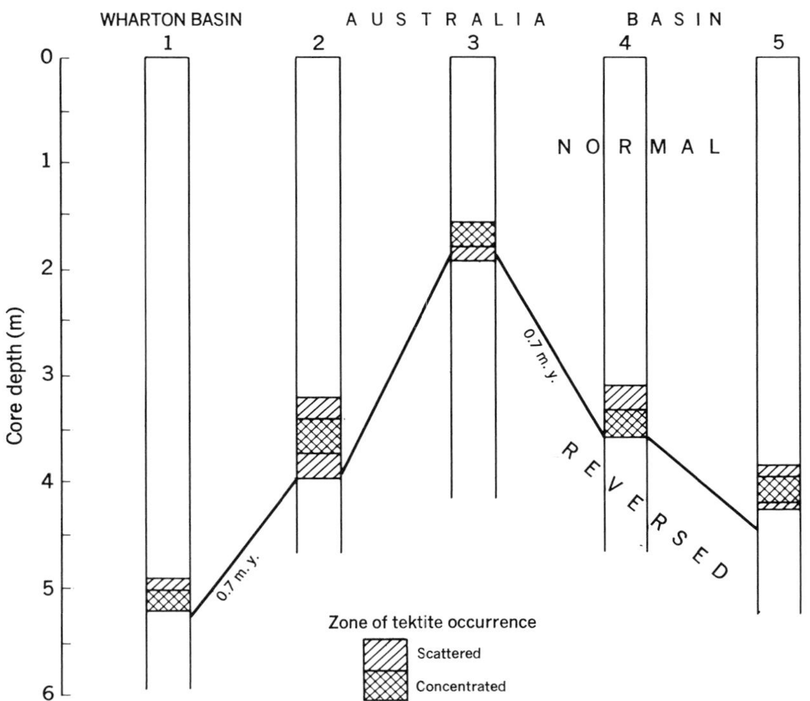

7.25 The tektite fall coincided with the last reversal of the earth's magnetic field. Both phenomena probably relate to a common cause (see Fig. 7.24 for core locations).

It seems probable that larger tektites lie buried with the smaller ones throughout their wide area of occurrence, which overlaps more than one-third of the length of the current-swept crest of the Mid-Oceanic Ridge of the Indian Ocean. Here, some sharp eye will one day recognize tear-drop or button-shaped tektites lying on a scoured rocky bottom.

ICE

Of all the larger objects consigned to the deep only ice-borne rocks are of any real significance. Even these are found in restricted areas. Glaciers formed of snow and ice on the continents carry large quantities of rock debris which they erode from the land. Icebergs carry with them the eroded material, and since they may float thousands of miles before melting, pebbles and boulders are dropped onto pelagic deposits far from land (7.26).[20] Sea ice formed through the freezing of sea water also plays an important role in the transportation of sediments, particularly in the Arctic where, in shallow water, ice may form from the sea surface to the bottom, even including the interstitial waters in the bottom sediments. In spring, melting commences from the surface; this causes the thinning ice to rise and lift the frozen sediment off the bottom. Later the rock-bearing ice is transported by wind and currents into the open ocean, where it breaks up and melts.

Virtually all icebergs of the North Atlantic originate from the tongues of the Greenland ice cap. These irregular masses of blue glacial ice, which float with about five-sixths of their mass below water, calve off the year around. In the winter, they are frozen fast in sea ice, but in the spring they move out into open water, and great numbers—swept along

7.26 Icebergs carry rocks that will eventually be consigned to the deep.

7.27 Ice-rafted boulder and rocks off Nova Scotia. This cluster of iceborne rocks may have reached the sea floor while still frozen in one mass, 4030 m, continental rise off Nova Scotia.

in the Greenland and Labrador currents—travel far south, reaching the shipping lanes of the North Atlantic. The last bergs finally melt upon reaching the Gulf Stream. Rocks borne by these bergs and by associated sea ice litter the continental margin (7.27) as well as the abyssal depths of the Atlantic down to about latitude thirty degrees North.[21] Grounded sea ice breaks off the Arctic shores and joins the great clockwise circulation of the sea ice which covers the Arctic Ocean. Occasionally a berg enters the Arctic, and becomes an ice island (7.28). This ice drops many rocks into the depths of the Arctic Basin, and they can be seen littering the sea floor[22] (7.29).

The Antarctic ice cap does not break up immediately upon reaching the sea, but pushes out over the continental shelf, forming an ice shelf dozens of miles wide. Enormous slabs, the largest reaching scores of miles in width, break off and float away. These wide snow-capped slabs of glacial ice are less dense than the Arctic bergs, and float higher in the water. They generally drift north as far as latitude forty-five degrees South in the Pacific, and latitude thirty-five degrees South in the Atlantic.

An extensive photographic survey of the floor of the southern ocean, including over 10,000 photographs at 500 locations, extending from the

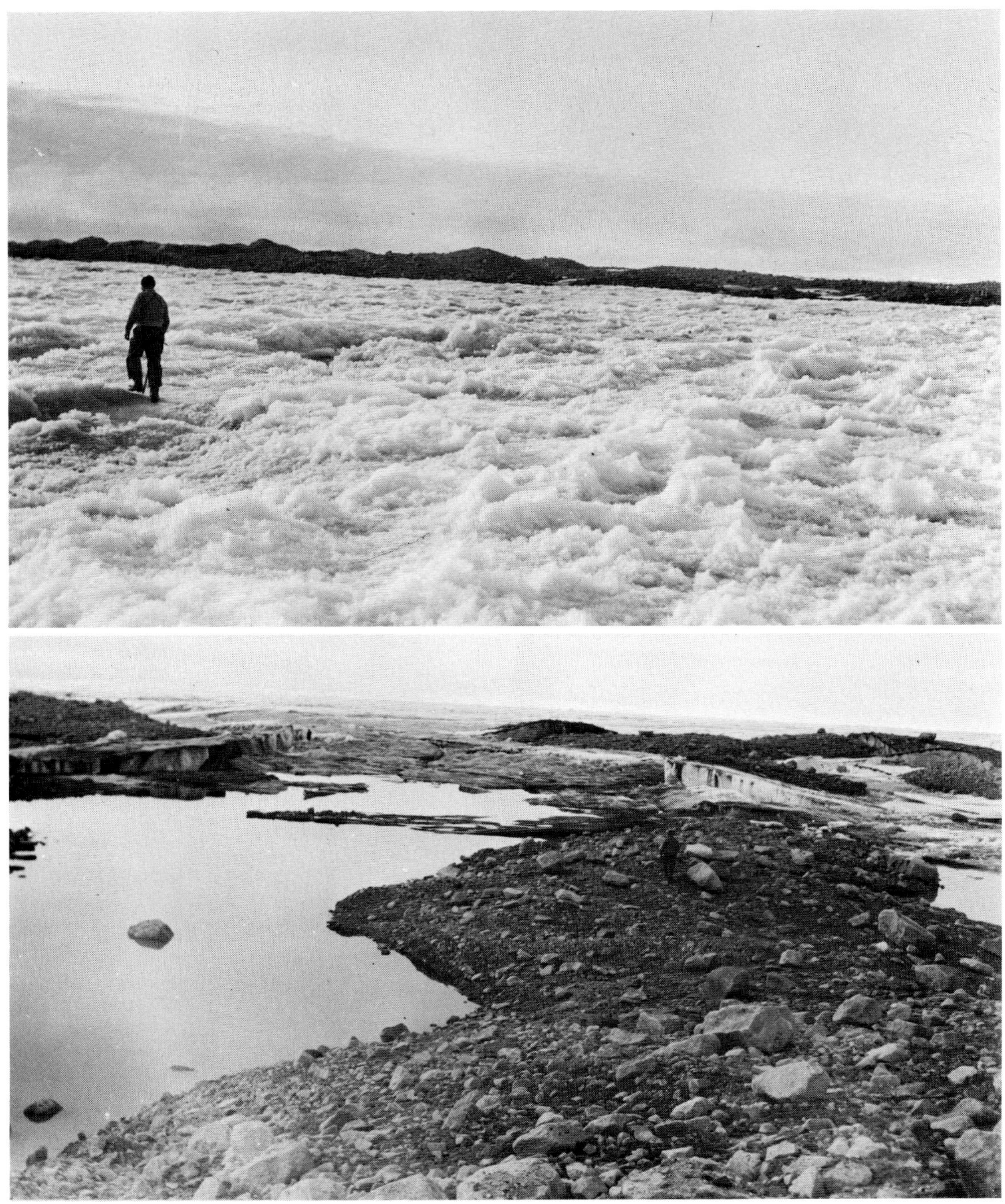

7.28 Sand, rocks, and boulders on an Arctic ice-island. As the ice-island melts, these rocks will bombard the denizens of the deep, Arlis Ice-Island, Arctic Ocean.

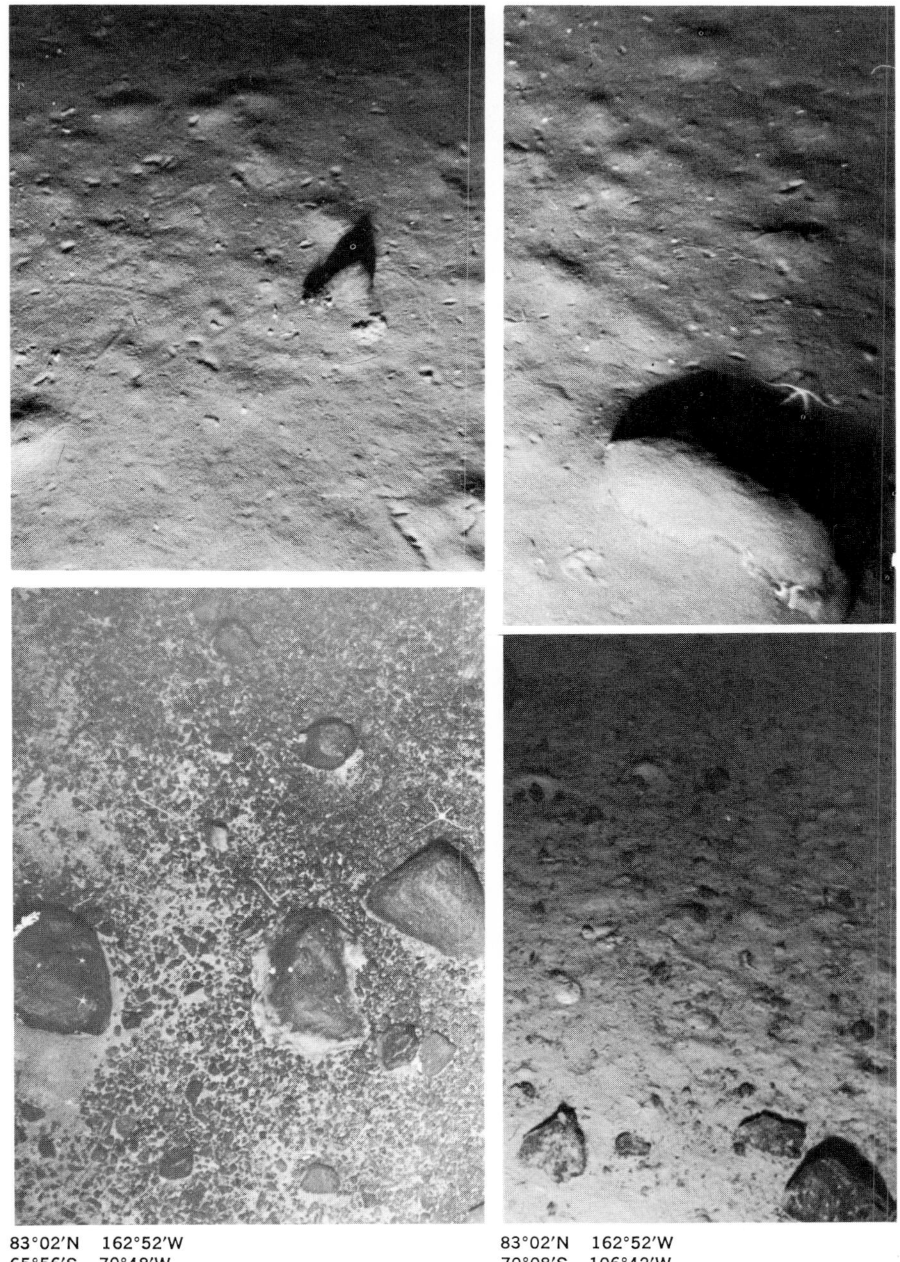

7.29 Rafted rocks from the polar seas. UL, UR, 3414 m, Arctic Ocean. LL, 2420 m, Pacific continental slope, Antarctic Peninsula. LR, 3619 m, continental rise, Marie Byrd Land, Antarctica.

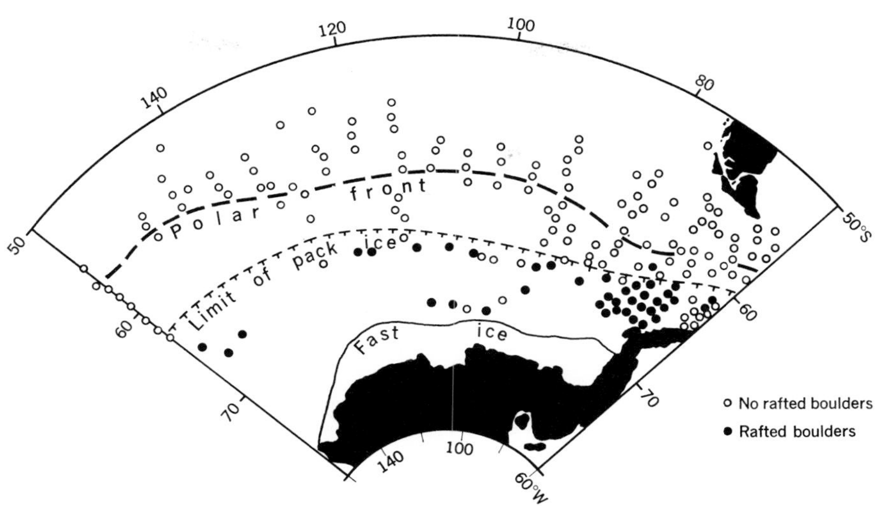

7.31 Large ice-rafted boulders are frequently photographed south of the limit of pack ice in the Bellingshausen Sea.

eastern Indian Ocean across the Pacific to the western Atlantic, has produced an impressive demonstration of the extent and importance of Ant-
70°25'S 99°36'W arctic ice-rafting. On the normally muddy bottom of the Antarctic continental rise, large angular boulders and pebbles of all shapes and sizes—some round and some angular—are frequently observed (7.30). They are much more abundant immediately west of the Antarctic Peninsula than they are further to the west off Marie Byrd Land (7.31). This dis-
63°58'S 71°13'W tribution may be related to the fact that on the western side of the Antarctic Peninsula pack ice is penetrable to the shore line each year, whereas further to the west fast ice surrounds the continent even during the Antarctic summer.

Most of the photographs obtained in the area immediately north of the polar front (approximately latitude sixty degrees South) show a bottom littered with rocks and manganese nodules (7.32). The surface productivity north of the front is lower than immediately to the south, thus rafted rocks remain unburied here for a longer period of time. Ice-rafted rocks are also abundant beneath the Ross Ice Shelf (7.33). At the present time, eighty million square kilometers of ocean floor are receiving glacial debris released by the melting of floating ice (7.34), and a much greater area was affected during the ice ages.[23]

◁ 7.30 Rafted boulders. U, 3680 m, continental rise, Marie Byrd Land, Antarctica. L, 3562 m, Drake Passage.

7.32 Rocks and nodules near Antarctic Polar Front. U, 3981 m, L, note disc-shaped coelenterate, 4825 m, Bellingshausen Basin. ▷

58°54′S 95°08′W

57°59′S 120°03 W

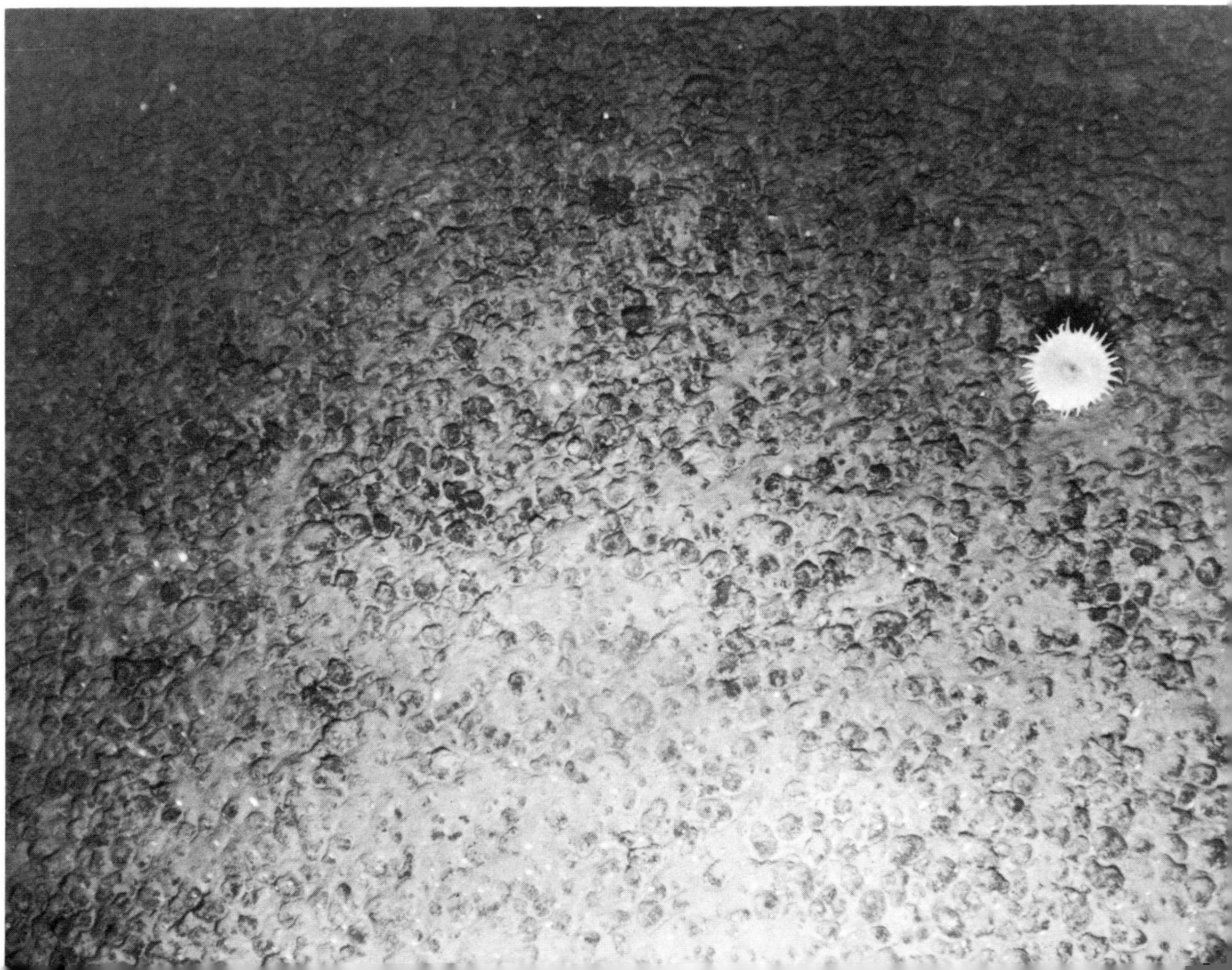

77°48′S 177°20′E

74°52′S 174°42′W

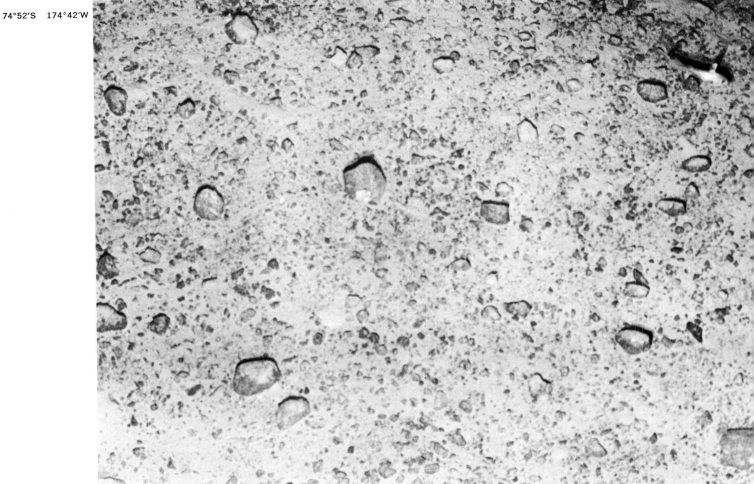

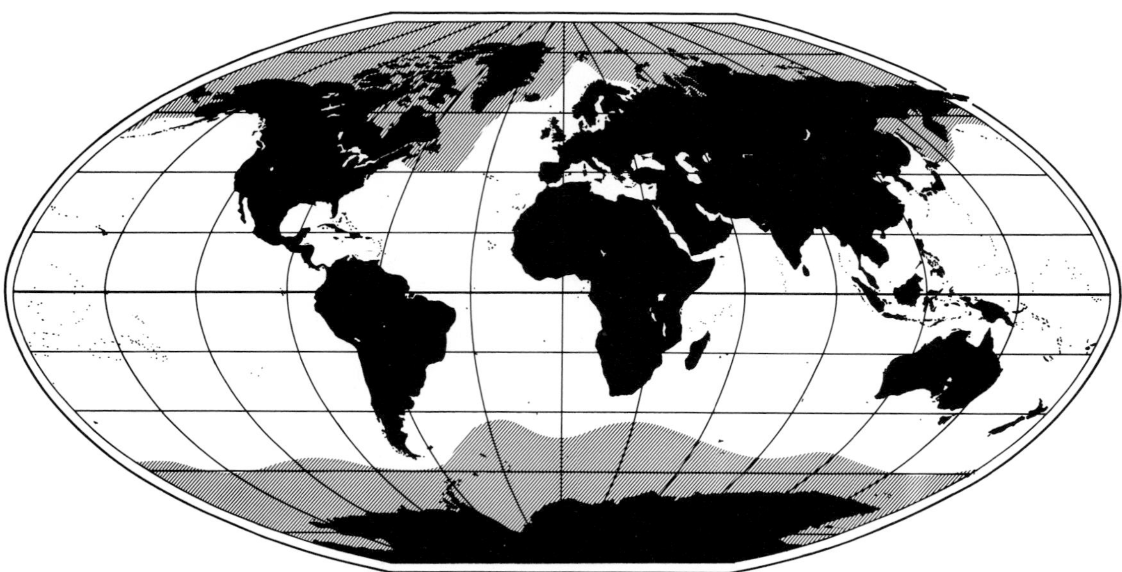

7.34 Occurrence of floating ice. The sea floor beneath areas covered with floating ice should receive occasional rafted pebbles, rocks, and boulders.

THE UNREMITTING DRIFT

> *When I think of the floor of the deep sea the single overwhelming fact that possesses my imagination is the accumulation of sediments. I see the steady, unremitting downward drift of materials from above, flake upon flake, layer upon layer, a drift that has continued for hundreds of millions of years, that will go on as long as there are seas and continents.*
>
> RACHEL CARSON

The heavy objects that occasionally plummet from above come to rest on a vastly more massive accumulation of fine particles.[24] Individually these particles are far below the threshold of our visual window (7.40), and therefore not in that sense relevant to a discussion of the visible abyss, but collectively they form the substance of the seascape and variations in their composition and rate of accumulation are thus among the most pertinent consideration in the geography of submarine scenery.

The rate at which these particles accumulate on the floor of the ocean has long intrigued geologists. Geochemists have calculated the rates of deposition on the basis of the radioactive decay over the past 30,000 years of the isotope carbon-14 or on the basis of the decay of ionium, uranium, and protactinium over the past few hundred thousands years.[25] Although radiocarbon dates are generally accepted as reliable, other methods have been considered less certain. Recently, however, it has

◁ 7.33 Melting Antarctic glaciers rain rocks upon the floor of the Ross Sea. U, L, Antartic continental shelf and slope, Ross Sea, 757 m, 2170 m.

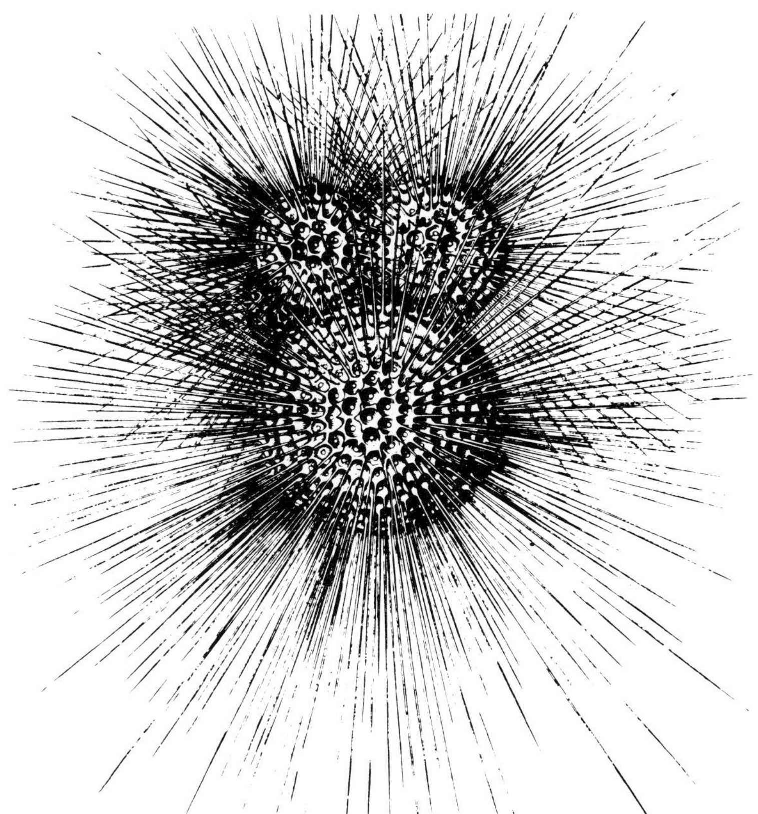

7.35 Living foraminifera (*Globigerina bulloides*). (x100)

been found that the remnant magnetization of deep-sea sediments is relatively strong and reasonably stable. Cores which penetrate sediment more than 700,000 years old may be readily correlated by the sequence of magnetic reversals.[26] The potassium-argon dates determined on volcanic rocks of the continents can now be applied to a refined dating of the reversals and therefore, under optimum conditions, it is possible to determine the average rates of deposition between reversals which occur every few hundred thousand years. It is now possible not only to correlate horizons in cores from the far corners of the earth but to determine with precision variations in the rate of sediment accumulation in the abyss.

WIND, RIVERS, AND SUN

The three principal sources of fine particles that eventually settle to the sea floor are the pelagic organisms which are sustained by the sun near the sea surface, the sediment-laden rivers which return the evaporated

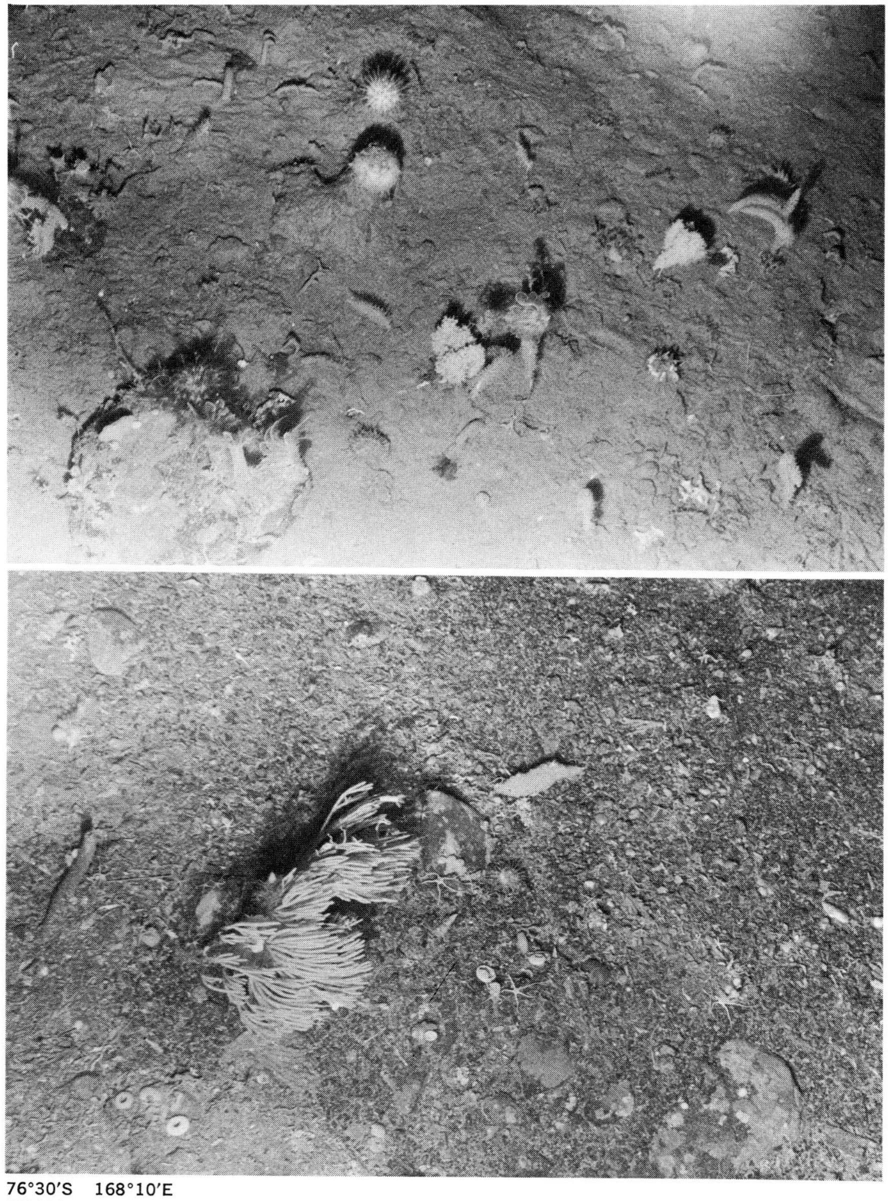

76°30′S 168°10′E
72°32′S 171°30′E

7.36 The life-covered sea floor beneath the nutrient-rich water of the Ross Sea. U, 750 m, and L, 348 m, Antarctic continental shelf in the Ross Sea.

and precipitated waters to the sea, and the winds which spread dust around the world. The microscopic calcareous tests of the single-celled planktonic foraminifera (7.35) are the principal constituent of the globigerina ooze that covers one-third of the ocean floor (Table 7.1,

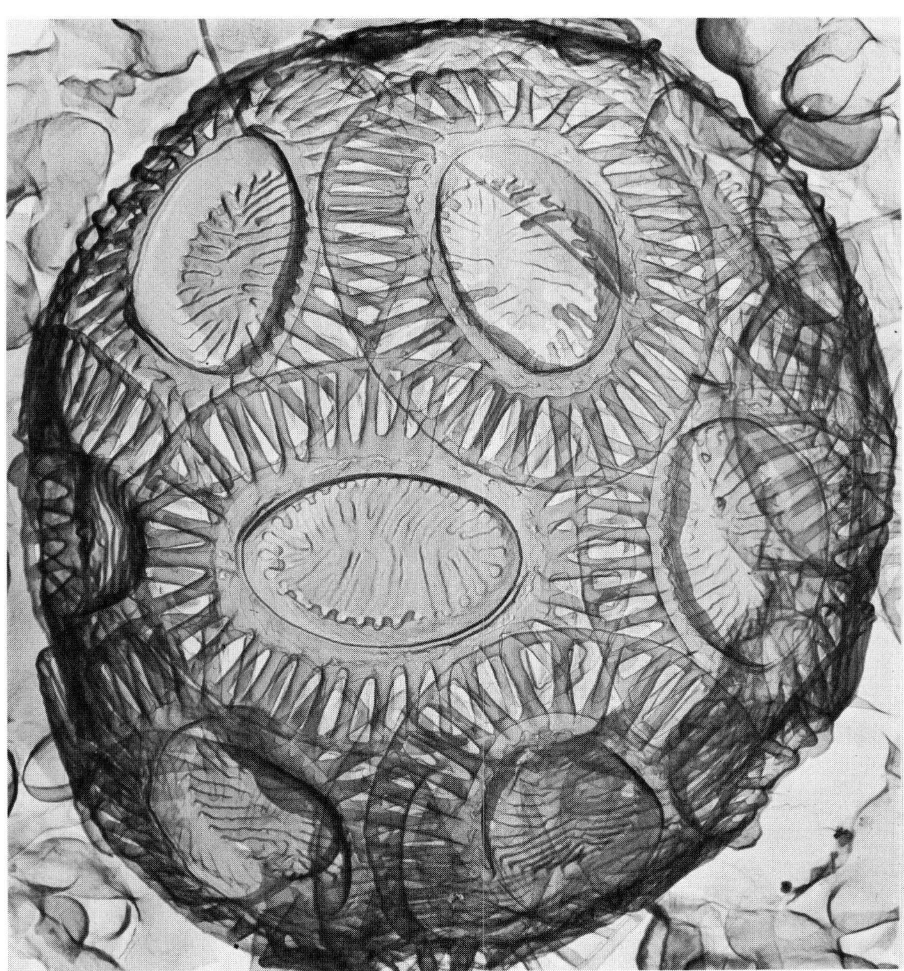

7.37 A coccolith. An electron micrograph. (x7500)

Table 7.1 Areas covered by pelagic sediments.

Type of sediment	Atlantic Ocean		Pacific Ocean		Indian Ocean		Total	
	Area, $\times 10^6$ km^2	%	Area, $\times 10^6$ km^2	%	Area, $\times 10^6$ km^2	%	Area, $\times 10^6$ km^2	%
Calcareous oozes								
Globigerina	40.1		51.9		34.4			
Pteropod	1.5							
Total	41.6	67.5	51.9	36.2	34.4	54.3	127.9	47.7
Siliceous oozes								
Diatom	4.1		14.4		12.6			
Radiolarian			6.6		0.3			
Total	4.1	6.7	21.0	14.7	12.9	20.4	38.0	14.2
Red clay	15.9	25.3	70.3	49.1	16.0	25.3	102.2	38.1
Grand total	61.6	100.0	143.2	100.0	63.3	100.0	268.1	100.0

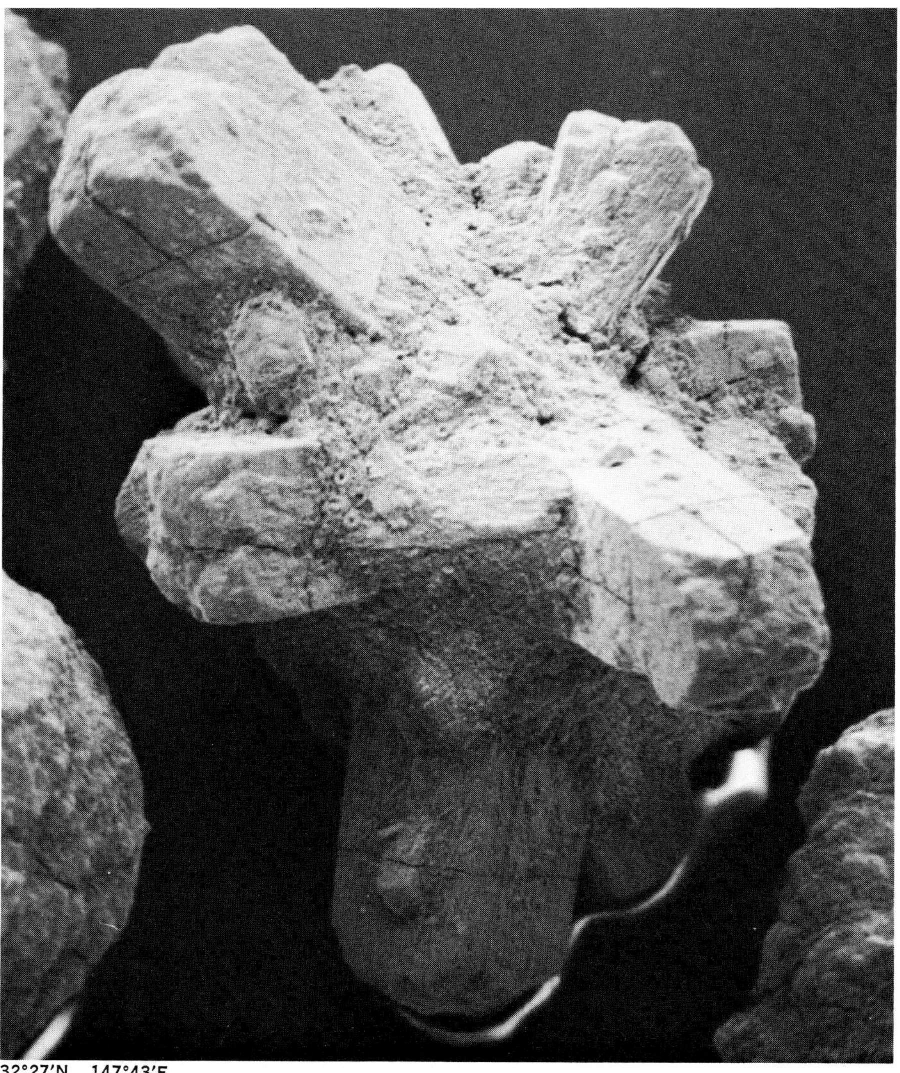

7.38 Zeolite crystals grew within the sediments. Donut shaped coccoliths are seen on the crystals. Scanning electron micrograph (x610), Deep-Sea Drilling Project hole 47, 50 meters below sea floor in 2690 meters, Shatsky Plateau.

7.46). These animals do not exceed 2 mm in maximum dimension and are thus never large enough to be seen in bottom photographs. The intricate plate-like remains of microscopic pelagic plants (coccoliths) (7.37), less than 10 microns in diameter, are also an important constituent of the calcareous ooze that forms the cream-colored substrate in moderate mid-ocean depths (7.38). The recent rate of deposition of calcareous ooze in the central equatorial Atlantic is approximately 2 cm per 1000 years.

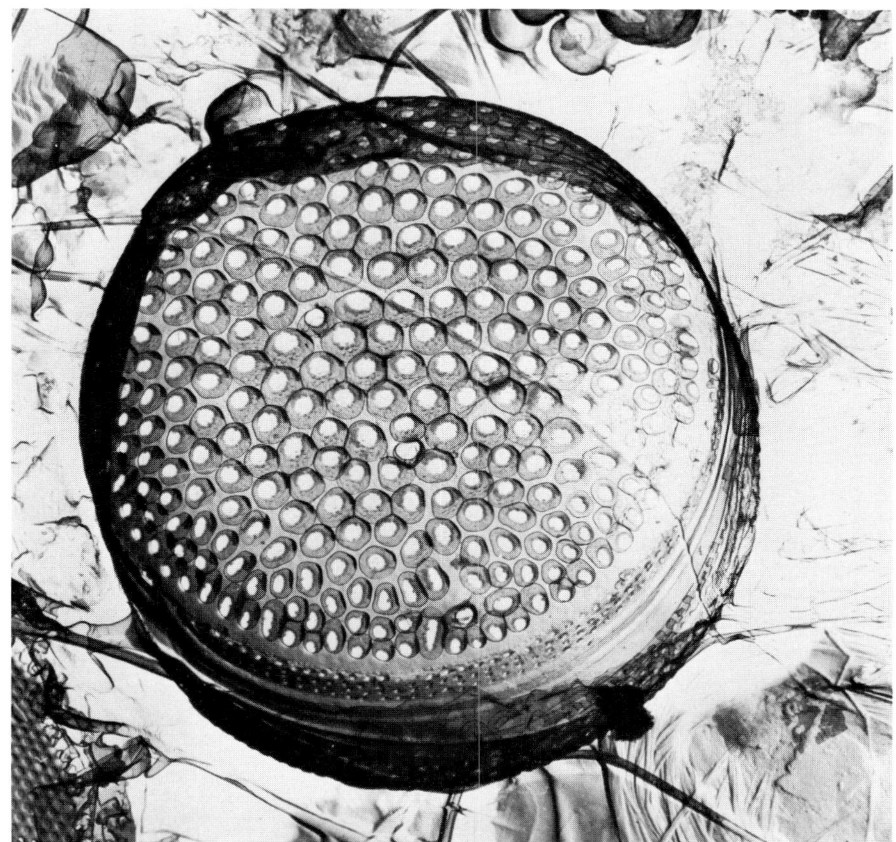

7.39 A diatom. Electron micrograph. (x5000)

The remains of the diatoms (7.39), together with the beautiful, radially symmetrical, discarded tests of the planktonic radiolaria (7.1), compose the siliceous oozes of the high latitudes. These tests, ten times smaller than the foraminifera, form the soft gray or green-gray carpet of the Antarctic abyss. Here the present rate of accumulation of siliceous ooze varies between about 0.2 cm and 1 cm per 1000 years.

Abyssal "red clay" or brown mud, found in the deepest part of the ocean basin, contains less than 30 per cent calcium carbonate and is composed predominantly of land-derived submicroscopic clay minerals (particles less than one micron in diameter) and insoluble inorganic residue, with minor amounts of inorganic precipitates (usually manganese micronodules less than 50 microns in diameter). Abyssal "red clay" is the predominant sediment covering the lower flanks of the Mid-Oceanic Ridge, the abyssal hills, the abyssal plains, and the oceanic rises. Rate of deposition of these fine-grained clays generally ranges from 0.2 mm to 2 mm per 1000 years.

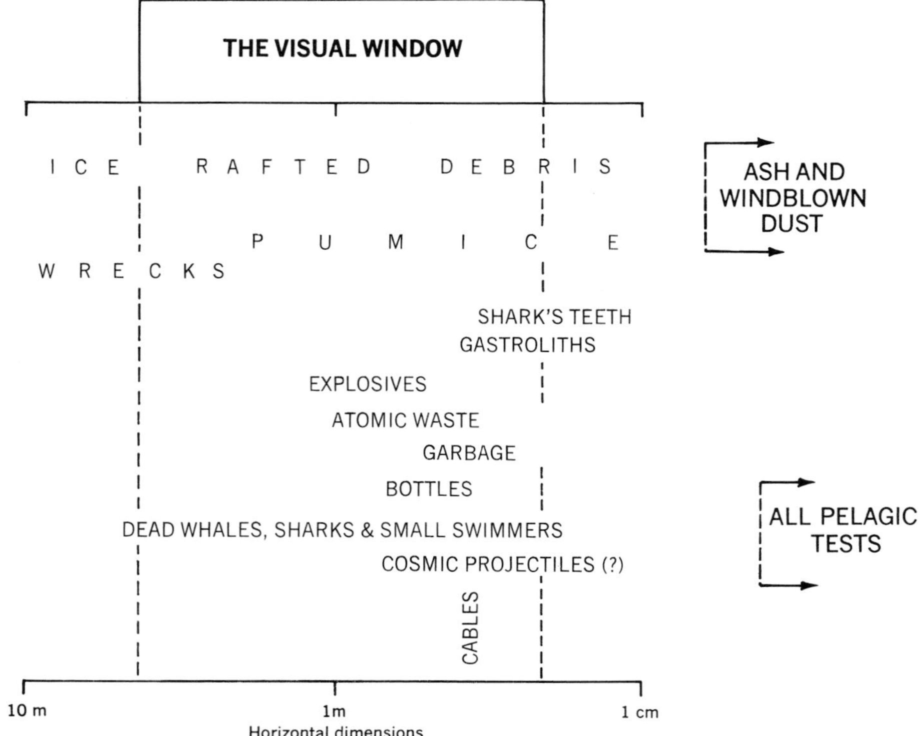

7.40 Sizes of things consigned to the deep.

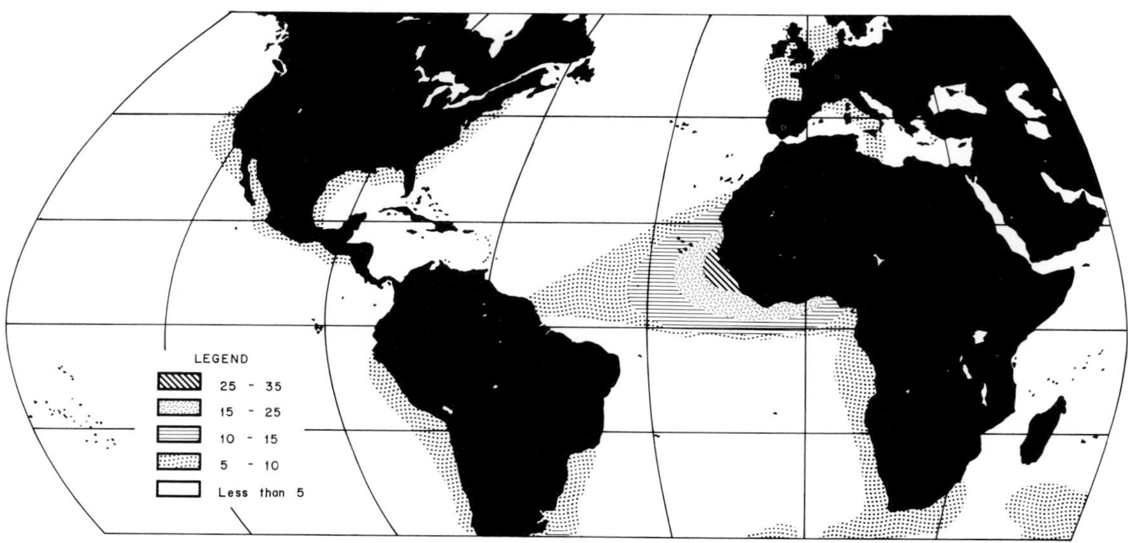

7.41 Hazy skies result from transport of dust in the atmosphere. Numbers are percent of total number of observations of haze in northern winter.

The predominant sediment covering the surface of the continental rise and continental slope is composed of a mixture of pelagic ooze and debris weathered from continents. This hemipelagic clay generally con-

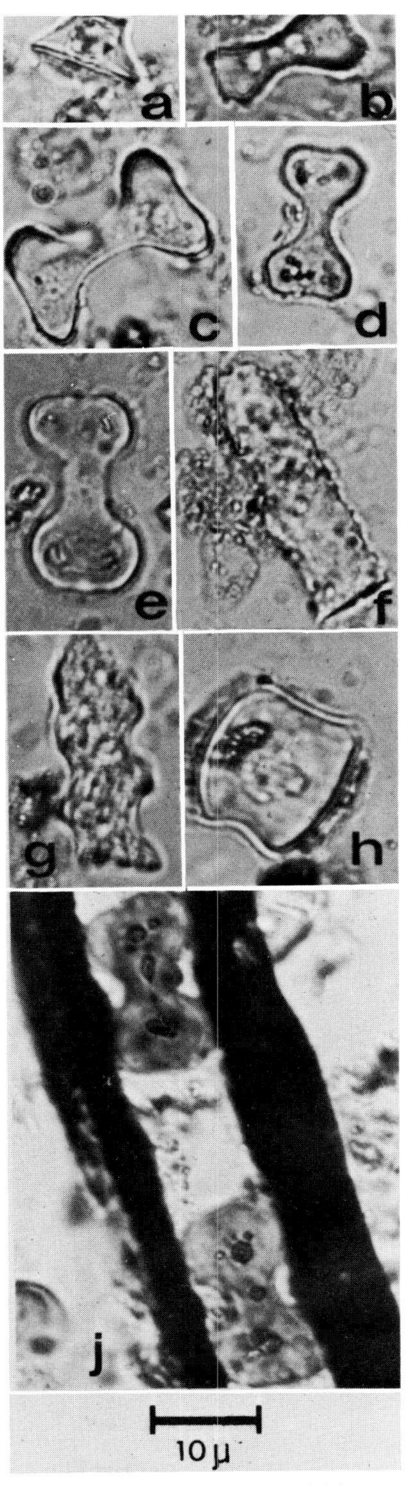

7.42 Glass from grass. Glassy dumbells from African grass settles from dust storms in the equatorial Atlantic. A few of these phytoliths are still bound together by original plant tissue (j).

tains as much as 10 to 20 per cent silt grains. Carbonate content is low and ranges between 20 and 30 per cent. When wet, the color is green to blue-gray. These tints are due to the low degree of oxidation of the relatively abundant finely divided organic matter. Rates of accumulation of hemipelagic clay are the highest of any deep-sea sediments. Rates determined from cores on the continental margin of eastern United States generally vary from 5 to 10 cm per 1000 years for the past 10,000 years; and much higher rates (often greater than 10 to 15 cm per 1000 years) predominated during glacial times.

The winds transport fine sediment far from shore and in certain areas wind-blown dust constitutes a significant proportion of abyssal sediments. In the equatorial Atlantic an appreciable quantity of dust is transported by the strong easterly winds blowing across the Sahara (7.41). Strong offshore wind also carries significant quantities of fresh-water diatoms as well as the siliceous remains of land plants (phytoliths) into the deep sea (7.42).

PATTERNS OF PRODUCTIVITY

The circulation of the waters of the sea is determined by thermal anomalies which produce systematic irregularities in the concentration of vital nutrients, and these in turn limit the productivity[27] of surface

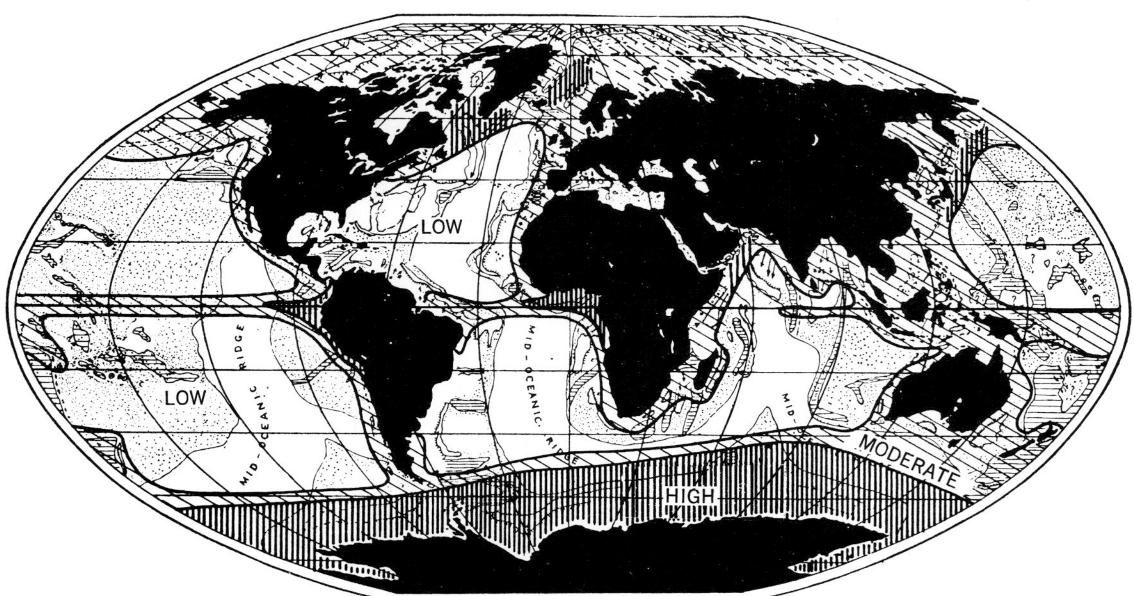

7.43 Organic productivity of the world ocean. A generalized interpretation based largely on oceanic circulation patterns.

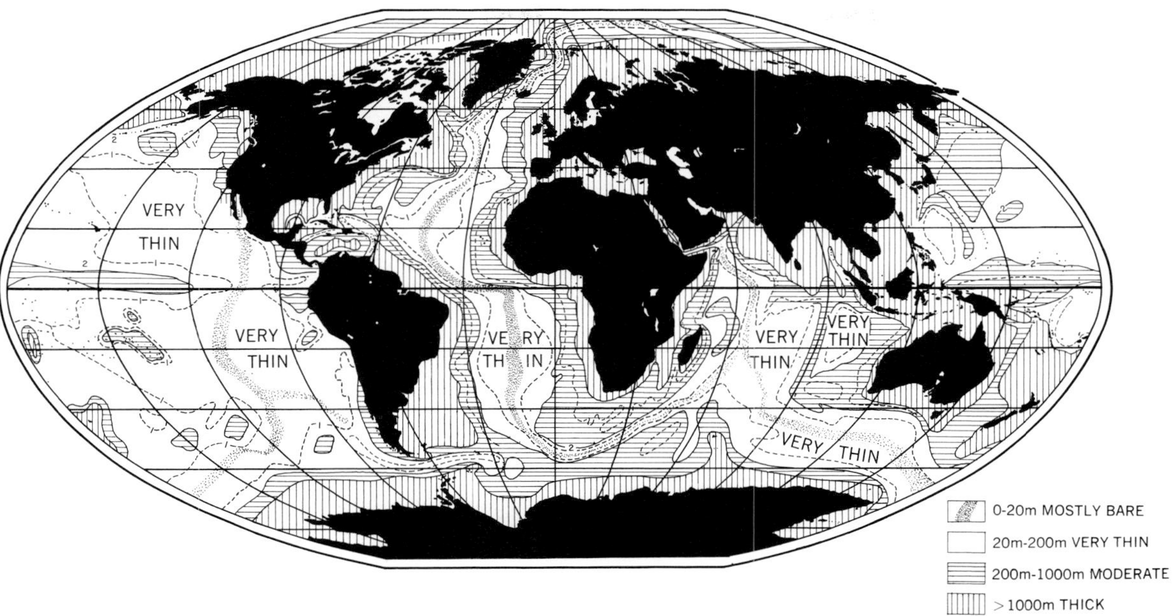

7.44 Sediment thickness based on seismic soundings and generalized on the basis of the smoothing of topography as observed on echo-sounding profiles. With a few exceptions, sediment is moderately thick (over 1000 meters) beneath the productive waters and relatively thin (less than 200 m) beneath the marine deserts.

waters. The patterns of productivity (7.43), which closely follow the patterns of horizontal and vertical circulation, determine the distribution of sediment type (7.46), sediment thickness (7.44), rates of accumulation (7.45), and abundance of bottom life (2.4).

The modest productivity of the warm, stable surface waters of the temperate latitudes is almost always nutrient-limited; whereas beyond the polar front, where the deep, nutrient-rich waters mix upward to the surface, productivity is limited by the available solar energy. Thus, there is a sharp contrast in productivity between the polar seas, where the upper waters have free circulation and communication with the deep, and the temperate seas, where a warm, stable, and partially spent surface layer bars the renewal of nutrients.

A polar divergence of the surface layers of the westerly equatorial current brings an upwelling of water from beneath. Thus a major zone of relatively high productivity follows the equator. Here the nineteenth-century New England whalers slaughtered sperm whales and here twentieth-century Japanese long-line tuna boats bring in bountiful catches. Beneath this narrow equatorial belt, the rate of sedimentation is ten times higher than in similar areas to the north or south. Sedimentation rates are also high

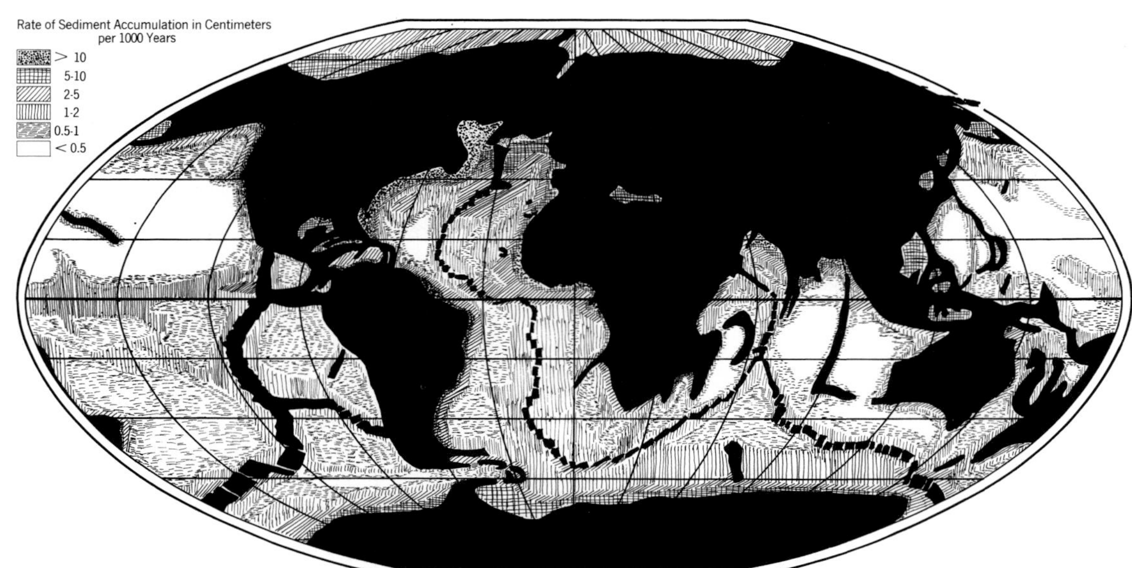

7.45 Rates of growth of the sediment blanket (in centimeters of thickness per thousand years).

where prevailing off-shore winds carry the warm surface waters seaward and upwelling draws the cold nutrient-rich waters to the surface.

Organic productivity and river discharge account for almost all the fine particles leaving the sea surface and descending to the deep; the waters, however, redissolve many of the discarded tests, the excreta, and the exuvia and return their constituents to the surface, providing nutrients for further generations of surface grazers and, in due course, for the animals that live on the sea floor below. The size of the benthic population, and consequently significant elements of submarine scenery, must be controlled principally by the quantity and type of organic detritus that rains down from above. An adequate supply of oxygen is needed to sustain life but the supply of other dissolved nutrients probably has no effect in the dark abyss, where no primary production takes place. Where oxygen is lacking in the bottom waters all life is snuffed out and the black floors of stagnant basins are without tracks, trails, or holes.

SCENIC DOMAINS OF OOZE AND CLAY

The calcareous shells of the planktonic foraminifera, pteropods, and coccoliths accumulate on the ocean floor and comprise a major proportion of the constituent particles of the organic ooze that blankets the floor of the only moderately deep portions of the abyss. As depths increase

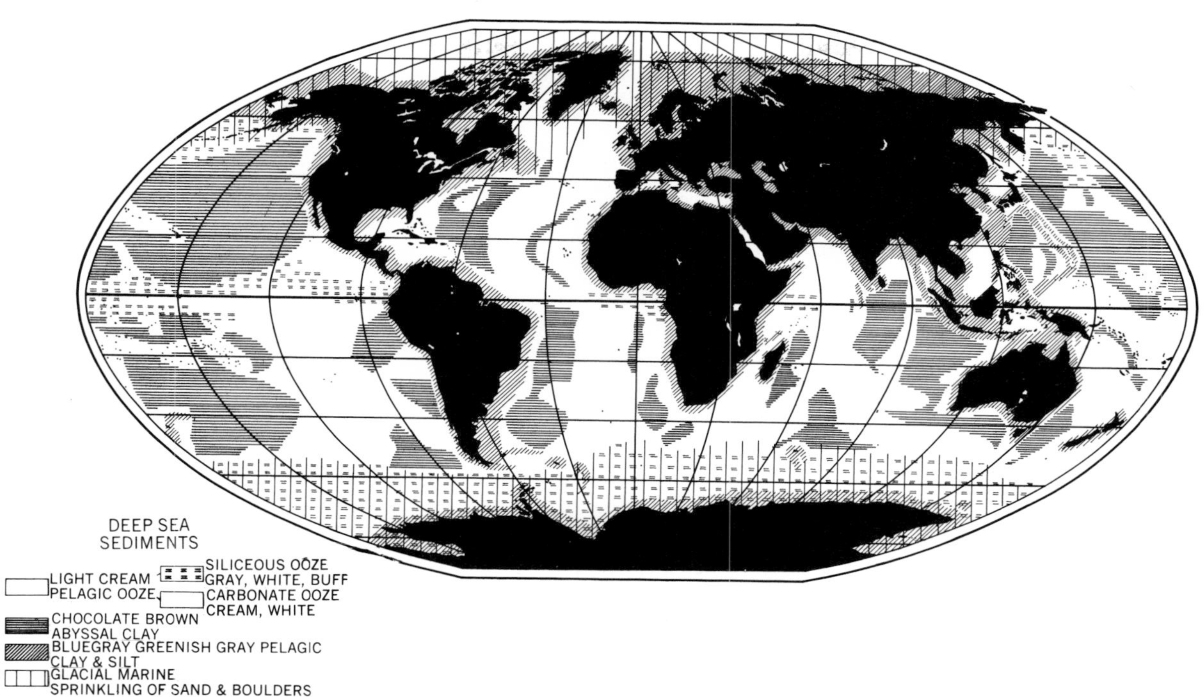

7.46 Distribution of sea-floor sediment.

over 4000 meters or as temperature drops below two-and-a-half degrees celsius the carbonate is redissolved by the deep and bottom waters, and in the frigid abyss below 4500 meters the proportion of carbonate in the bottom sediments rarely exceeds 10 per cent and usually falls below 2 per cent. In the transition zone between the carbonate ooze and the abyssal clay there is a decided shift in the foraminifera preserved. The thin-shelled fragile species disappear first at the upper limit while the heavier-shelled robust forms are the last to disappear as the lower limit of the carbonate zone is reached.

The carbonate ooze and the abyssal clay constitute the two basic types of substrate of the temperate abyss. The rate of accumulation of the ooze is in general ten times greater than the clay, and the coarse sandy texture of the foraminiferal ooze gives it decidedly different mechanical properties from the gelatinous clay. Thus in the search for an order in the world geography of submarine scenery the sediment map (7.46) offers an extremely significant key. The abyssal clay harbors less life and has fewer (and older) mounds, tracks, and holes. Those mounds that are seen are generally lower and less distinct than those of the carbonate ooze. Thus, in terms of the subtle scenery of the deep sea these two types of sub-sea soil are fundamental. The boundaries between the scenic domains of the ooze and clay have shifted through geologic time as the controlling factors of organic productivity at the sea surface, bottom-water circulation, and ocean depth have varied. These shifts in submarine scenery can be traced through a study of deep-sea cores which provide a record of past climates and past environments. The organic ooze preserves an exceedingly fine record of climatic changes at the sea surface.

An occasional catastrophe is recorded by a bed of volcanic ash, or laminae of wind-blown desert silt and diatoms, but in most mid-oceanic areas of ooze the principal characteristic is the monotonous uniformity over the thousands upon thousands of years represented by the accumulation. In the east equatorial Pacific the ooze boundary has shifted in response to fluctuations in the richness of equatorial productivity. Thus an inter-fingering of clay and ooze through the Pleistocene reflects the richer productivity of the ice ages, but the presence of middle Tertiary clay beneath the Pleistocene ooze and in a not too-distant spot the presence of early Tertiary ooze beneath the clay suggests that a large area of the eastern equatorial Pacific has undergone extensive shifts between the scenic realms of ooze and clay.

Climatic histories can be read from the ooze principally because various species of forminifera prefer cool waters, other species prefer the warm tropical waters, and still others have a variety of preferences. The three dozen species of foraminifera have shifted their patterns of distribution presumably in response to the changing temperature, salinity, and productivity patterns.

THICKNESS OF OCEAN SEDIMENTS

The layer of sediments that underlies the visible abyss and blankets the solid rocky foundations of the deep gradually accumulated during the span of geological time which separates the present day from that distant yesterday when the oceanic crust was born. Long before the ocean floor was explored, geologists had speculated on the probable average thickness of that water-soaked layer of mud. Assuming that the oceans were permanent and eternal all that was necessary was to estimate the rate of supply of the principal components of the sediment and to pick an appropriate date for the original creation of the present ocean basins. Alternately a rate of accumulation could be estimated on the basis of the 10- to 20-cm-thick layer of ooze deposited since that time when the shells of warm-water foraminifera began to outnumber the cold forms in and beneath temperate seas. This time interval between the ice age and the present is now known

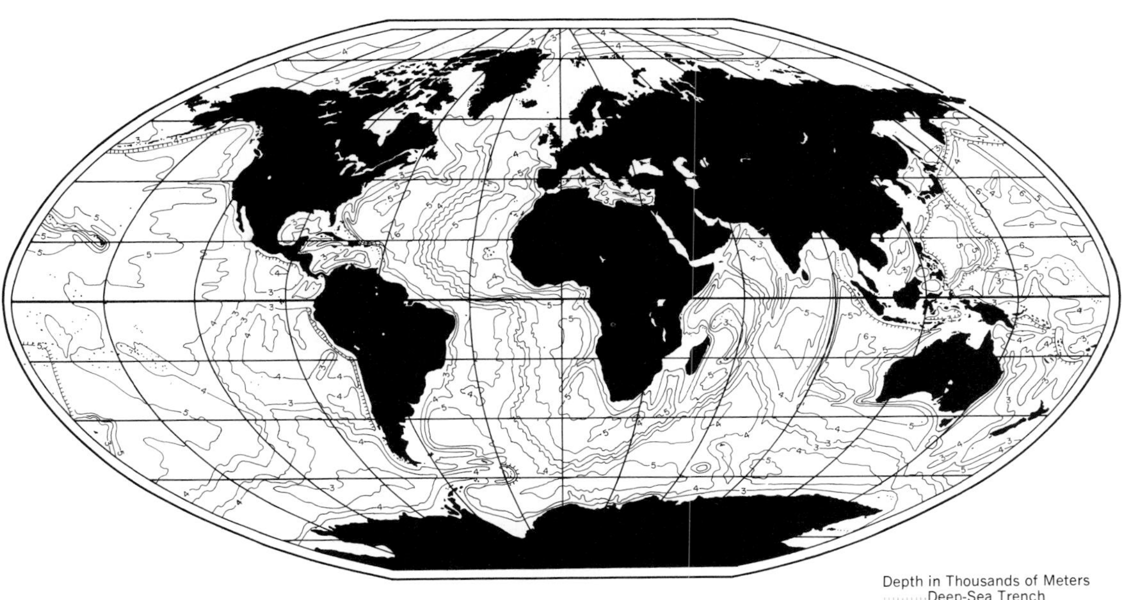

7.47 Generalized bathymetry of the world ocean.

to have been about 10,000 years but it was first assumed to be 20,000 years. This rate of accumulation was then applied to the total sedimentary blanket, which was estimated to have an average thickness of 3000 meters.

When echo-sounders revealed the rugged nature of the mid-oceanic abyss, there was concern over possible errors in the budget, but when seismic reflection profiles were obtained showing that the sediments over most of the floor of the world ocean were less than a few hundred meters thick this mild concern turned to near panic. Fundamental geological principles were at stake. Somebody was badly wrong. At first there was considerable revision of the estimates. Perhaps modern rates of erosion and deposition are exceptionally high; perhaps the Tertiary was also exceptional due to the increasing abundance of shell-bearing plankton in this latest period of earth history. Or perhaps there is a thick layer of consolidated sediments beneath the blanket of unconsolidated ooze which represents deposition during all previous geologic time. These simple considerations began a major crisis in oceanography. The seismic reflection measurements of sediment thickness made since World War II demonstrated a vast discrepancy between the measured thickness and the predicted thickness. Either rates of accumulation were vastly less for previous geologic epochs and periods or the ocean floor is not original and eternal. We shall explore the reasons for this startling discrepancy in later chapters but for now let us simply record that all was not well within the basic premises of deep-sea geology.

SUBSTANCE OF THE SUBSTRATE

We have in this chapter visually examined the objects which reach the deep-sea floor; both those huge in dimensions but volumetrically small and those fine and subtle but volumetrically important. It is these later components which make up the substance of the substrate in and on which animals live (7.46) and upon which the footprints, trails, mounds, feces, and holes are perceived. These features are the subject of our first six chapters.

Beginning in the next chapter, we turn to the physical processes that shape the sea floor and not only leave their mark in today's visible abyss but have through their activities over the past millions of years created or modified the topography of the deep-sea floor. We will first treat those processes associated with the smoother parts of the sea floor which produce their principal visual and topographic effects by the erosion, transportation, and redeposition of the materials we have just discussed.

REFERENCES AND NOTES

1. The study of sediments which accumulated on the floors of ancient seas occupies the majority of the world's geologists. The principles of geology are illustrated in thousands of texts; however, *Principles of Physical Geology* by Arthur Holmes (1965. Ronald Press, New York, pp. 287-345) is certainly one of the more engaging and is illustrated with excellent photographs of geologic phenomena taken from all parts of the world. Other outstanding texts include: Arthur Strahler. 1963. *The Earth Sciences.* Harper and Row, New York, 681 pp.; and C. R. Longwell, R. F. Flint, and J. E. Sanders. 1969. *Physical Geology.* Wiley, New York, 685 pp. The formation of sedimentary strata is thoroughly treated in the following classical works: A. W. Grabau. 1913. *Principles of Stratigraphy.* A. G. Seiler and Co., New York, 780 pp.; and W. H. Twenhofel, editor. 1932. *Treatise on Sedimentation.* Williams and Wilkins, Baltimore, 926 pp. This has been republished in paperback form in 1961 by Dover, New York.
2. The disposal of low-level radioactive waste in the sea has generated much controversy. One of the many studies of this problem is: D. E. Carritt, and others. 1959. Radioactive Waste Disposal into Atlantic and Gulf Coastal Waters. *U.S. Nat. Acad. Sci. and Nat. Res. Counc., Pub.* 655:37 pp.
3. Illustrated popular discussions of submarine archaeology are found in: N. C. Fleming. 1962. Sunken cities and forgotten wrecks, G. E. R. Deacon, editor. *Seas, Maps and Men.* Doubleday & Co., New York, pp. 123-73; J. Cousteau. 1954. To the depths of the sea by bathyscaphe. *Nat. Geog. Mag.,* 106:67-79; and in J. Dugan. 1967. *World Beneath the Sea.* Nat. Geog. Soc., Washington, D.C., 204 pp.
4. Wrecks have been visually identified in the abyss by use of cameras and deep submersibles (F. N. Spiess and A. E. Maxwell. 1964. Search for the *Thresher. Science,* 145:349-56.).

5. More than 250,000 miles of communication cable, both working and abandoned, has been laid on the ocean floor. A discussion of cable laying, cable equipment, and technique of repairing can be found in: C. Bright. 1898. *Submarine Telegraphs.* C. Lockwood and Son, London, 744 pp. A discussion of how the marine environment affects cables is found in: C. H. Elmendorf, B. C. Heezen, L. R. Snoke, and E. E. Zajac. 1957. Submarine Cables; Oceanography, Marine Biology and Cable Mechanics. *Bell Telephone System Monographs,* 2847:160 pp. Concerted efforts have been made to photograph and visually observe submarine cables in order to determine why trawlers so frequently snag them. It has been discovered that cables are often suspended across low and otherwise undetectable ridges on the sea floor. Because of these suspensions, trawls can plow beneath the suspended cables and become entangled with them.

6. A. C. Hardy. 1956. *The Open Sea. Its Natural History.* Houghton Mifflin, Boston, Pt. 1:335 pp.; and N. B. Marshall. 1954. *Aspects of Deep Sea Biology.* Hutchinson's, London, pp. 131-56.

7. Sharks' teeth and whale earbones are prominant among the larger objects described in this first comprehensive study of deep sea deposits: J. Murray and A. F. Renard. 1891. Report on deep-sea deposits based on specimens collected during the voyage of H. M. S. *Challenger* in the years 1872 to 1876. Challenger *Repts. Geology and Petrology,* 3:583 pp.

8. J. M. Peres. 1965. Aperçu sur les résultats de deux plongées effectuées dans le ravin de Puerto Rico par la bathyscaphe *Archimède. Deep-Sea Res.,* 12:883-91.

9. J. Knudsen. 1962. The bathyal and abyssal Xylophaga. Galathea Reports, 5:47 pp.

10. K. O. Emery. 1963. Organic transportation of marine sediments. In M. N. Hill, editor. *The Sea.* Wiley, New York, 3:776-93.

11. F. M. Bullard. 1962. *Volcanos.* Univ. of Texas Press, 441 pp.

12. R. V. Fisher. 1964. Maximum size, median diameter, and sorting of tephra. *J. Geophys. Res.,* 69:341-55.

13. Thorarinsson, S., 1967. *The Eruption of Hekla in Historical Time.* Rit Visindafj. Isl., 1:183 pp.

14. D. Ninkovich and B. C. Heezen. 1965. Santorini tephra. In W. F. Whittard and R. Bradshaw, editors. *Submarine Geology and Geophysics.* Butterworth, London, pp. 413-52; J. Lear. 1966. "The volcano that shaped the western world?" *Saturday Review,* 5 November, 57-66.

15. H. Pettersson. 1960. Cosmic spherules and meteoric dust. *Sci. American,* 202: 123-32.

16. J. A. O'Keefe, editor. 1963. *Tektites.* Univ. Chicago Press, Chicago, 228 pp.

17. E. Saurin and A. Millies-LaCroix. 1961. Tektites par 1270 m, de fond au large du Vietnam. *Compte. Rends, Soc. Geol. France,* 5:128-29.

18. B. Glass, D. B. Ericson, B. C. Heezen, N. D. Opdyke, and A. J. Glass. 1967. Geomagnetic reversals and Pleistocene chronology. *Nature,* 216:437-42. The earth's magnetic field reverses its polarity every few hundred thousand years. In a short period, certainly less than a few thousand years, the field flips and the poles exchange places.

19. B. Glass. 1967. Microtektites in deep-sea sediments. *Nature,* 214:372-74; and, B. Glass and B. C. Heezen. 1967. Tektites and geomagnetic reversals. *Nature,* 214:372. It has been suggested that an extraterrestrial body brought the tektites

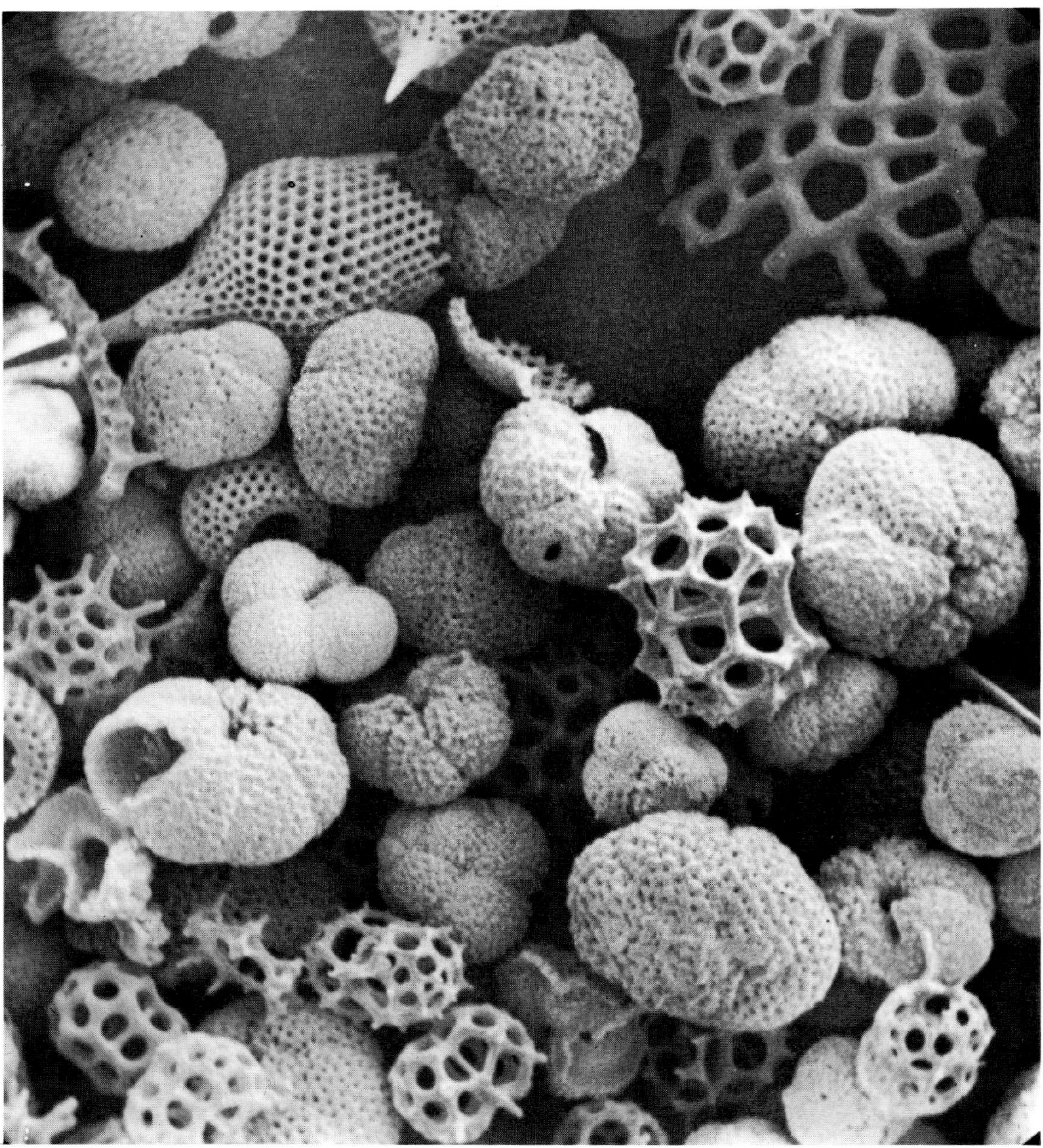

7.48 Foraminifera and radiolaria accumulate on the sea floor. Electron micrograph x250. 120 m below Caroline Ridge, western Pacific, 2850 m.

to earth and caused the magnetic field to reverse. The previous reversals which have occurred every few hundred thousand years over the late geological history of the earth might each have been caused or accompanied by such a cosmic encounter. Each may have affected the course of evolution and perhaps the total effect of these encounters may have in large measure determined the course of geologic history.

20. B. C. Heezen and C. Hollister. 1964. Turbidity Currents and Glaciation. In A. E. Nairin, editor. *Problems in Paleoclimatology*. Wiley, New York, 99-108. The areas affected by ice-rafting can be inferred from the *Ice Atlas of the Northern Hemisphere,* U.S. Navy Hydro. Off., Washington, D.C., 1946, Pub. 550.

21. K. Andree. 1920. *Geologie des Meeresbodens*. Borntrager, Leipzig, 2:689 pp.

22. W. Schwarzacher and K. Hunkins. 1961. Dredged gravels from the central Arctic Ocean. *Geology of the Arctic*. Univ. of Toronto Press, Toronto, pp. 666-77; K. L. Hunkins, M. Ewing, B. C. Heezen, and R. J. Menzies. 1960. Biological and geological observations on the first photographs of the Arctic Ocean deep-sea floor. *Limnology and Oceanography,* 5:154-61.

23. M. N. Bramelette and W. H. Bradley. 1941. Lithology and geologic interpretations. In M. N. Bradley, editor. Geology and biology of North Atlantic deep-sea cores between Newfoundland and Ireland. *U.S. Geol. Survey, Prof. Paper,* 196: 1-32.

24. For a general discussion of the composition and distribution of marine sediment, the reader is referred to: G. Arrhenius. 1963. Pelagic sediments. In M. N. Hill, editor. *The Sea*. Wiley, New York, 3:655-727: and E. D. Goldberg. 1963. Mineralogy and chemistry of marine sedimentation. In F. P. Shepard, *Submarine Geology,* 2nd edition, pp. 435-67.

25. K. K. Turekian. 1968. Stratigraphy and geochronometry of deep-sea deposits. *Oceans,* Prentice-Hall, Inc., Englewood Cliffs, N.J., pp. 51-72; and M. J. Keen. 1968. *An Introduction to Marine Geology*. Pergamon Press, New York, pp. 62-69.

26. D. Ninkovich, N. D. Opdyke, B. C. Heezen, and J. Foster. 1966. Paleomagnetic stratigraphy, rates of deposition and tephrachronology in north Pacific deep-sea sediments. *Earth and Planetary Science Letters,* 1:476-92.

27. E. Steemann Nielsen. 1963. Fertility of the oceans; productivity, definition and measurement. In M. N. Hill, editor. *The Sea*. Wiley, New York, 2:129-64.

41°17′N   66°01′W

8.1 Turbidity currents have carved the sedimentary rocks that now form the walls of Corsair Canyon, 1593 m, continental slope off New England.

8
Canyon Catastrophes

. . . it shoots the last dark canyon
to the plains of far away . . .
CONAN DOYLE

Submarine canyons constitute one of the most picturesque and intriguing phenomena of the continental margin. Discovered a century ago by some of the earliest sounding surveys, they immediately captured the imagination of scientists and laymen. The first detailed deep-sea hydrographic surveys were designed to delineate their morphology, and the first systematic rock dredging of the continental slope was conducted in an attempt to solve the problem of their origin and history. The first scientific use of research submarines beyond the edge of the continental shelf was to examine the walls of the canyons. To date submarine canyons have been visually examined to a greater extent than any other submarine phenomena beyond the continental shelf (8.1, 8.2).

Throughout the world, canyons indent the continental slope.[1] They are from a few kilometers to a few hundred kilometers long and from a few hundred meters to a few thousand meters wide. Although most are but a few hundred meters deep, some at their maximum development cut 2000 meters below the continental slope. Their walls are generally steeper than the slopes into which they cut but the declivity of the walls is difficult to ascertain (8.3); nearly vertical slopes (8.4) are certainly more common than the charts produced by echo-sounding suggest.[2] Canyons are generally V-shaped, but U-shaped and box canyons are also known. Most submarine canyons are limited to the continental slope, and neither indent the continental shelf nor extend seaward across the continental rise.

The term "submarine canyon" as used by most workers refers to any persistent valley found on the continental margin regardless of shape or size. Longitudinal gradients of the continental slope canyons range from

8.2 Vertical cliffs and giant talus blocks in submarine canyons suggest large-scale erosion. U, L, 2965 m, Mona Canyon west of Puerto Rico.

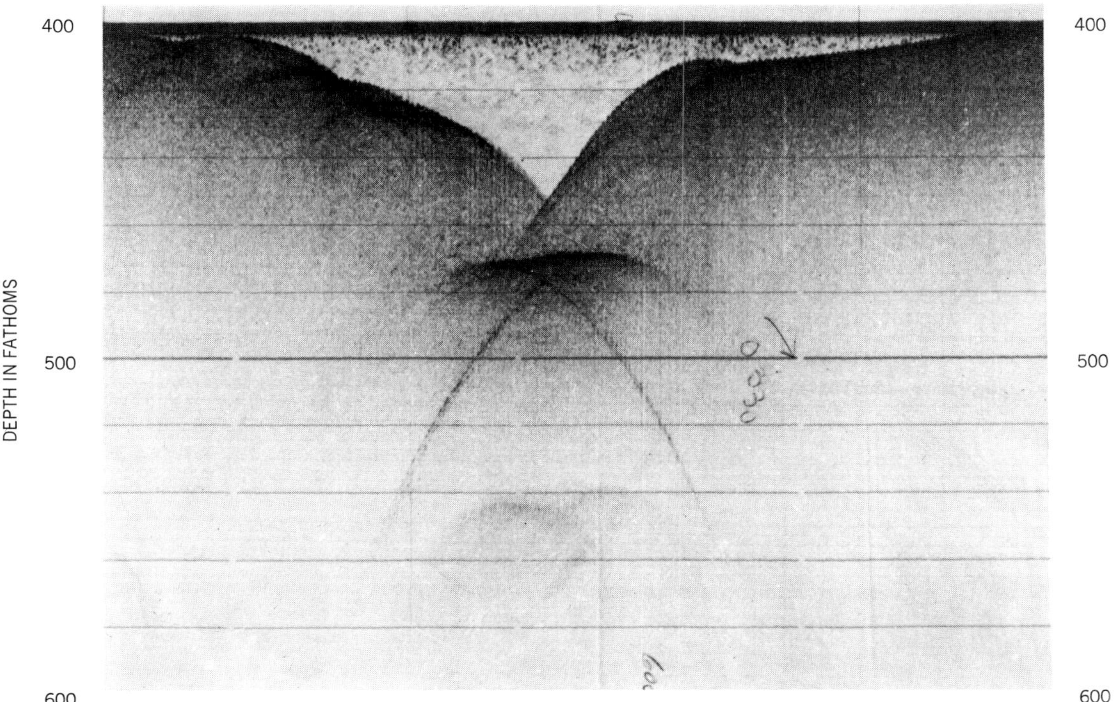

8.3 Echogram across a submarine canyon. Slopes greater than about fifteen degrees cannot be recorded with normal echo-sounding techniques.

one in three to one in one hundred; but such gradients as well as depth, width, and cross section are drastically reduced when the submarine canyons reach the continental rise. In those few of the largest canyons which extend further into the ocean basin, longitudinal gradient, depths, and widths are closely adjusted to the gradient of the continental rise. The Hudson Canyon, for instance, cuts 500 meters into the steeper seaward face of the upper continental rise, but on the low gradients of the lower continental rise it decreases to a feature only a few tens of meters deep. Large fan- or cone-shaped sediment accumulations flank the larger canyons. Virtually all canyons completely disappear before reaching the continental rise-abyssal plain boundary.

Where the continental shelf is narrow or nearly absent, subaerial canyons often continue beneath the sea as submarine canyons. Such continuations are well displayed in the French Riviera, Corsica, off southern California, and off areas where high relief borders the shore. Where the continental shelf is wide, certain of the large rivers are connected to the heads of major submarine canyons by drowned river channels. Often there is sufficient correspondence between the number and spacing of major rivers and major submarine canyons to suggest their former connection.

Numerous hypotheses on the origin of submarine canyons have appeared over the past century. A scientist who devoted much of his long career to the study of submarine canyons once observed that the authors of most of the hypotheses "had at least one thing in common; none of

23°22′N 109°25′W
22°52′N 109°54′W

8.4 Near the canyon's source. Sand falls have eroded these narrow gorges off Baja California, Mexico. U, 50 m, the head of Los Frailes Submarine Canyon. L, 39 m, San Lucas Submarine Canyon.

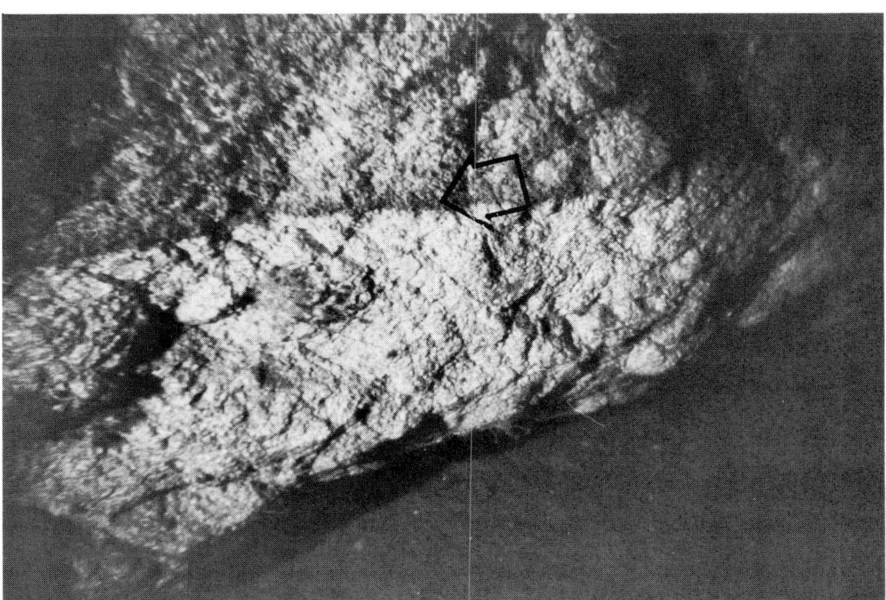

23°21′N 109°24′W

8.5 Re-excavated rock-walled canyons. The sharp break in animal growth (arrow) approximately one meter above the present floor of the canyon marks the former level of sediment fill. The re-excavated canyon wall is undercut and markedly smoother. 250 m, Los Frailes Canyon, Baja, California.

them had studied the canyons other than by examination of *published* charts." Additional data were needed in order to test and evaluate the numerous hypotheses. Such tests have recently been provided by direct sampling and direct visual observation (8.5, 8.6).

In the nineteenth century, New England fishermen are reported to have brought ashore curious fossiliferous rocks which they had recovered from the walls of submarine canyons. These marls and sandstones, which proved to be Tertiary and Cretaceous in age, gave the first clues to the nature and age of canyon walls. Later, when the rock walls of the New England canyons were systematically dredged,[3] it was found that they are cut into nearly horizontal beds of Tertiary and Mesozoic shallow-water sediments. Outcrops were eventually found in submarine canyons indenting the continental slopes of all continents. Contemporary, or at least recently active processes of erosion, were clearly called for.

THE FIRST PHOTOGRAPHS

The similarity in morphology between subaerial and submarine canyons was interpreted by many geologists as proof of their subaerial origin.[4] A sea-level lowering of several hundred meters as a consequence of water

32°52′N 117°15′W

8.6 Overhanging canyon wall. Solid walls of rock have been eroded by sand fall. Sand on the ledges is carried over the lip of the canyon during periods of strong storm swell. Large quantities of sand are diverted down the axis through tributaries. Mouth of south branch of Scripps Canyon where it enters Sumner branch, 40 m.

locked up in Pleistocene glaciers was postulated. Since these glaciers melted about 10,000 years ago, the rocky walls of the canyons, according to this hypothesis, should be covered by a thin layer of marine mud deposited on the subaerial erosion surface after its submergence beneath the rising sea.

The first photographs from the deep sea were obtained in the New England submarine canyons and the tranquil, muddy, tracked, and burrowed bottom observed was assumed to be the surface of the expected post-glacial layer of mud. The absence of obvious visual indications of contemporary processes of erosion was interpreted as further evidence

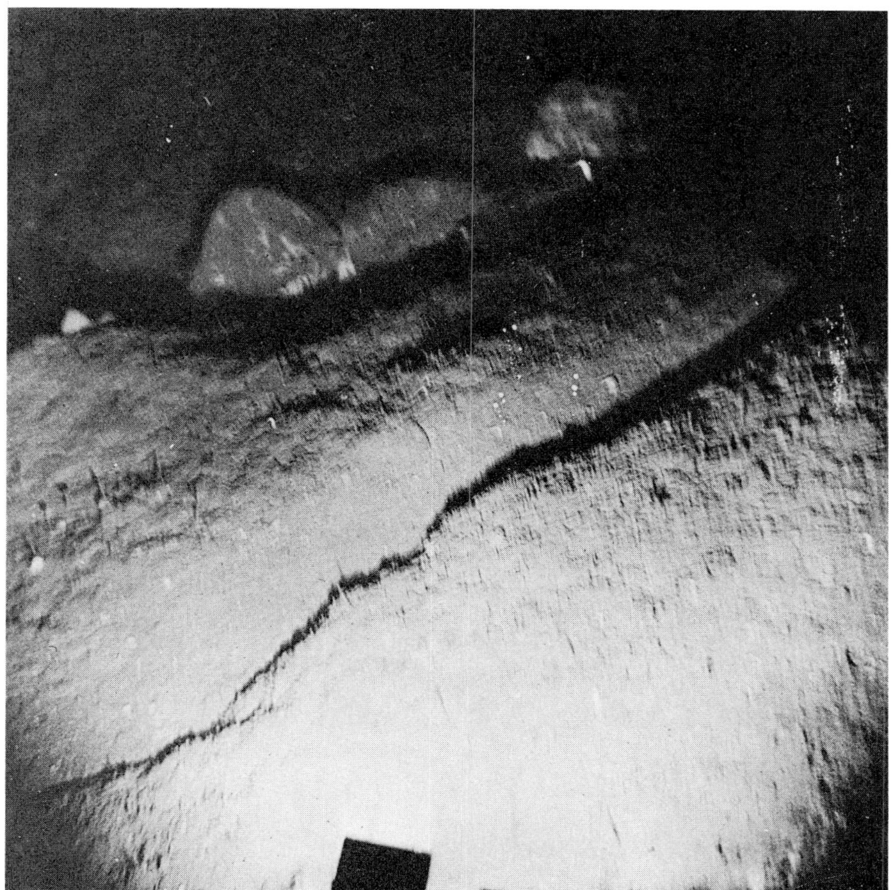

39°50′N 70°50′W

8.7 A recently eroded outcrop of Eocene marl. The first visual evidence of contemporary erosion, 1000 m, New England continental slope.

against the submarine formation of the canyons. However, in a small submarine canyon south of Rhode Island, a photograph and simultaneous core recorded a bare outcrop of unconsolidated Eocene marl; proof that erosion is occurring today deep on the continental slope (8.7).[5] This observation was the first of several post World War II discoveries which finally led to the rejection of the subaerial erosion hypothesis in favor of contemporary submarine processes. However, the puzzling fact remained that the first photographs taken in submarine canyons revealed little but a smooth muddy bottom, and this fact appeared to support the general opinion that the deep sea was devoid of currents or other steady-state processes capable of eroding canyons.

Since several submarine canyons seem to be related to great faults in the earth's crust, the general explanation of all submarine canyons as fault troughs gained some acceptance. However, sediment sampling in canyons revealed sands and silts, and rounded gravels, all of which bore clear evidence of extensive transportation, rather than broken and crushed rocks which would be predicted under the fault hypothesis. In fact, it was an investigation of the sands and gravels that lie beneath the muddy surface of the canyon floors which led to the present emphasis on downslope sediment transport through the canyons.

VIGOROUS BUT INTERMITTENT

The predominantly smooth, muddy, tranquil scene recorded by photographs of submarine canyons reveals that whatever contemporary process exposes and maintains the bare rock outcrops, and whatever process has eroded the canyons deeply into the ancient stratified rocks of the continental slope (8.8-8.13), this process operates intermittently—just how intermittently one cannot surely judge, for we know not how long it takes the deep-sea fauna to track and burrow the surface following either erosion or deposition. The coarseness of the displaced sediments

8.8. Seismic reflection profile of Laurentian Submarine Canyon. High-energy sound signals are sent to the sea floor and their reflections are recorded on depth recorders, thus revealing stratification within the upper few kilometers of unconsolidated sediments. U, horizontal beds have been eroded near the head of the Laurentian Submarine Canyon on the continental slope. L, this same canyon crossed again on the continental rise, appears to be formed by an upward migration of natural levees rather than by erosion of pre-existing deposits.

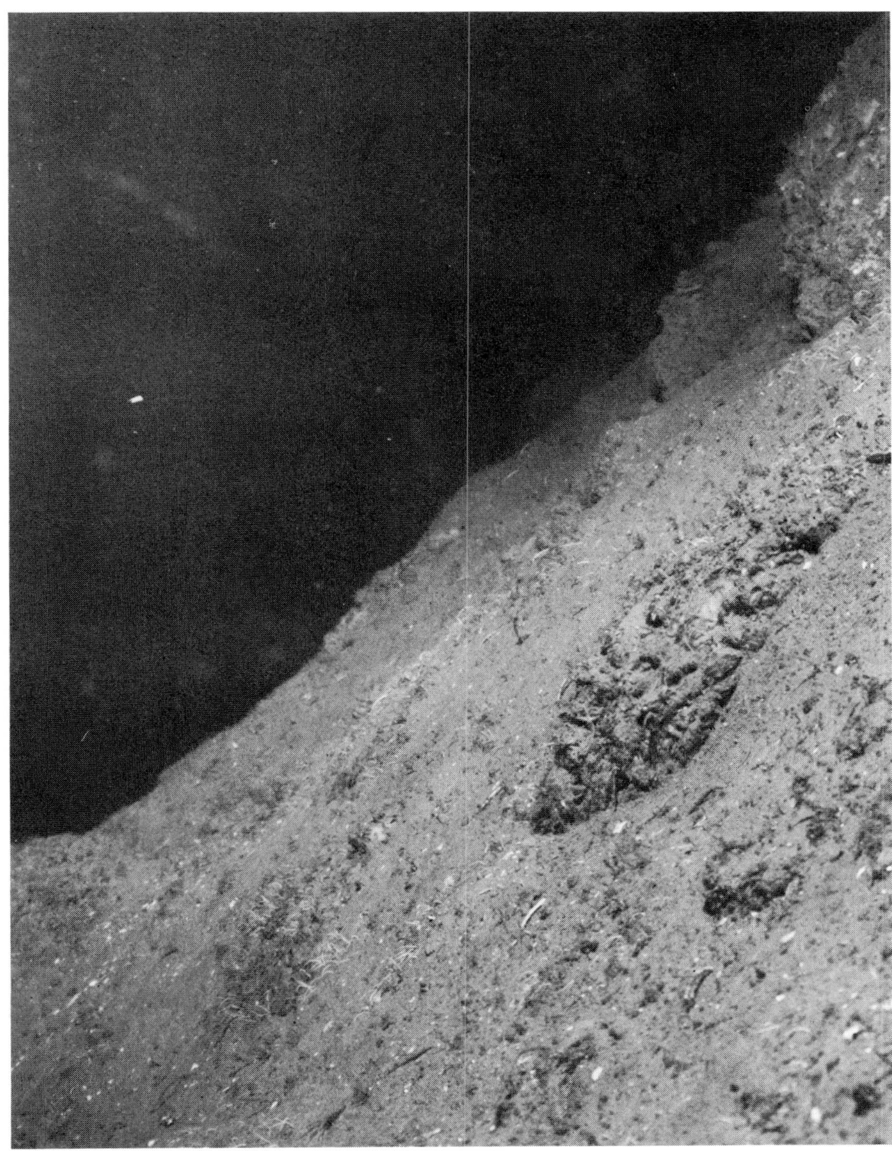

8.9 Sand and organic debris piles against a canyon wall. 800 m, north wall of Hudson Submarine Canyon.

which generally lie immediately beneath the surface film of mud in the floors of submarine canyons make it quite clear that the highly competent but intermittent processes involved may operate at relatively high velocities.

In the late nineteenth century it had been suggested that the sublacustrine channel of the River Rhone in eastern Lac Leman (Switzerland) was formed by a type of intermittent bottom current,[6] which might be

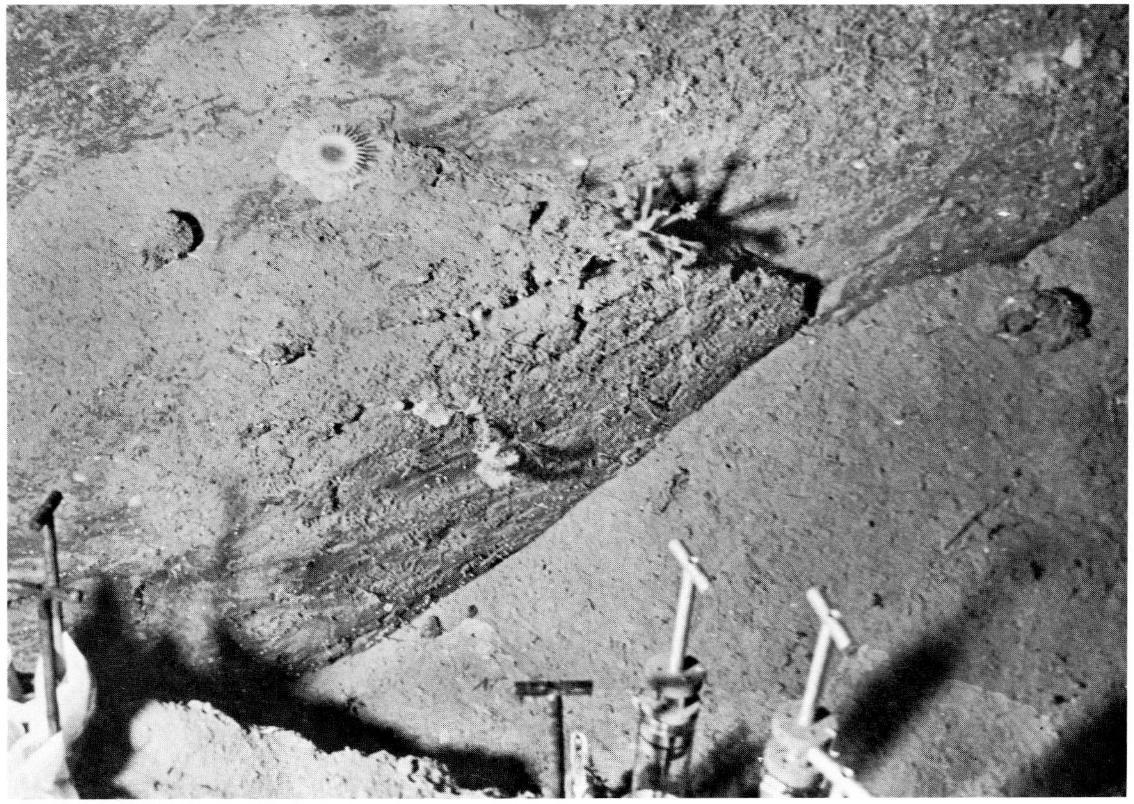

40°15′N 68°06′W

8.10 Outcrops in Oceanographer Canyon. The contact between the vertical rock wall of the canyon and the unconsolidated sediment on the canyon floor is abrupt. Photograph from Research Submarine *Alvin,* 1210 m, west wall of Oceanographer Canyon, continental slope off New England.

called a turbidity current. The mechanism envisaged was that the cold, sediment-laden river-water which seasonally flows on the lake floor beneath the lake waters produced the characteristic leveed channel. A half-century later, the idea was reintroduced into the submarine canyon controversy when it was suggested[7] that currents of sediment-laden water generated by breaking waves on ice age beaches had eroded submarine cayons as they flowed downslope into the abyss. In the late 1930's, model experiments[8] and investigations in fresh-water reservoirs revealed considerable new evidence in favor of the hypothesis. However, for ten or more years none of the experiments produced currents that could erode, and no evidence was found for the occurrence of such bottom-seeking currents in the modern ocean.

Sediment cores taken during the late 1940's in submarine canyons revealed beds of displaced sediment containing shallow-water foraminifera,

8.11 Results of a catastrophe. Scene of a collapse on the wall of a submarine canyon, 4000 m, continental rise off Cape Hatteras, western Atlantic.

coarse silts and sands, and even gravel. This material was first interpreted as evidence of a great lowering of sea level, but this idea had to be abandoned when it was found that normal pelagic sedimentation had continued without interruption in the shallower areas between the canyons at the same time the vigorous transportation intermittently occurred in the canyons.[9]

Meanwhile sedimentologists hypothesized that turbulent suspensions of sediment and water could have appreciable excess density and that they could flow at the relatively high velocities necessary to transport sand and gravel. However, many geologists and oceanographers remained unconvinced, and numerous alternate hypotheses for the explanation of the displaced sediments were put forward. Obviously, what was needed to confirm the role of modern turbidity currents was evidence of this activity on the deep-sea floor.

FULL-SCALE EXPERIMENTS

It was then recognized that a full-scale experiment had already been conducted. Cable failures that occurred following the 1929 Grand Banks

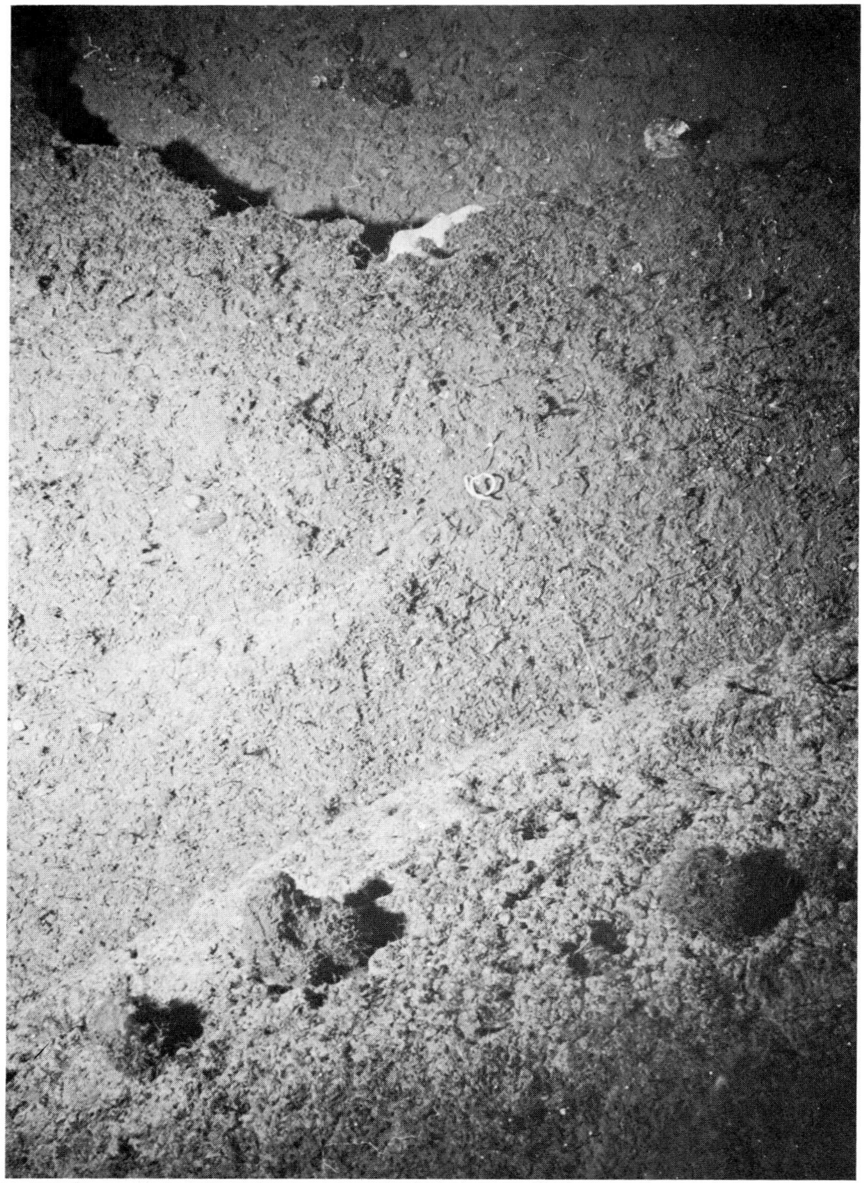

8.12 Ledges of ancient sedimentary rock lie exposed on the steep walls of "The Gully." A dense growth of benthic organisms covers rock, 819 m, northeast wall of "The Gully" Submarine Canyon, east of Nova Scotia.

earthquake appeared to be due to downslope motion of turbidity currents that converged from various sources near the epicenter and flowed south on a broad front four hundred kilometers wide for a distance of more than six hundred kilometers[10] (8.14). A series of sediment cores

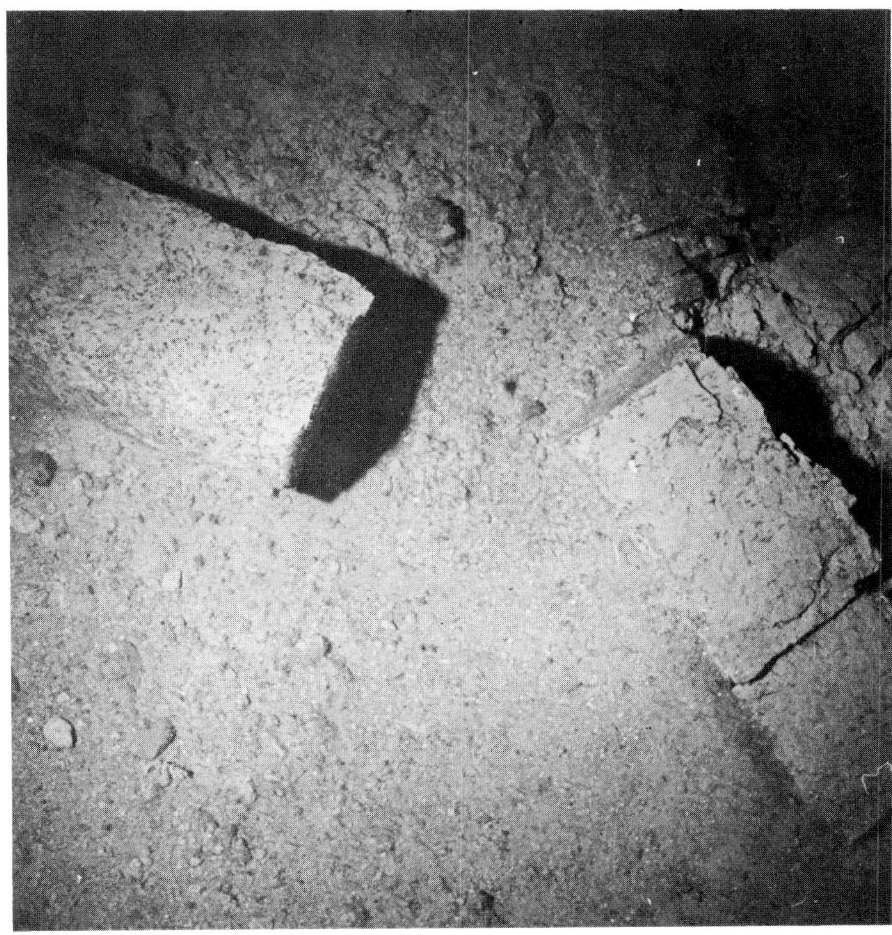

43°58′N 58°59′W

8.13 Fractured blocks of sedimentary rock on the wall of "The Gully." Absence of attached organisms on rock blocks suggest they were recently moved. 1334 m, northeast wall of "The Gully" Submarine Canyon, east of Nova Scotia.

taken on the abyssal plain south of the epicenter revealed an uppermost layer in which particle size graded upwards from fine sand to fine silt and clay. The sequence of the cable breaks and intervals between them made it possible to determine the speed of the current. The velocity turned out to be amazingly high, being over twenty-five meters per second on the continental slope and over seven meters per second at the base of the continental rise (8.15, 8.16). Such high velocities were hard to comprehend and were not at first accepted; some claimed that the sequence and pattern were merely coincidental.

In the year 1954, following an earthquake in Algeria, a roughly similarly sequence of cable breaks in the Mediterranean revealed similar

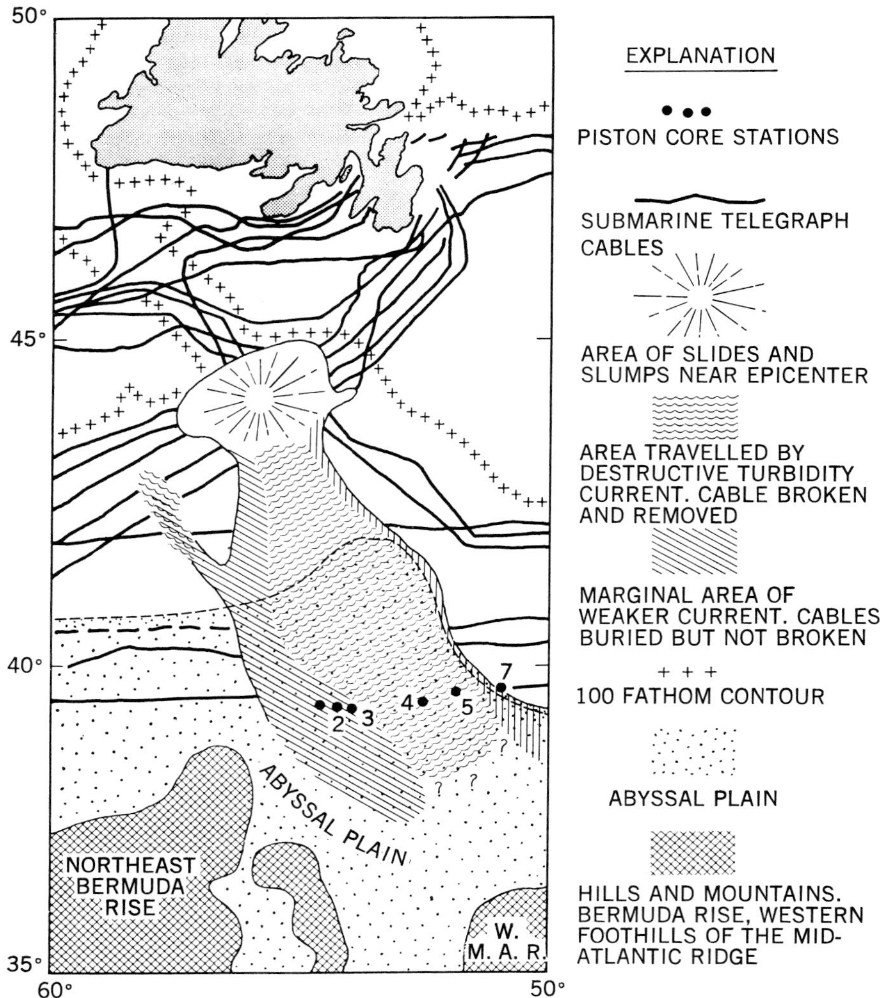

8.14 The 1929 Grand Banks turbidity current. Sediment cores obtained downslope of the earthquake epicenter contain graded, muddy sands which were deposited by the turbidity current. This catastrophic flow broke many submarine telegraph cables and deposited sand and silt and silty mud over an area of about 200,000 square miles.

velocities. A search of records revealed that the 1908 Messina earthquake had produced one later cable break which suggested a current traveling at an average velocity of more than five meters per second over a distance of two hundred kilometers. In 1966, and again in 1968, turbidity currents originating in the Markham River delta of New Guinea traveled down the axis of the New Britain Trench at velocities of over five meters per second, severing and burying a newly laid telephone cable (8.17, 8.18).

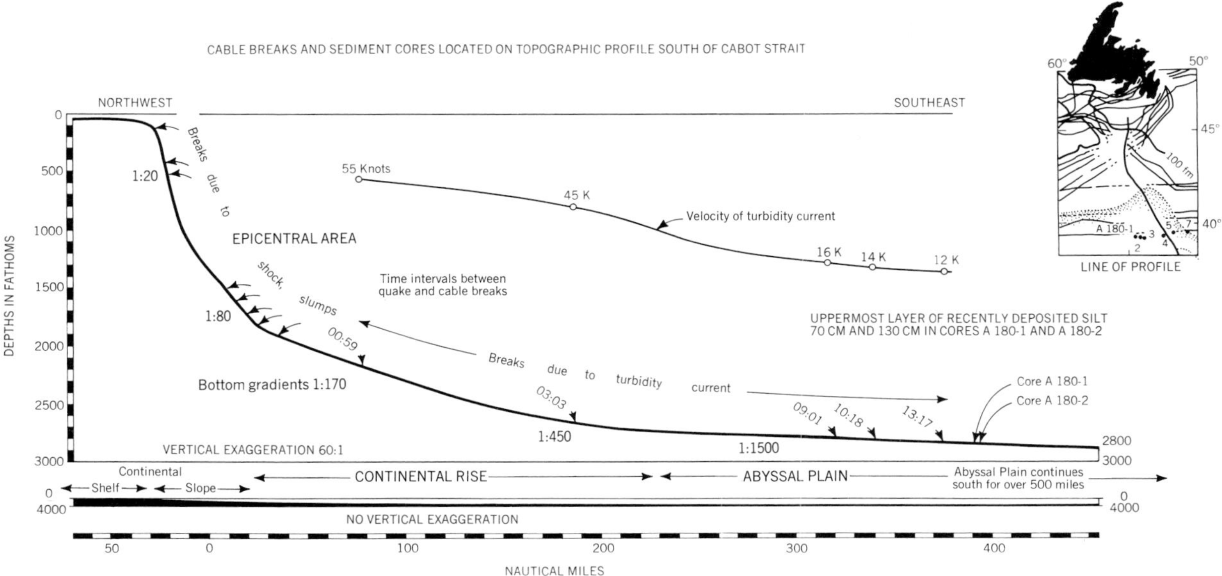

8.15 Turbidity currents flowing at high speed sever submarine cables. These catastrophic currents deposit sand and silt hundreds of miles from the epicentral area.

The St. Lawrence river was an important glacial discharge channel and during the lowered sea-level of the ice age built a thick submarine delta on the continental slope. Gravitational failure within this rapidly accumulated deposit was triggered by the 1929 Grand Banks earthquake (8.19-8.22). An extensive slump or overthrust 400 meters thick and over 100 kilometers wide and 100 kilometers long moved a few hundred meters, severing the submarine cables along the margin of the moving mass but leaving its internal stratification undisturbed. The turbidity currents began near the epicenter and flowed in part over, but mostly around, the large overthrust. Neither photographs nor cores have been obtained, either on the slump face or in the area in which the turbidity currents were apparently generated. Although it is dubious whether visual effects would be left after nearly half a century, cores should still reveal contorted, broken, and brecciated sediments.

Slumps have occasionally been photographed (8.23) and must be a rather common visual feature in areas where rapid deposition is occurring on relatively steep slopes. Cores containing angular mixtures of varicolored Tertiary clays are often found deep on steep submarine escarpments (8.24). Evidence of slumping is not limited to the steepest slopes, however, and has been found even on the lower gradients of the lower continental rise.

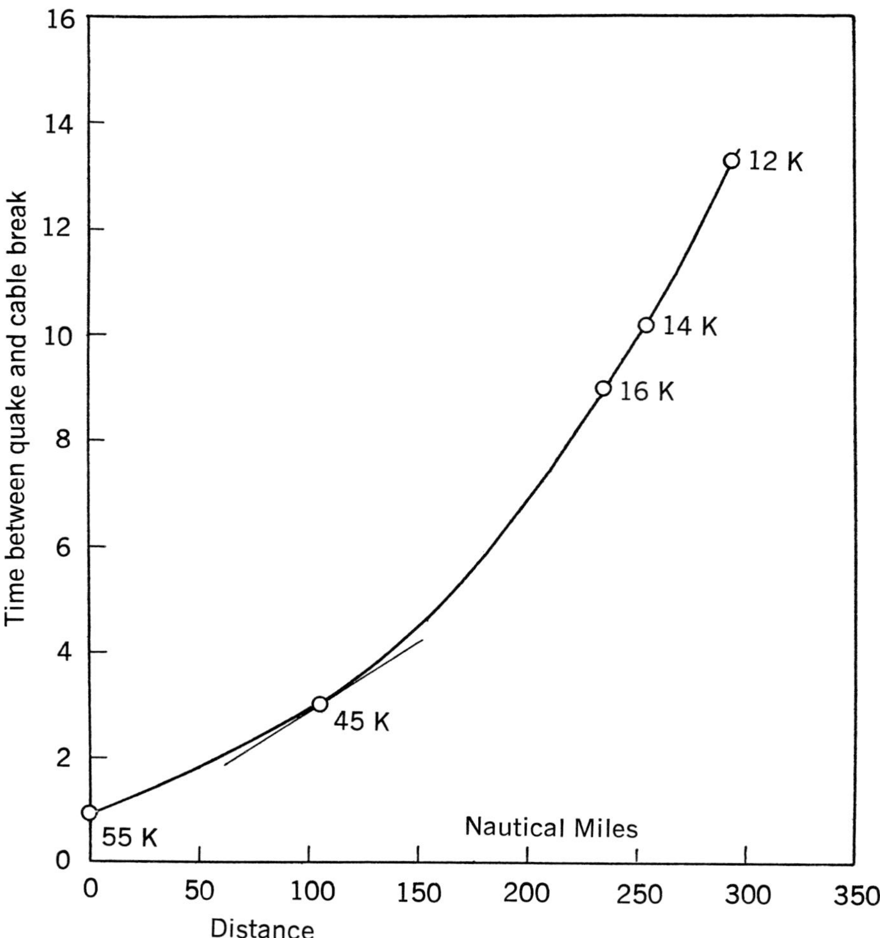

8.16 The velocity of the 1929 Grand Banks turbidity current was determined by the sequence of cable breaks. Velocities in knots, i.e. nautical miles per hour.

CONGO CABLES

The Congo Submarine Canyon is situated at the mouth of the Congo River on the west coast of Africa. Known to be at least 800 kilometers long, exclusive of meanders (8.25), it is one of the largest submarine canyons in the world. The heads of many submarine canyons are filled with sediment; in contrast, the Congo Canyon extends 30 kilometers into the mouth of the Congo River with steep sides and a V-shaped profile (8.26). A delta is not being formed at the river mouth. Instead, the bedload of the river is ultimately transported through the canyon and deposited on the continental rise and on the Angola Abyssal Plain to the

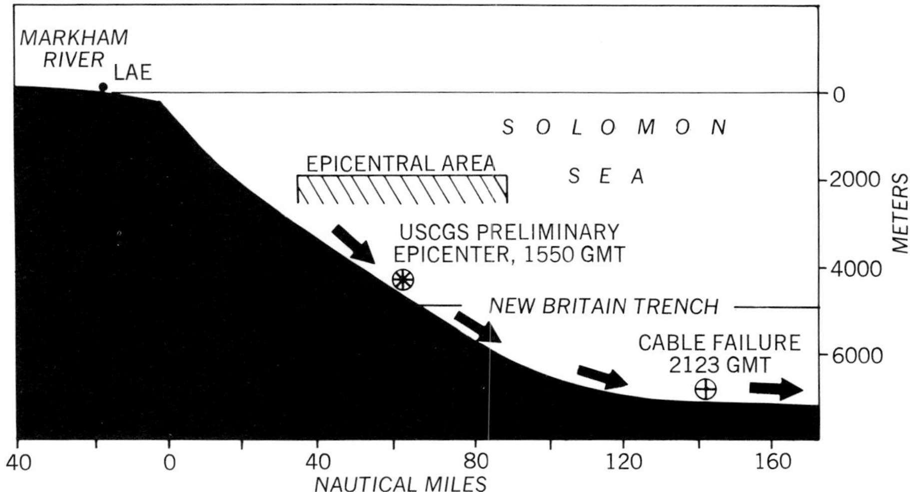

8.17 A violent earthquake-triggered turbidity current broke submarine cable in the New Britain Trench.

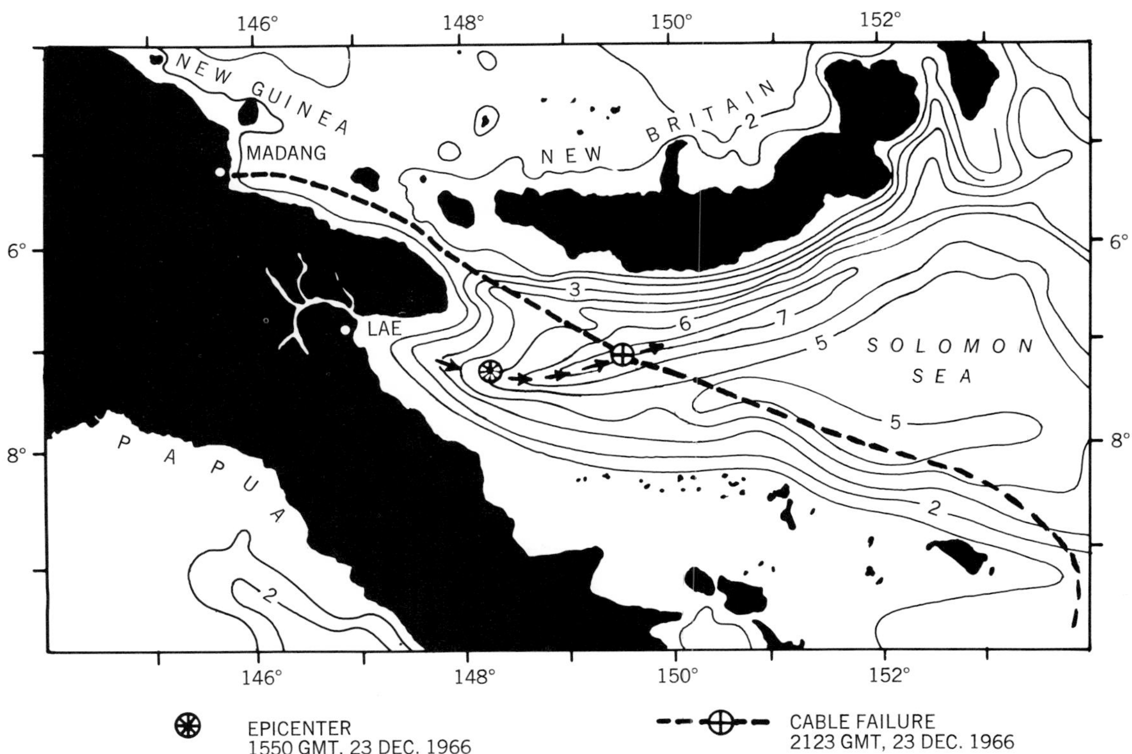

8.18 A turbidity current flowing from the continental slope off Lae into the New Britain Trench severed the Madang-Cairns telephone cable. Leaves and branches were wrapped around the broken cable by the catastrophic flow.

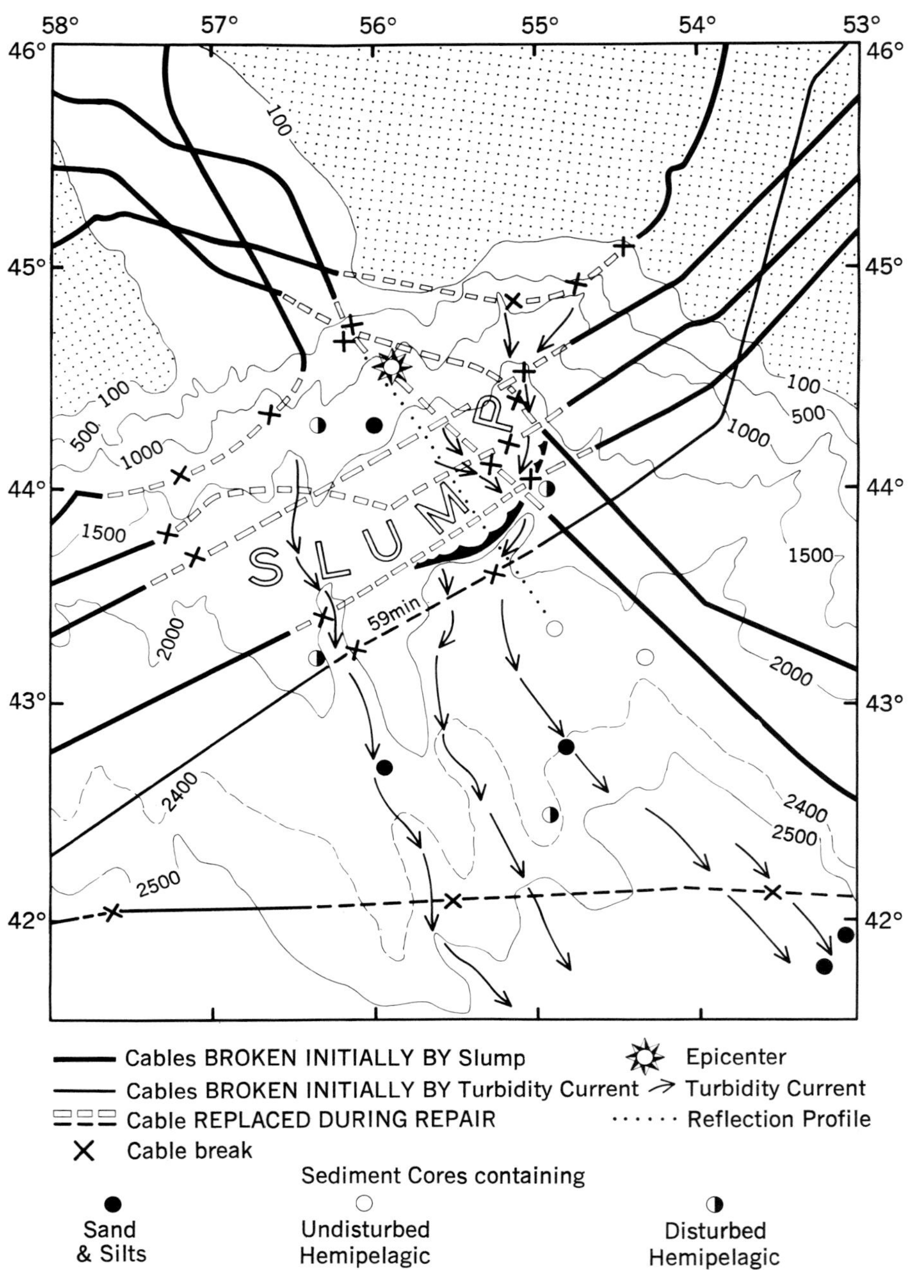

8.19 Grand Banks slump and turbidity currents severed submarine cables off Cabot Strait. All cables within about sixty miles south of the earthquake epicenter broke at the instant of the Grand Banks earthquake. A sequence of later cable failures occurred to the south, the first one occurring 59 minutes after the earthquake. The first two of the cables to break following the earthquake are indicated in this chart. The great slump is indicated by the thick scalloped line. Within the area of this map, turbidity currents flowed through at least three separate channels. Sediment cores taken between the channels indicate undisturbed or slightly disturbed sediment, while cores taken along the axes of these channels revealed turbidity current-deposited sands and silts.

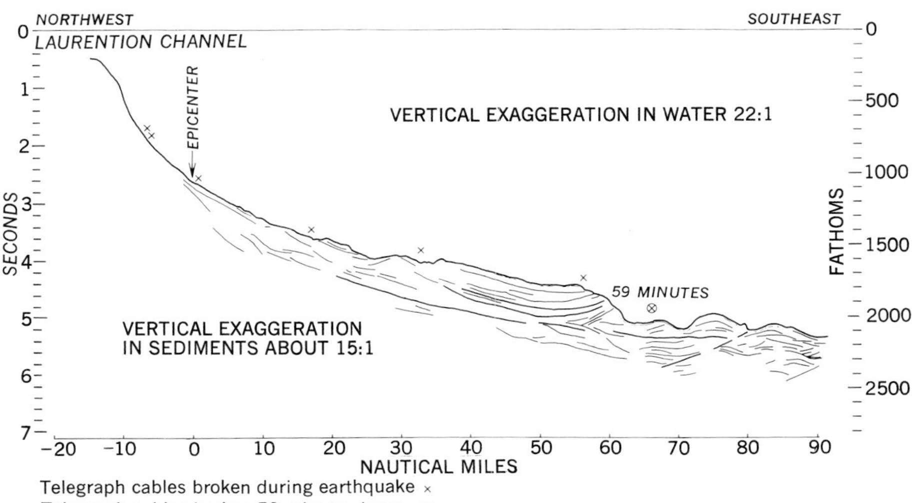

8.20 Grand Banks slump. This enormous upturned block of sediment slid downslope during the 1929 Grand Banks earthquake, severing all adjacent submarine cables. This profile is a tracing of the seismic reflection records made along a profile from the Laurentian Channel across the continental slope and continental rise south of the Grand Banks. The location of this profile is shown by the dotted line in Figure 8.19. All cables crossing the area of the slump were broken at the instant of the earthquake.

west. Here, an immense submarine distributory system was discovered. Intermittent transport of great quantities of silt and sand through the canyon must have eroded the deep canyon and formed an abyssal delta.

For fifty years a submarine cable crossing the canyon served as a monitor of turbidity currents (8.25). Cable breaks occurred during the two annual periods of maximum river discharge, when the greatest quantities of sediment were transported into the canyon head (8.27). Between 1892 and 1903, and between 1924 and 1928, when the river shifted its channel in the lower braided stream valley, turbidity currents were frequent. In the intervening years none occurred. Thus turbidity currents, even in this extremely active canyon, are highly intermittent. Although approximately fifty occur each century, evident visual effects on the sea floor probably could not be observed for more than a few months per century.

The upward decrease in particle size (size grading) in a turbidity current deposit (8.28) provides a soft muddy upper surface which will be rapidly tracked and burrowed by a host of migrating hungry beasts. How long they require to track the newly deposited mud is difficult to determine, and is probably highly variable, but the time must be measured in days and weeks and not in years. Photographs taken on the natural levees and in the floor of a distributory channel of the Congo Canyon revealed a muddy, burrowed, and tracked sea floor without obvious evidence of

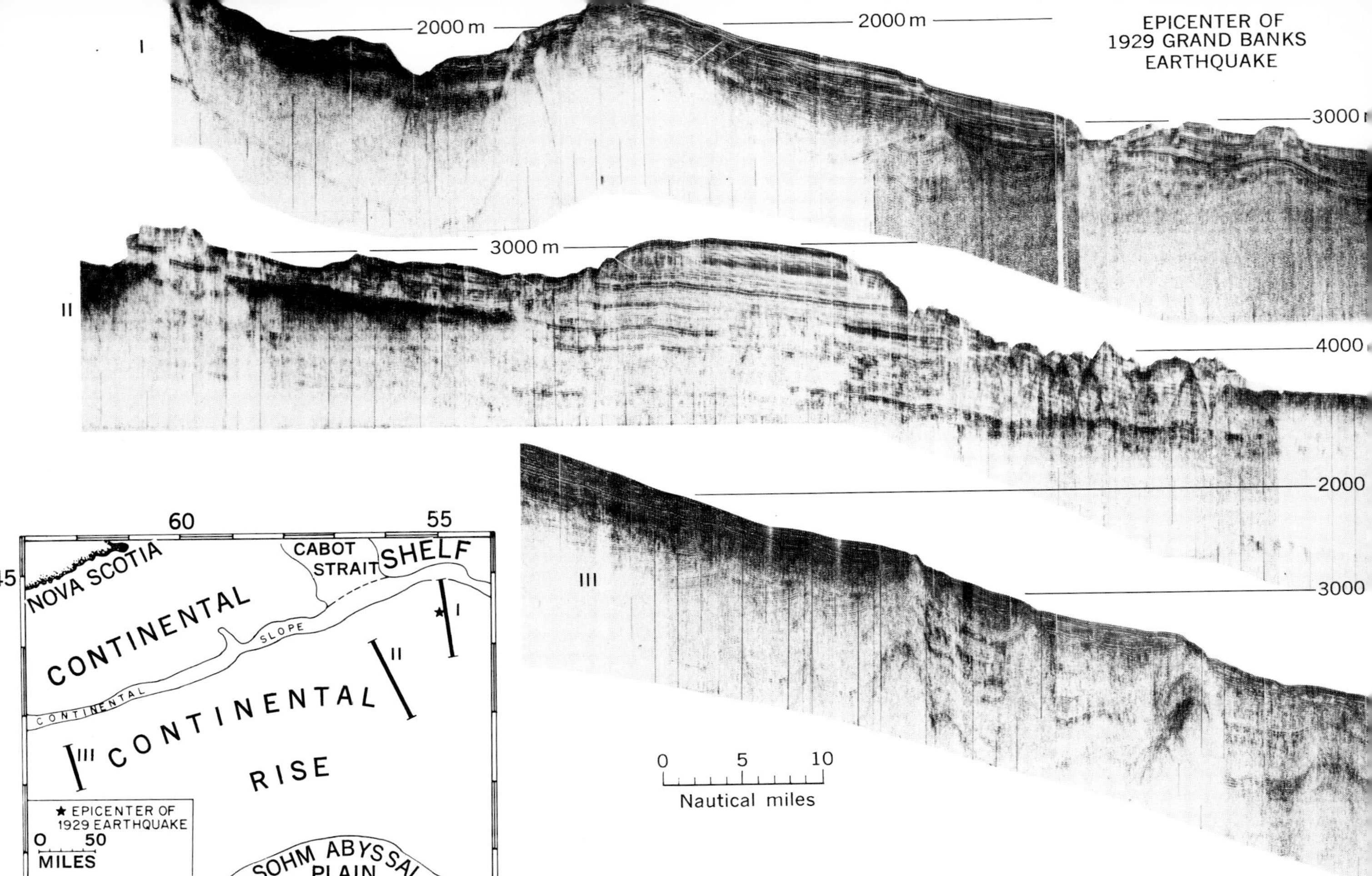

8.21 Faults (I) and massive slumps (II) are seen in the upper kilometers of sediment near the earthquake epicenter. Canyons have eroded sedimentary strata (I, 2200 m) and slumping has folded and contorted the sediment near the toe of the Grand Banks slump (II, 4000 m). Diapirs or piercement folds have disrupted the buried layers (III).

any recent catastrophic event (8.29). Although a turbidity current may not have traversed this particular distributory for several years, one might not have observed a very different seascape even if this channel had experienced a turbidity current a few weeks before the picture was taken. During or immediately following a turbidity current one would expect to see nothing but muddy water, and muddy water has been frequently observed over abyssal plains, the ultimate destination of the large turbidity currents.

"TO THE PLAINS OF FAR AWAY"

Gradients of the smooth, nearly horizontal surfaces of the abyssal plains which occupy the deepest portions of the ocean basins are less than one in one thousand. Abyssal plains appeared perfectly flat on the first primi-

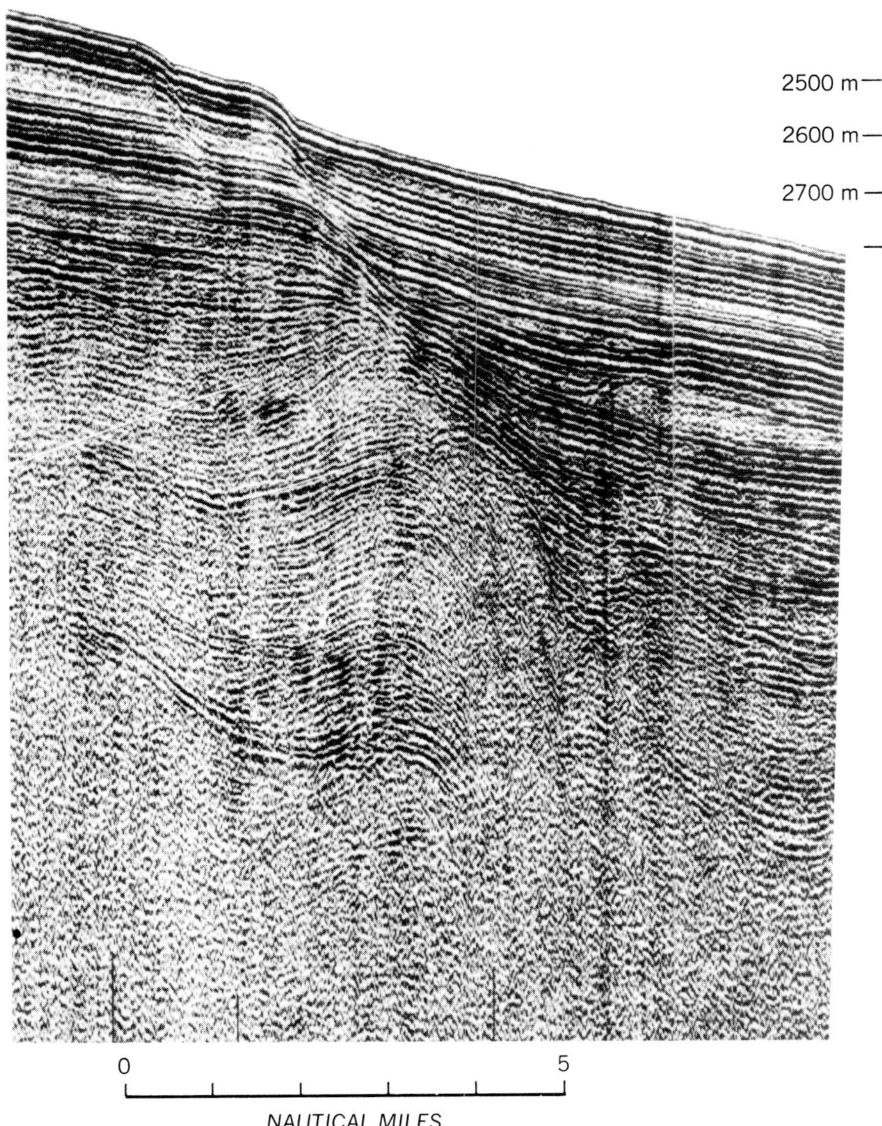

8.22 Fault near the epicenter of the 1929 Grand Banks earthquake. This enlarged portion of the seismic profile in Figure 8.21 (I) shows the detail of the submarine fault in the top kilometer of sediments on the continental rise near the earthquake epicenter.

tive low-resolution echo-sounding records. The high-resolution Precision Depth Recorder was designed specifically to study irregularities on the abyssal plains; but even with a resolution of one meter, no significant local irregularities could be detected and continuous seismic reflection records indicate that the numerous subbottom layers are nearly parallel

8.23 Slumped sediments. 4927 m, Mid-Indian Ocean Ridge.

to the present surface. Finally, sea-floor photography has shown that the smooth surface is devoid of significant irregularities even on a scale of centimeters.

The displaced sediments found in coarse graded beds beneath abyssal plains resemble the sands, silts, and gravels recovered from submarine canyons; and it appears certain that these characteristic beds were deposited by turbidity currents. On the Sohm Abyssal Plain, south of the Grand Banks, photographs have revealed very muddy bottom water, and it seems likely that some of the finest-grained clays have not yet settled out from the most recent turbidity current (8.30).

MUDDY MAGDALENA

The Magdalena River discharges its considerable load on the continental slope of South America. The bar, which often blocks the river mouth, intermittently slides down the continental slope into a prominent submarine canyon system. A submarine cable which crossed the canyon system thirty, thirty-five, forty, and ninety kilometers seaward of the river mouth was interrupted sixteen times in thirty-seven years (8.31). The cable was laid in 1930 at a time when engineers were building constricting jetties at the river mouth. On July 30, 1935, some 400 meters of the

8.24 Slump structures in multi-colored Tertiary clay. Core sections from 3615 m, Campeche Escarpment, Gulf of Mexico (core sections in centimeters).

western jetty disappeared along with the bar and a narrow shelf. The cable, which failed in the same night, was found fouled with large masses of green marsh grass when it was recovered by the repair ship from a depth of 1500 meters. One can imagine that if photographs had been taken a few days later, trestle work, railroad rails and ties, rip-rap and railroad gondolas would have been observed littering the canyon.

Seismic reflection records show evidence of repeated cut and fill in the canyon floor (8.32). The turbidity currents generated at the mouth of

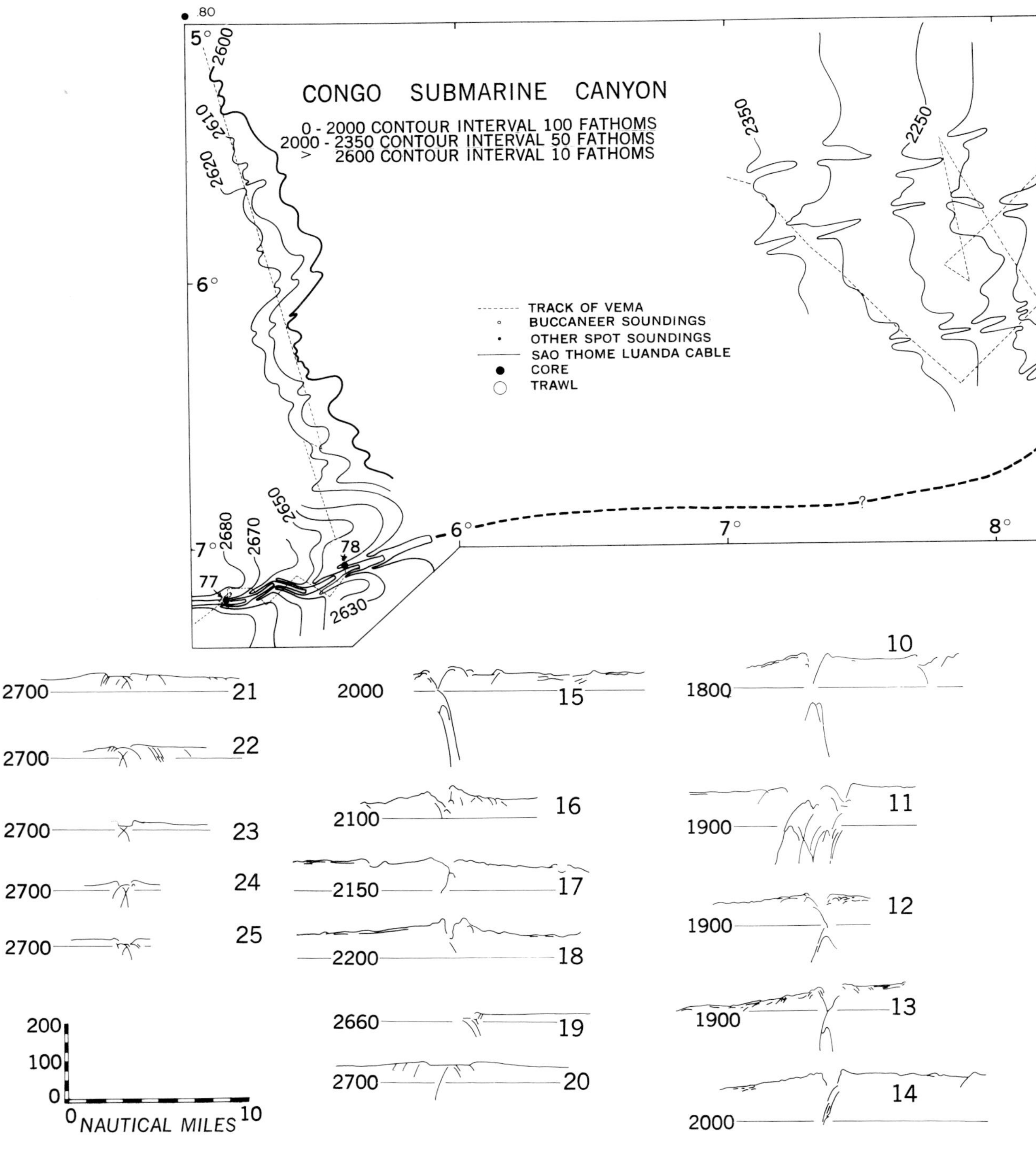
CONGO SUBMARINE CANYON
0 - 2000 CONTOUR INTERVAL 100 FATHOMS
2000 - 2350 CONTOUR INTERVAL 50 FATHOMS
> 2600 CONTOUR INTERVAL 10 FATHOMS
TRACK OF VEMA
BUCCANEER SOUNDINGS
OTHER SPOT SOUNDINGS
SAO THOME LUANDA CABLE
CORE
TRAWL
NAUTICAL MILES

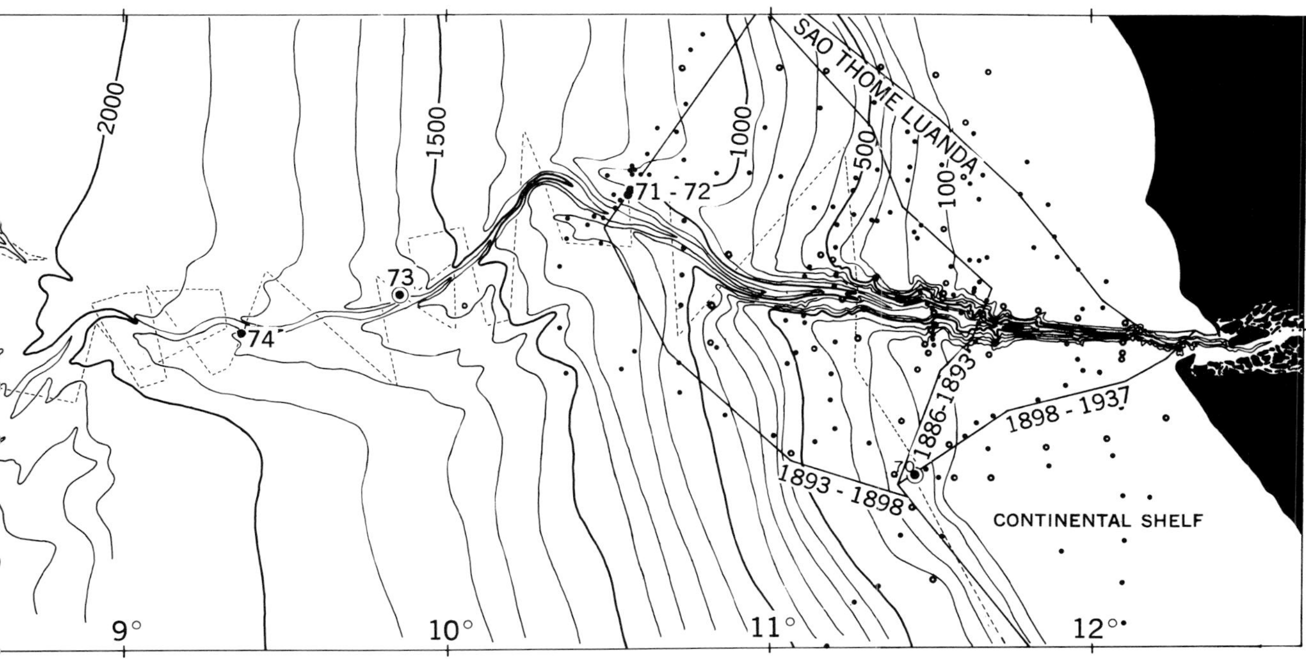

8.25 Congo Submarine Canyon. The canyon off this delta-free river cuts across the entire continental shelf. Turbidity currents periodically sever the São Thomé-Luanda telegraph cable.

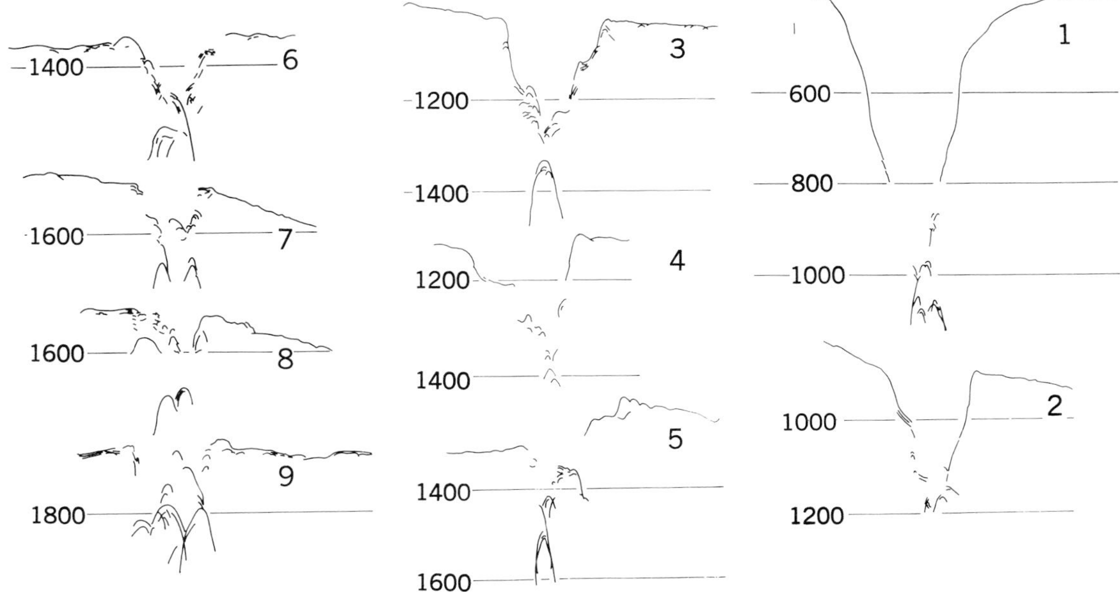

8.26 Profiles of Congo Submarine Canyon from the continental slope to the Congo Cone (9). Tracings from precision depth recorder echograms show the downslope change in shape from a deeply incised, nearly V-shape to a shallow notch associated with extensive, gently sloping, natural levees.

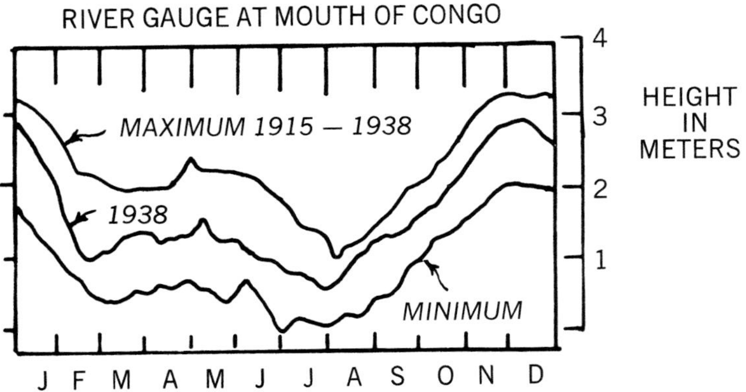

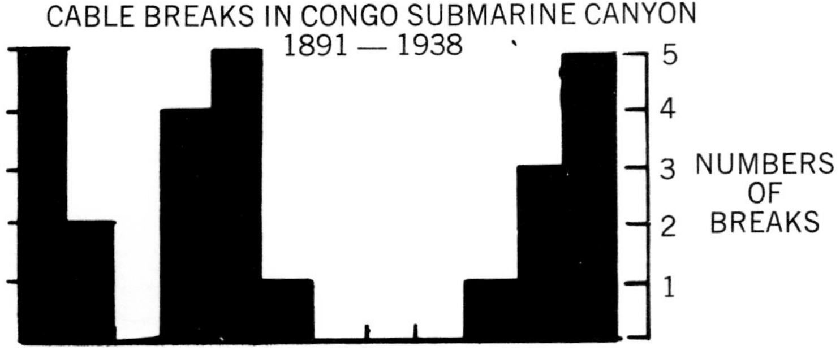

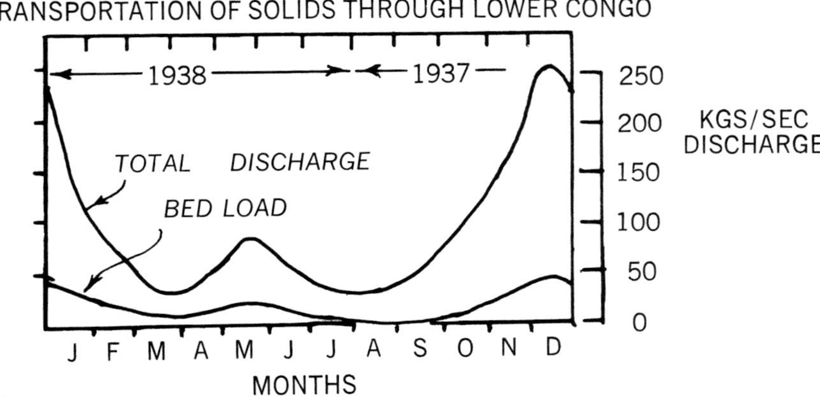

8.27 Cable failures and river discharge. Submarine cables are broken by turbidity currents which occur most frequently when total river discharge and bottom-transported sediment (bedload) are at a maximum.

the Magdalena flow far out on the Colombia Abyssal Plain, and even reach the Venezuela Abyssal Plain via Aruba Gap. Numerous beds of sand, rich in mica and topped by a thin layer of fragmented leaf debris, lie beneath the Colombia Abyssal Plain (8.33, 8.34). The light, broken,

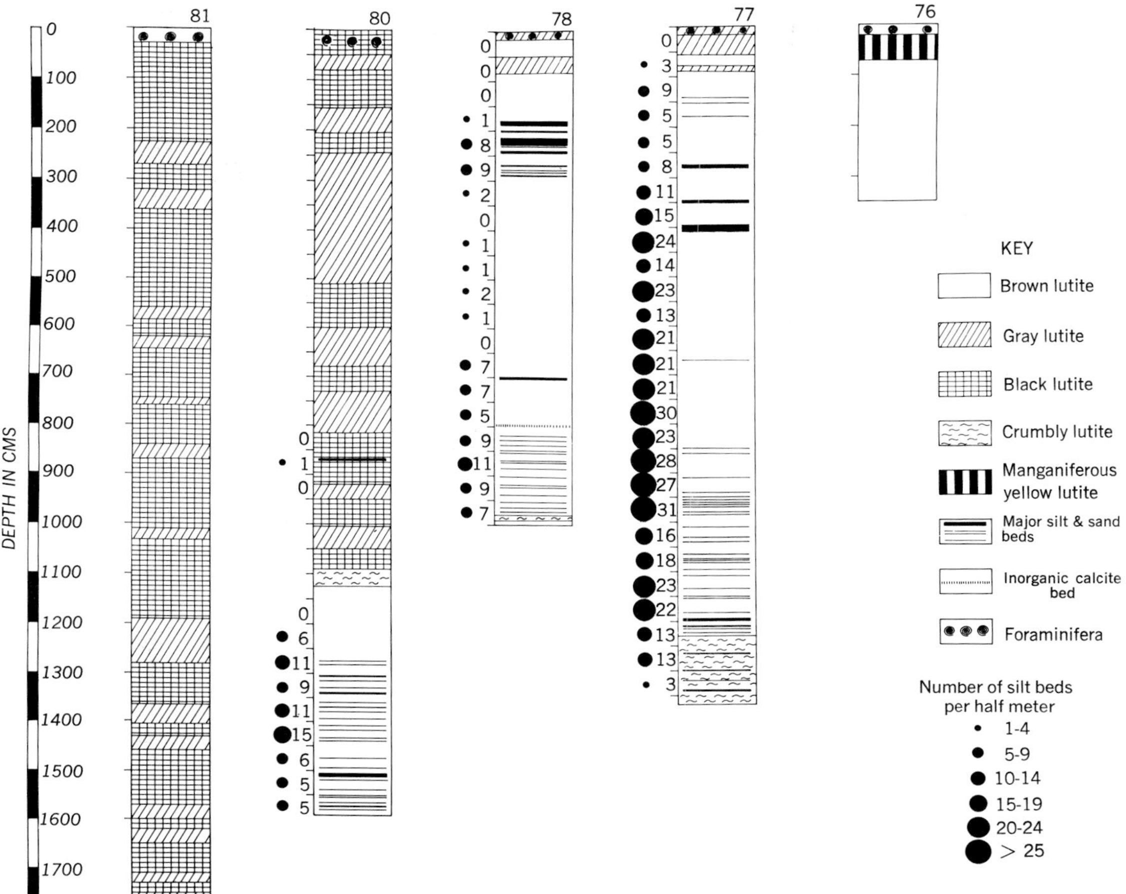

8.28 Many thin laminae of silt and sand interbedded with clay are deposited by turbidity currents on the natural levee. Core 81 is from an elevation north of the Congo Cone and 76 is from the abyssal hills west of the Cone. Cores 77, 78 are from the levee north of the active canyon and Core 80 is from an abandoned distributary channel.

and water-logged tree leaves deposited with the finer clays form the uppermost element of the graded beds, and must be visible on the sea floor following a turbidity current. It seems probable that someone will photograph a dark, leaf-covered bottom abundantly covered with detritus feeders. Logs, branches, and stumps are sometimes brought up entangled in broken communication cables (8.35), and masses of olive branches, up to five meters in diameter, were found entangled with the broken cables in the submarine canyons in the Gulf of Corinth and along the continental slope of Algeria. It has been argued that organic-rich turbidity currents may locally constitute an important factor in the nutrition of deep-sea fauna.[11]

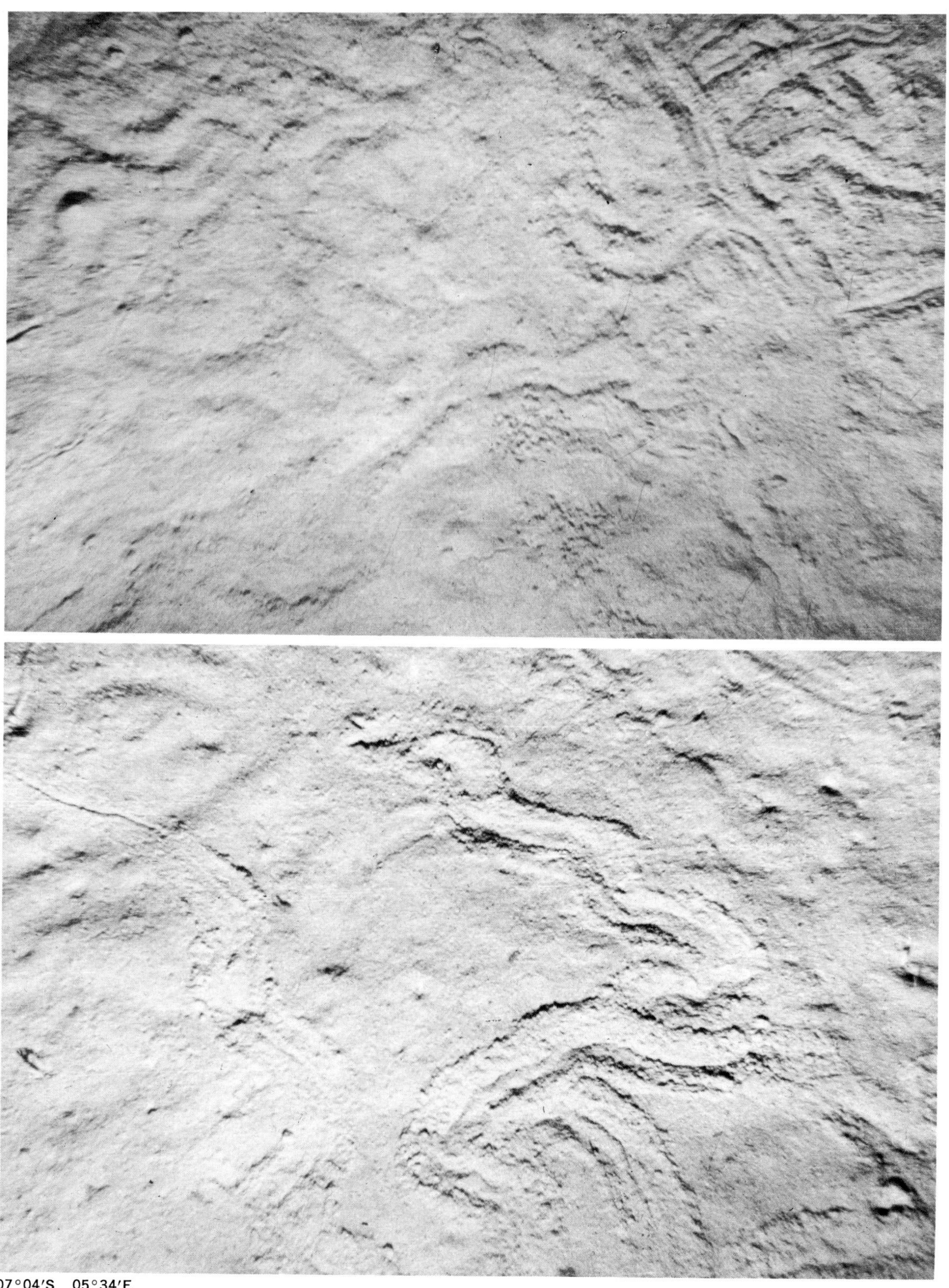

07°04′S 05°34′E
07°10′S 05°08′E

32°35′N 57°10′W

8.30 Suspended sediment from a recent turbidity current obscures the sea floor. 5785 m, southern end of Sohm Abyssal Plain, eastern North Atlantic.

SWATCH AND CONE

Two great abyssal cones dominate the northern Indian Ocean. One, formed by sediment transported through the Indus Canyon (The Swatch), has buried the flank of the Mid-Oceanic Ridge. The other, which spreads out from the Ganges Submarine Canyon (Swatch of No Ground), covers the entire deep-sea floor of the Bay of Bengal. (8.36). Both of these great cones with their system of distributory channels appear to be inactive. The several submarine cables which cross each of the

◁ 8.29 Plow marks and burrows on the now tranquil natural levee of the Congo Canyon. U, taken with Core 78 (see Fig. 8.28), 5050 m; L, taken with Core 77, 5132 m.

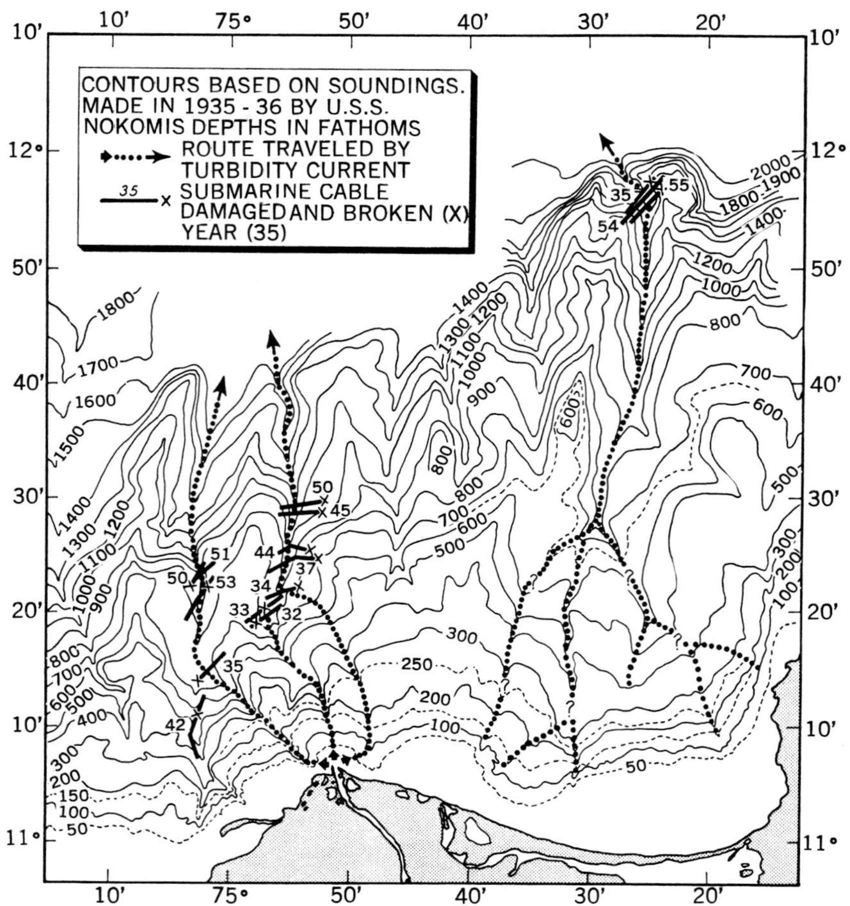

8.31 Turbidity currents break cables and erode channels off the Magdalena River.

channels have never broken in the over three-quarters of a century that they have monitored dynamic processes. Photographs taken on the wall of one of the Ganges distributories show a tranquil bottom devoid of current lineations and no evidence of exposed rock (8.37).

GAPS

Adjacent abyssal plains which lie at different levels are often connected by interplain channels which pass through constricted abyssal gaps. (8.38). These valleys, which somewhat resemble the distributory channels of continental margin submarine canyons, apparently begin and end on the abyssal floor. It is usually assumed that these mid-ocean canyons were cut and are maintained by eroding turbidity currents which flow

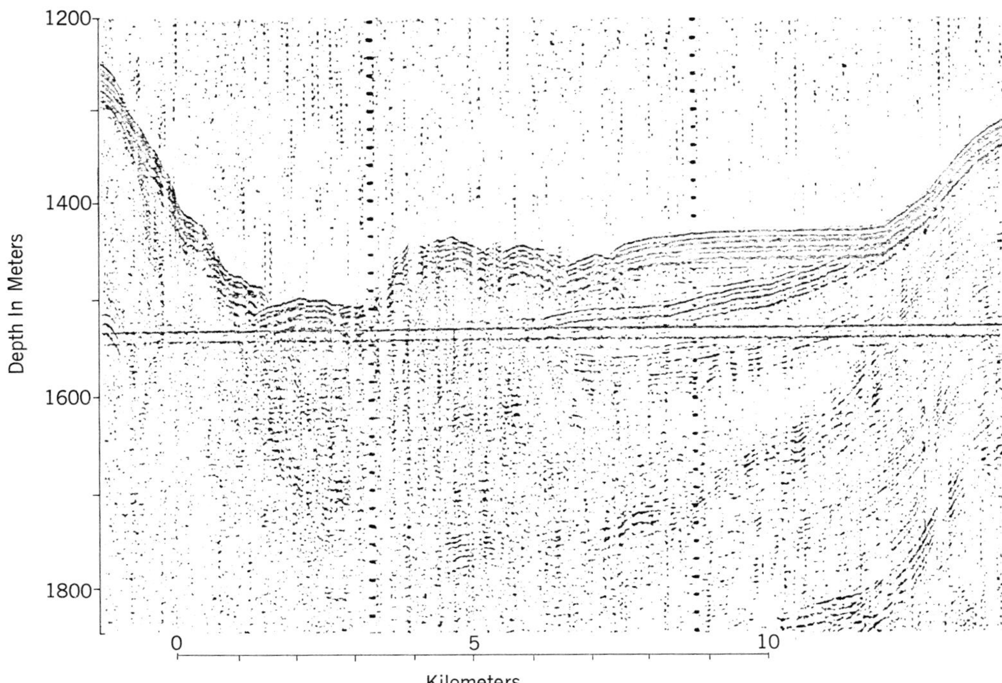

8.32 Layers of sediment are repeatedly eroded and deposited by turbidity currents off the Magdalena River.

down the steeper gradients of the abyssal gap from the higher to the lower abyssal plains. Semiconsolidated sediments crop out on the walls of interplain channels (8.39).

KIWA CANYON

The Hikurangi Trench is a minor oceanic trench which lies parallel to the eastern shore of the north island of New Zealand. Its extremely smooth floor is formed by an abyssal plain which is cut by the box-shaped Kiwa Mid-Ocean Canyon.[12] (8.40). The canyon in its southern end is three or four kilometers wide and over 200 meters deep. As the depth of the Hikurangi Trench increases to the north, the canyon widens and its walls become lower until at thirty-eight degrees South, the canyon is barely perceptible and its banks have less than twenty meters relief. Natural levees are strongly developed and the left bank is distinctly higher than the right.

Seismic reflection profiles show that the Kiwa Mid-Ocean Canyon bears no systematic relationship to the basement topography below. The

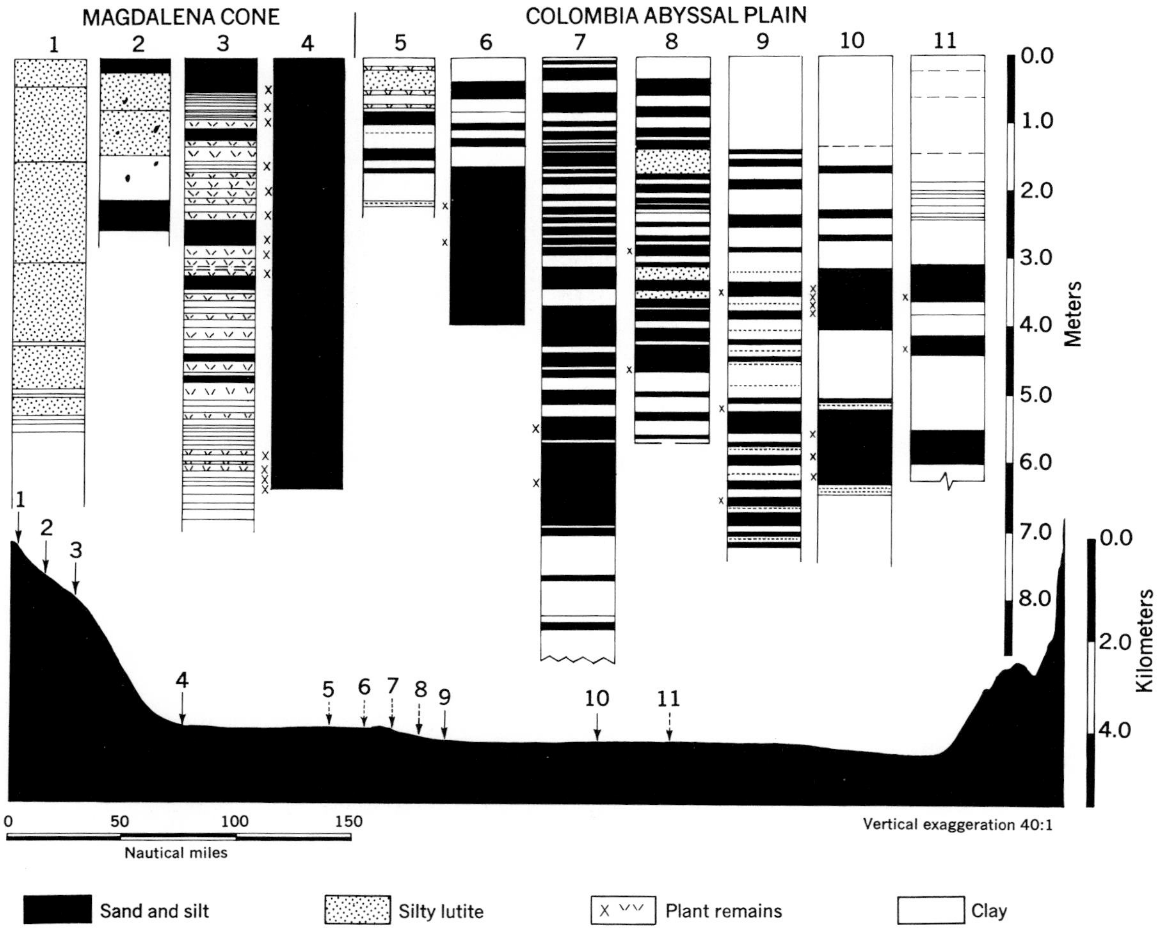

8.33 Sand and silt from the Magdalena River are spread across the Columbia Abyssal Plain by turbidity currents. Many of the beds grade in particle size from sand at the base, through silt to leaf fragments at the top.

canyon has in fact migrated to the east or to the right through time as former beds of the channel can be traced through the upper 800 meters of sediment (8.40).

THE LARGEST LEVEES

It has been noted that the right banks of northern hemisphere mid-ocean canyons are systematically higher than the left. However, in Kiwa Canyon, the left bank is systematically five to thirty meters higher than the right. In explanation of the higher banks, the Coriolis force has been in-

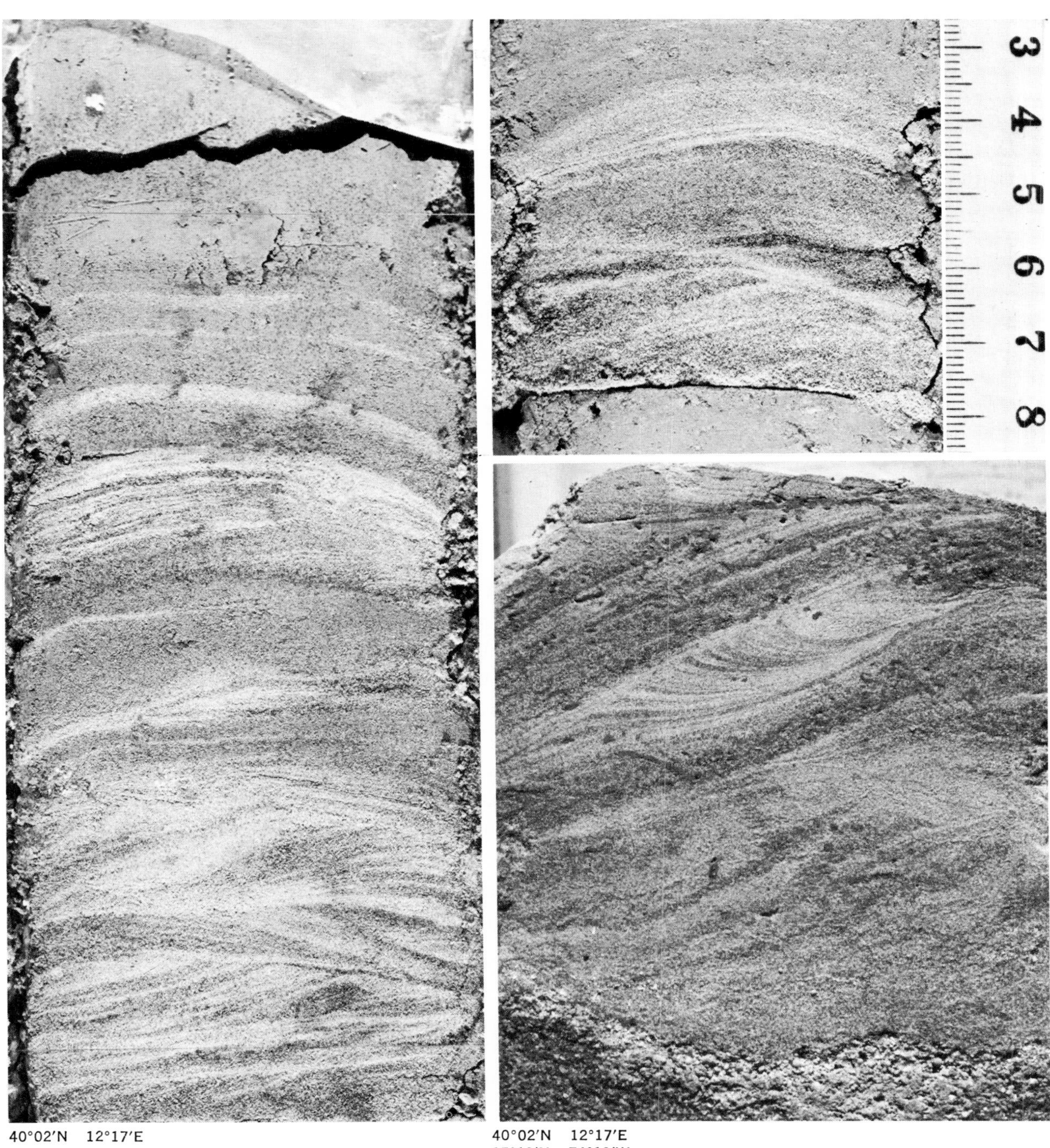

40°02′N 12°17′E

40°02′N 12°17′E
15°19′N 74°19′W

8.34 Abyssal plain turbidity current deposit (turbidite). Cross-stratification accentuated by concentration of clay are frequently seen in sand and silt layers from the abyssal plains. L, UR 3611 m, Tyrrhenian Abyssal Plain, north of Sicily; LR, 4177 m, Colombia Abyssal Plain, Caribbean Sea.

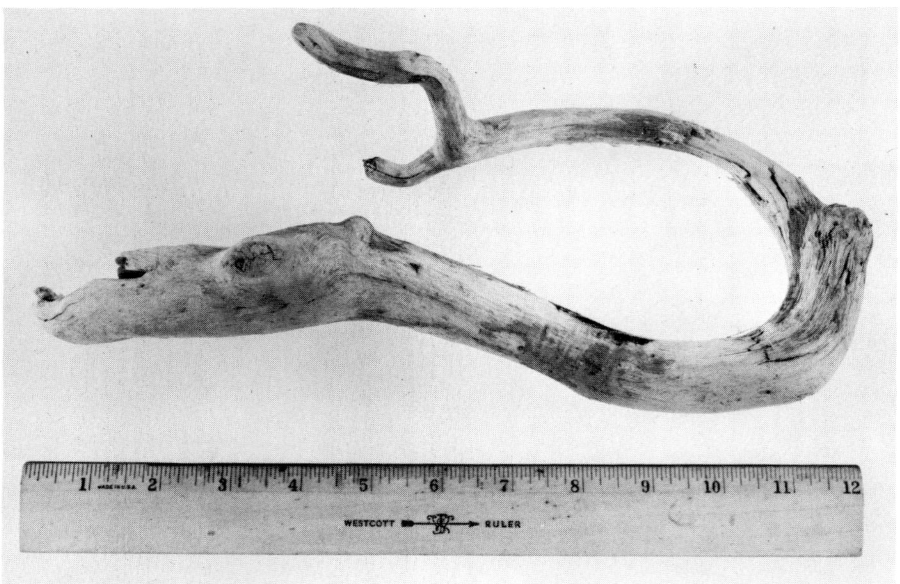

8.35 Carried into the abyss. This curved piece of wood was entangled with a telephone repeater of the new Cairns-Medang telephone cable in 7237 m. when it was repaired after having been severed by the 1966 Solomon Sea Turbidity Current.

voked. This force, which deflects moving bodies to the right in the northern hemisphere and to the left in the southern hemisphere, has long been debated as a morphological factor in stream erosion. But its apparent effect on the form of mid-ocean canyons and deep-sea channels is probably not related to erosion but to deposition.[13] The higher right bank of the northern hemisphere canyons, or the higher left bank of the southern hemisphere canyons, results because the deflecting force of the earth's rotation causes depositing currents within the channel to be deflected in this direction. The surface of the current will thus have a transverse slope. The thin lateral edges of each flow overtop the canyon banks and build the submarine natural levees. Migration of the Kiwa Canyon in the direction opposite to the direction of the Coriolis deflection must be related to the greater deposition on the preferred left bank, for if an erosional effect were involved the migration would be in the opposite direction. The banks of an active mid-ocean canyon or deep-sea distributary channel should repeatedly present a uniquely smooth seascape temporarily devoid of tracks, trails, or burrows. The smoothing effect should be more extensive on the higher bank due to the greater thickness of each successive layer. Erosion should be apparent on the walls, for seismic reflection records clearly indicate that the canyons have incised the earlier levee deposits.

8.36 The Great Ganges Cone dominates the northeast Indian Ocean.

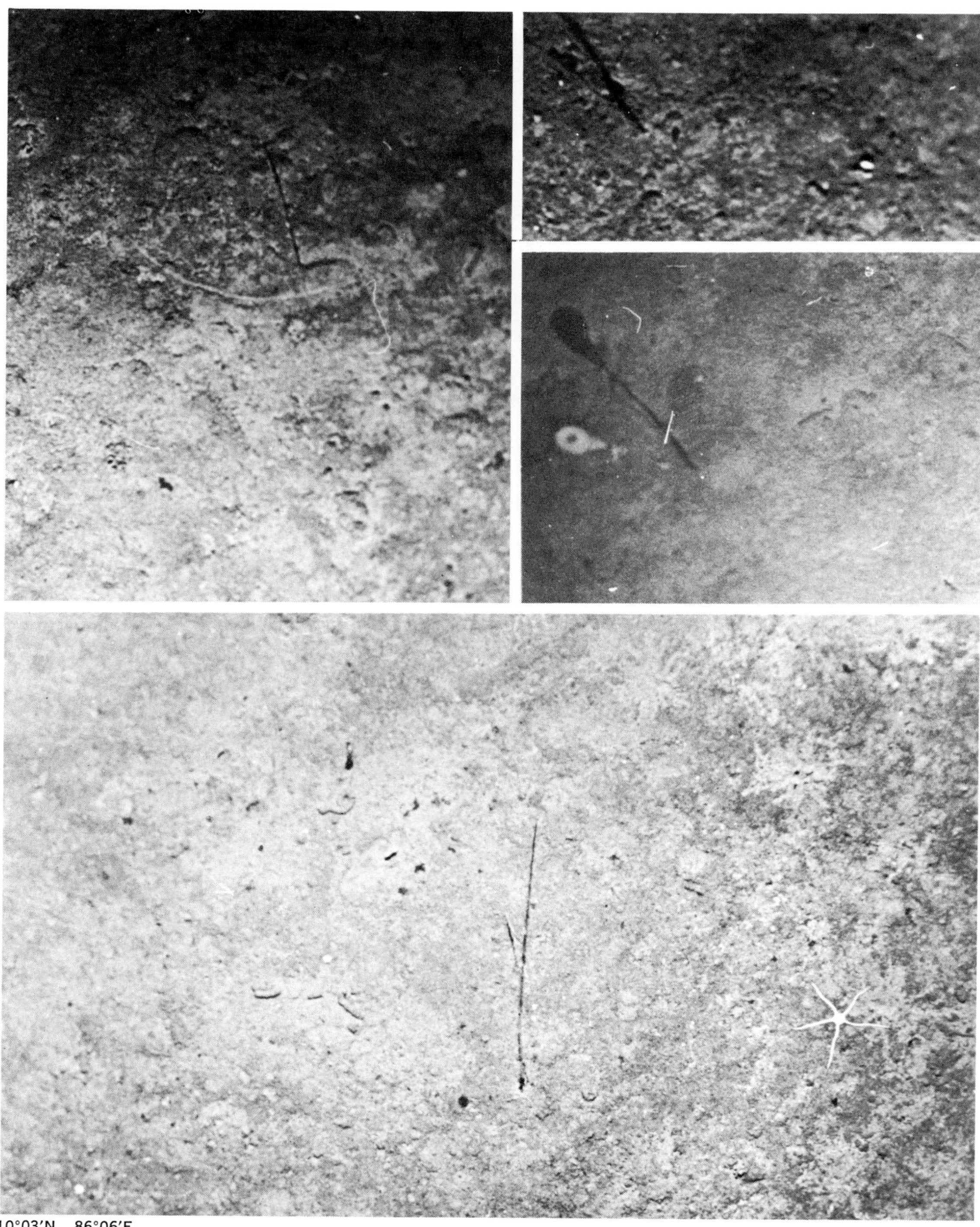

10°03′N 86°06′E

8.37 The floor of a meandering channel in the Ganges Cone. The sea floor does not appear to have been recently disturbed by currents, 3646 m.

8.38 Turbidity currents erode interplain channels between adjacent abyssal plains.

For over 3000 kilometers, a 5- to-10-kilometer-wide box-shaped mid-ocean canyon flanked by broad, low shoulders gently winds its way south from Davis Strait along the western Atlantic (8.41-8.43). Flowing first between the opposing margins of Greenland and Labrador, further south it lies between the Grand Banks and the Mid-Atlantic Ridge. It has no tributaries and, in fact, its levees stand slightly higher than the flanking basin floor throughout its length. A series of photographs taken a few years ago on the natural levee east of this canyon revealed a thin layer of muddy water moving over the sea floor. The bottom was almost obscured by the suspended material. Although the canyon largely owes its origin to the deposition of sediments on the soft muddy surface of the growing levees (8.44), the outcropping beds on the canyon wall revealed by seismic reflection profiles indicate that erosion as well has played a part in the evolution of the canyon and should be apparent in the seascape.[14]

8.39 Semi-consolidated sedimentary rocks crop out on cliffs of the current-eroded interplain channel. 5230 m, Theta Gap, eastern North Atlantic.

When photographed a few years ago, the levees of the Hatteras Transverse Canyon on the continental rise off North Carolina were exceedingly smooth, suggesting the recent emplacement of the uppermost layer of sediments. Although at present photographic evidence is sparse and often inconclusive, it may eventually be possible to recognize a distinct sequence of scenes reflecting the erosion, deposition, and repopulation of bottom sediments.

Turbidity current deposits in ancient rocks contain bounce and prod marks made by objects carried in the current and a variety of bed-forms of flute and convolute types are known. But these features are not part of the sea-floor scene for they lie at the base of the beds and we can only see the soft muddy tops of beds.

8.40 Thick accumulations of sediment have partially filled the Hikurangi Trench. These seismic reflection profiles reveal an eastward migration of the Kiwa Mid-Ocean Canyon. ▷

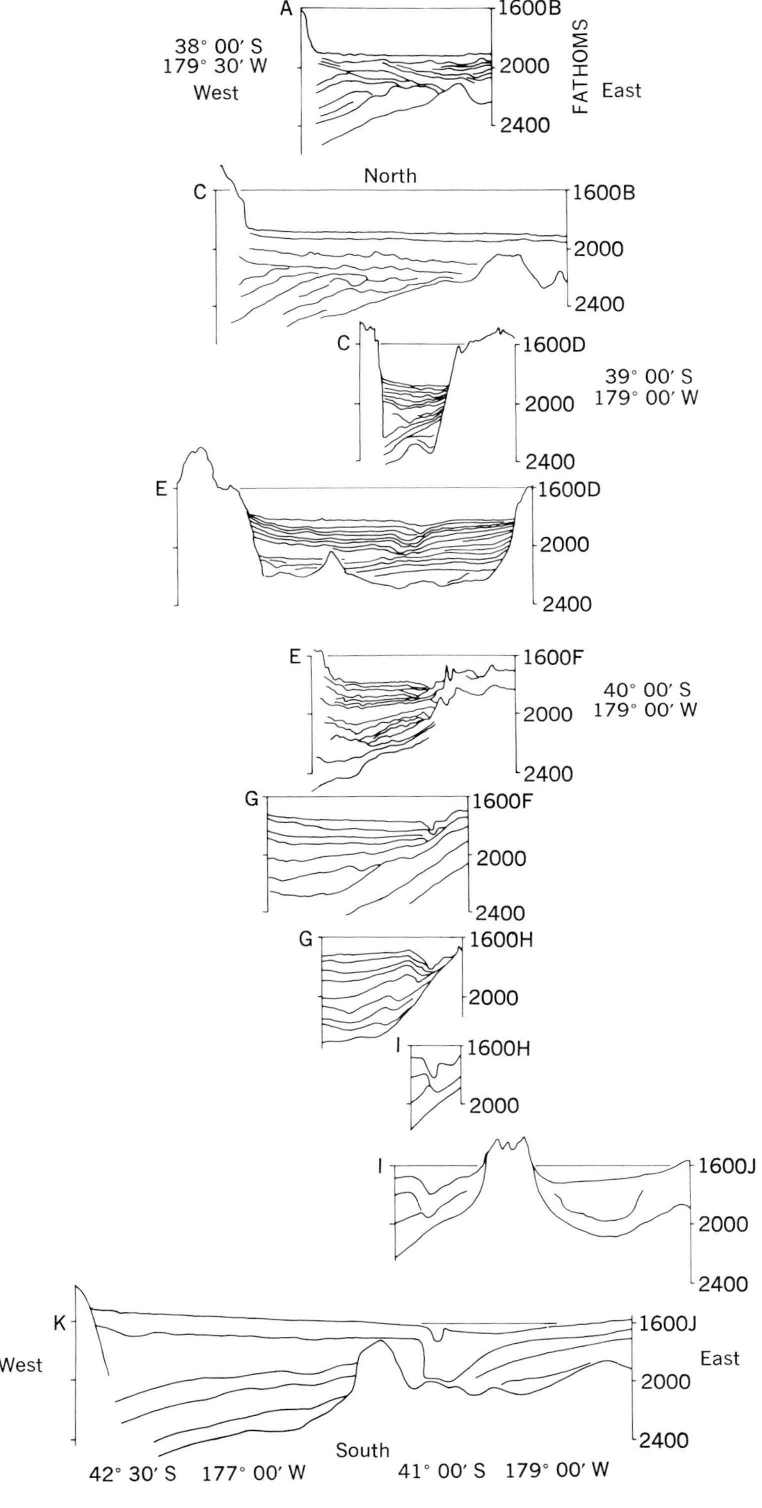
A
1600B
38° 00′ S
179° 30′ W
West
2000
FATHOMS
East
2400
North
C
1600B
2000
2400
C
1600D
39° 00′ S
179° 00′ W
2000
2400
E
1600D
2000
2400
E
1600F
40° 00′ S
179° 00′ W
2000
2400
G
1600F
2000
2400
G
1600H
2000
I
1600H
2000
I
1600J
2000
2400
K
1600J
West
East
2000
2400
South
42° 30′ S 177° 00′ W
41° 00′ S 179° 00′ W

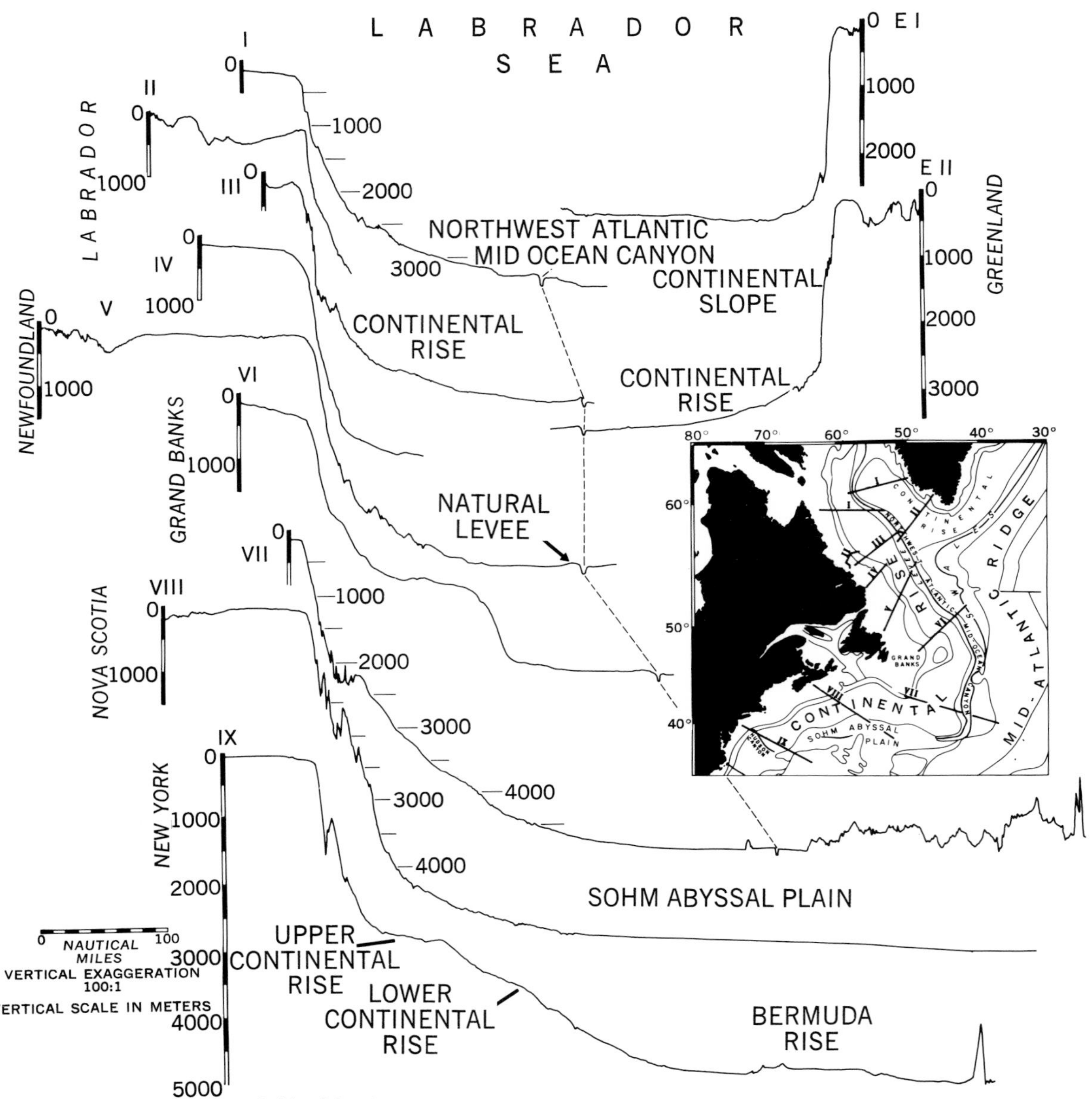

8.41 Northwest Atlantic Mid-Ocean Canyon. The canyon courses from the Davis Strait to the Sohm Abyssal Plain and its broad natural levees fill the floor of the Labrador-Newfoundland basin.

AT THE SCENE

On rare occasions bathyscaphe pilots have reported that they saw turbidity currents in action. In fact, one pilot claimed that he triggered a turbidity current by bumping into the canyon wall and was then carried

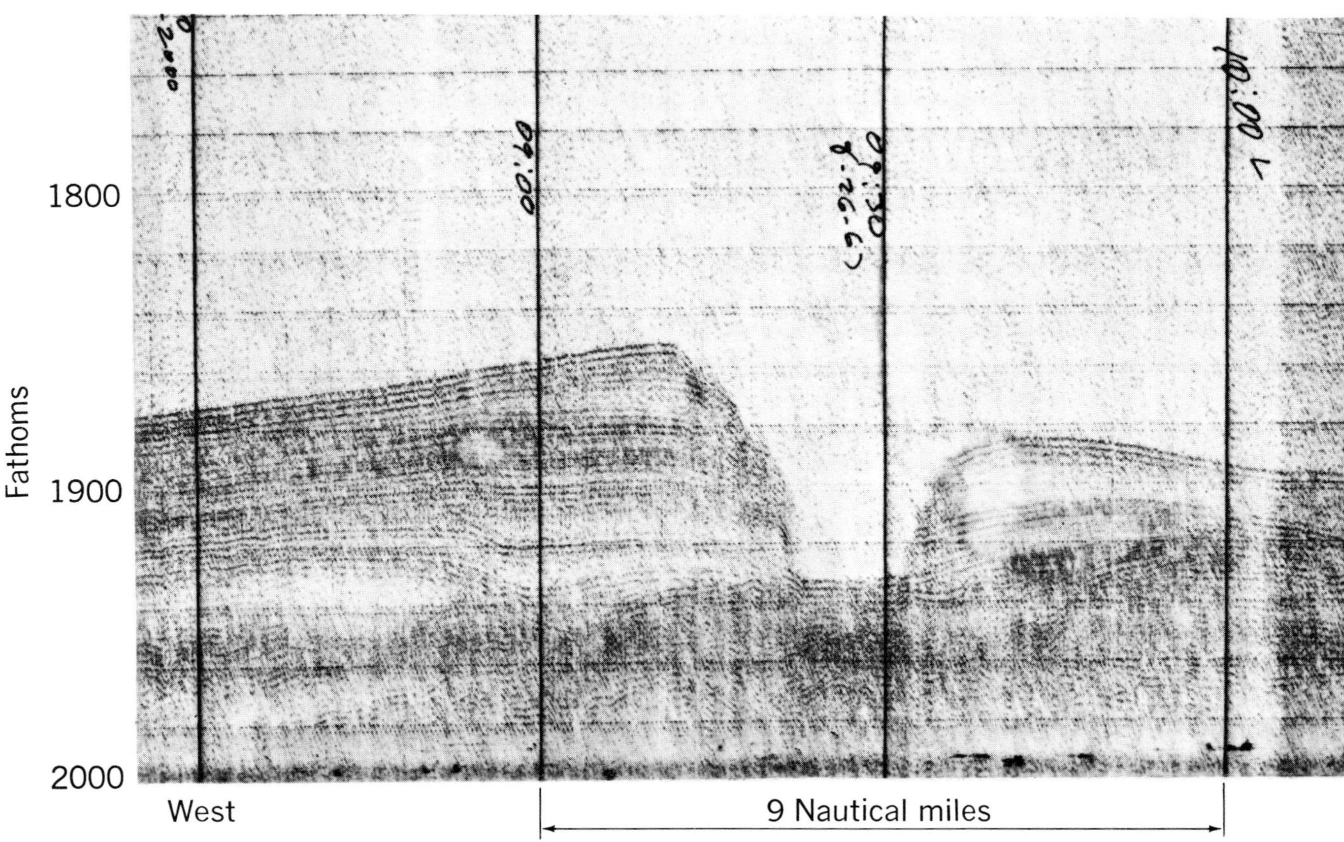

8.42 Natural levees have built upward on both sides of the Northwest Atlantic Mid-Ocean Canyon. Seismic profiler record. Length of the record is approximately 22 miles. Canyon crossed at 58°05′N, 51°40′W.

for a brief scary ride in a rapidly moving, visually impenetrable turbid mass of water. Everyone who has ever reached the sea floor in a submersible has observed the muddy blackout which occurs as the water-saturated sediment is stirred up when the submarine touches the bottom. The visual observation of a major turbidity current would hardly be worth the thrill, for one would be able to see nothing and the observer might not even survive.

Diving saucers have allowed examination to depths of 700 meters. A later model, introduced in 1966, extended the depth range to 1400 meters. The submarine canyons of southern California and of the French

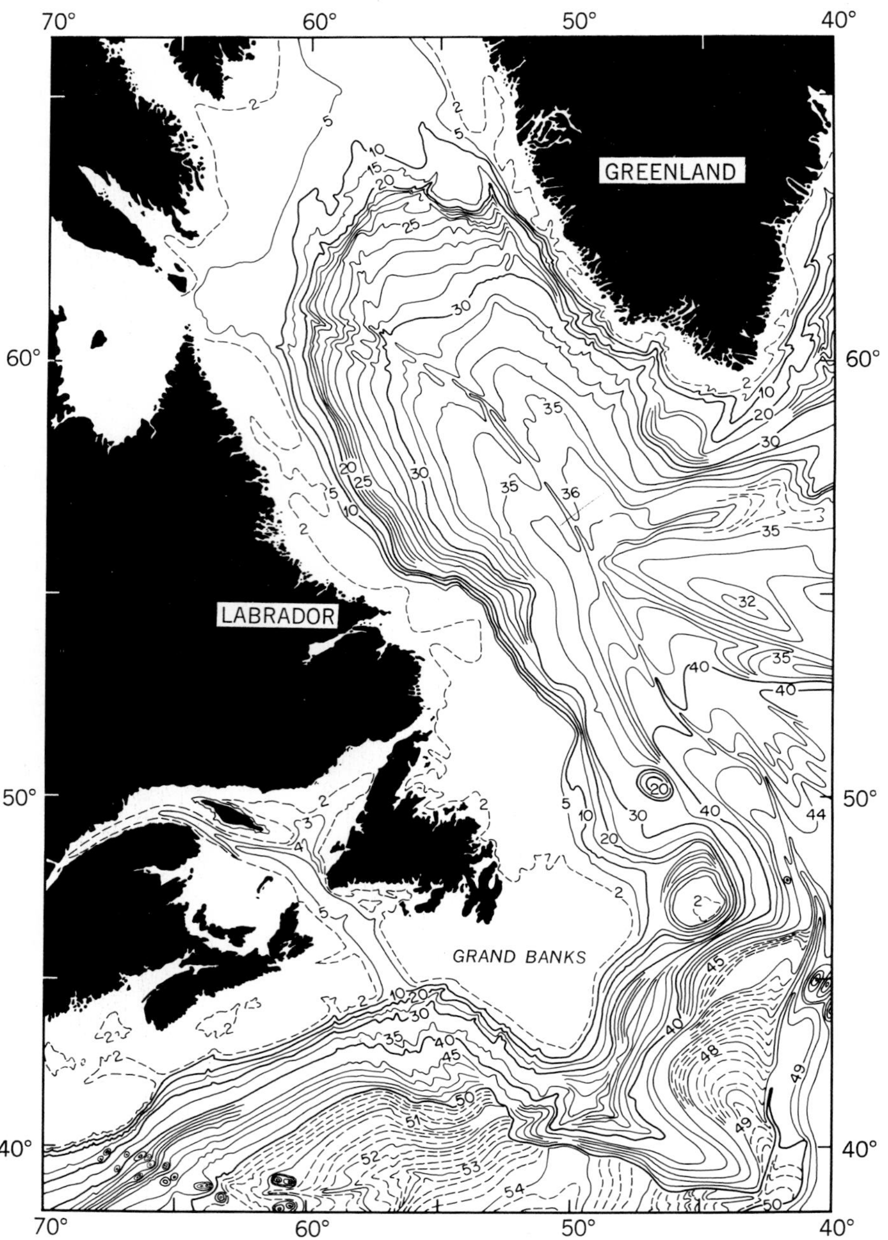

8.43 The Northwest Atlantic Mid-Ocean Canyon lies in the center of the Labrador Sea. Depths are in units of hundreds of meters. Note well developed natural levees.

Riviera have been extensively examined from diving saucers (8.45, 8.46). Rock walls are common, although generally there is a blanket of sediment which partially or completely covers the walls. As the observer proceeds to deeper and deeper water, outcrops are still observed along

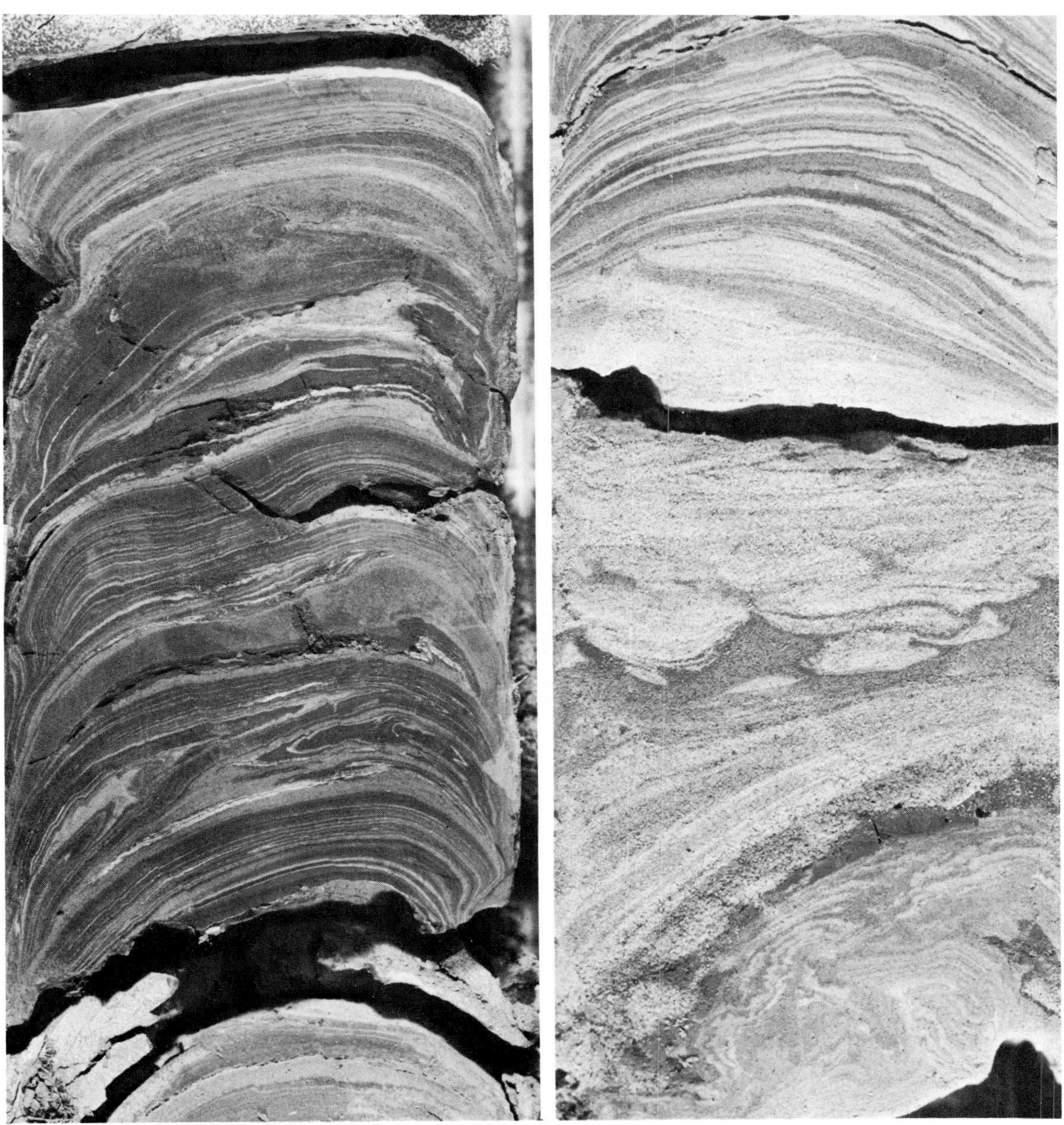

8.44 Laminations and contorted bedding from the natural levee of a mid-ocean canyon. Downwarping of layers near the sides is due to coring deformation; however, the horizontal lamina and folded bedding are current made structures. 3407 m, Western levee of Northwest Atlantic Mid-Ocean Canyon, Labrador Sea.

the canyon walls; but the minor features of the seascape are difficult, if not impossible, to distinguish from those of the adjacent basin floor.

In favored locations, submarine canyons extend into the sunlit waters and virtually reach the beach. Here, scuba divers and glass-bottomed

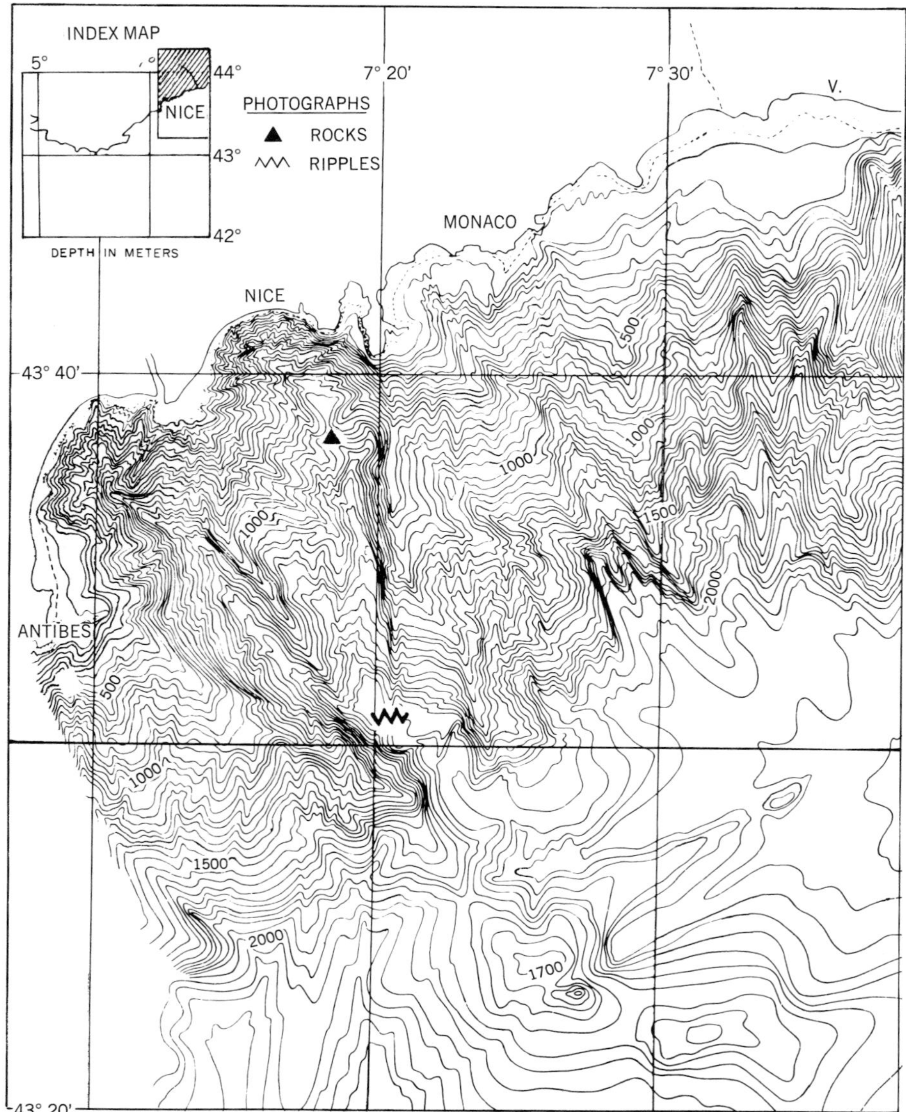

8.45 Active canyons of the French Riviera. Photographs of rocks and ripples in the Var Canyon are shown in 8.46.

boat observers can see the walls and floors of the submarine canyons. Although in such locations it is difficult to distinguish the processes unique to the canyons from those generally characteristic of shallow water, much insight has been gained. Sediment carried along the shore is intermittently dumped into the canyon heads, and makes its way either gradually or catastrophically to greater depths.

The visual effects of alternate fill and excavation on the canyon walls have been studied by several observers. By planting stakes in the sedi-

43°30′N 07°20′E
43°38′N 07°19′E

8.46 Fresh ripples and bare boulders indicate significant contemporary transportation in canyons off southern France. U, note plant debris, 1800 m and L, lee-side deposits attest to recent transport, 1000 m, both in Var Canyon off Nice.

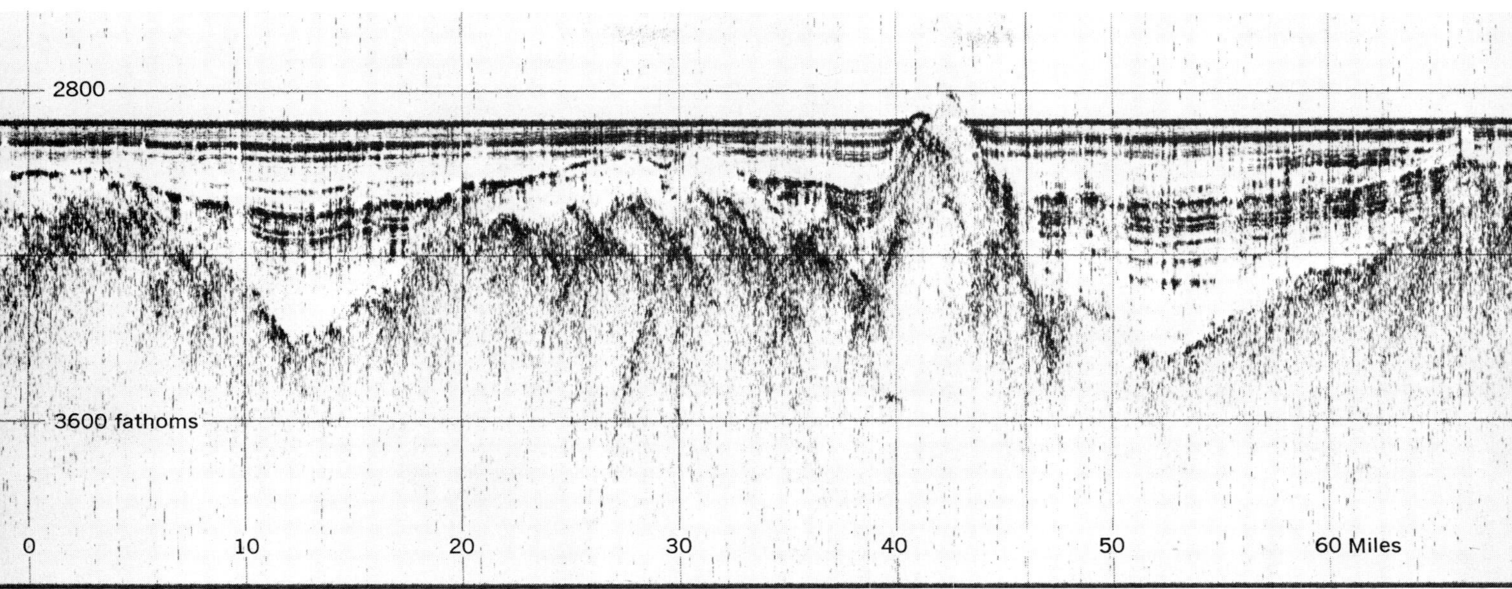

8.48 Abyssal plain deposits have buried one-hundred-million-year-old mountains. Seismic reflection profile. Northern Madeira Abyssal Plain.

ment, they have measured creep, erosion, and deposition which occurred between successive visual inspections.

Diving geologists have observed sand flowing from the beach into and down the San Lucas Canyon off Baja California. The sand was still flowing at velocities of ten centimeters per second when it reached the maximum depth of 100 meters to which the scuba-equipped observers could descend. It has been postulated that these relatively slow flows and creeping slumps maintain the nearly sediment-free canyons. Certainly sand flows are an important process and they are the only catastrophic process of excavation which has been visually observed in progress in submarine canyons.

NEITHER DRAMATIC NOR UNIQUE

Despite the fact that turbidity currents have had an immense physiographic effect on deep-sea topography, have eroded the submarine canyons, built the abyssal plains, and constructed the natural levees, the

◁ 8.47 The smoothed floor of an abyssal plain (U) contrasts markedly with the burrowed surface of the Mid-Oceanic Ridge. U, 5959 m, southern end of Sohm Abyssal Plain, western Atlantic. L, 4679 m, western flank of the Mid-Atlantic Ridge.

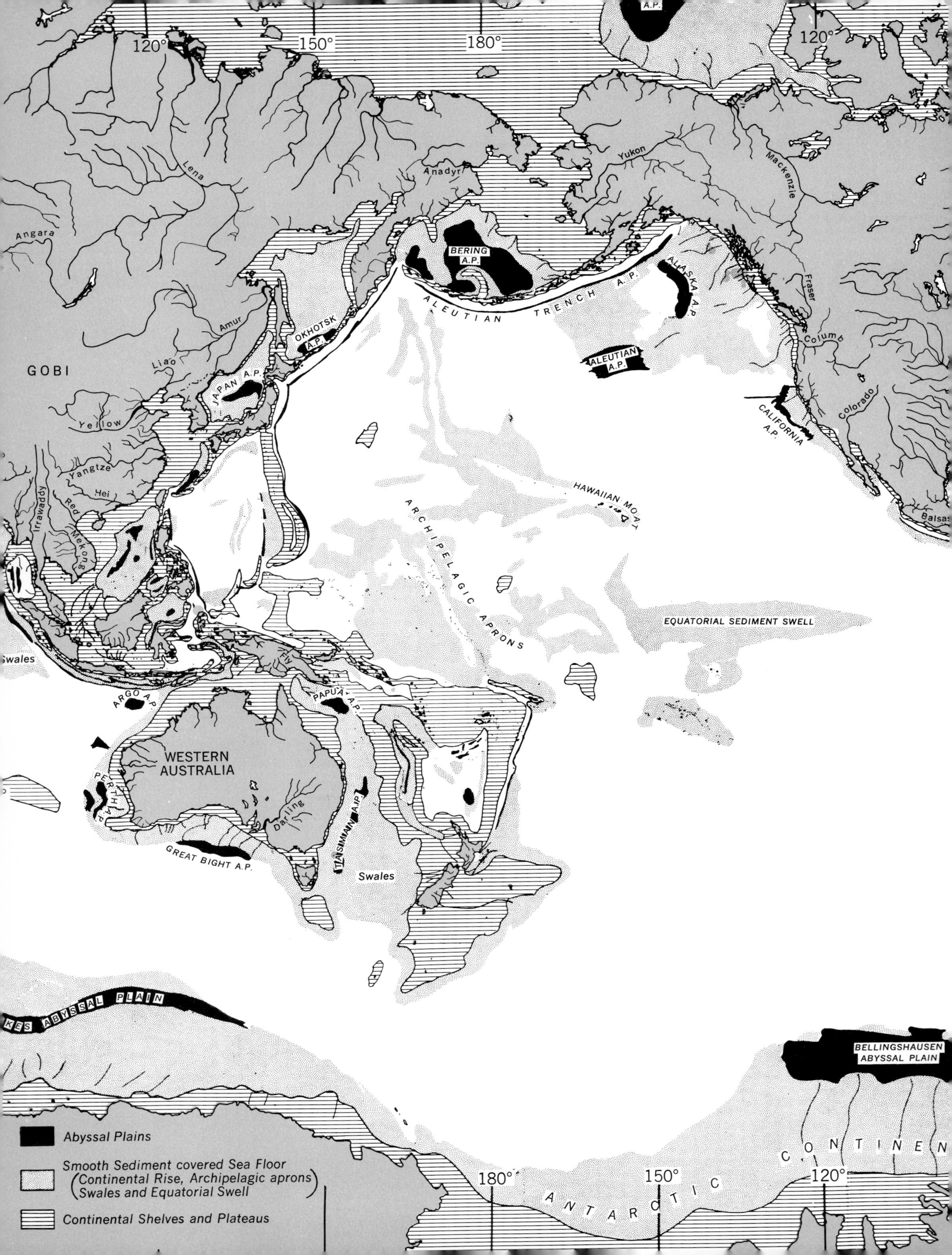

120°
150°
180°
120°
A.P.
Lena
Anadyr
Yukon
Mackenzie
Angara
BERING A.P.
Amur
ALEUTIAN TRENCH A.P.
ALASKA A.P.
Fraser
OKHOTSK A.P.
Columb
GOBI
Liao
JAPAN A.P.
ALEUTIAN A.P.
Yellow
Colorado
CALIFORNIA A.P.
Yangtze
Hei
Irrawaddy
Red
Mekong
HAWAIIAN MOAT
ARCHIPELAGIC APRONS
Balsas
EQUATORIAL SEDIMENT SWELL
Swales
Fly
ARGO A.P.
PAPUA A.P.
WESTERN AUSTRALIA
PERTH A.P.
Darling
TASMAN A.P.
GREAT BIGHT A.P.
Swales
KES ABYSSAL PLAIN
BELLINGSHAUSEN ABYSSAL PLAIN
Abyssal Plains
Smooth Sediment covered Sea Floor (Continental Rise, Archipelagic aprons Swales and Equatorial Swell)
Continental Shelves and Plateaus
180°
150°
120°
ANTARCTIC CONTINEN

60°
30°
0°
30°
60°
DUMSHAF A.P.
NORWAY A.P.
Yenisey
60°
Ob
Mid-Ocean Canyon
St. Lawrence
Hudson
LAURENTIAN CONE
SOHM A.P.
HATTERAS A.P.
Swales
Vema Gap
NARES A.P.
BISCAY A.P.
Theta Gap
IBERIA A.P.
TAGUS A.P.
MADEIRA A.P.
CAPE VERDE A.P.
CONTINENTAL RISE
Rhine
Rhone
Po
Danube
Dnieper
Volga
EXUNE A.P.
BALEARIC A.P.
Euphrates
Nile
Indus
30°
THAR
Ganges
SAHARA
ARABIA
COLOMBIA A.P.
DEMERARA A.P.
PARA A.P.
AMAZON CONE
CEARA A.P.
Magdalena
Orinoco
Amazon
SIERRA LEONE A.P.
GUINEA A.P.
Niger
INDUS CONE
INDIA A.P.
SOMALI A.P.
GANGES CONE
CEYLON A.P.
PERNAMBUCO A.P.
CONGO CONE
Congo
ANGOLA A.P.
MALAGASY A.P.
Zambezi
KALAHARI
Orange
VAZ A.P.
THE CORDILLERA
CHILE TRENCH A.P.
Platte
CONTINENTAL RISE
Swales
ARGENTINE A.P.
ARGENTINE RISE
CAPE A.P.
ORANGE CONE
MOZAMBIQUE A.P.
30°
Swales
SOUTH SANDWICH TRENCH A.P.
WEDDELL ABYSSAL PLAIN
Swales
RISE
60°
CONTINENTAL RISE
ANTARCTIC
60°
30°
0°
30°
60°
90

principal visual effects we can attribute to them are neither dramatic nor unique. The contemporary erosional slopes frequently found in canyons may in part result from their activity, and the smooth, muddy surface (8.47, 8.48) of the abyssal plains may represent the surface of their deposits.[15] The characteristic size gradation, ranging from sand or silt at the base to fine clay at the top of beds left by turbidity currents, clearly implies that their visual effects should be evasive and ephemeral. Thus, we should not be too surprised at the paucity of visual evidence of these important events.

REFERENCES AND NOTES

1. For a copiously illustrated and well-documented description of the world's submarine canyons, the reader is referred to: F. P. Shepard and R. F. Dill (1966. *Submarine Canyons and Other Sea Valleys.* Rand McNally, Chicago, 381 pp.).
2. D. C. Krause. 1962. Interpretation of echo sounding profiles. *Internat'l. Hydrograph. Rev.,* 39:65-123.
3. Interested fishermen advanced the science of marine geology by bringing fossiliferous rocks to the attention of paleontologists. (W. Upham. 1894. The fishing banks between Cape Cod and Newfoundland. *Am. Jour. Sci.,* 3d ser., 47:123-92; W. H. Dahl. 1925. Tertiary fossils dredged off the northeastern coast of North America. *Am. Jour. Sci.,* 5th ser. 10:213-18). However, it was not until the early 1930's that oceanographers began systematic investigations (H. C. Stetson. 1936. Geology and paleontology of Georges Bank canyons. *Bull. Geol. Soc. Amer.,* 47:339-66).
4. It is hard to discover a more hotly debated subject in geology or one that offers such a wide variety of theories as that of the origin of submarine canyons. Although now out-of-date and mainly of historical interest, the thorough and well-written discussion of D. Johnson (1939. *Origin of Submarine Canyons.* Columbia Univ. Press, New York, 216 pp); of F. P. Shepard and K. O. Emery (1941. Submarine topography off the California coast: canyons and tectonic interpretations. *Geol. Soc. America, Special Paper 31,* 171 pp.); and of Ph. H. Kuenen (1950. *Marine Geology.* Wiley, New York, 568 pp.) are still entertaining examples of deductive reasoning. Sea-level lowering of over 4000 meters due to water being locked in enormous Pleistocene continental glaciers has only recently been abandoned. For instance, compare the two editions of F. P. Shepard's textbook: 1948, *Submarine Geology,* 1st edition. 348 pp.; and, 1963, *Submarine Geology,* 2nd edition. Harper & Row, New York, 487 pp.
5. Exciting evidence of contemporary erosion was discovered in 1947 by two young students on their first deep-sea expedition (J. Northrop and B. C. Heezen. 1951. An outcrop of Eocene sediment on the continental slope. *J. Geol.,* 59:396-99).
6. F. A. Forel. 1885. Les ravins sous-lacoustres des fleuves glaciares. *Compt. Rend.* Acad. Sci. (Paris), 101:725-28.
7. R. A. Daly. 1936. Origin of submarine canyons. *Amer. J. Sci.,* 31:401-20.

◁ 8.49 Turbidity currents form flat, featureless abyssal plains, gently sloping submarine cones, and archipelagic aprons.

8. Ph. H. Kuenen. 1937. Experiments in connection with Daly's hypotheses on the formations of submarine canyons. *Leidsche Geol. Med.,* 8:327-35.
9. D. B. Ericson, M. Ewing, and B. C. Heezen. 1951. Deep-sea sands and submarine canyons. *Geol. Soc. Am. Bull.,* 62:961-65.; D. B. Ericson, M. Ewing, and B. C. Heezen. 1952. Turbidity currents and sediments in the North Atlantic. *Bull. Am. Assoc. Petrol. Geol.,* 36:489-511.
10. See review and references in: B. C. Heezen. 1959. Dynamic processes of abyssal sedimentation: erosion, transportation and re-deposition on the deep-sea floor. *Geophys. J. Roy. Astr. Soc.,* 2:142-63.
11. B. C. Heezen, M. Ewing, and R. J. Menzies. 1955. The influence of submarine turbidity currents on abyssal productivity. *Oikos,* 6:170-82.
12. Originally known only from a few fathograms, the Kiwa Canyon was initially considered a fault trough (J. W. Brodie and T. Hatherton. 1958. The morphology of Kermadec and Hikurangi trenches. *Deep-Sea Res.,* 5:18-28). Seismic reflection profile records in the Hikurangi Trench indicate sediment thicknesses up to 1500 meters. The minimum thicknesses of sediment occur toward the northern end of the trench and the sediments systematically thicken toward the southern end. The sediments of this trench appear to have originated in the region of Cook's Strait which separates the north and south islands of New Zealand, and it seems likely that much of this material was carried in by Pleistocene turbidity currents.
13. It has been suggested that the left hook characteristic of most California submarine canyons results from the migration of the channel under the influence of the Coriolis force, causing a greater deposition on the preferred bank (H. W. Menard, 1955. Deep sea channels, topography and sedimentation. *Amer. Assoc. Petrol. Geol. Bull.,* 39:236-55.). This proposal, made purely on the basis of the left hook, seems to be supported by the migration of the mid-ocean canyons. One might expect the higher bank to be smoother and that a discernible visual effect of the deflection might be seen in active canyon levees. This effect has also been noted in deep-sea channels in the Arctic Basin by H. Kutschale (1966. Arctic ocean geophysical studies: the southern half of the Siberia Basin. *Geophysics,* 31:683-709).
14. The canyon's course from the frigid Arctic south toward the deeper North America basin led to the speculation that dense Arctic bottom waters flowing south from the Davis Sea eroded its gorges and shaped its more than 100-kilometer-wide natural levees. Turbidity currents formed of glacial outwash offer another plausible explanation.
15. An immense literature exists on the supposed deposits of ancient turbidity currents. The term "turbidite" was coined for such deposits. The rock types included under the terms "flysch" and "graywacke" are considered by some to include deposits of turbidity currents. Modern treatments of supposed turbidity current deposits include: S. Dzulynski and E. K. Walton, 1965. *Sedimentary Features of Flysch and Graywackes.* Elsevier, Amsterdam, 265 pp.; A. H. Bouma. 1962. *Sedimentology of Some Flysch Deposits.* Elsevier, Amsterdam, 148 pp. An exhaustive bibliography on turbidity currents and their deposits has been prepared by Ph. H. Kuenen and F. L. Humbert (1964. Bibliography of turbidity currents and turbidites. In A. H. Bouma and A. Brouwer, editors. *Turbidites.* Elsevier, Amsterdam, pp. 222-46).

31°57′N 74°11′W

9.1 Unremitting circulation leaves its indelible marks. A short-stemmed sponge bends in the southwest current that smooths and sculpts the clay and ooze. 4902 m, Blake-Bahama Outer Ridge.

9

Noiseless Currents, Strong, Obscure, and Deep

Circulation is responsible for the aeration of the deeps without which all but the uppermost stratum would be a waste more desert than the Sahara.

HENRY BRYANT BIGELOW

There is a steady global circulation of the frigid deep-sea bottom waters, which spread and mix, along abyssal contours from their polar sources to the most remote of the far-flung abyssal basins.[1] These incessant contour currents stand in marked contrast to the ephemeral, catastrophic turbidity currents which intermittently rush downslope from their continental sediment sources to the abyssal plains. While turbidity currents offer little lasting visible evidence of their passing, the unremitting contour currents—which slowly circulate the bottom waters of the world along the slopes of the abyss—leave prominent and ubiquitous visible evidence of their dynamic presence (9.1). These effects[2] can be subtle (9.3) or strikingly dramatic.

LIKE A GENTLE WIND

Bottom currents too weak to produce any recognizable lineations deflect sea-pens, sponges, and other attached organisms, in a similar way as wheat is bent by a gentle wind. The mud thrown into suspension by the contour currents is sometimes observed drifting along the bottom. The gentlest current lineations are often evanescent features; and it is difficult in many cases to be certain that scour is really involved and that effects observed

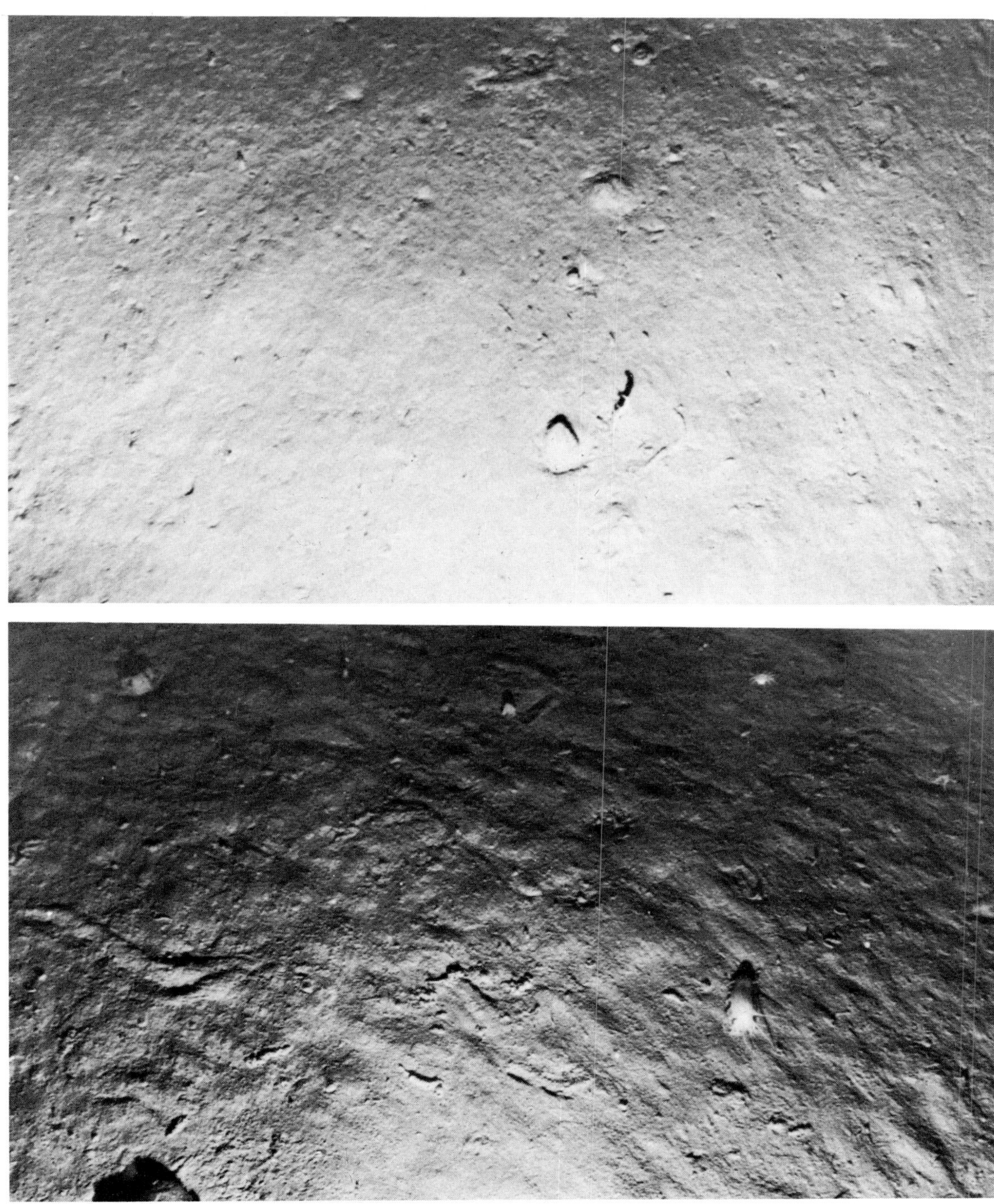

65°36′S 121°11′W
57°54′S 108°37′W

9.3 Smoothed. By beveling minor irregularities weak currents have subtly altered the abyssal seascape. U, 4879 m, Bellingshausen Basin. L, 2610 m, Mid-Oceanic Ridge, South Pacific.

12°02′S 168°53′W

◁ 9.2 Tranquil. This tracked and feces-covered sea floor reveals no evidence of currents. 5331 m, Samoa archipelagic apron, equatorial Pacific.

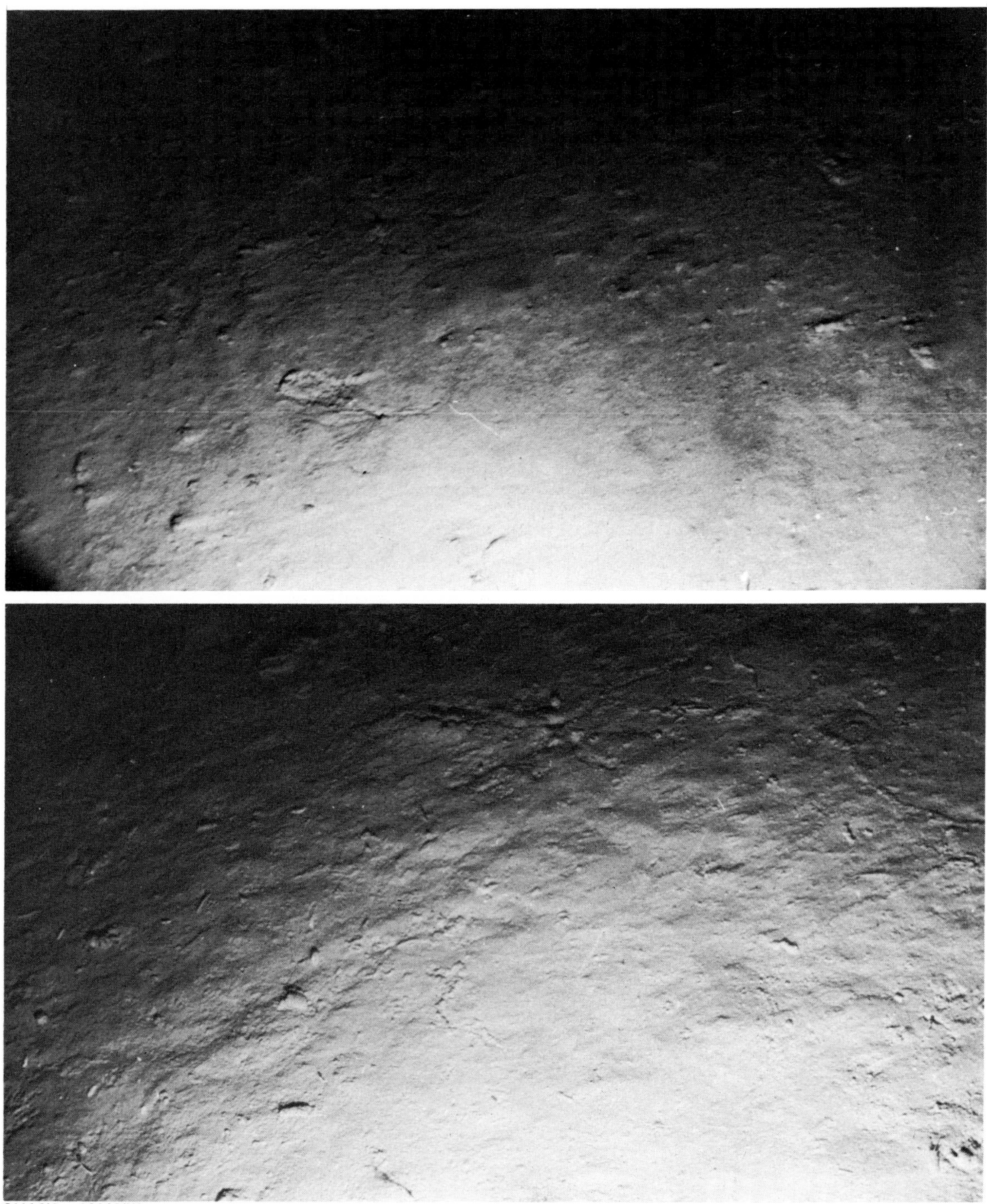

61°16′S 89°49′W
62°00′S 115°14′W

9.4 Lineated. Sediment is shaped into tails behind resistant objects by gentle currents. U, L, 4898 m, 5139 m, Bellingshausen Basin.

32°51′N 75°45′W
9.5 Textured. Subtle parallelism, elongated sediment tails and deflected organisms record a southerly current. 3183 m, Blake-Bahama Outer Ridge.

are not the result of bizarre lighting. However, since there are sufficient cases where gentle scour is transitional—within the same series of pictures—to stronger scour or ripples, there can be little doubt that the subtle lineations are current-induced. In some photographs, currents are indicated simply by the absence of burrows, mounds, and tracks. In other cases, mounds and burrows are deformed or partially destroyed. (9.3).

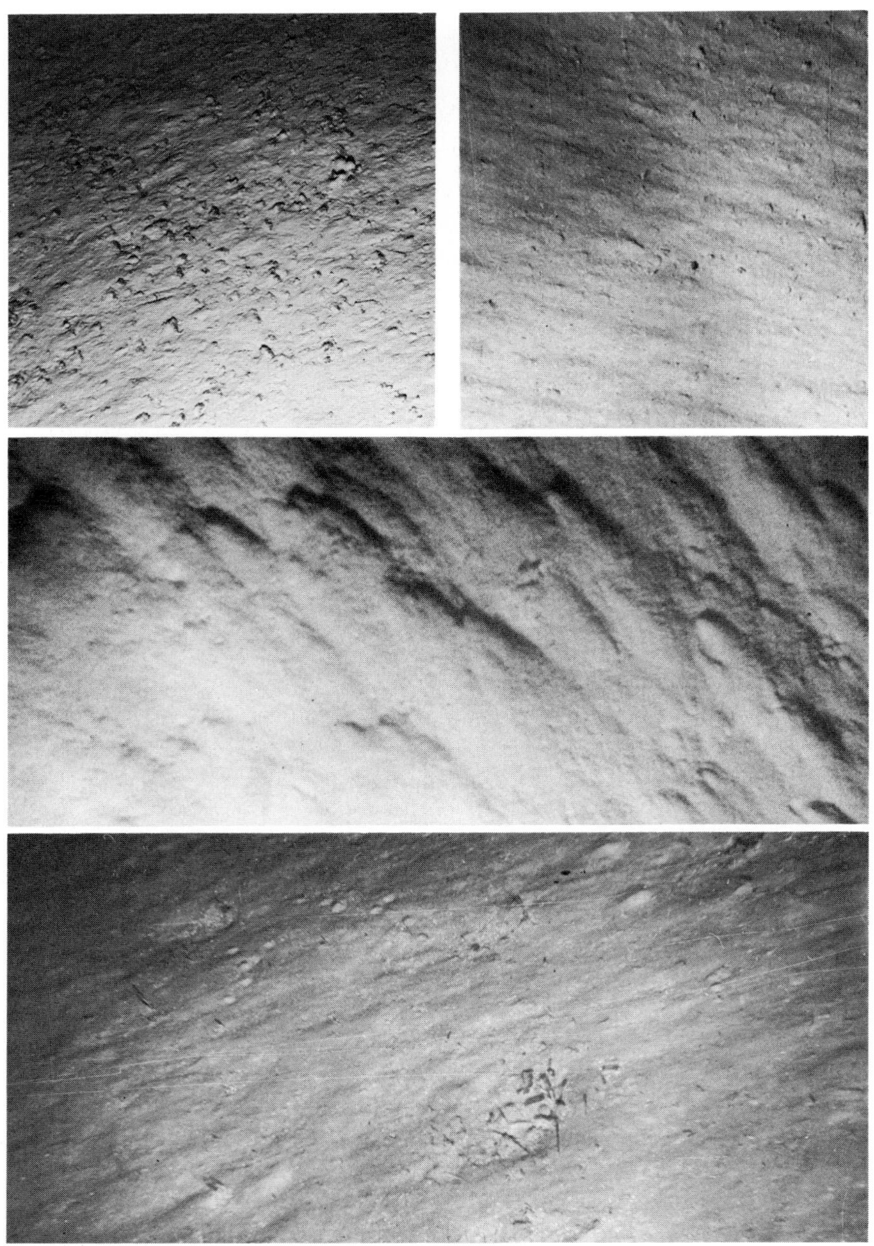

63°46′S 114°54′W 20°39′S 41°43′E
36°31′N 00°26′E
19°55′S 41°56′E

9.6 Sediment is scoured and deposited into elongated tails. UL, 5072 m, Bellingshausen Basin. UR, L, 3235 m, 2908 m, Mozambique Passage. C, 874 m, continental slope, Algeria.

The gentlest of current lineations consist of slight elongations of burrows and a noticeable linear texture which is accentuated by a parallelism of gentle sediment tails behind feces and other resistant objects

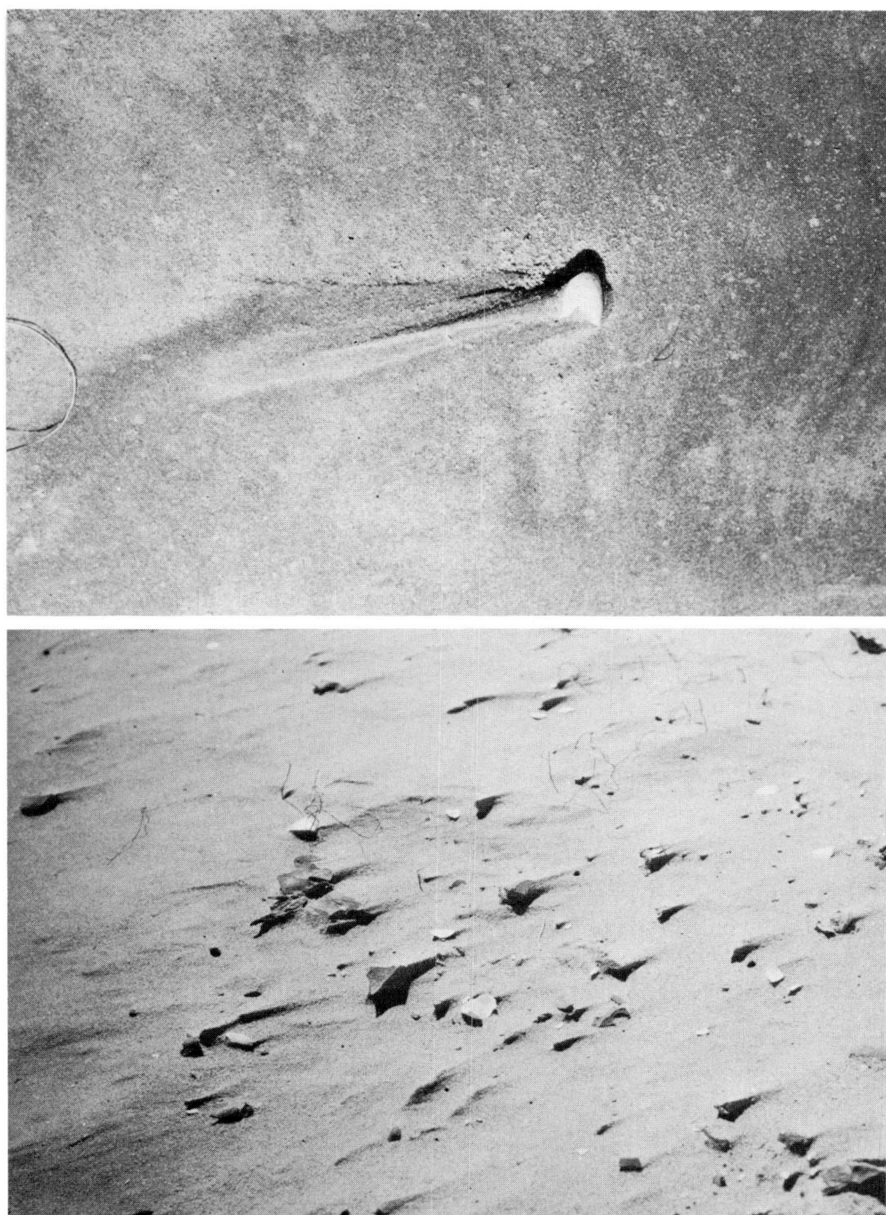

9.7 Deflation lineations. Wind deflation patterns on a beach resemble abyssal current lineations. Rancho Nuestra Señora del Refugio, Santa Barbara County, California.

(9.4). In most cases no very strong or definite features are seen. One simply has a general impression of a parallel arrangement of subtle features, any one of which is almost too small to detect or too poorly represented on photographs to be unequivocally identified (9.5). But these

32°32'N 66°29'W

9.9 Bowed by the current. A sea pen living on a lineated bottom is bent by the prevailing northeast current. 4916 m, western Bermuda Rise.

smoothed areas contrast markedly with the random irregularity of the normal ocean floor (9.2).

In areas of slightly faster currents, the features which we refer to as current lineations become more marked and one can discern definite individual drifts. There is a strong elongation of sediment behind burrows, pebbles, and other objects, and an appreciable accumulation of sediment in tails a centimeter or more thick is often revealed by a deepening of shadows (9.6-9.9).

Rocks, nodules, resistant lumps of mud and feces are obstacles to the flow of bottom currents. Commonly moat-like depressions are excavated on the upcurrent side of these obstacles, and a little ridge of sediment, narrowing and sloping downcurrent, forms on the lee side. These "current crescents" or "crag and tail" structures have been observed on tidal flats and beaches, and some have been photographed in abyssal depths (9.6). In areas where currents have higher velocity, the moats are deeper and the sediment tails may be destroyed. In areas affected by even

◁ 9.8 Sediment tails form behind rocks and feces. U, L, 3250 m, 3433 m, Mid-Oceanic Ridge south of Macquarie Island.

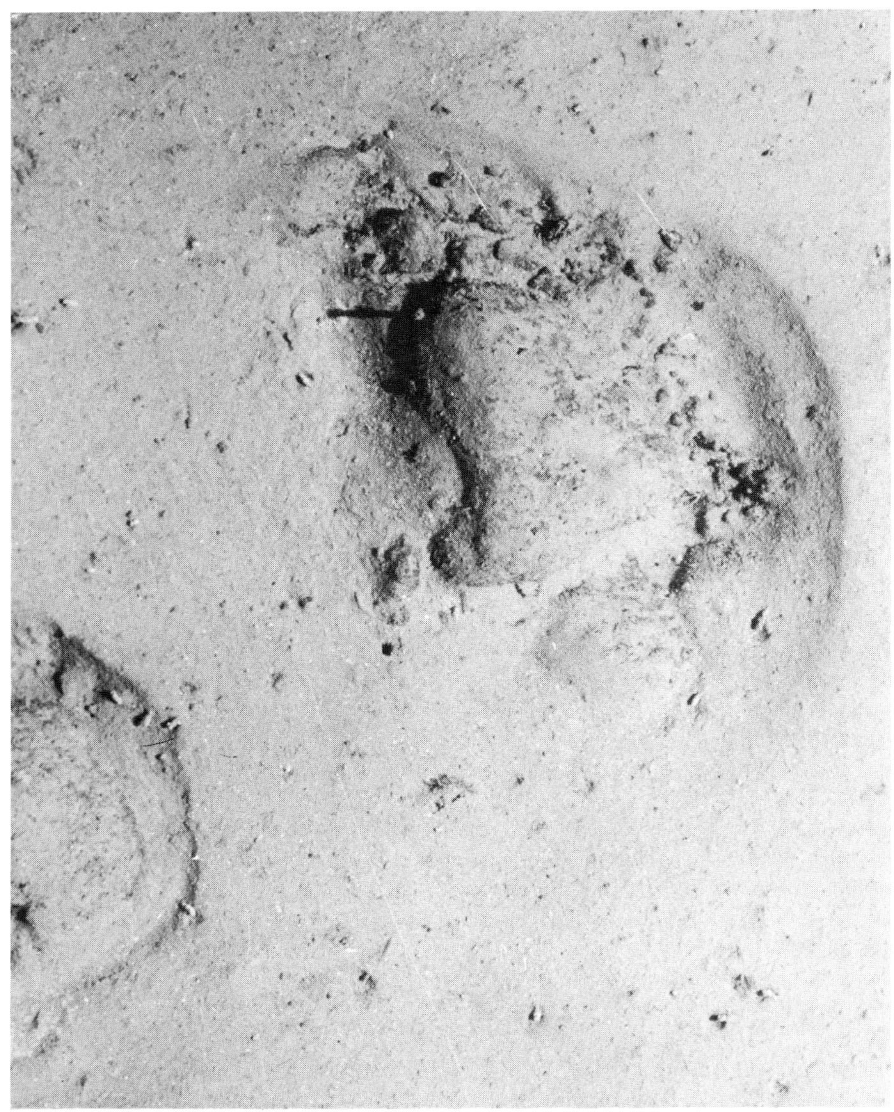

37°37′N 59°59′W
9.10 Nested rocks. Small pebbles lie in current-scoured moats which surround larger rocks. 4916 m, Kelvin Seamounts.

stronger currents, the moats appear to be partially filled with smaller pebbles or rock fragments, producing "rock nests" (9.10).

RIPPLES AND FLUTES

Flute marks (9.11), sculptured in clay or silty clay by strong bottom currents, are asymmetrical concavities having a steep upcurrent slope and a gentle downcurrent slope which gradually merges with the sur-

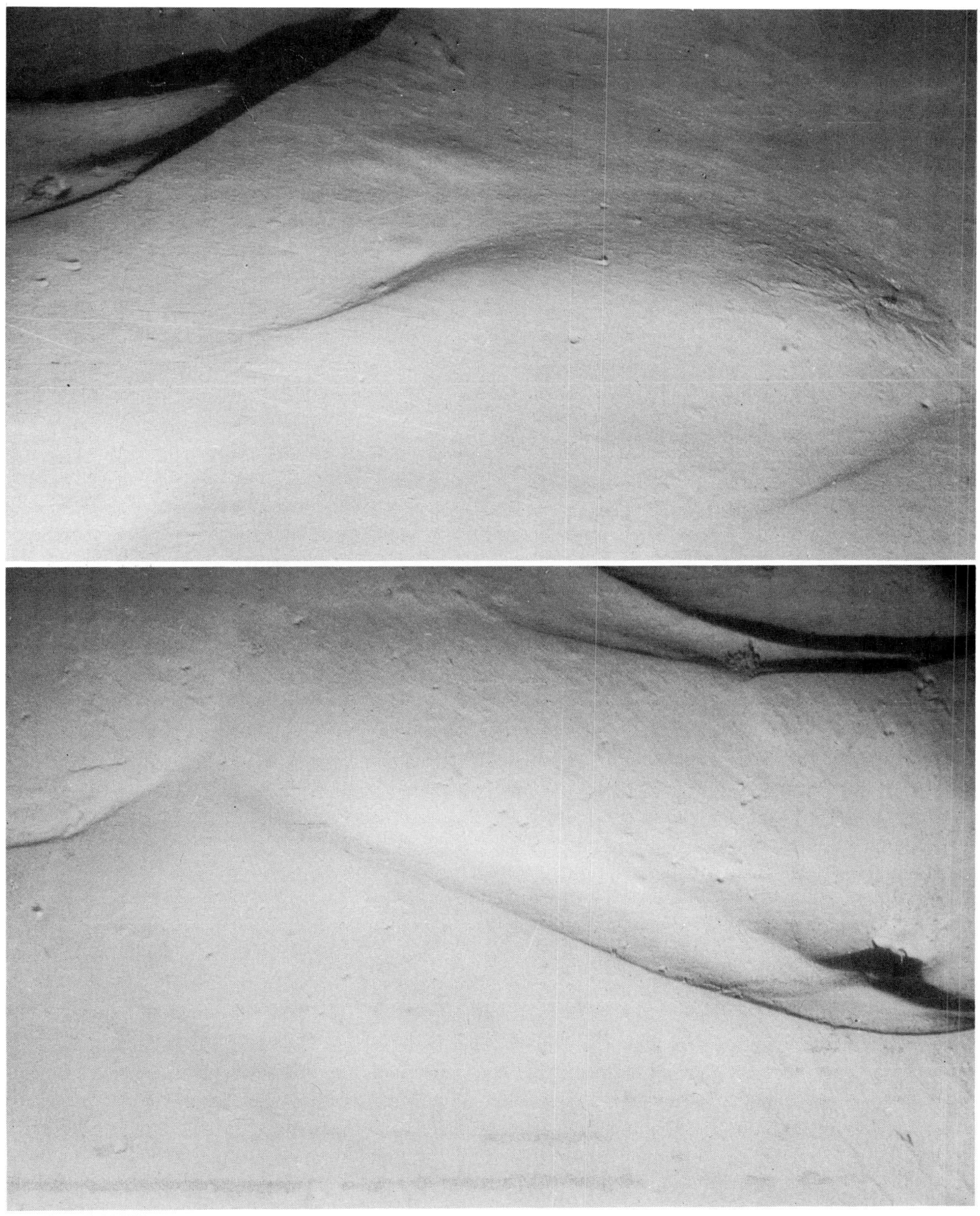

32°46′N 37°11′W
32°46′N 37°11′W

9.11 Fluted. Currents have sculpted the fine abyssal clay creating these fluted surfaces. 5202 m, Eastward Scarp, Bermuda Rise.

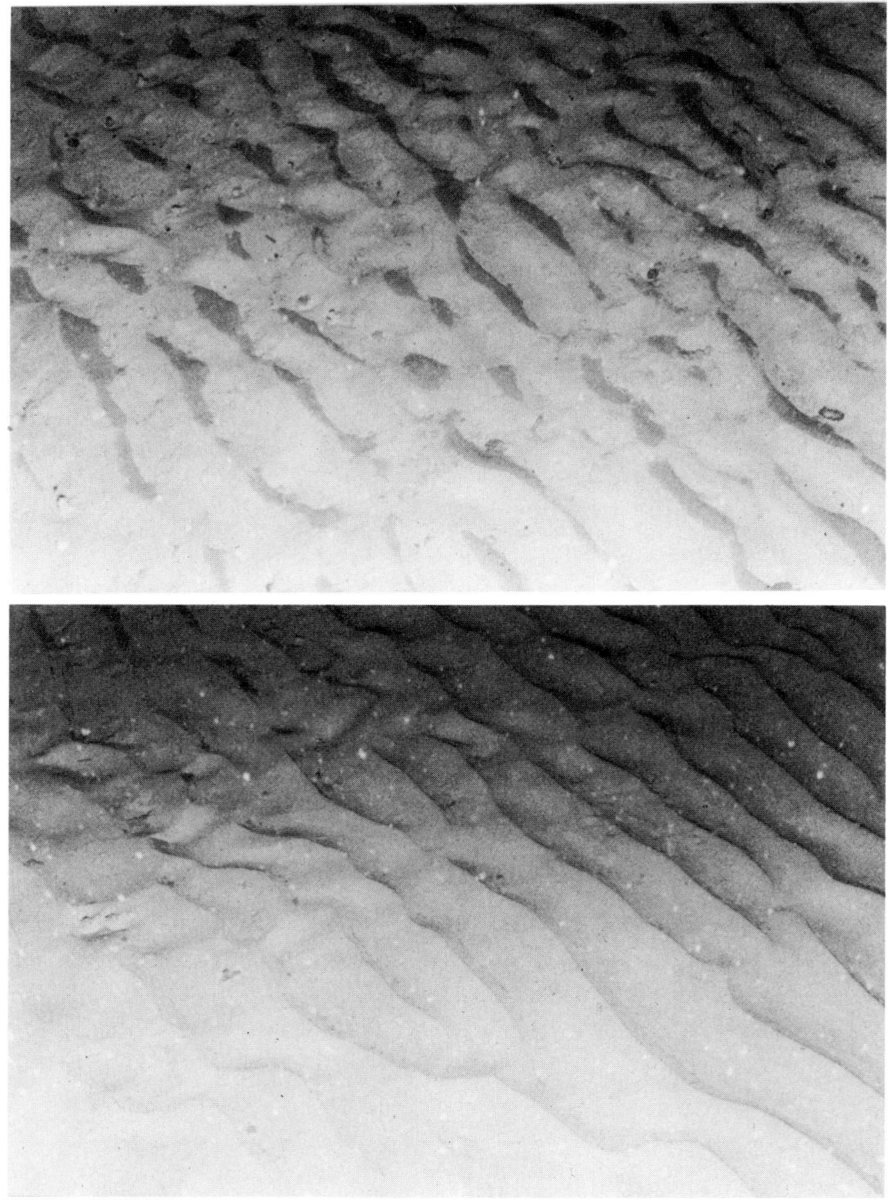

56°53′S 135°04′W

9.12 Strong sediment-laden currents ripple the ooze. Suspended particles carried in the current resemble snow, 3347 m, Mid-Oceanic Ridge, South Pacific.

rounding current-swept bottom. Flutes have been produced experimentally through erosion of the substrate by current vortices, and they have been photographed beneath contemporary deep-sea currents in various parts of the world ocean.

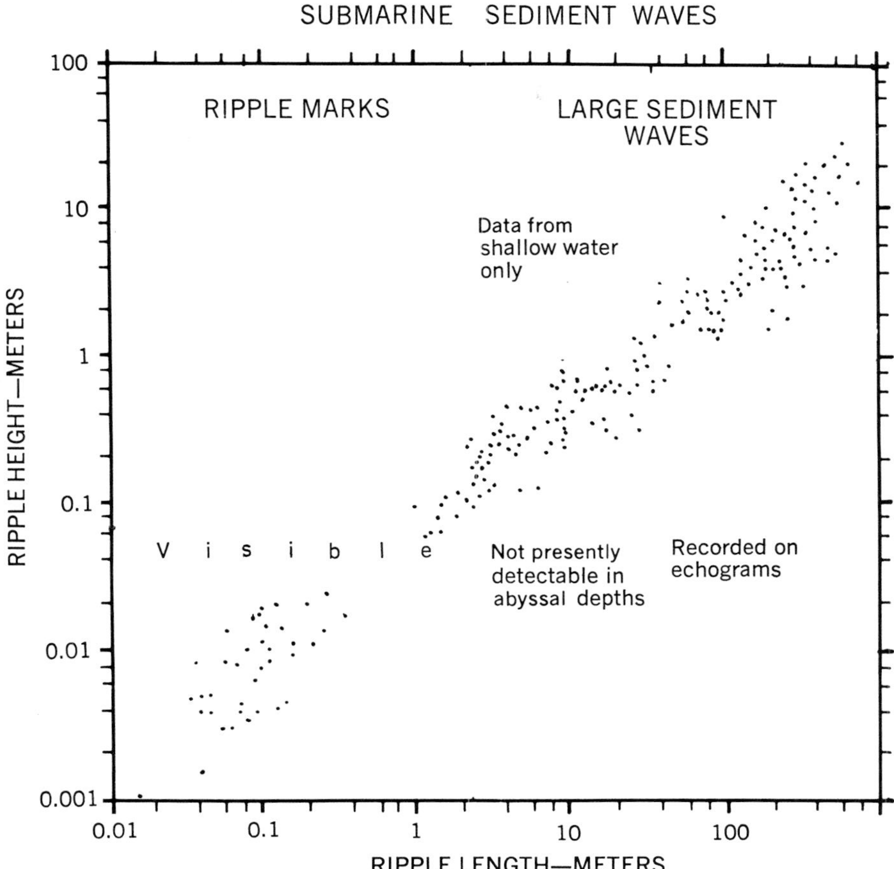

9.13 Submarine sediment waves. Height and wave-lengths vary by one hundred thousand times from the smallest ripple to the largest dunes.

Even stronger currents are indicated by the development of ripple marks (9.12). These periodic or rhythmic undulations that form on the sediment-fluid interface may be initiated by small sea-floor irregularities, or perhaps through instability of the boundary between the rapidly moving bottom water and the upper part of the sediment blanket. Current ripples, regardless of size, have a cross-bedded internal structure produced as the current moves the sediment and thus the ripples themselves in advancing waves.

Ripple marks essentially form the smaller end of a continuum of sediment waves on the sea floor (9.13). These waves range in size from wavelengths and amplitudes of a few centimeters up to amplitudes of tens of meters and wavelengths of thousands of meters (9.14). However, only those ripples with wavelengths of less than five or ten meters can be identified in underwater photographs (9.15-9.18).

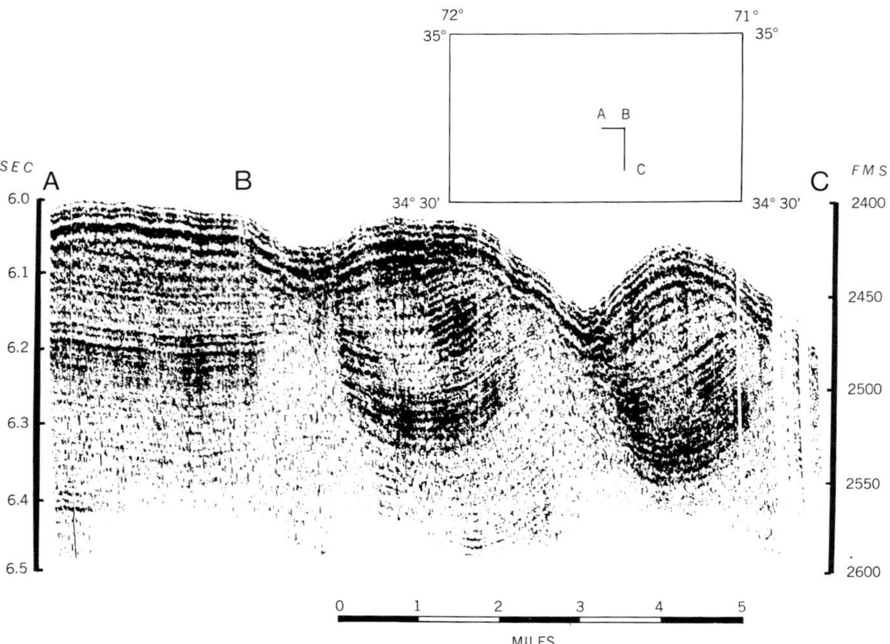

9.14 Giant sediment waves. These abyssal dunes result from deposition by strong bottom currents. Lower Continental Rise Hills, western North Atlantic.

Straight-crested ripple marks with symmetrical cross section (9.15), commonly referred to as oscillation ripple marks, were the first type of ripples photographed beneath the deep sea. Later work indicates that this type is somewhat rarer than early discoveries suggested. Straight-crested ripple marks may be symmetrical (9.15 U) or asymmetrical (9.16), transverse (9.12, 9.15 L, 9.16) or longitudinal (9.40). However, the vast majority of straight-crested ripple marks appear to be oriented transverse to the current direction, and the steeper side of an asymmetrical ripple faces downcurrent. Ripple marks with markedly curved crests (9.17) are also asymmetrical, and the steeper side faces downcurrent.

Attempts have been made to find a relationship of wavelengths to depth of water, but it is apparent from deep-sea photographs that no such simple correlation exists[3] (9.17). Underwater photographs have revealed ripple marks down to depths of 7000 meters (9.46), and although there are fewer ripple marks and scour marks in the greater depths, there appears to be no relationship whatsoever between depth of water and the size and shape of the ripples that do occur.

There probably is a relationship between the size and geometry of ripple marks and sediment composition. The largest ripples recognized in photographs are apparently formed in coarse debris or lag deposits

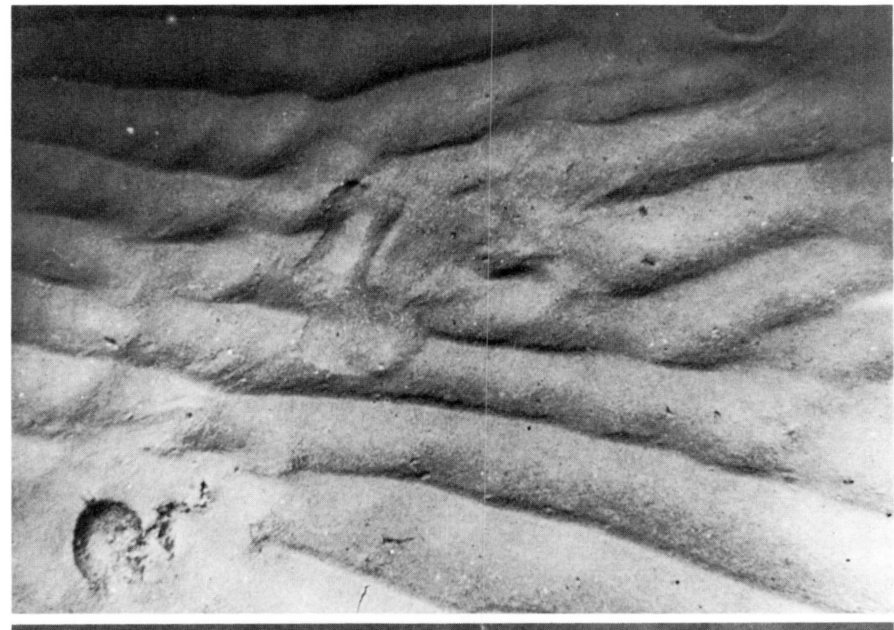

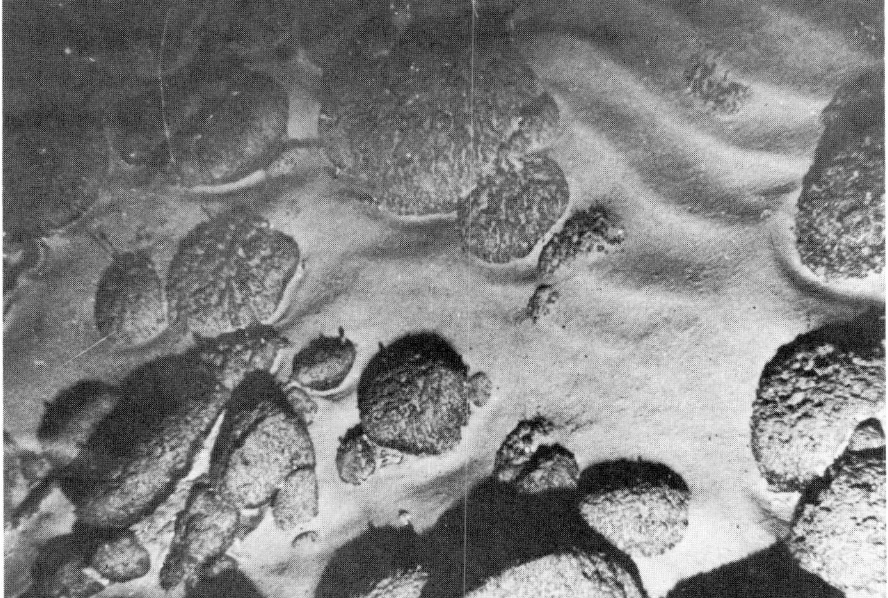

08°48′S 33°25′W

9.15 Ripples and scour moats forming in globigerina ooze. 3218 m, Bellefontaine Seamount.

near the crest of the Mid-Oceanic Ridge (9.18). It has been pointed out frequently that ripple marks are a phenomenon found almost exclusively in sand-size material, although we have photographs of ripples which appear to have formed in finer oozes and clays (9.46, 9.44).

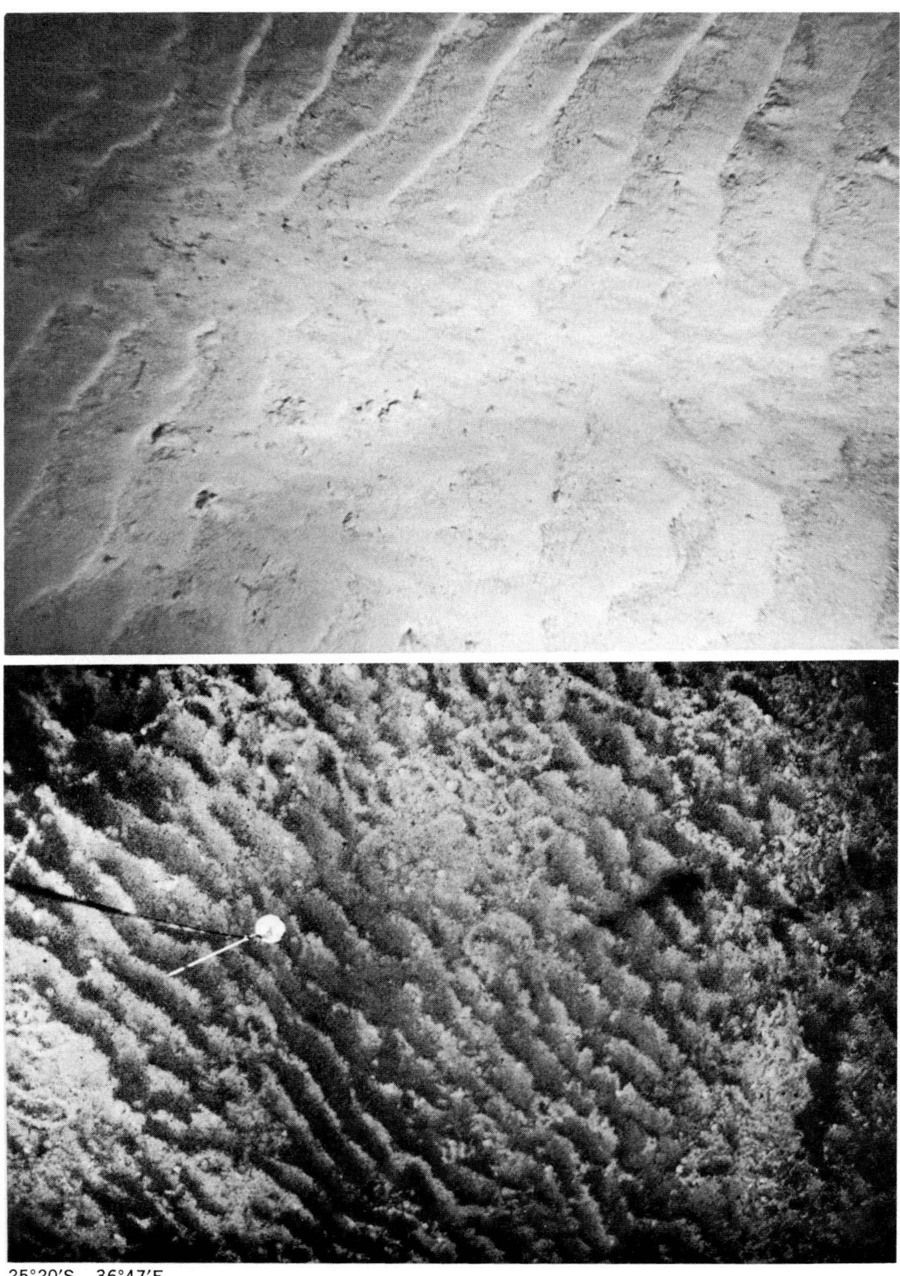

25°20′S 36°47′E
29°04′N 43°03′W

9.16 Starved asymmetrical ripples form on remote current-swept ridges. Current (U) flowing from left to right ripple and scour the bottom. The compass (L) and vane on the left indicate a current flowing transverse to the ripples in a southwesterly direction along the axis of the mid-Atlantic Rift Valley. U, 2195 m, Mozambique Ridge. L, 2311 m, Rift Valley, Mid-Atlantic Ridge.

30°52′N 78°41′W
57°06′S 63°16′W
55°15′S 64°56′W

9.17 Short-crested asymmetrical ripples form beneath strong currents. UL, 3895 m, Drake Passage. UR, 1934 m, continental slope off Cape Horn. L, 867 m, Blake Plateau.

Sediment dunes with wavelengths of hundreds to thousands of meters can be recognized only on echo-sounding records, and special sounding devices are needed to resolve sediment waves tens of meters in wave-

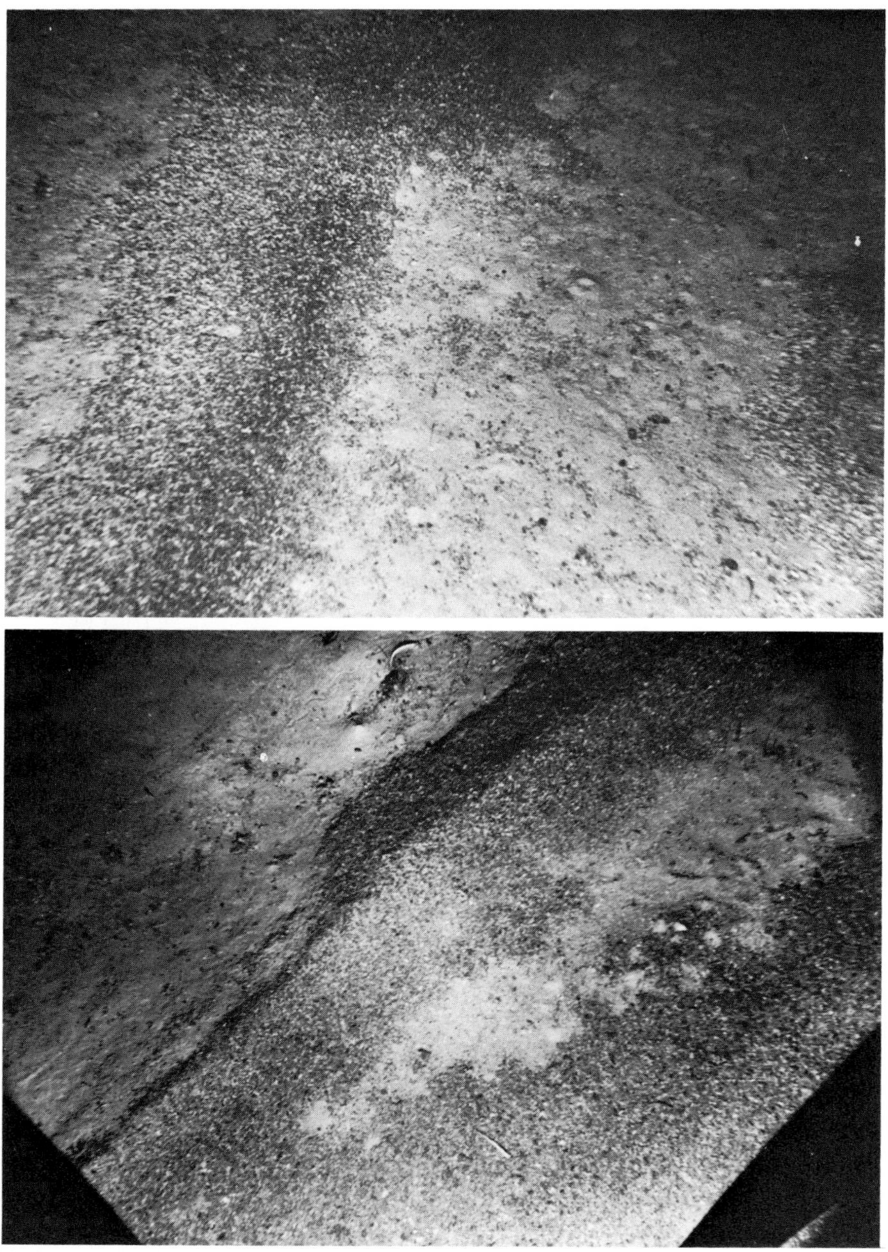

46°50′N 28°58′W
35°07′N 13°04′W

9.18 Coarse debris is swept into giant starved ripples. U, 2674 m, crest of Mid-Atlantic Ridge. L, 2065 m, Ampere Seamount.

length. Bottom photographs taken on sediment waves usually—but not always—show rippled or scoured bottom (9.57).

Current velocities in excess of the transport velocities of even the coarsest pelagic sediments (more than fifty centimeters per second) are

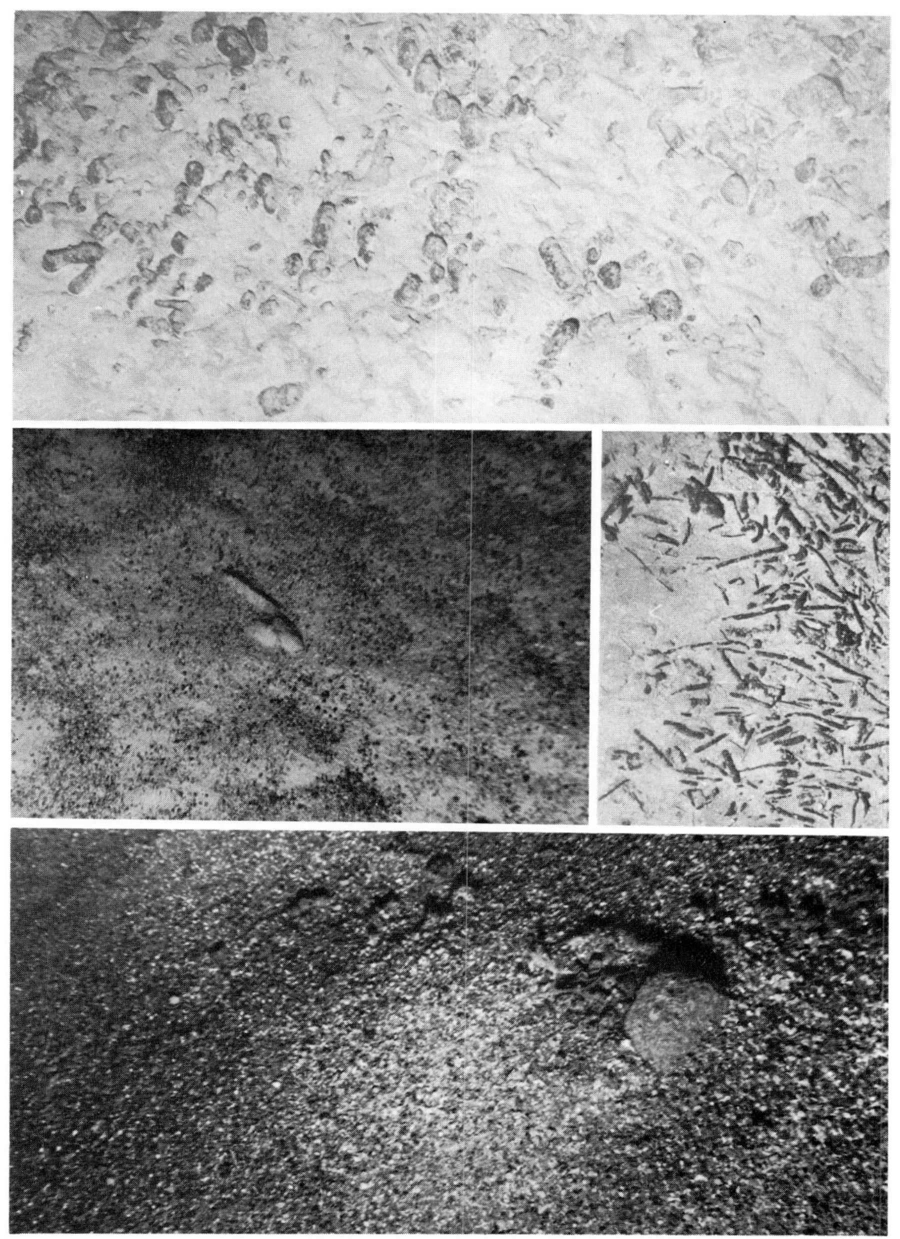

59°14′S 68°49′W
15°38′S 145°01′W
35°07′N 13°04′W
19°55′S 41°56′E

9.19 Coarse debris is left behind as currents winnow the clay and ooze. U, 3600 m, Drake Passage. LC, 1526 m, Tuamoto Archipelago. RC, 2908 m, Mozambique Passage. L, 2065 m, Ampere Seamount.

indicated where bottom photographs show lag deposits (9.19) and exposures of bare rock. In regions of very strong bottom currents, short-crested ripple marks are commonly seen in small pockets of coarse sand

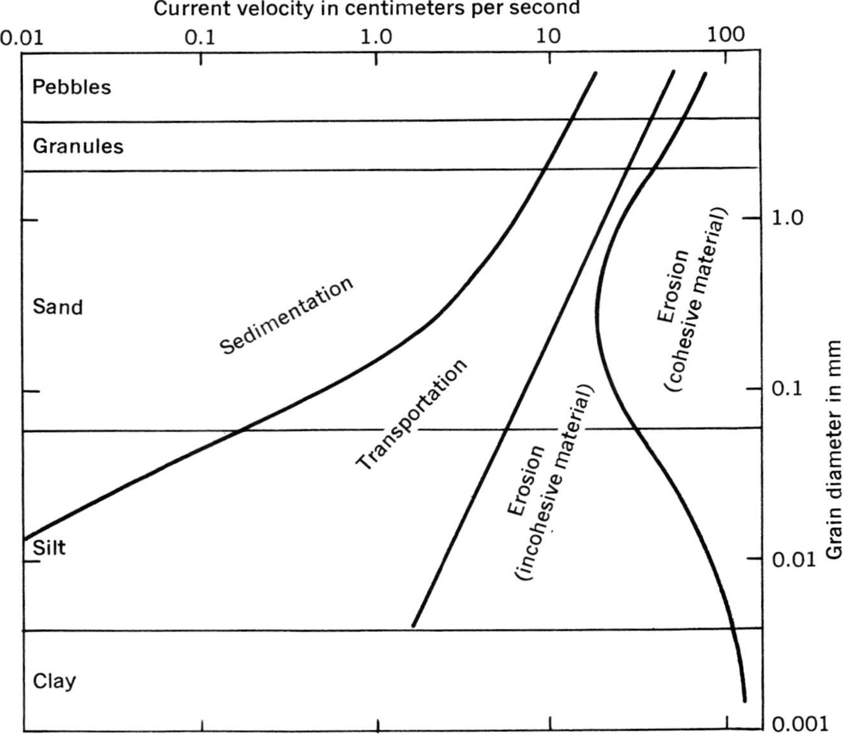

9.20 Current velocities required for erosion, transportation, and deposition. The vast majority of abyssal sediments are finer than sand. Experimentally determined erosion velocities for fine particles are uncertain as they depend on the degree of sediment cohesion.

between exposures of bare rock. Where bottom current velocity exceeds the erosion velocity of sand or gravel, only current-swept bare rock outcrops are observed.

WEATHER VANES

Most bottom current indicators reveal clear evidence of current direction, thus compass-oriented photographs can be used to map bottom current directions. Despite the fact that clear and unmistakable evidence of bottom currents was noted in the earliest photographs of the sea floor taken during and following World War II, it has only been in the past few years that this simple, direct tool has been employed in the mapping of bottom current directions.

The deflection of fauna and the drift of mud clouds give evidence of current direction and relative velocity at the moment the photographs

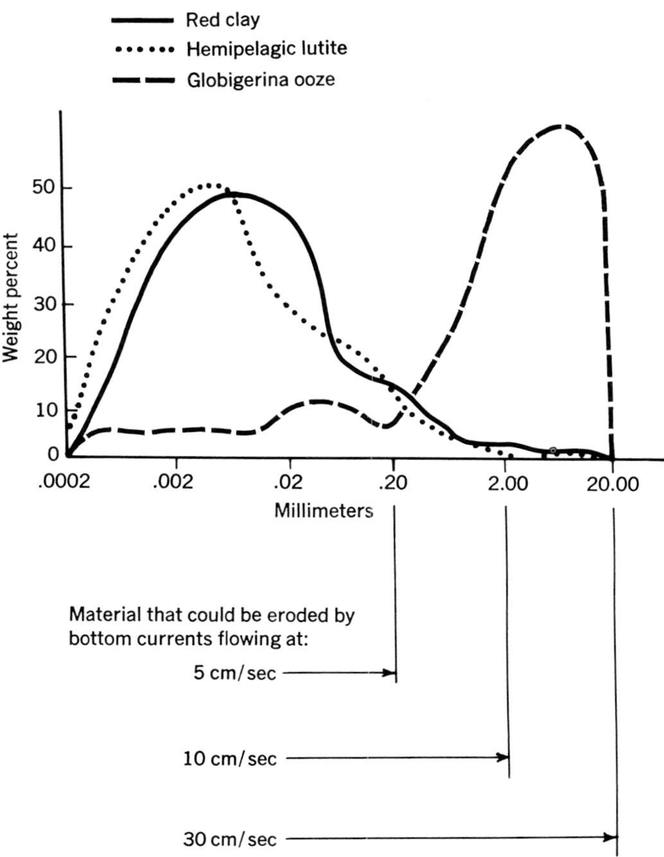

9.21 Minimum current velocities required for erosion of the principal deep-sea sediments.

were taken (9.1, 9.9). One can commonly see from other indicators, such as current lineations or ripples, that the currents observed are in the same direction as the prevailing current; but this need not always be the case. In one dramatic photograph (9.48), we see a deflected sponge which had at previous times undergone stronger deflection in a range of directions which were recorded by a short arc drawn in the bottom sediments. Such self-recording weathervanes, however, are infrequently photographed.

CURRENT COMPETENCE

Estimates can be made of current velocities implied by the presence of current lineations, scour marks, ripples, and cross beds on the basis of the particle sizes involved. Experimental studies indicate a nearly linear

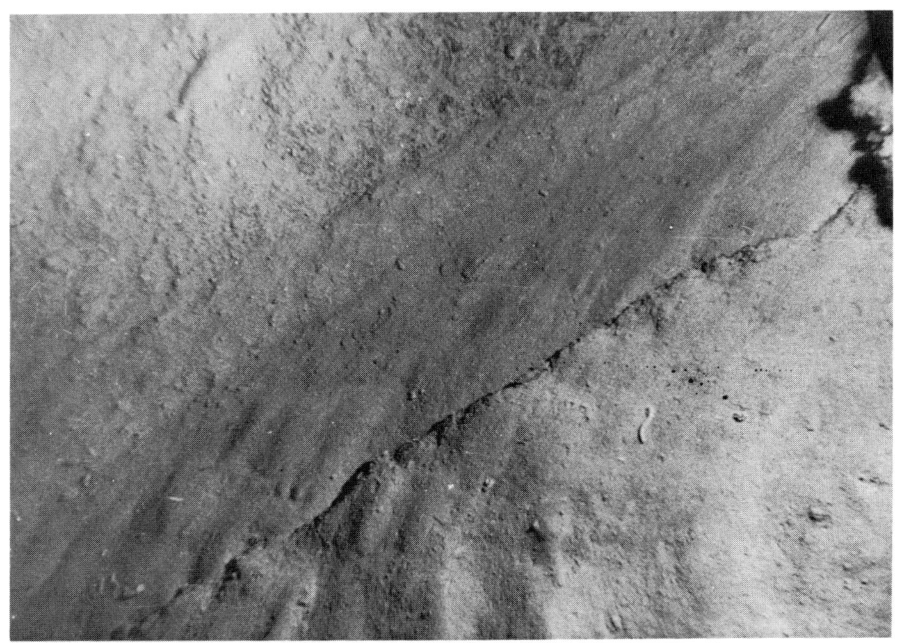

23°06′S 56°43′E
9.22 Currents erode the abyssal floor. 4909 m, floor of Mauritius Trench.

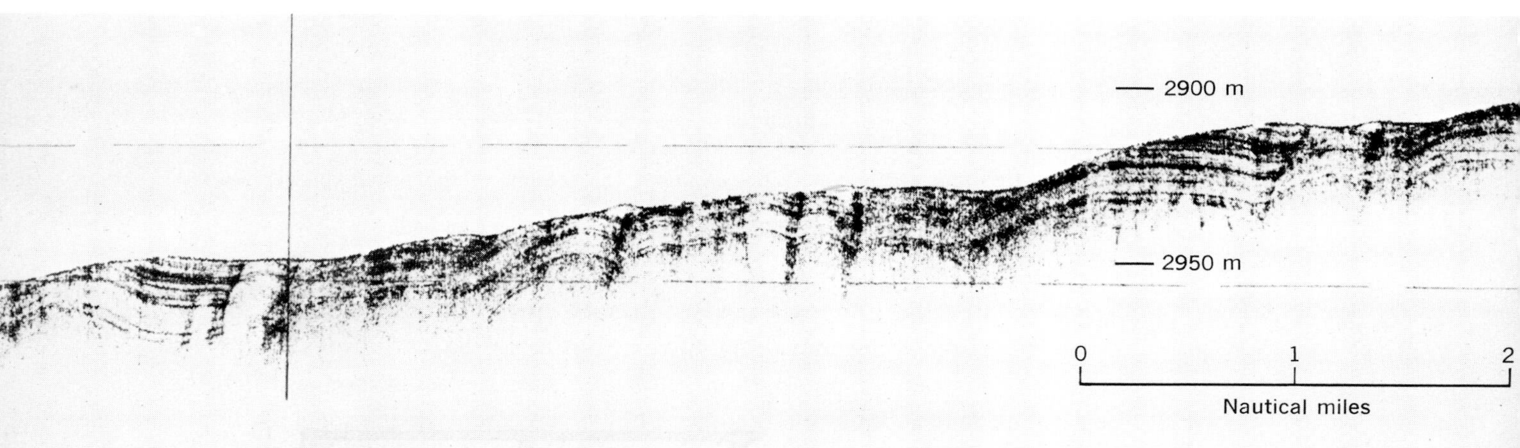

9.23 Currents have beveled the deformed sea-floor sediments. Continental slope off Louisiana, Gulf of Mexico.

relationship between particle size and velocity for sizes coarser than fine sand (9.20). For instance, the erosion of medium sand requires a velocity of at least twenty centimeters per second, whereas gravel requires velocities greater than thirty centimeters per second.[4] However, the lim-

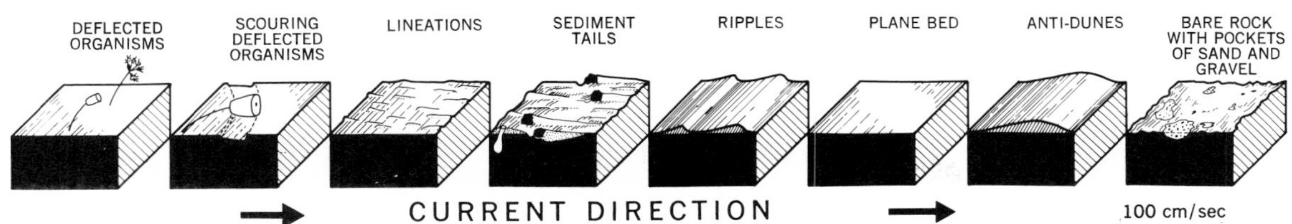

9.24 The effect of increasing current on the visual seascape.

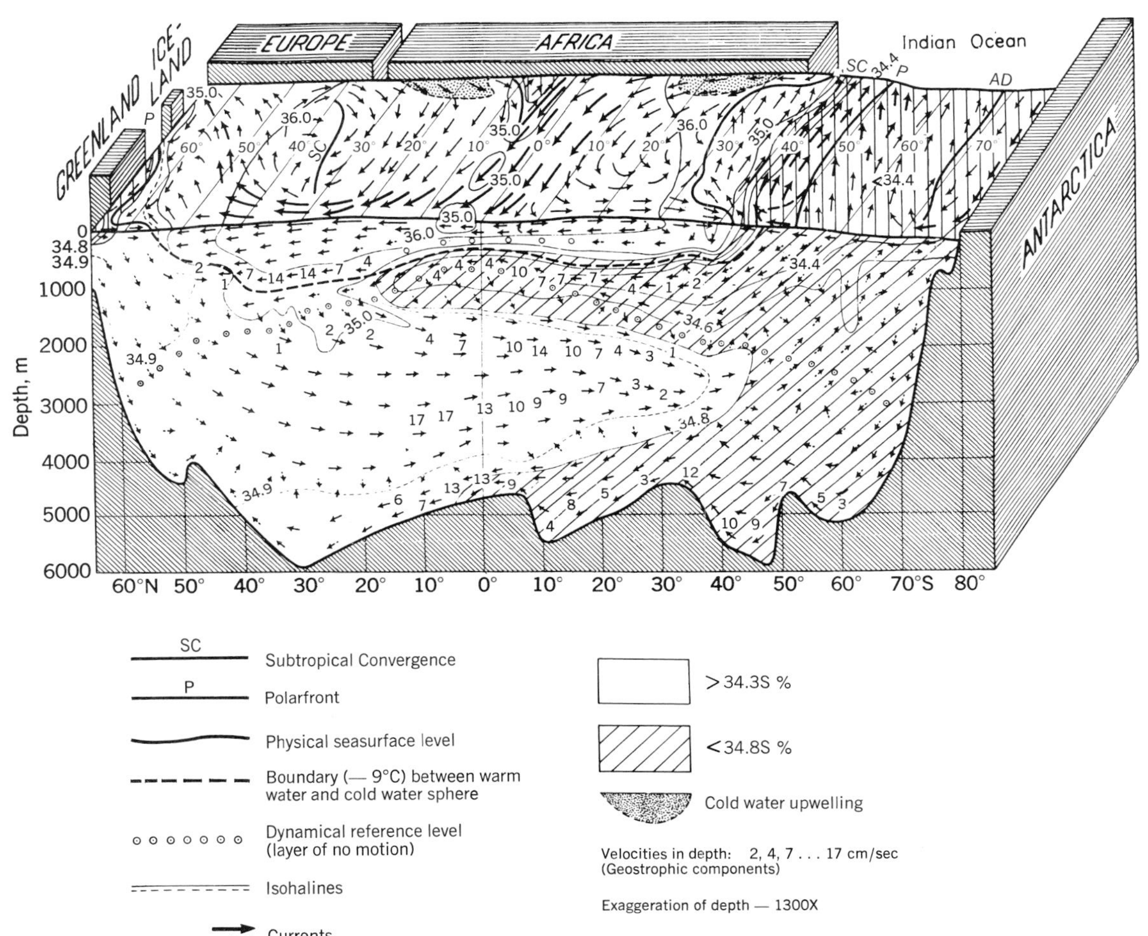

9.25 Abyssal circulation. Schematic block diagram of deep-sea circulation in the western Atlantic.

ited and conflicting data for smaller sizes found in normal abyssal sediments pose a more difficult problem. The inverse relationship between erosion velocity and grain size for grains finer than medium sand shown in textbook curves is probably not valid for modern abyssal sediments. In fact, the general validity of this relationship has often been ques-

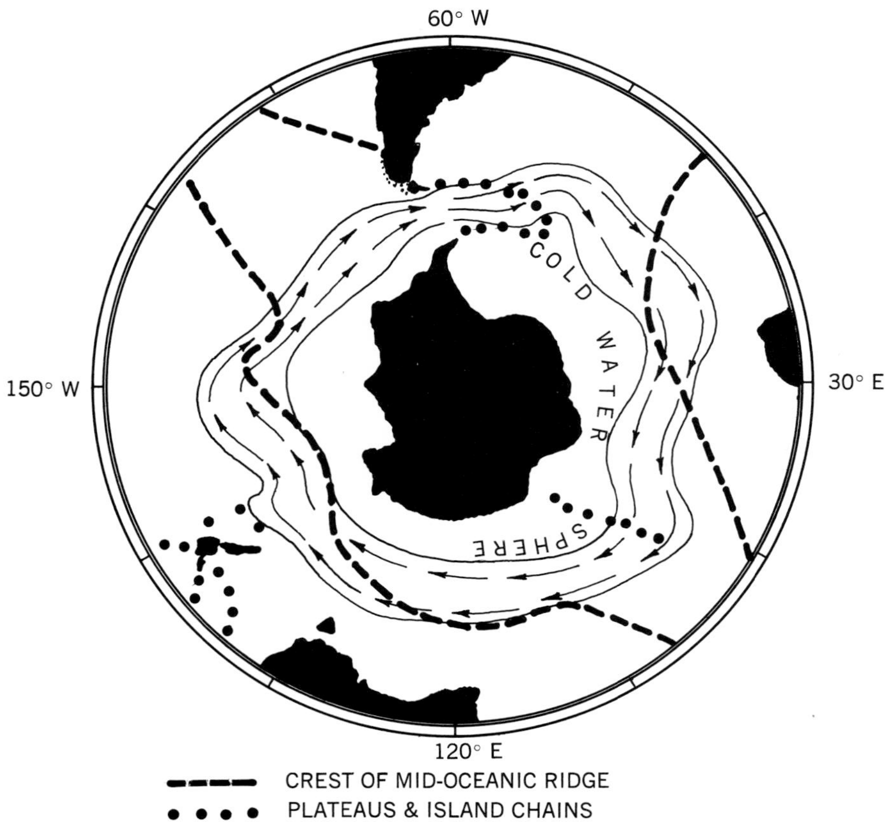

9.26 The Antarctic Circumpolar Current.

tioned.[5] For example, in recent experiments it was determined that fine silt (ten microns) was eroded at only four centimeters per second and that asymmetrical ripple marks were readily formed at current velocities ranging from about five to fifteen centimeters per second.[6] Thus, it is apparent that current marks observed in sediments of sizes normally present on the sea floor required bottom currents moving at velocities of at least five centimeters per second in the case of abyssal clay and hemipelagic lutite, and of thirty centimeters per second in the case of the coarsest globigerina ooze (9.21). Deep-sea tides have rarely been measured, but a few measurements from the abyss have indicated tidal velocities of about five centimeters per second.[7] Over a flat ocean floor the tidal currents should be elliptical; but where constrained by slopes, the horizontally stratified waters flow back and forth parallel to the contours and thus alternately augment and diminish other currents. A current of five centimeters per second cannot erode the bottom, and thus tidal currents alone probably cannot have a dramatic effect on the abyssal seascape. If

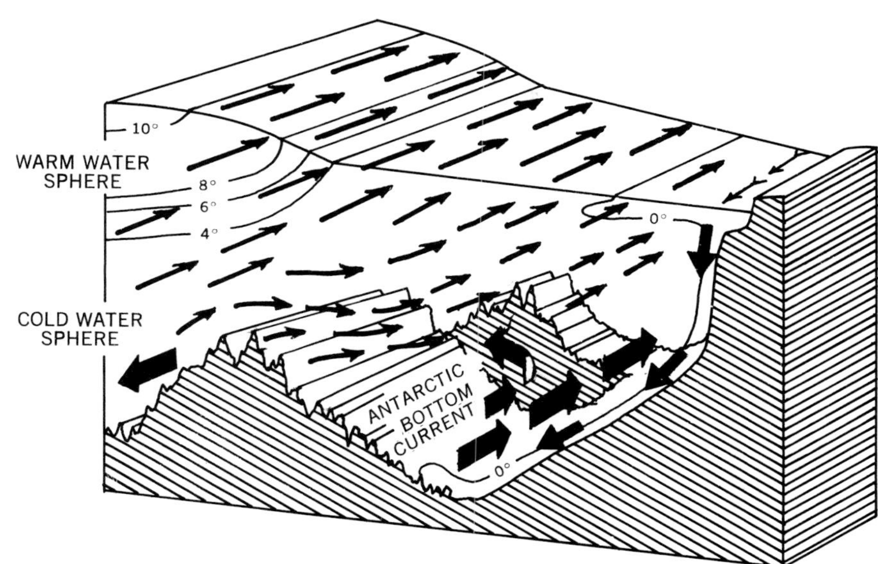

9.27 Deep circulation around Antarctica.

tides are shown by further measurements to attain higher velocities, even only occasionally, we may have to conclude that they are really more important in along-slope transportation than thermohaline currents, which are found mainly on the sides of basins where more rapid circulation occurs. Thus, the waters at the bottom of the sea are constantly in motion and only a slight nontidal current will allow erosion and net transportation of sediments, producing a notable visual effect (9.22).

The occurrence of deflected fauna on a bottom devoid of even the weakest lineations implies that velocities probably never exceed five centimeters per second. Velocities of this value have been observed for deep-sea tidal currents. The weaker current lineations probably require velocities greater than three to five centimeters per second. Ripple marks have been observed to form in fine silt under velocities as little as five centimeters per second, but ripples in medium sand probably form only at velocities greater than twenty centimeters per second. The bare rock slopes of the bold seamounts and ridge crests indicate velocities considerably in excess of twenty centimeters per second, for such current velocity is required to completely erode away the pelagic ooze.

Most oceanographers, until quite recently, considered the deep sea to be devoid of strong currents. Thus misled, geologists inferred that fossil ripple and scour marks found in rocks of all ages were infallible criteria for the recognition of ancient shallow-water deposits. In the early 1930's, German oceanographers had inferred relatively strong bottom currents in the western South Atlantic, calculating average velocities as high as

9.28 Sort-crested ripples beneath the Antarctic Circumpolar Current. U, L, 4010 m, this strong current scours the northern Drake Passage.

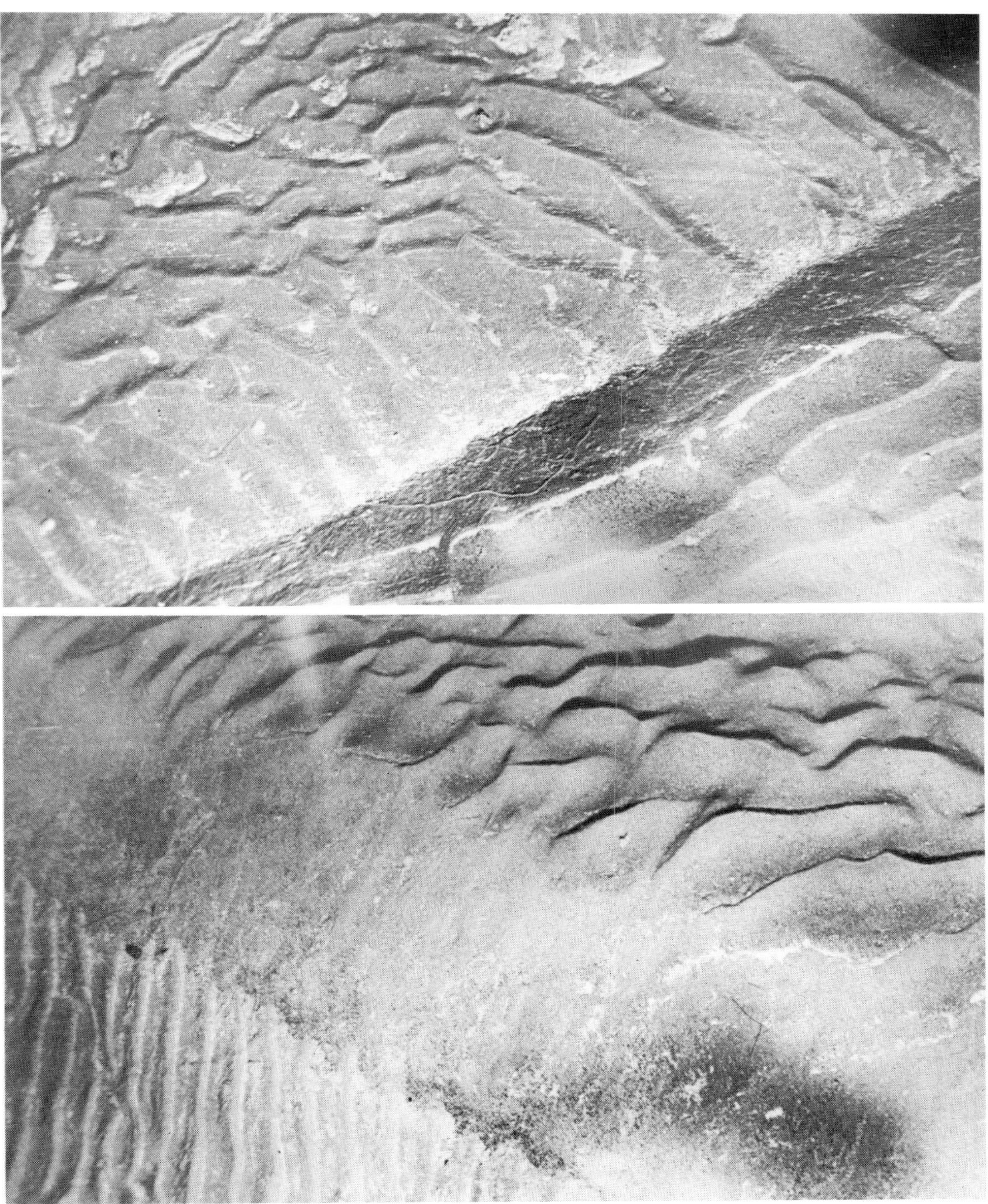

57°28′S 64°51′W

9.29 Confused ripple patterns. In areas of strong currents where well developed short-crested ripples prevail, abrupt changes in orientation are occasionally seen. U, L, 4531 m, Drake Passage.

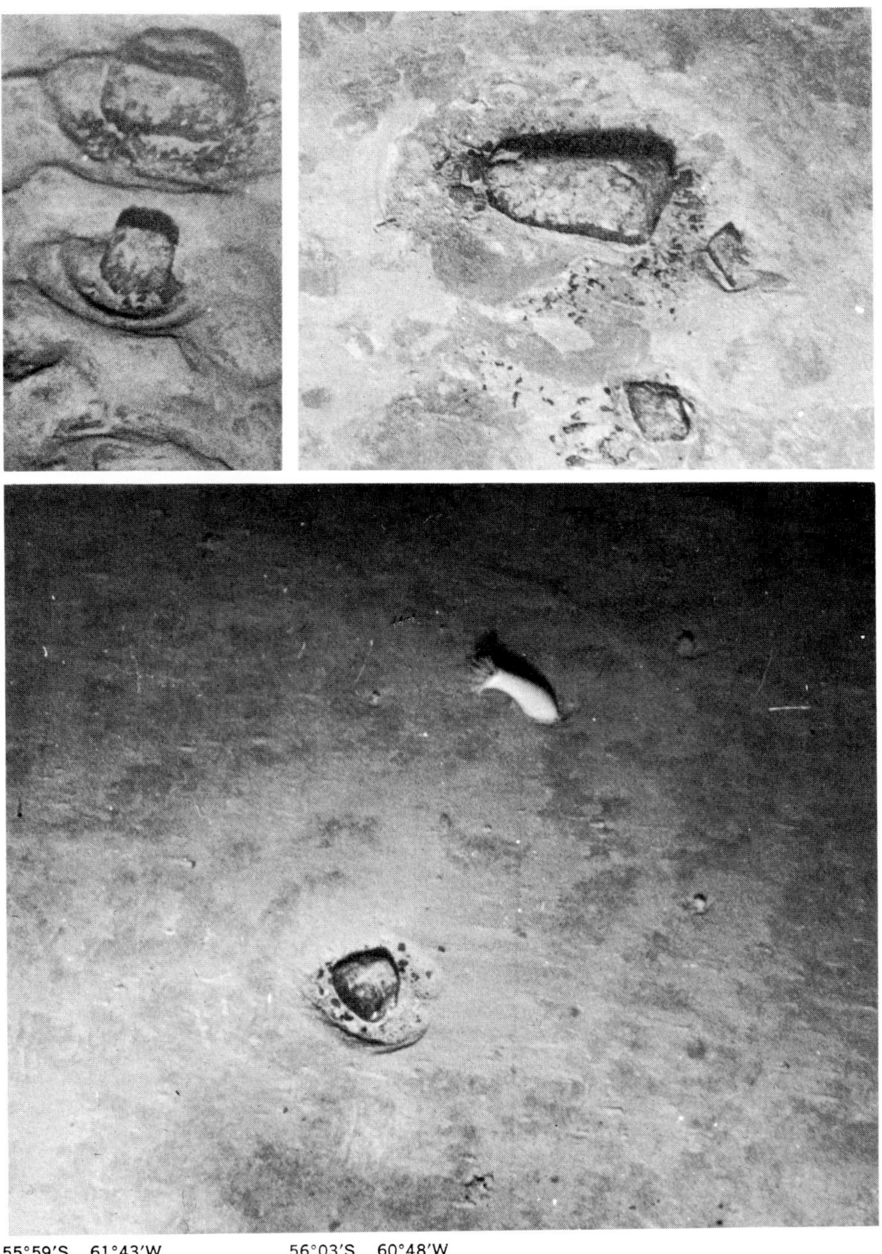

9.30 Rock nests and scour marks beneath the Circumpolar Current in the Drake Passage. UL, 4220 m. UR, L, 4190 m.

fifteen centimeters per second.[8] These revolutionary results, dependent on several computational assumptions but not supported by direct current measurements, were at first treated with some skepticism.[9] In the past few years, however, direct current measurements by neutrally buoyant floats,

59°35′S 155°17′E
57°58′S 153°58′E

9.31 The Antarctic Circumpolar Current scours the Mid-Indian Ocean Ridge south of Australia. U, 3245 m. L, 3433 m.

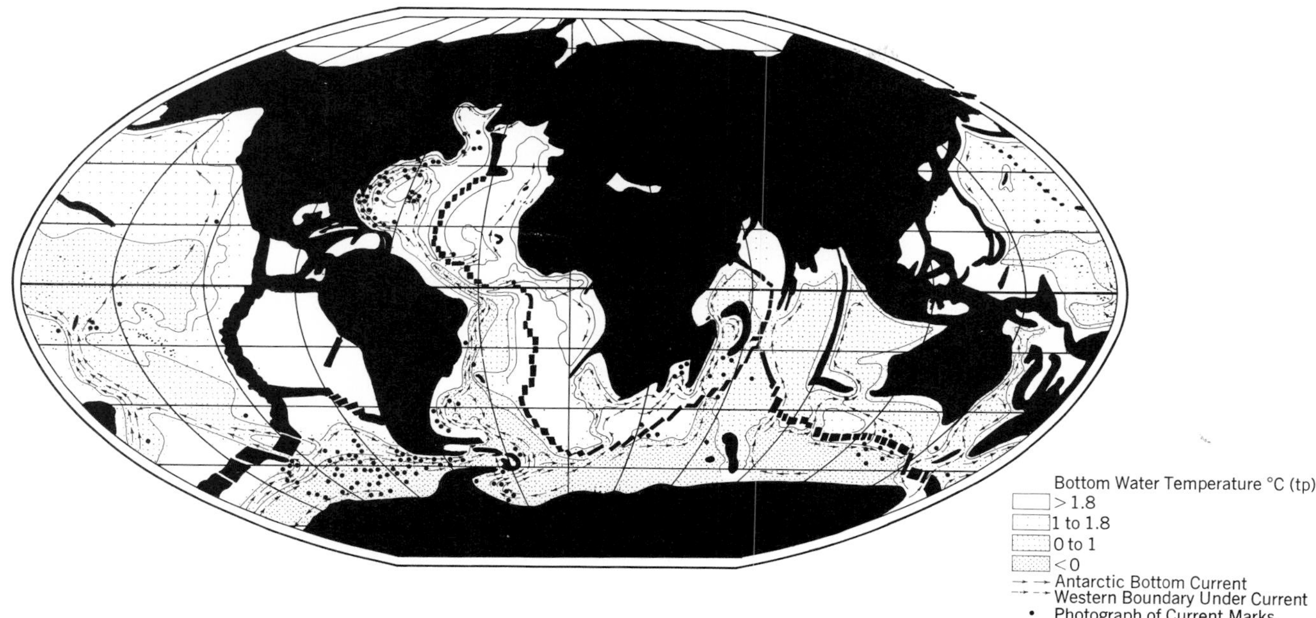

9.33 Abyssal circulation of the world ocean. Black areas less than 3000 meters water depth.

55°59′S 134°27′W

moored current meters, and bottom current meters have indicated the presence of relatively strong and variable currents (five to fifty centimeters per second) at great depths.[10] Thus, the current velocities implied by the sediment sizes present, and by their surface forms, are in general agreement with the directly observed velocities of bottom currents. All the sediment sizes present on the deep-sea floor could be transported by the observed deep currents, and certainly most were (9.23, 9.24).

55°59′S 134°27′W

FROM THE FRIGID POLES

The driving power for currents is drawn ultimately from the sun.[11] By the differential heating of air masses the sun creates wind which drives the vigorous surface circulation. Currents in the deep sea are driven by the earth's gravitational pull on water masses of differing density, which is in turn also controlled by the sun. The cold deep and bottom waters of the ocean mainly arise in the polar regions, where winter freezing leads to the formation of dense, cold, and relatively saline waters which sink down the continental slope and move steadily, but circuitously, toward lower latitudes (9.25). It was at first thought that the waters from both polar regions would rise at the equator, and from there begin their journey back to the poles. But since the waters formed in the antarctic are denser than

◁ 9.32 Ripples and rocks lie beneath the Antarctic Circumpolar Current in the South Pacific. U, L, 3157 m, Mid-Oceanic Ridge.

76°00'S 178°15'E
74°39'S 175°20'W

9.34 A frigid flow eminates from the Ross Sea and descends to the deep Pacific. U, 492 m, turbid waters of the Ross Sea shelf. L, 2280 m, rock trains and sediment streamers on the Antarctic continental slope near the edge of the Ross Sea.

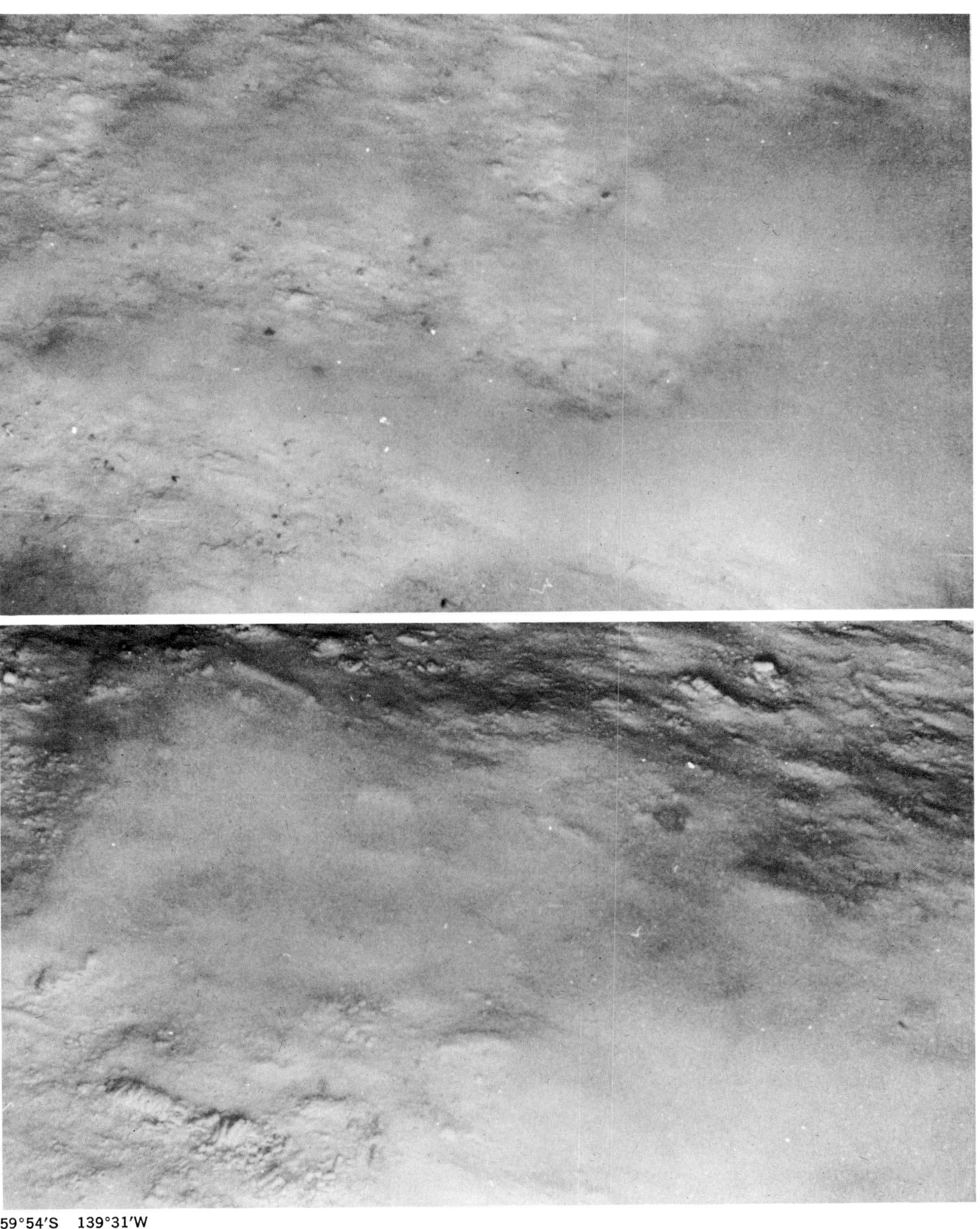

59°54′S 139°31′W
59°54′S 139°31′W

9.35 Turbid Antarctic water flowing over lineated bottom. U, L, 4080 m, Mid-Oceanic Ridge.

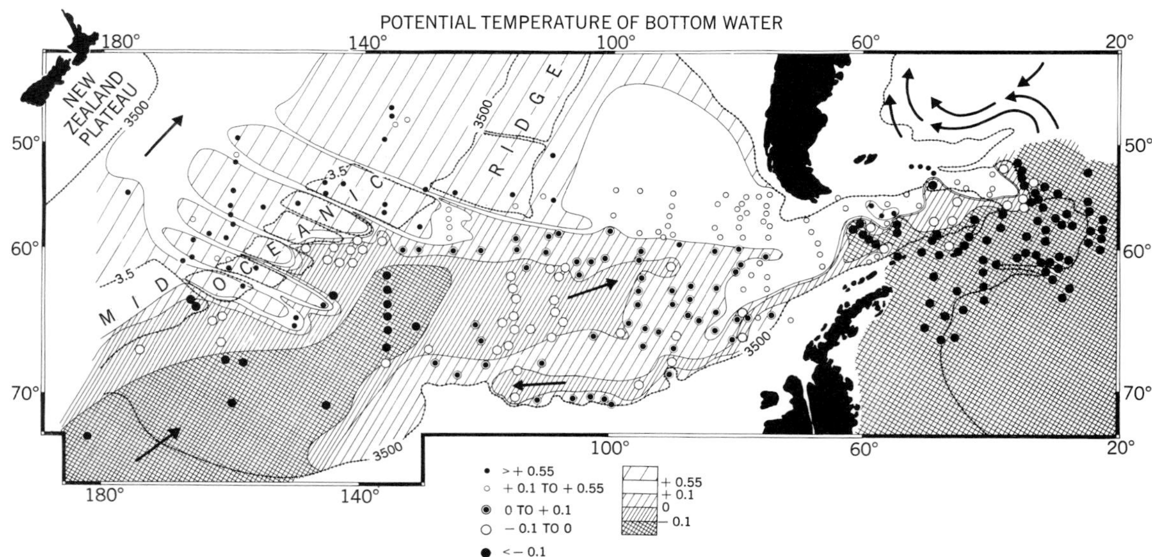

9.36 The distribution of bottom-water temperatures indicates that bottom water flows out from the Ross and Weddell Seas.

arctic waters, they flow as a wedge beneath the northern ones, reaching far into the northern hemisphere. The abyss is thus bathed by frigid polar waters which gradually mingle and eventually rise to the surface to begin again their poleward journey. These abyssal waters, which collectively constitute the cold-water sphere, are capped by the thin protective blanket of the solar-heated warm-water sphere which extends throughout the temperate latitudes. However, within the limits of the two polar fronts a warm surface layer is lacking, and the cold-water sphere extends to the surface (9.25). Here, the strong westerly winds of the southern ocean drive a vast, circumpolar current from west to east around the continent of Antarctica (9.26). In contrast to the surface currents of the temperate latitudes, this current extends deep into the abyss and in certain areas scours the deep-sea floor (9.27). On the southern flank of the Mid-Oceanic Ridge in the Bellingshausen Basin, the circumpolar ring and the clockwise contour-following deep currents flow in the same direction, thus augmenting each other. In this region, bottom photographs reveal the most violent and dramatic current evidence seen in abyssal basins.

In the northern hemisphere, the deep, southerly flowing currents flow counterclockwise. However, the circulation of the surface waters and particularly the concentrated flow of the warm western boundary currents, such as the Gulf Stream and the Kuroshio, flow clockwise. Thus, the surface gyres of the North Atlantic Basin generally flow in the opposite direction to the counterclockwise currents of the deep and bottom

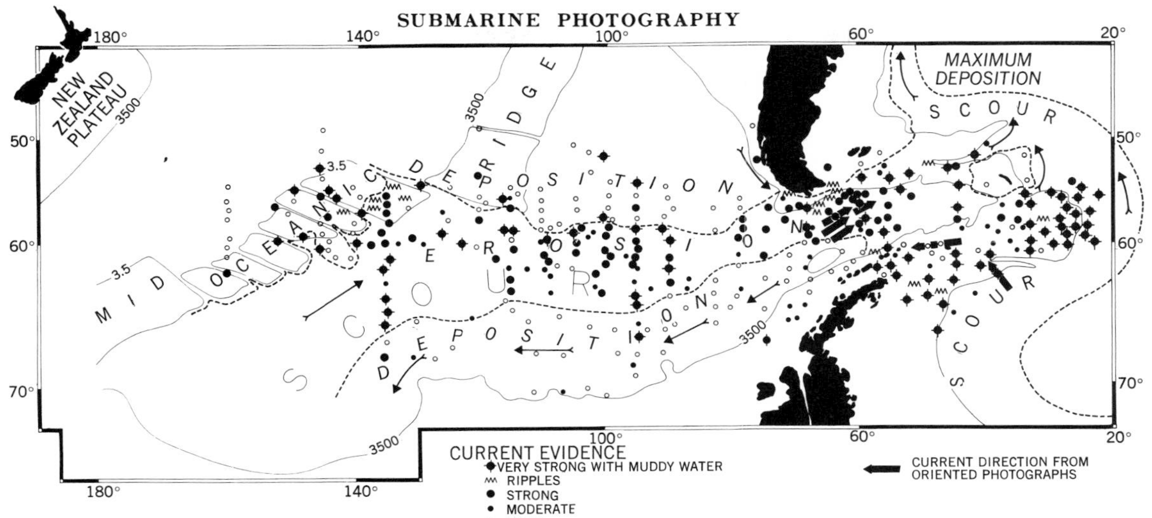

9.37 Visible current indications in the Bellingshausen Sea.

waters. When the surface currents flow deep and feel the bottom, particularly when they cross major ridges, the surface current is deflected to the right; and in such areas should also oppose the counterclockwise circulation of the deeper waters.

Current scour is a familiar phenomenon in narrow straits and, in fact, the coarse sediments produced by scour were early recognized and correctly interpreted by Agassiz, Weber, and others during the last century.[12] However, the Drake Passage—over 500 miles wide—might not be looked upon as a narrow constriction; but it very clearly is. Bare rock outcrops, linguoid and lunate ripples (9.28, 9.29), and deep rock nests (9.30) are clear evidence that the massive Pacific to Atlantic transport extends to the very bottom of the sea. The eastward moving waters scour the slopes of the ragged partial barrier thrown up by the Scotia Arc. The Antarctic Circumpolar Current moves through this greatest strait of the world at a rate of at least 200 million cubic meters per second. No wonder that some of the most dramatic current evidence ever observed from the abyss comes from the Scotia Sea.

The Antarctic Circumpolar Current is strongly deflected where it crosses major topographic barriers, being turned to the left while flowing over the upcurrent side of the barrier, and turned to the right on descending the downcurrent side. Rocks, ripples, and scour bear evidence of the vigor of this deep-reaching current which sweeps the Mid-Oceanic Ridge in the Southern Ocean (9.31, 9.32).

As Maury once wrote, "The agents which disturb the equilibrium of the sea, giving violence to its waves and force to its currents, all reside

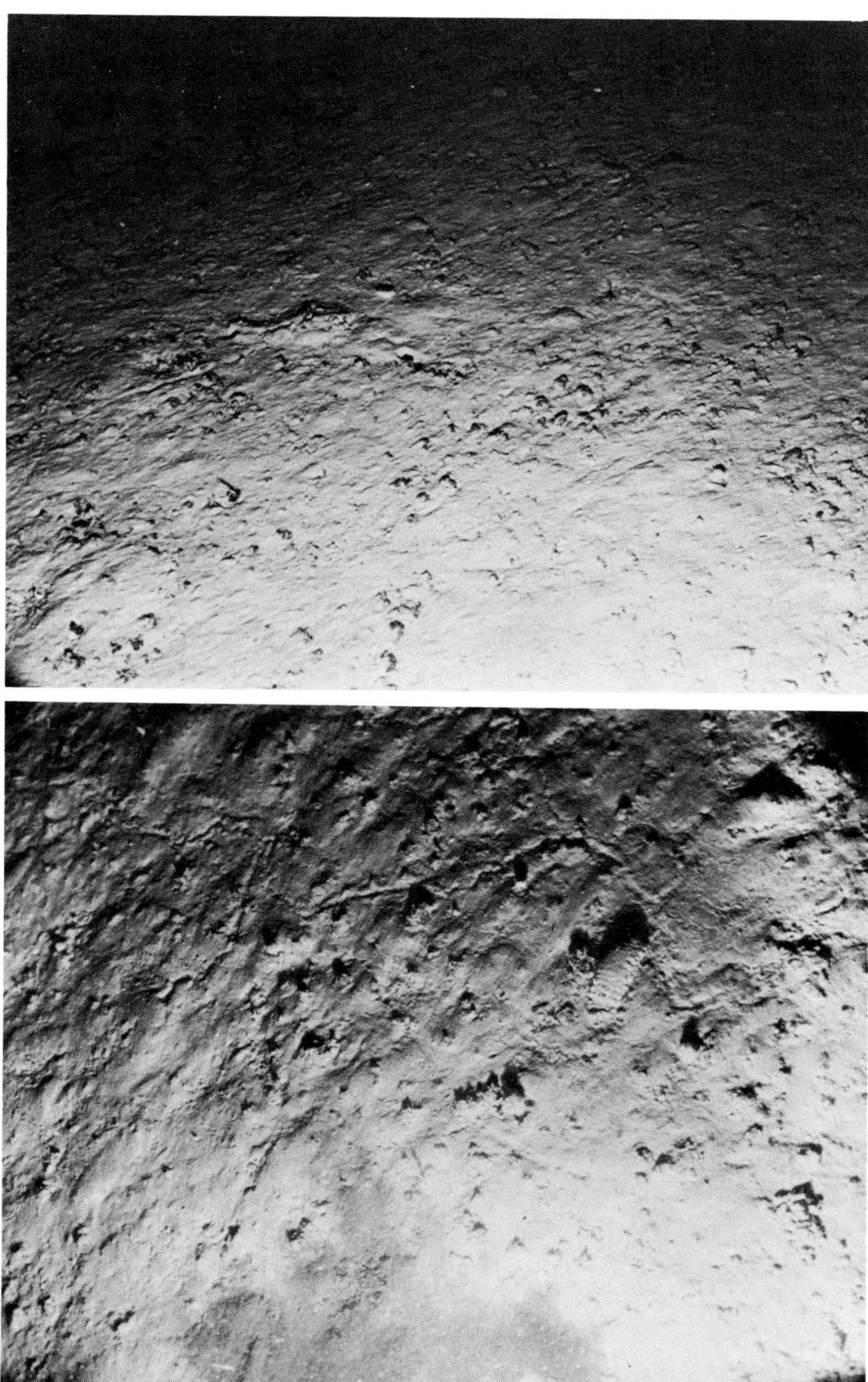

63°46′S 114°54′W
60°00′S 109°56′W

9.38 Sediment tails and current lineations. U, L, 5134 m, 5168 m, Bellingshausen Basin.

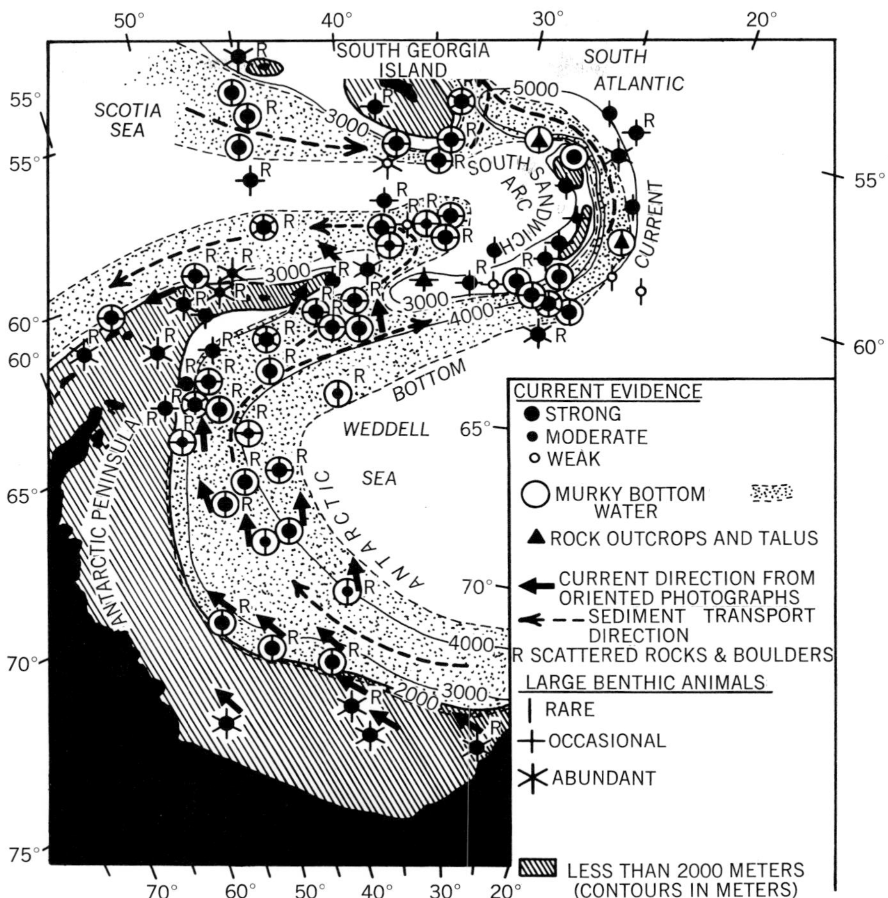

9.39 The Antarctic Bottom Current transports fine material into the Scotia Sea and South Atlantic. Distribution pattern of visual current evidence was determined by examining over 1200 sea-floor photographs at 80 locations. Current evidence was considered strong if lineations, ripples, or pronounced smoothing of the sea floor was apparent. In such cases, bottom-current velocities probably range between 15 and 30 centimeters per second. Velocities of about 10 centimeters per second (moderate) are sufficient to deflect attached organisms. Weak (less than 5 centimeters per second) bottom currents are probably capable of only slight smoothing of the muddy sea floor. Sediment stirred up and transported by the bottom current occasionally obscures the bottom.

near or above its surface; none have their home in its depths. These agents are its inhabitants, the moon, the winds, evaporation and precipitation, with changes in temperature, such as heating here and cooling there."[13] However, the warm-water sphere protects and isolates the abyss from the more familiar forces of weather, leaving as the only significant dynamic factors in the nearly closed abyssal system the thermohaline currents which spread and mix from pole to pole, the rotation of the earth which deflects these currents to the side of the basin, and the tides

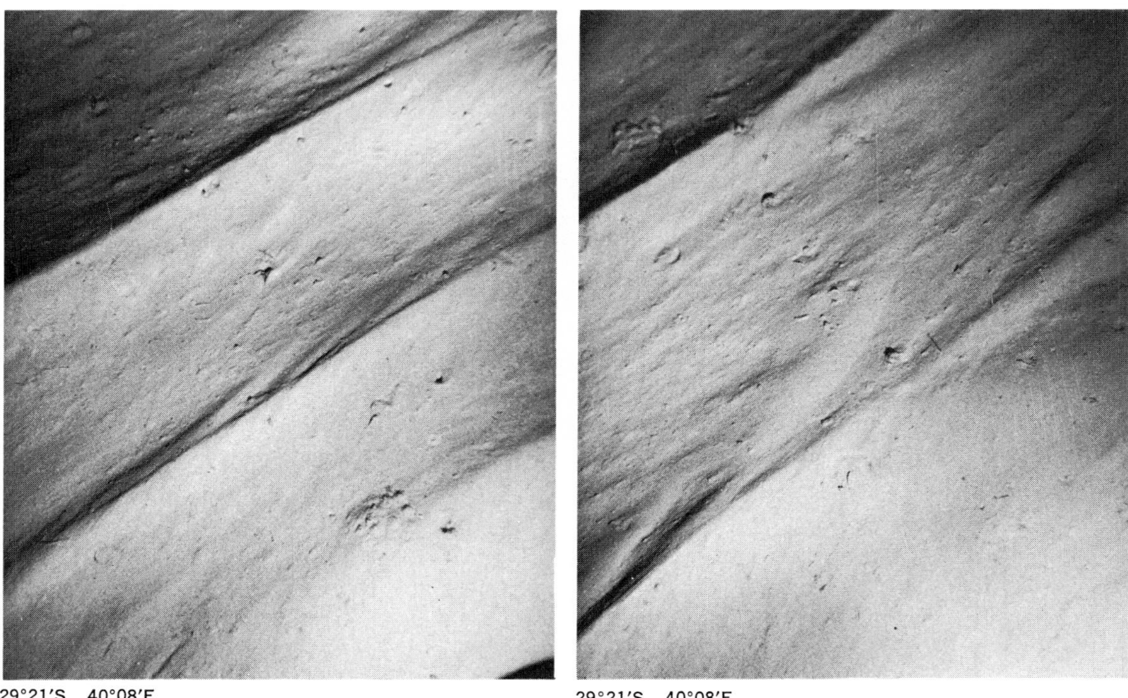

9.40 Longitudinal ripples beneath Antarctic Bottom Current south of Mozambique. Picture taken 40 meters above and a few miles east of the Mozambique Abyssal Plain. R, L, 4845 m.

of moon and sun which gently, but incessantly, caress the abyssal waters. Frost is unknown, desiccation unheard of, evaporation nonexistent, and the winds and rain far above are unfelt in the temperate abyss.

ANTARCTIC SOURCES

Water masses are recognized by distinctive combinations of temperature, salinity, and other chemical properties, and, thus, can be traced as they mix and mingle with the adjacent water masses along their extensive paths. The principal sources of Antarctic Bottom Water lie in the Weddell Sea, in the Ross Sea, and at the edge of the Antarctic continent. From these remote areas waters flow to the far corners of the earth, imprinting throughout the world ocean an indelible visual pattern (9.33).

The cold waters descending the continental slope (9.34) off the Ross Sea are deflected to the left by the Coriolis force against the southern flank of the Mid-Oceanic Ridge (9.35). The flow of these currents, from west to east along the northern edge of the basin and the lower flank of

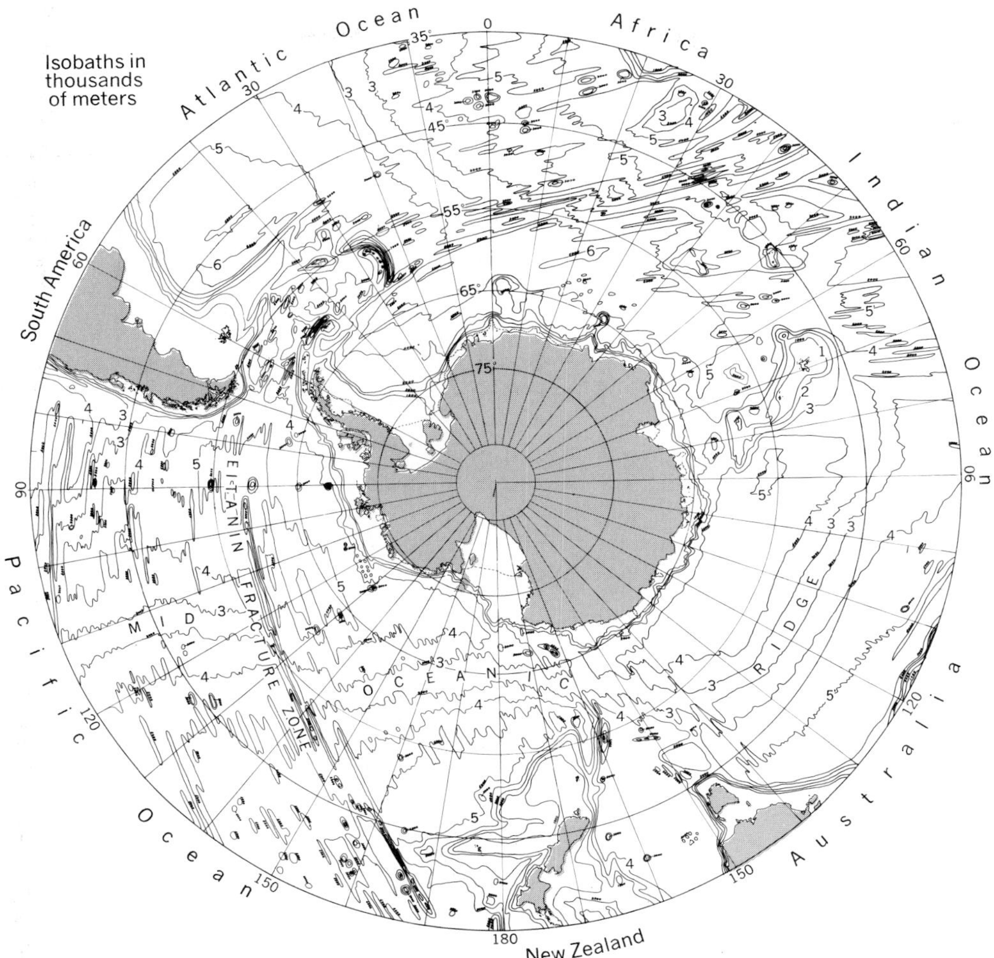

9.41 Bathymetric map of the Antarctic. The Mid-Oceanic Ridge forms a nearly continuous circular wall around the frigid polar waters. The Antarctic Bottom Water, however, leaks through the narrow fracture zones which serve as walled conduits for deep circulation. Contours in kilometers.

the Mid-Oceanic Ridge, can be inferred from both the distribution of current indications and the pattern of the bottom temperature (9.36, 9.37).

Less than a dozen of the more than five hundred camera stations taken in the Bellingshausen Sea employed a compass. Therefore, the orientation of the abundant lineations cannot be used to map current directions. However, the correspondence of the coldest waters and the strongest current marks (9.37) gives confirmation to the inferred easterly direction of flow. In the western Bellingshausen Sea, near-bottom water is frequently so sediment laden as to obscure the current-marked bottom (9.35).

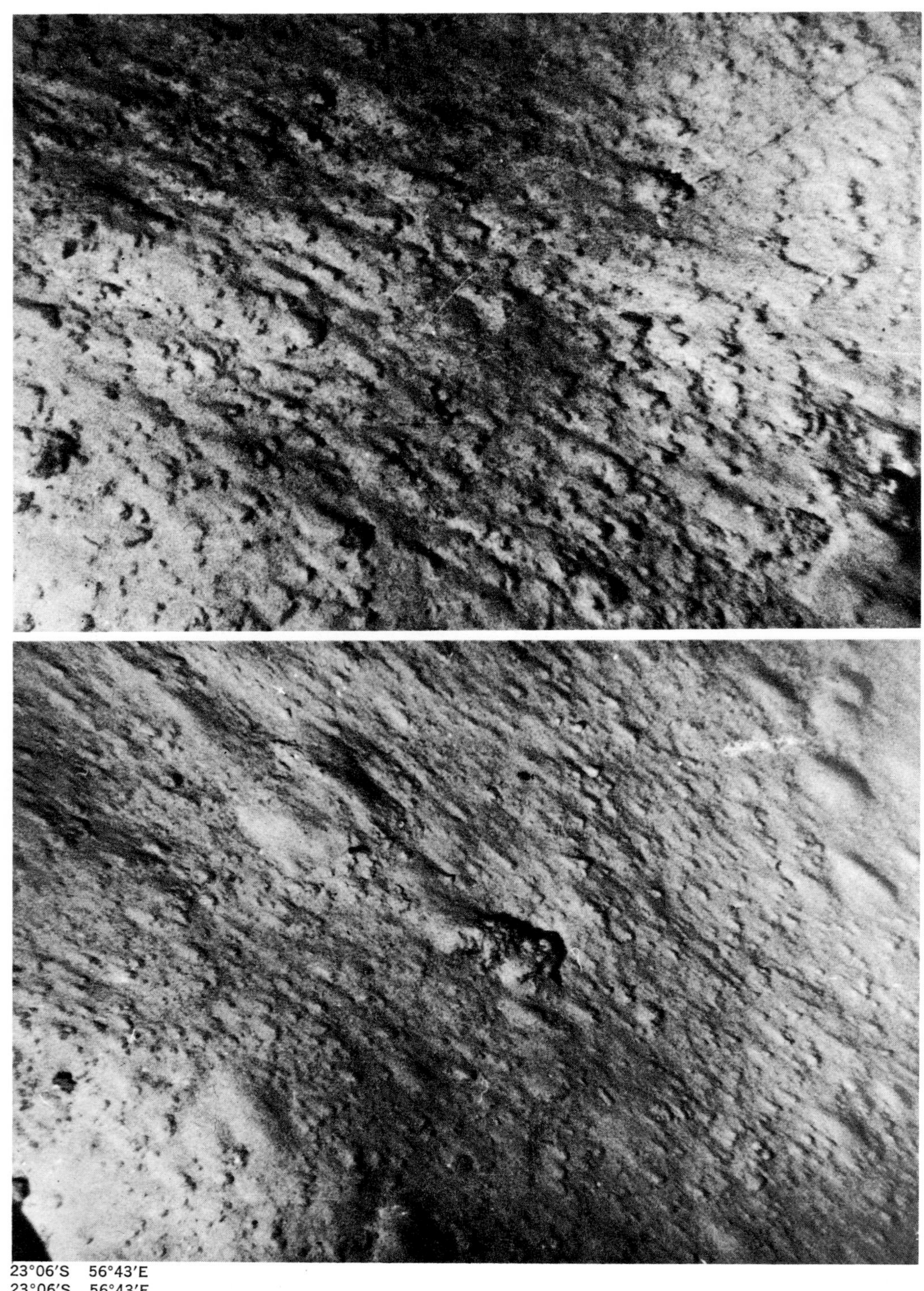

9.42 Erosion on the flat floor of the Mauritius Trench. U, L, 4909 m.

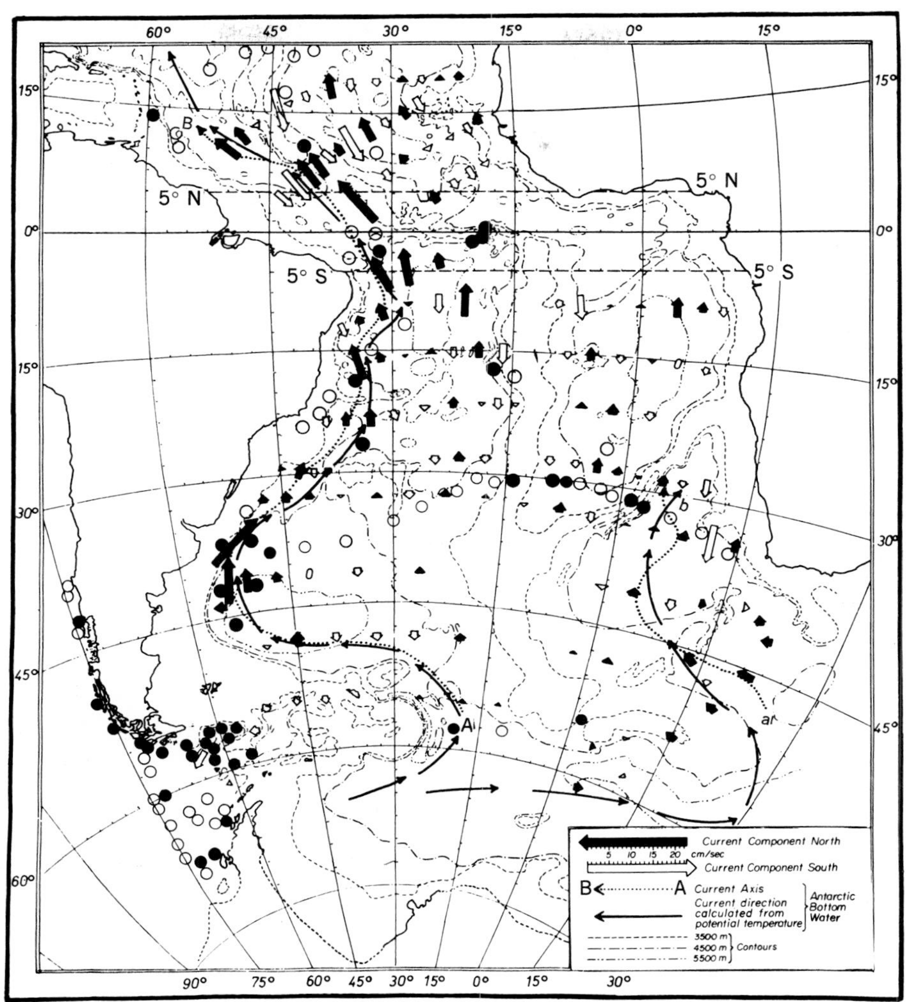

9.43 Ripples and current lineations (dots) occur near the axis of maximum velocity of the Antarctic Bottom Current.

THE NORTHERN JOURNEY

The cold waters leak through the narrow fracture zones which serve as walled conduits, allowing the Ross Sea water to reach the open passage of the southwest Pacific, from which point it joins the flow toward the North Pacific. The rocky western walls of the Tonga and Kermadec Trenches reveal abundant evidence of the northern flow of the Antarctic water (11.35). A principal south-to-north passage for the Antarctic Bottom Water lies east of the Manihiki Plateau. Here, abundant manganese nodules cover the over-five-thousand-meter-deep abyssal floor, and wild

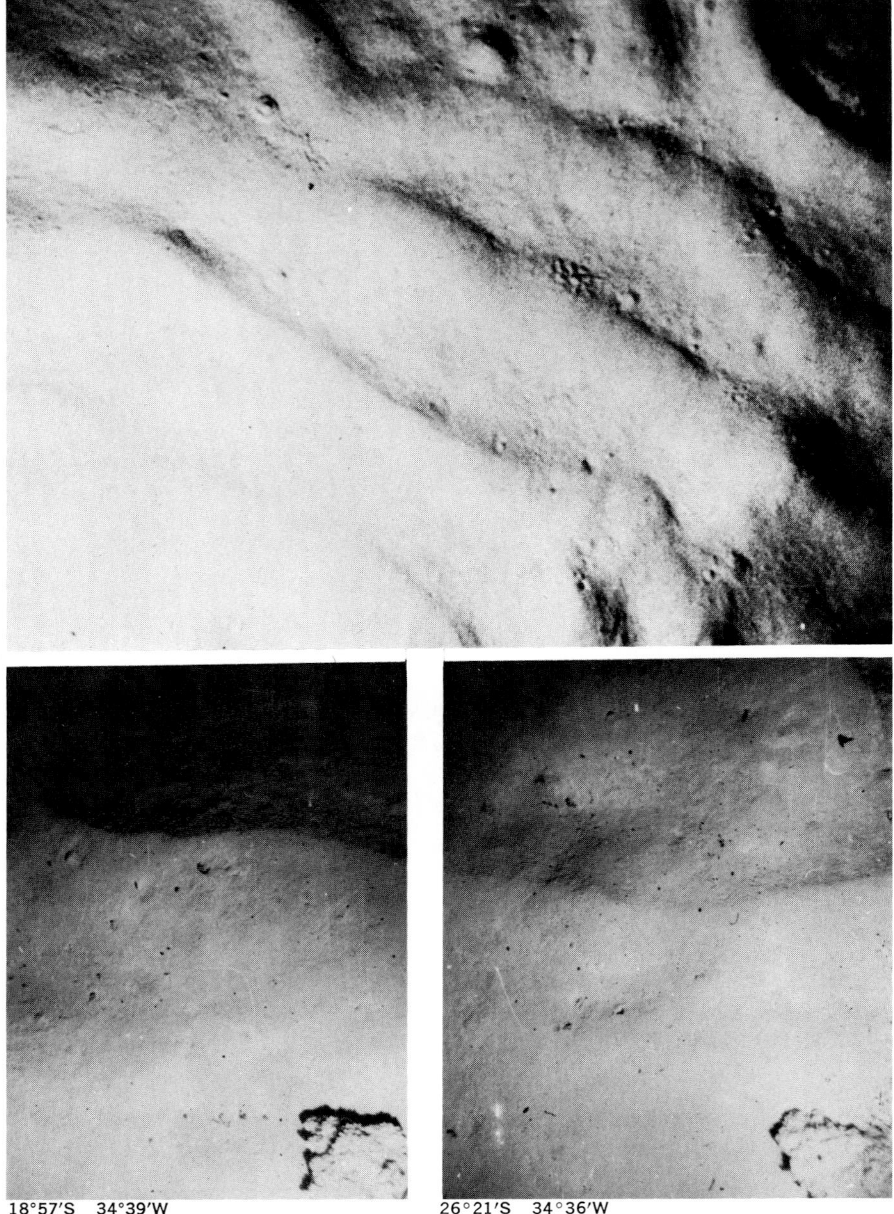

9.44 Rippled clay and ooze beneath the Antarctic Bottom Current off Brazil. U, L, 4150 m, 4452 m, continental rise off Brazil.

current scour and denuded outcrops along the eastern flank of the Manihiki Plateau give ample evidence of the vigor of this circulation.

In the Weddell Sea (9.39), relatively heavy Antarctic Bottom Water sinks to the floor of the Southern Ocean and from there spreads along the

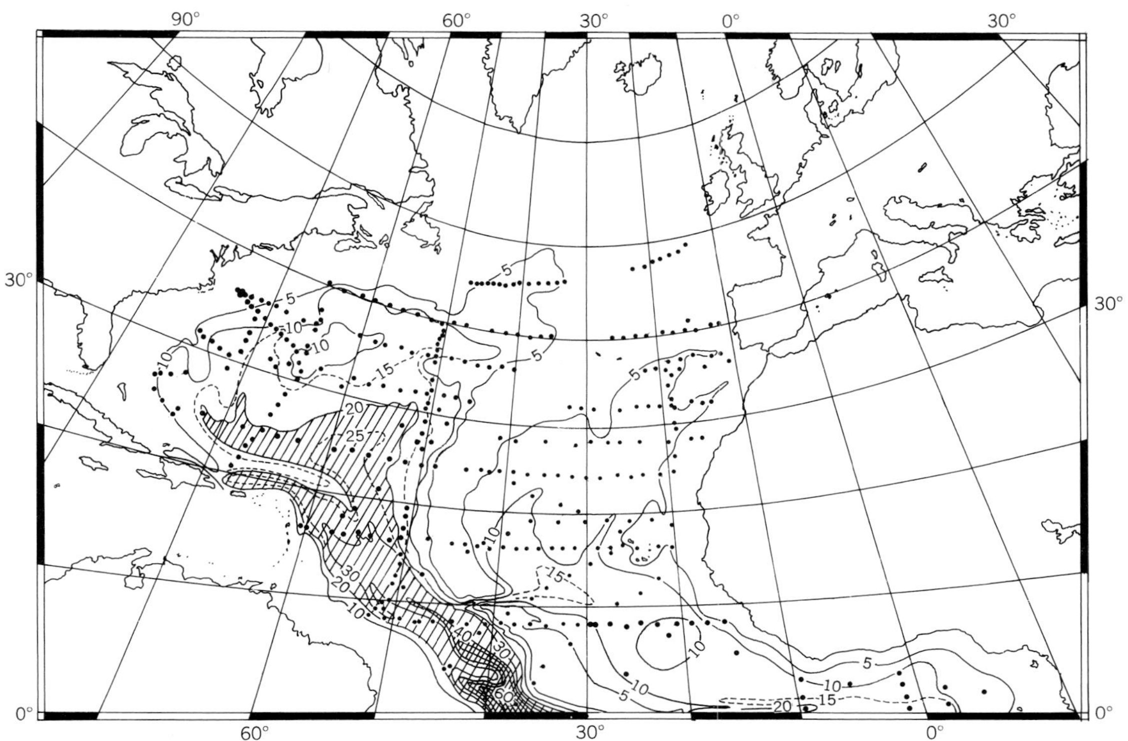

9.45 Spreading of Antarctic Bottom Water: Contours in percent Antarctic Water.

bottom of the Atlantic, Indian, and Pacific Oceans. The axis of spreading of the Antarctic Bottom Current is not along the axis of maximum depth, but is displaced to the left by the Coriolis force.[14] This "force," which arises through relative motion on a rotating earth, is proportional to the water velocity and the sine of the latitude and acts perpendicular to the velocity vector, to the left in the southern hemisphere and to the right in the northern hemisphere. Water originating in the Weddell Sea follows bathymetric contours along several routes. A principal branch follows the eastern flank of the Scotia Arc, eventually reaching the North Atlantic; another flows eastward along the southern flank of the Mid-Oceanic Ridge.

Fracture zones provide several tectonic avenues for this water to continue its northern journey. Fractures near the Greenwich meridian permit a flow into the Cape Basin which lies east of the Mid-Atlantic Ridge. But the Walvis Ridge blocks the northward flow, and the Antarctic current turns back—flowing south along the continental slope of South Africa, where, perhaps augmented by water entering from other fracture zones and by the eastward motion of the circumpolar ring, the current

19°51′N 63°56′W

9.46 Ripple marks at 7535 meters beneath the Antarctic Bottom Current, Puerto Rico Trench. Current lineation and ripple orientation indicate current flow from east to west, parallel to the spreading direction of the Antarctic Bottom Water. Lower north wall of Puerto Rico Trench.

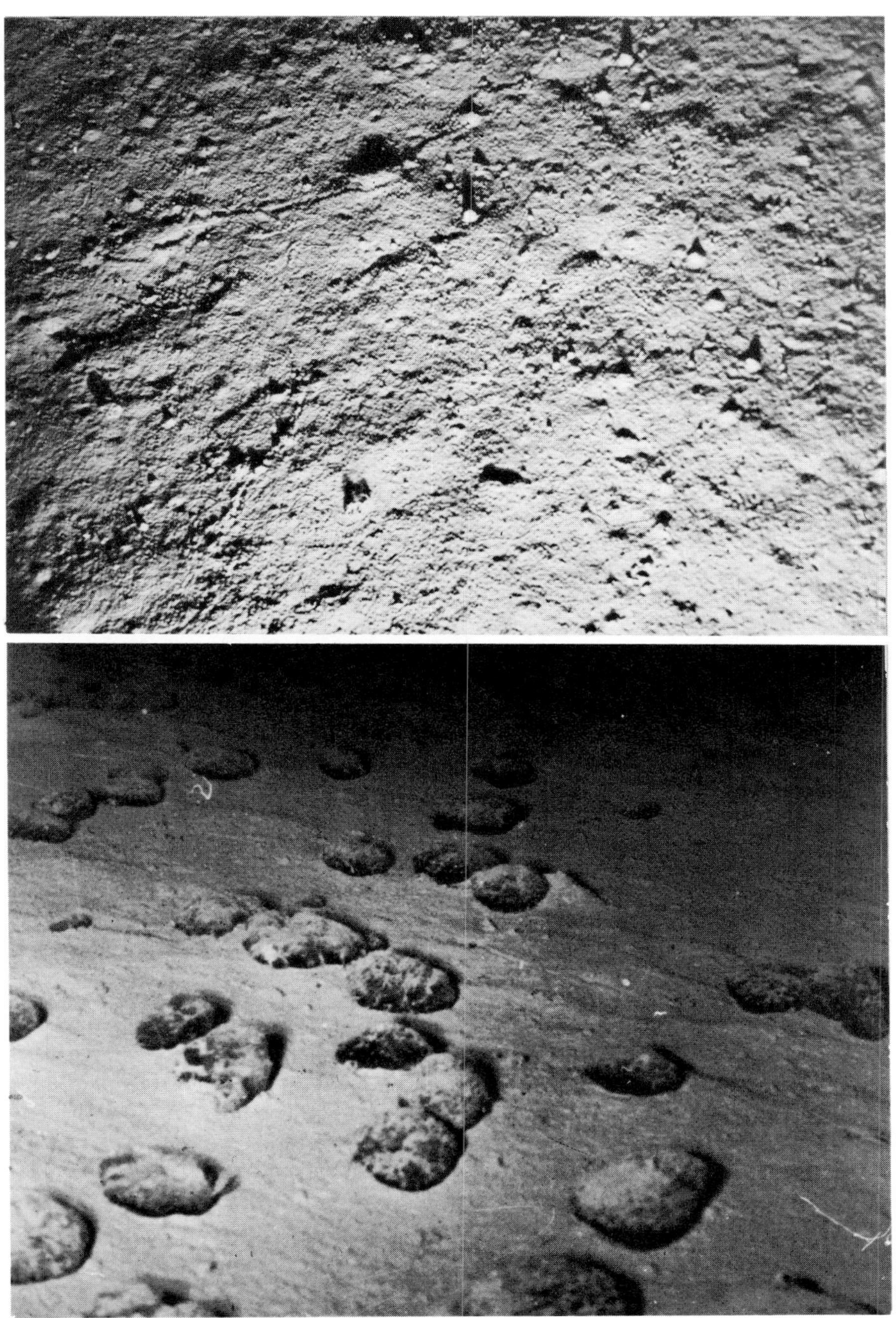

25°56′N 64°06′W
25°38′N 64°17′W

9.47 Sediment tails and manganese nodules on the southern flank of the Bermuda Rise. U, 5573 m. L, 5034 m.

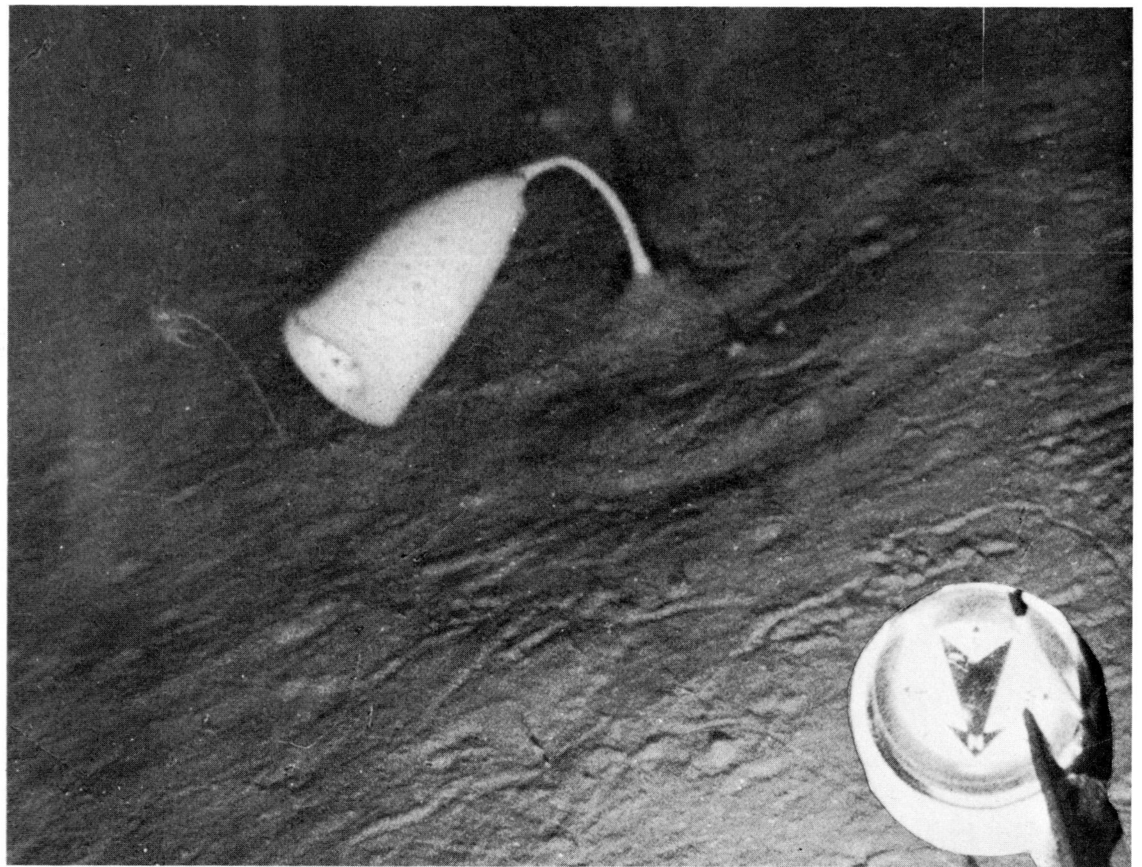

33°00′N 72°32′W

9.48 The Antarctic Bottom Current sweeps north along the western flank of the Bermuda Rise. This glass sponge serves as a recording current vane. Strong northeast to northwest currents have forced it to draw a short arc on the sea bed, 5378 m.

passes around the Cape and enters the Indian Ocean. Dramatic current effects are produced on the Agulhas Plateau. A steady and significant northward flow occurs along the coast of Natal and Mozambique (9.40), only to be again turned back by the shallow Mozambique Passage (9.6, 9.19). The waters flowing south around the Madagascar Ridge are joined perhaps by additional waters leaking through the Malagasy Fracture Zone, and then flow north again into the western equatorial Indian Ocean (9.41, 9.42).

Easterly flowing Antarctic Bottom Water moves along the southern flank of the forked Mid-Oceanic Ridge of the Indian Ocean, reaching new tectonic conduits. The area between thirty degrees East and one hundred and fifty degrees East longitude is so poorly mapped that we can but speculate on the number and location of significant sills. Antarctic Bottom Water reaching the Australia Basin continues through the gap between the Broken Ridge and the Naturaliste Plateau, and fills the Wharton Basin. The Ninetyeast Ridge forms a continuous barrier separating the colder Wharton Basin waters from the warmer Bengal Basin waters.

In the South Atlantic, the Antarctic Bottom Current flows along the continental rise of Argentina and Brazil. The calculated[8] average velocities of about fifteen centimeters per second tend to be minimal owing to the relatively large spacing of observations (9.43). Furthermore, tidal velocities of the order of five to ten centimeters per second are probably superimposed upon the thermohaline current and, therefore, the Antarctic Bottom Current velocities may reach twenty to twenty-five centimeters per second. Very recently, velocities of this magnitude have been measured.

A clear correlation between visual bottom current evidence and the axis of the Antarctic Bottom Current was first recognized in the South Atlantic (9.44), where a narrow ribbon defining the occurrence of ripple and scour marks lies along the continental rise of South America beneath the axis of the Antarctic Bottom Current.[10] After crossing the equator (where the horizontal component of the Coriolis force is zero) Antarctic Bottom Water is deflected toward the right against the western flank of the Mid-Atlantic Ridge. Some of this water leaks through the prominent current-scoured, rock-walled equatorial Atlantic fracture zones and becomes the principal source of bottom water for the eastern basins of the Atlantic. The invasion of cold Antarctic Bottom Water into the western basin of the North Atlantic takes place between the continental rise of Brazil and the Mid-Atlantic Ridge.

9.49 Giant cross bedding built by the easterly flowing Antarctic Bottom Current on the northern edge of the Bermuda Rise. An easterly bottom current of nearly 20 centimeters per second was measured near this seismic reflection profile.

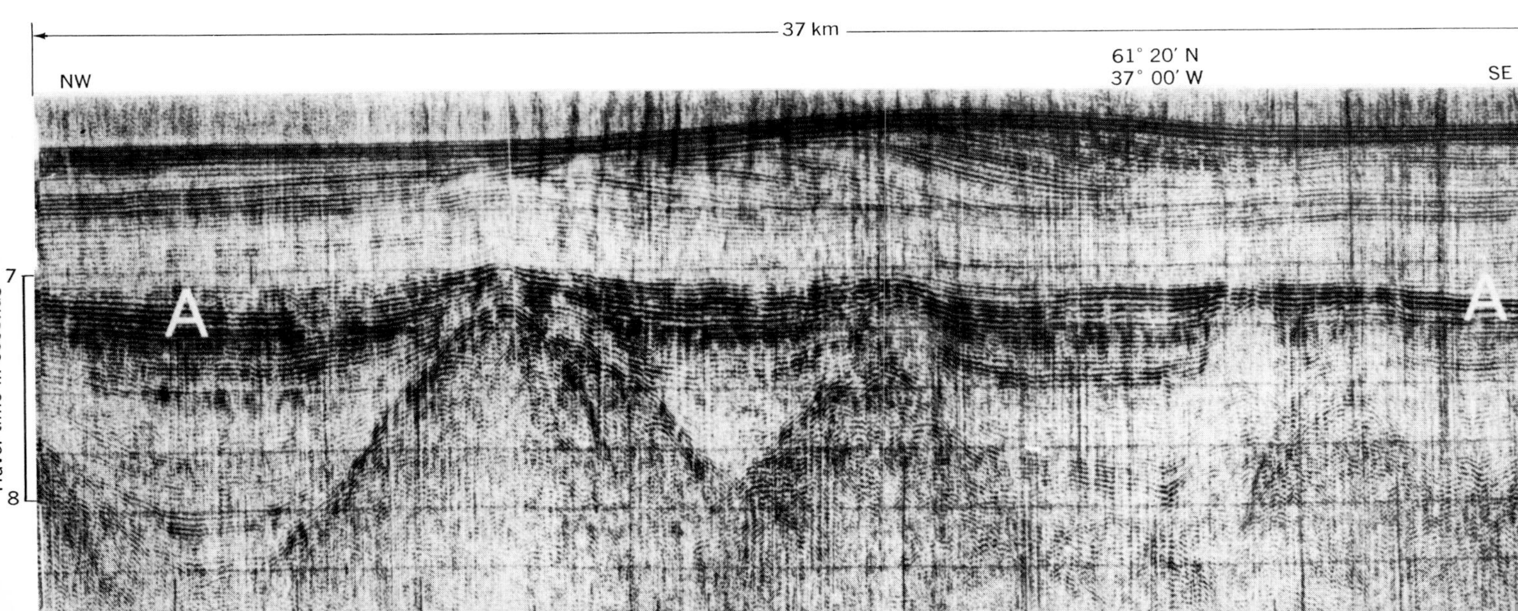

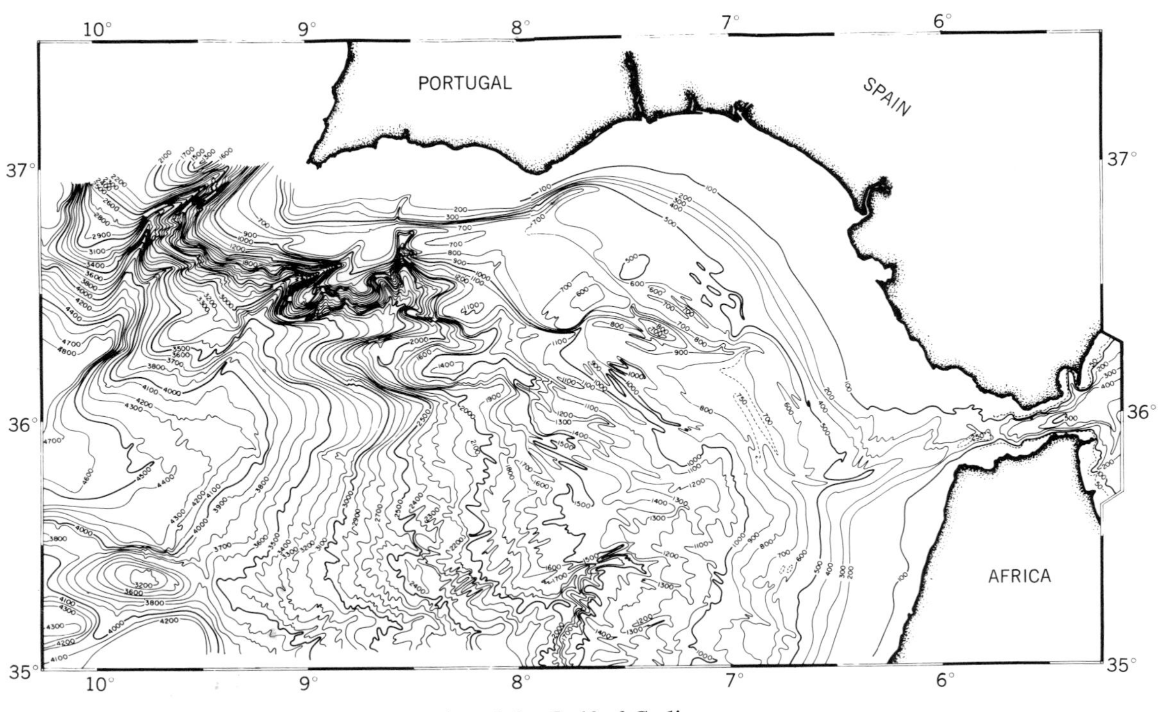

9.50 Topography of the Gulf of Cadiz.

TO BERMUDA AND BEYOND

Although the principal flow of Antarctic Bottom Water (9.45) continues along the flank of the Mid-Atlantic Ridge into the abyssal hills east of the Nares Abyssal Plain, a small but significant flow descends into the Puerto Rico Trench through a deep eastern extension associated with a fracture zone at about latitude eighteen degrees North. The visual effects of the westerly flow of this water along the northern wall of the Puerto Rico Trench has been observed. Remarkable ripple marks have been photographed in abyssal brown clay beneath this current in seven and one-half kilometers depth (9.46).

In the greatest depths of the North America Basin southeast of Bermuda, scour marks surrounding manganese nodules were early recognized as positive proof of the occurrence of appreciable currents in deep abyssal basins.[15] In this region, the Antarctic Bottom Waters split into two arms. One, still hugging the Mid-Atlantic Ridge, flows toward the northeast. The other, flowing westward along the slopes rising from the northern edge of the Nares Abyssal Plain, becomes a ring of very cold water which flows clockwise around the Bermuda Rise (9.45, 9.47, 9.48). The northerly flowing water on the western flank of the Bermuda

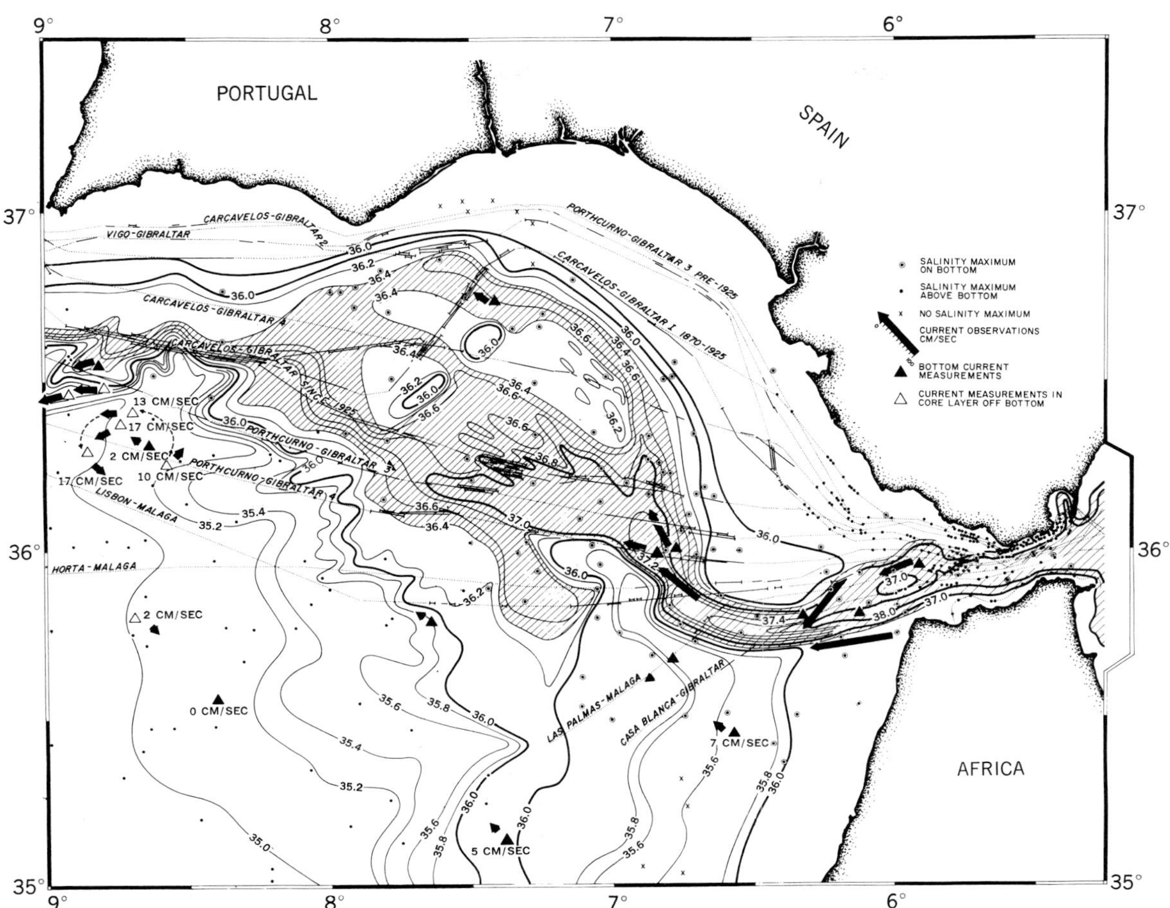

9.51 Cable failures occur beneath the strong Mediterranean Undercurrent. This long salty tongue of bottom water scours the sea floor off Spain and Portugal.

Rise is remarkably clear and contrasts sharply with the murky condition usually found within appreciable bottom currents on the continental margin. This clarity is somewhat surprising in view of the distinct lineations and scour marks seen in the area. Recent near-bottom direct current measurements made three meters off the bottom in 5092 meters on the western Bermuda Rise indicate current velocities as high as seventeen centimeters per second.[16]

The waters flowing around the northern edge of the Bermuda Rise turn and flow south again along the eastern scarps. Here, sediment is swept into giant cross bedding (9.49), flutes (9.11), ripples, and scour lineations by the strong, muddy current. None of the waters of the North America Basin contain much more than about 10 to 20 per cent of Antarctic water, and thus some oceanographers do not refer to this circum-Bermuda current as a portion of the Antarctic Bottom Current, although it does contain its final dregs.

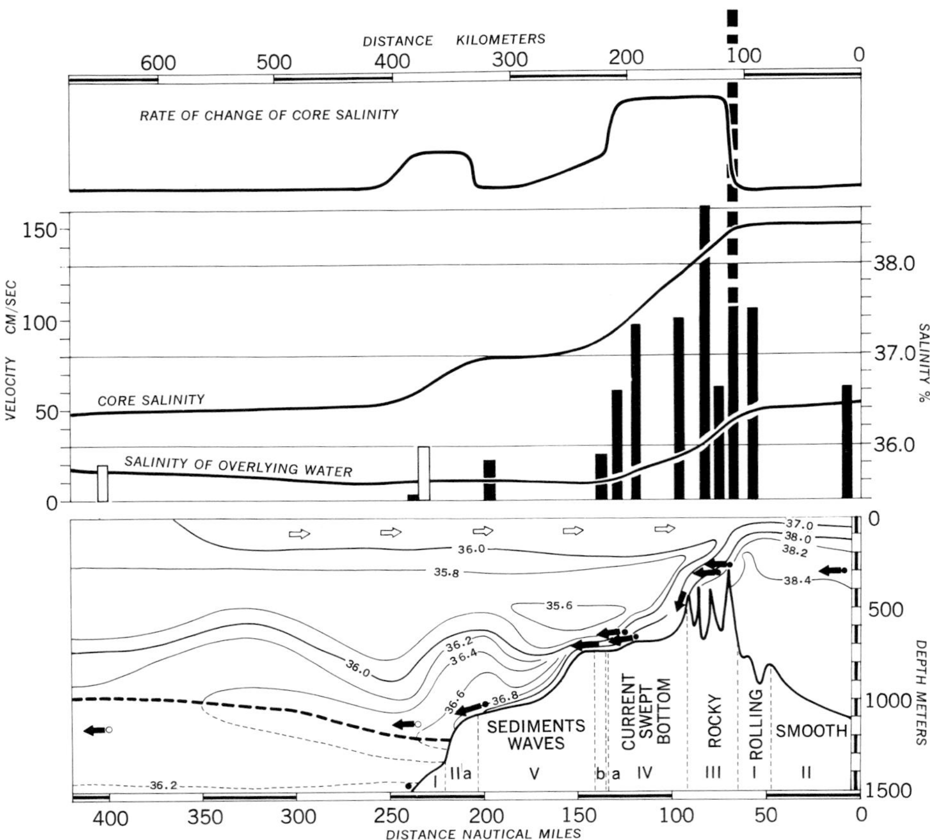

9.52 Current velocity and bottom shapes beneath the Mediterranean Undercurrent. Generalized profile along the core of Mediterranean Undercurrent from Gibraltar to Lisbon indicating: (a) rate of change of current's salinity; (b) current's salinity in units per mil; (c) salinity of overlying water; (d) current velocity measurements in centimeters per second; (e) vertical section showing location of current measurements and bottom types. The dashed line which begins to rise at about 1100 m represents the sea floor beneath the Mediterranean Undercurrent off the coast of the Iberian Peninsula.

A HOT SALTY TONGUE

The vigorous Mediterranean Undercurrent carries warm salty water through the Strait of Gibraltar and into the Atlantic (9.50).[17] These waters flow out directly on the sea floor as a thin, rapidly moving layer (9.51), reaching velocities of over one hundred centimeters per second. The flow turns sharply to the right on leaving the Strait and then, for a distance of two hundred and fifty kilometers, gradually descends to a depth of about 1200 meters. There, it leaves the bottom to become a

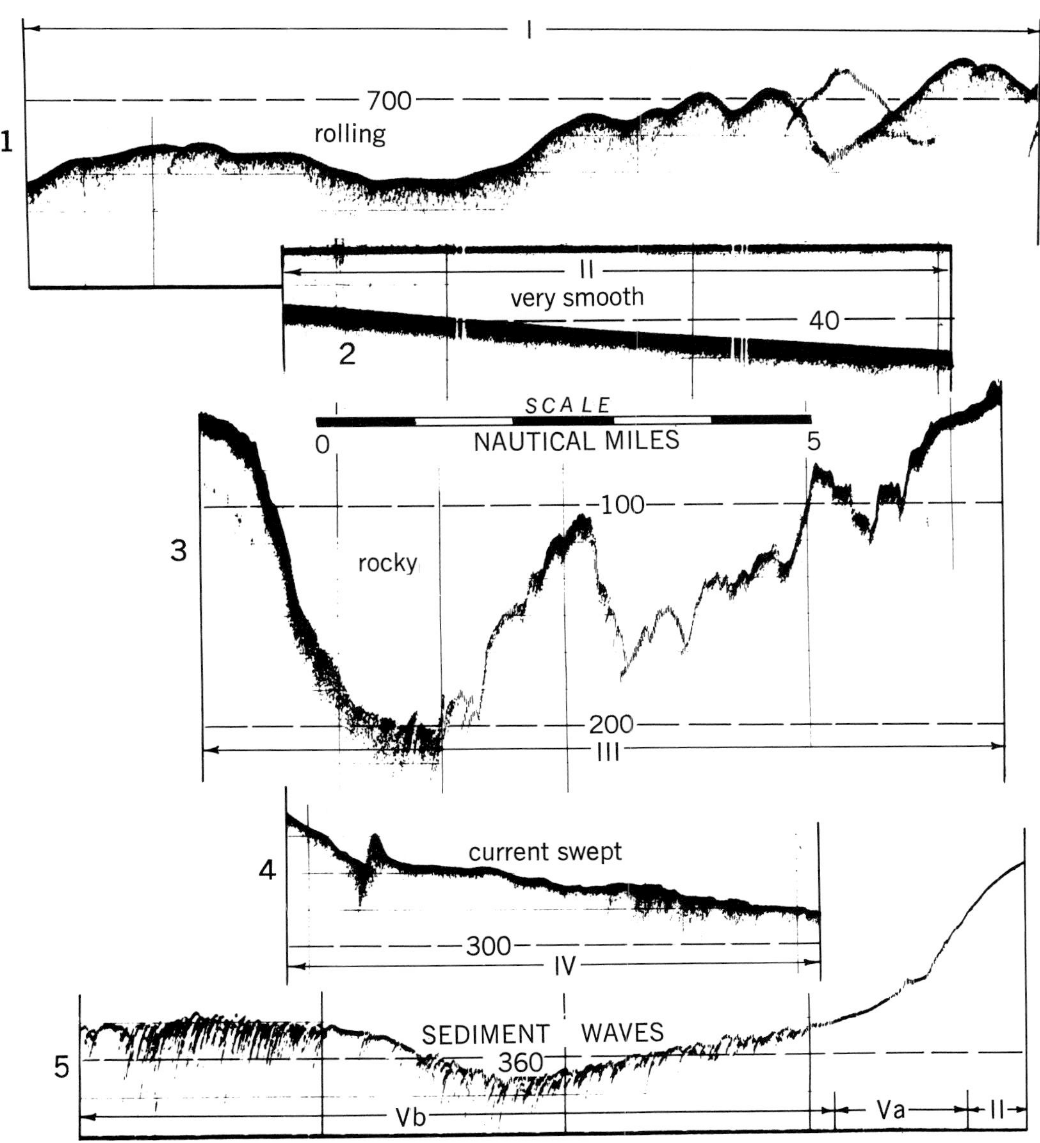

9.53 Bottom shapes in the Gulf of Cadiz. Photographs of precision echogram profiles illustrating 5 major types of microphysiography: Profile 1, *rolling;* Profile 2, *very smooth;* Profile 3, *rocky;* Profile 4, *current-swept;* Profile 5, *sediment waves.*

distinctive water mass which can be traced throughout the North Atlantic (9.52). The undercurrent maintains the sediment-free rock bottom in the Strait of Gibraltar. West of the Strait a tongue of sandy bottom with occasional small sand waves extends beneath the Undercurrent.

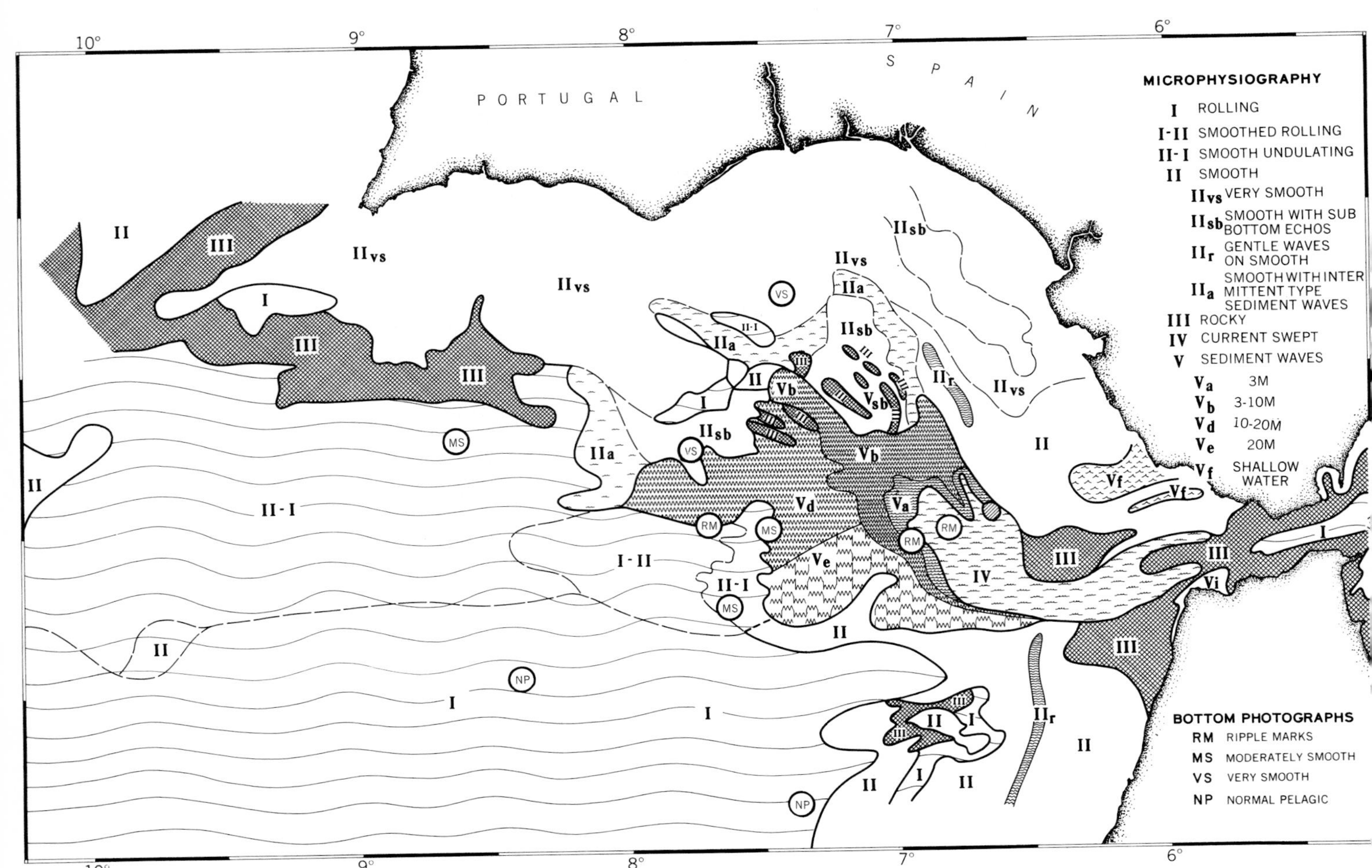

9.54 Microphysiography and the Mediterranean Undercurrent. Patterns determined from precision echograms reflect the scouring activity of this vigorous bottom current.

Commencing abruptly at 150 kilometers from the Strait, and continuing for 10 kilometers, symmetrical sediment waves of five-meter amplitude and 100-meter wavelength lie beneath the current. Further downcurrent amplitude and wavelength increase (maximum values 50-meter amplitude and one kilometer wavelength), and then at a distance of 250 kilometers the sediment waves decrease in size and eventually disappear (9.53, 9.54).

Sea-floor photographs taken in the rolling topography which occurs at depths between 1700 and 4200 meters show a typical, tranquil deep-sea floor, with mounds, burrows, and tracks virtually undisturbed by cur-

9.55 Tranquil and slightly smoothed bottom is found in areas of rolling or smooth and current-swept topography. U, 486 m, L, 630 m, Gulf of Cadiz.

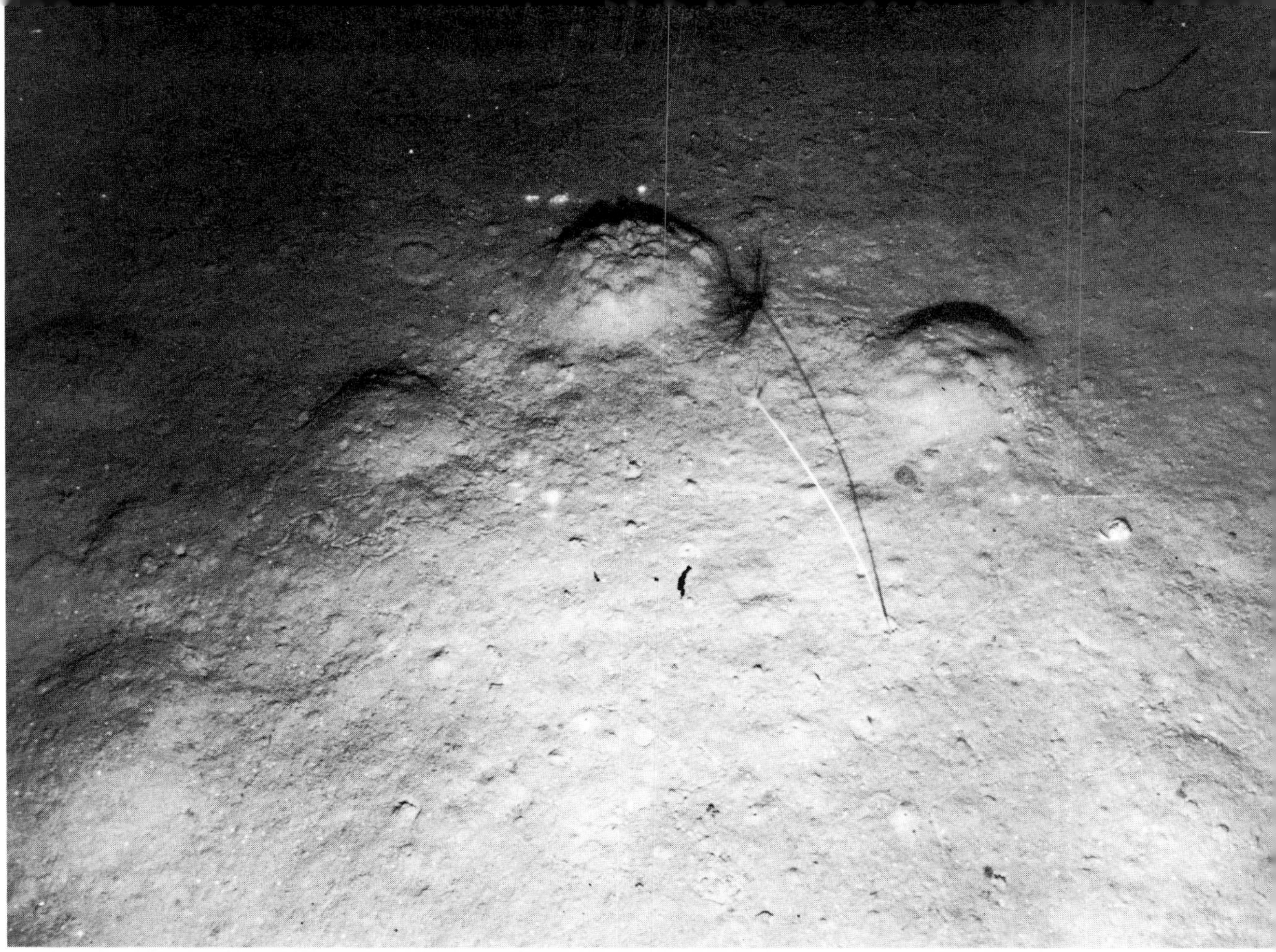

36°36′N 10°10′W

36°18′N 8°38′W

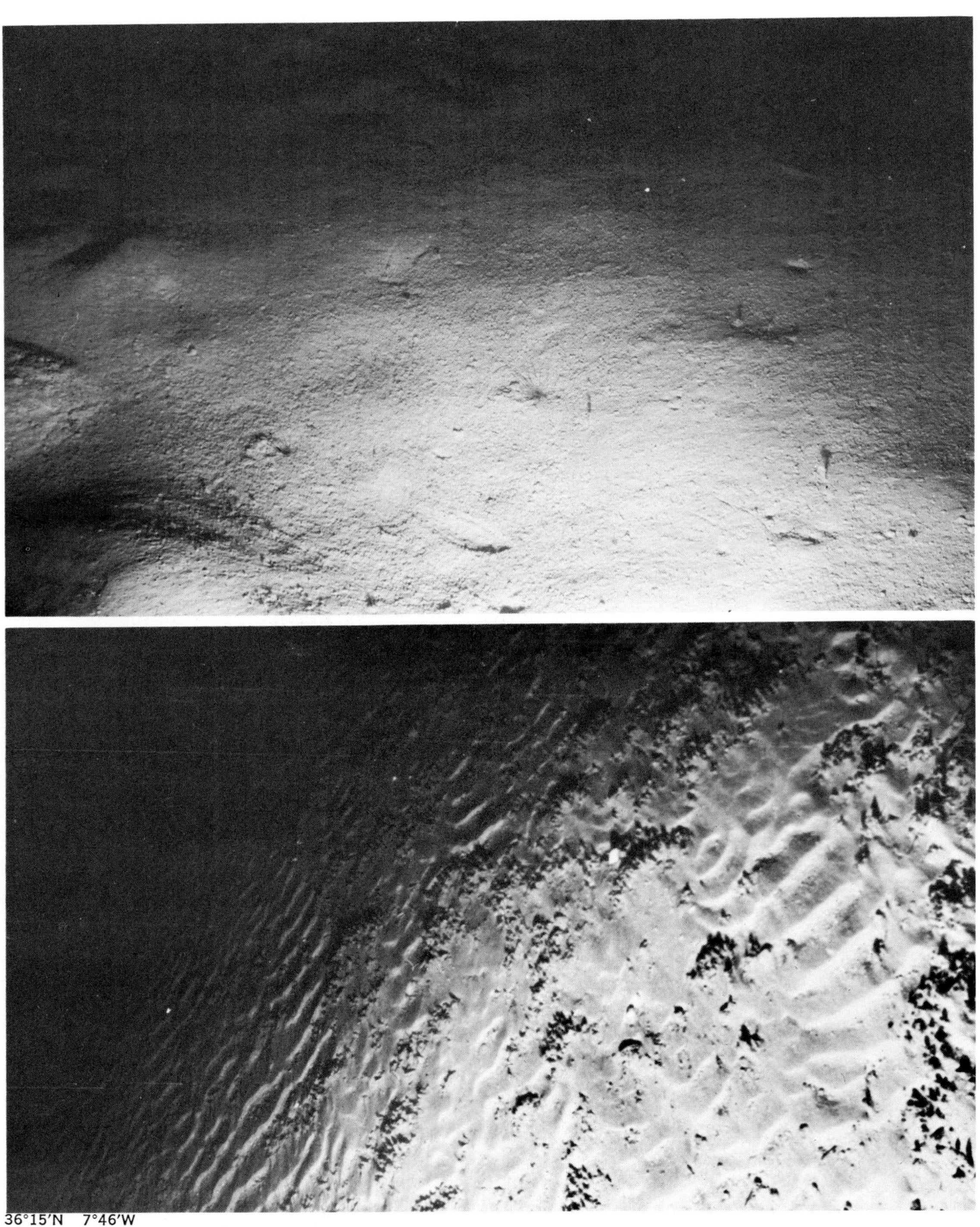

36°15′N 7°46′W
34°17′N 7°14′W

9.56 Current smoothing and starved asymmetrical ripples are typically seen on smooth and current-swept topography. U, 486 m, L, 630 m, Gulf of Cadiz.

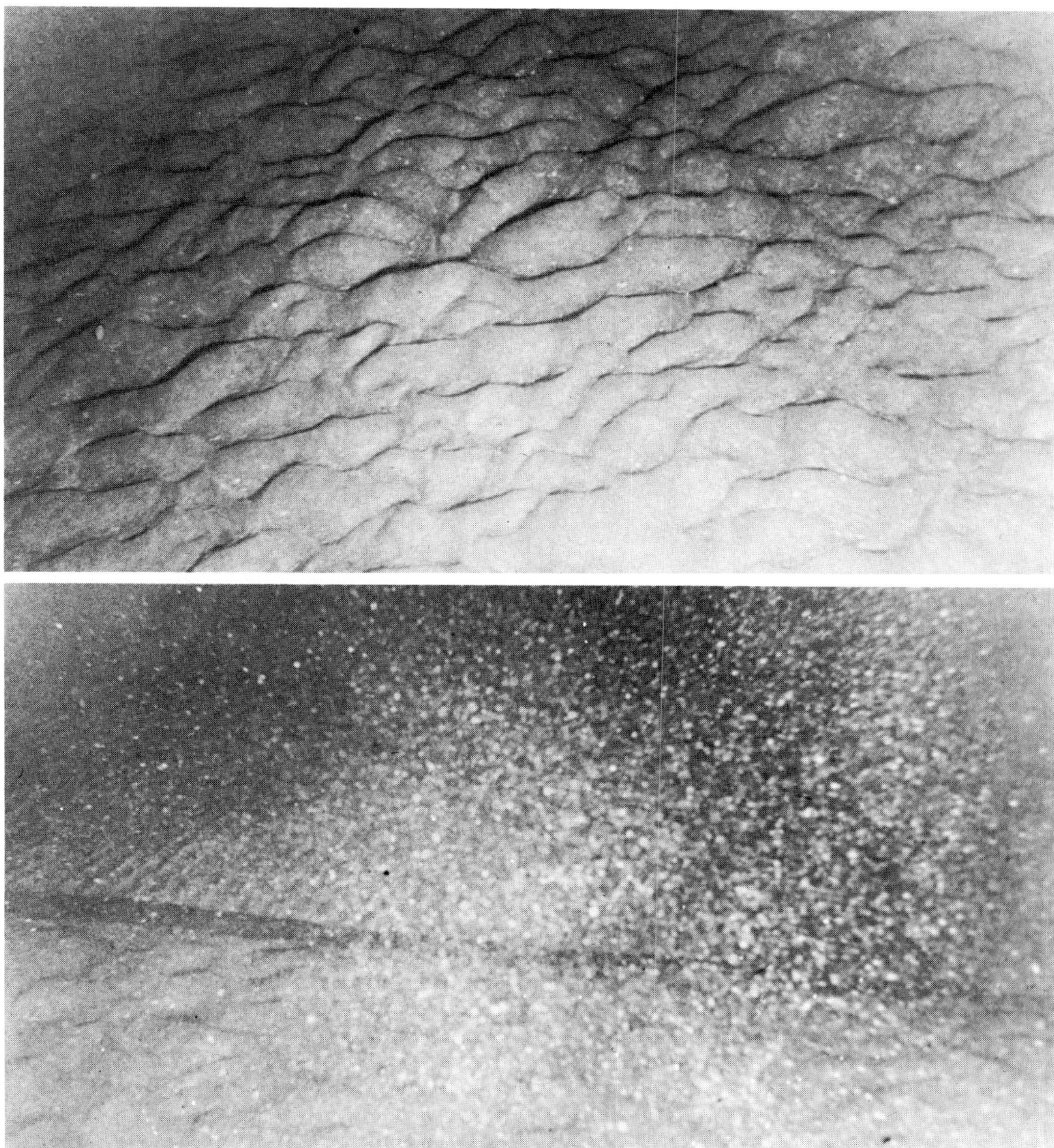

35°58′N 06°57′W
35°58′N 06°57′W

9.57 Ripples and suspended sediment beneath the Mediterranean Undercurrent. U, ripples in an area of sand waves. L, This first known *in situ* photograph of a deep-sea cable was taken accidentally in 1956, sixty miles west of the Strait of Gibraltar. It is not known whether it was a cable currently in use or one of the numerous scraps of abandoned cable that lie in this area of frequent cable failures. The ripples and submarine cable are partially obscured by suspended material, 744 m.

9.58 The course of the Western Boundary Undercurrent in the northern North Atlantic.

rents (9.55 U). Within topographically smooth areas an extremely smooth bottom with little indication of bioturbation, save an occasional mound or pit (9.56 U), is seen. The surface of the sediment waves are marked with well-developed rhomboid ripples (9.57). On the current-swept bottom starved, straight asymmetrical current ripples occur in patches on a gravel-strewn firm bottom (9.56 L).

At one location where sand ripples were observed on a current-swept bottom, a velocity of twenty-three centimeters per second was measured.

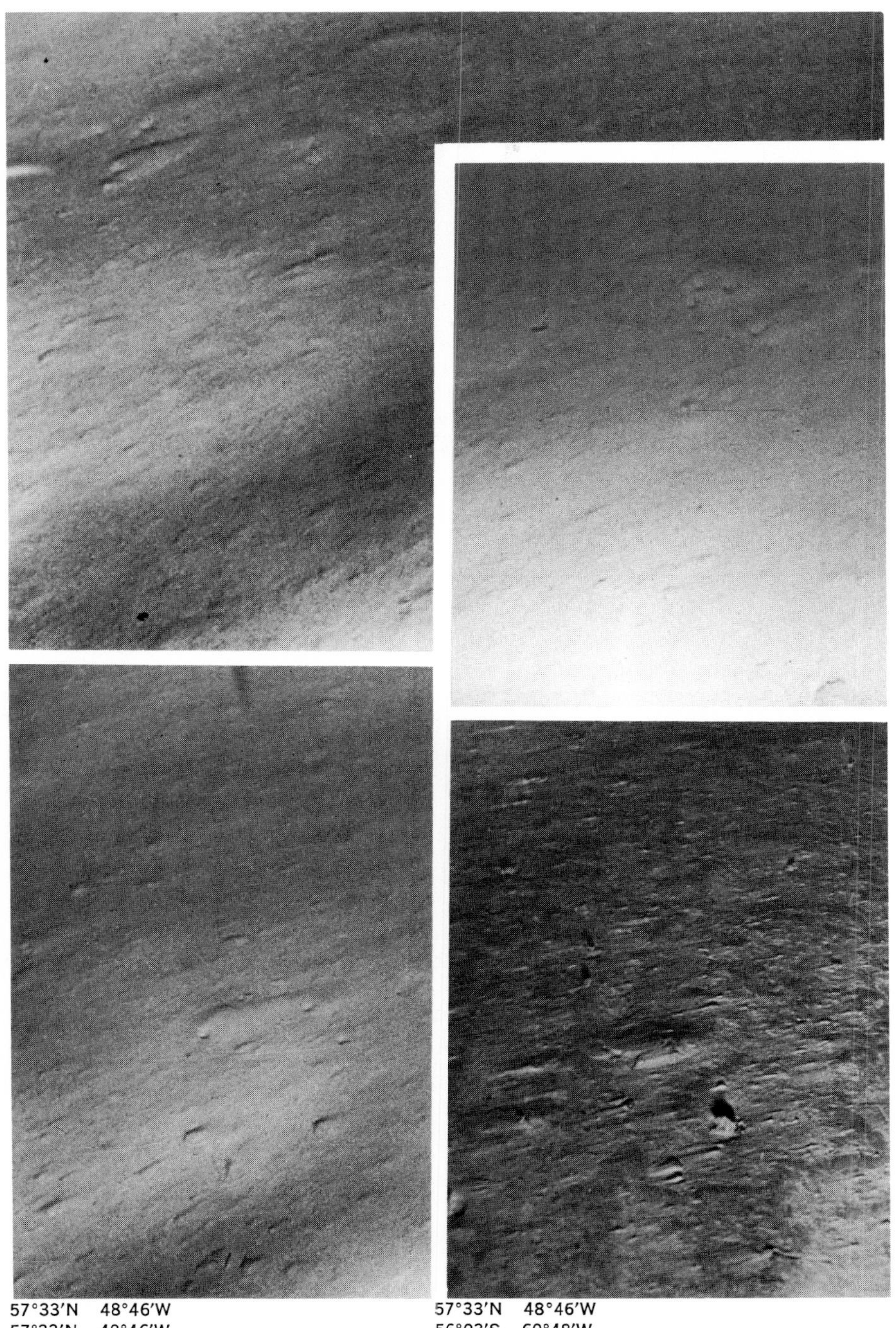

9.59 The turbid Western Boundary Undercurrent sweeps sediment into tails on the continental rise of Greenland. UL, UR, LL, a northwesterly bottom current of ten centimeters per second was measured near this station. 3426 m, Greenland continental rise southwest of Cape Farewell. LR, 4186 m, Drake Passage.

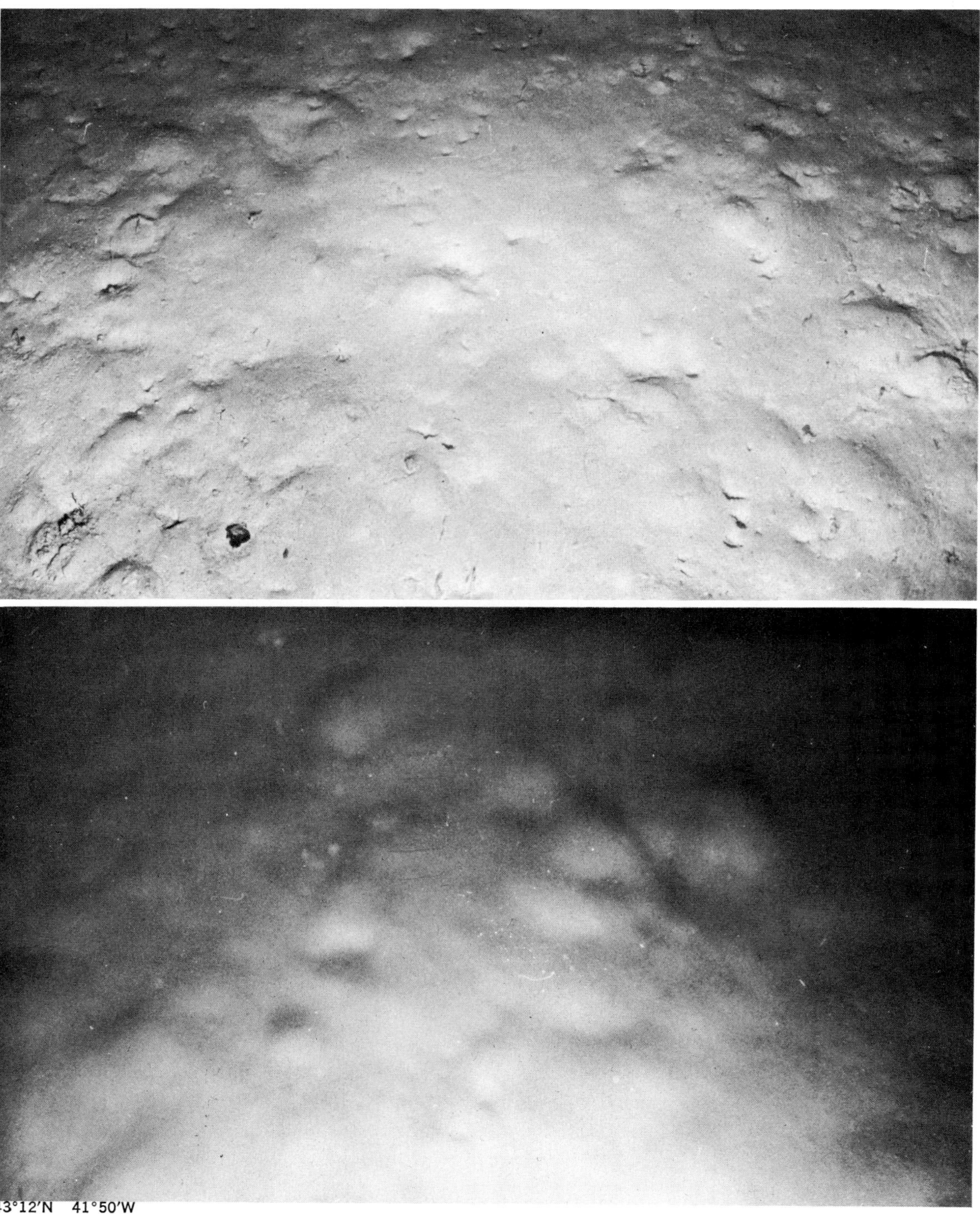

43°12′N 41°50′W
49°10′N 41°32′W

9.60 Scour marks, smoothing and drifting sediment clouds on the natural levee of the Northwest Atlantic Mid-Ocean Canyon. U, 4768 m, L, 4437 m.

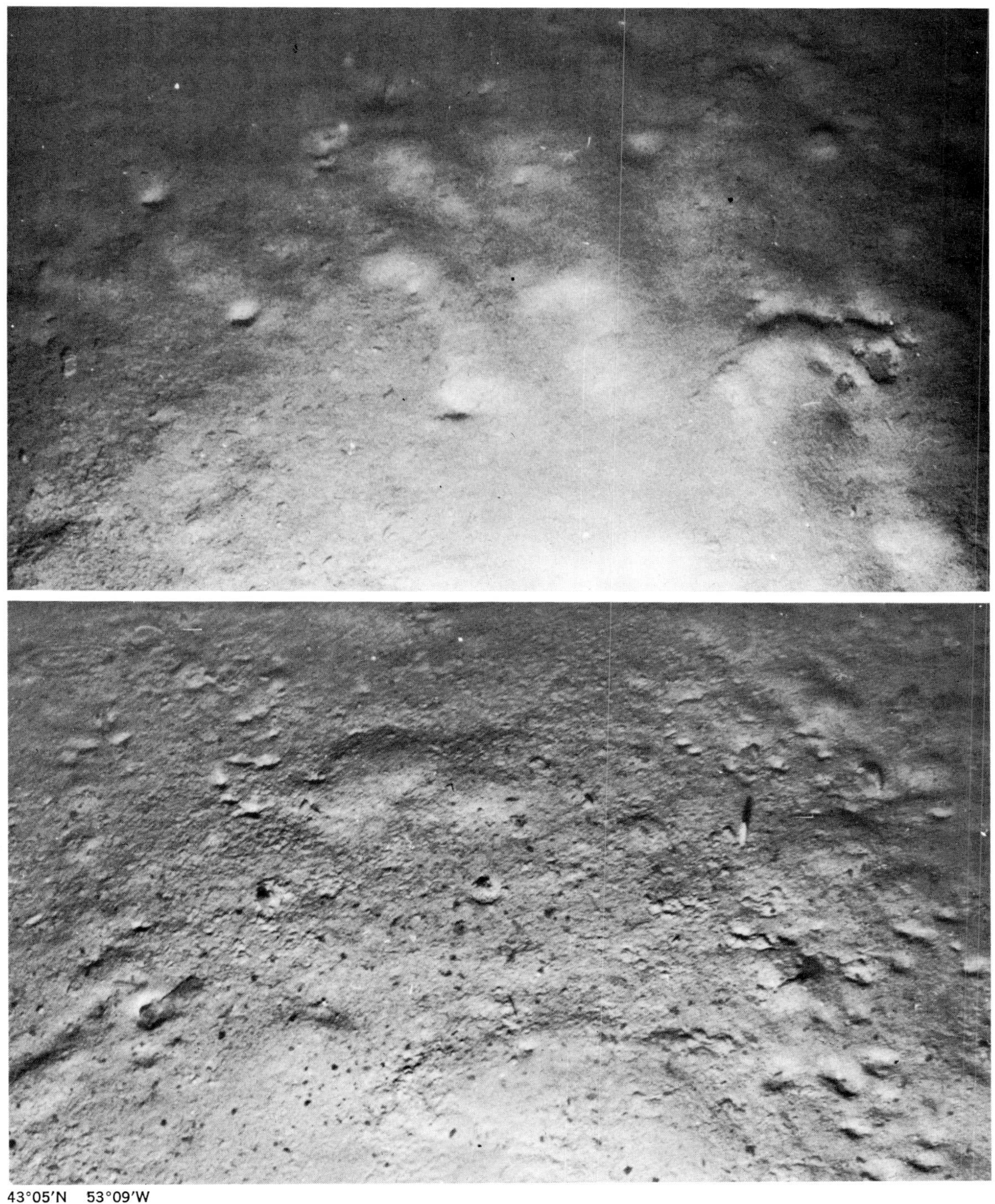

43°05′N 53°09′W
45°50′N 43°42′W

9.61 The Western Boundary Undercurrent sweeps around the Grand Banks. U, L, soft rounded ripple and scour are found beneath this contour current, 3910 m and 4656 m, continental rise east and south of the Grand Banks.

42°33′N 62°49′W
9.62 A gentle westerly current sweeps over a smooth muddy bottom at the base of the continental slope off Nova Scotia. The current vane, continually photographed during the recovery of the camera, recorded a westerly current from the sea floor to the sea surface, 1561 m.

At a location where a smooth, muddy bottom was photographed, a velocity of seventeen centimeters per second was found. Here sediment waves are shown on the echograms but ripples are not seen in the photographs. At another site, where the photographs showed smooth, muddy bottom, a velocity of eighteen centimeters per second was observed. In each case where tranquil, unsmoothed bottom was observed in photographs the velocities measured were less than five centimeters per second.

Chafe by sediment transported in the Mediterranean Undercurrent has resulted in the frequent failure of submarine cables in depths up to 1200 meters and at distances of up to 250 kilometers from the Strait of Gibraltar.

42°16′N 62°38′W
42°16′N 62°38′W

9.63 The Western Boundary Undercurrent ripples and scours the Nova Scotia continental rise. U, L, all of the nearly 100 photographs taken at this location revealed current lineations indicating a strong westerly flow, 2359 m.

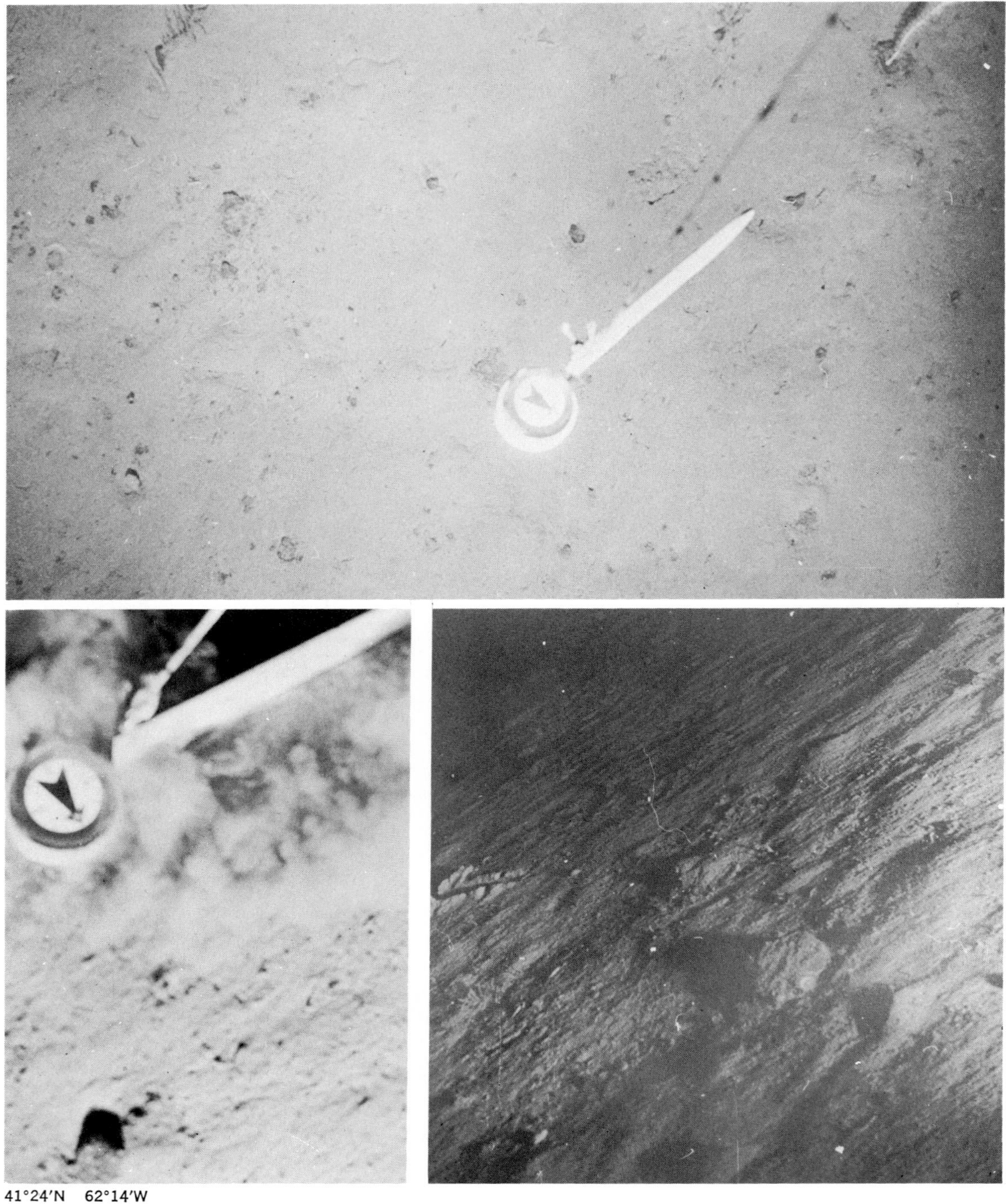

41°24′N 62°14′W
41°24′N 62°14′W
41°24′N 62°14′W

9.64 Scour marks and current lineations beneath the turbid westerly current. U, LL, LR, echo-sounding pulses return from a multitude of small and weak reflectors on this current-sculpted bottom. 4030 m, continental rise off Nova Scotia.

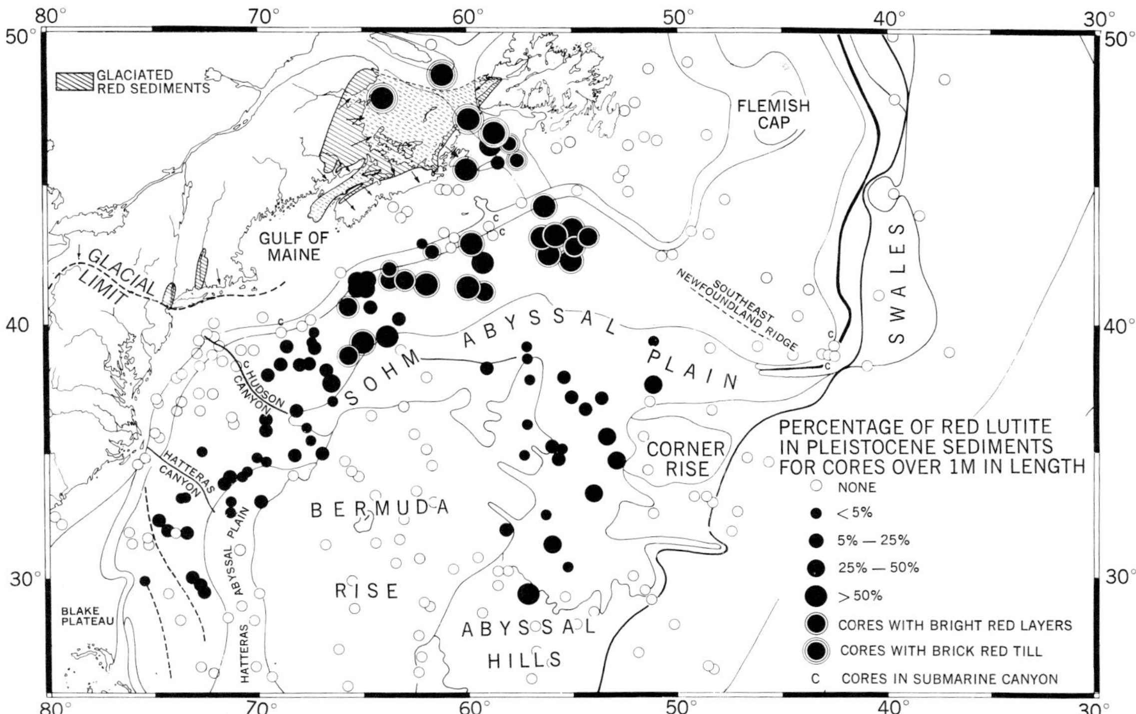

9.65 A bright red plume records the flow of the Pleistocene Western Boundary Undercurrent. A vast tracer of bright-red silt and clay was carried out of the Gulf of St. Lawrence and dumped into the Atlantic; some was carried downslope by turbidity currents but most drifted parallel to the contours for more than 3000 kilometers reaching as far south as the Bahamas. Percentage of total thickness of ice age sediment layers which are red in color.

With minor exceptions, the rolling topography seen in echograms is duplicated in a minute scale in the visual range. The smoothing seen in echograms is also seen in photographs for the same area, and the sediment waves far too large to be seen in photographs are found to be covered by smaller ripples. These morphological forms, which occupy a size range extending from centimeters to kilometers, are clearly related to the patterns, processes, and vigor of oceanic circulation.

FROM ARCTIC SOURCES

The cold waters of the Arctic, dammed in by ridges, spill over the deepest sills and flow toward the depths of the temperate seas. The North Atlantic Deep Water which forms in the northen North Atlantic mixes with this underlying Arctic Bottom Water and flows south through the mid-

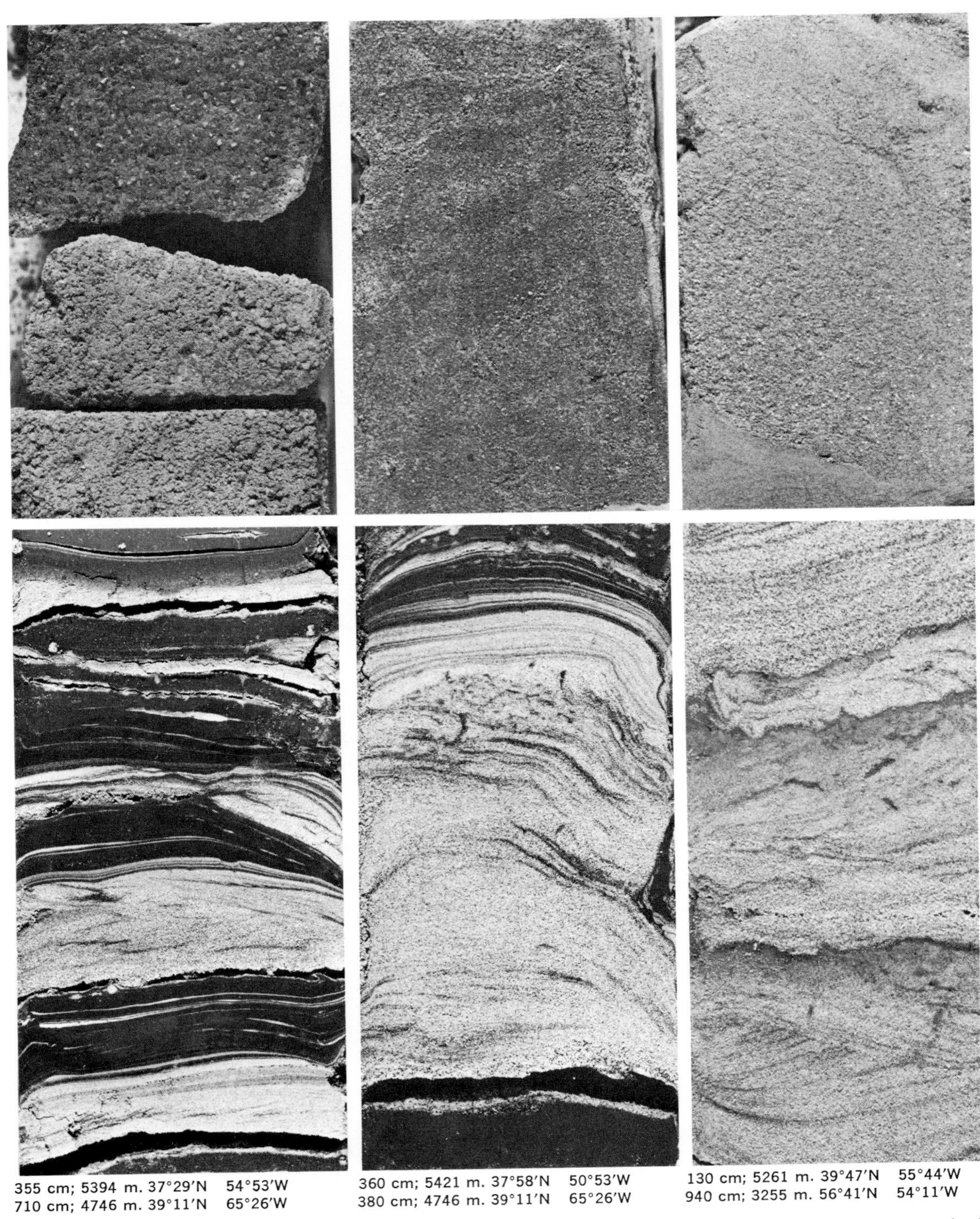

355 cm; 5394 m. 37°29′N 54°53′W
710 cm; 4746 m. 39°11′N 65°26′W

360 cm; 5421 m. 37°58′N 50°53′W
380 cm; 4746 m. 39°11′N 65°26′W

130 cm; 5261 m. 39°47′N 55°44′W
940 cm; 3255 m. 56°41′N 54°11′W

9.66 Muddy turbidity current-deposited sands and clean laminated silts deposited by the Western Boundary Undercurrent. UL, C, UR, graded, massive muddy sands from the Sohm Abyssal Plain. LL, LC, graded highly stratified, cross laminated, clean, fine sand and silt beds from the continental rise off New England, and LR, off Labrador (all photos x ¾).

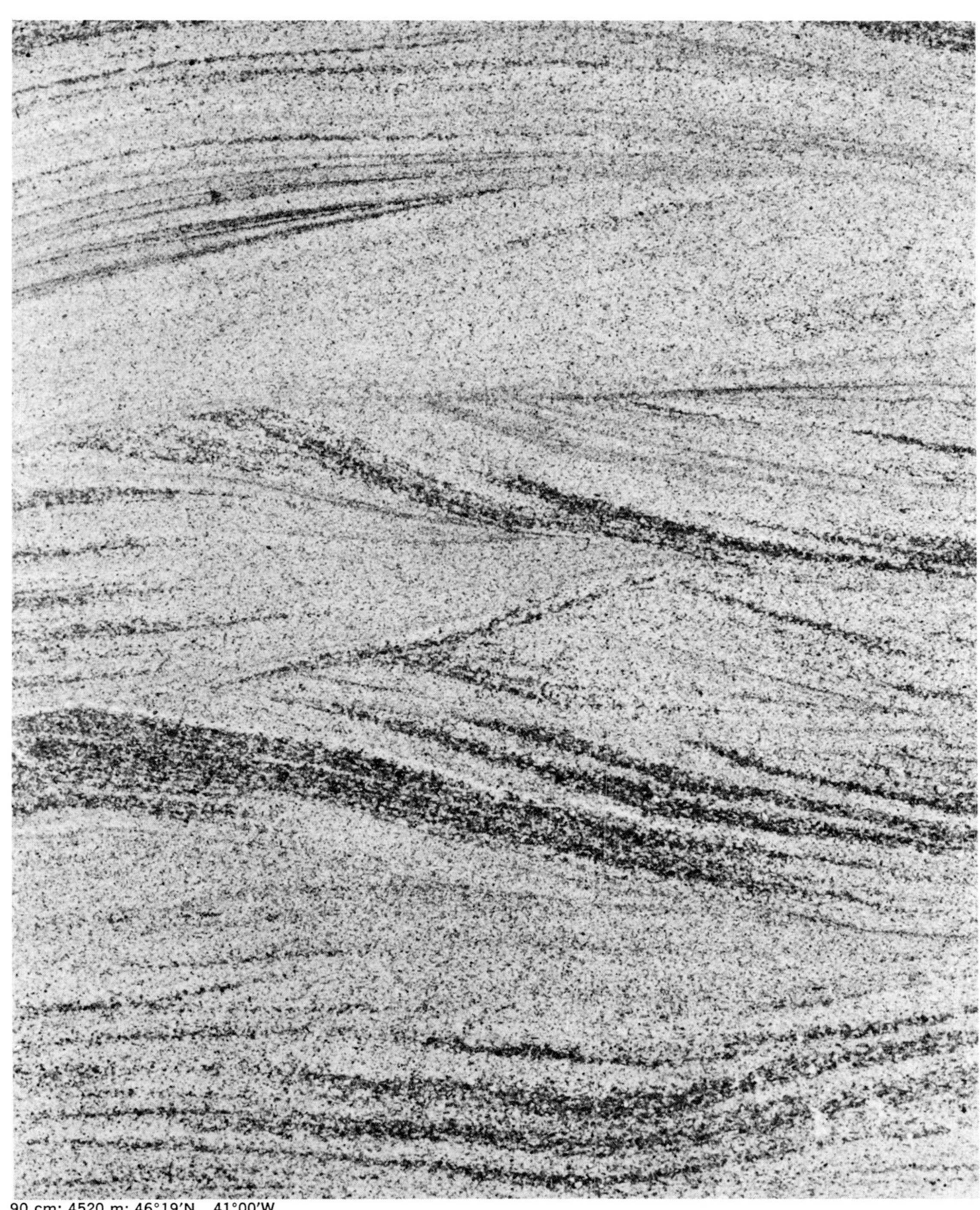

90 cm; 4520 m; 46°19′N 41°00′W

9.67 Clean cross-laminated sand. Cross laminations accentuated by concentrations of dark, heavy mineral grains, the Newfoundland continental rise (× 2-½). Virtually all of the comparatively thin (1-5 cm) sand and silt beds from the continental rise are cross laminated.

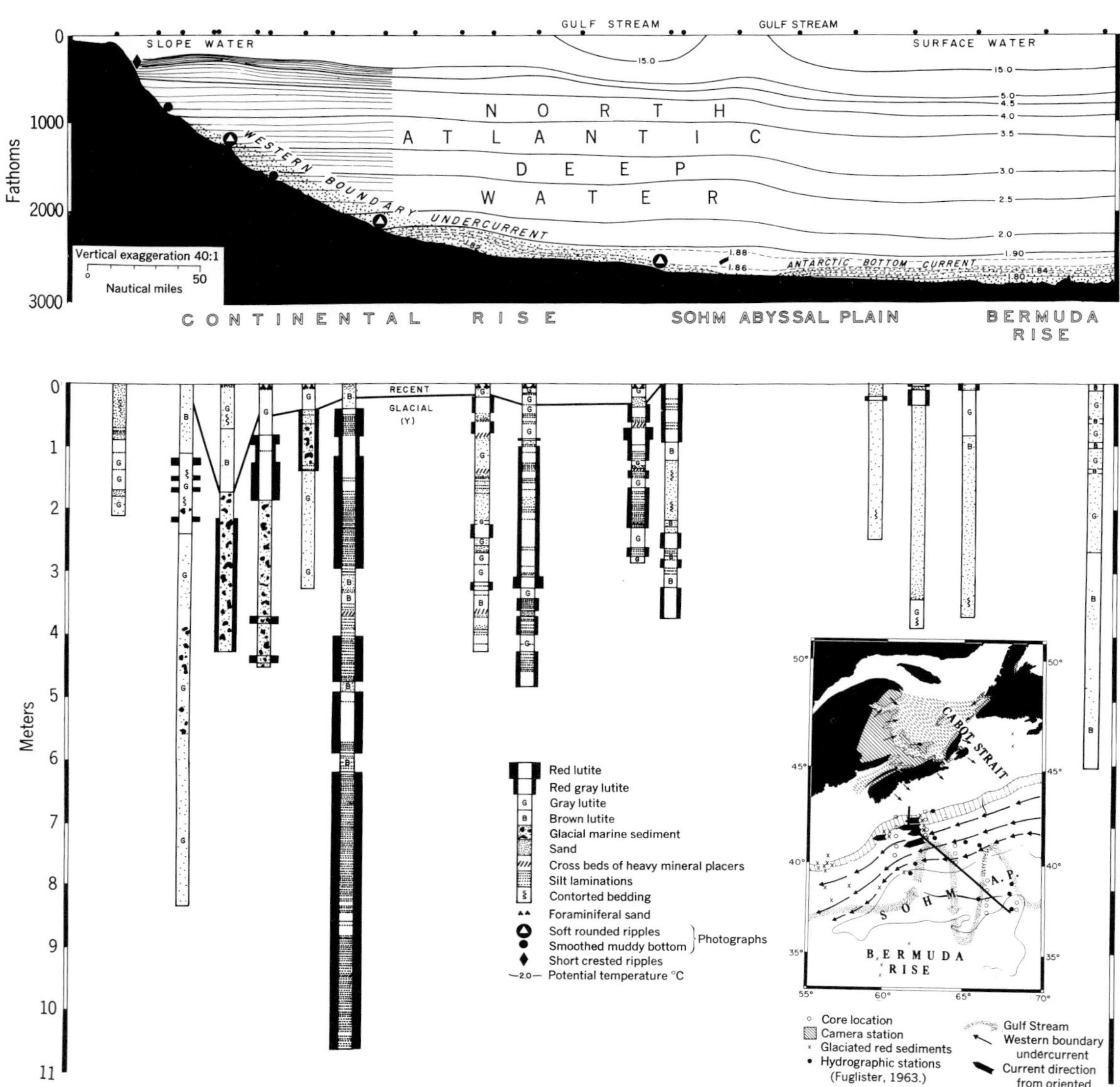

9.68 Innumerable silt laminae record continuing activity beneath the Western Boundary Undercurrent. Continental slope sediments are nearly unstratified and thick beds of muddy silt and sand underlie the flat abyssal plain. Post-glacial sediment is thickest near the base of the continental slope and thins to less than 5 cm near the continental rise-abyssal plain boundary (Core 10). The distribution of near-bottom temperature and current evidence seen in bottom photographs indicates that the strongest current occurs between Cores 6 and 10. In contrast to the coarse sandy sediments of the continental shelf and abyssal plain, sediment on the continental rise consists of numerous thin cross-bedded silt layers interbedded with red-colored lutite.

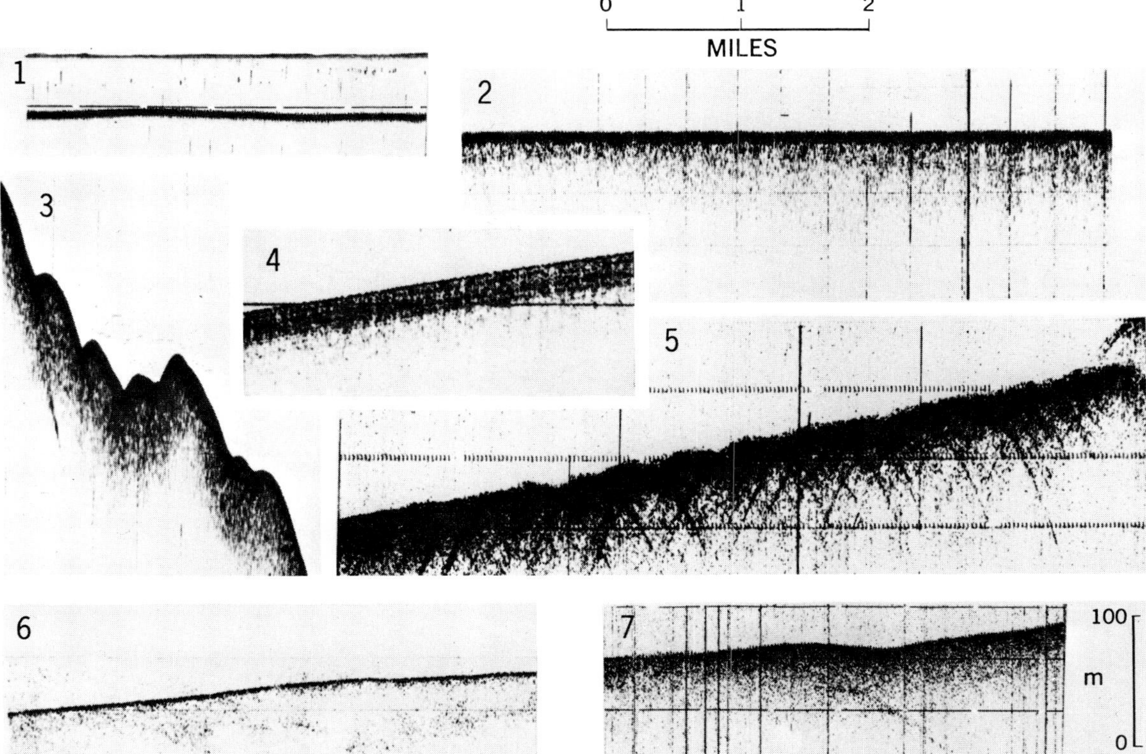

9.69 Characteristic echogram types off New England: (1) continental shelf; (2) abyssal plain; (3) large hyperbola found along the continental slope, Bermuda Pedestal and seamounts; (4) wedging sub-bottoms found on the upper continental rise; (5) low amplitude hyperbola on the lower continental rise; (6) coherent echo return from the Bermuda Rise; (7) incoherent echo typical of continental rise.

depths of the Atlantic, penetrating as far south as the Antarctic Polar Front. This southerly flowing water mass bathes the continental margins and then passes over and mixes with the northerly flowing Antarctic Bottom Current, which claims the deepest portions of the abyssal floor.[18]

Cold Arctic Bottom Water from the Norwegian Sea flows through the Faroe-Scotland Channel and leaks into the Atlantic via a narrow gap between the Faroe Islands and Lousy Bank. Velocities as high as twenty-three centimeters per second have been measured in this water mass along the southeast slope of Iceland in 1300 meters depth.[19] These currents, which are competent to transport particles as large as fine gravel, flow in a southwesterly direction parallel to the bathymetric contours along the eastern side of the Mid-Atlantic Ridge (9.58). At approximately latitude fifty-three degrees North this current escapes westward through a fracture zone in the Mid-Atlantic Ridge and enters the western North Atlantic.[20] This cold current is augmented by more Arctic bottom Water which flows intermittently through the Denmark Strait and cascades down into the Atlantic. The cold bottom current then flows south along the continental slope and continental rise east of Greenland, north along the western margin of Greenland, and then south along the continental rise of Labrador.

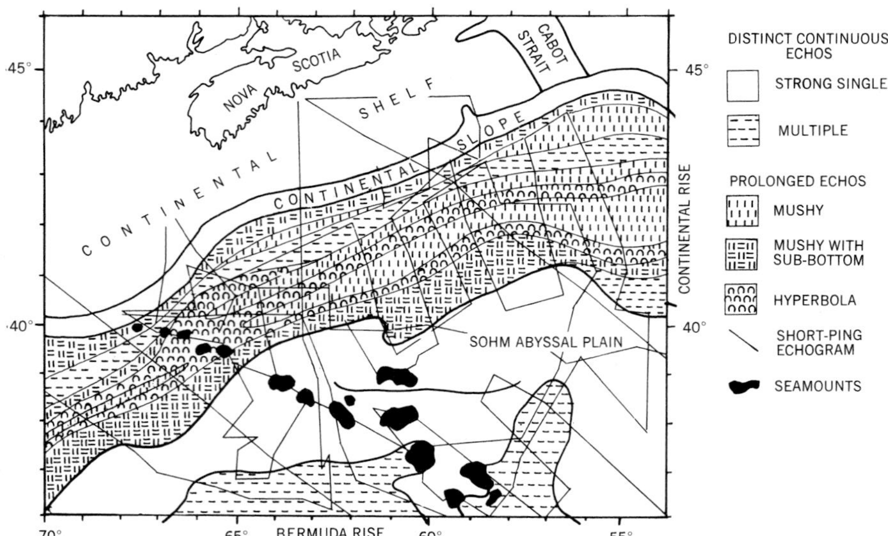

9.70 Echograms record the effect of sediment scour and drift by contour currents on the continental rise. Features too large to be seen on photographs but still too small to be seen on bathymetric maps can be inferred by subtle change in character of the echo returns.

Near-bottom direct current measurements made on the Greenland continental rise west of Cape Farewell indicated that this bottom current flows in a northwesterly direction at velocities of nearly ten centimeters per second.[21] (9.59). Ripples and scour marks, indicating a strong southerly current, have been observed beneath the current west of Greenland and east of the Grand Banks (9.60, 9.61).

After rounding the tail of the Grand Banks, this Western Boundary Undercurrent flows along the continental rise of Nova Scotia, and New England (9.61), where its effects are clearly evident in the visual seascape (9.62-9.64).

THE RED PLUME

The sediments of the continental rise contain evidence that the Western Boundary Undercurrent is a permanent and persistent feature. The Gulf of St. Lawrence is the source of bright-red sediments which in glacial times were introduced into the Atlantic through the Laurentian Channel, which cuts as a trough across the continental shelf (9.65). Although the modern sediments of the area are gray in color, the underlying glacial age sediments contain thick sequences of bright red sediments.[22] East of the Laurentian Channel these red sediments are absent, but to the south-

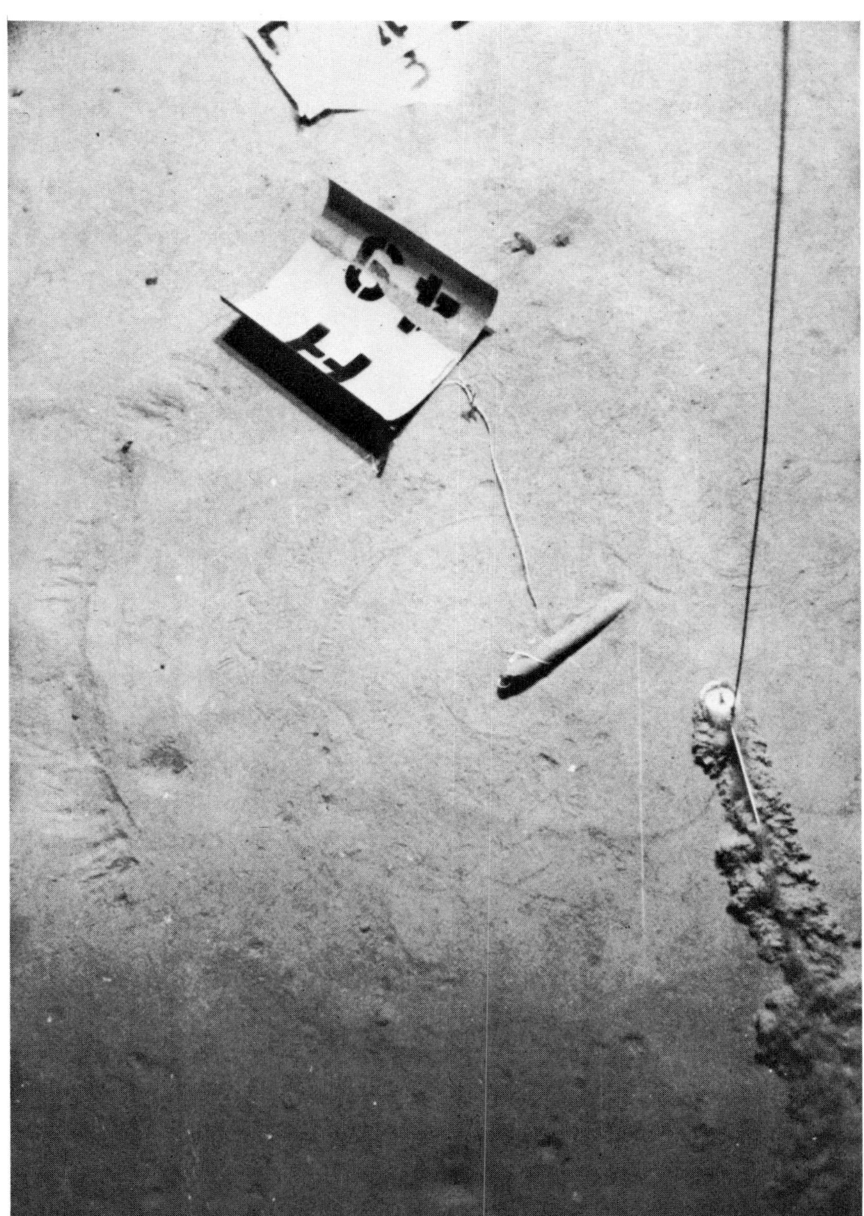

45°45′N 65°00′W
9.71 Drag marks of tethered placard indicate westerly flow of contour current. This marker, attached to a sash weight, was photographed more than a year after it had been dropped in connection with the *Thresher* search. 2500 m, upper continental rise off New England.

west they extend with gradually decreasing abundance and intensity of coloration for over 3000 kilometers, reaching the deep-sea floor off the Bahamas.

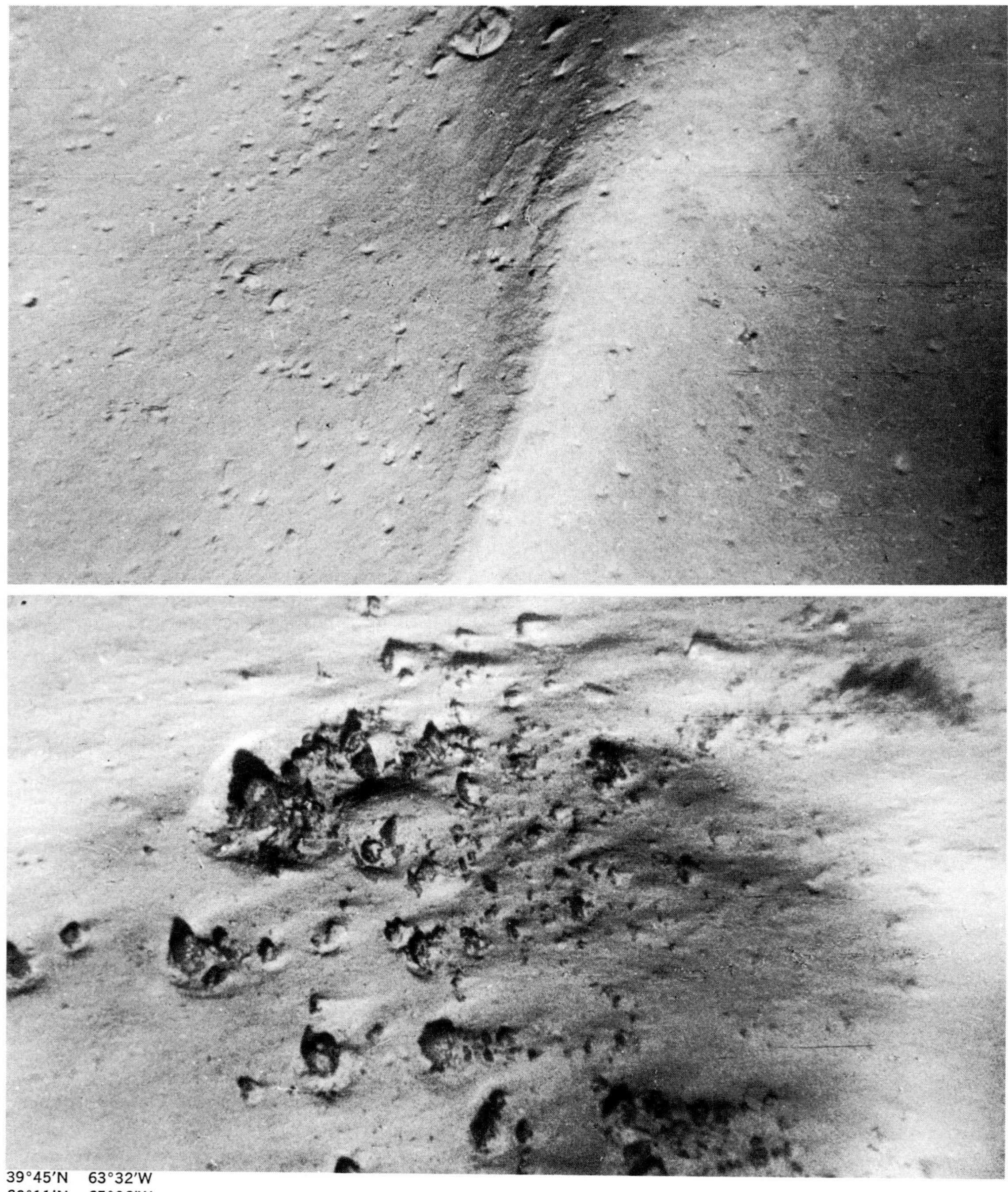

9.72 Ripples, moats, and tails are sculpted by the contour following Western Boundary Undercurrent near the lower edge of the continental rise off New England. U, 4954 m, near the boundary between the continental rise and the Sohm Abyssal Plain. L, 4754 m, between the Kelvin Seamounts, on the continental rise.

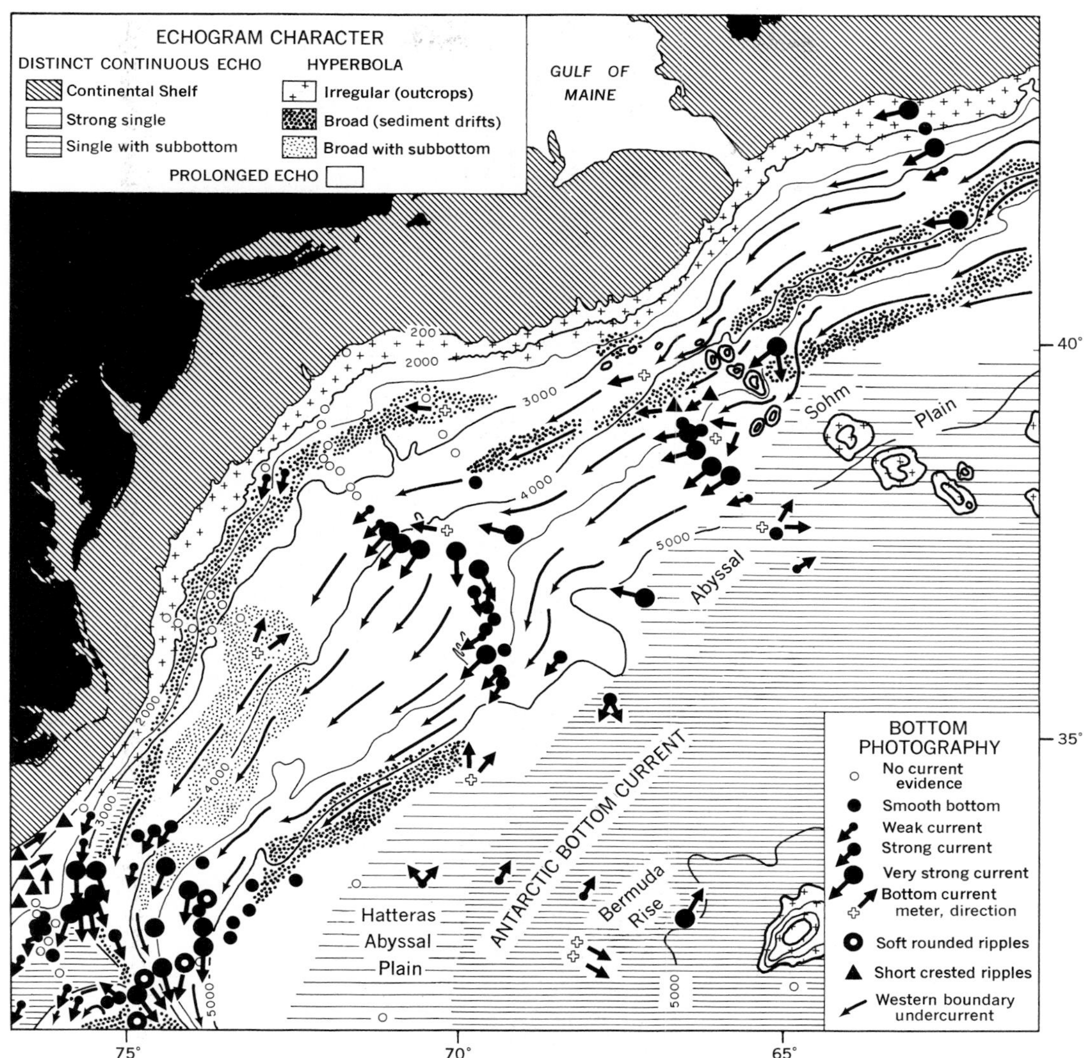

9.73 Direction and strength of Western Boundary Undercurrent inferred from bottom photographs. Strong coherent echos return from continental shelf and abyssal plains. On the continental rise, zones of prolonged echoes and hyperbola trend parallel to the regional contours. Above 3500 meters, tranquil, current-free bottom is seen, but below 3500 meters, swift contour currents transport sediment to the southwest. Photographs on the Hatteras Abyssal Plain show tranquil bottom or variable weak northerly flowing currents, while swifter northerly flow of the Antarctic Bottom Current is observed on the western Bermuda Rise (contours in meters).

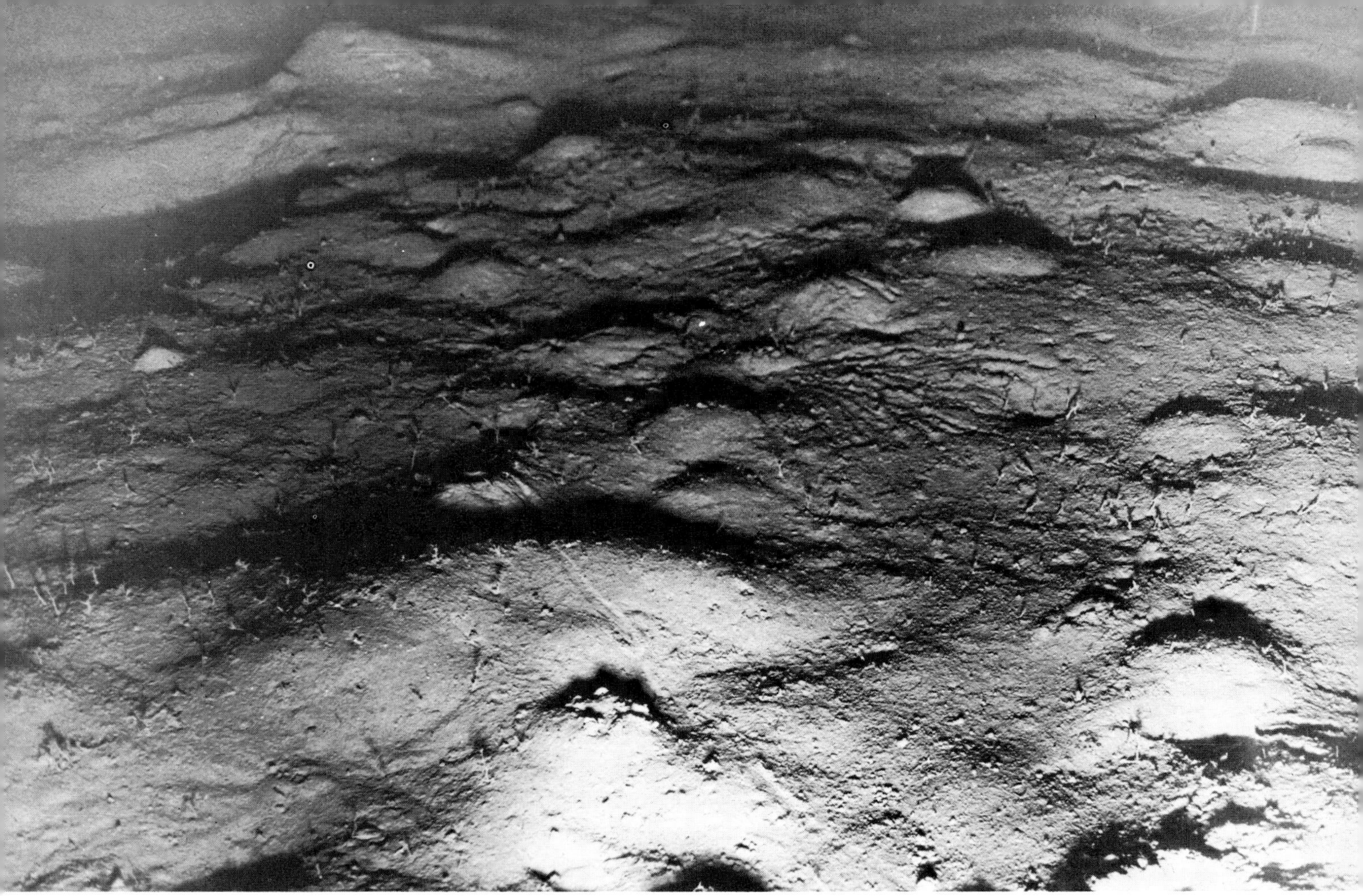

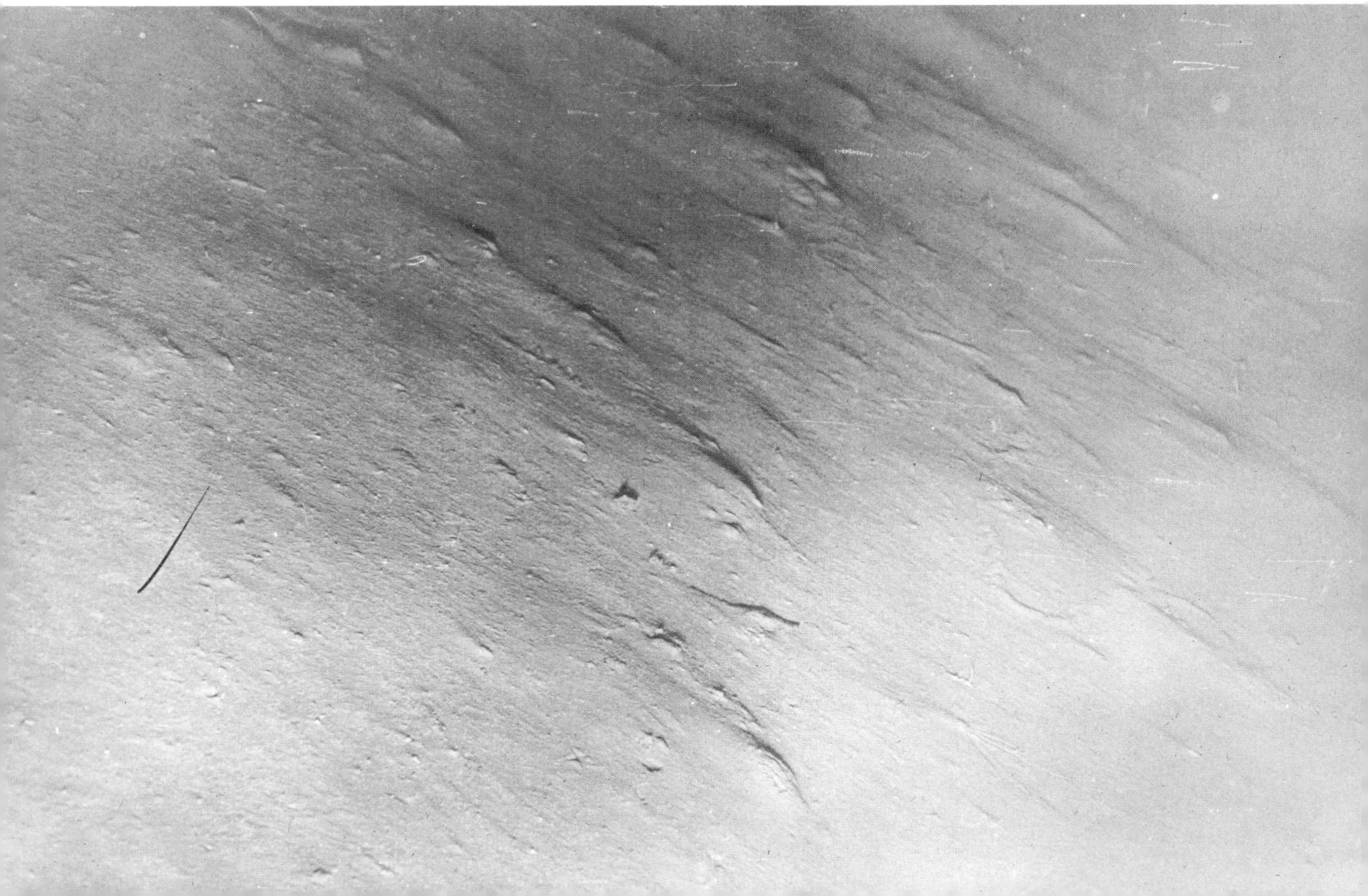

38°30′N 70°36′W

36°47′N 67°09′W

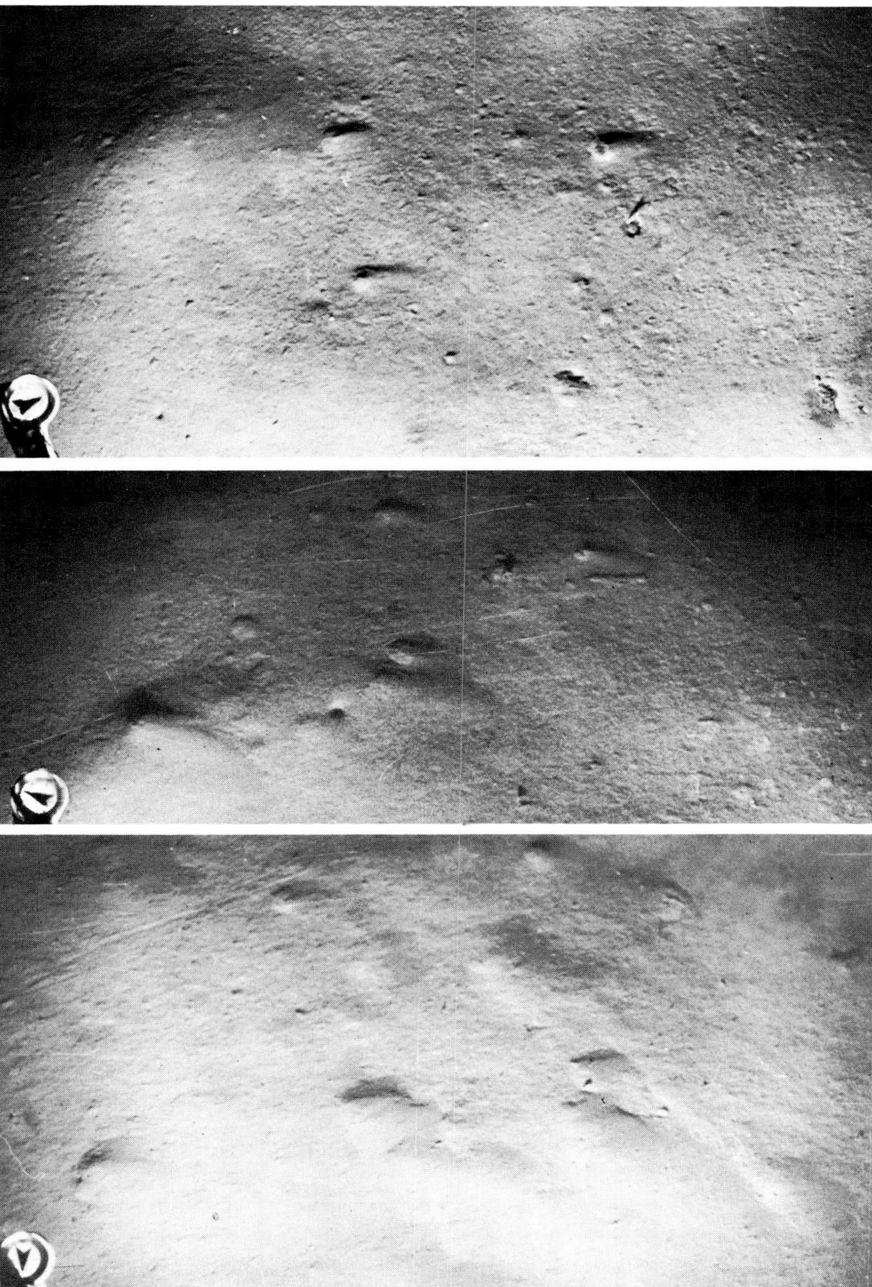

36°35′N 69°35′W
37°05′N 69°41′W
37°20′N 70°34′W

9.75 The Gulf Stream intermittently produces northward trending lineations on the deep-sea floor. U, sediment streamers trend NNE below the axis of the Gulf Stream, 4444 m, continental rise off New Jersey. C, L, lineations beneath the Western Boundary Undercurrent trends SSW, 4336 m and 4190 m, continental rise off New York.

◁ 9.74 The tranquil upper continental rise contrasts markedly with the current-smoothed and lineated lower continental rise beneath the Western Boundary Undercurrent. U, 3026 m, upper continental rise off New York; L, 5010 m, lower continental rise off New York.

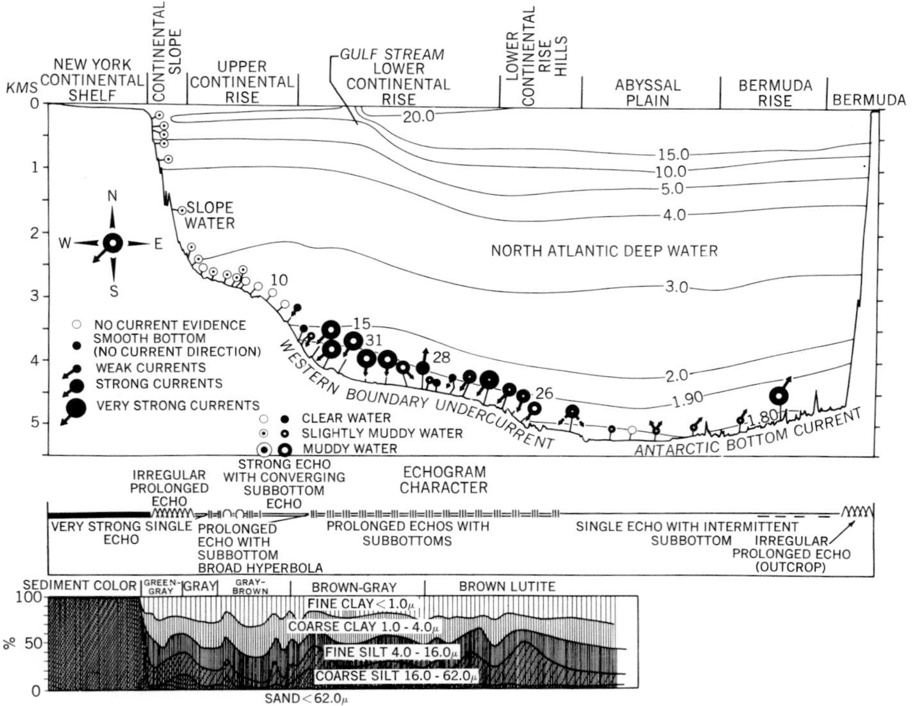

9.76 The activity of the Western Boundary Undercurrent can be studied in this profile of bottom current direction, bottom sediment, echogram character, and isotherms of potential temperature. Cold water (less than 2°C) lapping up on the continental rise and on the Bermuda Rise (less than 1.80°C) suggests vigorous circulation of deep water. Strong ocean currents visibly scour the seascape at the break in slope between the upper and lower continental rise, in the Lower Continental Rise Hills and above 5000 meters on the Bermuda Rise. Prolonged bottom echo sequences and an increase in the surface sand and silt-sized sediments are associated with the current-swept zones on the lower continental rise.

CROSS-BEDS AND HYPERBOLA

Distinctive thin (0.5 cm to 5 cm) current laminated beds of fine sand and silt are ubiquitous beneath the current-swept continental rise of eastern North America (9.66, 9.67). Sediment cores from this region contain approximately 200 laminae per ten centimeters of sediment (9.68). Virtually all silt laminations grade in grain size from coarser at the bottom to fine at the top and have sharp upper and lower contacts (9.66, 9.67).

Echo traces from flat, hard surfaces are sharp and well-defined and are called "hard" echoes. Poorly defined or weak echo traces are described as "mushy" echoes. Often an echogram reveals a multitude of hyperbolic echoes which have their tops or apexes tangent to the seafloor surface. These evenly spaced "hyperbolic echoes" are reflections

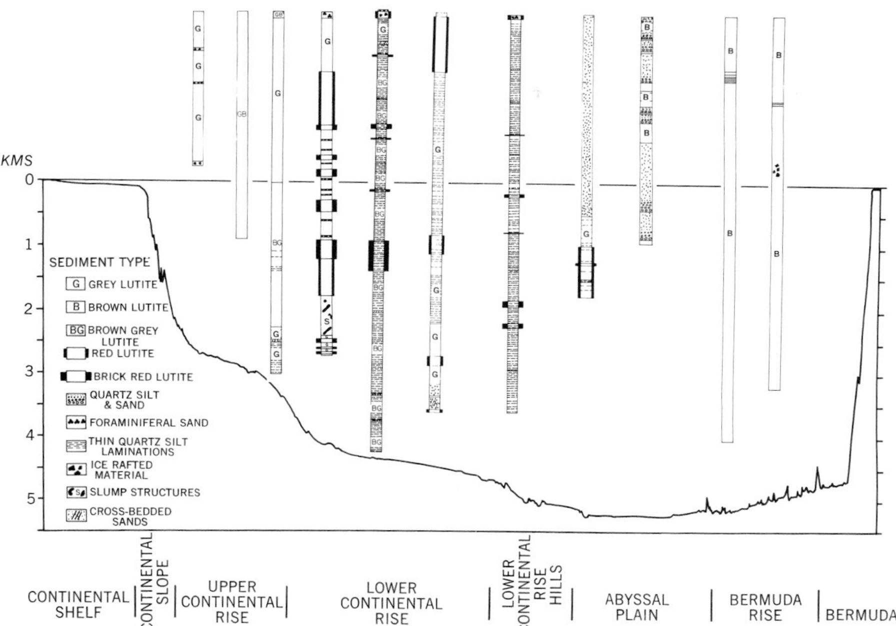

9.77 Homogeneous gray silty muds are cored on the upper continental rise while the lower continental rise is covered with many well-sorted thin silt beds and marked zones of red muds which have been transported south by contour currents from the Gulf of St. Lawrence region. Abyssal plain sediments consist of poorly sorted, graded sand and silt beds interbedded with brown clays; whereas Bermuda Rise sediments consist of homogeneous brown lutites. This characteristic change in sediment type marks the boundary between turbidity-current sedimentation (abyssal plains) and pelagic-bottom current sedimentation (continental rise and Bermuda Rise).

from a series of parallel linear elevations such as ripples or dunes (9.69). Two zones of small, even hyperbola occur on the continental rise of Nova Scotia—one at 4300 meters and another at 4700 meters (9.70).

In the constrictions between the Kelvin Seamounts on the continental rise off New England, echograms reveal exceptionally well-developed hyperbolic traces. Zones of predominantly mushy, indistinct echoes are found on both sides of the hyperbola zones, suggesting the presence of smaller sized lineations on a muddy sea floor.

The Western Boundary Undercurrent flows between the picket fence of the Kelvin Seamounts along the continental rise off New York and southward past Cape Hatteras (9.71-9.73). Off New York the continental rise is clearly divided into an upper and a lower portion separated by a steeper face. Currents are weak on the upper continental rise where a visually tranquil bottom (9.74 U) is underlain by parallel sub-bottom layering. At the outer edge of the upper continental rise, where sub-

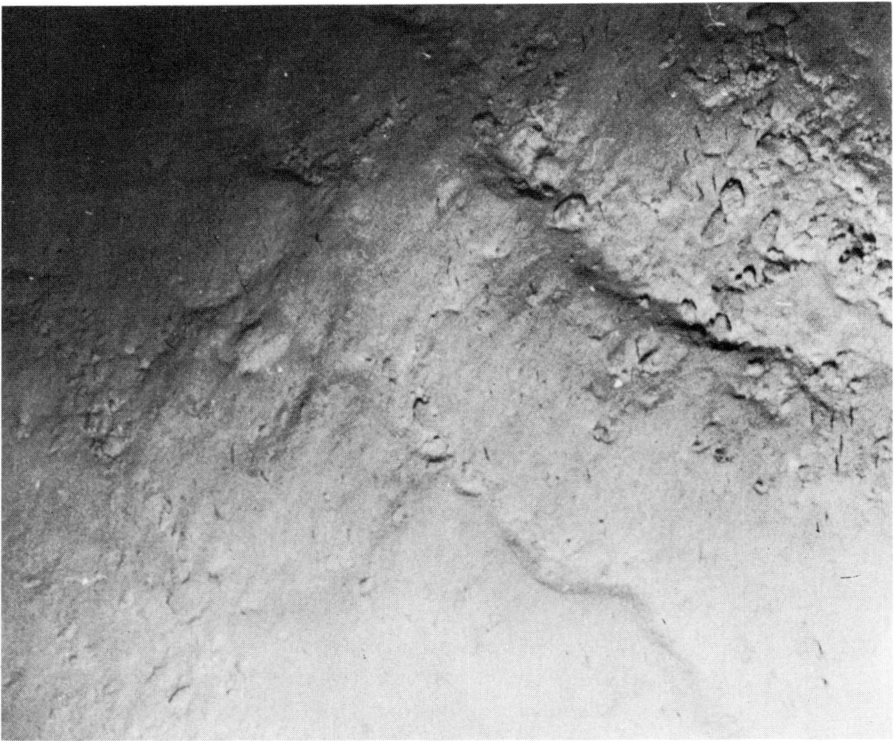

30°27′N 76°25′W

9.78 Ripples and lineations beneath the Western Boundary Undercurrent. 4163 m, continental rise north of Blake Plateau.

bottom layering converges toward the sea floor, visual current evidence becomes noticeable (9.74 L); and finally, where the sub-bottom layers crop out, hyperbola are seen on the echograms and strong southwesterly oriented current lineations are seen in the photographs (9.75 C).

On the more nearly level gradients on the mid-part of the lower continental rise, current indications are weaker and somewhat variable (9.75 U, C); but on the lower continental rise hills the visual effects of swifter currents are seen again (9.74 L) and hyperbola and truncated sub-bottom reflections are recorded by the echo-sounder. On the nearly perfect planar surface of the abyssal plain, current evidence is either absent or extremely weak and variable (9.76). On the continental slope and upper continental rise, where a tranquil bottom is observed in photographs, the sediments lack fine stratification (9.77) and brick-red lutite is absent. However, on the lower continental rise the Western Boundary Undercurrent has deposited numerous well-sorted silt laminations and has transported the striking brick-red lutite, found interbedded with these current bedded laminae, from the region of the Cabot Strait (9.65, 9.68, 9.78).

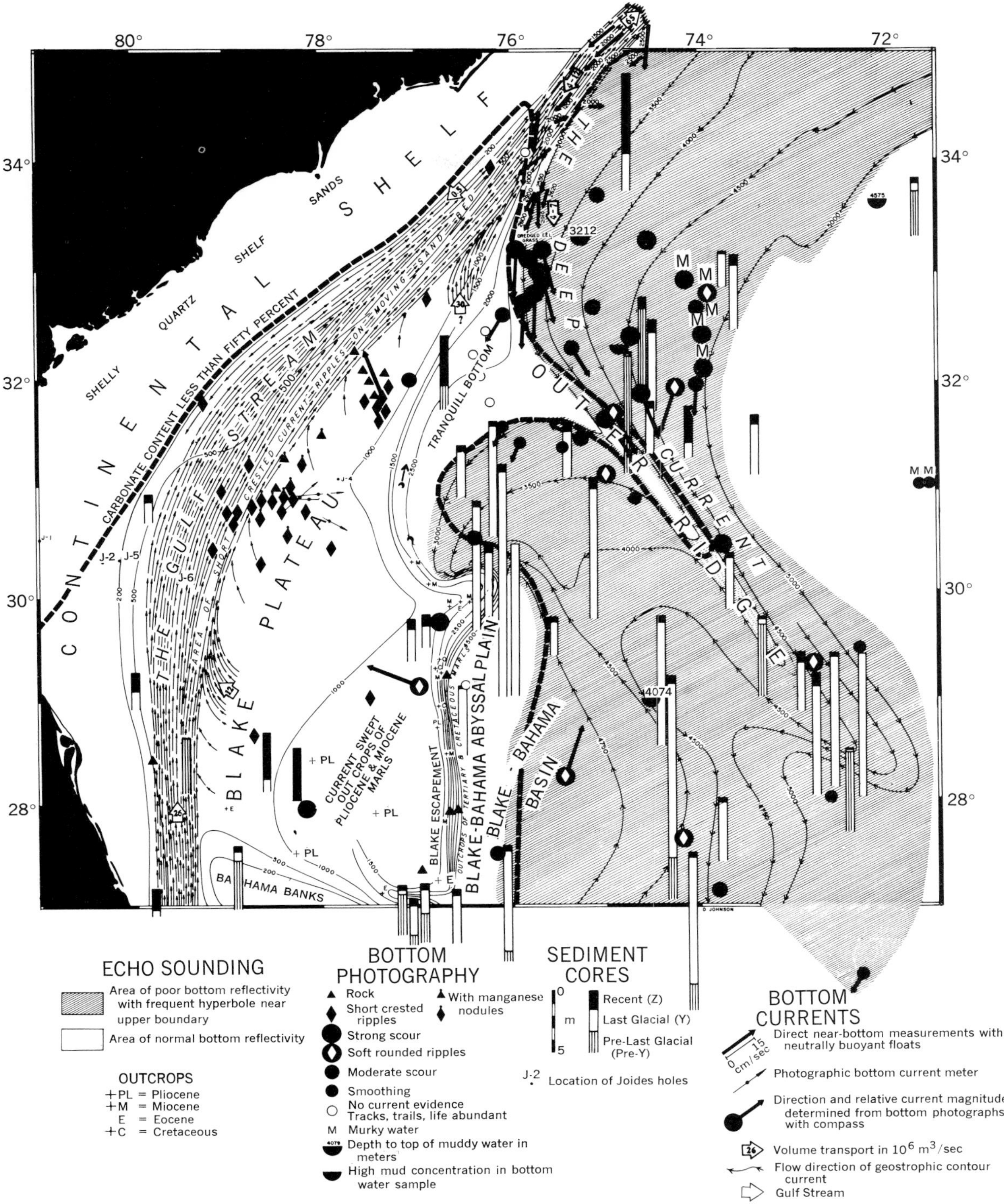

9.79 Bottom currents, sediments, and echogram character on the Blake Plateau and Blake-Bahama Outer Ridge. Short-crested ripples, manganese nodules, and Tertiary outcrops are found beneath the Gulf Stream which acts as a barrier to seaward transport of continental sediment. The Outer Ridge is formed by rapid deposition from the southerly flowing sediment-laden Western Boundary Undercurrent flowing parallel to the contours. Watery sediments that result from rapid deposition exhibit poor reflectivity.

GIANT DRIFTS

The continental rise off eastern United States merges, south of Cape Hatteras, with the broad southeasterly plunging Blake-Bahama Outer Ridge (9.79). Seismic investigations indicate that this southerly extension of the continental rise is an undeformed sediment wedge similar in geological structure to, and only slightly thinner than the normal continental rise sediment wedge found further north. The Outer Ridge is separated from the continent by a deep basin (the Blake-Bahama Basin) and by the broad (600-kilometer wide) Blake Plateau. Terrigenous sediments derived from southeastern United States are barred from the eastern Blake Plateau, the Blake Escarpment, and the western Blake-Bahama Basin by the vigorous northerly transport of the Gulf Stream which flows at velocities of 100-300 centimeters per second along the western margin of the Blake Plateau.[23] Thus, the existence of a continental-rise-type sediment accumulation 1000 kilometers seaward of Georgia and Florida suggests a north-to-south abyssal transport of terrigenous sediments along this southerly extension of the continental rise.[24]

Along the base of the continental slope off North Carolina and along the eastern flank of the Outer Ridge, current lineations consisting of streamers of sediment deposited in the lee of burrow mounds and other objects on the bottom have been universally observed (9.80 R). On both the eastern side of the Outer Ridge between 3000 and 5000 meters and at the base of the continental slope off North Carolina, abundant lineations indicate a southerly current which is flowing almost precisely parallel to the local contours (9.79). Where current lineations are abundant, the bottom is seen to be smooth and remarkably free of benthic life, and the water appears more or less muddy. Neither current lineations, ripples, nor turbid waters are observed on the Outer Ridge in depths of 2000-3000 meters. In such depths the bottom is marked by tracks and trails, and a relatively normal abundance of benthic life is observed (9.80 UL).

On the Blake Plateau, post-glacial (Recent) sediment is variable in thickness and consists of reworked sand and shell fragments on the landward side of the Gulf Stream, reworked coral sand and manganese nodules beneath the Gulf Stream, and pelagic ooze on the outer Blake Plateau. Near the seaward edge of the Blake Plateau the Pleistocene is absent and Pliocene or Miocene calcareous clay is either exposed at the surface, covered by a few centimeters of ooze, or coated with a manganese crust. The Outer Ridge, on the other hand, is covered by a thick sequence of post-glacial sediments (9.81). The thickness of this sedi-

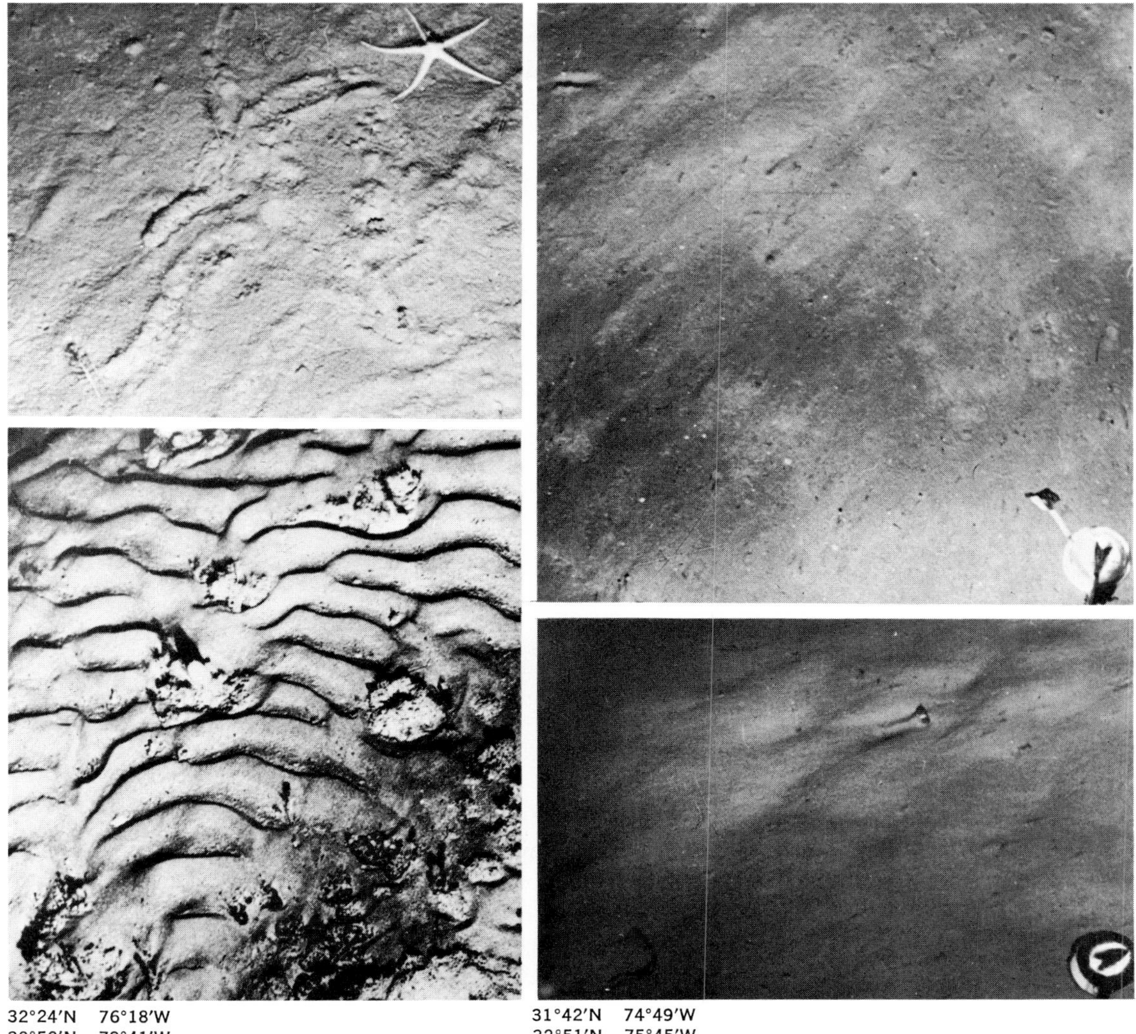

9.80 Bottom photographs of the Blake Plateau and Blake-Bahama Outer Ridge. UL, tranquil bottom is ubiquitous on the crest of the Outer Ridge near the base of continental slope. This photograph reveals abundant life and no current evidence, 2164 m. UR, current lineations are seen east of crest of the Outer Ridge. Photographs from both the eastern side of the Outer Ridge between 3000 and 5000 meters and from the base of the continental slope off North Carolina show abundant lineations that indicate a southerly current flowing precisely parallel to the contours, 3975 m. LL, short-crested current ripples occur beneath the Gulf Stream on the Blake Plateau. The surface of the Blake Plateau is characterized by rippled sand, manganese nodules, or manganese-encrusted tabular outcrops of Tertiary sediment, 872 m. LR, current lineations made by the southerly flowing Western Boundary Undercurrent east of the crest of the Blake-Bahama Outer Ridge near the base of the continental slope. Direct current measurements nearby indicate a southerly flowing near-bottom current of up to 18 centimeters per second, 3183 m.

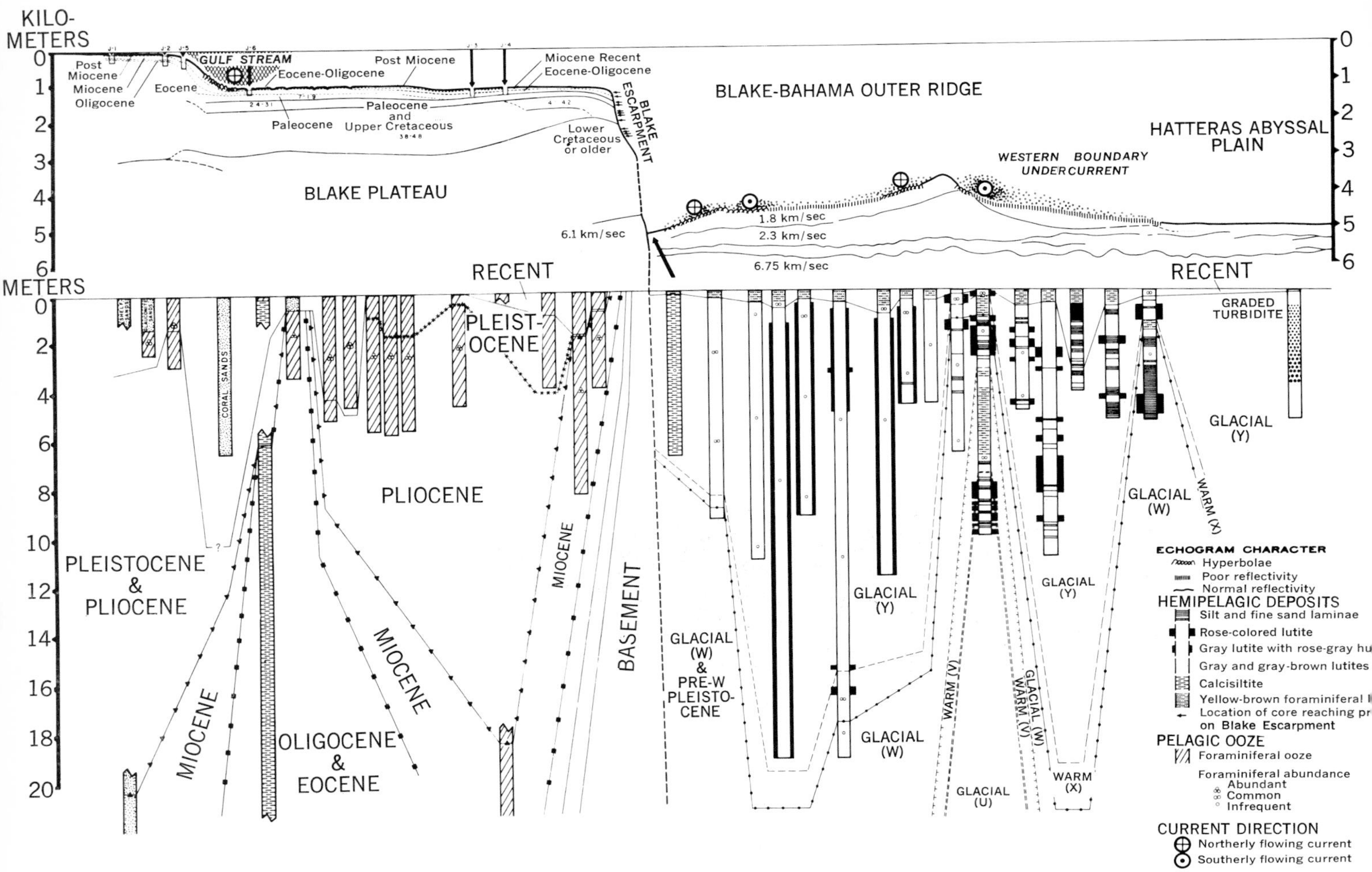

9.81 Profile across Blake Plateau and Blake-Bahama Outer Ridge. Thick Pleistocene and Recent wedges of clay on the Blake-Bahama Outer Ridge thin eastward toward the Hatteras Abyssal Plain and westward toward the Blake-Bahama Abyssal Plain in response to decreased volume transport of the Western Boundary Undercurrent. The greatest water depth west of the Outer Ridge occurs at the base of the Blake Escarpment, precluding any significant direct seaward sediment dispersal. Climatic zones are based on foraminiferal assemblages.

Years before present:

Z = Recent-warm

12,000

Y = Last glacial stage-cold

60,000

X = Last interglacial stage-warm

95,000

W = Next to last glacial stage-cold

ment increases from the Hatteras Abyssal Plain towards a maximum of over one meter on the eastern flank of the Outer Ridge and then decreases markedly, reaching a minimum east of the crest. West of the

9.82 Smoothed, lineated seascape produced by contour currents characterizes the continental rise and outer ridges of the western Atlantic, 4870 m.

crest the thickness of the Recent ranges from thirty to eighty centimeters, again decreasing toward the Blake-Bahama Abyssal Plain where its thickness is approximately twenty centimeters. The thickness of sediment deposited during the last glacial stage generally exceeds the 10- to 20-meter penetration of the cores. Near the apparent axis of the undercurrent, Recent and late glacial sediments are thin or absent, suggesting either slow deposition or considerable erosion along narrow linear belts displaced from the crest of the Outer Ridge and lying beneath the axis of the undercurrent at about 4500 meters.

A downslope thinning of sedimentary layers has been observed throughout the continental rise accumulation. This downslope thinning might be attributed solely to a decrease in rate of accumulation of continentally derived material with increasing distance from the continental sources, were it not for the presence of a similar wedging on both flanks of the Outer Ridge. This latter fact suggests that transport parallel to bathymetric contours by deep-sea currents must play an important role in the transportational history of continental rise deposits.

The area of tranquil bottom which lies on the Outer Ridge in depths less than 3000 meters appears to result from deposition in the absence of strong bottom currents.

The sediment carried in suspension by the Western Boundary Undercurrent reduces visibility due to the back-scattering of light and causes photographs to be somewhat cloudy. The back-scatter can actually be used to estimate relative concentrations of suspended matter and photographic devices have been constructed to make vertical profiles of the relative amounts of back-scattering. Such profiles show that from the abyssal plain to the upper continental rise a thick layer of turbid water several hundred meters thick overlies the sea floor.[25]

Approximately 150 cubic kilometers of land-derived sediment has been deposited in the Blake-Bahama Outer Ridge since the end of the Ice Age. If the Western Boundary Undercurrent has flowed at its present rate of approximately five million cubic meters per second[26] during this 10,000-year period, then a sediment concentration of only one part in ten million would be sufficient to supply the entire volume of sediments that comprise the last layer of this sedimentary drift. Since such concentrations have been measured in it the Western Boundary Undercurrent is clearly an adequate mechanism for the creation of the great sediment accumulation known as the Blake-Bahama Outer Ridge.

Having built this great spit-like ridge, the Western Boundary Undercurrent flows with renewed vigor from north to south along the precipitous Blake Escarpment. Tidal currents must vary to some degree with the slope of the sides of the confining basin, and this may perhaps explain the remarkable increase in current activity which is so dramatically revealed in photographs of the rocky escarpment (13.42).

The deep current which flows along the eastern flank of the Bahamas erodes the slopes as well as the basin far beyond, and has uncovered 100-million-year-old sediments. Where the current sweeps around the projecting ridge of San Salvador, the usual suite of large sediment dunes, outcropping sub-bottom layers, and visible scour and ripples offers clear evidence of continuing abyssal denudation. In the lee of San Salvador, another abyssal sediment spit is being built east of the Caicos Islands.

Appreciable sediment sources are remote from the Bahamas and as the current flows further to the southeast it sweeps clear the slopes of Silver Bank, Puerto Rico, and the Virgin Islands. It allows the deep-sea geologist to examine the bare rocky foundations of the Antilles Arc.

SMOOTHED SEASCAPE

The study of animal traces has enabled us to establish a norm which we have used to recognize anomalies in the visible seascape. The anomalies which generally appear as unusually smoothed and often lineated areas of the sea floor principally result from the activities of deep-sea currents (9.82). We have traced previously known, previously suspected, and unknown currents along the sea floor by recognizing patterns of current smoothing seen in underwater photographs. We have also noted that the shapes of many thick accumulations of sediment are in large measure controlled by the morphological activities of ocean circulation.

We have found a strong connection between large- and small-scale morphological forms. A visually undulating seascape is found to undulate at the larger scales observed on echograms. The surfaces of the vast abyssal plains are planar visually and topographically. We have further observed by examining the sediments and the sub-bottom layering recorded on echograms that contemporary processes have acted in the same way, in the same places, for millions of years; that, in fact, most of the major topographic features found on the smooth ocean floor have been created by processes still visibly active. This strong vindication of uniformitarianism reaffirms that the present truly is the key to the past.

In Chapters 8 and 9 we have examined the interplay of downslope and along-slope sediment transport in the shaping of the continental margin. Turbidity currents and contour currents,[27] acting through millions of years, have had a vast and over-riding effect on the smooth continental margins which predominantly occur in the Atlantic and Indian Oceans. Visual confirmation of the contemporary activity of the inferred process was amply provided by photographs and core sampling surveys. The net long-term result of these venerable processes was verified by seismic reflection and seismic refraction measurements which delineate the extent and characteristic internal stratification of the vast sediment bodies which border the continents and determine the shape of so many continental margins. In Chapter 11 we will turn to another type of continental margin where sediment deposition plays a barely visible role and where powerful forces acting from within the earth dominate the structure and scenery. In these broken and angular margins the yawning earth gapes, seemingly ready to receive its due measure of sediment but apparently waiting in vain and without reward. Later, we will see that the two basic types of continental margins so dramatically different in scenic and structural characteristics may form the earliest phases in the development of the world's most majestic scenery.

REFERENCES AND NOTES

1. A discussion of the circulation of the deep and bottom waters of the world ocean can be found in H. V. Sverdrup, M. W. Johnson, and R. H. Fleming. 1942. *The Oceans,* Prentice-Hall, Englewood Cliffs, N.J., Chap. 15, The water masses and currents in the oceans, pp. 605-761.

2. Sedimentary structures created by bottom currents are widely employed in the study of ancient sediments; for comprehensive works on current structures, see: P. E. Potter and F. P. Pettijohn. 1963. *Paleocurrents and Basin Analysis.* Academic Press, New York, 296 pp.; F. P. Pettijohn and P. E. Potter. 1964. *Atlas and Glossary of Primary Sedimentary Structures.* Springer-Verlag, New York, 370 pp.; and G. V. Middleton (Editor), 1965. Primary sedimentary structures and their hydrodynamic interpretation. *Soc. Econ. Paleon. and Mineralogists, Spec. Pub.* 12:265 pp.

3. J. R. L. Allen attempted to show a relation of wave length to depth of water (1963. Asymmetrical ripple marks and the origin of water-laid cosets of cross-strata. *Lpool. Manchr. Geol. J.,* 3:187-236), but deep-sea photographs (H. W. Menard. 1952. Deep ripple marks in the sea. *J. Sediment Petrol.,* 22:3-9) show that no such simple relationship exists.

4. F. Hjulstrom. 1935. Studies of the morphological activities of rivers illustrated by the River Fyris. *Bull. Geol. Inst. Univ. Upsala,* 25:221-527; F. A. Sundborg. 1956. The River Klaralven, a study on fluvial processes, *Geogr. Ann. Arg.,* 37:125-316; and H. Postma. 1967. Sediment transport and sedimentation in the estuarine environment. In: G. H. Lauff (Editor), *Estuaries.* American Assoc. Adv. of Sci., Washington, D.C., Publ. 83:158-179.

5. C. Nevin. 1946. Competency of moving water to transport debris. *Bull. Geol. Soc. Am.,* 57:651-674.

6. A. I. Rees. 1966. Some flume experiments with fine silt. *Sedimentology,* 6:209-239.

7. J. D. Isaacs, J. L. Reid, J. G. B. Schick, and R. A. Schwartzlose. 1966. Near-bottom currents measured in 4 kilometers depth off the Baja California coast. *Jour. Geophys. Res.,* 71:4297-4303; Ali A. Nowroozi, M. Ewing, J. E. Nafe, and M. Fliegel, 1968. Deep ocean current and its correlation with the ocean tide off the coast of northern California. *Jour. Geophys. Res.,* 73:1921-1931.

8. G. Wust. 1933. Das Bodenwasser und die Gliederung der Atlantischen Tiefsee, Die Stratosphare des Atlantischen Ozeans. Deut. Atlantische Expedition "METEOR," 1925-1927. *Wiss. Ergeb.,* 7(1):520 pp.; G. Wust. 1957. Quantitative untersuchungen zur Statik und Dynamik des Atlantischen Ozeans: Stromgeschwindigkeiten und Strommengen in den Tiefen des Atlantischen Ozeans. Deut. Atlantische Expedition "Meteor," 1925-1927. *Wiss. Ergeb.,* 6:261-420.

9. J. C. Swallow. 1962. Ocean circulation. *Pro. Roy. Soc. of London, Series A,* 265:325-328.

10. B. C. Heezen and C. D. Hollister. 1964. Deep-sea current evidence from abyssal sediments. *Mar. Geol.,* 1:141-174. Includes a table summarizing modern near-bottom deep-sea current measurements.

11. The reader is referred to the following texts which include discussions of deep ocean circulation: A. Defant. 1961. *Physical Oceanography,* Pergamon Press, New York, Chap. 17, Basic principles of the general oceanic circulation, 2:556-591; G. Neumann and W. J. Pierson, Jr. 1966. *Principles of Physical Oceanography,*

Prentice-Hall, Englewood Cliffs, N.J., Chap. 14, Circulation and stratification of the oceans, pp. 428-478; and G. Neumann. 1968. *Ocean Currents*. Elsevier, New York, 351 pp.

12. A. Agassiz. 1888. *Three Cruises of the BLAKE*. Riverside Press, Cambridge, 1:314 pp. 2:220 pp.; M. Weber. 1900. Die nederlandishe SIBOGA Expedition zur untersuchung der marien fauna und flora des Indischen Archipels., *Petermanns Geog. Mitt.*, 46:187.

13. M. F. Maury. 1855. *Physical Geography of the Sea*. Harper's, New York, 389 pp.

14. A general discussion of the Coriolis force can be found in: W. S. Von Arx. 1962. *An Introduction to Physical Oceanography*. Addison-Wesley, Reading, Mass., 422 pp.

15. The first photograph of current scour in depths over five kilometers was taken by D. M. Owen of the Woods Hole Oceanographic Institution in 1947. (D. M. Owen. 1949. ATLANTIS Cruise 151 to Mediterranean area, Scientific Report No. 2: Bottom Samples and Underwater Photography. *Woods Hole Oceanographic Institution Ref. No. 49-8*). This historic photograph showing scour moats around manganese nodules in the abyssal hills east of Bermuda was published by R. S. Dietz (1952. Geomorphic evolution of continental terrace, continental shelf and slope. *Bull. Am. Assoc. Petrol. Geologists*, 35:1802-1819).

16. J. Knauss. 1965. A technique for measuring deep ocean currents close to the bottom with an unattached current meter and some preliminary results. *J. Mar. Res.*, 23:237-245.

17. G. Schott. 1928. Die Wasserbewegungen im Gebiete der Gibraltarstrasse. *Conseil Perm. Internat. p. l'explor. de la mer., Jour. der Conseil.*, 3:139-175.

18. G. Wust. 1955. Stromgeschwindigkeiten im Tiefen-und Bodenwasser des Atlantischen Ozeans. *Deep-Sea Res.*, 3(Suppl.):373-397; F. C. Fuglister. 1960. *Atlantic Ocean Atlas of Temperature and Salinity Profiles and Data from the International Geophysical Year of 1957-1958. Volume I*. Woods Hole Oceanographic Institution, Woods Hole, Mass., 208 pp.

19. J. H. Steele, J. R. Barrett, and L. V. Worthington. 1962. Deep currents south of Iceland. *Deep-Sea Res.*, 9:465-474.

20. L. V. Worthington and G. H. Volkmann. 1965. The volume transport of the Norwegian Sea overflow water in the North Atlantic. *Deep-Sea Res.*, 12:667-676; G. Deitrich. 1957. Schichtung und Zirkulation der Irminger-See im Juni 1955. *Ber. It. Wiss. Kamm. Meeresforsch.*, 14:255-312.

21. J. C. Swallow and L. V. Worthington. 1969. Deep currents in the Labrador Sea. *Deep-Sea Res.*, 16:77-84.

22. Brick-red to rose-gray colored fine-grained sediment from the continental margin of the western North Atlantic were thought to inherit their peculiar color from nearby continental sources (D. B. Ericson, M. Ewing, G. Wollin, and B. C. Heezen. 1961. Atlantic deep-sea sediment cores. *Bull. Geol. Soc. Amer.*, 72:193-286). Subsequently, brick-red Pleistocene tills were reported from the Laurentian Channel (B. C. Heezen and C. L. Drake. 1964. Grand Banks slump. *Am. Assoc. Petrol. Geolog.*, 48:221-233.; and J. R. Conolly, H. D. Needham, and B. C. Heezen. 1969. Late Pleistocene and Holocene sedimentation in the Laurentian Channel, *J. Geol.*, 7:131-47). The tills were thought to represent glacial erosion of the red upper Paleozoic red-beds of New Brunswick and Nova Scotia. It was later

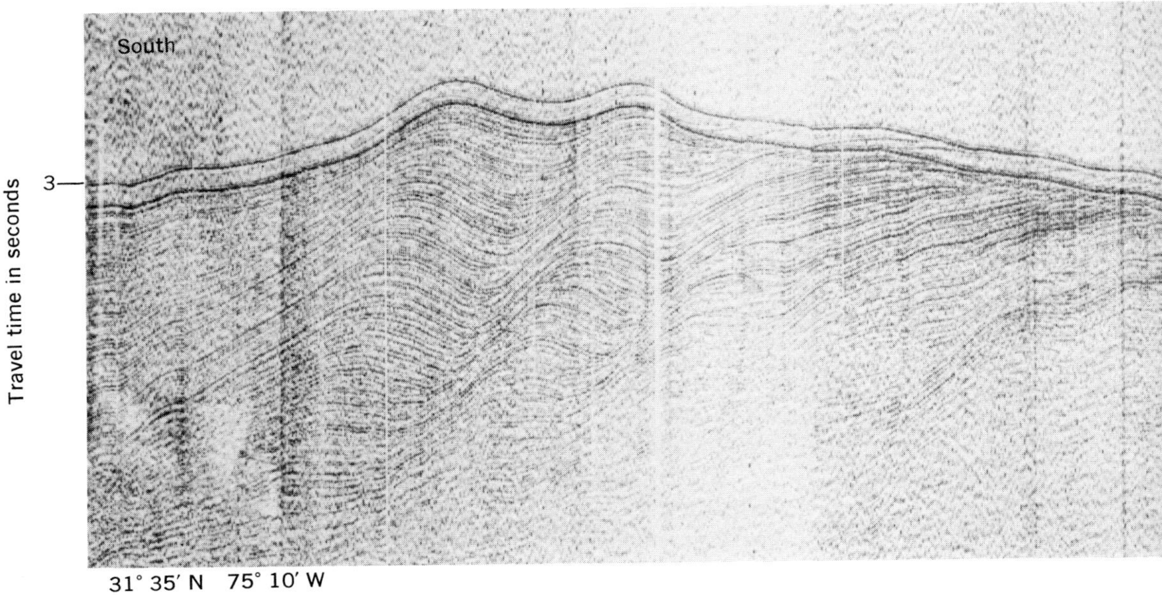

suggested by Needham, that the red deep-sea sediment found in the continental margin to the south came from this region. The Western Boundary Undercurrent was found to be the process transporting this distinctive red material parallel to bathymetric contours from the continental margin off Nova Scotia to the Bahamas. Recent work on pollen and spores has provided further confirmation (H. D. Needham, D. Habib, and B. C. Heezen. 1969. Upper Carbonniferous palynomorphs as a tracer of red sediment dispersal patterns in the northwest Atlantic. *J. Geol.,* 77:113-120).

23. H. Stommel. 1965. *The Gulf Stream: A Physical and Dynamical Description* (2nd ed.)., Univ. of California Press, Berkeley, 248 pp.

24. B. C. Heezen, C. D. Hollister, and W. F. Ruddiman. 1966. Shaping of the continental rise by geostrophic contour currents. *Science,* 151:502-508.

25. M. Ewing and E. M. Thorndike. 1965. Suspended matter in deep ocean water. *Science,* 147:1291-1294.

26. J. C. Swallow and L. V. Worthington. 1961. An observation of a deep countercurrent in the western North Atlantic. *Deep-Sea Res.,* 8:1-19.

27. The deposits of contour currents and turbidity currents (see Chapter 8) have often been confused. The ideal turbidity current deposit (*turbidite*) is a relatively thick bed, centimeters to meters thick, which grades in particle size from coarse at the base to finer toward the top. Bottom contact is sharp and the top diffuse. Turbidite sand is generally dirty with at least 10 per cent mud occupying the spaces between sand grains. The perfect deposit of the contour current (*contourite*) is a thin, millimeters to centimeters thick, bed of clean, cross-bedded silt. Both upper and lower contacts are sharp and there is little mud between the grains. Since contourites are often derived from turbidites, the two ideal extremes are separated by a complete transitional sequence.

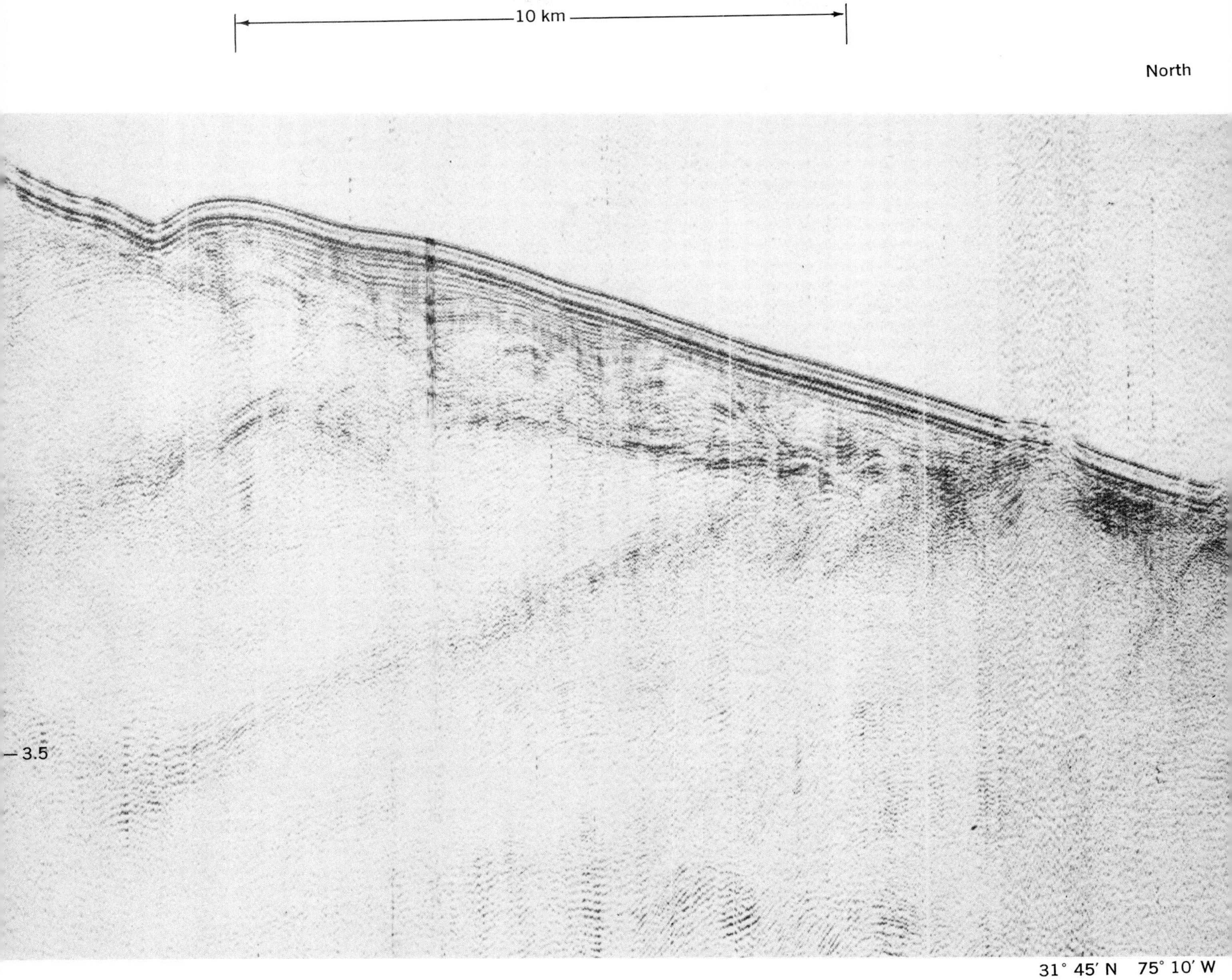

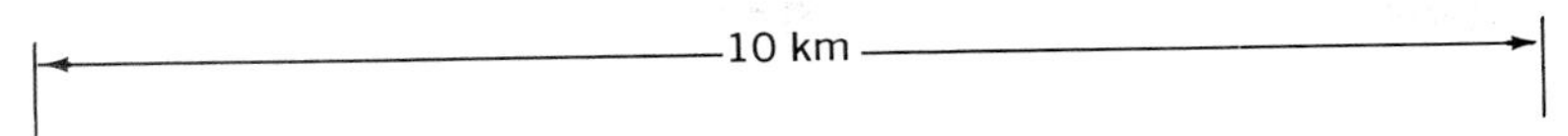

9.83 Bottom currents have built this migratory sediment drift (Blake-Bahama Outer Ridge) by preferentially eroding (right) and depositing (left) fine muds.

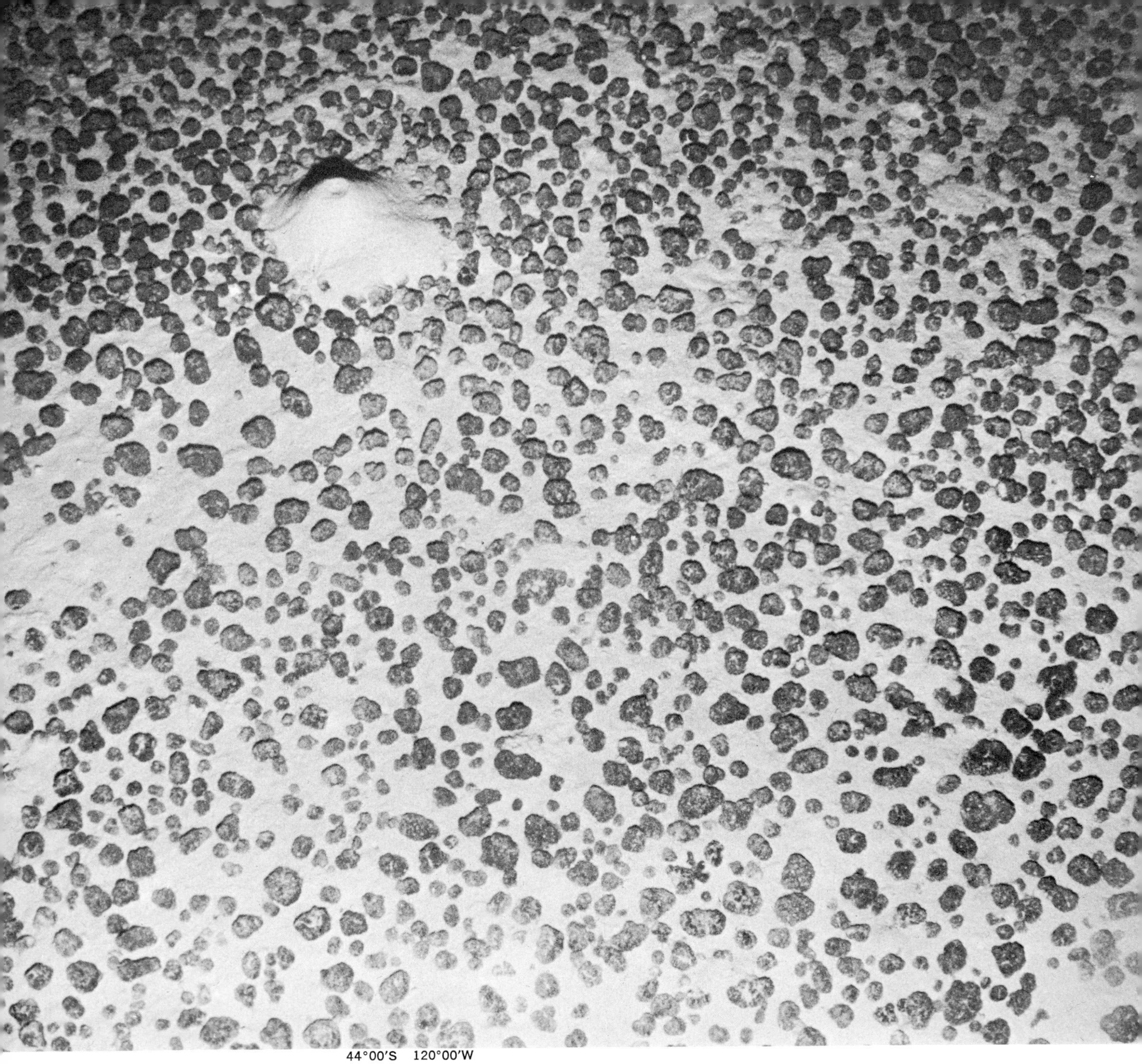

44°00′S 120°00′W

10.1 Small potatoes. Irregular potato-shaped nodules litter the flank of the Mid-Oceanic Ridge of the South Pacific. Sediment erupted from the animal volcano has swept toward the lower left and buried the smaller potatoes. On the right is an eroded stump of a former animal volcano, 4034 m, southwest Pacific.

10
Ion by Ion

After the natal season of the world,
The birthday of the sea and lands
and the uprising of the sun,
Many atoms have been added from without . . .
LUCRETIUS

While clay and ooze fall, like gentle snow, and rafted rocks, wrecks, and other heavy debris plummet to the sea floor, manganese, iron, cobalt, nickel, and copper invisibly migrate ion by ion to the deepest parts of the ocean (10.1). The rocks and other debris which reach the floor slowly become plated with a thin film of manganese oxide, assuming at first a reddish patina and later a dark earthy brown or black color as the coating gradually grows in thickness. Manganese nodules and coatings are generally lustrous and virtually jet black when recovered from the sea floor but upon drying they become brown in color and more earthy.

Ice-rafted debris, pumice, the earbones of whales, the teeth of sharks, and other nearly indestructible projectiles become the nuclei of the golf-ball to grapefruit-size manganese nodules which litter much of the deep-sea floor. It is estimated that about two billion metric tons of manganese nodules lie on the floor of the world ocean, and it is clear that these nodules comprise the largest mineral deposit on this planet.[1]

In detail, manganese nodules consist of alternate atomic layers of manganese oxide and iron hydroxide. In-between layers incorporate an important group of metallic ions such as nickel, copper, cobalt, and zinc. The growth of nodules is one of the slowest chemical reactions in nature, rates of accumulations being atomic layers per day, yet these mineral gardens of the abyss are vast, and despite their exceedingly slow rate of accumulation, they appear to be growing faster than we could ever expect to mine them.

10.2 Each paper-thin lamina took hundreds of thousands of years to grow. A nucleus of stone or bone or tooth or clay forms the center of each nodule.

Any hard object can serve as nucleus for a nodule. In the middle latitudes, tephra such as pumice and glassy volcanic bombs, in each case deeply altered, are the most common nuclei (10.2). Sharks' teeth (10.3) and teeth of other fish, otoliths, bones of whales and silicious and calcareous sponges may also serve. In high latitudes, ice-rafted rocks are by far the most common nuclei. Virtually all nodules obtained from the well-explored Scotia Sea and Bellingshausen Sea were found to have centers consisting of hard, glacially rafted rocks. In many cases, however, no identifiable nucleus is found, and microscopic grains of sediment, forminifera, or some now undetectable particle may have served. The accumulation of manganese on linear objects sometimes results in branching, stick-like forms with a central axis (10.4).

The composition of the manganese nodules is apparently unaffected by the chemical nature of the nucleus, and such centers of accumulation may consist of carbonate, phosphate, zeolite, clay, or various forms of silica. Manganese coatings also form on all hard rock surfaces, regardless of composition, on the deep-sea floor.

CANNON BALLS

There can never be any doubt as to the identification of the large cannon ball nodules which lie in evenly distributed fields; each nodule alike in shape and size (10.10, 10.5). In the case of these nearly perfectly symmetrical concretions, the shape of the nucleus is no longer preserved in

10.3 Sharks' teeth commonly form a nucleus for growth of manganese.

the external form. The upper surfaces—almost always sediment-free—often are covered by frail, hair-like growths which are not usually seen on dredged specimens (10.6 L, C).

Only a very small area of the under side of the nodule touches the soft underlying abyssal clay. They are generally not submerged in the sediment, but are either surrounded by scour moats or lie like golf balls on a green. In areas of the densest concentration they present the appearance of being carefully arranged as on a fruit-stand; however, concentrations are quite variable and, in a sequence of pictures over a limited area, densities can vary from one hundred per square meter to none at all.

POTATOES AND GRAPES

The small nodules often reveal more of the shape of the nucleus which constitutes a comparatively large proportion of the total volume. However, the potato shape is also found in relatively large nodules. Occasionally lobate nodules resemble a bunch of grapes (10.7, 10.8). Although the potatoes reach approximately the same size as the cannon

10.4 Manganese encrusts stick-like objects. 31°42′N 68°07′W, 5200 m.

balls, they are on the whole much smaller and tend to be much more irregular in shape (10.9). It is not always possible to identify surely the smallest potatoes visible in photographs (10.1). Since every hard ob- 58°11′S 79°11 ject on the sea floor eventually acquires a manganese coat, it is not possible accurately to estimate what proportion of the small fragments are made of manganese. The small potatoes are generally most abundant in the highest latitudes of ice-rafting and in the vicinity of current-scoured outcrops which provide a nearby source of angular fragments (10.11-10.13). 57°59′S 70°4

SLABS

Slabs of volcanic ash or consolidated sediments encrusted with ferromanganese oxides are commonly dredged from and photographed on the abyssal floor (10.14, 10.15).[2] Although the total accumulation on the upper surface of the slab is much greater, an accumulation on the underside, sometimes exceeding one-tenth of the growth on the upper surface, is often seen. The nucleus of a slab constitutes a much higher proportion of the total volume than in the case of the more symmetrical nodules (10.16).

10.5 Cannon-ball nodules form beneath the swift Antarctic Circumpolar Current. This unremitting current neither erodes nor allows sediments to bury the nodules in this area. Further to the west nodules become smaller and irregular, to the east currents erode the bottom U, L, 4705 m, 3924 m, eastern side Bellingshausen Basin, near entrance to Drake Passage.

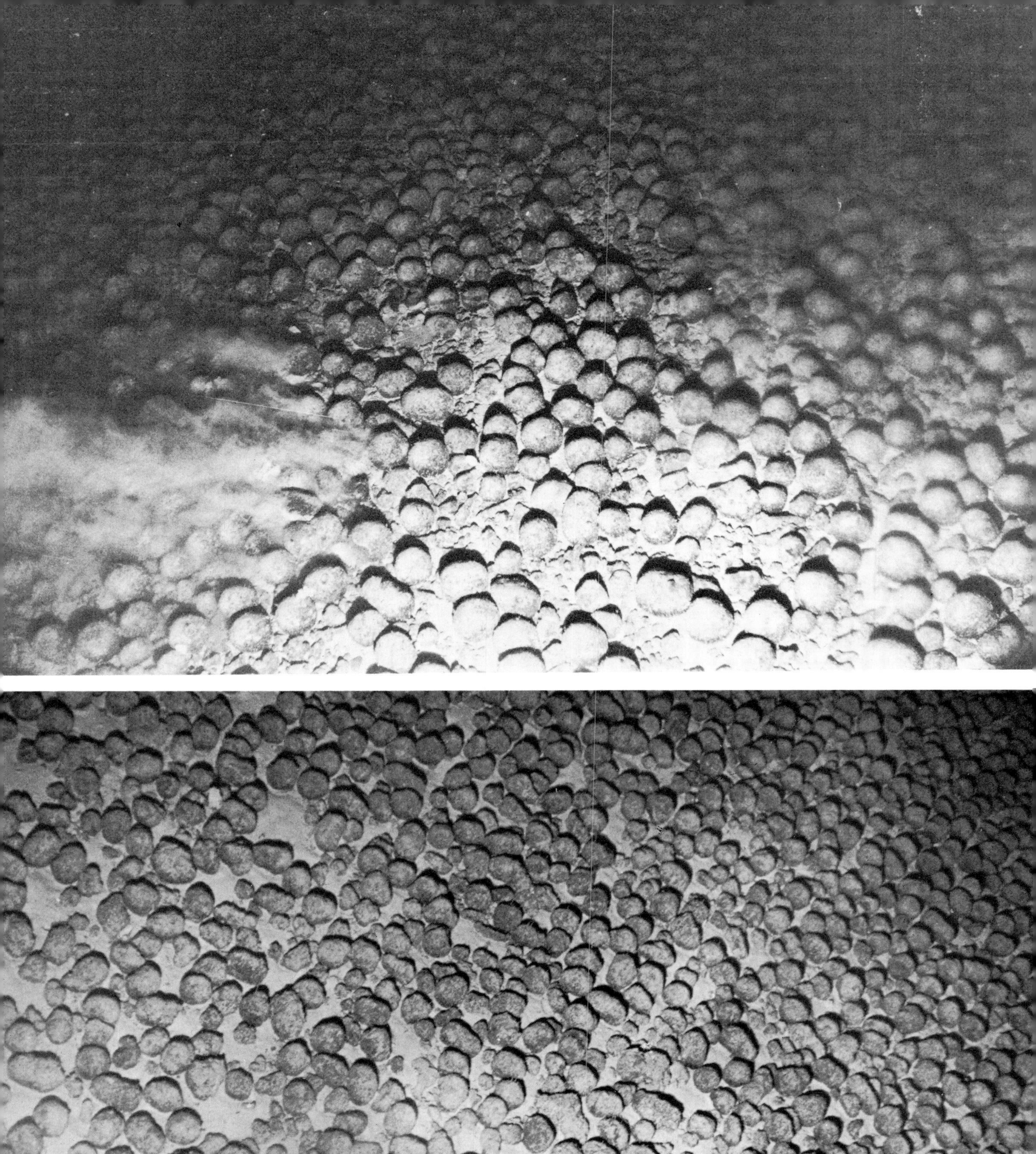

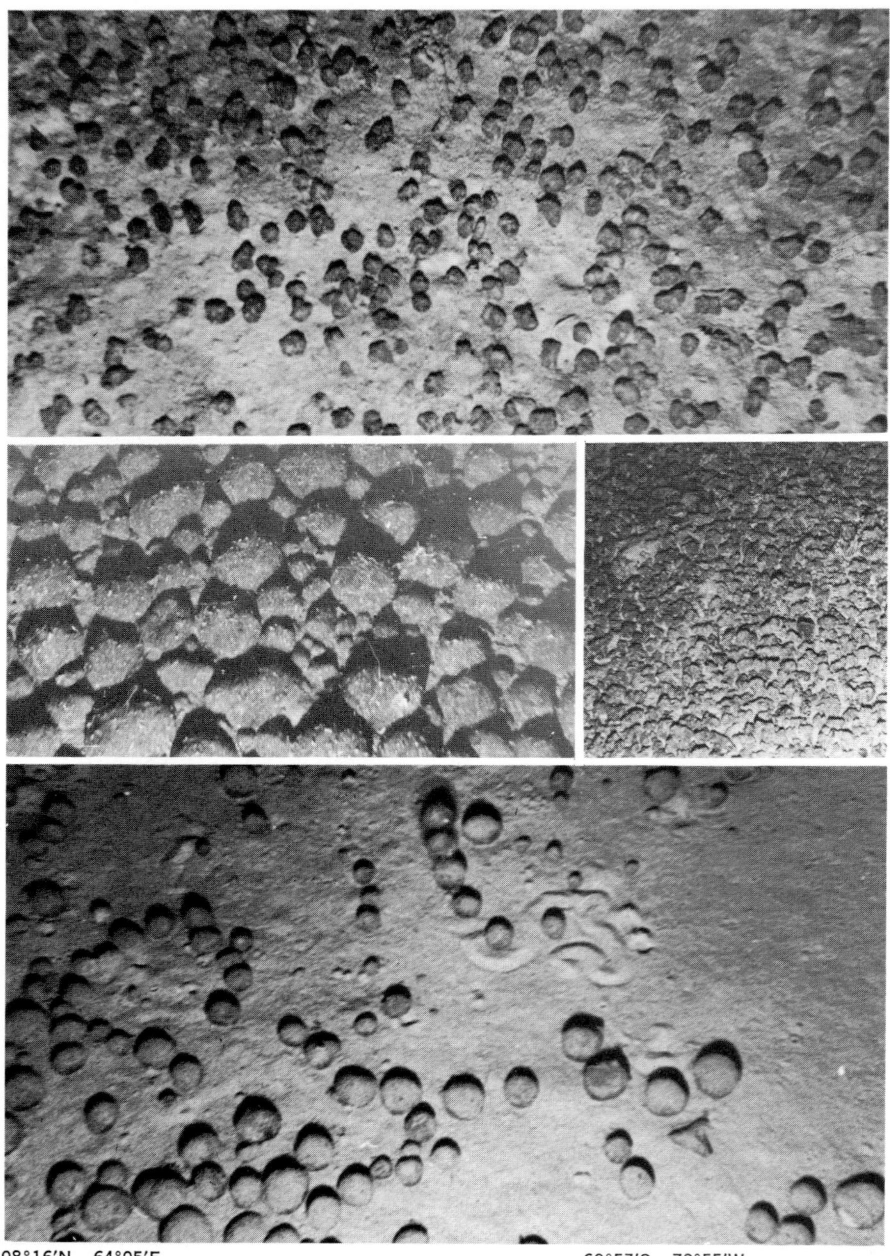

08°16′N 64°05′E
12°27′S 159°23′W
29°17′N 57°23′W
62°57′S 78°55′W

10.6 Cannon balls and potatoes. Nodules range from spherical to irregular and may be freely scattered or densely packed. U, 4080 m, abyssal hills east of the Carlsberg Ridge, Indian Ocean. LC, 4986 m, east of Manihiki Plateau, equatorial Pacific. RC, 4304 m, Pacific continental rise, Antarctic Peninsula. L, a shark's tooth lies in lower right-hand corner of photograph, 5830 m, abyssal hills southeast of Bermuda Rise.

58°11′S 79°11′W
31°03′N 78°23′W
12°43′S 89°08′W

10.7 Grapes and cannon balls. Nodules occasionally have irregular knobby outline sometimes resembling bunches of grapes. UL, 4559 m, outer ridge, southern Peru-Chile Trench. UR, 4202 m, east equatorial Pacific. L, 808 m, Blake Plateau.

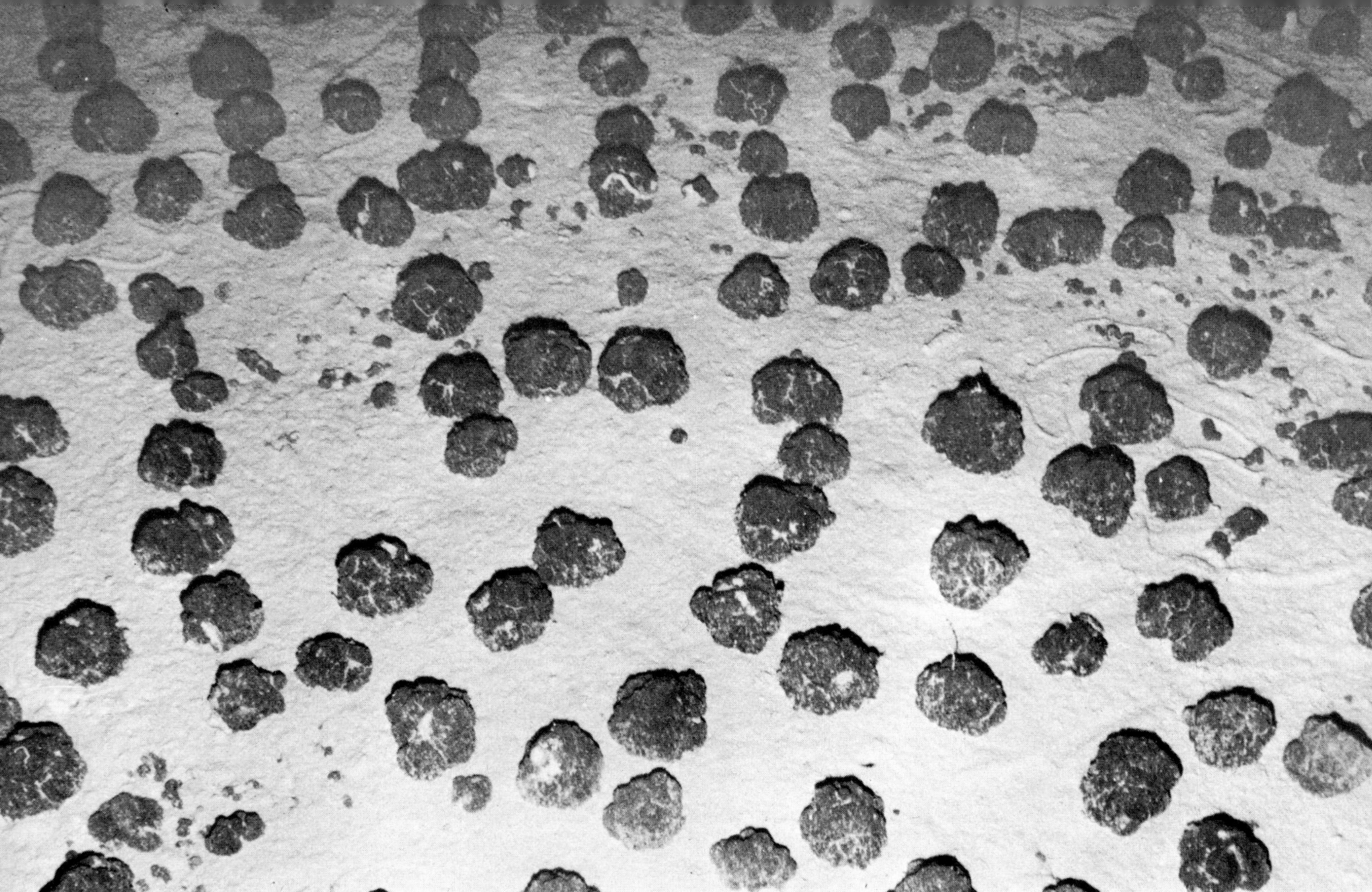

44°59′S 145°20′W

10.8 A field of grape nodules in mid-Pacific. Small hair-like organisms are often attached to irregular nodules, 5145 m, abyssal Pacific east of New Zealand.

PAINTED AND PLASTERED

Manganese films lightly coat rocks rafted by Pleistocene icebergs into the temperate Atlantic. A thicker manganese crust plasters Mesozoic lava-flows exposed on abyssal escarpments and a half-inch crust of manganese covers Miocene marls on the Blake Plateau. Manganese, in fact, paints—and with time, plasters—every sediment-free surface of the abyss (10.17, 10.18). In areas of the very strongest currents manganese growth appears to be inhibited. For example, Lower Cretaceous limestones recovered from the Blake Escarpment in 5000 meters beneath a swift current have a layer of manganese much thinner than that covering the much younger Pliocene and Miocene sediments on the Plateau.

10.9 Potatoes. Attached organisms lean in the gentle bottom current, (glass sponge UL and tunicate, UR), UL, UR, 5120 m, Bellingshausen Basin. LL, 4067 m, Mid-Oceanic Ridge, South Pacific. LR, 4832 m, Bellingshausen Basin. ▷

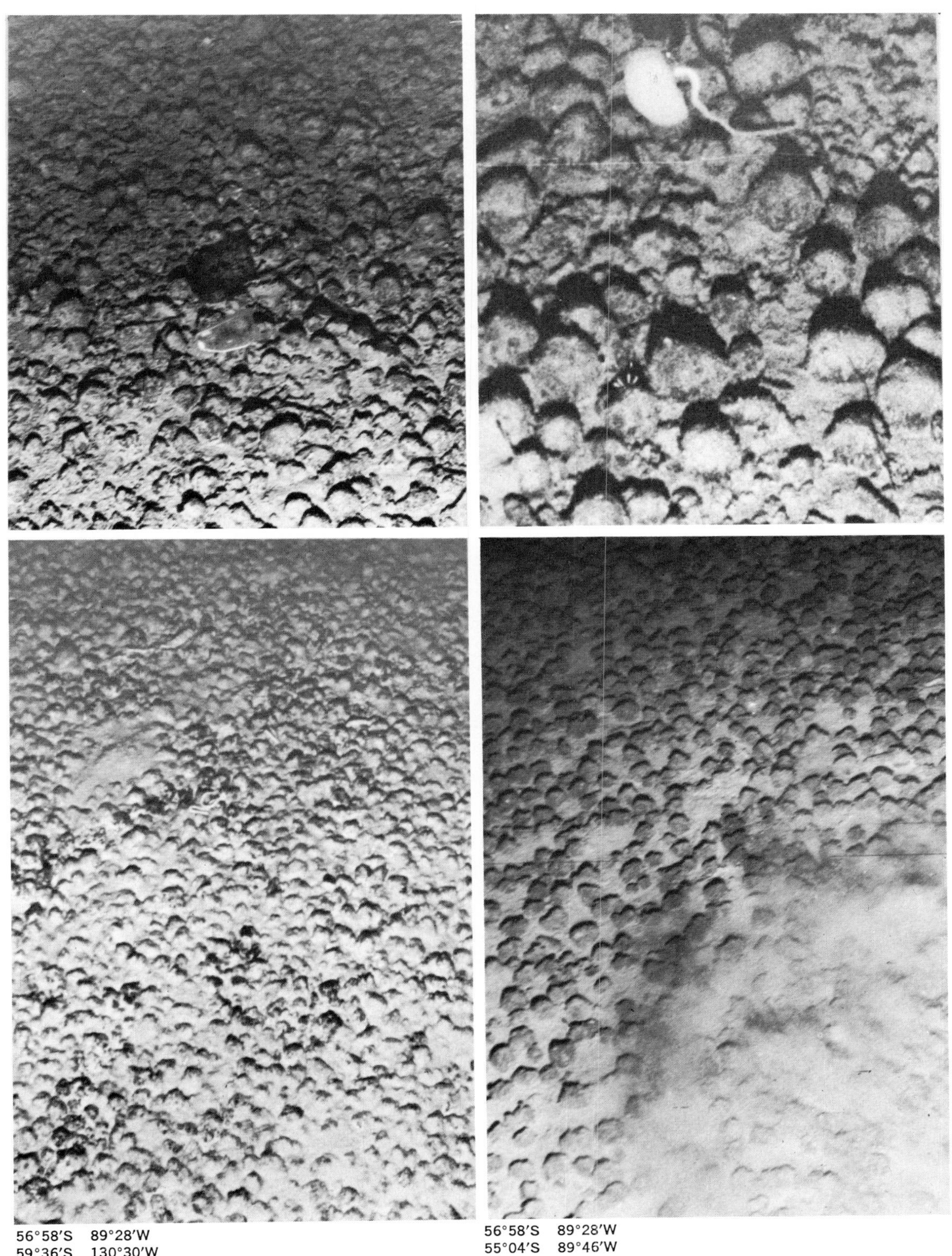

56°58′S 89°28′W
59°36′S 130°30′W

56°58′S 89°28′W
55°04′S 89°46′W

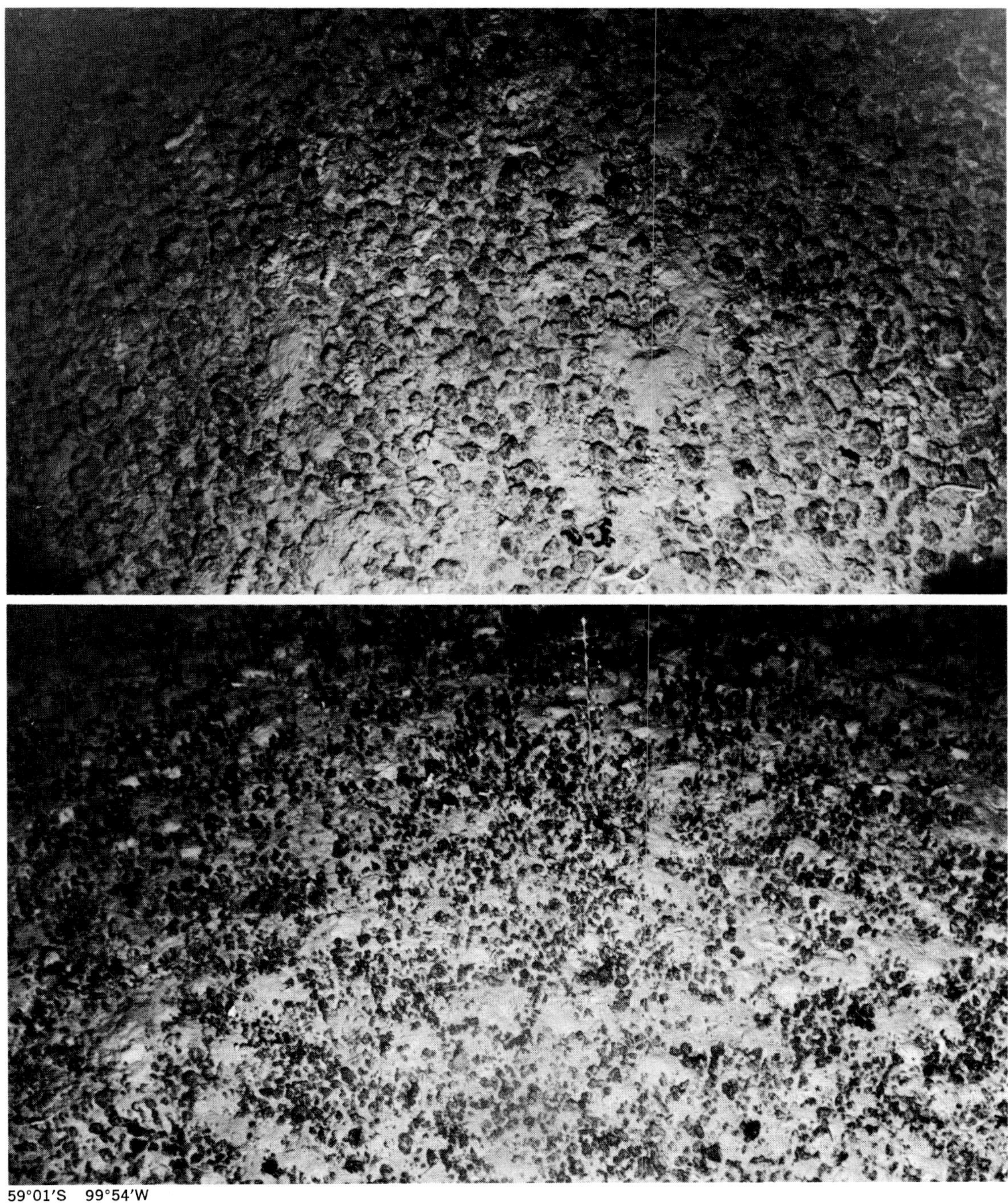

59°01′S 99°54′W
59°07′S 105°03′W

10.11 Small potatoes beneath Antarctic Circumpolar Current. Sediment is sifting through the nodule field, alternately burying and uncovering the nodules. Note antennae-like sponge (*Cladorhiza*) in lower photograph. U, L, 5072 m, 3904 m, Bellingshausen Basin.

43°01′S 139°37′W
42°31′S 145°06′W

10.10 Vast fields of cannon-ball nodules cover much of the abyssal Pacific. U, 5292 m, L, 5417, southwest Pacific.

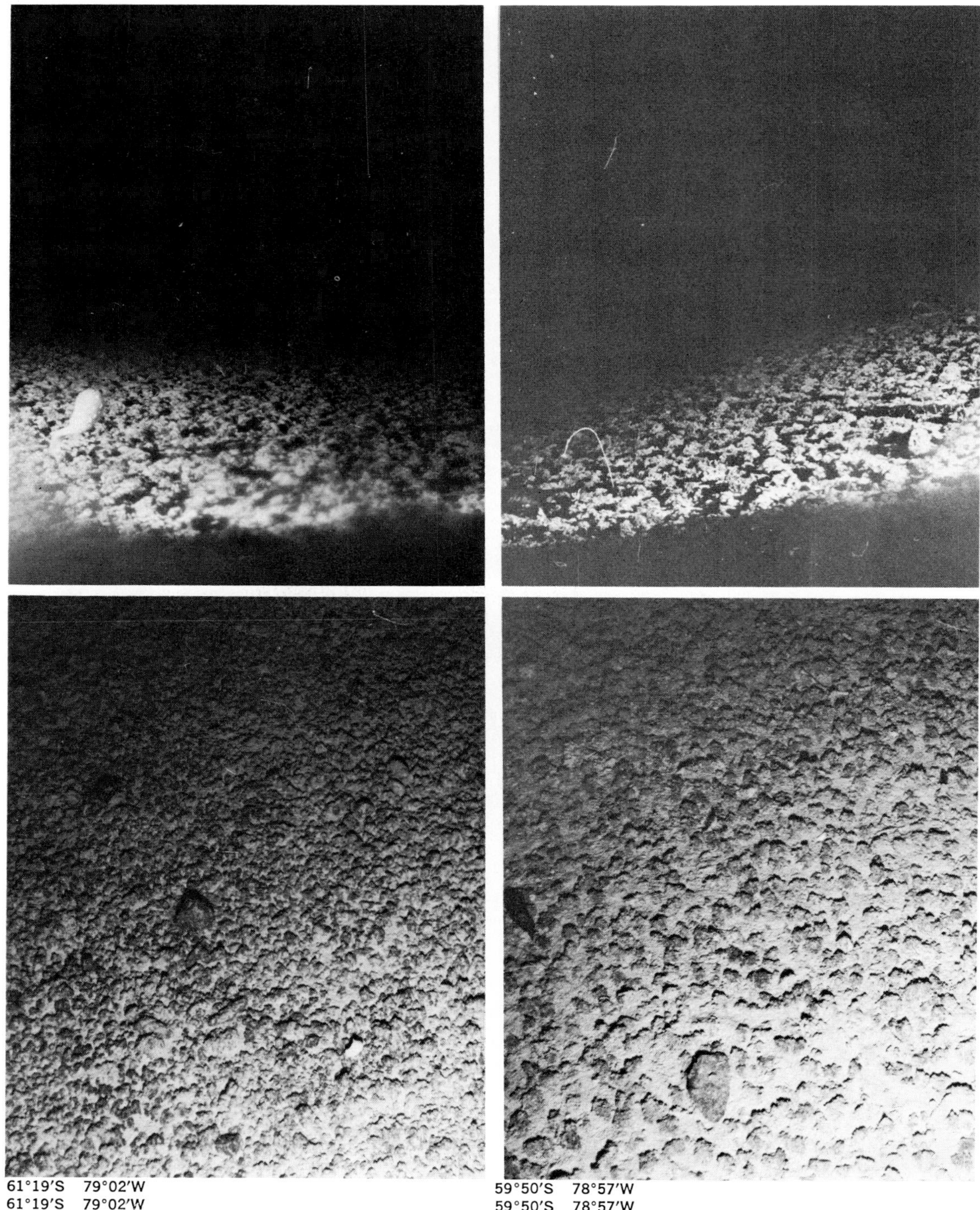

61°19′S 79°02′W
61°19′S 79°02′W

59°50′S 78°57′W
59°50′S 78°57′W

10.12 Potato nodules and rafted rocks in the Bellingshausen Sea. Profile views (upper) reveal abundant stalked organisms leaning in a gentle bottom current. UL, LL, 4646 m; UR, LR, 4871 m, Pacific continental rise, Antarctic Peninsula.

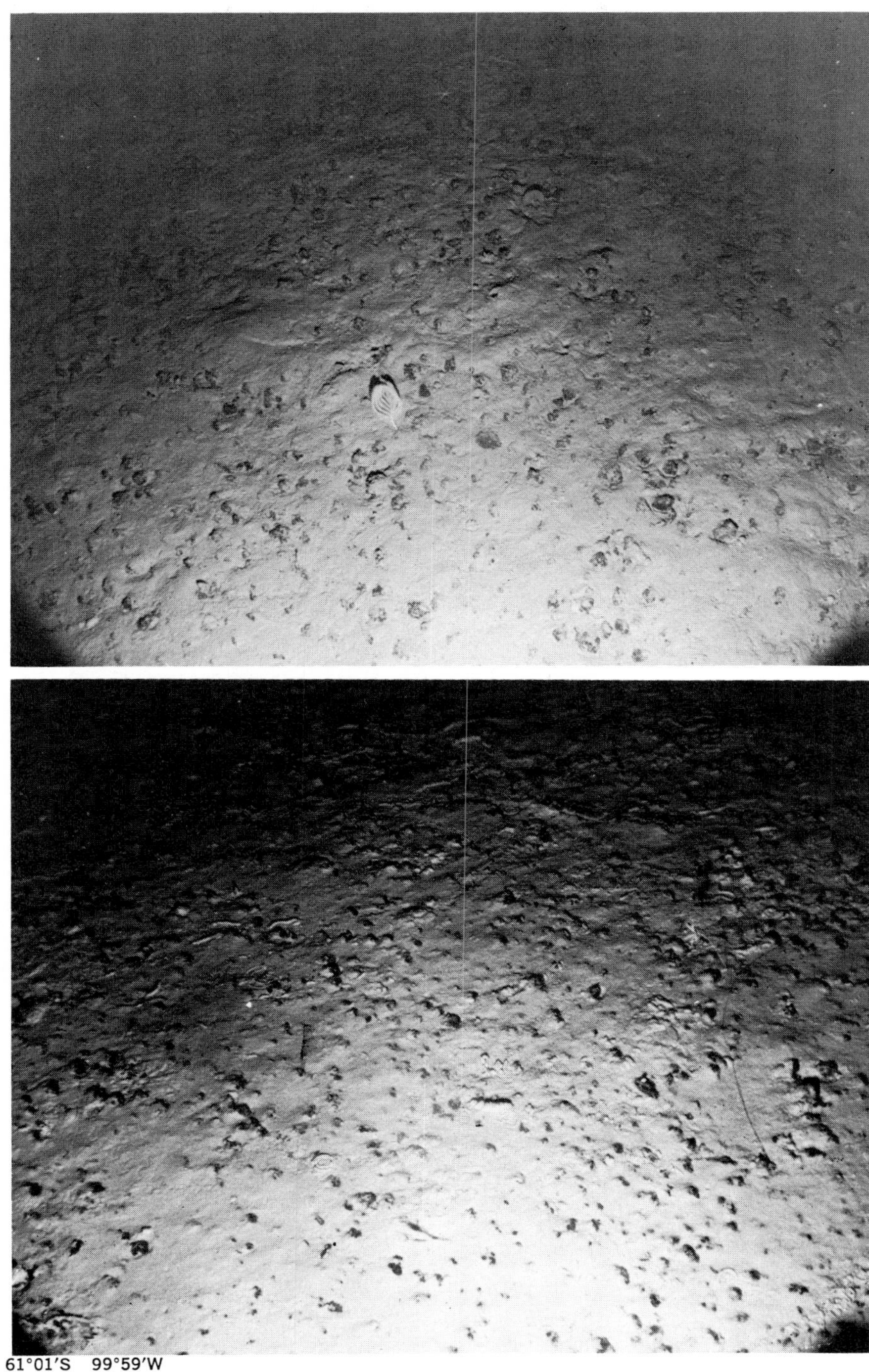

61°01′S 99°59′W
60°07′S 128°54′W

10.13 Vigorous bottom currents build sediment tails behind potato nodules. U, note the fan-like coral, 4966 m, Bellingshausen Basin. L, 4336 m, flank of Mid-Oceanic Ridge, South Pacific.

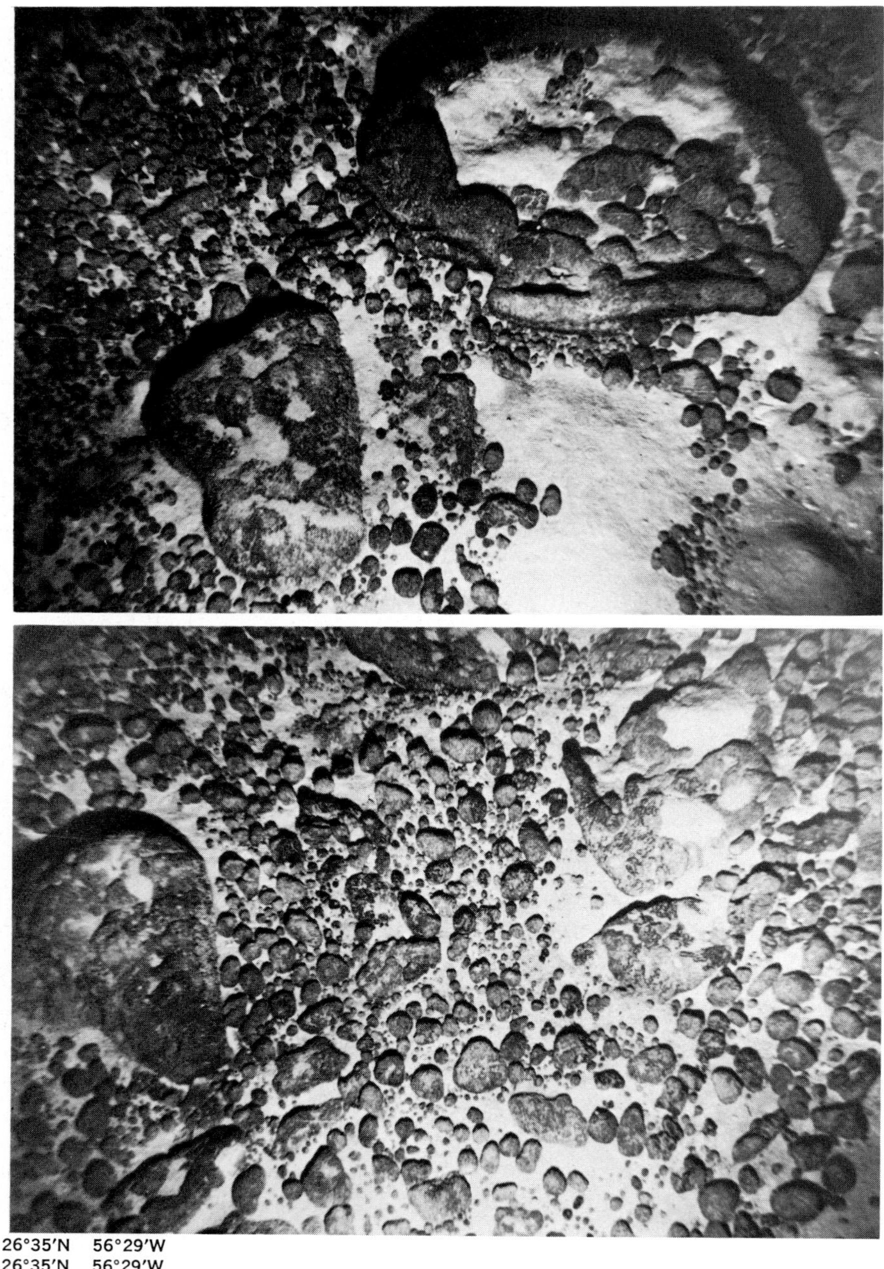

10.14 Slabs beneath the Antarctic Bottom Current. Manganese crusts form on irregular pieces of abyssal clay, volcanic ash, or hard rock surfaces. Slabs, weighing 15 to 20 kilograms, recovered near the location of these photographs were encrusted with two to three centimeters of manganese. U, L, 4700 m, abyssal hills east of the Bermuda Rise.

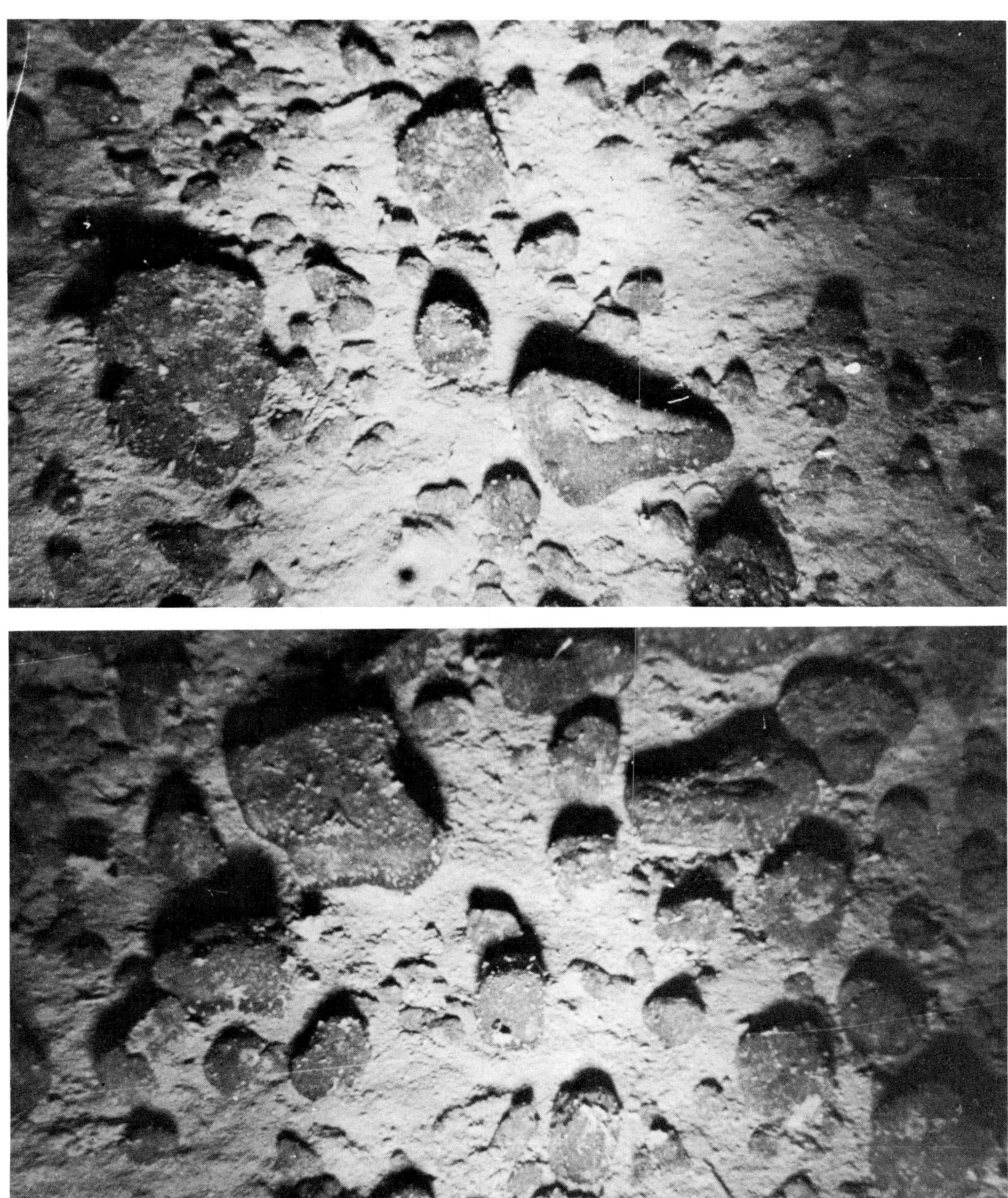

17°38′N 153°54′E
17°38′N 153°54′E

10.15 Lumps from the abyssal Pacific. Volcanic debris may form the nucleus of these broken slabs of manganese. U, L, 5718 m, east of the Mariana Trench, western North Pacific.

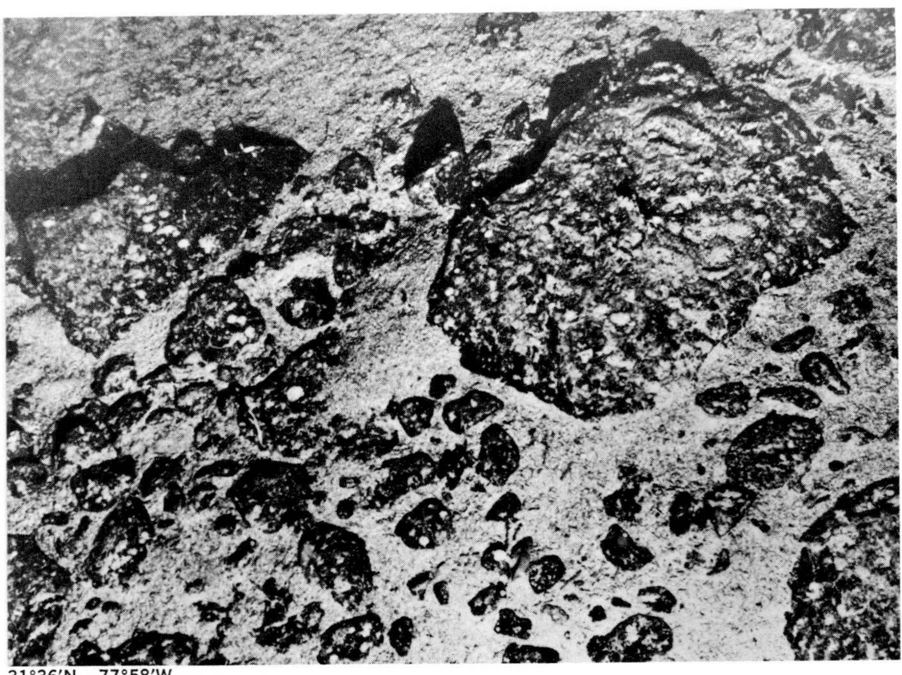

10.16 Slabs from the Blake Plateau. The Gulf Stream which reaches the bottom on the Blake Plateau supplies vast quantities of metallic ions to the growing mineral gardens of manganese nodules, slabs, and pavement, 666 m, eastern edge of Blake Plateau.

ION BY ION

Estimates of the rate of accumulation of manganese can be made by investigating the distribution of radium or thorium in the outermost concentric layers of nodules. Early work based on radium established that the rates of accumulation of nodules were less than the rates of accumulation of the sediments on which the nodules lay. Recent investigations indicate that the rate of growth of manganese nodules is two to four millimeters per million years; that is, one-thousandth of the average rate of accumulation of abyssal clay, one millimeter per thousand years. Further studies of the manganese content of abyssal clay indicates that the annual accumulation per unit area of sea floor is approximately the same in the sediments as in the nodules. Some geochemists have concluded that the rate of accumulation of manganese for a given area of the sea floor is constant in time and space.[3] However, applying this argument to sediments deposited in the rapidly accumulating Blake-Bahama Outer Ridge sediment drift, they arrived at rates of accumulation ten times too small as compared with those determined paleontologically.

57°59′S 120°03′W
58°54′S 95°08′W

10.17 Thin films of manganese lightly paint newly exposed rock surfaces on current-swept fracture zones and ridges. U, note suspended sediment carried by bottom currents. U, 4825 m, L, 3981 m, Eltanin Fracture Zone, South Pacific.

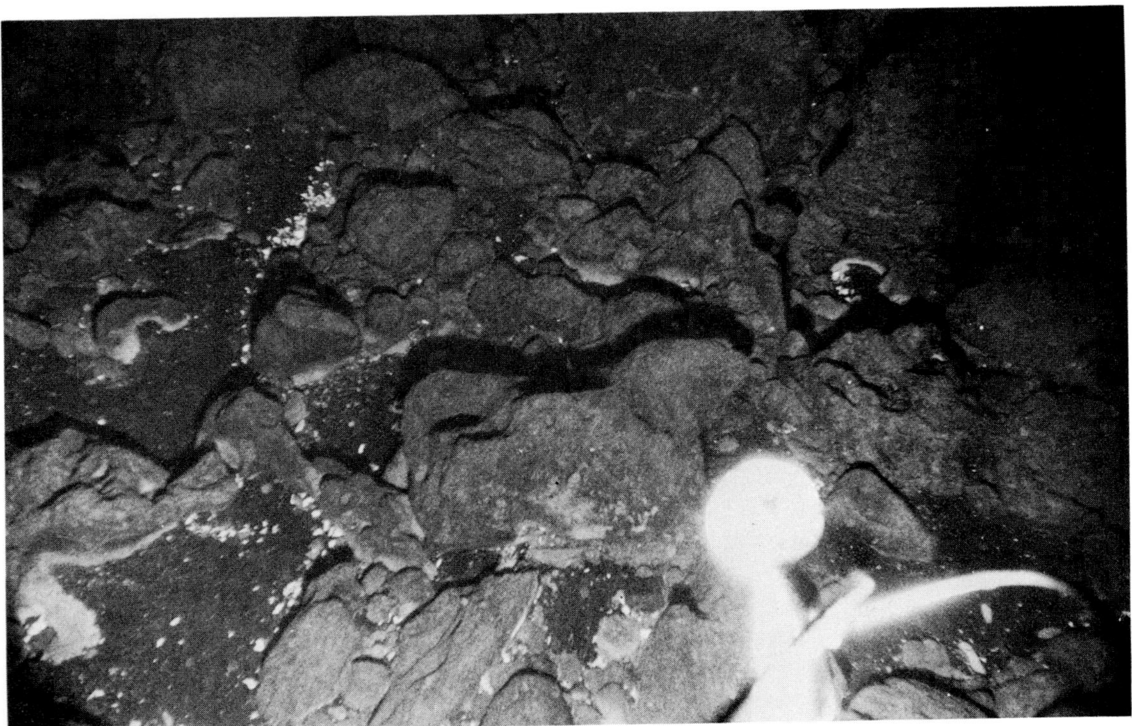

10.18 A thin veneer of manganese covers current abraded sandstone in the Luzon Strait. Coarse black sand has abraded the manganese coating at the edge of pockets in the rock, 2380 m, Luzon Straits, northeast of Calayan Bank.

The rate of accumulation of manganese may be a function of the concentration of manganese in the waters and the total quantity of water passing around the growing nodule. Although manganese concentrations in sea water appear to be fairly constant in mid-ocean, there may be significant local variations in the vicinity of the continental sources.

The presence of Miocene sharks' teeth, both within nodules and as uncoated fossils associated with the nodules, have long suggested that these objects remain on the sea floor for long periods of time. As has already been pointed out, sediment is not collecting on top of the nodules, nor is it seen drifted or banked against them. Thus they must be as mobile as the sediment and not constitute permanent obstructions to current flow. On the continental rise, drifts and streamers of sediment are formed behind mounds as large as a normal nodule; but such features are not found behind nodules lying on the deep-sea floor.

ROLL ON

Thus, the mineral gardens reveal a dramatic exception to the vast, even veil of sediment which was previously supposed to cover the entire abyss.

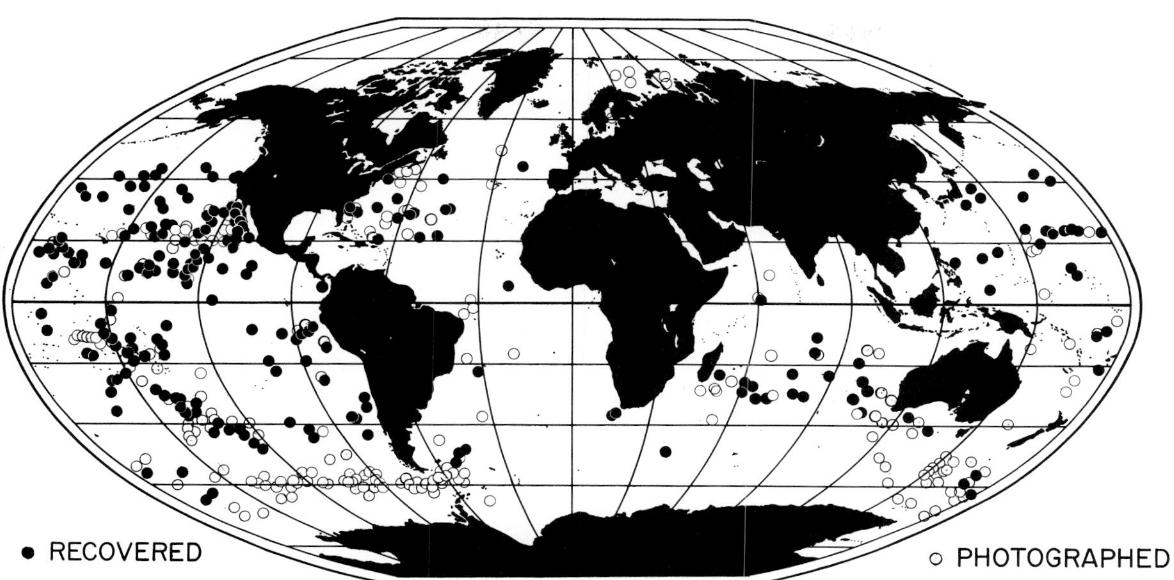

10.19 Distribution of manganese nodules from photographs and dredge hauls.

The richest mineral gardens are not found on the bold, current-swept peaks, but in the deepest abyssal hills of the ocean basins where one might have expected a thin, but continuous, blanket of slowly accumulating red oxidizing clay. The very existence of the mineral gardens implies attenuation of sedimentation, but peculiarities of the nodules themselves tell us that mere nondeposition is not enough. The nodules are round and grow much more slowly than the clay on which they lie. The larger nodules are, with a few exceptions, nearly perfectly concentric. In order to create the round shapes, the nodules must be frequently rolled over so as to allow uniform accumulation of a new layer. The nearly continuous concentric layers indicate that such rolling over occurs frequently in comparison with the rate of growth of individual layers.

The growth of the nodules requires a continually replenished source of manganese and iron, probably provided by the same currents which roll them about. It seems certain that fluctuations in the current would cause fluctuations in the rate of growth, since it would seem likely that the nodules are completely dependent on the currents for the supply of manganese and iron.

Although manganese accumulates in all depths of water and paints the rocks exposed on seamounts and escarpments, the vast fields of symmetrical nodules lie far from land within the greatest depths of the ocean, beneath the least productive surface waters and within the coldest bottom waters (10.19). The surface productivity of the oceans is exceedingly high in the cold waters beyond the polar fronts, and it is relatively high within the equatorial belt of upwelling. Pelagic deposition is high in such productive areas, and manganese fields are rarely observed in such areas even in the greatest depths. Nor are nodules usually seen in the rapidly accumulating sediment drifts which parallel the continents. In mid-ocean, between the equator and the polar front, pelagic and terrigenous debris accumulates exceedingly slowly; here, beneath the cold, polar-derived bottom waters the most extensive fields of nodules are seen.

The same pattern of circulation which we found to be so important in understanding the distribution of lineations and scour and in the shaping of the sediment bodies is found to be the best clue to the distribution of manganese nodules. The one-and-a-half degree Centigrade isotherm which can be taken as a rough measure of the limit of spreading of the Antarctic Bottom Water circumscribes virtually all the extensive manganese nodule fields of the deep-sea floor.

The principal source of the manganese contained in the nodules has been alternately attributed by various workers to (1) the decomposition of sea-floor igneous outcrops and debris; (2) submarine volcanic emanations; and (3) the manganese carried by streams into the sea. The patterns of distribution of manganese nodule fields might reveal a correlation with the outcrops or active vulcanism if the first two sources were exceptionally important. Active vulcanism appears to be concentrated either in the island arcs on the margins of the oceans, or along the Mid-Oceanic Ridge, yet the principal distribution of manganese nodules lies near the axis of maximum depth of the ocean basin. These areas have been inactive, both tectonically and volcanically, for at least fifty million years. Although outcrops do occur in the abyssal hills, a thin veneer of sediment generally protects the underlying igneous rocks from contact with sea water. It might be argued, that acidic emanations are spread from volcanic sources throughout the abyss in a thin layer of bottom water. However, the association of hot, volcanic emanations and the coldest water of the ocean somehow seems incongruous. Whatever the primary source of manganese, its transportation is effected principally by the thermohaline circulation of the deep and bottom waters of the oceans.

REFERENCES AND NOTES

1. Exploration of the shallow continental shelves for manganese nodules and other mineral deposits has accelerated during the last decade. In the deep sea, however, most efforts have yet to extend much beyond the planning stage. Information con-

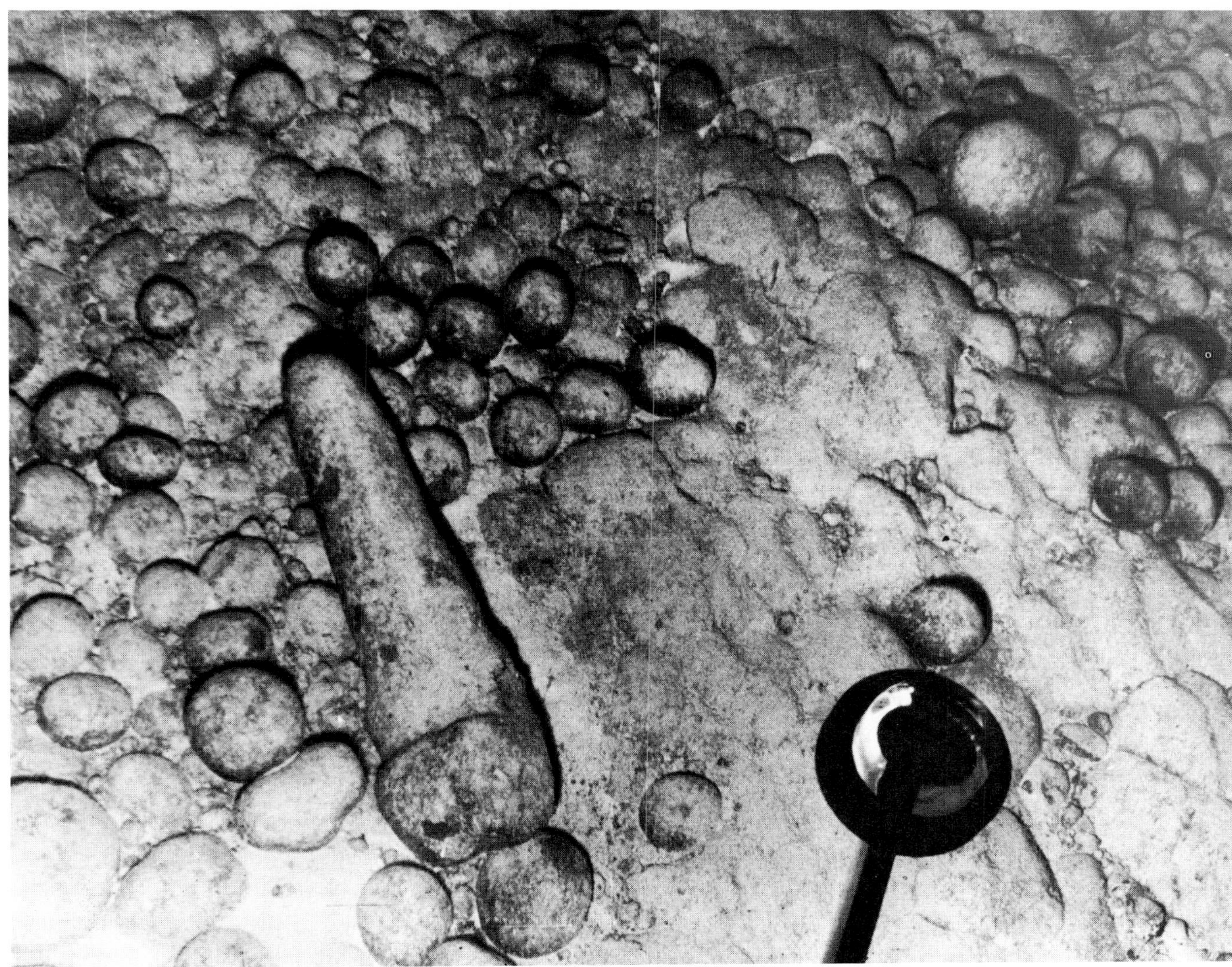

10.20 Manganese-encrusted whale bone. 3500 m.

cerning the composition, origin, rates of accumulation and distribution of manganese nodules as well as certain other valuable sea-floor deposits has been summarized by J. Mero (1965. *The Mineral Resource of the Sea.* Elsevier, Amsterdam, 312 pp). A modern discussion of manganese nodules from shallow water can be found in: F. T. Manheim. 1965. Manganese-iron accumulations in the shallow marine environment. *Narragansett Mar. Lab., Univ. Rhode Island, Occ. Publ.,* 3:217-275. Both of the references above include extensive bibliographies.

2. R. M. Pratt and P. F. McFarlin. 1966. Manganese pavements on the Blake Plateau. *Science,* 151:1080-1082.

3. M. L. Bender, T. L. Ku, and W. S. Broecker. 1966. Manganese nodules: their evolution. *Science,* 151:325-328.

19°07′N 65°23′W

11.1 Broken rock rubble, south wall, Puerto Rico Trench. L, R, 4144 m, shattered rocks (talus), broken loose by continuing deformation of the earth, stream down the inner walls of active trenches.

11

. . . and Tethys Shall Bear New Worlds . . .

An age shall come with late years when Ocean shall loosen the chains of things, and the earth be laid open in vastness, and Tethys shall bear new worlds . . .

SENECA

The face of the terrestrial globe bears welts of wrinkles and scars which record the massive movements that have deformed the earth's crust throughout geologic time. The highest, longest, and most prominent of these bands of deformation are the great lines of folded, overturned, and overthrust strata which constitute the earth's most recently created mountains. These are the cordillera—the backbone of the Americas—a slender belt extending from Chile to Alaska, and the narrow Alpine-Himalayan chain which extends across the breadth of our one remaining super continent, Eurasia. This enormous welt, which includes the earth's highest mountains, reaches its greatest breadth and height in Tibet and then, sweeping down through Burma and Malaysia, merges with the quaking and erupting island arcs and yawning deep-sea trenches of Indonesia and east Asia, giving the important clue that these three extreme phenomena may result from a common cause.

The arcuate folds which stretch around the southern and western margin of Eurasia can almost be seen to move as this gigantic continent comes in conflict with Africa, India, and Australia to the south and with the crust of the vast Pacific basin to the east. Indeed there is ample reason to believe that horizontal and vertical movement is still going on.

A nearly continuous garland of long, narrow, deep-sea trenches sharply separates the arcs of active volcanos and the deforming coastal ranges of Asia and America from the stable ocean basin floor which lies

120°
150°
180°
150°
120°
Okhotsk Sea
Bering Sea
ROCKY MOUNTAINS
Aleutian Trench
Kuril Trench
Japan Sea
Japan Tr.
Bonin Tr.
Ryukyu Trench
Philippine Sea
South China Sea
Philippine Tr.
Mariana Trench
Yap Trench
Palau Trench
Middle Ame
New Britain Trench
Vityaz Trench
Java Trench
Timor Ridge
Coral Sea
New Hebrides Tr.
Tonga Tr.
Kermadec Trench
Tasman Sea
30°
60°
120°
150°
180°
150°
120°

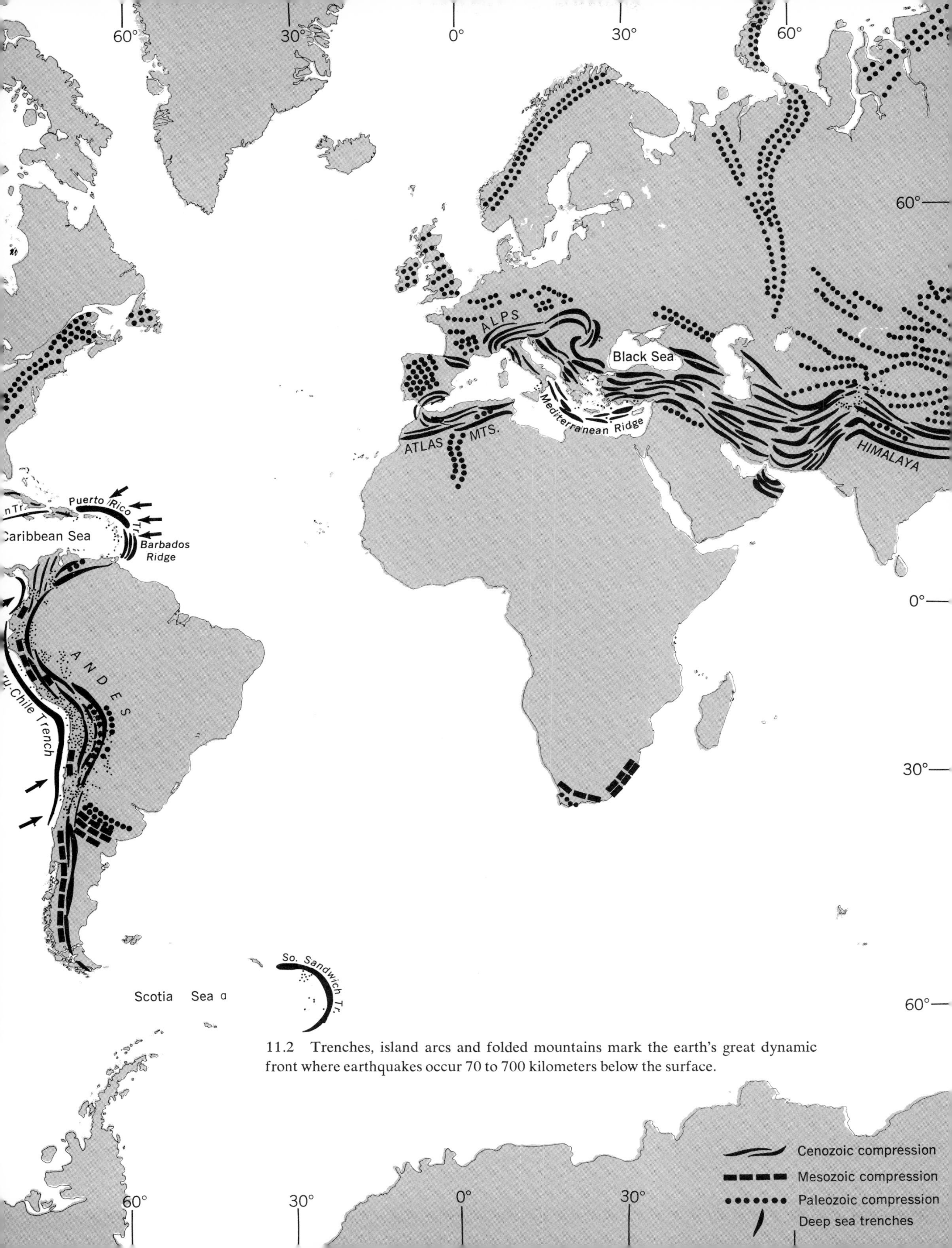

11.2 Trenches, island arcs and folded mountains mark the earth's great dynamic front where earthquakes occur 70 to 700 kilometers below the surface.

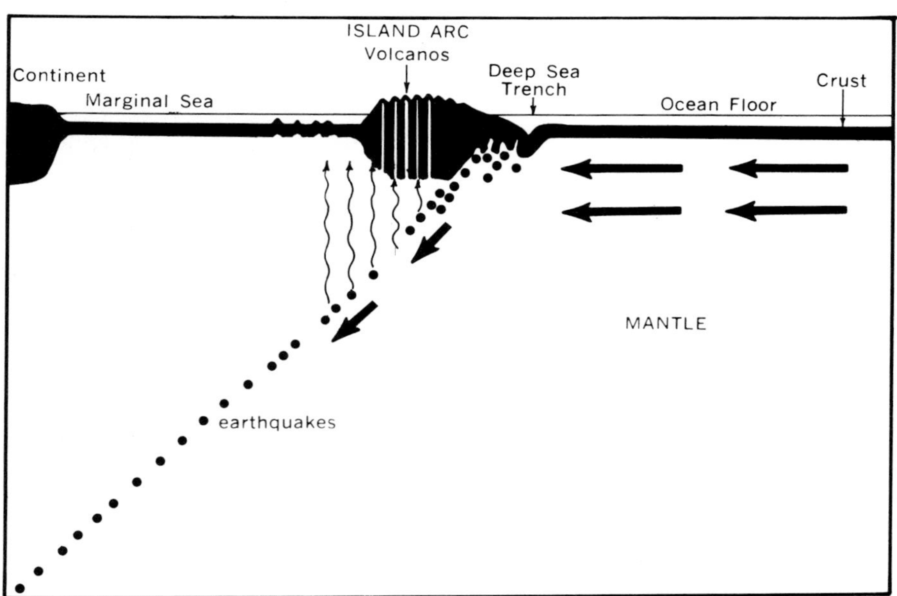

11.3 Earthquake epicenters lead from the trench floor along a sloping plane to depths of over 700 kilometers.

beyond. This narrow transition zone, this unstable continental margin, which includes the Indonesian arcs of Southeast Asia nearly rings the Pacific basin (11.1, 11.2). The greatest depths of the sea are found here in steep-sided narrow gashes which characteristically cut almost precisely ten kilometers into the earth's crust (11.3). The active arcs and trenches of the Pacific thus link together the great Eurasian and American mountains into one grand belt of crustal unrest. In this 60,000-kilometer long dynamic front, the earth's crust is raised to its greatest elevations and depressed to its greatest depths. The majority of the world's violent volcanic eruptions as well as most of its earthquakes originate here, deep beneath the arcs on dipping planes which extend from the earth's surface to 700 kilometers. They tell of the deepest deformation known on earth. The most beautiful of its scenery, the clearest air, the most inaccessible areas occur in this most extravagant belt of our planet.

That this girdle of folded, squeezed, and shattered rocks results from the pressing together of enormous elements of the earth's crust was clearly recognized long before the present century began.

This global pattern of compression required a general explanation, which for many nineteenth-century geologists was supplied by a cooling, shrinking earth. When this mechanism was shown to be inadequate to explain the amount of compression inferred from the mountains a supercritical reappraisal of the evidence of crustal shortening ensued. In the midst of the controversy a reaction set in and for the past several dec-

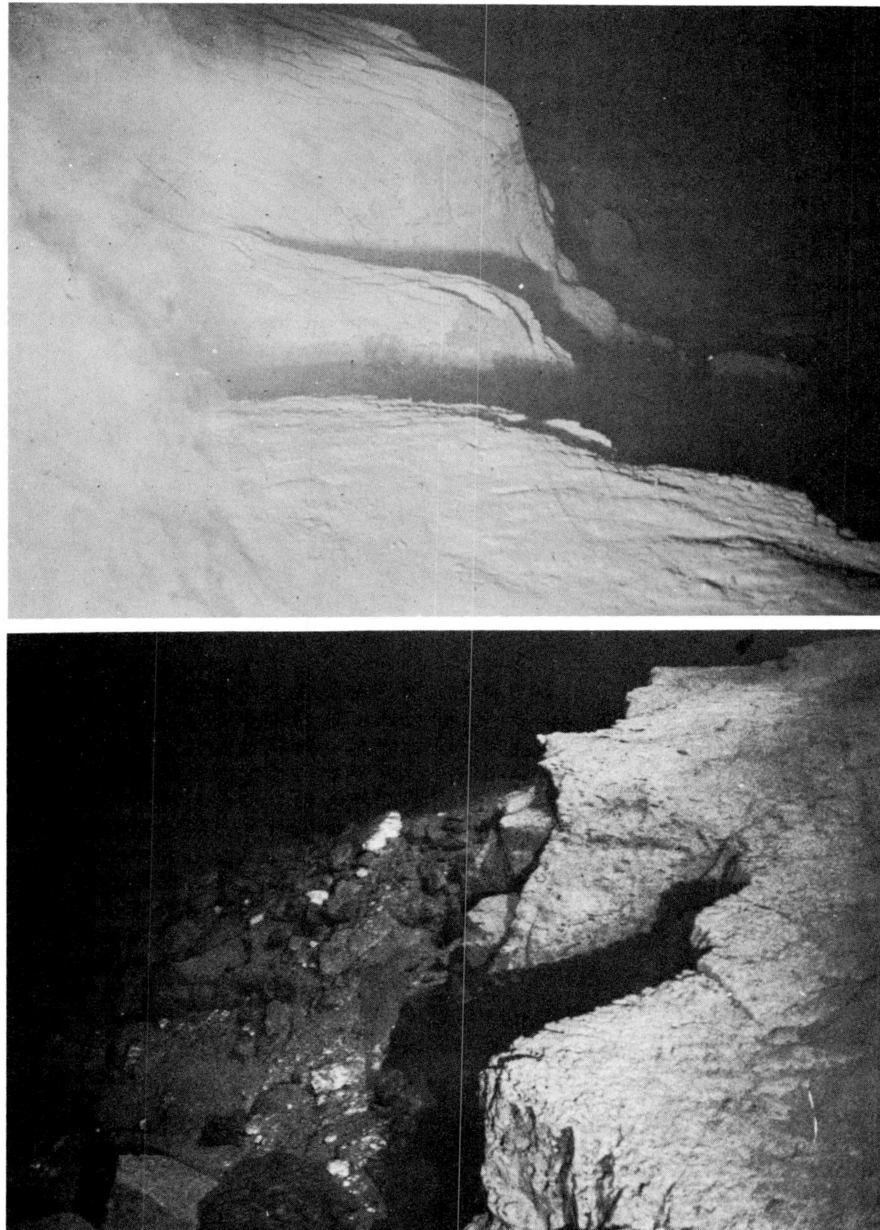

11.4 Jagged cliffs on the north wall of the Puerto Rico Trench. U, L, These photographs taken from the bathyscaphe, *Archimède* show outcrops of sedimentary rock at about 6600 meters.

ades numerous attempts have been made to interpret the evidence formerly used in support of crustal shortening as evidence for gravity-induced gliding of immensely large plates of strata down gentle inclines.

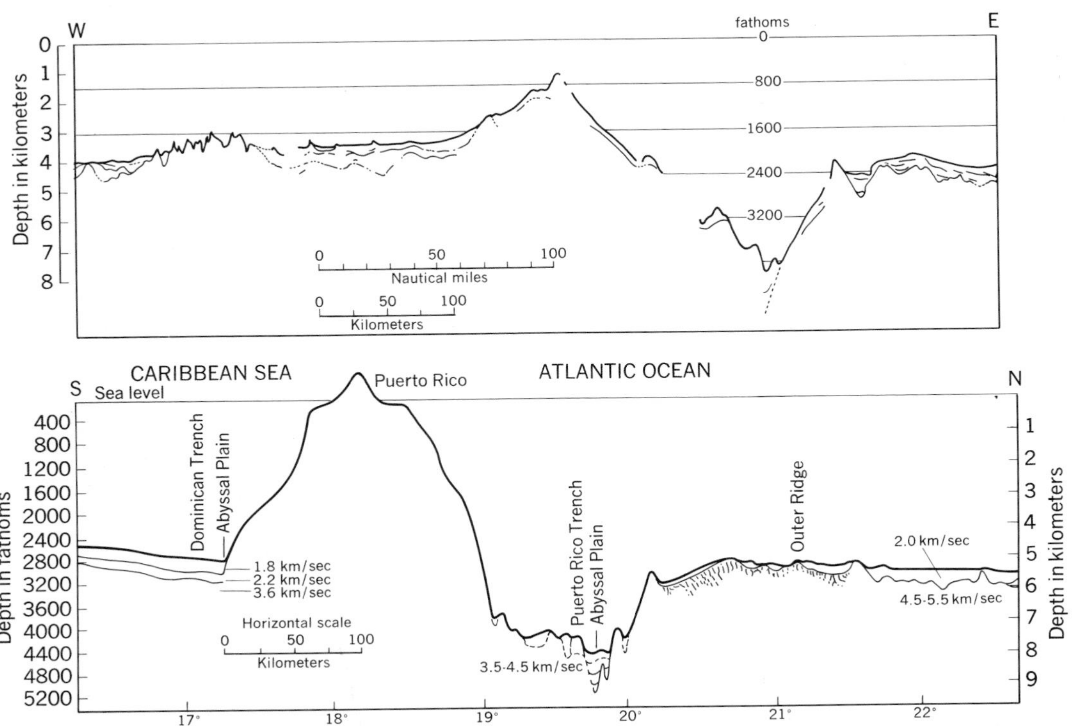

11.5 Steep-walled trenches border the two Atlantic island arcs. U, the South Sandwich Trench of the Scotia Arc lacks appreciable sediment filling; whereas, the Puerto Rico Trench (L) contains nearly two kilometers of sediment fill.

But today no one doubts that the Alps, the Jura, the Appalachians, or the Himalayas have been compressed. The real question is by how much and due to what cause?

Since the volcanic island arcs of the Pacific and Indian Oceans physically connect with the great folded mountain chains of Asia and Europe, most geologists early considered the arcs also to be basically compressional features.[1] But concerning the deep trenches which border the arcuate island chains there was less agreement. Must they too be formed by compression, perhaps by a great crustal downbuckle or underthrust or overthrust? Or might they be yawning cracks marking lines where the earth's crust is being torn asunder.[2]

Nearly everywhere the crust of the earth floats on the underlying mantle in nearly perfect equilibrium. The variations in the force of gravity which reflect inhomogeneities in mass and deviation from perfect

11.6 Tertiary and late Mesozoic rocks crop out on the north wall of the Puerto Rico Trench. U, L, Upper Cretaceous sedimentary rock was dredged within a few kilometers of these rock outcrops, 7261 m.

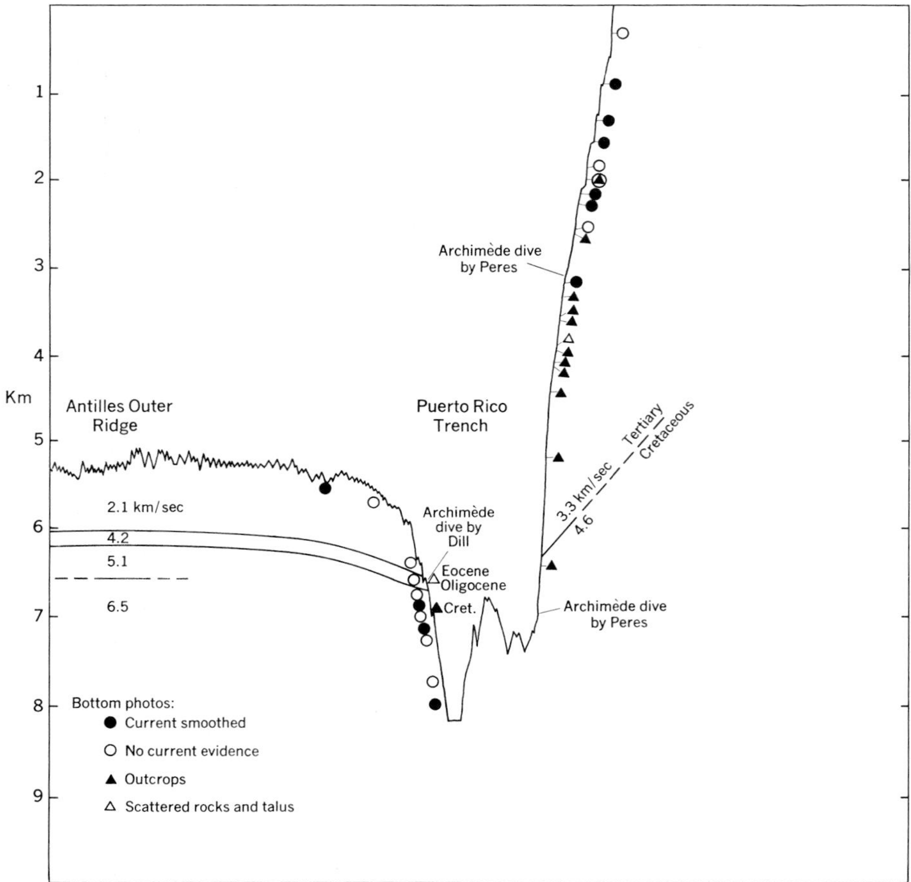

11.7 Rock outcrops and talus blocks photographed and observed directly on the walls of the Puerto Rico Trench suggest recent activity.

flotation are generally extremely small, hardly ever exceeding a hundred thousandth of the total force. But over the trenches the force of gravity pulls several ten-thousandths less than normal, indicating a vast deficiency in crustal mass. The highly disturbed gravity field suggests that the crust and upper mantle are deforming faster beneath the trenches than the earth can adjust to the new mass distributions. The world's principal belt of shallow earthquakes lies beneath the landward walls of the trenches in the very areas where the gravity field is most severely disturbed. Here active deformation of the crust must extend right up to the sea floor and here we should expect to see crushed and deformed rocks. This is in fact what has been observed. Masses of rubble, talus slopes, fractured, fragmented, pitted and corroded outcrops, all have been photographed on the inner walls of the Puerto Rico, Kermadec, Tonga, Peru-Chile, New Hebrides, West Solomon, New Britain, Palau, and South Sandwich Trenches.

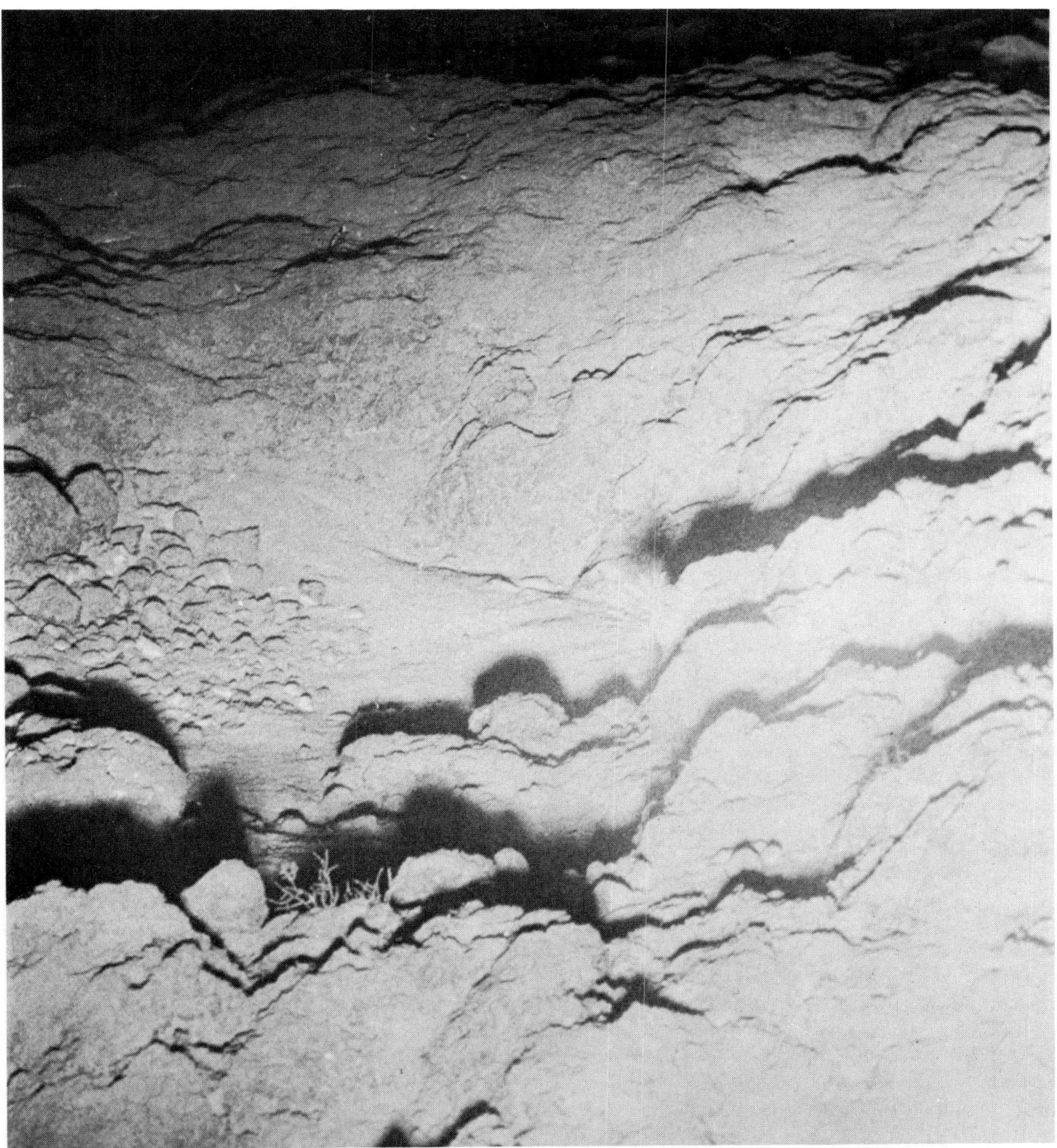

11.8 Pits and hollows. This subsided limestone has been corroded and pitted by cold deep currents. 4135 m, south wall, Puerto Rico Trench.

On the steep slopes bounding the trenches current activity is notable; and the fine sediments which under mid-ocean conditions would be deposited, are swept on. Since trenches border ocean basins and their landward walls form the sides of basins, they naturally are the locale of the contour currents which are also responsible for so much erosion and

19°09'N 65°23'W

11.9 Stratified rock is exposed on small cliffs which run north-south nearly perpendicular to the axis of the Puerto Rico Trench. 5202 m, south wall, Puerto Rico Trench.

transportation on the seismically quiet and mature continental margins. The visual evidence of the trench areas, however, indicates more than mere nondeposition. Deep-sea currents could not create the vast piles of shattered talus, nor produce the upturned and sometimes nearly vertical strata; although undoubtedly they make this evidence of contemporary earth-crushing movements more evident and more photogenic.

NO SIMPLE TASK

Interpretation of photographs of submarine outcrops (11.4) presents problems not normally encountered by earth scientists. The land geologist carries a hammer which he may use to pry loose a desired rock or to shape carefully a hand specimen, but mostly he uses it to whack hunks of rock from outcrops and break them in order to expose to view fresh unweathered and unworn surfaces. Even then he may not be able to identify the rock unless he looks for microscopic features with a hand lens.

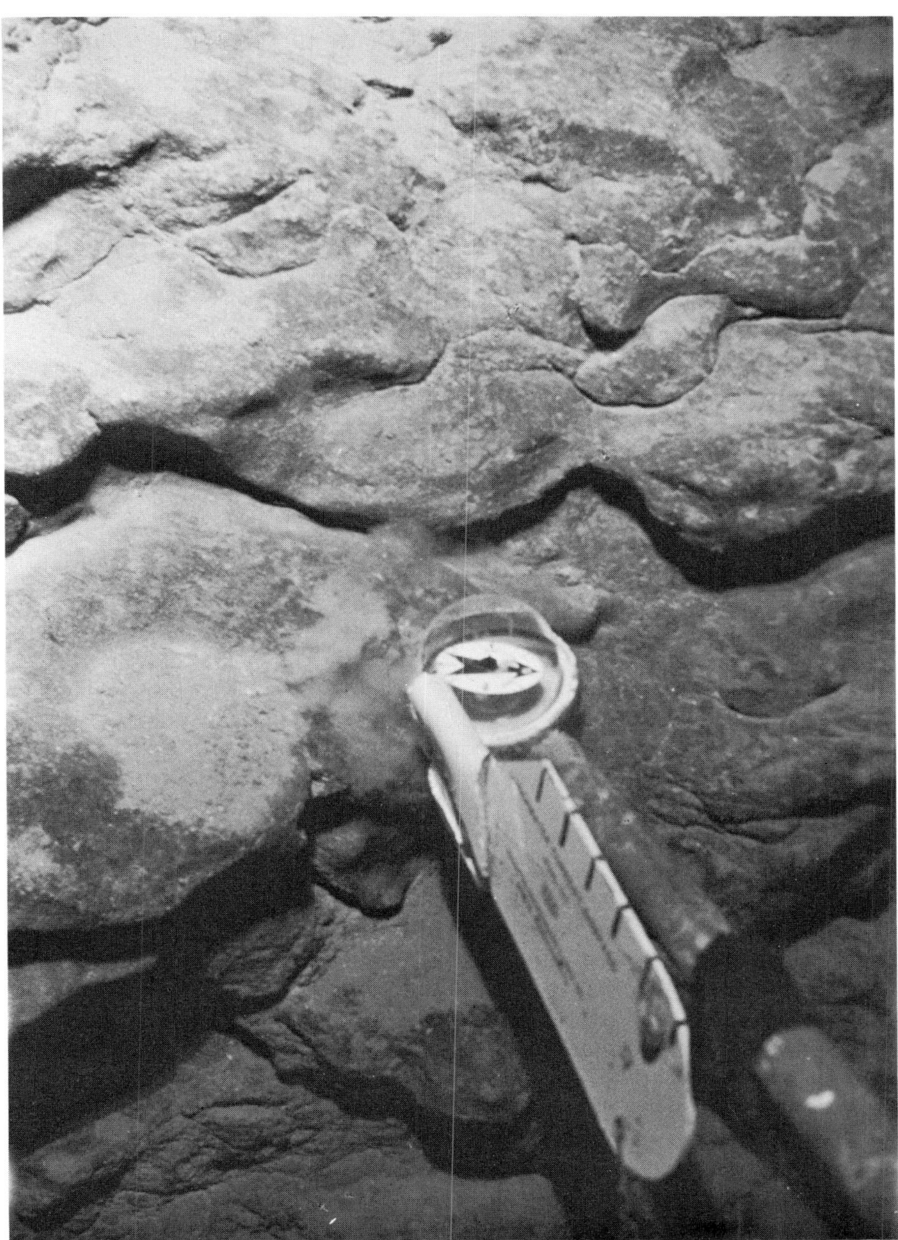

19°07′N 65°23′W
11.10 Vertical sediment-free cliffs on the trench walls are aligned north-south, perpendicular to the trench axis. 4450 m, south wall, Puerto Rico Trench.

It might seem a simple task for the marine observer to distinguish limestone from lava, granite from basalt, and sandstone from shale, but without specimens to break open and examine a few inches from his eyes such determination must be done on the basis of characteristics not usu-

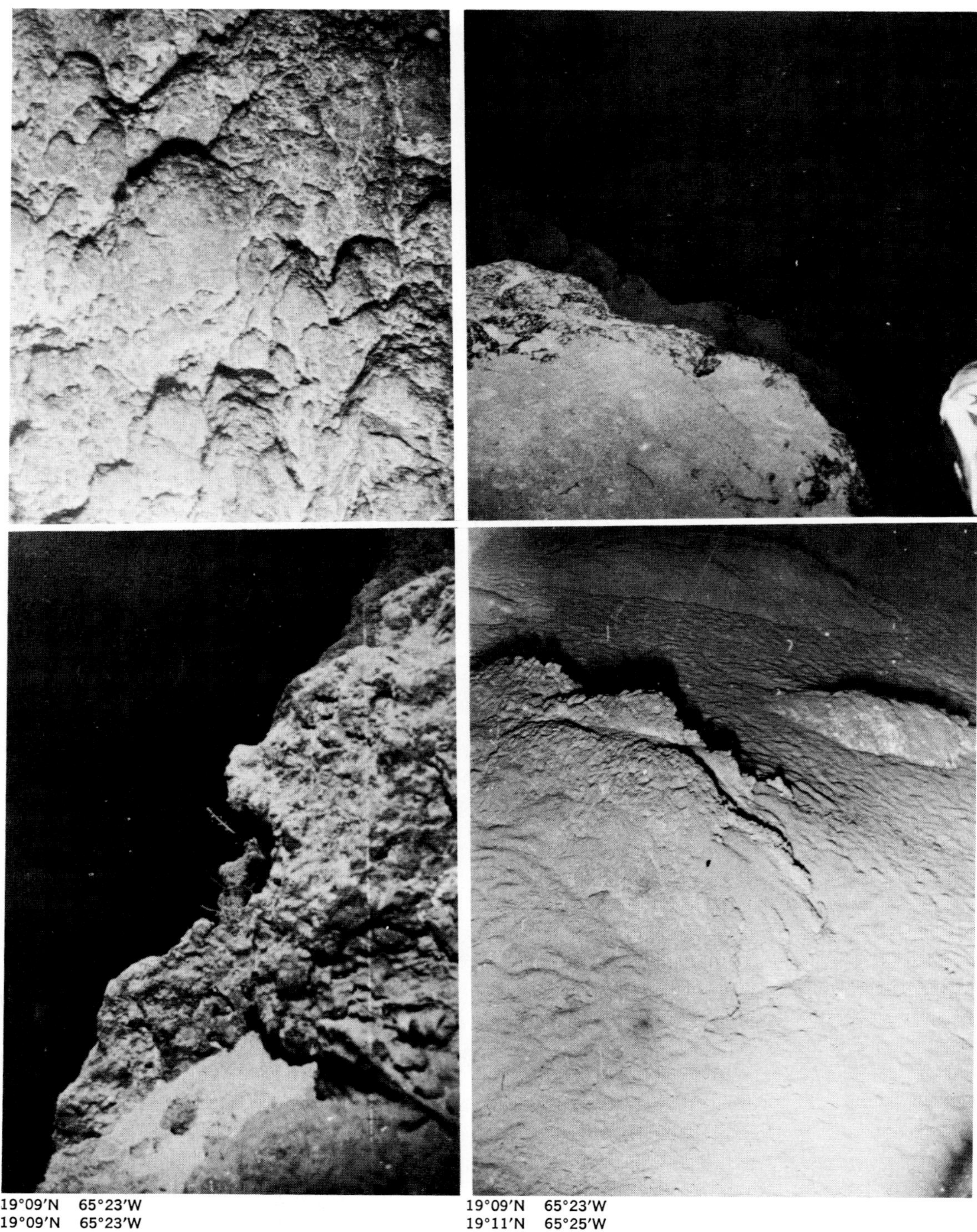

19°09′N 65°23′W
19°09′N 65°23′W

19°09′N 65°23′W
19°11′N 65°25′W

11.11 Nearly vertical exposures of rock are ubiquitous on the deeper portions of the Puerto Rico Trench's south wall. UL, LL, LR, 5202 m. UR, 6472 m.

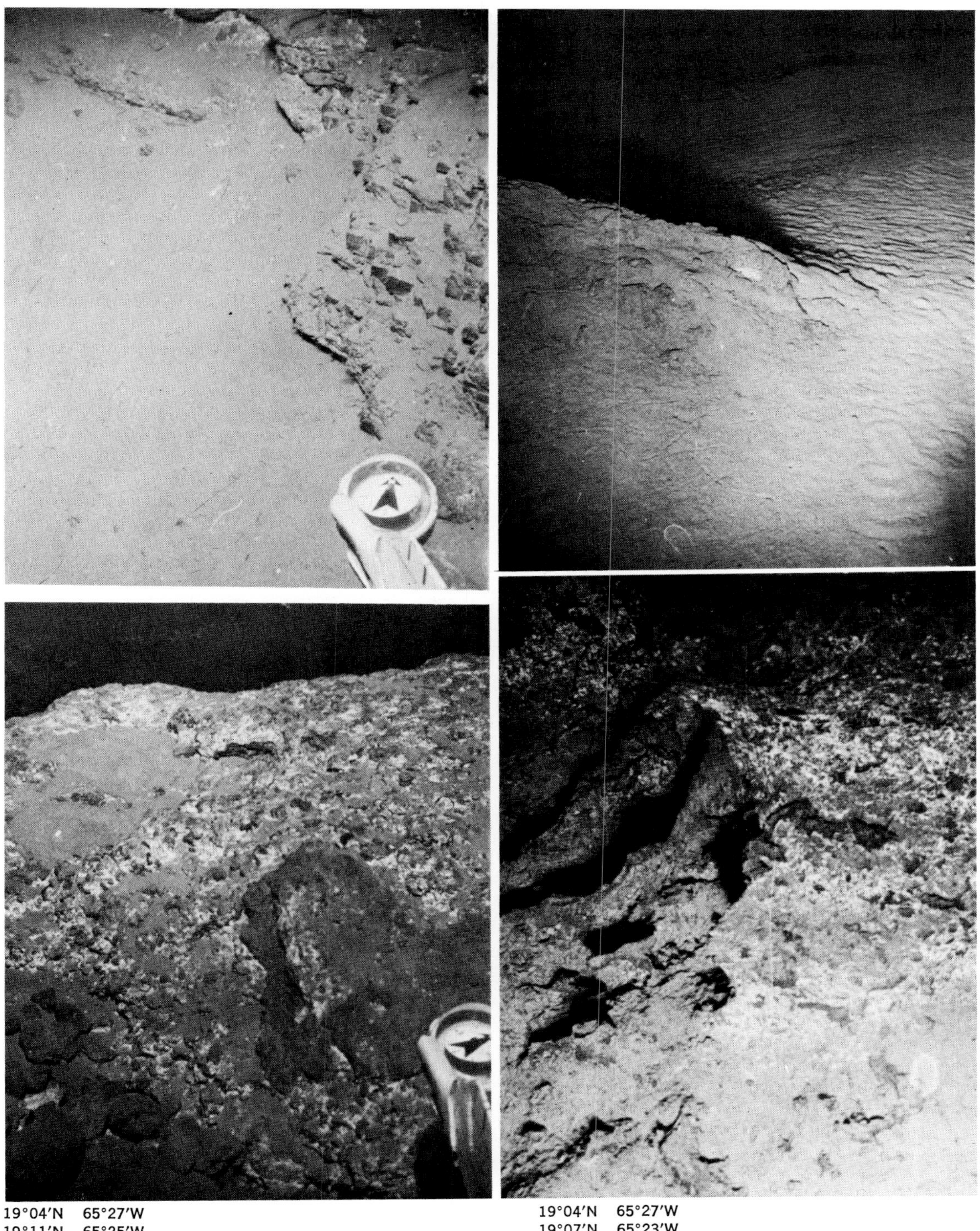

19°04′N 65°27′W
19°11′N 65°25′W

19°04′N 65°27′W
19°07′N 65°23′W

11.12 Sediment pockets and near vertical rock exposures on the trench wall. UL, UR, 3992 m. LL, 6472 m. LR, 4450 m, south wall, Puerto Rico Trench.

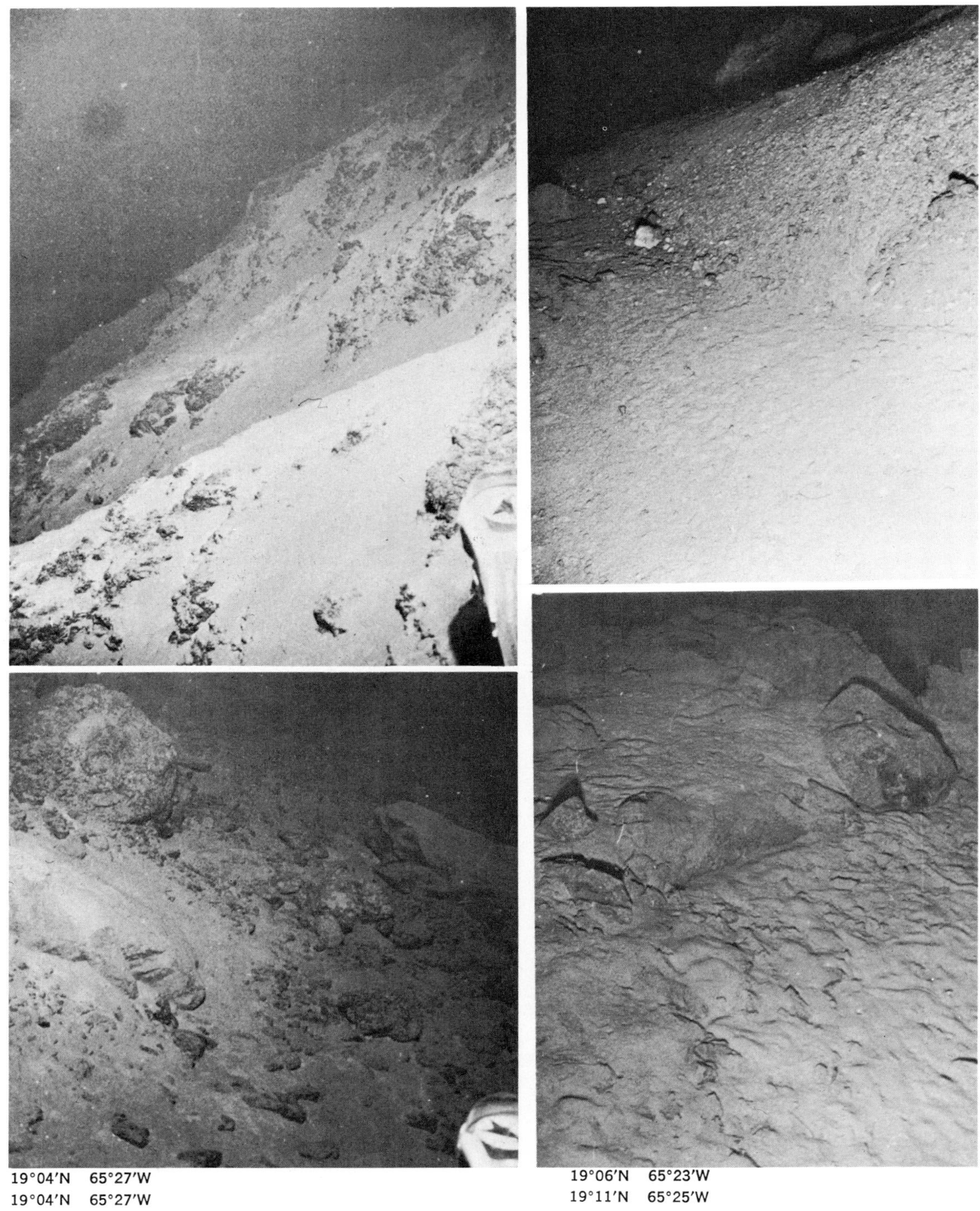

11.13 Talus blocks and rubble piles. UL, LL, 3992 m. UR, 4135 m. LR, 6472 m, south wall, Puerto Rico Trench.

19°04′N 65°27′W

11.14 Sediment pouring down the steep walls of the trench builds a tiny depositional apron. 3992 m, south wall, Puerto Rico Trench.

ally employed alone. For one thing, the ever-present manganese crust can be so thick as to round the outlines of all original shapes, so that a chilled lava pillow may not be distinguishable from an ancient sedimentary deposit coated with manganese. Even in fresh or only slightly coated rocks the job is not easy for there is generally enough weathering or manganese coating to make the recognition of mineral grains impossible. Thus robbed of crystal shapes and grain size, the two basic keys to all rock classifications, the submarine observer must make his identifications on the basis of grosser and less definitive secondary characteristics. The sub-

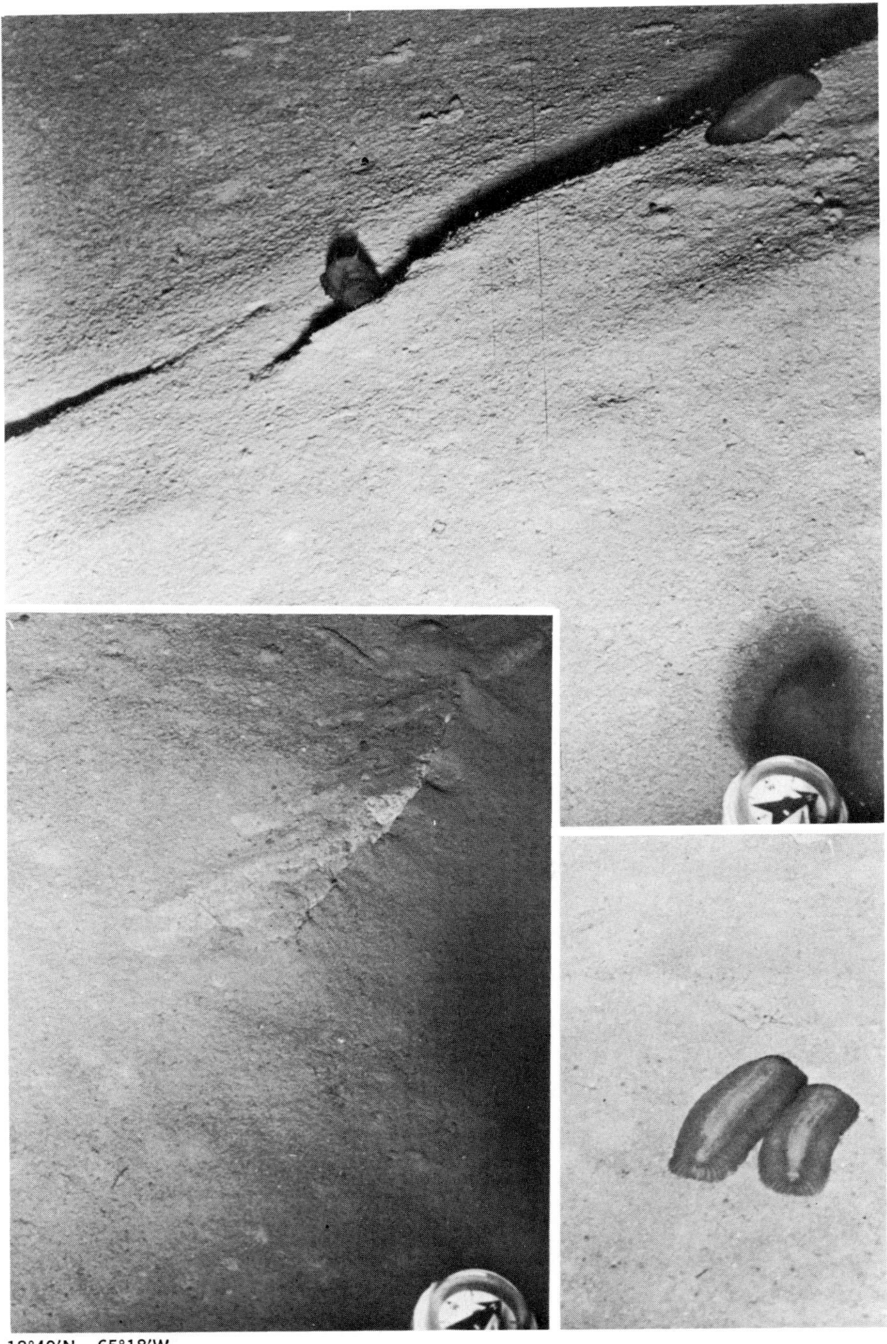

18°49′N 65°18′W
18°49′N 65°18′W
18°48′N 65°27′W

11.15 The upper, less precipitous slope of the south wall of the Puerto Rico Trench is covered by a thin blanket of sediment. An occasional north-south oriented rock ledge pokes through the thin sediment blanket. U, LL, 2016 m. LR, sea cucumbers on calcareous ooze, 2170 m, south wall, Puerto Rico Trench.

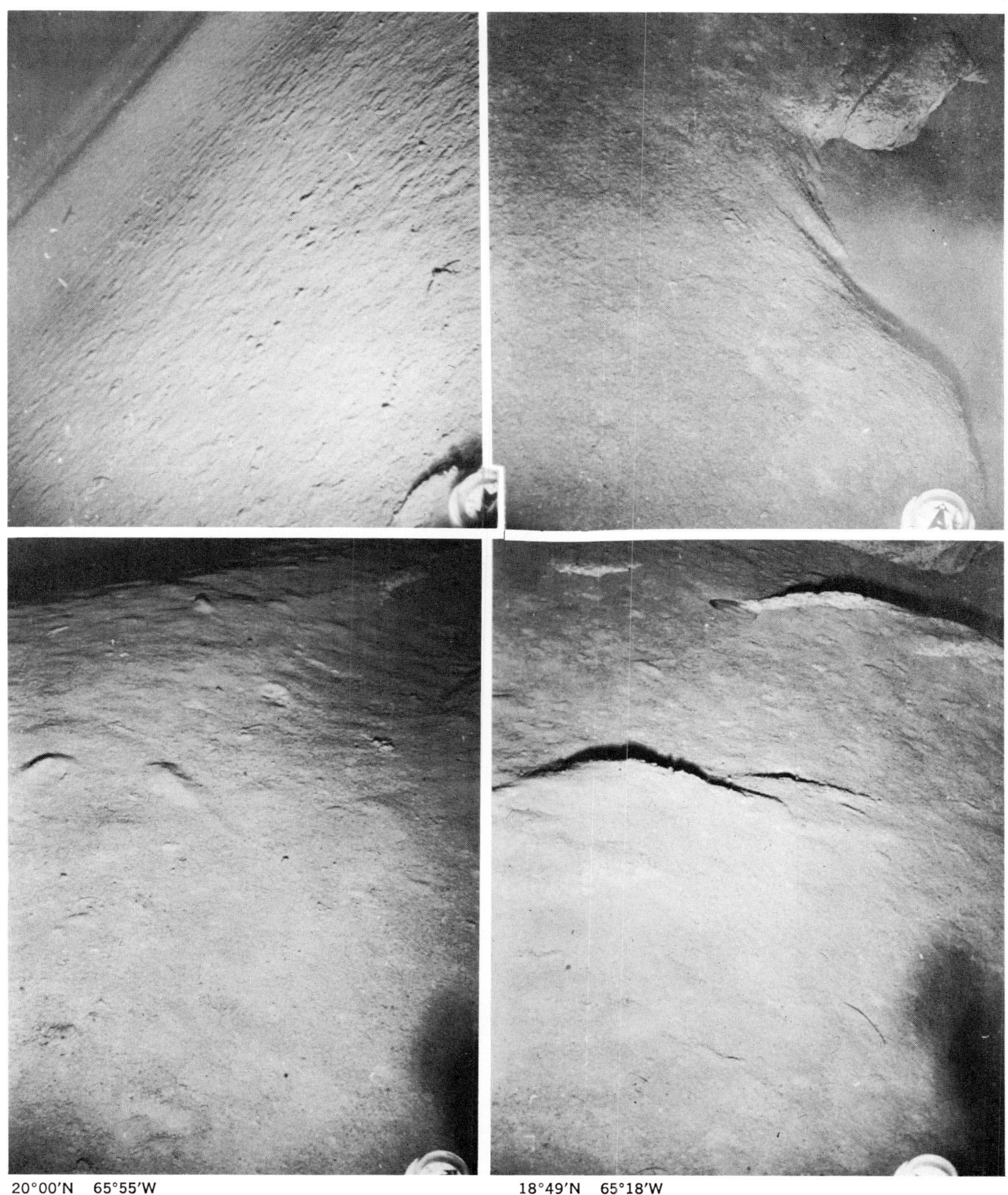

20°00'N 65°55'W
18°49'N 65°18'W

18°49'N 65°18'W
18°49'N 65°18'W

11.16 The sediment blanket is never very thick on the walls of the Puerto Rico Trench. UL, rock ledges are less frequently observed on the north wall of the Trench, 7360 m, north wall. UR, LL, LR, north-south oriented ledges and outcrops on the south wall of the Trench, 2016 m, south wall.

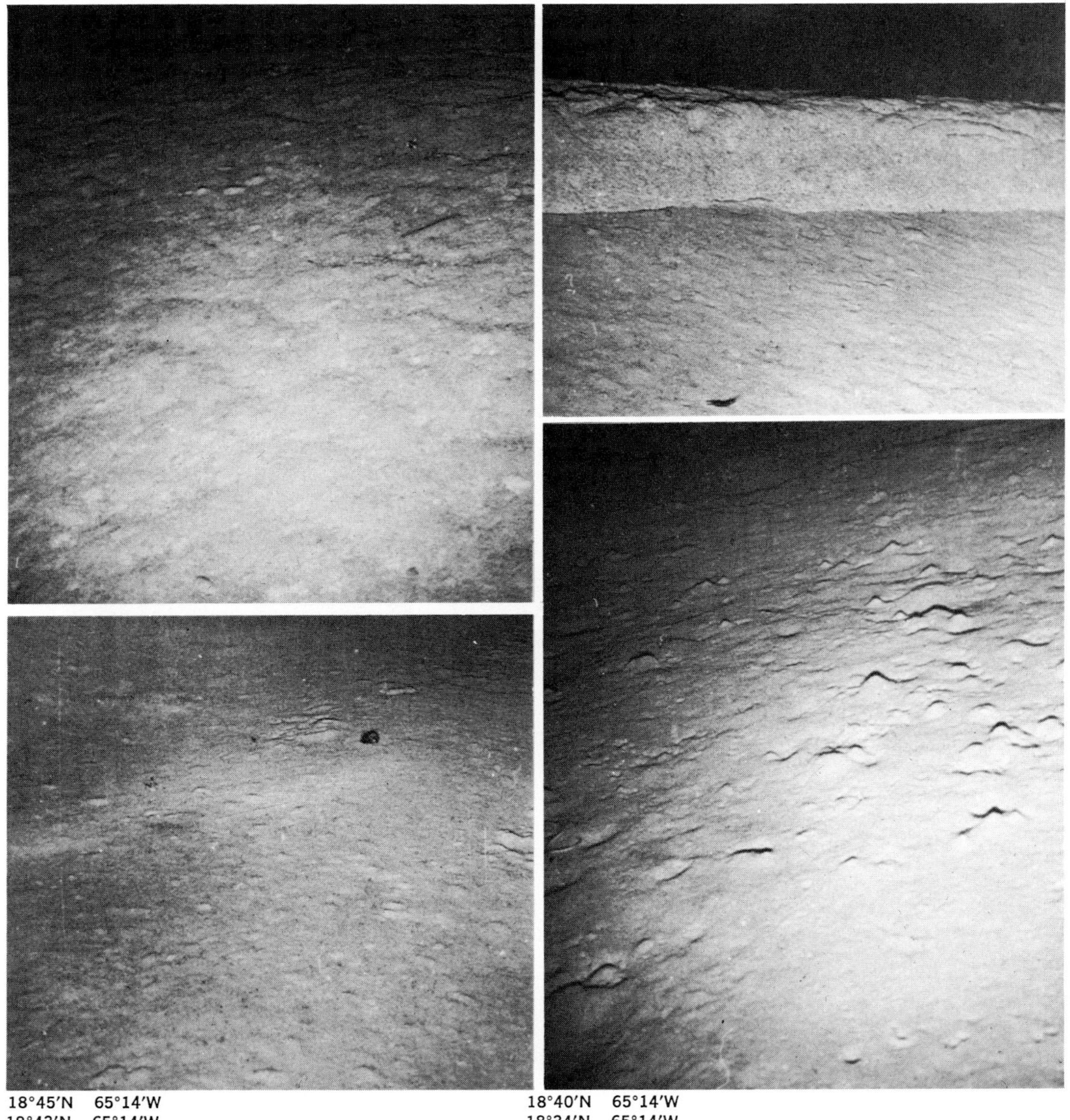

11.17 The sediment blanket locally becomes thicker on the uppermost portion of the south wall of the Puerto Rico Trench. UL, 1613 m. UR, 951 m. LL, 1352 m. LR, 327 m, south wall, Puerto Rico Trench.

marine lavas have their easily distinguished pillow-like surface, often with radial fractures. The limestone strata upturned in the wall of trenches have their thin-bedded tabular form. Some of the thinly bedded and platy metamorphic rocks and the peculiar rounded algal limestones

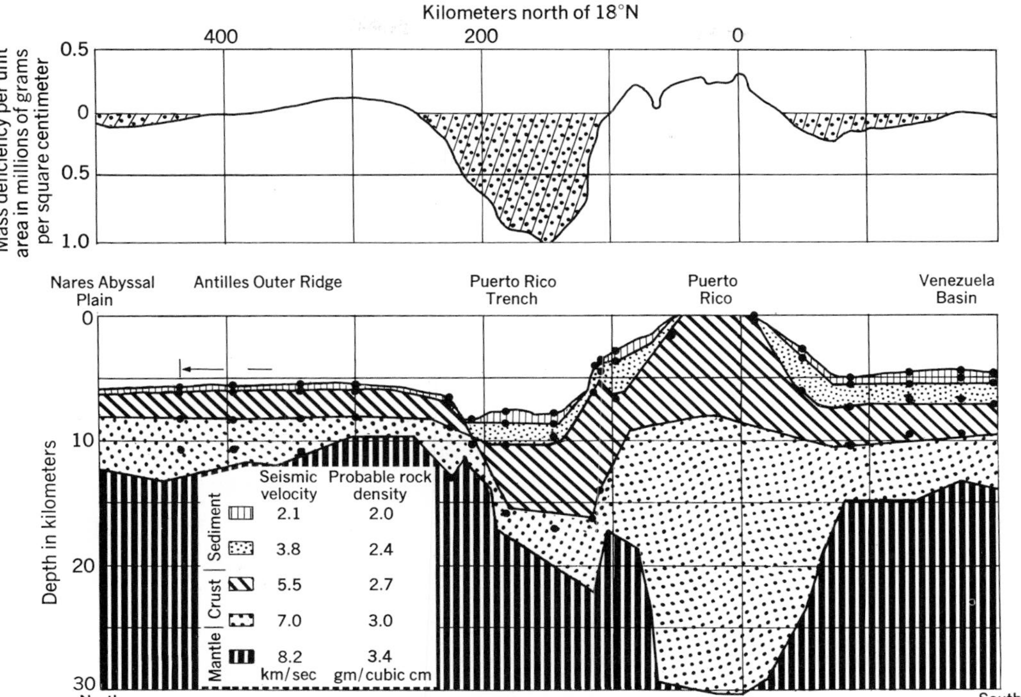

11.18 The Puerto Rico Trench is marked by an enormous deficit of crustal mass. The sediment accumulation in the south wall of the trench is presently being deformed. The north wall is relatively free of sediment.

could perhaps be recognized. Nevertheless, dredging and direct sampling must accompany visual observation before positive identifications can be made.

ANTILLEAN ARCS

Since more photographs of the Puerto Rico Trench are available for study than for any other trench, it is convenient to treat this visually dramatic locality in some detail. In passing from the tranquil muddy abyssal floor of the western North Atlantic, across the current-lineated Antilles Outer Ridge toward the rim of the Puerto Rico Trench, the seismic reflection profile records at first a gradual increase and then an abrupt decrease in sediment thickness (11.5). The persistent contour currents have marked this soft mud bottom with faint lineations and scour marks. However, the outer wall of the trench, which abruptly cuts into this long-accumulated wedge of sediment, presents a very different appearance with lightly veiled or even bare outcrops of flat-lying shale, sandstone and limestone strata, and crystalline rocks (11.4).

11.19 Cross-bedded and size-graded limey organic sand from the Puerto Rico Trench Abyssal Plain. Over half of this displaced debris consists of shallow-water coral and bryozoan fragments, while the remainder is composed of foraminifera and sponge spicules with about 10 per cent fine clay. 8347 m, eastern end of Puerto Rico Trench Abyssal Plain.

Contour currents leave gentle lineations and scour marks and occasionally ripples on the steep walls of the trench, but it seems highly unlikely that these currents have deeply eroded the bottom; and the wide-

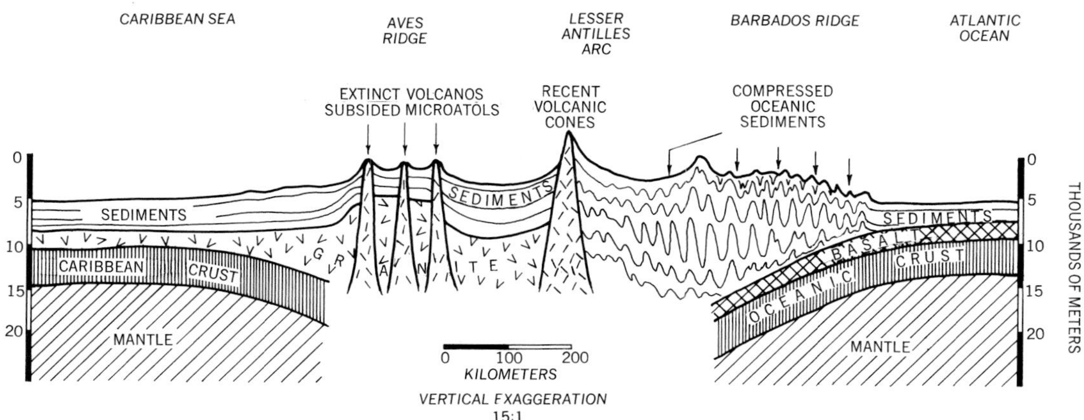

11.20 Compression of the earth's crust and subsequent deformation of thick sedimentary deposits have formed the Barbados Ridge.

spread outcrops and piles of crushed rock are clearly produced by continuing deformation of the earth's crust. Outcrops, although common on the north wall of the Puerto Rico Trench (11.6) are ubiquitous on the steeper, higher south wall (11.7). The precipitous scarp which extends from 4000 to 7000 meters depth is nearly sediment-free. Here, trains of coarse rubble stream down the rocky slopes (11.1). Outcropping rocks are often pitted, suggesting that the sea water may be attacking exposed limestone (11.8). Ledges of stratified rock are exposed in nearly vertical cliffs (11.9-11.14). The steep rocky wall is a poor seismic reflector, and a weak, lacy echo trace is characteristic of these broken outcrops. On the more gentle slopes between 1000 and 4000 meters, bare outcrops are less common; yet the tiny scarps and frequent rock bosses which peek through the sediment blanket show that this accumulation rarely reaches significant thickness (11.15-11.17). Although the major scarps trend east-west, many of the miniature scarplets seen on the upper portion of the inner wall trend nearly north-south (11.9, 11.10).

Layering of the earth's crust in the vicinity of the Puerto Rico Trench has been extensively investigated[4] (11.18). An unstratified (transaural)[5] layer of post-Cretaceous deep-sea sediment crops out on the north wall in depths above 6600 meters. Consolidated limestones and shales of Cretaceous age lie between these undeformed Tertiary deep-sea sediments and the underlying serpentized peridotite of the oceanic crust which is exposed on the lower wall of the trench. Beneath the trench floor the crustal layers lie beneath the stratified abyssal plain deposits (11.19) and therefore are inaccessible to camera and dredge.

A much more complex scene is observed on the south wall. Here the sequence, thickness, and attitude of the layers contrast sharply with the

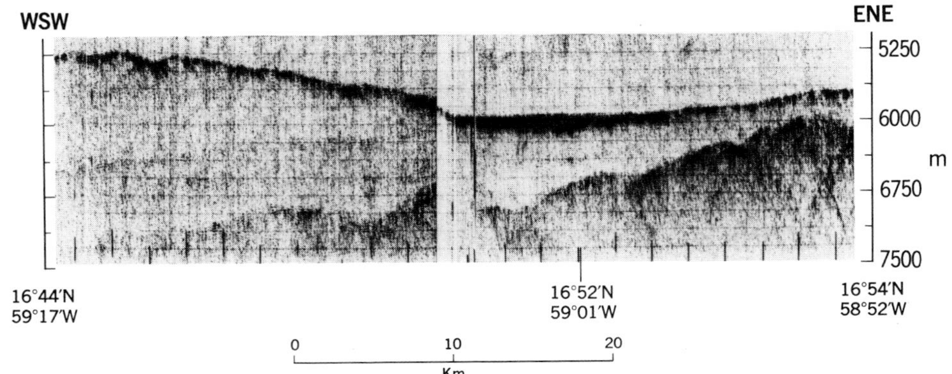

11.21 Sediment is piled up against the leading edge of the down-bending Atlantic Ocean crust as it plunges beneath the Antillean Island Arc. The deep-sea clays as well as the turbidites which are deposited on the depressed oceanic crust immediately ahead of the advancing prow of the arc will be overridden, compressed, and incorporated in the basement of the island arc.

more uniform and nearly flat-lying beds of the northern wall. The fifty-kilometer wide coastal plain wedge of northerly dipping Tertiary limestones and shales thickens seaward and finally crops out on the south wall in depths of over five kilometers. Continuing deformation is producing a steady stream of rock rubble that pours down the broken inner wall of the trench. No other areas of the ocean show evidence for more extensive and incessant deformation. The talus blocks appear very fresh, bearing no visible evidence of the normally ubiquitous manganese coating found on all submarine outcrops. These rocks must have only recently been broken and exposed to sea water. Indeed the outcrops and piles of crushed talus seen on the south wall beg to be dredged.

In 1964, the walls of the Puerto Rico Trench were observed from the French bathyscaphe *Archimède*. A series of vertical bare rock cliffs separated by ledges and twenty-degree to forty-degree rock and mud-covered ramps were seen near 6600 meters on the north wall (11.4). The first geologist[6] to view the trench wall, observing that the mixed rock rubble (up to eight inches in size) slid downslope when touched by the bathyscaphe, concluded that many talus slopes "were near their angle of repose." He saw vertical and even over-hanging walls of solid black rock, some of which "looked like poorly-bedded volcanic flows." In several places he observed "narrow channels cut back into the vertical rock slopes" which "contained mixed types of bare rocky blocks supported in the fine-grained sediment." This fill "appeared to be moving downslope confined to the bottom of the channels . . . The contact between the rock walls and the relatively flat-lying channel fill was sharp and nearly

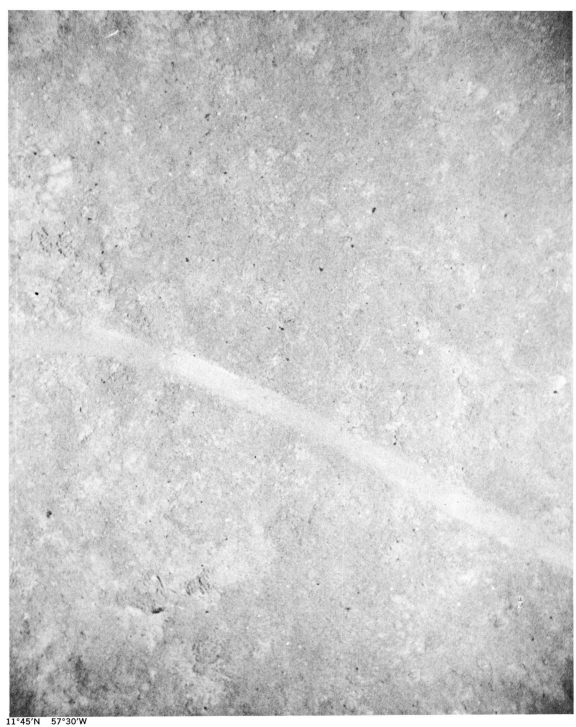

11°45′N 57°30′W

11.22 A thin layer of soft mud covers intensely deformed sediment layers of the Barbados Ridge. 3493 m, southeast of Barbados (vertical view).

11.23 Continuing compression in the earth's crust may eventually build a mountain range along the Antillean Arc.

at right angles." He was convinced that the straight, nearly vertical, undissected slopes are fault scarps. Currents up to eight centimeters per second were observed alternately flowing up and then down the north wall.

Exposures of soft yellow limestone were seen at 3100 meters' depth on the south wall of the Puerto Rico Trench. The rock was perforated by numerous holes one to one and a half centimeters in diameter. A marine biologist, observing that these burrows were uninhabited, at first wondered whether they had been formed in shallow water before the subsidence of the rock into the trench.[7] But he later concluded that "the corrosion seemed, if it is not going on at the present time, at least to be very recent; because one observes, in the immediate neighborhood of these rocky outcrops, an important proportion of pebbles (two to five centimeters in maximum dimension) of rather angular appearance in spite of the rather soft nature of the rocks." The biologists who dove were impressed with the abundance of life in the great depths of the trench, which they attributed to an ample supply of "organic particles derived from the adjacent continental shelf."

The Puerto Rico Trench is actively subsiding at the present time. The earthquake activity along the southern wall, the southerly dips observed

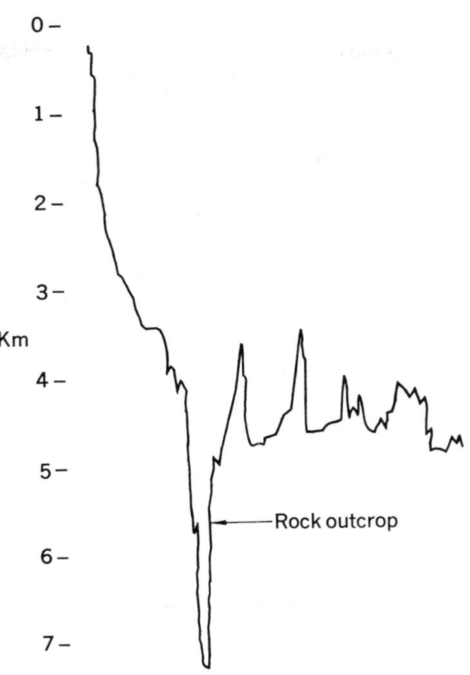

11.24 Rocks are exposed on the current-swept steep walls of the South Sandwich Trench. Vertical exaggeration of profile, 100:1. Fractured rock outcrop on outer wall of trench is shown in Fig. 11.26.

in sediments which underlie the trench abyssal plain and the extremely steep northerly dips of Tertiary strata along the south wall indicate continuing and contemporary subsidence.

As the Puerto Rico Trench curves around the eastern side of the Antillean Arc it shallows and its place with respect to the negative gravity anomaly belt is taken by the Barbados Ridge (11.20). Barbados has long held a special fascination for those concerned with the abyss for this small speck of land is one of the few places on earth where pelagic deposits can be seen above sea level. This low limestone island which lies astride a sedimentary ridge, wrapped around the volcanic arc of the Lesser Antilles, is composed of oceanic oozes and mudstones deposited in a mid-ocean pelagic realm. These distorted beds are capped by a perfect staircase of raised coral reefs which mark the intersection of the fluctuating sea level and the rising island. The highest terrace which lies 330 meters above sea level was cut approximately one million years ago.

That the Barbados Ridge is a thick accumulation of deformed sediments is evident from the geology of the island. Over most of the feature the complexity of the deformation defies the resolution of normal seismic reflection systems. However, one hundred miles east of Barbados along

Trinidade
Martin Vas
Falkland Islands
South Shetland Islands

11.26 Fractured and jointed rock is exposed on the steep walls of the South Sandwich Trench. The Antarctic Bottom Current scours the earthquake-wracked trench walls. Sediment carried in suspension clouds the picture. U, L, 5960 m, east wall of South Sandwich Trench.

◁ 11.25 The South Sandwich Island Arc and Trench, South Atlantic.

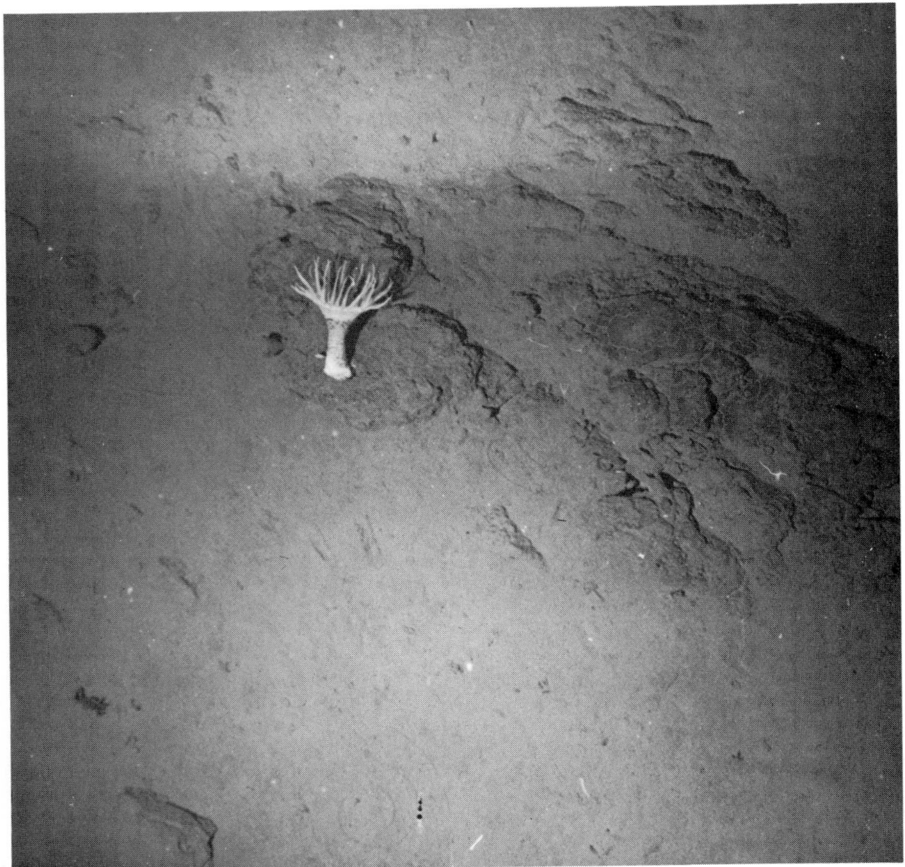

20°33′S 168°33′E
11.27 Steep rocky slopes suggest recent deformation. 6725 m, base of east wall, New Hebrides Trench, western Pacific.

a north-south escarpment the deformation ends abruptly. Here the nearly horizontal layers of sediment of the Atlantic floor can occasionally be observed to bend sharply down beneath the complexly deformed sediments of the Barbados Ridge (11.21). Thus the eastern limit of deformation of the Antilles Arc can be traced from South America along this escarpment east of Barbados and into the axis of the Puerto Rico Trench. The intensity of deformation increases from south to north. Directly east of Trinidad, the folds can be traced on the seismic reflection profiles, but just a few miles to the north the deformation is generally too complex to be resolved; and still further along this dynamic front, the deformed sediments no longer form a broad independent ridge but are squeezed against the inner wall of the trench.[8]

The folded and uplifted oceanic sediments of the Barbados Ridge, revealed by seismic reflection profiles and photographed both above and

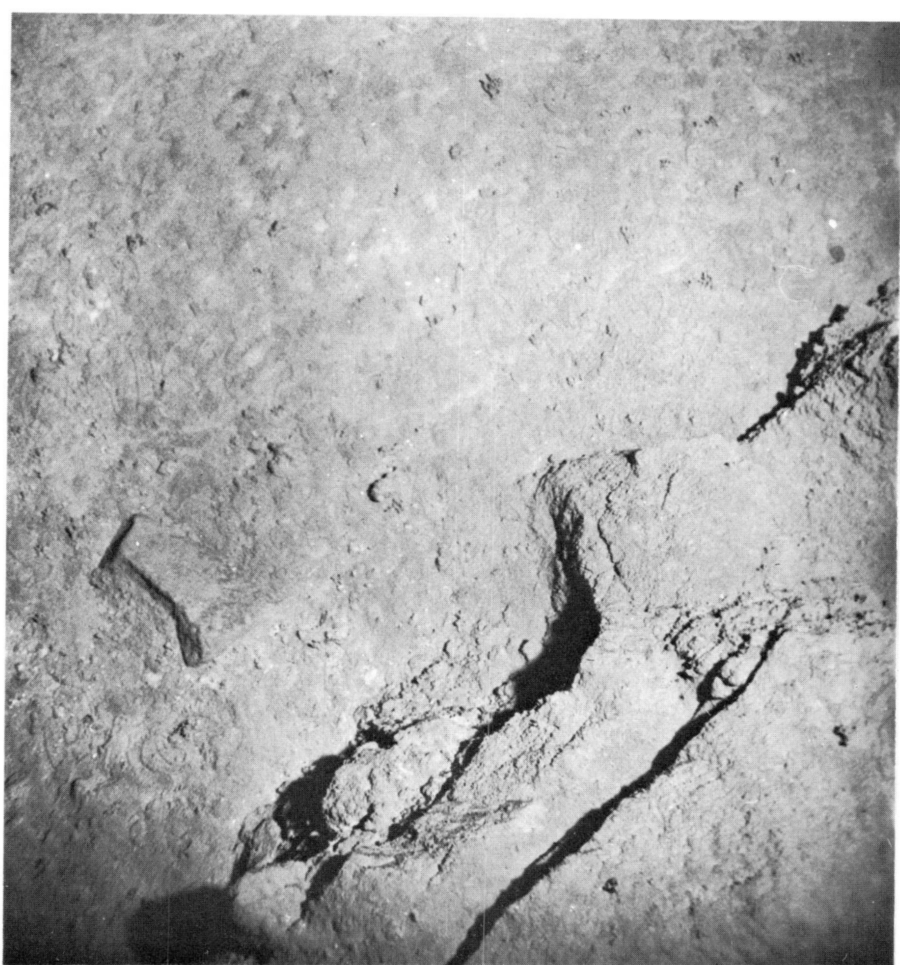

6°17′S 153°43′E
11.28 Shattered rock ledge on the steep wall of the Solomon Trench. 8625 m, base of southeast wall, western Pacific.

below the sea (11.22) thus offer support to the frequent assertion that island arcs, like most mountain ranges, result from the pressing together of large elements of the earth's crust (11.23).

The pattern of islands, ridges, and trenches so clearly displayed in the Caribbean is repeated with only slight modification in the South Sandwich Arc and Scotia Sea (11.24, 11.25) which form the Southern Antilles. However, in contrast to the northern Antilles, an empty trench and not a deforming sedimentary prism lies east of the arc. Bare rock crops out on the walls of the active South Sandwich Trench and pumice from recent volcanic eruptions has been seen littering the sea floor in this region. Visibility is poor due to the vigorous circulation of deep and bot-

8°43′N 135°12′E

11.29 Manganese-coated outcrops in the Palau Trench. 4555 m, upper part of east wall, western Pacific.

19°54′N 121°26′E

19°54′N 121°26′E

11.30 Intense deformation of the Philippine Arc has turned these sandstone beds on end. Strong currents through the Luzon Straits erode and abrade these bare outcrops. U,L, Luzon Straits, northeast of Calayan Bank, 2380 meters.

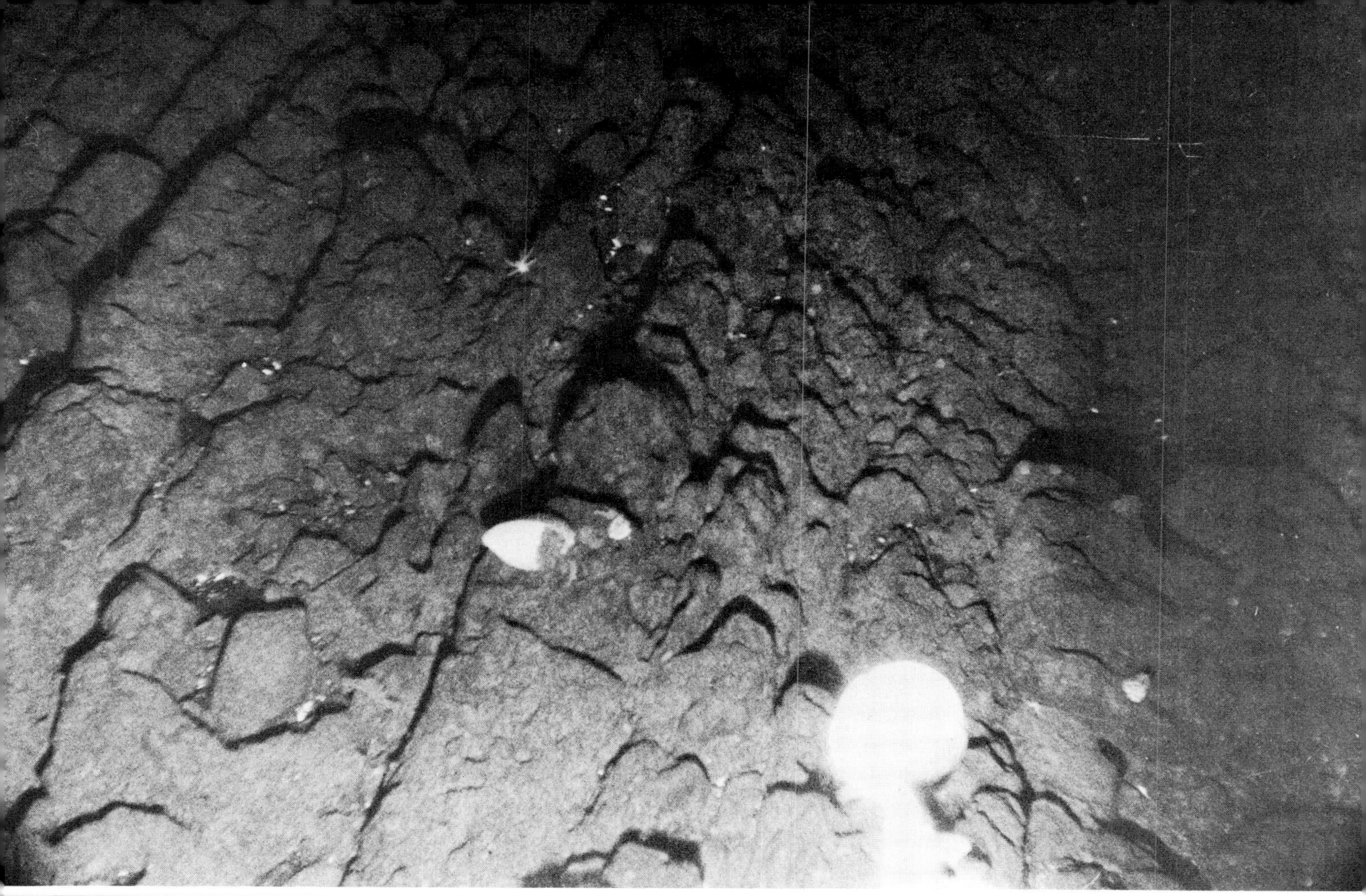

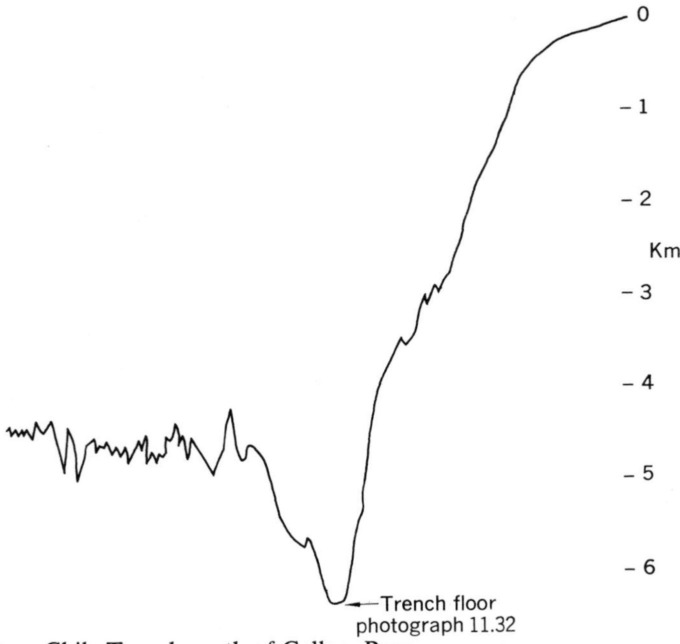

11.31 Peru-Chile Trench north of Callao, Peru.

tom waters and the high productivity of the surface waters. A contour current flows the length of the South Sandwich Trench from the Weddell Sea on the south to the Argentine Basin on the north, and the circumpolar current, which passes from west to east vigorously sweeps virtually every passage in the South Sandwich Arc (11.26).

WHEN THE DUST SETTLES

The volcanos of the island arcs often erupt with great violence, carrying immense quantities of fine ash far up into the stratosphere.[9] When this glass dust settles back to the sea and sinks to the abyss, layers of appreciable thickness are deposited on the deep-sea floor. The seascapes in the vicinity of island arcs should reveal evidence of such catastrophes either recent or contemporary. At first, the benthic life must be destroyed, but even after thousands of years, the presence of a thick layer of barren ash may impede or prevent the deeper burrowers from repopulating the area.

The greatest historical eruption was the 1883 explosion of Krakatao in the Indonesian Arc which spread ash over the adjacent sea floor. There have been six greater eruptions over the past million years which blanket the outer ridge and the adjacent basin south of the Java Trench. In contrast, the enormous eruptions of 1883 produced an insignificant

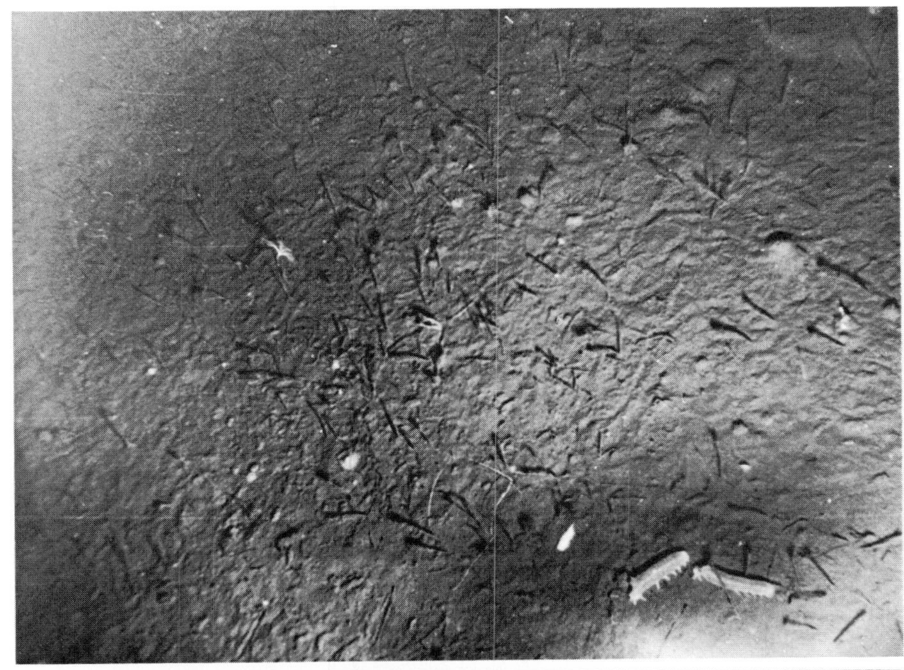

08°17′S 81°06′W
29°40′S 176°43′W

11.32 Pacific Trenches. U, a soft mud bottom with abundant life lies beneath the productive Humboldt Current on the floor of the Peru-Chile Trench, 6237 m, north of Callao, Peru (see Fig. 11.31). L, rock is exposed and life rarely seen on the east wall of the Kermadec Trench, 5069 m, southwest Pacific.

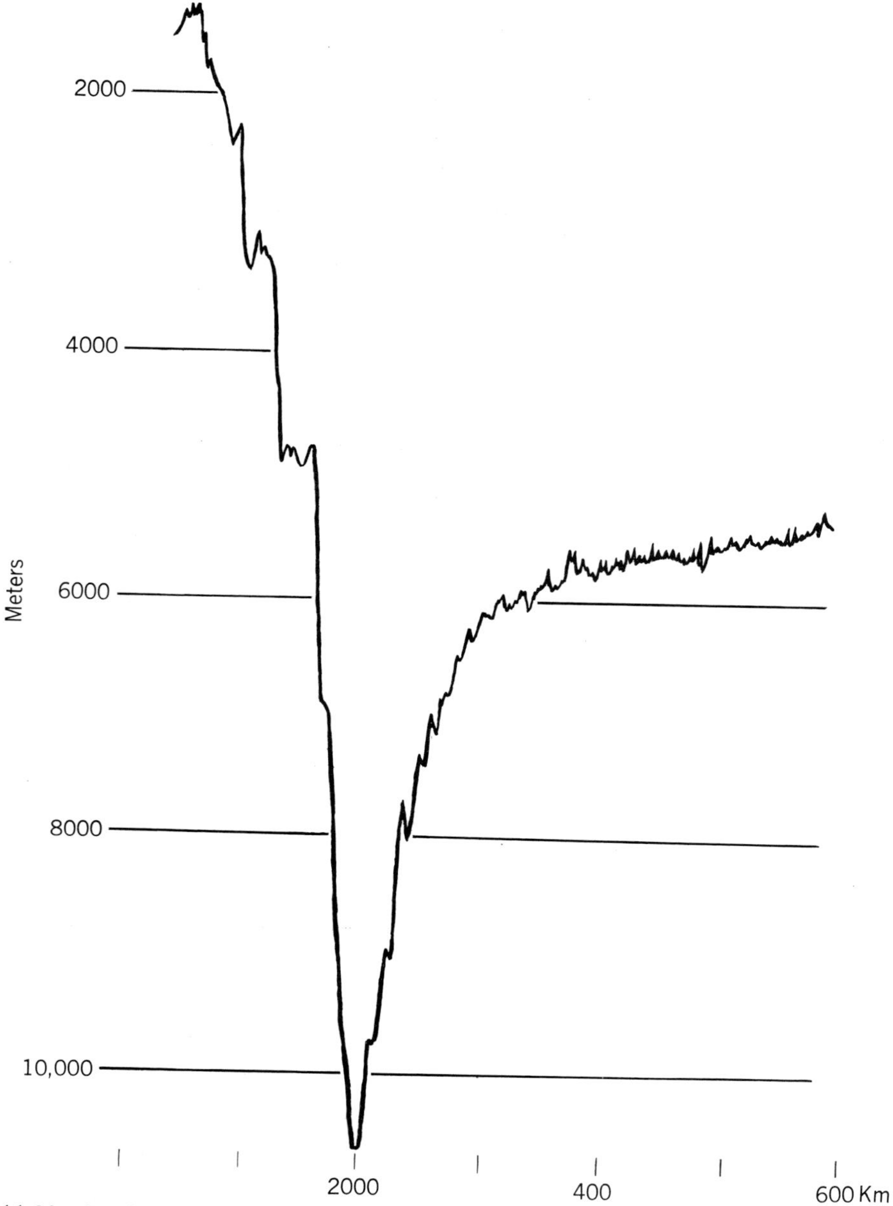

11.33 Profile of the Tonga Trench.

sprinkling of ash and it formed a measureable layer only a few score kilometers from the volcanic vent. Indeed, how great must have been the earlier eruptions if the greatest known to man was too small to produce a significant record? Powerful eruptions in the Japanese, Kurile, and Aleutian Arcs have produced so much ash that these airborne volcanic products dominate the sediments and modify the scenery of the northwest Pacific in a belt almost 1000 kilometers wide.

The great earthquakes which repeatedly jar the ocean trenches and cause long gravity waves to speed destruction to far-off shores must have

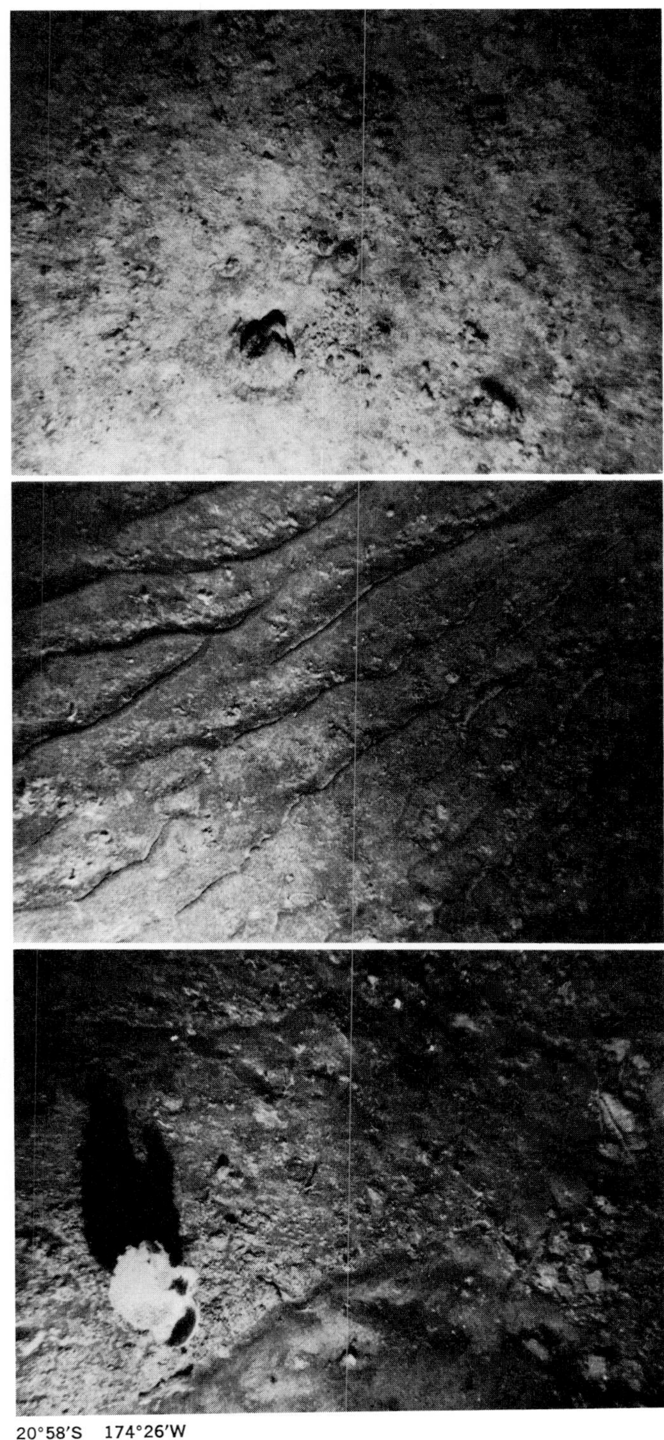

20°58′S 174°26′W
20°58′S 174°26′W
20°58′S 174°26′W

11.34 Coarse debris and ripples attest to vigorous currents along the west wall of the Tonga Trench. U, C, L, 1511 m, upper west wall.

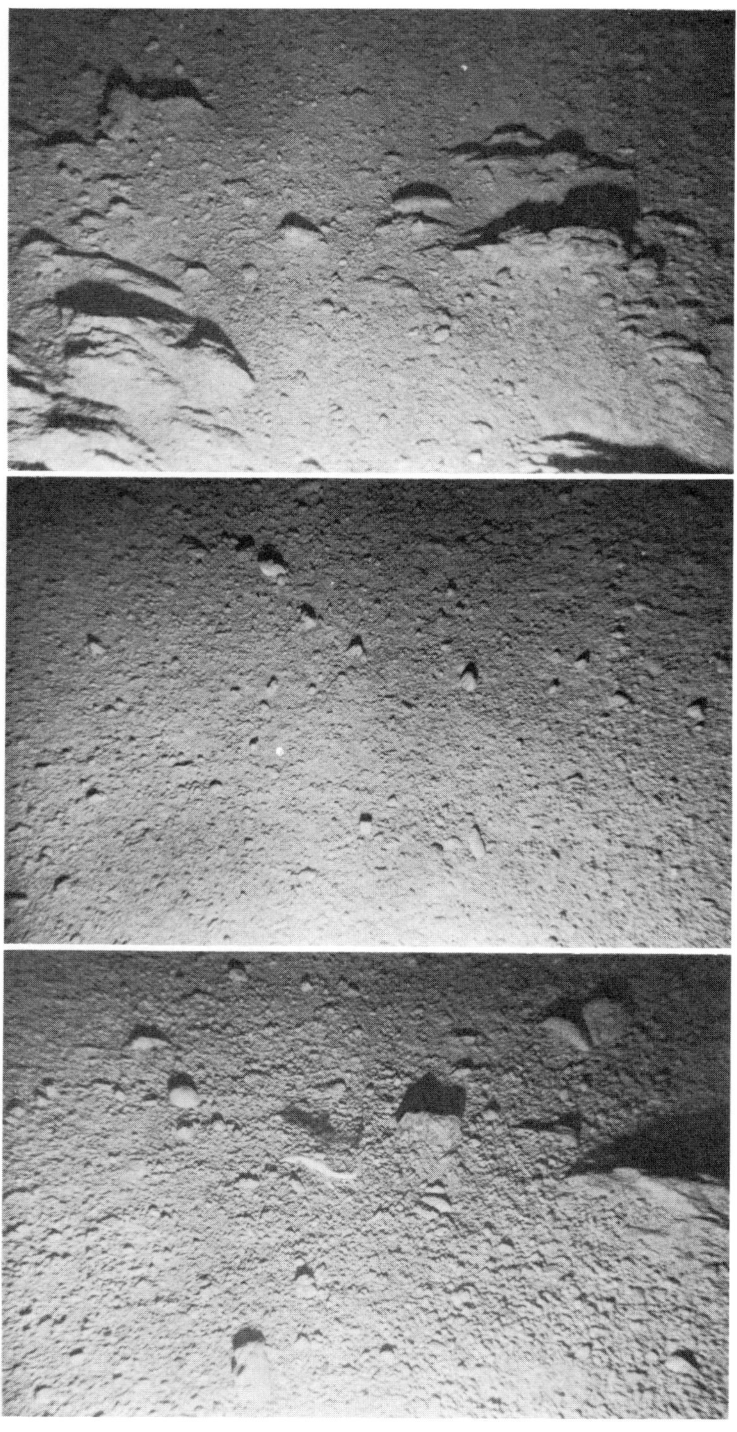

29°40′S 176°43′W
29°40′S 176°43′W
29°40′S 176°43′W

11.35 Rock outcrops and current-winnowed coarse debris in the Kermadec Trench, U, C, L, 5069 m, west wall.

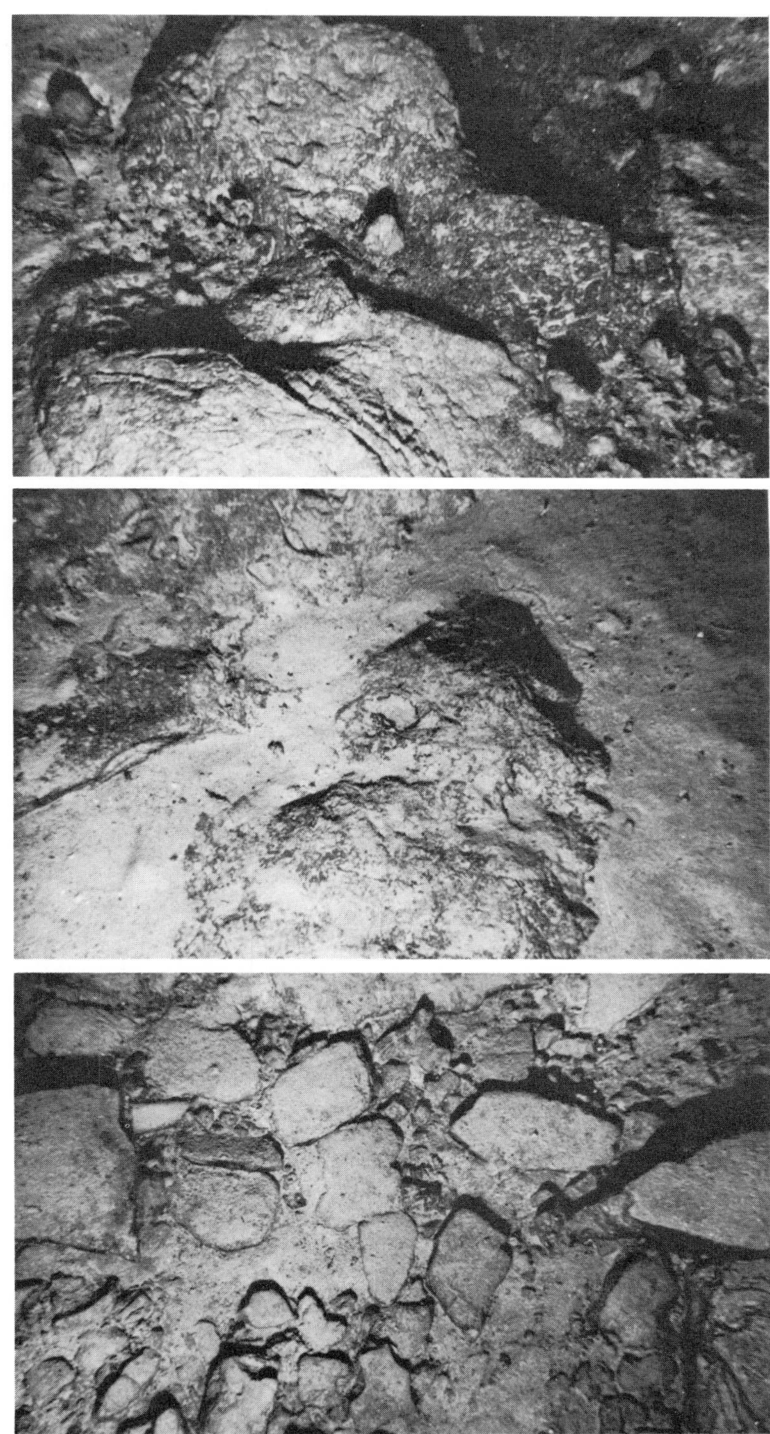

15°43′S 172°57′W
15°43′S 172°57′W
15°43′S 172°57′W

11.36 Manganese encrusted bare rock and talus on west wall of the Tonga Trench. U, C, L, 1929 m.

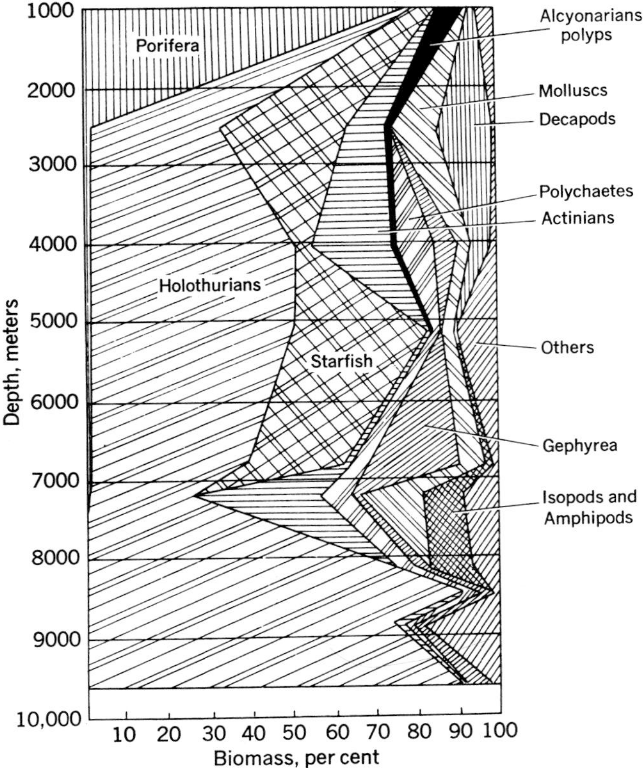

11.37 No unique group of animals is characteristic of the deep trenches. In hadal depths, greater than 8000 meters, holothurians are the dominate living organisms recovered in trawls.

an appreciable visible effect on the seascape. The broken rocks, of course, are tangible evidence of the physical forces, but the sloshing of the waters must stir up the muds and oozes and lower visibility until the sediment again settles to the sea floor and reaches a tranquil environment.

PACIFIC PATTERNS

Two basic types of trenches can be recognized in the Pacific. There are the great series of intersecting arcuate trenches which include the Aleutian, Kurile-Kamchatka, Japan, Bonin, Mariana, Yap, Palau, Philippine, and Java; each paralleling a volcanic island arc which in turn encloses a subsiding and filling marginal sea (11.27-11.30). The other, typified by the straighter Middle America and Peru-Chile Trenches (11.31, 11.32) parallel the continental margin without an intervening marginal sea.

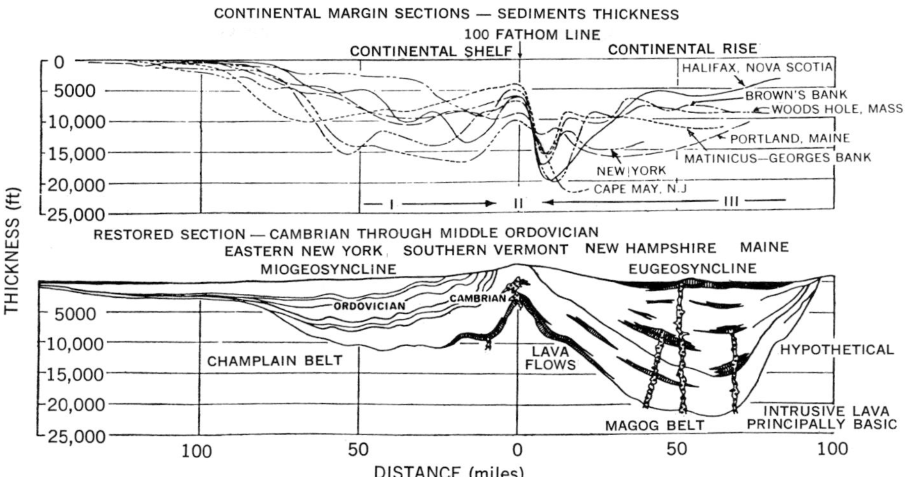

11.38 Great thicknesses of sediment are deposited in the continental margins.

We have few photographs of the great arcuate trenches of the north Pacific, but we suspect that their visual characteristics differ very little from those trenches we have seen. In fact, the reports of bathyscaphe observations confirm that rock crops out on the walls of the Japan Trench and that contour currents scour its walls and even its floor.

The Tonga-Kermadec Trench forms a straight and continuous, nearly north-south discontinuity between the subsided blocks of the former vast Melanesian continent and the oceanic crust of the South Pacific Basin. In passing east to west from the open ocean to the active Kermadec Island Arc the seismic reflection profile records a nearly uniform layer of unstratified sediment blanketing the crust below. The outer ridge is not separated from the trench by the usual escarpment. Instead, the crust seems to have broadly arched down toward the island arc without any of the usual fracturing. The virtual absence of a flat floor suggests that subsidence, perhaps accompanied by horizontal thrusting, is still proceeding for otherwise displaced debris should form a horizontal filling in the bottom of the trench. In the northern Kermadec Trench and in the Tonga Trench, which lies still further north, the outer ridge is fractured in the usual way to form a precipitous outer wall. Rock exposures have been photographed on both walls, but as in the case of the Puerto Rico Trench, they are more common and more frequently consist of shattered talus on the steeper higher landward side (11.34-11.36). Presumed mantle rocks (dunite) have been photographed and dredged from this precipice near the Tonga Islands.[10]

It is a general lack of sediment accumulation which is the most notable feature of all the deep-sea trenches. This lack, recorded by seismic reflec-

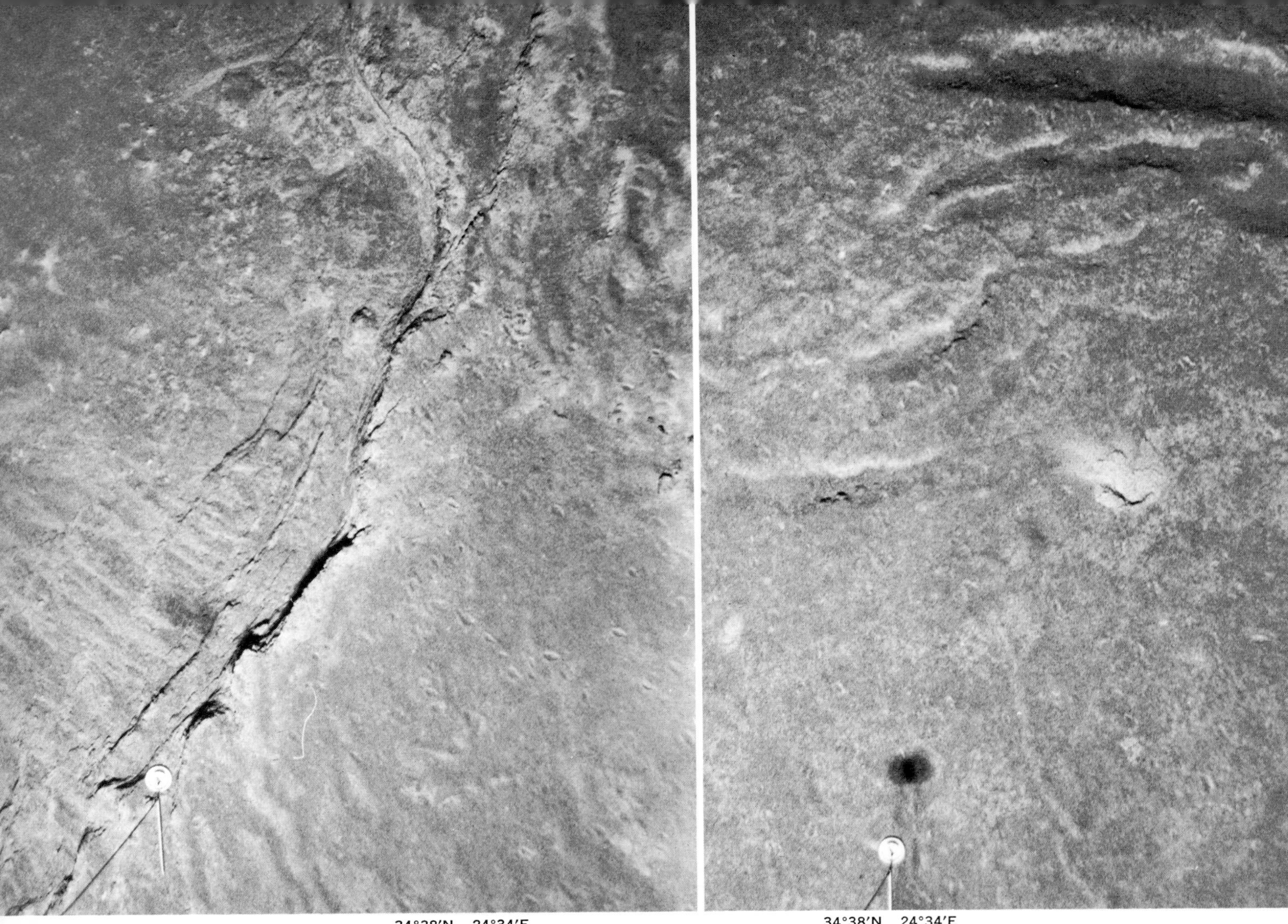

11.39 Steep sediment-covered slopes in the generally tranquil Mediterranean reveal fractures and slump scars. L, R, 1806 m, Ptolemy Mountains south of Crete.

tion profiles, inferred from coring and dredging, and visually observed in photographs, demands a recent origin of trench topography.

Although the existence of life on the abyssal floor has been well established since the *Challenger* expedition of the late nineteenth century, the lingering doubt that the deep-sea trenches might be azoic was not dispelled until after the Second World War when the *Galathea* and *Vityaz* expeditions demonstrated the existence of life in deep trenches throughout the world.[11] Few of the animals which inhabit the trenches are unique to this environment (11.37) and no discernible special effects in the visible seascape can be attributed to the trench or "hadal" animals. However, populations are frequently higher in the trenches due to the influ-

11.40 Small folds and faults attest to recent deformation of the Mediterranean Ridge. ▷

VESUVIUS
ETNA
STRAIT OF OTRANTO
STRAIT OF SICILY
SHELF
MESSINA CONE
MALTA ESCARPMENT
BOUNDARY CURRENT
ABYSSAL PLAIN
SANTORINI
MEDITERRANEAN RIDGE
PLINY TRENCH
STRABO TRENCH
ANAXIMANDER MOUNTAINS
NILE CONE
CM (7)
CM (4)
RECENT VOLCANIC ERUPTIONS PRODUCING TEPHRA
LIMIT OF NON-BURROWED UPPER SANTORINI TEPHRA LAYER
CONTOURED IN METERS
EFFECTED BY BOTTOM CONTOUR CURRENTS
ACTIVE SMOOTHING
RIPPLE MARKS
ORIENTATION OF LINEATIONS
CM (7) VELOCITY IN CM/SEC MEASURED BY BOTTOM CURRENT METER
NC NO CURRENT DETECTED
TRANQUIL ENVIRONMENTS
ANIMAL TRACKS & TRAILS
TEAR SHAPED BURROW MOUNDS
ANIMAL VOLCANOS
BURROWING COLONIES
SEA FLOOR LITTERED WITH CIRCULAR SPONGES
FRESH SCOOP MARKS PRODUCED BY FISH FEEDING IN THE SEDIMENT
TECTONICALLY DEFORMED
FAULTS, FOLDS, HORSTS, GRABENS
STRIKE OF TECTONIC LINEATION
R SEDIMENTARY OUTCROPS OR LOOSE BLOCKS
S FRESH SLUMP SCARS (SLICKENSIDES)

11.41 Mountain building forces are deforming the eastern Mediterranean. The sedimentary layers are severely deformed along the Mediterranean Ridge. In this region effects of contemporary compression can be seen in photographs.

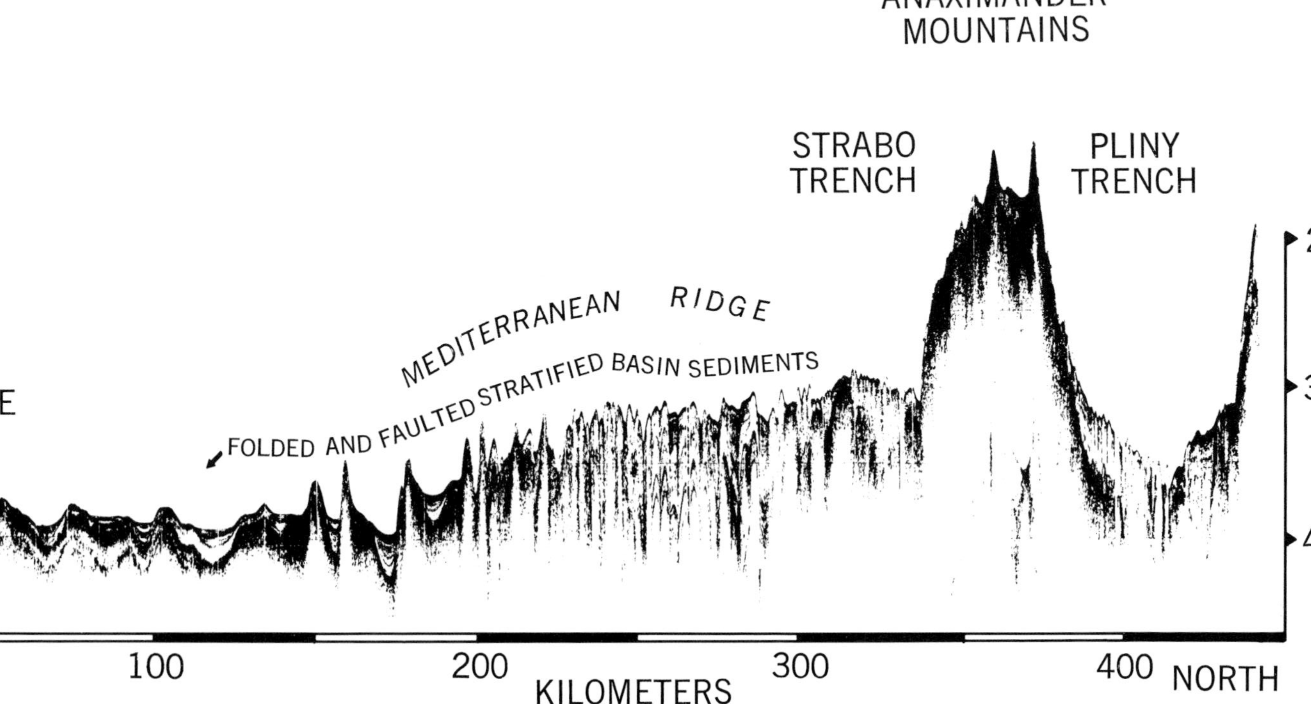

ence of the adjacent land barriers on oceanic circulation. Thus photographs of the floor of the Peru-Chile Trench,[12] which stretches almost the entire length of South America, reveal some of the highest benthic populations observed anywhere in the deep sea (11.32 U)—not because it is a trench, but because of the high surface productivity along the west coast of South America.

AND TETHYS SHALL BEAR NEW WORLDS

One of the basic generalizations of geology is that throughout the history of the earth, the thickest accumulation of sediments have tended to occur in long linear bodies and that these excessive accumulations, called geosynclines[13] (11.38), have been later deformed to produce mountains.

In the search for modern examples of geosynclines-in-the-making, the island arcs and trenches have often been discussed. The Java Trench, which lies seaward of the great Indonesian Arc, is clearly related to the Himalayan chain. It was over this trench that the characteristic huge gravity minimum now associated with all deep-sea trenches was first mapped. It was here that geologists first perceived that a relationship exists between the trench and the folded mountain range. The Indonesian islands seem to retain a history of former trenches running back two hundred million years or more. The island arc and the Indian Ocean floor have incessantly moved toward each other. The area of maximum conflict lies beneath the island slope and the trench floor marks the seaward limit of discernible interaction. The trench has continuously subsided and its contents have been successively accreted to the adjacent continent causing a slow growth of the Indonesian Arc toward the ocean.

The huge ridge of deformed sediments which lies between the Java Trench and the Indonesian Arc can be closely compared with the Barbados Ridge of the Antilles. This feature has often been identified as a geosyncline in the process of deformation. Similar but less well-known features exist in the Aleutian Trench; in fact, similar filled troughs of deforming sediments have been detected adjacent to or within the inner walls of all deep-sea trenches. There seems little doubt that these masses are our contemporary geosynclines and these will produce our future mountains.

It has been only a few million years since the great seaway, named after the goddess Tethys, stretched the length of what is now the Alpine-Himalaya mountain chain. An uplift from below sea level to the loftiest peaks on earth resulted when the great crustal blocks on either side pressed together and squeezed the thick accumulation of marine sediments into folded and overthrust mountains. From Indonesia and Burma across Pakistan, India, Nepal, Tibet, Iran, Iraq, and Turkey, the present dynamic front lies above the sea, bordered on the south by a series of plains that parallels the mountain system. In the Levant the thrust zone passes again beneath the sea. A minor ridge lies parallel to and south of the Greek archipelago extending through the eastern Mediterranean from Cyprus to the boot of Italy. Minor trenches separate it from the European continent and the Alpine-Himalayan belt. Compared with the great ocean trenches the topography of this eastern Mediterranean Arc seems extremely small but not insignificant. When examined in detail with echograms and seismic profiles, it is found to be intensely deformed on a fine scale. Many moving faults and folds involving the most recent deposits reach the sea floor where they have been frequently photographed (11.39-11.40). This contemporary deformation seems to result from the thrust of the Mediterranean sea floor beneath Crete, the Aegean Sea, and Greece, part of the continuing thrusting that is still building the Alpine-Himalayan mountain belt. Although much less is known about the trenches which rim the Pacific basin, we may presume that they too represent a zone of thrusting and folding, and that the crushed rock usually seen in trenches is a tangible visual demonstration of contemporary compression.

With respect to crustal layering, the Aleutian, Kurile-Kamchatka, Java, Middle America, and Peru-Chile Trenches are all strikingly similar. In each case the thin oceanic crust is bowed down toward the mass of deformed sediments which form the inner wall of the trench. Occasionally, fracturing has broken the outer ridge and produced steps similar to those sounded and photographed on the outer wall of the Puerto Rico Trench. Wherever bottom-seeking sediment transport has produced a level trench plain the tilt of the deeper structure shows that the downfaulted and downwarped crust has continued to subside along the shattered inner wall of the trench.

The rocks which constitute the islands of the arcs are principally volcanic, and the majority of the world's active volcanos lie in the arcs which constitute the Pacific's "ring of fire," but the volcanos spring from the arcs and not from the trenches. Although many of the rocks of the trenches may also be volcanic in origin, one is certainly not struck by the prevalence of billowy volcanic seascapes but rather by repeated and frequently dramatic evidences of contemporary deformation.

If one had considered the continents either as enormous snowplows moving outward over the ocean basins, or as great steamroller knives scraping the loose sediment from an underriding roller (11.41), one would have predicted the mass of tightly folded, shattered, and overthrust deep-sea sediments found in front of many arcs along the inner wall of the trench. But some of the continents and island arcs may act as great ice-breakers thrusting their prows up on the oceanic crust, applying their full weight to the crust, breaking segments of it off and forcing them down into the mantle beneath the continent. Since deformation on the inner walls of most trenches is confined to a narrow belt, the outcrop patterns resemble the Himalayan front where older consolidated and crystalline rocks are thrusting up and out over the underlying younger unconsolidated sediments of the Indo-Gangetic Plain.

The fracturing and faulting observed on the outer walls of the trenches may result from the bending down of the relatively strong oceanic crust, compression occurring on the lower side of the crustal layer and tension on the upper side. This would imply a basic structural and scenic difference between the two walls; the outer, dominated by tensional phenomena (i.e. nearly vertical faults and fissures) and the inner wall dominated by compressional (folds and thrusts). Our present knowledge of the seascape is at least compatible with this deductive view. The inner walls exhibit an enormously varied seascape with a prevalence of talus and frequently clear evidence of deformation while on the outer walls we see less talus and less deformation of the generally truncated horizontal beds.

We can watch the eroded sediments (Chapter 8) make their journey from the denuding continents into vast linear deposits (Chapter 9) which parallel the modern continental margins of the Atlantic and Indian Oceans. We can look at the rocky furrows which parallel the Pacific margins. We can see the broken surface of a deforming mass of sediments plastered on the landward wall and wonder if still more sediments have been swept from the nearly empty floor of the trench and shoved into the earth's mantle beneath the continents. Many of the ancient geosynclines which have repeatedly produced great mountain ranges on the earth must have once resembled the shattered trenches or looked like the current-lineated continental rises before eventually being compressed and uplifted into mountains. Perhaps we can anticipate that major mountain ranges will soon appear above the sea where the now deforming Barbados, Timor, and Mediterranean ridges now lie.

One of the most significant tasks which could be accomplished in deep submersibles is the examination and detailed mapping of the deformed rocks of the landward slope of the deep-sea trenches and the median sedimentary ridges in order to discern the nature of the contemporary deformation. Are the sediment layers of the ancient ocean floor being folded, crumpled and slid beneath the advancing continents? Do the shattered and deformed rocks which have been seen on the landward wall of the trenches represent the skimmed-off and contorted deep-sea sediment layers? Will Tethys bear new worlds—create new mountains—from the yawning deeps and muddy drifts of the abyss?

NOTES AND REFERENCES

1. Many of the larger islands of the arcs reveal ancient and deformed strata beneath younger volcanic outpourings and thus bear evidence of severe and even repeated compression during past eras (R. W. Van Bemmelen. 1949. *The Geology of Indonesia.* Govt. Printing Office, The Hague, Vol. IA, 732 pp.; M. Minato, M. Gorai, and Hunahashi. 1965. *The Geologic Development of the Japanese Islands.* Tsukiji Shokan, Tokyo).

2. In mid-century, reacting against an oversimplified compressional model, some geologists and geophysicists (including one of the present authors) attempted to interpret the trenches as purely tensional features (J. L. Worzel, and M. Ewing, 1954. Gravity anomalies and structure of the West Indies, Part II. *Geol. Soc. Amer. Bull.,* 65:195-199.; M. Ewing and B. C. Heezen. 1955. Puerto Rico Trench topographic and geophysical data. *Geol. Soc. Amer. Spec. Paper* 62:255-267).

3. The tiny parallel scratches and grooves which bear evidence of the direction of motion on fault scarps are known as slickensides. They have been observed on rocks dredged up from fault scarps and one is confident that when deep-sea photographic techniques are improved, slickensides will be observed on the minor scarplets which are seen in unstable areas. Since slickensides retain a record of the last movement on the fault, visual observations of these features in the abyss may be a common activity of the geological aquanaut of the future. In fault zones it is common that hot fluids flowing along fractures carrying calcite in solution eventually deposit this calcareous mineral in the fissures. These calcite veins have been dredged from submarine fault zones and will surely be easily recognized by aquanauts.

4. The structure of the Puerto Rico Trench has been studied by: M. Talwani, G. H. Sutton, and J. L. Worzel. 1959. Crustal section across the Puerto Rico Trench. *J. Geophys. Res.,* 64:1545-1555; E. T. Bunce. 1966. The Puerto Rico Trench. In: W. H. Poole (Ed.), Continental margins and island arcs, a symposium sponsored by the International Upper Mantle Committee. *Geol. Surv. Canada,* 66-15:165-175; and E. T. Bunce and D. A. Fahlquist. 1962. Geophysical Investigation of the Puerto Rico Trench and Outer Ridge. *Jour. Geophys. Res.,* 67:3955-3972. The crustal block which forms the floor of the Puerto Rico Trench resembles the dropped keystone of a rising ramp, which once bridged the transition from the thin oceanic crust to the thick foundation of the island arc. Perhaps the structure of the south flank of the island preserves the essential character of the pre-trench configuration of the now subsided crustal layers of the north.

5. Sediment bodies devoid of layering as recorded on seismic reflection records are usually termed transparent in the literature. We, however, choose to use the term transaural, which is a more accurate description of this characteristic.

6. R. F. Dill. Aboard *Archimède,* 1964.

7. Peres, J. M., 1965. Aperçu sur les résultats de deux plongées effectuées dans le ravin de Puerto Rico par la bathyscaphe *Archimède. Deep-Sea Res.,* 12:883-891.

Certain molluscs, echinoids, and sponges bore holes into solid rock and produce a riddled, honeycombed surface (R. R. Schrock. 1948. *Sequence in Layered Rocks.* McGraw-Hill, New York, pp. 184-187).

8. Granitic rocks have been dredged and photographed on the eastern flank of the Aves Ridge, a linear north-south trending plateau, which connects Venezuela and the Virgin Islands and lies approximately 200 miles west of the West Indian Island Arc. That the rocks were recently thoroughly shattered was obvious from the fragments dredged and from the broken and fractured expanses photographed. In fact, manganese crusts representing several million years of accumulation covered parts of the shattered blocks while other surfaces were fresh and hardly altered or coated. Thus, it appears that deformation is still going on.

9. D. Ninkovich, B. C. Heezen, J. R. Conolly, and L. H. Burckle. 1964. South Sandwich Tephra in deep-sea sediments. *Deep-Sea Res.,* 11:605-619.

10. R. L. Fisher and C. G. Engel. 1969. Ultramafic and basaltic rocks dredged from the near shore flank of the Tonga Trench. *Bull. Geol. Soc. Amer.,* 80:1367-1372.

11. A. F. Bruun. 1957. Deep sea and abyssal depths. In: J. W. Hedgepeth (Ed.). Treatise on marine ecology and paleocology. *Geol. Soc. Amer. Mem.,* 67(1):641-672; T. Wolff. 1961. Animal life from a single abyssal trawling. Galathea Rept., 5:129-162; L. Zenkevitch. 1963. *Biology of the Seas of the U.S.S.R.*, Allen and Unwin, London, 955 pp.

12. R. J. Menzies. 1963. General results of biological investigations U.S.N.S. Eltanin Cruise 3. *Int. Rev. Ges. Hydrobiol.,* 48:185-200.

13. This term cannot truly be applied to modern accumulations for lack of definite proof that deformation will ensue. Geosynclines are divided into a number of types depending on the composition of the sediments, proportion of volcanic material, and the style of subsequent deformation of the body. For present considerations we need only mention the parallel miogeosyncline–eugeosyncline association. The miogeosyncline is filled by limestones and sandstones composed of well-worn detritus from which all the more or less unstable minerals have been removed. The eugeosyncline which accumulated in deeper water has much volcanic derived sediments and the sands contain many unstable components. These generalizations were erected on the basis of a study of the Paleozoic deposits of the Appalachian Mountains of the eastern United States and of similar mountain ranges of the world (M. Kay. 1951. North American geosynclines. *Geol. Soc. Amer., Mem.,* 48:143 pp.). It has been suggested that the present margin of eastern North America has a similar sequence of sediment types and sediment bodies as the reconstructed Paleozoic geosyncline and that the Paleozoic geosyncline was deposited in a similar way in a similar environment as the Mesozoic and Tertiary deposits of the modern margin (C. L. Drake, M. Ewing, and G. H. Sutton. 1960. Continental margins and geosynclines; the east coast of North America north of Cape Hatteras. *Physics and Chemistry of the Earth,* 3:110-198; R. S. Dietz. 1963. Collapsing continental rises: an actualistic concept of geosynclines and mountain building. *Jour. Geology,* 71:314-333). Furthermore, the analogy implies that similar mountains will be erected by a similar deformation in the geological future. Thus the scenery of the Paleozoic miogeosyncline might have resembled the active modern shelves and reefs from Labrador to the Bahamas while the Paleozoic eugeosyncline may have resembled the continental rise with its contour current-shaped sea floor.

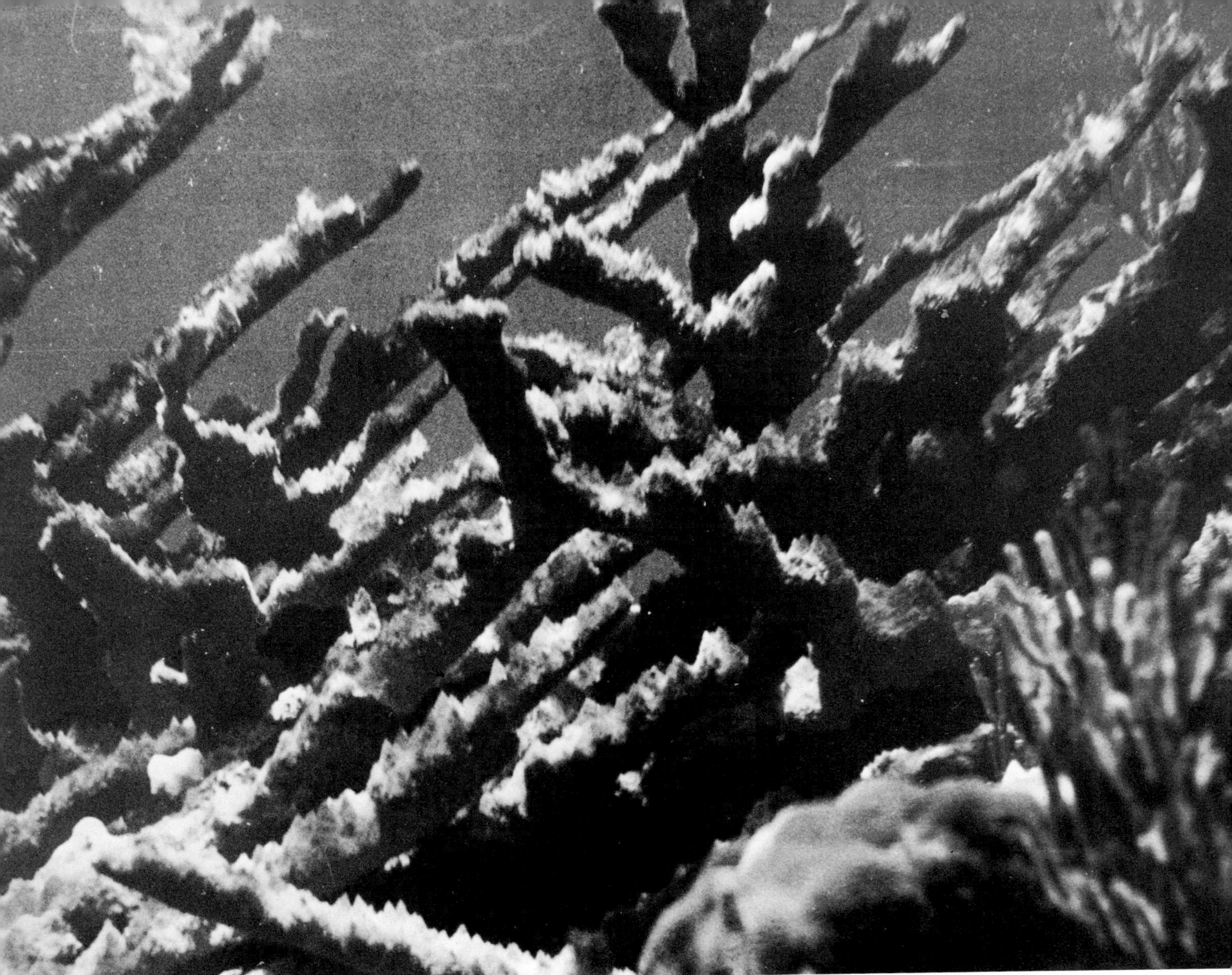

12.1 Coral gardens of the sunlit reefs of the tropics, Bahama Islands.

12
Pedestals and Plateaus

It had been strange to see it rushing forth for the first time; now it was almost as strange to see nothing but hard black rock where there had once been a molten stream. I felt as if my mountain had died. It had bled to death. Its golden burning heart had stopped beating.

SIGURDUR THORARINSSON

The explosions, violent surges of the sea, airborne rocks, dust, gas, and steam attending the birth of volcanic islands are awe-inspiring to behold (12.9). But we must remember that before the first bit of hot rock can appear above the waters, volcanic outpourings must have previously built an enormous volcanic mountain up from the deep-sea floor (12.2). Although several volcanic islands have been observed to form, no one has witnessed or photographed the construction of a deep-sea volcanic pedestal and no one can accurately describe the scene or say with certainty how long it takes to build one upward two or three miles above the abyssal floor.

The volcanos which rise above the sea can be divided into two distinct groups.[1] Those explosive vents which lie in arcuate rows on the continental side of the oceanic trenches produce comparatively light-colored and lightweight rocks,[2] but those which concern us here are the more tranquil vents which rise from the true oceanic abyss, lie in straight rows along vertical fractures, and calmly give forth, with little seismic fanfare, dark heavy lavas[3] (12.3). Thousands of bountiful volcanic vents have poured out sufficient lava from the earth's mantle to build the massive underpinnings of oceanic islands, coral atolls, and seamounts.[4] (12.4). However, millions of abyssal hills, knolls, and peaks have been produced by other less ample vents which failed to produce enough to build to the surface of the sea before their activity was snuffed out.

Lavas that erupt from vents above the sea's surface often contain large void spaces created by expanding pockets of trapped gas. This produces a sponge-cake texture and imparts a distinct visual characteristic to many subaerially erupted rocks. Those lavas that flow over damp ground are often dramatically roughened as a consequence of exploding bubbles of water vapor. Beneath the sea the pressure of the water constrains the formation of bubbles or vesicles and the rock often has a more compact appearance.

The most extreme example of gas bubble expansion is seen in pumice and ash, where bubbles claim so much of the volume that pumice can float. This effect, to a lesser degree, can be seen in many other surface-erupted rocks (12.5). The expansion of gas bubbles, which in the final thirty-five meters of ascent up the volcanic vent to the land surface must amount to ten times the original volume, in abyssal depths is negligible. Beneath the pressure of 5000 meters of water a 2 per cent change occurs in a similar ascent. Thus, there is a depth-dependent visual effect which, to some degree, controls the scenery of submarine volcanos.[5]

43°14′S 97°43′W

Studies of the gravitational attraction over several oceanic volcanos led to the conclusion that the average density of the pedestals is a great deal less than that of the lava flows emitted from subaerial vents; thus,

43°14′S 97°43′W

the submarine eruptions which build the volcanic pedestals must produce a greater proportion of low density rock than subaerial ones. Perhaps this is a result of a violent interaction of the hot lavas and the waters of the abyss or perhaps the result of interbedded sediments and quantities of chemically altered, low-density volcanic products. Thus, in attempts to visualize a submarine volcano, we can imagine not a solid mass, laid down dense flow upon dense flow, but a highly varied water-soaked and altered sequence of hard and soft layers shot with volcanic pipes and feeders. The scene during the growth of a volcano must be immensely varied and that preserved now still contains considerable variability. Dikes and sills, flows, ash and sediment layers are all visible on the flanks of volcanic pedestals (12.6).

When the photographic exploration of the ocean was just beginning, large extinct submarine volcanos (seamounts) received an inordinate share of the attention. Part of this was owing to their shallower depths which allowed the ship to save time while testing the still imperfect and frequently inoperative cameras; part to the early uncertainty of detecting bottom contact in true abyssal depths; but the delight of all viewers in the varied scene was surely a factor.

◁ 12.2 Corals now decorate the cooled lavas of a submarine volcano. U, L, 162 m, crest of Eltanin Seamount, southeast Pacific.

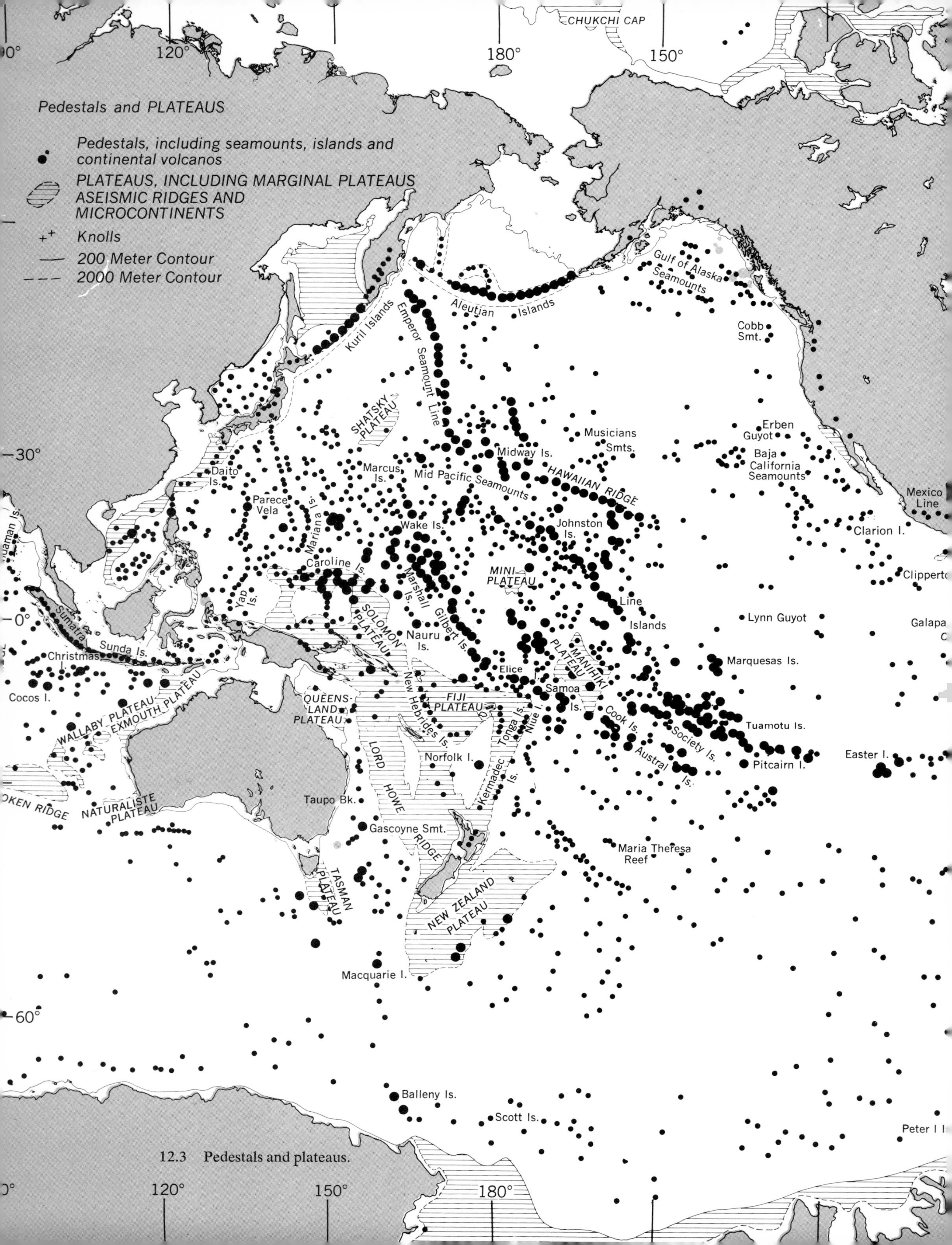

CHUKCHI CAP
120°
180°
150°
Pedestals and PLATEAUS
Pedestals, including seamounts, islands and continental volcanos
PLATEAUS, INCLUDING MARGINAL PLATEAUS ASEISMIC RIDGES AND MICROCONTINENTS
Knolls
200 Meter Contour
2000 Meter Contour
Gulf of Alaska Seamounts
Aleutian Islands
Kuril Islands
Emperor Seamount Line
Cobb Smt.
SHATSKY PLATEAU
Musicians Smts.
Erben Guyot
Baja California Seamounts
-30°
Midway Is.
HAWAIIAN RIDGE
Daito Is.
Marcus Is.
Mid Pacific Seamounts
Mexico Line
Parece Vela
Mariana Is.
Wake Is.
Johnston Is.
Clarion I.
Caroline Is.
MINI PLATEAU
Clipperton
Yap Is.
Marshall Is.
Line Islands
-0°
Sumatra
Sunda Is.
SOLOMON PLATEAU
Nauru Is.
Gilbert Is.
Lynn Guyot
Galapagos
Christmas I.
MANIHIKI PLATEAU
Marquesas Is.
Elice
Samoa Is.
Cocos I.
QUEENSLAND PLATEAU
FIJI PLATEAU
New Hebrides Is.
WALLABY PLATEAU
EXMOUTH PLATEAU
Tonga Is.
Niue I.
Cook Is.
Society Is.
Tuamotu Is.
Easter I.
LORD HOWE RIDGE
Norfolk I.
Austral Is.
Pitcairn I.
Kermadec Is.
Taupo Bk.
NATURALISTE PLATEAU
BROKEN RIDGE
Gascoyne Smt.
Maria Theresa Reef
TASMAN PLATEAU
NEW ZEALAND PLATEAU
Macquarie I.
-60°
Balleny Is.
Scott Is.
Peter I I.
120°
150°
180°

12.3 Pedestals and plateaus.

30°
0°
30°
90°
JAN MAYEN RIDGE
GREENLAND ICELAND FAEROE RIDGE
VORING PLATEAU
ROCKALL PLATEAU
PORCUPINE PLATEAU
60°
FLEMISH CAP
Cantabria Smt.
Galicia Bank
Kelvin Seamounts
Azores Is.
Horseshoe Smts.
Corner Smts.
Atlantis Cruiser
Bermuda I.
Great Meteor Smt.
Canary Is.
30°
BAHAMA BANKS
JAMAICA PLATEAU
AVES PLATEAU
Cape Verde Is.
DEMERARA PLATEAU
Sierra Leone Smts.
Fernando Po I.
São Tomè
Annabon I.
Cameroon Line
Rift Valley Volcanos
Seychelles Is.
Amirantes Is.
MASCARENE PLATEAU
Noronha Line
Ascension I.
LUANDA PLATEAU
Comores Is.
CHAGOS LACCADIVE PLATEAU
NINETYEAST RIDGE
Stocks Smt.
St. Helena I.
Trinidade Line
Trinidade I.
San Felix Is.
SANTOS PLATEAU
RIO GRANDE PLATEAU
WALFISCH RIDGE
MOZAMBIQUE PLATEAU
MADAGASCAR PLATEAU
Vema Smt.
andez Is.
Tristan da Cunha I.
Amsterdam I.
St. Paul I.
Gough I.
AGULHAS PLATEAU
Discovery Smt.
Crozet I.
Prince Edward I.
FALKLAND PLATEAU
KERGUELEN PLATEAU
Bouvet I.
Ob Smt.
Heard I.
SCOTIA RIDGE
S. Sandwich Is.
QUEEN MAUD RISE
30°
0°
30°
60°
90°

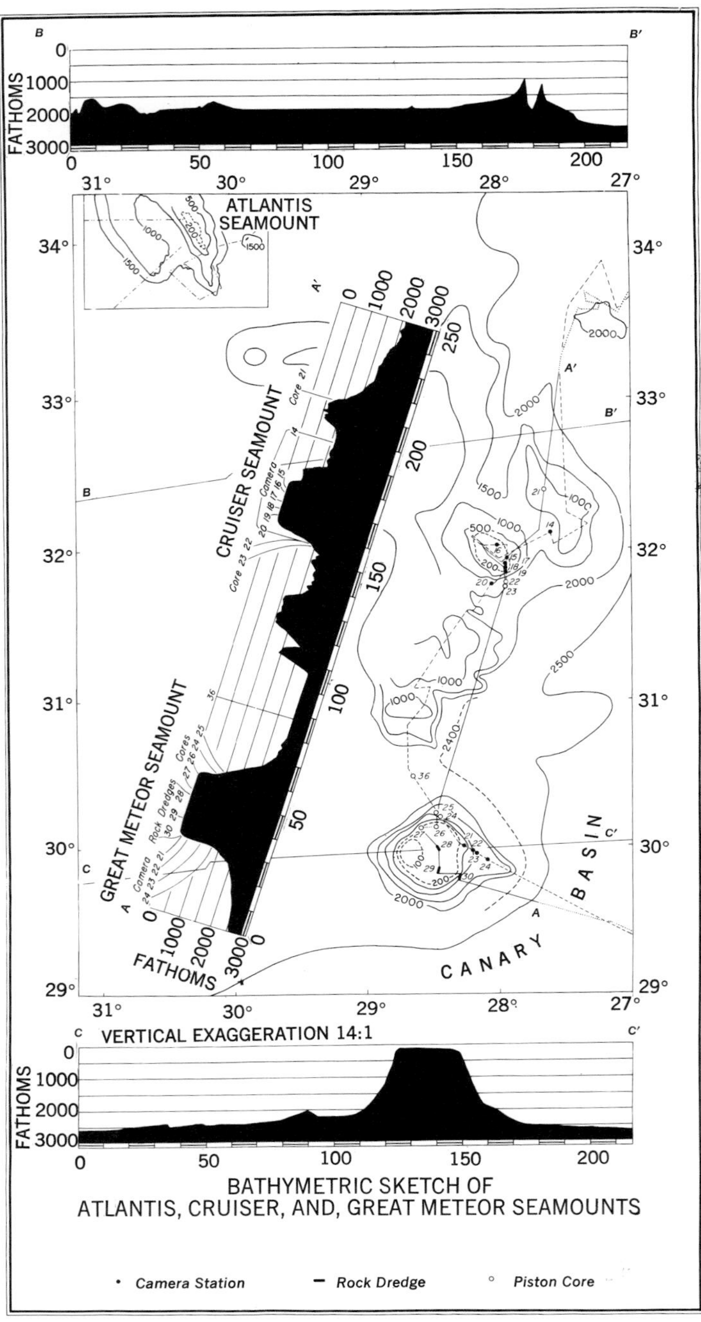

12.4 Ancient sunken islands of the eastern Atlantic. Rippled sand and limestone slabs have been photographed and dredged on the broad flat summits of these beveled volcanos. Reef rocks and lavas have been seen and sampled on their steep slopes.

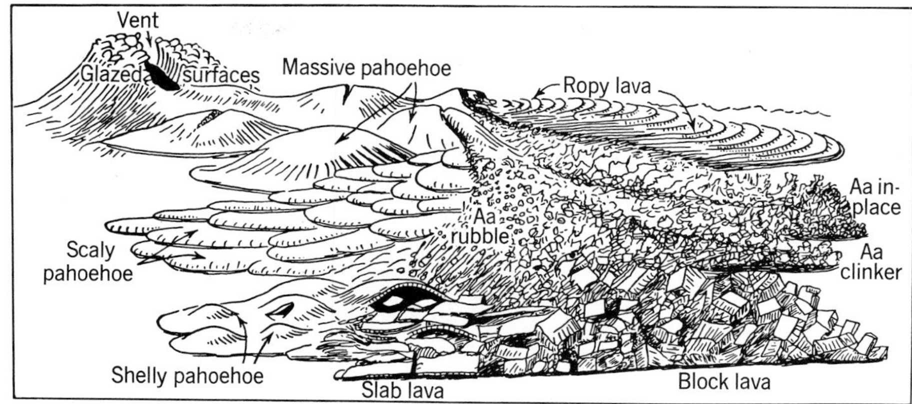

12.5 Types of lava surfaces seen above the sea. Pillow lava extruded beneath the sea resembles liquid filled balloons (see Fig. 13.3).

The overwhelming evidence for current scour (12.7) on seamounts was surprising to many oceanographers and geologists. A telegraph cable engineer would hardly have been surprised, for chafe and associated corrosion on rocky slopes account for most deep-sea cable failures not caused by man (12.8).

Volcanic peaks poke through and obstruct the flow of ocean waters, and as a result strong currents scour their steep slopes. The hard black rock of the freshly cooled volcano is coated with manganese films and crusts. Nooks and depressions between the barren broken rock and billowy pillows[6] are filled with current-rippled sand. Attached filter-feeding organisms such as sea pens, fans, and sponges soon congregate on the current-swept rock and spread their nets across the moving waters. Urchins and holothurians walk across patches of winnowed sand, and starfish burrow into the few areas of soft mud in search of smaller prey.

Volcanic peaks which have been successfully built above the surface of the sea are in constant battle with the ocean waves which batter and erode their new-born shores.[7] In tropical areas reefs begin to grow in the shallows (12.1), and the bottom soon becomes covered with beautiful coral gardens. After soil develops on the land, larger plants appear and the rocky spire develops a coastal fringe of trees, and people arrive to inhabit the island paradise (12.10). As the volcanic phase passes the island gradually subsides (12.11). In tropical waters, reefs build upwards, eventually creating a ring-like atoll as the volcanic base sinks (12.12). The lagoon widens, the subsiding peak claims less and less of the platform until it eventually is completely buried beneath the reef and lagoon sediments. The reef animals may build upwards for millions of years and

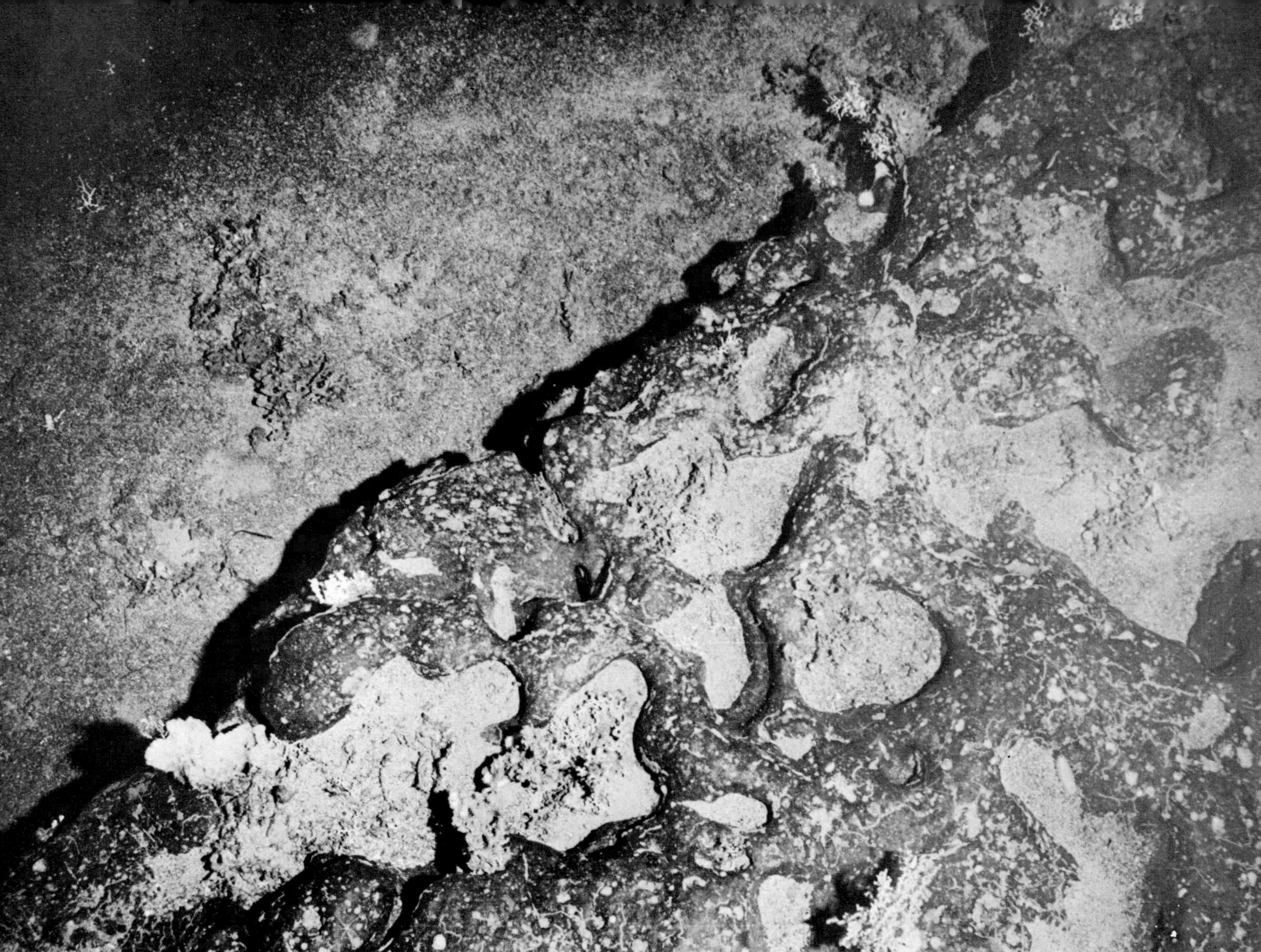

39°05′N 61°02′W
12.6 Pitted and polished lava decorated with deep-sea coral and bryozoan colonies are a familiar sight on seamounts. Patches of winnowed coarse sand and rock debris lie in depressions in the lava. 903 m, Kelvin Seamounts, western North Atlantic.

maintain an atoll, or they may die off and allow the flat-topped pedestal to disappear beneath the sea[8] (12.13-12.19).

Atolls are rings of coral, interrupted by narrow channels, which surround a lagoon of usually less than one hundred meters depth. The reef front generally falls off steeply, frequently at an angle exceeding forty-five degrees, and often the living coral overhangs the slope. The width of the reef, including islands, the seaward algal reef, and extensive tracts of dead coral lying near sea level, is usually only a few hundred meters.[9]

Ever since Charles Darwin proposed his elegant theory of the evolution of atolls, scientists' imaginations have been at work on the problem

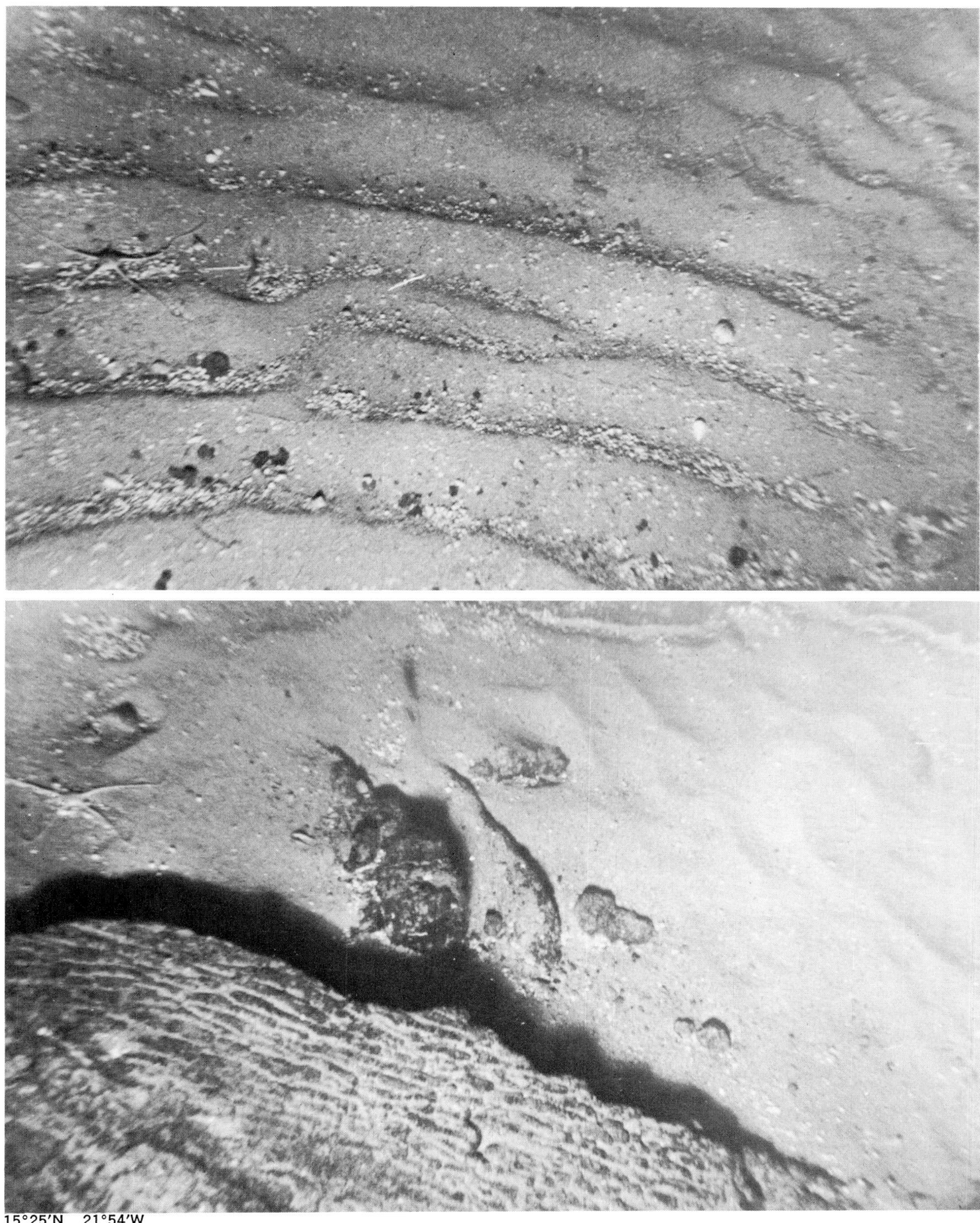

12.7 Currents scour the submerged flanks of oceanic islands. U, L, 2300 m, Maio Island, Cape Verde Islands, eastern Atlantic.

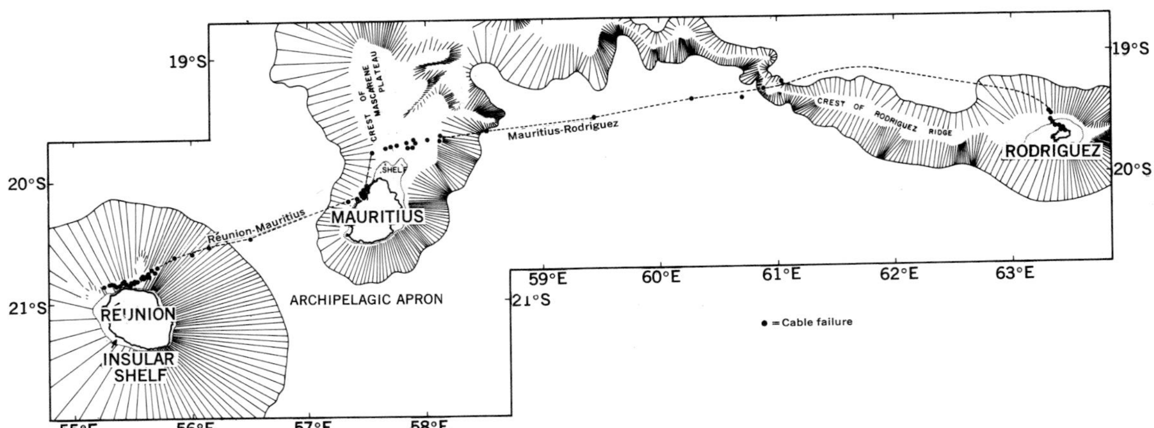

12.8 Submarine cables fail frequently on the rocky, current-swept island slopes. Strong bottom currents continually chaft the cable against sharp-edged rock.

of their origin. He suggested that atolls were constructed through the continued growth of a fringing reef initially formed around a volcano. The fringing reef built upwards at a growth rate equal to the rate of subsidence of the volcano. The volcano ultimately sank beneath the sea and the fringing reef became a circle of islands and bars surrounding a lagoon. This simple explanation was immediately criticized and more elaborate theories put forth. Sir John Murray advanced the idea that solution and erosion by currents of a solid mass of reef limestone produced the lagoon and that subsidence was not a factor. A few years later, J. D. Dana added strong support to Darwin's theory of subsidence by observing that the islands surrounded by barrier reefs reveal dramatic evidence of sinking in the form of drowned valleys and deep embayments. During the early 1900's, R. A. Daly and W. M. Davis recognized the significance of relative changes of sea level but thought that the existing form of atolls and lagoons resulted from glacial effects. They felt that cooling surface waters during glaciations killed the barrier reefs and allowed large-scale erosion of the reef and volcanic island. Daly underestimated the time needed to decapitate a volcano twenty to thirty miles wide, and both underestimated the importance of reef building by calcareous algae. The final test of theories on atoll formation had to wait for deep drilling on Eniwetok, which penetrated over one and a half kilometers of reef coral before reaching basalt, and for the result of seismic refraction studies on Bikini, which indicated a thick (nearly 2000 meter) cap of reef limestone resting on a basalt foundation. These investigations clearly showed that the amount of subsidence of the volcanos was matched by the steady upward growth of the coral, thus corroborating Darwin's simple explanation.[10]

12.9 "A blast of burning sand pours out in whirling clouds. Conspiring in their power, the rushing vapors carry up mountain blocks, black ash and dazzling fire" (Lucilius). The steaming hot Bayonaise Rocks blast forth from beneath the Pacific.

A large proportion of the volcanic pedestals of the abyss lie in relatively straight rows. Often they exhibit an evolutionary sequence, progressing from rugged active volcanos to gradually sinking eroded peaks, fringing reefs, atolls, and on to sunken seamounts. Such sequences, so well displayed from east to west in the Hawaiian Islands and the Society Islands and from west to east in the Samoan Islands, provide such a clear picture of pedestal evolution that the existence of flat-topped sunken islands, now known as "guyots," could have been anticipated a century before their final recognition on echograms during World War II.

A geologist on wartime cruises in the Pacific noted many flat-topped seamounts (guyots) on echograms. He hypothesized that they were not drowned atolls, but that they owed their flat tops to wave erosion near sea level, and that they sank in Pre-Cambrian time, before the develop-

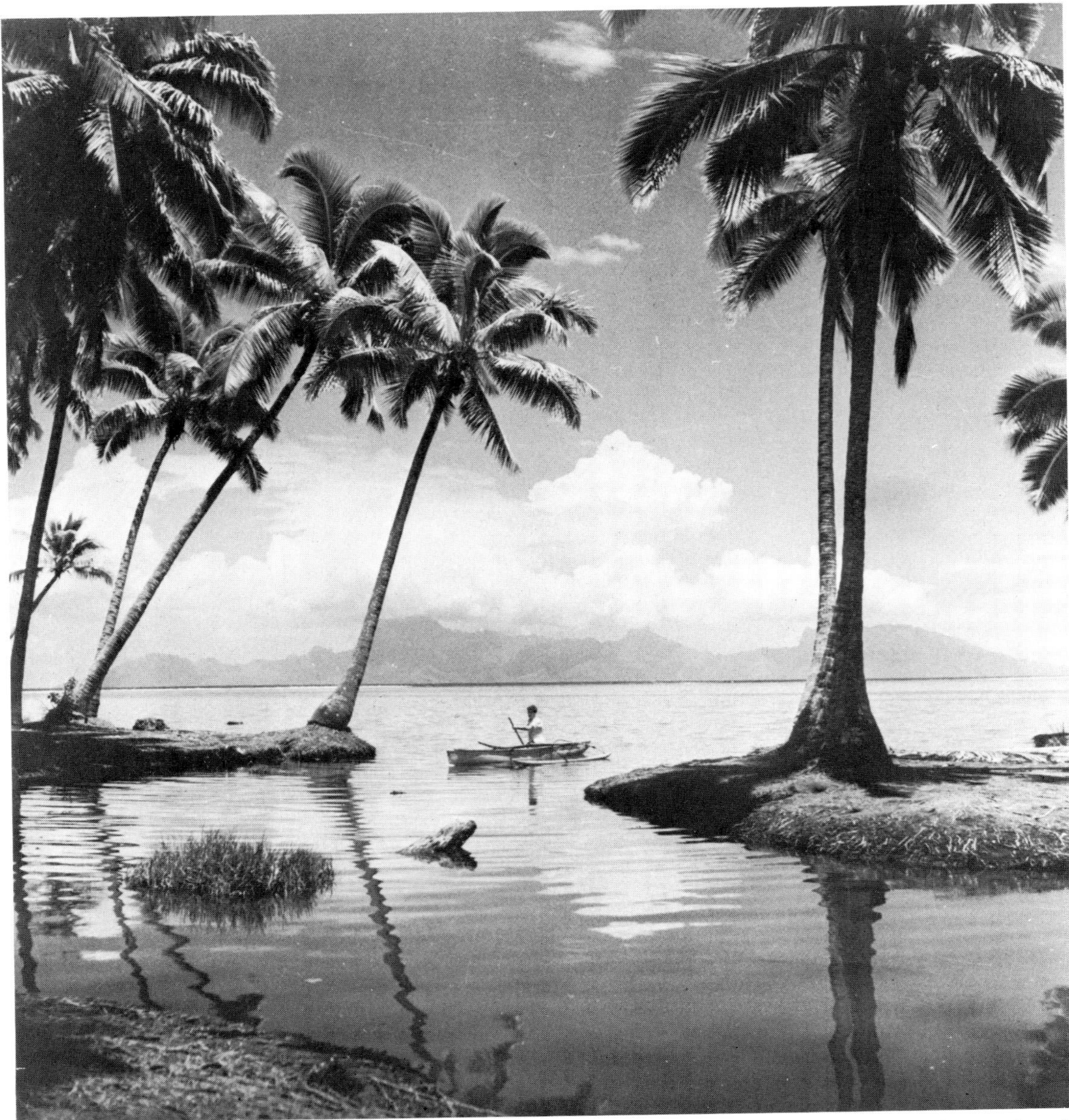

12.10 An island paradise. The eroded volcanic slopes of Morea rise from a broad lagoon. In the foreground, the peaceful lagoon of Tahiti is protected from ocean swell by the reefs.

ment of reef-building corals. Later, Cretaceous corals were recovered from the tops and sides of the guyots and it was concluded that the seamounts were ancient atolls and owed their flat tops to the growth of coral reefs and the formation of lagoons. They then sank faster than the corals could grow.[11]

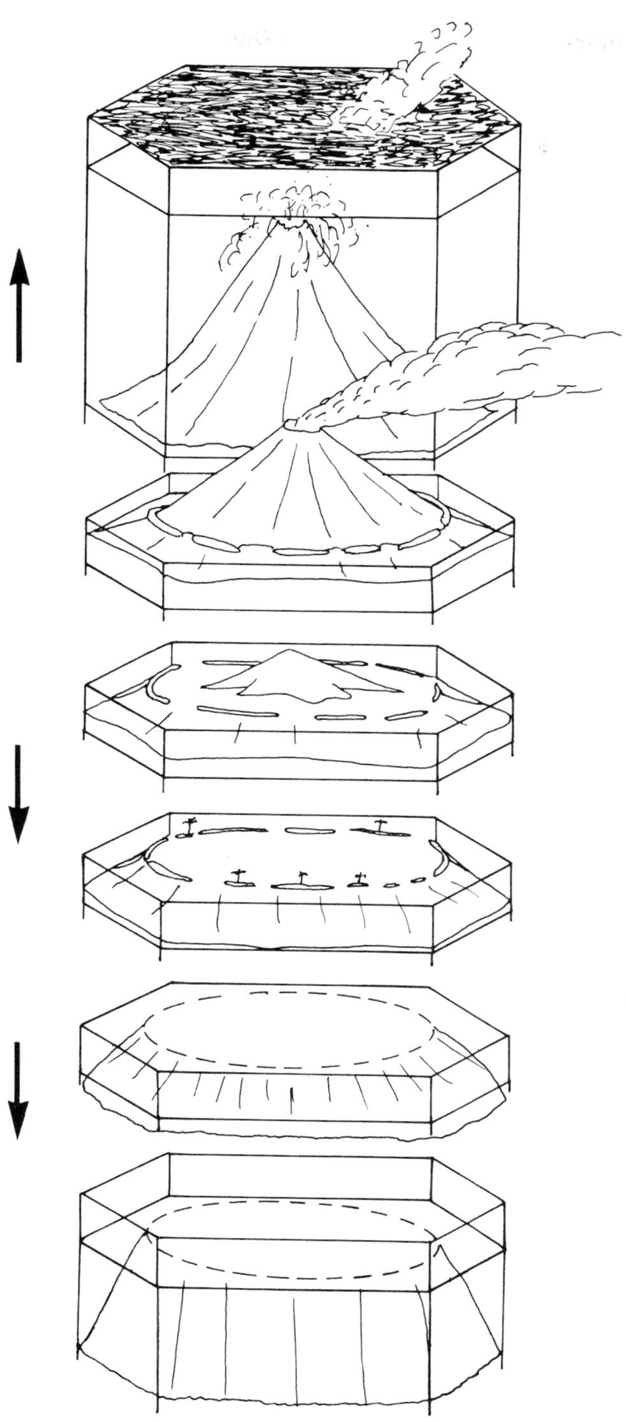

12.11 After a violent beginning, the volcano quietly sinks into the sea.

12.12 Kapingamaringi Atoll.

Exploration of the Pacific basin has led to the discovery of hundreds of sunken ancient islands and atolls which now lie in depths as great as 2500 meters. Fossil coral has been dredged and photographed from several such flat-topped seamounts southwest of Hawaii. In the course of future exploration remnants of the varied reef, lagoon, and island scenery will undoubtedly be recognized on these bare, current-swept summits.

ARCHIPELAGIC APRONS

The broad, smooth aprons that surround many seamounts and island groups represent the sediment-smoothed surface of wide volcanic accumulations which support the pedestal.[12] Although their profile resembles

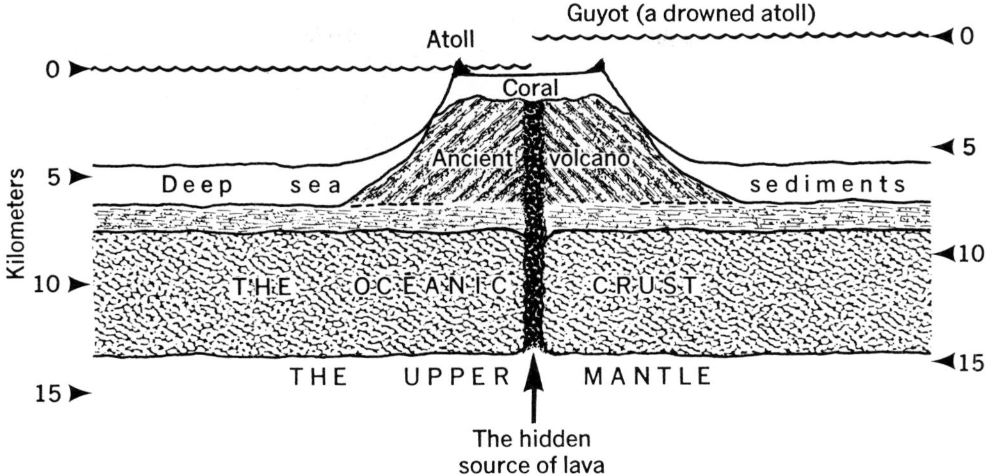

12.13 Structure of atolls and guyots.

in some ways that of the thick sediment aprons which fringe the continents, they contrast sharply in being composed principally of hard rock covered by a comparatively thin veneer of sediment hundreds rather than thousands of meters thick (12.20). In general, their surface is not marked by strong current scour or the prominent lineations which are so characteristic of the sediment drifts of the continental margins, but is instead relatively tranquil (12.21). Some archipelagic aprons form a circle hundreds of miles in diameter and the voluminous outpourings and deposited sediments contained in the discus-shaped accumulations vastly outweigh the generally ten-times smaller mass of the pedestals. Evidently, in these regions, the building of the pedestal was but the final crowning phase of a long period of volcanic outpouring. We cannot, however, exclude the possibility that in an earlier era continental-rise type environments may have prevailed and shaped the aprons.

Seamounts are commonly surrounded by moats which have been alternately attributed to varying local and limited subsidence of the volcanic mass into the underlying ocean crust or to the scour of sediments by ocean bottom currents accelerated in passing around the peak. Although subsidence may best explain the enormous moat which surrounds the Hawaiian Islands, the majority of moats appear to be the result of the interaction of currents and sediments. Acceleration of the moving water mass as it passes around the peak (9.10) can be expected to scour a moat, and the subsequent deceleration deposits the eroded sediment farther from the peak[13] (12.23).

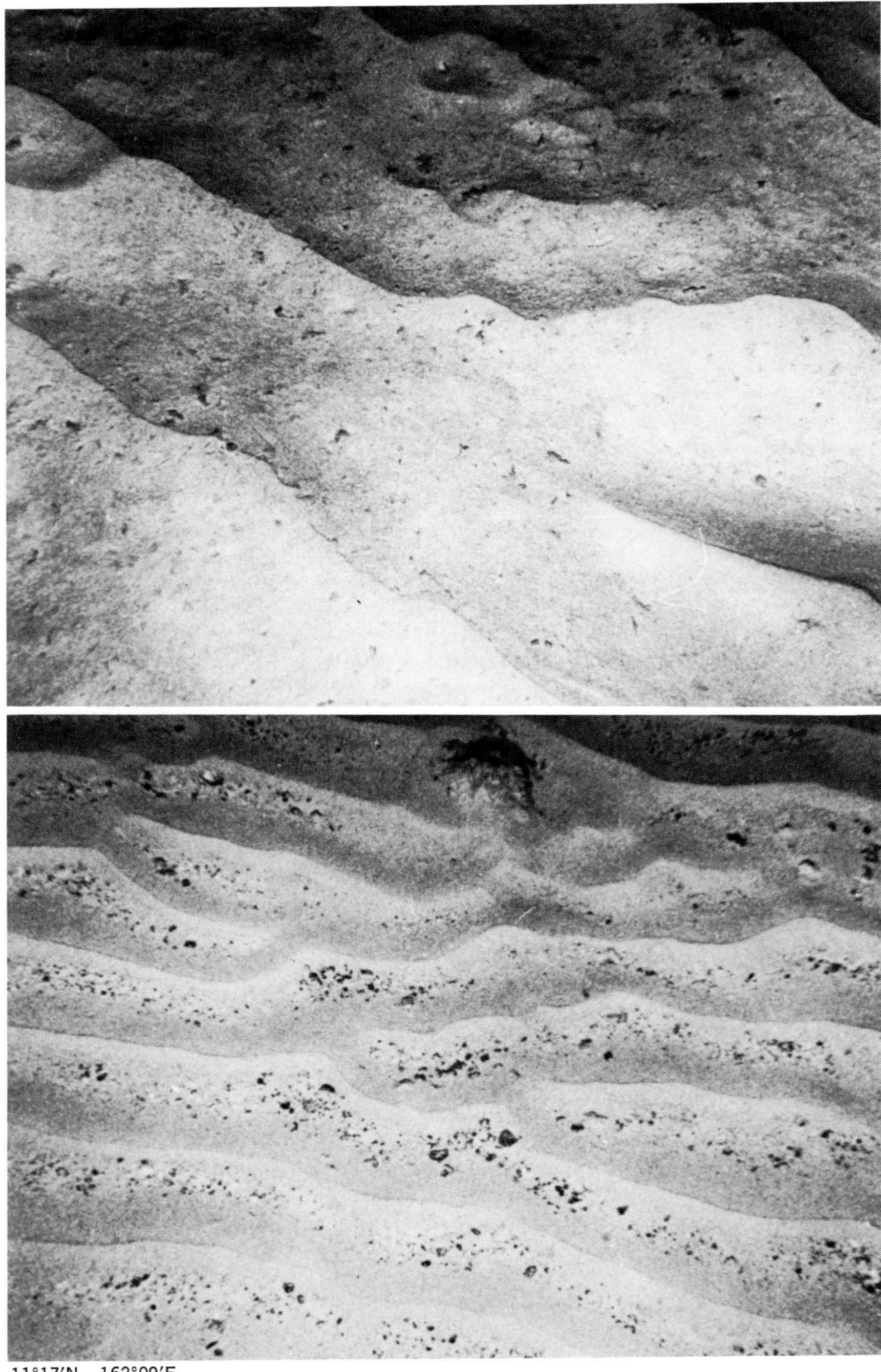

11°17′N 162°09′E
11°19′N 162°03′E
12.14 Currents ripple the sands on the flanks of the larger seamounts and islands. U, 1650 m; L, 2015 m, Eniwetok, Marshall Islands.

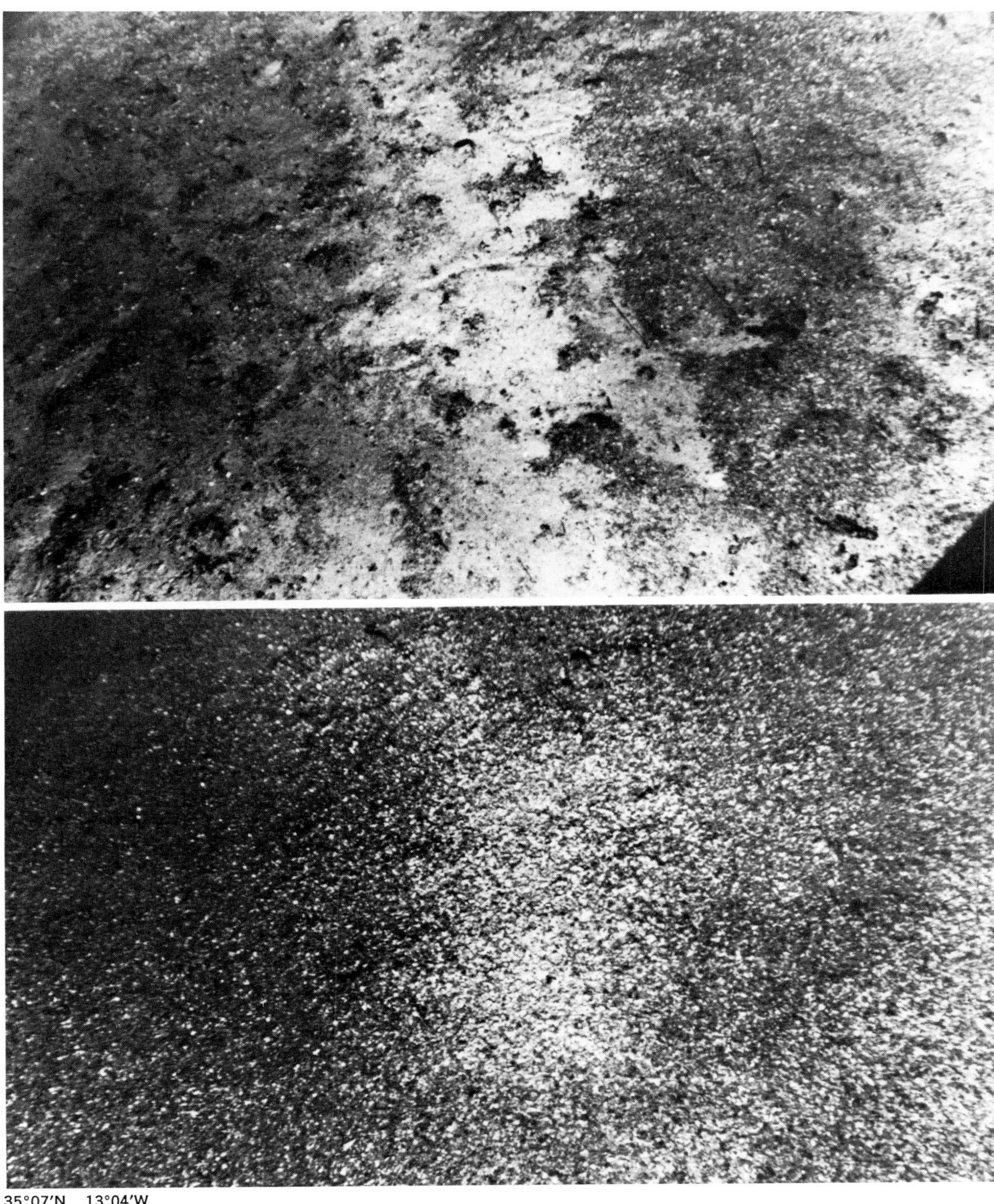

35°07′N 13°04′W
35°07′N 13°04′W

12.15 Coarse dark detritus covers the carbonate ooze on seamounts. The fine pelagic sediment is occasionally carried away entirely and what remains is reworked into windrows of coarse debris. U, L, 2065 m, Ampere Seamount, in North Atlantic.

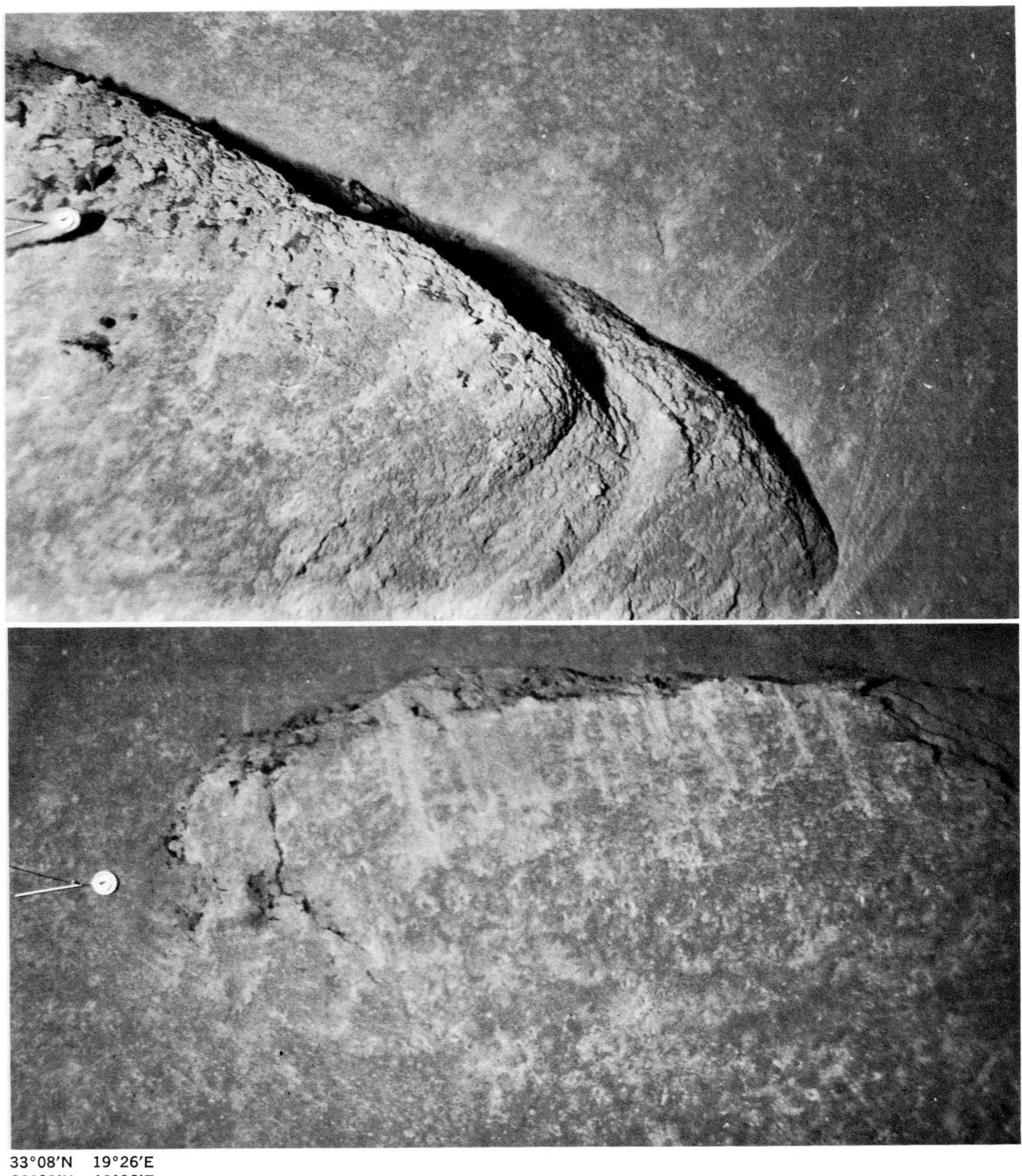

33°08′N 19°26′E
33°08′N 19°26′E

12.16 Deformed sediments are seen on the unstable mountains of the eastern Mediterranean. U, L, 2056 m, Takra Plateau, eastern Mediterranean.

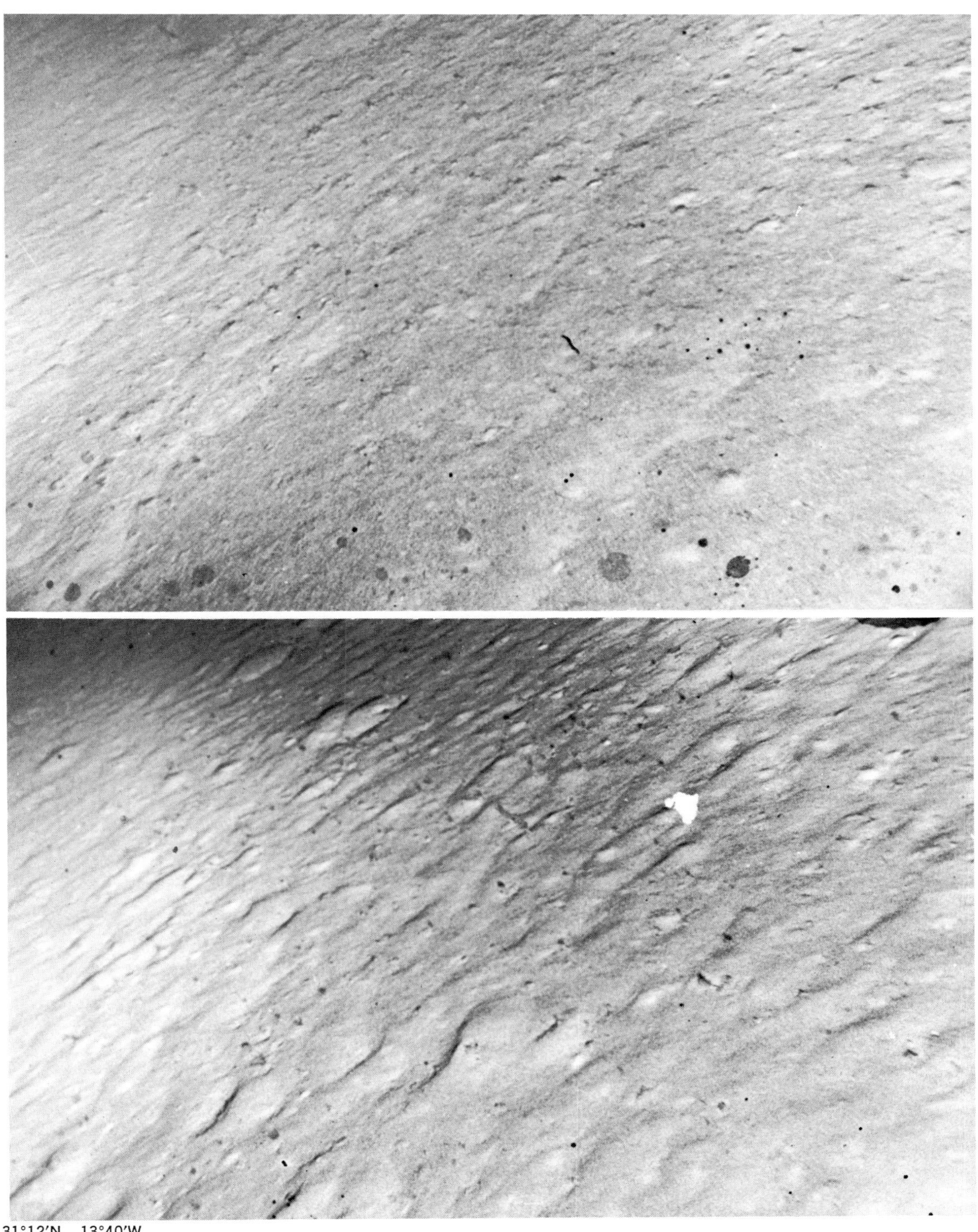

31°12′N 13°40′W

12.17 Expanses of current-smoothed limey sands are seen near the summits of seamounts. U, L, 358 m, near the top of Dacia Seamount.

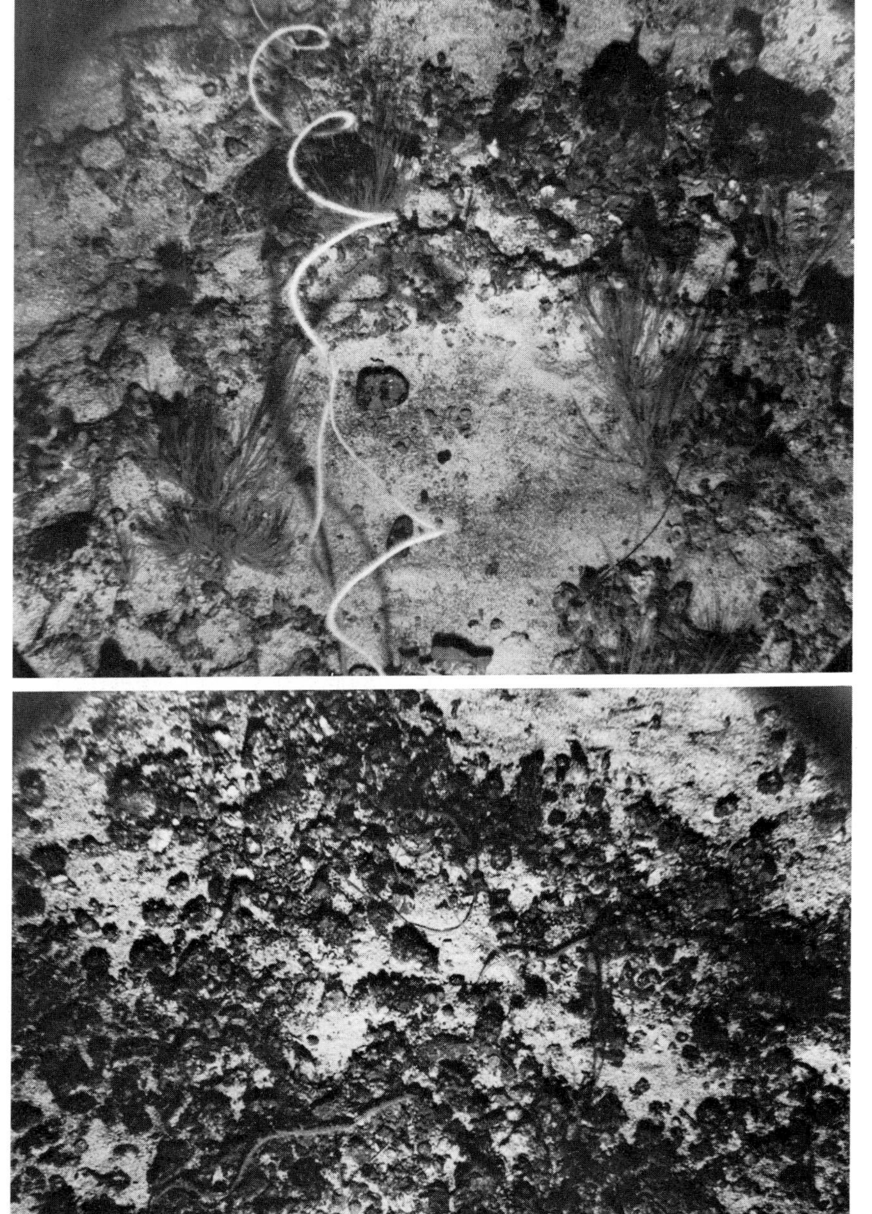

32°15′N 64°42′

32°15′N 64°42

35°10′N 12°55′W

12.18 Decorative animal life abounds on current-swept peaks. Fans, pens, and sponges are typically seen attached to hard black rocky surfaces. U, L, 143 m, top of Ampere Seamount.

12.19 Ripples and rock on the Bermuda Pedestal. This bold obstruction to the moving waters is scoured by strong bottom currents, 1541 m, south flank of Bermuda Pedestal.

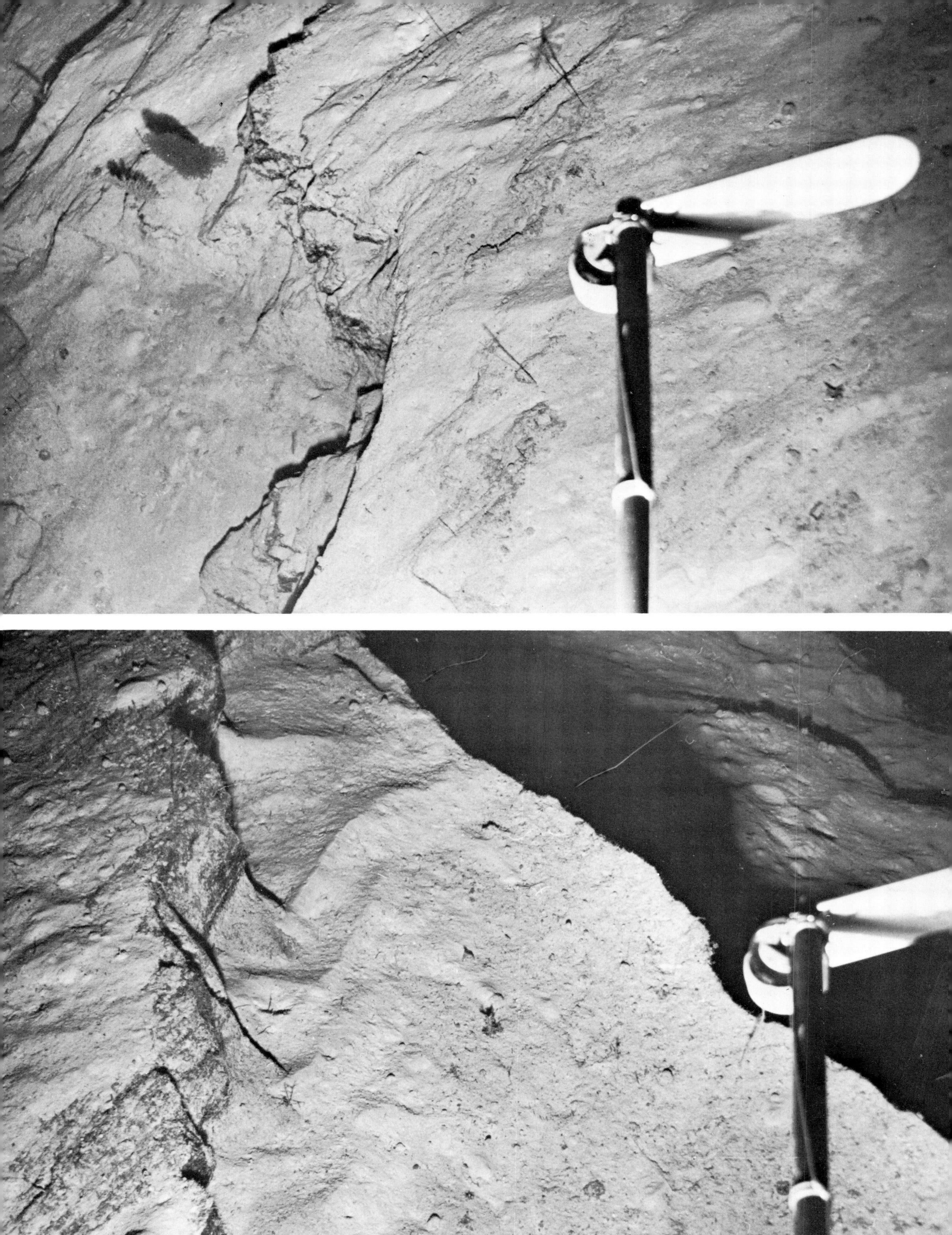

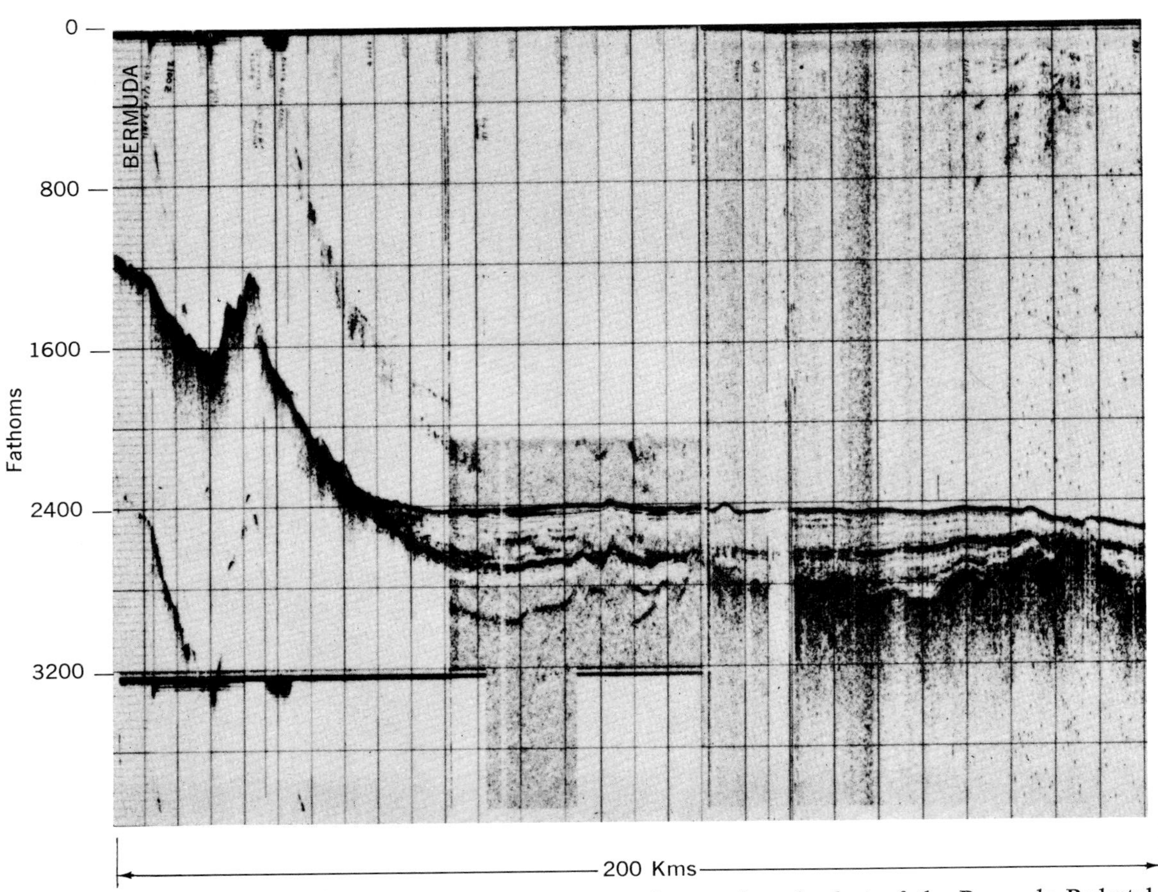

12.20 A thick apron of sediment laps against the foot of the Bermuda Pedestal.

SUBMERGED SHORES

The one-hundred-million-year-old fossil coral reefs seen and sampled on mid-Pacific seamounts represent but one example of the preservation of relics of former shores in the seascape of the deep sea.[14] The cuts sawed by former seas are preserved on the land and beneath the water, but the drowned shores better preserve their shape than those left high and dry. Some are so deeply cut that they were recognized from lead-line soundings long before the echosounder was developed. Others are so lightly drawn that they were unknown before geologists recognized them from the portholes of submersibles. Those lightly traced into the precipitous slopes off California are so similar to the modern wave-cut terraces on the adjacent rocky headlands that no one would fail to recognize the

12.21 The seascape of the archipelagic aprons reveals mounds, holes, and tracks. Current activity is very weak, 3938 m, archipelagic apron off Bora Bora.

form: the tiny undercut, the rounded boulders, the beach of broken shells, and the bold sea cliffs (albeit now partially covered with animals not characteristic of beaches) mark the submerged shores of the ice age Pacific (2.24). Among the distinguishing characteristics of the modern shore and the near shore are the striking colors, imparted largely by living things, dependent on light. The pinks and blues and oranges of the tropical shallows and the greens and browns of the cooler shelves all vanish when the sea deepens; colors fade when life departs and brown manganese paints out the lingering hues.

The beach forms but a fine line between the emerged coastal plain and the submerged continental shelf, but the visual remnants of former shores can be seen in a broad belt since many of the visual features of the continental shelves were produced by the migrating shore.[15] The visual aspects of the continental shelf contain many relic forms: bottom materials such as bones of mammoth, broken oyster shells, and peat are obviously quite out of place;[16] gravel and boulders litter the shelves of

38°04′N 62°10′W
12.22 Sponges, crinoids, and coral lean with the current as they screen the fertile waters for food. 1419 m, Kelvin Seamounts, western North Atlantic.

the high latitudes and beneath warmer shelf waters dead coral reefs are found.

Ever present is evidence of motion, for the shelf waters are never tranquil (12.25). In ancient marine strata, it has been frequently observed that the individual shells of dead bivalves were laid down with the convex side up, presumably as response to the action of the current to which the convex side offered least resistance. Much to the surprise of the early photographers of the continental shelf, this attitude was not observed, and if any preferred attitude was observed, the concave-up attitude was most frequent (2.65). Later studies have shown that the convex-up attitude is, in fact, found only within a short distance from the beach where waves touch the bottom and the bottom sediment washes to and fro.[17] The open shelf is an active environment as compared with the quieter abyss but does not today endure the violence of the beach. However, one need only to excavate a few inches or a few feet to find a buried surface which a few thousand years ago felt the violence of the shore.

There is no greater visual contrast in all of the inhabitated oceans than that between the continental shelves and the continental slopes. The history of ice-age sea levels is recorded not only in the notches representing ancient beaches up to a few hundred meters above and below the present shore but in both drowned and high-standing coral reefs, la-

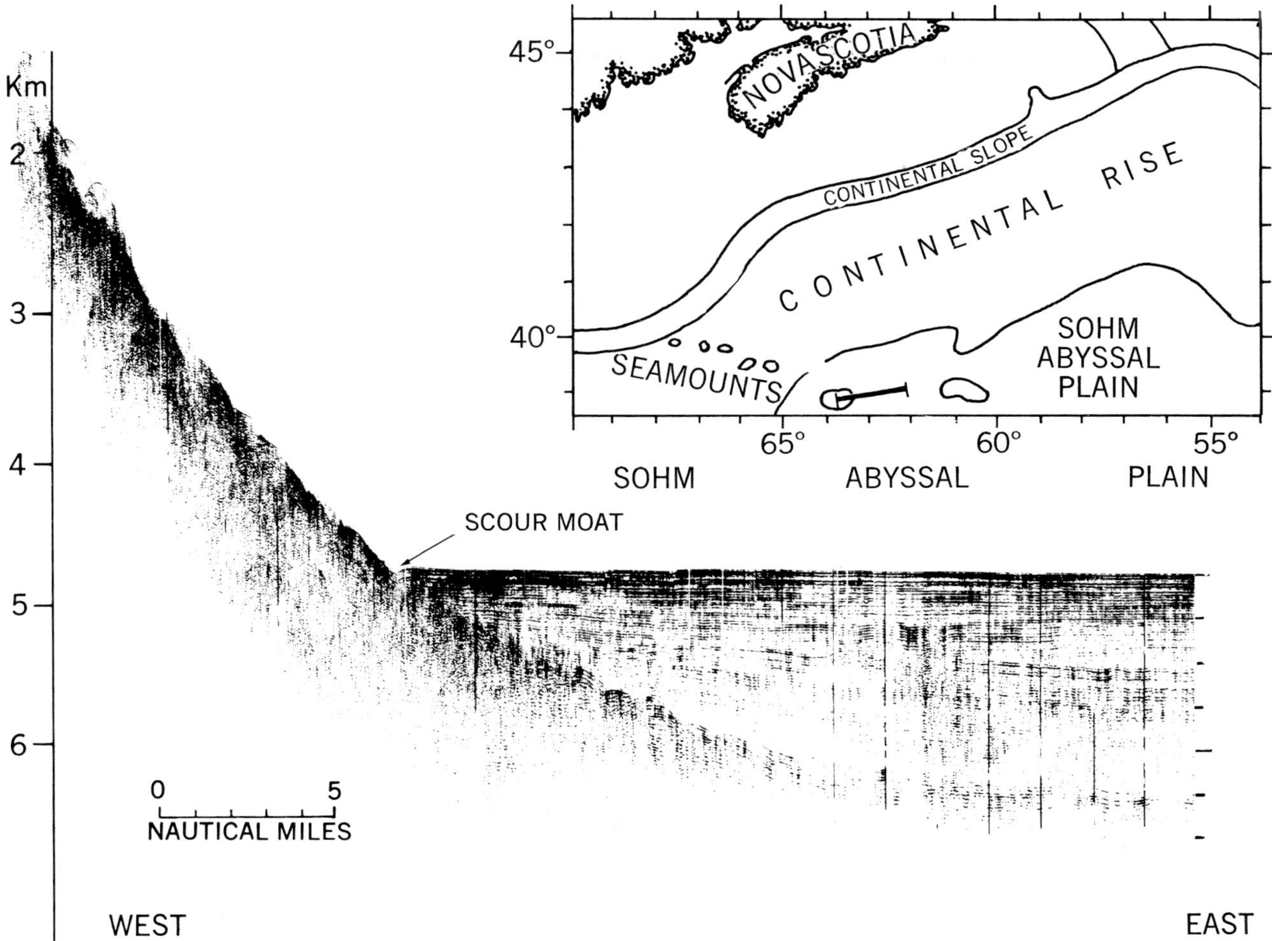

12.23 The growing abyssal plain has buried the archipelagic apron as well as the base of the seamount. The strong currents which prevent appreciable pelagic sediment from accumulating on the slopes of the seamount, has also scoured a moat from around its base.

goons, and marshes. The latter are particularly useful for studying the late Quaternary and Recent history of sea level as they provide adequate quantities of organic material suitable for radio-carbon dating. Several thousand ages have been determined and the resulting data points may be used to construct a historical record of the fluctuation of sea level (12.26).

Two different approaches have been applied to the construction of a sea-level curve. In one, a smooth line is drawn through the points on the assumption that sea level undergoes only slow, long-term variations, and it is assumed that the evidence for shorter oscillations can be accounted for by a variety of errors and local crustal movements. In the

117°20′W 32°45′N 12.24 Stalked anemones now grow on the drowned shores of the ice-age Pacific. These photographs were taken from *Deep Star 4000* on the continental slope of California. UL, UR, LL, LR, 230 m.

other approach, each point is connected to produce a jagged graph which is highly sensitive to the addition of new data or the rejection of older points. The first approach certainly overestimates the errors, while the second underestimates them, but basically the difference centers on the number and period of sea-level oscillations. On one hand, only those larger than 10,000 to 20,000 years are accepted; on the other hand, even those of a few score or a few hundred years' duration are accepted.

39°20′N 72°45′W

12.25 Starfish and shell fragments litter the sandy current-swept continental shelf. 84 m, south of Long Island, New York.

Visual observations could possibly resolve the controversy by indicating whether or not the numerous small notches predicted by the first interpretation are present.

Sea level is maintained in an uneasy equilibrium and would markedly rise or fall if the climate of Antarctica or Greenland were to suffer even a slight change. But fluctuations in the volume of sea water caused by the water locked in the waxing and waning glaciers of the last ice age

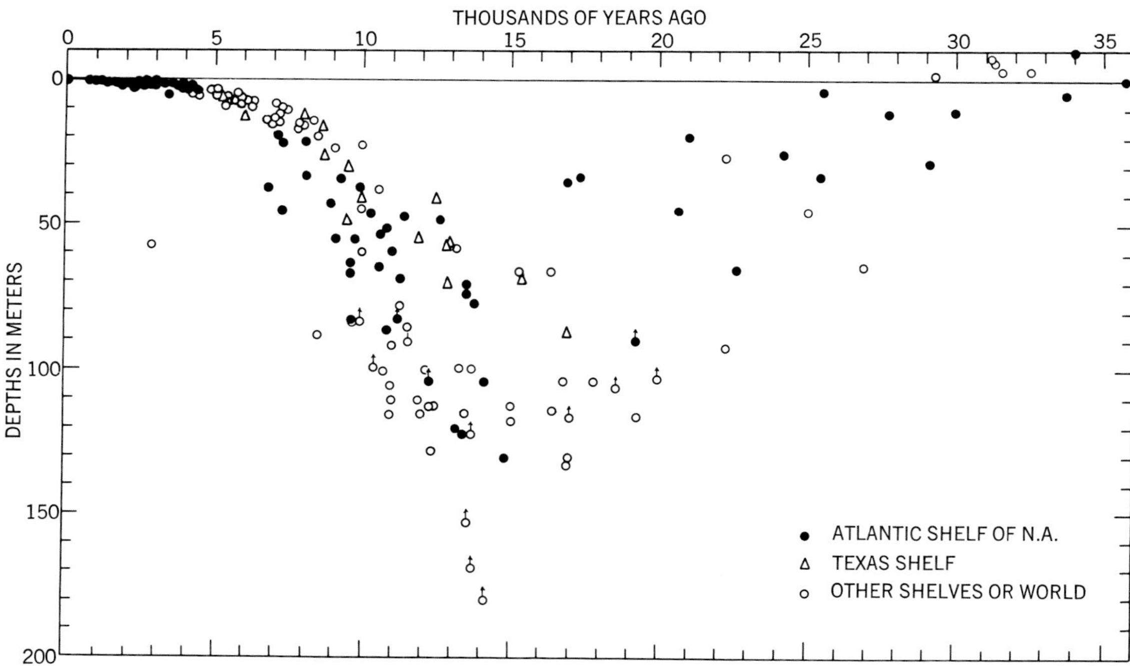

12.26 Sea level has risen more than one hundred meters in the past twenty thousand years. This curve, based on radio-carbon dates on drowned reefs and beaches, records the melting of the ice-age glaciers, the migration of the shore, and the progressive re-establishment of marine seascapes on the continental shelf.

have surely not exposed to view any of the surface of the globe which now forms part of the abyss. Those early attempts to explain submarine canyons as river valleys eroded during an ice-age sea-level dip of 4000 meters or more have long been discarded. Although there remains considerable uncertainty as to the maximum drop of ice-age sea level, it surely was much less than 1000 meters. Thus, the beaches of the past two million years lie far above the 3000-meter-deep boundary of the abyss. We can thus conclude that those beaches, beveled platforms, and reefs which lie more than a kilometer below sea level cannot be explained by fluctuations in the volume of sea water during the present geologic era and must really be quite old. The seamounts and guyots thus set important limits on the age and former depths of the ocean. For example, the fossil corals seen and dredged from the sunken islands of the mid-Pacific mountains prove that not only did the Pacific exist in early Cretaceous times but, given their height above the adjacent sea floor, that it was then at least 3000 meters deep. If the seamounts sank into the underlying crust of the earth, the depth of the ancient Pacific might have been greater but it could not have been shallower than the present height of the flat top above the adjacent floor. Thus, the flat-topped seamounts are ancient dip sticks which, when dated, give a measure of depth of the ancient oceans.

Some of the rocks photographed and dredged from the tops of seamounts have proved to be surprisingly young and have led geologists to wonder if sediments could be cemented and turned into rock on or just beneath the sea floor (12.27). Peculiar biscuits, composed of the cemented calcareous shells of clams, foraminifera, pteropods, worms, and bryozoans, have been photographed and dredged in depths of 300 to 400 meters on the beveled summits of several seamounts (12.28). The biscuits recovered from 500 meters' depth on one seamount have a radiocarbon age of 8000 to 12,000 years and imply either an unlikely high rate of subsidence or the operation of submarine processes of cementation which created these rocks out of the calcareous ooze which accumulates on shallow seamounts. In such a short period as 12,000 years subsidence is likely to be negligible. Thus, in order for the biscuits to be cemented in a lagoon or on a shore we need a 400-meter lowering of sea level 12,000 years ago. This conclusion is in conflict with the sea-level curve derived from a study of submerged beaches on the continental margin. But let it be said that there are many questions concerning ice-age sea level which await the diving geologist.

MICRO-CONTINENTS

The surface of the earth lies at two predominant elevations. One approximates present sea level and represents the interior lowlands, coastal plains, and continental shelves. The other lies approximately 4000 meters below sea level and represents the general level of the ocean basins.

The continents, steep-sided massive blocks surrounded by an enormous world-encircling sea, have deep roots which project 30,000 or 40,000 meters into the earth's mantle while the ocean crust is but a thin 5000-meter-thick film frozen over the earth's massive mantle. We have discussed the ocean trenches which cut deeply through the earth's crust and extend to as much as 10,000 meters below sea level and we have mentioned the terrestrial mountains which rise to similar heights above the sea and the tiny pedestals which prick through the waters to support islands, atolls and seamounts perched far above the abyssal floor. There is, however, another class of fundamental features which lie slightly submerged beneath the oceans and are supported by crustal underpinnings

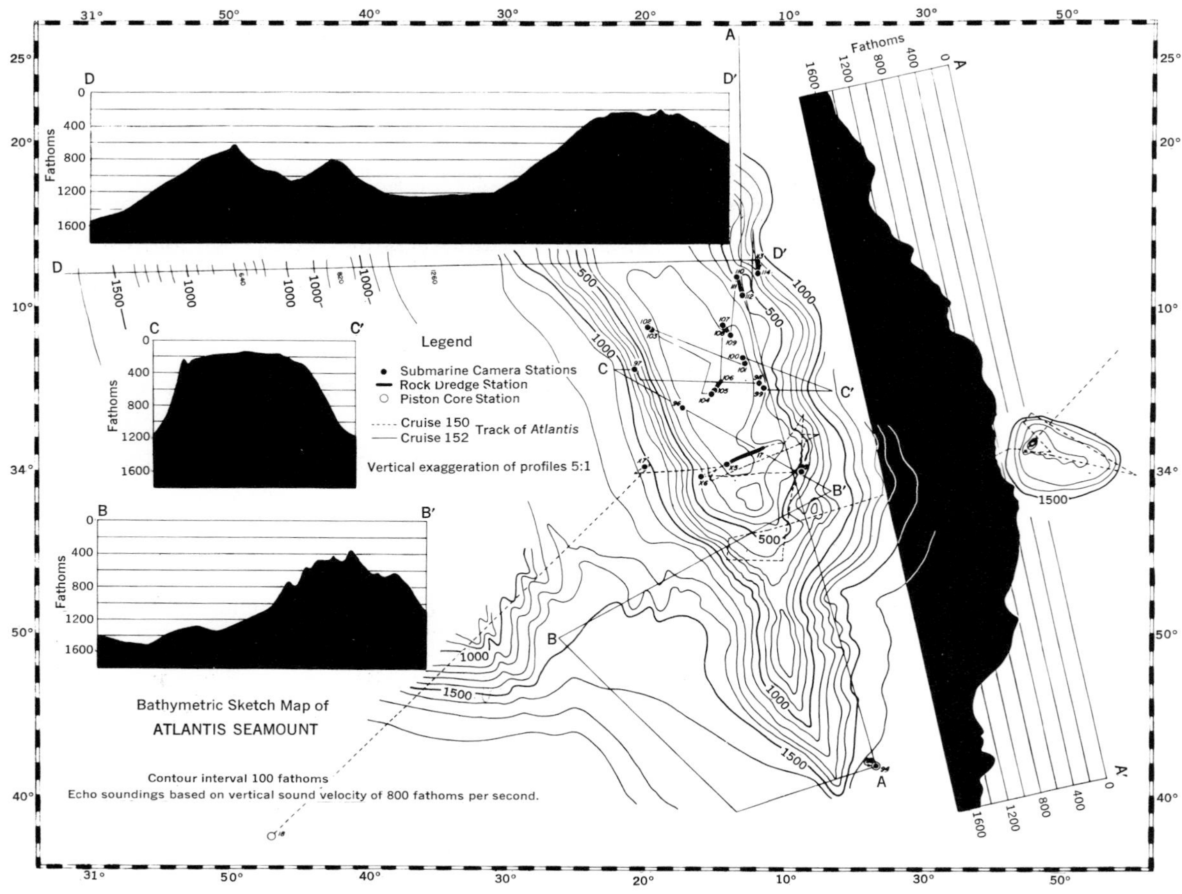

12.27 Limestone slabs litter the beveled current-swept summit of this eastern Atlantic seamount. (See Fig. 12.28)

nearly equivalent in draft to the continents. These are the micro-continents.[18] Small in size in comparison with the proverbial seven, and mostly covered by the sea, they constitute an enigmatic phenomenon. Drowned by present and former sea levels they have apparently lost their battle for survival as true continents and are gradually subsiding far beneath the waves. But whether they are fragments of former continents or unsuccessful or still struggling aspirants to continental rank is a debatable subject. Their beveled platforms were probably created at sea level. Some appear to be formed of oceanic rocks while others are in every sense continental, being composed of ancient granites. Their steep slopes and shallow summits are swept by strong currents which leave telltale marks in a visual seascape as varied as that of the margins of true

12.28 Limestone slabs from the summit of Atlantis Seamount. Shells of planktonic and benthic animals have been cemented together to form these peculiar "biscuits." U, 350 m (indicated as station 101 on figure 12.27), L, 350 m photograph of dredged "biscuits" (indicated as station 108 on figure 12.27). The largest slab is 30 cm wide and 5 cm thick.

34°08′N 30°12′W
34°09′N 30°14′W

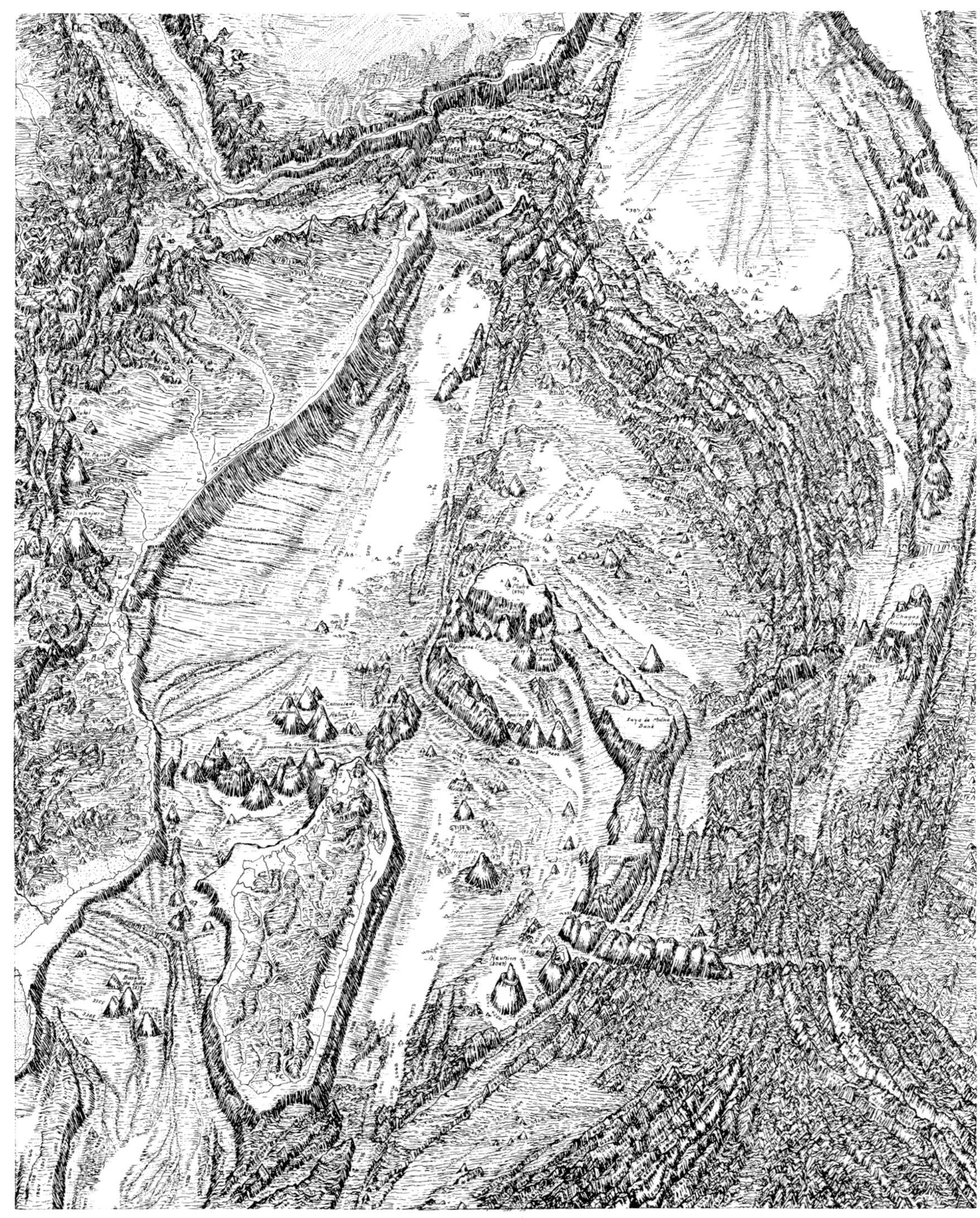

12.29 Western Indian Ocean. The Mascarene Plateau extends from Mahe toward Mauritius.

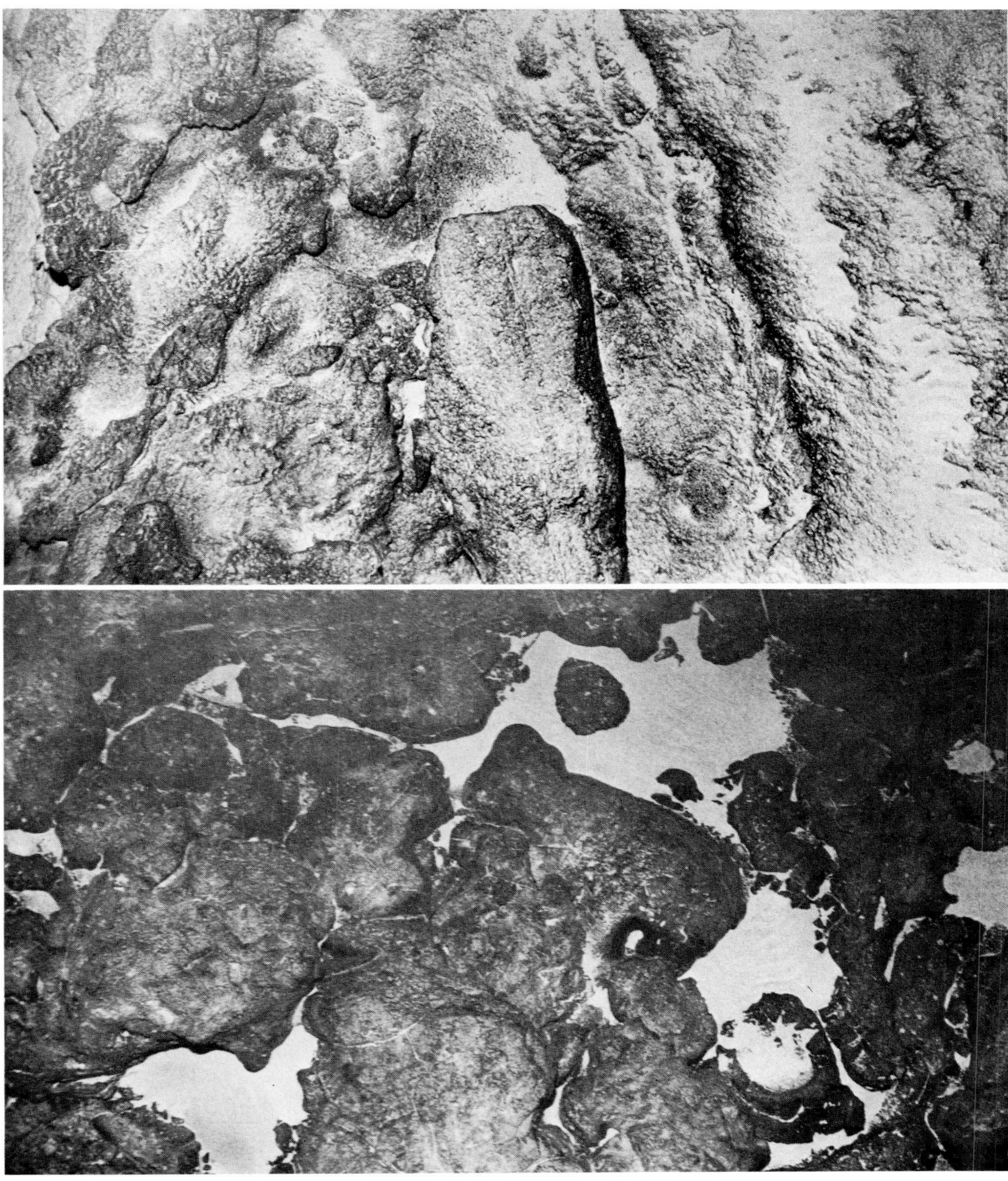

8°33′S 58°51′E
12°48′S 60°27′E

12.30 Manganese-encrusted limestone bedrock on the Mascarene Plateau. Vigorous bottom currents sweep the rocks of this microcontinent free of ooze and ripple the small pockets of carbonate sand. U, 1923 m, north of Saya de Malha Bank, northern Mascarene Plateau; L, 2397 m, northern end of Nazareth Bank, central portion Mascarene Plateau.

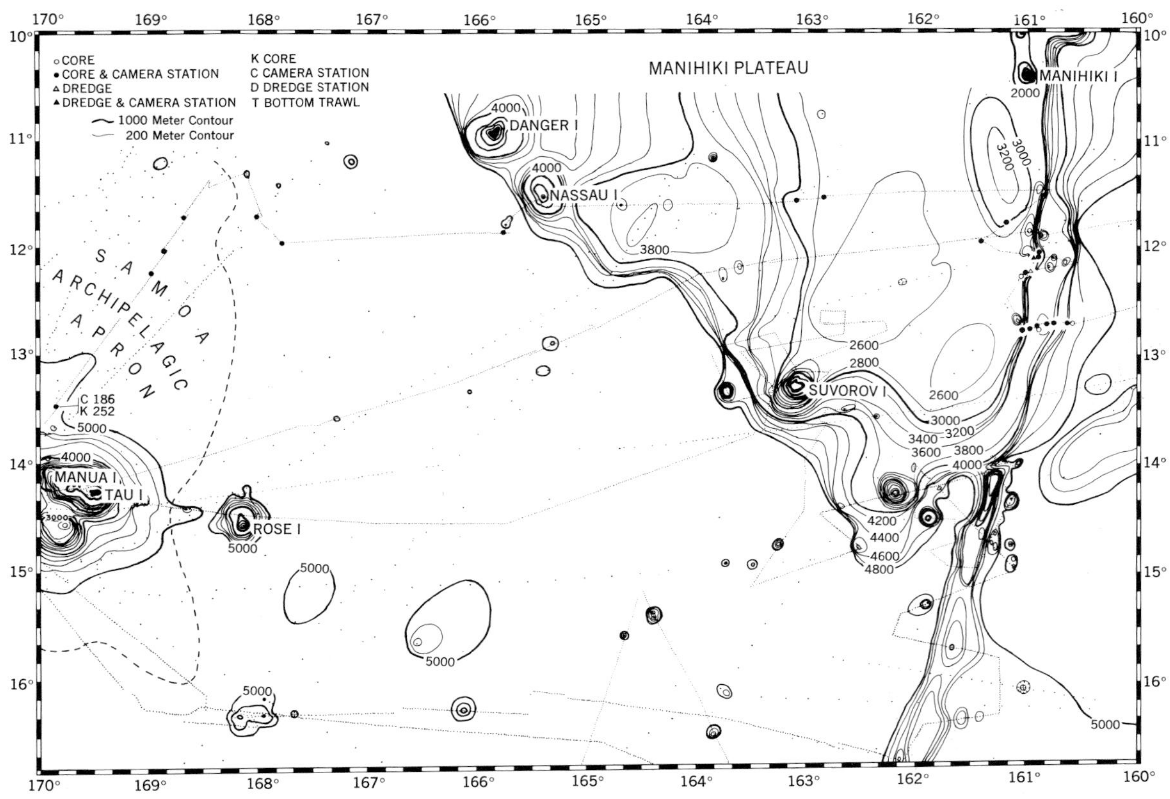

12.31 The Manihiki Plateau is a microcontinent in the western equatorial Pacific.

11°34′S 163°07′W

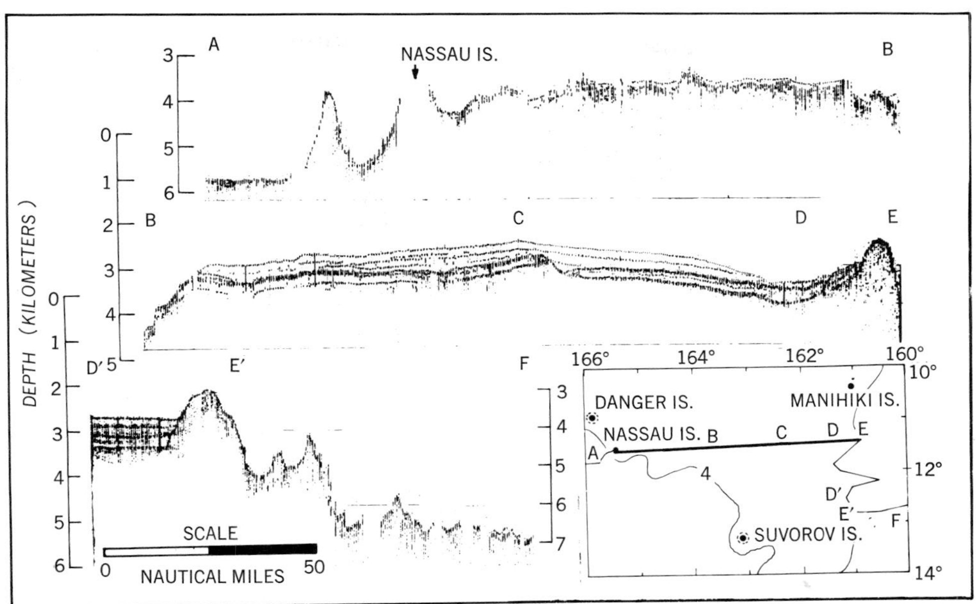

12.33 This seismic reflection profile across the Manihiki Plateau reveals a thick layer of sediment capping the central part of the plateau.

continents. Due to their generally remote, mid-oceanic locations, their sediment blanket is less complete and many characteristics of their underlying foundations are revealed to the echo-sounder and camera. Their flanks resemble those of the pedestals in the degree of current activity and in the presence of bare rock.

The Seychelles Islands, which poke their granite cores through the tropical waters of the western Indian Ocean, rise from the steep-sided Mascarene Plateau and establish this thousand-mile-long arcuate mass as the prime example of that class of crustal features known as micro-continents (12.29). The 650-million-year-old granites are almost completely beveled and only just peek through the engulfing coral and limestone strata. Saya de Malha, Nazareth, and Cargados Carajos, enormous 100- to 200-mile-wide atolls which lie astride the plateau grew up as the great micro-continent slowly sank toward abyssal depths. Those who have attempted to dredge and photograph the edge of the 2000-meter summit of the plateau between the Seychelles and Saya de Malha Banks concluded that the surface is nearly devoid of loose rock and consists of manganese-encrusted limestone bedrock with patches of rippled sand (12.30).

◁ 12.32 A thick blanket of sediments has accumulated on the tranquil top of the Manihiki Plateau. The ooze of the plateau has more and larger mounds than the fine red clay of the adjacent basin, 2939 m.

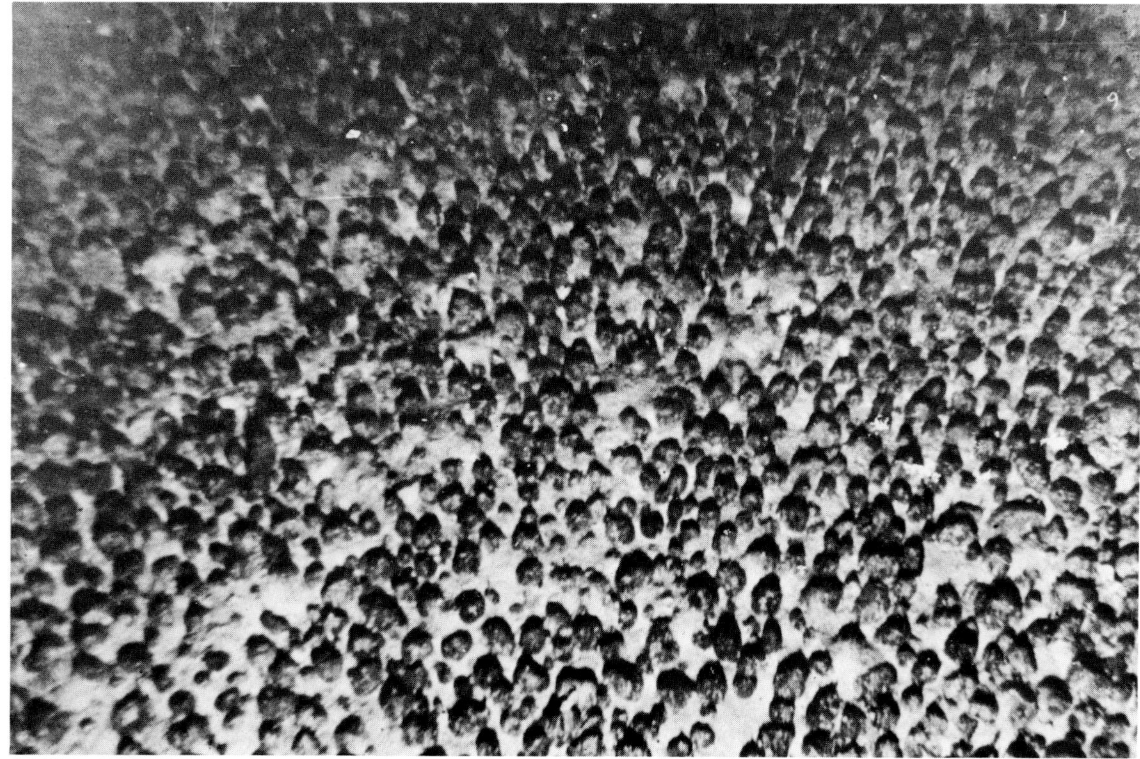

12.34 Manganese-encrusted rock, nodules, and rippled sand are ubiquitous on the current-swept scarp of the Manihiki Plateau, 3460 m.

Three hundred miles east of Samoa in the midst of the islands, atolls, and guyots of the equatorial Pacific lies the 2500- to 4000-meter-deep Manihiki Plateau (12.31). The tranquil tracked and burrowed surface of its nearly level summit (12.32) is underlain by evenly stratified beds of pelagic ooze which in turn lie on a beveled rock surface that can be traced on the seismic reflection profile to outcrops on the bare rocky escarpment which forms the abrupt boundaries of the plateau (12.33). Since this micro-continent sank beneath the waves of a Mesozoic sea, 1000 meters of pelagic frosting has been applied at a rate of about one micron per month to the central third of its 3800-meter beveled surface.

The currents which now scour the eastern escarpments have been active throughout the history of the plateau and probably began their work long before this micro-continent sank beneath the sea (12.34). In those favored locations where any sediment has accumulated at all we can see the results of this unceasing blizzard in the form of fluted, rippled drifts of pelagic sand, linear windrows, and scour marks. The remaining portion of the escarpment consists of black manganese-encrusted rocks

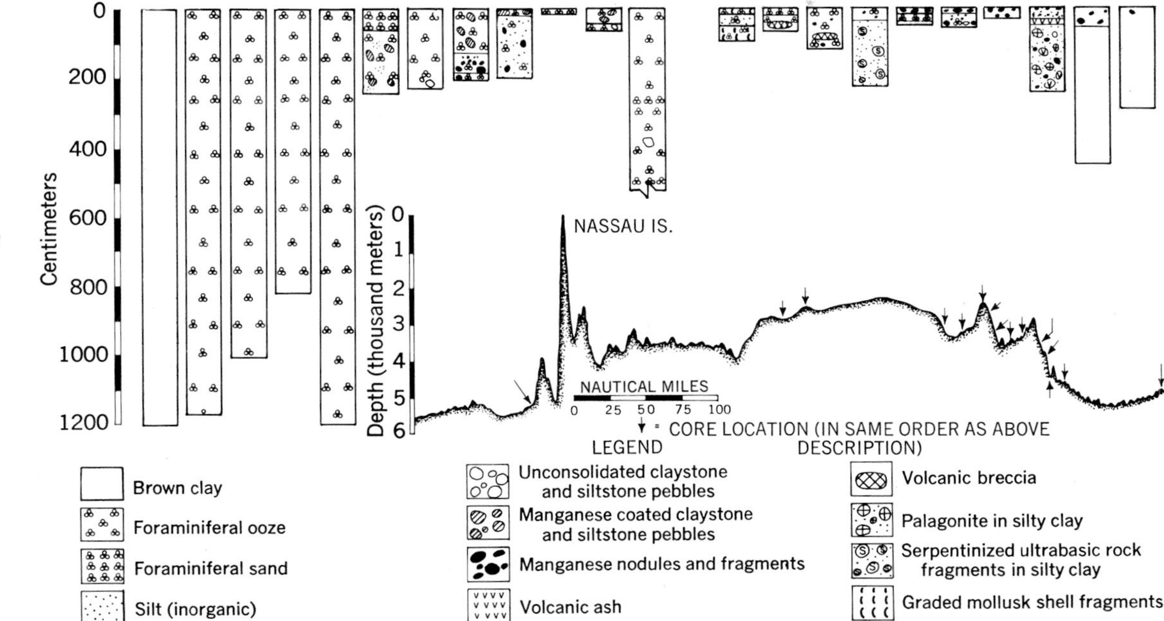

12.35 Fragments of volcanic rock are incorporated in the ooze near the peaks on the eastern top of the Manihiki Plateau. Manganese nodules and manganese-coated mud is found on steep current-swept slopes and abyssal brown clay is found in the ocean basin floor beyond. Mollusc shells (Core 271) may be remnants of a now-submerged beach or shallow shelf.

anomalously devoid of attached life (12.35, 12.36, 12.37).

The effect of intense scour has so often been seen on the crests and flanks of seamounts and micro-continents that it should not be in the least surprising that these environments constitute a most serious threat to submarine cables. The Madagascar Plateau, the Walvis Ridge, and the Mascarene Plateau are infamous in the annals of submarine telegraph maintenance, but for obscure reasons the great Ninetyeast Ridge, which extends 3000 miles as a great north-south barrier to abyssal circulation, has offered a more gentle environment. Cables have lain across this ridge for over fifty years and never suffered a failure. Yet photographs on the steep flanks of the ridge reveal scoured outcrops and rock has been dredged from its flanks at several locations.

Another broad plateau stretches 600 miles east of New Zealand and is capped by approximately 1000 meters of stratified sediment which has accumulated since it subsided.[19] Continental granite and metamorphic rocks, as well as oceanic basalts, are found on islands and rock prominences which protrude from the smooth surface of this foundered continental block.

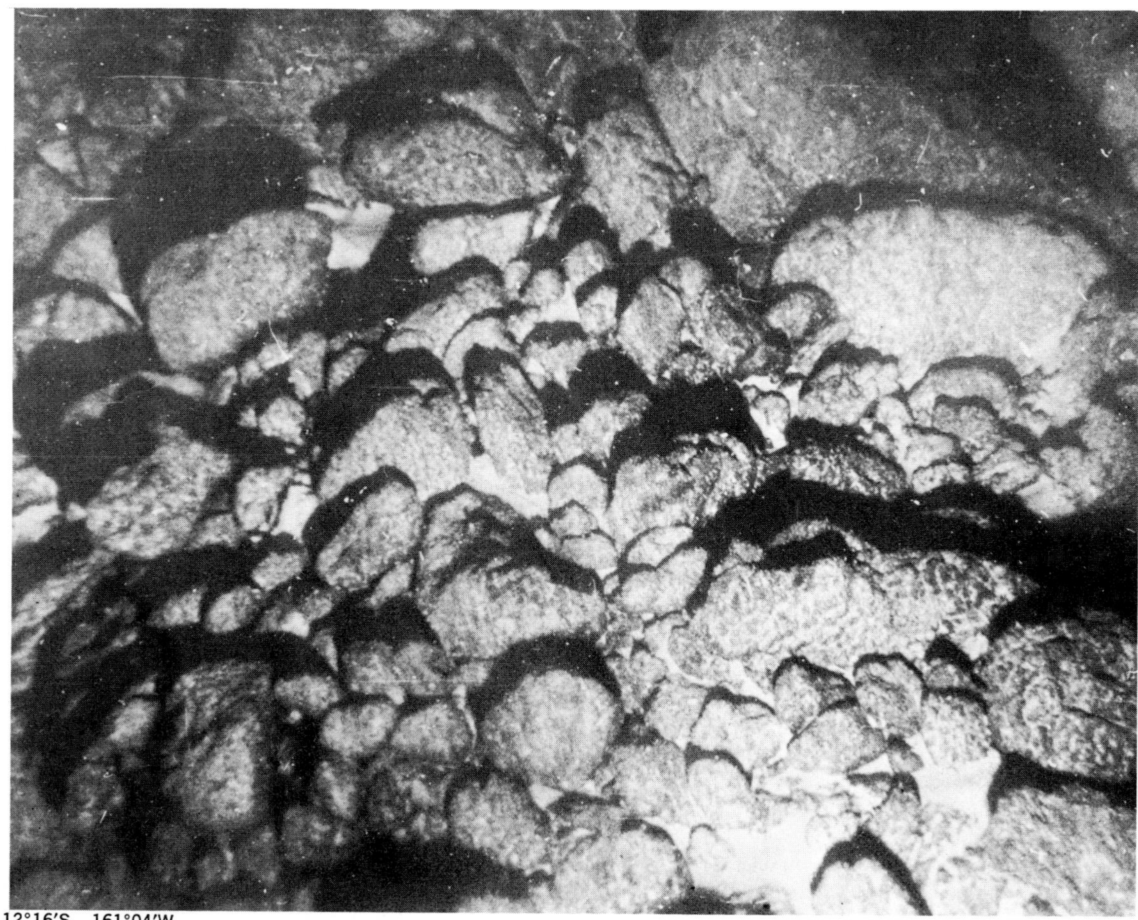

12.36 Scour marks around lava boulders and manganese-encrusted rock on the precipitous sides of the Manihiki Plateau. 2610 m, east flank of Manihiki Plateau.

Another ancient micro-continent is the sediment draped Shatsky Plateau of the northwest Pacific, where 140-million-year-old oozes have been sampled, near the base of the accumulation, in 4000 meters' depth[20] (12.38).

The guyots and micro-continents bear evidence of a slow but endless subsidence of the ocean basins which has carried Mesozoic terraces, shores, and reefs toward the abyss. We have recognized Mesozoic coastal features at the mean depth of modern oceans and who is to say that the remains of ancient landscapes do not lie hidden somewhere on the floor of the ancient abyssal basins? Perhaps there is even a place in the abyss where we may some day see the ancient land surface or at least sample its deposits.

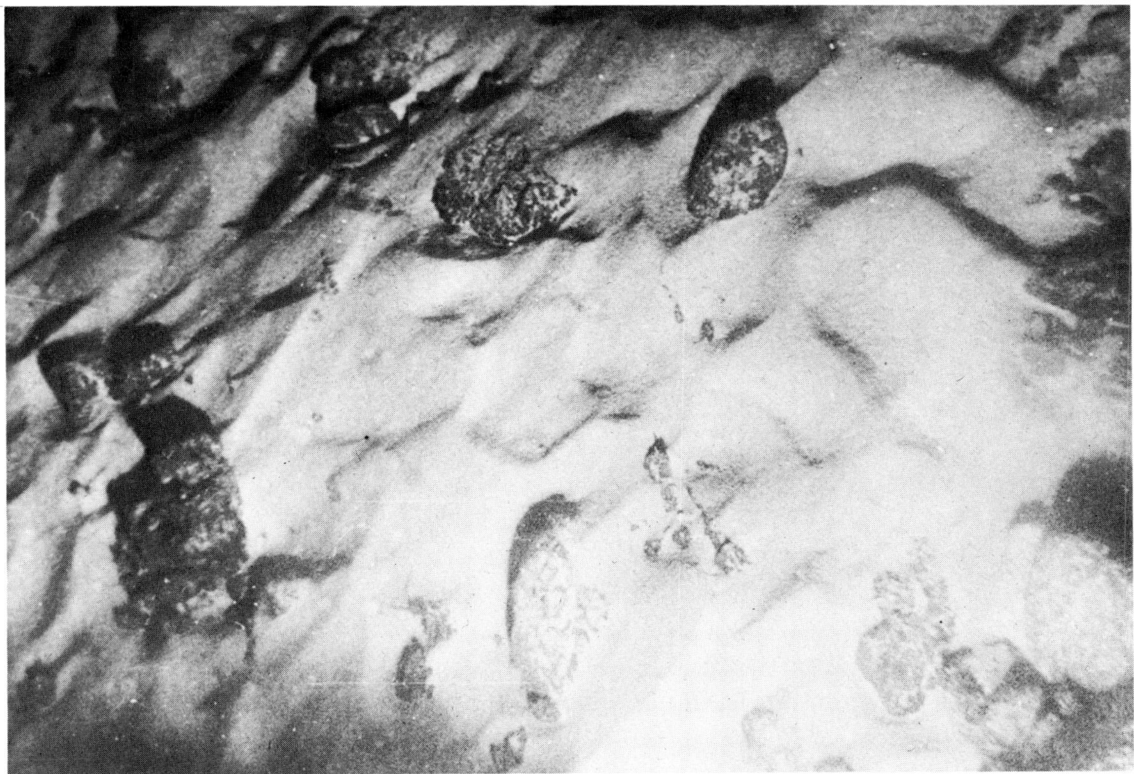

12.37 Violent bottom currents sweep the calcareous sand into ripples and drifts on the east flank or Manihiki Plateau. 2610 m.

We have viewed the results of compression along the earth's great dynamic front where mountains are forced up and trenches pressed down; where the earth's crust buckles as segments of crust override adjacent segments (Chapter 11). We have contemplated the construction of volcanos piled up from the deep-sea floor, have viewed the summits and flanks of the resulting islands and atolls—and have seen others which have sunk beneath the sea. We have viewed the result of the sinking of foundered and fragmented continents and have considered the changing scene resulting from this subsidence, from above sea level to the abyss. Thus far, in our exploration of the visual aspects of mountain building, we have reviewed the visual consequences of horizontal compression, volcanic upbuilding and vertical sinking, geological processes which have been discussed for more than a century. In the chapter that follows we will view a unique, visually dramatic, and newly discovered mid-oceanic type of mountain building and decay which appears to hold the basic key to the

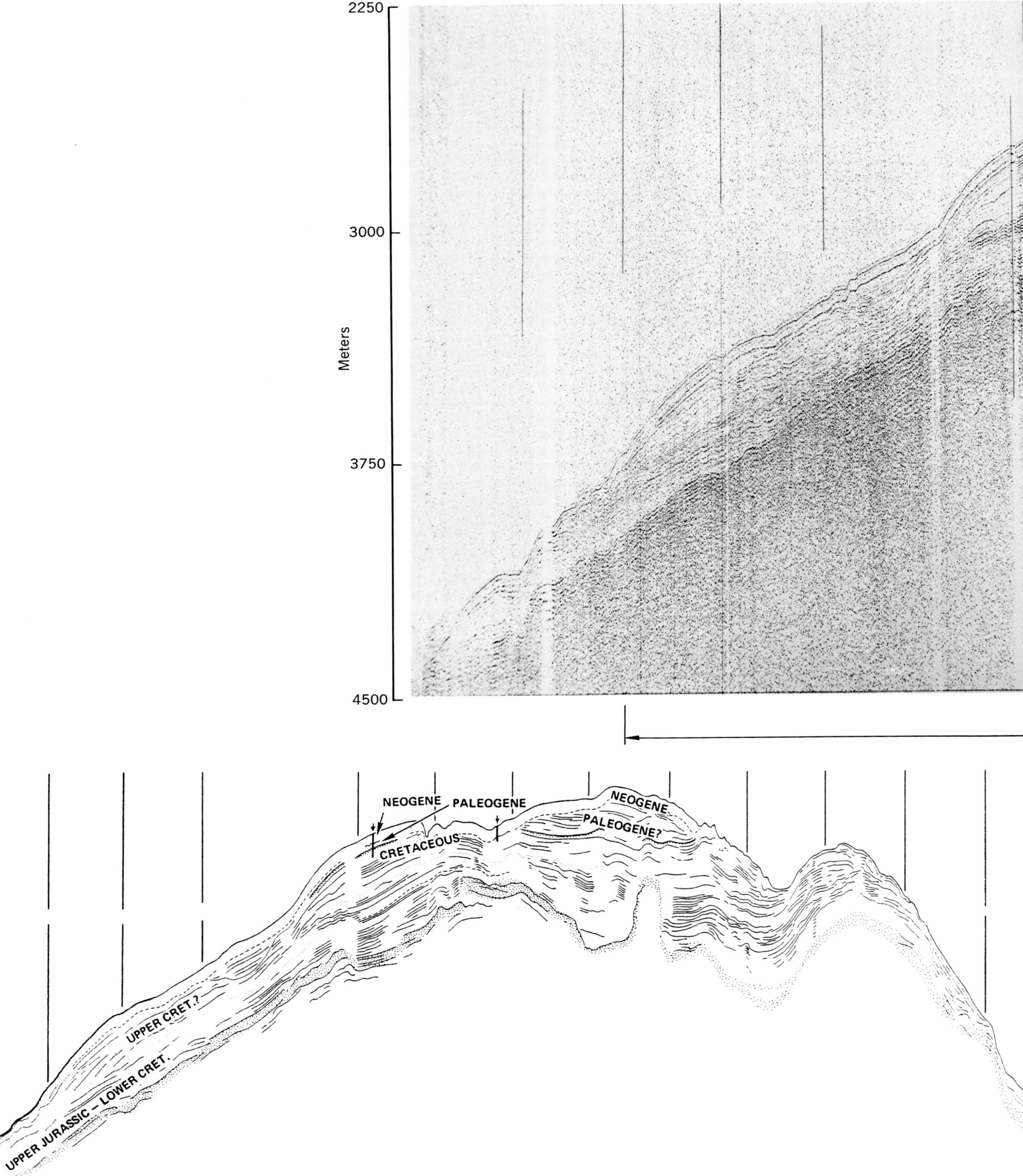
2250
3000
Meters
3750
4500
NEOGENE
PALEOGENE
CRETACEOUS
NEOGENE
PALEOGENE?
UPPER CRET.?
UPPER JURASSIC – LOWER CRET.

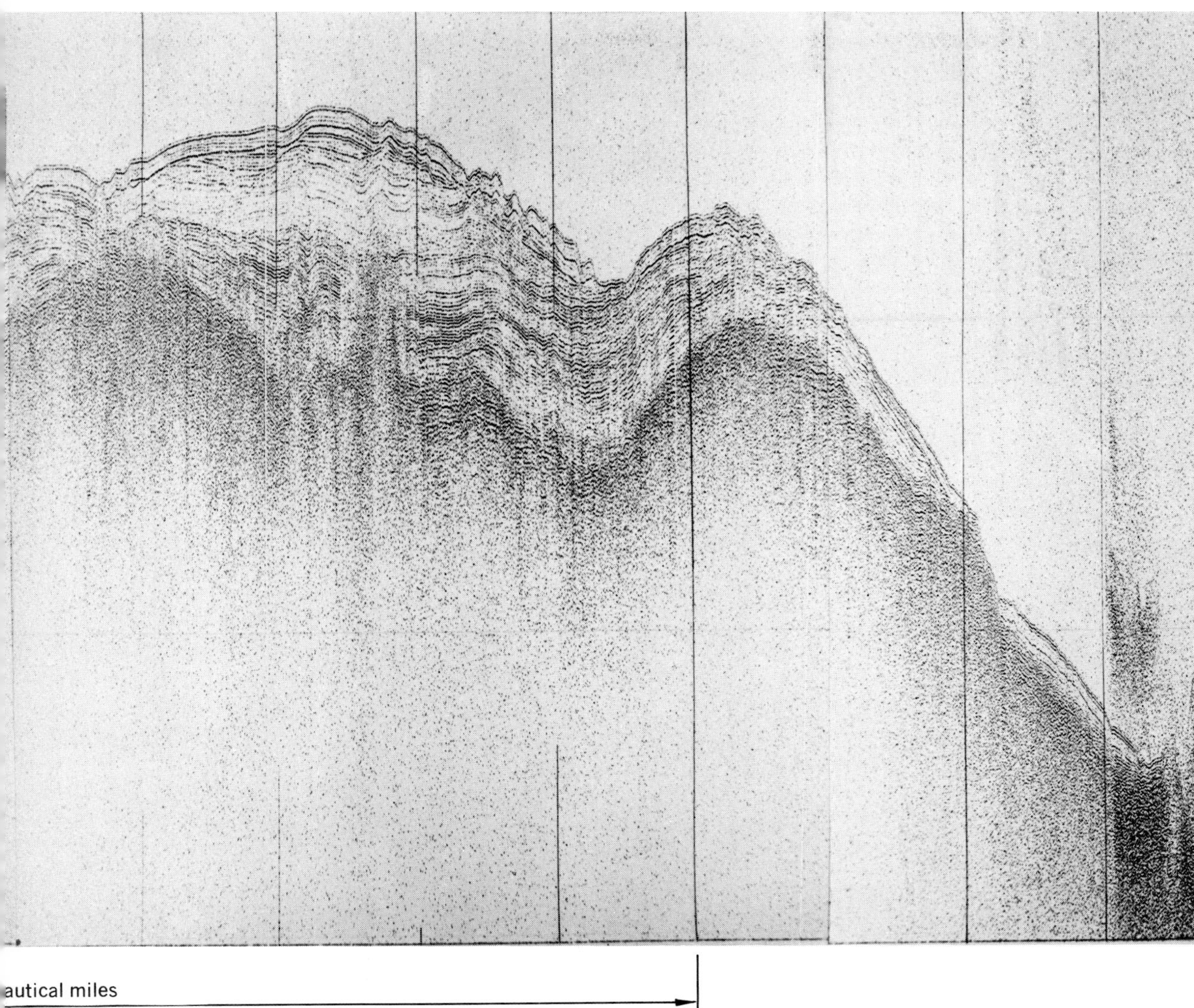

12.38 A thick accumulation of sediment caps the Shatsky Plateau. There is much similarity between the sediment thickness, layering, and surface and subsurface topography of this microcontinent and that of the Manihiki Plateau (see Fig. 12.33). A complex geologic history is revealed by the stratified Cretaceous and Tertiary oozes and cherts which overlay Jurassic volcanic foundations.

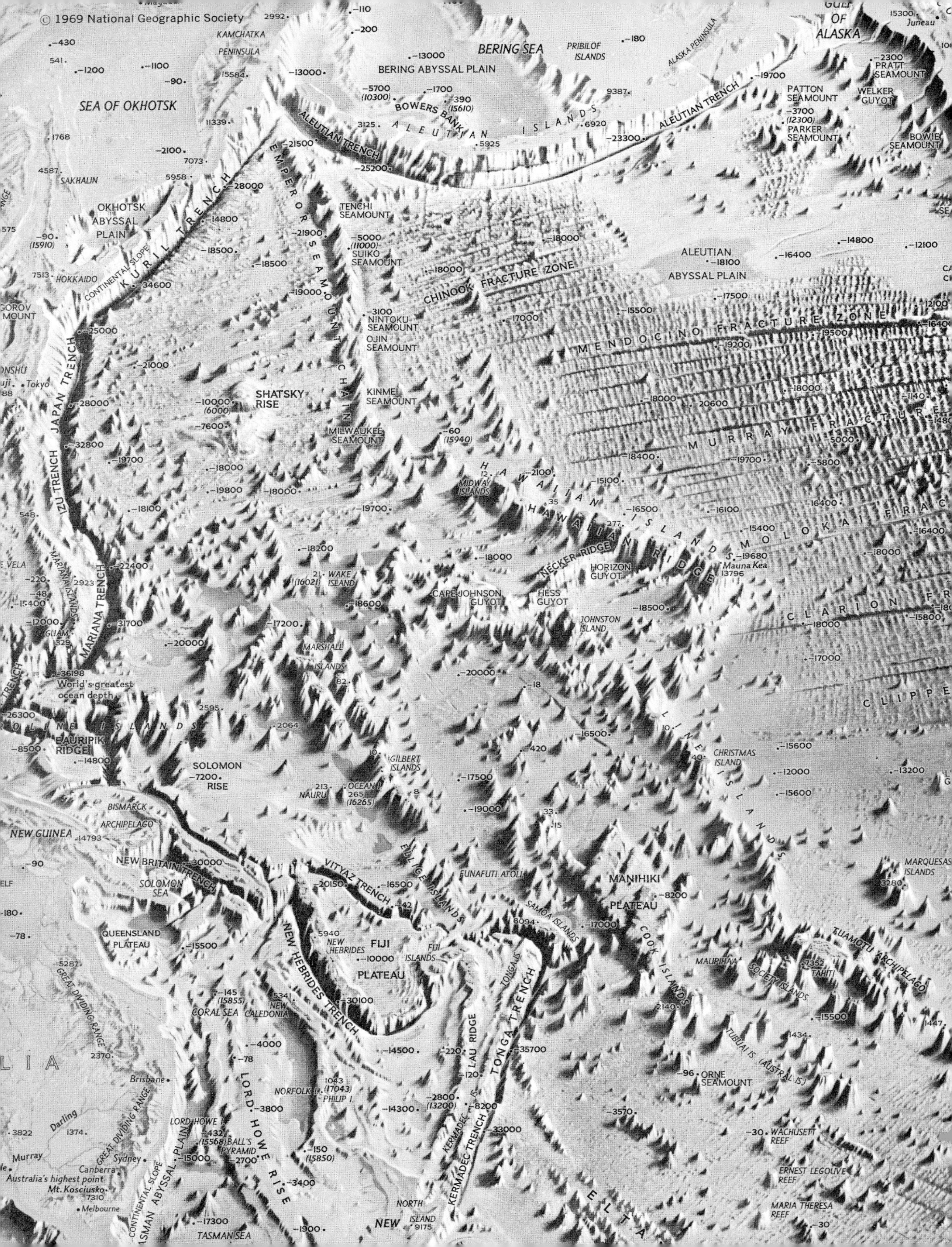

KAMCHATKA PENINSULA
BERING SEA
PRIBILOF ISLANDS
ALASKA PENINSULA
GULF OF ALASKA
Juneau
BERING ABYSSAL PLAIN
SEA OF OKHOTSK
BOWERS BANK
ALEUTIAN ISLANDS
ALEUTIAN TRENCH
PATTON SEAMOUNT
PRATT SEAMOUNT
WELKER GUYOT
PARKER SEAMOUNT
BOWIE SEAMOUNT
SAKHALIN
EMPEROR SEAMOUNT CHAIN
KURIL TRENCH
OKHOTSK ABYSSAL PLAIN
TENCHI SEAMOUNT
SUIKO SEAMOUNT
HOKKAIDO
CONTINENTAL SLOPE
CHINOOK FRACTURE ZONE
ALEUTIAN ABYSSAL PLAIN
NINTOKU SEAMOUNT
OJIN SEAMOUNT
MENDOCINO FRACTURE ZONE
Tokyo
JAPAN TRENCH
SHATSKY RISE
KINMEI SEAMOUNT
MILWAUKEE SEAMOUNT
MURRAY FRACTURE
IZU TRENCH
MIDWAY ISLANDS
HAWAIIAN ISLANDS
HAWAIIAN RIDGE
MOLOKAI FRAC
NECKER RIDGE
HORIZON GUYOT
Mauna Kea
WAKE ISLAND
CAPE JOHNSON GUYOT
HESS GUYOT
MARIANA ISLANDS
MARIANA TRENCH
JOHNSTON ISLAND
CLARION FR
GUAM
MARSHALL ISLANDS
World's greatest ocean depth
CLIPPE
LINE ISLANDS
EAURIPIK RIDGE
SOLOMON RISE
GILBERT ISLANDS
CHRISTMAS ISLAND
NAURU
OCEAN I.
BISMARCK ARCHIPELAGO
NEW GUINEA
ELLICE ISLANDS
NEW BRITAIN TRENCH
VITYAZ TRENCH
FUNAFUTI ATOLL
MANIHIKI PLATEAU
MARQUESAS ISLANDS
SOLOMON SEA
SAMOA ISLANDS
QUEENSLAND PLATEAU
NEW HEBRIDES
FIJI PLATEAU
FIJI ISLANDS
TONGA IS.
COOK ISLANDS
TUAMOTU ARCHIPELAGO
MAUPIHAA
SOCIETY ISLANDS
TAHITI
GREAT DIVIDING RANGE
CORAL SEA
NEW CALEDONIA
NEW HEBRIDES TRENCH
LAU RIDGE
TONGA TRENCH
LORD HOWE RISE
Brisbane
TUBUAI IS. (AUSTRAL IS.)
ORNE SEAMOUNT
NORFOLK I.
PHILIP I.
KERMADEC IS.
KERMADEC TRENCH
Darling
LORD HOWE I.
BALL'S PYRAMID
WACHUSETT REEF
Murray
Sydney
Canberra
Australia's highest point
Mt. Kosciusko
Melbourne
TASMAN ABYSSAL PLAIN
ERNEST LEGOUVE REEF
MARIA THERESA REEF
NORTH ISLAND
NEW
TASMAN SEA

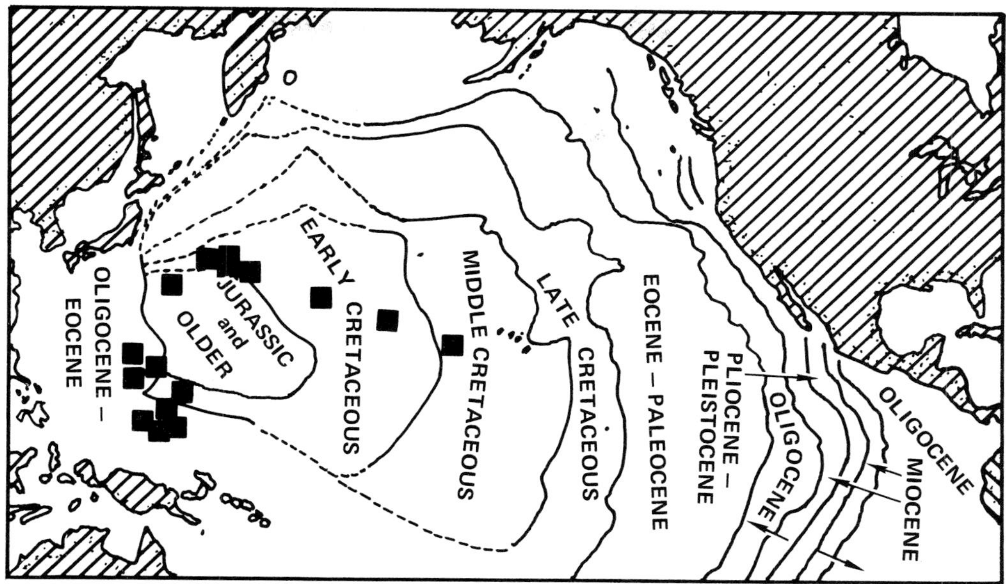

12.40 Age of the ocean floor in the western Pacific and deep-sea drill holes.

general explanation of the vast floor of the abyss and which, in addition, provides vital clues to the rearrangement of continents through geologic time.

REFERENCES AND NOTES

1. A well-illustrated description of volcanic phenomena is found in: A. Rittmann. 1962. *Volcanoes and Their Activity*. Wiley, New York, 305 pp.

2. F. J. Turner and J. Verhoogen, 1960. *Igneous and Metamorphic Petrology*. McGraw-Hill, New York; Chapter 15; "Environment, origin and evolution of magmas," pp. 431-450.

3. Seamount chains are discussed in: H. W. Menard. 1964. *Marine Geology of the Pacific*. McGraw-Hill, New York; Chapter 4: "Volcanism," pp. 55-96.

4. Marine geologists arbitrarily divide the roughly equidimensional submarine peaks into those which stand higher than 1000 meters: *seamounts,* and those which are smaller: *knolls or hills.*

5. The pressure of the overlying water is entirely sufficient throughout the abyss to prevent the escape of gases and dissolved water from the lava issuing onto the sea floor. In fact, water in considerable quantities must be absorbed by the lavas (G. C. Kennedy. 1955. Some aspects of the role of water in rock melts. *Geol. Soc. Am. Spec. Paper,* 62:489-503), and the resulting rock is composed of lighter minerals than the sub-aerial basalt flows. Evidence of this comes both from rocks dredged from submarine volcanos and from the contents of ancient troughs (geosynclines) which now lie exposed to view in mountain ranges.

◁ 12.39 Pedestals and plateaus abound in the ancient western Pacific.

6. Upon contact with chilling sea water, molten lavas characteristically form glass-encrusted bags which resemble a pile of pillows after cooling. Geologists when studying ancient rocks rely on these structures for positive proof of subaquatic extrusion.

7. As a volcanic pedestal builds closer to the sea surface, the heat of the volcano causes the surrounding water to rise and carry dissolved nutrients to the surface, engendering a bloom of plankton and the discolorization of the sea. Later, as the vent narrowly approaches the sea surface, a fiery display ensues, a scene which has been observed and photographed a few times (R. S. Dietz and M. J. Sheehy. 1954. Trans-Pacific detection of Myojin volcanic explosions by underwater sound. *Geol. Soc. Amer. Bull.*, 65:941-956).

8. In the Marshall Islands depths of the volcanic cores determined by the seismic refraction method are as much as 1500 meters, suggesting that the pedestals and perhaps the surrounding ocean floor have subsided at least that much. By extrapolating depths from the bottom of the drill hole to the volcanic core as determined by the refraction method it seems that the volcanos must have been active in the late Cretaceous. What then about the flat-topped sunken islands (guyots)? Dredging on them recovered lower Cretaceous corals.

9. Since we are concerned in this book with the abyss, we will not further discuss or describe the extensively varied and photogenic environment of the reef but refer to the following well-illustrated treatises: (K. O. Emery, J. I. Tracy, Jr., and H. S. Ladd, 1954. Geology of Bikini and nearby atolls. *U.S. Geol. Survey Prof. Paper,* 260A:265 pp.; and, H. J. Wiens. 1962. *Atoll Environment and Ecology.* Yale Univ. Press, New Haven, Conn., 532 pp.).

10. C. Darwin. 1842. *The Structure and Distribution of Coral Reefs.* Smith-Elder, London, 278 pp. J. Murray. 1880. On the structure of the coral reefs and islands. *Proc. Roy. Soc., Edinburgh,* 10:505-518. J. D. Dana. 1885. Origin of coral reefs and islands. *Am. Jour. Sci., Ser. 3.,* 30:89-105. R. A. Daly. 1910. Pleistocene glaciation and the coral reef problem. *Am. Jour. Sci., Ser. 4,* 30:297-308. W. M. Davis. 1928. The coral reef problem. *Am. Geog. Soc. Spec. Publ.,* 9:596 pp. H. S. Ladd and S. O. Schlanger. 1960. Drilling operations on Eniwetok Atoll. *U.S. Geol. Surv. Prof. Paper,* 260Y:863-905. R. W. Raitt. 1957. Seismic refraction studies of Eniwetok Atoll, Bikini, and nearby atolls, Marshall Islands. *U.S. Geol. Survey Prof. Paper,* 260-S:685-698. M. B. Dobrin. B. Perkins, Jr., and B. L. Snavely. 1949. Subsurface construction of Bikini Atoll as indicated by a seismic refaction survey. *Bull. Geol. Soc. Amer.,* 60:807-828.

11. H. Hess, 1946. Drowned ancient islands of the Pacific Basin. *Am. Jour. Sci.,* 244:772-791; E. L. Hamilton. 1956. Sunken islands of the mid Pacific mountains. *Geol. Soc. Amer. Mem.,* 64:97 pp.

12. Exceptionally smooth topography bordering island groups was recorded on some of the first continuously recording echo-sounding profiles obtained. These archipelagic aprons grade from a level plain at their seaward limit to slopes on the order of one degree near the base of the much steeper (10°) island slope (H. W. Menard. 1956. Archipelagic aprons. *Bull. Amer. Assoc. Petrol. Geol.,* 49:2195-2210.; H. W. Menard. 1964. *Marine Geology of the Pacific.* McGraw-Hill, New York, pp. 82-87).

13. R. S. Dietz and H. W. Menard. 1953. Hawaiian swell, deep, arch and subsidence of the Hawaiian Islands. *J. Geol.,* 61:99-113; B. C. Heezen and G. L.

Johnson. 1963. A moated knoll in the Canary Passage. *Deut. Hydrog. Zeit.,* 16(6):269-272.

14. The profound influence of changes in sea level on the scenery of the earth is the basic theme of a classic treatise by L. King (1967. *Morphology of the Earth.* Oliver and Boyd, Edinburgh, 726 pp.) For a discussion of evidence for fluctuating sea levels, see: R. W. Fairbridge. 1961. Eustatic changes in sea level. *Physics and Chemistry of the Earth,* 4:99-185.

15. A. Guilcher. 1958. *Coastal and Submarine Morphology.* Wiley, New York, 274 pp.; K. O. Emery. 1960. *The Sea Off Southern California.* Wiley, New York, 366 pp.

16. K. O. Emery, R. L. Wigley, A. S. Bartlett, and M. Rubin, 1967. Freshwater peat on the continental shelf. *Science,* 158:1301-1306; F. C. Whitmore, Jr., K. O. Emery, H. B. S. Cooke, D. J. P. Swift. 1967. Elephant teeth from the Atlantic continental shelf. *Science,* 156:1477-1481.

17. K. O. Emery, 1968. Positions of empty pelecypod valves on the continental shelf. *Jour. Sed. Pet.,* 38:1264-1269.

18. B. C. Heezen, and M. Tharp, 1965. Tectonic fabric of the Indian Ocean. *Phil. Trans. Roy. Soc. A,* 259:137-149; R. L. Fisher, G. L. Johnson, and B. C. Heezen, 1967. Mascarene Plateau, Western Indian Ocean. *Bull. Geol. Soc. Am.,* 78:1247-1266.

19. R. Houtz, J. Ewing, M. Ewing, and A. G. Lonardi. 1967. Seismic reflection profiles of the New Zealand Plateau. *Jour. Geophys. Res.,* 72:4713-4729; J. W. Brodie. 1964. Bathymetry of the New Zealand region. *Mem., New Zealand Oceanogr. Inst.,* 11:54 pp.

20. J. Ewing, M. Ewing, T. Aitken, and W. Ludwig. 1968. North Pacific sediment layers measured by seismic profiling. In: L. Knopoff, C. L. Drake, P. J. Hart (Eds.). *The Crust and Upper Mantle of the Pacific Area.* Amer. Geophys. Union, Geophysical Monograph, 12:147-173; M. Ewing, T. Saito, J. Ewing, L. H. Burckle. 1966. Lower Cretaceous sediments from the northwest Pacific. *Science,* 152:751-755; A. G. Fisher, B. C. Heezen, R. E. Boyce, D. Bukry, R. G. Douglas, R. E. Garrison, S. A. Kling, V. Krasheninnikov, A. P. Lisitzin, A. C. Pimm (1971). Initial Reports of the Deep Sea Drilling Project, Leg VI, Western North Pacific. *National Science Foundation.* 1329 pp.

32°N 40°W

13.1 Lava wells up into the floor of the widening mid-oceanic rift valley. Hot lava suddenly quenched by the chilling waters form glass-encrusted pillows. These wrinkled, fractured flows, only lightly dusted by the ooze, were formed in a recent yesterday and are still measurably warm. This photograph was made by a movie camera. Although motion picture photography has been only rarely used in the deep sea, a notable and interesting development was the "Troika" underwater camera of Edgerton-Cousteau, which has produced some extremely interesting cinematic footage of the Mid-Atlantic Ridge. Two large light sources are provided on this sleigh-like device which is towed from the stern of a research vessel. 3000 m, rift valley, Mid-Atlantic Ridge.

13

The Very Ribs of the Solid Earth

Let there be a firmament in the midst of the waters and let it divide the waters from the waters.

In the dark, secluded recess of a world-girdling mid-oceanic valley Mother Earth relentless tries to mend a chronic, never-healing wound. It is indeed startling that there we can still behold the birth of that firmament which forms the foundations of the deep. The rough, rocky skin of the earth beneath the sea, created out of hot fluids rising from the earth's interior, is engendered there as scar tissue in an ever-continuing violent confrontation between the white hot lavas and frigid abyssal waters (13.1-13.3). We know not how or when in the dim past, millions or billions of years ago, this wound was first inflicted and we can see no prospect of it ever completely healing (13.4). As the great sea gash which separates continents grows steadily wider, the newly born crust of the earth incessantly marches outward from the perpetual wound.

The earth trembles and shakes as molten rock wells upward into the ever-widening rift valley of the great Mid-Oceanic Ridge (13.5, 13.6), and seismologists, by locating such convulsions, allow us to foresee a narrow belt of shattered lava-covered submarine scenery more than 30,000 miles long.[1] But one need not descend into the abyss to view the quaking wound, for this birth zone of the earth's crust also crosses Iceland and penetrates East Africa.

That this unhealing wound is in reality the womb of the ocean floor is a recent revelation. Many prominent and knowledgeable scientists will rightfully insist that it is not yet proven, and others will flatly deny that it is so. We need look back only a few years to our first pronouncement

55°59′S 134°27′W

55°59′ 134°27′W

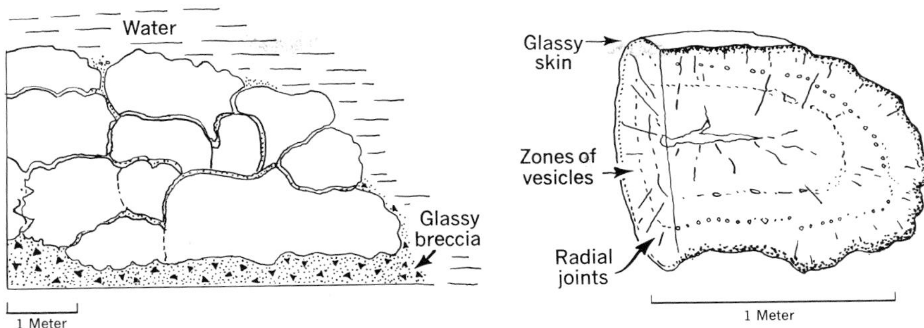

13.3 Pillows resemble liquid-filled balloons. Radial jointing (R) is occasionally seen in fractured pillows on the Mid-Oceanic Ridge.

that the crust of the ocean floor is continuously created at its center line.[2] But the background of thinking which laid the way began in the distant past. Alfred Wegener envisioned the continents as great blocks of granite, remnants of a former greater mass all floating and drifting on a sea of denser basalt. Wegener pointed out that this theory of continental drift, which generally bears his name, had been considered on and off for several hundred years, always initially because of the striking geometrical fit of the opposing coasts of South America and Africa. His writings generated a surge of enthusiasm which was rapidly followed in the 1930's and '40's by a bitter reaction which made rational discussion of drift virtually impossible. One either was a drifter or a nondrifter; there were two incompatible religions, two militant opposing camps. Critics complained that, if true, the theory would require the rewriting of all geology and the majority were clearly not willing to grant that they had been so grossly in error. For many years in America and parts of Europe to even mention the word "Drift" was to court professional or academic disaster. Thus, there developed two separate literatures—that of the drifters and that of the advocates of permanence.

Even today the term "continental drift" evokes so many bad memories that modern advocates often support it under other names such as continental displacement, sea-floor expansion, sea-floor spreading, or plate tectonics. Although they originally had differences of meaning, these terms, through imprecise usage, have become synonymous. To many, the word "drift" still implies both a rather random process and a mechanical impossibility. Yet during the past few years a great shift in opinion has taken place, and many scientists have become converts to drift. Each, how-

◁ 13.2 New crust for the earth. These quickly quenched pillows shattered by radial fractures welled up in mid-ocean. They are the most recent addition to the expanding sea floor. U, L, 3166 m, crest of Mid-Oceanic Ridge, South Pacific.

13.4 The most recent addition to the ever expanding Mid-Oceanic Ridge. The new volcano Surtsey burst forth beneath the sea in 1963 south of Iceland.

ever, retains certain of his previous prejudices and tends to consider ideas published before his conversion with some of the same contempt he acquired when a member of the opposing camp. It is, therefore, difficult to trace the history of ideas in the literature, difficult also to explain numerous recent "discoveries" of already well-known or well-documented phenomena.

Both Wegener and his eminent follower, Du Toit, believed that the Mid-Atlantic Ridge was composed of lighter rock similar to, and probably derived from, the continents, and neither considered the ridge to represent the newly formed crust of the earth. Both imagined that the sites of rifting in this great rift ocean were not on the ridge but in the deep basins. Although neither was sure that drift was still going on, presumably if either had been asked to predict where in the oceans long strips of fresh lava-covered scenery would be found, they would have picked the abyssal basins.[3]

Following World War II, the first modern expeditions set out to explore the deep-sea floor employing underwater cameras, continuously recording echo-sounders, deep seismic profilers, and magnetometers. By 1952, it was realized that an axial median valley cuts the crest of the Mid-Atlantic Ridge throughout its length[4] (13.5). By 1955, it began to be recognized that this median valley had several unique morphological, geophysical, and visual characteristics and that it could be traced by its seismicity through a world-wide belt 45,000 miles long. The realization that the widening rift valleys of Africa and the fissured and also widening median valley of Iceland (13.7, 13.8) were continental extensions of one world-girdling submarine tectonic belt gave the initial clue that tension rather than compression dominated the origin of the great mountain range known as the Mid-Oceanic Ridge. Had it not been for the mutual contempt shown between the drifters and the predominantly anti-drift marine geophysicists, this discovery should have led immediately to a general recognition that the generation of new crust required by drift was occurring in the mid-oceanic rift valley and that drift was still going on. But it took time to convert and almost a decade elapsed before the significance of these sea-floor discoveries began to be generally recognized.

The turning point in the continental drift controversy actually came in the middle 1950's, when studies of the history of the earth's magnetic field began to demand differential movements of the continents.[5] These studies indicated that not only had the pole apparently wandered with time but that the paths determined for individual continents were sufficiently different that it had to be concluded that each must also have

13.5 The rugged crest of the Mid-Oceanic Ridge is cleft by an expanding valley. ▷

55°
10°
20°
80°
70°
60°
50°
Orinoco
Rio Negro
Rio Caqueta
Rio Içá
Amazon
Rio Juruá
Rio Purus
Rio Madeira
Rio Parana
San Felix I.
San Ambrosio I.

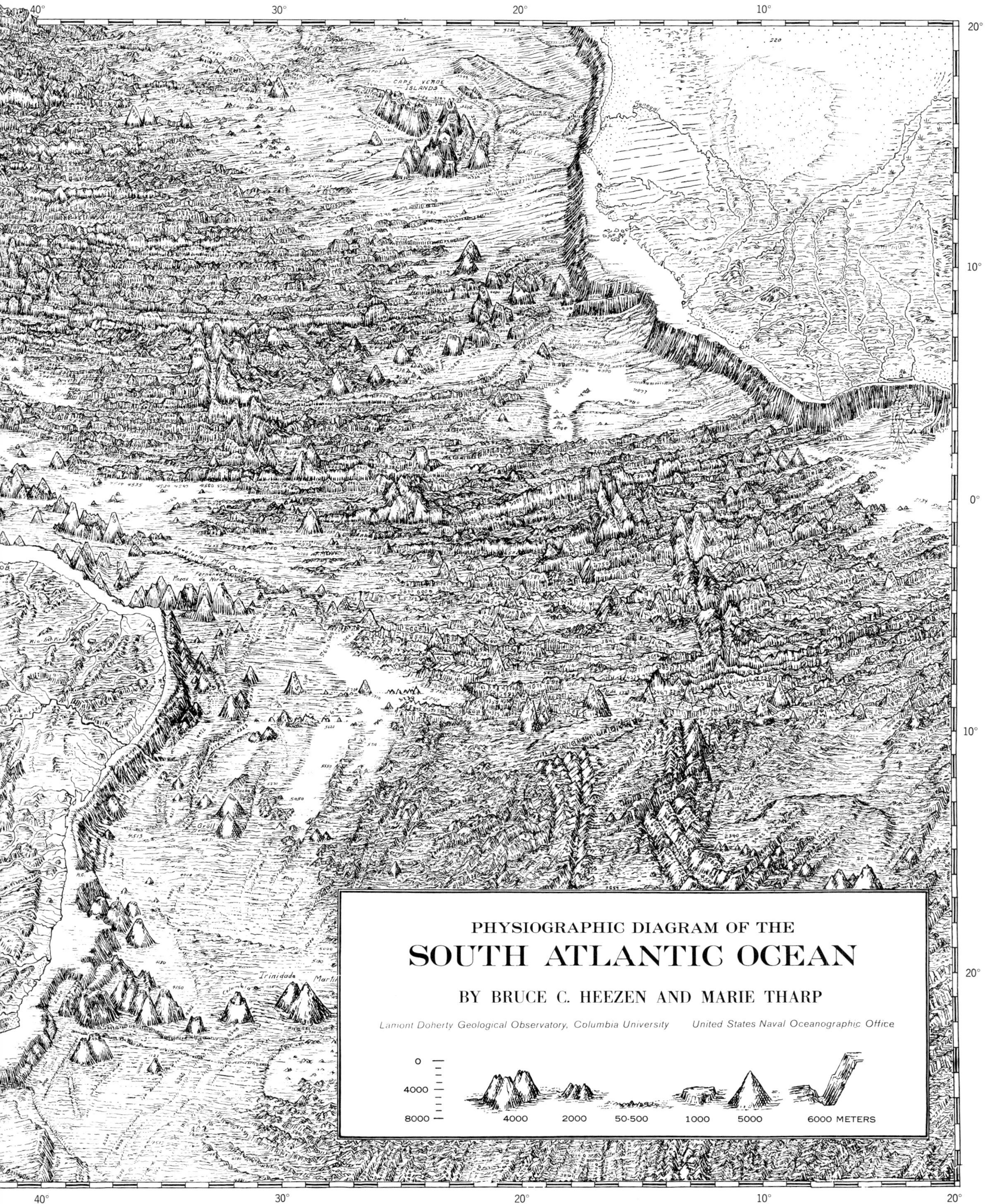

PHYSIOGRAPHIC DIAGRAM OF THE
SOUTH ATLANTIC OCEAN
BY BRUCE C. HEEZEN AND MARIE THARP
Lamont Doherty Geological Observatory, Columbia University
United States Naval Oceanographic Office
0
4000
8000
4000
2000
50-500
1000
5000
6000 METERS
40°
30°
20°
10°
20°
10°
0°
10°
20°
CAPE VERDE ISLANDS
St. Helena
Trinidade

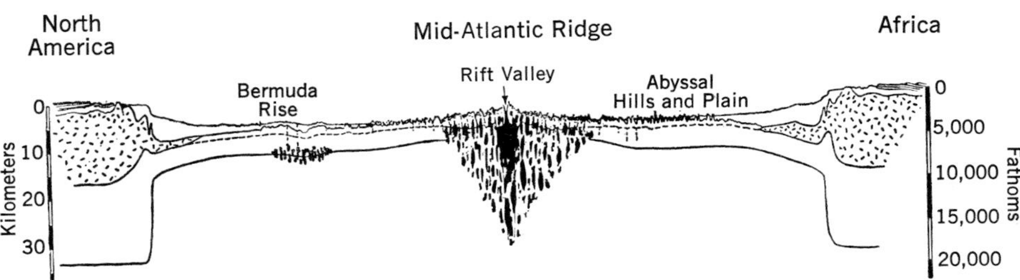

13.6 Crustal section across the North Atlantic. The central third of the ocean is occupied by the Mid-Atlantic Ridge underlain by a mixture of crustal and mantle rock. The first layer under the oceans represents sediments; the second, possibly consolidated sediments or, more probably, volcanic rocks; the third is oceanic crustal rock (basement) which is probably basalt. Beneath this layer lies the mantle.

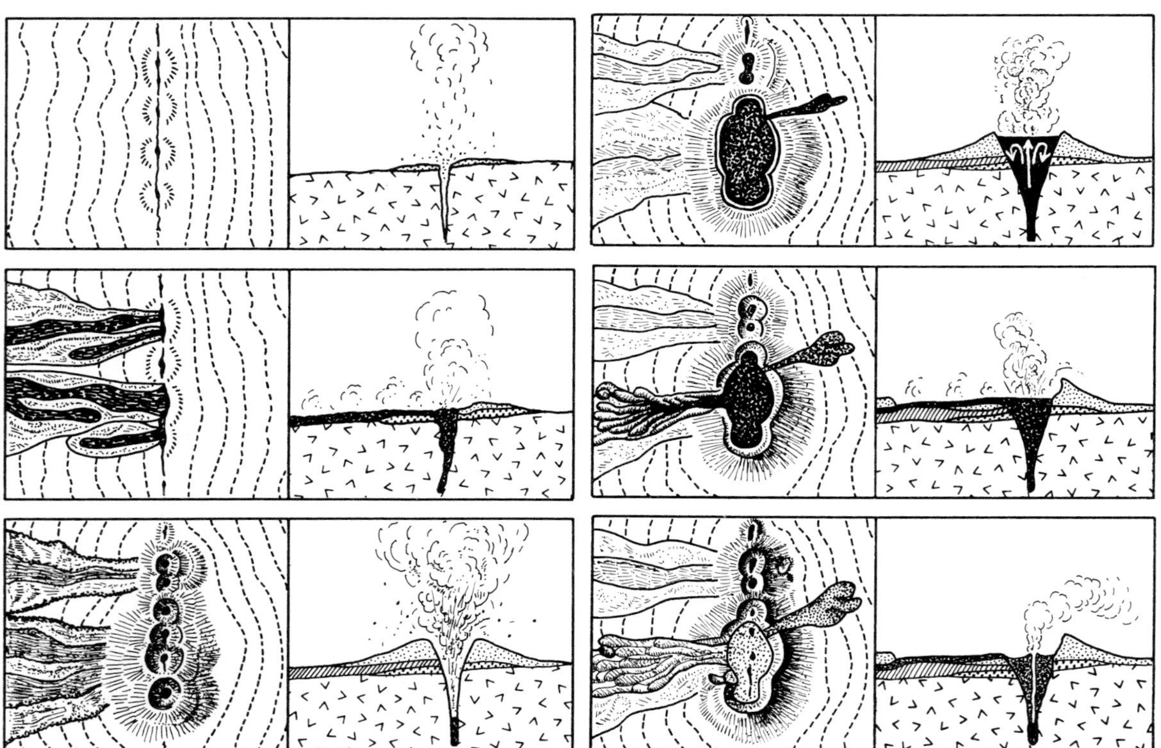

13.7 Lava issues from volcanic vents along a deep crack in the World Rift System exposed on Iceland.

moved with respect to the others. The anti-drifters initially refused to accept the evidence, feeling that obvious errors would certainly be found or claiming that the results were unfairly biased, or that they were simply fraudulent. It was a time when much rethinking had to be done. Much

13.8 Deep fissures mark the widening rift valley. This cleft (Almannagja) parallels the median rift and lies along the active earthquake belt of central Iceland.

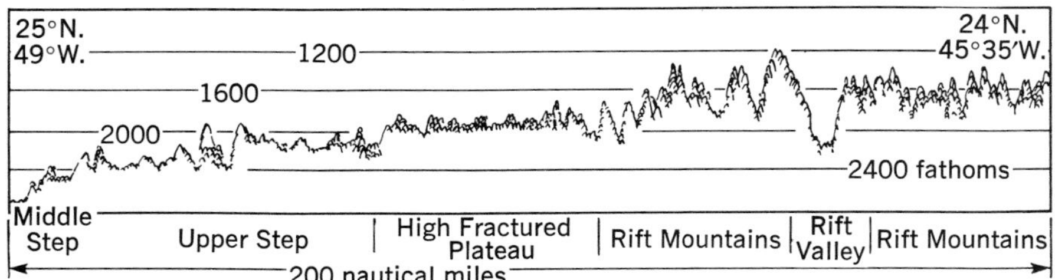

13.9 In the Rift Valley as well as on the ruggest Rift Mountains sediment rarely covers the fractured pillows which form the seascape.

to the dismay of the anti-drifters paleomagnetic data supporting continental displacements[6] continued to pour in, and impressive converts were made within the establishment of geophysics. But it is well to remember that the discovery of the mid-oceanic rift valley and the recognition of its tensional origin came just before the magnetic results began to support drift and long before they could be considered compelling evidence.

The student of the continents need not concern himself unduly with continental drift for it infrequently affects his daily work. But for the submarine geologist, continental drift is vital and basic and of constant concern. For example, if the Atlantic basin was formed by the drifting apart of the continents, virtually every significant and insignificant feature of underlying rock surface must owe its origin to the drift. One could not intelligently proceed in the interpretation of the morphology or structure of the ocean floor or, in fact, understand almost any geological aspect of the seascape until this question was resolved. For this reason students of global submarine morphology had to take a stand in order to come to any general conclusions while the students of continental phenomena could continue their work without waiting for the controversy to be resolved.

13.10 No smoothing is recorded either on echograms or on photographs on these new ribs of the solid earth. These profiles illustrate the nature of bottom information obtained by echo-sounding. (A) Precision-Depth-Recorder record of a peak in the Mid-Altantic Ridge. Record shows multiple 400-fathom scales. On original record 400-fathom range is represented by 18 inches and one hour (or about 10 miles) by 24 inches. Light horizontal lines are at 20-fathom intervals. (B) Same profile with no vertical exaggeration, with corrections for slope. (C) Profile at 40:1 exaggeration plotted from first echoes shown in A. Although depth variations of one meter can be measured, precision echo-soundings cannot give detailed information on ocean-floor features less than 100 meters wide. Variations in the reflectivity of the sea floor are related to variations in the composition of the bottom (soft sediment, ooze, sand, rock) and to topographic features too small to be detected on normal echograms. The fuzzy echo between points C and D suggests a rocky steep slope.

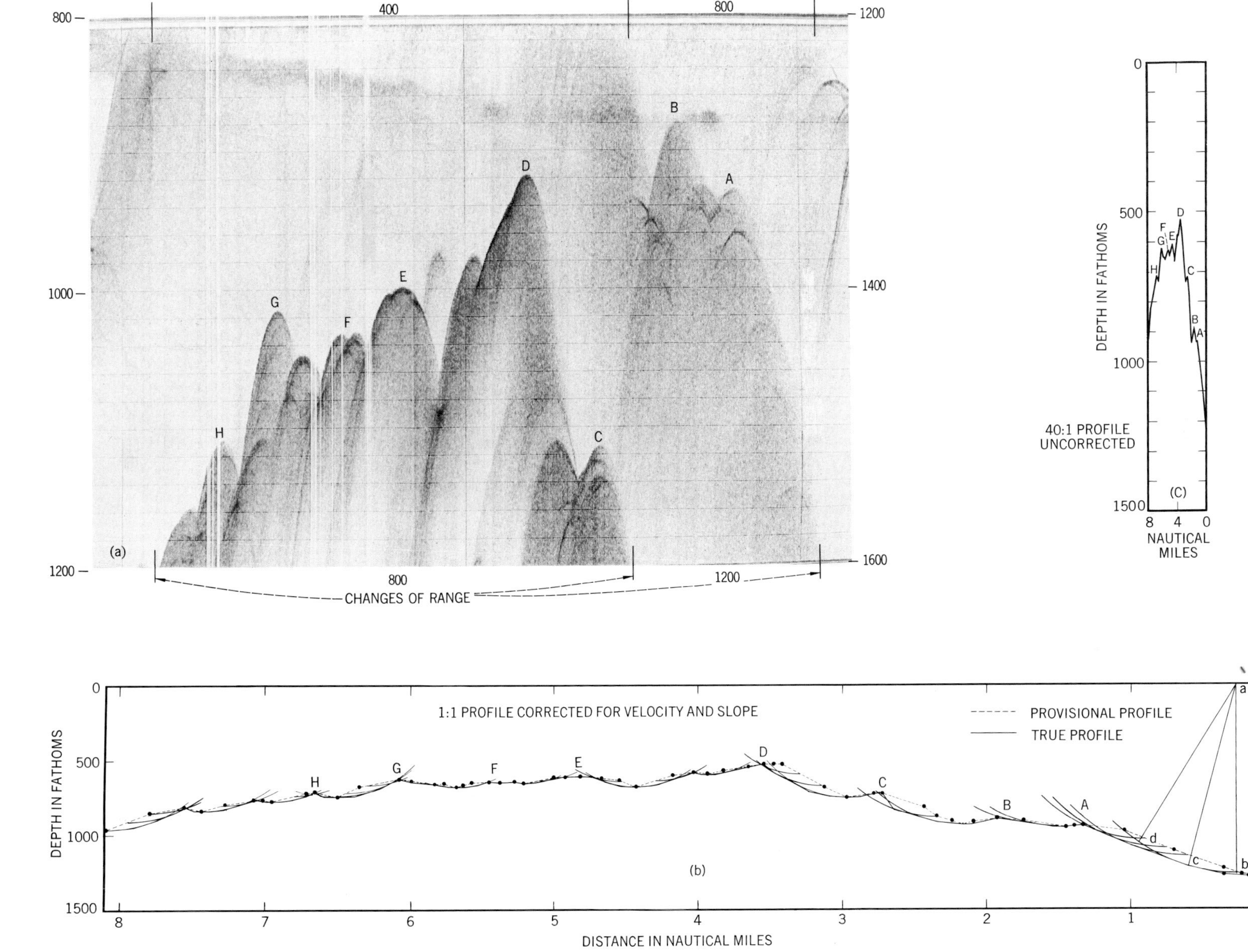
800
400
800
1200
1000
1400
1200
1600
(a)
A
B
C
D
E
F
G
H
800
1200
CHANGES OF RANGE
DEPTH IN FATHOMS
0
500
1000
1500
(C)
8 4 0
NAUTICAL MILES
40:1 PROFILE UNCORRECTED
1:1 PROFILE CORRECTED FOR VELOCITY AND SLOPE
PROVISIONAL PROFILE
TRUE PROFILE
a
b
c
d
(b)
DISTANCE IN NAUTICAL MILES
8
7
6
5
4
3
2
1
0

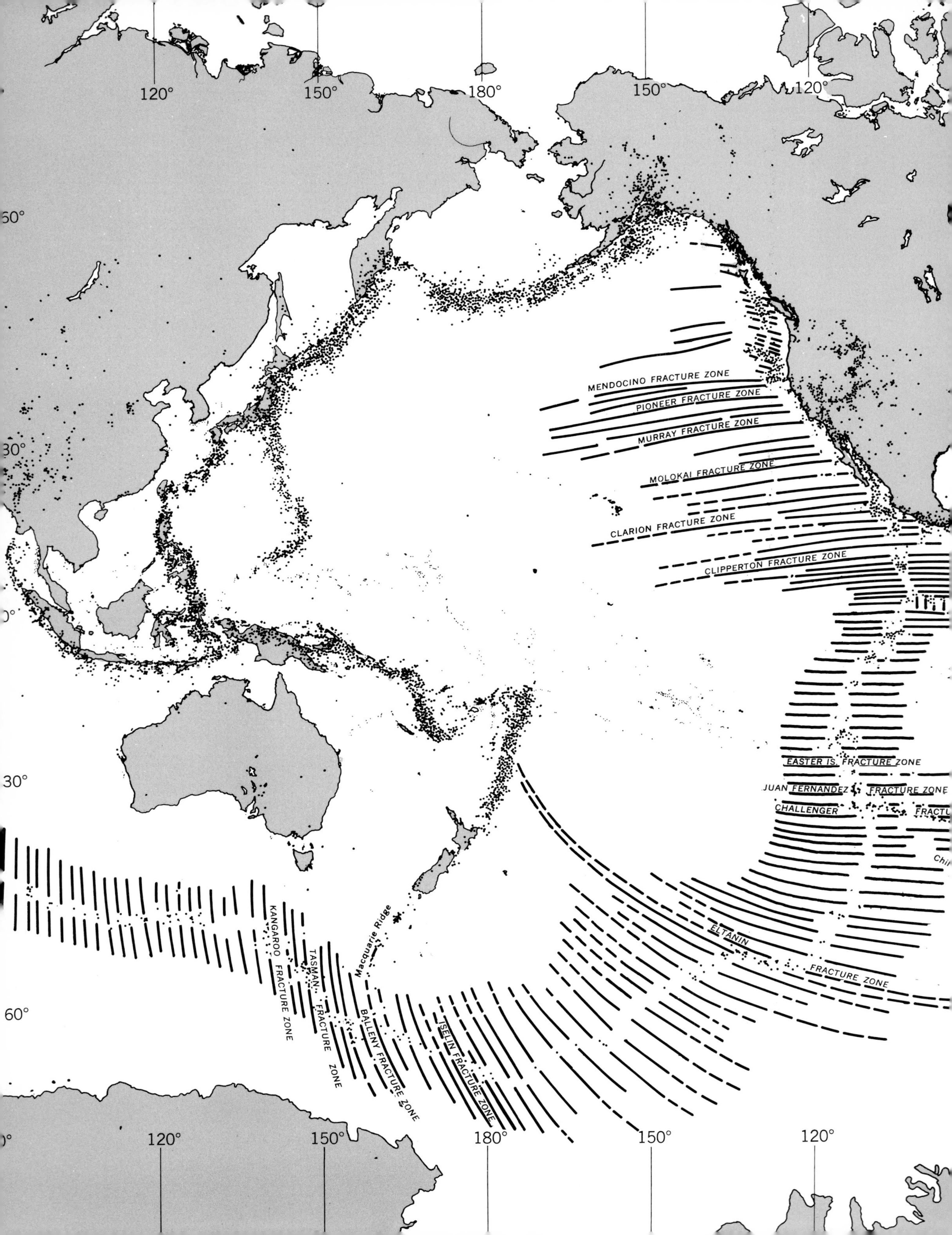

120°
150°
180°
150°
120°
60°
30°
0°
30°
60°
MENDOCINO FRACTURE ZONE
PIONEER FRACTURE ZONE
MURRAY FRACTURE ZONE
MOLOKAI FRACTURE ZONE
CLARION FRACTURE ZONE
CLIPPERTON FRACTURE ZONE
EASTER IS. FRACTURE ZONE
JUAN FERNANDEZ FRACTURE ZONE
CHALLENGER
ELTANIN
FRACTURE ZONE
KANGAROO FRACTURE ZONE
TASMAN FRACTURE ZONE
Macquarie Ridge
BALLENY FRACTURE ZONE
ISELIN FRACTURE ZONE
120°
150°
180°
150°
120°

JAN MAYEN FRACTURE ZONE
SPAR F.Z.
ICELAND
GIBBS
FRACTURE ZONE
Azores
Gibraltar Ridge
OCEANOGRAPHER
FRACTURE ZONE
ATLANTIS
FRACTURE ZONE
KANE
FRACTURE
ZONE
VEMA
FRACTURE ZONE
DOLDRUMS
FRACTURE ZONE
ST. PAUL
FRACTURE ZONE
ROMANCHE FRACTURE ZONE
CHAIN
FRACTURE ZONE
ASCENSION
FRACTURE ZONE
ST. HELENA
FRACTURE ZONE
HOTSPUR
FRACTURE ZONE
MARTIN VAZ
FRACTURE ZONE
RIO GRANDE
FRACTURE ZONE
WALFISCH FRACTURE ZONE
TRISTAN DA CUNHA
FRACTURE ZONE
GOUGH
FRACTURE ZONE
FALKLAND FRACTURE ZONE
Bristol-Bouvet Ridge
SANDWICH F.Z.
Dead Sea
Red Sea
Gulf of Aden
OWEN FRACTURE ZONE
East African Rift Valleys
Chagos Trench
Vema Trench
AMSTERDAM FRACTURE ZONE
MALAGASY F.Z.
MOZAMBIQUE F.Z.
60°
30°
30°
60°
60°
30°
0°
30°
60°
60°
30°
0°
30°
60°

If the American submarine geologist of the 1950's put aside for a moment his American prejudice against drift and wondered where in the Atlantic the new crust demanded by continental drift must be forming, there was only really one possibility—the mid-oceanic rift valley—for only there had they seen a belt of fresh lava-covered scenery (13.1-13.11), totally lacking of sediment cover, only there had echo-sounders detected the high shattered relief of young mountains (13.10); only there (and in the trenches) had seismographs recorded continuing instability beneath the sea; and from the entire ocean floor only there had temperature probes recorded anomalously high heat flow (13.13). The broad, undeformed sediment aprons of the continental margin and the undeformed expanses of the ocean basin floor denied the possibility of either wholesale extension or significant compression in these broad belts.

Of course, there remained the question of whether drift was still going on, a point of particular relevence to the interpretation of the visual seascape. American paleomagnetists, true to their tradition, made a valiant attempt to explain away all indications of drift over the past seventy million years as errors in measurement—and there was a general feeling that if drift had occurred it had happened long ago.[7] Those of this persuasion saw no need of identifying a zone of active crustal growth.

Two general views developed in the late 1950's concerning the origin of the Mid-Oceanic Ridge. Both recognized the essential median position of the ridge. One group[2], accepting the evidence of continental displacement as compelling, considered the ridge to be a permanent feature growing wider in a widening ocean (13.14). Those of this persuasion could place significance on the gradation in scenic features from the rocky volcanic ridge axis to the ever more tranquil sea floor stretching out on either side. The other group, rejecting continental displacements, considered the ridge an ephemeral uplift of ancient crust in an ocean of essentially constant width,[8] a position which ignored the visual pattern. Both groups appealed to upwelling of mantle material, in the first case[2] simply to fill the growing void, in the second case[8] to cause the uplift. The concept of the widening ocean which must continuously grow along a median line gave rise to two further schools of thought. At first it was contended that since the amount of crustal growth inferred from the geology of the Mid-Oceanic Ridge vastly exceeded the amount of crustal

◁ 13.11 Lava rises up from the depths of the earth into the 60,000 kilometer-long World Rift System which is marked by a line of shallow earthquakes.

13.12 As the rift expands, its floor is broken into long narrow blocks which are tilted and upturned. The crest of the Mid-Oceanic Ridge must greatly resemble this faulted landscape seen where the World Rift System passes through East Africa and Iceland. U, the Gregory Rift near Lake Magadi, Kenya. L, Southern Iceland.

13.13 The recently emplaced lavas at the crest of the Mid-Oceanic Ridge produce a narrow belt of high heat flow from the earth's interior. Units are in micro-calories per square centimeter per second.

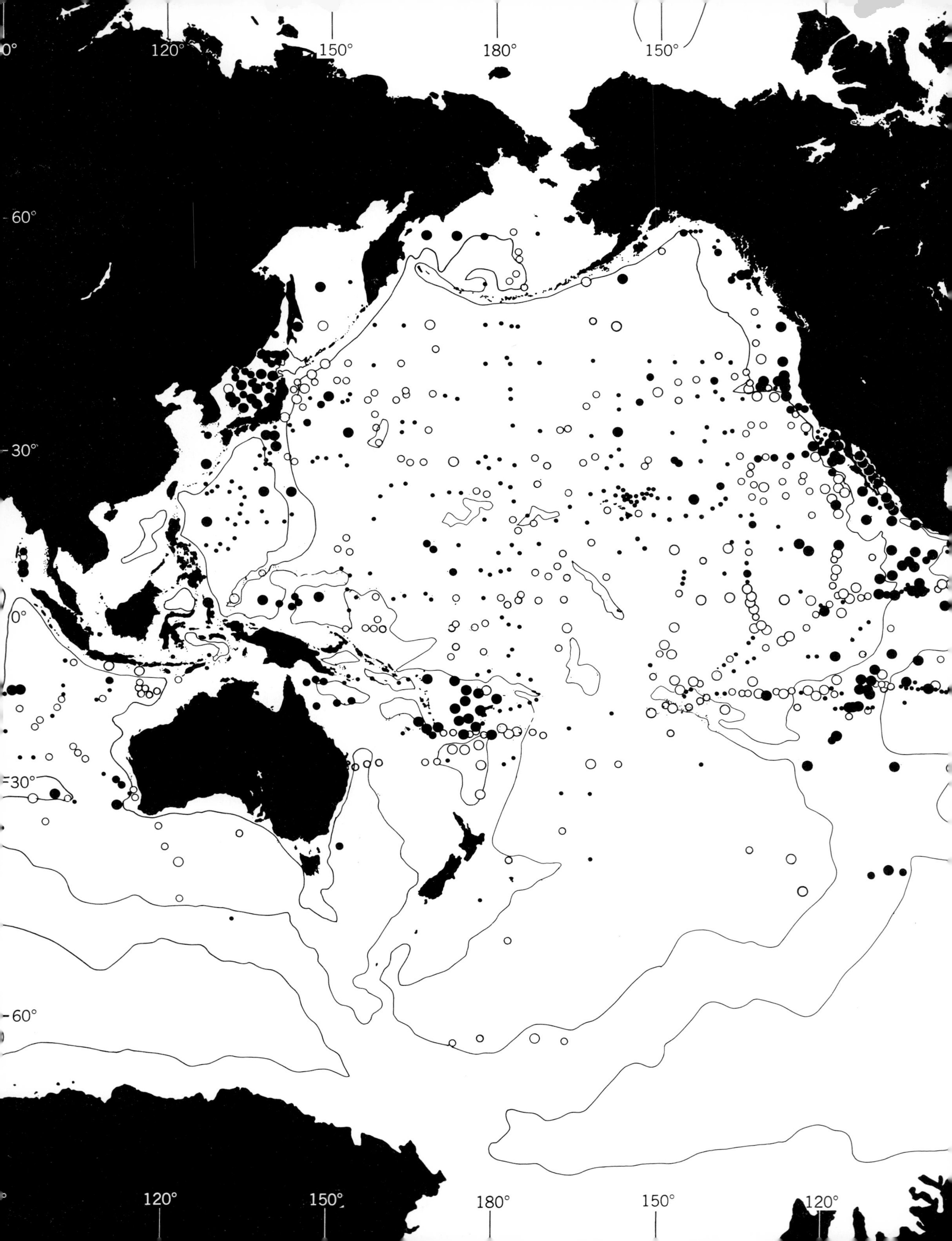

120°
150°
180°
150°
60°
30°
0°
30°
60°
120°
150°
180°
150°
120°

60°
30°
0°
30°
60°
Heat Flow
Hot
> 2.25
1.75 – 2.25
normal
1.25 – 1.75
Cold
0.75 – 1.25
< 0.75
Value in millionths of a calorie from one square centimeter per second:
Micro Calorie/CM²/Sec.
4000 Meter Contour
60°
30°
0°
30°
60°
60°
30°
0°
30°
60°

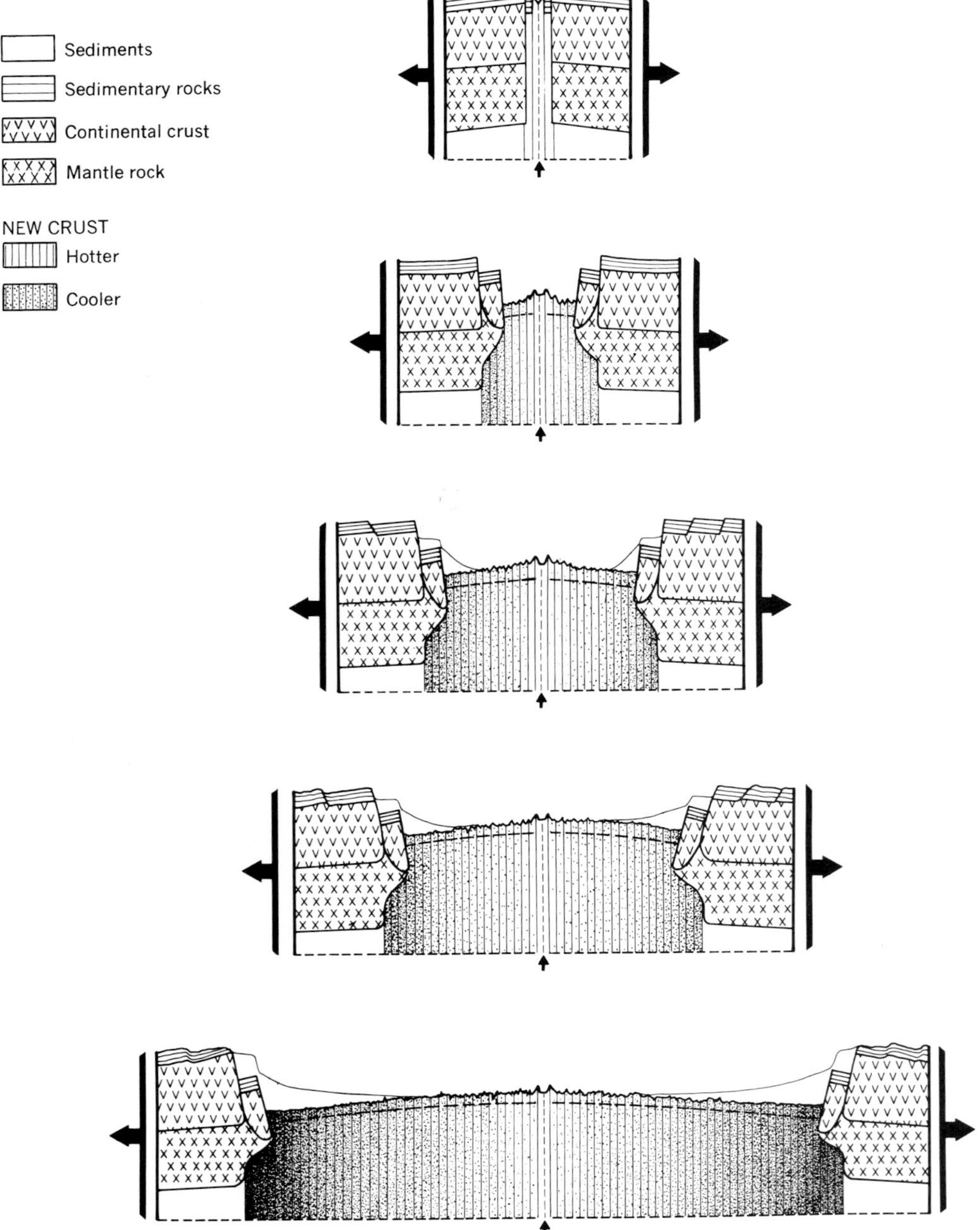

13.14 Evolution of the ocean floor. Top profile represents an initial continental rift such as the modern East African Rift Valleys or the Triassic Atlantic. The second profile represents a young rift ocean such as the modern Red Sea or the Jurassic Atlantic. The third profile represents an ocean in a later stage of expansion such as the modern Gulf of Aden or the Neocomian (Lower Cretaceous) Atlantic. The fourth profile indicates a still later stage which might be represented by the Norwegian Sea or the Cenomanian (Middle Cretaceous) Atlantic.

45°12′N 27°59′W

13.15 Large attached organisms are rare on the very recently emplaced additions to the growing Mid-Oceanic Ridge. 3282 m, floor of Rift Valley in Mid-Atlantic Ridge.

shortening for the entire earth allowed by most structural geologists, the earth necessarily must be growing larger.[9] But later another group, avoiding the radical implications of global expansion, held that most of the world's geologists and geophysicists were completely wrong in their estimates of crustal shortening; this group postulated that the construction of crust is precisely compensated by exactly the same amount of crustal destruction.[10] The latter controversy is not yet resolved, but let it be said that the more conservative group has the larger following.

CLUES

During recorded history more lava has poured forth above the sea in Iceland than in all the rest of the earth's volcanic belts combined. Yet to comprehend more fully this fact we must remember that Iceland's volcanic belt comprises less than one-half of one per cent of the total length of the growing world-encircling rift.

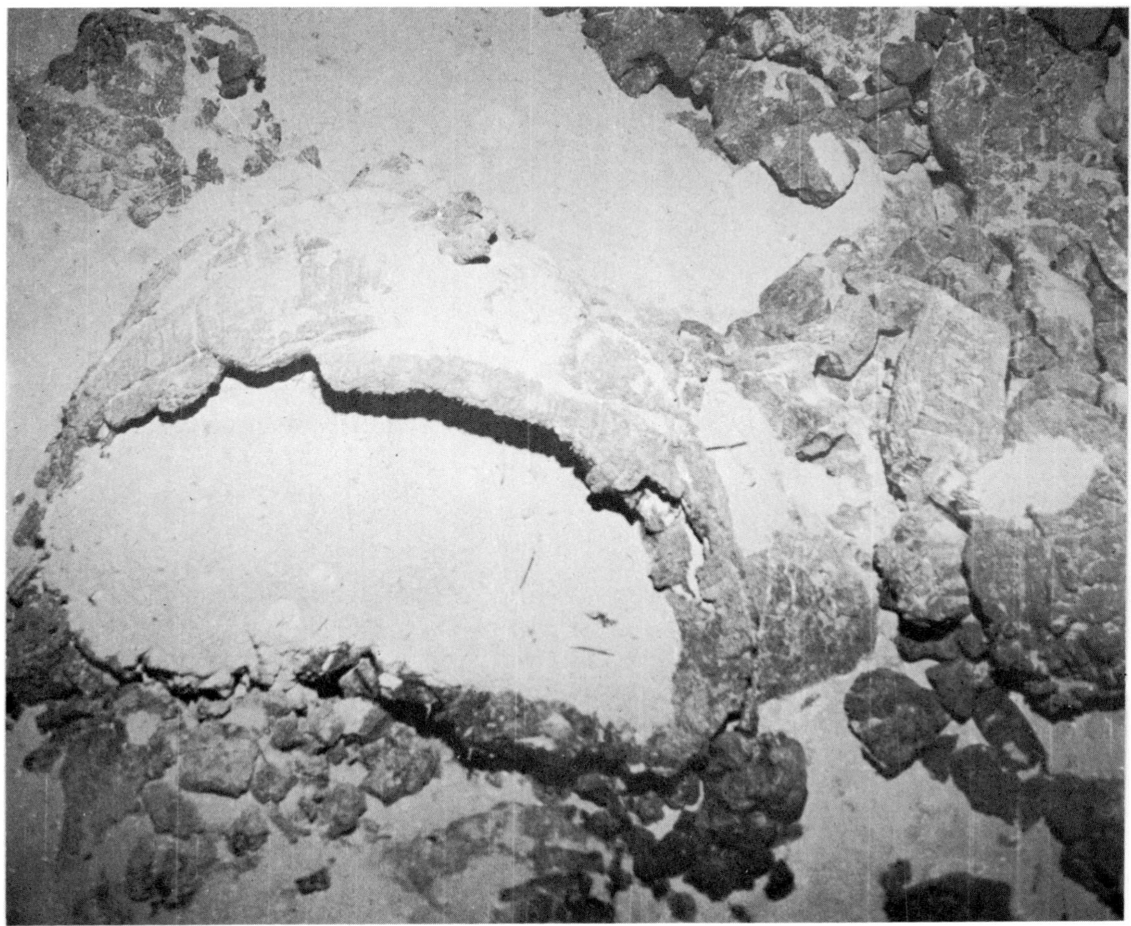

13.16 A broken pillow of basalt. At the growing center of the widening rift where hot lavas meet the chilly ocean and noxious volcanic emanations are carried up through the shattered rock by hot rising water, life is rarely seen. But it begins to flourish as the rocks cool, the emanations cease, and the new-born rock is carried up to form the bold mountain peaks. 3188 m, floor of rift valley, Mid-Atlantic Ridge.

A visit to Iceland is a necessary experience in the education of a submarine geologist, for here one can examine features of the earth's suboceanic crust nowhere else exposed above the waves. Volcanos of diverse types abound but elongate and linear patterns predominate. The parallel vertical-walled fissures, meters to kilometers wide, which repeatedly stretch out across the treeless countryside (13.8) tell so clearly that the central valley is growing wider that hardly an Icelander, no matter what his pursuit, would fail to consider it so. But if in looking across this cen-

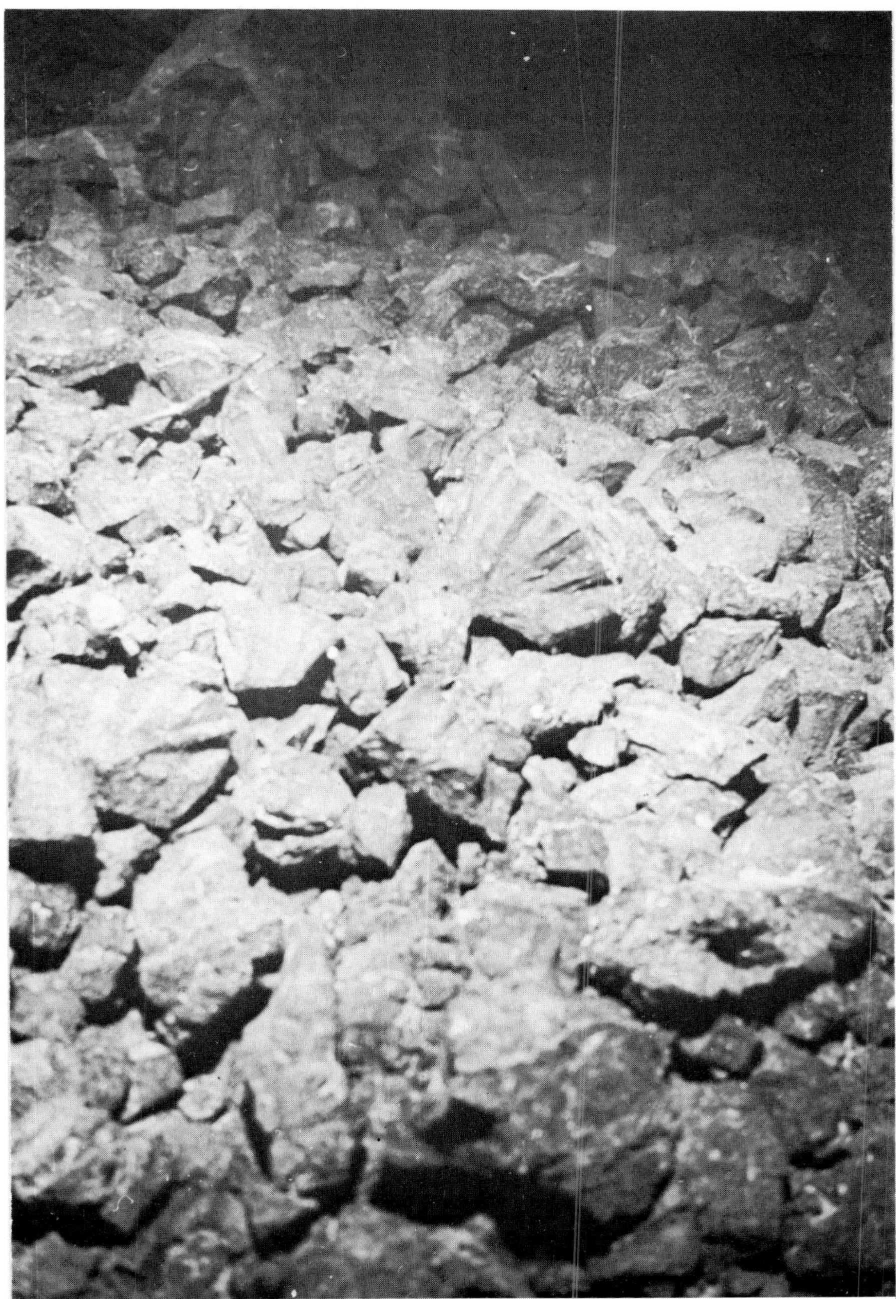

45°20′N 28°02′W

13.17 Steep slopes composed of the shattered fragments of pillow lavas are characteristic of the walls of the Rift Valley. Wedge-shaped fragments in center reveal the characteristic radial jointing of pillows. 1890 m, west wall of rift valley, Mid-Atlantic Ridge.

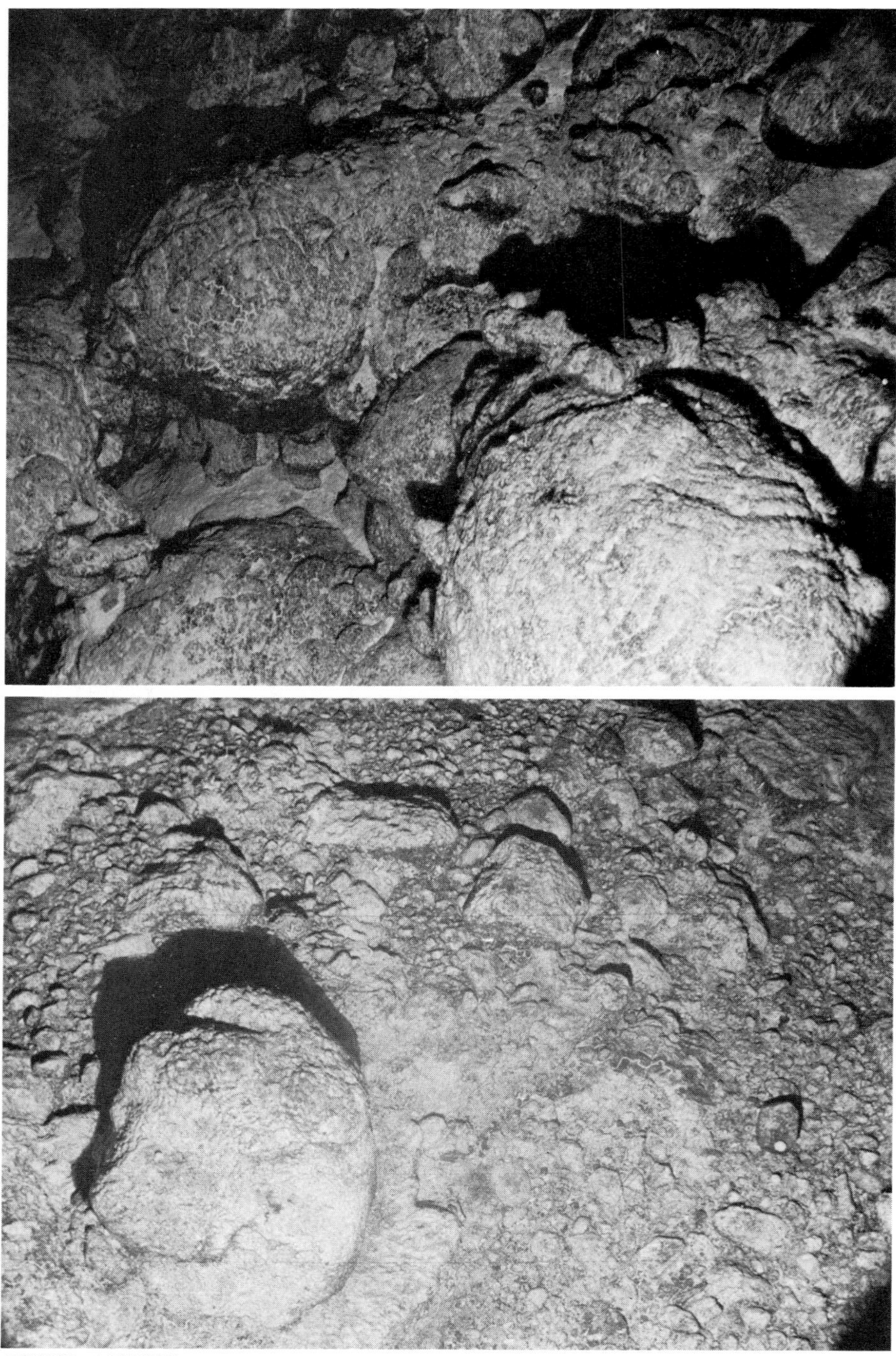

56°07′S 144°59′W
57°35′S 138°51′W

13.18 These pillowed lavas which recently rose from the depths of the earth and flowed out in mid-Pacific, form the foundations of the deep, the very ribs of the solid earth. U, L, 2638 m, 2925 m, crest of Mid-Oceanic Ridge.

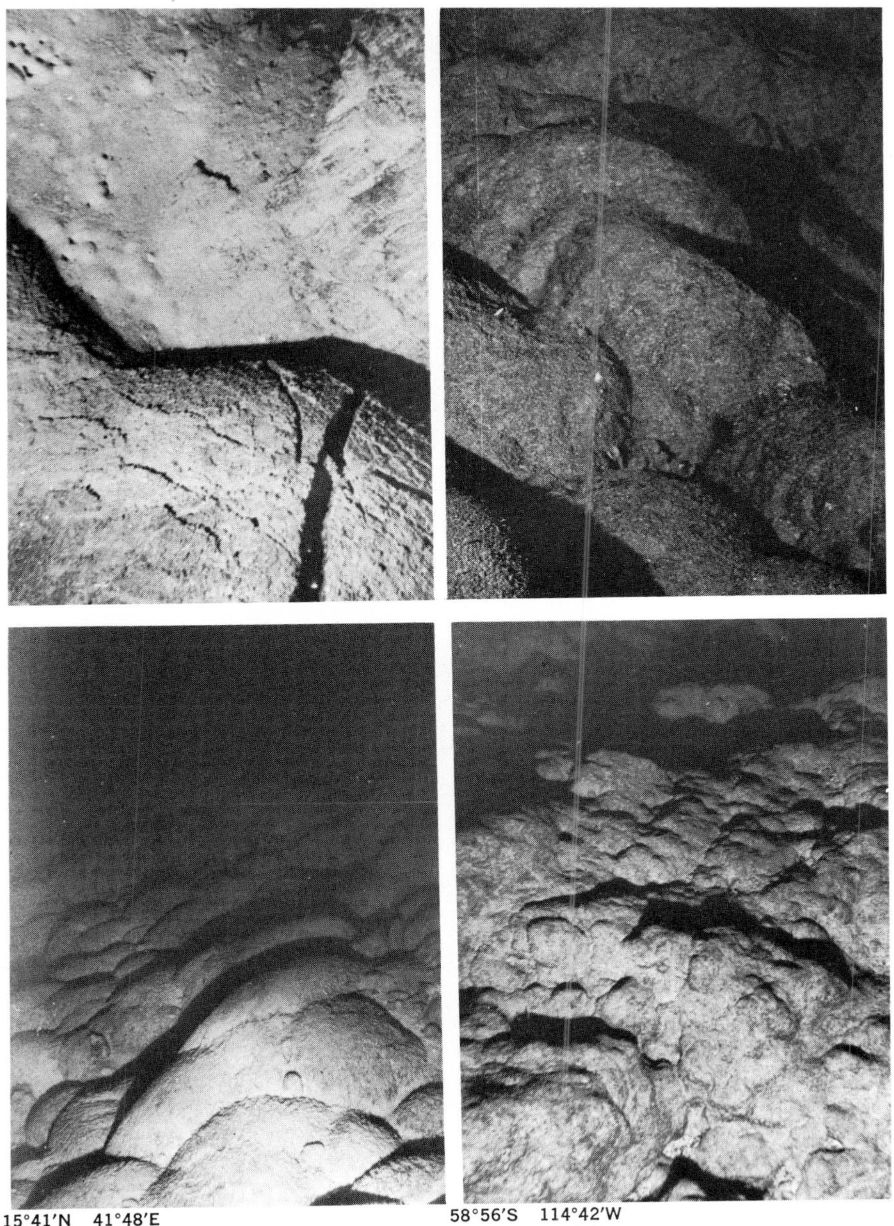

13.19 Rounded manganese-encrusted outcrops are seen where molten rocks have been recently emplaced or where strong bottom currents prevent deposition of sediments. UL, fractured pillow lavas, 1061 m, east of Asmara, Red Sea. UR, current-swept manganese-encrusted lava, 5014 m, eastern end of Eltanin Fracture Zone, Bellingshausen Sea. LL, current-swept bedrock, 4172 m, Drake Passage, south of Tierra del Fuego. LR, recent addition to the growing Mid-Oceanic Ridge lies exposed to abyssal circulation, 5058 m, north wall, Vema Fracture Zone, equatorial Atlantic.

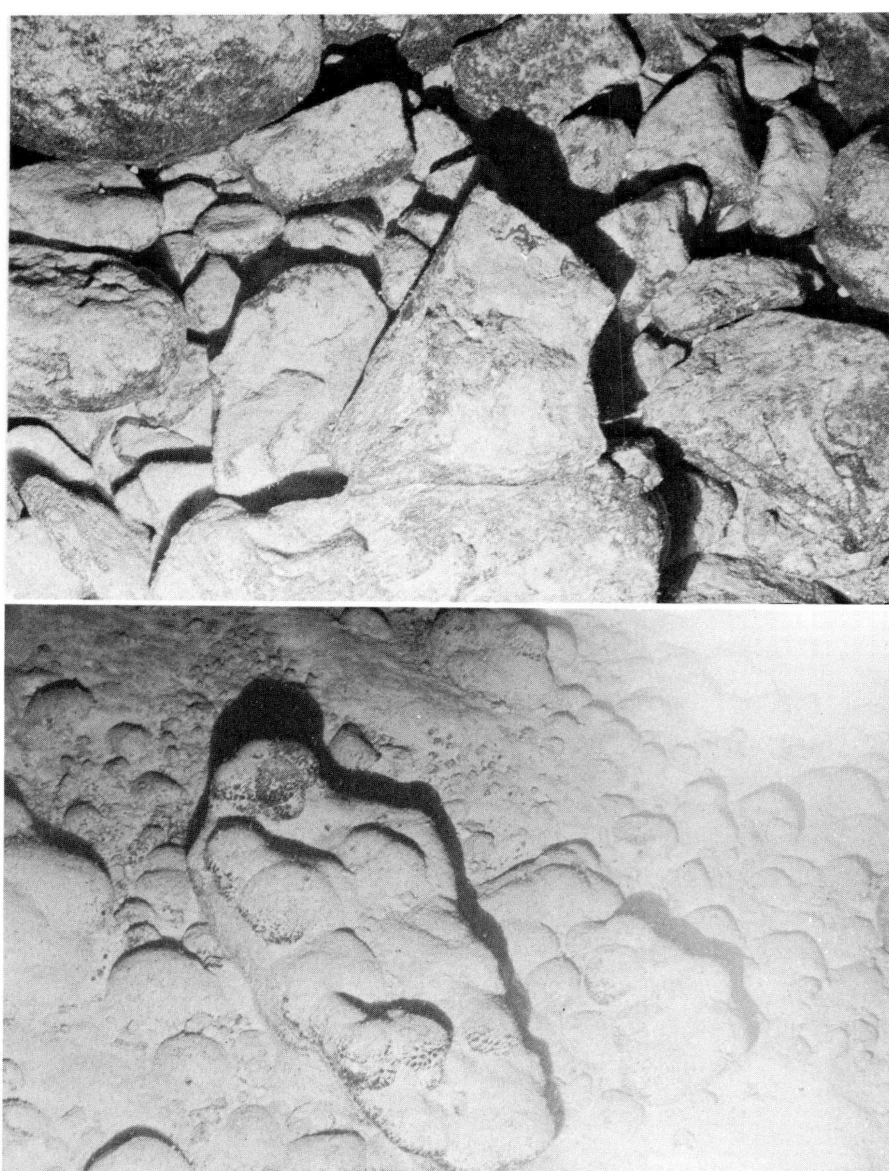

54°00′S 151°15′E
51°57′S 150°15′E

13.20 Fractured blocks on the Mid-Oceanic Ridge beneath the Circumpolar Current are gradually coated with manganese as they recede from the rift. Beneath this swift current the flanks as well as the crest of the ridge are swept clean of sediment. The manganese has taken tens of millions of years to produce the rounding and smoothing seen in the lower photograph for only a few millimeters of manganese paint the rock each million years. U, L, 3852 m, and 4334 m, flank of Mid-Oceanic Ridge, south of Tasmania.

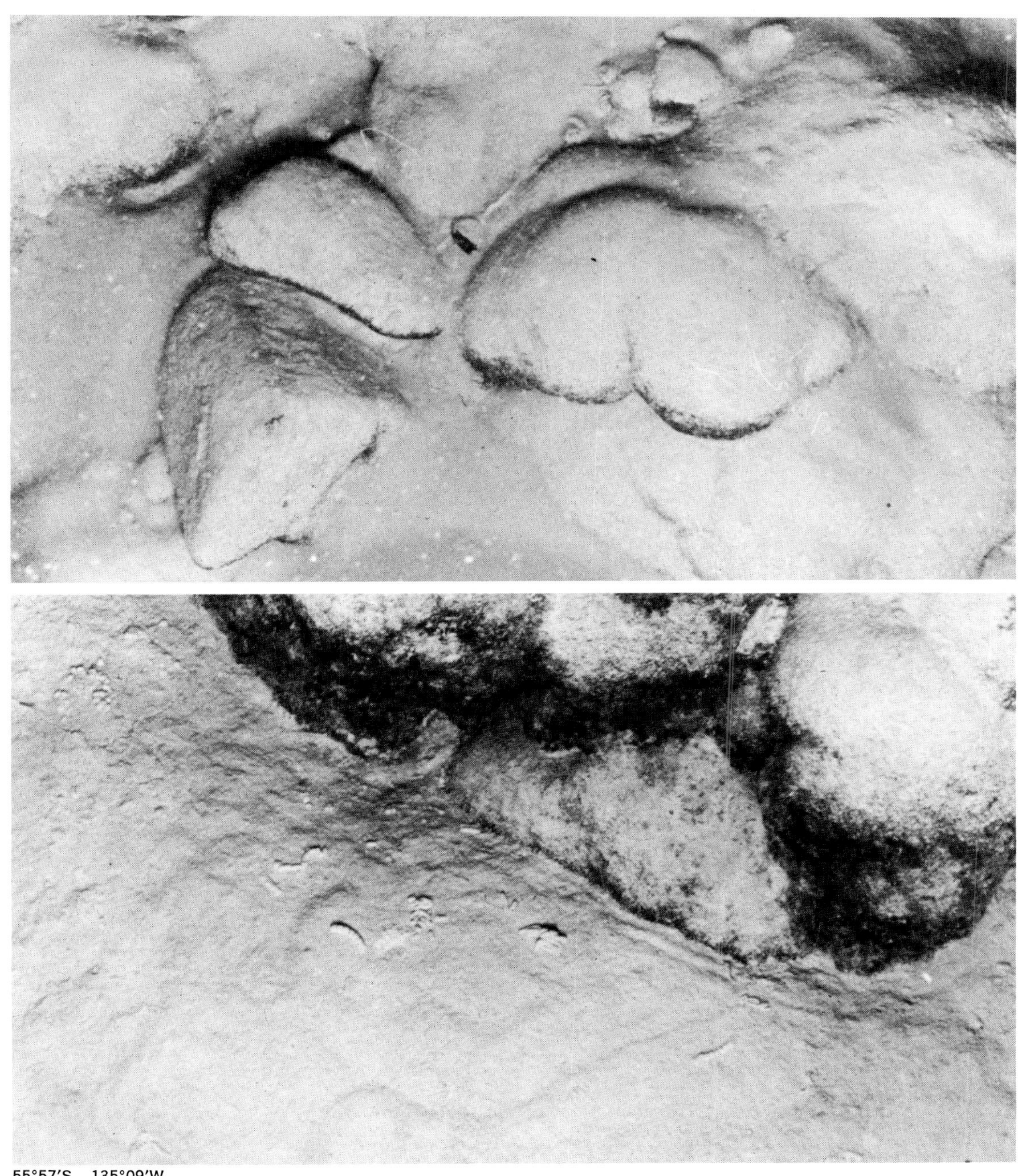

55°57′S 135°09′W
58°58′S 135°29′W

13.21 An unrelenting downward drift of clay and ooze casts a thin veil over the cooling lavas. As the new crust marches outward from the crest of the expanding ridge this thickening veil eventually blankets and hides the ribs of the earth. U, L, 3280 m, 3800 m, upper flanks of Mid-Oceanic Ridge, South Pacific.

46°50′N 28°58′W
46°50′N 28°58′W

13.22 Coarse volcanic debris swept from the crest of the ridge forms huge ripples over the growing blanket of globigerina ooze. Volcanic sand and gravel interbedded with abyssal ooze caps the now cooled crust. U, L, 2674 m, near the crest of Mid-Atlantic Ridge.

45°29′N 28°32′W

13.23 Pens, fans and sponges adorn the current-swept craggy peaks of the Rift Mountains. 1798 m, crest of Mid-Atlantic Ridge.

tral, newly created valley of Iceland we try to imagine what it would have been like if during its growth sea level had accidentally been a few hundred meters higher, we have to make certain mental adjustments. Probably the most important consideration is the effect sea water would have had in arresting the flow of lava. Even above the sea we can gain some insight by examining the wildly contorted lava flows which have run over damp ground.

The enormous flows of 1783 which poured forth from the fissure Làkigja ran fifty kilometers before reaching the chilling sea. No such broad and sweeping flows can be expected in the abyss. Lava flowing from fissures should build linear mountains which extend very little distance on either side of the nourishing crack. Flows beneath the sea must be quickly quenched and the resulting submarine topography must thus be rougher than that of the land. Yet anyone who has walked over the more

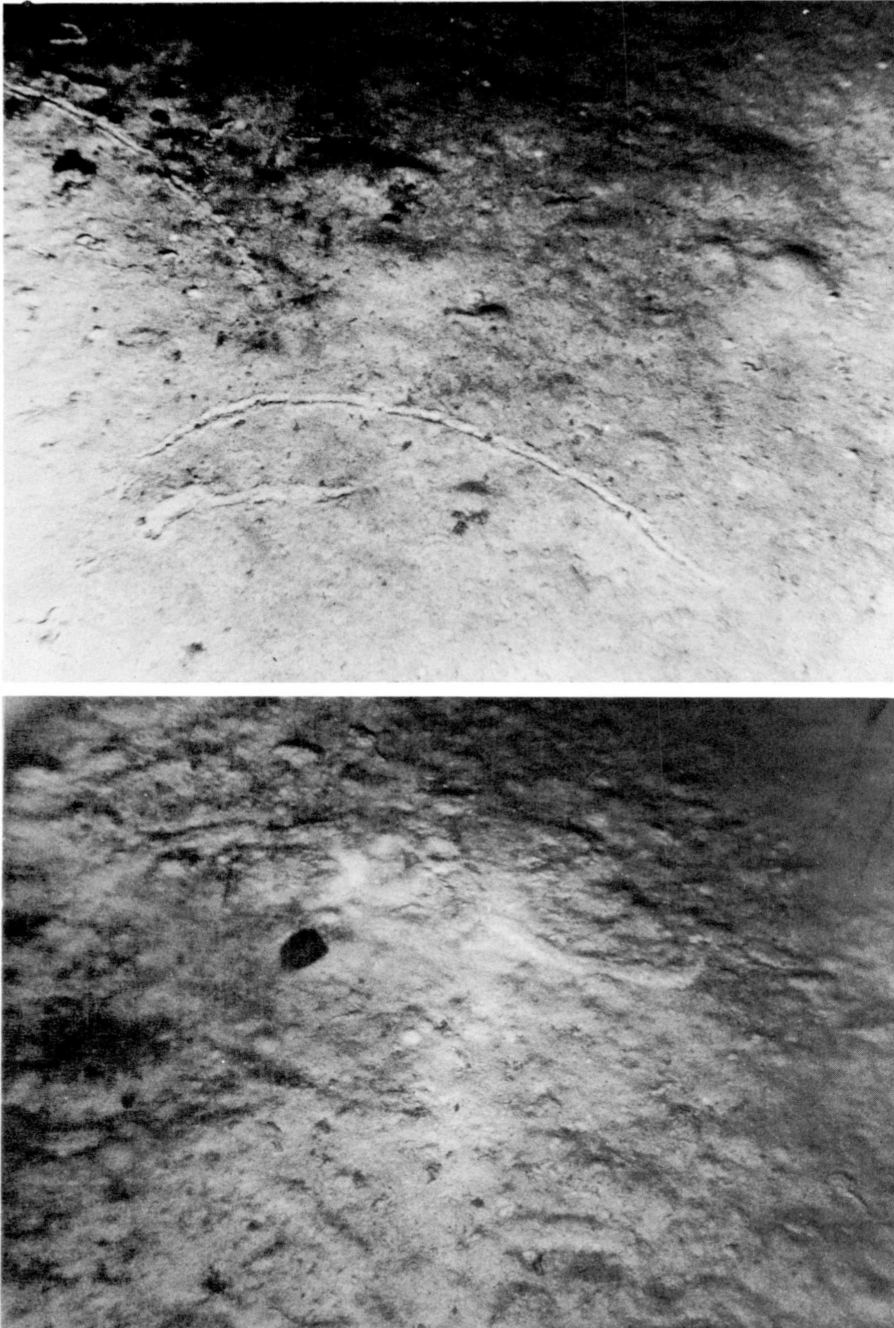

46°04′N 17°43′W
48°36′N 22°17′W

13.24 On the flanks of the ridge the growing blanket of ooze has buried the cooled dark lavas. Tranquil, tracked, and burrowed calcareous ooze, U, L. 4004 m, 4014 m, east flank of the Mid-Atlantic Ridge.

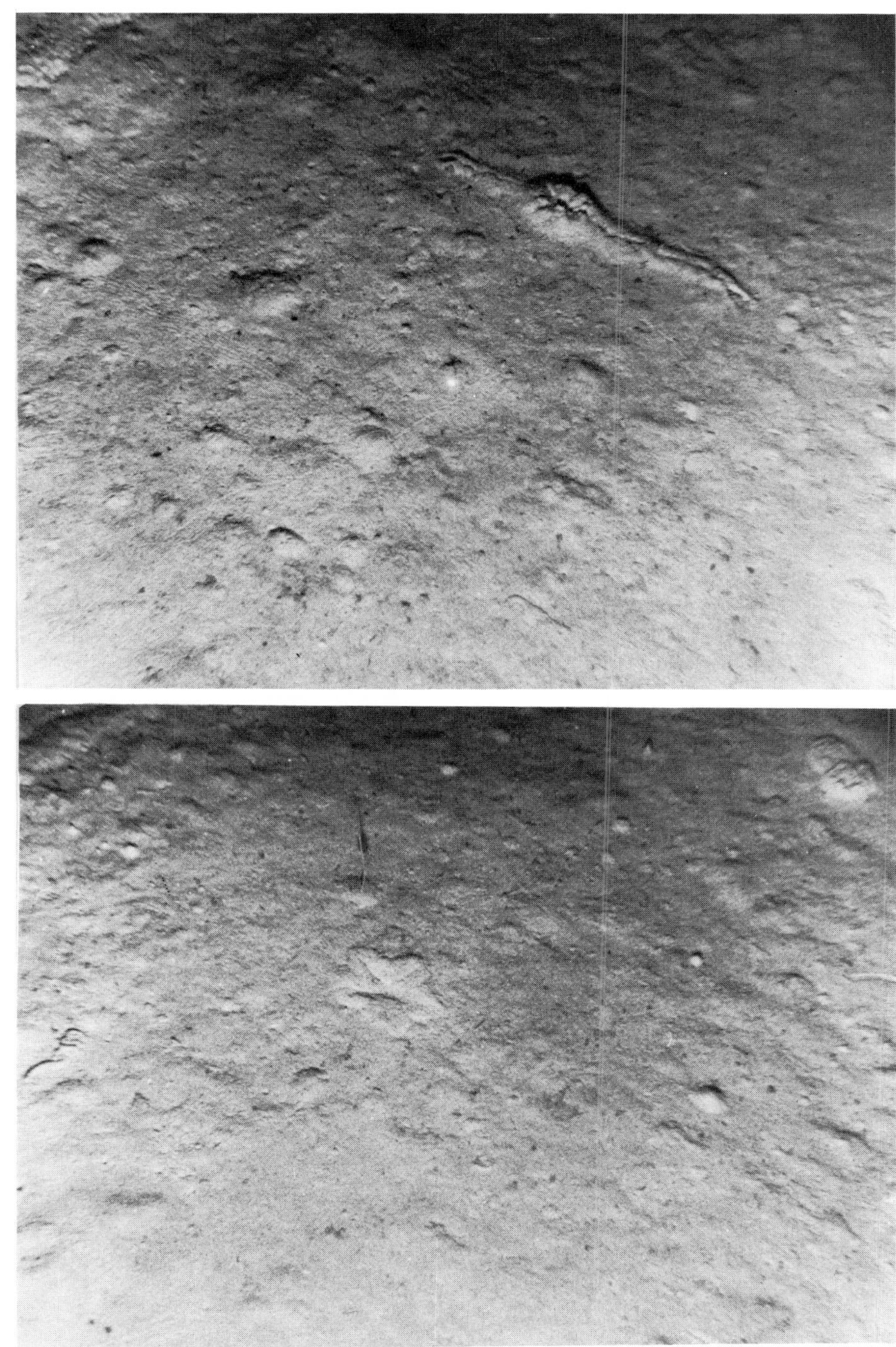

45°42′N 20°38′W
45°42′N 20°38′W
13.25 On the lower flanks of the Mid-Oceanic Ridge a thick blanket of ooze and clay subdues the once sharp and craggy peaks. U, L, 4732 m, east flank Mid-Atlantic Ridge.

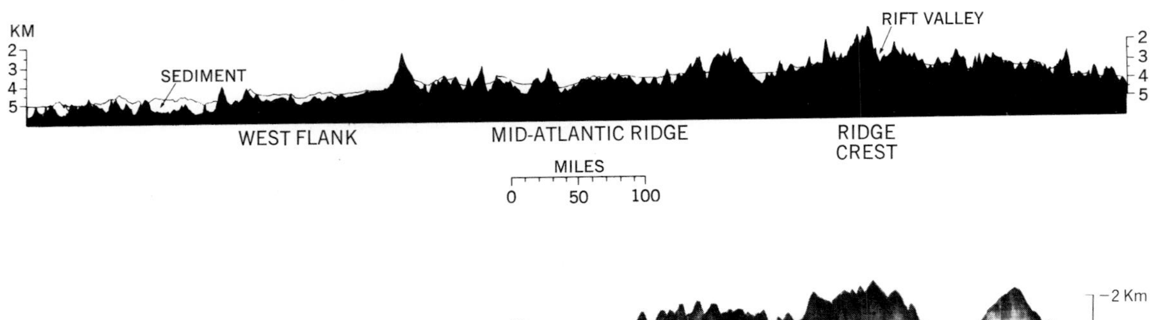

13.26 The sediment blanket gradually thickens toward the ocean basin. This seismic reflection profile shows that on the eastern flank of the Mid-Atlantic Ridge the higher and sharper peaks protrude from beneath the thickening sediments.

recent flows in Iceland might find it hard to believe that anything could be more irregular on a scale of tens of meters. The undersea landscape of the Mid-Oceanic Ridge which we see in photographs must be more linear and of higher relief and more broken in detail than that exposed above the sea.

It is surprising that the scenery west of Nairobi, Kenya, and that east of Reykjavik, Iceland, is so similar; surprising until one realizes that both are parts of the same world rift system and that in these two areas so removed from one another, similar rocks have reacted in similar ways to similar forces.[11] One can stand on the rim of the Gregory Rift Valley on a clear day and see the same lava flow repeated dozens of times in the multitude of tilted, fractured, and faulted blocks which fill the rift valley floor (13.12). We can imagine for a moment that we have been granted a privileged peek through an obscuring ocean. But as probably anomalous as these areas are, they give us our principal clue as to the interpretation of the submarine scenery of the world rift system and provide our principal visual background for understanding deep-sea photographs of the Mid-Oceanic Ridge.

CHILLED PILLOWS

Along the crest of the rugged mountain range which bisects the Atlantic, Arctic, Indian, and South Pacific Oceans freshly chilled pillowed surfaces of submarine lava flows have been repeatedly photographed (13.1-

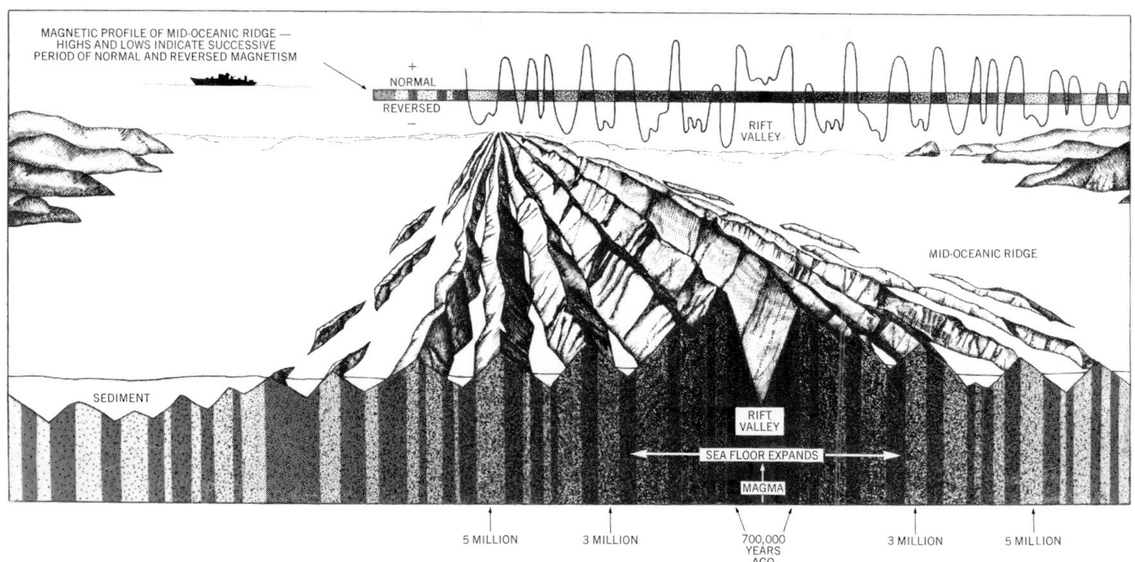

13.27 Reversals in the earth's magnetic field are preserved in the cooling lavas issuing from the expanding Rift Valley.

13.3). These rocks recently emplaced are still measurably warm along this narrow belt and here the escape of heat from the earth's interior is several times the ocean average (13.13).[12] It is therefore not surprising that the chilled lavas look fresh and are hardly coated with manganese or draped with sediment (13.15). The molten rock is quickly quenched by the sea, producing glassy surfaced billowy pillows (13.16) which are often thoroughly shattered (13.17). The insides of the pillows remain liquid after the surface has chilled and the fluid escaping from cracks in the skin forms new pillows which are linked to their parents by tails. The resulting deposit resembles a pile of liquid-filled balloons (13.18).

Pillows observed in ancient rocks range in size from a few centimeters to as much as three meters across. Those photographed on the sea floor tend to be one-half meter to two meters across, but the smaller sizes if present probably could not be recognized in photographs and the largest ones exceed the width of our "visual window." Although the dramatic pillows broken by radial fractures are easily recognized in photographs, the smaller, rounded, and less fractured types can be identified visually only in very fresh flows. With time, manganese crusts form over the devitrified glass rinds, and it becomes increasingly difficult to positively identify the pillows, although frequently the billowy shapes of manganese-coated bottom suggests the existence of an underlying flow (13.19-13.21).

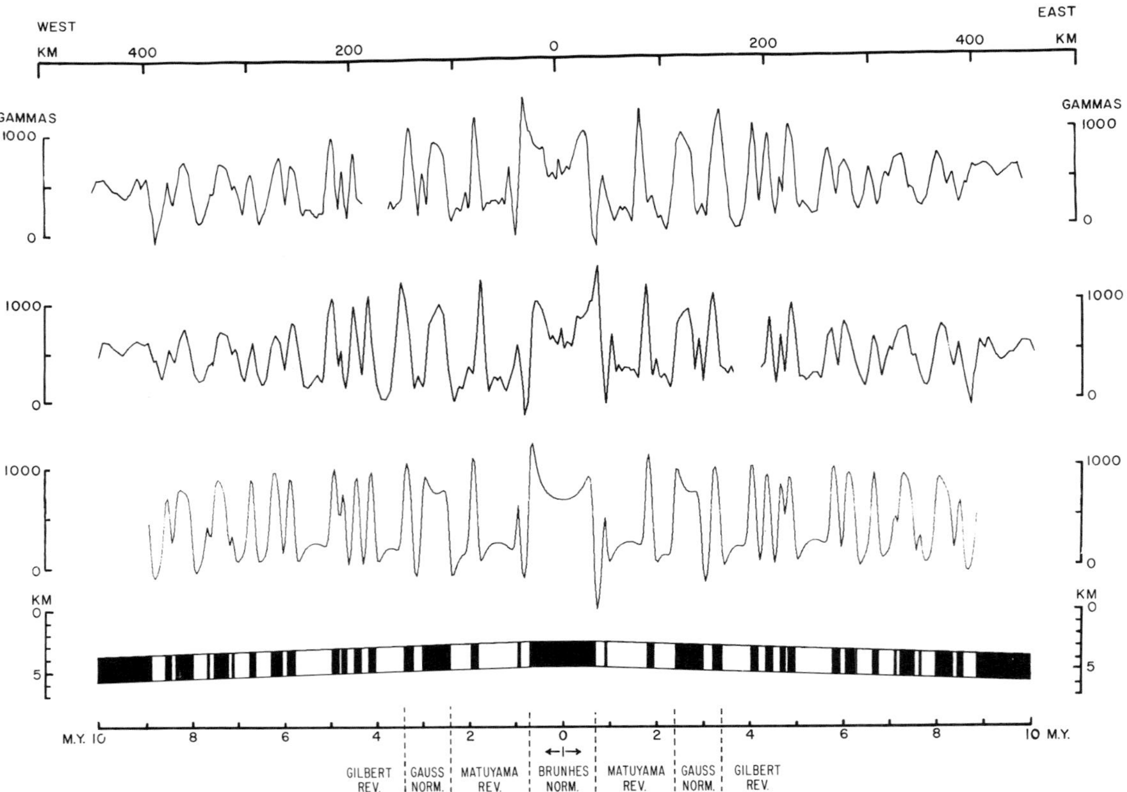

13.28 Rates of expansion of the oceans determined by correlation of magnetic reversals. The upper two profiles are from the Mid-Oceanic Ridge in the South Pacific. The middle profile is a reverse copy of the upper profile, and the similarity illustrates that sea-floor growth is symmetrical about the rift valley. Black areas on the bar represent normally magnetized material—white areas represent material with reverse magnetization.

Repeated extrusion of lava and subsequent fissuring of the widening rift have produced the characteristic topography, not only of the modern Mid-Oceanic Ridge but the vast expanse of ocean floor beyond. Steep scarps face the modern rift, whereas the lava plateaus dip more gently away from the active zone until rent by another inward-facing scarp. Volcanic eruptions build lines of cones along the fissures. These processes have resulted in a regular and symmetrical topography consisting of long parallel lines of volcanos and scarps which persist for dozens of miles (13.5, 13.9).

Pillows seen in the rift valley may represent eruptions which occurred days, months, or years ago, but those exposed on the flanking rift mountains must be thousands or millions of years old. One is at first puzzled by the general absence of a sediment blanket on the older rift mountains.

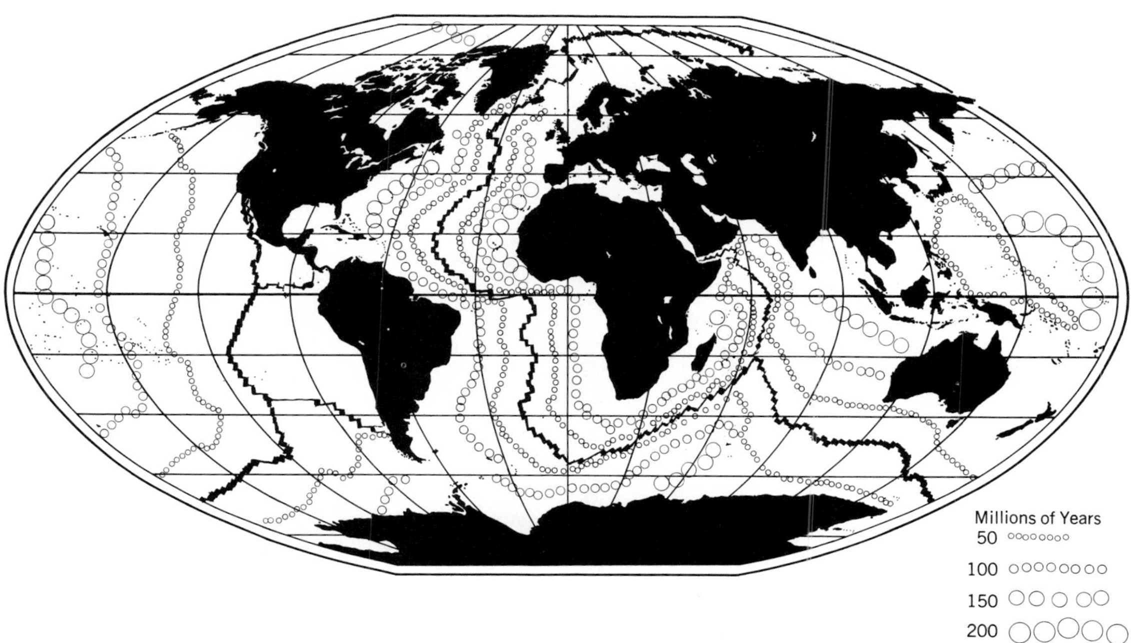

13.29 The age of the earth's crust beneath the sea increases from the cooling rift mountains toward the continents—spanning about 180 to 200 million years.

But one reason for this absence soon becomes visibly evident, for the currents which sweep the ridge crest leave dramatic indications of their presence. Patches of winnowed gravel, scour marks, and ripple marks which usually have the appearance of being starved are omnipresent (13.22). Often what appears to be the finer debris of volcanic eruptions is streamed across the ooze-covered sediment pockets. Current-loving sessile filter-feeders such as sponges, sea pens, tunicates, and corals are seen attached to the black rock (13.23).

To explain the absence of sediments from small hills near the crest of the Mid-Oceanic Ridge, it has been suggested that bottom-living animals continually throw sediment in suspension and that occasionally the normally quiet bottom waters move rapidly enough to transport this sediment to more tranquil depressions nearby. Since velocities required for erosion are much higher than those sufficient for transportation, this mechanism has the advantage in allowing the generally weak current to assume a greater role. It cannot be denied that this mechanism must operate, but the current scour and ripple marks frequently seen near the crest of the Ridge demonstrate so clearly that currents erode the sediments that the animal suspension mechanism might assume a significant role in the less dynamic domains of the ridge flanks.

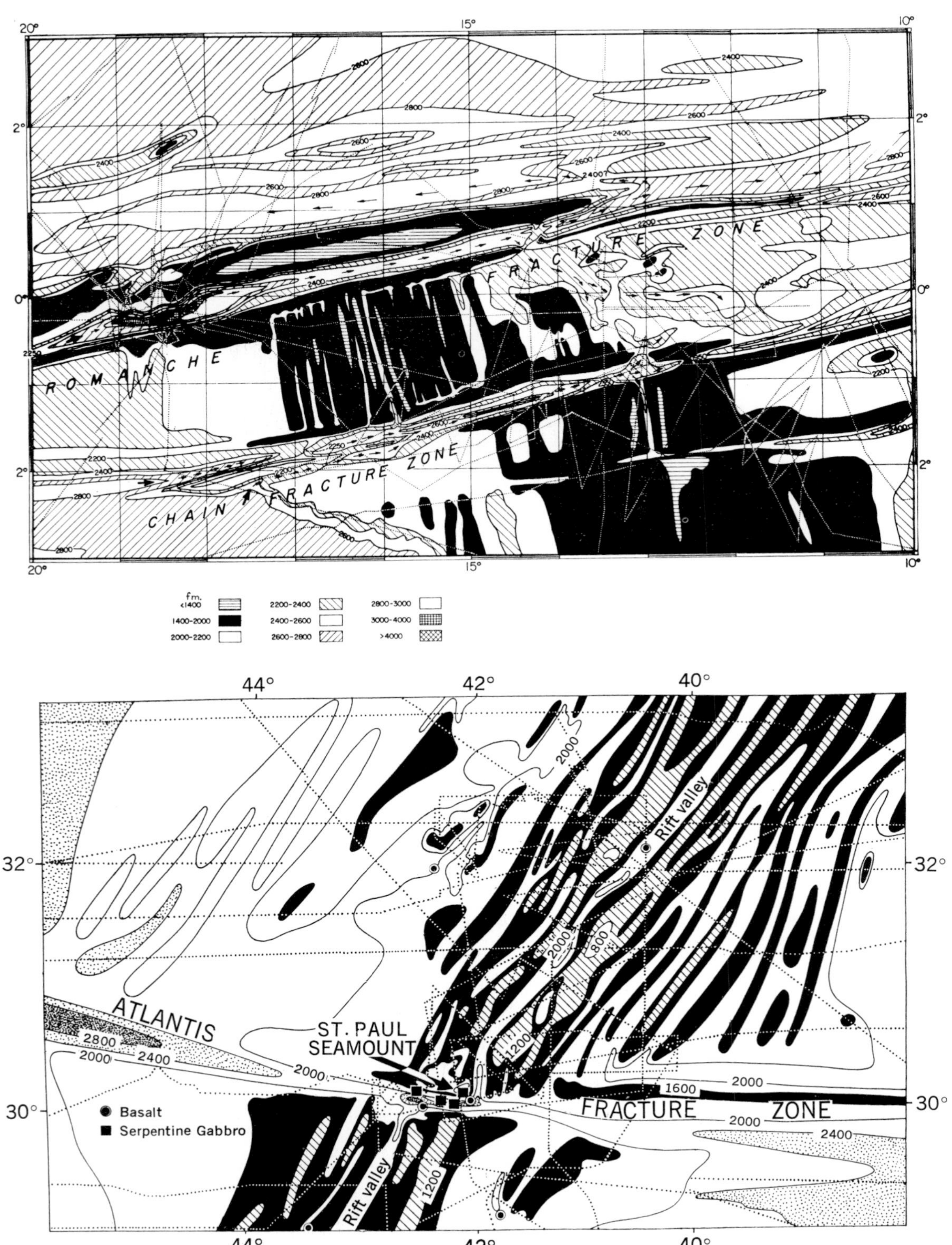

20°
15°
10°
2°
0°
2°
ROMANCHE
FRACTURE ZONE
CHAIN FRACTURE ZONE
fm.
<1400
1400-2000
2000-2200
2200-2400
2400-2600
2600-2800
2800-3000
3000-4000
>4000
44°
42°
40°
32°
30°
ATLANTIS
ST. PAUL
SEAMOUNT
FRACTURE
ZONE
Rift valley
Rift valley
Basalt
Serpentine Gabbro
2000
2400
2800
1200
1600

13.31 Fracture zones in the ancient basins. As the aging sea floor is buried under a growing blanket of sediment the steep-sided fracture zones are among the last rocky areas to be engulfed. Seismic reflection profile in the western Pacific east of the Shatsky Plateau.

Evidences of current become less and less frequent and less dramatic with increasing distance from the crest zone. In depths between 2500 and 3500 meters, photographs typically show somewhat smoothed and occasionally scoured, light-colored ooze, but dark-colored coarse debris and soft rounded ripples are also occasionally photographed here on the outer flanks of the rift mountains. Below 3500 meters current evidence becomes rarer and burrows, mounds, tracks, trails and other bioturbations dominate the generally tranquil seascape (13.24, 13.25).

The Mid-Oceanic Ridge lies successively beneath the ice-covered Arctic, the highly productive north polar front, the deserts of the north temperate latitudes, the equatorial productivity belt, the southern temperate deserts, and the rich pelagic gardens of the southern polar front (7.43). It passes close by the deltas of the great Siberian rivers in the Arctic and lies farthest from all sediment sources in the central South Pacific. The flanks of the ridge are swept by extremely vigorous currents in some areas, and in other areas lie beneath tranquil waters. The differing rates of deposition produce the varying thickness of the sediment blanket, and cause discernible differences in topography. The smoothed relief of the extreme northern and extreme southern portions of the Mid-Atlantic Ridge is explained by the blanketing effect of the thicker sediment layer

◁ 13.30 Great built-in offsets displace the crest of the Mid-Oceanic Ridge. The deep troughs, which follow these fracture zones serve as conduits for the flow of deep and bottom water.

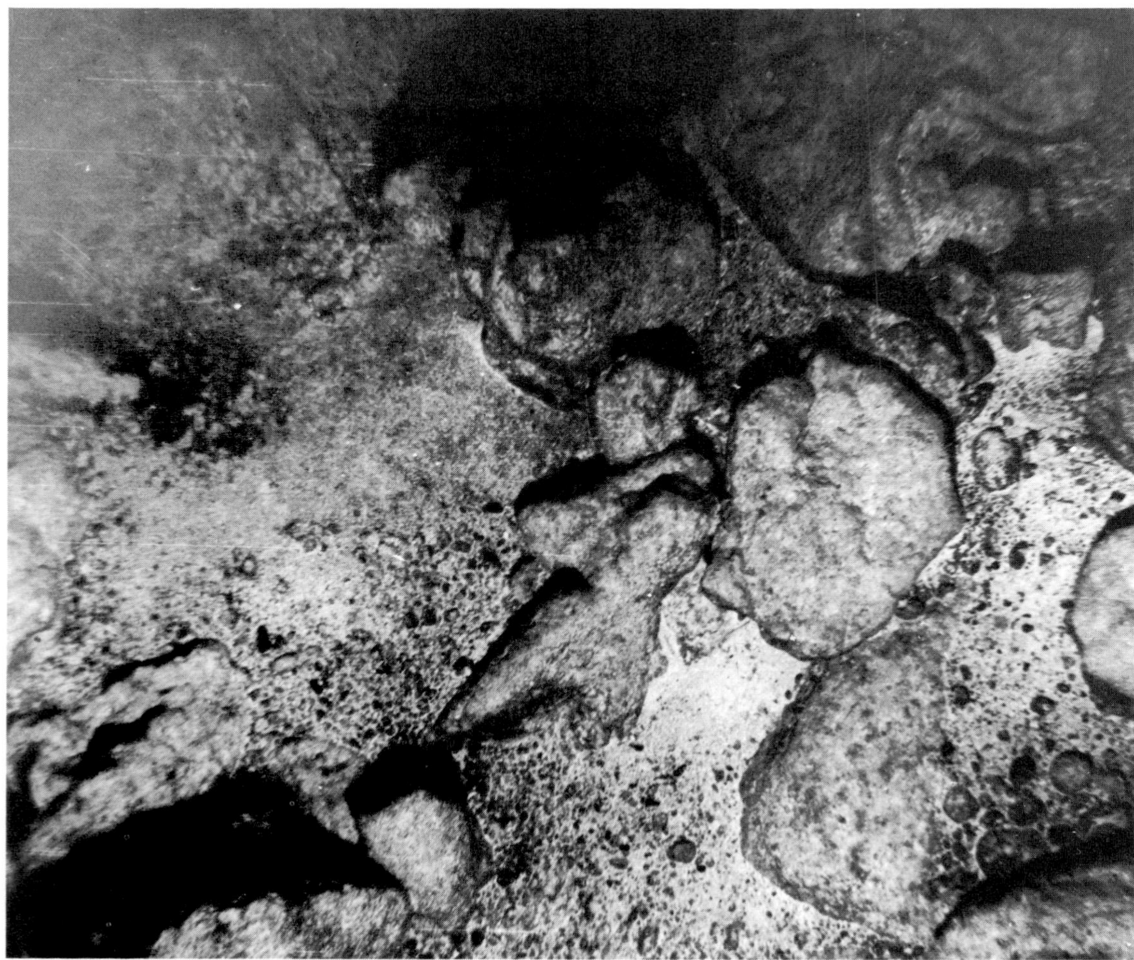

10°45′N 40°30′W

13.32 Current-swept fractured rocks cover the walls of the Vema Fracture Zone. This narrow gap in the Mid-Atlantic Ridge allows a significant flow of Antarctic Bottom Water to enter the eastern basin of the Atlantic. 5116 m. Vema Fracture Zone, Equatorial Atlantic.

which results from the greater rate of deposition beneath the more productive polar waters. The effect of the varying rates of deposition are often visibly discernible. The increased deposition rate supports a larger fauna and produces in some cases a more granular sediment often of a distinctive color.

If the mid-oceanic rift is indeed the womb of the ocean floor, then one should expect accumulated sediments to thicken gradually from the recently formed flanks of the rocky rift mountains toward the continents and this is approximately what has been found to be the case[13] (13.26). Sediment is of a negligible thickness within a narrow belt approximately

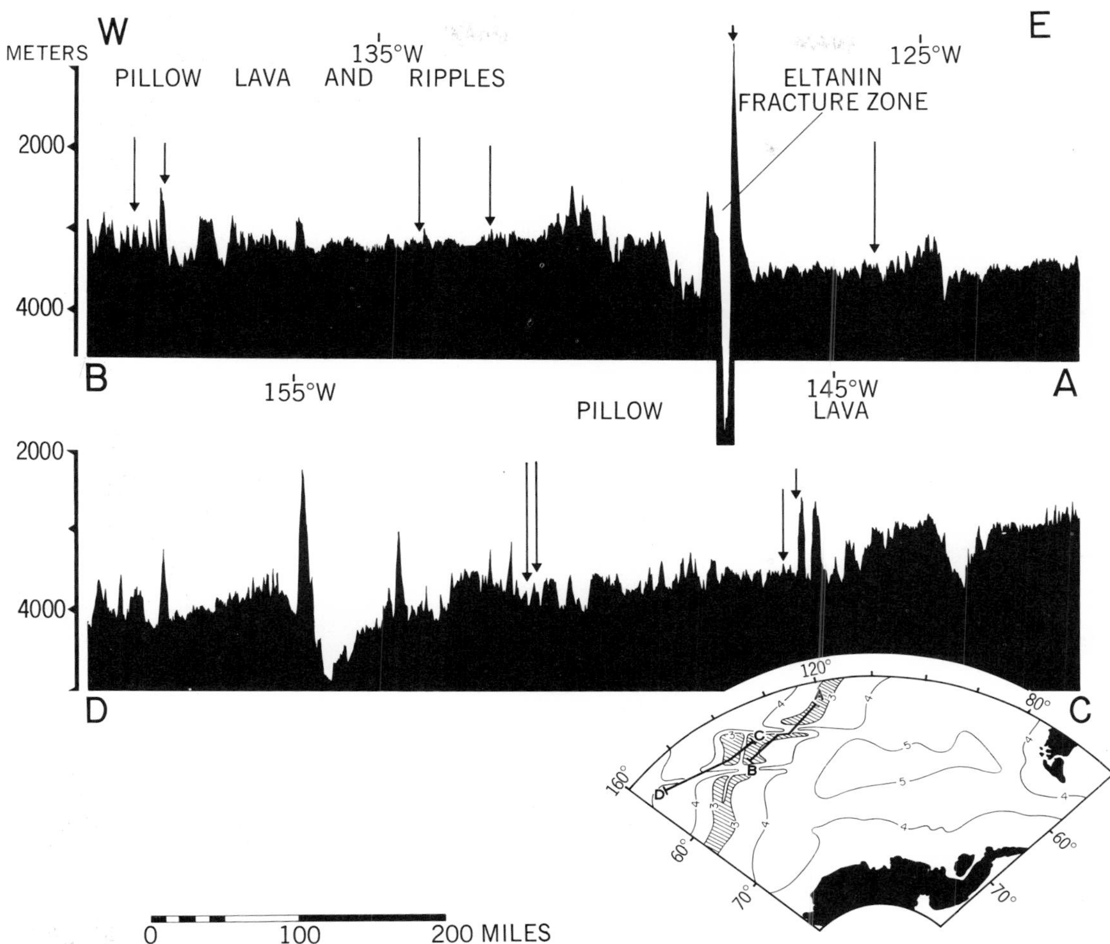

13.33 A great fracture cuts across the South Pacific from New Zealand to the Drake Passage. Profile of Eltanin Fracture Zone at a vertical exaggeration of 100:1.

200 kilometers wide which corresponds to the rugged crest of the ridge.[14] Here depths are less than about 3500 meters. The available photographs taken near the crest of the Mid-Oceanic Ridge indicate that the principal zone in which current effects are visible corresponds to the zone of thin sediments as determined by seismic reflection profiles and as inferred from the quantitative analysis of bottom slopes. Thus, the sediment-free zone seems more satisfactorily accounted for by a steady state uniformitarian current regimen than by an erratic pattern of crustal catastrophes.

As the flanks of the ridge drop into progressively deeper water the rapidly accumulating organic oozes of the crest are replaced by slowly accumulating abyssal clays with a corresponding visible contrast. The

60°01'S 104°52'W

58°54'S 95°08'W

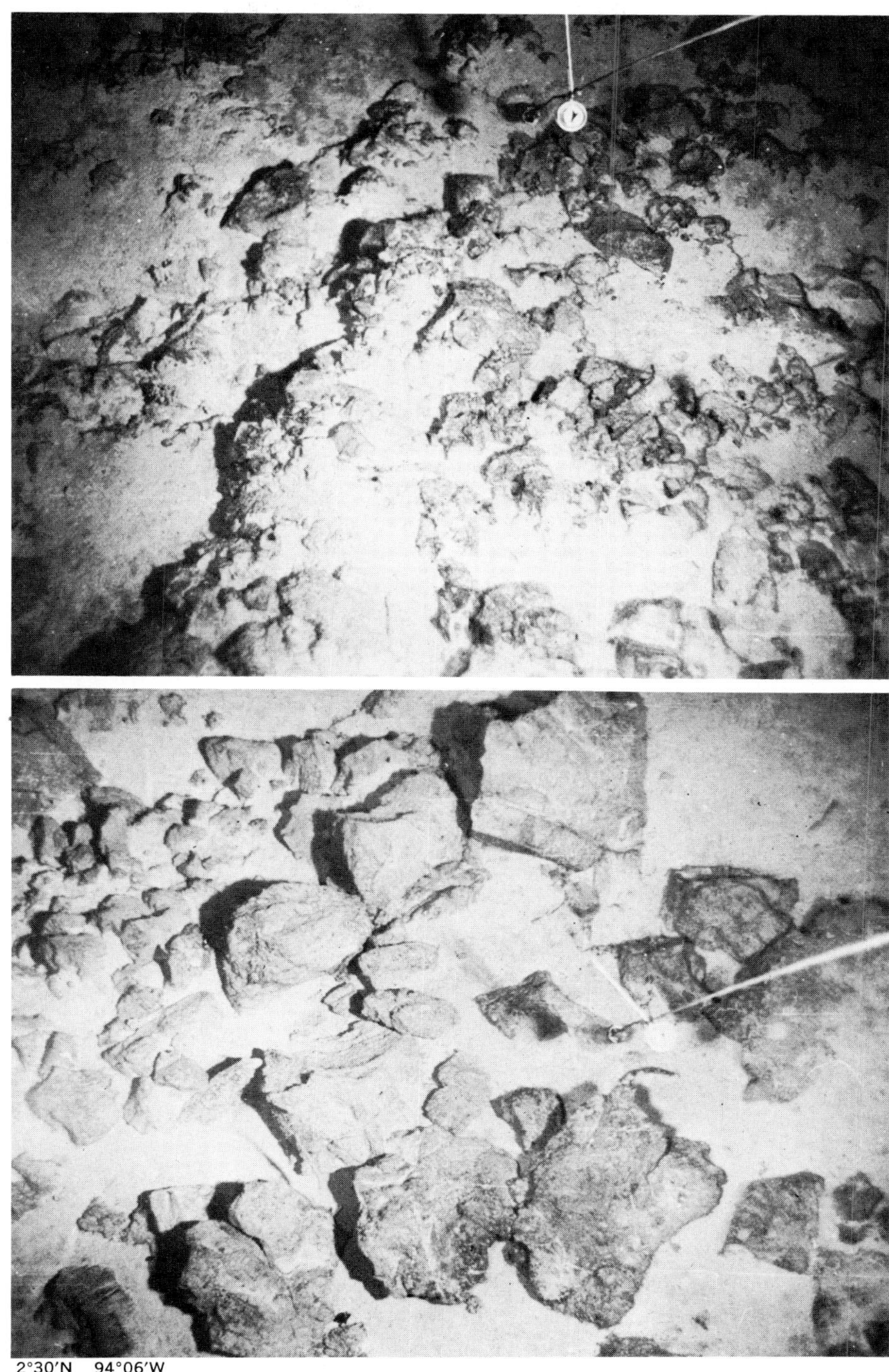

13.35 Ooze collects between angular blocks of broken basalt in the Galapagos Rift Zone. U, L, 2700 m.

◁ 13.34 Fractured angular blocks and manganese rounded cobbles, broken by tectonic movements of the past, are kept clean by present-day currents. U, L, 4802 m, 3990 m, Eltanin Fracture Zone in the Bellingshausen Basin.

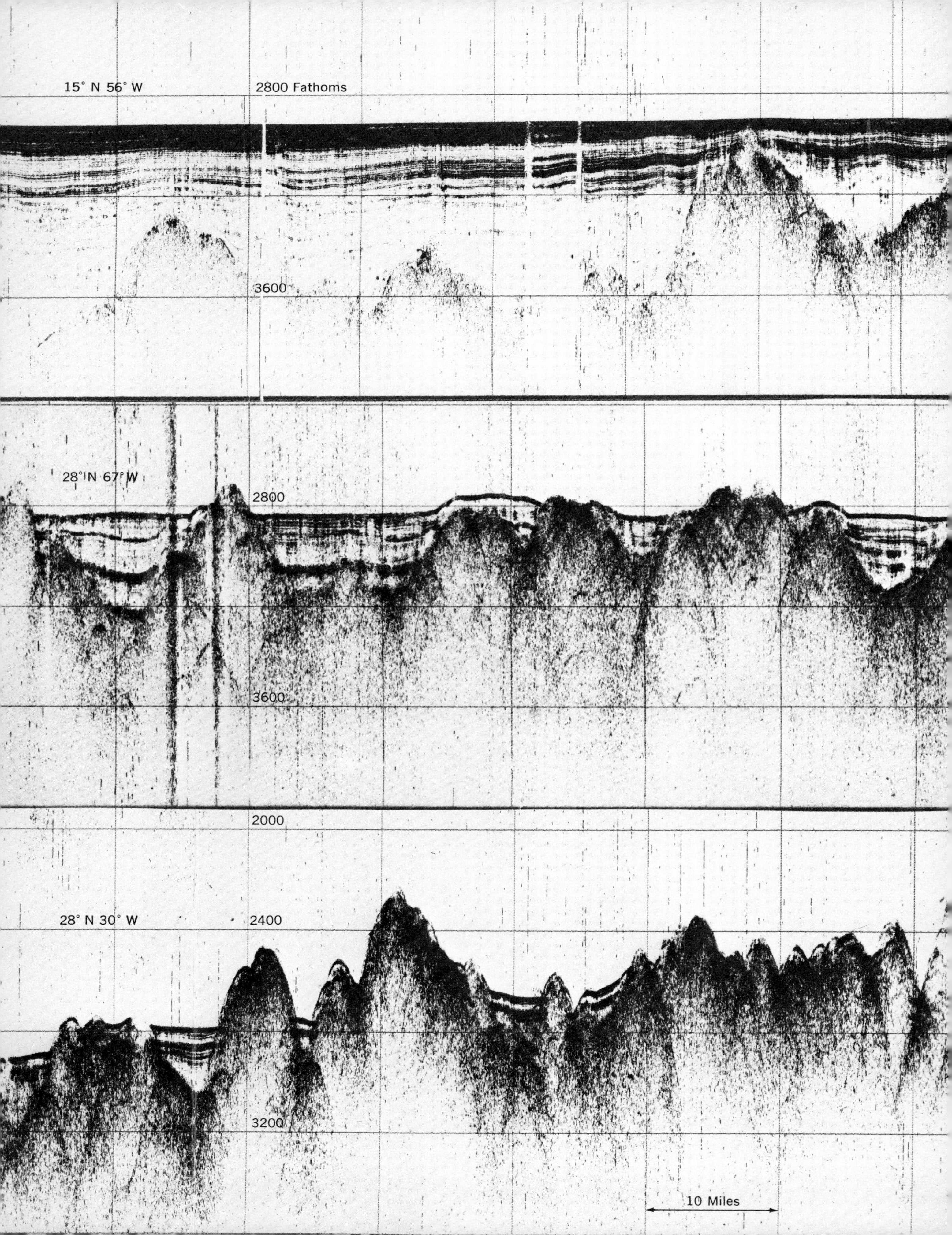
15° N 56° W
2800 Fathoms
3600
28° N 67° W
2800
3600
2000
28° N 30° W
2400
3200
10 Miles

seascape probably does not reflect variations in the thickness of the sediment blanket but the effects of variations in the rate of deposition may be discernible. One sees little difference between the seascape recorded in photographs taken hundreds of miles apart on the flanks of the ridge, and up to now little correlation with major structural provinces has been found. Thus there is no visible evidence for the existence of contemporary processes of sedimentation which might offer an alternate explanation of the observed gradual thickening in the sediment blanket from the upper flanks of the ridge toward the abyssal basins. But the thickening from the ridge crest to the basin floor is in fact so slight that several observers have denied that it exists and they have used the apparent uniformity as an argument against axial evolution of the oceanic crust and continental drift. We need only consider the fact that in ten million years near the crest of the Mid-Oceanic Ridge the crust receives as much sediment as it does in one hundred million years deep on the ridge flank. Since the crust appears to be continuously moving into deeper water the higher rates of ooze accumulation on the new crust are compensated by the lower rates of clay accumulation on the subsiding deeper flanks, resulting in a layer which increases in thickness very gradually toward the continental margins.

It has been shown that the Mid-Oceanic Ridge lacks a prominent underlying sedimentary layer which is found throughout the adjacent basins.[15] By extrapolating modern rates of deposition it was concluded that the top of this layer was formed approximately seventy-five million years ago.[16] Subsequently, by studying fossils obtained by coring current-denuded outcrops of this layer, the age of its top was established at several places as Maestrichian.[17] This stage of the upper Cretaceous began seventy-two million years ago and ended sixty-three million years ago. This observation not only supports ocean floor expansion but with the general agreement of extrapolated and interpolated rates of sedimentation indicates that the same processes that are observed creating the modern seascape must have continued without interruption and without significant change in rate since the oceanic crust was formed.[16]

Where the Mid-Oceanic Ridge is 1500 kilometers wide the average rate of expansion of the ridge (assuming the above seventy-million-year date) would have been two centimeters per year; and where the ridge reaches 3000 kilometers in width the rate of growth would have been four centimeters per year. If we extrapolate these rates backward in time we arrive at a zero width for the Atlantic and Indian Oceans at about two hundred million years ago. According to this reasoning these oceans were formed during the Triassic period.

◁ 13.36 The rugged relief created in the Mid-Oceanic Rift valley is gradually smothered by slowly accumulating deep-sea sediments. Seismic reflection profiles, North Atlantic.

Only a few years ago, small-scale geographical anomalies in the magnitude of the earth's magnetic force were thought to be entirely the result of variations in the magnetic susceptibility and the depth of burial of the rocks of the earth's crust. When a magnetometer was first towed across the ocean it was discovered that the magnetic anomalies showed little correlation to topography except in the case of the largest peaks. Geomagnetists thus concluded that large geographical variations in composition must occur in the oceanic crust. Subsequently, an enormous positive anomaly, amounting to approximately one per cent of the total field, was discovered on each mid- and high-latitude crossing of the mid-oceanic rift valley.[18] Debate raged between the hypothesis that the rift valley positive anomaly resulted from rocks of unique magnetic properties, a view obviously favored by anti-drifters, and the then completely unorthodox view that the alternate strips of magnetic positive and negative anomalies was largely the result of fossil magnetism and that these strips recorded reversals in the polarity of the earth's magnetic field as the Mid-Oceanic Ridge grew wider through geologic time[19] (13.27). Part of the difficulty of this idea's gaining acceptance stemmed from a general refusal to accept continental drift in any form and in part to a similar refusal to believe that the earth's magnetic poles could reverse. Instead, the rocks were thought to reverse their magnetic polarity internally for some reason. But in the 1960's true reversals became better and better documented and it was no longer possible to dismiss all reversals as self-reversals, although it was found that in a very few cases this had occurred. The magnetic reversals over the past few million years are recorded in geomagnetic traverses, sediment cores, and volcanic flows on the continents. The latter have been radio-chemically dated, providing a time scale for the reversals that occurred during the past five million years and a base for the extrapolation of earlier dates.

The recent application of the dated magnetic reversal sequence to the interpretation of geomagnetic traverses of the Mid-Oceanic Ridge has led to a further striking confirmation of ocean-floor expansion and has clearly shown that the widening of the ocean has continued steadily and essentially uninterruptedly even when considering periods of time as short as 30,000 years[20] (13.28). The rates of widening observed for the past five million years are in agreement with those cruder estimates obtained by extrapolating rates of deposition and are also in agreement with a variety of other evidence for continental drift observed on the continents. The pattern of growth implied by the extrapolated magnetic pattern (13.29) is subject to confirmation by dredging and drilling. But the rocks of the ridge flanks have hardly ever been sampled and here lies one of the most crucial tests of ocean-floor evolution.

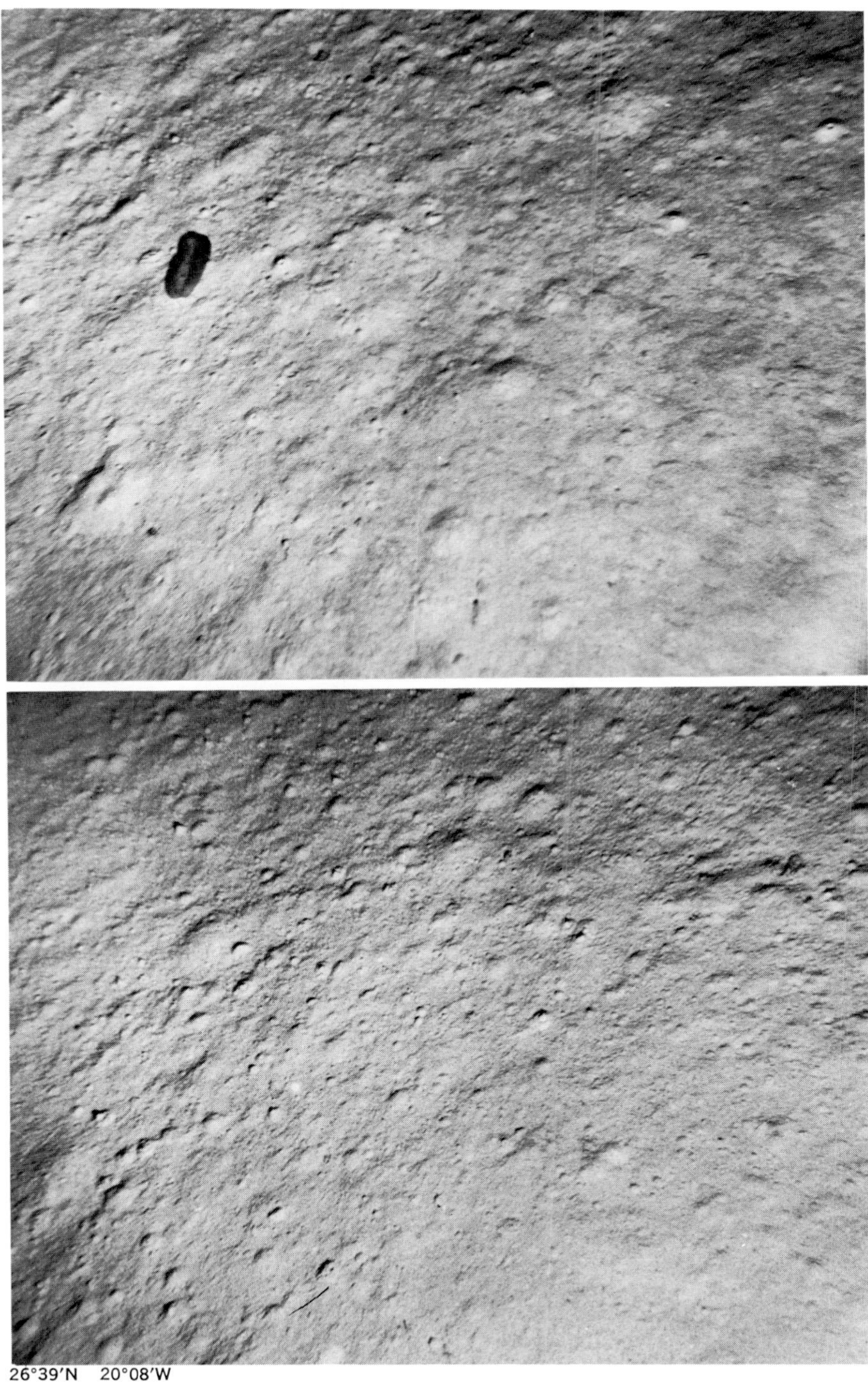

26°39′N 20°08′W
25°15′N 25°45′W
13.37 The tranquil continental rise off the Sahara is burrowed and tracked by benthic life. U, black object in upper left is a holothurian, 4338 m, continental rise west of the Canary Islands. L, 5292 m, lower continental rise west of the Canary Islands.

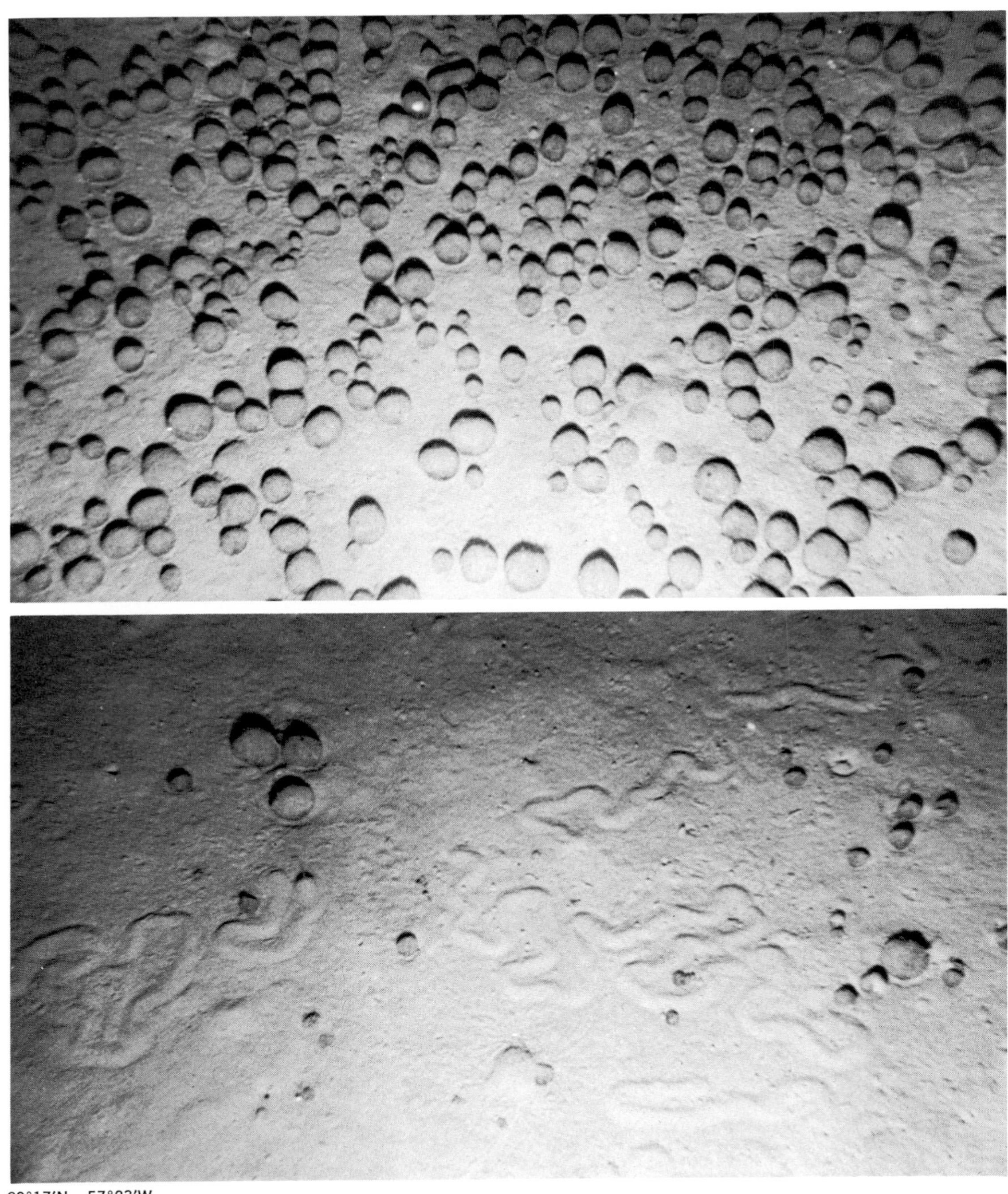

29°17′N 57°23′W
29°17′N 57°23′W

13.38 Manganese nodules lie on the current-smoothed abyssal clay which drapes the abyssal hills of the Western Atlantic. U, L, the nodules are surrounded by moats scoured by the Antarctic bottom current, 5830 m, abyssal hills southeast of the Bermuda Rise.

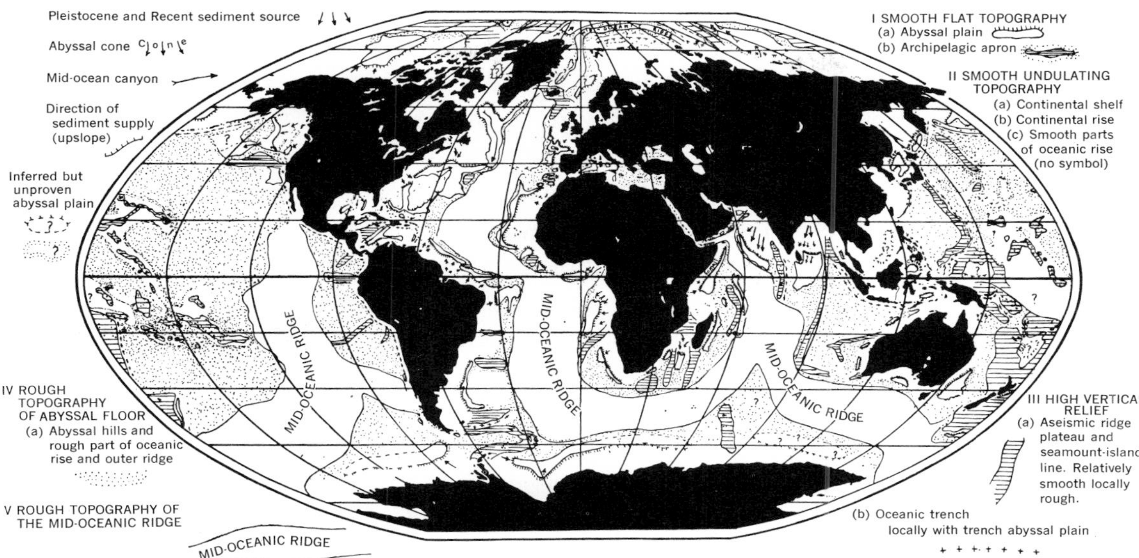

13.39 Distribution of smooth and rough topography of the world ocean.

So far the rocks dredged further from the ridge crest are too weathered for radio-chemical analysis. However, the oldest fossils found in sediment cores show a general increase in age with distance from the crest and the ages inferred roughly agree with the extrapolated magnetic dates.[21] More recently, drilling through the entire sediment blanket to the rocks beneath has given further support to axial accretion, and at present we can consider the axial expansion of the oceans as proved by the assembled facts including those provided by visual observations of the seascape.

TELL-TALE FRACTURES

The crust of the earth beneath the sea is broken into long narrow strips by persistent fractures (13.30) which extend for thousands of kilometers across the Mid-Oceanic Ridge and adjacent basins. In the progress of geologic time these enormous fault zones have steadily lengthened at the crest of the Mid-Oceanic Ridge as the oceans grew wider. The fracture pattern and the complimentary rift pattern intersect at nearly right angles. The ten- to twenty-kilometer spacing of the ridge-rift texture and the fourty- to eighty-kilometer spacing of the fractures establish the fundamental structural fabric of over half of the earth's crust (13.5). Studies of submarine physiography over the past decade gradually revealed this world pattern of fracture zones. The major ones, which are spaced every few hundred miles, were the first to be traced. Those along which horizontal movements have produced large displacements of the rift valley were the easiest to find, and conversely those which caused a negligible displacement were the hardest to detect. It now appears that there are one or more facture zones for each 100 kilometers along the entire length of the Mid-Oceanic Ridge. The earthquake belt which coincides with the axial rift valley clearly indicates the presence of fractures by abrupt displacement of the belt even in areas where no soundings have been made.[22] The epicenter map upon which the pattern of the Mid-Oceanic Ridge was first based included all larger earthquakes recorded since the beginning of instrumental seismology. Despite the fifty-year length of the record, accuracy was poor and sensitivity low, and thus the scatter of plotted epicenters was often more than 100 miles wide. Consequently, only a few of the largest fracture zones could be detected. The use of seismology as a political and military tool brought a technological revolution in the late 1950's, which resulted in earthquake maps that presented the location of the quakes of the past decade with a high degree of accuracy. These improvements allowed the detection of many more fracture zones through the geographical patterns of seismic activity. At the same time the increase in the number of sounding profiles and their careful analysis has also led to the discovery of more and more fracture zones extending far out from the central zone of seismicity.

Visually, the fracture zones are extremely varied, but except when completely buried beneath the continental rise or abyssal plains they present a rocky aspect. Photographs taken in fracture zones cutting the Mid-Oceanic Ridge reveal pebble- or sand-strewn bottoms and precipitous bare rock walls (13.32). Serpentine, gabbro, and metamorphosed basic and ultra basic rocks, possibly from exposures of the earth's mantle, have been dredged from the long scarps.

The presence of precipitous bare rock slopes in fracture zones is in some cases certainly due to continuing crustal deformation and to the recent origin of the topography. However, since fracture zones often determine the maximum sill depth of the Mid-Oeanic Ridge, they frequently form conduits for the exchange of deep and bottom waters from one basin to another. Flow accelerated through the restricted passages of fracture zones thus tends to sweep the underlying rocks clean of unconsolidated sediment.

Since the two halves of the ocean basin are moving apart under continental drift there must be horizontal slippage along a fracture zone where it separates the displaced axes of the ridge. The pattern of earthquake activity in these offsets clearly indicates that such is the case.[23] Here the visual scene is most rugged and the escarpments highest, and boldest,

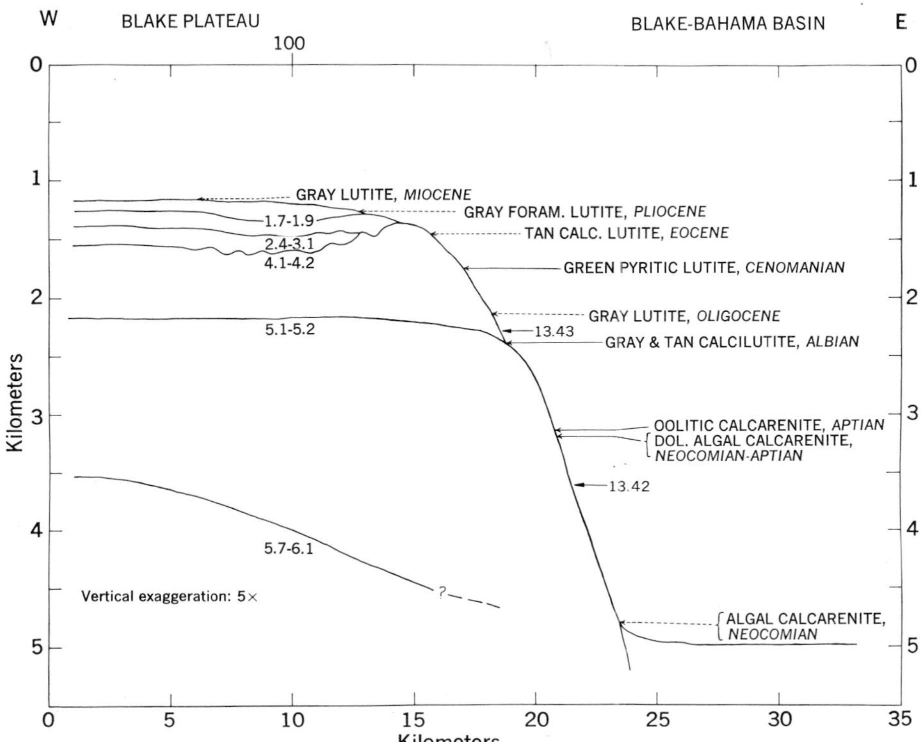

13.40 The shallow-water algal rocks that lie exposed at the foot of the Blake Escarpment suggest that the sea floor has subsided nearly 5000 meters during the past 150 million years.

and here slickensides, fault gouge, and sheared rocks are most frequently seen (13.33-13.35). Further out on the flanks, past the displaced axis, the shearing may cease or drastically diminish. Here the fracture may become filled with sediments which exhibit little or no evidence of deformation; or there may be little sediment ponding, possibly because of continuing slippage and consequent deformation.[24]

Although visually fracture zones are similar in the general presence of current evidence at major sills and on steep slopes, as they become buried beneath the growing blanket of sediment farther and farther from the axis of the Mid-Oceanic Ridge, their visual characteristics become almost completely indistinguishable from those of the adjacent basin.

Lines of large extinct and active volcanos also mark major lineaments and these generally rocky eminences remain as topographic and scenic features long after the smaller fault scarps have been buried beneath the mud. The lava which flows out of a vent in older oceanic crust is emitted from a magma source in the underlying mantle of the earth. As the oceanic crust drifts by an active magma chamber, a succession of volcanos is built

13.41 Shallow-water Cretaceous algal reef material dredged from abyssal depths on the Blake Escarpment. U, gray and tan calcareous mudstone of Aptian-Albian age (120 million years old), 2400 m. M, dolomitic algal sandstone of Neocomian-Aptian age (130 million years old), 3200 m. L, algal sandstone of Neocomian-Aptian age, 4800 m.

on the overlying moving crust. Such volcano lines do not mark fundamental fractures in the earth's crust but rather the islands, atolls, and guyots record the direction which the crust has drifted with respect to the mantle.[25] The major central vents which built the huge oceanic islands and seamounts became active at long and variable intervals after the crust which underlies them was formed. Most of their growth must necessarily

13.42 Outcrops of Lower Cretaceous shallow-water algal sandstone. Dredged rocks from near this photograph station were Neocomian-Aptian in age (130 million years old), 3539 m, Blake Escarpment, western Atlantic.

have been accomplished far from the crest of the Mid-Oceanic Ridge in depths approximating the average depth of the ocean basins.[26] Such bold lineaments record crustal motions which occurred long after the underlying crust and its primeval fracture zones were formed. It is thus entirely expectable that the volcanic lines cross the trends of the older fracture zones at various angles.

The ages of oceanic islands tend to decrease toward mid-ocean and it should be noted that their number similarly tends to decrease with decreasing age. If volcanism is rather randomly distributed in space and

28°59′N 76°42′W

13.43 Tabular outcrop of Lower Cretaceous mudstone. Rocks dredged near this photograph location were Aptian-Albian in age (120 million years old), 2340 m, Blake Escarpment, western Atlantic.

time except to the extent that it is controlled by location of lines of weakness, this is the distribution one would expect; the oldest crust would be decorated by more large volcanos simply because it had been there longer to receive them.[27]

The fracture zones are fundamental tools in continental drift reconstruction, for the fractures indicate the precise course followed by the continents. When combined with evidence of speed derived from magnetic and paleontologic methods, the fracture zones define the tracks (13.11) of the drifting continents[28] and reveal the precise pattern of growth from which the scenic evolution of the ocean floor can be inferred.

In a visual sense the lower flanks of the Mid-Oceanic Ridge usually

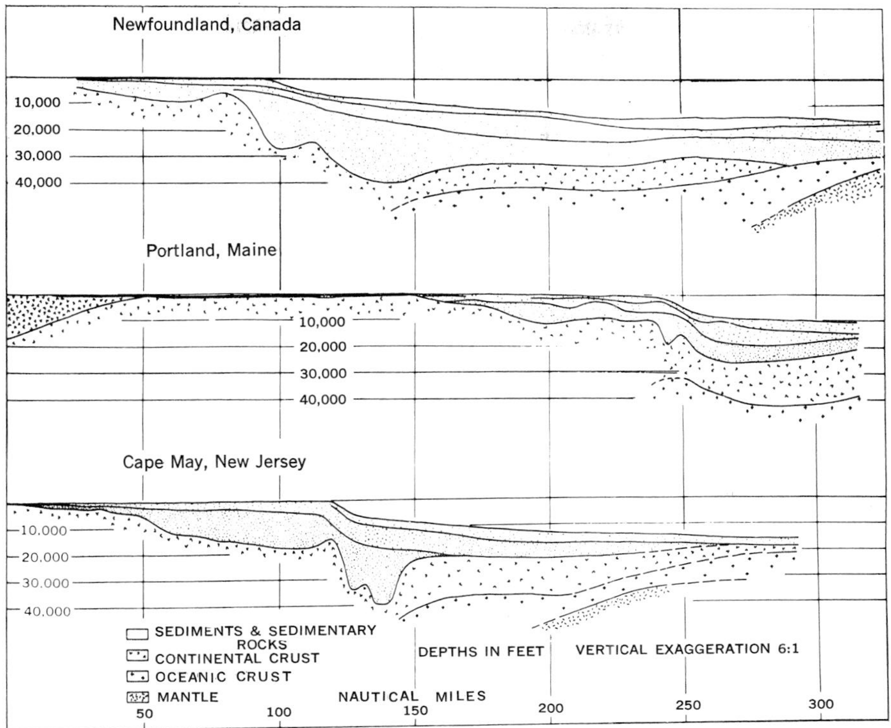

13.44 Massive accumulation of sediments form the continental margin off northeastern North America. Sediment thicknesses decrease seaward toward the abyssal plains.

cannot be distinguished from the adjacent abyssal hills or oceanic rises. Due to the vigorous circulation of cold bottom waters through the deeper parts of the ocean basins, current effects are in some areas more common on the abyssal floor than on the flanks of the Mid-Oceanic Ridge. As we have previously pointed out, the flat, nearly featureless abyssal plains which usually flank the ridge are often covered by murky water (8.30) and may have a characteristic seascape (8.47). The oceanic rises of the Atlantic are commonly current-marked, bearing evidence of the dynamic processes which have heaped up the thick blankets of sediments covering these features (9.75-9.80).

Let us continue our visual excursion across the ocean basins (13.37, 13.38) and return to the continental margin where the ribs exposed to view present a seascape entirely different from the rifted volcanic terrain of the mid-oceanic realm.

We have in a previous chapter shown that on the continental margin current evidence is common and often extremely dramatic and that the combined work of downslope turbidity currents, along-slope contour cur-

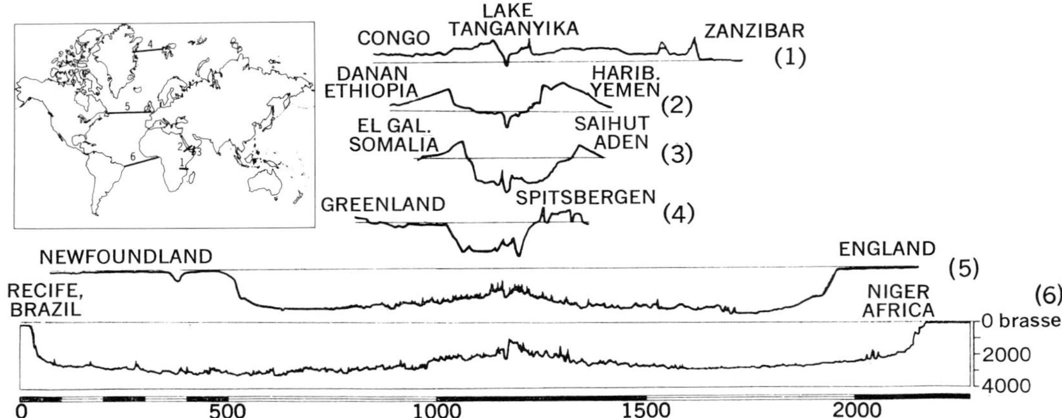

13.45 An evolutionary sequence is recorded in this series of profiles across the World Rift System. There is a marked similarity of each profile, despite the large difference in profile lengths. This sequence could represent a genetic series in which the rift valleys of Africa represent an early stage in the development of an ocean, and the Atlantic shown in profiles 5 and 6 represents later stages.

rents, and the settling—particle by particle—of sediments derived from adjacent sources produces the characteristic smoothed relief which borders the continents (13.39). Currents flowing along the precipitous declivities which form the broken edges of the continental blocks have often swept these bulwarks bare, and here the eroded, nearly horizontal sedimentary strata exposed to view record a long and fascinating story which reaches farther back in geologic time than the history book of abyssal sediments which lie beyond and below this lofty perch.

The precipitous Blake Escarpment which falls off at gradients of 1 : 3 from the eastward lip of the Blake Plateau is supported by underlying horizontal beds (13.40). The high velocity attained by seismic waves traveling through these strata had indicated that the rocks are well consolidated. Cores raised from the upper parts of the escarpment had recovered unconsolidated Tertiary and Upper Cretaceous marls which had been deposited in moderately deep water far from shore. The much steeper lower escarpment below 3000 meters has recently yielded well-consolidated lowermost Cretaceous algal limestones which had been deposited in the sunlit waters of a shallow sea (13.41). Photographs show stratified as well as occasionally massive outcrops (13.42, 13.43). Over 5000 meters of subsidence in the past 130 million years is evidenced by these deposits, most of the subsidence occurring before the close of the Lower Cretaceous.[29]

The outcrops on the continental margin occur in the submarine canyons and on the straighter stretches of the continental slope, on the mar-

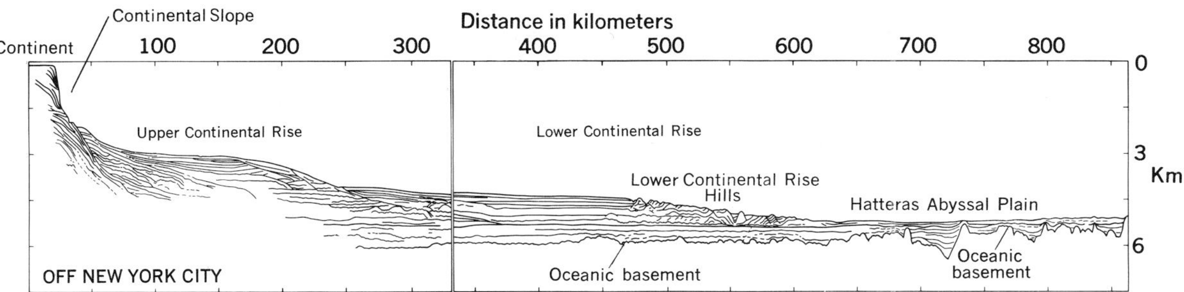

13.46 The sediments steadily thicken toward the continent. This tracing of reflections from a seismic reflection profile show stratification within the upper few kilometers of sediment.

ginal escarpments and in the marginal trenches. The mapping of these outcrops constitutes one of the most attractive and significant tasks awaiting the deep-diving geologists. Dredging, coring, and bottom photography can result in a rough yet fairly complete reconnaissance but detailed investigations must await the manned undersea survey vehicles of the future.

VISUAL HISTORY

> *Amid all the revolutions of the globe, the economy of nature has been uniform and her laws are the only things which have resisted the general movement. The ravines and the rocks, the seas and the continents have been changed in all their parts; but the laws which direct those changes and the rules to which they are subject, have remained invariably the same.*
>
> JOHN PLAYFAIR

Geologists love this guiding principle of uniformitarianism. No grander demonstration of this *modus operandi* could be imagined than that provided by the shaping of submarine topography. We not only refer to the demonstration that currents have in the past smoothed, and are still smoothing and shaping the great sediment drifts, but also the continuous creation of the foundations of the deep in the mid-oceanic rift valley where lava has continuously welled up year after year for millions of years, and may continue to do so forever.

Let us for the moment accept the evidence for the expansion of the oceans and try through modern analogy to interpret the meager but simple data in order to construct a visual history of an ocean floor. It is convenient to choose the relatively familiar Atlantic for this imaginary visual trip through geologic time.

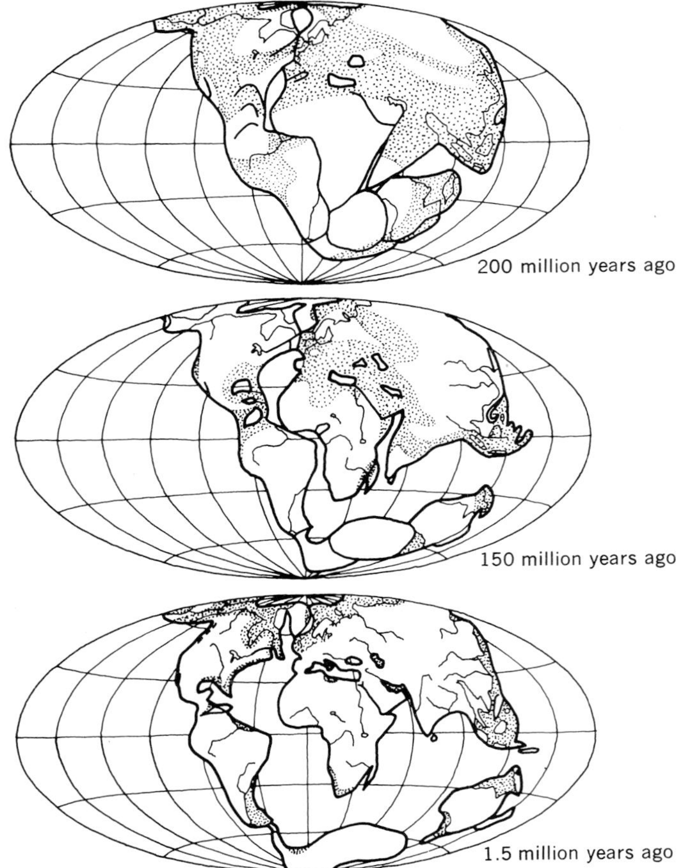

13.47 Wegener's classic diagram of the drifting continents. Shaded areas represent shallow seas.

In eastern North America the Triassic period was a time when lava poured out on generally barren and arid expanses of red sands, clays, and gravels. The sea was far away. The Triassic scenery along the present continental margin of North America may have been somewhat similar to that now seen in the modern Gregory Rift of Kenya (13.12). The emplacement of extensive basaltic dikes and sills into the red Triassic sands and shales of the eastern United States may well mark the beginning of rifting which led to the birth of the Atlantic. During the Jurassic period, the width of the Atlantic grew to over 1000 kilometers, and the sea invaded the evolving basin. Sediments poured in from the adjacent land; the original rocky seascape was smoothed and smothered and as a result may have resembled the muddy floor of the modern Gulf of Suez. As the ocean grew wider, the newly formed margins of the continents were upturned due, at least in part, to buoyant effects on the toes of the continental blocks. We would expect this slender, early Mesozoic Atlantic to have been relatively shallow and to have resembled the present Red Sea.

Circulation in this narrow, low-latitude sea must have been imperfect, with occasional stagnation of the bottom waters and consequent extermination of bottom life. The seascape must have alternately resembled the black trackless barrens of the Cariaco Trench and the well-tracked muddy continental slopes. Invasion and extermination must have followed one another until in late Cretaceous a permanent, viable circulation permitted the establishment of ventilation in the modern pattern. We may thus speculate that the sediments of this proto-Atlantic which now lie buried beneath the huge sediment wedges of the continental rise are rich in hydrocarbons (13.44). Thus potential oil reserves may be preserved in ancient anaerobic sediments which were deposited before the establishment of a permanent pole-to-pole ventilation of the abyss. The sediments may also contain peculiar mineral products emplaced by the volcanic emanations in this early rift ocean. The red, blue, purple, and green mineralized sediments and salty anaerobic brines found in the hot, deep holes of the modern Red Sea may represent a common phenomenon of the early Atlantic; and vast mineral deposits emplaced by juvenile waters seeping out of the earth's mantle may also lie beneath the huge embankments of sediment which border the continents.

Jurassic deposits are absent along the continental margin of eastern North America probably indicating that the broken edges of the continental blocks still stood relatively high, and may have resembled the eroded and up-turned Arabian and African margins of the modern Red Sea.

The oldest sediments recovered to date from the abyssal sea floor of the Atlantic are shallow-water sandstones and limestones of upper Jurassic age. The current-swept Lower Cretaceous (Neocomian) algal reef beds exposed at the base of the Blake Escarpment were obtained from a re-excavated reef at a point only a few kilometers distant and only 600 meters higher in elevation than the basement layer of the adjacent basin. In other words, the Atlantic Basin east of the Lower Cretaceous Blake Reef was no more than 600 meters deep and must have presented a shelly, rippled, and populous seascape not unlike that observed in the modern shelf seas (12.25).

The Atlantic must have been at least 2000 kilometers wide by mid-lower Cretaceous time and the adjacent continental margins must have begun to escape the influence of the 2000-kilometer-wide (more or less) central elevation which characterizes the Mid-Oceanic Ridge welt.

13.48 Pillows exposed on this sharp cleft are covered with millions of years' accumulation of manganese. Nearly five centimeters of manganese crust were measured on rocks dredged nearby, 5067 m, scarp D, south of Bermuda.

Throughout the early Cretaceous, the edge of the continent warped down toward a rapidly deepening Atlantic, in which the seascape was acquiring a modern aspect.

Comparative morphologic studies suggest that as the ocean widens it steadily deepens until it reaches a width of 2000 or 3000 kilometers (13.45), at which point its subsidence slows and its basin floor approaches a depth of 5000 or 6000 meters. Bermuda is an extinct volcano which was truncated in late Cretaceous or early Tertiary time, and has not subsided since. The depth of the Atlantic in the vicinity of Bermuda could not have been very much different in late Cretaceous time than the present 5000 to 6000 meters. Thus, Bermuda testifies that the subsidence of the Atlantic floor had been entirely accomplished in this region prior to the Tertiary and that the surface of the Mesozoic Bermuda Rise could probably not have been visually distinguished from that now observed (9.48).

The uplifted edges of the rifted continents were eroded, and the Cretaceous seas invaded the edges of the eroded and subsided continents. The margin continued to subside, and sediment continued to be deposited on the continental shelf which was created in middle Cretaceous time after the final filling of the former linear epicontinental basins which now lie buried beneath the continental shelf (13.44). The continental rise began to grow at the base of the continental slope by the accumulation of sediment injected into the sea through the water column and carried in along the bottom by turbidity currents. These sediments were then transported parallel to the continent by contour currents which in turn shaped the great sediment wedges which constitute the current-lineated continental rise and outer ridge accumulations (13.46). These sedimentary drifts began to build upward in the Tertiary, signaling the commencement of a vigorous, thermohaline, abyssal circulation in the modern pattern. Although these drifts probably steadily evolved, there was certainly repeated filling and recutting as the vigor of the thermohaline circulation of the Atlantic fiuctuated and as local geologic events altered the specific path of the flow.

The visual aspect of the Atlantic probably has not changed since the Cretaceous. The processes and the agents continued without interruption, and the only significant change has been a gradual increase in the total width of the basin (13.47), and of the width, slope, and height of the sedimentary drifts surrounding the continent. Although submarine canyons probably had existed throughout the history of the Atlantic, the late Cenozoic regression brought a great influx of continental sediments which were transported to abyssal depths through the submarine canyons and poured out onto the abyssal floor, causing the ultra-smooth abyssal plains to reach their maximum Tertiary extension. Thus, the rocky Atlantic continental margin created and uplifted during a Triassic convulsion was eroded, mantled, and subsided, and finally transgressed by late Cretaceous and Tertiary seas as the Atlantic grew to its present width and depth.

The evolution of the Indian and Pacific Oceans must have been similar to that which we have just hypothesized for the Atlantic. The resulting pattern of fracture zones and intersecting ancient axial growth

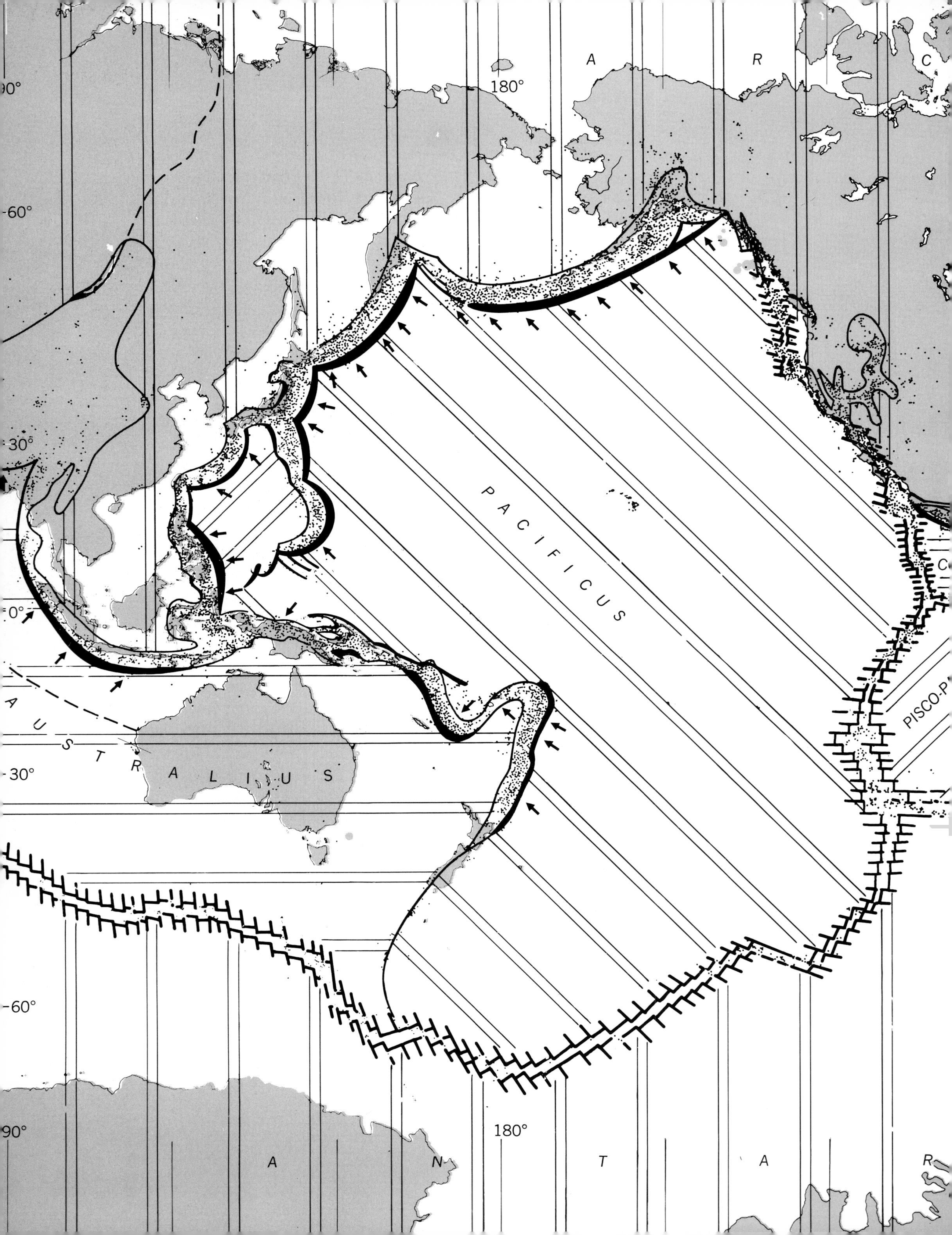

A
R
C
180°
90°
60°
30°
0°
P A C I F I C U S
PISCO-P
A U S T R A L I U S
30°
60°
90°
180°
A
N
T
A
R

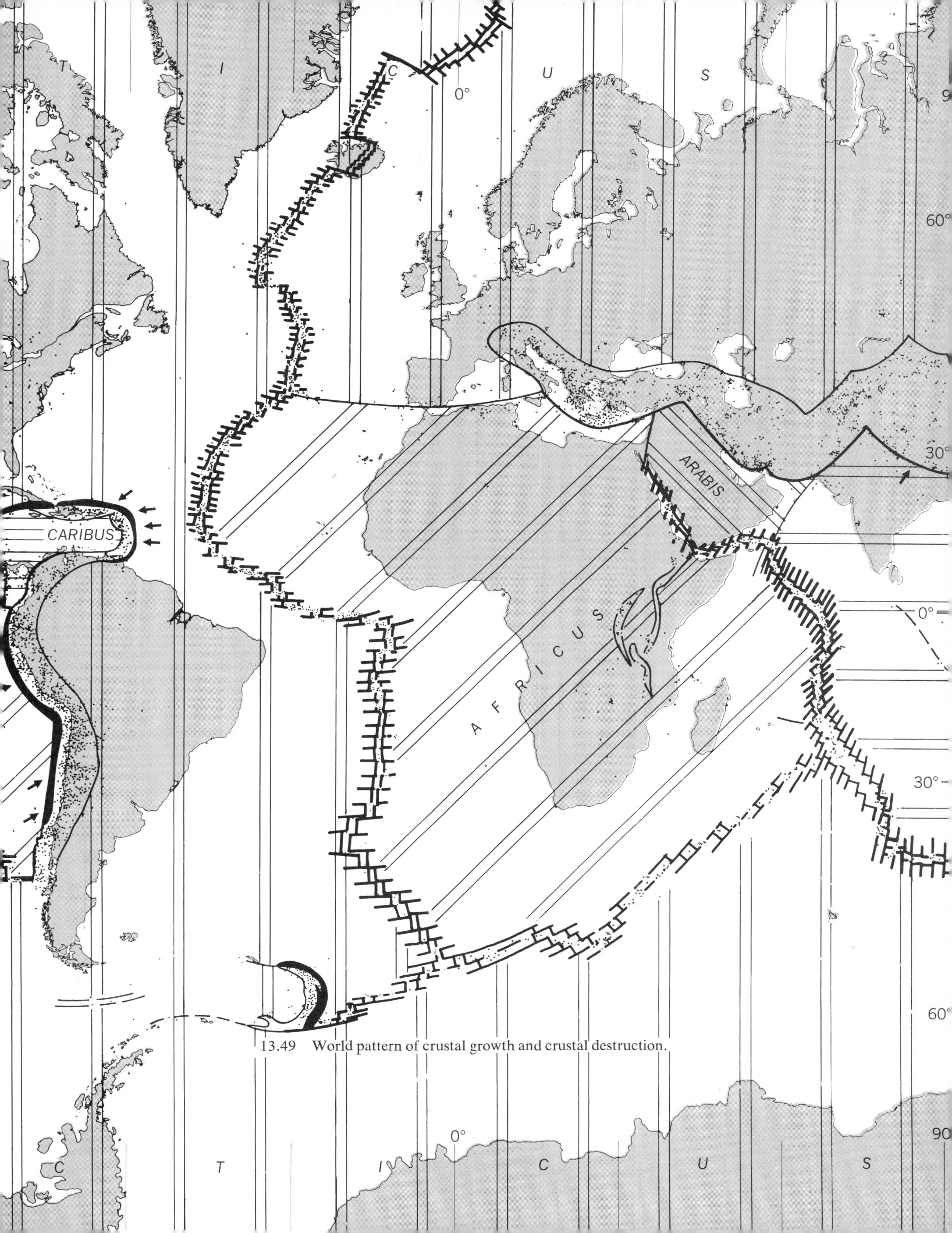

13.49 World pattern of crustal growth and crustal destruction.

lines is, however, more complicated in these other seas. The deformation of the borders of the Pacific may have destroyed the rocks which might otherwise tell us of the early visual history. The pattern of magnetic anomalies traced through the world ocean confirms the earlier, less certain, conclusion based on rates of sedimentation and sediment thickness that the present elevated Mid-Oceanic Ridge was built by axial accretion between drifting blocks over the past seventy-five to one hundred million years. It is clear from visual observation, as well as geological measurements, that the two types of margins contrast principally in sediment accumulation and deformation. The Peru-Chile Trench, if filled with sediment, would certainly closely resemble a normal Atlantic continental margin. The lack of sediment along the Pacific margin can partially be attributed to the small drainage areas of the Pacific rivers and off Peru and Chile, to the arid conditions. But this is clearly insufficient to explain the near absence of sediments in the trenches. Where are the sediments which should have been derived from the adjacent continents? Where are the continental rise accumulations? We either have to propose a super-efficient ocean current which sweeps them on or a mobile ocean floor which carries them away. In both cases, the question is, whither? The efficient ocean current would somewhere have to deposit its load, and we can see no obvious drifts which represent the sediments excavated from the trenches. If the ocean floor is carrying the sediments away, it could either be taking them into the earth beneath the trench or out to sea. In the latter case, the sediments should thin from the ocean basins toward the trench floor, and there should be some evidence of a decreasing age of the underlying crust toward the trench axis. This motion would conflict with our initial generalization that the folded mountains and the island arcs form one continuous belt of crustal compression. But if we assume that the missing sediments have been swallowed into the earth's crust beneath the landward walls of the trenches, we can see a global simplicity in the grand belt of crustal unrest.

We should search the many bare rock scarps of the deep-sea floor (13.48); for the discovery in the abyss of the lithified remains of a Paleozoic or lower Mesozoic abyssal, bathal, or neritic seascape or landscape would allow someone to build a wonderful new hypothesis. As Mark Twain once observed, "There is something fascinating about science. One gets such a wholesale return of conjecture out of such a trifling investment of facts."

The evolution of the ocean floor as pictured here calls for the creation of one-third of the ocean floor in the past 75 million years and, in fact, the creation of two-thirds of the earth's surface in the past 150 to 200 million years. This brings us back to the topics we considered in Chapter 11, for the axial growth of the ocean crust provides a quantitative prediction of the amount of crustal shortening which must have simultaneously occurred in the earth's compressional belts, if we can make the single assumption that the earth has neither contracted nor expanded. The length of the earth's rugged compressional front is approximately the same as the present-day Mid-Oceanic Ridge. Since the belt of new crust formed in the past ten million years at the crest of the Mid-Oceanic Ridge is on the average 200 kilometers wide, a simultaneous crustal shortening averaging 200 kilometers must have occurred along the compressional front.

In these last few paragraphs we have seemingly strayed far from the visual seascape, but in actual fact, the virgin lava-covered scenery of the Mid-Oceanic Ridge, and the old crushed rocks viewed in the trenches, can best be understood in this context of complimentary global patterns and these scenes of incessant growth and endless destructions add some modest contemporary evidence which bears on the grander plans of crustal evolution.

REFERENCES AND NOTES

1. The realization that a continuous ridge occupies the center one-third of the Atlantic, Indian, and South Pacific Oceans came as a result of post-World War II ocean-floor studies (M. Ewing and B. C. Heezen. 1956. Some problems of Antarctic submarine geology. Antarctica in the I.G.Y., *Am. Geophysical Union Geophysical Monograph #1,* 75-81; C. H. Elmendorf and B. C. Heezen. 1957. Oceanographic information for engineering submarine cable systems. *The Bell System Technical Journal,* 36(3):1047-1093; B. C. Heezen, M. Tharp, and M. Ewing. 1959. The floors of the oceans I. The North Atlantic. *Geol. Soc. Amer. Spec. Paper 65,* 83-104 and Plate 19). B. C. Heezen and M. Ewing. 1961. The Mid-Oceanic Ridge and its extension through the Arctic Basin. In: G. O. Raasch (Ed.), *The Geology of the Arctic.* Univ. of Toronto Press, Toronto, 622-642.

2. B. C. Heezen. 1957. Deep-sea Physiographic provinces and crustal structure. *Transactions American Geophysical Union,* 38:394; B. C. Heezen. 1959. Geologie sous-marine et deplacements des continents. In: La Topographie et la geologie des profondeurs oceaniques, *LXXXIII, Colloques Internationaux du Centre National de la Recherche Scientifique,* 295-304.

3. A. Wegener. 1915, 1923, 1929, 1966. *The Origin of the Continents and Oceans.* Dover, New York, 212 pp; A. L. Du Toit. 1937. *Our Wandering Continents.* Oliver and Boyd, Edinburgh, 366 pp.

4. The story of this discovery has been told several times. One of the more accurate accounts is given by John Lear (1965. The New Island of Surtsey—child of an expanding earth. *Sat. Review,* July 3:33-39). Marie Tharp, only a few years ago, discovered the mid-oceanic rift valley, that basic key in this scientific detective

story which led directly to the present understanding of the style and historical sequence of mid-ocean mountain building.

5. S. K. Runcorn. 1956. Paleomagnetic comparisons between Europe and North America. *Geol. Assoc. Canada, Proc.,* 8:77-85; E. Irving. 1964. *Paleomagnetism.* Wiley, New York, 399 pp.

6. P. M. S. Blackett, J. A. Clegg, and P. H. S. Stubbs. 1960. An analysis of rock magnetic data. *Proc. Royal Soc.,* A263- : 1-30; P. M. S. Blackett. 1965. A symposium on continental drift. *Phil. Trans. Roy. Soc., London,* 1088:323 pp. A delightful semi-popular account of the impact of paleomagnetic investigations on the continental displacement controversy is given by: H. Takeuchi, S. Uyeda, H. Kanamori, 1964. *Debate about the Earth.* Freeman-Cooper, San Francisco, 253 pp.

7. A. Cox and R. R. Doell. 1960. Review of paleomagnetism. *Geol. Soc. Amer. Bull.,* 71:645-768.

8. Widespread subsidence in the western Pacific was interpreted as evidence that a former mid-oceanic ridge had existed there and had disappeared when the supposed convection current pattern in the mantle suddenly shifted to the eastern Pacific (H. W. Menard. 1960. The East Pacific rise. *Science,* 132:1737-1746; H. W. Menard. 1964. *Marine Geology of the Pacific.* McGraw-Hill, New York, 117-152; H. W. Menard. 1966. Sea floor relief and mantle convection. *Physics and Chemistry of the Earth,* 6:315-364).

9. S. W. Carey. 1958. The tectonic approach to continental drift. In: *Continental Drift, A Symposium,* Univ. of Tasmania, Hobart, 177-355; B. C. Heezen. 1960. The rift in the ocean floor. *Scientific American,* 203(4):98-110; P. Jordan. 1966. *Die Expansion der Erde.* Vieweg, Braunschweig, 182 pp.

10. R. S. Dietz. 1961. Continent and ocean basin evolution. *Nature,* 190:854-857; H. H. Hess. 1962. History of Ocean Basins. *Petrologic Studies.* Geol. Soc. Amer., New York, 599-620.

11. Sveinbjorn Bjornsson (Ed.). 1967. *Iceland and Mid-Ocean Ridges.* Soc. Scient. Islandica, 209 pp.; S. Thorarinsson. 1966. The median zone of Iceland. In: T. N. Irvine (Ed.), *The world rift system.* Geol. Surv. Canada, 66-14:187-211.

12. The first heat flow measurements made in the Atlantic were made by E. C. Bullard (1954. The flow of heat through the floor of the Atlantic Ocean. *Proc. Roy. Soc. London, A,* 222:408-429) and in the Pacific by R. Revelle and A. E. Maxwell (1952. Heat flow through the floor of the eastern North Pacific Ocean. *Nature,* 170:199-200). A recent summary is given by R. P. Von Herzen and M. G. Langseth (1966. Present status of oceanic heat-flow measurements. *Physics and Chemistry of the Earth,* 6:365-408).

13. A. Lowrie and E. Escowitz (Eds.) 1969. *KANE Nine* (data report). U.S. Naval Oceanog. Office, Wash., D.C., 975 pp.

14. This observation has recently given rise to hypotheses of discontinuous growth of the ridge crest (J. Ewing, and M. Ewing. 1967. Sediment distribution on the mid-ocean ridges with respect to spreading of the sea floor. *Science,* 156:1590-1592). The last episode, some believe, started ten million years ago after an extremely long stoppage.

15. M. Ewing, J. Ewing, and M. Talwani. 1964. Sediment distribution in the oceans: The Mid-Atlantic Ridge. *Geol. Soc. Amer. Bull.,* 75:17-36.

16. B. C. Heezen. 1962. The deep sea floor. In: S. K. Runcorn (Ed.), *Continental Drift,* Academic, New York, pp. 235-288.

17. J. Ewing, J. L. Worzel, E. Ewing, and C. Windisch. 1966. Ages of Horizon A and the oldest Atlantic sediments. *Science,* 154:1125-1132. Results of deep sea drilling suggest that the boundary between the upper and lower beds varies in age from place to place ranging from less than 50 million to greater than 100 million years.

18. B. C. Heezen, M. Ewing, and E. T. Miller. 1953. Trans-Atlantic profile of total magnetic intensity and topography, Dakar to Barbados. *Deep-Sea Res.,* 1:25-33.; M. Ewing, B. C. Heezen, and J. Hirschman. 1957. Mid-Atlantic Ridge seismic belt and magnetic anomalies. *Comm. No. 110 Bis. Assoc. Seismol. Ass. Gen. U.G.G.I.,* Toronto; M. Ewing, J. Hirshman, and B. C. Heezen. 1959. Magnetic anomalies of the Mid-Oceanic Rift. *Int. Oceanog. Congress.* 1:24-25.

19. In New York this latter view was so ridiculed that it failed to pass the critical appraisal of local geomagnetists. From Toronto the idea was submitted to international journals and soundly rejected by reviewers (J. T. Wilson. 1967. Advice for the establishment. *Sat. Rev.,* 2 Sept.:50-51), so that credit for the initial publication must be accorded to workers at Cambridge who got the unorthodox idea past the scientific reviewers and into print (F. J. Vine, and D. H. Matthews, 1963. Magnetic anomalies over oceanic ridges. *Nature,* 199:947).

20. W. C. Pitman, III. 1967. Magnetic anomalies in the Pacific. Thesis, Columbia University. W. E. Pitman and J. R. Heirtzler. 1966. Magnetic anomalies in the Pacific. Science, 154:1164.

21. Pillow lavas ranging in age from Recent to Miocene have been dredged from the crest zone of the Mid-Oceanic Ridge, the age of the flows having been determined by the fossil foraminifera found in the baked ooze incorporated in the lava (T. Saito, M. Ewing, and L. H. Burckle, 1966. Tertiary sediment from the Mid-Atlantic Ridge. *Science,* 151:1075-1079) and by potassium-argon analysis of the lava (G. P. Ericson and J. L. Kulp. 1961. Potassium-argon dates on basaltic rocks. *Ann. N.Y. Acad. Sci.,* 91:321-323).

22. B. C. Heezen and M. Tharp. 1961. *Physiographic Diagram of the South Atlantic.* Geological Society of America, New York, New York); M. Ewing and B. C. Heezen. 1956. Mid-Atlantic Ridge seismic belt. *Trans. Amer. Geophys. Union,* 37:343; C. H. Elmendorf, and B. C. Heezen. 1957. Oceanographic information for engineering submarine cable systems. *Bell System Technical Jour.,* XXXVI (5):1047-1093). Recently the epicenters of the U.S. Coast and Geodetic Survey's world seismic network were machine-plotted on a set of 1 : 40,000,000 scale maps (M. Barazangi and J. Dorman. 1969. World seismicity maps compiled from ESSA, Coast and Geodetic Survey, epicenter data, 1961-1967. *Bull. Seismol. Soc. Amer.,* 59:369-380.).

23. The initial motion of earthquakes also provides impressive confirmation of continental drift movements along the portion of the fracture zones which displace the rift valley. (L. R. Sykes. 1967. Mechanisms of earthquakes and nature of faulting on the mid-oceanic ridge. *Jour. Geophys. Res.,* 72:2131-2153.)

24. The fact that fracture zones thousands of miles long appeared to be active along only a small part of their length was perplexing and embarrassing to the anti-drifters who proposed the convenient but unlikely hypothesis that on the flanks of the ridges faults are so well lubricated that earthquakes no longer occur although motion still continues.

25. The prime example is the Hawaiian chain where the sequence from old to young is from west to east. Hawaii, the active eastern island, is 3000 miles from the Mid-

Oceanic Ridge. The trend of the Hawaiian Ridge seems to be nearly at right angles to the fracture zones.

26. Attempts have been made to interpret the evidence of widespread subsidence which the guyots and bevelled micro-continents provide in terms of episodic regional uplift and collapse of enormous ancient welts raised on the oceanic crust by maladies suffered by the underlying mantle. However, the data presented in support of the existence of ancient linear and symmetrical uplifts such as the hypothetical Darwin Rise are by no means compelling, and the idea has not been widely accepted. Despite present-day evidence of systematic regional differences in age of the volcanos, atolls and guyots arranged along single lines, the dubious assumption was made that virtually all volcanos of the Pacific were formed during a single short period. Hence the deepest summits were assumed to represent areas suffering the greatest subsidence and to have once been on the crest of the former crustal welt. Finally, the sketchy pattern observed was assumed to be but half of a symmetrical distribution the west flank of which had not yet been detected or had not been recorded due to lack of volcanos. We do not wish to imply that wide-scale subsidence of the oceanic crust did not occur for it very definitely did, but evidence for the alternate uplift and collapse of the linear symmetrical welts is lacking and thus, despite an auspicious origin, the proud name Darwin Rise must pass into oblivion.

27. If we were to predict the age of the ocean floor on the basis of the frequency of volcanos, we should conclude that the North America and Canary Basins, which have numerous large volcanos, are much older than the Mid-Atlantic Ridge, which has few large cones, and that the areas of islands and seamounts of the western Pacific are vastly older than the East Pacific Ridge.

28. In order to determine the pattern of fracture zones and to employ this information in the study of the motions of the continents and the evolution of the ocean floor, several of the major ones have been traced in some detail far out from the crest of the Mid-Oceanic Ridge. It was found that some fracture zones undergo abrupt changes in trend which seem to indicate successive changes in the world pattern of continental drift. As yet, no single fracture has been traced from continent to continent and thus there is considerable uncertainty as to the pattern of the fractures in the basement relief beneath the continental margins. A fracture zone at eight degrees north in the Atlantic, however, has been traced from the African continent three-quarters of the distance to the West Indies (B. C. Heezen, P. J. Fox, G. L. Johnson, M. Tharp, and A. Ballard. 1969. A fracture zone at 8°N. *Trans. Amer. Geophys. Union,* 50:211).

29. B. C. Heezen and R. E. Sheridan, 1966. Lower Cretaceous rocks (Neocomian-Albian) dredged from Blake Escarpment. *Science,* 154:1644-1647.

30. It is one thing to establish that shortening is occurring but it is immensely more difficult to establish the amount of shortening which has occurred. If one straightens out all the folds and corrects this measurement for stretching by exactly the correct amount, and if one detects all the thrusts and measures the horizontal displacement of all of them, one still could arrive at a figure for crustal shortening which was several times too small, for hundreds of kilometers of oceanic crust could conceivably disappear without a trace. The deformation seen in the mountains can only set a lower limit on the amount of crustal shortening which has occurred in a zone of compression. Alpine geologists have estimated

shortening of 600 to 1000 kilometers in late Tertiary time, admitting that in the more complexly deformed areas they could make no estimate despite the belief that extensive shortening was implied by the obscure structure. One may make a rough estimate of the amount of crustal shortening in the Andes region by estimating the width which the smooth continental margin should have occupied. South of Valpariso the trench is, in fact, filled and a modest continental rise and even an abyssal plain is present. Off Peru the trench is empty where the Andes reach their highest general level and mass. Here one might have expected a continental rise 200 or 300 miles wide and thus one can infer that at least that much crustal shortening has occurred here in the Tertiary. The result of such considerations are generally inconclusive. Although it might seem probable that crustal growth is equal to crustal shortening it can by no means yet be proven.

Lost in antiquity is the name of the first person who seriously considered that the great driving force which moulded the earth's face might be thermal convection in the mantle. However, clear and forceful expositions of the proposition are found in scientific works of such prominent men of science as A. Holmes (1928. Radioactivity and earth movements. *Trans. Geol. Soc. Glasgow,* 18:559-606), F. A. Vening-Meinesz (1947. Major tectonic phenomena and the hypothesis of convection currents in the earth. *Geol. Soc. London, Quart. Jour.,* 103:191-207), D. Griggs (1939. A theory of mountain building. *Amer. Jour. Sci.,* 237:611-650), and C. L. Pekeris (1935. Thermal convection in the interior of the earth. *Monthly Not. R. Astr. Soc. Geoph. Suppl.,* 3:343-367), writing in the second and third decades of this century. The discussion of mantle convection given by Osmond Fisher (1889. *Physics of the Earth's Crust, Second Edit.,* Macmillan, London, 391 pp.), although primitive by modern standards, is not too oblique to be easily discounted by today's impatient and less scholarly geophysicists. Nevertheless, the theory did not find a broad following until relatively recently. It is a perfectly natural mechanism which anyone can observe in a cup of tea or a pot of porridge. Its main disadvantage stems from the fact that its application is *ad hoc*. Despite numerous attempts no compelling evidence of convection can be demonstrated save the evidence of crustal movements which the convection cells are invoked to explain. This objection is mainly practical. There is yet no clear way to obtain independent evidence of their existence or location within the earth.

14.1 The foundations of the sea.

14
Summing Up

The sea folds away from you like a mystery.
You can look and look at it and mystery never leaves it.
CARL SANDBURG

We can now view the visible abyss with less mystery and more real understanding. A vast unremitting snowfall of sediment has cast a veil, sometimes a thick blanket, over the rugged, grand, imposing ribs of the solid earth which forms the foundations of the sea. This oozy bed has become the frugal home of creatures specially adapted to conditions of life so precarious that before they were discovered, it was widely believed that none would be found.

The universal, dominant, and in the majority of cases, the only features seen in deep-sea photographs are mounds, depressions, and irregularities that appear to have been produced by animal life. Biological sampling has repeatedly shown the existence of benthic organisms in the abyss but cannot even suggest the magnitude or manner in which this life affects the landscape of the sea floor.

The creatures of the abyss are at the end of a long food chain which reaches down from the sunlit pelagic gardens of the surface waters to the lightless skin-deep bacterial pastures on the endless refuse heap of the deep-sea floor.

The largest and most abundant of these creatures are those "carpet sweepers" that skim off the microscopic epidermal slime, converting it to large translucent and presumably delectable chunks up to a foot long. These "housemaids" of the underworld sometimes tread lightly, but often track up their freshly swept carpet. Every few tens of feet they empty the sweeper bag leaving neat little knots and strings everywhere they go. This untidy habit detracts from their character as "housemaids," and leads one to consider whether they shouldn't be thought of as the stock of a huge abyssal cattle ranch. Some people probably would prefer to consider it a pork farm for some of our little abyssal "housemaids" physically resemble pigs more closely than cows, but we prefer to think of them as cattle gently grazing on bacterial pastures rather than pigs rooting in a garbage dump. One might consider them a type of advanced space-age harvester which converts the grass to a super-digestible jelly and leaves the rejected straw in little bales littered in the field.

Our combined "carpet sweeper," "maid," "cow," and "combine" produces not only the most dramatic features of the seascape but leaves a permanent record in the history book of the abyss. That is to say, their record is kind of a nonrecord, since they, together with their cohorts, till and mix the abyssal epidermis, smoothing out the fine variations in the abyssal record book. Their work in this regard is not all bad, for without their help in creating a running average, the poor paleontologist would have to examine each millimeter of all deep-sea sediment cores individually, and in some detail, just as he must count and analyze each annual lamina in cores from the anaerobic and nearly azoic basins.

There are some vegetarians among us who have chosen their way of life rather than be responsible for the death of a steer, but most of us are not so squeamish, so we need not feel sorry for our abyssal herds who provide food for our friends, the fishes, as well as their friends and enemies. We say friends because, usually, people reserve certain tender, gentle feelings toward fishes that they deny the starfish, spiders, and crabs. These animals must be the shepherds, the slaughterers, and the consumers of the abyssal trepang herds.

Other creatures of the deep are more commonplace, for the clams, snails, and worms, so familiar to any visitor to the seashore are also found in the abyss and are preyed on there by starfish, sea urchins, and other more or less familiar enemies.

The result of all this commotion in the ocean is seen in our pictures: the footprints, the burrows and furrows, the vast piles of manure which litter the bacterial pastures of the deep.

Photographs have been presented which illustrate representatives of twenty-three of the thirty-seven (60 per cent) nonparasitic groups that are large enough to be seen with present-day methods of photography. Members representing eighteen of the twenty-five taxa (70 per cent) that might be considered important bottom markers have been photographed in the process of producing tracks, trails, impressions, burrows, or mounds (Table 2.1). The zoological record (based on trawl samples) indicates that the Echinodermata should be the most common phylum of large abyssal epifauna. This abundance is clearly shown in the photographic record which indicates that holothurians and ophiuroids are the most abundant classes of large epifauna seen on the deep-sea floor. Many polychaete worms are too small to be identified; however, large representatives are sometimes seen in profusion in the greatest depths and they are probably more abundant than the photographic record indicates. Gorgonians and pennatulids are often seen attached to rocks in moderate depths but are rather uncommon in the abyss.

The vast majority of walking trails seen on the deep-sea floor are the work of holothurians. The plowmarks, or bilobate grooves, in deep-sea sediments are largely the creation of echinoids. The large feces and coils of remoulded sediment are left by holothurians, while the larger spiral feces appear to be produced by hemichordates. The myriads of mounds are less definitely assigned, for except for an occasional worm bristle, one can almost never see the animal producing the cone or mound.

The exceedingly deliberate pace at which our marine snow accumulates allows us to see the results of hundreds of years of abyssal commotion superimposed. Of course it is easy to see that one mound looks older than another owing to its softer outlines, just as it is easy to tell the features resulting from the first snowfall of the winter from those of the second. But our abyssal snow never melts; its fall is continuous. This complicates the interpretation.

It would seem reasonable to suppose a clear relationship between the abundance and type of deep-sea life, and thus of seascape, with the richness of the pelagic gardens above. We can, in fact, recognize several different types of records. The extremely fine red clay which lies beneath the deepest marine deserts is so soft that it preserves few marks and its nutrients are so scant that it could support little life in any case. The soft chocolate outlines are easily recognized as a distinct type. The limy or siliceous oozes of the shallow, or more productive, areas are typically covered with mounds, holes, tracks, furrows but, except beneath the richest waters, most of these undulations appear to be exhausted relics of the past. The continental margins often reveal the richest and clearest new-appearing bumps and dumps on the sea floor, but in this same area beneath equally productive waters are some of the smoothest barrens. Thus, the seascapes of the abyss are governed only partly by the richness of the pelagic gardens above and additional factors must be reckoned with in explaining the distribution of bumps on the bottom.

We have seen that this additional factor is circulation, which is nearly as steady and unremitting as the snowfall which it sweeps into huge drifts. Just as winds striking the mountains drive the snows from the boldest, highest peaks, so the deep-sea currents sweep the sediment from the

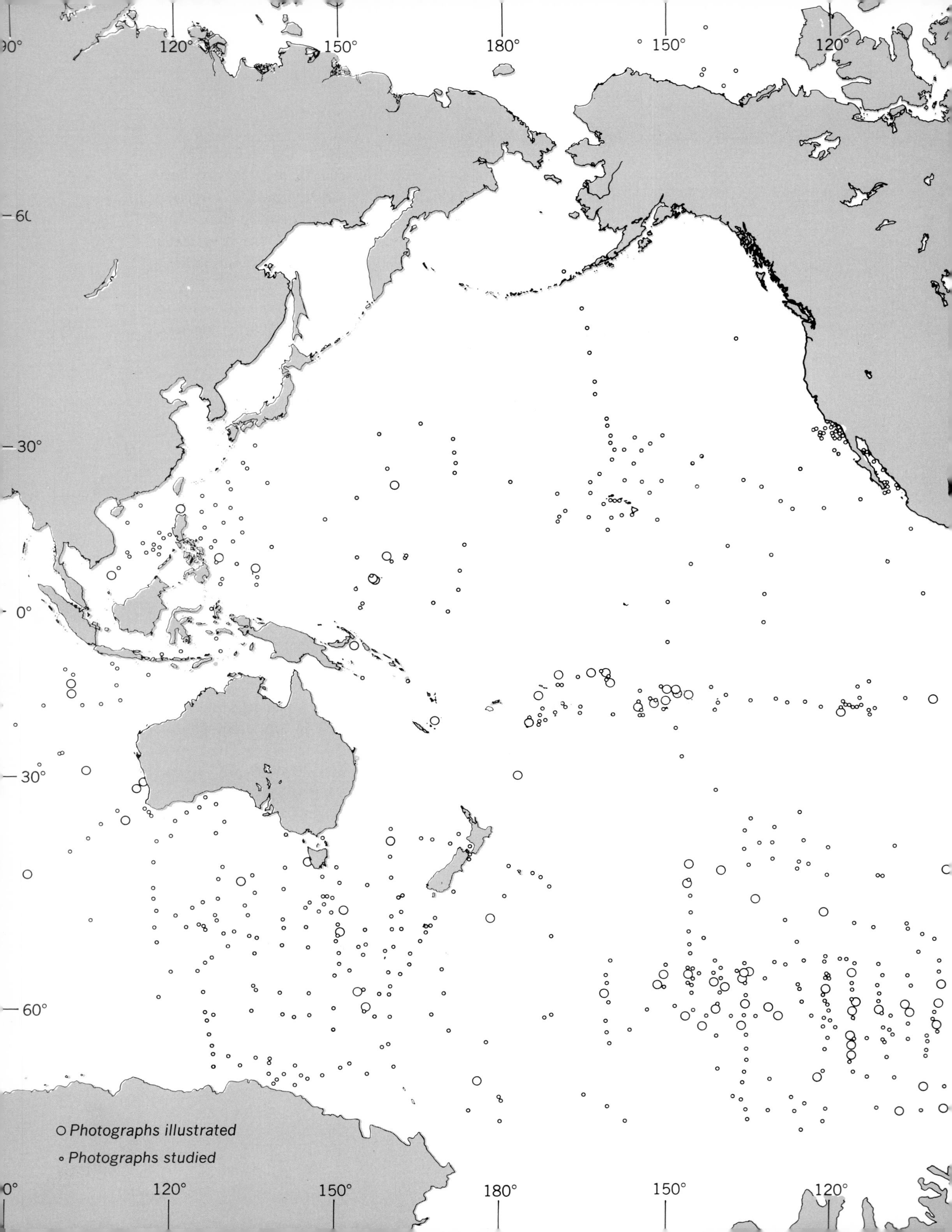

90°
120°
150°
180°
150°
120°
60
30°
0°
30°
60°
Photographs illustrated
Photographs studied
0°
120°
150°
180°
150°
120°

14.2 World distribution of photographs studied and photographs reproduced in this book (large circles).

peaks to the lower slopes below. However, this great pattern of circulation—which is so necessary to the aeration of the deeps and without which the abyss would be a desert more barren than the Sahara—flows according to planetary laws in a definite and simple pattern, creating as it moves a global pattern of abyssal snowdrifts. Thus, the Arctic and Antarctic waters cooled in their frigid polar seas sink and flow toward the equator. Since they are not equally dense, they pass over one another, each extending to the opposite polar area.

In the abyss there are no winds of air; there is no evaporation, no rain, no warming by the sun or cooling by radiation. The abyss is protected by a thick blanket of warm upper waters. Thus, when sinking takes place near the poles and the massive descent of denser cool waters begins, its flow is controlled by only a few factors. The most important is the rotation of the earth which causes any moving body—train, car, ship, river, or ocean current—to be deflected slightly. The deflection is to the right in the northern hemisphere and to the left in the southern hemisphere. This deflection is not noticeable to most humans and is not a normal part of "common sense reasoning." However, to the massive currents of the air and the water, it is of immense importance. Thus, as the frigid flow creeps from pole to equator, it is strongly deflected toward the side of the ocean basin where it rests against the floor of the sea. Motions are variable and differ from place to place, but this current system, although steady, is slow and deliberate, reaching velocities of only five to fifteen centimeters per second. Such a rate is perhaps not impressive, since it is only one-fifth as fast as one walks on his Sunday afternoon stroll. But it is a relentless massive motion which continues day and night as long as there is water in the oceans, as long as there are frigid polar seas, and as long as the earth rotates on its axis.

Rivers discharge mud into the sea. Some of this is returned to the delta by waves, and that which reaches the shallow shelf is generally picked up again and carried farther. For in this rugged current and wave-swept environment, little or no fine sediment can survive for any length of time. Upon reaching the quieter waters of the continental slope and upon sinking to the bottom, this rain of organic and inorganic debris is swept on by the weak contour-following boundary under-currents. These currents are not sufficiently swift to hold the load in suspension indefinitely and by gradual attrition the debris, if not renewed by further rivers downcurrent, eventually all drops out within 1000 to 5000 kilometers of the point it joined the undercurrent.

Very little terrigenous debris reaches past this formidable barrier which encircles all continents in all seas, except that carried by swift, dense, bottom-seeking turbidity currents which sweep down the slope like powder avalanches in the Alps, smothering and leveling the lower slopes and creating the vast flat abyssal plains which fill the deepest depressions of the sea.

The effect of the steady, unremitting contour currents on the bottom is distinct, often dramatic, and unmistakable. The normal bumpy bottom is smoothed out into streamers; each animal volcano is a long oval instead of a cone; depressions are cut around scattered rocks; stalked animals are bent with the current; tracks, furrows, and mounds are decidedly rare despite the usually high surface productivity near the margins of the sea.

Through a study of the normal seascape, we have identified many of the factors responsible for the normal bumpy bottom and can now recognize anomalies in this pattern and relate them to such factors as deep sea currents.

A good many characteristics of the seascape must be essentially unchanging. We have seen that on the continental rise currents are transporting sediment and creating streamers and lineations on the bottom. Beneath this area of current streamers, the upper strata form thin wedges which diminish seaward from the base of the continental slope. These wedges compose thicker wedges which in turn form the immense kilometers-thick wedge which is the continental rise. It seems hard to escape the conclusion that the transportational processes which we see in the bottom photographs have been operative throughout the accumulation of this entire wedge. Again, we don't know when the construction of the continental rise began, but it certainly was no less than one hundred million years ago and it may have been longer than that.

We have seen that in the areas of manganese nodules nearly sediment-free currents are creating an ionic plating of iron and manganese in the form of concentric nodules. The association of these nodules with sharks' teeth which are at least mid-Tertiary in age indicates that these mineral gardens have existed in the same place, under relatively the same conditions, for tens of millions of years.

The correlation of bottom smoothing seen on echo-sounders and the patterns of present-day productivity, together with the patterns of terrestrial river discharge, indicate that the locations of the greatest sedimentation correlate with the areas of the greatest production of sediments, and that the vast pelagic deserts such as the Sargasso Sea are underlain by relatively thin sediments. There are a number of anomalies in this pattern which required explanation but, by and large, the global pattern is consistent and uniform. Thus, it would appear that the accumulation of sediments on the solid ribs of the foundation of the abyss has taken place under a current pattern and productivity pattern virtually identical to the one that exists today. Thus, by examining the modern depositional surface in detail and contrasting the various environments observed, one can use this present environment as a key to predicting the past much in the way the geologist uses this basic concept of uniformitarianism to deduce the paleo-ecology of early geological periods.

During the Pleistocene glacial stages, patterns of productivity of the oceans were undoubtedly modified. It has been suggested that higher winds of the glacial stages produced greater upwelling in the equatorial Pacific, thus resulting in greater productivity of planktonic organisms and a distinct shift in the type of sediment accumulating on the deep-sea floor. In certain areas the rate of deposition doubled and in other areas changed by as much as tenfold. The general effect of the higher productivity of the equatorial Pacific would be to spread the carbonate ooze into greater depths and to cause an overlapping of glacial globigerina ooze over interglacial or pre-glacial red clay. This would, of course, locally cause noticeable changes in the seascape. The rate of deposition in the equatorial Atlantic was two or three times higher during the glacial stages than it is now, but this higher rate of deposition may have been accompanied by a greater benthic population and, therefore, Pleistocene photographs would have indicated greater life and perhaps more extensive bioturbation. Ice-rafted rocks would be seen at lower latitudes than at present.

During the Pleistocene glacial stages the abyssal plains may have received turbidity currents at intervals of months rather than decades or centuries. This should have produced a noticeable effect in the seascape. The Gulf of Mexico, which was flooded by turbidity currents from the Mississippi River, must have had a very different sea floor than seen at present. In the area seaward of Cabot Strait the great outwash of the Laurentian glaciers produced a brick-red bottom quite distinct from the modern light grayish-green bottom.

Volcanism and tectonism, if more episodic than we presently believe, may have caused great revolutions in the seascape of the past. A tephra fall must have had a profound effect on the bottom. The deposition of a bed of ash several centimeters thick over a wide area must obliterate much of the bottom life. It would have been difficult for the grazers to reinvade the area of the thickest ash until a new deposit of sediment was laid down. The smaller infauna may have been wiped out, and the nutrition of the benthos would have been so vastly altered as to temporarily create an entirely different seascape. However, burrows have been noted in ash beds, indicating that certain animals can survive these catastrophes.

Periodically during the Pleistocene, the deeper waters of the eastern Mediterranean became stagnated due to a stable surface stratification. The oxygen was soon used up and the sea floor was without life. These events are recorded in a series of black azoic muds which contain the unique assemblage of planktonic foraminifera without benthonic foraminifera, fine stratification without evidence of burrowing, fine fish bones and delicate spicules. During these stagnations the seascape of the eastern Mediterranean must have resembled the present floor of the Black Sea or the Cariaco Trench or other stagnant basins.

The deeper waters of the Cariaco Trench at the present time are anaerobic due to a strong density stratification in the surface waters which allows only a small trickle of deep cold water to enter the trench. This stratification and slow circulation coupled with the high surface productivity exhausts the oxygen supply of the deep waters. At the present time no marine animals are found in this basin; the bottom is a dark smooth surface devoid of bioturbation. However, during the late glacial time the surface density stratification over the trench was destroyed and mixing occurred from the surface to the greater depths. Although the basin at that time was poorly ventilated, it was far from stagnant, and benthic forms must have populated the bottom, probably giving it a seascape similar to the modern continental slopes.

If during the Tertiary period the deep and bottom waters of the abyss gradually cooled and ventilation gradually improved, as several investigators have proposed, there should have been a continuing change in the seascape due to increasing current scour, growing benthic population, and a gradual modification in patterns of sediment distribution.

Numerous outcrops of pillow lava spread over the narrow crest of the Mid-Oceanic Ridge. The frequent occurrence of fresh basalt, both in photographs and in dredges, suggests that the Mid-Oceanic Ridge is still being actively formed. This, together with the pattern delineated by the earthquake epicenters, defines an area where the foundations of the deep have been gradually created though geological time. This appears to be the fundamental insight which we need to understand the creation of the rock surface beneath the sediments throughout the width of the ocean. Throughout most of the width and depth of the ocean a simple environment nearly unchanging in time and space has prevailed throughout the time required for deposition of the sedimentary blanket which covers the rugged volcanic rock surface beneath. Over mid-latitude—mid-oceanic—reaches, sediments are so uniform in space and time that the thickness of the blanket is a measure of the age of the underlying ribs of the earth and records a steady evolution of an ever-widening and ever-filling median rift valley which has created the bilaterally symmetrical rocky foundations of the deep. Once created, the ocean floor has seemingly undergone a simple evolution, governed by such basic facts as heat and water balance of the earth, deep circulation of the sea and rotation of the earth. Sediments have been injected into this system, then transported and deposited through various agencies. But the changes brought about by the above processes which act through the agencies of atmosphere and hydrosphere alone are outstripped in sheer grandeur by the sensational series of changes which, as a result of forces acting in the lithosphere below, lead to the evolution of a mountain range. Progressing from a primeval pillow-lava terrain which forms the base of the sediment accumulation through the realm of turbidity currents and the visual sequences of contour-current lineated sea floor to the yawning earth crushers of the rugged trenches, the sequence culminates in great compressions that produce the majestic Cordellera, Himalaya, and Alps. Of this long history, only the latest stage is directly visible to terrestrial man, for all the early development occurred deep within the abyss.

Ocean

The Sea, our sea, thou great and glorious sea,
Yield up thy secrets to our weak and fumbling band
Whose probing passion and bright eyes doth bring a joy, a glory,
An overwhelming magnificence to many a trifling detail
 of thy vast dark deep interior's plan.
The slime, the filth, the excrement of eons becomes a glorious history
To those whose minds can conjure from these bare
 bits, a living teeming mass of life of yesteryears,
A fiery blast of Vulcan or a cosmic comet's searing fall.
The earth's alive to all who care to read its rustic
 book and ponder past and future.
But 'tis not the knowing but the learning to which
 all our thoughts, ambitions and desires aspire.
For life is to live and not to hoard; our striving,
 driving, living days are themselves just and due reward.
Honors, titles and epithets are but empty words for
 joy of teaching, joy of learning,
Joy at the instants of revelation are our life's real rewards.

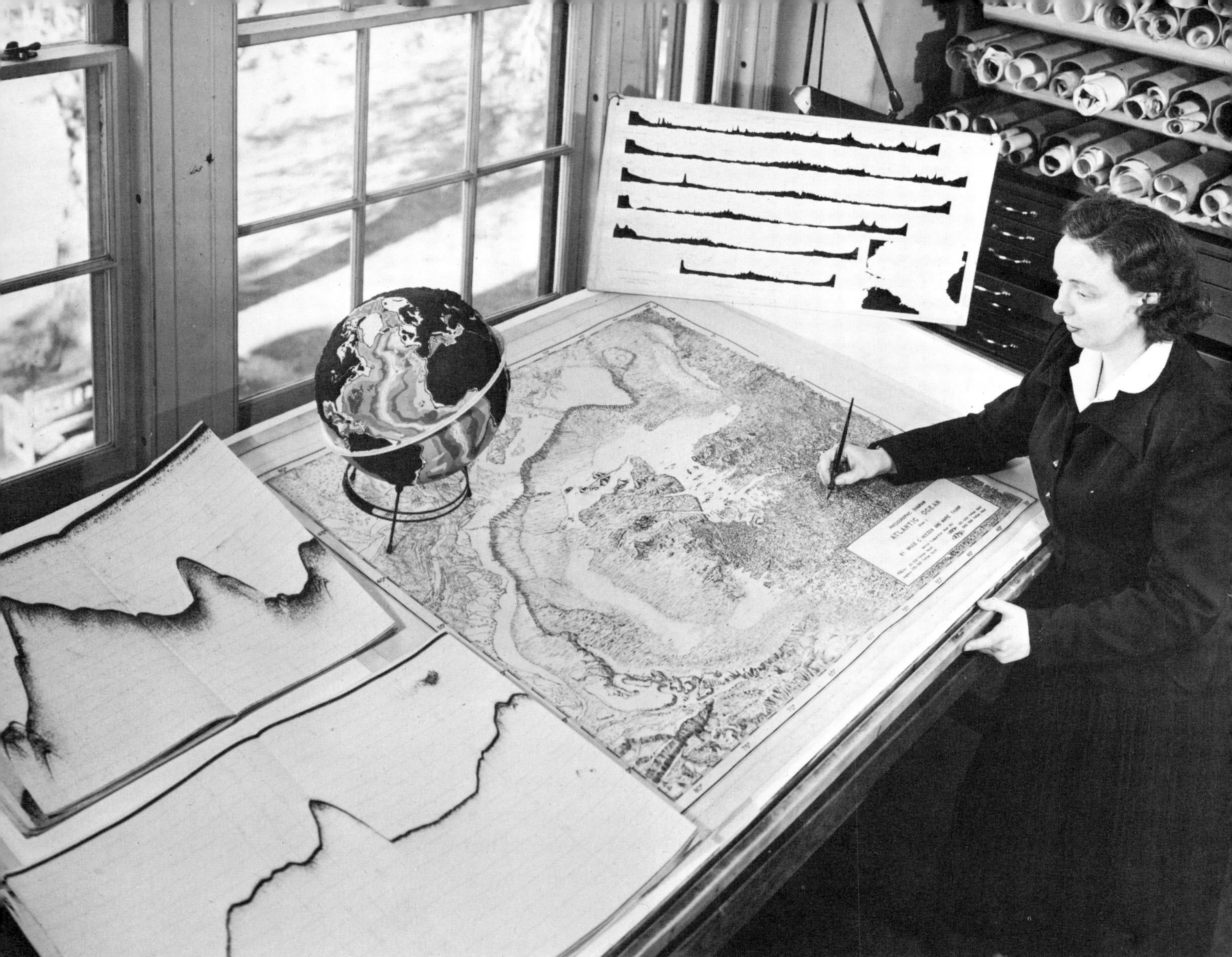

A1.1 Exploration and explanation. The larger view of the ocean floor is of necessity an abstract and continuously evolving construction incorporating fact, theory, and hypothesis.

APPENDIX 1

Deep-Sea Exploration

The exploration of the deep-sea floor did not begin in earnest until the mid-nineteenth century. Naval Lt. Matthew Fontaine Maury has left us an eloquent testimony of the state of knowledge in mid-century in his delightful work, *The Physical Geography of the Sea* (1855. Harper and Bros., New York, 389 pp.). Sir John Murray's thumbnail history of ocean exploration provides a handy guide to the expeditions and leading explorers that played major roles in the rapidly developing science of oceanography during the latter part of the last century (in T. H. Tizard, H. N. Moseley, J. Y. Buchanan, and J. Murray. 1885. Narrative of the Cruise of H.M.S. *Challenger*. Challenger Reports, *Narrative*, 1: Introduction, pp. xxxi-liv). This lengthy report has been condensed in: J. Murray and J. Hjort. 1912. *Depths of the Ocean*. Macmillan, London, Chap. I, A brief historical review of oceanographical investigations, 1-22.

The turning point in the study of submarine morphology came just before the First World War when depth determination by echo-sounding was proved an effective method. No real picture of the detailed morphology of the abyssal floor was or could have been obtained before the early 1920's when echo-sounders were first used (Anon., 1939. A summary of echo-sounding apparatus. *Int. Hydro. Bureau, Spec. Publ.*, 20:137 pp.). The development of precision high resolution deep-sea echo-sounders did not occur until the fifties (B. Luskin, B. C. Heezen, M. Ewing, and M. Landisman. 1954. Precision measurement of ocean depth. *Deep-Sea Res.*, 1:131-40). A variety of instruments are now available, most of which have been described only in manufacturers' manuals. Today, depth differences of two meters can be recorded. In addition powerful sound sources are employed to obtain echo profiles of layers a mile or more below the sea floor, thus allowing geologists to study the deeper structure of the earth beneath the sea.

Soundings are measured in units of echo time and converted to depths (Table A1-1) through a knowledge of the vertical velocity of sound as computed from a formula relating pressure, temperature, and salinity to sound velocity. The sounding unit in modern use is the 400th of a second (t = tau). This unit is used on all U.S. Navy charts of the deep sea. Several tables for the conversion of travel time to depth are employed but the one almost universally used is known as the Matthews Tables (D. J. Matthews. 1939. *Tables of the Velocity of Sound in Pure Water and Sea Water for Use in Echo Sounding and Echo Ranging.* Admiralty Hydrographic Dept., London, 52 pp.).

Exploration by sound and sight is given tangible meaning through direct sampling of the sea floor by dredging and coring apparatus. Dredging is a rewarding, but, unfortunately, a neglected method of exploring the material which forms the sea bed. The introduction of piston coring by B. Kullenberg (1955. Deep Sea Coring. *Reports, Swedish Deep-Sea Exped.*, 4:37-96; R. S. Dietz. 1952. Methods of exploring the ocean floor. In J. D. Isaacs and C. O'D. Iselin, editors. Oceanographic

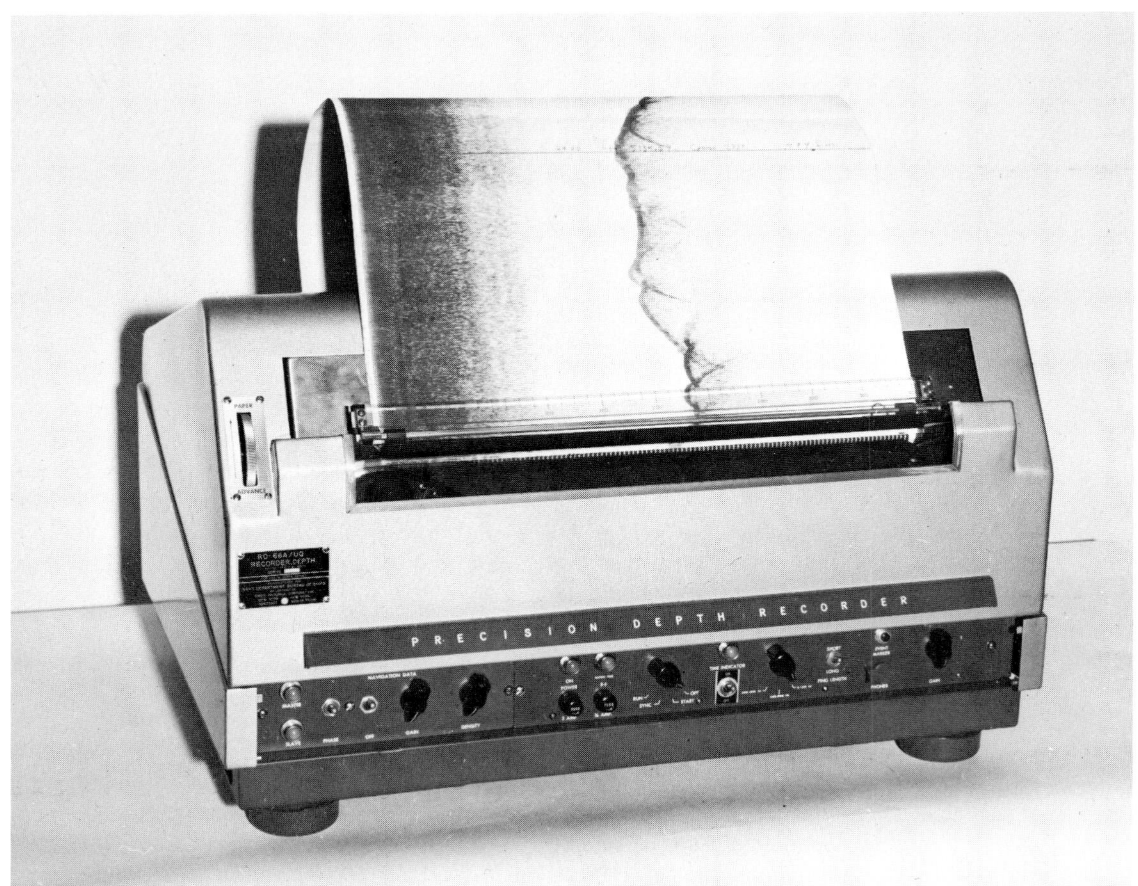

A1.2 Precision depth recorder traces detailed profiles of the ocean floor.

Instrumentation. *Nat. Res. Council. Publ.,* 309:194-209; and T. L. Hopkins. 1964. A survey of marine bottom samplers. *Prog. in Oceanog.,* 2:215-55.) has led to great advances in our knowledge of the past history of the sea (G. Arrhenius. 1963. Pelagic sediments. In M. N. Hill, editor. *The Sea.* Wiley, New York, 3:655-727). In addition to the methods illustrated in Figure 1.2, other important aspects of the nature of the sea floor can be inferred from perturbations of the magnetic and gravity fields of the earth. Continuously recording magnetometers (B. C. Heezen, M. Ewing, and E. T. Miller. 1953. Trans-Atlantic profile of total magnetic intensity and topography, Dakar to Barbados. *Deep-Sea Res.,* 1:25-33; E. C. Bullard and R. G. Mason. 1963. The magnetic field over the oceans. In M. N. Hill, editor. *The Sea.* Wiley, New York, 3:175-210) and gravity meters (J. C. Harrison, 1960. The measurement of gravity at sea. In S. K. Runcorn, editor. *Methods and Techniques in Geophysics.* Interscience, New York, 1:211-229) are employed on most expeditions exploring the dep-sea floor. Recently deep-ocean drilling has been added to the list of important tools used for submarine geology (M. N. A. Peterson and N. T. Edgar. 1969. Deep ocean drilling with *Glomar Challenger. Oceans,* 1(5): 18-32).

Table A1.1

	Depths			Soundings	
	METERS	FATHOMS	FEET	SECONDS	1/400th SECOND*
BATHYAL	1000	547	3280	1.34	535
	2000	1094	6561	2.68	1073
ABYSSAL	3000	1640	9842	4.02	1606
	4000	2187	13123	5.34	2135
	5000	2734	16404	6.64	2656
HADAL	6000	3280	19684	7.93	3171
	10000	5468	32808	12.93	5173

* In the western Pacific

1 meter = 3.2808 feet 1 meter = 0.54681 fathoms
1 fathom = 1.829 meters 1 fathom = 6 feet

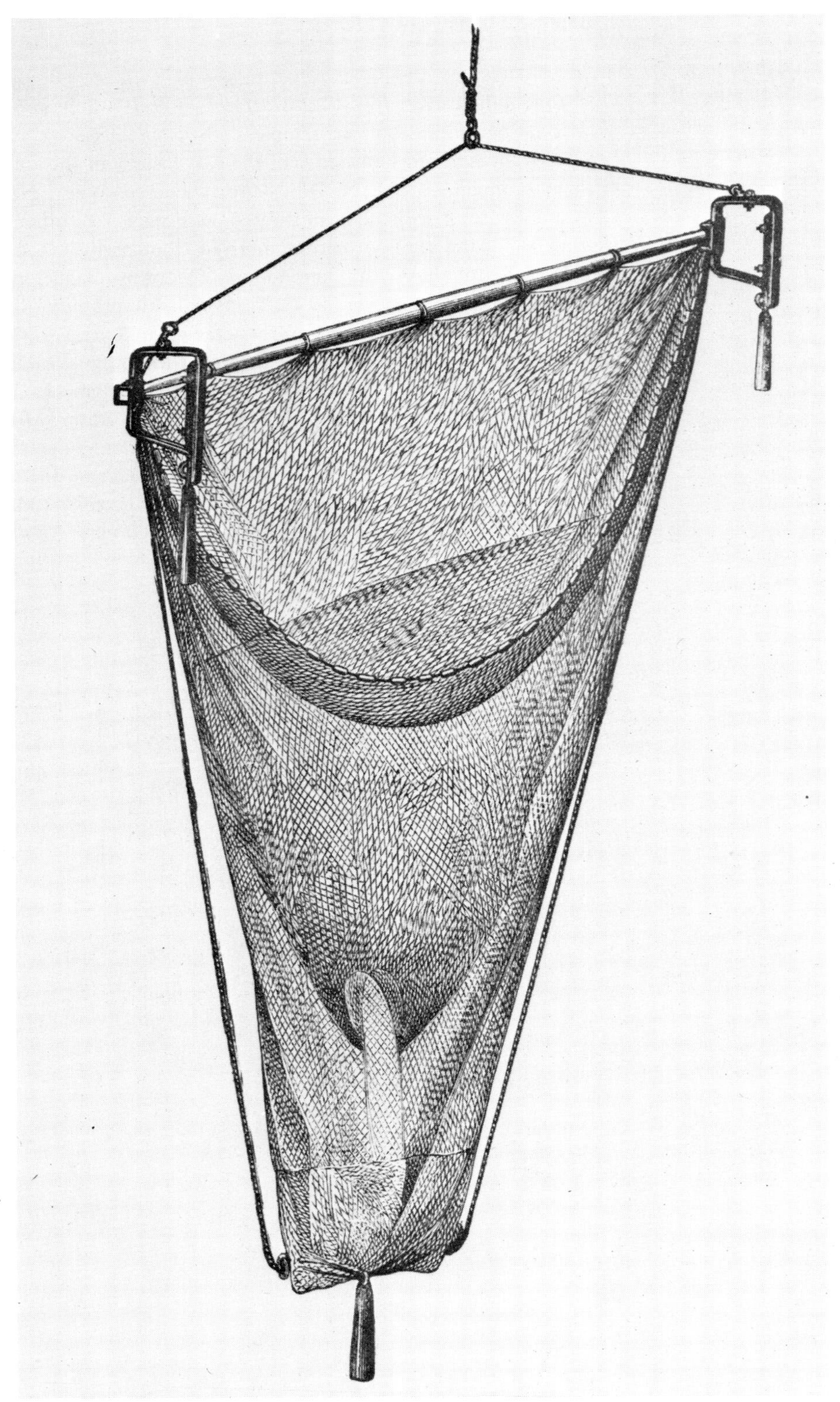

A2.1 Deep-sea trawl.

APPENDIX 2

Deep-Sea Fauna

The late nineteenth century was a time of particularly vigorous investigation of deep-sea life. Study of the deep-sea fauna reached its peak then, and the foremost biologists of the world devoted their talents to this exciting and rewarding pursuit. The best general descriptions of the deep-sea fauna are found in the following chronological list of publications:

1873 C. W. Thomson. *The Depths of the Sea.* Macmillan, London, 527 pp. Describes the early investigation of the continental slope and adjacent abyss of the northeast Atlantic and the Mediterranean. This investigation led to the organization of the great *Challenger* expedition.

1878 C. W. Thomson. *The Atlantic: The Voyage of the H.M.S.* Challenger. Harper, New York, 1:391 pp.; 2:329 pp. A semi-popular narrative of the Atlantic portion of the cruise of *Challenger.* Includes excellent woodcuts and a good summary of the deep-sea fauna.

1888 A. Agassiz. *Three Cruises of the* Blake. Riverside Press, Cambridge, 1:314 pp.; 2:220 pp. Although out of date in many respects, these volumes still comprise one of the best summaries available of the deep-sea fauna. Excellent illustrations.

1895 J. Murray. Summary of the scientific results obtained at the sounding and dredging stations of H.M.S. *Challenger.* Challenger *Reports, Summary,* 5:1665 pp.

1912 J. Murray and J. Hjort. *The Depths of the Ocean.* Macmillan, London, 821 pp. (reprinted 1965, Stechert and Hafner, New York). This classic, written at the close of the period of great exploring expeditions, contains the best of all summaries of the biological results of these efforts. Out of date in many respects, it is still an invaluable reference.

1912 G. H. Fowler. Editor. *Science of the Sea.* John Murray, London, 452 pp. (2nd edition by G. H. Fowler and E. J. Allen, editors. 1928. Clarendon Press, Oxford, 502 pp.). This semi-popular book contains a brief but interesting chapter (pp. 270-306 in the 2nd edition) about deep-sea life written by G. P. Farran and W. T. Calman.

1948 E. L. Le Danois. *Les Profondeurs de la Mer.* Payot, Paris, 303 pp. A summary of the results of dredging on the shelf, slope, and abyss off the Atlantic coasts of France and Spain. Two hundred geographic regions are defined and faunal lists presented. A few sketches of the bottom communities are presented. These are interesting from two aspects: (1) most of the asemblages noted by Le Danois have now been observed in photographs; (2) the bottom is never as densely populated as shown in his schematic drawings.

1953 S. Ekman. *Zoogeography of the Sea.* Sedgwick and Jackson, London, 417 pp. Originally published in German in 1935, it was extensively rewritten before the appearance of this English translation in 1953. Contains a good summary of the major endemic fauna; only a few drawings and maps.

1954 N. B. Marshall. *Aspects of Deep Sea Biology.* Hutchinson, London, 380 pp. A good summary of deep-sea biology. Contains good figures including color paintings of fish, but can be read to better advantage with Agassiz (1888) or Murray and Hjort (1912) at your side.

1956 A. C. Hardy. *The Open Sea.* Houghton Mifflin, Boston, 1:335 pp.; 2:322 pp.

1956 A. F. Bruun. Animal life of the deep-sea bottom. In A. Brunn, S. V. Greve, H. Mielche, and R. Sparck, editors. The *Galathea Deep-Sea Expedition 1950-1952.* Macmillan, New York, pp. 149-95.

1956 K. Gunther and K. Deckert. *Creatures of the Deep Sea.* Scribner's, New York, 222 pp. This popular treatment, translated from an original 1950 German edition, contains a moderate number of good line drawings.

1957 J. W. Hedgepeth and H. S. Ladd. Treatise on marine ecology and paleocology. *Geol. Soc. Am., Memoir 67,* 1:1296 pp.; 2:1076 pp., with annotated bibliographies on each of the major groups.

1961 T. Wolff. Animal life from a single abyssal trawling. Galathea *Rept.,* 5:129-62. Color reproductions of three paintings illustrate hypothetical seascapes.

1963 L. Zenkevitch. *Biology of the Seas of the U.S.S.R.* George Allen and Unwin, London, 955 pp. This standard work, for which the author received the Lenin Prize, is largely concerned with the shallow seas; however, it includes an excellent summary of the northwest Pacific with many maps and profiles but few drawings of animals.

1964 C. P. Idyll. *The Abyss: The Deep Sea and the Creatures That Live in It.* Crowell, New York, 396 pp. Popular.

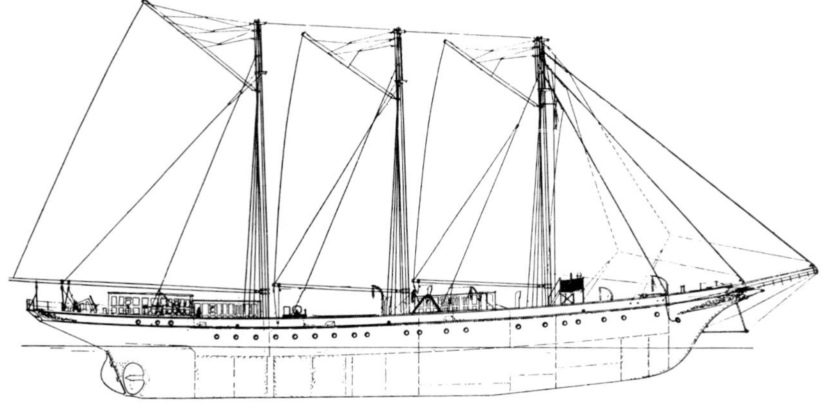

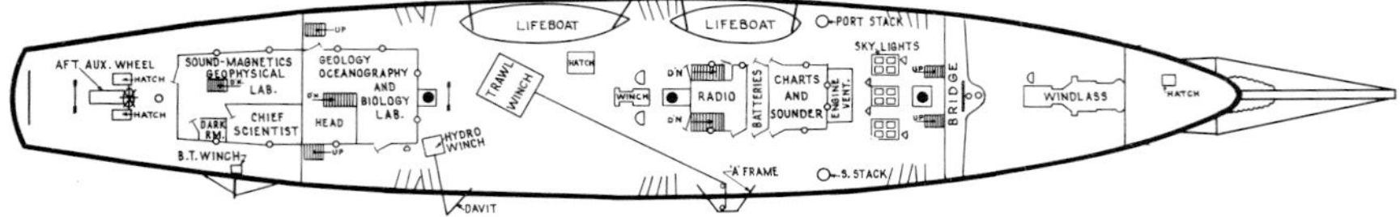

A2.2 Research vessel

APPENDIX 3

Illustrations of Large Abyssal Animals

The drawings prepared by the marine biologists who studied and described the animals trawled by the early exploring expeditions provide the best, and in many cases the only, guide to the identification of animals seen or photographed on the deep-sea floor. The following list includes reports, most over fifty years old, that contain the best illustrations of the larger abyssal animals.

SPONGES

1883 N. Polejaeff. Report on the Calcarea. Challenger *Rept., zool.,* 8 (XXIV): 89 pp. Two plates of whole specimens are reproduced.

1887 F. E. Schulze. Report on the Hexactinellida. Challenger *Rept., zool.,* 8 (LIII):624 pp. Approximately seventy-five beautiful drawings show whole specimens (with scale).

1888 W. J. Sollas. Report on the Tetractinellida. Challenger *Rept., zoöl.,* 25 (LXIII):673 pp. Forty-four excellent colored plates of entire animals.

1940 L. H. Hyman. *The Invertebrates:* Protozoa through Ctenophora. McGraw-Hill, New York, 726 pp. A comprehensive summary of the sponges, hydroids, gorgonians, sea pens, anemones, and black corals. Many simple sketches, unfortunately none with a scale.

1964 C. Levi. Spongiaires des zones bathyale, abyssale et hadale. Galathea *Rept.,* 7:63-112. Levi's comprehensive list of all bathal, abyssal, and hadal sponges recovered from the deep sea show that thirty-five genera from five families of the order Hexactinellida and thirteen genera from eight families of Demospongiae have been found below 3000 meters. Ten photographic plates illustrate the variety of forms of sponges. A good bibliography is also included.

COELENTERATES

Hydroids

1883 and 1888 G. J. Allman, Report on the Hydroida. Challenger *Rept., zool.,* 7 (XX): 79 pp. and 23 (LXX):202 pp. Contain approximately twenty and forty plates respectively of hydroids, all of which were found in less than 1800 meters.

1951 P. L. Kramp. Hydrozoa and Scyphozoa. *Repts. Swedish Deep Sea Exped.,* 2:121-27. Includes a list of the twelve species of tiny hydroids dredged from below 3000 meters.

Gorgonians and Pennatulids

1880 A. V. Kolliker. Report on the Pennatulida. Challenger *Rept., zool.,* 1 (II):45 pp. Eleven excellent plates of entire animals.

1889 T. Studer. Report on the Alcyonaira (Suppl.). Challenger *Rept., zool.,* 32 (LXXXI):41 pp. Four plates, two in color, show whole specimens.

1889 E. P. Wright and T. Studer. Report on the Alcyonaria. Challenger *Rept., zool.,* 31 (LXIV):439 pp. Contains thirty-two plates of whole specimens.

Actiniarians

1882 R. Hertwig. Report on the Actiniaria. Challenger *Rept., zool.,* 5 (XV): 154 pp. Three plates illustrate entire animals. The largest in the collection measured five centimeters.

1951 O. Carlgren. Actiniaria. *Repts. Swedish Deep Sea Exped.,* 2:101-4. A list of species dredged below 3000 meters before 1951 is included.

Corals

1881 H. N. Moseley. Report on certain Hydroid, Alcyonarian, and Madreporarian Corals. Challenger *Rept., zool.,* 2 (VII):252 pp. Contains eighteen plates showing entire animals and a number of sketches.

1889 G. Brook. Report on the Antipatharia. Challenger *Rept., zool.,* 32 (LXXX): 245 pp. Seven plates of entire animals.

1959 D. Squires. Deep sea corals collected by the Lamont Geological Observatory, 2, Scotia Sea Corals. *Am. Mus. Novitates,* 2045:48 pp. Twenty-nine drawings show whole specimens. Five sea-floor photographs in depths less than 400 meters on the Falkland Plateau are illustrated.

1962 T. R. Stetson, D. F. Squires, and R. M. Pratt. Coral banks occurring in deep water on the Blake Plateau. *Am. Mus. Novitates,* 2114:39 pp. Eight photographs of coral are reproduced.

BRYOZOANS

1884 and 1886 G. Busk. Report on the Polyzoa. Challenger *Rept., zool.,* 10 (XXX): 257 pp. and 17 (L):69 pp. Contain twenty-five and nine plates, respectively, illustrating entire colonies.

1961 L. Silen. Bryzoa. *Repts. Swedish Deep Sea Exped.,* 2:63-69. Includes a list of the forty-eight species dredged in depths of 3000 meters prior to 1951. A colony approximately ten centimeters high is illustrated.

ECHINODERMS

1955 L. H. Hyman. *The Invertebrates: Echinodermata.* McGraw-Hill, New York, 761 pp. An extensive review of the phylum with many sketches (none with scale).

Crinoids

1884 P. H. Carpenter. Report on the Crinoidea-stalked crinoids. Challenger *Rept., zool.,* 11 (XXXII):520 pp. Thirty plates show complete specimens. Fourteen of the specimens illustrated are larger than ten centimeters in maximum dimension.

1888 P. H. Carpenter. Report on the Crinoidea–*Comatulae,* Challenger *Rept., zool.,* 25 (LX):483 pp. Contains forty plates showing complete specimens. Over half of the specimens illustrated are larger than ten centimeters.

1892 A. Agassiz. *Calamocrinus diomedae*–a new stalked crinoid. *Mem. Mus. Comp. Zool.,* 17(2):95 pp. One colored plate of complete specimen (yellow) is included.

1957 Torsten Gislen. Crinoidea, with a survey of the bathymetric distribution of the deep-sea crinoids. *Repts. Swedish Deep Sea Exped.,* 2:49-61. Includes a list of crinoids reported from depths greater than 3000 meters.

Asteroids

1889 W. P. Sladen. Report on the Asteroidea (plates only). Challenger *Rept., zool.,* 30 (LI):119 pl. Approximately fifty plates show nearly complete specimens.

1935 I. Lieberkind. Asteroidea, Part I, Porcellanasteridae. *Danish* Ingolf *Exped.,* 4(10):37 pp. One plate shows nine complete specimens.

1951 F. J. Madsen. Asteroidea. *Repts. Swedish Deep Sea Exped.,* 2:73-92. Includes a list of species dredged in depths greater than 3000 meters.

1961 F. J. Madsen. The Porcellanasteridae. Galathea *Repts.,* 4:33-176. Contains distribution maps, bibliography, and thirteen plates showing the ventral and dorsal sides of forty complete specimens.

Ophiuroids

1882 T. Lyman. Report on the Ophiuroidea. Challenger *Rept., zool.,* 5 (XIV): 386 pp. Eleven plates show nearly complete specimens.

1933 T. Mortensen. Ophiuroidea. *Danish* Ingolf *Exped.,* 4(8):121 pp. Three plates show entire specimens. Many line drawings. Good bibliography.

1951 F. J. Madsen. Ophiuroidea. *Repts. Swedish Deep Sea Exped.,* 2:105-19. Includes list of species dredged below 3000 meters.

Echinoids

1881 A. Agassiz. Report on the Echinoidea. Challenger *Rept., zool.,* 3 (IX): 325 pp. Forty-nine finely executed plates of entire echinoids.

1903 and 1907 T. Mortensen. Echinoidea. *Danish* Ingolf *Exped.,* 4(1 and 2):193 and 200 pp. Six plates of complete animals including three in color (1903) and eight black and white plates of complete animals (1907).

1928-1951 T. Mortensen. *A Monograph of the Echinoidea.* C. Reitzel, Copenhagen, 4433 pp., 5 vols., 15 parts, 551 plates, 2458 figs. The largest and most complete work on the Echinoidea.

1951 T. Mortensen. Echinoidea. *Repts. Swedish Deep Sea Exped.,* 2:47-48. Includes a list of echinoids dredged below 3000 meters.

Holothurians

1882 and 1886 H. Theel. Report on the Holothurioidea. Challenger *Rept., zool.,* 4 (XIII): 176 pp. and 14 (XXXIX):310 pp. Contain thirty plates showing complete specimens of the order Elasapoda and eight plates showing complete specimens of the order Apoda.

1886b H. Theel. Report on the Holothurioidea. *Bull. Mus. Comp. Zool.,* 13:1-21. One plate showing five complete specimens.

1894 H. Ludwig. The Holothurioidea. *Mem. Mus. Comp. Zool.,* 17(3):183 pp. Ten colored paintings made by Agassiz at sea are reproduced in the excellent plates.

1902 E. Herouard. Holothuries des campagnes de la Princesse-Alice (1892-1897). *Resultats des Camp. Scie. du Prince de Monaco,* 66:161 pp. Seven plates show complete specimens, two of these are in color.

1902 Remy Perrier. *Exped. Sci. du* Travailleur *et du* Talisman *(1880-1883): Holothuries.* G. Masson, Paris, 281 pp.

1907 H. L. Clark. The Apodous holothurians. *Smithsonian Contr. to Knowledge.* 35 (1723):231 pp. Includes three colored plates of six individual specimens and eight black and white plates showing entire organisms.

1908 C. Vaney. Les holothuries de l'expedition Antarctique Nationale Ecossaise. *Trans. Royal Soc. Edinburgh,* 46:405-41. Two plates illustrate ten holothurians. Good ventral-side illustration.

1920 H. L. Clark. Tropical Pacific Holothurioidea. *Mem. Mus. Comp. Zool.,* 39:115-54. Contains thirteen beautiful colored paintings by A. Agassiz of specimens dredged by the *Albatross.*

1921 J. A. Grieg. Echinodermata. *Rep. Sci. Res.* Michael Sars *Exp.,* 3(2):47 pp. Photographs show upper, lower, and side views of six elasipod holothurians, one in color.

1927 S. Ekman. Holothurien aus der Ostantarkis und von Kerguelen. *Deutsche Sudpolar Exp. 1901-03, zool.,* 11:359-419. Includes three line drawings in the text, no plates.

1930 E. Deichmann. The holothurians of the western part of the Atlantic Ocean. *Bull. Mus. Comp. Zool.,* 71:44-229. Good bibliography. No illustrations of whole specimens.

1935 S. G. Heding. Holothurioidea, Part I. Ingolf *Exp. Rep.,* 4(9):84 pp. Figures show six partially dissected specimens. Emphasis is on mesentary track.

1942 S. G. Heding. Holothurioidea, Part II. Ingolf *Exp. Rep.,* 4(13):39 pp. One plate illustrates two complete specimens.

1955 F. J. Madsen. Holothurioidea. *Repts. Swedish Deep Sea Exped.,* 2:149-75. Includes a list of species dredged below 3000 meters.

MOLLUSKS AND BRACHIOPODS

1880 T. Davidson. Report on the Brachiopoda. Challenger *Rept., zool.,* 1 (I): 67 pp. Many complete specimens are illustrated in the four plates. The largest specimen is only about six centimeters in maximum dimension.

1884 R. Bergh. Report on the Nudibranchiata. Challenger *Rept., zool.,* 10 (XXVI):172 pp. One plate shows a complete specimen.

1885 E. A. Smith. Report on the Lamellibranchiata. Challenger *Rept., zool.,* 13 (XXXV):342 pp. Includes twenty-five plates of complete specimens.

1886 R. B. Watson. Report on the Scaphopoda and Gastropoda. Challenger *Rept., zool.,* 15 (XIII): 756 pp. Includes three plates showing complete specimens of scaphopods and forty-seven plates showing complete specimens of gastropods.

WORMS

1885 W. C. McIntosh. Report on the Annelida Polychaeta. Challenger *Rept., zool.,* 12 (XXXIV):554 pp. Contains thirty-three plates showing entire specimens.

1885 E. Selenka. Report on the Gephyrea. Challenger *Rept., zool.,* 13 (XXXVI): 24 pp. Contains four plates showing entire specimens.

1930 E. Wesenberg-Lund. Priapulidea and Sipunculidea. Ingolf *Exp. Rep.,* 4 (7):42 pp. Contains three plates of entire specimens.

1951 A. Eliason. Polychaeta. *Repts. Swedish Deep Sea Exped.,* 2:131-148. Includes list of all species dredged below 3000 meters, a bibliography, and one plate showing a complete specimen.

1955 E. Wesenberg-Lund. Sipunculidae. *Repts. Swedish Deep Sea Exped.,* 2: 199-201. Includes a list of the sixteen species dredged from below 3000 meters and illustrates three specimens in line drawings.

ARTHROPODS

1881 P. P. C. Hoek. Report on the Pycnogonida. Challenger *Rept., zool.,* 3 (X):167 pp. Twelve plates show entire specimens.

1884 and 1886 F. E. Beddard. Report on the Isopoda. Challenger *Rept., zool.,* 11 (XXXIII):85 pp., and 17 (XLVIII):207 pp. Thirty-five plates show entire specimens.

1888 T. Stebbing. Report on Amphipoda. Challenger *Rept., zool.,* 29 (LXVII): 212 pp. Two hundred and twelve plates show nearly two hundred complete specimens.

1948 J. W. Hedgepeth. The Pycnogonida of the western North Atlantic and the Caribbean. *Proc. U.S. Natl. Mus.,* 97:157-342. Includes distribution table and extensive bibliography. Only a few sketches of partial specimens are reproduced.

1955 I. Gordon. Crustacea Decapoda. *Repts. Swedish Deep Sea Exped.,* 2:239-45. Includes a list of the twenty-seven species of eight genera which have been dredged from depths exceeding 3000 meters before 1955 and one photographic plate of a complete specimen.

1955 C. A. Nilsson-Cantell. Cirripedia. *Repts. Swedish Deep Sea Exped.,* 2:215-30. Lists thirty-four species of four genera of barnacles found below 3000 meters.

1956 E. Sivertsen and L. B. Holthius. Crustacea Decapoda. *Report of* Michael Sars *Exped.,* 5(12):54 pp. Four beautiful colored plates of crabs.

1956 T. Wolff. Isopoda from depths exceeding 6000 meters. Galathea *Repts.,* 2:85-157. Simple sketches of ten nearly complete specimens.

1961 J. L. Barnard. Gammaridean Amphipoda from depths of 400 to 6000 meters. Galathea *Rept.,* 5:23-128. Contains sketches of fifty-seven specimens.

1962 R. J. Menzies. The isopods of abyssal depths in the Atlantic Ocean. *Vema Research Series,* Columbia University Press, 1:79-206. Sixty-four figures illustrate complete or nearly complete specimens.

1962 T. Wolff. The systematics and biology of bathyal and abyssal Isopoda *Asellota.* Galathea *Repts.,* 5:320 pp. Contains nineteen plates of good photographs and lists of species with depth and size. Most isopods are too small to be seen in photographs. Only one species of *Asellota* is known to be greater than five centimeters in length.

TUNICATES AND HEMICHORDATES

1882 and 1886 W. A. Herdman. Report on the Tunicata. Challenger *Rept., zool.,* 6 (XVII):337 pp. and 14 (XXXVIII):485 pp. Contains seventy-three plates showing complete specimens.

1893 J. W. Spengel. Die Enteropneusten. *Fauna und Flora des Golfes von Neapel, Monograph,* 18:756 pp.

1955 R. H. Millar. Ascidiacea. *Repts. Swedish Deep Sea Exped.,* 2:223-36. Includes a list of the thirty-eight species of twenty-three genera dredged from below 3000 meters and six diagramatic sketches showing complete specimens.

1965 E. J. W. Barrington. *The Biology of Hemichordata and Protochordata.* W. H. Freeman, San Francisco, 176 pp. Contains many line drawings, sections on life histories and habit and 114 references.

FISH

1887 A. Gunther. Report on deep-sea fishes. Challenger *Rept., zool.,* 22 (LVII): 335 pp. Seventy-three plates show entire specimens.

1888 L. Vaillant. *Exped. Sci. du* Travailleur *et du* Talisman *(1880-1883): Poissons.* G. Masson, Paris, 406 pp. This volume contains twenty-eight plates showing entire specimens.

1899 S. Garmen. The fishes. *Mem. Mus. Comp. Zool.,* 24(2):97 pp. Contains sixty-four excellent plates showing entire specimens (twelve are in color) dredged by *Albatross* in 1891.

1912 J. Murray and J. Hjort. *The Depth of the Ocean.* Macmillan, London. 821 pp. Chapter Seven (pp. 387-456), written by J. Hjort, includes numerous sketches of the important species of bottom fish.

1957 O. Nybelin. Deep sea bottom fishes. *Repts. Swedish Deep Sea Exped.,* 2:247-346. Includes a list of sixty-nine species found below 3600 meters.

APPENDIX 4

Tracks and Trails

Some of the earlier workers on fossil animal traces employed "genera" and "species" to classify and identify the various morphologically distinguishable forms. However, the variability of traces created by an individual animal makes such a classification of questionable use in the modern environment. Non-morphological classifications which are based principally on function combine surface burrows and burrow fillings and cannot easily be applied to the visual seascape. For instance, Lessertisseur divided all traces of biological activity into *exogene* (tracks and trails on the surface) and *endogene* (burrows). He then divided both into functional classes; features related to (1) locomotion (tracks and trails); (2) nutrition (feces, holes and mounds); and (3) repose (body impressions). He further classified on simple morphological grounds c.f., biolobate, trilobate, spiral, etc.). The biogenic traces which concern us in the visual seascapes of the modern deep-sea floor are those larger, evident tracks and trails (*exogene*) produced in *locomotion* by the larger members of the mobile benthos (Chaps. 3 and 4); feces or remolded sediment (Chap. 5), mounds and holes resulting from the *nutritional* activities of the larger members of the larger benthos, either mobile or hemisessile; and the *repose* traces of larger forms (Chap. 6).

The principal general works on trace fossils are: O. Abel. 1936. *Verzeitlich Lebensspuren.* Fischer, Jena, 644 pp., a classic treatise on trace fossils including many plates showing ancient and modern tracks, trails, burrows, and feces; A. Seilacher. 1953. Studient zur Palichnologie I. Uber die Methoden der Palichnologie. *Neues Jb. Geol. U. Palaeontol.,* 96:421-52, a study of features and structures useful for determining top and bottom in bedded and tabular rocks; J. Lessertisseur. 1955. Traces fossiles d'activité animale et leur signification paléobiologique. *Mem., Soc. Geol. France,* 74:148 pp., a report containing eleven plates of ancient and modern animal traces, numerous text figures, and a useful classification of trace fossils based on functional as well as morphological criteria; W. Hantzchel. 1962. Trace fossils and problematica. In R. C. Moore, editor. *Treatise on Invertebrate Paleontology, Part W, Miscellanae.* Geol. Soc. Am., New York, pp. 177-245, an annotated list of types of trace fossils which have been described and illustrated; and E. A. R. Ennion and N. Tinbergen. 1967. *Tracks.* Oxford University Press, London, 63 pp., a collection of photographs and sketches showing many familiar tracks and trails from beaches and dunes.

APPENDIX 5

Deep-Sea Sediments

Classifications of deep-sea sediment depend primarily on color, texture, composition, and origin (J. Murray and A. F. Renard. 1891. Report on deep-sea deposits based on specimens collected during the voyage of H.M.S. *Challenger* in the years 1872 to 1876. Challenger *Repts., Geology and Petrology,* 3:583 pp.; G. Arrhenius. 1959. Sedimentation on the ocean floor. *Researches in Geochemistry*. Wiley, New York).

MAJOR TYPES OF OCEAN SEDIMENT

Red Clay: A chocolate-brown, extremely fine-grained sediment consisting of particles, over 80 per cent of which are less than thirty microns (.030 mm) in diameter. It contains less than 30 per cent calcium carbonate. Found in depths greater than 5000 meters, it covers half of the Pacific floor and a quarter of the Atlantic and Indian oceans. It is composed of clay minerals, residue from dissolved plankton shells, wind-borne continentally derived silt, volcanic particles, and in high latitudes red clay contains an admixture of ice-rafted pebbles, rocks, and sand. Accumulation rates are the lowest of any deep-sea sediment, ranging from one-tenth to one millimeter per thousand years.

Globigerina Ooze: This milky white, rose-yellow, or brown chalky sediment is the second most important deep-sea sediment. It is composed primarily of the shells of planktonic foraminifera and is generally found in mid-ocean areas at depths less than 4000 meters. Particles finer than about 30 microns comprise less than 50 per cent of the sediment. The finer fraction often consists of the small platelets of planktonic plants called coccoliths. Rates of accumulation vary between one and three centimeters per thousand years.

Diatom Ooze: Yellowish straw-or-cream-colored siliceous sediment composed of about 40 per cent diatom shells. More than half of the material exceeds 30 microns in diameter. It is abundant near the highly productive waters surrounding Antarctica and the northern North Pacific and Atlantic. Rates of accumulation vary between one and two centimeters per thousand years.

Radiolarian Ooze: The soft pale greenish to greenish-yellow sediment composed of over 40 per cent radiolarian shells. Approximately 30 per cent of the material exceeds 30 microns in diameter. Like diatom ooze, radiolarian ooze is found in areas of high productivity, and in relatively deep water. Radiolarian ooze covers less than 10 per cent of the deep ocean floor and accumulates at rates varying between one and two centimeters per thousand years.

Terrigenous or Hemipelagic Mud: A sediment comprised of more than 30 per cent continentally derived sand and silt grains, it is often green, black, or slightly red, due to varying degrees of oxidation of the abundant organic matter. This sediment is generally over 50 per cent material coarser than 30 microns in diameter and it covers continental slopes and continental rises in most of the world oceans. Sedimentation rates vary between five and one hundred centimeters per thousand years.

BOTTOM TRANSPORTED SEDIMENTS

Turbidite: A hemipelagic sediment on abyssal plains and in and around submarine canyons, transported and deposited by turbidity currents. A turbidite bed which may range in average grain size from gravel to fine silt and clay is graded from coarser material at the bottom to finer at the top. A single bed may be ten to greater than one hundred centimeters thick. Turbidite sediment contains at least 10 per cent fine (less than 2 microns) clay mixed with sand and silt. Well-preserved displaced plant and shell fragments are common.

Contourite: Hemipelagic sediment transported and deposited by contour currents. In contract to the material transported by turbidity currents (which flow downhill), contourite is transported parallel to bathymetric contours. Size grading is fairly common and particle-size sorting is well developed. Contourites are more thinly bedded than turbidites. Primary current structures are common and the amount of clay between silt and sand grains is less than 5 per cent. The coarsest grain size of this sediment ranges from very fine sand to very fine silt. Like turbidites, contourite can be composed of virtually any type of sediment. Contourites are found where deep thermohaline circulation is present, that is, principally along the western margins of the world oceans and along continental rises. Rates of accumulation may exceed one meter per thousand years.

RAFTED AND EJECTED SEDIMENTS

Glacial Marine: Material deposited in the deep sea from the melting of icebergs. Glacial marine sediment is extremely poorly sorted with respect to grain size and millionfold range of particle size is not uncommon. Found predominantly in high latitudes, it constitutes an important constituent of diatom and radiolarian ooze.

Volcanic Sediment: Light-colored, porous volcanic ejecta of all sizes is found on the deep-sea floor in areas close to volcanic sources, where it may constitute a major component of the sediment. Volcanic material ranges in size from large blocks found within a few kilometers of the source to very fine ash which may be found thousands of kilometers from the volcanic source. Wind plays a large role in the distribution pattern of volcanic ash.

APPENDIX 6

Current Velocities

The velocities of fluid motions at the deep-sea floor range from the steady deliberate contour currents to rapid sporadic turbidity currents.

	cm/sec	MPH	Knots	Feet/Sec	km/day	Millions of km/Century*
Contour Currents	1	.02	.02	.03	.86	.03
	5	.11	.01	.16	4.3	.16
	10	.22	.19	.33	8.6	.32
	15	.33	.29	.49	12.9	.48
	20	.44	.38	.66	17.2	.64
	25	.55	.48	.82	21.5	.80
	50	1.1	.9	1.6	43.0	1.60

* Assume continuous undirectional flow.

	cm/sec	MPH	Knots	Feet/Sec	km/day	Millions of km/Century*
Turbidity Currents	500	11	9	16	430	.0004**
	1000	22	19	33	864	.0008
	2000	44	38	66	1720	.0017
	3000	66	57	99	2584	.0026
	4000	88	76	132	3440	.0034

** Assume one turbidity current of a day's duration per century.

APPENDIX 7

Geologic Time

There is no record in the abyss which reaches back as far as 200 million years, and either there was no abyss then or the relicts of these ancient seas have been completely destroyed. The deposits of earlier seas are found exclusively on the continents.

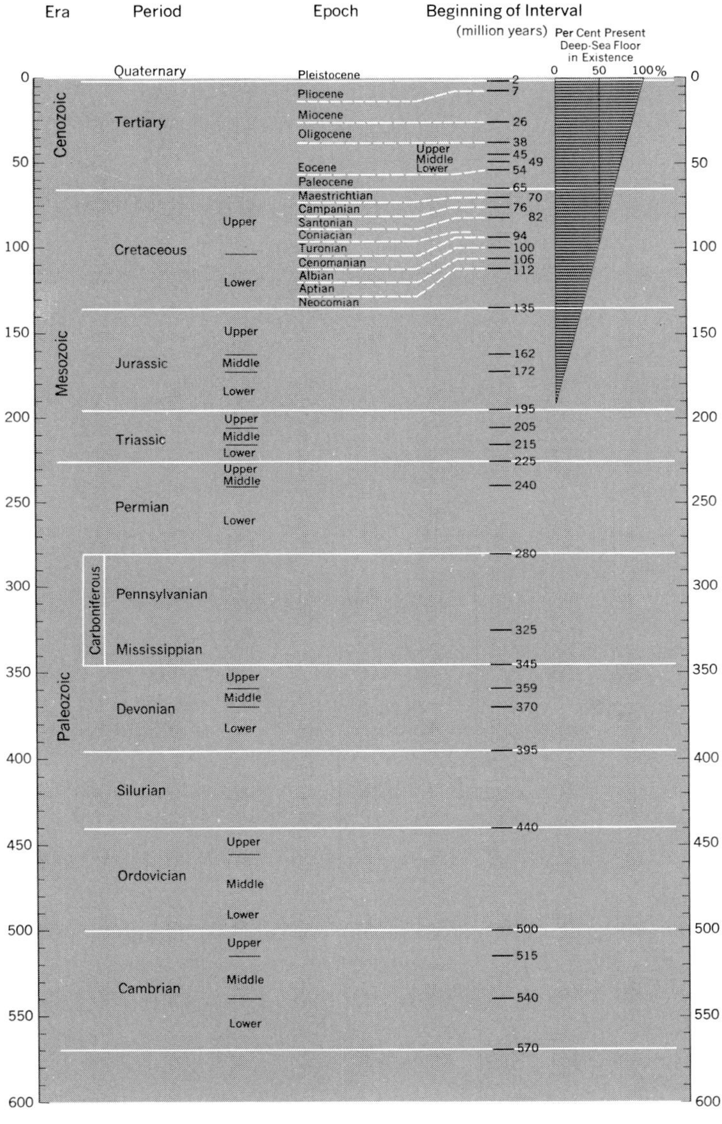

A7.1 The geologic time scale.

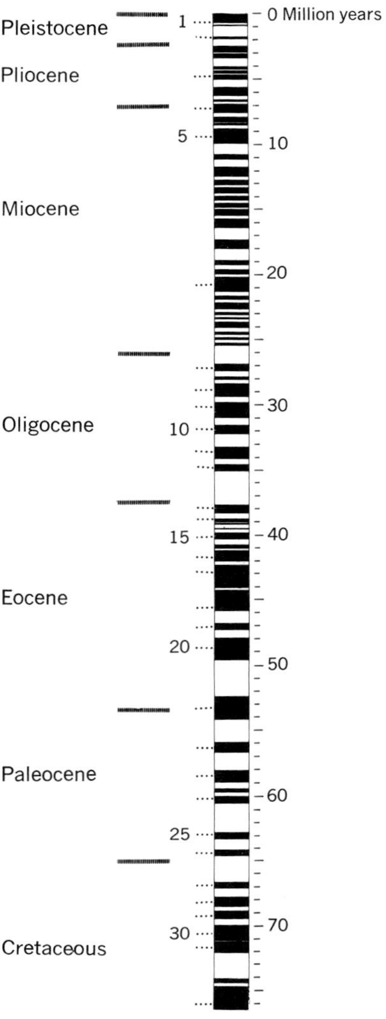

A7.2 The sequence of polarity reversals of the earth's magnetic field. This sequence, determined from profiles of magnetic intensity run across the width of the expanding oceans and dated by correlations with vertical sequences in sediments and lavas of known ages, has provided a powerful tool in the unraveling of ocean floor history. Black represents normal polarity; white, reversed polarity.[13.20]

Illustration Acknowledgments

Photographs were provided by: American Telephone and Telegraph Company, AT&T; Bedford Institute of Oceanography, BIO; Bell Telephone Laboratories, BTL; Cable and Wireless, Ltd., C&W; Duke University Marine Laboratory, DML; Lamont-Doherty Geological Observatory of Columbia University, LDGO; National Institute of Oceanography of the United Kingdom, NIO; National Science Foundation, NSF, in particular, the United States Antarctic Research Program, USARP; North Atlantic Treaty Organization, NATO, in particular, Project NAVADO; The Scripps Institution of Oceanography, SIO; United States Navy, in particular, The Naval Oceanographic Office, NAVOCEANO, and The Naval Undersea Research and Development Center, NUC; U.S.S.R. Academy of Sciences, in particular, The Institute of Oceanology, USSR; Woods Hole Oceanographic Institution, WHOI.

1.1, NSF (USARP). *1.3,* B. C. Heezen and M. Tharp. 1968. *Physiographic Diagram of the North Atlantic.* Geol. Soc. Am., Boulder, Colo. *1.5,* B. C. Heezen, M. Tharp, and M. Ewing. 1959. *The floors of the oceans,* I. Geol. Soc. Am., Spec. Paper 65, Fig. 9. *1.6* ibid. Fig. 8. *1.12,* UL,* AT&T (B.C.H.); LL, NSF (USARP); UR, LR, C&W (C.D.H.). *1.13,* W. Fedukowicz.

2.1, LDGO (B.C.H.). *2.2,* redrawn from E. L. Le Danois. 1948. *Les Profondeurs de la Mer.* Payot, Paris, Figs. 45, 46. *2.3,* ibid. Fig. 56. *2.5,* BIO (B. Loncarevic). *2.6,* C. W. Thomson. 1878. *The Atlantic: Voyage of the H.M.S.* Challenger. Harper, New York, 1:Fig. 29. *2.7,* NAVOCEANO (B.C.H.). *2.8,* NSF (USARP). *2.9,* UL, UR, LR, LDGO (B.C.H.); LL, LDGO (R. Markl). *2.10,* redrawn from F. E. Schulze. 1887. Report on the Hexactinellida. Challenger *Rept., zool.,* 8:Pl. 34. *2.11,* UL, DML (B.C.H.); UR, LL, LDGO (B.C.H.); LR, WHOI (R. Pratt). *2.12,* redrawn from C. W. Thomson. 1878. Op. cit. Fig. 28. *2.13,* redrawn from J. Murray and J. Hjort. 1912. *The Depths of the Ocean.* Macmillan, London, Fig. 383. *2.14,* BIO (B. Loncarevic). *2.15,* redrawn from A. Agassiz. 1888. *Three Cruises of the* Blake. Riverside Press, Cambridge, 2:Fig. 541. *2.16,* NSF (USARP). *2.17,* UL, UR, LDGO (B.C.H.); L, LDGO (R. Wall). *2.18,* redrawn from A. Agassiz. 1888. Op. cit. 2:Fig. 458. *2.19,* UL, LDGO (M. Langseth); UR, LL, DML (B.C.H.); LR, NSF (USARP). *2.20,* U, LDGO (B.C.H.); LL, LR, NSF (USARP); *2.21,* L, NSF (USARP); R, NAVOCEANO (W. Jahns). *2.22,* redrawn from A. Agassiz. 1888. Op. cit. 2:Fig. 449. *2.23,* BIO (B. Loncarevic). *2.24-2.25,* WHOI (R. Pratt). *2.26,* redrawn from J. Murray and J. Hjort. 1912. Op. cit. Fig. 341. *2.27,* C. W. Thomson. 1878. Op. cit. 1:Fig 36. *2.28,* U, LDGO (J. Nafe); LC, LL, LR, NSF (USARP). *2.29,* redrawn from E. Haeckel. 1889. Deep-sea Keratosa. Challenger *Rept., zool.,* 32:Pl. 8. *2.30,* LDGO (R. Markl). *2.31,* NSF (USARP). *2.32,* UL, AT&T (B.C.H.); UR, LL, LC, NSF (USARP); LR, LDGO (M. Langseth). *2.33,* LDGO (B.C.H.). *2.34,* WHOI (B.C.H.). *2.35,* WHOI (R. Pratt). *2.36,* UL, UR, LDGO (E. Thorndike); L, WHOI (R. Pratt). *2.37,* C. W. Thomson. 1878. Op. cit. 1:Fig. 23. *2.38,* NSF (USARP). *2.39,* C. W. Thomson. 1878. Op. cit. 1:Fig. 31. *2.40,* BTL (R. Leopold). *2.41,* UL, LDGO (B.C.H.); UC, UR, LC, RC, NSF (USARP); L, WHOI

* UL—Upper Left　L—Lower　LC—Left Center
UR—Upper Right　U—Upper　RC—Right Center

(M. Ewing). *2.42,* C. W. Thomson. 1878. Op. cit. 1:Fig. 98. *2.43,* UL, LDGO (R. Markl); UR, WHOI (R. Pratt); LL, NSF (USARP); LR, LDGO (B.C.H.). *2.44,* U, LR, NSF (USARP); LL, WHOI (R. Pratt). *2.46,* U, C, WHOI (R. Pratt); L, LDGO (R. Markl). *2.47,* NSF (USARP). *2.48,* C. W. Thomson. 1878. Op. cit. 1:Figs. 33, 34. *2.49,* AT&T (B.C.H.). *2.50,* LDGO (R. Markl), *2.51,* redrawn from D. Nichols. 1962. *Echinoderms.* Hutchinson, London, Fig. 11. *2.52,* UL, UR, RC, LL, LR, NSF (USARP); LC, LDGO (M. Langseth). *2.54,* NSF (USARP). *2.55,* redrawn from A. Agassiz. 1888. Op. cit. 2:Fig. 341. *2.56,* UL, LR, NSF (USARP); UR, LDGO (B.C.H.); LL, LDGO (M. Talwani). *2.57,* redrawn from H. Theel. 1882. Report on the Holothurioidea. Challenger *Rept., zool.,* 4:Pl. 29. *2.58,* WHOI (E. Bunce). *2.59,* WHOI (K. O. Emery). *2.60,* NUC (R. Dill). *2.61,* U, LL, RC, C, AT&T (B.C.H.); LR, NSF (USARP). *2.62,* NSF (USARP). *2.63,* UL, NSF (USARP); UC, LDGO (M. Langseth); UR, WHOI (R. Pratt); LL, LDGO (J. Nafe); LR, WHOI (B.C.H.). *2.64,* U, NSF (USARP); L, DML (B.C.H.). *2.65,* BTL (R. Allen). *2.66,* NSF (USARP). *2.67,* U, L, WHOI (B.C.H.). *2.68,* WHOI (R. Hessler). *2.69,* U, L, AT&T (B.C.H.). *2.70,* redrawn from A. Agassiz. 1888. Op. cit. 2:Fig. 232. *2.71,* UL, UR, AT&T (B.C.H.); LL, NSF (USARP); LR, BIO (C.D.H.). *2.72,* redrawn from R. J. Menzies. 1962. *The Isopods of Abyssal Depths in the Atlantic Ocean.* Columbia University Press, Vema Research Series, 1:Fig. 79. *2.73,* UL, UR, RC, L, NSF (USARP); LC, WHOI (D. Owen). *2.74,* redrawn from T. Wolfe. 1961. Animal life from a single abyssal trawling. Galathea *Rept.,* 5:Pl. 10. *2.75,* U, C, NSF (USARP); L, WHOI (D. Owen). *2.76,* WHOI (R. Hessler). *2.77,* NAVOCEANO (B.C.H.). *2.78,* redrawn from W. A. Herdman. 1882. Challenger *Rept., zool.,* 6:Pl. 7. *2.79,* LDGO (B.C.H.). *2.81,* SIO (J. Isaacs). *2.82,* LDGO (R. Gerrard). *2.83,* C. W. Thomson. 1878. Op. cit. 1:Fig. 23. *2.84,* BIO (C.D.H.). *2.85,* redrawn from N. B. Marshall and D. W. Bourne. 1964. A photographic survey of benthic fishes in the Red Sea and Gulf of Aden with observations on their populations, density, diversity and habits. *Bull. Mus. Comp. Zool.,* 232:Fig. 4. *2.86,* Westinghouse (R. Church). *2.87,* C&W (C.D.H.). *2.88,* UL, NSF (USARP); UR, LL, LDGO (B.C.H.); LR, WHOI (R. Pratt). *2.89,* UL, LDGO (B.C.H.); R, WHOI (B.C.H.); LL, NSF (USARP). *2.90,* UL, C&W (C.D.H.); UR, L, NUC (R. Dill). *2.91,* NSF (USARP). *2.92,* Naval Research Lab. (W. Brundage).

3.1, DML (B.C.H.). *3.3,* redrawn from J. Lessertisseur. 1955. Traces fossiles d'activité animale et leur signification paléobiologique, *Mem., Soc. Geol. France,* 74:Fig. 16. *3.4,* UL, UR, LDGO (B.C.H.); L, USSR (N. L. Zenkevich). *3.5,* U, L, C&W (C.D.H.). *3.6,* redrawn from A. F. Bruun. 1956. Animal life of the deep sea bottom. In A. F. Bruun, S. V. Greve, H. Mielche, and R. Sparck, editors. *The* Galathea *Deep Sea Expedition, 1950-1952.* Macmillan, New York, p. 173. *3.7,* Westinghouse (R. Church); *3.8,* U, L, LDGO (B.C.H.). *3.9,* redrawn from N. B. Marshall and D. W. Bourne. 1964. Op. cit. Fig. 3. *3.10,* U, L, WHOI (R. Pratt). *3.12,* U, CL, CR, NSF (USARP); L, LDGO (R. Wall). *3.13,* UL, LDGO (B.C.H.); R, WHOI (R. Pratt); LL, LDGO (R. Wall). *3.14,* redrawn from H. Theel. 1882. Op. cit. Pl. 30. *3.15-3.16,* redrawn from R. Koehler and C. Vaney. 1905. An account of the deep-sea holothurioidea. *Echinoderma of the Indian Museum, Calcutta,* Pls. 7, 5. *3.17,* redrawn from H. Theel. 1882. Op. cit. Pl. 26. *3.18,* LDGO (B.C.H.). *3.19,* U, LC, LR, LDGO (B.C.H.); LL, WHOI (J. B. Hersey). *3.20,* WHOI (B.C.H.). *3.21,* UL, L, LDGO (B.C.H.); UR, NSF (USARP). *3.22-3.24,* redrawn from H. Theel. 1882. Op. cit. Pls. 12, 22, 10. *3.25,* NSF (USARP). *3.26,* redrawn from H. Theel. 1882. Op. cit. Pl. 19. *3.27,* NAVOCEANO (Alpine). *3.28,* redrawn from H. Theel. 1882. Op. cit. Pl. 4. *3.29,* U, LDGO (B.C.H.).

4.1, WHOI (R. Pratt). *4.2,* UL, LDGO (B.C.H.); UR, L, NSF (USARP); RC, WHOI (J. Graham). *4.3,* G. H. Parker. 1921. The locomotion of the holothurian: *Stichopus panimensis* (Clark). *J. Exper. Zool.,* 33:p. 206. *4.4,* redrawn from J. Lessertisseur. 1955. Op. cit. Pl. 2. *4.5,* NSF (USARP). *4.6-4.7,* redrawn from J. Lessertisseur. 1955. Op. cit. Fig. 4B, Pl. 2. *4.8,* LDGO (R. Menzies). *4.9,* UL, UR, WHOI (R. Pratt); L, LDGO (B.C.H.). *4.10,* DML (B.C.H.). *4.11,* NSF (USARP). *4.12,* LDGO (K. Hunkins). *4.13,* LDGO (B.C.H.). *4.14,* NSF (USARP). *4.15-4.16,* B. C. Heezen. 1957. Whales entangled in deep sea cables. *Deep-Sea Res.,* 4:Figs. 3, 5. *4.18,* UL, LDGO (M. Langseth); UR, C&W (C.D.H.); L, NUC (R. Dill). *4.19,* U, NSF (USARP); LL, WHOI (J. B. Hersey);

LR, WHOI (M. Ewing). *4.20, 4.21,* U, NSF (USARP); L, WHOI (J. B. Hersey). *4.22,* NSF (USARP). *4.23,* UL, AT&T (B.C.H.); UR, CR, L, NSF (USARP). *4.24,* T. Mortensen. 1938-1951. *A Monograph of the Echinoidea: Spatangoids.* C. Reitzel, Copenhagen, 2:Pl. 40. *4.25, 4.26, 4.27,* NSF (USARP). *4.28, 4.29,* LDGO (B.C.H.). *4.30,* NSF (USARP).

5.1, LDGO (B.C.H.). *5.2* D. W. Bourne and B. C. Heezen. 1965. A wandering enteropneust from the abyssal Pacific; and the distribution of "spiral" tracks on the sea floor. *Science,* 150:Fig. 1. *5.3,* T. H. Tizard, H. N. Mosely, J. V. Buchanan, and J. Murray. 1885. Challenger *Repts. Narrative,* 1:Fig. 78. *5.4,* J. W. Spengel. 1893. Die Enteropneusten. *Fauna und Flora des Golfes von Neapel,* 18:Pl. 1. *5.5,* UL, UR, LR, NSF (USARP); LL, LDGO (R. Markl). *5.6,* SIO (R. Fisher). *5.7,* redrawn from A. Seilacher. 1958. Zur Ökologischen Characteristik von Flysch und Molasse. *Ecologae Geol. Helv.,* 51: 1062-1078, Fig. 1. *5.8,* U, LR, LDGO (B.C.H.); RC, LL, LDGO (R. Wall); LC, NSF (USARP). *5.9-5.13,* NSF (USARP). *5.15,* LDGO (K. Hunkins). *5.16,* LDGO (G. Mathieu). *5.17, 5.18,* NSF (USARP). *5.19,* U, LDGO (R. Wall); LC, L, LDGO (B.C.H.). *5.20,* U, WHOI (J. B. Hersey); L, LDGO (M. Langseth). *5.21,* redrawn from J. Lessertisseur. 1955. Op. cit. Fig. 16.

6.1, J. Y. Cousteau and J. Dugan. 1953. *The Living Sea.* Harper and Row, New York, p. 228. *6.2,* redrawn from A. N. Clark. 1962. *Starfishes and Their Relatives.* British Museum, London, Fig. 30. *6.6,* redrawn from G. Stiasny. 1910. Zur Kenntnis dei lebensweise von *Balanoglossus clarigerus* Belle Chiage. *Zool. Anz.,* 35:p. 562. *6.7,* redrawn from J. Lessertisseur. 1955. Op. cit. Fig. 15. *6.8,* redrawn from R. R. Shrock and W. H. Twenhofel. 1953. *Principles of Invertebrate Paleontology.* McGraw-Hill, New York, Fig. 10-13. *6.9,* UL, LDGO (R. Markl); UR, WHOI (M. Ewing); L. LDGO (B.C.H.). *6.10,* redrawn from J. Lessertisseur. 1955. Op. cit. Fig. 17. *6.11,* WHOI (R. Pratt). *6.12,* redrawn from A. N. Clark. 1962. Op. cit. P. 112. *6.13,* U, LDGO (B.C.H.); L, NSF (USARP). *6.14,* NSF (USARP). *6.15,* redrawn from J. Lessertisseur. 1955. Op. cit. Fig. 30. *6.16,* UL, UR, LL, LDGO (B.C.H.). RC, WHOI (R. Pratt); LR, NSF (USARP). *6.17,* UL, UR, LDGO (B.C.H.); LL, LDGO (M. Langseth); LR, Keil Univ. (E. Seibold). *6.18,* AT&T (B.C.H.). *6. 19,* LDGO (B.C.H.). *6.20,* UL, RC, NSF (USARP); LC, LL, UR, LR, LDGO (B.C.H.). *6.21,* DML (B.C.H.). *6.22,* NSF (USARP). *6.23,* WHOI (E. Zarudski). *6.24,* LDGO (B.C.H.). *6.25,* redrawn from J. Lessertisseur. 1955. Op. cit. Fig. 8. *6.26,* LDGO (J. Worzel). *6.27,* LDGO (B.C.H.). *6.28,* LDGO (B.C.H.). *6.29,* redrawn from J. Lessertisseur. 1955. Op. cit. Fig. 8. *6.30,* U, WHOI (R. Pratt); LL, LR, LDGO (B.C.H.). *6.31,* NSF (USARP). *6.32,* U, WHOI (R. Pratt); L, NSF (USARP). *6.33,* DML (H. D. Needham). *6.35,* redrawn from B. C. Heezen, R. J. Menzies, W. S. Broecker, and M. Ewing. 1959. Stagnation of the Cariaco Trench. *Internat. Oceanogr. Congress,* 1:Fig. 2. *6.36-6.40,* LDGO (B.C.H.). *6.41,* U, NASA (Ranger); L, LDGO (B.C.H.).

7.1, S. A. Kling. *7.2,* U, AT&T (B.C.H.); L, DML (J. Cason). *7.3,* NUC (R. Dill). *7.4,* LDGO (B.C.H.). *7.6,* U, DML (W. Ruddiman); L, WHOI (E. Zarudski). *7.7,* AT&T (B.C.H.). *7.8,* J. Y. Cousteau and J. Dugan. 1963. Op. cit. P. 192. *7.9,* WHOI (R. Tirey). *7.10,* WHOI (W. Rainnie). *7.11,* LDGO (R. Gerrard). *7.13,* AT&T (L. Schindel). *7.14,* BTL (R. Leopold). *7.15,* NAVOCEANO. *7.16,* SIO (R. Fisher). *7.17,* AT&T (B.C.H.). *7.20-7.21,* D. Ninkovitch and B. C. Heezen. 1965. Santorini Tephra. In W. F. Whittard and R. Bradshaw, editors. *Submarine Geology.* Butterworths, London, Fig. 161, Pl. 38. *7.24,* W. A. Cassidy, B. Glass, and B. C. Heezen. 1969. Physical and chemical properties of Australasian microtektites. *Jour. Geophys. Res.,* 74:Fig. 1. *7.25,* redrawn from B. Glass. 1967. Microtektites in deep-sea sediments. *Nature,* 214:374, Fig. 1. *7.26,* J. Prestwick. 1886. *Geology.* Oxford. *7.27,* BIO (C.D.H.). *7.28,* NAVOCEANO (W. Whitman). *7.29,* UL, UR, LDGO (K. Hunkins); LL, LR, NSF (USARP). *7.30,* NSF (USARP). *7.32-7.33,* NSF (USARP). *7.35,* C. W. Thomson. 1878. Op. cit. Fig. 46. *7.36,* NSF (USARP). *7.37,* LDGO (A. McIntyre). *7.39,* LDGO (A. McIntyre). *7.40,* R. E. Garrison. *7.42,* D. Folger, L. Burckle, and B. C. Heezen. 1967. Opal phytoliths in a North Atlantic dust fall. *Science,* 155:1243-44, Fig. 2. *7.48,* S. A. Kling.

8.1, WHOI (D. Ross). *8.2,* WHOI (E. Bunce). *8.4-8.6,* NUC (R. Dill). *8.7,* LDGO (B.C.H.). *8.8,* K O. Emery, E. Uchupi, J. D. Phillips, C. O. Bowin, E. T. Bunce, and S. T. Knott. 1970. The continental rise off eastern North America. *Bull. Am. Assoc. Pet. Geol.,* 54:Fig. 6. *8.9,* WHOI (R. Pratt). *8.10,* WHOI (J. Hathaway). *8.11,* DML (B.C.H.). *8.12-8.13,* BIO (B. Loncarevic). *8.14-8.15,* B. C. Heezen, D. B. Ericson, and M. Ewing. 1954. Further evidence for a turbidity current following the 1929 Grand Banks earthquake. *Deep-Sea Res.,* 1:Figs. 1, 4. *8.16,* B. C. Heezen and M. Ewing. 1952. Turbidity currents and submarine slumps and the Grand Banks earthquake. *Am. J. Sci.,* 250:Fig. 3. *8.19-8.20,* B. C. Heezen and C. L. Drake. 1964. Grand Banks slump. *Am. Assoc. Pet. Geol.,* 48:Figs. 2, 1. *8.21-8.22,* K. O. Emery et al. 1970. Op. cit. Figs. 8, 6. *8.23,* LDGO (M. Langseth). *8.25-8.29,* B. C. Heezen, R. J. Menzies, E. D. Schneider, M. Ewing, and N. C. L. Granelli. 1964. Congo Submarine Canyon. *Bull. Am. Assoc. Pet. Geol.,* 48:Figs. 2, 3, 16, 11, 12. *8.30,* DML (B.C.H.). *8.31,* B. C. Heezen, 1956. Corrientes de turbidez del Rio Magdalena. *Boletin de la Sociedad Geografica de Columbia,* Bogota, Fig. 1. *8.36,* B. C. Heezen and M. Tharp. 1964. *Physiographic Diagram of the Indian Ocean. Geol. Soc. Am.,* Boulder, Colo. *8.37,* C&W (W. B. F. Ryan). *8.38,* B. C. Heezen and M. Tharp. 1968. Op. cit. *8.39,* NIO (A. Laughton). *8.45,* J. Bourcart. *8.46,* Inst. Oceano. Monaco (M. Gennesseux).

9.1, DML (B.C.H.). *9.2,* LDGO (B.C.H.). *9.3-9.4,* NSF (USARP). *9.5,* DML (B.C.H.). *9.6,* UL, NSF (USARP); UR, L, C, LDGO (M. Langseth). *9.8,* NSF (USARP). *9.9,* DML (O. Pilkey). *9.10,* WHOI (R. Pratt). *9.11,* DML (B.C.H.). *9.12,* NSF (USARP). *9.14,* Record obtain on U.S.N.S. *Silas Bent* by Billy P. Glass. In P. J. Fox, A. Harian, and B. C. Heezen. 1968. Abyssal anti-dunes. *Nature,* 229:Fig. 3. *9.15,* B. C. Heezen and C. D. Hollister. 1964. Deep sea current evidence from abyssal sediments. *Marine Geology,* 1:Fig. 4. *9.16,* U, LDGO (M. Langseth); L, WHOI (J. B. Hersey). *9.17,* UL, UR, NSF (USARP); L, DML (B.C.H.). *9.18,* LDGO (B.C.H.). *9.19,* U, NSF (USARP); LC, L, LDGO (B.C.H.); RC, LDGO (M. Langseth). *9.20,* redrawn from B. C. Heezen and C. D. Hollister. 1964. Op. cit. Fig. 18. *9.22,* LDGO (M. Langseth). *9.25,* G. Wust. 1949. Blockdiagramme der Atlantischen Zirkulation auf Grund der "Meteor." *Erg. Kieler Meeresforschungen,* 7:Fig. 1. *9.28-9.32,* NSF (USARP). *9.34-9.35* NSF (USARP). *9.38,* NSF (USARP). *9.40,* B. C. Heezen and C. D. Hollister. 1964. Op. cit. Fig. 10. *9.41,* B. C. Heezen, C. R. Bentley, and M. Tharp. 1971. *Morphology of the Earth. Antarctic Serial Atlas,* folio 16. Amer. Geogr. Soc., New York. *9.42-9.44,* B. C. Heezen and C. D. Hollister. 1964. Op. cit. Figs. 5, 13, 14. *9.46-9.47,* C&W (C.D.H.). *9.48,* DML (E. Schneider). *9.49,* WHOI (E. Uchupi). *9.50-9.54,* B. C. Heezen and G. L. Johnson. 1969. Mediterranean undercurrent and microphysiography west of Gibraltar. *Bull. Inst. Oceanogr.,* 67(1382):Figs. 1, 24, 31, 30, 5, 4. *9.55-9.56,* NATO (NAVADO). *9.57,* LDGO (B.C.H.). *9.58,* B. C. Heezen, M. Tharp, and H. C. Berann. 1968. Atlantic Ocean floor. *Nat. Geog. Mag.,* 134 (map supplement). *9.59,* NSF (USARP). *9.60-9.61,* NATO (NAVADO). *9.62-9.64,* BIO (C.D.H.). *9.69,* E. D. Schneider, P. J. Fox, C. D. Hollister, D. Needham, and B. C. Heezen. 1967. Further evidence for contour currents in the western North Atlantic. *Earth and Planetary Science Letters,* 2:Fig. 5. *9.71,* NUC (W. Brundage). *9.72,* LDGO (C. Drake). *9.73-9.77,* E. D. Schneider et al. 1967. Op. cit. Figs. 1, 3, 4, 2, 6. *9.78,* DML (B. C. H.). *9.79-9.81,* B. C. Heezen, C. D. Hollister, and W. F. Ruddiman. 1966. Shaping of the continental rise by geostrophic contour currents. *Science,* 152:503, Figs. 1-3. *9.82,* DML (Ruddiman).

10.1 NSF (USARP). *10.5,* NSF (USARP). *10.6,* U, LDGO (M. Langseth); LC, LDGO (B.C.H.); RC, NSF (USARP); L, LDGO (B.C.H.). *10.7,* UL, NSF (USARP); UR, NSF (USARP); L, DML (B.C.H.). *10.8-10.13,* NSF (USARP). *10.14,* LDGO (R. Gerrard). *10.15,* USSR (N. L. Zenkevich). *10.16,* LDGO (R. Gerrard). *10.17,* NSF (USARP). *10.18,* C&W (A. Laughton).

11.1, AT&T (B.C.H.). *11.4,* NUC (R. Dill) *11.5,* B. C. Heezen and G. L. Johnson. 1965. The South Sandwich Trench. *Deep-Sea Res.,* 12:Fig. 10. *11.6,* WHOI (E. Bunce). *11.8-11.17,* AT&T (B.C.H.) *11.18,* redrawn from M. Talwani, G. H. Sutton, and J. L. Worzel. 1959. Crustal section across the Puerto Rico Trench. *J. Geophys. Res.,* 64:Fig.

3. *11.21,* R. L. Chase and E. T. Bunce. 1969. Underthrusting of the eastern margin of the Antilles by the floor of the western North Atlantic Ocean and origin of the Barbados Ridge. *J. Geophys. Res.,* 74:Fig. 3. *11.22,* WHOI (E. Bunce). *11.24,* B. C. Heezen and G. L. Johnson. 1965. Op. cit. Fig. 7. *11.25,* B. C. Heezen and M. Tharp. *Physiographic Diagram of the South Atlantic.* Geol. Soc. Am., Boulder, Colo. *11.26,* NSF (USARP). *11.27-11.29,* SIO (R. Fisher). *11.30,* C&W (A. Laughton). *11.32,* B. C. Heezen and C. D. Hollister. 1964. Op. cit. Fig. 12. *11.34-11.36,* LDGO (B.C.H.). *11.37,* L. Zenkevitch. 1963. *Biology of the Seas of the U.S.S.R.* George Allen & Unwin, London, Fig. 348. U, 3:Fig. 23; L, 3:Fig. 30. *11.39,* WHOI (E. Zarudski). *11.40,* W. B. F. Ryan. 1970. Ph.D. thesis, Columbia Univ.

12.1, Am. Mus. Nat. History (N. Newell). *12.2,* NSF (USARP). *12.5,* redrawn from R. Compton, 1962. *Manual of field geology.* J. Wiley, New York, Fig. 13-12. *12.6,* BIO (B. Loncarevic). *12.7,* Univ. R.I. (D. Krause). *12.8,* R. L. Fisher, G. L. Johnson, and B. C. Heezen. 1967. Mascarene Plateau, Western Indian Ocean. *Geol. Soc. Am. Bull.,* 78:Fig. 6. *12.9,* Asahi Press (R. Dietz). *12.10,* French Tourist Office. *12.12,* H. J. Wiens. *12.14,* NUC (C. Shipek). *12.15,* LDGO (B.C.H.). *12.16, WHOI* (E. Zarudski). *12.17-12.18,* LDGO (B.C.H.). *12.19,* C&W (C.D.H.). *12.21,* LDGO (B.C.H.). *12.22,* BIO (B. Loncarevic). *12.23,* WHOI (K. O. Emery). *12.24,* NUC (R. Dill). *12.25,* AT&T (B.C.H.). *12.26,* WHOI (K. O. Emery). *12.28,* WHOI (B.C.H.). *12.29,* B. C. Heezen and M. Tharp. 1964. *Physiographic Diagram of the Indian Ocean.* Geol. Soc. Am., Boulder, Colo. *12.30,* WHOI (R. Chase). *12.31-12.37,* B. C. Heezen, B. Glass, and H. W. Menard. 1966. The Manihiki Plateau. *Deep-Sea Res.,* 13:Figs. 1, 7, 3, 10, 4, 11, 12. *12.38,* SIO (G. Shor). *12.39,* B. C. Heezen, M. Tharp, and H. C. Berann. 1969. *Pacific Ocean Floor.* Nat. Geog. Soc. *12.40,* B. C. Heezen and A. G. Fischer. 1971. Regional problems. *Initial Rept. Deep Sea Drilling Project,* 6:1301-1305.

13.1, J. Y. Cousteau and J. Dugan, 1963. *The Living Sea.* Harper, New York, p. 239. *13.2,* NSF (USARP). *13.3,* redrawn from R. R. Shrock. 1948. *Sequence in Layered Rocks.* McGraw-Hill, New York, Fig. 123. *13.4,* S. Thorarinsson. *13.5,* B. C. Heezen and M. Tharp. 1961. *Physiographic Diagram of the South Atlantic.* Geol. Soc. Am., Boulder, Colo. *13.7,* redrawn from A. Rittmann. 1962. *Volcanoes and Their Activity.* John Wiley, New York, Fig. 51. *13.8-13.9,* B. C. Heezen, M. Tharp, and M. Ewing. 1959. Op. cit. Pl. 19. *13.10,* C. H. Elmendorf, and B. C. Heezen. 1957. Oceanographic information for engineering submarine cable systems. *The Bell System Technical Journal,* 36:1047-1093, Fig. 2. *13.12,* B.C.H. *13.14,* B. C. Heezen. 1960. The rift in the ocean floor, *Sci. Am.,* 203(4):98-110, p 108. *13.15, 13.16-13.17,* BIO (B. Loncarevic). *13.18,* NSF (USARP). *13.19,* UL, LDGO (M. Langseth); UR, LL, NSF (USARP); LR, LDGO (R. Gerrard). *13.20-13.21,* NSF (USARP). *13.22,* LDGO (B.C.H.). *13.23,* BIO (B. Loncarevic). *13.24-13.25,* LDGO (B.C.H.). *13.26,* WHOI (E. Bunce). *13.28,* W. C. Pitman III, and J. R. Heirtzler. 1966. Magnetic anomalies over the Pacific-Antarctic Ridge. *Science,* 154: Fig. 2. *13.30,* B. C. Heezen and M. Tharp. 1965. Tectonic fabric of the Atlantic and Indian oceans and continental drift. *Phil. Trans. Roy. Soc. A,* 259:Figs. 3, 6. *13.32,* LDGO (R. Gerrard). *13.33,* B. C. Heezen, M. Tharp, and C. D. Hollister. 1966. Illustrations of the marine geology of the Southern Ocean. *Symposium on Antarctic Oceanography.* Fig. 1. *13.34,* NSF (USARP). *13.35,* NAVOCEANO (Alpine). *13.36,* LDGO (C. Drake). *13.37-13.38,* LDGO (B.C.H). *13.39,* B. C. Heezen and M. Tharp. 1965. Tectonic fabric of the Atlantic and Indian Oceans and continental drift. *Phil. Trans. Roy. Soc. A,* 259:90-106, Fig. 1. *13.40-13.42,* B. C. Heezen and R. E. Sheridan. 1966. Lower Cretaceous rocks (Neocomian-Albian) dredged from Blake Escarpment. *Science,* 154:1645, Figs. 3, 2, 2. *13.43,* DML (B.C.H.). *13.44,* redrawn from C. L. Drake, M. Ewing, and G. H. Sutton. 1959. Op. cit. fig. 30. *13.45,* B. C. Heezen. 1959. Géologie sous-marine et déplacements des continents. In *Topographie et la Geologie des Profondeurs Oceaniques, Colloques Int., Centre Nat. Recher, Sci.,* 83:295-361, Fig. 5. *13.46* WHOI (K. Emery). *13.48* DML (B.C.H.).

14.1, B. C. Heezen and M. Tharp. 1971. *Physiographic Diagram of the Equatorial Atlantic.* Geol. Soc. Am., Boulder, Colo.

Name Index

Page numbers which refer to the text are in ordinary type and those which refer to the bibliographical references listed at the end of each chapter are in italics. Additional names are found in the Illustration Acknowledgments, pp. 635-639.

Subject Index

Page numbers which refer to illustrations are in italics.